MACQUARIE

AUSTRALIA'S NATIONAL DICTIONARY

BUDGET DICTIONARY

MACQUARIE

AUSTRALIA'S NATIONAL DICTIONARY

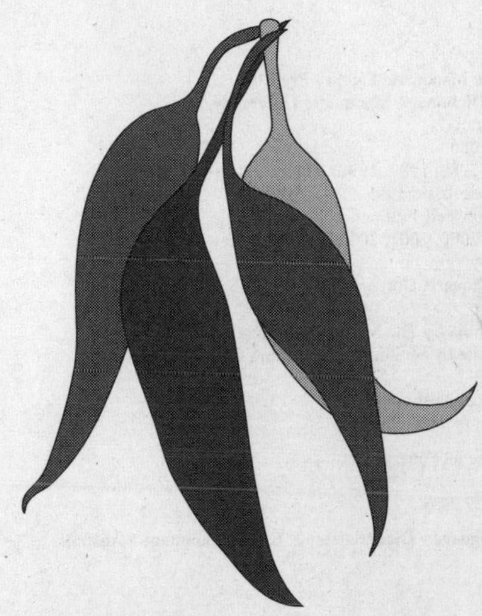

BUDGET DICTIONARY

Published by The Macquarie Library Pty Ltd
The Macquarie Dictionary, Macquarie University,
NSW 2109 Australia
First published 1985
Reprinted 1986, 1988, 1989, 1990, 1991, 1992, 1993, 1994
Second edition published 1995
Third edition published 1998
Reprinted 1999, 2000, 2001, 2002 (twice), 2003

Typeset in Australia by The Macquarie Library Pty Ltd
Printed in Australia by McPherson's Printing Group

National Library of Australia
cataloguing in publication data

The Macquarie dictionary
3rd budget ed.
ISBN 1 876429 04 6.

1. English language - Dictionaries. 2. English language - Australia.

423

A number of words entered in this dictionary are derived from trademarks.
However, the presence or absence of this indication of derivation should not
be regarded as affecting the legal status of any trademark.

Contents

Explanatory notes

THE ENTRY

All information within one complete entry has been arranged for the convenience of the user. In general, information about spelling and pronunciation comes first, meanings next, and run-on headwords last.

Abbreviations used in this dictionary have been limited as far as possible to familiar ones. All abbreviations can be found on page x.

HEADWORD

The headword is the word or words which are being defined in a particular entry; it appears in large bold-face type at the left, slightly farther into the left margin than the usual line of text.

Words which, though spelt identically, are of quite distinct derivation, are given separate entries; in such cases, each headword is followed by a small superscript number. (Example: **gum**^{1} and **gum**^{2}.) Entries are arranged under headwords in strict alphabetical order. A particular headword can be located by taking each successive letter of the headword in alphabetical order, ignoring hyphens, apostrophes and word spaces. For example, **bush band** is found between **bush** and **bushcraft**.

PRONUNCIATION

The prounuciation follows the headword within slant brackets. It is given in the International Phonetic Alphabet, for which keys may be found on the following pages. For some headwords more than one pronunciation is given, the first of these being the one more widely used.

Headwords made up of two or more separate words are generally not given pronunciations, unless one of the words does not appear as a headword in its own right. In these cases, the pronunciation of that word only is given.

PARTS OF SPEECH

The pronunciation is usually followed by an abbreviation in italics which indicates the part of speech of the headword, for example, *n.*, *adj.*

If the headword is used in more than one grammatical form, the part-of-speech label precedes each set of definitions to which it applies.

INFLECTED FORMS

If a headword has irregularly inflected forms (any form not made by the simple addition of the suffix to the main entry), the summary of these forms is given immediately after the pronunciation. Regularly inflected forms, not generally shown, include:

1. Nouns forming a plural merely by the addition of *s* or *-es*, such as *dog* (*dogs*) or *class* (*classes*);
2. Verbs forming the past tense by adding *-ed*, such as *halt* (*halted*);
3. Verbs forming the present tense by adding *-s* or *-es*, such as *talk* (*talks*) or *smash* (*smashes*);
4. Verbs forming the present participle by adding *-ing*, such as *walk* (*walking*);
5. Adjectives forming the comparative and superlative by adding *-er*, *-est*, such as *black* (*blacker*, *blackest*).

Regular forms are given, however, when necessary for clarity or the avoidance of confusion.

The past tense, past participle and present participle are given as the inflected forms of verbs; where, as commonly happens, the past tense and past participle are the same in form, this form is shown once. Example: the inflected forms indicated for **put** are **put**, **putting**, where **put** is both the past tense and past participle.)

If necessary, variants of inflected forms are labelled as to level of usage or distribution.

RESTRICTIVE LABELS

Entries that are limited in usage as to the level, region, time, or subject, are marked with such labels as *Colloquial*, *US*, *Obsolete*, *Electronics*, etc. If the restrictive label applies to the entire entry, it appears before the definition(s).

If, however, the restrictive label applies to only one grammatical form, it appears after that part-of-speech label but before the definition numbers to which it applies. If the restrictive label applies to only one definition, it appears before that definition, after the definition number.

DEFINITIONS

Definitions are individually numbered; numbers appear in a single sequence which does not begin afresh with each grammatical form. In some cases in which two definitions are very closely related, usually within the same field of information, they are marked with bold-face letters of the alphabet under the same definition number.

SECONDARY HEADWORDS

Idiomatic phrases, prepositional verb phrases, etc., are usually listed in bold face under main headwords. Such entries are usually placed under the difficult or key word.

VARIANT SPELLINGS

Definitions always appear under the most common spelling of a word. Less common variants cross-refer to the main headword. Variants regarded as equally acceptable appear in the headword itself, separated by an equals sign (for example **colour = color**). Other variants are given after the definitions.

RUN-ON HEADWORDS

Words which are derivatives of the headword and which are a simple extension of the meaning are run on after the last definition in the entry. Such headwords appear in secondary bold-face type followed by an indication of their grammatical form.

CROSS-REFERENCING

There are several forms of cross-referencing in this dictionary. The arrow → indicates that the headword which precedes it is not defined in this place but that a suitable definition is to be found under the headword which follows the arrow.

The word 'See' directs the reader to information relevant to the current definition but to be found within a different part of the dictionary. The abbreviation 'Cf.' is similar in function but limited to those cases where the information is in some way complementary or matching.

International Phonetic Alphabet used in the Dictionary

(a) *Vowels*

i	as in "peat"	/pit/
ɪ	as in "pit"	/pɪt/
ɛ	as in "pet"	/pɛt/
æ	as in "pat"	/pæt/
a	as in "part"	/pat/
ɒ	as in "pot"	/pɒt/
ʌ	as in "putt"	/pʌt/
ɔ	as in "port"	/pɔt/
ʊ	as in "put"	/pʊt/
u	as in "pool"	/pul/
ɜ	as in "pert"	/pɜt/
ə	as in "apart"	/ə'pat/
ɒ̃	as in "bon voyage"	/bɒ̃ vwa'jaʒ/

(b) *Diphthongs*

aɪ	as in "buy"	/baɪ/
eɪ	as in "bay"	/beɪ/
ɔɪ	as in "boy"	/bɔɪ/
aʊ	as in "how"	/haʊ/
oʊ	as in "hoe"	/hoʊ/
ɪə	as in "here"	/hɪə/
ɛə	as in "hair"	/hɛə/
ʊə	as in "tour"	/tʊə/

(c) *Consonants*

(i) *Plosives*

p	as in "pet"	/pɛt/
b	as in "bet"	/bɛt/
t	as in "tale"	/teɪl/
d	as in "dale"	/deɪl/
k	as in "came"	/keɪm/
g	as in "game"	/geɪm/

(ii) *Fricatives*

f as in "fine" /faɪn/
v as in "vine" /vaɪn/
θ as in "thin" /θɪn/
ð as in "then" /ðɛn/
s as in "seal" /sil/
z as in "zeal" /zil/
ʃ as in "show" /ʃoʊ/
ʒ as in "pleasure" /ˈplɛʒə/
h as in "heal" /hil/
r as in "real" /ril/

(iii) *Affricatives*

tʃ as in "choke" /tʃoʊk/
dʒ as in "joke" /dʒoʊk/

(iv) *Nasals*

m as in "mail" /meɪl/
n as in "nail" /neɪl/
ŋ as in "sing" /sɪŋ/

(v) *Semi-vowels*

j as in "you" /ju/
w as in "woo" /wu/

(vi) *Laterals*

l as in "love" /lʌv/

(d) *Stress*

ˈ as in "clatter" /ˈklætə/
ˌ as in "encyclopedia" /ɛnˌsaɪkləˈpidɪə/

Abbreviations used in the Dictionary

abbrev.	abbreviation	*orig.*	originally
adj.	adjective	*pl.*	plural
adv.	adverb	*p.p.*	past participle
aux.	auxiliary	*prep.*	preposition
Brit	British	*pres.*	present
conj.	conjunction	*pres. part.*	present participle
def.	definition	*pron.*	pronoun
e.g.	for example	*pt.*	past tense
esp.	especially	*Qld*	Queensland
etc.	et cetera	*SA*	South Australia
fol.	followed	*sing.*	singular
i.e.	that is	*Tas.*	Tasmania
indic.	indicative	*US*	United States of America
interj.	interjection		
n.	noun	*v.*	verb
NSW	New South Wales	*v.i.*	intransitive verb
NT	Northern Territory	*Vic.*	Victoria
NZ	New Zealand	*v.t.*	transitive verb
oft.	often	*WA*	Western Australia

A a

A, a /eɪ/ *n., pl.* **A's**, **a's** *or* **As**. **1.** the first letter of the English alphabet. **2.** the first in any series.

a[1] /ə/, *emphatic* /eɪ/ – *indefinite article* used especially before nouns beginning with a consonant sound to mean: **1.** some (indefinite singular referring to one individual of a class). **2.** another. **3.** one. **4.** any (a single). **5.** indefinite plural. Also (*before a vowel sound*), **an**.

a[2] /eɪ/, *weak form* /ə/ – *indefinite article* each; every.

a-[1] a prefix, meaning 'on', 'in', 'into', 'to', 'towards', as in *aside*, etc.

a-[2] a prefix, a reduced form of Old English *of*, as in *akin*, *afresh*, *anew*.

a-[3] a prefix indicating: **1.** up, out, or away, as in *arise*, *awake*. **2.** intensified action, as in *abide*, *amaze*.

a-[4] variant of **ab-** before *m*, *p*, and *v*, as in *avert*.

a-[5] variant of **ad-**, used: **1.** before *sc*, *sp*, *st*, as in *ascend*. **2.** in words of French derivation (often with the sense of increase, addition), as in *amass*.

a-[6] variant of **an-**[1] before consonants.

aardvark /'advak/ *n.* a large, nocturnal, burrowing mammal of Africa.

ab- a prefix meaning 'off', 'away', 'from', as in *abduct*, *abjure*.

aback /ə'bæk/ *adv. in the phr.* **taken aback,** suddenly disconcerted.

abacus /'æbəkəs/ *n., pl.* **-ci** /-si/. a contrivance for calculating, consisting of beads or balls strung on wires or rods set in a frame.

abalone /æbə'louni/ *n.* any of the various univalve, marine molluscs of the genus *Haliotis*.

abandon[1] /ə'bændən/ *v.t.* **1.** to leave completely and finally; forsake utterly; desert. **2.** to give up (something begun) without finishing.

abandon[2] /ə'bændən/ *n.* a giving up to natural impulses; freedom from constraint or conventionality.

abase /ə'beɪs/ *v.t.,* **abased**, **abasing**. to reduce or lower, as in rank, office, estimation; humble; degrade.

abashed /ə'bæʃt/ *adj.* embarrassed; mortified.

abate /ə'beɪt/ *v.,* **abated**, **abating**. – *v.t.* **1.** to reduce in amount, intensity, etc.; lessen. **2.** *Law* to put an end to or suppress (a nuisance); suspend or extinguish (an action); annul (a writ). – *v.i.* **3.** to decrease or become less in strength or violence.

abattoir /'æbətwa, -tɔ/ *n.* a building or place where animals are slaughtered for food. Also, **abattoirs**.

abbess /'æbɛs/ *n.* the female superior of a convent.

abbey /'æbi/ *n., pl.* **-beys**. the religious body or establishment under an abbot or abbess; a monastery or convent.

abbot /'æbət/ *n.* the head or superior of a monastery.

abbreviate /ə'brivieɪt/ *v.t.,* **-ated**, **-ating**. to make brief; make shorter by contraction or omission. – **abbreviator**, **abbreviation**, *n.*

abdicate /'æbdəkeɪt/ *v.i., v.t.,* **-cated**, **-cating**. to renounce a throne or some claim; relinquish a right, power, or trust.

abdomen /'æbdəmən, əb'doumən/ *n.* that part of the body of a mammal between the thorax and the pelvis; the belly. – **abdominal**, *adj.*

abduct /əb'dʌkt, æb-/ *v.t.* to carry off surreptitiously or by force, especially to kidnap. – **abduction**, *n.*

aberrant /'æbərənt, ə'bɛrənt/ *adj.* **1.** straying from the right or usual course. **2.** deviating from the ordinary or normal type.

aberration /æbə'reɪʃən/ *n.* **1.** the act of wandering from the usual way or normal course. **2.** deviation from truth or moral rectitude. **3.** lapse from a sound mental state.

abet /ə'bɛt/ *v.t.,* **abetted**, **abetting**. to encourage or countenance by aid or approval (used chiefly in a bad sense). – **abetment**, *n.* – **abetter**; *Law*, **abettor**, *n.*

abeyance /ə'beɪəns/ *n.* temporary inactivity or suspension.

abhor /əb'hɔ/ *v.t.,* **-horred**, **-horring**. to regard with repugnance; loathe or abominate. – **abhorrer**, *n.*

abhorrent /əb'hɒrənt/ *adj.* **1.** utterly opposed (fol. by *to*). **2.** exciting horror; detestable.

abide /ə'baɪd/ *v.,* **abode** /ə'boud/ *or* **abided**, **abiding**. – *v.i.* **1.** to remain; continue; stay. **2.** to continue in a certain condition; remain steadfast or faithful. – *v.t.* **3.** to stand one's ground against; await or sustain defiantly. **4.** *Colloquial* to put up with; tolerate.

ability /ə'bɪləti/ *n., pl.* **-ties**. power or capacity to do or act in any relation.

abject /'æbdʒɛkt/ *adj.* **1.** utterly humiliating or disheartening. **2.** contemptible; despicable. **3.** humble; servile.

abjure /əb'dʒuə/ *v.t.,* **-jured**, **-juring**. **1.** to renounce or repudiate; retract, especially with solemnity. **2.** to forswear.

ablation /ə'bleɪʃən/ *n.* **1.** *Medicine* removal of organs, growths, etc., from the body, as by surgery. **2.** the melting or wearing away of a solid body.

ablaze /ə'bleɪz/ *adj., adv.* **1.** gleaming as if on fire. **2.** excited.

able /'eɪbəl/ *adj.,* **abler**, **ablest**. **1.** having sufficient power, strength, or qualifications; qualified. **2.** showing talent or knowledge. – **ably**, *adj.*

-able a suffix used to form adjectives to denote ability, liability, tendency, worthiness, or likelihood, as in *teachable*, *perishable*, *obtainable*.

able-bodied seaman /'eɪbəl-bɒdid/ *n.* an experienced seaman who has passed certain tests in the practice of seamanship. Also, **able seaman**.

ablution /ə'bluʃən/ *n.* **1.** a cleansing with water or other liquid, as in ceremonial purification. **2.** (*pl.*) the act of washing oneself.

abnegate /'æbnəgeɪt/ *v.t.,* **-gated**, **-gating**. to refuse or deny to oneself; reject; renounce.

abnormal /æb'nɔməl/ *adj.* not conforming to rule; deviating from the type or standard.

aboard /ə'bɔd/ *adv.* **1.** on board; on or in a ship, train, bus, etc. **2.** alongside.

abode /ə'boʊd/ *n.* **1.** a dwelling place. **2.** continuance in a place; sojourn; stay. – *v.* **3.** past tense and past participle of **abide**.

abolish /ə'bɒlɪʃ/ *v.t.* to put an end to; annul; destroy.

abolition /æbə'lɪʃən/ *n.* utter destruction; annulment. – **abolitionary**, *adj.*

abominable /ə'bɒmənəbəl, ə'bɒmnəbəl/ *adj.* detestable; loathsome.

abominate /ə'bɒməneɪt/ *v.t.*, **-nated**, **-nating**. **1.** to abhor. **2.** to dislike strongly.

abomination /əbɒmə'neɪʃən/ *n.* **1.** an object greatly disliked or abhorred. **2.** intense aversion. **3.** a detestable action; shameful vice.

aboriginal /æbə'rɪdʒənəl/ *adj.* **1.** (*usu. cap.*) of or relating to the Australian Aborigines. **2.** of or relating to an aborigine (def. 2); indigenous. – *n.* **3.** (*usu. cap.*) an Australian Aborigine.

Aboriginal law *n.* the traditional laws of the Australian Aborigines. Also, **Aboriginal customary law**.

aborigine /æbə'rɪdʒəni/ *n.* **1.** (*usu. cap.*) one of a race of tribal peoples, the earliest known to live in Australia. **2.** (generally) one of a people living in a country or place from the earliest known times.

abort /ə'bɔt/ *v.i.* **1.** to miscarry before the foetus is viable. **2.** to come to nothing; fail. – *v.t.* **3.** to cause to abort. – **abortive**, *adj.*

abortion /ə'bɔʃən/ *n.* **1.** the expulsion or removal of a human foetus before it is viable. **2.** anything which fails in its progress before it is matured or perfected. – **abortionist**, *n.*

abound /ə'baʊnd/ *v.i.* **1.** to be in great plenty. **2.** to be rich (fol. by *in*). **3.** to be filled; teem (fol. by *with*). – **abounding**, *adj.*

about /ə'baʊt/ *prep.* **1.** of; concerning; in regard to. **2.** near; close to. **3.** on every side of; around. **4.** on the point of (followed by an infinitive). **5.** concerned with; engaged in doing. – *adv.* **6.** near in time, number, degree, etc.; approximately. **7.** on every side in every direction. **8.** half round; in the reverse direction. **9.** to and fro; here and there. **10.** in rotation or succession; alternately. – *adj.* **11. up and about,** astir; active (after sleep).

about-face /əbaʊt-'feɪs/ *n., v.,* **-faced**, **-facing**. – *n.* **1.** a complete, sudden change in position, principle, attitude, etc. – *v.i.* **2.** to turn in the opposite direction. Also, **about-turn**.

above /ə'bʌv/ *adv.* **1.** in or to a higher place; overhead. **2.** higher in rank or power. **3.** before in order, especially in a book or writing. – *prep.* **4.** in or to a higher place than. **5.** more in quantity or number than. **6.** superior to, in rank or authority. **7.** not capable of (an undesirable thought, action, etc.). – *adj.* **8.** said, mentioned, or written above.

aboveboard /əbʌv'bɔd/ *adv., adj.* openly; without tricks, deceit or disguise.

abrade /ə'breɪd/ *v.,* **abraded**, **abrading**. – *v.t.* **1.** to scrape off. – *v.i.* **2.** to wear down by friction.

abrasion /ə'breɪʒən/ *n.* **1.** the result of rubbing or abrading; an abraded spot or place. **2.** the act or process of abrading.

abrasive /ə'breɪsɪv, -zɪv/ *n.* **1.** any material or substance used for grinding, polishing, lapping, etc., as emery or sand. – *adj.* **2.** tending to produce abrasion.

abreast /ə'brɛst/ *adv.* **1.** side by side. **2.** alongside, in progress or attainment; equally advanced (fol. by *of* or *with*).

abridge /ə'brɪdʒ/ *v.t.,* **abridged**, **abridging**. to shorten by condensation or omission; rewrite or reconstruct on a smaller scale.

abroad /ə'brɔd/ *adv.* **1.** in or to a foreign country or countries. **2.** astir; at large; in circulation.

abrogate /'æbrəgeɪt/ *v.t.,* **-gated**, **-gating**. to abolish summarily; annul by an authoritative act; repeal.

abrupt /ə'brʌpt/ *adj.* **1.** terminating or changing suddenly. **2.** sudden; unceremonious.

abs- variant of **ab-** before *c, q, t,* as in *abscond.*

abscess /'æbsəs/ *n.* a localised collection of pus in a cavity. – **abscessed**, *adj.*

abscind /əb'sɪnd/ *v.t.* to cut off; sever.

abscission /əb'sɪʒən/ *n.* the act of cutting off; sudden termination.

abscond /æb'skɒnd, əb-/ *v.i.* to depart in a sudden and secret manner, especially to avoid legal process.

absent /'æbsənt/ *adj.,* /əb'sɛnt/ *v.* – *adj.* **1.** not in a certain place at a given time; away (opposed to *present*). **2.** lacking. **3.** absentminded. – *v.t.* **4.** to take or keep (oneself) away. – **absence**, *n.*

absentee /æbsən'ti/ *n.* someone who is absent.

absenteeism /æbsən'tiɪzəm/ *n.* the practice of absenting oneself from duties, studies, employment, etc., often for inadequate reasons.

absent-minded /æbsənt-'maɪndəd/ *adj.* forgetful of one's immediate surroundings; preoccupied.

absolute /'æbsəlut/ *adj.* **1.** free from imperfection; complete; perfect. **2.** free from restriction or limitation; unqualified. **3.** arbitrary or despotic. **4.** viewed independently; not comparative or relative. **5.** positive. **6.** *Physics* **a.** as nearly independent as possible of arbitrary standards or of properties of special substances or systems. **b.** relating to a system of units based on some primary units, especially units of length, mass, and time. – **absolutely**, *adv.*

absolute zero *n.* the lowest possible temperature at which the particles whose motion constitutes heat would be at rest, being defined as **zero kelvin** or -273.15 degrees Celsius (or -459.67 degrees Fahrenheit). Cf. **absolute** (def. 6a).

absolution /æbsə'luʃən/ *n.* **1.** release from consequences, obligations, or penalties. **2.** the state of being absolved.

absolve /əb'zɒlv/ *v.t.,* **-solved**, **-solving**. **1.** to free from the consequences or penalties of actions (fol. by *from*). **2.** to set free or release, as from some duty, obligation, or responsibility (fol. by *from*).

absorb /əb'sɔb, -'zɔb/ *v.t.* **1.** to swallow up the identity or individuality of. **2.** to engross wholly. **3.** to suck up or drink in (liquids). **4.** to assimilate (ideas, knowledge, etc.). – **absorbent**, *adj.*

absorption /əb'sɔpʃən, -'zɔp-/ *n.* **1.** assimilation. **2.** a taking in or reception by molecular or chemical action. **3.** preoccupation.

abstain /əb'steɪn/ *v.i.* to refrain voluntarily, especially from doing or enjoying something (fol. by *from*). – **abstention**, *n.*

abstemious /əb'stimiəs/ *adj.* sparing in diet; moderate in the use of food and drink; temperate.

abstinence /'æbstənəns/ *n.* forbearance from any indulgence of appetite, especially from the drinking of alcohol. – **abstinent**, *adj.* – **abstinently**, *adv.*

abstract /'æbstrækt/ *adj., n.*; /əb'strækt/ *for defs 5 and 6*, /'æbstrækt/ *for def. 7 v.* – *adj.* **1.** theoretical; not applied. **2.** difficult to understand; abstruse. – *n.* **3.** a summary of a statement, document, speech, etc. **4.** an idea or term considered apart from some material basis or object. – *v.t.* **5.** to draw or take away; remove. **6.** to consider as a general object apart from special circumstances. **7.** to summarise.

abstracted /əb'stræktəd/ *adj.* lost in thought; preoccupied.

abstraction /əb'strækʃən/ *n.* **1.** an abstract or general idea or term. **2.** the act of taking away or separating; withdrawal. **3.** absent-mindedness; reverie.

abstract of title *n.* a chronological statement of the instruments and events, traced back to the original grant of title, under which a person is currently entitled to property; not applicable to property held under Torrens Title, title to which depends upon registration.

abstruse /əb'strus/ *adj.* difficult to understand; esoteric.

absurd /əb'sɜd, -'zɜd/ *adj.* contrary to reason or common sense; ridiculous. – **absurdity**, *n.*

abundant /ə'bʌndənt/ *adj.* **1.** present in great quantity; fully sufficient. **2.** possessing in great quantity; abounding (fol. by *in*). – **abundance**, *n.*

abuse /ə'bjuz/ *v.*, **abused**, **abusing**; /ə'bjus/ *n.* – *v.t.* **1.** to use wrongly or improperly; misuse. **2.** to revile; malign. – *n.* **3.** wrong or improper use; misuse. **4.** insulting language. – **abuser**, *n.* – **abusive**, *adj.*

abut /ə'bʌt/ *v.i.*, **abutted**, **abutting**. to be adjacent to (often fol. by *on*, *upon*, or *against*). – **abuttal**, *n.*

abysmal /ə'bɪzməl/ *adj.* **1.** immeasurable. **2.** immeasurably bad.

abyss /ə'bɪs/ *n.* **1.** any deep, immeasurable space. **2.** anything profound and unfathomable. – **abyssal**, *adj.*

ac- variant of **ad-**(by assimilation) before *c* and *qu*, as in *accede*, *acquire*, etc.

-ac an adjective suffix meaning 'pertaining to', as in *cardiac*.

AC /eɪ 'si/ **1.** Companion of the Order of Australia. **2.** *Electricity* alternating current.

acacia /ə'keɪʃə, ə'keɪsiə/ *n.* any tree or shrub of the genus *Acacia*, native in warm regions; usually known as wattle in Australia.

academic /ækə'dɛmɪk/ *adj.* **1.** relating to an advanced institution of learning; relating to higher education. **2.** relating to those university subjects which are concerned with the refinement of the mind rather than the learning of skills (opposed to *technical*). **3.** theoretical; not practical. – *n.* **4.** a member of a college or university.

academy /ə'kædəmi/ *n., pl.* **-mies**. **1.** an association or institution for the promotion of literature, science, or art. **2.** a school for instruction in a particular art or science.

accede /ək'sid/ *v.i.*, **-ceded**, **-ceding**. **1.** to give consent; agree; yield. **2.** to attain, as an office or dignity; arrive at (fol. by *to*).

accelerate /ək'sɛləreɪt, æk-/ *v.*, **-rated**, **-rating**. – *v.t.* **1.** to cause to move or advance faster. **2.** *Physics* to change the magnitude and/or direction of the velocity of a body. – *v.i.* **3.** to become faster; increase in speed. – **acceleration**, *n.*

accelerator /ək'sɛləreɪtə, æk-/ *n.* *Motor Vehicles* a device which increases the speed of the machine by opening and closing the throttle, especially one operated by the foot.

accelerator principle *n.* an economic principle which states that an increase (or decrease) in the rate of consumer demand will cause an acceleration (or deceleration) in the rate of investment in machines to produce these consumer goods.

accent /'æksɛnt/ *n.*, /æk'sɛnt/ *v.* – *n.* **1.** the distinctive character of a vowel or syllable determined by its degree or pattern of stress or musical tone. **2.** a mark indicating stress, musical tone, or vowel quality. **3.** *Prosody* regularly recurring stress. **4.** characteristic style of pronunciation as of a dialect. **5.** *Music* stress or emphasis given to certain notes. – *v.t.* **6.** to pronounce (a vowel, syllable, or word) with one of the distinctive accents of the language, especially with a stress accent. **7.** to mark with a written accent or accents.

accentuate /ək'sɛntʃueɪt/ *v.t.*, **-ated**, **-ating**. to emphasise.

accept /ək'sɛpt/ *v.t.* **1.** to take or receive (something offered); receive with approval or favour. **2.** to admit and agree to. **3.** to accommodate oneself to. **4.** to understand. **5.** *Commerce* to acknowledge, by signature, as calling for payment, and thus to agree to pay, as a draft. – **acceptance**, *n.*

acceptable /ək'sɛptəbəl/ *adj.* capable or worthy of being accepted.

acceptance house *n.* a bank which specialises in handling bills of exchange for foreign trade.

accepted /ək'sɛptəd/ *adj.* customary; established; approved.

access /'æksɛs/ *n.* **1.** the act or privilege of coming (fol. by *to*); admittance; approach. **2.** way, means, or opportunity of approach. **3.** a parent's right to see a child. **4.** an attack, as of disease. – *v.t.* **5.** *Computers* to locate and provide means of getting (information) out of or into a computer storage. – *adj.* **6.** *Radio*, *TV*, *etc.* run by special-interest or minority groups who wish to transmit their own programs.

accessible /ək'sɛsəbəl/ *adj.* **1.** easy of access; approachable. **2.** attainable.

3. open to the influence of (fol. by *to*).

accession /ək'sɛʃən/ *n.* **1.** the act of coming into the possession of a right, dignity, office, etc. **2.** an increase by something added. **3.** consent. **4.** *International Law* formal acceptance of an agreement between states.

accessory /ək'sɛsəri/ *n., pl.* **-ries**. **1.** something added or attached for convenience, attractiveness, etc. **2.** Also, **accessary**. *Law* the person who is not the chief actor at a felony, nor present at its perpetration, but yet is in some way concerned therein (either before or after the fact committed).

access time *n.* the time taken to reach information stored in a computer.

accident /'æksədənt/ *n.* **1.** an undesirable or unfortunate happening; mishap. **2.** anything that happens unexpectedly, without design, or by chance. – **accidental**, *adj.*

acclaim /ə'kleɪm/ *v.t.* **1.** to salute with words or sounds of joy or approval; applaud. **2.** to announce or proclaim by acclamation. -*n.* **3.** strong approval or applause.

acclamation /æklə'meɪʃən/ *n.* **1.** a shout or other demonstration of welcome, goodwill, or applause. **2.** the act of acclaiming. – **acclamatory**, *adj.*

acclimatise = acclimatize /ə'klaɪmətaɪz/ *v.*, **-tised**, **-tising**. – *v.t.* **1.** to habituate to a new climate or environment. – *v.i.* **2.** to become habituated to a new climate or environment.

accolade /'ækəleɪd/ *n.* **1.** a ceremony used in conferring knighthood. **2.** any award; honour.

accommodate /ə'kɒmədeɪt/ *v.t.*, **-dated**, **-dating**. **1.** to do a kindness or a favour to. **2.** to provide suitably. **3.** to make suitable or consistent; adapt. **4.** to bring into harmony; adjust; reconcile. **5.** to find or provide space for (something).

accommodation /əkɒmə'deɪʃən/ *n.* **1.** the act or result of accommodating. **2.** lodging, or food and lodging.

accommodation bill *n.* a bill, draft, note, etc., drawn, accepted or endorsed by one person for another without consideration, to enable the second person to obtain credit or raise money.

accompaniment /ə'kʌmpnimənt/ *n.* **1.** something incidental or added for ornament, symmetry, etc. **2.** *Music* that part of a composition which provides the harmonic and rhythmic backing to a melodic line, especially a song.

accompany /ə'kʌmpəni, ə'kʌmpni/ *v.t.*, **-nied**, **-nying**. **1.** to go or be in company with. **2.** *Music* to play or sing an accompaniment to.

accomplice /ə'kʌmpləs, -'kɒm-/ *n.* an associate in a crime; partner in wrongdoing.

accomplish /ə'kʌmplɪʃ, -'kɒm-/ *v.t.* to bring to pass; carry out; finish.

accomplished /ə'kʌmplɪʃt, -'kɒm-/ *adj.* **1.** completed; effected. **2.** perfected; expert. **3.** perfected in the graces and attainments of polite society.

accomplishment /ə'kʌmplɪʃmənt, -'kɒm-/ *n.* **1.** the act of carrying into effect; fulfilment. **2.** anything accomplished; achievement. **3.** (*often pl.*) an acquired art or grace; polite attainment.

accord /ə'kɔd/ *v.i.* **1.** to be in correspondence or harmony; agree. – *v.t.* **2.** to grant; concede. – *n.* **3.** just correspondence of things; harmony of relation. **4.** consent or concurrence of opinions or wills; agreement. **5. of one's own accord,** voluntarily. **6. with one accord,** with spontaneous agreement.

according /ə'kɔdɪŋ/ *adv.* **1. according to, a.** in accordance with. **b.** proportionately. **c.** on the authority of; as stated by. **2. according as,** conformably or proportionately as. – *adj.* **3.** agreeing.

accordion /ə'kɔdiən/ *n.* **1.** a portable wind instrument with bellows and button-like keys sounded by means of metallic reeds. – *adj.* **2.** having folds like the bellows of an accordion.

accost /ə'kɒst/ *v.t.* to approach, especially with a greeting or remark.

accouchement /ə'kutʃmənt, -'kuʃ-/ *n.* period of confinement in childbirth; labour.

account /ə'kaʊnt/ *n.* **1.** a verbal or written recital of particular transactions and events; narrative. **2.** a statement of reasons, causes, etc., explaining some event. **3.** a statement of pecuniary transactions. **4.** *Bookkeeping* **a.** a formal record of debits and credits. **b.** a balance of a specified period's receipts and expenditures. **5. bring** (or **call**) **to account,** to demand explanation or justification of actions. **6. in account with,** having a credit arrangement with. **7. on account of, a.** because of; by reason of. **b.** for the sake of. **8. on** (or **to**) **account,** as an interim payment. – *v.i.* **9.** to give an explanation (fol. by *for*). **10.** to answer concerning one's conduct, duties, etc. (fol. by *for*). **11.** to cause death, capture, etc. (fol. by *for*). **12.** to render an account, especially of money. – *v.t.* **13.** to count; consider as.

accountant /ə'kaʊntənt/ *n.* a person whose profession is analysing and communicating economic information for the judgment and decision-making of individuals and organisations who seek it. – **accountancy**, *n.*

accounting /ə'kaʊntɪŋ/ *n.* the art of analysing the financial position and operating results of a business firm from a study of its sales, purchases, overheads, etc.

accredit /ə'krɛdət/ *v.t.* **1.** to ascribe or attribute to (fol. by *with*). **2.** to furnish (an officially recognised agent) with credentials. **3.** to certify as meeting official requirements. **4.** to believe.

accretion /ə'kriʃən/ *n.* **1.** an increase by natural growth or by gradual external addition. **2.** an extraneous addition. **3.** the growing together of separate parts into a single whole.

accrue /ə'kru/ *v.i.*, **-crued**, **-cruing**. to happen or result as a natural growth; come or fall as an addition or increment. – **accrual**, **accruement**, *n.*

accrued interest *n.* the amount of interest accumulated at a given time but not yet paid (or received).

acculturation /əkʌltʃə'reɪʃən/ *n.* the process of borrowing between cultures, resulting in new and blended patterns.

accumulate /ə'kjumjəleɪt/ *v.*, **-lated**, **-lating**. – *v.t.* **1.** to heap up; gather as into a mass. – *v.i.* **2.** to grow into a heap or mass; form an increasing quantity. – **accumulation**, *n.* – **accumulative**, *adj.*

accumulator /ə'kjumjəleɪtə/ *n.* an electric device in arithmetic machines, as the main register of a digital computer, where the arithmetic operations are performed.

accurate /'ækjərət/ *adj.* in exact conformity to truth, to a standard or rule, or to a model; free from error or defect. – **accuracy**, **accurateness**, *n.* – **accurately**, *adv.*

accursed /ə'kɜsəd, ə'kɜst/ *adj.* **1.** subject to a curse; ruined. **2.** worthy of curses; detestable.

accusation /ˌækju'zeɪʃən/ *n.* **1.** a charge of wrongdoing; imputation of guilt or blame. **2.** the specific offence charged.

accusatory /ə'kjuzətəri, -tri/ *adj.* containing an accusation; accusing.

accuse /ə'kjuz/ *v.t.*, **-cused**, **-cusing**. **1.** to bring a charge against; charge with the fault or crime (*of*). **2.** to blame.

accustom /ə'kʌstəm/ *v.t.* to familiarise by custom or use; habituate.

accustomed /ə'kʌstəmd/ *adj.* customary; habitual.

ace /eɪs/ *n.* **1.** a single spot or mark on a card or die. **2.** (in tennis, badminton, etc.) a serve which the opponent fails to touch. **3.** a highly skilled person. – *adj. Colloquial* **4.** excellent.

-aceous a suffix of adjectives used in scientific terminology, indicating: **1.** of or relating to. **2.** of the nature of, or similar to. **3.** belonging to a scientific grouping, especially a botanic family.

acerbity /ə'sɜbəti/ *n.*, *pl.* **-ties**. **1.** sourness, with roughness or astringency of taste. **2.** harshness or severity, as of temper or expression. – **acerbic**, *adj.*

acetate /'æsəteɪt/ *n.* a salt or ester of acetic acid. – **acetated**, *adj.*

acetone /'æsətoʊn/ *n.* a colourless, volatile, flammable liquid, used as a solvent and in varnishes, etc.

acetylene /ə'sɛtəlin, -lən/ *n.* a colourless gas, used in metal welding, as an illuminant, and in organic synthesis.

ache /eɪk/ *v.*, **ached**, **aching**, *n.* – *v.i.* **1.** to have or be in continuous pain. – *n.* **2.** pain of some duration, in opposition to sudden twinges or spasmodic pain.

achieve /ə'tʃiv/ *v.t.*, **achieved**, **achieving**. to bring to a successful end; accomplish.

achievement /ə'tʃivmənt/ *n.* **1.** something accomplished; a great or heroic deed. **2.** the act of achieving; accomplishment.

acid[1] /'æsəd/ *n.* **1.** *Chemistry* a compound which reacts with an alkali to form a salt. **2.** a substance with a sour taste. – *adj.* **3.** sharp or sour. – **acidic**, *adj.* – **acidity**, *n.*

acid[2] /æsəd/ *n. Colloquial* LSD.

acidulous /ə'sɪdʒələs/ *adj.* slightly acid.

-acious an adjective suffix made by adding **-ous** to nouns ending in **-acity** (the *-ty* being dropped), indicating a tendency towards or abundance of something, as *audacious.*

-acity a suffix of nouns denoting quality or a state of being, and the like.

acknowledge /ək'nɒlɪdʒ/ *v.t.*, **-edged**, **-edging**. **1.** to admit to be real or true; recognise the existence, truth, or fact of. **2.** to express recognition or realisation of. **3.** to recognise the authority or claims of. **4.** to indicate appreciation or gratitude for. **5.** to admit or certify the receipt of. – **acknowledgeable**, *adj.* – **acknowledger**, *n.* – **acknowledgment = acknowledgement**, *n.*

acme /'ækmi/ *n.* the highest point; culmination.

acne /'ækni/ *n.* an inflammatory disease of the sebaceous glands, characterised by an eruption (often pustular) of the skin, especially of the face.

acolyte /'ækəlaɪt/ *n.* an attendant; an assistant.

acorn /'eɪkɔn/ *n.* the fruit of the oak, a nut in a hardened scaly cup.

acoustic /ə'kustɪk/ *adj.* **1.** Also, **acoustical**. relating to the sense or organs of hearing, or to the science of sound. **2.** *Music* of or relating to instruments whose sound is not electronically amplified.

acquaint /ə'kweɪnt/ *v.t.* to make more or less familiar or conversant (fol. by *with*).

acquaintance /ə'kweɪntəns/ *n.* **1.** a person (or persons) known to one, especially a person with whom one is not on terms of great intimacy. **2.** the state of being acquainted; personal knowledge.

acquiesce /ˌækwi'ɛs/ *v.i.*, **-esced**, **-escing**. to assent tacitly; comply quietly; agree; consent (often fol. by *in*).

acquire /ə'kwaɪə/ *v.t.*, **-quired**, **-quiring**. to come into possession of; get as one's own. – **acquisition**, *n.*

acquired immune deficiency syndrome *n.* → **AIDS**.

acquisitive /ə'kwɪzətɪv/ *adj.* fond of acquiring possessions.

acquit /ə'kwɪt/ *v.t.*, **-quitted**, **-quitting**. **1.** to relieve from a charge of fault or crime. **2.** to release or discharge (a person) from an obligation. – **acquittal**, *n.*

acreage /'eɪkərɪdʒ/ *n.* extent in acres.

acrid /'ækrəd/ *adj.* sharp or biting.

acrimony /'ækrəməni/ *n.*, *pl.* **-nies**. sharpness or severity of temper; bitterness of expression proceeding from anger or ill nature. – **acrimonious**, *adj.*

acro- a word element meaning 'tip', 'top', 'apex', or 'edge'.

acrobat /'ækrəbæt/ *n.* a skilled performer who can walk on a tightrope, perform on a trapeze, or do other similar feats. – **acrobatic**, *adj.* – **acrobatically**, *adv.*

acronym /'ækrənɪm/ *n.* a word formed from the initial letters of other words, as *radar* (from *radio detection and ranging*) or *ANZAC* (from *Australian and New Zealand Army Corps*).

acropolis /ə'krɒpələs/ *n.* the citadel of an ancient Greek city.

across /ə'krɒs/ *prep.* **1.** from side to side of. **2.** on the other side of. **3.** so as to meet or fall in with. – *adv.* **4.** from one side to another. **5.** on the other side. **6.** crosswise.

acrostic /ə'krɒstɪk/ *n.* a series of lines or verses in which the first, last, or other particular letters form a word, phrase, the alphabet, etc.

acrylic /ə'krɪlɪk/ *adj.* of or relating to fibres formed by the polymerisation of acrylonitrile, or to fabrics woven from such fibres.

acrylonitrile /əˌkrɪloʊ'naɪtraɪl/ *n.* a colourless toxic organic chemical used in the manufacture of acrylic fibres, thermoplastics, synthetic rubber, etc.

act /ækt/ *n.* **1.** anything done or performed; a doing; deed. **2.** the process of doing. **3.** a decree, edict, law, statute, judgment, resolve, or award. **4.** one of the main divisions of a play or opera. **5.** an individual performance forming part of a variety show, radio program, etc. **6.** behaviour which is contrived and artificial, somewhat in the manner of a theatrical performance. – *v.i.* **7.** to do something; exert energy or force; be employed or operative. **8.** to behave. **9.** to pretend. **10.** to perform as an actor. **11.** to serve or substitute (fol. by *for*). **12. act up,** *Colloquial* **a.** to play up; take advantage. **b.** (of a car, etc.) to malfunction. – *v.t.* **13.** to represent (a fictitious or historical character) with one's person. **14.** to feign; counterfeit. **15.** to behave as.

actinium /æk'tɪniəm/ *n.* a radioactive chemical element occurring in pitchblende. *Symbol*: Ac

action /'ækʃən/ *n.* **1.** the process or state of acting or of being active. **2.** something done; an act; deed. **3.** way or manner of moving. **4.** military and naval combat. **5.** the main subject or story, as distinguished from an incidental episode. **6.** *Law* **a.** a proceeding instituted by one party against another. **b. take action,** to commence legal proceedings.

actionable /'ækʃənəbəl/ *adj.* furnishing ground for a law suit. – **actionably**, *adv.*

activate /'æktəveɪt/ *v.t.*, **-vated**, **-vating**. **1.** to make active. **2.** *Physics* to render radioactive. **3.** to aerate (sewage) as a purification measure. – **activation**, *n.*

activist /'æktəvəst/ *n.* a zealous worker for a cause, especially a political cause.

activity /æk'tɪvəti/ *n.*, *pl.* **-ties**. **1.** the state of action; doing. **2.** a specific deed or action; sphere of action. **3.** liveliness; agility.

act of God *n. Law* a direct, sudden, and irresistible action of natural forces, such as could not humanly have been foreseen or prevented.

actor /'æktə/ *n.* someone who plays the part of a character in a dramatic performance.

actress /'æktrəs/ *n.* a female actor.

actual /'æktʃuəl/ *adj.* **1.** existing in act or fact; real. **2.** now existing; present.

actuality /æktʃu'æləti/ *n.*, *pl.* **-ties**. **1.** actual existence; reality. **2.** (*pl.*) actual conditions or circumstances; facts.

actually /'æktʃuəli, 'æktʃəli/ *adv.* as an actual or existing fact; really.

actuary /'æktʃuəri/ *n.*, *pl.* **-ries**. a statistician who computes risks, rates, etc., according to probabilities indicated by recorded facts. – **actuarial**, *adj.* – **actuarially**, *adv.*

actuate /'æktʃueɪt/ *v.t.*, **-ated**, **-ating**. **1.** to incite to action. **2.** to put into action.

acuity /ə'kjuəti/ *n.* sharpness; acuteness.

acumen /'ækjəmən/ *n.* quickness of perception; mental acuteness; keen insight.

acupressure /'ækjəprɛsə, 'ækə-/ *n.* the massage of muscles and application of pressure to acupuncture points to promote well-being or to cure illness; shiatsu.

acupuncture /'ækjəpʌŋktʃə, 'ækə-/ *n.* a Chinese medical practice to treat disease, establish diagnosis or relieve pain, by puncturing specific areas of skin with long sharp needles. – **acupuncturist**, *n.*

acute /ə'kjut/ *adj.* **1.** sharp at the end; ending in a point (opposed to *blunt* or *obtuse*). **2.** sharp in effect; intense; poignant. **3.** severe; crucial. **4.** brief and severe, as disease (opposed to *chronic*). **5.** sharp or penetrating in intellect, insight, or perception. **6.** having quick sensibility. **7.** *Geometry, etc.* (of an angle) less than 90°.

-acy a suffix of nouns of quality, state, office, etc., many of which accompany adjectives in *-acious* or nouns or adjectives in *-ate*, as in *efficacy*, etc., *advocacy*, etc., *accuracy*, etc.

ad /æd/ *n. Colloquial* an advertisement.

adage /'ædɪdʒ/ *n.* a proverb.

adamant /'ædəmənt/ *adj.* firm in purpose or opinion; unyielding.

adapt /ə'dæpt/ *v.t.* **1.** to make suitable to requirements; adjust or modify fittingly. – *v.i.* **2.** to adjust oneself. – **adaptive**, *adj.* – **adaptation**, *n.*

adaptable /ə'dæptəbəl/ *adj.* **1.** capable of being adapted. **2.** able to adapt oneself easily to new conditions.

A-D converter /'eɪ-di/ *n.* → **analog-to-digital converter**. Also, **A-to-D converter**.

add /æd/ *v.t.* **1.** to unite or join so as to increase the number, quantity, size, or importance. **2.** to find the sum of (often fol. by *up*). **3.** to say or write further. **4.** to include (fol. by *in*). – *v.i.* **5.** to perform the arithmetical operation of addition. **6.** to be or serve as an addition (fol. by *to*). **7. add up, a.** to amount (*to*). **b.** to make the desired or expected total. **c.** *Colloquial* to make sense, be logically consistent.

ADD /eɪ di 'di/ *n.* → **attention deficit disorder**.

addendum /ə'dɛndəm/ *n.*, *pl.* **-da** /-də/. a thing to be added; an addition.

adder /'ædə/ *n.* the common viper.

addict /'ædɪkt/ *n.* someone who is addicted to a practice or habit.

addicted /ə'dɪktəd/ *adj.* devoted or given up (to a practice, habit, or substance) (fol. by *to*).

addiction /ə'dɪkʃən/ *n.* the state of being addicted to some habit, practice, or substance, especially to narcotics. – **addictive**, *adj.*

addition /ə'dɪʃən/ *n.* **1.** the act or process of adding or uniting. **2.** the process of uniting two or more numbers into one sum, denoted by the symbol + . **3.** the result of adding; anything added. – **additional**, *adj.*

additive /'ædətɪv/ *n.* something added.

address /ə'drɛs, 'ædrɛs/ *n.*, /ə'drɛs/ *v.* – *n.* **1.** a formal speech or writing directed to a person or a group of persons. **2.** a direction as to name and residence inscribed on a letter, etc. **3.** a place where a person lives or may be reached. **4.** *Computers* a number or symbol which identifies a particular register in the memory of a digital computer. **5.** manner of speaking to persons; personal bearing in conversation. **6.** skilful management; adroitness. – *v.t.* **7.** to speak to a person in an official position, such as a judge, governor-general, etc., using their formal title. **8.** to direct to the ear or attention. **9.** to direct the energy or force of (used reflexively, fol. by *to*). – **addresser = addressor**, *n.* – **addressee**, *n.*

addressograph /ə'drɛsəgræf, -graf/ *n.* a machine that prints addresses upon envelopes, etc., from stencils.

adduce /ə'djus/ *v.t.*, **-duced**, **-ducing**. to bring forward in argument; cite as pertinent or conclusive.

-ade[1] **1.** a suffix found in nouns denoting action or process, product or result of action, person or persons acting, often irregularly attached, as in *blockade*, *escapade*, *masquerade*. **2.** a noun suffix indicating a drink made of a particular fruit, as in *lemonade*.

-ade[2] a collective suffix, as in *decade*.

adeno- a word element meaning 'gland'. Also (*before vowels*), **aden-**.

adenoid /'ædənɔɪd/ *n.* (*usu. pl.*) a mass of lymphoid tissue in the upper pharynx; enlargement can prevent nasal breathing, especially in young children.

adept /ə'dɛpt/ *adj.* highly skilled; proficient; expert.

adequate /'ædəkwət/ *adj.* fully sufficient, suitable, or fit (often fol. by *to* or *for*). – **adequacy**, *n.*

ADHD /eɪ di eɪtʃ 'di/ *n.* → **attention deficit hyperactive disorder**.

adhere /əd'hɪə/ *v.i.*, **-hered**, **-hering**. **1.** to stick fast; cleave; cling (fol. by *to*). **2.** to be devoted; be attached as a follower or upholder (fol. by *to*). – **adhesion**, *n.*

adherent /əd'hɪərənt, -'hɛrənt/ *n.* **1.** someone who follows or upholds a leader, cause, etc.; supporter; follower (fol. by *of*). – *adj.* **2.** sticking; clinging; adhering.

adhesive /əd'hisɪv, -'hizɪv/ *adj.* **1.** clinging; tenacious; sticking fast. – *n.* **2.** a substance for sticking things together.

ad hoc /æd 'hɒk/ *adj.* **1.** for this (special purpose); an **ad hoc committee** is one set up to deal with one subject only. **2.** impromptu; an **ad hoc decision** is one made with regard to the exigencies of the moment. – *adv.* **3.** with respect to this (subject or thing).

ad infinitum /ˌæd ɪnfə'naɪtəm/ *adv.* to infinity; endlessly; without limit.

adipose /'ædəpoʊs/ *adj.* fatty.

adjacent /ə'dʒeɪsənt/ *adj.* lying near, close, or contiguous; adjoining; neighbouring. – **adjacency**, *n.*

adjective /'ædʒəktɪv/ *n. Grammar* one of the major parts of speech of many languages, comprising words used to modify or limit a noun. – **adjectival**, *adj.*

adjoin /ə'dʒɔɪn/ *v.t.* **1.** to be in connection or contact with; abut on. – *v.i.* **2.** to lie or be next, or in contact. – **adjoining**, *adj.*

adjourn /ə'dʒɜn/ *v.t.* **1.** to suspend the meeting of, as a public or private body, to a future day or to another place. – *v.i.* **2.** to postpone, suspend, or transfer proceedings. – **adjournment**, *n.*

adjudge /ə'dʒʌdʒ/ *v.t.*, **-judged**, **-judging**. **1.** to pronounce formally; decree. **2.** to award judicially; assign.

adjunct /'ædʒʌŋkt/ *n.* **1.** something added to another thing but not essentially a part of it. **2.** a person joined to another in some duty or service. – *adj.* **3.** joined to a thing or person, especially subordinately; associated; auxiliary.

adjure /ə'dʒuə/ *v.t.*, **-jured**, **-juring**. **1.** to charge, bind, or command, earnestly and solemnly, often under oath or the threat of a curse. **2.** to entreat or request earnestly.

adjust /ə'dʒʌst/ *v.t.* **1.** to make correspondent or conformable; adapt. **2.** to put in working order; bring to a proper state or position. **3.** to settle or bring to a satisfactory state, so that parties are agreed in the result. **4.** *Insurance* to fix (the sum to be paid on a claim); settle (a claim). – *v.i.* **5.** to adapt oneself; become adapted. – **adjustable**, *adj.* – **adjustment**, *n.*

adjutant /'ædʒətənt/ *n.* **1.** *Military* a staff officer who assists the commanding officer. **2.** an assistant. – **adjutancy**, *n.*

ad lib /æd 'lɪb/ *adv.* **1.** in an impromptu manner. – *adj.* **2.** of or relating to an improvised performance.

administer /æd'mɪnəstə, əd-/ *v.t.* **1.** to manage (affairs, a government, etc.). **2.** to bring into use or operation; dispense. **3.** to tender or impose. – *v.i.* **4.** to contribute assistance. **5.** to perform the duties of an administrator.

administration /ədmɪnəs'treɪʃən/ *n.* **1.** the management or direction of any office or employment. **2.** the function of a political state in exercising its governmental duties. **3.** any body of people entrusted with administrative powers.

administrative /əd'mɪnəstrətɪv/ *adj.* relating to administration; executive.

administrator /əd'mɪnəstreɪtə/ *n.* **1.** someone who directs or manages affairs of any kind. **2.** *Law* a person appointed by a court to take charge of the estate of a person who died without appointing an executor.

admirable /'ædmərəbəl/ *adj.* worthy of admiration, exciting approval, reverence or affection. – **admirably**, *adv.*

admiral /'ædmərəl/ *n.* a naval officer of high rank. – **admiralty**, *n.*

admire /əd'maɪə/ *v.t.*, **-mired**, **-miring**. to regard with wonder, pleasure, and approbation. – **admiration**, *n.* – **admirer**, *n.*

admissible /əd'mɪsəbəl/ *adj.* **1.** that may be allowed or conceded; allowable. **2.** *Law* allowable as evidence.

admission /əd'mɪʃən/ *n.* **1.** the act of allowing to enter. **2.** the price paid for entrance, as to a theatre, etc. **3.** the act or condition of being received or accepted in a position or office; appointment. **4.** a point or statement admitted; concession.

admit /əd'mɪt/ *v.t.*, **-mitted**, **-mitting**. **1.** to allow to enter; grant or afford entrance to. **2.** to permit; allow. **3.** to permit to exercise a certain function or privilege. **4.** to allow as valid. **5.** to have capacity for the admission of at one time. **6.** to acknowledge;

confess. – **admittance**, *n.*

admittedly /əd'mɪtədli/ *adv.* by acknowledgment.

admonish /əd'mɒnɪʃ/ *v.t.* **1.** to counsel against something; caution or advise. **2.** to notify of or reprove for a fault, especially mildly. **3.** to recall or incite to duty; remind. – **admonition**, *n.*

ad nauseam /æd 'nɔziəm, -si-/ *adv.* to a sickening or disgusting extent.

ado /ə'du/ *n.* activity; fuss.

adolescence /ædə'lɛsəns/ *n.* the transition period between puberty and adult stages of development; youth. – **adolescent**, *adj.*, *n.*

adopt /ə'dɒpt/ *v.t.* **1.** to choose for or take to oneself; make one's own by selection or assent. **2.** to take as one's own child, specifically by a formal legal act. **3.** to vote to accept. – **adoptable**, *adj.* – **adopter**, *n.* – **adoption**, *n.*

adoptive /ə'dɒptɪv/ *adj.* **1.** related by adoption. **2.** tending to adopt. **3.** (of children) for adoption. – **adoptively**, *adv.*

adorable /ə'dɔrəbəl/ *adj.* worthy of being adored.

adoration /ædə'reɪʃən/ *n.* **1.** worship. **2.** fervent and devoted love.

adore /ə'dɔ/ *v.t.*, **adored**, **adoring**. **1.** to regard with the utmost esteem, love, and respect. **2.** to honour as divine; worship.

adorn /ə'dɔn/ *v.t.* **1.** to make pleasing or more attractive. **2.** to increase or lend beauty to, as by dress or ornaments; decorate.

adrenalin /ə'drɛnələn, -lin/ *n.* a whitish hormone, which, when purified, is used as a drug to speed heart action, etc. Also, **adrenaline**.

adrift /ə'drɪft/ *adj.* **1.** not fastened by any kind of moorings; at the mercy of winds and currents. **2.** swayed by any chance impulse. **3.** *Colloquial* confused; wide of the mark.

adroit /ə'drɔɪt/ *adj.* expert in the use of the hand or mind.

adsorb /əd'sɔb/ *v.t.* to gather (a gas, liquid, or dissolved substance) on a surface in a condensed layer, as is the case when charcoal adsorbs gases.

adulate /'ædʒəleɪt, 'ædjuleɪt/ *v.t.*, **-lated**, **-lating**. to show pretended or undiscriminating devotion to; flatter servilely. – **adulation**, *n.* – **adulater**, *n.* – **adulatory**, *adj.*

adult /ə'dʌlt, 'ædʌlt/ *adj.* **1.** having attained full size and strength; mature. **2.** relating to or designed for adults. – *n.* **3.** a person who is of age. **4.** a full-grown animal or plant.

adulterate /ə'dʌltəreɪt/ *v.t.*, **-rated**, **-rating**. to make impure by admixture. – **adulterator**, **adulterant**, **adulteration**, *n.*

adultery /ə'dʌltəri/ *n.*, *pl.* **-teries**. voluntary sexual intercourse between a married person and any other than the lawful spouse. – **adulterous**, *adj.*

ad valorem /æd və'lɔrəm/ *adj.* in proportion to the value. An *ad valorem* duty charged on goods entering a country is fixed at a percentage of the customs value as stated on the invoice.

advance /əd'væns, -'vans/ *v.*, **-vanced**, **-vancing**, *n.* – *v.t.* **1.** to move or bring forwards in place. **2.** to bring to view or notice; propose. **3.** to improve; further. **4.** to raise in rate. **5.** to bring forwards in time; accelerate. **6.** to supply beforehand; furnish on credit, or before goods are delivered or work is done. **7.** to supply or pay in expectation of reimbursement. – *v.i.* **8.** to move or go forwards; proceed. **9.** to improve or make progress; grow. **10.** to increase in quantity, value, price, etc. – *n.* **11.** a moving forwards; progress in space. **12.** (*usu. pl.*) an effort to bring about acquaintance, accord, understanding, etc. **13.** addition to price; rise in price. **14.** *Commerce* **a.** a giving beforehand; a furnishing of something before an equivalent is received. **b.** a loan against securities, or in advance of payment due.

advantage /əd'væntɪdʒ, -'van-/ *n.*, *v.*, **-taged**, **-taging**. – *n.* **1.** any state, circumstance, opportunity, or means specially favourable to success, interest, or any desired end. **2.** benefit; gain; profit. **3.** *Tennis* the first point scored after deuce, or the resulting state of the score. **4. take advantage of,** to make use of. – *v.t.* **5.** to be of service to; yield profit or gain to; benefit. – **advantageous**, *adj.*

advent /'ædvɛnt/ *n.* a coming into place, view, or being; arrival.

adventitious /ædvɛn'tɪʃəs/ *adj.* accidentally or casually acquired; added extrinsically; foreign.

adventure /əd'vɛntʃə/ *n.*, *v.*, **-tured**, **-turing**. – *n.* **1.** an undertaking of uncertain outcome; a hazardous enterprise. **2.** an exciting experience. **3.** participation in exciting undertakings or enterprises. **4.** a commercial or financial speculation of any kind; a venture. – *v.i.* **5.** to venture. – **adventurous**, *adj.*

adverb /'ædvɜb/ *n.* a part of speech comprising words used to limit a verb, adjective, or another adverb, by expressing time, manner, place, cause, degree, etc. – **adverbial**, *adj.*

ad verbum /æd 'vɜbəm/ *adv.* exact in wording according to an original.

adversary /'ædvəsri, -səri/ *n.*, *pl.* **-saries**. an opponent in a contest.

adverse /'ædvɜs, əd'vɜs/ *adj.* **1.** antagonistic in purpose or effect. **2.** opposing one's interests or desire. – **adversity**, *n.*

advert[1] /əd'vɜt/ *v.i.* to make a remark or remarks (about or in relation to); refer (fol. by *to*).

advert[2] /'ædvɜt/ *n.* *Colloquial* an advertisement.

advertise /'ædvətaɪz/ *v.*, **-tised**, **-tising**. – *v.t.* **1.** to give information to the public about (something). **2.** to praise the good qualities of, by advertisement, to induce the public to buy. – *v.i.* **3.** to ask (*for*) by placing an advertisement in a newspaper, magazine, etc.

advertisement /əd'vɜtəsmənt/ *n.* any device or public announcement designed to attract public attention, bring in custom, etc.

advice /əd'vaɪs/ *n.* **1.** an opinion recommended, or offered, as worthy to be followed. **2.** a communication, especially from a distance, containing information. **3.** a formal or professional opinion given, especially by a barrister.

advisable /əd'vaɪzəbəl/ *adj.* proper to be advised or to be recommended.

advise /əd'vaɪz/ *v.*, **-vised**, **-vising**. – *v.t.* **1.** to give counsel to; offer an opinion to, as worthy or expedient to be followed. **2.** to recommend as wise, prudent, etc. **3.** to give (a person, etc.) information or notice (fol. by *of*). – *v.i.* **4.** to offer counsel; give advice. – **adviser**, *n.* – **advisory**, *adj.*

advocate /'ædvəkeɪt/ *v.*, **-cated**, **-cating** /'ædvəkət, -keɪt/ *n.* – *v.t.* **1.** to plead in favour of; support or urge by argument; recommend publicly. – *n.* **2.** someone who defends, vindicates, or espouses a cause by argument; an upholder; a defender (fol. by *of*). – **advocacy**, **advocator**, *n.* – **advocatory**, *adj.*

adze /ædz/ *n.* a heavy chisel-like tool fastened at right angles to a wooden handle, used to dress timber, etc.

ae- For words with initial **ae-**, see also **e-**.

aegis /'idʒəs/ *n.* protection; sponsorship.

-aemia a suffix referring to the state of the blood. Also, **-emia**, **-haemia**, **-hemia**.

aeon = eon /'iən/ *n.* an indefinitely long period of time; an age.

aerate /'ɛəreɪt/ *v.t.*, **-rated**, **-rating**. to charge or treat with air or a gas, especially with carbon dioxide.

aerial /'ɛəriəl/ *n.* **1.** *Radio* that part of a radio system designed to radiate or receive electromagnetic waves into or from free space; an antenna. – *adj.* **2.** of, in, or produced by the air. **3.** inhabiting or frequenting the air. **4.** unsubstantial; visionary. **5.** having a light and graceful beauty; ethereal. **6.** relating to or used for, against, or in aircraft. – **aerially**, *adv.*

aero- a word element indicating: **1.** air; atmosphere. **2.** gas. **3.** aeroplane

aerobics /ɛə'roʊbɪks/ *pl. n.* physical exercises which stimulate the respiratory and circulatory systems to improve and maintain physical fitness.

aerodrome /'ɛərədroʊm/ *n.* a landing field for aeroplanes, especially private aeroplanes, usually smaller than an airport.

aerodynamics /ˌɛəroʊdaɪ'næmɪks/ *n.* the study of air in motion and of the forces acting on solids in motion relative to the air through which they move.

aerogram /'ɛərəgræm/ *n.* a sheet of lightweight paper (sold only by post offices) which serves both as the envelope and the writing paper for an airmail letter. Also, **aerogramme**.

aeronautics /ɛərə'nɔtɪks/ *n.* the science or art of flight. – **aeronautic**, *adj.*

aeroplane /'ɛərəpleɪn/ *n.* an aircraft, heavier than air, kept aloft by the upward thrust exerted by the passing air on its fixed wings, and driven by propellers, jet propulsion, etc.

aerosol container /'ɛərəsɒl/ *n.* a small metal container for storing under pressure, and subsequently dispensing as a spray, such products as insecticides, waxes, lacquers, etc.

aesthetic = esthetic /əs'θɛtɪk, is-/ *adj.* relating to the sense of the beautiful or the science of aesthetics.

aesthetics = esthetics /əs'θɛtɪks, is-/ *n.* *Philosophy* the science which deduces from nature and taste the rules and principles of art; the theory of the fine arts. – **aesthetical**, *adj.* – **aesthetically**, *adv.*

aetiology = etiology /iti'ɒlədʒi/ *n.* the study of the causes of anything, especially of diseases.

af- variant of **ad-** (by assimilation) before *f*, as in *affect*.

afar /ə'fa/ *adv.* from a distance (usually preceded by *from*).

affable /'æfəbəl/ *adj.* easy to talk to or to approach; polite; friendly.

affair /ə'fɛə/ *n.* **1.** anything done or to be done; that which requires action or effort; business; concern. **2.** (*pl.*) matters of interest or concern; particular doings or interests. **3.** an event or a performance; a particular action, operation, or proceeding. **4.** a sexual relationship.

affect[1] /ə'fɛkt/ *v.t.* **1.** to act on; produce an effect or a change in. **2.** to impress; move (in mind or feelings).

affect[2] /ə'fɛkt/ *v.t.* **1.** to make a show of; feign. **2.** to use or adopt by preference.

affectation /ˌæfɛk'teɪʃən/ *n.* **1.** pretence. **2.** artificiality of manner or conduct; effort to attract notice by pretence, assumption, or any assumed peculiarity.

affected[1] /ə'fɛktəd/ *adj.* **1.** acted upon; influenced. **2.** influenced injuriously; impaired; attacked, as by climate or disease. **3.** moved; touched.

affected[2] /ə'fɛktəd/ *adj.* **1.** assumed artificially. **2.** assuming or pretending to possess characteristics which are not natural.

affection /ə'fɛkʃən/ *n.* **1.** a settled goodwill, love, or attachment. **2.** *Pathology* a disease. **3.** the act or result of affecting.

affectionate /ə'fɛkʃənət/ *adj.* characterised by or manifesting affection; possessing or indicating love; tender.

affiance /æfi'ɒns, ə'faɪəns/ *v.t.*, **-anced**, **-ancing**. to bind by promise of marriage; betroth.

affidavit /æfə'deɪvət/ *n.* a written statement on oath, sworn to before an authorised official, often used as evidence in court proceedings.

affiliate /ə'fɪlieɪt/ *v.*, **-ated**, **-ating**, /ə'fɪliət/ *n.* – *v.t.* **1.** to attach as a branch or part; unite; associate (fol. by *with*). **2.** to bring into association or close connection. – *v.i.* **3.** to associate oneself; be intimately united in action or interest. – *n.* **4.** someone who or that which is affiliated; associate or auxiliary. – **affiliation**, *n.*

affinity /ə'fɪnəti/ *n.*, *pl.* **-ties**. **1.** a natural liking for, or attraction to, a person or thing. **2.** close resemblance or connection. **3.** relationship by marriage. **4.** *Chemistry* that force by which the atoms of bodies of dissimilar nature unite in certain definite proportions to form a compound.

affirm /ə'fɜm/ *v.t.* **1.** to state or assert positively; maintain as true. **2.** to establish, confirm, or ratify. – *v.i.* **3.** to declare positively; assert solemnly. **4.** *Law* to declare solemnly before a court or magistrate, but without oath (a practice allowed where the affirmant has scruples, usually religious, against taking an oath). – **affirmant**, *n.*

affirmative /ə'fɜmətɪv/ *adj.* **1.** giving affirmation or assent; not negative. – *n.* **2.** an affirmative word or phrase, as *yes* or *I do.*

affix /ə'fɪks/ *v.,* /'æfɪks/ – *n., v.t.* **1.** to fix; fasten, join, or attach (often fol. by *to*). – *n.* **2.** that which is joined or attached. **3.** *Grammar* any meaningful element (prefix, infix, or suffix) added to a stem or base, as *-ed* added to *want* to form *wanted.* – **affixation**, *n.*

afflict /ə'flɪkt/ *v.t.* to distress with mental or bodily pain; trouble greatly or grievously. – **affliction**, *n.*

affluent /'æfluənt/ *adj.* rich. – **affluence**, *n.*

afford /ə'fɔd/ *v.t.* **1.** to have the means (often preceded by *can* or *may* and followed by an infinitive). **2.** to be able to meet the expense of; spare the price of (often preceded by *can* or *may*). **3.** to be able to give or spare (often preceded by *can* or *may*). **4.** to give or confer upon.

affreightment /ə'freɪtmənt/ *n.* a contract made by a shipowner to carry goods for payment.

affront /ə'frʌnt/ *n.* **1.** a personally offensive act or word; an intentional slight. – *v.t.* **2.** to offend by an open manifestation of disrespect or insolence. **3.** to put out of countenance.

afield /ə'fild/ *adv.* **1.** abroad; away from home. **2.** off the beaten path; far and wide.

afloat /ə'floʊt/ *adj., adv.* **1.** borne on the water; in a floating condition. **2.** flooded. **3.** passing from place to place; in circulation. **4. stay afloat,** to survive financially.

afoot /ə'fʊt/ *adj.* astir; in progress.

afraid /ə'freɪd/ *adj.* **1.** feeling fear. **2.** reluctantly or regretfully of the opinion (sometimes fol. by *that*).

afresh /ə'frɛʃ/ *adv.* anew; again.

aft /aft/ *adv. Nautical* at, in, or towards the stern.

after /'aftə/ *prep.* **1.** behind in place or time. **2.** in pursuit of; in search of; with or in desire for. **3.** concerning. **4.** subsequent to and in consequence of. **5.** below in rank or excellence; next to. **6.** in imitation of, or in imitation of the style of. **7.** with name of. **8.** in proportion to; in accordance with. **9.** according to the nature of; in agreement or unison with; in conformity to. – *adv.* **10.** behind. – *adj.* **11.** later in time; next; subsequent; succeeding. **12.** *Nautical* farther aft, or towards the stern of the ship. – *conj.* **13.** subsequent to the time that.

after-acquired property *n. Law* property acquired by a bankrupt after sequestration, usually vested in the trustee.

afterbirth /'aftəbɜθ/ *n.* the placenta and foetal membranes expelled from the uterus after parturition.

aftermath /'aftəmæθ, -maθ/ *n.* resultant conditions, especially of a catastrophe.

afternoon /aftə'nun/ *n.* the time from noon until evening.

after-sales service *n.* the service given by a company after the sale of goods, especially during the period of warranty.

afterwards /'aftəwədz/ *adv.* in later or subsequent time; subsequently. Also, **afterward** /'aftəwəd/.

ag- variant of **ad-** (by assimilation) before *g*, as in *agglutinate.*

again /ə'gɛn, ə'geɪn/ *adv.* **1.** once more; in addition; another time; anew. **2.** in an additional case or instance; moreover; besides; furthermore. **3.** on the other hand. **4.** in the opposite direction; to the same place or person.

against /ə'gɛnst, ə'geɪnst/ *prep.* **1.** in an opposite direction to, so as to meet; towards; upon. **2.** in contact with, or in pressure upon. **3.** in opposition to; adverse or hostile to. **4.** in resistance to or defence from. **5.** in preparation for; in provision for. **6.** in contrast with; having as background. **7.** in exchange for; in return for; as a balance to. **8.** instead of, as an alternative to, in contrast with, (sometimes preceded by *as*).

agape /ə'geɪp/ *adv.* **1.** in an attitude of wonder or eagerness; with the mouth wide open. – *adj.* **2.** wide open.

agate /'ægət/ *n.* a variegated variety of quartz showing coloured bands or other markings.

age /eɪdʒ/ *n., v.,* **aged**, **ageing** *or* **aging**. -*n.* **1.** the length of time during which a being or thing has existed. **2.** the lifetime of an individual, or of the individuals of a class or species on an average. **3. of age,** being in possession of full adult rights and responsibilities. **4.** one of the periods or stages of human life. **5.** old age. **6.** a particular period of history, as distinguished from others; a historical epoch. **7.** a generation or a succession of generations. **8.** *Colloquial* a great length of time. **9.** *Geology* a long or short part of the world's history distinguished by special features. – *v.t., v.i.* **10.** to make or become old or mature.

-age a noun suffix, forming: **1.** collective nouns as in *leafage.* **2.** nouns denoting condition, rank, service, fee, etc., as in *bondage, parsonage.* **3.** nouns expressing various relations, from verbs, as in *breakage, cleavage.* **4.** nouns denoting an amount or charge as in *postage, corkage.*

ageism /'eɪdʒɪzəm/ *n.* an attitude which stereotypes a person, especially an elderly person, according to age.

agency /'eɪdʒənsi/ *n., pl.* **-cies**. **1.** a commercial or other organisation furnishing some form of service for the public. **2.** the office of agent; the business of an agent entrusted with the concerns of another. **3.** the state of being in action or of exerting power; action; operation. **4.** a mode of exerting power; a means of producing effects.

agenda /ə'dʒɛndə/ *pl. n., sing.* **-dum**. **1.** things to be done. **2.** (*construed as sing.*) a program or list of things to be done, discussed, etc.

agent /'eɪdʒənt/ *n.* **1.** a person acting on behalf of another. **2.** someone who or that which acts or has the power to act. **3.** someone who acts for a buyer or seller of stock or wool, etc., and who usually represents a firm supplying manufactured rural requirements for the farmer. **4.** a representative of a business firm, especially a commercial traveller; a canvasser.

agent provocateur /ˌaʒɔ̃ prəvɒkə'tɜ/ *n., pl.* **agents provocateurs** /ˌaʒɔ̃ prəvɒkə'tɜz/. any person who tries to incite dissatisfaction or unrest, especially someone who incites to an illegal action.

agglomerate /ə'glɒməreɪt/ *v.*, **-rated**, **-rating** /ə'glɒmərət/. *n.* – *v.t.* **1.** to collect or gather into a mass. – *n.* **2.** a rock formation composed of large angular volcanic fragments. – **agglomeration**, *n.*

agglutinate /ə'glutəneɪt/ *v.t.*, **-nated**, **-nating**. to unite or cause to adhere, as with glue. – **agglutination**, *n.*

aggrandise = aggrandize /ə'grændaɪz/ *v.t.*, **-dised**, **-dising**. **1.** to make great or greater in power, wealth, rank, or honour. **2.** to make (something) appear greater. Also, **aggrandize**. – **aggrandisement**, *n.* – **aggrandiser**, *n.*

aggravate /'ægrəveɪt/ *v.t.*, **-vated**, **-vating**. **1.** to make worse or more severe; intensify, as anything evil, disorderly, or troublesome. **2.** *Colloquial* to provoke; irritate; exasperate.

aggregate /'ægrəgət/ *adj.*, *n.*; /'ægrəgeɪt/ *v.*, **-gated**, **-gating**. – *adj.* **1.** formed by the conjunction or collection of particulars into a whole mass or sum; total; combined. – *n.* **2.** a sum, or assemblage of particulars; a total or gross amount. **3.** any hard material added to cement to make concrete. – *v.t.* **4.** to bring together; collect into one sum, mass, or body. **5.** to amount to (the number of).

aggression /ə'grɛʃən/ *n.* **1.** any offensive action or procedure; an inroad or encroachment. **2.** *Psychology* the emotional drive to attack; an offensive mental attitude (rather than defensive). – **aggressive**, *adj.* – **aggressor**, *n.*

aggrieve /ə'griv/ *v.t.*, **-grieved**, **-grieving**. to oppress or wrong grievously; injure by injustice (used now chiefly in the passive). – **aggrieved**, *adj.*

aghast /ə'gast/ *adj.* struck with amazement; stupefied with fright or horror.

agile /'ædʒaɪl/ *adj.* **1.** quick and light in movement. **2.** active; lively. – **agility**, *n.*

agio /'ædʒioʊ/ *n.*, *pl.* **-os**. **1.** a premium on money in exchange. **2.** an allowance for the difference in value of two currencies. **3.** an allowance given or taken on bills of exchange from other countries, to balance out exchange expenses. **4.** → **agiotage**.

agiotage /'ædʒətɪdʒ/ *n.* **1.** the business of exchange. **2.** speculative dealing in securities. Also, **agio**.

agist /ə'dʒɪst/ *v.t.* to take in and feed or pasture (livestock) for payment.

agitate /'ædʒəteɪt/ *v.*, **-tated**, **-tating**. – *v.t.* **1.** to move or force into violent irregular action; shake or move briskly. **2.** to disturb, or excite into tumult; perturb. – *v.i.* **3.** to arouse or attempt to arouse public feeling as in some political or social question.

agnostic /æg'nɒstɪk/ *n.* someone who holds that the ultimate cause (God) and the essential nature of things are unknown or unknowable, or that human knowledge is limited to experience.

ago /ə'goʊ/ *adv.* in past time.

agog /ə'gɒg/ *adj.* highly excited by eagerness or curiosity.

-agogue a word element meaning 'leading' or 'guiding', found in a few agent nouns (often with pejorative value), as in *demagogue*, *pedagogue*.

agony /'ægəni/ *n.*, *pl.* **-nies**. **1.** extreme, and generally prolonged, pain; intense suffering. **2.** the struggle preceding natural death. – **agonise = agonize**, *v.*

agrarian /ə'grɛəriən/ *adj.* **1.** relating to land, land tenure, or the division of landed property. **2.** rural; agricultural.

agree /ə'gri/ *v.*, **agreed**, **agreeing**. – *v.i.* **1.** to yield assent; consent (often fol. by *to*, especially with reference to things and acts). **2.** to be of one mind; harmonise in opinion or feeling (often fol. by *with*, especially with reference to persons). **3.** to come to one opinion or mind; come to an arrangement or understanding; arrive at a settlement (sometimes fol. by *upon*). **4.** to be accommodated or adapted; suit (fol. by *with*). – *v.t.* **5.** to concede; grant: *I agree that she is the ablest of us.* **6.** to determine; settle: *to agree a price*; *to agree that a meeting should be held.* – **agreed**, *adj.*

agreeable /ə'griəbəl/ *adj.* **1.** to one's liking; pleasing. **2.** willing or ready to agree or consent.

agreement /ə'grimənt/ *n.* **1.** (the act of coming to) a mutual arrangement. **2.** the state of being in accord; concord; harmony; conformity.

agriculture /'ægrəkʌltʃə/ *n.* the cultivation of land, including crop-raising, forestry, stock-raising, etc.; farming. – **agricultural**, *adj.*

agro- a word element meaning 'soil', 'field'.

agronomy /ə'grɒnəmi/ *n.* the applied aspects of both soil science and the several plant sciences, often limited to applied plant sciences dealing with crops.

ahead /ə'hɛd/ *adv.* **1.** in or to the front; in advance; before. **2.** forward; onward.

ahoy /ə'hɔɪ/ *interj.* (a call used in hailing, especially on ships).

aid /eɪd/ *v.t.* **1.** to afford support or relief to; help. – *n.* **2.** help; support; assistance.

aide-de-camp /eɪd-də-'kɒ̃/ *n.*, *pl.* **aides-de-camp**. a military or naval officer acting as a confidential assistant to a superior, especially a general, governor, etc.

AIDS /eɪdz/ *n.* a disease caused by a virus (HIV) which destroys the body's white cells, resulting in reduced immunity, and therefore severe infections, tumours, and ultimately death.

ail /eɪl/ *v.t.* **1.** to affect with pain or uneasiness; trouble. – *v.i.* **2.** to feel pain; be ill (usually in a slight degree); be unwell. – **ailing**, *adj.* – **ailment**, *n.*

aim /eɪm/ *v.t.* **1.** to direct or point (something) at something. – *v.i.* **2.** to level a gun; give direction to a blow, missile, etc. **3.** to direct efforts towards an object. – *n.* **4.** the act of aiming or directing anything at or towards a particular point or object. **5.** something intended or desired to be attained by one's efforts; purpose.

air /ɛə/ *n.* **1.** a mixture of oxygen, nitrogen and other gases, which surrounds the earth and forms its atmosphere. **2.** the general character or complexion of anything; appearance. **3.** (*pl.*) affected manner; manifestation of pride or vanity; assumed haughtiness. **4.** *Music* a tune; a melody. **5. off (the) air,** no longer being broadcast;

not on the air. **6. on (the) air,** in the act of broadcasting; being broadcast. – *v.t.* **7.** to expose to the air; give access to the open air; ventilate. **8.** to expose ostentatiously; bring into public notice; display.

airbag /ˈɛəbæg/ *n.* a safety device in a motor vehicle consisting of a bag which inflates instantly before the driver or front-seat passenger on collision.

airconditioning /ˈɛəkəndɪʃənɪŋ/ *n.* a system of treating air in buildings or vehicles to assure temperature, humidity, dustlessness, and movement at levels most conducive to personal comfort, manufacturing processes, or preservation of items stored.

air corridor /ˈɛə kɒrədɔ/ *n.* an air route established by international agreement or government regulation.

aircraft /ˈɛəkraft/ *n., pl.* **-craft**. any machine supported for flight in the air by buoyancy (such as balloons and other lighter-than-air craft) or by dynamic action of air on its surfaces (such as aeroplanes, helicopters, gliders, and other heavier-than-air craft).

aircraft carrier *n.* a large naval ship, designed to serve as an air base at sea, with a long strip of deck for the taking off and landing of aircraft.

air force /ˈɛəfɔs/ *n.* the branch of the armed forces of any country concerned with military aircraft.

airlift /ˈɛəlɪft/ *n.* a system of transporting people, supplies, equipment, etc., by aircraft when surface routes are blocked, as during a military blockade, or at a time of national emergency.

airline /ˈɛəlaɪn/ *n.* **1.** a system furnishing scheduled air transport between specified points. **2.** a company that owns or operates such a system.

airlock /ˈɛəlɒk/ *n. Engineering* an obstruction to or stoppage of a flow of liquid in a pipe caused by an air bubble.

airmail /ˈɛəmeɪl/ *n.* the system of transmitting mail by aircraft.

airplay /ˈɛəpleɪ/ *n.* the amount of public exposure a recording receives on radio or television.

air pocket /ˈɛə pɒkət/ *n. Aeronautics* a downward current of air, usually causing a sudden loss of altitude.

airport /ˈɛəpɔt/ *n.* a large airfield usually equipped with a control tower, hangars, and accommodation for the receiving and discharging of passengers and cargo.

airspace /ˈɛəspeɪs/ *n.* **1.** the space directly above a building which can be sold for the construction of another building on or over the first. **2.** the part or region of the atmosphere above the territory of a nation or other political division which is considered under its jurisdiction.

airtight /ˈɛətaɪt/ *adj.* so tight or close as to be impermeable to air.

airy /ˈɛəri/ *adj.*, **airier**, **airiest**. **1.** open to a free current of air. **2.** light in appearance; thin. **3.** light in manner; sprightly; lively. **4.** visionary; speculative. **5.** casual, offhand; superficial, flippant.

aisle /aɪl/ *n.* a passageway between seats in a church, hall, etc.

ajar /əˈdʒa/ *adv.* **1.** neither quite open nor shut; partly opened. – *adj.* **2.** partly open.

akimbo /əˈkɪmboʊ/ *adv.* with hand on hip and elbow bent outwards.

akin /əˈkɪn/ *adj.* **1.** of kin; related by blood. **2.** allied by nature; partaking of the same properties.

al- variant of **ad-** before *l*, as in *allure*.

-al[1] an adjective suffix meaning 'having to do with', 'connected with', 'being', 'like', 'befitting', etc., occurring in numerous adjectives and in many nouns of adjectival origin, as *annual, choral, equal, regal.*

-al[2] a suffix forming nouns of action from verbs, as in *refusal, denial, recital, trial.*

-al[3] a suffix indicating that a compound includes an alcohol.

alabaster /ˈæləbæstə/ *n.* a finely granular variety of gypsum, often white and translucent, used for ornamental objects or work, such as lamp bases, figurines, etc.

alacrity /əˈlækrəti/ *n.* **1.** liveliness; briskness; sprightliness. **2.** cheerful readiness or willingness.

alarm /əˈlam/ *n.* **1.** a sudden fear or painful suspense excited by an apprehension of danger; apprehension; fright. **2.** any sound, outcry, or information intended to give notice of approaching danger. **3.** a self-acting contrivance of any kind used to call attention, rouse from sleep, warn of danger, etc. – *v.t.* **4.** to surprise with apprehension of danger; disturb with sudden fear.

alas /əˈlæs, əˈlas/ *interj.* (an exclamation expressing sorrow, grief, pity, concern, or apprehension of evil).

albatross /ˈælbətrɒs/ *n.* any of various large web-footed seabirds related to the petrels.

albeit /ɔlˈbiɪt, æl-/ *conj.* although; notwithstanding that.

albino /ælˈbinoʊ/ *n., pl.* **-nos**. a person with a pale, milky skin, light hair, and pink eyes, resulting from a congenital absence of pigmentation.

album /ˈælbəm/ *n.* **1.** a book consisting of blank leaves for the insertion or preservation of photographs, stamps, autographs, etc. **2.** a long-playing recording on which there is a collection of songs or pieces.

alcohol /ˈælkəhɒl/ *n.* **1.** a colourless, flammable liquid (**ethyl alcohol**, C_2H_5OH), the intoxicating principle of fermented liquors. **2.** any intoxicating liquor containing this spirit. **3.** *Chemistry* any of a class of compounds derived from the hydrocarbon by replacement of a hydrogen atom by the hydroxyl radical, OH.

alcoholic /ælkəˈhɒlik/ *adj.* **1.** of or relating to alcohol. – *n.* **2.** a person suffering from alcoholism. **3.** one addicted to intoxicating drinks.

alcoholism /ˈælkəhɒlɪzəm/ *n.* a diseased condition due to the excessive use of alcoholic beverages.

alcove /ˈælkoʊv/ *n.* a recess opening out of a room.

alderman /ˈɔldəmən/ *n., pl.* **-men**. a local government representative elected by constituents of a municipality.

ale /eɪl/ *n.* beer.

aleatory /æliˈeɪtəri/ *adj.* **1.** dependent on chance. **2. aleatory contract,** a contract or agreement of which the effects with respect both to the advantages and the losses depend on uncertain events; a wagering contract.

alert /ə'lɜt/ *adj.* **1.** vigilantly attentive. – *n.* **2.** an attitude of vigilance, wariness or caution. – *v.t.* **3.** to prepare (troops, etc.) for action.

alga /'ælgə/ *n., pl.* **-gae** /-dʒi, -gi/ any of various chlorophyll-containing plants such as seaweed, etc., of varying form and size.

algebra /'ældʒəbrə/ *n.* the mathematical art of reasoning about (quantitative) relations by means of a systematised notation including letters and other symbols; the analysis of equations, combinatorial analysis, theory of fractions, etc. – **algebraic**, *adj.*

-algia a noun suffix meaning 'pain'.

algo- a word element meaning 'pain'.

ALGOL /'ælgɒl/ *n.* an internationally accepted language in which computer programs are written.

algorithm /'ælgərɪðəm/ *n.* an effective procedure for solving a particular mathematical problem in a finite number of steps. Also, **algorism**.

alias /'eɪliəs/ *adv., n., pl.* **aliases**. – *adv.* **1.** known sometimes as: *Simpson alias Smith.* – *n.* **2.** an assumed name; another name: *living under an alias.*

alibi /'æləbaɪ/ *n., pl.* **-bis**. *Law* a defence by an accused person that they were elsewhere at the time the offence with which they are charged was committed.

alien /'eɪliən/ *n.* one born in or belonging to another country who has not acquired citizenship by naturalisation and is not entitled to the privileges of a citizen.

alienate /'eɪliəneɪt/ *v.t.,* **-nated**, **-nating**. **1** to make indifferent or averse; estrange. **2.** to turn away.

alight /ə'laɪt/ *v.i.,* **alighted** *or* **alit** /ə'lɪt/, **alighting**. to get down from a horse or out of a vehicle.

align /ə'laɪn/ *v.t.* **1.** to adjust to a line; lay out or regulate by line; form in line. – *v.i.* **2.** to fall or come into line; be in line.

alike /ə'laɪk/ *adv.* **1.** in the same manner, form, or degree; in common; equally. – *adj.* **2.** having resemblance or similarity; having or exhibiting no marked or essential difference (used regularly of a plural substantive or idea, and only in the predicate).

alimentary canal /ælə'mɛntri/ *n.* the digestive passage in any animal from mouth to anus. Also, **alimentary tract**.

alimony /'æləməni/ *n. US* → **maintenance** (def. 2).

alive /ə'laɪv/ *adj.* **1.** (*rarely used attributively*) in life or existence; living. **2.** in a state of action; in force or operation. **3.** full of life; lively.

alkali /'ælkəlaɪ/ *n., pl.* **-lis**, **-lies**. *Chemistry* any of various bases, the hydroxides of the alkali metals and of ammonium, which neutralise acids to form salts and turn red litmus paper blue. – **alkaline**, *adj.* – **alkalinity**, *n.*

all /ɔl/ *adj.* **1.** the whole of (with reference to quantity, extent, duration, amount, or degree). **2.** the whole number of (with reference to individuals or particulars, taken collectively). – *pron.* **3.** the whole quantity or amount. – *n.* **4.** a whole; a totality of things or qualities. **5.** one's whole interest, concern, or property. – *adv.* **6.** wholly; entirely; quite. **7.** only; exclusively. **8.** each; apiece. **9.** by so much; to that extent (fol. by *the* and a comparative adjective).

allay /ə'leɪ/ *v.t.,* **-layed**, **-laying**. **1.** to put at rest; quiet (tumult, fear, suspicion, etc.); appease (wrath). **2.** to mitigate; relieve or alleviate.

allege /ə'lɛdʒ/ *v.t.,* **-leged**, **-leging**. **1.** to assert without proof. **2.** to declare before a court, or elsewhere as if upon oath. **3.** to declare with positiveness; affirm; assert. – **allegation**, *n.*

allegiance /ə'lidʒəns/ *n.* **1.** the obligation of a subject or citizen to their sovereign or government; duty owed to a sovereign or state. **2.** observance of obligation; faithfulness to any person or thing.

allegory /'æləgəri, -gri/ *n., pl.* **-ries**. figurative treatment of one subject under the guise of another; a presentation of an abstract or spiritual meaning under concrete or material forms. – **allegorical**, *adj.*

allergy /'ælədʒi/ *n., pl.* **-gies**. a state of physical hypersensitivity to certain things, as pollens, food, fruits, etc., which are normally harmless. – **allergic**, *adj.*

alleviate /ə'livieɪt/ *v.t.,* **-ated**, **-ating**. to make easier to be endured; lessen; mitigate.

alley /'æli/ *n., pl.* **alleys**. a narrow backstreet or lane.

alliance /ə'laɪəns/ *n.* **1.** the state of being allied or connected; relation between parties allied or connected. **2.** any joining of efforts or interests by persons, families, states, or organisations.

alligator /'æləgeɪtə/ *n.* the broad-snouted representative of the crocodile group.

alliteration /əlɪtə'reɪʃən/ *n.* the commencement of two or more words of a word group with the same sound.

allo- a word element indicating difference, alternation, or divergence.

allocate /'æləkeɪt/ *v.t.,* **-cated**, **-cating**. to set apart for a particular purpose; assign or allot. – **allocation**, *n.*

allonge /ə'lɒndʒ/ *n.* a slip of paper attached to a bill of exchange to take further endorsements.

all-ordinaries index *n.* a weighted average given by a stock exchange of ordinary share prices of a specified large group of companies expressed in relation to a base period. Also, **all-ords**.

allot /ə'lɒt/ *v.t.,* **-lotted**, **-lotting**. to divide or distribute as by lot; distribute or parcel out; apportion.

allotment /ə'lɒtmənt/ *n.* **1.** a portion, share, or thing allotted. **2.** a block of land.

allotrope /'ælətroʊp/ *n.* one of two or more existing forms of a chemical element.

allow /ə'laʊ/ *v.t.* **1.** to grant permission to or for; permit. **2.** to admit; acknowledge; concede. – *v.i.* **3.** **allow for,** to make concession, allowance, or provision for.

allowance /ə'laʊəns/ *n.* **1.** a definite amount or share allotted; a ration. **2.** an addition on account of some extenuating or qualifying circumstance. **3.** sanction; tolerance.

alloy /'ælɔɪ/ *n.* a substance composed of two or more metals (or, sometimes, a metal and a non-metal) which have been intimately mixed by fusion, electrolytic deposition, or the like.

allspice /'ɔlspaɪs/ *n.* **1.** the berry of a tropical American tree. **2.** a mildly sharp and fragrant spice made from it.

allude /ə'lud/ *v.i.,* **-luded**, **-luding**. to make an allusion, refer casually or indirectly (fol. by *to*).

all-up /'ɔl-ʌp/ *adj.* total; inclusive.

allure /ə'luə, ə'ljuə/ *v.,* **-lured**, **-luring**, *n.* – *v.t.* **1.** to attract by the offer of some real or apparent good; tempt by something flattering or acceptable. – *n.* **2.** fascination; charm.

allusion /ə'luʒən/ *n.* a passing or casual reference; an incidental mention of something, either directly or by implication.

alluvial /ə'luviəl/ *adj.* **1.** of or relating to alluvium. **2.** of or relating to a mine, claim, diggings, etc., on alluvial soil.

alluvion /ə'luviən/ *n.* **1.** → **alluvium**. **2.** *Law* land gained gradually on a shore or a river bank through the recent action or recession of water, whether from natural or artificial causes. **3.** overflow; flood.

alluvium /ə'luviəm/ *n., pl.* **-via** /-viə/, **-viums**. **1.** a deposit of sand, mud, etc., formed by flowing water. **2.** the sedimentary matter deposited thus within recent times, especially in the valleys of large rivers.

ally /ə'laɪ/ *v.,* **-lied**, **-lying**; /'ælaɪ/ *n., pl.* **-lies**. – *v.t.* **1.** to unite by marriage, treaty, league, or confederacy; connect by formal agreement (fol. by *to* or *with*). – *n.* **2.** one united or associated with another, especially by treaty or league; an allied nation, sovereign, etc. **3.** someone who cooperates with another; supporter; associate.

almanac /'ɔlmənæk, 'æl-/ *n.* a calendar of the days of the year, in weeks and months, indicating the time of various events or phenomena during the period, as anniversaries, sunrise and sunset, changes of the moon and tides, etc.

almighty /ɔl'maɪti/ *adj.* possessing all power; omnipotent.

almond /'amənd/ *n.* a kind of nut, grown in warm temperate regions.

almost /'ɔlmoʊst/ *adv.* very nearly; all but.

alms /amz/ *n.* (*sing. or pl.*) that which is given to the poor or needy; anything given as charity.

aloft /ə'lɒft/ *adv., adj.* high up; in or into the air; above the ground.

alone /ə'loʊn/ *adj.* (*used in the predicate or following the noun*) **1.** apart from another or others. **2.** to the exclusion of all others or all else. – *adv.* **3.** solitarily. **4.** only; merely.

along /ə'lɒŋ/ *prep.* **1.** by the length of; parallel to or in a line with the length of. – *adv.* **2.** in a line, or with a progressive motion; onwards. **3.** by the length; lengthways. **4.** in company; together (fol. by *with*).

alongside /əlɒŋ'saɪd/ *adv.* **1.** along or by the side; at or to the side of anything. – *prep.* **2.** beside; by the side of.

aloof /ə'luf/ *adv.* **1.** at a distance; not participating. – *adj.* **2.** reserved; unsympathetic; disinterested.

aloud /ə'laʊd/ *adv.* **1.** with the natural tone of the voice as distinguished from in a whisper or silently. **2.** with a loud voice; loudly.

alp /ælp/ *n.* **1.** a high mountain. **2.** (*pl.*) a high mountain system, usually with snowy peaks, as the Australian Alps, the Swiss Alps, etc. – **alpine**, *adj.*

alphabet /'ælfəbɛt/ *n.* **1.** the letters of a language in their customary order. **2.** any system of characters or signs for representing sounds or ideas. – **alphabetical**, *adj.*

already /ɔl'rɛdi/ *adv.* by this (or that) time; previously to or at some specified time.

Alsatian /æl'seɪʃən/ *n.* → **German shepherd**.

also /'ɔlsoʊ/ *adv.* in addition; too; further.

alt- variant of **alto-** before vowels.

altar /'ɔltə, 'ɒl-/ *n.* an elevated place or structure, on which sacrifices are offered or at which religious rites are performed.

alter /'ɔltə, 'ɒl-/ *v.t.* to make different in some particular; modify. – **alteration**, *n.*

altercation /'ɔltəkeɪʃən, 'ɒl-/ *n.* a heated or angry dispute; a noisy wrangle.

alternate /'ɔltəneɪt, 'ɒl-/ *v.,* **-nated**, **-nating**, /ɔl'tɜnət, ɒl-/ *adj.* – *v.i.* **1.** to follow one another in time or place reciprocally (usually fol. by *with*). **2.** to change about by turns between points, states, actions, etc. – *v.t.* **3.** to perform by turns, or one after another. – *adj.* **4.** arranged or following each after the other, in succession. **5.** every other one of a series.

alternating current *n.* a current that reverses direction in regular cycles. *Abbrev.*: AC, a.c.

alternative /ɔl'tɜnətɪv, ɒl-/ *n.* **1.** a possibility of one out of two (or, less strictly, more) things. – *adj.* **2.** affording a choice between two things, or a possibility of one thing out of two. **3.** offering standards and criteria of behaviour of a minority group within and opposed to an established western society.

although /ɔl'ðoʊ/ *conj.* even though (practically equivalent to *though*, but often preferred to it in stating fact). Also, **altho'**.

altimeter /'æltəmitə/ *n.* an instrument for measuring height.

altitude /'æltətʃud/ *n.* **1.** the height above sea level of any point on the earth's surface or in the atmosphere. **2.** extent or distance upwards.

alto /'æltoʊ/ *n., pl.* **-tos**. *Music* **1.** the lowest female voice; contralto. **2.** the highest male voice.

alto- a word element meaning 'high'. Also, **alt-**, **alti-**.

altogether /ɔltə'gɛðə/ *adv.* **1.** wholly; entirely; completely; quite. **2.** in all. **3.** on the whole. – *n.* **4.** a whole.

altruism /'æltruˌɪzəm/ *n.* the principle or practice of seeking the welfare of others (opposed to *egoism*). – **altruistic**, *adj.*

aluminium /ˌæljə'mɪniəm/ *n.* a silver-white, ductile, malleable, metallic element, which is not readily oxidised. *Symbol*: Al

always /'ɔlweɪz, -wəz/ *adv.* **1.** all the time. **2.** every time; on every occasion (opposed to *sometimes* or *occasionally*).

Alzheimer's disease /'æltshaɪməz/ *n.* a brain disease which usually appears in old age and which results in confusion, memory failure, disorientation, etc.

am /æm/, *weak forms* /əm, m/ – *v.* 1st person singular present indicative of **be**.

amalgam /ə'mælgəm/ *n.* **1.** a mixture or combination. **2.** an alloy of mercury with another metal or metals.

amalgamate /ə'mælgəmeɪt/ *v.t.*, **-mated**, **-mating**. **1.** to mix so as to make a combination; blend; unite; combine. **2.** *Metallurgy* to mix or alloy (a metal) with mercury. – **amalgamation**, *n.*

amanuensis /əmænju'ɛnsəs/ *n., pl.* **-enses** /-ɛnsiz/. a person employed to write or type what another dictates or to copy what has been written by another; secretary.

amass /ə'mæs/ *v.t.* to collect into a mass or pile; bring together.

amateur /'æmətə, 'æmətʃə/ *n.* **1.** someone who cultivates any study or art or other activity for personal pleasure instead of professionally or for gain. **2.** an athlete who has never competed for money.

amatory /'æmətri/ *adj.* relating to lovers or lovemaking; expressive of love.

amaze /ə'meɪz/ *v.t.*, **amazed**, **amazing**. to overwhelm with surprise; astonish greatly.

amazon /'æməzən/ *n.* a tall, physically strong woman.

ambassador /æm'bæsədə/ *n.* a diplomatic agent of the highest rank who represents his or her country's interests in another country.

amber /'æmbə/ *n.* **1.** a pale yellow, sometimes reddish or brownish, fossil resin of vegetable origin, translucent, brittle, and capable of gaining a negative electrical charge by friction. – *adj.* **2.** resembling amber.

ambergris /'æmbəgris, -grɪs/ *n.* an opaque, ash-coloured substance, a morbid secretion of the sperm whale, fragrant when heated, usually found floating on the ocean or cast ashore, used chiefly in perfumery.

ambi- a word element meaning 'both', 'around', 'on both sides'.

ambidextrous /æmbi'dɛkstrəs/ *adj.* able to use both hands equally well. – **ambidexter**, *n.*

ambience /'æmbiəns/ *n.* environment; surrounding atmosphere.

ambient /'æmbiənt/ *adj.* **1.** completely surrounding. **2.** circulating.

ambiguous /æm'bɪgjuəs/ *adj.* open to various interpretations; having a double meaning; equivocal. – **ambiguity**, *n.*

ambit /'æmbət/ *n.* **1.** boundary; limits; sphere. **2.** scope; extent.

ambit claim *n.* a claim made by employees to a conciliation and arbitration court which anticipates bargaining and compromise with the employer and is therefore extreme in its demands.

ambition /æm'bɪʃən/ *n.* **1.** an eager desire for distinction, preferment, power, or fame. **2.** the object desired or sought after. – **ambitious**, *adj.*

ambivalence /æm'bɪvələns/ *n.* **1.** the coexistence in one person of opposite and conflicting feelings towards someone or something. **2.** uncertainty or ambiguity, especially due to inability to make up one's mind. – **ambivalent**, *adj.*

amble /'æmbəl/ *v.*, **-bled**, **-bling**, *n.* – *v.i.* **1.** to move with the gait of a horse, when it lifts first the two legs on one side and then the two on the other. **2.** to go at an easy pace. – *n.* **3.** an ambling gait.

ambulance /'æmbjələns/ *n.* a vehicle specially equipped for carrying sick or wounded persons.

ambush /'æmbuʃ/ *n.* **1.** the act of attacking unexpectedly from a concealed position. – *v.t.* **2.** to attack from ambush.

ameliorate /ə'miliəreɪt, ə'miljəreɪt/ *v.t., v.i.*, **-rated**, **-rating**. to make or become better; improve.

amen /eɪ'mɛn, a-/ *interj.* it is so; so be it (used after a prayer, creed, or other formal statement).

amenable /ə'mɛnəbəl, ə'min-/ *adj.* **1.** disposed or ready to answer, yield, or submit; submissive; tractable. **2.** liable to be called to account; answerable; legally responsible. **3.** liable or exposed (to charge, claim, etc.).

amend /ə'mɛnd/ *v.t.* **1.** to alter (a motion, bill, constitution, etc.) by due formal procedure. **2.** to change for the better; improve. **3.** to remove or correct faults in; rectify. – **amendment**, *n.*

amends /ə'mɛndz/ *n.* (*sing. or pl.*) reparation or compensation for a loss, damage, or injury of any kind; recompense.

amenity /ə'mɛnəti, ə'min-/ *n., pl.* **-ties**. **1.** (*pl.*) agreeable features, circumstances, ways, etc. **2.** (*pl.*) public toilets.

amethyst /'æməθəst/ *n.* *Mineralogy* a crystallised purple or violet quartz used in jewellery.

amiable /'eɪmiəbəl/ *adj.* having or showing agreeable personal qualities, as sweetness of temper, kindheartedness, etc.

amicable /'æmɪkəbəl/ *adj.* characterised by or exhibiting friendliness; friendly; peaceable.

amid /ə'mɪd/ *prep.* in the midst of or surrounded by; among; amidst.

amidst /ə'mɪdst/ *prep.* amid.

amino acid /əˌminoʊ 'æsəd, ˌæmənoʊ/ *n.* an organic compound from which proteins are formed.

amiss /ə'mɪs/ *adv.* out of the proper course or order; in a faulty manner; wrongly.

amity /'æməti/ *n., pl.* **-ties**. friendship; harmony; good understanding, especially between nations.

ammeter /'æmitə/ *n.* an instrument for measuring the strength of electric currents in amperes.

ammonia /ə'moʊniə, -jə/ *n.* **1.** a colourless, pungent, suffocating gas, NH_3, a compound of nitrogen and hydrogen, very soluble in water. **2.** Also, **ammonia water** or **aqueous ammonia**. this gas dissolved in water, the common commercial form.

ammunition /ˌæmjə'nɪʃən/ *n.* **1.** projectiles that can be discharged from firearms, etc., as bullets, shrapnel, etc. **2.** *Colloquial* evidence used to support an argument.

amnesia /æm'niʒə, -ziə/ *n.* loss of a memory.

amnesty /'æmnəsti/ *n., pl.* **-ties**. a general

pardon for offences against a government.

amoeba = ameba /ə'mibə/ *n., pl.* **-bas, -bae** /-bi/. a microscopic, one-celled animal. – **amoebic**, *adj.*

amok /ə'mʌk/ *adv. in the phr.* **run amok,** to rush about wildly. Also, **amuck**.

among /ə'mʌŋ/ *prep.* **1.** in or into the midst of; in association or connection with; surrounded by. **2.** to each of; by or for distribution to. **3.** each with the other; mutually.

amongst /ə'mʌŋst/ *prep.* among.

amoral /eɪ'mɒrəl, æ-/ *adj.* without moral quality; neither moral nor immoral.

amorous /'æmərəs/ *adj.* **1.** inclined or disposed to love. **2.** in love; enamoured.

amorphous /ə'mɔfəs/ *adj.* lacking definite form; having no specific shape.

amortise = amortize /ə'mɔtaɪz, 'æmətaɪz/ *v.t.,* **-tised, -tising**. to liquidate or extinguish (an indebtedness or charge) usually by periodic payments (or by entries) made to a sinking fund, to a creditor, or to an account.

amount /ə'maʊnt/ *n.* **1.** quantity or extent. **2.** the sum of the principal and interest of a loan. – *v.i.* **3.** to reach, extend, or be equal in number, quantity, effect, etc. (fol. by *to*).

ampere /'æmpɛə/ *n.* the base SI unit of current. *Symbol*: A

ampersand /'æmpəsænd/ *n.* the character *&*, meaning *and*.

amphetamine /æm'fɛtəmin, -mən/ *n.* a drug which, diluted with water, is used as a spray or inhaled to relieve nasal congestion and is taken internally to stimulate the central nervous system.

amphi- a word element meaning 'on both sides', 'on all sides', 'around', 'round about'.

amphibian /æm'fɪbiən/ *n.* **1.** a vertebrate animal that lives on land but breeds in water, as a frog, salamander, etc. **2.** a vehicle which can be used on both land and water, as a tank. – **amphibious**, *adj.*

amphitheatre /'æmfiθɪətə/ *n.* **1.** a level area of oval or circular shape surrounded by rising ground. **2.** any place for public contests or games; an arena. **3.** a semi-circular sloping gallery in a modern theatre.

amphora /'æmfərə/ *n., pl.* **-rae** /-ri/. a two-handled, narrow-necked vessel, used by the ancient Greeks and Romans for holding wine, oil, etc.

ample /'æmpəl/ *adj.,* **-pler, -plest**. **1.** in full or abundant measure; copious; liberal. **2.** rather bulky or full in form or figure.

amplify /'æmpləfaɪ/ *v.t.,* **-fied, -fying**. **1.** to make larger or greater; enlarge; extend. **2.** to expand in stating or describing, as by details, illustration, etc. **3.** *Electricity* to increase the amplitude of (impulses or waves). **4.** to make louder; magnify (the sound of). – **amplifier**, *n.* – **amplification**, *n.*

amplitude /'æmplə,tjud/ *n.* **1.** extension in space, especially breadth or width; largeness; extent. **2.** large or full measure; abundance; copiousness. **3.** *Physics* the distance or range from one extremity of an oscillation to the middle point or neutral value.

amputate /'æmpjəteɪt/ *v.t.,* **-tated, -tating**. to cut off (a limb, arm, etc.) by a surgical operation.

amulet /'æmjələt/ *n.* an object superstitiously worn to ward off evil; a protecting charm.

amuse /ə'mjuz/ *v.t.,* **amused, amusing**. **1.** to hold the attention of agreeably; entertain; divert. **2.** to excite mirth in. – **amusement**, *n.*

an /æn/, *weak form* /ən/ – *indefinite article* the form of **a** before an initial vowel sound. See **a**[1].

an-[1] a prefix meaning 'not', 'without', 'lacking', used before vowels and *h*, as in *anarchy*. Also, **a-**[6].

an-[2] variant of **ad-**, before *n*, as in *announce*.

an-[3] variant of **ana-**, used before vowels.

-an a suffix meaning: **1.** 'belonging to', 'pertaining or relating to', 'adhering to', as in *Australian, Christian*. **2.** *Zoology* 'relating to a certain class of organisms'.

ana- a prefix meaning 'up', 'throughout', 'again', 'back'.

-ana = -iana a noun suffix denoting a collection of material relating to a given subject, as in *Australiana*.

anachronism /ə'nækrənɪzəm/ *n.* something placed or occurring out of its proper time. – **anachronistic**, *adj.*

anaemia = anemia /ə'nimiə/ *n.* a reduced number of red blood cells, causing pallor, weakness, and breathlessness. – **anaemic**, *adj.*

anaesthesia = anesthesia /ænəs'θiʒə, -ziə/ *n. Medicine* general or local insensibility, as to pain and other sensation, induced by certain drugs.

anaesthetic = anesthetic /ænəs'θɛtɪk/ *n.* a substance such as ether, chloroform, cocaine, etc., that produces anaesthesia. – **an(a)esthetise = an(a)esthetize**, *v.* – **anaesthetist**, *n.*

anagram /'ænəgræm/ *n.* a transposition of the letters of a word or sentence to form a new word or sentence, as *caned* is an anagram of *dance*.

anal /'eɪnəl/ *adj.* of, relating to, or near the anus.

analgesic /ænəl'dʒizɪk, -sɪk/ *n.* a remedy that relieves or removes pain.

analog /'ænəlɒg/ *adj.* **1.** *Electronics* relating to the use of physical quantities (such as voltages, etc.) as analogues to the variables in a mathematical problem, as in an analog computer. **2.** of or relating to any device which represents a variable by a continuously moving or varying entity, as a clock, the hands of which move to represent time. Cf. **digital**. Also, **analogue**.

analog computer *n.* a type of computer in which information is represented by directly measurable, continuously varying quantities.

analogous /ə'næləgəs, -dʒəs/ *adj.* having analogy; corresponding in some particular.

analog-to-digital converter /,ænəlɒg-tə-,dɪdʒətl kən'vɜtə/ *n.* a device which converts an analog signal to a digital equivalent. Also, **analog-digital converter**.

analogue /'ænəlɒg/ *n.* **1.** something having analogy to something else. – *adj.* **2.** → **analog**.

analogy /əˈnælədʒi/ *n., pl.* **-gies**. an agreement, likeness, or correspondence between the relations of things to one another; a partial similarity in particular circumstances on which a comparison may be based.

analyse /ˈænəlaɪz/ *v.t.,* **-lysed**, **-lysing**. **1.** to resolve into elements or constituent parts; determine the elements or essential features of. **2.** to examine critically, so as to bring out the essential elements or give the essence of.

analysis /əˈnæləsəs/ *n., pl.* **analyses** /əˈnæləsiz/. **1.** separation of a whole, whether a material substance or any matter of thought, into its constituent elements (opposed to *synthesis*). **2.** this process as a method of studying the nature of a thing or of determining its essential features. **3.** a brief presentation of essential features; an outline or summary, as of a book; a synopsis. – **analyst**, *n.* – **analytic**, *adj.*

anarchy /ˈænəki/ *n.* **1.** a state of society without government or law. **2.** confusion in general; disorder. – **anarchic**, *adj.* – **anarchist**, **anarchism**, *n.*

anathema /əˈnæθəmə/ *n., pl.* **-mas**. **1.** any imprecation of divine punishment. **2.** a person or thing detested or loathed.

anatomy /əˈnætəmi/ *n., pl.* **-mies**. **1.** the structure of an animal or plant, or of any of its parts. **2.** the science of the structure of animals and plants. **3.** any analysis or minute examination. – **anatomical**, *adj.*

-ance a suffix of nouns denoting action, state, or quality, as in *brilliance, distance.*

ancestor /ˈænsɛstə/ *n.* one from whom a person is descended, usually distantly; a forefather; a progenitor. – **ancestral**, *adj.*

ancestry /ˈænsəstri, -sɛs-/ *n., pl.* **-tries**. ancestral descent.

anchor /ˈæŋkə/ *n.* **1.** a device for holding boats, vessels, floating bridges, etc., in place. **2.** a means of stability. **3. weigh anchor,** to take up the anchor. – *v.t.* **4.** to hold fast by an anchor. **5.** to fix or fasten; affix firmly. – *v.i.* **6.** to drop anchor. **7.** to keep hold or be firmly fixed. – **anchorage**, *n.*

anchorite /ˈæŋkəraɪt/ *n.* someone who has retired to a solitary place for a life of religious seclusion; a hermit; a recluse.

anchovy /ˈæntʃəvi, ænˈtʃoʊvi/ *n., pl.* **-vies**. any of a number of small, herring-like fishes, much used pickled and in the form of a salt paste.

ancient /ˈeɪnʃənt, ˈeɪntʃənt/ *adj.* **1.** of or in time long past, especially before the end of the Western Roman Empire, A.D. 476. **2.** dating from a remote period; of great age. **3.** *Law* having been in existence for a statutory period of time, often 20 years. -*n.* **4.** a person who lived in ancient times, especially one of the ancient Greeks, Romans, Hebrews, etc.

ancillary /ænˈsɪləri/ *adj.* accessory; auxiliary.

-ancy an equivalent of **-ance**, used chiefly in nouns denoting state or quality, as in *buoyancy.*

and /ænd/, *weak forms* /ənd, ən, n/ – *conj.* **1.** with; along with; together with; besides; also; moreover (used to connect grammatically coordinate words, phrases, or clauses). **2.** as well as. **3.** *Colloquial* to (used between verbs).

andro- a word element meaning 'man', 'male', as contrasted with 'female'. Also, **andr-**.

-androus a word element meaning 'male'.

-ane 1. a noun suffix used in chemical terms, especially names of hydrocarbons of the methane or paraffin series. **2.** an adjective suffix used when a similar form (with a different meaning) exists in **-an**, as *human, humane.*

anecdote /ˈænəkdoʊt/ *n.* a short narrative of a particular incident or occurrence of an interesting nature. – **anecdotal**, *adj.*

anemo- a word element meaning 'wind'.

anemone /əˈnɛməni/ *n.* **1.** a plant with mostly red and blue flowers. **2.** → **sea anemone**.

aneurism = aneurysm /ˈænjərɪzəm/ *n.* a permanent cardiac or arterial dilatation usually caused by weakening of the vessel wall by diseases such as syphilis or arteriosclerosis. Also, **aneurysm**.

anew /əˈnju/ *adv.* **1.** over again; once more. **2.** in a new form or manner.

angel /ˈeɪndʒəl/ *n.* **1.** *Theology* one of a class of spiritual beings, attendants of God. **2.** a messenger, especially of God. **3.** a person who resembles an angel in beauty, kindliness, etc. – **angelic**, *adj.*

anger /ˈæŋgə/ *n.* **1.** a strongly felt displeasure aroused by real or supposed wrongs, often accompanied by an impulse to retaliate; wrath; ire. – *v.t.* **2.** to excite to anger or wrath.

angio- a word element meaning 'vessel', or 'container'.

angle[1] /ˈæŋgəl/ *n., v.,* **-gled**, **-gling**. – *n.* **1.** *Mathematics* the space within two lines or three planes diverging from a common point, or within two planes diverging from a common line. **2.** an angular projection or recess. **3.** a point of view; standpoint. **4.** *Colloquial* a devious, artful scheme, method, etc. – *v.t.* **5.** to move, direct, bend or present at an angle or in an angular course.

angle[2] /ˈæŋgəl/ *v.i.,* **-gled**, **-gling**. to fish with hook and line. – **angler**, *n.*

Anglo /ˈæŋgloʊ/ *n.* **1.** an Australian of Anglo-Celtic ancestry. **2.** (in some countries) a white person whose first language is English.

Anglo- a word element meaning 'relating to England or the English'.

Angora /æŋˈgɔrə/ *n.* (yarn or fabric made from) the long, silky hair of certain goats and rabbits.

angry /ˈæŋgri/ *adj.,* **-grier**, **-griest**. **1.** feeling or showing anger or resentment (*with* or *at* a person, *at* or *about* a thing). **2.** *Medicine* inflamed, as a sore; exhibiting inflammation. – **angrily**, *adv.*

anguish /ˈæŋgwɪʃ/ *n.* **1.** excruciating or agonising pain of either body or mind; acute suffering or distress. – *v.t., v.i.* **2.** to affect with or suffer anguish.

angular /ˈæŋgjələ/ *adj.* **1.** having an angle or angles. **2.** consisting of, situated at, or forming an angle. **3.** bony; gaunt. **4.** stiff in manner; unbending. – **angularity**, *n.*

animadvert /ænəmæd'vɜt/ *v.i.* to comment critically; make remarks by way of criticism or censure (fol. by *on* or *upon*).

animal /'ænəməl/ *n.* **1.** any living thing that is not a plant, generally capable of voluntary motion, sensation, etc. **2.** any animal other than a human. **3.** a brutish or beastlike person. – *adj.* **4.** of, relating to, or derived from animals. **5.** relating to the physical or carnal nature of humans, rather than their spiritual or intellectual nature.

animate /'ænəmeɪt/ *v.*, **-mated**, **-mating**; /'ænəmət/ *adj.* – *v.t.* **1.** to give life to; make alive. **2.** to make lively, vivacious, or vigorous. **3.** to move to action; actuate. **4.** to cause to appear or move as if alive, as in an animated cartoon. – *adj.* **5.** alive; possessing life. – **animation**, *n.*

animosity /ænə'mɒsəti/ *n.*, *pl.* **-ities**. a feeling of ill will or enmity animating the conduct, or tending to display itself in action (fol. by *between* or *towards*).

anion /'ænaɪən/ *n.* a negatively charged ion which is attracted to the anode in electrolysis.

aniseed /'ænəsid/ *n.* the aromatic seed of the anise, used in medicine, in cookery, etc.

aniso- a word element meaning 'unlike' or 'unequal'.

ankle /'æŋkəl/ *n.* **1.** the aggregate joint connecting the foot with the leg. **2.** the slender part of the leg above the foot.

ankle-biter /'æŋkəl-baɪtə/ *n.* *Colloquial* a child.

annals /'ænəlz/ *pl. n.* history or relation of events recorded year by year.

anneal /ə'nɪəl/ *v.t.* to heat (glass, earthenware, metals, etc.) to remove or prevent internal stress.

annex /'ænɛks, ə'nɛks/ *v.*, /'ænɛks/ *n.* – *v.t.* **1.** to attach, join, or add, especially to something larger or more important; unite; append. **2.** to take possession of, take to one's own use permanently. – *n.* **3.** something annexed or added, especially a supplement to a document. – **annexation**, *n.*

annexe /'ænɛks/ *n.* a subsidiary building or an addition to a building.

annihilate /ə'naɪəleɪt/ *v.t.*, **-lated**, **-lating**. to reduce to nothing; destroy utterly.

anniversary /ænə'vɜsəri/ *n.*, *pl.* **-ries**. the yearly recurrence of the date of a past event.

annotate /'ænəteɪt/ *v.t.*, **-tated**, **-tating**. to supply with notes; remark upon in notes. – **annotator**, *n.* – **annotation**, *n.*

announce /ə'naʊns/ *v.t.*, **-nounced**, **-nouncing**. **1.** to make known publicly; give notice of. **2.** to state the approach or presence of. – **announcement**, *n.*

annoy /ə'nɔɪ/ *v.t.* to disturb (a person) in a way that is displeasing, troubling, or slightly irritating. – **annoyance**, *n.* – **annoying**, *adj.*

annual /'ænjuəl/ *adj.* **1.** of, for, or relating to a year; yearly. – *n.* **2.** a plant living only one year or season.

annuity /ə'njuəti/ *n.*, *pl.* **-ties**. **1.** a specified income payable at stated intervals for a fixed or a contingent period, often for the recipient's life, in consideration of a stipulated premium paid either in prior instalment payments or in a single payment. **2.** the right to receive such an income, or the duty to make such a payment or payments. – **annuitant**, *n.*

annul /ə'nʌl/ *v.t.*, **annulled**, **annulling**. to make void or null; abolish (used especially of laws or other established rules, usages, and the like). – **annulment**, *n.*

annular /'ænjələ/ *adj.* having the form of a ring.

annunciate /ə'nʌnsieɪt/ *v.t.*, **-ated**, **-ating**. to announce.

annunciation /ənʌnsi'eɪʃən/ *n.* *Bible* (*often cap.*) the announcement by the angel Gabriel to the Virgin Mary of the incarnation of Christ.

anode /'ænoʊd/ *n.* the positive pole of a battery or other source of current.

anoint /ə'nɔɪnt/ *v.t.* **1.** to put oil on; apply an unguent or oily liquid to. **2.** to consecrate by applying oil.

anomaly /ə'nɒməli/ *n.*, *pl.* **-lies**. deviation from the common rule or analogy. – **anomalous**, *adj.*

anonymous /ə'nɒnəməs/ *adj.* **1.** without any name acknowledged, as that of author, contributor, or the like. **2.** lacking individuality; without distinguishing features; without identity. – **anonymity**, **anonymousness**, *n.* – **anonymously**, *adv.*

anorak /'ænəræk/ *n.* → **parka**.

another /ə'nʌðə/ *adj.* **1.** a second; a further; an additional. **2.** a different; a distinct; of a different kind. – *pron.* **3.** one more; an additional one.

answer /'ænsə, 'an-/ *n.* **1.** a reply to a question, request, letter, etc., or to an accusation. **2.** a solution to a doubt or problem, especially in mathematics. – *v.i.* **3.** to make answer; reply. **4.** to respond (to a stimulus, direction, command, etc.); obey; acknowledge (fol. by *to*). **5.** to be or declare oneself responsible or accountable (fol. by *for*). **6.** to act or suffer in consequence of (fol. by *for*). **7.** to correspond; conform (fol. by *to*). – *v.t.* **8.** to make answer to; to reply or respond to. **9.** to give as an answer. **10.** to make a defence against (a charge); meet or refute (an argument).

answerable /'ænsərəbəl/ *adj.* **1.** accountable, responsible (*for* a person, act, etc.). **2.** liable to be called to account or asked to defend one's actions (*to* a person).

ant /ænt/ *n.* any of certain small, usually wingless, insects, very widely distributed in thousands of species, all of which have some degree of social organisation.

ant- variant of **anti-**, especially before a vowel or *h*, as in *antacid*.

-ant **1.** adjective suffix, originally participial, as in *ascendant*, *pleasant*. **2.** noun suffix used in words of participial origin, denoting agency or instrumentality, as in *servant*, *irritant*. Cf. **-ent**.

antagonise = antagonize /æn'tægənaɪz/ *v.t.*, **-nised**, **-nising**. to make hostile.

antagonism /æn'tægənɪzəm/ *n.* **1.** the activity or the relation of contending parties or conflicting forces; active opposition. **2.** an opposing force, principle, or tendency. – **antagonist**, *n.*

ante /'ænti/ *n.* a payment, usually monetary, extracted as part of a bargain.

ante- a prefix meaning 'before in space or time'.

anteater /'æntitə/ *n.* any of the echidnas or spiny anteaters of Australia and New Guinea.

antecedent /æntə'sidənt/ *adj.* **1.** going or being before; preceding; prior (often fol. by *to*). – *n.* **2.** (*pl.*) **a.** ancestry. **b.** one's past history. **3.** a preceding circumstance, event, etc. **4.** *Grammar* the word or phrase, usually a noun, which is replaced by a pronoun later in the sentence.

antedate /'æntideɪt, ænti'deɪt/ *v.t.*, **-dated**, **-dating**. **1.** to be of older date than; precede in time. **2.** to affix a date earlier than the true one to (a document, etc.).

antelope /'æntəloʊp/ *n., pl.* **-lopes**, (*esp. collectively*) **-lope**. a slenderly built, hollow-horned ruminant allied to cattle, sheep, and goats, found chiefly in Africa and Asia.

ante meridiem /ˌænti mə'rɪdiəm/ **1.** before noon. **2.** the time between 12 midnight and 12 noon. *Abbrev.*: a.m., am – **antemeridian**, *adj.*

antenna /æn'tɛnə/ *n., pl.* **-tennae** /-'tɛni/ *for def. 1* **-tennas** *for def. 2* – **1.** *Zoology* one of the jointed appendages occurring in pairs on the heads of insects, crustaceans, etc., often called feelers. **2.** a radio or television aerial.

antepenultimate /ˌæntipə'nʌltəmət/ *adj.* last but two.

anterior /æn'tɪəriə/ *adj.* **1.** placed before; situated more to the front (opposed to *posterior*). **2.** going before in time; preceding; earlier.

anthem /'ænθəm/ *n.* a hymn, as of praise, devotion, or patriotism.

antho- a word element meaning 'flower'.

anthology /æn'θɒlədʒi/ *n., pl.* **-gies**. a collection of literary pieces, especially poems, of varied authorship.

anthropo- a word element meaning 'human being'. Also, **anthrop-**.

anthropoid /'ænθrəpɔɪd/ *adj.* resembling a human being.

anthropology /ænθrə'pɒlədʒi/ *n.* the science that deals with the origin, development (physical, intellectual, cultural, moral, etc.) and varieties of humanity. – **anthropologist**, *n.* – **anthropological**, *adj.*

anti- a prefix meaning 'against', 'opposed to'. Also, **ant-**.

antibiotic /ˌæntibaɪ'ɒtɪk/ *n.* a chemical substance used in the treatment of bacterial infections.

antibody /'æntibɒdi/ *n., pl.* **-bodies**. any of various substances existing in the blood or developed in immunisation which counteract bacterial or viral poisons or destroy bacteria in the system.

antic /'æntɪk/ *n.* (*often pl.*) a grotesque, fantastic, or ludicrous gesture or posture.

anticipate /æn'tɪsəpeɪt/ *v.t.*, **-pated**, **-pating**. **1.** to realise beforehand; foretaste or foresee. **2.** to consider or mention before the proper time. – **anticipation**, *n.*

anticlimax /ænti'klaɪmæks/ *n.* **1.** a noticeable or ludicrous descent in discourse from lofty ideas or expressions to what is much less impressive. **2.** an abrupt descent in dignity; an inglorious or disappointing conclusion.

anticlockwise /ænti'klɒkwaɪz/ *adv., adj.* in a direction opposite to that of the rotation of the hands of a clock.

antidote /'æntidoʊt/ *n.* a medicine or other remedy for counteracting the effects of poison, disease, etc.

antilogy /æn'tɪlədʒi/ *n., pl.* **-gies**. a contradiction in terms or ideas.

antinomy /æn'tɪnəmi/ *n., pl.* **-mies**. opposition between laws and principles; contradiction in law.

antipathy /æn'tɪpəθi/ *n., pl.* **-thies**. **1.** a natural or settled dislike; repugnance; aversion. **2.** an instinctive contrariety or opposition in feeling.

antiperspirant /ænti'pɜspərənt/ *n.* any preparation for decreasing or preventing perspiration.

antipodes /æn'tɪpədiz/ *pl. n.* points diametrically opposite to each other on the earth or any globe. – **antipodean**, *adj., n.*

antiquary /'æntəkwəri/ *n., pl.* **-quaries**. an expert on ancient things; a student or collector of antiquities.

antiquate /'æntəkweɪt/ *v.t.*, **-quated**, **-quating**. **1.** to make old and useless by substituting something newer and better. **2.** to make antique. – **antiquated**, *adj.*

antique /æn'tik/ *adj.* **1.** belonging to former times as contrasted with modern. – *n.* **2.** an object of art or a furniture piece of a former period.

antiquity /æn'tɪkwəti/ *n., pl.* **-ties**. **1.** the quality of being ancient; great age. **2.** (*usu. pl.*) something belonging to or remaining from ancient times.

antiseptic /æntə'sɛptɪk/ *n.* an agent which destroys the micro-organisms that produce septic disease.

antisocial /ænti'soʊʃəl/ *adj.* **1.** unwilling or unable to associate normally with one's fellows. **2.** opposed, damaging, or motivated by antagonism to social order, or to the principles on which society is constituted.

antithesis /æn'tɪθəsəs/ *n., pl.* **-theses** /-θəsiz/. **1.** opposition; contrast. **2.** the direct opposite (fol. by *of* or *to*).

antitoxin /ænti'tɒksən/ *n.* a substance which counteracts a specific toxin. – **antitoxic**, *adj.*

antitrust /ænti'trʌst/ *adj.* of or relating to trade practices law regulating commercial agreements and practices which restrict or impede competition in a market economy.

antivenene /ˌæntivə'nin/ *n.* **1.** an antitoxin produced in the blood by repeated injections of venom, as of snakes. **2.** the antitoxic serum obtained from such blood. Also, **antivenin**.

antler /'æntlə/ *n.* one of the solid deciduous horns, usually branched, of an animal of the deer family.

antonym /'æntənɪm/ *n.* a word opposed in meaning to another (opposed to *synonym*).

anus /'eɪnəs/ *n.* the opening at the lower end of the alimentary canal, through which the solid refuse of digestion is excreted.

anvil /'ænvəl/ *n.* a heavy iron block with a smooth face, frequently of steel, on which metals, usually red-hot or white-hot, are hammered into desired shapes.

anxiety /æŋ'zaɪəti/ *n., pl.* **-ties**. distress or uneasiness of mind caused by apprehension of danger or misfortune.

anxious /'æŋʃəs, 'æŋk-/ *adj.* **1.** full of anxiety or solicitude; greatly troubled or solicitous. **2.** earnestly desirous (followed by infinitive or *for*).

any /'ɛni/ *adj.* **1.** one, a, an, or (with plural noun) some; whatever or whichever it may be. **2.** in whatever quantity or number, great or small. **3.** every. **4.** a great or unlimited (amount). – *pron.* **5.** (*construed as sing.*) any person; anybody, or (*construed as pl.*) any persons. **6.** any single one or any one's; any thing or things; any quantity or number. – *adv.* **7.** in any degree; to any extent; at all.

anybody /'ɛnibɒdi, -bədi/ *pron., n., pl.* **-bodies**. **1.** any person. **2.** a person of little importance.

anyhow /'ɛnihaʊ/ *adv.* **1.** in any case; at all events. **2.** in a careless manner. **3.** in any way whatever.

anyone /'ɛniwʌn/ *pron.* any person; anybody.

anything /'ɛniθɪŋ/ *pron.* **1.** any thing whatever; something, no matter what. – *n.* **2.** a thing of any kind. – *adv.* **3.** in any degree; to any extent.

any way *adv.* **1.** in any way or manner. **2.** carelessly; haphazardly; anyhow.

anyway /'ɛniweɪ/ *adv.* in any case; anyhow.

anywhere /'ɛniwɛə/ *adv.* in, at, or to any place.

anywise /'ɛniwaɪz/ *adv.* in any way or respect.

A-1 /eɪ-'wʌn/ *adj.* **1.** registered as a first-class vessel in a shipping register, as Lloyd's Register. **2.** *Colloquial* first-class; excellent. Also, **A1**.

aorta /eɪ'ɔtə/ *n., pl.* **-tas**, **-tae** /-ti/. *Anatomy* the main trunk of the arterial system, conveying blood from the left ventricle of the heart to all of the body except the lungs.

ap- variant of **ad-**, before *p* as in *appear*.

apart /ə'pat/ *adv.* **1.** in pieces, or to pieces. **2.** separately or aside in motion, place, or position. **3.** to or at one side, with respect to purpose or function. **4.** separately or individually in consideration. **5.** aside (used with a gerund or noun). – *adj.* **6.** separate; independent.

apartheid /ə'pateɪt/ *n.* (especially in South Africa) racial segregation.

apartment /ə'patmənt/ *n.* **1.** a single room in a building. **2.** a home unit.

apathy /'æpəθi/ *n., pl.* **-thies**. lack of feeling; absence or suppression of passion, emotion, or excitement. – **apathetic**, *adj.*

ape /eɪp/ *n., v.,* **aped**, **aping**. – *n.* **1.** a tailless monkey or a monkey with a very short tail. – *v.t.* **2.** to imitate servilely; mimic.

aperture /'æpətʃə/ *n.* a hole, slit, crack, gap, or other opening.

apex /'eɪpɛks/ *n., pl.* **apexes**, **apices** /'eɪpəsiz/. the tip, point, or vertex of anything; the summit.

aphid /'eɪfəd/ *n.* a plant-sucking insect.

aphorism /'æfərɪzəm/ *n.* a terse saying embodying a general truth.

aphrodisiac /æfrə'dɪziæk/ *n.* a drug or food that arouses sexual desire.

apiary /'eɪpiəri/ *n., pl.* **-ries**. a place in which bees are kept; a stand or shed containing a number of beehives. – **apiarist**, *n.*

apical /'æpɪkəl, 'eɪ-/ *adj.* of, at, or forming the apex.

apices /'eɪpəsiz/ *n.* a plural of **apex**.

apiece /ə'pis/ *adv.* for each piece, thing, or person; for each one; each.

aplomb /ə'plɒm/ *n.* **1.** imperturbable self-possession, poise, or assurance. **2.** a perpendicular position.

apocalypse /ə'pɒkəlɪps/ *n.* revelation; discovery; disclosure. – **apocalyptic**, *adj.*

apocryphal /ə'pɒkrəfəl/ *adj.* **1.** of doubtful authorship or authenticity. **2.** false; spurious. **3.** fabulous; fictitious; mythical.

apolitical /eɪpə'lɪtɪkəl/ *adj.* **1.** having no interest in political issues. **2.** not involving obligations to a particular political party.

apologia /æpə'loʊdʒiə/ *n.* a formal defence or justification in speech or writing, as of a cause or doctrine.

apologise = apologize /ə'pɒlədʒaɪz/ *v.i.,* **-gised**, **-gising**. **1.** to offer excuses or regrets for some fault, insult, failure, or injury. **2.** to make a formal defence in speech or writing. – **apologetic**, *adj.*

apology /ə'pɒlədʒi/ *n., pl.* **-gies**. **1.** an expression of regret offered for some fault, failure, insult, or injury. **2.** a poor specimen or substitute; a makeshift.

apoplexy /'æpəplɛksi/ *n.* marked loss of bodily function due to cerebral haemorrhage. – **apoplectic**, *adj.*

apostasy /ə'pɒstəsi/ *n., pl.* **-sies**. a total desertion of, or departure from, one's religion, principles, party, cause, etc.

apostle /ə'pɒsəl/ *n.* a vigorous and zealous upholder (of a principle, cause, etc.). – **apostolic**, *adj.*

apostrophe /ə'pɒstrəfi/ *n.* the sign (') used to indicate: **1.** the omission of one or more letters in a word, as in *o'er* for *over*, *halo'd* for *haloed*. **2.** the possessive case, as in *lion's*, *lions'*. **3.** certain plurals, as in *several M.D.'s*. – **apostrophic**, *adj.*

apothecary /ə'pɒθəkri, -kəri/ *n., pl.* **-ries**. *Archaic* a chemist; a pharmacist.

appal /ə'pɔl/ *v.t.,* **-palled**, **-palling**. **1.** to overcome with fear; fill with consternation and horror. **2.** *Colloquial* to shock; dismay; displease.

apparatus /æpə'ratəs, -'reɪtəs/ *n., pl.* **-tus**, **-tuses**. an assemblage of instruments, machinery, appliances, materials, etc., for a particular use.

apparel /ə'pærəl/ *n.* a person's outer clothing; raiment.

apparent /ə'pærənt/ *adj.* **1.** capable of being clearly perceived or understood; plain or clear. **2.** seeming; ostensible. **3.** exposed to the sight; open to view.

apparition /æpə'rɪʃən/ *n.* **1.** a ghostly appearance; a spectre or phantom. **2.** anything that appears, especially something remarkable or phenomenal.

appeal /ə'pil/ *n.* **1.** a call for aid, support, mercy, etc.; an earnest request or entreaty. **2.** application or reference to some person or authority for corroboration, vindication, decision, etc. **3.** power to attract or to move the feelings. – *v.i.* **4.** to make an appeal. **5.** to resort for proof, decision, or settlement. **6.** to offer a peculiar attraction, interest, enjoyment, etc.

appear /ə'pɪə/ *v.i.* **1.** to come into sight; become visible. **2.** to have an appearance; seem; look. **3.** to be obvious; be clear or made clear by evidence. **4.** to come or be placed before the public. **5.** *Law* to come formally before a tribunal, authority, etc. – **appearance**, *n.*

appease /ə'piz/ *v.t.*, **-peased**, **-peasing**. **1.** to bring to a state of peace, quiet, ease, or content. **2.** to satisfy.

appellant /ə'pɛlənt/ *n.* someone who appeals.

appellate /ə'pɛlət/ *adj.* *Law* relating to appeals.

appellation /æpə'leɪʃən/ *n.* **1.** a name, title, or designation. **2.** the act of naming.

append /ə'pɛnd/ *v.t.* to add, as an accessory; annex. – **appendage**, *n.* – **appendant**, *adj.*

appendicitis /əpɛndə'saɪtəs/ *n.* inflammation of the appendix.

appendix /ə'pɛndɪks/ *n.*, *pl.* **-dixes**, **-dices** /-dəsiz/. **1.** matter which supplements the main text of a book, generally explanatory, statistical, or bibliographic material. **2.** *Anatomy* a narrow, blind tube at the beginning of the large intestine.

appertain /æpə'teɪn/ *v.i.* to belong as a part, member, possession, attribute, etc.; pertain (fol. by *to*).

appetising = appetizing /'æpətaɪzɪŋ/ *adj.* exciting or appealing to the appetite.

appetite /'æpətaɪt/ *n.* **1.** a desire for food or drink. **2.** a desire to supply any bodily want or craving.

applaud /ə'plɔd/ *v.i.* **1.** to express approval by clapping the hands, shouting, etc. **2.** to give praise; express approval. – **applause**, *n.*

apple /'æpəl/ *n.* an edible fruit, usually round and with red, yellow or green skin.

appliance /ə'plaɪəns/ *n.* **1.** an instrument, apparatus, or device, especially one operated by electricity and designed for household use. **2.** the act of applying; application.

applicable /ə'plɪkəbəl, 'æp-/ *adj.* capable of being applied; fit; suitable; relevant.

applicant /'æpləkənt/ *n.* someone who applies; a candidate.

application /æplə'keɪʃən/ *n.* **1.** the act of putting to a special use or purpose. **2.** the quality of being useable for a particular purpose or in a special way; relevance. **3.** something applied, as a salve. **4.** a written or spoken request or appeal. **5.** close attention; persistent effort.

apply /ə'plaɪ/ *v.*, **-plied**, **-plying**. – *v.t.* **1.** to lay on; bring into physical proximity or contact. **2.** to put into practical operation, as a principle, law, rule, etc. **3.** to put to use; employ. **4.** to give with earnestness or assiduity. – *v.i.* **5.** to have a bearing or reference; be pertinent. **6.** to make application or request; ask.

appoint /ə'pɔɪnt/ *v.t.* **1.** to nominate or assign to a position, or to perform a function. **2.** to determine by authority or agreement; fix; settle. **3.** to provide with what is requisite; equip.

appointment /ə'pɔɪntmənt/ *n.* **1.** the act of appointing, designating, or placing in office. **2.** an office held by a person appointed. **3.** the act of fixing by mutual agreement.

apportion /ə'pɔʃən/ *v.t.* to distribute or allocate proportionally.

apposite /'æpəzət/ *adj.* suitable; well-adapted; pertinent.

apposition /æpə'zɪʃən/ *n.* the act of adding to or together; a placing together; juxtaposition.

appraise /ə'preɪz/ *v.t.*, **-praised**, **-praising**. **1.** to estimate generally, as to quality, size, weight, etc. **2.** to value in current money; estimate the value of. – **appraisal**, *n.*

appreciable /ə'priʃəbəl/ *adj.* **1.** capable of being perceived or estimated; noticeable. **2.** fairly large.

appreciate /ə'priʃieɪt, ə'prisi-/ *v.*, **-ated**, **-ating**. – *v.t.* **1.** to place a sufficiently high estimate on. **2.** to be fully conscious of; be aware of; detect. **3.** to be pleased with or grateful for. **4.** to raise in value. – *v.i.* **5.** to increase in value. – **appreciation**, *n.* – **appreciative**, *adj.*

apprehend /æprə'hɛnd/ *v.t.* **1.** to take into custody; arrest by legal warrant or authority. **2.** to grasp the meaning of; understand; conceive.

apprehension /æprə'hɛnʃən/ *n.* **1.** anticipation of adversity; dread or fear of coming evil. **2.** the faculty of apprehending; understanding. **3.** a view, opinion, or idea on any subject. **4.** the act of arresting; seizure. – **apprehensible**, *adj.*

apprentice /ə'prɛntəs/ *n.* **1.** someone who works for another with obligations to learn a trade. **2.** a learner; a novice.

apprise = apprize /ə'praɪz/ *v.t.*, **-prised**, **-prising**. to give notice to; inform; advise (often fol. by *of*).

approach /ə'proʊtʃ/ *v.t.* **1.** to come nearer or near to. **2.** to make advances or a proposal to. – *v.i.* **3.** to come nearer; draw near. – *n.* **4.** the act of drawing near. **5.** any means of access. **6.** the method used or steps taken in setting about a task, problem, etc.

approachable /ə'proʊtʃəbəl/ *adj.* **1.** capable of being approached; accessible. **2.** (of a person) easy to approach.

approbation /æprə'beɪʃən/ *n.* approval; commendation. – **approbatory**, *adj.*

appropriate /ə'proʊpriət/ *adj.*, /ə'proʊprieɪt/ *v.*, **-ated**, **-ating**. – *adj.* **1.** suitable or fitting for a particular purpose, person, occasion, etc. – *v.t.* **2.** to set apart for some specific purpose or use. **3.** to take to or for oneself; take possession of.

appropriation /əproʊpri'eɪʃən/ *n.* **1.** anything appropriated. **2.** the act of appropriating. **3.** an act of a legislature authorising money to be paid from the treasury for a special use.

approval /ə'pruvəl/ *n.* **1.** the act of approving; approbation. **2.** sanction; official permission. **3. on approval,** for examination, without obligation to buy.

approve /ə'pruv/ *v.*, **-proved**, **-proving**. – *v.t.* **1.** to confirm or sanction officially; ratify. – *v.i.* **2.** to speak or think favourably (usually fol. by *of*).

approximate /ə'prɒksəmət/ *adj.*, /ə'prɒksəmeɪt/ *v.*, **-mated**, **-mating**. – *adj.* **1.** nearly exact, equal, or perfect. **2.** inaccurate; rough. – *v.t.* **3.** to come near to; approach closely to.

appurtenance /ə'pɜtənəns/ *n.* something accessory to another and more important thing; an adjunct. – **appurtenant**, *adj.*

apricot /'eɪprikɒt, -prə-/ *n.* **1.** a downy yellow fruit, somewhat resembling a small peach. **2.** a pinkish yellow or yellowish pink.

apron /'eɪprən/ *n.* a piece of clothing made in various ways for covering, and usually also protecting, the front of the person more or less completely.

apropos /æprə'poʊ/ *adv.* **1.** to the purpose; opportunely. **2.** with reference or regard. – *adj.* **3.** opportune; pertinent.

apse /æps/ *n.* a vaulted recess in a building, especially a church.

apt /æpt/ *adj.* **1.** inclined; disposed; prone. **2.** unusually intelligent; quick to learn. **3.** suited to the purpose or occasion.

aptitude /'æptətʃud/ *n.* **1.** a natural tendency or acquired inclination. **2.** readiness in learning; intelligence; talent. **3.** the state or quality of being apt; special fitness.

aqualung /'ækwəlʌŋ/ *n.* an apparatus enabling a diver to breathe underwater.

aquamarine /ækwəmə'rin/ *n.*, *adj.* light blue-green or greenish blue.

aquarium /ə'kwɛəriəm/ *n.*, *pl.* **aquariums**, **aquaria** /ə'kwɛəriə/. a pond, tank, or establishment in which living aquatic animals or plants are kept, as for exhibition.

aquatic /ə'kwɒtɪk/ *adj.* **1.** of or relating to water. **2.** living or growing in water.

aqueduct /'ækwədʌkt/ *n.* *Civil Engineering* a conduit or artificial channel for conducting water from a distance, the water usually flowing by gravity.

aqueous /'ækwiəs, 'eɪkwi-/ *adj.* of, like, or containing water; watery.

aquifer /'ækwəfə/ *n.* a geological formation which holds water and allows water to percolate through it.

aquiline /'ækwəlaɪn/ *adj.* **1.** of or like the eagle. **2.** (of the nose) curved like an eagle's beak; hooked.

ar- variant of **ad-** before *r*.

-ar[1] **1.** an adjective suffix meaning 'of or relating to', 'of the nature of', 'like'. **2.** a suffix forming adjectives not directly related to nouns.

-ar[2] a noun suffix, as in *vicar*, *scholar*, *collar*.

-ar[3] a noun suffix denoting an agent (replacing regular **-er**[1]), as in *beggar*, *liar*.

Arabic numerals /ærəbɪk/ *pl. n.* the characters 0, 1, 2, 3, 4, 5, 6, 7, 8, 9, introduced into general Western use since the 12th century.

arable /'ærəbəl/ *adj.* capable, without much modification, of producing crops by means of tillage.

arachnid /ə'ræknɪd/ *n.* any arthropod of the class which includes the spiders, scorpions, mites, etc.

arbiter /'abətə/ *n.* **1.** a person empowered to decide points at issue. **2.** someone who has the sole or absolute power of judging or determining.

arbitrage /'abətrɪdʒ/ *n.* the simultaneous purchase and sale of the same securities, commodities, or moneys in different markets to profit from unequal prices. – **arbitrageur**, **arbitrager**, *n.*

arbitrary /'abətrəri, 'abətri/ *adj.* **1.** subject to individual will or judgment. **2.** not attributable to any rule or law; accidental. **3.** capricious; uncertain; unreasonable. **4.** selected at random or by convention.

arbitrate /'abətreɪt/ *v.t.*, **-trated**, **-trating**. **1.** to decide as arbiter or arbitrator; determine. **2.** to submit to arbitration; settle by arbitration. – **arbitrator**, *n.*

arbitration /abə'treɪʃən/ *n.* **1.** *Law* the hearing or determining of a dispute between parties by a person or persons chosen, agreed between them, or appointed by virtue of a statutory obligation. **2.** *Industrial Law* the presentation of legal argument by parties (for whom conciliation has failed), before a government-appointed arbitrator who is empowered to make a binding decision.

arboreal /a'bɔriəl/ *adj.* **1.** of or relating to trees. **2.** *Zoology* adapted for living in trees.

arbour = arbor /'abə/ *n.* a bower formed by trees, shrubs, or vines, often on a trellis.

arc /ak/ *n.* **1.** any part of a circle or other curved line. **2.** *Electricity* the luminous bridge formed by the passage of a current across a gap between two conductors or terminals. **3.** anything bow-shaped.

arcade /a'keɪd/ *n.* a pedestrian way with shops on one side or both sides.

arcane /a'keɪn/ *adj.* mysterious; secret; obscure.

arch[1] /atʃ/ *n.* **1.** a curved structure resting on supports at both extremities. – *v.t.* **2.** to cover with a vault, or span with an arch. **3.** to throw or make into the shape of an arch or vault; curve.

arch[2] /atʃ/ *adj.* **1.** chief; most important; principal. **2.** cunning; sly; roguish.

arch- a prefix meaning 'first', 'chief'.

-arch a suffix meaning 'chief'.

archaeo- = archeo- a word element meaning 'primeval', 'primitive', 'ancient'. Also (*esp. before a vowel*), **archae-**, **archeo-**.

archaeology = archeology /aki'ɒlədʒi/ *n.* the scientific study of any culture, especially a prehistoric one, by excavation and description of its remains.

archaic /a'keɪɪk/ *adj.* **1.** marked by the characteristics of an earlier period; old-fashioned. **2.** no longer used in ordinary speech or writing; borrowed from older usage (distinguished from *obsolete*).

archaism /'akeɪˌɪzəm/ *n.* something archaic, as a word or expression.

archangel /'akeɪndʒəl/ *n.* a chief or principal angel.

archbishop /atʃ'bɪʃəp/ *n.* a bishop of the highest rank.

archenemy /atʃ'ɛnəmi/ *n.*, *pl.* **-mies**. a chief enemy.

archer /'atʃə/ *n.* someone who shoots with a bow and arrow. – **archery**, *n.*

archetype /'akitaɪp/ *n.* the original pattern or model after which a thing is made. – **archetypal**, **archetypical**, *adj.*

archipelago /akə'pɛləgoʊ/ *n., pl.* **-gos, -goes**. any large body of water with many islands.

architect /'akətɛkt/ *n.* one whose profession it is to design buildings and superintend their construction.

architecture /'akətɛktʃə/ *n.* **1.** the art or science of building, including plan, design, construction, and decorative treatment. **2.** the style of building. **3.** the structure or design of something, as a computer, a novel, etc.

architrave /'akətreɪv/ *n.* a band of mouldings or other ornamentation about a rectangular door or other opening or a panel.

archive /'akaɪv/ *n.* (*often pl.*) **1.** the non-current documents or records relating to the activities, rights, claims, treaties, constitutions, etc., of a family, corporation, community, or nation. **2.** a place where public records or other historical documents are kept.

-archy a word element meaning 'rule', 'government'.

arctic /'aktɪk/ *adj.* **1.** of, at, or near the North Pole. **2.** extremely cold.

-ard a noun suffix, often depreciative, as in *coward, drunkard, wizard.* Also, **-art**.

ardent /'adənt/ *adj.* **1.** glowing with feeling, earnestness, or zeal; passionate; fervent. **2.** burning, fiery, or hot.

ardour = ardor /'adə/ *n.* warmth of feeling; fervour; eagerness; zeal.

arduous /'adʒuəs/ *adj.* requiring great exertion; laborious; difficult.

are[1] /a/, *weak form* /ə/ – *v.* present indicative plural of the verb **be**.

are[2] /ɛə/ *n.* a hundredth of a hectare.

area /'ɛəriə/ *n.* **1.** any particular extent of surface; region; tract. **2.** extent, range or scope. **3.** a piece of unoccupied ground; an open space. **4.** *Mathematics* two dimensional extent. – **areal**, *adj.*

area code *n.* a sequence of numbers or letters preceding a telephone subscriber's number, indicating the area or exchange. Also, **S.T.D. code**.

arena /ə'rinə/ *n.* **1.** an enclosure for sports contests, shows, etc. **2.** a field of conflict or endeavour.

areola /ə'rɪələ/ *n., pl.* **-lae** /-li/. a small ring of colour, as around a pustule or the human nipple.

argon /'agɒn/ *n.* a colourless, odourless, chemically inactive, gaseous element. *Symbol*: Ar

argot /'agoʊ/ *n.* the peculiar language or jargon of any class or group.

arguable /'agjuəbəl/ *adj.* **1.** capable of being maintained; plausible. **2.** open to dispute or argument. **3.** capable of being argued. – **arguably**, *adv.*

argue /'agju/ *v.,* **-gued, -guing**. – *v.i.* **1.** to present reasons for or against a thing. **2.** to contend in argument; dispute. – *v.t.* **3.** to state the reasons for or against. **4.** to argue in favour of; support by argument.

argument /'agjəmənt/ *n.* **1.** an argumentation; debate. **2.** a matter of contention. **3.** a statement or fact tending to support a point. **4.** *Computers* a datum or value used while transferring information from part to part of a program.

argumentation /agjəmən'teɪʃən/ *n.* **1.** debate; discussion; reasoning. **2.** the setting forth of reasons together with the conclusion drawn from them; formal or logical reasoning.

argumentative /agjə'mɛntətɪv/ *adj.* **1.** given to argument. **2.** controversial.

aria /'ariə/ *n.* an elaborate melody for a single voice, with accompaniment, in an opera, oratorio, etc.

-arian a compound suffix of adjectives and nouns, often referring to pursuits, doctrines, etc.

arid /'ærəd/ *adj.* dry; without moisture; parched with heat.

-arious an adjective suffix meaning 'connected with', 'having to do with'.

arise /ə'raɪz/ *v.i.,* **arose, arisen, arising**. **1.** to come into being or action; originate; appear. **2.** to move upwards. **3.** to rise; get up from sitting, lying, or kneeling.

aristo- a word element meaning 'best', 'superior'.

aristocracy /ærə'stɒkrəsi/ *n., pl.* **-cies**. a class of hereditary nobility.

aristocrat /'ærəstəkræt/ *n.* **1.** someone who has the tastes, manners, etc., of the members of a superior group or class. **2.** (one of) the best of its kind. – **aristocratic**, *adj.*

arithmetic /ə'rɪθmətɪk/ *n.,* /ærəθ'mɛtɪk/ *adj.* – *n.* **1.** the art or skill of computation with figures (the most elementary branch of mathematics). – *adj.* **2.** of or relating to arithmetic. – **arithmetical**, *adj.*

arithmetic unit *n.* the section of a computer which does arithmetical processes.

ark /ak/ *n.* **1.** a wooden chest or coffer. **2.** a large, floating vessel resembling this, as Noah's Ark.

arm[1] /am/ *n.* **1.** the upper limb of the human body from the shoulder to the hand. **2.** this limb, exclusive of the hand. **3.** the forelimb of any four-legged vertebrate. **4.** any arm-like part. **5.** a covering for the arm, as the sleeve of a garment.

arm[2] /am/ *n.* **1.** (*usu. pl.*) a weapon. – *v.t.* **2.** to equip with arms. **3.** to fit or prepare (a thing) for any specific purpose or effective use.

armada /a'madə/ *n.* a fleet of warships.

armadillo /amə'dɪloʊ/ *n., pl.* **-los**. an armoured, burrowing mammal of Central and South America.

armament /'aməmənt/ *n.* the weapons with which a military unit, especially an aeroplane, vehicle, or warship, is equipped.

armature /'amətʃə/ *n.* protective covering.

armchair /'amtʃɛə/ *n.* a chair with arms to support the forearms or elbows.

armistice /'aməstəs/ *n.* a truce.

armorial /a'mɔriəl/ *adj.* belonging to heraldry or to heraldic bearing.

armour = armor /'amə/ *n.* **1.** defensive equipment; any covering worn as a protection against offensive weapons. **2.** that which serves as a protection or safeguard.

armoury = armory /'aməri/ *n., pl.* **-ries**. a storage place for weapons and other war equipment.

armpit /'ampɪt/ *n.* the hollow under the arm

at the shoulder.

arms /amz/ *pl. n.* **1.** → **arm²** (def. 1). **2.** *Military* small arms. **3.** heraldic bearings.

army /'ami/ *n., pl.* **-mies**. **1.** (*cap. or lower case*) the military forces of a nation. **2.** a large body of people trained and armed for war.

aroma /ə'roumə/ *n.* a smell, especially an agreeable smell; fragrance. – **aromatic**, *adj.*

aromatherapy /əroumə'θɛrəpi/ *n.* a type of massage using scented oils.

arose /ə'rouz/ *v.* past tense of **arise**.

around /ə'raund/ *adv.* **1.** in a circle or sphere; round about; on every side. **2.** here and there; about. – *prep.* **3.** about; on all sides; encircling; encompassing. **4.** *Colloquial* approximately; near in time, amount, etc.

arouse /ə'rauz/ *v.,* **aroused**, **arousing**. – *v.t.* **1.** to excite into action; stir or put in motion; call into being. **2.** to wake from sleep. – **arousal**, *n.*

arraign /ə'reɪn/ *v.t.* *Law* to call or bring before a court to answer to a charge or accusation.

arrange /ə'reɪndʒ/ *v.t.,* **-ranged**, **-ranging**. **1.** to place in proper, desired, or convenient order; adjust properly. **2.** to come to an agreement or understanding regarding. **3.** to prepare or plan. – **arrangement**, *n.*

arrant /'ærənt/ *adj.* downright; thorough.

array /ə'reɪ/ *v.t.* **1.** to place in proper or desired order, as troops for battle. **2.** to clothe with garments, especially of an ornamental kind; deck. – *n.* **3.** regular order or arrangement. **4.** attire; dress.

arrear /ə'rɪə/ *n.* **1.** (*usu. pl.*) that which is behind in payment; a debt which remains unpaid, though due. **2. in arrear** or **in arrears,** behind in payments.

arrest /ə'rɛst/ *v.t.* **1.** to seize (a person) by legal authority or warrant. **2.** to capture; seize. **3.** to bring to a standstill; stop; check. – *n.* **4.** the taking of a person into custody in connection with a legal proceeding.

arresting /ə'rɛstɪŋ/ *adj.* catching the attention; striking.

arrive /ə'raɪv/ *v.i.,* **-rived**, **-riving**. **1.** to come to a certain point in the course of travel; reach one's destination. **2.** to reach in any course or process; attain (fol. by *at*). – **arrival**, *n.*

arrogant /'ærəgənt/ *adj.* making unwarrantable claims or pretensions to superior importance or rights. – **arrogance**, **arrogancy**, *n.*

arrow /'ærou/ *n.* **1.** a slender, straight, generally pointed, missile weapon made to be shot from a bow. **2.** a figure of an arrow used to indicate direction.

arrowroot /'ærərut/ *n.* a tropical American plant whose rhizomes yield a nutritious starch.

arse /as/ *n.* *Colloquial* rump; bottom; buttocks; posterior.

arsenal /'asənəl/ *n.* a repository or magazine of arms and military stores.

arsenic /'asənɪk/ *n.* a greyish-white element having a metallic lustre, and forming poisonous compounds. *Symbol*: As

arson /'asən/ *n.* the malicious burning of any building.

art /at/ *n.* **1.** the production or expression of what is beautiful (especially visually), appealing, or of more than ordinary significance. **2.** (*pl.*) a branch of learning or university study. **3.** skilled workmanship, execution, or agency (often opposed to *nature*). **4.** a skill or knack; a method of doing a thing, especially if it is difficult. **5.** craft; cunning. **6.** studied action; artificiality in behaviour. **7.** learning or science.

-art variant of **-ard**, as in *braggart*.

arterial /a'tɪəriəl/ *adj.* **1.** *Anatomy* of, relating to, or resembling the arteries. **2.** having a main channel and many branches. **3.** carrying the main flow of traffic between large towns.

arteriosclerosis /a,tɪəriousklə'rousəs/ *n.* *Pathology* an arterial disease characterised by inelasticity and thickening of the vessel walls, with lessened blood flow.

artery /'atəri/ *n., pl.* **-teries**. **1.** *Anatomy* a blood vessel which conveys blood from the heart to any part of the body. **2.** a main channel, as in drainage or roads.

artesian bore /a'tiʒən/ *n.* a bore in which the water level, under pressure, rises above ground. Also, **artesian well**.

arthritis /a'θraɪtəs/ *n.* *Pathology* inflammation of a joint, as in gout or rheumatism. – **arthritic**, *adj., n.*

arthro- *Anatomy* a word element meaning joint, as in *arthropod*. Also, **arthr-**.

arthropod /'aθrəpɒd/ *n.* any of the Arthropoda, the phylum of segmented invertebrates, having jointed legs, as the insects, arachnids, and crustaceans.

artichoke /'atətʃouk, 'atɪtʃouk/ *n.* a herbaceous, thistlelike plant with an edible flower head.

article /'atɪkəl/ *n., v.,* **-cled**, **-cling**. – *n.* **1.** a piece of writing on a specific topic. **2.** an individual piece or thing of a class; an item or particular. **3.** a thing, indefinitely. **4.** in English, the words *a*, *an* and *the*. **5.** a clause, item, point, or particular in a contract, treaty, etc. **6.** a separate clause or provision of a statute. **7.** (*pl.*) a document drawn up in articles; an agreement or code. – *v.t.* **8.** to set forth in articles; charge or accuse specifically. **9.** to bind by articles of covenant or stipulation. **10.** to bind by articles of agreement.

articled clerk /,atɪkəld/ *n.* a person under articles of agreement to serve a solicitor in return for training.

articles of association *pl. n.* (a document containing) the regulations and constitution of a registered company.

articulate /a'tɪkjələɪt/ *v.,* **-lated**, **-lating** /a'tɪkjələt/. *adj.* – *v.t.* **1.** to utter articulately. **2.** *Phonetics* to make the movements and adjustments of the speech organs necessary to utter (a speech sound). **3.** to unite by a joint or joints. – *v.i.* **4.** to utter distinct syllables or words. **5.** *Phonetics* to articulate a speech sound. – *adj.* **6.** clear; distinct. **7.** uttered clearly in distinct syllables. **8.** capable of speech; eloquent. **9.** Also, **articulated**. having joints; composed of segments. – **articulation**, *n.*

artifice /'atəfəs/ *n.* **1.** a crafty device or

expedient; a clever trick or stratagem. **2.** craft; trickery.

artificial /atə'fɪʃəl/ *adj.* **1.** made by human skill and labour (opposed to *natural*). **2.** made in imitation of or as a substitute; not genuine. **3.** feigned; fictitious; assumed.

artificial intelligence *n.* decision-making computers.

artificial respiration *n.* a method for restarting the breathing of a person who has been half-drowned or otherwise asphyxiated, as by alternately pressing on and releasing the rib cage.

artillery /a'tɪləri/ *n.* mounted guns, movable or stationary, light or heavy, as distinguished from small arms.

artisan /'atəzən/ *n.* one skilled in an industrial or applied art; a craftsman.

artist /'atəst/ *n.* **1.** a person who practises one of the fine arts, especially a painter or sculptor. **2.** a person who practises one of the performing arts, as an actor or singer.

artistic /a'tɪstɪk/ *adj.* **1.** conformable to the standards of art; aesthetically excellent or admirable. **2.** stormy, emotional, and capricious, as temperament or behaviour popularly ascribed to artists. – **artistically**, *adv.*

artistry /'atəstri/ *n., pl.* **-tries**. **1.** artistic workmanship, effect, or quality. **2.** artistic pursuits.

art union *n.* a lottery.

-ary[1] **1.** an adjective suffix meaning 'pertaining to', attached chiefly to nouns (*honorary*) and to stems appearing in other words (*voluntary*). **2.** a suffix forming nouns from other nouns or adjectives indicating location or repository (*dictionary, granary, apiary*), officers (*functionary, secretary*), or other relations (*adversary*). **3.** a suffix forming collective numeral nouns, especially in time units (*centenary*).

-ary[2] variant of **-ar**[1], as in *exemplary, military.*

as /æz/, *weak form* /əz/ – *adv.* **1.** to such a degree or extent. **2. as well as,** as much or as truly as; just as; equally as; as also; in addition to. **3. as well, a.** equally; also; too. **b.** as well as not; equally well; better; advisable. – *conj.* **4.** the consequent in the correlations *as* (or *so*) ... *as, same* ... *as*, etc., denoting degree, extent, manner, etc. (*as good as gold, in the same way as before*), or in the correlations *so as, such as*, denoting purpose or result (followed by infinitive). **5.** (without antecedent) in the degree, manner, etc., of or that. **6.** though. **7.** as if; as though. **8.** when or while. **9.** since; because. **10.** for instance. **11. as for** or **as to,** with regard or respect to; for the matter of. **12. as if** or **as though,** as it would be if. **13. as it were,** in some sort; so to speak. **14. as yet, a.** up to now; even yet. **b.** for the moment; in the near future; just yet. – *relative pron.* **15.** that; who; which (especially after *such* and *the same*). **16.** (of) which fact, contingency, etc. (referring to a statement). – *prep.* **17.** in the role, function, status, or manner of.

as- variant of **ad-** before *s*, as in *assert.*

asbestos /əs'bɛstəs, æs-/ *n.* **1.** *Mineralogy* a fibrous amphibole, used for making incombustible or fireproof articles. **2.** a fire-resistant fabric woven from asbestos fibres.

ascend /ə'sɛnd/ *v.i.* **1.** to climb or go upwards; mount; rise. – *v.t.* **2.** to go or move upwards upon or along; climb; mount. – **ascension**, *n.*

ascendancy /ə'sɛndənsi/ *n.* the state of being in the ascendant; governing or controlling influence; domination. Also, **ascendency**, **ascendance**, **ascendence**.

ascendant /ə'sɛndənt/ *n.* **1.** a position of dominance or controlling influence; superiority; predominance. – *adj.* **2.** superior; predominant.

ascent /ə'sɛnt/ *n.* **1.** the act of ascending; upward movement; rise. **2.** the act of climbing or travelling up. **3.** gradient.

ascertain /æsə'teɪn/ *v.t.* to find out by trial, examination, or experiment, so as to know as certain; determine.

ascetic /ə'sɛtɪk/ *n.* **1.** a person who leads an abstemious life. – *adj.* **2.** rigorously abstinent; austere.

ASCII /æski/ *n.* a standard computer code for representing alphabetical and numerical characters.

asco- a word element meaning 'bag'.

ascorbic acid /əskɔbɪk 'æsəd/ *n.* a water-soluble vitamin, vitamin C, occurring naturally in citrus fruits, tomatoes, capsicum, and green vegetables, but also made industrially, and used in the treatment of scurvy.

ascribe /ə'skraɪb/ *v.t.,* **ascribed**, **ascribing**. to attribute, impute, or refer, as to a cause or source; assign.

-ase a noun suffix used in names of enzymes.

asexual /eɪ'sɛkʃuəl/ *adj.* **1.** not sexual. **2.** having no sex or no sexual organs. **3.** independent of sexual processes. **asexuality**, *n.*

ash[1] /æʃ/ *n.* (*usu. pl., used as sing. chiefly in scientific and commercial language*) the powdery residue of matter that remains after burning.

ash[2] /æʃ/ *n.* **1.** a tree of the Northern Hemisphere. **2.** any of many Southern Hemisphere trees whose timber or foliage resembles that of the ash.

ashamed /ə'ʃeɪmd/ *adj.* **1.** feeling shame; abashed by guilt. **2.** unwilling or restrained through fear of shame. **3.** loath to acknowledge (fol. by *of*).

ashore /ə'ʃɔ/ *adv.* **1.** to shore; on or to the land. – *adj.* **2.** on land (opposed to *aboard* or *afloat*).

aside /ə'saɪd/ *adv.* **1.** on or to one side; to or at a short distance; apart; away from some position or direction. **2.** away from one's thoughts or consideration. – *n.* **3.** words spoken in an undertone, so as not to be heard by some of the people present. **4.** a remark or comment which is incidental to the main subject.

asinine /'æsənaɪn/ *adj.* stupid; obstinate.

ask /ask/ *v.t.* **1.** to put a question to. **2.** to seek to be informed about. **3.** to seek by words to obtain; request. **4.** to call for; require. **5.** to invite. – *v.i.* **6.** to make inquiry; inquire. **7.** to request or petition (fol. by *for*).

askance /əs'kæns/ *adv.* **1.** with suspicion, mistrust, or disapproval. **2.** with a side glance; sideways.

askew /əs'kju/ *adv.* **1.** to one side; out of line; obliquely; awry. – *adj.* **2.** oblique.

asking price *n.* the price demanded by a seller, usually considered as subject to bargaining or discount.

asleep /ə'slip/ *adv.* **1.** in or into a state of sleep. – *adj.* **2.** sleeping. **3.** (of the foot, hand, leg, etc.) numb.

asp /æsp/ *n.* **1.** any of several poisonous snakes. **2.** the common European viper or adder.

asparagus /ə'spærəgəs/ *n.* a plant cultivated for its edible shoots.

aspect /'æspɛkt/ *n.* **1.** appearance to the eye or mind; look. **2.** a way in which a thing may be viewed or regarded. **3.** view commanded; exposure. **4.** *Grammar* (in some languages) a category of verb inflection denoting various relations of the action or state of the verb to the passage of time, as duration, repetition, or completion.

aspen /'æspən/ *n.* any of various species of poplar.

asperity /æs'pɛrəti, əs-/ *n., pl.* **-ties**. **1.** roughness or sharpness of temper; severity; acrimony. **2.** hardship; difficulty; rigour. **3.** roughness of surface; unevenness.

aspersion /ə'spɜʒən, -spɜʃən/ *n.* a damaging imputation; a derogatory criticism.

asphalt /'æʃfɛlt, 'æsfɛlt/ *n.* any of various dark-coloured, solid bituminous substances, composed mostly of mixtures of hydrocarbons, occurring native in various parts of the earth.

asphyxia /əs'fɪksiə/ *n. Pathology* the extreme condition caused by lack of oxygen and excess of carbon dioxide in the blood, caused by sufficient interference with respiration, as in choking. – **asphyxiant**, *adj., n.* – **asphyxiate**, *v.*

aspic /'æspɪk/ *n.* **1.** a cold dish of meat, fish, etc., served set in a jellied mould. **2.** the jellied garnish, made from fish or meat stock, sometimes with added gelatine.

aspiration /æspə'reɪʃən/ *n.* **1.** the act of aspiring; lofty or ambitious desire. **2.** a breath.

aspire /ə'spaɪə/ *v.i.,* **-spired**, **-spiring**. to long, aim, or seek ambitiously; be eagerly desirous, especially for something great or lofty (fol. by *to*, *after*, or an infinitive).

aspirin /'æsprən/ *n.* **1.** a white crystalline substance, used to relieve the pain of headache, rheumatism, gout, neuralgia, etc. **2.** a tablet of aspirin.

ass /æs/ *n.* **1.** a long-eared, usually ash-coloured mammal related to the horse; the donkey. **2.** a fool; a blockhead.

assail /ə'seɪl/ *v.t.* **1.** to set upon with violence; assault. **2.** to set upon vigorously with arguments, entreaties, abuse, etc. – **assailant**, *n., adj.*

assassin /ə'sæsən/ *n.* someone who undertakes to murder, especially from fanaticism or for a reward.

assassinate /ə'sæsəneɪt/ *v.t.,* **-nated**, **-nating**. **1.** to kill by sudden or secret, premeditated assault, especially for political or religious motives. **2.** to blight or destroy treacherously. – **assassination**, *n.* – **assassinator**, *n.*

assault /ə'sɒlt, -'sɔlt/ *n.* **1.** the act of assailing; an attack; onslaught. **2.** *Law* an unlawful physical attack upon another; an attempt or offer to do violence to another, with or without a battery, as by holding a weapon in a threatening manner. – *v.t.* **3.** to make an assault upon; attack. – **assaulter**, *n.*

assay /ə'seɪ/ *v.t.* **1.** to examine by trial; put to test or trial. **2.** to judge the quality of; evaluate.

assemblage /ə'sɛmblɪdʒ/ *n.* a number of persons or things assembled; an assembly.

assemble /ə'sɛmbəl/ *v.,* **-bled**, **-bling**. – *v.t.* **1.** to bring together; gather into one place, company, body or whole. **2.** to put or fit (parts) together; put together the parts of (a mechanism, etc.). – *v.i.* **3.** to come together; gather; meet.

assembler /ə'sɛmblə/ *n. Computers* a program which converts symbolic language to machine language on a word for word basis.

assembly /ə'sɛmbli/ *n., pl.* **-blies**. **1.** a company of persons gathered together, usually for the same purpose, whether religious, political, educational, or social. **2.** (*cap.*) *Government* a legislative body, sometimes especially a lower house of a legislature. **3.** the putting together of complex machinery, as aeroplanes, from interchangeable parts of standard dimensions.

assent /ə'sɛnt/ *v.i.* **1.** to express agreement or concurrence (often fol. by *to*). – *n.* **2.** agreement, as to a proposal; acquiescence; concurrence. **3.** Also, **royal assent**. the formal act of recognition by the sovereign's representative which transforms a parliamentary bill into an act of parliament. – **assenter**, *n.*

assert /ə'sɜt/ *v.t.* **1.** to state as true; affirm; declare. **2.** to maintain or defend (claims, rights, etc.). **3.** to put (oneself) forward boldly and insistently. – **assertion**, *n.* – **assertive**, *adj.*

assess /ə'sɛs/ *v.t.* **1.** to estimate officially the value of (property, income, etc.) as a basis for taxation (fol. by *at*). **2.** to fix or determine the amount of (damages, a tax, a fine, etc.). **3.** to impose a tax or other charge on. **4.** to measure or evaluate.

assessor /ə'sɛsə/ *n.* **1.** someone who makes assessments, as of damage for insurance purposes, or of property, etc., for taxation purposes. **2.** an advisory associate or assistant.

asset /'æsɛt/ *n.* **1.** a useful thing or quality. **2.** a single item of property.

asset backing *n.* support for a commercial enterprise provided by its assets.

assets /'æsɛts/ *pl. n.* **1.** *Commerce* resources of a person or business consisting of such items as real property, machinery, inventories, notes, securities, cash, etc. **2.** property or effects (opposed to *liabilities*). **3.** any property available for paying debts, etc. **4.** *Accounting* the detailed listing of property owned by a firm and money owing to it.

asset-stripping /'æsɛt-strɪpɪŋ/ *n.* the practice of identifying and selling off the readily separable assets of a company, especially one that has been acquired through a recent takeover.

asseverate /ə'sɛvəreɪt/ *v.t.*, **-rated**, **-rating**. to declare earnestly or solemnly; affirm positively.

assiduous /ə'sɪdʒuəs/ *adj.* **1.** constant; unremitting. **2.** constant in application; attentive; devoted. – **assiduity**, *n.*

assign /ə'saɪn/ *v.t.* **1.** to make over or give, as in distribution; allot. **2.** to appoint, as to a post or duty. **3.** (formerly) to allocate (a convict) for employment by an officer or settler. **4.** to designate; specify. **5.** to ascribe; attribute; refer. – **assigner**; *Chiefly Law*, **assignor**, *n.*

assignation /æsɪg'neɪʃən/ *n.* **1.** an appointment for a meeting, now especially an illicit love-meeting. **2.** the act of assigning; assignment.

assignee /əsaɪ'ni/ *n.* **1.** *Law* someone to whom some right or interest is transferred, either for their own enjoyment or in trust. **2.** (formerly) a convict assigned as a servant.

assignment /ə'saɪnmənt/ *n.* something assigned, as a particular task or duty.

assimilate /ə'sɪməleɪt/ *v.*, **-lated**, **-lating**. – *v.t.* **1.** to take in and incorporate as one's own; absorb (fol. by *to* or *with*). **2.** *Physiology* to convert (food, etc.) into a substance suitable for absorption into the system. **3.** to make like; cause to resemble (fol. by *to* or *with*). – *v.i.* **4.** to be or become absorbed. **5.** to become or be like; resemble (fol. by *to* or *with*). – **assimilable**, *adj.* – **assimilation**, *n.*

assist /ə'sɪst/ *v.t.* **1.** to give support, help, or aid to in some undertaking or effort, or in time of distress. **2.** to be associated with as an assistant. – *v.i.* **3.** to give aid or help. – **assister**; *Law*, **assistor**, *n.* – **assistance**, *n.*

assistant /ə'sɪstənt/ *n.* **1.** someone who assists a superior in some office or work; helper. – *adj.* **2.** assisting; helpful. **3.** associated with a superior in some office or work.

associate /ə'souʃieɪt, ə'sousieɪt/ *v.*, **-ated**, **-ating** /ə'souʃiət, -siət/ *n.*, *adj.* – *v.t.* **1.** to connect by some relation, as in thought. **2.** to join as a companion, partner, or ally. **3.** to unite; combine. – *v.i.* **4.** to enter into a league or union; unite. **5.** to keep company, as a friend or intimate. – *n.* **6.** a partner in interest, as in business or in an enterprise or action. – *adj.* **7.** having subordinate membership; without full rights and privileges.

association /əsousi'eɪʃən/ *n.* **1.** an organisation of people with a common purpose and having a formal structure. **2.** companionship or intimacy. **3.** connection or combination. **4.** the connection of ideas in thought, or an idea connected with or suggested by a subject of thought.

assonance /'æsənəns/ *n.* **1.** resemblance of sounds. **2.** partial agreement.

assort /ə'sɔt/ *v.t.* **1.** to distribute according to sort or kind; classify. **2.** to furnish with a suitable assortment or variety of goods; make up of articles likely to suit a demand.

assortment /ə'sɔtmənt/ *n.* **1.** the act of assorting; distribution; classification. **2.** an assorted collection.

assuage /ə'sweɪdʒ/ *v.t.*, **-suaged**, **-suaging**. **1.** to make milder or less severe; mitigate; ease. **2.** to appease; satisfy.

assume /ə'sjum/ *v.t.*, **-sumed**, **-suming**. **1.** to take for granted or without proof; suppose as a fact. **2.** to take upon oneself; undertake. **3.** to pretend to have or be; feign. **4.** to appropriate or arrogate. – **assumption**, *n.*

assuming /ə'sjumɪŋ/ *adj.* arrogant; presuming. – **assumingly**, *adv.*

assurance /ə'ʃɔrəns, -'ʃʊə-/ *n.* **1.** a positive declaration intended to give confidence. **2.** pledge; guarantee; surety. **3.** full confidence or trust; freedom from doubt; certainty. **4.** freedom from timidity; self-reliance; courage. **5.** insurance (now usually restricted to life insurance).

assure /ə'ʃɔ/ *v.t.*, **-sured**, **-suring**. **1.** to declare earnestly to; inform or tell positively. **2.** to make (one) sure or certain; convince, as by a promise or declaration. **3.** to make (a future event) sure; ensure. **4.** to secure or confirm; render safe or stable. **5.** to give confidence to; encourage. **6.** to insure, especially against death.

-aster a suffix used to form nouns denoting something that imperfectly resembles or merely apes the true thing, or an inferior or petty instance of something.

asterisk /'æstərɪsk/ *n.* **1.** the figure of a star (*), used in writing and printing as a reference mark or to indicate omission, doubtful matter, etc. **2.** something in the shape of a star or asterisk. – *v.t.* **3.** to identify or mark by means of this sign.

asteroid /'æstərɔɪd/ *n.* **1.** *Zoology* any of the Asteroidea, a class of echinoderms characterised by a starlike body with radiating arms or rays, as the starfishes. **2.** *Astronomy* one of several hundred planetoids with orbits lying mostly between those of Mars and Jupiter.

asthma /'æsmə/ *n.* a paroxysmal disorder of respiration with laboured breathing, a feeling of constriction in the chest, and coughing. – **asthmatic**, *adj.*, *n.*

astonish /ə'stɒnɪʃ/ *v.t.* to strike with sudden and overpowering wonder; surprise greatly; amaze.

astound /ə'staʊnd/ *v.t.* to overwhelm with amazement; astonish greatly.

astral /'æstrəl/ *adj.* relating to or proceeding from the stars; consisting of or resembling stars; starry; stellar.

astray /ə'streɪ/ *adv.* out of the right way or away from the right; straying; wandering.

astride /ə'straɪd/ *adv.* **1.** in the posture of striding or straddling. – *prep.* **2.** with a leg on each side of.

astringent /ə'strɪndʒənt/ *adj.* **1.** (as affecting the skin) refreshing, tightening, drying. **2.** severe, sharp, austere. – *n.* **3.** an astringent agent (especially cosmetic).

astro- a word element meaning 'star', as in *astrology*.

astrology /əs'trɒlədʒi/ *n.* **1.** a study which assumes, and professes to interpret, the influence of the heavenly bodies on human affairs. **2.** (formerly) practical astronomy, the earliest form of the science. – **astrologer**, *n.* – **astrological**, **astrologic**, *adj.*

astronaut /'æstrənɔt/ *n.* a person trained as a pilot, navigator, etc., to take part in the flight of a spacecraft.

astronomy /əs'trɒnəmi/ *n.* the science of the celestial bodies, their motions, positions, distances, magnitudes, etc. – **astronomer**, *n.*

astute /əs'tjut/ *adj.* of keen penetration or discernment; sagacious; shrewd; cunning.

asunder /ə'sʌndə/ *adv.* into separate parts; in or into pieces.

asylum /ə'saɪləm/ *n.* **1.** an institution for the maintenance and care of the insane, the blind, orphans or the like. **2.** an inviolable refuge, as formerly for criminals and debtors; a sanctuary. **3.** *International Law* a temporary refuge granted political offenders, especially in a foreign legation.

at /æt/, *weak form* /ət/ – *prep.* a particle specifying a point occupied, attained, sought, or otherwise concerned, as in place, time, order, experience, etc., and hence used in many idiomatic phrases expressing circumstantial or relative position, degree or rate, action, manner: *at noon, at home, at length.*

at- variant of **ad-** before *t*, as in *attend.*

atavism /'ætəvɪzəm/ *n.* reversion to an earlier type. – **atavistic**, *adj.*

ate /eɪt, ɛt/ *v.* past tense of **eat**.

-ate[1] a suffix forming: **1.** adjectives equivalent to **-ed** (in participial and other adjectives), as in *accumulate, separate.* **2.** nouns denoting especially persons charged with some duty or function, or invested with some dignity, right, or special character, as in *advocate, candidate, curate, legate, prelate.* **3.** nouns denoting some product or result of action, as in *mandate* (lit., a thing commanded). **4.** verbs, originally taken from Latin past participles but now formed from any Latin or other stem, as in *actuate, agitate, calibrate.*

-ate[2] a suffix forming nouns denoting a salt formed by action of an acid on a base, especially where the name of the acid ends in *-ic*, as in *acetate.*

-ate[3] a suffix forming nouns denoting condition, estate, office, officials, or an official, etc., as in *consulate, senate.*

atheism /'eɪθiˌɪzəm/ *n.* **1.** the doctrine that there is no god. **2.** disbelief in the existence of a god (or gods) (opposed to *theism*). – **atheist**, *n.*

athlete /'æθlit/ *n.* **1.** anyone trained to exercises of physical agility and strength. **2.** one trained for track and field events only.

athletic /æθ'lɛtɪk/ *adj.* **1.** physically active and strong. **2.** of, like, or befitting an athlete.

athletics /æθ'lɛtɪks/ *n.* (*usu. construed as pl.*) athletic sports, as running, rowing, boxing, etc.

-ation a suffix forming nouns denoting action or process, state or condition, a product or result, or something producing a result. See **-ion**, **-tion**.

-ative an adjective suffix expressing tendency, disposition, function, bearing, connection, etc., as in *affirmative, demonstrative, talkative.* See **-ive**.

atlas /'ætləs/ *n.* **1.** a bound collection of maps. **2.** a volume of plates or tables illustrating any subject.

ATM /eɪ ti 'ɛm/ automatic teller machine.

atmosphere /'ætməsfɪə/ *n.* **1.** the gaseous fluid surrounding the earth; the air. **2.** environing or pervading influence. – **atmospheric**, *adj.*

atoll /'ætɒl/ *n.* a ringlike coral island enclosing a lagoon.

atom /'ætəm/ *n. Physics, Chemistry* the smallest unitary constituent of a chemical element, composed of a more or less complex aggregate of protons, neutrons, and electrons, whose number and arrangement determine the element.

atomic /ə'tɒmɪk/ *adj.* **1.** relating to atoms. **2.** propelled or driven by atomic energy. **3.** using or having developed atomic weapons.

atomic energy *n.* **1.** the energy obtained from changes within the atomic nucleus, chiefly from nuclear fission, or fusion. **2.** this energy regarded as a source of power, as for industrial usage.

atomic mass *n.* the mass of an isotope of an element.

atomic number *n.* the number of protons in the nucleus of an atom of a given element. *Abbrev.*: at. no.

atomic power *n.* energy released in nuclear reactions.

atomic weight *n.* → **relative atomic mass**.

atomiser = atomizer /'ætəmaɪzə/ *n.* an apparatus for reducing liquids to a fine spray, as for medicinal application.

atone /ə'toun/ *v.i.*, **atoned**, **atoning**. to make amends or reparation, as for an offence or a crime, or for an offender (fol. by *for*). – **atonement**, *n.*

atrium /'ætriəm, 'eɪ-/ *n.*, *pl.* **-tria** /-triə/. **1.** *Architecture* **a.** the central main room of an ancient Roman private house. **b.** an open area which is central to the design of a building. **2.** *Zoology* an internal cavity or space; applied variously to different cavities in different organisms.

atrocious /ə'trouʃəs/ *adj.* **1.** extremely or shockingly wicked or cruel; heinous. **2.** shockingly bad or lacking in taste; execrable.

atrocity /ə'trɒsəti/ *n.*, *pl.* **-ties**. **1.** the quality of being atrocious. **2.** an atrocious deed or thing.

atrophy /'ætrəfi/ *n.*, *v.*, **-phied**, **-phying**. – *n.* **1.** *Pathology* wasting away of the body or of an organ or part, as from defective nutrition or other cause. **2.** degeneration; reduction in size and functional power through lack of use. – *v.t.* **3.** to affect with atrophy. – *v.i.* **4.** to undergo atrophy.

attach /ə'tætʃ/ *v.t.* **1.** to fasten to; affix; join; connect. **2.** to join in action or function. **3.** to connect as an adjunct; associate. **4.** to assign or attribute. **5.** to bind by ties of affection or regard. – **attachment**, *n.*

attaché /ə'tæʃeɪ/ *n.* one attached to an official staff, especially that of an embassy or legation.

attaché case *n.* a small rectangular case with a hinged lid, for documents, etc.

attack /ə'tæk/ *v.t.* **1.** to set upon with force or weapons; begin hostilities against. **2.** to direct unfavourable criticism, argument, etc., against; blame or abuse violently. **3.** to set about (a task) or go to work on (a thing) vigorously. **4.** (of disease, destructive agencies, etc.) to begin to affect. – *n.* **5.** the act of attacking; onslaught; assault. **6.** criticism; abuse; calumny.

attain /ə'teɪn/ *v.t.* **1.** to reach, achieve, or accomplish by continued effort. **2.** to come to or arrive at in due course. – *v.i.* **3. attain to,** to arrive at; succeed in reaching or obtaining.

attempt /ə'tɛmpt, ə'tɛmt/ *v.t.* **1.** to make an effort at; try; undertake; seek. **2.** to attack; make an effort against. – *n.* **3.** effort put forth to accomplish something; a trial or essay. **4.** an attack or assault.

attend /ə'tɛnd/ *v.t.* **1.** to be present at. **2.** to go with as a concomitant or result; accompany. **3.** to minister to; devote one's services to. – *v.i.* **4.** to give attention; pay regard or heed. **5.** to apply oneself. **6.** to take care or charge of. **7.** to be consequent (*on*). **8.** to wait (*on*) with service.

attendance /ə'tɛndəns/ *n.* **1.** the act of attending. **2.** the (number of) persons present.

attendant /ə'tɛndənt/ *n.* **1.** someone who attends another, as for service or company. **2.** someone employed to take care or charge of someone or something, especially when this involves directing or assisting the public. – *adj.* **3.** concomitant; consequent.

attention /ə'tɛnʃən/ *n.* **1.** observant care; consideration; notice. **2.** civility or courtesy. **3.** (*pl.*) acts of courtesy indicating regard, as in courtship.

attention deficit disorder *n.* a genetic disorder especially marked in children who may have a short attention span and display aberrant social behaviour. Also, **ADD**.

attention deficit hyperactive disorder *n.* a type of attention deficit disorder which has hyperactivity as a symptom. Also, **ADHD**.

attentive /ə'tɛntɪv/ *adj.* **1.** characterised by or giving attention; observant. **2.** assiduous in service or courtesy; polite; courteous. – **attentiveness**, *n.*

attenuate /ə'tɛnjueɪt/ *v.*, **-ated**, **-ating**. – *v.t.* **1.** to make thin; make slender or fine; rarefy. – *v.i.* **2.** to grow less; weaken.

attest /ə'tɛst/ *v.t.* **1.** to bear witness to; certify; declare the truth of, in words or writing; especially, affirm in an official capacity. **2.** to give proof or evidence of; manifest. – *v.i.* **3.** to certify to the genuineness of a document by signing as witness. – **attestor**, **attester**, *n.* – **attestation**, *n.*

attic /'ætɪk/ *n.* that part of a building, especially a house, directly under a roof; garret.

attire /ə'taɪə/ *v.*, **-tired**, **-tiring**, *n.* – *v.t.* **1.** to dress, array, or adorn, especially for special occasions, ceremonials, etc. – *n.* **2.** clothes or apparel, especially rich or splendid garments.

attitude /'ætətjud/ *n.* **1.** position, disposition, or manner with regard to a person or thing. **2.** position of the body appropriate to an action, emotion, etc.

attorney /ə'tɜni/ *n.*, *pl.* **-neys**. **1.** someone duly appointed or empowered by another to transact any business for him or her (**attorney in fact**). **2. power of attorney,** Also, **letter of attorney**, **warrant of attorney**. a formal document by which one person authorises another to act for him or her.

attorney-general /ətɜni-'dʒɛnrəl/ *n.*, *pl.* **attorneys-general**, **attorney-generals**. the chief law officer of a government and the minister responsible for the administration of justice.

attract /ə'trækt/ *v.t.* **1.** to act upon by a physical force causing or tending to cause approach or union (opposed to *repel*). **2.** to draw by other than physical influence; invite or allure; win. – *v.i.* **3.** to possess or exert the power of attraction. – **attraction**, *n.*

attractive /ə'træktɪv/ *adj.* appealing to one's liking or admiration; engaging; alluring; pleasing.

attribute /ə'trɪbjut/ *v.*, **-uted**, **-uting** /'ætrəbjut/. *n.* – *v.t.* **1.** to consider as belonging; regard as owing, as an effect to a cause (often fol. by *to*). – *n.* **2.** something attributed as belonging; a quality, character, characteristic, or property. – **attributive**, *adj.*

attrition /ə'trɪʃən/ *n.* **1.** a rubbing against; friction. **2.** a wearing down or away by friction; abrasion. **3.** a natural, gradual reduction in membership or personnel, as by retirement, resignation or death.

attune /ə'tjun, ə'tʃun/ *v.t.*, **-tuned**, **-tuning**. to adjust to tune or harmony; bring into accord.

atypical /eɪ'tɪpɪkəl/ *adj.* not typical; not conforming to the type; irregular; abnormal. Also, **atypic**. – **atypically**, *adv.*

aubergine /'oʊbədʒɪn/ *n.* → **eggplant**.

auburn /'ɔbən/ *n.* a reddish-brown or golden-brown colour.

auction /'ɒkʃən/ *n.* a public sale at which property or goods are sold to the highest bidder. – **auctioneer**, *n.*

audacious /ɔ'deɪʃəs/ *adj.* **1.** bold or daring; adventurous. **2.** reckless or bold in wrongdoing; impudent and presumptuous. – **audacity**, *n.*

audible /'ɔdəbəl/ *adj.* capable of being heard; actually heard.

audience /'ɔdiəns/ *n.* **1.** an assembly of hearers or spectators. **2.** *Government* admission of a diplomatic representative to a sovereign or high officer of government; formal interview. **3.** the act of hearing or attending to words or sounds.

audio- a word element meaning 'hear', 'of or for hearing', as in *audiology*.

audiology /ɔdi'ɒlədʒi/ *n.* the study of the hearing mechanism, especially the diagnosis and measurement of impaired function.

audit /'ɔdət/ *n.* **1.** an official examination and verification of accounts and records, especially of financial accounts. **2.** an account or a statement of account. **3.** a calling to account. – *v.t.* **4.** to make audit of; examine (accounts, etc.) officially.

audition /ɔ'dɪʃən/ *n.* **1.** the act, sense, or power of hearing. **2.** a hearing given to a musician, actor, etc., to test voice qualities, performance, etc.

auditor /'ɔdətə/ *n.* **1.** a hearer; listener. **2.** a person appointed and authorised to examine accounts and accounting records, compare the charges with the vouchers, verify balance sheet and income items, and state the result.

auditorium /ɔdə'tɔriəm/ *n., pl.* **-toriums**, **-toria** /-'tɔriə/. **1.** the space for the audience in a concert hall, theatre, school, or other building. **2.** a large building or room for meetings, assemblies, theatrical performances, etc.

auditory /'ɔdətri, -təri/ *adj.* relating to hearing, to the sense of hearing, or to the organs of hearing.

auger /'ɔgə/ *n.* a carpenter's tool for boring holes in wood.

aught /ɔt/ *n.* anything whatever; any part.

augment /ɔg'mɛnt/ *v.t.* to make larger; enlarge in size or extent; increase.

augur /'ɔgə/ *n.* **1.** any soothsayer; prophet. – *v.t.* **2.** to divine or predict, as from omens; prognosticate.

august /ɔ'gʌst/ *adj.* **1.** inspiring reverence or admiration; of supreme dignity or grandeur; majestic. **2.** venerable.

aunt /ant/ *n.* **1.** the sister of one's father or mother. **2.** the wife of one's uncle.

aura /'ɔrə/ *n., pl.* **auras**, **aurae** /'ɔri/. **1.** a distinctive air, atmosphere, character, etc. **2.** a subtle emanation proceeding from a body and surrounding it as an atmosphere.

aural /'ɔrəl/ *adj.* of, or perceived by, the organs of hearing. – **aurally**, *adv.*

aureole /'ɒrioʊl, 'ɔ-/ *n.* a radiance surrounding the head or the whole figure in the representation of a sacred personage.

auric /'ɔrɪk/ *adj.* of or containing gold, especially in the trivalent state.

auricle /'ɔrɪkəl, 'ɒr-/ *n.* **1.** *Anatomy* **a.** the projecting outer portion of the ear; the pinna. **b.** a chamber of the heart. **2.** *Botany, Zoology* a part like or likened to an ear.

auriferous /ɔ'rɪfərəs/ *adj.* yielding or containing gold.

aurora /ə'rɔrə/ *n.* a display in the skies of moving bands of light, visible at high latitudes.

auspice /'ɔspəs/ *n.* **1.** (*usu. pl.*) favouring influence; patronage. **2.** a propitious circumstance.

auspicious /ɔ'spɪʃəs, ə-/ *adj.* of good omen; betokening success; favourable.

austere /ɒs'tɪə, ɔs-/ *adj.* **1.** harsh in manner; stern in appearance. **2.** severe in disciplining or restraining oneself; morally strict. **3.** severely simple; without ornament. – **austerity**, *n.*

Australian Rules /əstreɪljən 'rulz/ *pl. n.* a code of football requiring two teams of 18 players, which originated in Australia, though based on Gaelic football. Also, **Australian National Football**, **Australian Football**, **Aussie Rules**.

Australian salute *n. Colloquial* (*humorous*) the movement of hand and arm to brush away flies from one's face.

aut- variant of **auto-**[1] before most vowels.

autarchy /'ɔtaki/ *n., pl.* **-chies**. **1.** absolute sovereignty. **2.** self-government.

autarky /'ɔtaki/ *n., pl.* **-kies**. the condition of self-sufficiency, especially economic, as applied to a state.

authentic /ɔ'θɛntɪk/ *adj.* **1.** entitled to acceptance or belief; reliable; trustworthy. **2.** of the authorship or origin reputed; of genuine origin. **3.** *Law* executed with all due formalities. – **authenticity**, *n.*

authenticate /ɔ'θɛntəkeɪt/ *v.t.*, **-cated**, **-cating**. **1.** to make authoritative or valid. **2.** to establish as genuine.

author /'ɔθə/ *n.* a person who writes a novel, poem, essay, etc.; the composer of a literary work, as distinguished from a compiler, translator, editor, or copyist.

authorise = authorize /'ɔθəraɪz/ *v.t.*, **-rised**, **-rising**. **1.** to give authority or legal power to; empower (to do something). **2.** to establish by authority or usage. **3.** to afford a ground for; warrant; justify. – **authorisation**, *n.*

authoritarian /ɔ,θɒrə'tɛəriən, ə-/ *adj.* favouring the principle of subjection to authority as opposed to that of individual freedom.

authority /ɔ'θɒrəti, ə-/ *n., pl.* **-ties**. **1.** the right to determine, adjudicate, or otherwise settle issues or disputes; the right to control, command, or determine. **2.** a person or body with such rights. **3.** an accepted source of information, advice, etc. **4.** a statute, court rule, or judicial decision which establishes a rule or principle of law; a ruling. **5.** title to respect or acceptance; commanding influence. **6.** a warrant for action; justification. – **authoritative**, *adj.*

autism /'ɔtɪzəm/ *n. Psychiatry* a syndrome of unknown aetiology, chiefly characterised by some degree of inability to comprehend or communicate, failure to relate affectively, and inappropriate or obsessive behaviour. – **autistic**, *adj.*

auto-[1] a word element meaning 'self', 'same', as in *autograph*. Also, **aut-**.

auto-[2] a combining form of **automobile**.

autobiography /,ɔtəbaɪ'ɒgrəfi/ *n., pl.* **-phies**. an account of a person's life written by himself or herself.

autocracy /ɔ'tɒkrəsi/ *n., pl.* **-cies**. **1.** uncontrolled or unlimited authority over others, invested in a single person; the government or power of an absolute monarch. **2.** independent or self-derived power. – **autocrat**, *n.* – **autocratic**, *adj.*

auto-electrician /,ɔtoʊ-ɛlɛk'trɪʃən/ *n.* someone who specialises in the repair and servicing of the electrical circuits of motor cars.

autograph /'ɔtəgræf, -graf/ *n.* **1.** a person's own signature. – *v.t.* **2.** to write one's name on or in.

auto-immune system /ɔtoʊ-ɪm'jun sɪstəm/ *n.* the system within the body which produces antibodies.

automate /'ɔtəmeɪt/ *v.t.*, **-mated**, **-mating**. to apply the principles of automation to (a mechanical process).

automatic /,ɔtə'mætɪk/ *adj.* **1.** having the power of self-motion; self-moving or self-acting; mechanical. **2.** *Physiology* occurring independently of volition, as certain muscular actions. **3.** done unconsciously or from force of habit; mechanical (opposed to *voluntary*). – *n.* **4.** a machine which operates automatically, as a motor car with automatic gear shift. – **automatically**, *adv.*

automatic data processing *n.* the use of computers and other information-handling machines to store, organise, and perform calculations on large quantities of numerical data with the minimum of human intervention. *Abbrev.*: ADP

automatic teller machine *n.* computerised equipment located outside banks and building societies, in shopping areas, etc., offering basic banking facilities and operated by inserting a plastic card with a magnetised strip and keying in a personal identification number. Also, **ATM**, **automated teller machine**.

automation /ɔtə'meɪʃən/ *n.* **1.** the science of applying automatic control to industrial processes; the replacement of manpower by sophisticated machinery. **2.** the process or act of automating a mechanical process. **3.** the degree to which a mechanical process is automatically controlled.

automaton /ɔ'tɒmətən/ *n., pl.* **-tons**, **-ta** /-tə/. **1.** a mechanical figure or contrivance constructed to act as if spontaneously through concealed motive power. **2.** a person who acts in a monotonous routine manner, without active intelligence.

automotive /ɔtə'moʊtɪv/ *adj.* **1.** propelled by a self-contained power plant. **2.** of or relating to motor vehicles.

autonomics /ɔtə'nɒmɪks/ *n.* (*construed as sing.*) the science, study, or practice of developing a number of self-governing systems, as within a large business organisation.

autonomous /ɔ'tɒnəməs/ *adj.* self-governing; independent. – **autonomy**, *n.*

autopsy /'ɔtɒpsi/ *n., pl.* **-sies**. inspection and dissection of a body after death, as for determination of the cause of death; a post-mortem examination.

autumn /'ɔtəm/ *n.* the season of the year between summer and winter.

auxiliary /ɒg'zɪljəri, ɔg-/ *adj., n., pl.* **-ries**. – *adj.* **1.** giving support; helping; aiding; assisting. **2.** subsidiary; additional. – *n.* **3.** person or thing that gives aid of any kind; helper. **4.** a group or organisation which assists or is supplementary to a larger one. **5.** (*pl.*) foreign troops in the service of a nation at war.

auxiliary verb *n.* a verb customarily preceding certain forms of other verbs, used to express distinctions of time, aspect, mood, etc., as *do*, *am*, etc., in I *do* think; I *am* going; we *have* spoken; *may* we go?; *can* they see?; we *shall* walk.

avail /ə'veɪl/ *v.i.* **1.** to have force or efficacy; be of use; serve. **2.** to be of value or profit. – *v.t.* **3.** to be of use or value to; profit; advantage. **4. avail oneself of,** to give oneself the advantage of; make use of. – *n.* **5.** efficacy for a purpose; advantage to an object or end.

available /ə'veɪləbəl/ *adj.* suitable or ready for use; at hand; of use or service. – **availability**, *n.*

avalanche /'ævəlæntʃ, -lanʃ/ *n.* a large mass of snow, ice, etc., detached from a mountain slope and sliding or falling suddenly downwards.

avarice /'ævərəs/ *n.* insatiable greed for riches; inordinate, miserly desire to gain and hoard wealth. – **avaricious**, *adj.*

avenge /ə'vɛndʒ/ *v.t.*, **avenged**, **avenging**. to take vengeance or exact satisfaction for.

avenue /'ævənju/ *n.* **1.** a double row of trees, whether lining a road or not. **2.** means of access or attainment.

aver /ə'vɜ/ *v.t.*, **averred**, **averring**. to affirm with confidence; declare in a positive or peremptory manner.

average /'ævərɪdʒ, -vrɪdʒ/ *n., adj., v.*, **-raged**, **-raging**. – *n.* **1.** an arithmetical mean. **2.** the ordinary, normal, or typical amount, rate, quality, kind, etc.; the common run. **3.** *Commerce* **a.** a small charge paid by the master on account of the ship and cargo, such as pilotage, towage, etc. **b.** an expense, partial loss, or damage to ship or cargo. **c.** the incidence of such an expense or loss on the owners or their insurers. **d.** an equitable apportionment among all the interested parties of such an expense or loss. – *adj.* **4.** of or relating to an average; estimated by average; forming an average. – *v.t.* **5.** to find an average value for; reduce to a mean.

averse /ə'vɜs/ *adj.* disinclined, reluctant, or opposed.

aversion /ə'vɜʒən, -vɜʃən/ *n.* **1.** an averted state of the mind or feelings; repugnance, antipathy, or rooted dislike (usually fol. by *to*). **2.** a cause of dislike; an object of repugnance.

avert /ə'vɜt/ *v.t.* **1.** to turn away or aside. **2.** to ward off; prevent.

avi- a word element meaning 'bird'.

avian /'eɪviən/ *adj.* of or relating to birds.

aviary /'eɪvəri, 'eɪvjəri/ *n., pl.* **-ries**. a large cage or enclosure in which birds are kept.

aviation /ˌeɪvi'eɪʃən/ *n.* the act, art, or science of flying by mechanical means, especially with heavier-than-air craft.

aviator /'eɪvieɪtə/ *n.* a pilot of an aeroplane or other heavier-than-air craft.

avid /'ævəd/ *adj.* keenly desirous; eager; greedy (often fol. by *of* or *for*).

AVO /eɪ vi 'oʊ/ *n. Law* apprehended violence order; an injunction issued by a local court, which protects a person fearing molestation, etc., by forbidding the named party to approach or contact the protected person.

avocado /ævə'kadoʊ/ *n., pl.* **-dos**. **1.** a tropical American fruit, green to black in colour and commonly pear-shaped, eaten raw, especially as a salad fruit. **2.** the tree. Also, **avocado pear**.

avocation /ævə'keɪʃən/ *n.* **1.** minor or occasional occupation; hobby. **2.** (*also pl.*) one's regular occupation, calling, or vocation. **3.** diversion or distraction.

avoid /ə'vɔɪd/ *v.t.* to keep away from; keep clear of; shun; evade. – **avoidance**, *n.*

avoirdupois /ævwadju'pwa/ *adj.* of or relating to a system of weights formerly used for goods other than gems, precious metals, and drugs.

avow /ə'vaʊ/ *v.t.* to admit or acknowledge frankly or openly; own; confess. – **avowal**, *n.*

avuncular /ə'vʌŋkjələ/ *adj.* like or characteristic of an uncle.

await /ə'weɪt/ *v.t.* **1.** to wait for; look for or expect. **2.** to be in store for; be ready for.

– *v.i.* **3.** to wait, as in expectation.

awake /ə'weɪk/ *v.*, **awoke** *or* **awaked**, **awoken**, **awaking**, *adj.* – *v.t.* **1.** to rouse from sleep; wake up. **2.** to stir the interest of; excite. **3.** to stir, disturb (the memories, fears, etc.). – *v.i.* **4.** to wake up. **5.** to come to a realisation of the truth; to rouse to action, attention, etc. – *adj.* **6.** waking, not sleeping. **7.** vigilant; alert.

awakening /ə'weɪkənɪŋ/ *adj.* **1.** rousing; alarming. – *n.* **2.** the act of awaking from sleep. **3.** an arousal or revival of interest or attention; a waking up, as from indifference, ignorance, etc.

award /ə'wɔd/ *v.t.* **1.** to adjudge to be due or merited; assign or bestow. **2.** to bestow by judicial decree; assign or appoint by deliberate judgment, as in arbitration. – *n.* **3.** something awarded, as a medal, rate of pay, particular working conditions, etc.

award wage *n.* a wage arrived at by mutual consent or arbitration and fixed by an industrial court, payable by law to all employees in a particular occupation.

aware /ə'wɛə/ *adj.* cognisant or conscious (*of*); informed. – **awareness**, *n.*

away /ə'weɪ/ *adv.* **1.** from this or that place; off. **2.** apart; at a distance. **3.** aside. **4.** out of possession, notice, use, or existence. **5.** continuously; on. **6.** without hesitation. **7.** immediately; forthwith. – *adj.* **8.** absent. **9.** distant. **10.** *Colloquial* on the move; having started; in full flight.

awe /ɔ/ *n.*, *v.*, **awed**, **awing**. – *n.* **1.** respectful or reverential fear, inspired by what is grand or sublime. – *v.t.* **2.** to inspire with awe. **3.** to influence or restrain by awe.

awesome /'ɔsəm/ *adj.* inspiring awe.

awful /'ɔfəl/ *adj.* **1.** *Colloquial* extremely bad; unpleasant; ugly. **2.** *Colloquial* very great. **3.** inspiring fear; dreadful; terrible. – **awfully**, *adv.* – **awfulness**, *n.*

awhile /ə'waɪl/ *adv.* for a short time or period.

awkward /'ɔkwəd/ *adj.* **1.** lacking dexterity or skill; clumsy; bungling. **2.** ungraceful; ungainly; uncouth. **3.** ill-adapted for use or handling. **4.** requiring caution; somewhat hazardous. **5.** difficult to handle; dangerous. **6.** embarrassing or trying. **7.** deliberately obstructive, difficult, or perverse.

awl /ɔl/ *n.* a pointed instrument for piercing small holes in leather, wood, etc.

awning /'ɔnɪŋ/ *n.* **1.** a rooflike shelter of canvas, etc., before a window or door, over a deck, etc., as for protection from the weather. **2.** a shelter.

awoke /ə'woʊk/ *v.* past tense of **awake**.

awry /ə'raɪ/ *adv.* **1.** with a turn or twist to one side; askew. **2.** away from reason or the truth. **3.** amiss; wrong.

axes[1] /'æksiz/ *n.* plural of **axis**.

axes[2] /'æksəz/ *n.* plural of **axe**.

axial /'æksiəl/ *adj.* **1.** of, relating to, or forming an axis. **2.** situated in an axis or on the axis.

axilla /æk'sɪlə/ *n.*, *pl.* **axillae** /æk'sɪli/. *Anatomy* the armpit.

axiom /'æksiəm/ *n.* **1.** a recognised truth. **2.** an established and universally accepted principle or rule. – **axiomatic**, *adj.*

axis /'æksəs/ *n.*, *pl.* **axes** /'æksiz/. **1.** the line about which a rotating body, such as the earth, turns. **2.** a fixed line adopted for reference, as in plotting a curve on a graph, in crystallography, etc.

axle /'æksəl/ *n.* *Machinery* the pin, bar, shaft, or the like, on which or with which a wheel or pair of wheels rotate.

aye /aɪ/ *adv.*, *n.*, *pl.* **ayes**. – *adv.* **1.** yes. – *n.* **2.** an affirmative vote or voter. Also, **ay**.

azalea /ə'zeɪljə/ *n.* any of various plants with handsome, variously coloured flowers.

azo- a prefix indicating the presence of a divalent nitrogen group.

azure /'eɪʒə, æ'zjʊə/ *adj.* of a sky blue colour.

B b

B, b /bi/ *n., pl.* **B's** *or* **Bs**, **b's** *or* **bs**. the second letter of the English alphabet.

babaco /bə'bakoʊ/ *n.* a seedless, five-sided fruit similar to the pawpaw.

babble /'bæbəl/ *v.,* **-led**, **-ling**, *n. – v.i.* **1.** to utter words imperfectly or indistinctly. **2.** to make a continuous murmuring sound. *– n.* **3.** inarticulate speech. **4.** a murmuring sound.

baboon /bæ'bun, bə-/ *n.* a large, terrestrial monkey.

baby /'beɪbi/ *n., pl.* **-bies**. **1.** an infant; young child of either sex. **2.** *Colloquial* an invention or creation of which one is particularly proud.

baby boomer *n.* a person born in the period following World War II when a sudden and marked increase in the number of babies born occurred.

babysit /'beɪbisɪt/ *v.t.,* **babysat**, **babysitting**. to mind (a child).

bachelor /'bætʃələ/ *n.* **1.** an unmarried man of any age. **2.** a person who has taken the first or lowest degree at a university.

bacillus /bə'sɪləs/ *n., pl.* **-cilli** /-'sɪli/. any of the group of rod-shaped bacteria which produce spores in the presence of free oxygen.

back[1] /bæk/ *n.* **1.** the hinder part of the human body, extending from the neck to the end of the spine. **2.** the part of the body of animals corresponding to the human back. **3.** the part opposite to or farthest from the face or front; the hinder side; the rear part. *– v.t.* **4.** to support, as with authority, influence, or money (often fol. by *up*). **5.** to cause to move backwards; reverse the action of. **6.** to bet in favour of. *– v.i.* **7.** to go backwards (often fol. by *up*). *– adj.* **8.** lying or being behind. **9.** away from the front position or rank; remote.

back[2] /bæk/ *adv.* **1.** at, to, or towards the rear; backwards. **2.** towards the past. **3.** towards the original starting point, place, or condition. **4.** in reply; in return.

backbench /'bækbɛntʃ/ *n.* the non-office-holding parliamentary membership of a political party. – **backbencher**, *n.*

back bond *n.* a bond of indemnity given to a surety.

backbone /'bækboʊn/ *n.* **1.** the spinal or vertebral column; the spine. **2.** strength of character; resolution.

backdate /'bækdeɪt/ *v.t.,* **-dated**, **-dating**. to date (something) earlier; apply retrospectively.

backfire /bæk'faɪə/ *v.i.,* **-fired**, **-firing**. **1.** (of an internal-combustion engine) to have a premature explosion in the cylinder or in the admission or exhaust passages. **2.** to bring results opposite to those planned.

backgammon /'bækgæmən, bæk'gæmən/ *n.* a game played by two persons at a board with pieces moved in accordance with throws of dice.

background /'bækgraʊnd/ *n.* **1.** the portions of a picture represented as in the distance. **2.** the social, historical and other antecedents which explain an event or condition. **3.** *Computers* a program tolerant of interrupts, which continues on an extended task unless there is an interrupt task to be performed. *– adj.* **4.** of or relating to the background; in the background. **5.** *Computers* of or relating to a program of low priority.

backhand /'bækhænd/ *n.* a stroke, as in tennis, by a right-handed player from the left of the body (or the reverse for a left-handed player).

backing store /'bækɪŋ/ *n.* an auxiliary memory store attached to a digital computer.

backlash /'bæklæʃ/ *n.* any sudden, violent, or unexpected reaction.

backlog /'bæklɒg/ *n.* **1.** an accumulation of business resources, stock, etc., acting as a reserve. **2.** an accumulation of work, correspondence, etc., awaiting attention.

backpack /'bækpæk/ *n.* **1.** a light, strong bag designed to be carried on the back. **2.** portable equipment carried on the back, as television or film cameras, or fire-fighting, hiking, camping equipment, etc.

back-seat driver /'bæk-sit/ *n.* **1.** a passenger in a car who offers unsolicited advice to the driver. **2.** someone who gives advice or orders in matters which are not their responsibility.

backside /bæk'saɪd/ *n.* the buttocks.

backspace /'bækspeɪs/ *v.i.,* **-spaced**, **-spacing**. (in keyboarding) to move back in the text one space at a time, by depressing a particular key.

backstage /bæk'steɪdʒ/ *adv.* out of the view of the audience in a theatre; in the wings or dressing rooms, or behind the curtain on the stage.

backstop /'bækstɒp/ *n.* **1.** *Sport* a person, screen, or fence placed to prevent a ball going too far. **2.** a person who or a thing which is relied on for assistance when all else fails.

backstroke /'bækstroʊk/ *n.* *Swimming* a stroke in which the swimmer is on his or her back.

backtrack /'bæktræk/ *v.i.* **1.** to return over the same course or route. **2.** to withdraw from an undertaking, position, etc.; pursue a reverse policy.

backup /'bækʌp/ *n.* **1.** a pent-up accumulation, especially of a liquid. **2.** a reserve supply or resource; a second means of support.

backwardation /bækwə'deɪʃən/ *n.* *Stock Exchange* the position in a futures market where the more distantly traded contracts are selling at a discount to the nearer dated contracts.

backwards /'bækwədz/ *adv.* **1.** towards the back or rear. **2.** with the back foremost. **3.** towards the past. **4.** towards a worse or less advanced condition.

backwater /'bækwɔtə/ *n.* **1.** a body of stagnant water connected to a river. **2.** a place or state considered to be stagnant or backward.

backwoods /'bækwʊdz/ *pl. n.* any unfamiliar or unfrequented area.

backyard /bæk'jad/ *n.* **1.** an area, often of some size with gardens and lawn, at the back of a building, usually a house. – *adj.* **2.** illegal, illicit, improper or unqualified.

bacon /'beɪkən/ *n.* meat from the back and sides of the pig, salted and dried or smoked.

bacteri- a word element meaning 'bacteria' or 'bacterial'. Also, **bacter-**, **bacterio-**, **bactero-**.

bacteria /bæk'tɪəriə/ *n.* (*pl. of bacterium*) microscopic organisms, various species of which produce disease.

bad /bæd/ *adj.*, **worse**, **worst**. **1.** not good. **2.** unsatisfactory; poor; below standard; inadequate. **3.** regretful; contrite; sorry; upset. **4.** severe. **5.** rotten; decayed.

bade /bæd/ *v.* past tense of **bid**.

badge /bædʒ/ *n.* a mark, token or device worn as a sign of allegiance, membership, authority, achievement.

badger /'bædʒə/ *n.* **1.** a burrowing carnivorous mammal. – *v.t.* **2.** to harass; torment.

badminton /'bædmɪntən/ *n.* a game, similar to tennis, but played with a high net and shuttlecock.

baffle /'bæfəl/ *v.t.*, **-fled**, **-fling**. **1.** to thwart or frustrate disconcertingly; baulk; confuse. **2.** to puzzle or mystify.

bag /bæg/ *n.*, *v.*, **bagged**, **bagging**. – *n.* **1.** a receptacle of leather, cloth, paper, etc. **2.** (*pl.*) *Colloquial* a lot; an abundance (of). **3.** a sac, as in the body of an animal or insect. – *v.i.* **4.** to swell or bulge. **5.** to hang loosely like an empty bag. – *v.t.* **6.** to put into a bag. **7.** to kill or catch, as in hunting.

baggage /'bægɪdʒ/ *n.* luggage.

bagpipes /'bægpaɪps/ *n.* a reed instrument consisting of a melody pipe and one or more accompanying drone pipes protruding from a windbag into which the air is blown by the mouth or a bellows.

bail[1] /beɪl/ *n.* **1.** (in criminal proceedings) the release of a prisoner from legal custody into the custody of persons acting as sureties, undertaking to produce the prisoner to the court at a later date or forfeit the security deposited as a condition of the release. **2.** property given as security that a person released on bail will appear in court at the appointed time. **3.** the person acting as surety or providing security for a person released on bail. – *v.t.* **4.** to deliver possession of (goods, etc.) for storage, hire or other special purpose, without transfer of ownership.

bail[2] /beɪl/ *n.* **1.** *Cricket* either of the two small bars or sticks laid across the tops of the stumps which form the wicket. **2.** a framework for securing a cow's head during milking. **3.** Also, **bail rod** or **paper bail**. (in a typewriter) the rod which holds paper in place. – *v.t.* **4. bail up,** to hold up.

bait /beɪt/ *n.* **1.** food or some substitute used as a lure in fishing, trapping, etc. **2.** food containing a harmful additive such as poison or razor blades used to lure and kill animals considered pests. – *v.t.* **3.** to prepare (a hook or trap) with bait. **4.** to add harmful substances to (food) to kill or drug animals. **5.** to goad to anger; torment (someone) for amusement.

bake /beɪk/ *v.t.*, **baked**, **baking**. **1.** to cook by dry heat in an oven, under coals, or on heated metals or stones. **2.** to harden by heat.

baker /'beɪkə/ *n.* someone who bakes; someone who makes and sells bread, cake, etc. – **bakery**, *n.*

balance /'bæləns/ *n.*, *v.*, **-anced**, **-ancing**. -*n.* **1.** an instrument for weighing, typically a bar poised or swaying on a central support according to the weights borne in scales (pans) suspended at the ends. **2.** a state of equilibrium; equal distribution of weight, amount, etc. **3.** mental steadiness; habit of calm behaviour, judgment, etc. **4.** harmonious arrangement or adjustment, especially in the arts of design. **5.** something used to produce equilibrium. **6.** the act of balancing; comparison as to weight, amount, importance, etc.; estimate. **7.** the remainder or rest. **8.** *Commerce* **a.** equality between the totals of the two sides of an account. **b.** the difference between the debit total and the credit total of an account. **c.** unpaid difference represented by the excess of debits over credits. **9.** an adjustment of accounts. – *v.t.* **10.** to weigh in a balance. **11.** to estimate the relative weight or importance of; compare. **12.** to arrange, adjust, or proportion the parts of symmetrically. **13.** to be equal or proportionate to. **14.** *Commerce* **a.** to add up the two sides of (an account) and determine the difference. **b.** to make the necessary entries in (an account) so that the sums of the two sides will be equal. **c.** to settle by paying what remains due on an account. – *v.i.* **15.** *Commerce* to reckon or adjust accounts.

balance of payments *n.* the difference between a nation's total payments to foreign countries (debits) and its total receipts from foreign sources (credits).

balance of trade *n.* the difference between the value of the exports and imports of a country, said to be favourable or unfavourable as exports are greater or less than imports.

balance sheet *n.* the analysis at a given date of an enterprise's financial position, in accordance with which the total equities listed on one side are balanced by the assets listed on the other.

balcony /'bælkəni/ *n.*, *pl.* **-nies**. a raised and railed platform projecting from the wall of a building.

bald /bɔld/ *adj.* **1.** lacking hair on some part of the scalp. **2.** (of pneumatic tyres) having the rubber tread worn off. **3.** bare; plain; unadorned.

bale[1] /beɪl/ *n.* a large bundle or package prepared for storage or transportation, especially one closely compressed and secured by cords, wires, hoops or the like, sometimes with a wrapping.

bale[2] /beɪl/ *v.*, **baled**, **baling**, *n.* – *v.t.* **1.** to remove (water) especially from a boat, as with a bucket or a can. – *v.i.* **2.** to bale water. **3. bale out, a.** to make a parachute-jump from a plane. **b.** *Colloquial* to abandon a dangerous position or course. -*n.* **4.** a bucket or other vessel for baling. Also, **bail**.

baleful /'beɪlfəl/ *adj.* full of menacing or

malign influences; pernicious.

ball[1] /bɔl/ *n.* **1.** a spherical or approximately spherical body; a sphere. **2.** a round or roundish body, of different materials and sizes, hollow or solid, for use in various games, as cricket, football, tennis, or golf. **3.** *Colloquial* a testicle. **4. on the ball,** *Colloquial* alert; sharp.

ball[2] /bɔl/ *n.* **1.** a social gathering (usually formal) at which people dance. **2.** an enjoyable occasion.

ballad /'bæləd/ *n.* **1.** a simple narrative poem, often of popular origin, composed in short stanzas, especially one of romantic character and adapted for singing. **2.** a slick and sentimentalised pop song.

ballast /'bæləst/ *n.* **1.** any heavy material carried by a ship or boat for ensuring proper stability, so as to avoid capsizing and to secure the greatest effectiveness of the propelling power. **2.** anything that gives mental, moral, or political stability or steadiness.

ballerina /bælə'rinə/ *n., pl.* **-nas**. **1.** the principal female dancer in a ballet company. **2.** any female ballet-dancer.

ballet /'bæleɪ/ *n.* (performance of) an intricate style of dance using a formal technique and marked by grace and precision of movement.

ballistic /bə'lɪstɪk/ *adj.* relating to projectiles.

balloon /bə'lun/ *n.* a usually spherical bag made of some material impermeable to gas and filled with some gas lighter than air.

ballot /'bælət/ *n.* **1.** a ticket or paper used in voting. **2.** Also, **secret ballot**. the system or practice of secret voting by means of printed or written ballots or voting machines.

balm /bam/ *n.* **1.** any aromatic or fragrant ointment. **2.** anything which heals, soothes, or mitigates pain.

balmy /'bami/ *adj.,* **balmier**, **balmiest**. mild and refreshing; soft; soothing.

balsam /'bɔlsəm, 'bɒl-/ *n.* **1.** any of various fragrant exudations from certain trees. **2.** a common garden plant often with red, pink or white flowers. **3.** any aromatic ointment. **4.** any healing or soothing agent or agency.

bamboo /bæm'bu/ *n., pl.* **-boos**. **1.** any of various woody or treelike tropical and semitropical grasses. **2.** the hollow woody stem of such a plant, used for building purposes and for making furniture, poles, etc. *– adj.* **3.** made with bamboo: *bamboo ladder.*

bamboozle /bæm'buzəl/ *v.t.,* **-zled**, **-zling**. **1.** to deceive by trickery; impose upon. **2.** to perplex; mystify.

ban[1] /bæn/ *v.,* **banned**, **banning**, *n. – v.t.* **1.** to prohibit; interdict. *– n.* **2.** a prohibition by law or decree.

ban[2] /bæn/ *n.* a public proclamation or edict.

banal /'beɪnəl, bə'nal/ *adj.* hackneyed; trite. – **banality**, *n.*

banana /bə'nanə/ *n.* the pulpy, yellow-skinned, elongated fruit of a tropical plant.

band[1] /bænd/ *n.* **1.** a group of people or animals. **2.** a company of musicians constituted according to the kind of music played, usually playing for performance or as an accompaniment to dancing. *– v.i.* **3.** to unite; form a group; confederate (usually fol. by *together*).

band[2] /bænd/ *n.* **1.** any strip that contrasts with its surroundings in colour, texture or material. **2.** *Radio* a range of frequencies lying between any two well-defined limits.

band[3] /bænd/ *n.* (*usu. pl.*) anything which binds.

bandage /'bændɪdʒ/ *n.* a strip of cloth or other material used to bind up a wound, hold a dressing in place, etc.

bandicoot /'bændikut/ *n.* any of various small omnivorous somewhat ratlike Australian marsupials.

bandit /'bændət/ *n.* **1.** a robber, especially one who robs by violence. **2.** an outlaw.

bandy /'bændi/ *v.,* **-died**, **-dying**, *adj. – v.t.* **1.** to pass from one to another, or back and forth; give and take. *– adj.* **2.** (of legs) having a bend or crook outward.

bane /beɪn/ *n.* a person or thing that ruins or destroys.

bang /bæŋ/ *n.* **1.** a loud, sudden explosive noise, as the discharge of a gun. **2.** a knock; a bump. *– v.t.* **3.** to strike or beat resoundingly. **4.** to slam. **5.** to knock or bump. *– v.i.* **6.** to strike violently or noisily. *– adv.* **7.** exactly; precisely; just.

bangle /'bæŋgəl/ *n.* a bracelet in the form of a ring, without a clasp.

banish /'bænɪʃ/ *v.t.* to condemn to exile; expel from or relegate to a country or place by authoritative decree.

banister /'bænəstə/ *n.* one of the supports of a stair rail, either plain or resembling a pillar. Also, **bannister**.

banjo /'bændʒoʊ/ *n., pl.* **-jos**. a musical instrument of the guitar family, having a circular body.

bank[1] /bæŋk/ *n.* **1.** a long pile or mass. **2.** a slope or acclivity. **3.** *Physical Geography* the slope immediately bordering the course of a river along which the water normally runs. **4.** lateral inclination during a curve. *– v.i.* **5.** to rise in or form banks, as clouds or snow. **6.** to tip or incline laterally, as of an aeroplane, a road, a cycle racing track, etc. as an aircraft or a road.

bank[2] /bæŋk/ *n.* **1.** an institution for receiving and lending money (in some cases, issuing notes or holding current accounts that serve as money) and transacting other financial business. **2.** any store or reserve. *– v.i.* **3.** to exercise the functions of a bank or banker. **4.** to keep money in, or have an account with, a bank. **5.** *Colloquial* to rely or count (fol. by *on* or *upon*). **6. bank up,** to accumulate. *– v.t.* **7.** to deposit in a bank.

bank[3] /bæŋk/ *n.* **1.** an arrangement of objects in line. **2.** a row or tier of oars.

bank acceptance *n.* a draft endorsed or otherwise formally acknowledged by a bank on which it is drawn.

bank bill *n.* a commercial bill which has been accepted or endorsed by a trading bank.

bank charge *n.* a charge for bank services debited to a customer's account.

bank cheque *n.* a cheque issued by a bank in its own name.

bank-draft /'bæŋk-draft/ *n.* a draft drawn by one bank on another, payable on demand or at a specified future date.

banker /ˈbæŋkə/ *n.* **1.** someone who manages a bank or is in the banking business. **2.** someone who holds or supplies money for another.

banker's order *n.* a customer's written order to a bank to make a payment or a series of payments on their behalf.

banknote /ˈbæŋknoʊt/ *n.* a promissory note, payable on demand, issued by a bank and intended to circulate as money.

bank rate *n.* the rate at which the central bank of a country, as the Reserve Bank, is prepared to discount bills.

bankroll /ˈbæŋkroʊl/ *n.* **1.** a roll of money notes. – *v.t.* **2.** to provide funds for; act as backer for.

bankrupt /ˈbæŋkrʌpt/ *n.* **1.** *Law* a person who upon his or her own petition or that of his or her creditors is adjudged insolvent by a court, and whose property is therefore to be administered by a trustee for the benefit of the creditors in accordance with bankruptcy legislation. **2.** any insolvent debtor; one unable to satisfy any just claims made upon him or her. **3.** a person completely depleted of some human quality or resource. – *adj.* **4.** *Law* subject to having (one's) property administered by a trustee in accordance with bankruptcy legislation. **5.** completely depleted of some human quality or resource. **6.** relating to bankrupts. – *v.t.* **7.** to make bankrupt. – **bankruptcy**, *n.*

banksia /ˈbæŋksiə/ *n.* any of various shrubs and trees with leathery leaves and dense cylindrical heads of flowers, sometimes called a bottlebrush.

bank statement *n.* a printed sheet bearing a complete record of a current account, sent periodically to a customer.

banner /ˈbænə/ *n.* the flag of a country, army, troop, etc.

banquet /ˈbæŋkwət/ *n.* a formal and ceremonious meal, often one given to celebrate an event or to honour a person.

bantam /ˈbæntəm/ *n.* (*often cap.*) a domestic fowl of any of certain varieties or breeds characterised by very small size.

banter /ˈbæntə/ *n.* **1.** playfully teasing language; good-humoured raillery. – *v.i.* **2.** to use banter.

baptism /ˈbæptɪzəm/ *n.* **1.** a ceremonial immersion in water, or application of water, as an initiatory rite or sacrament of the Christian church. **2.** any similar ceremony or action of initiation, dedication, etc. – **baptise = baptize**, *v.*

bar /ba/ *n.*, *v.*, **barred**, **barring**, *prep.* – *n.* **1.** a relatively long and evenly shaped piece of some solid substance. **2.** a band or stripe. **3.** a ridge of sand or gravel in coastal waters. **4.** anything which obstructs, hinders, or impedes; an obstacle; a barrier. **5.** *Music* Also, **bar-line**. the vertical line drawn across the stave to mark the metrical accent. **6.** a counter or a room where alcoholic drinks, etc., are served to customers. **7.** practising barristers collectively. **8.** *Law* **a.** an objection which nullifies an action or claim. **b.** a stoppage or defeat of an alleged right of action. **9.** any tribunal. – *v.t.* **10.** to provide or fasten with a bar or bars. **11.** to block (a way, etc.) as with a barrier; prevent or hinder, as access. **12.** to forbid; preclude. – *prep.* **13.** except; omitting; but.

barb /bab/ *n.* **1.** a point or pointed part projecting backwards from a main point, as of a fishhook, an arrowhead, or a fence wire. **2.** a sharp or unkind implication in a remark; cutting comment.

barbarian /baˈbɛəriən/ *n.* an ignorant, uncouth and cruel person. – **barbaric**, **barbarous**, *adj.*

barbecue /ˈbabəkju/ *n.*, *v.t.*, **-cued**, **-cuing**. – *n.* **1.** a metal frame for cooking meat, etc., above an open fire of coals, wood, etc. **2.** a social occasion, usually out of doors, where barbecued food is served. – *v.t.* **3.** to cook on a barbecue. Also, **barbeque**, **bar-b-q**.

barber /ˈbabə/ *n.* one whose occupation it is to cut and dress the hair of customers and to shave or trim the beard.

bar code *n.* a product code containing information about prices, etc., in the form of a series of bars of varying thickness, designed to be read by an optical scanner.

bard /bad/ *n.* *Archaic* a poet.

bare /bɛə/ *adj.*, **barer**, **barest**, *v.*, **bared**, **baring**. – *adj.* **1.** without covering or clothing; naked or nude. **2.** without the usual furnishings, contents, etc. **3.** open to view; unconcealed; undisguised. **4.** unadorned; bald; plain. **5.** scarcely or just sufficient. – *v.t.* **6.** to make bare.

bargain /ˈbagən/ *n.* **1.** an agreement between parties settling what each shall give and take, or perform and receive, in a transaction. **2.** *Stock Exchange* an agreement to sell or to purchase; a sale or purchase. **3.** an advantageous purchase. – *v.i.* **4.** to discuss the terms of a bargain; haggle over terms.

barge /badʒ/ *n.*, *v.*, **barged**, **barging**. – *n.* **1.** a large flat-bottomed vessel, usually moved by towing, used for transporting freight. – *v.i.* **2.** to move aggressively or with undue energy often knocking others out of the way.

baritone /ˈbærətoʊn/ *n.* a male voice or voice part intermediate between tenor and bass.

barium /ˈbɛəriəm/ *n.* a whitish, malleable, active, divalent, metallic element. *Symbol*: Ba

bark[1] /bak/ *n.* **1.** the abrupt, explosive cry of a dog. – *v.i.* **2.** to utter an abrupt, explosive cry or a series of such cries, as a dog. **3.** to speak or cry out sharply or gruffly.

bark[2] /bak/ *n.* the external covering of the woody stems, branches, and roots of plants, as distinct and separable from the wood itself.

barley /ˈbali/ *n.* a cereal plant whose grain is used as food and in the making of whisky.

barn /ban/ *n.* a building for storing hay, grain, etc., and often for stabling livestock.

barnacle /ˈbanəkəl/ *n.* any of certain crustaceans which attach themselves to marine rocks.

barney /ˈbani/ *n.* *Colloquial* an argument; fight.

baro- a word element meaning 'weight', 'pressure'.

barometer /bəˈrɒmətə/ *n.* **1.** an instrument for measuring atmospheric pressure, thus determining height, weather changes, etc. **2.** anything that indicates changes.

baron /'bærən/ *n.* **1.** a man holding a peerage of the lowest titular rank. **2.** a rich and powerful man; magnate.

baronet /'bærənət, -nɛt/ *n.* a member of a British hereditary order of honour, ranking below the barons.

baroque /bə'rɒk, bə'roʊk/ *adj.* **1.** *Music* of or relating to the ornate style of composition of the 17th and early 18th centuries. **2.** extravagantly ornamented.

barrack[1] /'bærək/ *n.* (*usu. pl.*) a building or range of buildings for lodging soldiers, especially in garrison.

barrack[2] /'bærɪk/ *v.i.* to support; shout encouragement and approval (fol. by *for*).

barracouta /bærə'kutə/ *n.* an elongated, cold water, sport and food fish.

barracuda /bærə'kudə/ *n.* **1.** any of various species of elongated, predacious, tropical and subtropical marine fishes. **2.** → **barracouta**.

barrage /'bæraʒ, -adʒ/ *n.* **1.** *Military* a barrier of artillery fire. **2.** any overwhelming quantity.

barratry /'bærətri/ *n.* *Law* **1.** a wrongful act of a ship's master or crew at the expense of the owner or charterer, reckoned as one of the perils of the seas in marine insurance. **2.** the obsolete common-law offence of exciting and maintaining suits and quarrels.

barrel /'bærəl/ *n.* **1.** a wooden cylindrical vessel having slightly bulging sides and flat parallel ends. **2.** the tube of a gun.

barren /'bærən/ *adj.* **1.** incapable of producing, or not producing, offspring; sterile. **2.** unproductive; unfruitful.

barricade /'bærəkeɪd, bærə'keɪd/ *n.*, *v.*, **-caded**, **-cading**. – *n.* **1.** a defensive barrier hastily constructed, as in a street, to stop an enemy. – *v.t.* **2.** to obstruct or block with a barricade. **3.** to shut in and defend with or as with a barricade.

barrier /'bæriə/ *n.* anything that bars passage or access.

barrister /'bærəstə/ *n.* a lawyer allowed to plead cases in any court.

barrow /'bæroʊ/ *n.* a pushcart or horsedrawn cart used by street vendors, especially those selling fruit and vegetables.

barter /'batə/ *v.i.* to trade by exchange of commodities rather than by the use of money.

basalt /'bæsɔlt/ *n.* a dark, dense igneous rock.

base[1] /beɪs/ *n.*, *v.*, **based**, **basing**. – *n.* **1.** the bottom of anything, considered as its support; that on which a thing stands or rests. **2.** the principal element or ingredient of anything, considered as its fundamental part. **3.** *Military* a fortified or protected area or place used by any of the armed services. **4.** *Mathematics* **a.** the number which serves as a starting point for a logarithmic or other numerical system. **b.** the side or face of a geometric figure to which an altitude is thought to be drawn. **5.** *Chemistry* any of numerous compounds which react with an acid to form a salt. -*v.t.* **6.** to make or form a base or foundation for. **7.** to establish, as a fact or conclusion (fol. by *on* or *upon*). **8.** to place or establish on a base or basis; ground; found; establish.

base[2] /beɪs/ *adj.*, **baser**, **basest**. **1.** morally low; without dignity of sentiment; mean-spirited; selfish; cowardly. **2.** debased or counterfeit.

baseball /'beɪsbɔl/ *n.* a game played with a wooden bat and a hard ball.

basement /'beɪsmənt/ *n.* a storey of a building partly or wholly underground.

bash /bæʃ/ *v.t.* to strike with a crushing or smashing blow.

bashful /'bæʃfəl/ *adj.* uncomfortably diffident or shy; timid and easily embarrassed.

basic /'beɪsɪk/ *adj.* **1.** of, relating to, or forming a base; fundamental. – *n.* **2.** something that is basic or essential. – **basically**, *adv.*

basic wage *n.* the minimum wage payable to an adult employee under an award or agreement.

basil /'bæzəl/ *n.* any of various herbs having aromatic leaves used in cookery.

basin /'beɪsən/ *n.* **1.** a circular container of greater width than depth, contracting towards the bottom, used chiefly to hold water or other liquid, especially for washing. **2.** a small circular container of approximately equal width and depth, used chiefly for mixing, cooking, etc. **3.** *Physical Geography* a hollow or depression in the earth's surface, wholly or partly surrounded by higher land.

basis /'beɪsəs/ *n.*, *pl.* **bases** /'beɪsiz/. **1.** the bottom or base of anything, or that on which it stands or rests. **2.** a groundwork or fundamental principle. **3.** the principal constituent; a fundamental ingredient.

bask /bask/ *v.i.* to lie in or be exposed to a pleasant warmth.

basket /'baskət/ *n.* **1.** a receptacle made of twigs, rushes, thin strips of wood, or other flexible material, woven together. **2.** *Economics* a list of retail goods from which the consumer price index is calculated.

basketball /'baskətbɔl/ *n.* a ball game, the object of which is to throw the ball through an elevated basket.

bass[1] /beɪs/ *adj.* low in pitch; of the lowest pitch or range.

bass[2] /bæs/ *n.* an Australian freshwater fish.

basset /'bæsət/ *n.* a long-bodied, short-legged dog resembling a dachshund but larger and heavier. Also, **basset hound**.

bassinette /bæsə'nɛt/ *n.* a basket in which a baby sleeps.

bassoon /bə'sun/ *n.* a double-reed woodwind instrument.

bastard /'bastəd/ *n.* **1.** an illegitimate child. **2.** something irregular, inferior, spurious, or unusual. **3.** *Colloquial* an unpleasant or despicable person or thing.

baste[1] /beɪst/ *v.t.*, **basted**, **basting**. to sew with temporary stitches, as a garment in the first stages of making; tack.

baste[2] /beɪst/ *v.t.*, **basted**, **basting**. to moisten (meat, etc.) while cooking, with dripping, butter, etc.

bastion /'bæstiən/ *n.* **1.** a fortified place. **2.** any person or object which affords support or defence.

bat[1] /bæt/ *n., v.,* **batted**, **batting**. – *n.* **1.** *Sport* **a.** the club used in certain games, as cricket and baseball, to strike the ball. **b.** a racquet, especially one used in table tennis. **2.** *Colloquial* rate of motion. – *v.t.* **3.** to strike or hit with or as with a bat or club.

bat[2] /bæt/ *n.* **1.** a nocturnal or flying mammal characterised by modified forelimbs which serve as wings and are covered with a membranous skin extending to the hind limbs. **2.** *Colloquial* a cranky or silly woman.

bat[3] /bæt/ *v.t.,* **batted**, **batting**. to wink or flutter (one's eyelids).

batch /bætʃ/ *n.* **1.** a quantity or a number taken together; a group. **2.** the quantity of material prepared or required for one operation or that quantity produced by one operation.

batch costing *n. Commerce* a form of job costing in which a convenient unit or quantity of production is treated as a batch or job.

bate /beɪt/ *v.t.,* **bated**, **bating**. to moderate or restrain (the breath).

bath /baθ/ *n., pl.* **baths** /baθs/ *or especially def. 3* /baðz/; *v.t.,* /baθ/ – *n.* **1.** a washing of the body in, or an exposure of it to the action of, water or other liquid, or vapour, etc., as for cleaning, refreshment, medical treatment, etc. **2.** a vessel for containing this. **3.** (*pl.*) a public swimming pool. – *v.t.* **4.** to put or wash in a bath.

bathe /beɪð/ *v.t.,* **bathed**, **bathing**. **1.** to immerse in water or other liquid for cleansing, refreshment, etc. **2.** to apply water or other liquid to, with a sponge, cloth, etc.

batho- a word element meaning 'deep'.

batik /'bætɪk, 'batik/ *n.* a method of printing cloth using a wax deposit to achieve the desired pattern.

baton /'bætn/ *n.* **1.** a staff, club, or truncheon, especially as a mark of office or authority. **2.** *Music* the wand used by a conductor. **3.** *Athletics* (in relay racing) a metal or wooden tube, handed on by one relay runner to the next.

battalion /bə'tæljən/ *n. Military* a ground-force unit composed of three or more companies or similar units.

batten /'bætn/ *n.* **1.** a light strip of wood usually having an oblong cross-section and used to fasten main members of a structure together. – *v.t.* **2.** *Nautical* to fasten (as hatches) with battens and tarpaulins (usually fol. by *down*).

batter[1] /'bætə/ *v.t.* **1.** to beat persistently or hard; pound. **2.** to damage by beating or hard usage.

batter[2] /'bætə/ *n.* a mixture of flour, milk or water, eggs, etc., beaten together for use in cookery.

battery /'bætəri, -tri/ *n., pl.* **-ries**. **1.** *Electricity* either of two chemical cells or groups of cells: **a.** one which produces electrical energy. **b.** one which stores electrical energy. **2.** a group of similar items used together. **3.** a large number of cages in which chickens etc., are reared for intensive productivity. **4.** *Law* unlawful and intentional interference with the person of another.

battle /'bætl/ *n., v.,* **battled**, **battling**. – *n.* **1.** a hostile encounter or engagement between opposing forces. **2.** any extended or intense fight, struggle or contest. – *v.i.* **3.** to engage in battle. – *v.t.* **4.** to fight.

battleaxe block /'bætəlæks/ *n.* a block or section of land, behind those with street frontages and accessible through a drive or lane.

bauble /'bɔbl/ *n.* a cheap piece of ornament; trinket.

baulk /bɔk/ *v.i.* **1.** to stop, as at an obstacle. **2.** *Sport* to make an incomplete or misleading move, especially an illegal one.

bauxite /'bɔksaɪt/ *n.* a rock, the principal ore of aluminium.

bawdy /'bɔdi/ *adj.* rollickingly vulgar; lewd.

bawl /bɔl/ *v.i.* to cry loudly and vigorously.

bay[1] /beɪ/ *n.* a recess or inlet in the shore of a sea or lake between two capes or headlands, not as large as a gulf but larger than a cove.

bay[2] /beɪ/ *n.* **1.** a recessed space projecting outwards from the line of a wall, as to contain a window. **2.** the aisle between parallel shelvings as in a library.

bay[3] /beɪ/ *n.* a deep, prolonged bark, as of a hound or hounds in hunting.

bay[4] /beɪ/ *n.* a reddish brown colour.

bayonet /'beɪnət/ *n.* a stabbing or slashing instrument of steel, made to be attached to or at the muzzle of a rifle.

bazaar /bə'za/ *n.* a marketplace.

bazooka /bə'zukə/ *n.* a cylindrical rocket-launcher, an individual infantry weapon that fires a rocket.

be /bi/ *v., present indicative sing. 1* **am**; *2* **are**; *3* **is**, *pl.* **are**, *past indicative 1* **was**; *2* **were**; *3* **was**, *pl.* **were**, *present subjunctive* **be**, *past subjunctive* **were**, *past participle* **been**, *present participle* **being**. – *substantive* **1.** to exist; have reality; live; take place; occur; remain as before. – *v. (cop)* **2.** (a link connecting a subject with predicate or qualifying words in assertive, interrogative, and imperative sentences, or serving to form infinitive and participial phrases). – *v. (aux)* **3.** (used with the present participle of a principal verb to form the progressive tense (*I am waiting*), or with a past participle in passive forms, regularly of transitive verbs (*the date was fixed*; *it must be done*) and formerly, as still to some extent, of intransitives (*I am done*; *he is come*)).

be- a prefix meaning 'about', 'around', 'all over', as in *besiege*.

beach /bitʃ/ *n.* **1.** the sand or loose water-worn pebbles of the seashore. **2.** that part of the shore of the sea, or of a large river or lake, washed by the tide or waves. **3.** the seaside as a place of recreation. – *v.t.* **4.** *Nautical* to run or haul up (a ship or boat) on the beach.

beacon /'bikən/ *n.* a guiding or warning signal, such as a lighthouse, fire, etc.

bead /bid/ *n.* **1.** a small ball of glass, pearl, wood, etc., with a hole through it, strung with others like it, and used as an ornament or in a rosary. **2.** a drop of liquid.

beagle /'bigəl/ *n.* one of a breed of small hounds with short legs and drooping ears, used especially in hunting.

beak /bik/ *n.* the horny bill of a bird; the neb.

beaker /'bikə/ *n.* a large drinking vessel with a wide mouth.

beam /bim/ *n.* **1.** a thick, long piece of timber, shaped for structural use. **2.** *Nautical* the side of a vessel, or the direction at right angles to the keel, with reference to the wind, sea, etc. **3.** the widest part. **4.** the transverse bar of a balance from the ends of which the scales or pans are suspended. **5.** a ray, or bundle of parallel rays, of light or other radiation. **6.** a gleam; suggestion. **7.** *Radio, Aeronautics* a signal transmitted along a narrow course, used to guide pilots through darkness, bad weather, etc. – *v.i.* **8.** to emit beams, as of light. **9.** to look or smile radiantly.

bean /bin/ *n.* **1.** the edible fruit or seed of various plants. **2.** any of various other beanlike seeds or plants, as the coffee bean.

bean curd /'bin kɜd/ *n.* → **tofu**. Also, **beancurd**.

beanie /'bini/ *n. Colloquial* a small close-fitting knitted cap, often having a pompom or other decoration on top.

bean sprout /'bin spraʊt/ *n.* the very young shoot of any of certain beans, used in Chinese and some other Asian cookery and as a salad vegetable. Also, **beansprout**, **bean shoot**.

bear[1] /bɛə/ *v.*, **bore**, **borne** *or* **born**, **bearing**. – *v.t.* **1.** to hold up; support. **2.** to carry. **3.** to render; afford; give. **4.** to undergo; suffer. **5.** to be fit for or worthy of. **6.** to possess as a quality, characteristic, etc.; have in or on. **7.** to manage (oneself, one's body, head, etc.). **8.** to give birth to. **9.** to produce by natural growth. **10. bear out,** to confirm; prove right. – *v.i.* **11.** to hold, or remain firm, as under pressure (often fol. by *up*). **12.** to be patient (fol. by *with*). **13.** to press (fol. by *on, against*, etc.). **14.** to have an effect, reference, or bearing (fol. by *on*). **15.** to have relevance to. **16.** to tend in course or direction; move; go. **17.** to be located or situated. **18.** to bring forth young, fruit, etc.

bear[2] /bɛə/ *n., adj., v.,* **beared**, **bearing**. – *n.* **1.** a carnivorous or omnivorous mammal, having a massive body, coarse, heavy fur, relatively short limbs, and an almost rudimentary tail. **2.** (in general business) someone who believes that conditions are or will be unfavourable. – *adj.* **3.** *Stock Exchange* of, having to do with, or caused by declining prices in stocks, etc. – *v.i.* **4.** *Stock Exchange* to operate in stocks for a decline in price.

beard /bɪəd/ *n.* the growth of hair on the face of an adult male, sometimes exclusive of the moustache.

bearing /'bɛərɪŋ/ *n.* **1.** the manner in which one bears or carries oneself, including posture, gestures, etc. **2.** reference, relation, or relevance (fol. by *on*). **3.** *Machinery* a part in which a journal, pivot, or the like, turns or moves. **4.** (*often pl.*) direction or relative position. **5.** *Geography* a horizontal angle measured from 0° to 90° fixing the direction of a line with respect to either the north or south direction.

bear market *n. Stock Exchange* a gloomy period of trading during and after a decline in share prices when traders consider there is little prospect of immediate recovery.

beast /bist/ *n.* **1.** any animal except a human being, especially a large four-footed one. **2.** a coarse, filthy, or otherwise beastlike human.

beastly /'bistli/ *adj.*, **beastlier**, **beastliest**. **1.** of or like a beast; bestial. **2.** *Colloquial* nasty; disagreeable.

beat /bit/ *v.*, **beat**, **beaten** *or* **beat**, **beating**, *n., adj.* – *v.t.* **1.** to strike repeatedly and usually violently, especially as a punishment. **2.** to whisk; stir, as in order to thicken or aerate. **3.** to flutter or flap. **4.** to sound as on a drum. **5.** to hammer (metal) thin; flatten (usually fol. by *out*). **6.** to make (a path) by repeated treading. **7.** *Music* to mark (time) by strokes, as with the hand or a metronome. **8.** to overcome in a contest; defeat. **9.** to be superior to. – *v.i.* **10.** to strike repeated blows; pound. **11.** to throb or pulsate. **12.** to radiate intense light or heat; glare. **13.** to resound under blows, as a drum. – *n.* **14.** a stroke or blow. **15.** a throb or pulsation. **16.** a beaten path or habitual round, as of a police officer. **17.** *Music* **a.** the audible, visual, or mental marking of the metrical divisions of music. **b.** a stroke of the hand, baton, etc., marking time division or accent for music during performance. – *adj.* **18.** *Colloquial* exhausted; worn out.

beatific /biə'tɪfɪk/ *adj.* **1.** bestowing blessedness or beatitude. **2.** blissful.

beatify /bi'ætəfaɪ/ *v.t.*, **-fied**, **-fying**. **1.** to make blissfully happy. **2.** *Roman Catholic Church* to declare (a deceased person) to be among the blessed, and thus entitled to specific religious honour.

beaut /bjut/ *Colloquial* – *adj.* **1.** fine; good. – *interj.* **2.** Also, **you beaut!**. (an exclamation of approval, delight, enthusiasm, etc.).

beauteous /'bjutiəs/ *adj.* beautiful.

beautician /bju'tɪʃən/ *n.* a person skilled in cosmetic treatment and beauty aids.

beautiful /'bjutəfʊl/ *adj.* **1.** having or exhibiting beauty. **2.** very pleasant.

beautify /'bjutəfaɪ/ *v.t.*, **-fied**, **-fying**. to decorate, adorn or make more beautiful.

beauty /'bjuti/ *n., pl.* **-ties**. **1.** that quality or characteristic which excites an admiring pleasure, or delights the eye or the aesthetic sense. **2.** something or someone beautiful. **3.** *Colloquial* an excellent or remarkable example of its kind. **4.** *Colloquial* a particular advantage. – *interj.* **5.** (an exclamation of approval, delight, etc.).

beaver /'bivə/ *n.* an amphibious rodent noted for its ingenuity in damming streams with branches, mud, etc.

became /bə'keɪm/ *v.* past tense of **become**.

because /bi'kɔz, -'kɒz, bə-/ *conj.* **1.** for the reason that; due to the fact that. – *adv.* **2.** by reason; on account (fol. by *of*).

beck /bɛk/ *n. in the phr.* **at someone's beck and call,** ready to obey someone immediately; subject to someone's slightest wish.

beckon /'bɛkən/ *v.t.* **1.** to signal, summon, or direct by a gesture of the head or hand. **2.** to lure; entice.

become /bə'kʌm, bi-/ *v.*, **became**, **become**, **becoming**. – *v.i.* **1.** to come into being; come or grow to be (as stated). **2.** to be the fate (of). – *v.t.* **3.** to befit; suit.

becoming /bəˈkʌmɪŋ, bi-/ *adj.* **1.** attractive. **2.** suitable; proper.

bed /bɛd/ *n.* **1.** a piece of furniture upon which or within which a person sleeps. **2.** a piece of ground (in a garden) in which plants are grown. **3.** a piece or part forming a foundation or base.

bedlam /ˈbɛdləm/ *n.* a scene of wild uproar and confusion.

bedraggle /bəˈdrægəl, bi-/ *v.t.*, **-gled**, **-gling**. to make limp and soiled as with wet or dirt.

bedridden /ˈbɛdrɪdn/ *adj.* confined to bed.

bedrock /ˈbɛdrɒk/ *n.* **1.** *Geology* unbroken solid rock, overlaid in most places by soil or rock fragments. **2.** any firm foundation.

bee /bi/ *n.* **1.** a four-winged, usually stinging insect which gathers pollen. **2.** a local gathering for work, entertainment, contests, etc.

beech /bitʃ/ *n.* a type of tree growing in temperate regions.

beef /bif/ *n.* **1.** the flesh of an animal of the genus *Bos*, used for food. – *v.i.* **2.** *Chiefly US Colloquial* to complain; grumble.

beefy /ˈbifi/ *adj.*, **beefier**, **beefiest**. fleshy; brawny; solid; heavy.

beeline /ˈbilaɪn/ *n.* a direct line, like the course of bees returning to a hive.

been /bin/ *v.* past participle of **be**.

beer /bɪə/ *n.* an alcoholic beverage made by brewing and fermentation from cereals, usually malted barley and flavoured with hops, etc., to give a bitter taste.

beet /bit/ *n.* any of various biennial plants including the red beet, which has a fleshy edible root, and the sugar beet, which yields sugar.

beetle /ˈbitl/ *n.* any insect characterised by having forewings modified as hard, horny structures, not vibrated in flight.

beetroot /ˈbitrut/ *n.* the edible root of the red beet.

befall /bəˈfɔl, bi-/ *v.*, **-fell**, **-fallen**, **-falling**. – *v.i.* **1.** to happen or occur. – *v.t.* **2.** to happen to.

befit /bəˈfɪt, bi-/ *v.t.*, **-fitted**, **-fitting**. to be fitting or appropriate for; be suited to.

before /bəˈfɔ, bi-/ *adv.* **1.** in front; in advance; ahead. **2.** earlier or sooner. – *prep.* **3.** in front of; ahead of; in advance of. **4.** previously to; earlier than. **5.** in preference to; rather than. **6.** in precedence of, as in order or rank. **7.** in the presence or sight of. **8.** under the jurisdiction or consideration of. – *conj.* **9.** previously to the time when. **10.** sooner than; rather than.

beforehand /bəˈfɔhænd, bi-/ *adv.* in anticipation; in advance; ahead of time.

befriend /bəˈfrɛnd, bi-/ *v.t.* to act as a friend to; aid.

befuddle /bəˈfʌdl, bi-/ *v.t.*, **-dled**, **-dling**. **1.** to make stupidly drunk. **2.** to confuse, as with glib argument.

beg /bɛg/ *v.*, **begged**, **begging**. – *v.t.* **1.** to ask for in charity; ask as alms. **2.** to ask for, or of, with humility or earnestness, or as a favour. – *v.i.* **3.** to ask alms or charity; live by asking alms. **4.** to ask humbly or earnestly.

began /bəˈgæn, bi-/ *v.* past tense of **begin**.

beget /bəˈgɛt, bi-/ *v.t.*, **begot**, **begotten** *or* **begot**, **begetting**. to procreate or generate (used chiefly of the male parent).

beggar /ˈbɛgə/ *n.* **1.** someone who begs alms, or lives by begging. **2.** a penniless person. **3.** (in playful use) a wretch or rogue.

begin /bəˈgɪn/ *v.*, **began**, **begun**, **beginning**. – *v.i.* **1.** to enter upon an action; take the first step; commence; start. **2.** to come into existence; arise; originate. – *v.t.* **3.** to take the first step in; set about; start; commence. **4.** to originate; be the originator of. – **beginning**, *n.*

beginner /bəˈgɪnə/ *n.* someone who has recently begun to learn a skill; a novice.

begrudge /bəˈgrʌdʒ, bi-/ *v.t.*, **-grudged**, **-grudging**. to be discontented at seeing (a person) have (something).

beguile /bəˈgaɪl, bi-/ *v.t.*, **-guiled**, **-guiling**. **1.** to influence by guile; mislead; delude. **2.** to charm or divert.

begun /bəˈgʌn, bi-/ *v.* past participle of **begin**.

behalf /bəˈhaf, bi-/ *n.* side, interest, or aid (preceded by *on*).

behave /bəˈheɪv, bi-/ *v.i.*, **-haved**, **-having**. **1.** to conduct oneself or itself; act. **2.** to act in a socially acceptable manner. – **behaviour**, *n.*

behead /bəˈhɛd, bi-/ *v.t.* to cut off the head of; kill or execute by decapitation.

behest /bəˈhɛst, bi-/ *n.* bidding or injunction; mandate or command.

behind /bəˈhaɪnd, bi-/ *prep.* **1.** at the back of; at the rear of. **2.** after; later than. **3.** less advanced than; inferior to. **4.** on the farther side of; beyond. **5.** supporting; promoting. **6.** hidden or unrevealed by. – *adv.* **7.** at or towards the back; in the rear. **8.** in arrears; behindhand. – *n.* **9.** the buttocks.

behindhand /bəˈhaɪndhænd, bi-/ *adj.* **1.** late. **2.** behind in progress; backward.

behold /bəˈhoʊld, bi-/ *v.t.*, **-held**, **-holding**. to observe; look at; see.

behove /bəˈhoʊv, bi-/ *v.t.*, **-hoved**, **-hoving**. to be needful or proper for or incumbent on (now only in impersonal use).

beige /beɪʒ/ *n.*, *adj.* very light brown.

being /ˈbiɪŋ/ *n.* **1.** existence, as opposed to non-existence. **2.** conscious existence; life. **3.** substance or nature. **4.** a living thing.

belated /bəˈleɪtəd, bi-/ *adj.* coming or being late or too late.

belch /bɛltʃ/ *v.i.* **1.** to eject wind spasmodically and noisily from the stomach through the mouth; burp. **2.** to emit contents violently, as a gun, geyser, or volcano. – *v.t.* **3.** to eject spasmodically or violently; give forth. – *n.* **4.** a belching.

belfry /ˈbɛlfri/ *n.*, *pl.* **-fries**. a belltower, either attached to a church or other building or standing apart.

belie /bəˈlaɪ, bi-/ *v.t.*, **-lied**, **-lying**. **1.** to misrepresent. **2.** to show to be false.

belief /bəˈlif, bi-/ *n.* **1.** that which is believed; an accepted opinion. **2.** conviction of the truth or reality of a thing, based upon grounds insufficient to afford positive knowledge. **3.** confidence; faith; trust.

believe /bəˈliv, bi-/ *v.*, **-lieved**, **-lieving**. – *v.i.* **1.** to have confidence (*in*); trust; rely through faith (*on*). **2.** to be persuaded of the truth of anything; accept a doctrine, principle, system, etc. (fol. by *in*). – *v.t.* **3.** to have belief in; credit; accept as true. **4.** to think. – **believable**, *adj.* – **believer**, *n.*

belittle /bəˈlɪtl, bi-/ *v.t.*, **-tled**, **-tling**. to make little or less important; depreciate; disparage.

bell /bɛl/ *n.* **1.** a sounding instrument, usually of metal, cup-shaped with a flaring mouth, rung by the strokes of a clapper, tongue, or hammer suspended within it. **2.** any instrument emitting a ringing signal, especially an electrical device as a doorbell. **3. ring a bell,** *Colloquial* to remind one; jog the memory. **4.** *Nautical* the half-hourly subdivisions of a watch of four hours, each being marked by single or double strokes of a bell.

bellbird /ˈbɛlbɜd/ *n.* a yellowish-green honeyeater with a distinctive, tinkling, bell-like call.

bellicose /ˈbɛləkoʊs/ *adj.* inclined to war; warlike; pugnacious.

belligerent /bəˈlɪdʒərənt/ *adj.* **1.** warlike; given to waging war. **2.** relating to war, or to those engaged in war. – *n.* **3.** a state or nation at war, or a member of the military forces of such a state.

bellow /ˈbɛloʊ/ *v.i.* **1.** to make a hollow, loud, animal cry, as a bull or cow. **2.** to roar; bawl.

bellows /ˈbɛloʊz/ *n.* (*sing. and pl.*) an instrument which produces a strong current of air when the air-chamber inside is contracted.

belly /ˈbɛli/ *n.*, *pl.* **-lies**. the front or underpart of a vertebrate body from the breastbone to the pelvis, containing the abdominal viscera; the abdomen.

belong /bəˈlɒŋ, bɪ-/ *v.i.* **1.** to have one's rightful place; to bear relation as a member, adherent, inhabitant, etc. (fol. by *to*). **2.** to be proper or due.

belongings /bəˈlɒŋɪŋz, bi-/ *pl. n.* possessions.

beloved /bəˈlʌvəd, -ˈlʌvd, bi-/ *adj.* **1.** greatly loved; dear to the heart. – *n.* **2.** someone who is greatly loved.

below /bəˈloʊ, bi-/ *adv.* **1.** in or to a lower place; lower down; beneath. **2.** at a later point on a page or in writing. **3.** in a lower rank or grade. – *prep.* **4.** lower down than. **5.** too low or base to be worthy of.

belt /bɛlt/ *n.* **1.** a band of flexible material, as leather, worn around the waist to support clothing, for decoration, etc. **2.** any encircling or transverse band, strip, or strips. **3.** *Machinery* a flexible band or cord connecting and pulling about each of two or more wheels, pulleys or the like, to transmit or change the direction of motion. **4.** *Boxing* an imaginary line round the body at the level of the navel below which the boxer must not strike. – *v.t.* **5.** to gird or furnish with a belt. **6.** *Colloquial* to give a thwack or blow to. **7.** to sing very loudly and often raucously (fol. by *out*). – *v.i.* **8.** *Colloquial* to move quickly or expeditiously. **9. belt up,** *Colloquial* be quiet; shut up.

bemused /bəˈmjuzd, bi-/ *adj.* **1.** confused; muddled; stupefied. **2.** lost in thought; preoccupied.

bench /bɛntʃ/ *n.* **1.** a long seat with or without a back to accommodate several people. **2.** a seat on which members sit in a house of parliament. **3.** the strong work-table of a carpenter or other mechanic. **4. the bench, a.** the position or office of a judge: *appointed to the bench.* **b.** the body of persons sitting as judges.

benchmark /ˈbɛntʃmak/ *n.* **1.** a point of reference from which quality or excellence is measured. – *v.t.* **2.** to set a benchmark for: *this case will benchmark all future judgments in the wages area.*

benchmarking /ˈbɛntʃmakɪŋ/ *n.* the practice whereby companies compare their performance in a variety of different management and manufacturing fields with that of other companies.

bend /bɛnd/ *v.*, **bent**, **bending**, *n.* – *v.t.* **1.** to force into a different or particular, especially curved, shape, as by pressure. **2.** to cause to submit. **3.** to turn in a particular direction. **4.** to incline mentally (fol. by *to* or *towards*). – *v.i.* **5.** to become curved, crooked, or bent. **6.** to bow in submission or reverence; yield; submit. **7.** to turn or incline in a particular direction; be directed. – *n.* **8.** the act of bending. **9.** the state of being bent. **10.** a bent thing or part; curve; crook.

bene- a word element meaning 'well'.

beneath /bəˈniθ, bi-/ *adv.* **1.** below; in a lower place, position, state, etc. – *prep.* **2.** below; under. **3.** unworthy of; below the level or dignity of.

benediction /bɛnəˈdɪkʃən/ *n.* *Ecclesiastical* the act of uttering a blessing.

benefactor /ˈbɛnəfæktə, bɛnəˈfæktə/ *n.* **1.** someone who confers a benefit; kindly helper. **2.** someone who makes a bequest or endowment.

beneficent /bəˈnɛfəsənt/ *adj.* doing good or causing good to be done; conferring benefits; kindly in action or purpose.

beneficial /bɛnəˈfɪʃəl/ *adj.* **1.** conferring benefit; advantageous; helpful. **2.** *Law* helpful in the meeting of needs.

beneficiary /bɛnəˈfɪʃəri/ *n.*, *pl.* **-aries**. – *n.* **1.** someone who receives benefits, profits, or advantages. **2.** *Law* a person designated as the recipient of funds or other property under a trust, will, insurance policy, etc.

benefit /ˈbɛnəfət/ *n.*, *v.*, **-fited**, **-fiting**. – *n.* **1.** an act of kindness. **2.** anything that is for the good of a person or thing. **3.** a payment or other assistance given by an insurance company, mutual benefit society, or public agency. – *v.t.* **4.** to do good to; be of service to. – *v.i.* **5.** to gain advantage; make improvement.

benevolent /bəˈnɛvələnt/ *adj.* **1.** desiring to do good for others. **2.** intended for benefits rather than profit.

benighted /bəˈnaɪtəd/ *adj.* intellectually or morally ignorant; unenlightened.

benign /bəˈnaɪn/ *adj.* **1.** of a kind disposition; kind. **2.** *Pathology* not malignant.

bent /bɛnt/ *adj.* **1.** curved; crooked. **2.** determined; set; resolved (fol. by *on*). **3.** *Colloquial* diverging from what is considered to be normal or conservative behaviour. – *n.* **4.** direction taken; inclination; bias.

bequeath /bəˈkwið, ˈ-kwiθ/ *v.t.* *Law* to dispose by last will of (personal property, especially money). – **bequest**, *n.*

berate /bə'reɪt/ *v.t.*, **-rated**, **-rating**. to scold.

bereave /bə'riv, bi-/ *v.t.*, **-reaved** *or* **-reft**, **-reaving**. to make desolate through loss (*of*), especially by death.

bereft /bə'rɛft/ *adj.* **1.** suffering loss; deprived of possession. **2.** lacking.

beret /'bɛreɪ/ *n.* a soft, round, peakless cap that fits closely.

berry /'bɛri/ *n., pl.* **-ries**. **1.** any small, (usually) stoneless and juicy fruit, as the gooseberry, strawberry, holly berry, rose hip, etc. **2.** a dry seed or kernel, as of wheat.

berserk /bə'zɜk/ *adj.* violently and destructively frenzied.

berth /bɜθ/ *n.* a shelf-like space, bunk, or whole room allotted to a traveller on a vessel or a train as a sleeping space.

beseech /bə'sitʃ, bi-/ *v.t.*, **-sought** *or* **-seeched**, **-seeching**. **1.** to implore urgently. **2.** to beg eagerly for; solicit.

beset /bə'sɛt, bi-/ *v.t.*, **-set**, **-setting**. to attack on all sides; assail; harass.

beside /bə'saɪd, bi-/ *prep.* **1.** by or at the side of; near. **2.** compared with.

besides /bə'saɪdz, bi-/ *adv.* **1.** moreover. **2.** in addition. **3.** otherwise; else. – *prep.* **4.** over and above; in addition to. **5.** other than; except.

besiege /bə'sidʒ, bi-/ *v.t.*, **-sieged**, **-sieging**. **1.** to lay siege to. **2.** to assail or ply, as with requests, etc.

besot /bə'sɒt, bi-/ *v.t.*, **-sotted**, **-sotting**. **1.** to infatuate. **2.** to make stupid or foolish. **3.** to stupefy with drink.

bespoke /bə'spoʊk, bi-/ *adj.* made to order.

best /bɛst/ *adj.* (*superlative of good*) **1.** of the highest quality, excellence, or standing. **2.** most advantageous, suitable, or desirable. **3.** favourite. – *adv.* (*superlative of well*) **4.** most excellently or suitably; with most advantage or success. **5.** in or to the highest degree; most fully. – *n.* **6.** the best thing, state, or part. **7.** utmost or best quality. – *v.t.* **8.** to defeat; beat. **9.** to outdo; surpass.

bestial /'bɛstiəl/ *adj.* **1.** of or belonging to a beast. **2.** brutal; inhuman; irrational.

bestiality /bɛsti'æləti/ *n.* sexual relations of a human with an animal.

best man *n.* the chief attendant of the bridegroom at a wedding.

bestow /bə'stoʊ, bi-/ *v.t.* to present as a gift; give; confer.

best practice /bɛst 'præktəs/ *n.* the set of operations achieving world-class results in business performance, especially resulting from the cooperation of management and employees in all key processes of the business.

bet /bɛt/ *v.*, **bet** *or* **betted**, **betting**, *n.* – *v.t.* **1.** to pledge as a forfeit to another who makes a similar pledge in return, in support of an opinion; stake; wager. – *v.i.* **2.** to lay a wager. **3.** to make a practice of betting. – *n.* **4.** a pledge of something to be forfeited, in case one is wrong, to another who has the opposite opinion.

betide /bə'taɪd, bi-/ *v.t.*, **-tided**, **-tiding**. *Archaic* to happen; befall; come to.

betray /bə'treɪ, bi-/ *v.t.* **1.** to deliver or expose to an enemy by treachery or disloyalty. **2.** to be unfaithful in keeping or upholding. **3.** to reveal or disclose in violation of confidence. **4.** to show; exhibit. **5.** to deceive; mislead. – **betrayal**, *n.*

betrothed /bə'troʊðd, bi-/ *adj.* **1.** engaged to be married. – *n.* **2.** an engaged person.

better /'bɛtə/ *adj.* (*comparative of good*) **1.** of superior quality or excellence. **2.** of superior value, use, fitness, desirability, acceptableness, etc. **3.** larger; greater. – *adv.* (*comparative of well*) **4.** in a more excellent way or manner. **5.** in a superior degree. **6. had better,** would be wiser, safer, etc., to. **7. better off,** in better circumstances. – *v.t.* **8.** to make better; improve; increase the good qualities of. – *n.* **9.** that which has superior excellence, etc. **10.** (*usu. pl.*) one's superior in wisdom, wealth, etc.

between /bə'twin, bi-/ *prep.* **1.** in the space separating (two or more points, objects, etc.). **2.** intermediate to, in time, quantity, or degree. **3.** connecting. **4.** distinguishing one thing from another. – *adv.* **5.** in the intervening space or time; in an intermediate position or relation.

bevel /'bɛvəl/ *n.* the inclination that one line or surface makes with another when not at right angles.

beverage /'bɛvrɪdʒ, 'bɛvərɪdʒ/ *n.* a drink of any kind.

bevy /'bɛvi/ *n., pl.* **bevies**. a flock.

beware /bə'wɛə, bi-/ *v.* (*now only used as imperative or infinitive*) – *v.i.* **1.** to be wary, cautious, or careful (fol. by *of* or a clause). – *v.t.* **2.** *Archaic* be wary of.

bewilder /bə'wɪldə, bi-/ *v.t.* to confuse or puzzle completely; perplex.

bewitch /bə'wɪtʃ, bi-/ *v.t.* to affect by witchcraft or magic; throw a spell over.

beyond /bə'jɒnd, bi-/ *prep.* **1.** on or to the farther side of. **2.** farther on than; more distant than. **3.** outside the understanding, limits, or reach of; past. **4.** more than; in excess of; over and above. – *adv.* **5.** farther on or away.

bi- a prefix meaning 'twice, doubly, two', as in *bilateral, binocular, biweekly*. Also, **bin-**.

biannual /baɪ'ænjuəl/ *adj.* occurring twice a year.

bias /'baɪəs/ *n., v.*, **biased**, **biasing**. – *n.* **1.** an oblique or diagonal line of direction, especially across a woven fabric. **2.** a particular tendency or inclination, especially one which prevents unprejudiced consideration of a question. – *v.t.* **3.** to influence, usually unfairly; prejudice; warp.

bib /bɪb/ *n.* an article of clothing worn under the chin by a child, especially while eating, to protect the clothes.

biblio- a word element meaning 'book'.

bibliography /bɪbli'ɒgrəfi/ *n., pl.* **-phies**. **1.** a complete or selective list of literature on a particular subject. **2.** a list of works by a given author. **3.** a list of source materials used or consulted in the preparation of a work.

bicameral /baɪ'kæmərəl/ *adj.* having two branches, chambers, or houses, as a legislative body.

bicentenary /baɪsən'tinəri, -'tɛnəri/ *n.* a

200th anniversary.

bicentennial /baɪsən'tɛniəl/ *adj.* **1.** consisting of or lasting 200 years. **2.** recurring every 200 years.

biceps /'baɪsəps, -sɛps/ *n.* a muscle having two heads of origin, especially the muscle on the front of the upper arm, which bends the forearm.

bicker /'bɪkə/ *v.i.* to engage in petulant argument; wrangle.

bicycle /'baɪsɪkəl/ *n.* a vehicle with two wheels, one in front of the other, and having a saddle-like seat for the rider.

bid /bɪd/ *v.,* **bade** /bæd/ *or* **bad** /bæd/ *for defs 1 and 2 or* **bid** *for defs 3 and 4*; **bidden** *or* **bid**, **bidding**, *n.* *– v.t.* **1.** to command; order; direct. **2.** to say as a greeting or benediction. **3.** *Commerce* to offer, as a price at an auction or as terms in a competition to secure a contract. **4.** *Commerce* **a.** to overbid all offers for (property) at an auction in order to retain ownership (fol. by *in*). **b.** to increase (the market price) by increasing bids (fol. by *up*). *– n.* **5.** the act of someone who bids. **6.** an offer, as at an auction. **7.** an attempt to attain some goal or purpose.

biddy /'bɪdi/ *n., pl.* **-dies**. *Colloquial* an old woman.

bide /baɪd/ *v.t.,* **bided**, **biding**.*– in the phr.* **bide one's time,** to wait for a favourable opportunity.

bidet /'bideɪ/ *n.* a small low bath, straddled by the user, for washing the genitals.

biennial /baɪ'ɛniəl/ *adj.* happening every two years.

bier /bɪə/ *n.* a frame or stand on which a corpse, or the coffin containing it, is laid before burial.

bifocal /baɪ'foukəl/ *adj.* **1.** *Chiefly Optics* having two foci. **2.** (of spectacle lenses) having two portions, one for near and the other for far vision.

big /bɪg/ *adj.,* **bigger**, **biggest**. **1.** large in size, height, width, amount, etc. **2.** large in compass or conception; magnanimous; generous; liberal.

bigamy /'bɪgəmi/ *n.* the offence of purporting to marry while a valid prior marriage subsists. – **bigamist**, *n.* – **bigamous**, *adj.*

bight /baɪt/ *n.* **1.** the loop or bent part of a rope, as distinguished from the ends. **2.** a bend or curve in the shore of a sea or a river.

bigot /'bɪgət/ *n.* a person who is intolerantly convinced of the rightness of a particular creed, opinion, practice, etc.

big-time /'bɪg-taɪm/ *Colloquial – adj.* **1.** at the top level in any business or pursuit. *-n.* **2.** the top level, especially in business or society.

bigwig /'bɪgwɪg/ *n. Colloquial* a very important person.

bike /baɪk/ *n. Colloquial* a bicycle, tricycle, or motorcycle.

bikini /bə'kini/ *n.* a very brief, two-piece swimming costume.

bilateral /baɪ'lætrəl/ *adj.* **1.** relating to, involving, or affecting two sides or parties. **2.** *Law, etc.* (of a contract) binding the parties to reciprocal obligations.

bile /baɪl/ *n.* **1.** *Physiology* a bitter yellow or greenish liquid secreted by the liver and aiding in digestion, principally by emulsifying fats. **2.** ill nature; peevishness.

bilge /bɪldʒ/ *n. Nautical* **1.** the lowest portion of a ship's interior. **2.** foul water that collects there.

bilingual /baɪ'lɪŋgwəl/ *adj.* able to speak one's native language and another with approximately equal facility.

bilious /'bɪljəs/ *adj.* **1.** *Physiology, Pathology* relating to bile or to an excess secretion of bile. **2.** peevish; testy; cross. **3.** sick; nauseated. **4.** sickly; nauseating.

-bility a suffix forming nouns from adjectives in *-ble*, as in *nobility*.

bill[1] /bɪl/ *n.* **1.** an account of money owed for goods or services supplied. **2.** *Government* a form or draft of a proposed statute presented to a legislature, but not yet enacted or passed and made law. **3.** a written or printed public notice or advertisement. **4.** a bill of exchange. **5.** program; entertainment. *– v.t.* **6.** to announce by bill or public notice. **7.** to schedule as part of a program. **8.** to render an account of money owed.

bill[2] /bɪl/ *n.* that part of the jaws of a bird covered with a horny sheath; a beak.

billabong /'bɪləbɒŋ/ *n.* a waterhole, originally part of a river, formed when the channel connecting it to the river dries up.

billboard /'bɪlbɔd/ *n.* → **hoarding**.

billet /'bɪlət/ *n.* **1.** lodging for a soldier, especially lodging in private or non-military public buildings. **2.** private, usually unpaid, temporary lodgings arranged for members of a group or team.

billiards /'bɪljədz/ *n.* a game played by two or more persons on a rectangular table, with balls driven by means of cues.

billing /'bɪlɪŋ/ *n.* **1.** the relative position in which a performer or act is listed on handbills, posters, etc. **2.** the total business of an advertising agency during a given period.

billion /'bɪljən/ *n.* **1.** a thousand times a million, or 10^9. **2.** *Obsolescent* a million times a million, or 10^{12}.

bill of exchange *n.* a written authorisation or order to pay a specified sum of money to a specified person.

bill of lading *n.* a document recording particulars of a contract for the carriage of goods by sea, serving also as a document of title to the goods.

bill of sale *n.* a document transferring title in personal property from one person to another, either temporarily as security against a loan or debt (**conditional bill of sale**), or permanently (**absolute bill of sale**).

billow /'bɪlou/ *n.* **1.** a great wave or surge of the sea. *– v.i.* **2.** to rise or roll in or like billows; surge.

billposter /'bɪlpoustə/ *n.* someone who pastes up bills and advertisements.

billy /'bɪli/ *n., pl.* **-lies**. a cylindrical container for liquids, sometimes enamelled, usually having a close-fitting lid.

billycart /'bɪlikat/ *n.* a small four-wheeled cart.

billygoat /'bɪligout/ *n.* a male goat.

bimbo /'bɪmbou/ *n. Originally US Colloquial*

an attractive but empty-headed young woman.

bimensal /baɪ'mɛnsəl/ *adj.* occurring once in two months; bimonthly.

bimonthly /baɪ'mʌnθli/ *adj., adv.* **1.** every two months. **2.** twice a month.

bin /bɪn/ *n.* **1.** a box or enclosed space used for storing grain, wool as it is shorn, coal, refuse, etc. **2.** a partitioned stand used by a winemaker for storing wine in bottles.

binary /'baɪnəri/ *adj.* **1.** consisting of, indicating, or involving two. **2.** using, involving, or expressed in the binary number system. **3.** *Mathematics* having two variables.

binary code *n.* any means of representing information by a sequence of the digits 1 and 0.

binary digit *n.* a single digit in a binary number.

binary number system *n.* a number system which uses only the digits 1 and 0, based on the rules 1 + 0=1, 1 + 1=10. Also, **binary system**.

bind /baɪnd/ *v.*, **bound**, **binding**, *n.* – *v.t.* **1.** to make fast with a band or bond. **2.** to swathe or bandage (often fol. by *up*). **3.** to unite by any legal or moral tie. **4.** to hold to a particular state, place, employment, etc. **5.** (*usu. passive*) to place under obligation or compulsion. **6.** *Law* to put under legal obligation (fol. by *over*). **7.** to indenture as an apprentice (often fol. by *out*). **8.** to fasten or secure within a cover, as a book. – *v.i.* **9.** to become compact or solid; cohere. **10.** to have power to oblige. – *n.* **11.** something that binds. **12.** *Colloquial* a nuisance; bore.

bindi-eye /'bɪndi-aɪ/ *n.* any of a number of plants with small, burrlike fruits. Also, **bindii**, **bindy-eye**, **bindy**.

binge /bɪndʒ/ *n.* *Colloquial* a spree; a period of excessive indulgence, as in eating or drinking.

binocular /bə'nɒkjələ/ *adj.* **1.** involving (the use of) two eyes. – *n.* **2.** (*pl.*) a double telescope used by both eyes at once; field-glasses.

binomial /baɪ'noʊmiəl/ *n.* *Mathematics* an expression which is a sum or difference of two terms, as $3x + 2y$ and $x^2 - 4x$.

bio- a word element meaning 'life', 'living things'.

biodegradable /ˌbaɪoʊdə'greɪdəbəl/ *adj.* capable of being decomposed by the action of living organisms, especially of bacteria.

bioethics /ˌbaɪoʊ'ɛθɪks/ *n.* the study of ethical implications of medical, biological and environmental research. – **bioethical**, *adj.*

biography /baɪ'ɒgrəfi/ *n., pl.* **-phies**. a written account of a person's life. – **biographer**, *n.* – **biographical**, *adj.*

biological clock *n.* a hypothetical mechanism controlling the timing of the development of an organism through the various stages of its life span.

biology /baɪ'ɒlədʒi/ *n.* the science of life or living matter in all its forms and phenomena, especially with reference to origin, growth, reproduction, structure, etc. – **biologist**, *n.* – **biological**, *adj.*

biopsy /'baɪɒpsi/ *n.* *Medicine* the excision and diagnostic study of a piece of tissue from a living body.

biorhythms /'baɪoʊrɪðəmz/ *pl. n.* the three internal cycles, the physiological, emotional, and intellectual, that theoretically affect our well being.

-biosis a word element meaning 'way of life'.

bipartite /baɪ'pataɪt/ *adj.* *Law* being in two corresponding parts.

bipolar affective disorder *n.* a mental disorder marked by alternating periods of excitation and depression; manic depression. Also, **bipolar mood disorder**.

birch /bɜtʃ/ *n.* a tree or shrub with a smooth, outer bark and close-grained wood.

bird /bɜd/ *n.* **1.** any of the class of warm-blooded vertebrates having a body more or less completely covered with feathers, and the forelimbs so modified as to form wings by means of which most species fly. **2.** *Colloquial* a girl; a girlfriend.

bird's-eye /'bɜdz-aɪ/ *adj.* seen from above.

biro /'baɪroʊ/ *n.* a ballpoint pen.

birth /bɜθ/ *n.* **1.** the fact of being born. **2.** the act of bearing or bringing forth. **3.** lineage; extraction; descent. **4.** supposedly natural heritage. **5.** any coming into existence; origin.

birth certificate *n.* a certificate issued by a registrar upon the birth of each person, recording sex and parentage.

birth control *n.* the regulation of birth through the deliberate control or prevention of conception.

birthday /'bɜθdeɪ/ *n.* **1.** the day of one's birth. **2.** the anniversary of one's birth or the origin of something.

birthmark /'bɜθmak/ *n.* a congenital mark on the body.

birthright /'bɜθraɪt/ *n.* any right or privilege to which a person is entitled by birth.

birthstone /'bɜθstoun/ *n.* a precious stone associated with a person's month of birth and worn as a lucky charm.

biscuit /'bɪskət/ *n.* a mixture of flour, liquid, shortening, etc., baked in small pieces.

bisect /baɪ'sɛkt/ *v.t.* to cut or divide into two parts.

bisexual /baɪ'sɛkʃuəl/ *adj.* **1.** of both sexes. – *n.* **2.** a person sexually attracted to either sex.

bishop /'bɪʃəp/ *n.* a member of the clergy consecrated for the spiritual direction of a diocese.

bison /'baɪsən/ *n., pl.* **-son**. *Zoology* a large North American bovine ruminant.

bistro /'bɪstroʊ/ *n.* **1.** a wine bar. **2.** a small restaurant.

bit[1] /bɪt/ *n.* **1.** the metal mouthpiece of a bridle, with the adjacent parts to which the reins are fastened. **2.** anything that curbs or restrains. **3.** *Machinery* the cutting or penetrating part of various tools.

bit[2] /bɪt/ *n.* **1.** a small piece or quantity of anything. **2.** share or part of a duty, task, etc.

bit[3] /bɪt/ *n.* a single, basic unit of information, used in connection with computers and communication theory.

bitch /bɪtʃ/ *n.* **1.** a female dog. **2.** *Colloquial* a woman, especially a disagreeable or malicious one. **3.** *Colloquial* a complaint. **4.** *Colloquial* something which is giving rise to difficulties and dissatisfaction. – **bitchy,** *adj.*

bite /baɪt/ *v.,* **bit, bitten** *or* **bit, biting,** *n.* – *v.t.* **1.** to cut into or wound, or cut (*off, out,* etc.) with the teeth. **2.** to sting, as an insect. **3.** *Colloquial* to trouble; worry; disturb. **4.** to cheat; deceive. – *v.i.* **5.** to press the teeth (*into, on,* etc.); snap. **6.** *Angling* (of fish) to take the bait. **7.** to accept a deceptive offer or suggestion. – *n.* **8.** the act of biting. **9.** a wound made by biting. **10.** *Dentistry* the angle at which the upper and lower teeth meet. **11.** pungency; sharpness.

bitter /ˈbɪtə/ *adj.* **1.** having a harsh, disagreeable taste, like that of quinine. **2.** hard to bear; grievous; distressful. **3.** characterised by intense animosity.

bittersweet /bɪtəˈswit/ *adj.* **1.** both bitter and sweet to the taste. **2.** both pleasant and painful.

bitumen /ˈbɪtʃəmən/ *n.* **1.** any of various natural substances, as asphalt, etc., consisting mainly of hydrocarbons. **2. the bitumen,** a tarred or sealed road.

bivalve /ˈbaɪvælv/ *n.* a mollusc having two shells hinged together.

bivouac /ˈbɪvuæk/ *n.* a temporary camp, especially a military one, made out in the open with little or no equipment.

biweekly /baɪˈwikli/ *adj., adv.* **1.** every two weeks. **2.** twice a week.

bizarre /bəˈza/ *adj.* singular in appearance, style, or general character; whimsically strange; odd.

blab /blæb/ *v.t.,* **blabbed, blabbing.** to reveal indiscreetly and thoughtlessly.

black /blæk/ *adj.* **1.** without brightness or colour; absorbing all or nearly all the rays emitted by a light source. **2.** *Anthropology* relating or belonging to an ethnic group characterised by dark skin pigmentation. **3.** soiled or stained with dirt. **4.** gloomy; dismal. **5.** indicating censure, disgrace, or liability to punishment. **6.** illicit. **7.** prohibited or banned by a trade union. – *n.* **8.** a colour without hue at one extreme end of the scale of greys, opposite to white. A black surface absorbs light of all hues equally. **9.** (*sometimes cap.*) a member of a dark-skinned people; an Aborigine; a Negro. **10. in the black,** financially solvent. – *v.t.* **11.** to make black; put black on. **12.** (of a trade union) to ban or prevent normal industrial working in (a factory, industry, or the like.). – *v.i.* **13.** to become black; take on a black colour. **14. black out,** to lose consciousness.

blackball /ˈblækbɔl/ *v.t.* **1.** to ostracise. **2.** to vote against.

black ban *n.* a refusal by a group interest, as of producers, trade unions, consumers, to supply or purchase goods or services. – **black-ban,** *v.*

blackberry /ˈblækbəri, -bri/ *n., pl.* **-ries.** a black or very dark purple fruit.

blackbird /ˈblækbɜd/ *n.* a European songbird of the thrush family.

blackboard /ˈblækbɔd/ *n.* a smooth dark board, used in schools, etc., for writing or drawing on with chalk.

blackcurrant /blækˈkʌrənt/ *n.* **1.** a small, black edible fruit. **2.** the shrub itself.

black economy *n.* a system of cash payments for goods or services, where the receiver of the cash does not disclose it as income.

black eye *n.* bruising round the eye, resulting from a blow, etc.

blackguard /ˈblægad/ *n.* a coarse, despicable person; a scoundrel.

blackhead /ˈblækhɛd/ *n.* a small, black-tipped, fatty mass in a follicle, especially of the face.

blackleg /ˈblæklɛg/ *n.* **1.** → **scab** (def. 2). **2.** a swindler especially in racing or gambling.

black light *n.* ultraviolet light.

black list *n.* a list of persons under suspicion, disfavour, censure, etc., or a list of fraudulent or unreliable customers or firms.

black magic *n.* magic used for evil purposes.

blackmail /ˈblækmeɪl/ *n.* **1.** *Law* **a.** any payment extorted by intimidation, as by threats of injurious revelations or accusations. **b.** the extortion of such payment. – *v.t.* **2.** to extort blackmail from.

black maria /məˈraɪə/ *n.* *Colloquial* a closed vehicle used for conveying prisoners to and from jail. Also, **Black Maria**.

black market *n.* an illegal market violating price controls, rationing, etc.

blackout /ˈblækaʊt/ *n.* **1.** the extinguishing of all visible lights in a city, etc., as a wartime protection. **2.** the extinguishing or failure of light as in a power failure. **3.** temporary loss of consciousness or vision, especially in aviation due to high acceleration.

black power *n.* a movement originating in the US advocating the advancement of blacks (in Australia especially of the Aborigines) through violence or political means.

black sheep *n.* a person regarded as worthless despite a good background.

blacksmith /ˈblæksmɪθ/ *n.* **1.** a person who makes horseshoes and shoes horses. **2.** an artisan who works in iron.

black swan *n.* a large, stately swimming bird, with black plumage and a red bill.

bladder /ˈblædə/ *n.* **1.** *Anatomy, Zoology* a distensible pelvic sac with membranous and muscular walls, for storage and expulsion of urine excreted by the kidneys. **2.** any similar sac or receptacle, as the inflatable inner bag of a football.

blade /bleɪd/ *n.* **1.** the flat cutting part of sword, knife, etc. **2.** a sword. **3.** the leaf of a plant, especially of a grass or cereal. **4.** a thin, flat part of something, as of a bone, an oar, a propeller, a bat, etc. **5.** a dashing, swaggering, or rakish young fellow.

blame /bleɪm/ *v.,* **blamed, blaming,** *n.* – *v.t.* **1.** to lay the responsibility of (a fault, error, etc.) on a person. **2. to blame,** responsible for a fault or error; blamable; culpable. – *n.* **3.** imputation of fault; censure. **4.** responsibility for a fault, error, etc.

blanch /blænʃ, blanʃ/ *v.i.* to become white;

turn pale.

bland /blænd/ *adj.* **1.** (of a person's manner) suave; deliberately agreeable or pleasant but often without real feeling. **2.** soothing or balmy, as air. **3.** mild, as food or medicines.

blandish /'blændɪʃ/ *v.t.* to treat flatteringly; coax; cajole.

blank /blæŋk/ *adj.* **1.** (of paper, etc.) free from marks; not written or printed on. **2.** not filled in. **3.** unrelieved or unbroken by ornament or opening. **4.** lacking some usual or completing feature; empty. **5.** complete, utter, or unmitigated. – *n.* **6.** a place where something is lacking. **7.** a void; emptiness. **8.** a space left (to be filled in) in written or printed matter. **9.** *Machinery* a piece of metal prepared to be stamped or cut into a finished object, such as a coin or key. **10. in blank,** (of a document) with spaces left to be filled in.

blank cheque *n.* a cheque bearing a signature but no stated amount.

blank endorsement *n.* an endorsement on a cheque or note naming no payee, and payable to bearer.

blanket /'blæŋkət/ *n.* **1.** a large rectangular piece of soft, loosely woven fabric, usually wool, used especially as a bed covering. **2.** any heavy concealing layer or covering. – *adj.* **3.** covering or intended to cover a group or class of things, conditions, etc.

blare /blɛə/ *v.i.,* **blared**, **blaring**. to emit a loud raucous sound.

blasé /bla'zeɪ, 'blazeɪ/ *adj.* indifferent to and bored by pleasures of life.

blaspheme /blæs'fim/ *v.,* **-phemed**, **-pheming**. – *v.t.* **1.** to speak impiously or irreverently of (God or sacred things). – *v.i.* **2.** to utter impious words. – **blasphemy**, *n.* – **blasphemous**, *adj.*

blast /blast/ *n.* **1.** a sudden blowing or gust of wind. **2.** the blowing of a trumpet, whistle, etc. **3.** a forcible stream of air from the mouth, from bellows, or the like. **4.** the act of exploding; explosion. **5.** severe criticism. – *v.t.* **6.** to blow (a trumpet, etc.). **7.** to affect with any pernicious influence; ruin; destroy. **8.** to tear (rock, etc.) to pieces with an explosive. **9.** to criticise (someone) abusively. – *interj.* **10.** (an exclamation of anger or irritation).

-blast a combining form meaning 'embryo', 'sprout', 'germ'.

blast furnace *n.* a vertical, steel cylindrical furnace using a forced blast to produce molten iron for conversion into steel, etc.

blatant /'bleɪtnt/ *adj.* (of actions, etc.) flagrantly obvious or undisguised.

blaze[1] /bleɪz/ *n., v.,* **blazed**, **blazing**. – *n.* **1.** a bright flame or fire. **2.** a sudden, intense outburst, as of fire, passion, fury. – *v.i.* **3.** to burn brightly.

blaze[2] /bleɪz/ *n.* **1.** a spot or mark made on a tree, as by removing a piece of the bark, to indicate a boundary or a path in a forest. **2.** a white spot on the face of a horse, cow, etc.

blazer /'bleɪzə/ *n.* a jacket.

blazon /'bleɪzən/ *v.t.* to set forth conspicuously or publicly; display; proclaim.

-ble variant of **-able**, as in *noble.*

bleach /blitʃ/ *v.t.* **1.** to make white, pale, or colourless. – *n.* **2.** a bleaching agent.

bleak /blik/ *adj.* **1.** bare, desolate, and windswept. **2.** cold and piercing.

bleary /'blɪəri/ *adj.,* **blearier**, **bleariest**. (of the eyes) dim from a watery discharge, or from tiredness.

bleat /blit/ *v.i.* **1.** to cry as a sheep, goat, or calf. **2.** to complain; moan.

bleed /blid/ *v.,* **bled** /blɛd/, **bleeding**. – *v.i.* **1.** to lose blood, from the body or internally from the vascular system. **2.** to exude sap, juice, etc. – *v.t.* **3.** to cause to lose blood, especially surgically. **4.** *Colloquial* to obtain, as in excessive amount, or extort money from.

blemish /'blɛmɪʃ/ *v.t.* **1.** to destroy the perfection of. – *n.* **2.** a defect; a disfigurement; stain.

blench /blɛntʃ/ *v.i.* to shrink; flinch; quail.

blend /blɛnd/ *v.,* **blended**, **blending**, *n.* – *v.t.* **1.** to mix smoothly and inseparably together. **2.** to mix (various sorts or grades) in order to obtain a particular kind or quality. – *n.* **3.** a mixture or kind produced by blending.

blended family /ˌblɛndəd/ *n.* a family formed from the members of separate families, usually as a result of the parents' remarriage.

bless /blɛs/ *v.t.,* **blessed** *or* **blest**, **blessing**. **1.** to consecrate by a religious rite; make or pronounce holy. **2.** to request of God the bestowal of divine favour on. **3.** to bestow good of any kind upon.

blew /blu/ *n.* past tense of **blow**.

blight /blaɪt/ *n.* **1.** any cause of destruction, ruin, or frustration. – *v.t.* **2.** to destroy; ruin; frustrate.

blind /blaɪnd/ *adj.* **1.** lacking the sense of sight. **2.** unwilling or unable to try to understand. **3.** lacking all awareness. **4.** having no outlets. **5.** made without knowledge in advance. – *v.t.* **6.** to make blind, as by injuring, dazzling, or bandaging the eyes. – *n.* **7.** something that obstructs vision or keeps out light. **8.** a shade for a window, as a strip of cloth on a roller, or a venetian blind. **9.** a cover for masking action or purpose; decoy. – *adv.* **10.** without being able to see one's way. **11.** without assessment or prior consideration.

blindfold /'blaɪndfoʊld/ *v.t.* to prevent sight by covering (the eyes); cover the eyes of.

blink /blɪŋk/ *v.i.* **1.** to wink, especially rapidly and repeatedly. – *n.* **2.** a glance or glimpse. **3. on the blink,** *Colloquial* not working properly.

blinker /'blɪŋkə/ *n.* either of two flaps on a bridle, to prevent a horse from seeing sideways or backwards.

bliss /blɪs/ *n.* **1.** lightness of heart; blitheness; gladness. **2.** supreme happiness or delight.

blister /'blɪstə/ *n.* **1.** a thin vesicle on the skin, containing watery matter or serum, as from a burn or other injury. **2.** any similar swelling, as an air bubble in a casting or a paint blister. – *v.i.* **3.** to rise in blisters; become blistered.

blithe /blaɪð/ *adj.* joyous, merry, or happy in disposition; glad; cheerful.

blithering /ˈblɪðərɪŋ/ *adj.* nonsensical; jabbering.

blitz /blɪts/ *n.* **1.** *Military* war waged by surprise, swiftly and violently, as by the use of aircraft. **2.** any swift, vigorous attack.

blizzard /ˈblɪzəd/ *n.* a violent windstorm with dry, driving snow and intense cold.

bloat /bloʊt/ *v.t.* **1.** to make distended, as with air, water, etc.; cause to swell. **2.** to puff up; make vain or conceited. – *v.i.* **3.** to become swollen; be puffed out or dilated.

bloated /ˈbloʊtəd/ *adj.* **1.** swollen: *bloated features.* **2.** suffering from flatulence. **3.** suffering from excessive size: *a bloated bureaucracy.*

bloc /blɒk/ *n.* a group of states or territories united by some common factor.

block /blɒk/ *n.* **1.** a solid mass of wood, stone, etc., usually with one or more plane or approximately plane faces. **2.** a mould or piece on which something is shaped or kept in shape, as a hat block. **3.** a piece of wood prepared for cutting, or as cut, for wood engraving. **4.** *Printing* a letter-press printing plate mounted on a base to make it type-high. **5.** *Mechanics* **a.** a device consisting of one or more grooved pulleys mounted in a casing or shell, to which a hook or the like is attached, used for transmitting power, changing direction of motion, etc. **b.** the casing or shell holding the pulley. **6.** a blocking or obstructing, or blocked or obstructed state or condition. **7.** *Computers* a set of data or instructions. **8. a.** a fairly large area of land, especially for settlement, mining, farming, etc. **b.** a section of land, frequently suburban, as for building a house, etc. **9.** one large building, divided into offices, apartments, etc.: *an office block, a block of flats.* **10.** a portion of a city, town, etc., enclosed by (usually four) neighbouring and intersecting streets. **11.** a large number of shares taken together, as on the stock exchange. **12.** a writing or sketching pad. – *v.t.* **13.** to fit with blocks; mount on a block. **14.** to shape or prepare on or with a block. **15.** to sketch or outline roughly or in a general plan, without details (fol. by *out* or *in*). **16.** to obstruct (a space, progress, etc.); check or hinder (a person, etc.) by placing obstacles in the way.

blockade /blɒˈkeɪd/ *n.* any obstruction of passage or progress.

blockage /ˈblɒkɪdʒ/ *n.* an obstruction.

blockbuster /ˈblɒkbʌstə/ *n.* *Colloquial* anything large and spectacular, as a lavish theatrical production.

block letter *n.* a plain capital letter. Also, **block capital**.

bloke /bloʊk/ *n.* *Colloquial* a man; fellow; guy.

blond /blɒnd/ *adj.* **1.** light-coloured. **2.** (of a person) having light-coloured hair and skin. – *n.* **3.** a blond person.

blonde /blɒnd/ *n.* **1.** a female with light-coloured hair. – *adj.* **2.** (of a female) having light-coloured hair and skin.

blood /blʌd/ *n.* **1.** the fluid that circulates in the arteries and veins or principal vascular system of animals, in humans being of a red colour and consisting of a pale yellow plasma containing semisolid corpuscles. **2.** man's fleshly nature. **3.** physical and cultural extraction. **4.** descent from a common ancestor. **5. in cold blood,** calmly, coolly, and deliberately.

blood bank *n.* a place where blood is stored for later use.

bloodbath /ˈblʌdbaθ/ *n.* a massacre.

bloodhound /ˈblʌdhaʊnd/ *n.* one of a breed of large, powerful dogs with a very acute sense of smell, used for tracking game, human fugitives, etc.

blood pressure *n.* the pressure of the blood against the inner walls of the blood vessels.

bloodshed /ˈblʌdʃɛd/ *n.* destruction of life; slaughter.

bloodshot /ˈblʌdʃɒt/ *adj.* (of the eyes) red from dilated blood vessels.

bloodstream /ˈblʌdstrim/ *n.* the blood flowing through a circulatory system.

bloodthirsty /ˈblʌdθɜsti/ *adj.* eager to shed blood; murderous.

blood vessel *n.* any of the vessels (arteries, veins, capillaries) through which the blood circulates.

bloody /ˈblʌdi/ *adj.*, **bloodier**, **bloodiest**, *v.*, **bloodied**, **bloodying**, *adv.* – *adj.* **1.** stained with blood. **2.** attended with bloodshed. **3.** *Colloquial* (an intensifier signifying approval, as in *bloody beauty*, or disapproval, as in *bloody bastard*). **4.** *Colloquial* difficult; obstinate; cruel. – *v.t.* **5.** to stain with blood. – *adv.* **6.** *Colloquial* very; extremely.

bloom /blum/ *n.* **1.** the flower of a plant. **2.** a flourishing, healthy condition. **3.** a whitish, powdery surface coating or appearance. – *v.i.* **4.** to produce or yield blossoms. **5.** to flourish.

bloomers /ˈblumәz/ *n.* **1.** loose trousers gathered at the knee, formerly worn by women as part of gymnasium, riding, or other such dress. **2.** a woman's undergarment so designed.

blossom /ˈblɒsəm/ *n.* *Botany* **1.** the flower of a plant, especially of one producing an edible fruit. – *v.i.* **2.** to flourish; develop (often fol. by *out*).

blot /blɒt/ *n.*, *v.*, **blotted**, **blotting**. – *n.* **1.** a spot or stain, especially of ink on paper. -*v.t.* **2.** to spot, stain, or bespatter. **3.** to make indistinguishable (fol. by *out*). **4.** to dry with absorbent paper or the like. – *v.i.* **5.** (of ink, etc.) to spread in a stain. **6.** to become blotted or stained.

blotch /blɒtʃ/ *n.* a large irregular spot or blot.

blouse /blaʊz/ *n.*, *v.*, **bloused**, **blousing**. -*n.* **1.** a light, loosely fitting bodice or shirt, especially one that is gathered or held in at the waist. – *v.i.* **2.** to hang loose and full.

blow[1] /bloʊ/ *n.* **1.** a sudden stroke with hand, fist, or weapon. **2.** a sudden shock, or a calamity or reverse.

blow[2] /bloʊ/ *v.*, **blew** /blu/, **blown**, **blowing**, *n.* – *v.i.* **1.** (of the wind or air) to be in motion. **2.** to produce or emit a current of air, as with the mouth, a bellows, etc. **3.** *Music* (of horn, trumpet, etc.) to give out sound. **4.** (of a fuse, gasket, light bulb, radio valve, tyre, etc.) to burn out or perish; become unusable (often fol. by *out*). **5.** to be extinguished, as by the wind (fol. by *out*). **6. blow up, a.** to come into being. **b.** to explode. **c.** *Colloquial* to lose one's temper. *– v.t.* **7.** to drive by means of a current of air. **8.** to extinguish (a flame, etc.) with a puff of air (fol. by *out*). **9.** to shape (glass, etc.) with a current of air. **10.** to cause to sound, especially by a current of air. **11.** to cause to explode (fol. by *up, to bits*, etc.). **12.** *Photography* to reproduce by enlargement (fol. by *up*). **13.** *Colloquial* to waste; squander. **14.** *Colloquial* to fail in.

blowfly /'bloʊflaɪ/ *n., pl.* **-flies**. any of various flies which deposit their eggs or larvae on carcasses or meat, or in sores, wounds, etc.

blowlamp /'bloʊlæmp/ *n.* a small portable apparatus which gives a hot flame by forcing kerosene under pressure through a small nozzle and burning it in air.

blow-out /'bloʊ-aʊt/ *n.* a rupture of a motor-car tyre.

blowtorch /'bloʊtɔtʃ/ *n.* a portable apparatus which gives an extremely hot flame.

blowzy /'blaʊzi/ *adj.,* **blowzier**, **blowziest**. dishevelled; unkempt.

blubber /'blʌbə/ *n.* **1.** *Zoology* the fat found between the skin and muscle of whales and other cetaceans, from which oil is made. *– v.i.* **2.** to weep, usually noisily and with contorted face.

bludge /blʌdʒ/ *v.,* **bludged**, **bludging**, *n. Colloquial – v.i.* **1.** to evade responsibilities. **2.** to impose on others (fol. by *on*). *– v.t.* **3.** to cadge. *– n.* **4.** a job which entails next to no work. – **bludger**, *n.*

bludgeon /'blʌdʒən/ *n.* **1.** a short, heavy club with one end loaded, or thicker and heavier than the other. *– v.t.* **2.** to strike or fell with a bludgeon. **3.** to force (someone) into something; bully.

blue /blu/ *n., adj.,* **bluer**, **bluest**. *– n.* **1.** the pure hue of clear sky (between green and violet in the spectrum). **2.** *Colloquial* a fight; dispute. **3.** *Colloquial* a mistake. **4.** *Colloquial* (a nickname for a red-headed person). *– adj.* **5.** of the colour blue. **6.** depressed in spirits. **7.** obscene, or relating to obscenity.

blue blood *n.* aristocratic descent.

bluebottle /'blubɒtl/ *n.* a coelenterate found in warm seas and having an elongated, deep blue, gas-filled bladder, from which trail numerous stinging tentacles.

blue chip *n.* **1.** *Stock Exchange* a stock in which investment is secure. **2.** a valuable asset.

blue-collar /'blu-kɒlə/ *adj.* belonging or relating to workers other than white-collar, as factory, production line workers, etc.

blueprint /'bluprɪnt/ *n.* a process of photographic printing in which the prints are white on a blue ground.

blue-ribbon /'blu-rɪbən/ *adj.* **1.** (of an electorate) sure to be held by a particular party or candidate; safe; certain. **2.** of or relating to a prize-winner.

blue-ringed octopus /'blu-rɪŋd/ *n.* a small octopus of eastern Australia, with a highly venomous bite and blue to purple bands on the tentacles appearing when the octopus is disturbed.

blues /bluz/ *pl. n.* **1.** despondency; melancholy, saddness. **2.** a type of song, of American Negro origin, predominantly melancholy in character and usually performed in slow tempo.

blue-tongue /'blu-tʌŋ/ *n.* **1.** Also, **blue-tongue lizard**. any of several large, stout-bodied Australian skinks which are harmless but display their broad blue tongues in a threatening manner when disturbed. **2.** → **rouseabout**.

bluff[1] /blʌf/ *adj.* **1.** somewhat abrupt and unconventional in manner; hearty; frank. *-n.* **2.** a cliff, headland, or hill with a broad, steep face.

bluff[2] /blʌf/ *v.t.* to mislead by presenting a bold front.

blunder /'blʌndə/ *n.* **1.** a gross or stupid mistake. *– v.i.* **2.** to move or act blindly, stupidly, or without direction or steady guidance.

blunt /blʌnt/ *adj.* **1.** having an obtuse, thick, or dull edge or tip; rounded; not sharp. **2.** abrupt in address or manner; forthright; plain-spoken.

blur /blɜ/ *v.,* **blurred**, **blurring**, *n. – v.t.* **1.** to obscure by making confused in form or outline; make indistinct. *– v.i.* **2.** to become indistinct. *– n.* **3.** a blurred condition; indistinctness.

blurb /blɜb/ *n.* an announcement or advertisement, usually an effusively laudatory one, especially on the jacket flap of a book or the cover of a record.

blurt /blɜt/ *v.t.* to utter suddenly or inadvertently; divulge unadvisedly (usually fol. by *out*).

blush /blʌʃ/ *v.i.* **1.** to redden as from embarrassment, shame, or modesty. *– n.* **2.** a rosy or pinkish tinge.

bluster /'blʌstə/ *v.i.* **1.** to roar and be tumultuous, as wind. *– n.* **2.** noisy, empty menaces or protests; inflated talk.

BO /bi 'oʊ/ *n. Colloquial* body odour, especially due to excessive perspiration.

boa /'boʊə/ *n., pl.* **boas**. **1.** any of various non-venomous snakes notable for their vestiges of hind limbs, as the **boa constrictor** of the American tropics. **2.** a long, snake-shaped wrap of silk, feathers, or other material.

boar /bɔ/ *n.* an uncastrated male pig.

board /bɔd/ *n.* **1.** a piece of timber sawn thin, and of considerable length and breadth compared with the thickness. **2.** daily meals, especially as provided for pay. **3.** an official body of persons who direct or supervise some activity, as a business. **4.** the border or edge of anything, as in *seaboard*. **5.** **on board,** on or in a ship, aeroplane, or vehicle. *– v.t.* **6.** to cover or close with boards. **7.** to go on board of or enter (a ship, train, etc.). *– v.i.* **8.** to take one's meals, or be supplied with food and lodging at a fixed price.

board of reference *n.* a committee appointed to deal with industrial disputes arising from a particular award.

boardroom /'bɔdrum/ *n.* a room in which a board (def. 3) meets to carry out business.

boast /boʊst/ *v.i.* **1.** to speak exaggeratedly and objectionably, especially about oneself. **2.** to speak with pride (fol. by *of*). *– v.t.* **3.** to be proud in the possession of.

boat /boʊt/ *n.* a vessel for transport by water, constructed to provide buoyancy by excluding water and shaped to give stability and permit propulsion.

boater /'boutə/ *n.* a straw hat with a flat hard brim.

bob[1] /bɒb/ *n., v.,* **bobbed**, **bobbing**. – *n.* **1.** a short jerky motion. **2.** a quick curtsy. – *v.i.* **3.** to move up and down with a bouncing motion, as a boat.

bob[2] /bɒb/ *n. Colloquial* (formerly) a shilling.

bobbin /'bɒbən/ *n.* a reel, cylinder, or spool upon which yarn or thread is wound, as used in spinning, machine sewing, etc.

bobble /'bɒbəl/ *n.* any small ball which dangles or bobs.

bode /boud/ *v.t.,* **boded**, **boding**. to be an omen of; portend.

bodice /'bɒdəs/ *n.* the fitted upper part of or body of a woman's dress.

bodkin /'bɒdkən/ *n.* a blunt needle-like instrument for drawing tape, cord, etc., through a loop, hem, or the like.

body /'bɒdi/ *n., pl.* **bodies**. **1.** the physical structure of an animal (and sometimes, of a plant) living or dead. **2.** a corpse; carcass. **3.** the trunk or main mass of a thing. **4.** a number of things or people taken together. **5.** consistency or density; substance; strength as opposed to thinness. **6.** matter or physical substance (as opposed to *spirit* or *soul*).

body corporate *n.* the governing body of a block of home units consisting of the home unit owners or their representatives.

bodyguard /'bɒdigad/ *n.* a personal or private guard, as for a high official.

body hire *n. Colloquial* the practice of recruiting casual labour for short periods from a central pick-up spot.

body shop *n. Colloquial* an agency for computer programmers.

bog[1] /bɒg/ *n., v.,* **bogged**, **bogging**. – *n.* **1.** wet, spongy ground, with soil composed mainly of decayed vegetable matter. – *v.t., v.i.* **2.** to sink in or as in a bog (often fol. by *down*).

bog[2] /bɒg/ *n. Colloquial* a toilet or latrine.

bogey[1] /'bougi/ *n., pl.* **-geys**, *v.,* **-geyed**, **-geying**. *Golf* – *n.* **1.** *Originally US* a score of one over par. – *v.t.* **2.** to score a bogey on (a certain hole).

bogey[2] /'bougi/ *n. Colloquial* **1.** a swim or bath. **2.** a swimming hole. Also, **bogie**.

boggle /'bɒgəl/ *v.i.,* **-gled**, **-gling**. to take alarm; start with fright.

bogie[1] /'bougi/ *n.* a low truck or trolley.

bogie[2] /'bougi/ *n.* → **bogey**[2].

bogus /'bougəs/ *adj.* counterfeit; spurious; sham.

bogy /'bougi/ *n., pl.* **bogies**. **1.** a hobgoblin; evil spirit. **2.** anything that haunts, frightens or annoys one.

bohemian /bou'himiən/ *n.* **1.** a person with artistic or intellectual tendencies or pretensions who lives and acts without regard for conventional rules of behaviour. – *adj.* **2.** relating to or characteristic of bohemians.

boil[1] /bɔɪl/ *v.i.* **1.** to change from liquid to gaseous state, producing bubbles of gas that rise to the surface of the liquid, agitating it as they rise. **2.** to be agitated by angry feeling. **3.** *Colloquial* to feel very hot. – *v.t.* **4.** to cause to boil. **5.** to cook by boiling.

boil[2] /bɔɪl/ *n.* a painful, suppurating, inflammatory sore forming a central core.

boiler /'bɔɪlə/ *n.* **1.** a closed vessel together with its furnace, in which steam or other vapour is generated for heating or for driving engines. **2.** a vessel for boiling or heating, especially a copper one.

boisterous /'bɔɪstrəs/ *adj.* rough and noisy; clamorous; unrestrained.

bold /bould/ *adj.* **1.** not hesitating in the face of actual or possible danger or rebuff. **2.** not hesitating to breach the rules of propriety; forward. **3.** *Printing* (of type, etc.) with heavy lines.

bolster /'boulstə/ *n.* **1.** a long ornamental pillow for a bed, sofa, etc. **2.** a support, as one for a bridge truss. – *v.t.* **3.** to support with or as with a pillow. **4.** to prop, support, or uphold (something weak, unworthy, etc.) (often fol. by *up*).

bolt /boult/ *n.* **1.** a movable bar which when slid into a socket fastens a door, gate, etc. **2.** a strong metal pin, often with a head at one end and with a screw thread at the other to receive a nut. **3.** a woven length of cloth. **4.** any sudden dash, run, flight, etc. – *v.t.* **5.** to fasten with or as with bolts. **6.** to swallow (one's food) hurriedly or without chewing. – *v.i.* **7.** to run away in alarm and uncontrollably, especially of horses and rabbits. – *adv.* **8.** suddenly; with sudden meeting or collision. **9. bolt upright,** stiffly upright.

bomb /bɒm/ *n.* **1.** a hollow projectile filled with an explosive charge. **2.** *Colloquial* an old car. **3.** *Colloquial* a failure, as in an examination. – *v.t.* **4.** to hurl bombs at; drop bombs upon, as from an aeroplane; bombard. **5.** to jump onto (someone) in water. **6.** to fail; perform badly at. – *v.i.* **7.** to explode a bomb or bombs. **8.** to hurl or drop bombs. **9.** to err; to fail (often fol. by *out*).

bombard /bɒm'bad/ *v.t.* to assail vigorously.

bombardier /bɒmbə'dɪə/ *n. Military* the member of a bomber crew who operates the bomb release mechanism.

bombast /'bɒmbæst/ *n.* high-sounding and often insincere words; verbiage. – **bombastic**, *adj.*

bombshell /'bɒmʃɛl/ *n.* **1.** a bomb. **2.** a sudden or devastating action or effect. **3.** *Colloquial* a very attractive woman.

bona fide /ˌbounə 'faɪdi/ *adj.* **1.** genuine; real. **2.** undertaken in good faith; without fraud. Also, **bona-fide**.

bond /bɒnd/ *n.* **1.** something that binds, fastens, confines, or holds together. **2.** something that unites individual people into a group. **3.** a sealed document under which a person or corporation guarantees to pay a stated sum of money on or before a specified day. **4.** any written obligation under seal. **5.** a written undertaking to work for a specified period, or to pay back an agreed sum of money in default, as a condition for accepting certain scholarships, awards or privileges from an employer. **6.** *Law* **a.** a contract under seal to pay a debt, or to to pay a sum of money in default of fulfilling some condition. **b.** an undertaking by an offender to be of good behaviour for a certain period. **7.** the state of dutiable goods on which the duties are unpaid (especially in phrase *in bond*). **8.** *Finance* a fixed-term security, esp. one issued by government or semi-government authorities, that pays a fixed rate of interest during its life and repays the principal at maturity. Cf. **debenture**. **9.** *Insurance* **a.** a surety agreement. **b.** the money deposited, or the promissory arrangement entered into, under any such agreement. **10.** → **bond money**. **11.** a substance that causes particles to adhere; a binder. **12.** *Chemistry* any linkage between atoms in a compound. – *v.t.* **13.** to put (goods, an employee, official, etc.) in or under bond. **14.** *Finance* to place a bonded debt on; mortgage. **15.** *Building Trades* to cause (bricks or other building materials) to hold together firmly by laying them in some overlapping pattern. – *v.i.* **16.** to hold together by being bonded, as bricks in a wall.

bondage /'bɒndɪdʒ/ *n.* the state of being bound by or subjected to external control.

bondholder /'bɒnd-hoʊldə/ *n.* a holder of bonds issued by a government or corporation.

bond money *n.* money additional to any rent which a new tenant pays as surety against damages to the premises rented.

bond store *n.* a warehouse licensed under the Customs Act for the storage of goods on which duty has not yet been paid.

bone /boʊn/ *n.*, *v.*, **boned**, **boning**. – *n.* **1.** *Anatomy, Zoology* any of the separate pieces of which the skeleton of a vertebrate is composed. **2.** any of various similar substances, such as ivory, whalebone, etc. **3.** an off-white colour. **4. bone of contention,** a matter which causes disagreement. – *v.i.* **5. bone up,** *Colloquial* to study hard; acquire information (fol. by *on*).

bone marrow *n.* → **marrow** (def. 1).

bonfire /'bɒnfaɪə/ *n.* a large fire in an open place, for entertainment, celebration, or as a signal.

bongo /'bɒŋgoʊ/ *n., pl.* **-gos**, **-goes**. one of a pair of small drums, played by beating with the fingers.

bonkers /'bɒŋkəz/ *adj. Colloquial* crazy.

bonnet /'bɒnət/ *n.* **1.** a woman's or child's outdoor head covering, commonly fitting down over the hair, and often tied under the chin. **2.** any of various hoods, covers, or protective devices.

bonny /'bɒni/ *adj.*, **-ier**, **-iest**. radiant with health; handsome; pretty.

bonus /'boʊnəs/ *n.* **1.** something given or paid over and above what is due. **2.** *Insurance* **a.** dividend. **b.** free additions to the sum assured.

bonus issue *n.* a free issue of shares to shareholders of a company. Also, **bonus**.

bonzer /'bɒnzə/ *adj. Colloquial* excellent, attractive, pleasing. Also, **bonza**.

boob[1] /bub/ *n. Colloquial* a fool; a dunce.

boob[2] /bub/ *n. Colloquial* a woman's breast.

booby prize /'bubi/ *n.* a prize given in consolation or good-natured ridicule to the worst player in a game or contest.

booby trap *n.* an object so placed as to fall on or trip up an unsuspecting person.

boogie board /'bugi bɔd/ *n.* a small surfboard, usually ridden lying down.

book /bʊk/ *n.* **1.** a written or printed work of some length, as a treatise or other literary composition, especially on consecutive sheets fastened or bound together. **2.** a number of sheets of writing paper bound together and used for making entries, as of commercial transactions. **3. the books,** a record of commercial transactions. **4.** a set of tickets, cheques, stamps, etc., bound together like a book. **5.** a number of mares, bitches, etc., to be mated with the one sire. **6.** anything that serves for the recording of facts or events. – *v.t.* **7.** to enter in a book or list; record; register. **8.** to engage (a place, passage, etc.) beforehand. **9.** to put (somebody, something) down for a place, passage, etc. **10.** to engage (a person or company) for a performance or performances. **11.** to record the name of, with a view to possible prosecution for a minor offence. – *v.i.* **12.** to register one's name (fol. by *in*). **13.** to engage a place, services, etc.

book debt *n.* a debt due in connection with the carrying on of a profession, trade or business.

bookish /'bʊkɪʃ/ *adj.* given to reading or study.

bookkeeping /'bʊkkipɪŋ/ *n.* the work or skill of keeping account books or systematic records of money transactions. – **bookkeeper**, *n.*

booklet /'bʊklət/ *n.* a little book, especially one with paper covers; pamphlet.

bookmaker /'bʊkmeɪkə/ *n.* a professional betting person, who accepts the bets of others, as on horses in racing.

book of prime entry *n.* a book of account in which transactions are initially recorded before being transferred to the ledger, as a cashbook or daybook. Also, **book of original entry**, **book of originating entry**.

books closing date *n.* the date on which a company closes its books to determine those shareholders registered for a dividend, new issue, etc. See **ex date**.

book value *n. Economics* the amount which a trader shows in his or her accounts as the value of an item.

bookworm /'bʊkwɜm/ *n.* a person fond of reading or study.

boom[1] /bum/ *v.i.* **1.** to make a deep, prolonged, resonant sound; make a rumbling, humming, or droning noise. **2.** to progress or flourish vigorously, as a business, a city, etc. – *n.* **3.** a deep, hollow, continued sound. **4.** a rapid increase in prices, business activity, etc.

boom[2] /bum/ *n. Nautical* a long pole or spar used to extend the foot of certain sails.

boomer /'bumə/ *n.* **1.** *Colloquial* something large, as a surfing wave. **2.** *Colloquial* something successful or popular, as a party or song. **3.** a large male kangaroo.

boomerang /'bumərӕŋ/ *n.* **1.** a bent or curved piece of hard wood used as a missile by Aborigines, one form of which can be thrown so as to return to the thrower. **2.** *Colloquial* that which is expected to be returned by a borrower. – *v.i.* **3.** to return to, or recoil upon, the originator.

boon /bun/ *n.* a benefit enjoyed; a thing to be thankful for; a blessing.

boor /bɔ, bʊə/ *n.* a rude or unmannerly person.

boost /bust/ *v.t.* **1.** to lift or raise by pushing from behind or below. **2.** to increase; push up. – *n.* **3.** an upward shove or push. **4.** an aid or encouragement to success.

booster /ˈbustə/ *n.* **1.** someone who or that which boosts. **2.** *Electricity* a device connected in series with a current for increasing or decreasing the nominal circuit voltage. **3.** *Pharmaceutical* a substance, usually injected, for prolonging a person's immunity to a specific infection.

boot[1] /but/ *n.* **1.** a heavy shoe, especially one reaching above the ankle. **2.** a place for baggage, usually at the rear of a vehicle. **3.** a kick. **4. get the boot,** to be discharged.

boot[2] /but/ *n. in the phr.* **to boot,** into the bargain; in addition.

boot[3] /but/ *v.t.* **1.** Also, **boot up**. to start (a computer) from a primitive state progressing to a fully operational state. **2. boot up,** (of a computer) to become operational.

booth /buð, buθ/ *n.* a small compartment for a telephone, film projector, etc.

bootleg /ˈbutlɛg/ *v.t.*, **-legged**, **-legging**. to deal in (spirits or other goods) illicitly.

bootscoot /ˈbutskut/ *v.i.* to dance in a line-dance. – **bootscooting**, *n.*

bootstrap /ˈbutstræp/ *n. Computers* a program or procedure by which a computer can be made to translate progressively more complex programs.

booty /ˈbuti/ *n., pl.* **-ties**. spoil taken from an enemy in war; plunder; pillage.

booze /buz/ *n. Colloquial* alcoholic drink.

booze bus *n. Colloquial* a bus used by a mobile police unit engaged in breath analysis.

bordello /bɔˈdɛloʊ/ *n.* a brothel.

border /ˈbɔdə/ *n.* **1.** a side, edge, or margin. **2.** the line that separates one country, state, or province from another; frontier line. – *v.i.* **3. border on** (or **upon**), **a.** to touch or abut at the border. **b.** to approach closely in character; verge.

borderline /ˈbɔdəlaɪn/ *adj.* **1.** on or near a border or boundary. **2.** (in examinations, etc.) qualifying or failing to qualify by a narrow margin.

bore[1] /bɔ/ *v.*, **bored**, **boring**, *n.* – *v.t.* **1.** to pierce (a solid substance) or make (a round hole, etc.) with an auger, drill, or other rotated instrument. **2.** to force by persistent forward thrusting. – *n.* **3.** a deep hole of small diameter through which water is obtained from beneath the ground. **4.** the inside diameter of a hollow cylindrical object or device, such as a bush or bearing, or the barrel of a gun.

bore[2] /bɔ/ *v.*, **bored**, **boring**, *n.* – *v.t.* **1.** to weary by tedious repetition, dullness, unwelcome attentions, etc. – *n.* **2.** a dull, tiresome, or uncongenial person. – **boredom**, *n.*

bore[3] /bɔ/ *v.* past tense of **bear**[1].

borer /ˈbɔrə/ *n. Entomology* any insect that burrows in trees, fruits, etc., especially any beetle of certain groups.

born /bɔn/ *adj.* **1.** brought forth by birth. **2.** possessing from birth the quality or character stated.

borne /bɔn/ *v.* past participle of **bear**[1].

boron /ˈbɔrɒn/ *n.* a non-metallic element. *Symbol*: B

boronia /bəˈroʊniə/ *n.* any of a number of Australian shrubs.

borough /ˈbʌrə/ *n. Vic.* an area of land corresponding to a municipality in the other states of Australia.

borrow /ˈbɒroʊ/ *v.t.* **1.** to take or obtain (a thing) on the promise to return it or its equivalent; obtain the temporary use of. **2.** to get from another or from a foreign source; appropriate or adopt. **3.** *Arithmetic* (in subtraction) to take from one column to add to the next lower.

bosom /ˈbʊzəm/ *n.* **1.** the breast of a human being, especially a woman. **2.** the breast, conceived of as the seat of thought or emotion. – *adj.* **3.** intimate or confidential.

boss /bɒs/ *n. Colloquial* **1.** someone who employs or superintends workers; a foreperson or manager. **2.** anyone who asserts mastery, especially one who controls a political or other body. – *v.i.* **3.** to be domineering.

bot /bɒt/ *v.t., v.i.,* **botted**, **botting**. to cadge.

botany /ˈbɒtəni/ *n., pl.* **-nies**. the science of plants; the branch of biology that deals with plant life. – **botanist**, *n.* – **botanical**, *adj.*

botch /bɒtʃ/ *v.t.* to spoil by poor work; bungle.

both /boʊθ/ *adj., pron.* **1.** the one and the other; the two together. – *adv.* **2.** alike; equally.

bother /ˈbɒðə/ *v.t.* **1.** to give trouble to; annoy; pester; worry. – *v.i.* **2.** to trouble oneself. – *n.* **3.** an annoying disturbance. **4.** worried or perplexed state. **5.** someone who bothers. – **bothersome**, *adj.*

bottle /ˈbɒtl/ *n., v.*, **-tled**, **-tling**. – *n.* **1.** a portable vessel with a neck or mouth, now commonly made of glass, used for holding liquids. – *v.t.* **2.** to put into or seal in a bottle; to preserve (fruit or vegetables) in bottles.

bottlebrush /ˈbɒtlbrʌʃ/ *n.* an Australian plant whose flower spikes resemble a cylindrical brush.

bottleneck /ˈbɒtlnɛk/ *n.* **1.** a place, or stage in a process, where progress is retarded. **2. a.** a narrow part of a road between two wide stretches. **b.** a congested junction, road, town, etc., fed by several roads, where traffic is likely to be held up.

bottom /ˈbɒtəm/ *n.* **1.** the lowest or deepest part of anything, as distinguished from the top. **2.** the underside. **3.** the ground under any body of water. **4.** the buttocks. **5.** the fundamental part; basic aspect. – *v.i.* **6.** to be based; rest. **7.** to strike against the bottom or end; reach the bottom. **8. bottom out,** to reach the lowest level of economic activity thought likely. – *adj.* **9.** lowest.

bottom line *n.* the last line of a financial statement where overall cost, profit, loss, etc., is likely to be found.

bougainvillea /boʊgənˈvɪliə/ *n.* a shrub or spiny climber with brightly coloured bracts.

bough /baʊ/ *n.* a branch of a tree, especially one of the larger of the main branches.

bought /bɔt/ *v.* past tense and past participle of **buy**.

boulder /'boʊldə/ *n.* a detached and rounded or worn rock, especially a large one.

boulevard /'buləvad/ *n.* **1.** a broad avenue of a city, often having trees and used as a promenade. **2.** a street.

bounce /baʊns/ *v.*, **bounced**, **bouncing**, *n.* – *v.i.* **1.** to move with a bound, and rebound, as a ball. **2.** to burst ebulliently (*into* or *out of*). **3.** *Colloquial* (of cheques) to be dishonoured; to be returned unpaid. – *v.t.* **4.** to cause to bound or rebound. **5.** *Colloquial* to eject or discharge summarily. **6.** *Colloquial* to arrest. – *n.* **7.** a rebound or bound. **8.** ability to bounce; resilience.

bound[1] /baʊnd/ *adj.* **1.** tied; in bonds: *a bound prisoner.* **2.** made fast as by a band or bond. **3.** secured within a cover, as a book. **4.** under obligation, legally or morally. **5.** destined or sure.

bound[2] /baʊnd/ *v.i.* **1.** to move by leaps; leap; jump; spring. – *n.* **2.** a leap onwards or upwards; a jump.

bound[3] /baʊnd/ *n.* **1.** (*usu. pl.*) a limiting line, or boundary. **2. out of bounds,** forbidden of access to certain persons or to the general public. – *v.t.* **3.** to form the boundary or limit of.

bound[4] /baʊnd/ *adj.* going or intending to go; on the way (*to*); destined (*for*).

boundary /'baʊndri/ *n., pl.* **-ries**. something that indicates bounds or limits; a limiting or bounding line.

bounteous /'baʊntiəs/ *adj.* **1.** giving or disposed to give freely; generously liberal. **2.** freely bestowed; plentiful; abundant.

bountiful /'baʊntəfəl/ *adj.* **1.** liberal in bestowing gifts, favours, or bounties; munificent; generous. **2.** abundant; ample.

bounty /'baʊnti/ *n., pl.* **-ties**. **1.** generosity in giving. **2.** whatever is given bounteously; a benevolent, generous gift. **3.** a premium or reward, especially one offered by a government.

bouquet /bu'keɪ, boʊ'keɪ/ *n.* **1.** a bunch of flowers. **2.** the characteristic aroma of wine, liqueurs, etc.

bourbon /'bɜbən/ *n.* a kind of whisky distilled from a mash containing 51 per cent or more maize. Also, **bourbon whisky**.

bourgeois /'bʊəʒwa, 'bu-/ *n., pl.* **-geois**, *adj.* – *n.* **1.** a member of the middle class. **2.** one whose outlook is said to be determined by a concern for property values; a capitalist, as opposed to a member of the wage-earning class. – *adj.* **3.** lacking in refinement or elegance; conventional. – **bourgeoisie**, *n.*

bout /baʊt/ *n.* **1.** a contest, especially a boxing or wrestling match; a trial of strength. **2.** period; spell.

boutique /bu'tik/ *n.* a small shop selling fashionable or luxury articles, especially for women.

bovine /'boʊvaɪn/ *n.* **1.** an animal of the ox family. – *adj.* **2.** oxlike. **3.** stolid; dull.

bovver /'bɒvə/ *n. Brit Colloquial* rowdiness, violence, especially street violence.

bow[1] /baʊ/ *v.i.* **1.** to bend or curve downwards; stoop. **2.** to yield; submit. **3.** to bend the body or head in worship, reverence, salutation, respect, or submission. – *v.t.* **4.** to bend or incline in worship, submission, respect, civility, or agreement. **5.** to cause to submit; subdue; crush. – *n.* **6.** an inclination of the head or body in salutation, assent, thanks, reverence, respect, or submission.

bow[2] /boʊ/ *n.* **1.** a strip of flexible wood or other material bent by a string stretched between its ends, used for shooting arrows. **2.** something curved or arc-shaped. **3.** a looped knot, as of ribbon, composed of one or two loops and two ends. **4.** *Music* an implement, originally curved, but now almost always straight, with horsehairs stretched upon it, designed for playing any stringed instrument. – *adj.* **5.** curved; bent like a bow. – *v.t.* **6.** to bend into the form of a bow; curve.

bow[3] /baʊ/ *n.* (*sometimes pl.*) the front or forward part or end of a ship, boat, airship, etc.

bowdlerise = bowdlerize /'baʊdləraɪz/ *v.t.*, **-rised**, **-rising**. to expurgate prudishly.

bowel /'baʊəl/ *n.* **1.** *Anatomy* **a.** an intestine. **b.** (*usu. pl.*) the parts of the alimentary canal below the stomach; the intestines or entrails. **2.** the inward or interior parts.

bower /'baʊə/ *n.* a leafy shelter or recess; an arbour.

bowerbird /'baʊəbɜd/ *n.* **1.** any of various birds which build bowerlike structures, used, not as nests, but as places of resort to attract the females. **2.** someone who collects useless objects.

bowl[1] /boʊl/ *n.* **1.** a rather deep, round dish or basin, used chiefly for holding liquids, food, etc. **2.** any bowl-shaped depression or formation.

bowl[2] /boʊl/ *n.* **1.** one of the biased or weighted balls used in the game of bowls. **2.** a cast or delivery of the ball in bowling. – *v.i.* **3.** to play with bowls, or at bowling. – *v.t.* **4.** to roll or trundle, as a ball, hoop, etc. **5.** to knock or strike, as by the ball in bowling (fol. by *over* or *down*). **6.** to disconcert; upset (fol. by *over*). **7.** *Cricket* to dismiss (the person batting) by delivering a ball which breaks their wicket.

bowler /'boʊlə/ *n.* a hard felt hat with a rounded crown and narrow brim.

bowls /boʊlz/ *n.* **1.** → **lawn bowls**. **2.** a similar game (**carpet bowls**) played indoors. **3.** skittles, ninepins, or tenpin bowling.

bowser /'baʊzə/ *n.* a petrol pump.

box[1] /bɒks/ *n.* **1.** a case or receptacle, usually rectangular, of wood, metal, cardboard, etc., with a lid or removable cover. **2.** a compartment or place shut or railed off for the accommodation of a small number of people in a public place, especially in theatres, opera houses, sporting venues, etc. **3.** (in a court of law) a stand or pew reserved for witnesses, the accused or the jury. **4.** part of a page of a periodical set off by lines, border, or white space. **5.** *Cricket, etc.* a lightweight padded shield worn to protect the genitals. – *v.t.* **6.** to put into a box. **7.** to enclose or confine as in a box (often fol. by *up* or *in*).

box² /bɒks/ *n.* **1.** a blow as with the hand or fist. – *v.t.* **2.** to strike with the hand or fist, especially on the ear. **3.** to fight in a boxing match.

boxer /'bɒksə/ *n.* **1.** someone who boxes. **2.** the person who looks after the bets in a two-up game. **3.** a smooth-coated, brown dog of medium size, related to the bulldog and terrier.

boxing /'bɒksɪŋ/ *n.* the act or art of fighting with the fists.

box office *n.* the office in which tickets are sold at a theatre or other place of public entertainment.

box seat *n. Colloquial* any position of vantage.

boy /bɔɪ/ *n.* **1.** a male child, from birth to full growth, but especially to the beginning of youth. **2.** a young servant; a page. – *interj.* **3.** (an exclamation of surprise, delight, etc.).

boycott /'bɔɪkɒt/ *v.t.* **1.** to combine in abstaining from, or preventing dealings with, as a means of intimidation or coercion. **2.** to abstain from buying or using. – *n.* **3.** the practice or an instance of boycotting.

boyfriend /'bɔɪfrɛnd/ *n.* **1.** a man with whom one has a steady romantic relationship. **2.** any young male friend.

bra /bra/ *n.* → **brassiere**.

brace /breɪs/ *n., v.,* **braced**, **bracing**. – *n.* **1.** something that holds parts together or in place, as a clasp or clamp. **2.** anything that imparts rigidity or steadiness. **3.** *Machinery* a device for holding and turning tools for boring or drilling. **4.** *Building Trades* a piece of timber, metal, etc., used to support or position another piece or portion of a framework. **5.** (*often pl.*) *Dentistry* a round or flat metal wire placed against surfaces of the teeth, and used to straighten irregularly arranged teeth. **6.** *Medicine* an appliance for supporting a weak joint or joints. **7.** (*pl.*) straps or bands worn over the shoulders for holding up the trousers. **8.** a pair; a couple. **9. a.** Also, **curly bracket**. one of two characters, { or }, for connecting written or printed lines. **b.** (*pl.*) *Mathematics* → **bracket** (def. 3). – *v.t.* **10.** to furnish, fasten, or strengthen with or as with a brace. **11.** to fix firmly; make steady. **12.** to make tight; increase the tension of. **13.** to act as a stimulant to.

bracelet /'breɪslət/ *n.* **1.** an ornamental band or circlet for the wrist or arm. **2.** *Colloquial* a handcuff.

bracken /'brækən/ *n.* a large, coarse fern.

bracket /'brækət/ *n.* **1.** a wooden, metal, etc., support of triangular outline placed under a shelf or the like. **2.** one of two marks, [or], used in writing or printing to enclose parenthetical matter, interpolations, etc. **3.** (*pl.*) *Mathematics* parentheses of various forms indicating that the enclosed quantity is to be treated as a unit. **4.** a grouping of persons, especially as based on the amount of their taxable income. **5.** a small group of musical items. – *v.t.* **6.** to furnish with or support by a bracket or brackets. **7.** to associate or mention together, implying equality of some kind.

bracket creep *n.* the gradual shift as a result of inflation of an income subject to a progressive income tax from one tax bracket to another where more tax is paid despite the real level of the income (its purchasing power) remaining unchanged.

brackish /'brækɪʃ/ *adj.* slightly salt; having a salty or briny flavour.

bract /brækt/ *n.* a specialised leaf-like part, usually situated at the base of a flower.

brag /bræg/ *v.i.,* **bragged**, **bragging**. to use boastful language; boast. – **braggart**, *n.*

braid /breɪd/ *v.t.* to weave together strips or strands of; plait.

braille /breɪl/ *n.* a system of writing or printing for the blind, in which combinations of tangible points are used to represent letters, etc.

brain /breɪn/ *n.* **1.** (*sometimes pl.*) the soft convoluted mass of greyish and whitish nerve substance which fills the cranium of humans and other vertebrates; centre of sensation, body coordination, thought, emotion, etc. **2.** (*usu. pl.*) understanding; intellectual power; intelligence. **3.** *Colloquial* a highly intelligent or well-informed person.

brainstorm /'breɪnstɔm/ *n.* **1.** a sudden, violent attack of mental disturbance. **2.** *Colloquial* a sudden inspiration, idea, etc.

brainwashing /'breɪnwɒʃɪŋ/ *n.* systematic indoctrination that changes or undermines one's convictions, especially political.

brainy /'breɪni/ *adj.,* **brainier**, **brainiest**. having brains; intelligent; clever.

braise /breɪz/ *v.t.,* **braised**, **braising**. to cook (meat or vegetables) by sautéing in fat and then cooking slowly in very little moisture.

brake¹ /breɪk/ *n.* **1.** any mechanical device for arresting the motion of a wheel, a motor, or a vehicle, chiefly by means of friction or pressure. **2.** a heavy kind of harrow. – *v.i.* **3.** to use or apply a brake. **4.** to run a hoisting machine.

brake² /breɪk/ *n.* a place overgrown with bushes, shrubs, brambles, or cane; a thicket.

bramble /'bræmbəl/ *n.* **1.** the common blackberry. **2.** any rough prickly shrub.

bran /bræn/ *n.* the ground husk of wheat or other grain, separated from flour or meal by bolting.

branch /bræntʃ/ *n.* **1.** *Botany* a division or subdivision of the stem or axis of a tree, shrub, or other plant (the ultimate or smaller ramifications being called branchlets, twigs, or shoots). **2.** a limb, offshoot, or ramification. **3.** any member or part of a body or system; a section or subdivision. **4.** *Geography* a tributary stream. – *v.i.* **5.** to put forth branches; spread in branches. **6.** to divide into separate parts or subdivisions; diverge.

brand /brænd/ *n.* **1.** a trademark or trade name to identify a product, as that of a distributor, or a manufacturer or other producer. **2.** a mark made by burning or otherwise, to indicate kind, grade, make, ownership, etc. **3.** any mark of infamy; a stigma.

brandish /'brændɪʃ/ *v.t.* **1.** to shake or wave, as a weapon; flourish. – *n.* **2.** a wave or flourish, as of a weapon.

brandy /'brændi/ *n., pl.* **-dies**. the spirit distilled from the fermented juice of grapes or, sometimes, of apples, peaches, plums, etc.

brash /bræʃ/ *adj.* impertinent; impudent; forward.

brass /bras/ *n.* **1.** a durable, malleable, and ductile yellow alloy, consisting essentially of copper and zinc. **2.** a collective term for musical instruments of the trumpet and horn families (brass instruments), usually made of brass and having a funnel-shaped mouthpiece without a reed. **3.** Also, **top brass**. *Colloquial* high-ranking people. **4.** *Colloquial* excessive assurance; impudence; effrontery. **5.** *Colloquial* money.

brassiere /'bræziə, -siə/ *n.* a woman's undergarment which supports the breasts.

brat /bræt/ *n.* a child (used usually in contempt or irritation).

bravado /brə'vadoʊ/ *n., pl.* **-does**, **-dos**. boasting; swaggering pretence.

brave /breɪv/ *adj.*, **braver**, **bravest**, *n., v.,* **braved**, **braving**. – *adj.* **1.** possessing or exhibiting courage or courageous endurance. – *n.* **2.** a North American Indian or other savage warrior. – *v.t.* **3.** to meet or face courageously. **4.** to defy; challenge; dare. – **bravery**, *n.*

bravo /bra'voʊ/ *interj.* well done! good!

brawl /brɔl/ *n.* a noisy quarrel; a squabble.

brawn /brɔn/ *n.* **1.** well-developed muscles. **2.** meat, especially pork, boiled, pickled, and pressed into a mould.

bray /breɪ/ *n.* a harsh, breathy cry, as of the donkey.

brazen /'breɪzən/ *adj.* **1.** made of brass. **2.** like brass, as in sound, colour, strength, etc. **3.** shameless or impudent.

brazier[1] /'breɪziə/ *n.* a person who works in brass. Also, **brasier**.

brazier[2] /'breɪziə/ *n.* a metal receptacle for holding burning charcoal or other fuel. Also, **brasier**.

brazil nut /brə'zɪl/ *n.* a triangular edible nut.

breach /britʃ/ *n.* **1.** the act or result of breaking; a break or rupture. **2.** a gap made in a wall, dyke, fortification, etc.; rift; fissure. **3.** an infraction or violation, as of law, trust, faith, promise, etc. **4.** a severance of friendly relations.

breach of contract *n.* the breaking, by action or omission, of an obligation imposed by a contract.

breach of privilege *n.* an abuse of any of the privileges accorded to members of parliament.

bread /brɛd/ *n.* **1.** a food made of flour or meal, milk or water, etc., made into a dough or batter, with or without yeast or the like, and baked. **2.** food or sustenance; livelihood. **3.** *Colloquial* money; earnings.

breadline /'brɛdlaɪn/ *n. in the phr.* **on the breadline,** living at subsistence level.

breadth /brɛdθ/ *n.* **1.** *Mathematics* the measure of the second principal diameter of a surface or solid, the first being length, and the third (in the case of a solid) thickness; width. **2.** freedom from narrowness or restraint. **3.** size in general; extent.

breadwinner /'brɛdwɪnə/ *n.* someone who earns a livelihood for a family or household.

break /breɪk/ *v.*, **broke**, **broken**, **breaking**, *n.* – *v.t.* **1.** to divide into parts violently; reduce to pieces or fragments. **2.** to violate. **3.** to dissolve or annul (often fol. by *off*). **4.** to fracture a bone of. **5.** to destroy the regularity of. **6.** to put an end to; overcome. **7.** to exchange for a smaller amount or smaller units. **8.** to make one's way through; penetrate. **9.** *Law* to open or force one's way into (a dwelling, store, etc.). **10.** to disable or destroy by or as by shattering or crushing. **11.** to ruin financially, or make bankrupt. **12.** to impair or weaken in strength, spirit, force, or effect. **13.** to publish (a news item). **14.** to defeat the purpose of (a strike). **15.** to train to obedience; tame (often fol. by *in*). **16.** *Electricity* to render (a circuit) incomplete; stop the flow of (a current). – *v.i.* **17.** to become broken; separate into parts or fragments, especially suddenly and violently. **18.** to become suddenly discontinuous or interrupted; leave off abruptly (fol. by *off*, etc.) **19.** to dissolve and separate (fol. by *up*). **20.** to sever relations (fol. by *up* or *with*). **21.** (of a wave) to topple forward after developing a crest through the opposing pull of an undertow in shallow water. **22.** to free oneself or escape suddenly, as from restraint (often fol. by *away*). **23.** to force a way (fol. by *in*, *through*, *out*, etc.). **24.** to burst (fol. by *in*, *forth*, *from*, etc.). **25.** to change state or activity (fol. by *into*). **26.** to dawn, as the day. **27.** (of the heart) to be crushed or overwhelmed, especially by grief. **28.** (of stock-exchange prices) to drop quickly and considerably. **29.** (of the voice) to vary between two registers, especially in emotion or during adolescence. **30.** (in a race) to start before the signal to do so has been given. – *v.* **31. break down, a.** to take down or destroy by breaking. **b.** to overcome. **c.** to analyse. **d.** to collapse. **e.** to cease to function. **32. break in, a.** to interrupt. **b.** to adapt to one's convenience by use. **c.** to accustom a horse to harness and use. **d.** to enter (a house or the like) forcibly, as a burglar. **33. break out, a.** to issue forth; arise. **b.** *Pathology* (of certain diseases) to appear in eruptions. **c.** to have a sudden appearance of various eruptions on the skin. **34. break up, a.** to separate; disband (especially of a school at end of term). **b.** (of a marriage) to cease. **c.** to put an end to; discontinue. **d.** to cut up (fowl, etc.). **e.** *Colloquial* to collapse with laughter. – *n.* **35.** a forcible disruption or separation of parts; a breaking; a fracture, rupture, or shattering. **36.** an opening made by breaking; a gap. **37.** a rush away from a place; an attempt to escape. **38.** an interruption of continuity; suspension, stoppage. **39.** an abrupt or marked change, as in sound or direction. **40.** *Colloquial* an opportunity; chance. **41.** a brief rest, as from work, especially a midmorning pause, usually of fifteen minutes, between school classes. **42.** *Stock Exchange* a sudden drop in prices. **43.** any continuous run, especially of good fortune. **44.** *Billiards* the shot that breaks or scatters the balls at the beginning of the game. **45.** a premature start in racing.

breakage /'breɪkɪdʒ/ *n.* **1.** an act of breaking; a break. **2.** the amount or quantity of things broken. **3.** an allowance or compensation for loss or damage of articles broken in transit or in use.

breakaway /'breɪkəweɪ/ *n.* **1.** the formation of a splinter group in a political party, or similar group. **2.** a panic rush of or among a mob of cattle, horses, etc.

break dancing *n.* a form of street dancing which involves spectacular movements such as spinning the body on the ground.

breakfast /'brɛkfəst/ *n.* the first meal of the day; a morning meal.

breakneck /'breɪknɛk/ *adj.* dangerous; hazardous.

breakpoint /'breɪkpɔɪnt/ *n.* **1.** an instruction inserted by a debug program. **2.** the point in a program at which such an instruction operates.

breakthrough /'breɪkθru/ *n.* any development, as in science, technology, or diplomacy, which removes a barrier to progress.

bream /brɪm/ *n.* a marine food and sport fish.

breast /brɛst/ *n.* **1.** *Anatomy, Zoology* the outer front part of the thorax, or the front part of the body from neck to belly; the chest. **2.** *Anatomy, Zoology* a mammary or milk gland, especially of a woman, or of female animals whose milk glands are similarly formed. **3.** the bosom regarded as the seat of thoughts and feelings.

breast stroke *n. Swimming* a stroke made in the prone position in which both hands move simultaneously forwards, outwards and rearwards from in front of the chest, and the legs move in a frog-like manner.

breath /brɛθ/ *n.* **1.** the air inhaled and exhaled in respiration. **2.** ability to breathe, especially freely. **3.** the brief time required for it; an instant. **4.** a light current of air.

breathalyser /'brɛθəlaɪzə/ *n.* a breath-analysing device which contains chemicals in ampoules which react with alcohol and which change colour in proportion to the amount of alcohol in the breath.

breathe /brið/ *v.*, **breathed** /briðd/, **breathing**. – *v.i.* **1.** to inhale and exhale air. **2.** to blow lightly, as air. **3.** to live; exist. **4.** to be redolent (*of*). – *v.t.* **5.** to inhale and exhale in respiration. **6.** to give utterance to; whisper.

breathtaking /'brɛθteɪkɪŋ/ *adj.* causing amazement.

breathy /'brɛθi/ *adj.* (of the voice) characterised by excessive emission of breath.

bred /brɛd/ *v.* past tense and past participle of **breed**.

breech /britʃ/ *n.* **1.** the lower part of the trunk of the body behind; the posterior or buttocks. **2.** the hinder or lower part of anything.

breeches /'brɪtʃəz/ *pl. n.* **1.** a garment worn by men (and by women for riding, etc.), covering the hips and thighs. **2.** trousers.

breed /brid/ *v.*, **bred**, **breeding**, *n.* – *v.t.* **1.** to produce (offspring). **2.** to procure by the mating of parents; propagate. **3.** *Horticulture* to cause to reproduce by controlled pollination. **4.** to cause; occasion; produce. – *v.i.* **5.** to produce offspring. – *n.* **6.** *Genetics* a relatively homogeneous group of animals within a species, developed and maintained by humans. **7.** race; lineage; strain.

breeding /'bridɪŋ/ *n.* **1.** the rearing of livestock to improve their quality or merit. **2.** the results of training as shown in behaviour and manners; good manners.

breeze /briz/ *n.*, *v.*, **breezed**, **breezing**. – *n.* **1.** a wind or current of air, especially a light or moderate one. **2.** *Colloquial* an easy task. – *v.i.* **3.** *Colloquial* to move or proceed in a casual, quick, carefree manner (often fol. by *along*, *in*). **4. breeze through**, *Colloquial* to perform without effort.

brethren /'brɛðrən/ *n.* **1.** *Archaic* plural of **brother**. **2.** fellow members.

brevi- a word element meaning 'short'.

brevity /'brɛvəti/ *n.*, *pl.* **-ties**. shortness of time or duration; briefness.

brew /bru/ *v.t.* **1.** to make (beer, ale, etc.) from malt, etc., by steeping, boiling, and fermentation. **2.** to make (tea) (often fol. by *up*). **3.** to concoct or contrive; bring about. – *v.i.* **4.** to be in preparation; be forming or gathering (often fol. by *up*). – *n.* **5.** a quantity brewed in a single process. – **brewery**, *n.*

briar /'braɪə/ *n.* a prickly shrub or plant. Also, **brier**.

bribe /braɪb/ *n.*, *v.*, **bribed**, **bribing**. – *n.* **1.** any valuable consideration given or promised for corrupt behaviour in the performance of official or public duty. – *v.t.* **2.** to influence or corrupt by a bribe. – **bribery**, *n.*

brick /brɪk/ *n.* **1.** a block of clay, usually rectangular, hardened by drying in the sun or burning in a kiln, and used for building, paving, etc. **2.** *Colloquial* a person who has gained one's special admiration. **3. like a ton of bricks**, heavily.

brick veneer *n.* a building whose external walls each consist of a timber framework faced with a single skin of bricks, the brickwork being non-structural.

bride /braɪd/ *n.* a woman newly married, or about to be married. – **bridal**, *adj.*

bridegroom /'braɪdgrum/ *n.* a man newly married, or about to be married.

bridesmaid /'braɪdzmeɪd/ *n.* a young unmarried woman who attends the bride at a wedding.

bridge[1] /brɪdʒ/ *n.*, *v.*, **bridged**, **bridging**. – *n.* **1.** a structure spanning a river, chasm, road, or the like, and affording passage. **2.** *Anatomy* the ridge or upper line of the nose. – *v.t.* **3.** to make a bridge over; span.

bridge[2] /brɪdʒ/ *n. Cards* a game for four players, derived from whist, in which the trump suit is decided by bidding amongst players and in which one partnership plays to fulfil a certain declaration against the other partnership which tries to prevent this.

bridging finance *n. Building Trades* a temporary loan at high interest, usually to someone who has disposed of one asset, as a house, but who has not yet been paid for it, and who is obliged to pay for another.

bridle /'braɪdl/ *n.*, *v.*, **-dled**, **-dling**. – *n.* **1.** the part of the harness of a horse, etc., around the head, used to restrain and guide the animal. – *v.i.* **2.** to draw up the head and draw in the chin, as in disdain or resentment; to be resentful or annoyed (often fol. by *at*).

brief /brif/ *adj.* **1.** of little duration. **2.** using few words; concise; succinct. – *n.* **3.** an outline, the form of which is determined by set rules, of all the possible arguments and information on one side of a controversy. – *v.t.* **4.** *Law* to retain as advocate in a suit.

briefcase /'brifkeɪs/ *n.* a flat, rectangular leather case used for carrying documents, books, manuscripts, etc. Also, **dispatch case**.

briefing /'brifɪŋ/ *n.* a short, accurate summary of the details of a plan or operation, as one given to a military unit, crew of an aeroplane, etc., before it undertakes the operation.

brigade /brə'geɪd/ *n.* **1.** a large body of troops. **2.** a body of individuals organised for a special purpose.

brigand /'brɪgənd/ *n.* a bandit.

bright /braɪt/ *adj.* **1.** radiating or reflecting light; luminous; shining. **2.** vivid or brilliant, as colour. **3.** quick-witted or intelligent. **4.** animated; lively; cheerful, as a person. – *adv.* **5.** in a bright manner.

brilliant /'brɪljənt/ *adj.* **1.** shining brightly; sparkling; glittering; lustrous. **2.** distinguished; illustrious. **3.** having or showing great intelligence or mental ability. – **brilliance**, *n.*

brim /brɪm/ *n., v.,* **brimmed, brimming**. – *n.* **1.** the upper edge of anything hollow; rim. **2.** a projecting edge. – *v.i.* **3.** to be full to the brim; to be full to overflowing.

brindled /'brɪndld/ *adj.* grey or tawny with darker streaks or spots. Also, **brinded** /'brɪndəd/.

brine /braɪn/ *n.* water saturated or strongly impregnated with salt.

bring /brɪŋ/ *v.t.,* **brought** /brɔt/, **bringing**. **1.** to cause to come with oneself; conduct or convey. **2.** to lead or induce. **3.** *Law* to put forward before a tribunal; declare in or as if in court. **4. bring about,** to cause; accomplish. **5. bring down, a.** to shoot down or cause to fall (a plane, animal, footballer, etc.) **b.** to reduce (a price); lower in price. **c.** to humble or subdue. **d.** introduce proposed legislation. **6. bring forward, a.** to produce to view. **b.** *Accounting* to transfer (a figure) to the top of the next column. **7. bring in, a.** to introduce. **b.** to pronounce (a verdict). **8. bring off,** to bring to a successful conclusion; achieve. **9. bring out, a.** to expose; show; reveal. **b.** to encourage (a timid or diffident person) **c.** to induce (workers, etc.) to leave work and go on strike. **10. bring up, a.** to care for during childhood; rear. **b.** to introduce to notice or consideration. **c.** to vomit.

brink /brɪŋk/ *n.* any extreme edge; verge.

brinkmanship /'brɪŋkmənʃɪp/ *n. Colloquial* the practice of courting disaster, especially nuclear war, to gain one's ends.

briny /'braɪni/ *adj.,* **brinier, briniest**. of or like brine; salty.

brisk /brɪsk/ *adj.* quick and active; lively.

bristle /'brɪsəl/ *n., v.,* **-tled, -tling**. – *n.* **1.** one of the short, stiff, coarse hairs of certain animals, especially swine, used in making brushes, etc. – *v.i.* **2.** to stand or rise stiffly, like bristles. **3.** to erect the bristles, as an irritated animal. **4.** to be visibly roused to anger, hostility, or resistance.

brittle /'brɪtl/ *adj.* breaking readily with a comparatively smooth fracture, as glass.

broach /broʊtʃ/ *v.t.* to mention or suggest for the first time.

broad /'brɔd/ *adj.* **1.** of great breadth. **2.** of great extent; large. **3.** widely diffused; open; full. **4.** not limited or narrow; liberal. **5.** of extensive range or scope. **6.** main or general. **7.** (of pronunciation) strongly dialectal. – *adv.* **8.** fully. – *n.* **9.** *Colloquial* a woman.

broadcast /'brɔdkast/ *v.,* **-cast** *or* **-casted, -casting**, *n.* – *v.t.* **1.** to send (messages, speeches, music, etc.) by radio. **2.** to spread or disseminate widely. – *n.* **3.** that which is broadcast.

broadsheet /'brɔdʃit/ *n.* **1.** a sheet of paper, especially of large size, printed on one side only, as for distribution or posting. **2.** a newspaper printed on the standard sheet size of paper, usually giving greater depth of reporting than a tabloid.

broadside /'brɔdsaɪd/ *n.* **1.** *Nautical* the whole side of a ship above the waterline, from the bow to the quarter. **2.** an attack, as of criticism.

brocade /brə'keɪd/ *n.* fabric woven with an elaborate design from any yarn. The right side has a raised effect.

broccoli /'brɒkəli, -laɪ/ *n.* a plant of the mustard family, resembling the cauliflower.

brochure /'broʊʃə, brə'ʃʊə/ *n.* → **pamphlet**.

brogue[1] /broʊg/ *n.* a broad accent, especially Irish, in the pronunciation of English.

brogue[2] /broʊg/ *n.* a strongly made, comfortable type of ordinary shoe.

broil /brɔɪl/ *v.t.* to cook by direct radiant heat, as on a gridiron or griller, or under an electric coil, gas grill or the like; grill; pan fry.

broke /broʊk/ *v.* **1.** past tense of **break**. – *adj.* **2. flat broke,** *Colloquial* completely out of money.

broken /'broʊkən/ *v.* **1.** past participle of **break**. – *adj.* **2.** having undergone breaking. **3.** uneven; (of ground) rough; (of water) with a disturbed surface as choppy water, surf, etc.; (of weather) patchy, unsettled. **4.** imperfectly spoken, as language.

broker /'broʊkə/ *n.* **1.** an agent who buys or sells for a principal on a commission basis without having title to the property. **2.** a middleman or agent. – **brokerage**, *n.*

brolga /'brɒlgə/ *n.* a large, silvery-grey crane.

brolly /'brɒli/ *n. Colloquial* an umbrella.

bromine /'broʊmin, -aɪn/ *n.* an element, a dark-reddish fuming liquid, resembling chlorine and iodine in chemical properties. *Symbol*: Br

bronchitis /brɒŋ'kaɪtəs/ *n.* a inflammation of the membrane lining of the bronchial tubes.

broncho- a word element meaning 'bronchial'. Also, **bronch-**.

bronchus /'brɒŋkəs/ *n., pl.* **-chi** /-kaɪ/. either of the two main branches of the trachea. – **bronchial**, *adj.*

bronze /brɒnz/ *n. Metallurgy* a durable brown alloy, consisting essentially of copper and tin.

brooch /broʊtʃ/ *n.* a clasp or ornament for

the dress, having a pin at the back for passing through the clothing and a catch for securing the pin.

brood /brud/ *n.* **1.** a number of young creatures produced or hatched at one time; a family of offspring or young. – *v.i.* **2.** to meditate with morbid persistence.

brook[1] /brʊk/ *n.* a small, natural stream of fresh water; creek.

brook[2] /brʊk/ *v.t.* to bear; suffer; tolerate (usually in a negative sentence).

broom /brum/ *n.* a sweeping implement consisting of a flat brush of bristles, nylon, etc., on a long handle.

broth /brɒθ/ *n.* thin soup of concentrated meat or fish stock.

brothel /'brɒθəl/ *n.* a house of prostitution.

brother /'brʌðə/ *n., pl.* **brothers**, **brethren**. – *n.* **1.** a male child of the same parents as another, (**full brother** or **brother-german**). **2.** a male child of only one of one's parents (**half-brother**). **3.** a male member of the same kinship group, nationality, profession, etc.; an associate; a fellow countryman, fellow man, etc. **4.** *Ecclesiastical* a male lay member of a religious organisation which has a priesthood.

brother-in-law /'brʌðər-ɪn-lɔ/ *n., pl.* **brothers-in-law**. **1.** one's husband's or wife's brother. **2.** one's sister's husband. **3.** the husband of one's wife's or husband's sister.

brought /brɔt/ *v.* past tense and past participle of **bring**.

brow /braʊ/ *n.* the ridge over the eye.

browbeat /'braʊbit/ *v.t.*, **-beat**, **-beaten**, **-beating**. to intimidate by overbearing looks or words; bully.

brown /braʊn/ *n.* **1.** a dark shade with yellowish or reddish hue. – *adj.* **2.** of the colour brown. **3.** having skin of that colour. **4.** sunburned or tanned. – *v.t.* **5.** to make brown.

brown bomber *n. Obsolete Colloquial* an officer employed to enforce parking and other associated traffic regulations.

browse /braʊz/ *v.i.*, **browsed**, **browsing**. **1.** to glance though merchandise in a shop. **2.** to glance at random through a book or books.

bruise /bruz/ *v.*, **bruised**, **bruising**, *n.* – *v.t.* **1.** to injure by striking or pressing, without breaking the skin or drawing blood. **2.** to injure or hurt superficially. – *v.i.* **3.** to develop a discoloured spot on the skin as the result of a blow, fall, etc. – *n.* **4.** an injury due to bruising; a contusion.

brumby /'brʌmbi/ *n.* a wild horse, especially one descended from runaway stock.

brunch /brʌntʃ/ *n.* a midmorning meal that serves as both breakfast and lunch.

brunette /bru'nɛt/ *adj.* (of a person) having dark or brown hair, often with brown eyes and olive skin.

brunt /brʌnt/ *n.* the shock or force of an attack, etc.; the main stress, force, or violence.

brush[1] /brʌʃ/ *n.* **1.** an instrument consisting of bristles, hair, or the like, set in or attached to a handle, used for painting, cleaning, polishing, rubbing, etc. **2.** an act of brushing; an application of a brush. **3.** the bushy tail of an animal, especially of a fox. **4.** a slight skimming touch or contact. **5.** a brief hostile encounter; argument; skirmish. – *v.t.* **6.** to sweep, rub, clean, polish, etc., with a brush. **7.** to touch lightly in passing; pass lightly over. **8.** to remove by brushing or by lightly passing over (usually fol. by *aside*).

brush[2] /brʌʃ/ *n.* a dense growth of bushes, shrubs, etc.; scrub; a thicket.

brush-tailed possum /'brʌʃ-teɪld/ *n.* any of various strongly-built, medium sized possums.

brusque /brʌsk, brʊsk/ *adj.* abrupt in manner; blunt; rough.

brussels sprout *n.* a plant with small edible heads or sprouts along the stalk, which resemble miniature cabbage heads.

brutal /'brutl/ *adj.* **1.** savage; cruel; inhuman. **2.** crude; coarse; harsh. – **brutality**, *n.*

brute /brut/ *n.* **1.** a non-human animal; beast. **2.** a brutal person.

bubble /'bʌbəl/ *n., v.*, **-bled**, **-bling**. – *n.* **1.** a small globule of gas in a liquid or solid. **2.** a small globule of gas in a thin liquid envelope. – *v.i.* **3.** to send up bubbles; effervesce.

bubblegum /'bʌbəlgʌm/ *n.* a type of chewing gum which can be blown into bubbles.

bubbler /'bʌblə/ *n. Chiefly NSW* a drinking fountain.

buccaneer /bʌkə'nɪə/ *n.* a pirate.

buck[1] /bʌk/ *n.* the male of certain animals, as the deer, antelope, rabbit, or hare.

buck[2] /bʌk/ *v.i.* **1.** (of a saddle or pack animal) to leap with arched back and come down with head low and forelegs stiff, in order to dislodge rider or pack. **2.** *Colloquial* to resist obstinately; object strongly: *to buck at improvements.* **3.** *Colloquial* to become more cheerful, vigorous, etc. (fol. by *up*).

buck[3] /bʌk/ *n. in the phr.* **pass the buck,** *Colloquial* to shift the responsibility or blame to another person.

buck[4] /bʌk/ *n. Colloquial* a dollar.

bucket /'bʌkət/ *n.* **1.** a vessel, usually round with flat bottom and a semicircular handle, for carrying water, sand, etc. **2. kick the bucket,** *Colloquial* to die.

bucket seat *n.* (in a car, etc.) a seat with a rounded or moulded back, to hold one person. Also, **bucket**.

bucket shop *n.* a stockbroking firm, usually small, which offers to transact its clients' orders at reduced commission rates.

buckle /'bʌkl/ *n., v.*, **-led**, **-ling**. – *n.* **1.** a clasp consisting of a rectangular or curved rim with one or more movable tongues, used for fastening together two loose ends, as of a belt or strap. **2.** a bend, bulge, or kink, as in a saw blade. – *v.t.* **3.** to fasten with a buckle or buckles. **4.** to bend and shrivel, by applying heat or pressure; warp; curl. – *v.i.* **5.** to set to work with vigour (fol. by *to* or *down to*). **6.** to bend, warp, or give way suddenly, as with heat or pressure.

Buckley's /'bʌkliz/ *n. Colloquial* a very slim chance; forlorn hope. Also, **Buckley's chance**.

bucks party *n.* a party in which only the bridegroom and his male associates participate, held as part of the preliminaries to a wedding. Also, **bucks' party**, **bucks' night**.

bucktooth /bʌk'tuθ/ *n., pl.* **-teeth** /-'tiθ/. a projecting tooth.

bucolic /bju'kɒlɪk/ *adj.* rustic; rural.

bud /bʌd/ *n. Botany* a small axillary or terminal protuberance on a plant, containing rudimentary foliage (**leaf bud**), the rudimentary inflorescence (**flower bud**), or both (**mixed bud**).

buddy /'bʌdi/ *n., pl.* **-dies**. *Colloquial* comrade; mate.

budge /bʌdʒ/ *v.,* **budged**, **budging**. *– v.i.* **1.** to move slightly; give way (usually with negative). *– v.t.* **2.** to cause to budge (usually with negative).

budgerigar /'bʌdʒəri͵ga/ *n.* a small yellow and green parakeet that has been widely domesticated and bred in many coloured varieties.

budget /'bʌdʒət/ *n.* an estimate, often itemised, of expected income and expenditure, or operating results, for a given period in the future. – **budgetary**, *adj.*

budget account *n.* an account with a department store, etc., enabling a customer to obtain goods of a specified value, and pay for them over a specified period.

buff[1] /bʌf/ *n.* **1.** a kind of thick leather. **2.** yellowish brown; medium or light tan. **3.** *Colloquial* the bare skin. **4.** *Colloquial* an enthusiast; an expert (sometimes self-proclaimed). *– v.t.* **5.** to polish (metal) or to give a grainless finish of high lustre to (plated surfaces).

buff[2] /bʌf/ *v.t.* to reduce or deaden the force of, as a buffer.

buffalo /'bʌfəloʊ/ *n., pl.* **-loes**, **-los**, (*esp. collectively*) **-lo**. any of several mammals of the ox kind, especially those valued as draught animals.

buffer[1] /'bʌfə/ *n.* **1.** anything serving to neutralise the shock of opposing forces. **2.** *Computers* an area of temporary storage where data is held during computer operations.

buffer[2] /'bʌfə/ *n.* a device for polishing.

buffet[1] /'bʌfət/ *n., v.,* **-feted**, **-feting**. *– n.* **1.** a blow, as with the hand or fist. *– v.t.* **2.** to strike, as with the hand or fist.

buffet[2] /'bʌfeɪ, 'bʊfeɪ/ *n.* **1.** a counter, bar, or the like, for lunch or refreshments. **2.** a sideboard or cabinet for holding china, plate, etc. *– adj.* **3.** (of a meal) spread on tables or buffets from which the guests serve themselves.

buffoon /bə'fun/ *n.* someone who amuses others by tricks, odd gestures and postures, jokes, etc.

bug /bʌg/ *n., v.t.,* **bugged**, **bugging**. *– n.* **1.** any insect. **2.** *Colloquial* an illness caused by bacteria or viruses. **3.** *Computers* an error in a program or the machine itself, often undetected by the most stringent tests. **4.** *Colloquial* an idea or belief with which one is obsessed. **5.** *Colloquial* a microphone hidden in a room to tap conversation. *– v.t.* **6.** *Colloquial* to install a bug in (a room, etc.). **7.** *Colloquial* to cause annoyance or distress to (a person).

bugbear /'bʌgbɛə/ *n.* any source, real or imaginary, of needless fright or fear.

bugger /'bʌgə/ *n.* **1.** someone who practises bestiality or sodomy. **2.** *Colloquial* a contemptible person. **3. bugger all,** *Colloquial* nothing. *– v.t.* **4.** *Colloquial* to cause damage, frustration or inconvenience to (fol. by *up*). *– interj.* **5.** (a strong exclamation of annoyance, disgust, etc.). – **buggery**, *n.*

buggy /'bʌgi/ *n., pl.* **-gies**. a two-wheeled horse-drawn carriage with or without a hood.

bugle /'bjugəl/ *n.* a cornet-like military wind instrument, usually metal, used for sounding signals and sometimes furnished with keys or valves.

build /bɪld/ *v.,* **built**, **building**, *n. – v.t.* **1.** to construct (something relatively complex) by assembling and combining parts. **2.** to establish, increase, and strengthen (often fol. by *up*). **3.** to base; form; construct. **4.** to obstruct the view from (a building) by erecting another building close to it (fol. by *out*). *– v.i.* **5.** to engage in the art or business of building. **6.** to form or construct a plan, system of thought, etc. (fol. by *on* or *upon*). *– n.* **7.** manner or form of construction.

building society *n.* an organisation which uses money subscribed by its members as a fund for lending money to members, as for the purchase of homes.

built-up area *n.* an area of dense habitation within which speed-limits apply to traffic.

bulb /bʌlb/ *n.* **1.** *Botany* a storage organ, having fleshy leaves and usually subterranean, in which the stem is reduced to a flat disc, rooting from the underside, as in the onion, lily, etc. **2.** *Electricity* the glass housing which contains the filament of an incandescent electric light globe. – **bulbous**, *adj.*

bulge /bʌldʒ/ *n., v.,* **bulged**, **bulging**. *– n.* **1.** a rounded projecting or protruding part; protuberance; hump. *– v.i.* **2.** to swell out; be protuberant.

bulk /bʌlk/ *n.* **1.** magnitude in three dimensions. **2.** the greater part; the main mass or body. **3. in bulk, a.** unpackaged. **b.** in large quantities. – **bulky**, *adj.*

bull[1] /bʊl/ *n.* **1.** the male of a bovine animal, with sexual organs intact and capable of reproduction. **2.** the male of certain other animals. **3.** *Stock Exchange* someone who buys in the hope of selling later at a profit due to a rise in prices (opposed to *bear*).

bull[2] /bʊl/ *n. Colloquial* nonsense.

bulla /'bʊlə, 'bʌlə/ *n., pl.* **bullae** /'bʊli, 'bʌli/. a seal attached to an official document.

bulldog /'bʊldɒg/ *n.* a large-headed, short-haired, heavily built variety of dog, of comparatively small size but very muscular and vigorous.

bulldozer /'bʊldoʊzə/ *n.* a powerful caterpillar tractor having a vertical blade at the front end for moving earth, tree stumps, rocks, etc.

bullet /'bʊlət/ *n.* a small metal projectile, part of a cartridge, for firing from small arms.

bulletin /'bʊlətən/ *n.* **1.** a brief account or statement, as of news or events, issued for the information of the public. **2.** a periodical publication, as of a learned society.

bull-headed /bʊl-'hɛdəd/ *adj.* obstinate;

blunderingly stubborn; stupid.

bullion /'bʊljən/ *n.* **1.** gold or silver in the mass. **2.** gold or silver in the form of bars or ingots.

bullish /'bʊlɪʃ/ *adj.* (in the stock exchange, etc.) tending to cause a rise in price.

bull market *n. Stock Exchange* a buoyant period of trading during and immediately after a rise in share prices when traders consider that there are strong prospects of further price rises.

bullock /'bʊlək/ *n.* **1.** a castrated male of a bovine animal, not having been used for reproduction; ox; steer. – *v.t.* **2.** to force.

bullseye /'bʊlzaɪ/ *n.* the central spot, usually black, of a target.

bullshit /'bʊlʃɪt/ *n. Colloquial* nonsense.

bull-terrier /bʊl-'tɛriə/ *n.* one of a breed of dogs produced by crossing the bulldog and the terrier.

bully /'bʊli/ *n., pl.* **-lies**, *v.,* **-lied**, **-lying**. – *n.* **1.** a blustering, quarrelsome, overbearing person who brow-beats smaller or weaker people. – *v.i.* **2.** to be loudly arrogant and overbearing.

bum /bʌm/ *n.* **1.** the rump; buttocks. **2.** a shiftless or dissolute person.

bumble /'bʌmbəl/ *v.i.,* **bumbled**, **bumbling**. *Colloquial* to proceed clumsily or inefficiently.

bumblebee /'bʌmbəlbi/ *n.* any of various large, hairy social bees. Also, **humblebee**.

bummer /'bʌmə/ *n. Colloquial* something which causes disappointment.

bump /bʌmp/ *v.t.* **1.** to come more or less heavily in contact with; strike; collide with. **2.** *Colloquial* to increase (in extent, etc.) (fol. by *up*). – *v.i.* **3. a.** to come in contact with; collide (often fol. by *against*, *into*). **b.** to meet by chance (fol. by *into*). – *n.* **4.** the act of bumping; a blow. **5.** a dull thud; the noise of collision. **6.** a small area raised above the level of the surrounding surface, as on the skull or on a road.

bumper bar *n.* a horizontal bar affixed to the front or rear of a vehicle to give some protection in collisions.

bumpkin /'bʌmpkən/ *n.* an awkward, clumsy yokel.

bumptious /'bʌmpʃəs/ *adj.* offensively self-assertive.

bun /bʌn/ *n.* **1.** a kind of bread roll, usually slightly sweetened and round-shaped, and sometimes containing spice, dried currants, citron, etc. **2.** hair arranged at the back of the head in a bun shape.

bunch /bʌntʃ/ *n.* **1.** a connected group; cluster. – *v.t.* **2.** to group together; make a bunch of.

bundle /'bʌndl/ *n., v.,* **-dled**, **-dling**. – *n.* **1.** a group loosely held together. **2.** something wrapped for carrying; package. – *v.t.* **3.** to dress snugly (fol. by *up*). **4.** to send away hurriedly or unceremoniously (fol. by *off*, *out*, etc.).

bundling /'bʌndlɪŋ/ *n. Computers* the practice of including some software with a hardware purchase for the same price.

bundy /'bʌndi/ *n. Colloquial* a clock which marks the time on a card inserted in it, used to record arrival and departure times of employees; time clock.

bung[1] /bʌŋ/ *n.* **1.** a stopper, as for the hole of a cask. – *v.t. Colloquial* **2.** to put. **3. bung it on, a.** to behave temperamentally. **b.** to act in a pretentious or ostentatious manner.

bung[2] /bʌŋ/ *adj. Colloquial* not in good working order; impaired; injured.

bungalow /'bʌŋgəloʊ/ *n.* a house or cottage of one storey.

bungle /'bʌŋgəl/ *v.t.,* **-gled**, **-gling**. to do clumsily and awkwardly; botch.

bunion /'bʌnjən/ *n.* a swelling on the foot.

bunk[1] /bʌŋk/ *n.* a built-in platform bed, as on a ship.

bunk[2] /bʌŋk/ *n. Colloquial* humbug; nonsense.

bunker[1] /'bʌŋkə/ *n.* **1.** a chest or box; a large bin or receptacle. **2.** *Golf* a shallow excavation, usually at the side of a green, which has been nearly filled with sand.

bunker[2] /'bʌŋkə/ *n.* a bombproof shelter, often underground.

bunkum /'bʌŋkəm/ *n.* insincere talk; humbug.

bunny /'bʌni/ *n., pl.* **-nies**. *Colloquial* **1.** a rabbit. **2.** someone who accepts the responsibility for a situation, sometimes willingly.

bunting /'bʌntɪŋ/ *n.* **1.** a coarse open fabric of worsted or cotton used for flags, signals. **2.** festive decorations made from bunting, paper, etc., usually in the form of draperies, wide streamers, etc.

bunyip /'bʌnjəp/ *n.* an imaginary creature of Aboriginal legend, said to haunt rushy swamps and billabongs.

buoy /bɔɪ/ *n.* **1.** *Nautical* a distinctively marked and shaped anchored float, sometimes carrying a light, whistle, or bell, marking a channel or obstruction. – *v.t.* **2.** to support by or as by a buoy; keep afloat in a fluid. **3.** to bear up or sustain, as hope or courage does.

buoyant /'bɔɪənt/ *adj.* **1.** tending to float or rise in a fluid. **2.** not easily depressed; cheerful. **3.** (of production levels, prices, etc.) having the capacity of recovering from a reverse.

burble /'bɜbəl/ *v.t.,* **-bled**, **-bling**. to make a bubbling sound; bubble.

burden /'bɜdn/ *n.* **1.** that which is carried; a load. **2.** that which is borne with difficulty. **3.** *Commerce* the duty to discharge an obligation or responsibility. – *v.t.* **4.** to load heavily. – **burdensome**, *adj.*

bureau /'bjuroʊ, bju'roʊ/ *n., pl.* **-reaus**, **-reaux** /-roʊz/. **1.** a desk or writing table with drawers for papers. **2.** a division of a government department or independent administrative unit.

bureaucracy /bju'rɒkrəsi/ *n., pl.* **-cies**. **1.** government by officials against whom there is inadequate public right of redress. **2.** the body of officials administering bureaus. **3.** excessive governmental red tape and routine. – **bureaucrat**, *n.* – **bureaucratic**, *adj.*

burgeon /'bɜdʒən/ *v.i.* to begin to grow, as a bud; to put forth buds, shoots, as a plant (often fol. by *out*, *forth*).

burghul /'bɜgəl/ *n.* crushed wheat that has been hulled, parboiled, dried, and then ground, used especially in Lebanese cookery. Also, **bourghul**.

burglary /'bɜgləri/ *n., pl.* **-ries**. the offence of breaking into and entering the house of another with intent to commit a felony therein. – **burglar**, *n.*

burgundy /'bɜgəndi/ *n., pl.* **-dies**. **1.** wine of many varieties, red and white, mostly still, full, and dry, produced in the Burgundy region of France. **2.** dull reddish blue (colour).

burial /'bɛriəl/ *n.* the act of burying.

burl /bɜl/ *n. Colloquial* an attempt.

burlesque /bɜ'lɛsk/ *n.* a theatrical or cabaret entertainment featuring coarse, crude, often vulgar comedy and dancing.

burly /'bɜli/ *adj.,* **-lier**, **-liest**. **1.** great in bodily size; stout; sturdy. **2.** bluff; brusque.

burn /bɜn/ *v.,* **burnt** *or* **burned**, **burning**, *n.* – *v.i.* **1.** to be on fire. **2.** to feel heat or a physiologically identical sensation. **3.** to give light. **4.** to feel strong passion. **5.** to become discoloured, tanned, or charred through heat. – *v.t.* **6.** to consume, partly or wholly, with fire. **7.** to injure, discolour, char, or treat with heat. **8.** to produce with fire. **9.** to pass through or over quickly and easily (fol. by *up*). **10.** to clear or improve (land) by burning the cover (often fol. by *off*). – *n.* **11.** *Pathology* an injury produced by heat or by abnormal cold, chemicals, poison gas, electricity, or lightning.

burnish /'bɜnɪʃ/ *v.t.* to polish (a surface) by friction.

burnt /bɜnt/ *v.* a past tense and past participle of **burn**.

burp /bɜp/ *n., v.i. Colloquial* → **belch** (defs 1 and 4).

burr[1] /bɜ/ *n. Botany* the rough, prickly case around the seeds of certain plants.

burr[2] /bɜ/ *n.* **1.** any of various tools and appliances for cutting or drilling. **2.** to form a rough point or edge on. Also, **bur**.

burrow /'bʌroʊ/ *n.* **1.** a hole in the ground made by a rabbit, fox, or similar small animal, for refuge and habitation. – *v.i.* **2.** to make a hole or passage (*in*, *into*, or *under* something).

bursar /'bɜsə/ *n.* **1.** a treasurer or business officer, especially of a college or university. **2.** a student holding a bursary.

bursary /'bɜsəri/ *n., pl.* **-ries**. a scholarship.

burst /bɜst/ *v.,* **burst**, **bursting**, *n.* – *v.i.* **1.** to fly apart or break open with sudden violence; explode. **2.** to issue forth suddenly and forcibly from or as from confinement. **3.** to break or give way from violent pain or emotion. **4.** to be extremely full, as if ready to break open. – *v.t.* **5.** to cause to burst; break suddenly and violently. – *n.* **6.** the act of bursting. **7.** a sudden display of activity or energy. **8.** a sudden expression or manifestation of emotion, etc.

bury /'bɛri/ *v.t.,* **buried**, **burying**. **1.** to put in the ground and cover with earth. **2.** to cover in order to conceal from sight. **3.** to occupy (oneself) completely.

bus /bʌs/ *n., pl.* **buses**, **busses**. **1.** a vehicle with a long body equipped with seats or benches for passengers, usually operating as part of a scheduled service. **2.** *Computers* a circuit or group of circuits which provide a communication path between two or more devices, as between a central processor, a memory bank, and peripherals.

bush /bʊʃ/ *n.* **1.** a woody plant, especially a low one, with many branches which usually arise from or near the ground. **2.** something resembling or suggesting this, as a thick, shaggy head of hair. **3.** *Geography* a stretch of land covered with bushy vegetation or trees. **4.** **go bush, a.** to turn one's back on civilisation; adopt a way of life close to nature. **b.** Also, **take to the bush**. to disappear suddenly from one's normal surroundings or circle of friends. **5. the bush,** the countryside in general, as opposed to the towns. – *v.t.* **6.** to cover with bushes; protect with bushes set round about; support with bushes. – *adj.* **7.** found in or typical of the bush: *a bush nurse*; *a bush pub*; *bush hospitality*. **8.** uncivilised; rough; makeshift: *a bush bed*; *bush carpentry*.

bush band *n.* a band which performs Australian folk music, usually with such instruments as the accordion, tea-chest bass, guitar, etc.

bushcraft /'bʊʃkraft/ *n.* the ability to live in and travel through the bush with a minimum of equipment and assistance.

bushed /bʊʃt/ *adj. Colloquial* **1.** lost. **2.** exhausted. **3.** confused.

bushel /'bʊʃəl/ *n.* a unit of dry measure in the imperial system equal to 36.368 72 × 10^{-3} m^3 (8 gal).

bushfire /'bʊʃfaɪə/ *n.* a fire in forest or scrub country.

bushland /'bʊʃlænd/ *n.* natural, uncultivated land.

bushman /'bʊʃmən/ *n.* someone skilled in bushcraft.

bushranger /'bʊʃreɪndʒə/ *n.* (formerly) a bandit or criminal who hid in the bush and stole from settlers and travellers at gunpoint.

bush telegraph *n. Colloquial* an unofficial chain of communication by which information is conveyed and rumour spread, as by word of mouth. Also, **bush wireless**.

bushwalking /'bʊʃwɔkɪŋ/ *n.* the sport of making one's way on foot through the bush, often on tracks designed for this but sometimes for longer periods through virgin terrain.

bushwhacker /'bʊʃwækə/ *n. Colloquial* someone who lives in the bush. Also, **bushwacker**.

business /'bɪznəs/ *n.* **1.** one's occupation, profession, or trade. **2.** *Economics* the purchase and sale of goods in an attempt to make a profit. **3.** *Commerce* a person, partnership, or corporation engaged in this; an established or going enterprise or concern. **4.** volume of trade; patronage. **5.** that with which one is principally and seriously concerned. **6.** that with which one is rightfully concerned. **7.** affair; matter.

business college *n.* a private institution where subjects of use commercially, as shorthand, typing, book-keeping etc., are taught.

businesslike /'bɪznəslaɪk/ *adj.* conforming to the methods of business or trade; methodical; systematic.

businessman /'bɪznəsmən/ *n., pl.* **-men** /-mən/. a man who engages in business or commerce.

businessperson /ˈbɪznəspɜsən/ *n., pl.* **-people**. a person engaged in business or commerce.

businesswoman /ˈbɪznəswʊmən/ *n., pl.* **-women**. a woman who engages in business or commerce.

busker /ˈbʌskə/ *n.* an entertainer who gives impromptu performances in streets, parks, markets, etc.

bust[1] /bʌst/ *n.* **1.** the head and shoulders of a person done in sculpture, either in the round or in relief. **2.** the chest or breast; the bosom.

bust[2] /bʌst/ *Colloquial* – *v.i.* **1.** to burst. **2.** to go bankrupt (often fol. by *up*). **3.** to part finally; quarrel and part (fol. by *up*). – *v.t.* **4.** to burst (often fol. by *in*). **5.** to smash (fol. by *up*). **6.** to bankrupt; ruin (often fol. by *up*). **7.** to interrupt violently a political meeting or other gathering (fol. by *up*). **8.** to reduce in rank or grade; demote. – *n.* **9.** a complete failure; bankruptcy. **10.** a police raid. – *adj.* **11.** Also, **busted**. broken; ruined. **12.** bankrupt.

bustard /ˈbʌstəd/ *n.* a large, heavy bird inhabiting grassy plains and open scrub country of Australia; plain turkey.

bustle[1] /ˈbʌsəl/ *v.i.*, **-tled**, **-tling**. to move or act with a great show of energy (often fol. by *about*).

bustle[2] /ˈbʌsəl/ *n.* (formerly) a pad, cushion, or wire framework worn by women on the back part of the body below the waist, to expand and support the skirt.

busy /ˈbɪzi/ *adj.*, **busier**, **busiest**, *v.*, **busied**, **busying**. – *adj.* **1.** actively and attentively engaged. **2.** full of or characterised by activity. – *v.t.* **3.** to keep occupied; make or keep busy.

busybody /ˈbɪzibɒdi/ *n., pl.* **-bodies**. a person who pries into and meddles in the affairs of others.

but /bʌt/, *weak form* /bət/ – *conj.* **1.** on the contrary; yet. **2.** except, rather than, or save. **3.** except that (followed by a clause, often with *that* expressed). **4.** without the circumstance that, or that not. **5.** otherwise than. **6.** that (especially after *doubt*, *deny*, etc., with a negative). **7.** who or which not. – *prep.* **8.** with the exception of; except; save. – *adv.* **9.** only; just. – *n.* **10.** a restriction or objection.

butane /ˈbjuteɪn, bjuˈteɪn/ *n.* a hydrocarbon used as a fuel.

butch /bʊtʃ/ *adj. Colloquial* (of a man or woman) exhibiting masculine characteristics.

butcher /ˈbʊtʃə/ *n.* **1.** a retail dealer in meat. **2.** a person guilty of cruel or indiscriminate slaughter. – *v.t.* **3.** to murder indiscriminately or brutally. – **butchery**, *n.*

butcherbird *n.* any of several birds so called because they impale their prey of small birds, etc., on spikes or thorns or wedge it in the forks of trees.

butler /ˈbʌtlə/ *n.* the head male servant of a household.

butt[1] /bʌt/ *n.* **1.** the end or extremity of anything, especially the thicker, larger, or blunt end, as of a rifle, fishing rod, whip handle, arrow, log, etc. **2.** an end which is not used up. **3.** *Colloquial* the buttocks; bottom.

butt[2] /bʌt/ *n.* **1.** a person or thing that is an object of wit, ridicule, sarcasm, etc., or contempt. **2.** the target for archery practice. – *v.i.* **3.** to have an end or projection (*on*); be adjacent (*to*).

butt[3] /bʌt/ *v.t.* **1.** to strike with the head or horns. **2.** to project. **3. butt in,** *Colloquial* to interrupt; interfere; intrude. **4. butt out,** *Colloquial* to mind one's own business and not interfere in something which is not one's proper concern.

butter /ˈbʌtə/ *n.* **1.** the fatty portion of milk, separating as a soft whitish or yellowish solid when milk or cream is agitated or churned. – *v.t.* **2.** to put butter on or in. **3.** *Colloquial* to flatter grossly (often fol. by *up*).

butterfly /ˈbʌtəflaɪ/ *n., pl.* **-flies**. **1.** an insect with large, broad wings often conspicuously coloured and marked. **2.** (*pl.*) nervousness. **3.** → **butterfly stroke**.

butterfly stroke *n.* a swimming stroke in which both arms are lifted simultaneously out of the water and flung forward.

buttermilk /ˈbʌtəmɪlk/ *n.* the liquid remaining after the butter has been separated from milk or cream.

butterscotch /ˈbʌtəskɒtʃ/ *n.* a kind of toffee made with butter.

buttock /ˈbʌtək/ *n. Anatomy* either of the two protuberances which form the rump.

button /ˈbʌtn/ *n.* **1.** a disc or knob on a piece of cloth which, when passed through a slit or loop either in the same piece or another, serves as a fastening. **2.** anything resembling a button. **3.** a disc pressed to close an electric circuit, as in ringing a bell. – *v.t.* **4.** to fasten with a button or buttons.

buttonhole /ˈbʌtnhoʊl/ *n.* **1.** the hole, slit, or loop through which a button is passed. **2.** a small flower or nosegay worn in the buttonhole in the lapel of a jacket.

buttress /ˈbʌtrəs/ *n.* **1.** *Architecture* a structure built against a wall or building for the purpose of giving it stability. **2.** any prop or support.

buxom /ˈbʌksəm/ *adj.* (of a woman) full-bosomed, plump, and attractive because of radiant health.

buy /baɪ/ *v.*, **bought**, **buying**, *n.* – *v.t.* **1.** to acquire the possession of, or the right to, by paying an equivalent, especially in money. **2.** to get rid of (a claim, opposition, etc.) by payment; purchase the non-intervention of; bribe (fol. by *off*). **3.** to secure all of (an owner's or partner's) share or interest in an enterprise (fol. by *out*). **4.** to buy as much as one can of (fol. by *up*). **5.** to acquire shares in; become involved in (fol. by *in*, *into*). **6.** *Colloquial* to accept. – *v.i.* **7.** to be or become a purchaser. **8. buy in, a.** *Stock Exchange* (of a broker) to obtain a share scrip from another broker to cover his or her position after a third broker fails to deliver shares. **b.** to join in; become involved. **9. buy into,** to choose to become involved in. – *n.* **10.** *Colloquial* a purchase, esp. a good purchase.

buyback /ˈbaɪbæk/ *n.* an agreement between two participants, especially in the money or stock market, whereby the first party sells securities to the second party and at the same time undertakes to buy them back at a specified price at some agreed time in the future. Also, **buy-back**.

buyer /ˈbaɪə/ *n.* **1.** someone who buys; a purchaser. **2.** a purchasing agent, as for a chain-store.

buyers' market *n.* a market in which the buyer is at an advantage because of oversupply.

buyout /ˈbaɪaʊt/ *n.* → **management buyout**. Also, **buy-out**.

buzz /bʌz/ *n.* **1.** a low, vibrating, humming sound, as of bees. **2.** *Colloquial* a telephone call. **3.** *Colloquial* **a.** a feeling of exhilaration or pleasure, especially as induced by drugs. **b.** a similar experience of pleasure, delight, etc.: *I get a real buzz out of going sailing.* – *v.i.* **4.** to make a low, vibrating, humming sound. **5.** to move busily from place to place (usually fol. by *about*). **6.** *Colloquial* to go; leave (usually fol. by *off* or *along*). – *v.t.* **7.** to make a buzzing sound with. **8.** *Aeronautics Colloquial* **a.** to fly an aeroplane very low over. **b.** to signal or greet (someone) by flying an aeroplane low and slowing the motor spasmodically.

buzzard /ˈbʌzəd/ *n.* any of various carrion-eating birds, as the honey buzzard and the turkey buzzard.

buzz word *n.* *Colloquial* a word used for its emotive value or its ability to impress the listener.

by /baɪ/ *prep.* **1.** near to. **2.** using as a route. **3.** through or on as a means of conveyance. **4.** not later than. **5.** to the extent of. **6.** through evidence or authority of. **7.** in conformity with. **8.** before; in the presence of. **9.** through the agency or efficacy of. **10.** after; in serial order. **11.** combined with in multiplication or relative dimension. **12.** involving as unit of measure. – *adv.* **13.** near to something. **14.** to and past a point near something. **15.** aside. **16.** over; past. **17. by and by,** at some time in the future; before long; presently. **18. by and large,** in general; on the whole.

by- a prefix meaning: **1.** secondary; incidental, as in *by-product.* **2.** out of the way; removed, as in *byway.* **3.** near, as in *by-stander.* Also, **bye-**.

bye /baɪ/ *n.* *Sport* the state of having no competitor in a contest where several competitors are engaged in pairs, conferring the right to compete in the next round in a competition. Also, **by**.

by-election /ˈbaɪ-əlɛkʃən/ *n.* a parliamentary election held between general elections, to fill a vacancy. Also, **bye-election**.

bygone /ˈbaɪgɒn/ *adj.* **1.** past; gone by; out of date. – *n.* **2.** that which is past.

by-law /ˈbaɪ-lɔ/ *n.* **1.** an ordinance of an authority having legal effect only within the boundaries of that authority's jurisdiction. **2.** subordinate legislation, generally at the level of local government. **3.** a standing rule, as of a company or society, not in its constitution. Also, **bye-law**.

by-line /ˈbaɪ-laɪn/ *n.* *Journalism* a line under the heading of a newspaper or magazine article giving the writer's name.

byname /ˈbaɪneɪm/ *n.* **1.** a secondary name. **2.** a nickname.

bypass /ˈbaɪpas/ *n.* **1.** a road enabling motorists to avoid towns and other heavy traffic points or any obstruction to easy travel on a main road. **2.** *Medicine* **a.** a channel inserted by surgery in order to avoid the normal passage of fluids in the circulatory or digestive systems. **b.** → **bypass operation**. – *v.t.* **3.** to avoid (obstructions, etc.) by following a bypass. **4.** to go over the head of (one's immediate supervisor, etc.).

bypass operation *n.* *Medicine* an operation in which a diseased or obstructed segment of the circulatory or digestive systems of the body is circumvented; particularly used to circumvent diseased blood vessels in the heart.

by-product /ˈbaɪ-prɒdʌkt/ *n.* a secondary or incidental product, as in a process of manufacture.

byre /ˈbaɪə/ *n.* a cowhouse or shed; a cattle pen.

bystander /ˈbaɪstændə/ *n.* a person present but not involved; a chance looker-on.

byte /baɪt/ *n.* a unit of information, usually eight bits, stored by a computer. See **bit**[3].

byway /ˈbaɪweɪ/ *n.* **1.** a secluded, or obscure road. **2.** a subsidiary or obscure field of research, endeavour, etc.

byword /ˈbaɪwɜd/ *n.* **1.** the name of a quality or concept which characterises some person or group; the epitome (of). **2.** a word or phrase used proverbially; a common saying; a proverb.

C c

C, c *n., pl.* **C's** *or* **Cs**, **c's** *or* **cs**. the third letter of the English alphabet.

cab /kæb/ *n.* **1.** → **taxi**. **2.** the covered part of a truck, etc., where the driver sits.

cabal /kə'bal, kə'bæl/ *n.* the secret schemes of a small group of plotters.

cabaret /'kæbəreɪ/ *n.* a form of musical entertainment at a restaurant, nightclub, etc.

cabbage /'kæbɪdʒ/ *n.* a vegetable with a short stem and leaves formed into a compact, edible head.

caber /'keɪbə/ *n.* a pole or beam, especially one thrown as a trial of strength in the Scottish Highland game of **tossing the caber**.

cabin /'kæbən/ *n.* **1.** a small temporary house. **2.** an apartment or room in a ship, aircraft, etc.

cabinet /'kæbənət, 'kæbnət/ *n.* **1.** (*also cap.*) a council advising a sovereign or chief executive; the group of ministers responsible for the government of a nation. **2.** a piece of furniture with shelves, drawers, etc.

cable /'keɪbəl/ *n.* **1.** a thick, strong rope. **2.** a telegram sent abroad, especially by submarine cable.

caboodle /kə'budl/ *n. in the phr.* **the whole (kit and) caboodle,** *Colloquial* the whole lot, pack, or crowd.

cabotage /'kæbətaʒ/ *n.* trade or navigation in coastal waters.

cacao /kə'keɪoʊ, -'kaoʊ/ *n., pl.* **-caos**. a small evergreen tree, cultivated for its seeds, the source of cocoa, etc.

cache /kæʃ/ *n.* a hiding place.

cache memory *n.* a section of computer memory which can be accessed at high speed and in which information is stored for fast retrieval.

cackle /'kækəl/ *v.,* **-led**, **-ling**.– *v.i.* to utter a shrill, broken sound or cry, as a hen after laying an egg.

cacophony /kə'kɒfəni/ *n., pl.* **-nies**. a harsh sound.

cactus /'kæktəs/ *n., pl.* **-ti** /-ti, -taɪ/ **-tuses**. any of various fleshy-stemmed plants of the family Cactaceae.

cad /kæd/ *n.* a contemptible person.

CAD /si eɪ 'di/ computer-aided design.

cadastre /kə'dæstə/ *n.* an official register of property, with details of boundaries, ownership, etc.

cadaver /kə'dævə, -'davə/ *n.* a corpse.

caddie /'kædi/ *n. Golf* an attendant, hired to carry the player's clubs, find the ball, etc.

caddy /'kædi/ *n., pl.* **-dies**. a small box, tin, or chest, especially one for holding tea.

cadence /'keɪdəns/ *n.* **1.** rhythmic flow, as of verses; rhythm. **2.** the general modulation of the voice.

cadet /kə'dɛt/ *n.* a person undergoing training, especially in the armed services.

cadge /kædʒ/ *v.t.,* **cadged**, **cadging**. to borrow without intent to repay.

cadmium /'kædmiəm/ *n.* a white, ductile, divalent metallic element, like tin in appearance, used in plating and in making certain alloys. *Symbol*: Cd

cadre /'kadə, 'keɪdə/ *n.* a unit within an organisational framework, especially personnel.

CAE /si eɪ 'i/ computer-aided engineering.

caesarean section /sə'zɛəriən/ *n.* the operation by which a foetus is taken from the womb by cutting through the walls of the abdomen and womb.

caesium /'siziəm/ *n.* a rare, extremely active, soft, monovalent metallic element. *Symbol*: Cs

cafe /'kæfeɪ/ (*humorous*) /keɪf/ *n.* a room or building where coffee and light refreshments are served. Also, **café**.

cafeteria /kæfə'tɪəriə/ *n.* an inexpensive restaurant or snack-bar, usually self-service.

caffeine /'kæfin/ *n.* a bitter substance, a stimulant and diuretic, obtained from coffee, tea, etc.

cage /keɪdʒ/ *n., v.,* **caged**, **caging**. – *n.* **1.** a box-shaped receptacle or enclosure for confining birds or other animals. – *v.t.* **2.** to put or confine in or as in a cage.

cagey = cagy /'keɪdʒi/ *adj.,* **cagier cagiest**. *Colloquial* cautious; secretive. Also, **cagy**.

cahoots /kə'huts/ *n. in the phr.* **in cahoots,** in partnership; in league.

caino- a word element meaning 'new', 'recent'. Also, **ceno-**, **caeno-**.

cajole /kə'dʒoʊl/ *v.,* **-joled**, **-joling**. to persuade by flattery or promises. – **cajolery**, **cajolement**, **cajoler**, *n.*

cake /keɪk/ *n.* a sweet baked food in loaf or layer form.

calamari /kælə'mari/ *n.* squid, especially as used for food.

calamine /'kæləmaɪn/ *n.* a liquid soothing to the skin. Also, **calamine lotion**.

calamity /kə'læməti/ *n., pl.* **-ties**. a disaster. – **calamitous**, *adj.*

calcareous /kal'kɛəriəs/ *adj.* chalk-like.

calcify /'kælsəfaɪ/ *v.i.,* **-fied**, **-fying**. *Physiology* to become chalky or bony.

calcium /'kælsiəm/ *n.* a silver-white divalent metal. *Symbol*: Ca

calculate /'kælkjəleɪt/ *v.t.,* **-lated**, **-lating**. to ascertain by mathematical methods. – **calculation**, *n.* – **calculable**, *adj.*

calculating /'kælkjəleɪtɪŋ/ *adj.* shrewd.

calculator /'kælkjəleɪtə/ *n.* a machine that performs mathematical operations.

calculus /'kælkjələs/ *n., pl.* **-luses** *for def. 1* **-li** /-laɪ/. *for def. 2* – **1.** a method of calculation. **2.** *Pathology* a stone in the body.

calendar /'kæləndə/ *n.* any of various systems of reckoning time, especially with reference to the beginning, length, and divisions of the year.

calf[1] /kaf/ *n., pl.* **calves**. the young of the cow or certain other animals.

calf[2] /kaf/ *n., pl.* **calves**. the fleshy part of the back of the human leg below the knee.

calibrate /'kæləbreɪt/ *v.t.,* **-brated**, **-brating**. to determine, check, or rectify the graduation or accuracy of.

calibre /'kæləbə/ *n.* **1.** the diameter of something of circular section, especially that of the inside of a tube, as the bore of a gun. **2.** personal character.

calico /'kælɪkoʊ/ *n., pl.* **-coes**, **-cos**. white cotton cloth.

call /kɔl/ *v.t.* **1.** to cry out in a loud voice. **2.** (of a bird or other animal) to utter (its characteristic cry). **3.** to command or request to come. **4.** *Economics* to ask for payment of (all or part of the unpaid part of a company's share capital). **5.** to give a name to. *– v.i.* **6.** to speak loudly, as to attract attention; shout. **7.** (of a bird or animal) to utter its characteristic cry. **8.** to make a short visit; stop at a place on some errand or business. **9. call in, a.** to collect. **b.** to withdraw from circulation. *– n.* **10.** a cry or shout. **11.** the cry of a bird or other animal. **12.** a short visit. **13.** a telephone conversation. **14.** a summons; invitation. **15.** a demand or claim. **16.** a demand for payment of an obligation, especially where payment is at the option of the creditor. **17.** *Stock Exchange* the option of claiming stock at or before a given date. **18. on call, a.** *Commerce* Also, **at call**. payable or subject to return without advance notice. **b.** (of doctors, etc.) available for duty at short notice. *– adj.* **19.** *Commerce* repayable on demand.

callgirl /'kɔlgɜl/ *n.* a prostitute who makes herself available for appointments by telephone.

calli- a word element meaning 'beauty'.

calligraphy /kə'lɪgrəfi/ *n.* handwriting.

calling /'kɔlɪŋ/ *n.* a vocation, profession, or trade.

calliper /'kæləpə/ *n.* **1.** (*usu. pl.*) a tool for measuring diameters. **2.** *Medicine* a limb brace.

callisthenics /kæləs'θɛnɪks/ *pl. n.* light gymnastic exercises.

call option *n. Stock Exchange* the right to buy a specified parcel of shares at an agreed price within a specified period of time.

callous /'kæləs/ *adj.* hardened.

callow /'kæloʊ/ *adj.* immature or inexperienced.

callus /'kæləs/ *n., pl.* **-luses**. *Pathology, Physiology* a hardened or thickened part of the skin.

calm /kam/ *adj.* **1.** without rough motion; still. **2.** free from excitement or passion; tranquil. *– v.t.* **3.** to make calm.

calorie /'kæləri/ *n.* **1.** a non-SI unit equal to the large calorie, used to express the heat output of an organism or the energy value of a food. The recommended SI unit is the kilojoule; 1 calorie is equivalent to 4.1868 kJ. *– phr.* **2. count calories,** to be watchful of the amount of food consumed in order to control one's weight.

calumny /'kæləmni/ *n., pl.* **-nies**. slander. – **calumniate**, *v.*

calve /kav/ *v.i.,* **calved**, **calving**. to give birth to a calf.

calves /kavz/ *n.* plural of **calf**.

calyx /'keɪlɪks, 'kæl-/ *n., pl.* **calyces** /'kæləsiz, 'keɪ-/ **calyxes**. the outermost parts of a flower, usually green.

CAM /kæm/ computer-aided manufacturing.

camaraderie /kæmə'radəri/ *n.* comradeship; close friendship.

cambist /'kæmbəst/ *n.* **1.** a dealer in the foreign exchange market. **2.** a manual giving the moneys, weights, and measures of different countries with their equivalents.

came /keɪm/ *v.* past tense of **come**.

camel /'kæməl/ *n.* **1.** a large humped ruminant quadruped. **2.** a brown colour somewhat lighter than fawn.

cameo /'kæmioʊ/ *n., pl.* **-os**. an engraving in relief upon a gem, stone, etc.

camera /'kæmrə, 'kæmərə/ *n., pl.* **-eras** *for def. 1* **-erae** /-əri/. *for def. 2 –* **1.** a photographic apparatus in which sensitive plates or film are exposed, the image being formed by means of a lens. **2. in camera, a.** *Law* in the privacy of a judge's chambers, with the public excluded. **b.** in private; in secret.

camisole /'kæməsoʊl/ *n.* an ornamental underbodice, worn under a thin outer bodice.

camomile /'kæməmaɪl/ *n.* → **chamomile**.

camouflage /'kæməflaʒ, -fladʒ/ *n.* the means by which any object or creature renders itself indistinguishable from its background.

camp[1] /kæmp/ *n.* **1.** a group of tents, caravans, or other temporary shelters in one place. **2.** a group of people favouring the same ideals, doctrines, etc. *– v.i.* **3.** to establish or pitch a camp. **4.** to live temporarily in a tent (often fol. by *out*).

camp[2] /kæmp/ *adj.* homosexual.

campaign /kæm'peɪn/ *n.* any course of aggressive activities for some special purpose.

camphor /'kæmfə/ *n.* **1.** a whitish, translucent, crystalline substance used in medicine, etc. **2.** any of various similar substances, for household use as an insect deterrent.

campus /'kæmpəs/ *n.* the grounds of a university or other such institute.

can[1] /kæn/, *weak forms* /kən, kn/ *or* (*if followed by k or g*) /kŋ/ *v., present singular1* **can**; *2* **can**; *3* **can**; *past,* **could**. *– v. (aux)* **1.** to know how to; be able to; have the ability, power, right, qualifications, or means to. **2.** *Colloquial* may; have permission.

can[2] /kæn/ *n., v.,* **canned**, **canning**. *– n.* **1.** a container made of sheet iron coated with tin or other metal. **2.** *Colloquial* the blame for something. *– v.t.* **3.** to put in a container, usually sealed for preservation.

canal /kə'næl/ *n.* an artificial waterway.

canary /kə'nɛəri/ *n., pl.* **-ries**. a cage bird, usually yellow.

canasta /kə'næstə/ *n.* a card game.

cancel /'kænsəl/ *v.t.,* **-celled**, **-celling**. *– v.t.* **1.** to decide not to proceed with (an appointment, a meeting, an event, etc.). **2.** to cross out (writing, etc.) by drawing a line or lines over. **3.** to make void.

cancer /'kænsə/ *n. Pathology* a malignant and invasive growth or tumour. – **cancerous**, *adj.*

candela /kæn'dilə, -'deɪlə/ *n.* the SI base unit of luminous intensity. *Symbol*: cd

candelabrum /kændə'labrəm/ *n., pl.* **-bra**

/-brə/. an ornamental branched candlestick.

candid /'kændəd/ *adj.* frank; outspoken; open and sincere.

candidate /'kændədeɪt, -dət/ *n.* someone who seeks an office, an honour, etc.

candle /'kændl/ *n.* a long, usually slender, piece of tallow, wax, etc., with an embedded wick, burnt to give light.

candour = candor /'kændə/ *n.* frankness; sincerity; honesty.

candy /'kændi/ *n., pl.* **-dies**, *v.,* **-died**, **-dying**. – *n.* **1.** a sweet made of sugar crystallised by boiling. – *v.t.* **2.** to cook in heavy syrup until transparent, as fruit, fruit peel, or ginger.

cane /keɪn/ *n.* **1.** a long, hollow or pithy, jointed woody stem, as that of bamboo, rattan, sugar cane, certain palms, etc. **2.** the stem of a bamboo, etc., used as a rod for punishing school children. **3.** a walking stick.

canine /'keɪnaɪn/ *adj.* relating to or characteristic of dogs.

canister /'kænəstə/ *n.* a small box, usually of metal, for holding tea, coffee, etc.

canker /'kæŋkə/ *n.* **1.** *Pathology* a gangrenous or ulcerous sore, especially in the mouth. **2.** anything that corrodes, corrupts, destroys, or irritates.

cannabis /'kænəbəs/ *n.* hashish.

cannibal /'kænəbəl/ *n.* any animal that eats its own kind.

cannon /'kænən/ *n., pl.* **-nons**, (*esp. collectively*) **-non**. **1.** a large ancient gun for firing heavy projectiles, mounted on a carriage. **2.** any strike and rebound, as a ball striking a wall and glancing off.

cannot /'kænɒt, kæ'nɒt/ *v.* a form of **can not**.

canny /'kæni/ *adj.,* **-nier**, **-niest**. careful; cautious; wary.

canoe /kə'nu/ *n.* any light and narrow boat that is propelled by paddles.

canon[1] /'kænən/ *n.* **1.** an ecclesiastical rule or law. **2.** the body of ecclesiastical law. **3.** a fundamental principle. – **canonical**, *adj.*

canon[2] /'kænən/ *n.* a member of the chapter of a cathedral or collegiate church.

canoodle /kə'nudl/ *v.i.,* **-dled**, **-dling**. *Colloquial* to indulge in fondling and petting.

canopy /'kænəpi/ *n., pl.* **-pies**. a covering suspended or supported over a throne, bed, etc.

cant[1] /kænt/ *n.* **1.** insincere statements. **2.** the words, phrases, etc., peculiar to a particular class, party, profession, etc.

cant[2] /kænt/ *n.* **1.** a salient angle. **2.** a sudden movement that tilts or overturns a thing. **3.** an oblique or slanting face of anything.

can't /kant/ *v.* contraction of **cannot**.

cantaloupe /'kæntəlup/ *n.* → **rockmelon**. Also, **cantaloup**.

cantankerous /kæn'tæŋkərəs/ *adj.* ill-natured; quarrelsome.

canteen /kæn'tin/ *n.* **1.** a restaurant or cafeteria attached to a factory, office, etc. **2.** a box containing a set of plate or cutlery. **3.** a small container used by soldiers and others for carrying water or other liquids.

canter /'kæntə/ *n.* **1.** an easy gallop. – *v.i.* **2.** to go or ride at a canter.

canton /'kæntɒn, kæn'tɒn/ *n.* a small territorial district, especially in Switzerland.

canvas /'kænvəs/ *n.* **1.** a closely woven, heavy cloth used for tents, sails, etc. **2.** a piece of this material on which an oil painting is made. **3.** a tent, or tents collectively. **4.** sails collectively.

canvass /'kænvəs/ *v.t.* to solicit votes, subscriptions, opinions, etc., from (a district, group of people, etc.).

canyon /'kænjən/ *n.* a deep valley with steep sides.

cap /kæp/ *n., v.,* **capped**, **capping**. – *n.* **1.** a covering for the head, especially one fitting closely and made of softer material than a hat, and having little or no brim, but often having a peak. **2.** a close-fitting waterproof headdress worn when swimming, etc. **3.** the detachable protective top of a fountain pen, jar, etc. **4.** a noisemaking device for toy pistols. – *v.t.* **5.** to provide or cover with or as with a cap. **6.** to surpass.

capable /'keɪpəbəl/ *adj.* **1.** having much intelligence or ability; competent; efficient; able. **2. capable of,** qualified or fitted for. – **capability**, *n.*

capacious /kə'peɪʃəs/ *adj.* capable of holding much.

capacity /kə'pæsəti/ *n., pl.* **-ties**. **1.** cubic contents; volume. **2.** power, ability, or possibility of doing something. **3.** position; function; relation.

cape[1] /keɪp/ *n.* a sleeveless garment fastened round the neck and falling loosely over the shoulders.

cape[2] /keɪp/ *n.* a piece of land jutting into the sea or some other body of water.

caper[1] /'keɪpə/ *v.i.* **1.** to leap or skip about in a sprightly manner. – *n.* **2.** a prank; capricious action.

caper[2] /'keɪpə/ *n.* the pickled flower bud of a shrub, used in cookery.

capillary /kə'pɪləri/ *adj., n., pl.* **-laries**. – *adj.* **1.** relating to or occurring in or as in a tube of fine bore. – *n.* **2.** *Anatomy* one of the minute blood vessels between the terminations of the arteries and the beginnings of the veins.

capital /'kæpətl/ *n.* **1.** the city or town which is the official seat of government in a country, state, etc. **2.** any form of wealth employed or capable of being employed in the production of more wealth. **3.** *Commerce* the ownership interest in a business. **4.** any source of profit, advantage, power, etc. – *adj.* **5.** relating to capital. **6.** principal; highly important. **7.** (of letters) of the large size. **8.** involving the loss of the head or life, usually as punishment; punishable by death.

capital account *n.* **1.** a business account showing the owner's or shareholder's interest in the assets. **2.** (*pl.*) *Accounting* accounts showing the net worth, as in a business enterprise, as assets minus liabilities.

capital appreciation *n.* an increase in the value of an asset over a period of time.

capital distribution *n.* the issue of bonus shares to shareholders in a company.

capital expenditure *n.* an addition to the value of a fixed asset, as by the purchase of a new building.

capital gains *pl. n.* profits from the sale of capital assets.

capital gains tax *n.* a tax paid on the increased value of capital invested.

capital goods *pl. n.* goods used in the production of other goods.

capital-intensive /ˈkæpətl-ɪnˌtɛnsɪv/ *adj.* of or relating to an industry which, while requiring relatively little labour, requires a high capital investment in plant, etc. (opposed to *labour-intensive*).

capitalise = capitalize /ˈkæpətəlaɪz/ *v.t.*, **-lised**, **-lising**. **1.** to write or print in capital letters, or with an initial capital. **2.** to authorise a certain amount of stocks and bonds in the corporate charter. **3.** to convert (floating debt) into stock or shares. **4.** *Accounting* to set up (expenditures) as business assets in the books of account instead of treating as expense. **5.** to supply with capital. **6.** to estimate the value of (a stock or an enterprise). **7.** to take advantage of; turn to one's advantage (often fol. by *on*). – **capitalisation**, *n.*

capitalism /ˈkæpətəlɪzəm/ *n.* **1.** a system under which the means of production, distribution, and exchange are in large measure privately owned and directed. **2.** the concentration of capital in the hands of a few, or the resulting power or influence. **3.** a system favouring such concentration of wealth.

capitalist /ˈkæpətələst/ *n.* **1.** someone who has capital, especially extensive capital, in business enterprises. – *adj.* **2.** founded on or believing in capitalism.

capital levy *n.* a tax based on total assets.

capital stock *n.* **1.** the total shares issued by a company. **2.** the book value of all the shares of a company, including unissued shares and those not completely paid in.

capital sum *n.* the sum stated to be payable on the happening of some event against which insurance has been effected.

capital surplus *n.* the surplus of a business, exclusive of its earned surplus.

capitation /kæpəˈteɪʃən/ *n.* **1.** a numbering or assessing by the head. **2.** a poll tax. **3.** a fee or payment of a uniform amount for each person.

capitulate /kəˈpɪtʃəleɪt/ *v.i.*, **-lated**, **-lating**. to surrender unconditionally or on stipulated terms. – **capitulation**, *n.*

caprice /kəˈpris/ *n.* a whim. – **capricious**, *adj.*

capsicum /ˈkæpsəkəm/ *n.* the common pepper of the garden, with mild to hot, pungent seeds enclosed in a bell-shaped fruit.

capsize /kæpˈsaɪz/ *v.t.*, *v.i.*, **-sized**, **-sizing**. to overturn.

capsule /ˈkæpʃul, -ʃəl/ *n.* **1.** a gelatinous case enclosing a dose of medicine; the dose itself. **2.** the compartment of a spacecraft containing the crew or instruments.

captain /ˈkæptn/ *n.* someone who is in authority over others; a chief; leader.

caption /ˈkæpʃən/ *n.* **1.** *Printing* an inscription for a picture or illustration. **2.** *Film* the title of a scene, the text of a speech, etc., shown on the screen.

captivate /ˈkæptəveɪt/ *v.t.*, **-vated**, **-vating**. to enthral by beauty or excellence.

captive /ˈkæptɪv/ *n.* **1.** a prisoner. – *adj.* **2.** made or held prisoner, especially in war. – **captivity**, *n.*

captor /ˈkæptə/ *n.* a person who captures.

capture /ˈkæptʃə/ *v.*, **-tured**, **-turing**, *n.* – *v.t.* **1.** to take prisoner; seize. – *n.* **2.** the act of capturing. **3.** the thing or person captured.

car /ka/ *n.* **1.** a motor car. **2.** a vehicle of various kinds running on rails, as a restaurant car, tramcar, etc.

carafe /kəˈraf, -ˈræf, ˈkærəf/ *n.* a glass bottle for water, wine, etc.

caramel /ˈkærəməl/ *n.* burnt sugar, used for colouring and flavouring food, etc.

carat /ˈkærət/ *n.* **1.** Also, **metric carat**. a unit of weight in gem stones, 0.2×10^{-3} kg. *Abbrev.*: CM **2.** a twenty-fourth part (used in expressing the fineness of gold, pure gold being 24 carats fine).

caravan /ˈkærəvæn/ *n.* **1.** a vehicle in which people may live, usually having two wheels and designed to be drawn by a motor car. **2.** a group of merchants or others travelling together, especially over deserts, etc.

caraway /ˈkærəweɪ/ *n.* a herb bearing aromatic seedlike fruit used in cookery and medicine.

carbide /ˈkabaɪd/ *n.* a compound of carbon with a more electropositive element or radical.

carbine /ˈkabaɪn, ˈkabən/ *n.* (formerly) a short rifle for cavalry use.

carbo- a word element meaning 'carbon'. Also, **carb-**.

carbohydrate /kabəˈhaɪdreɪt/ *n.* any of a class of organic compounds including sugars, starch, and cellulose, which are important food for animals.

carbon /ˈkabən/ *n.* *Chemistry* a widely distributed element which forms organic compounds in combination with hydrogen, oxygen, etc., and which occurs in a pure state as charcoal. *Symbol*: C

carbonate /ˈkabəneɪt, -nət/ *n.*, /ˈkabəneɪt/ *v.*, **-nated**, **-nating** – *v.t.* to charge or impregnate with carbon dioxide. – **carbonated**, *adj.* – **carbonation**, *n.*

carbon dioxide *n.* a colourless, odourless, incombustible gas, CO_2, used extensively in industry as dry ice, and in fizzy drinks, fire extinguishers, etc.

carbon monoxide *n.* a colourless, odourless, poisonous gas, CO.

carbon paper *n.* paper faced with a preparation of carbon or other material, used between two sheets of plain paper in order to reproduce upon the lower sheet that which is written or typed on the upper.

carbuncle /ˈkabʌŋkəl/ *n.* a painful circumscribed inflammation of the subcutaneous tissue.

carburettor /ˈkabjərɛtə, kabjəˈrɛtə/ *n.* a device in an internal-combustion engine for mixing a volatile fuel with the correct proportion of air in order to form an explosive gas. Also, **carburetter**.

carcass /ˈkakəs/ *n.* **1.** the dead body of an animal. **2.** (*usually humorous or derogatory*) a person's body.

carcinogen /ka'sɪnədʒən/ *n.* any substance which tends to produce a cancer in a body. – **carcinogenic**, *adj.*

card[1] /kad/ *n.* **1.** a piece of stiff paper or thin pasteboard, usually rectangular, for various uses. **2.** one of a set of small pieces of cardboard with spots or figures, used in playing various games. **3.** *Colloquial* a likeable, amusing, or facetious person.

card[2] /kad/ *n.* an implement used in disentangling and combing out fibres of wool, flax, etc., preparatory to spinning.

cardboard /'kadbɔd/ *n.* thin, stiff pasteboard.

cardi- variant of **cardio-** before vowels.

cardiac /'kadiæk/ *adj.* relating to the heart.

cardigan /'kadɪgən/ *n.* a knitted jacket.

cardinal /'kadənəl/ *adj.* **1.** of prime importance; chief; principal; fundamental. – *n.* **2.** one of the members of the Sacred College of the Roman Catholic Church, ranking next to the pope.

cardinal number *n. Mathematics* a number such as *one*, *two*, *three*, etc., which indicates how many things are in a given set, and not the order in which those things occur (the latter is indicated by the ordinal numbers, *first*, *second*, *third*, etc.).

cardio- a word element meaning 'heart'. Also, **cardi-**.

card reader /'kad ridə/ *n. Computers* a device which reads data on a card by sensing or analysing the information coded on it and converting it into electronic messages.

care /kɛə/ *n.*, *v.*, **cared**, **caring**. – *n.* **1.** worry; anxiety; concern. **2.** serious attention; heed; caution. **3.** protection; charge. **4. care of**, Also, **c/o**. at the address of. – *v.i.* **5.** to be troubled; to be affected emotionally. **6.** to be concerned or solicitous; have thought or regard. **7.** to have a fondness or affection (fol. by *for*). **8.** to look after; make provision (fol. by *for*).

careen /kə'rin/ *v.i.* to lean, sway, or tip to one side, as a ship.

career /kə'rɪə/ *n.* **1.** general course of action or progress of a person through life. **2.** an occupation, profession, etc., followed as one's lifework. **3.** speed; full speed.

caress /kə'rɛs/ *n.* **1.** an act or gesture expressing affection. – *v.t.* **2.** to touch or pat gently to show affection.

caret /'kærət/ *n.* **1.** a mark (ʌ) made in written or printed matter to show the place where something is to be inserted. **2.** *Computers* the symbol ^.

caretaker /'kɛəteɪkə/ *n.* **1.** a person who takes care of a thing or place, especially one whose job is to maintain and protect a building or group of buildings. – *adj.* **2.** holding office temporarily until a new appointment, election, etc., can be made, as an administration.

cargo /'kagoʊ/ *n.*, *pl.* **-goes**. **1.** the lading or freight of a ship. **2.** load.

caricature /'kærəkətʃʊə/ *n.* a picture, description, etc., ludicrously exaggerating the peculiarities or defects of persons or things.

caries /'kɛəriz/ *n.* decay, as of bone or teeth, or of plant tissue.

carillon /kə'rɪljən/ *n.* a set of stationary bells hung in a tower and sounded by manual or pedal action, or by machinery.

cark /kak/ *v.i. Colloquial* to collapse; die.

carmine /'kamaɪn/ *n.* crimson.

carnage /'kanɪdʒ/ *n.* the slaughter of a great number, as in battle.

carnal /'kanəl/ *adj.* **1.** relating to the flesh or the body, its passions and appetites; sensual. **2.** sexual.

carnal knowledge *n.* sexual intercourse especially with one under the age of consent.

carnation /ka'neɪʃən/ *n.* any of numerous cultivated plants with fragrant flowers of various colours.

carnival /'kanəvəl/ *n.* **1.** a festive procession. **2.** a fair or amusement show, especially one erected temporarily. **3.** a series of sporting events as a racing carnival, etc.

carnivore /'kanəvɔ/ *n. Zoology* a flesh-eating animal or plant. – **carnivorous**, *adj.*

carob /'kærəb/ *n.* the fruit of a tree used as animal fodder, and in cookery as a substitute for chocolate.

carol /'kærəl/ *n.* a song, especially of joy.

carotid /kə'rɒtəd/ *n.* either of the two great arteries, one on each side of the neck, which carry blood to the head.

carouse /kə'raʊz/ *n.*, *v.*, **-roused**, **-rousing**. – *n.* **1.** a noisy or drunken feast; jovial revelry. – *v.i.* **2.** to engage in a carouse.

carousel /kærə'sɛl/ *n.* → **merry-go-round**.

carp[1] /kap/ *v.i.* to find fault.

carp[2] /kap/ *n.*, *pl.* **carp**. a large, coarse, freshwater food fish.

-carp a noun termination meaning 'fruit', used in botanical terms.

carpenter /'kapəntə/ *n.* someone who erects and fixes the wooden parts, etc., in the building of houses and other structures. – **carpentry**, *n.*

carpet /'kapət/ *n.* a heavy fabric, commonly of wool, for covering floors.

-carpic a word element related to **-carp**.

carpo- a word element meaning 'fruit'.

-carpous a combining form related to **-carp**.

carrel /kə'rɛl, 'kærəl/ *n.* (in a library) a small area or cubicle used by students and others for individual study; a stall.

carriage /'kærɪdʒ/ *n.* **1.** a wheeled vehicle for conveying persons. **2.** manner of carrying the head and body; bearing. **3.** a part of a machine, etc., designed for carrying something.

carriage return *n.* **1.** (on a typewriter) a key or lever which causes the carriage (def. 3) to return to the starting position so that the next character typed is positioned at the left margin and down a line. **2.** (on a computer) a key or character which performs a similar function.

carrier pigeon /'kæriə/ *n.* a pigeon trained to fly home from great distances and thus transport written message.

carrion /'kæriən/ *n.* dead and putrefying flesh.

carrot /'kærət/ *n.* a plant valued for its reddish edible root.

carry /'kæri/ *v.,* **-ried, -rying.** – *v.t.* **1.** to convey from one place to another. **2.** to bear the weight, burden, etc., of; sustain. **3.** to hold (the body, head, etc.) in a certain manner. **4.** to secure the election of (a candidate) or the adoption of (a motion or bill). **5.** to support or give validity to (a related claim, etc.). **6.** *Commerce* **a.** to keep on hand or in stock. **b.** to keep on one's account books, etc. – *v.i.* **7.** to be transmitted, propelled, or sustained. – *v.* **8. carry away, a.** to influence greatly or beyond reason. **9. carry forward, a.** *Bookkeeping* to transfer (an amount, etc.) to the next column, page, etc. **10. carry off, a.** to face consequences boldly. **11. carry on, a.** to manage; conduct. **b.** to behave in an excited, foolish, or improper manner; flirt. **12. carry out,** to accomplish or complete (a plan, scheme, etc.). **13. carry over, a.** to postpone; hold off until later. **b.** *Stock Exchange* to defer completion of (a contract) so that it falls under a different account.

cart /kat/ *n.* a heavy horse-drawn vehicle.

carte blanche /kat 'blɒntʃ/ *n., pl.* **cartes blanches** /kats 'blɒntʃ/. unconditional authority; full power.

cartel /ka'tɛl/ *n.* an international syndicate formed to regulate prices and output in some field of business.

cartilage /'katəlɪdʒ, 'katlɪdʒ/ *n. Anatomy, Zoology* a firm, elastic, flexible substance of a translucent whitish or yellowish colour, consisting of a connective tissue; gristle.

cartography /ka'tɒgrəfi/ *n.* the production of maps.

carton /'katən/ *n.* a cardboard box, especially one in which food is packaged and sold.

cartoon /ka'tun/ *n.* **1.** a sketch or drawing as in a newspaper or periodical, symbolising or caricaturing some subject or person of current interest. **2.** an animated cartoon.

cartridge /'katrɪdʒ/ *n.* **1.** Also, **cartridge case**. a cylindrical case for holding a complete charge of powder, and often also the bullet or the shot, for a rifle, etc. **2.** anything resembling a cartridge, as the disposable container of ink for some types of fountain pen. **3.** (in a tape recorder) a plastic container enclosing recording tape usually in the form of an endless loop.

carve /kav/ *v.t.,* **carved, carving. 1.** to fashion by cutting. **2.** to cut into slices or pieces, as meat.

cascade /kæs'keɪd/ *n., v.,* **-caded, -cading.** – *n.* **1.** a waterfall over steep rocks. – *v.i.* **2.** to fall in or like a cascade.

case[1] /keɪs/ *n.* **1.** an instance of the occurrence, existence, etc., of something. **2.** the actual state of things. **3.** a statement of facts, reasons, etc. **4.** *Law* a suit or action at law. **5.** *Grammar* a category in the inflection of nouns, pronouns, and adjectives, denoting the syntactic relation of these words to other words in the sentence, indicated by the form or the position of the words. **6. in case,** if; if it should happen that.

case[2] /keɪs/ *n., v.,* **cased, casing.** – *n.* **1.** a receptacle. **2.** a sheath or outer covering. – *v.t.* **3.** to put or enclose in a case. **4.** *Colloquial* to examine or survey (a house, bank, etc.) in planning a crime.

case law *n.* law established by judicial decisions in particular cases, instead of by legislation.

casement /'keɪsmənt/ *n.* a window sash opening on hinges.

cash /kæʃ/ *n.* **1.** money, especially money on hand, as opposed to a money equivalent (as a cheque). – *v.t.* **2.** to give or obtain cash for (a cheque, etc.). **3. cash up,** (of shopkeepers, etc.) to add up the takings.

cash account *n.* **1.** current account. **2.** *Bookkeeping* a record kept of cash transactions.

cashbook /'kæʃbʊk/ *n.* a book in which to record money received and paid out.

cash crop *n.* a crop which, when harvested, offers a quick return of money.

cash economy *n.* the part of a country's economy in which payment for goods and services is made in cash without receipts, often as a means of tax evasion.

cashew /'kæʃu/ *n.* (a tropical tree yielding) a small, edible kidney-shaped nut (**cashew nut**).

cash flow *n.* (of a company) the amount of cash generated by a company in a given period. It equals the net profit after tax, less dividends paid out, plus depreciation in that period.

cashier /kæ'ʃɪə/ *n.* someone who has charge of cash or money, especially someone who superintends monetary transactions.

cash management trust *n.* a trust that pools the relatively small investments of individuals and invests the funds it receives in short-dated securities, such as treasury notes and bank bills, which have traditionally required large minimum investments.

cashmere /'kæʃmɪə/ *n.* the fine downy wool at the roots of the hair of Kashmir goats of India.

cash register /'kæʃ rɛdʒəstə/ *n.* a till with a mechanism for indicating amounts of sales, etc.

casino /kə'sinoʊ/ *n., pl.* **-nos.** a building or large room used for gambling, etc.

cask /kask/ *n.* **1.** a barrel-like container for holding liquids, etc. **2.** a lightweight container, usually cardboard with a plastic lining and small tap, used for holding and serving wine for domestic use.

casket /'kaskət/ *n.* **1.** a small chest or box, as for jewels. **2.** a coffin.

cassava /kə'savə/ *n.* any of several tropical plants cultivated for their tuberous roots. Also, **manoic**.

casserole /'kæsəroʊl/ *n.* **1.** a baking dish of glass, pottery, etc., usually with a cover. **2.** any food, usually a mixture, baked in such a dish.

cassette /kə'sɛt, kæ'sɛt/ *n.* **1.** (in a tape recorder) a plastic container enclosing both a recording tape and two hubs about which it winds. **2.** (in a video recorder, computer, etc.) a device of similar principle with wider tape.

cassia /'kæsiə/ *n.* an ornamental tropical tree with clusters of bright yellow flowers and long pods whose pulp is a mild laxative.

cassock /'kæsək/ *n.* a long, close-fitting garment worn by ecclesiastics.

cassowary /'kæsəwəri/ *n., pl.* **-ries**. a large, three-toed, flightless, bird of Australasian regions, superficially resembling the ostrich.

cast /kast/ *v.,* **cast**, **casting**, *n.* – *v.t.* **1.** to throw; fling; hurl (often fol. by *away, off, out*, etc.) **2.** to direct (the eye, a glance, etc.) **3.** to shed or drop (hair, fruit, etc.), especially prematurely. **4.** to deposit (a vote, etc.) **5.** to compute or calculate astrologically, as a horoscope; forecast. **6.** *Nautical* to let go or let loose, as a vessel from a mooring (fol. by *loose, off*, etc.). – *v.i.* **7.** to throw a fishing line or the like (often fol. by *out*). **8.** to consider; plan or scheme (often fol. by *about*). **9. cast off, a.** to discard or reject. **b.** *Knitting* to make the final row of stitches. **10. cast on,** *Knitting* to make the initial row of stitches. – *n.* **11.** the act of casting or throwing. **12.** the form in which something is made or written; arrangement. **13.** *Theatre* the actors to whom the parts in a play are assigned. **14.** something shaped in a mould while in a fluid or plastic state; a casting. **15.** any impression or mould made from an object. **16.** *Medicine* rigid surgical dressing usually made of plaster-of-Paris bandage. **17.** a permanent twist or turn, especially a squint. **18.** a conjecture; forecast.

castanet /kæstə'nɛt/ *n.* a pair or one of a pair of shells held in the palm of the hand and struck together as an accompaniment to music and dancing.

castaway /'kastəweɪ/ *n.* **1.** a ship-wrecked person. **2.** an outcast.

caste /kast/ *n.* **1.** *Sociology* a social group. **2.** one of the artificial hereditary divisions or social classes into which the Hindus are rigidly separated.

castigate /'kæstəgeɪt/ *v.t.,* **-gated**, **-gating**. to punish in order to correct.

casting vote /kastɪŋ/ *n.* the deciding vote of the presiding officer when votes are equally divided.

cast iron *n.* an alloy of iron, carbon, and other elements.

castle /'kasəl, 'kæsəl/ *n.* a fortified residence.

castor = caster /'kastə/ *n.* a small wheel on a swivel, set under a piece of furniture, etc.

castor oil *n.* a viscid oil used as a cathartic, lubricant, etc.

castrate /'kæstreɪt, 'kas-/ *v.t.,* **-trated**, **-trating**. to deprive of the testicles; emasculate.

casual /'kæʒjuəl/ *adj.* **1.** happening by chance. **2.** unpremeditated; offhand. **3.** careless; negligent; unconcerned. **4.** irregular; occasional. **5.** informal. **6.** employed only irregularly.

casualty /'kæʒjuəlti/ *n., pl.* **-ties**. **1.** an unfortunate accident, especially one involving bodily injury or death. **2.** *Military* a soldier who is missing in action, or who has been killed, wounded, or captured. **3.** someone who is injured or killed in an accident. **4.** Also, **casualty ward**. the section of a hospital to which accident or emergency cases are taken.

casuarina /kæʒjə'rinə/ *n.* a group of trees and shrubs characterised by jointed stems with leaves reduced to whorls of teeth at the joints.

cat /kæt/ *n.* any of the carnivorous feline mammals, as the domesticated cat, or the lion, tiger, etc.

cata- a prefix meaning 'down', 'against', 'back'.

cataclysm /'kætəklɪzəm/ *n.* any violent upheaval. – **cataclysmic**, *adj.*

catacomb /'kætəkoum, -kum/ *n.* a series of underground tunnels and caves, especially for burial.

catalogue /'kætəlɒg/ *n., v.,* **-logued**, **-loguing**. – *n.* **1.** a list, usually in alphabetical order, with brief notes on the names, articles, etc., listed. – *v.t.* **2.** to enter in a catalogue.

catalyst /'kætələst/ *n.* **1.** *Chemistry* a substance which causes or accelerates a chemical change without being itself permanently affected by the reaction. **2.** the manipulating agent of any event, unaffected by the completion of the event or by its consequences.

catamaran /'kætəmərən/ *n.* *Nautical* any craft with twin parallel hulls.

catapult /'kætəpʌlt/ *n.* a Y-shaped stick with an elastic strip between the prongs for propelling stones, etc.

cataract /'kætərækt/ *n.* **1.** a waterfall, especially one of considerable size. **2.** an abnormality of the eye, characterised by opacity of the lens.

catarrh /kə'ta/ *n.* inflammation of a mucous membrane, especially of the respiratory tract, accompanied by excessive secretions.

catastrophe /kə'tæstrəfi/ *n.* **1.** a sudden and widespread disaster. **2.** a final event or conclusion, usually an unfortunate one. – **catastrophic**, *adj.*

catch /kætʃ/ *v.,* **caught**, **catching**, *n.* – *v.t.* **1.** to capture, especially after pursuit; take captive. **2.** to ensnare, entrap, or deceive. **3.** to be in time to reach (a train, boat, etc.). **4.** to come upon suddenly; surprise or detect, as in some action. **5.** to strike; hit. **6.** to intercept and seize (a ball, etc.). **7.** to get, receive, incur, or contract (often used figuratively). – *v.i.* **8.** to become fastened or entangled. **9.** to take hold. **10.** to become lit, take fire, ignite. **11.** to spread or be communicated, as a disease. – *n.* **12.** the act of catching. **13.** anything that catches, especially a device for checking motion. **14.** that which is caught, as a quantity of fish. **15.** anything worth getting.

catchcry /'kætʃkraɪ/ *n.* an ear-catching expression or group of words, voicing a popular sentiment.

catchment area *n.* *Geography* a drainage area, especially of a reservoir or river. Also, **catchment basin**.

catchphrase /'kætʃfreɪz/ *n.* a phrase caught up and repeated because it is fashionable.

catch 22 /ˌkætʃ twɛnti-'tu/ *n.* a rule or condition which prevents the completion of a sequence of operations and which may establish a futile, self-perpetuating cycle.

catch-up /'kætʃ-ʌp/ *adj.* of or relating to a price rise, award increase, etc., which is an attempt to compensate for related increases elsewhere in the economy.

catechism /'kætəkɪzəm/ *n.* *Ecclesiastical* an

elementary book containing a summary of the principles of the Christian religion in the form of questions and answers.

categorical /kætə'gɒrɪkəl/ *adj.* not involving a condition, qualification, etc.

category /'kætəgəri, -təgri/ *n., pl.* **-ries**. **1.** a classificatory division in any field of knowledge. **2.** any general or comprehensive division; a class.

cater /'keɪtə/ *v.i.* **1.** to provide food and service, means of amusement, or the like at functions (fol. by *for*). **2.** to go out of one's way to placate or provide for (fol. by *to*).

caterpillar /'kætəpɪlə/ *n.* **1.** the wormlike larva of a butterfly or a moth. **2.** a tractor having the driving wheels moving inside endless tracks on either side.

caterwaul /'kætəwɔl/ *v.i.* to cry as cats on heat.

cath- variant of **cata-** before an aspirate, as in *cathode*.

catharsis /kə'θasəs/ *n.* **1.** *Psychology* an effective discharge with symptomatic relief. **2.** *Medicine* a purging. – **cathartic**, *adj.*

cathedral /kə'θidrəl/ *n.* the principal church of a diocese.

catheter /'kæθətə/ *n. Medicine* a flexible or rigid hollow tube employed to drain fluids from body cavities or to distend body passages.

cathode /'kæθoʊd/ *n.* the negative pole of a battery or other source of current (opposed to *anode*). Also, **kathode**.

catholic /'kæθlɪk, -əlɪk/ *adj.* universal in extent.

cation /'kætaɪən/ *n. Physical Chemistry* a positively charged ion.

cattle /'kætl/ *n.* ruminants of the bovine kind, of any age, breed, or sex.

catwalk /'kætwɔk/ *n.* **1.** any narrow walking space. **2.** a long narrow platform on which fashion models parade clothes.

caucus /'kɔkəs/ *n.* **1.** the parliamentary members of a political party or faction of a political party. **2.** a private meeting of the parliamentary members of a political party or faction to discuss policy or tactics.

caught /kɔt/ *v.* past tense and past participle of **catch**.

caul /kɔl/ *n.* a part of the amnion sometimes covering the head of a child at birth.

cauldron /'kɔldrən/ *n.* a large kettle or boiler.

cauliflower /'kɒliflaʊə/ *n.* a cultivated plant with a compact, fleshy head, which is used as a vegetable.

caulk /kɔk/ *v.t.* to fill or close (a seam, joint, etc.), as in a boat.

causal /'kɔzəl/ *adj.* of, constituting, or implying a cause.

causality /kɔ'zæləti/ *n., pl.* **-ties**. **1.** the relation of cause and effect. **2.** causal quality or agency.

causation /kɔ'zeɪʃən/ *n.* **1.** the action of causing or producing. **2.** the relation of cause to effect. **3.** anything that produces an effect.

cause /kɔz/ *n., v.,* **caused**, **causing**. – *n.* **1.** that which produces an effect; the thing, person, etc., from which something results. **2.** the ground of any action or result; reason; motive. **3.** any subject of discussion or debate. **4.** that side of a question which a person or party supports; the aim, purpose, etc., of a group. – *v.t.* **5.** to be the cause of; bring about.

causeway /'kɔzweɪ/ *n.* a raised road or path, as across low or wet ground.

caustic /'kɒstɪk/ *adj.* **1.** capable of burning, corroding, or destroying living tissue. **2.** severely critical or sarcastic.

cauterise = cauterize /'kɔtəraɪz/ *v.t.,* **-rised**, **-rising**. to burn, especially for curative purposes.

caution /'kɔʃən/ *n.* **1.** prudence in regard to danger or evil; carefulness. **2.** a warning. – *v.t.* **3.** to give warning to. – **cautionary**, *adj.* – **cautious**, *adj.*

cavalcade /kævəl'keɪd/ *n.* any procession.

cavalier /kævə'lɪə/ *n.* **1.** a courtly gentleman. – *adj.* **2.** haughty, disdainful, or supercilious. **3.** offhand; casual. **4.** reckless.

cavalry /'kævəlri/ *n., pl.* **-ries**. *Military* part of an army, formerly mounted on horseback, and now equipped with armoured vehicles.

cave /keɪv/ *n., v.,* **caved**, **caving**. – *n.* **1.** a hollow in the earth, especially one opening more or less horizontally into a hill, mountain, etc. – *v.i.* **2.** to fall or sink, as ground (fol. by *in*).

caveat /'keɪviət/ *n.* **1.** *Law* a notice to suspend a proceeding until the notifier is given a hearing. **2.** any warning or caution.

caveat emptor /keɪviət 'ɛmptɔ/ let the buyer beware (since he or she buys without recourse).

cavern /'kævən/ *n.* a cave, especially a large, deep cave. – **cavernous**, *adj.*

caviar /'kævia, kævi'a/ *n.* the roe of sturgeon or other large fish, pressed and salted, considered a great delicacy.

cavil /'kævəl/ *v.i.,* **-illed**, **-illing**. to raise irritating and trivial objections.

cavity /'kævəti/ *n., pl.* **-ties**. any hollow place.

cavort /kə'vɔt/ *v.i. Colloquial* to prance or caper about.

CBD /si bi 'di/ *n.* the central business district of a city.

CB radio /si bi 'reɪdioʊ/ *n.* citizen band radio. Also, **CB**.

CD /si 'di/ *n.* → **compact disc**.

CD-ROM /si di 'rɒm/ *n.* a laser disc designed for storing digitised text and graphics which can be displayed on a visual display unit.

cease /sis/ *v.,* **ceased**, **ceasing**. – *v.i.* **1.** to stop. – *v.t.* **2.** to put a stop or end to. – **ceaseless**, *adj.*

cease-fire /sis-'faɪə/ *n.* a cessation of active hostilities; truce.

cedar /'sidə/ *n.* any of several coniferous trees.

cede /sid/ *v.t.,* **ceded**, **ceding**. to yield or formally resign and surrender to another.

ceiling /'silɪŋ/ *n.* **1.** the overhead interior lining of a room. **2.** top limit.

-cele[1] a word element meaning 'tumour'.

-cele[2] variant of **-coele**.

celebrant /'sɛləbrənt/ *n.* **1.** the priest who

officiates at the performance of a religious rite. **2.** a participant in any celebration.

celebrate /'sɛləbreɪt/ *v.*, **-brated**, **-brating**. – *v.t.* **1.** to observe (a day) or commemorate (an event) with ceremonies or festivities. **2.** to make known publicly. **3.** to sound the praises of. – *v.i.* **4.** to observe a day or commemorate an event with ceremonies or festivities.

celebrated /'sɛləbreɪtəd/ *adj.* famous; renowned; well-known.

celebrity /sə'lɛbrəti/ *n., pl.* **-ties**. a famous or well-known person.

celerity /sə'lɛrəti/ *n.* swiftness; speed.

celery /'sɛləri/ *n.* a plant whose leafstalks are used raw for salad, and cooked as a vegetable.

celestial /sə'lɛstiəl/ *adj.* **1.** relating to the spiritual or invisible heaven; divine. **2.** relating to the sky or visible heaven.

celibacy /'sɛləbəsi/ *n., pl.* **-cies**. **1.** the unmarried state. **2.** (of priests, etc.) abstention by vow from marriage. **3.** abstention from sexual intercourse; chastity. – **celibate**, *n., adj.*

cell /sɛl/ *n.* **1.** a small room in a convent, prison, etc. **2.** a small group acting as a unit within a larger organisation. **3.** *Biology* the structural unit of plant and animal life. **4.** *Electricity* a device which generates electricity. **5.** *Physical Chemistry* a device for producing electrolysis. – **cellular**, *adj.*

cellar /'sɛlə/ *n.* an underground room or store; basement.

cello /'tʃɛlou/ *n., pl.* **-los**, **-li**. a four-stringed instrument of the violin family. Also, **'cello**, **violoncello**. – **cellist**, *n.*

cellophane /'sɛləfeɪn/ *n.* a transparent, paper-like product used to wrap sweets, tobacco, etc.

cellular telephone *n.* a type of telephone, usually portable or for use in a car, which sends and receives signals by a radio transmitter, each transmitter covering a specific area (**cell**) but linked to other such areas by a computer network. Also, **cellular phone**.

cellulite /'sɛljəlaɪt/ *n.* fatty deposits, resulting in a dimply appearance of the skin.

celluloid /'sɛljəlɔɪd/ *n.* **1.** *Chemistry* a type of plastic. **2.** films; the cinema.

cellulose /'sɛljəlous/ *n.* *Chemistry* the chief constituent of the cell walls of plants.

Celsius /'sɛlsiəs/ *adj.* denoting or relating to a scale of temperature on which the boiling point of water under a pressure of 101.325 kPa is approximately 100°C. *Symbol*: C

cement /sə'mɛnt/ *n.* any of various substances which are soft when first prepared but later become hard or stonelike.

cemetery /'sɛmətri/ *n., pl.* **-teries**. a burial ground.

-cene a word element meaning 'recent', 'new'.

ceno-[1] variant of **caino-**.

ceno-[2] variant of **coeno-**. Also (*before vowels*), **cen-**.

cenotaph /'sɛnətaf/ *n.* a municipal, civic or national memorial to those killed in war.

censor /'sɛnsə/ *n.* **1.** an official who examines books, plays, news reports, films, radio programs, etc., for the purpose of suppressing parts deemed objectionable on moral, political, military, or other grounds. – *v.t.* **2.** to examine and act upon as a censor does.

censorious /sɛn'sɔriəs/ *adj.* fault-finding; carping.

censure /'sɛnʃə/ *n., v.*, **-sured**, **-suring**. – *n.* **1.** an expression of disapproval. – *v.t.* **2.** to criticise adversely.

census /'sɛnsəs/ *n.* an official enumeration of inhabitants, with details as to age, sex, pursuits, etc.

cent /sɛnt/ *n.* **1.** the hundredth part of the dollar. **2.** a coin of this value.

cent- /sɛnt-/ → **centi-**.

centenary /sɛn'tinəri, -'tɛn-/ *adj., n., pl.* **-ries**. – *adj.* **1.** of or relating to a 100th anniversary. – *n.* **2.** a 100th anniversary. **3.** a period of 100 years; a century.

centennial /sɛn'tɛniəl/ *adj.* consisting of, or marking the completion of, 100 years.

centi- /'sɛnti-/ a prefix denoting 10^{-2} of a given unit, as in *centigram*. *Symbol*: c Also (*before vowels*), **cent-**.

Centigrade /'sɛntəgreɪd/ *n.* **1.** (*lower case*) a non-SI unit of plane angle, equal to 10^{-4} of a right angle. – *adj.* **2.** *Obsolete* → **Celsius**. *Symbol*: C

centigram /'sɛntəgræm/ *n.* a unit of mass equal to 0.01 gram. *Symbol*: cg

centimetre /'sɛntəmitə/ *n.* a unit of length equal to 0.01 metre. *Symbol*: cm

centipede /'sɛntəpid/ *n.* a small, segmented arthropod with a pair of legs attached to each segment.

centr- variant of **centro-** before vowels.

central /'sɛntrəl/ *adj.* **1.** of or forming the centre. **2.** in, at, or near the centre. **3.** principal; chief; dominant.

centralise = centralize /'sɛntrəlaɪz/ *v.*, **-lised**, **-lising**. – *v.t.* **1.** to draw to or towards a centre. **2.** to bring under one control, especially in government. – *v.i.* **3.** to come together at a centre.

central nervous system *n.* the brain and spinal cord considered together.

central processor unit *n.* → **CPU**. Also, **central processing unit**.

centre /'sɛntə/ *n., v.*, **-tred**, **-tring**. – *n.* **1.** *Geometry* the middle point. **2.** a point, pivot, axis, etc., round which anything rotates or revolves. **3.** a building or building complex which houses a number of related specified services: *shopping centre*; *sports centre*; *medical centre*. – *v.t.* **4.** to place in or on a centre.

centrefold /'sɛntəfould/ *n.* the folded pages in the centre of a magazine, designed to be lifted out and unfolded.

centre of gravity *n.* that point of a body (or system of bodies) from which it could be suspended or on which it could be supported and be in equilibrium in any position in a uniform gravitational field.

centri- variant of **centro-**, as in *centrifugal*.

centrifugal force /sɛn'trɪfəgəl/ *n.* the force exerted outwards by a body moving in a curved path; the reaction of centripetal force. Also, **centrifugal action**.

centripetal force /sɛn'trɪpətl/ *n.* a force

acting on a body, which is directed towards the centre of a circle or curve, which causes it to move in the circle or curve. Also, **centripetal action**.

centro- a word element meaning 'centre'. Also, **centr-**, **centri-**.

century /'sɛntʃəri/ *n., pl.* **-ries**. **1.** a period of one hundred years. **2.** any group or collection of 100.

cephalic /sə'fælɪk/ *adj.* of or relating to the head.

-cephalic a word element meaning 'head'.

cephalo- a word element denoting the 'head'.

cephalopod /'sɛfələpɒd/ *n.* a type of mollusc with tentacles attached to the head, as the octopus.

-cephalous a word element related to **cephalo-**.

-ceptor a word element meaning 'taker', 'receiver'.

cer- variant of **cero-**, used before vowels.

ceramic /sə'ræmɪk/ *adj.* **1.** relating to products made from clay and similar materials, such as pottery, brick, etc., or to their manufacture. – *n.* **2.** such a product. – **ceramics**, *n.*

cereal /'sɪəriəl/ *n.* **1.** any grasslike plant yielding an edible farinaceous grain, as wheat, rye, oats, rice, maize, etc. **2.** some edible preparation of it, especially a breakfast food made from some grain.

cerebral /'sɛrəbrəl/ *adj.* **1.** of or relating to the brain. **2.** intellectual.

ceremony /'sɛrəməni/ *n., pl.* **-monies**. **1.** the formalities observed on some solemn or important public or state occasion. **2.** a solemn rite. **3.** any formal act or observance, especially a meaningless one. – **ceremonious**, *adj.* – **ceremonial**, *adj., n.*

cerise /sə'ris, -riz/ *adj., n.* mauve-tinged cherry red.

cero- a word element meaning 'wax'.

certain /'sɜtn/ *adj.* **1.** having no doubt; confident; assured. **2.** sure; inevitable. **3.** unquestionable; indisputable. **4.** definite or particular, but not named or specified. **5.** some though not much. – **certainty**, *n.*

certificate /sə'tɪfəkət/ *n.* a writing on paper certifying to the truth of something or to status, qualifications, privileges, etc.

certificate of deposit *n. Economics* a short-term, negotiable, interest-bearing note acknowledging indebtedness, issued mainly by trading banks and merchant banks.

certified cheque /'sɜtəfaɪd/ *n.* a cheque bearing a guarantee of payment by the bank on which it is drawn.

certify /'sɜtəfaɪ/ *v.t.,* **-fied**, **-fying**. **1.** to guarantee as certain; give reliable information of. **2.** to declare insane.

cervical /'sɜvɪkəl, sɜ'vaɪkəl/ *adj.* relating to the cervix or neck.

cervico- variant of **cervic-** used before consonants.

cervix /'sɜvɪks/ *n., pl.* **cervixes**, **cervices** /sə'vaɪsiz/. *Anatomy* **1.** the neck. **2.** the neck of the uterus, which dilates just before giving birth.

cessation /sɛ'seɪʃən/ *n.* a ceasing; pause.

cession /'sɛʃən/ *n.* **1.** the act of ceding, as by treaty. **2.** the voluntary surrender by a debtor of his or her effects to creditors.

cesspool /'sɛspul/ *n.* **1.** a cistern, well, or pit for retaining the sediment of a drain or for receiving the filth of a water closet, etc. **2.** any filthy receptacle or place.

cetacean /sə'teɪʃən/ *n.* one of the order of aquatic mammals including the whales, dolphins, porpoises, etc. – **cetaceous**, *adj.*

chablis /'ʃæbli, 'ʃabli/ *n.* a very dry white table wine.

chafe /tʃeɪf/ *v.t.,* **chafed**, **chafing**. **1.** to warm by rubbing. **2.** to wear or abrade by rubbing. **3.** to irritate; annoy.

chaff[1] /tʃaf/ *n.* the husks of grains and grasses separated from the seed.

chaff[2] /tʃaf/ *v.t.* to ridicule or tease good-naturedly.

chagrin /'ʃægrən, ʃə'grin/ *n.* a feeling of vexation and disappointment or humiliation.

chain /tʃeɪn/ *n.* **1.** a connected series of metal or other links. **2.** something that binds or restrains. **3.** a series of things connected or following in succession. **4.** a surveying measure. – *v.t.* **5.** to fasten or secure with or as with a chain.

chain reaction *n. Colloquial* a series of reactions provoked by one event.

chair /tʃɛə/ *n.* **1.** a seat with a back and legs or other support, usually for one person. **2.** a seat of office or authority. **3.** the person occupying a seat of office, especially the chairperson of a meeting. **4. take the chair,** to assume the position of chair (def. 3) of a meeting; begin or open a meeting. – *v.t.* **5.** to preside over.

chairlift /'tʃɛəlɪft/ *n.* a series of chairs suspended from an endless cable driven by a motor, for conveying people up or down mountains.

chairman /'tʃɛəmən/ *n., pl.* **-men**. **1.** → **chairperson**. **2.** a male chairperson.

chairperson /'tʃɛəpɜsən/ *n.* the presiding officer of a meeting, committee, board, etc.

chalet /'ʃæleɪ/ *n.* a kind of cottage, low and with wide eaves, common in alpine regions.

chalice /'tʃæləs/ *n. Ecclesiastical* a cup for the wine of the eucharist or mass.

chalk /tʃɔk/ *n.* **1.** *Geology* a soft, white, pure limestone. **2.** a prepared piece of chalk or chalk-like substance for marking. – *v.t.* **3.** to mark or write with chalk. **4. chalk up, a.** to score. **b.** to ascribe to.

chalkie /'tʃɔki/ *n. Stock Exchange* the person who records transactions on the board. Also, **chalky**.

challenge /'tʃæləndʒ/ *n., v.,* **-lenged**, **-lenging**. – *n.* **1.** a call to engage in a contest of skill, strength, etc. **2.** something that makes demands upon one's abilities, endurance, etc. **3.** a calling to account or into question. – *v.t.* **4.** to summon to a contest. **5.** to make demands, especially stimulating demands, upon. **6.** to call in question.

chamber /'tʃeɪmbə/ *n.* **1.** a room or apartment, usually a private room, and especially a bedroom. **2.** the meeting hall of a legislative or other assembly. **3.** (*pl.*) a place where a judge hears matters not requiring action in court. **4.** (*pl.*) a suite of rooms of barristers and others. **5.** a legislative, judicial, or other like body. **6.** a compartment or enclosed space.

chamber magistrate *n.* a qualified solicitor employed in a Court of Petty Sessions, who gives free legal advice.

chambermaid /ˈtʃeɪmbəmeɪd/ *n.* a female servant who takes care of bedrooms.

chamber of commerce *n.* an association, primarily of businessmen, to protect and promote the business activities of a city, etc.

chamber-pot /ˈtʃeɪmbə-pɒt/ *n.* a portable vessel used chiefly in bedrooms as a toilet.

chameleon /kəˈmiliən, ʃə-/ *n.* a slow-moving lizard noted for its power of changing skin colour and its projectile tongue.

chamois /ˈʃæmwa/ *for def. 1*, /ˈʃæmi/ *for def. 2 n., pl.* **-ois. 1.** an agile, goatlike antelope. **2.** Also, **chammy**. a soft, pliable leather.

chamomile /ˈkæməmaɪl/ *n.* a herb with strongly scented foliage and flowers which are used medicinally. Also, **camomile**.

champ[1] /tʃæmp/ *v.t.* to bite upon, especially impatiently.

champ[2] /tʃæmp/ *n. Colloquial* a champion.

champagne /ʃæmˈpeɪn/ *n.* a sparkling white wine.

champignon /ˈʃæmpɪnjɔ̃/ *n.* a very small mushroom.

champion /ˈtʃæmpiən/ *n.* **1.** someone who holds first place in any sport, etc., having defeated all opponents. **2.** someone who fights for or defends any person or cause. *– v.t.* **3.** to act as champion of; defend; support.

chance /tʃæns, tʃans/ *n., v.,* **chanced, chancing**, *adj. – n.* **1.** the absence of any known reason why an event should turn out one way rather than another, spoken of as if it were a real agency. **2.** fortune; fate; luck. **3.** a possibility or probability of anything happening. **4.** an opportunity. **5.** a risk or hazard. *– v.i.* **6.** to come by chance (fol. by *on* or *upon*). *– v.t.* **7.** *Colloquial* to take the chances or risks of; risk (usually followed by impersonal *it*). *– adj.* **8.** due to chance.

chancellor /ˈtʃænsələ, ˈtʃansələ/ *n.* **1.** the title of various important judges and other high officials. **2.** the titular, honorary head of a university.

chandelier /ʃændəˈlɪə/ *n.* a branched support for a number of lights, especially one suspended from a ceiling.

change /tʃeɪndʒ/ *v.,* **changed, changing**, *n. – v.t.* **1.** to alter in condition, appearance, etc. **2.** to substitute another or others for; exchange for something else. **3.** to remove and replace the coverings of. *– v.i.* **4.** to become different; alter (sometimes fol. by *to* or *into*). **5.** to change trains or other conveyances. **6.** to change one's clothes. *– n.* **7.** variation; alteration. **8.** the substitution of one thing for another. **9.** variety or novelty. **10.** the passing from one place, state, form, or phase to another. **11.** a balance of money that is returned when the sum tendered is larger than the sum due. **12.** coins of low denomination. **13.** (*often cap.*) *Commerce* a place where merchants meet for business transactions; an exchange.

channel /ˈtʃænəl/ *n., v.,* **-nelled, -nelling**. *– n.* **1.** the bed and banks of a stream or waterway. **2.** the deeper part of a waterway. **3.** a route through which anything passes or progresses. **4.** a frequency band for one-way communication (as radio, television, etc.). *– v.t.* **5.** to convey through a channel. **6.** to direct towards or into some particular course.

chant /tʃænt, tʃant/ *n.* **1.** a short, simple melody. *– v.t.* **2.** to sing to a chant, or in the manner of a chant.

chaos /ˈkeɪɒs/ *n.* utter confusion or disorder. – **chaotic**, *adj.*

chap[1] /tʃæp/ *v.,* **chapped, chapping**. *– v.t.* **1.** (of cold or exposure) to crack, roughen, and redden (the skin). *– v.i.* **2.** to become chapped.

chap[2] /tʃæp/ *n. Colloquial* a fellow.

chapel /ˈtʃæpəl/ *n.* a separately dedicated part of a church, or a small, independent, churchlike edifice, devoted to special services.

chaperone = chaperon /ˈʃæpəroʊn/ *n.* an older person who, for propriety, attends a young unmarried woman in public or accompanies a group of young people on public outings, etc.

chaplain /ˈtʃæplən/ *n.* an ecclesiastic attached to the chapel of a royal court, or to a college, school, etc.

chapter /ˈtʃæptə/ *n.* **1.** a main division, usually numbered, of a book, treatise, or the like. **2.** a branch, usually localised, of a society or fraternity.

char[1] /tʃa/ *v.t.,* **charred, charring**. **1.** to burn or reduce to charcoal. **2.** to burn slightly; scorch.

char[2] /tʃa/ *n. Colloquial* a woman paid to do housework.

char[3] /tʃa/ *n.* tea.

character /ˈkærəktə/ *n.* **1.** the aggregate of qualities that distinguishes one person or thing from others. **2.** good moral constitution or status. **3.** a formal statement from an employer concerning the qualities and habits of a former employee. **4.** a person. **5.** *Colloquial* an odd or interesting person. **6.** a person represented in a drama, story, etc. **7.** a symbol as used in a writing system, as a letter of the alphabet. **8.** *Computers* a group of bits representing such a symbol or a numeral.

characterise = characterize /ˈkærəktəraɪz/ *v.t.,* **-rised, -rising**. **1.** to mark or distinguish as a characteristic; be a characteristic of. **2.** to describe the characteristic or peculiar quality of.

characteristic /kærəktəˈrɪstɪk/ *adj.* **1.** typical; distinctive. *– n.* **2.** a distinguishing feature or quality.

charade /ʃəˈrad/ *n.* **1.** a game in which a player or players act out in pantomime a word or phrase which the others try to guess. **2.** a ridiculous or pointless act or series of acts.

charcoal /ˈtʃakoʊl/ *n.* the carbonaceous material obtained by the imperfect combustion of wood etc.

chardonnay /ˈʃadəneɪ/ *n.* (*sometimes cap.*) a dry white wine.

charge /tʃadʒ/ *v.,* **charged, charging**, *n. – v.t.* **1.** to put a load or burden on or in. **2.** to fill or furnish (something) with the appropriate quantity of that which it is designed to receive. **3.** to supply a quantity of electricity to (a battery) usually sufficient to make it fully operational again. **4.** to lay a command or injunction upon. **5.** to lay blame upon; blame; accuse (usually fol. by *with*). **6.** to hold liable for payment. **7.** to postpone payment on (a service or purchase) by having it recorded on one's charge account. **8.** to impose or ask as a price. **9.** to attack by rushing violently against. – *v.i.* **10.** to rush, as to an attack. – *n.* **11.** a load or burden. **12.** the quantity of anything which an apparatus is fitted to hold, or holds, at one time. **13.** *Electricity* an electric charge. **14.** care, custody, or superintendence. **15.** anything or anybody committed to one's care or management. **16.** a command or injunction. **17.** an accusation or imputation of guilt. **18.** a sum or price charged. **19.** an impetuous onset or attack, as of soldiers. **20.** the quantity of energy stored in a capacitor or electrical storage battery. **21. in charge,** having supervisory powers.

charge account *n.* a credit arrangement with a department store, service station, etc., whereby the purchase of goods is charged to the customer's account.

chargé d'affaires /ˌʃaʒeɪ dəˈfɛə/ *n., pl.* **chargés d'affaires**. **1.** (in full: **chargé d'affaires ad interim**) an official placed in charge of diplomatic business during the temporary absence of the ambassador or minister. **2.** an envoy to a state to which a diplomat of higher grade is not sent. Also, **chargé**.

chariot /ˈtʃæriət/ *n.* a two-wheeled vehicle.

charisma /kəˈrɪzmə/ *n., pl.* **-mata** /-mətə/. those special personal qualities that give an individual influence or authority over large numbers of people. – **charismatic**, *adj., n.*

charitable /ˈtʃærətəbəl/ *adj.* **1.** generous in gifts to relieve the needs of others. **2.** kindly or lenient in judging others.

charity /ˈtʃærəti/ *n., pl.* **-ties**. **1.** almsgiving; the private or public relief of unfortunate or needy people. **2.** a charitable fund, foundation, or institution. **3.** benevolent feeling, especially towards those in need.

charlatan /ˈʃalətən/ *n.* someone who pretends to more knowledge or skill than they possesses; a quack.

charm /tʃam/ *n.* **1.** a power to please and attract. **2.** a trinket to be worn on a chain, bracelet, etc. **3.** a verse or formula credited with magical power. – *v.t.* **4.** to attract powerfully by beauty, etc.; please greatly. **5.** to act upon with or as with a charm; enchant.

chart /tʃat/ *n.* **1.** a sheet exhibiting information in tabulated or methodical form. **2.** a map, especially a marine map. – *v.t.* **3.** to make a chart of. **4.** to plan.

charter /ˈtʃatə/ *n.* **1.** a written instrument or contract, especially relating to land transfers. **2.** a written document, granted by a sovereign or legislature giving privileges, rights, the benefit of a new invention, a peerage, etc. **3.** Also, **charter party**. a contract by which part or all of a ship is leased for a voyage or a stated time, and safe delivery of the cargo is agreed. – *v.t.* **4.** to establish by charter. **5.** to hire a vehicle, etc. – *adj.* **6.** founded, granted, or protected by a charter. **7.** hired for a particular purpose or journey.

chartered accountant *n.* an accountant who is a full member of one of the institutes of accountants granted a royal charter which have branches in Australia.

charter member *n.* one of the original members.

chartist /ˈtʃatəst/ *n.* *Economics* **1.** a share market analyst who plots the price trends of shares on charts. **2.** someone who interprets these price patterns.

chary /ˈtʃɛəri/ *adj.,* **charier**, **chariest**. **1.** careful; wary. **2.** shy.

chase[1] /tʃeɪs/ *v.,* **chased**, **chasing**, *n.* – *v.t.* **1.** to pursue in order to seize, overtake, etc. – *v.i.* **2.** to follow in pursuit. – *n.* **3.** the act of chasing. **4.** a flora and fauna reserve.

chase[2] /tʃeɪs/ *v.t.,* **chased**, **chasing**. to ornament (metal) by engraving or embossing.

chasm /ˈkæzəm/ *n.* a deep cleft in the earth's surface.

chassis /ˈʃæzi/ *n., pl.* **chassis** /ˈʃæziz/. the frame, wheels, and machinery of a motor vehicle, on which the body is supported.

chaste /tʃeɪst/ *adj.* **1.** virgin, especially when considered as being virtuous. **2.** pure in style; simple. – **chastity**, *n.*

chasten /ˈtʃeɪsən/ *v.t.* to chastise.

chastise /tʃæsˈtaɪz/ *v.t.,* **-tised**, **-tising**. to punish, especially physically.

chat /tʃæt/ *v.,* **chatted**, **chatting**, *n.* – *v.i.* **1.** to converse in a familiar or informal manner. – *v.t.* **2.** *Colloquial* to talk persuasively to or flirt with (fol. by *up*). – *n.* **3.** informal conversation.

chattel /ˈtʃætl/ *n.* a movable article of property.

chatter /ˈtʃætə/ *v.i.* **1.** to utter a succession of quick, inarticulate, speechlike sounds. **2.** to talk rapidly and to little purpose; jabber.

chatterbox /ˈtʃætəbɒks/ *n.* a very talkative person.

chauffeur /ˈʃoʊfə, ʃoʊˈfɜ/ *n.* **1.** a person employed as a driver for a private motor car. – *v.t.* **2.** to act as chauffeur to.

chauvinism /ˈʃoʊvənɪzəm/ *n.* zealous and belligerent patriotism or devotion to any cause, as male chauvinism.

cheap /tʃip/ *adj.* **1.** of a relatively low price; at a bargain. **2.** of poor quality.

cheat /tʃit/ *n.* **1.** a fraud; swindle; deception. **2.** a person who cheats or defrauds. – *v.t.* **3.** to defraud; swindle.

check /tʃɛk/ *v.t.* **1.** to stop or arrest the motion of suddenly or forcibly. **2.** to restrain; hold in restraint or control. **3.** to investigate or verify as to correctness. **4.** to leave in temporary custody (fol. by *in*). **5.** to mark in a pattern of checks or squares. **6.** *Chess* to place (an opponent's king) under direct attack. – *v.i.* **7.** to prove to be right; to correspond accurately. **8.** to make an inquiry or investigation for verification, etc. (usually fol. by *up* or *on*). **9. check in,** to register one's arrival. **10. check out,** to register one's departure. – *n.* **11.** a person or thing that checks or restrains. **12.** a sudden arrest or stoppage; repulse; rebuff. **13.** control with a view to ascertaining performance or preventing error. **14.** a means or standard to insure against error, fraud, etc. **15.** a pattern formed of squares, as on a draughtboard. **16.** *US* → **cheque. 17.** *US* → **bill**[1] (def. 1).

checkmate /ˈtʃɛkmeɪt/ *n. Chess* the act of putting the opponent's king into an inextricable check, thus winning the game.

check-up /ˈtʃɛk-ʌp/ *n.* **1.** an examination or close scrutiny for purposes of verification as to accuracy, comparison, etc. **2.** a comprehensive physical examination.

cheddar /ˈtʃɛdə/ *n.* a firm white or yellow cheese.

cheek /tʃik/ *n.* **1.** either side of the face below eye level. **2.** the side wall of the mouth between the upper and lower jaws. **3.** a buttock. **4.** *Colloquial* impudence or effrontery.

cheeky /ˈtʃiki/ *adj.,* **cheekier, cheekiest.** *Colloquial* impudent; insolent.

cheep /tʃip/ *v.i.* to chirp; peep.

cheer /tʃɪə/ *n.* **1.** a shout of encouragement, approval, congratulation, etc. **2.** gladness, gaiety, or animation. – *v.t.* **3.** to salute with shouts of approval, congratulation, etc. **4.** to inspire with cheer; gladden (often fol. by *up*). **5.** to encourage or incite (fol. by *on*).

cheerful /ˈtʃɪəfəl/ *adj.* full of or promoting good spirits; pleasant.

cheese /tʃiz/ *n.* **1.** the curd of milk separated from the whey and prepared in many ways as a food. **2. hard** (or **stiff**) **cheese,** *Colloquial* bad luck.

cheetah /ˈtʃitə/ *n.* an animal of the cat family resembling the leopard; reputed to be the fastest four-legged animal.

chef /ʃɛf/ *n.* a cook, especially a head cook.

cheiro- variant of **chiro-**.

cheli- a word element meaning 'claws'.

chem- a word element representing chemic or chemical used before vowels. Also (*esp. before a consonant*), **chemo-**.

chemical /ˈkɛmɪkəl/ *adj.* **1.** of or concerned with the science or the operations or processes of chemistry. – *n.* **2.** a substance produced by or used in a chemical process.

chemical warfare *n.* warfare with asphyxiating, poisonous, and corrosive gases, oil flames, etc.

chemist /ˈkɛməst/ *n.* **1.** one versed in chemistry or professionally engaged in chemical investigations. **2.** a retailer of medicinal drugs and toilet preparations.

chemistry /ˈkɛməstri/ *n., pl.* **-tries. 1.** the science concerned with the composition of substances, the various elementary forms of matter, and the interactions between them. **2.** chemical properties, reactions, etc.

cheque /tʃɛk/ *n.* **1.** *Banking* a written order, usually on a standard printed form directing a bank to pay a specified sum of money to, or to the order of, some particular person or the bearer, either *crossed* (payable only through a bank account), or *uncrossed* (payable on demand). **2.** wages, pay.

cheque account *n.* a bank account from which money may be withdrawn by cheque at any time by the customer.

cherish /ˈtʃɛrɪʃ/ *v.t.* to hold or treat as dear.

cheroot /ʃəˈrut/ *n.* a cigar having open, unpointed ends.

cherry /ˈtʃɛri/ *n., pl.* **-ries**. the fruit of any of various trees, consisting of a red-coloured, pulpy, globular drupe enclosing a one-seeded smooth stone.

cherub /ˈtʃɛrəb/ *n., pl.* **cherubim** /tʃɛrəbɪm, kɛ-/ *for def. 1* **cherubs** *for def. 2* – **1.** *Bible* a kind of celestial being. **2.** a beautiful or innocent person, especially a child.

chess /tʃɛs/ *n.* a game played by two persons, each with sixteen pieces, on a chequered board.

chest /tʃɛst/ *n.* **1.** the trunk of the body from the neck to the belly. **2.** a box, usually a large, strong one, for the safekeeping of valuables.

chestnut /ˈtʃɛsnʌt/ *n.* **1.** the edible nut of trees, of the beech family. **2.** reddish brown.

chew /tʃu/ *v.t.* **1.** to crush or grind with the teeth; masticate. **2.** to damage or destroy by or as if by chewing (fol. by *up*). **3.** to meditate on; consider deliberately (fol. by *over*).

chewing gum /ˈtʃuɪŋ ˌgʌm/ *n.* a preparation for chewing, usually made of sweetened and flavoured gum.

chewy /ˈtʃuI/ *adj.* requiring chewing; tough.

chic /ʃik/ *adj.* stylish.

chicanery /ʃəˈkeɪnəri/ *n., pl.* **-ries**. legal trickery, quibbling, or sophistry.

chick /tʃɪk/ *n.* **1.** a young chicken or other bird. **2.** *Colloquial* a young woman.

chicken /ˈtʃɪkən/ *n.* **1.** the young of the domestic fowl (or of certain other birds). **2.** *Colloquial* a coward. – *v.i.* **3. chicken out,** to withdraw because of cowardice, tiredness, etc.

chickenpox /ˈtʃɪkənpɒks/ *n.* a mild, contagious eruptive disease, commonly of children, caused by a virus.

chide /tʃaɪd/ *v.,* **chided, chiding**. – *v.i.* **1.** to scold; find fault. – *v.t.* **2.** to drive, impel, etc., by chiding.

chief /tʃif/ *n.* **1.** the head or ruler of a clan, tribe, or military or youth organisation, etc. **2.** *Colloquial* boss. – *adj.* **3.** highest in rank or authority. **4.** most important.

chieftain /ˈtʃiftən/ *n.* a leader of a group, band, etc.

chiffon /ʃəˈfɒn, ˈʃɪfɒn/ *n.* sheer fabric of silk, nylon, or rayon in plain weave.

chil- variant of **chilo-**, used before vowels.

chilblain /ˈtʃɪlbleɪn/ *n.* (*usu. pl.*) *Pathology* an inflammation on the hands and feet caused by exposure to cold and moisture.

child /tʃaɪld/ *n., pl.* **children**. **1.** a baby or infant. **2.** a boy or girl. **3.** a childish person. **4.** any descendant.

childish /ˈtʃaɪldɪʃ/ *adj.* like a child; weak or foolish.

children /ˈtʃɪldrən/ *n.* plural of **child**.

child restraint *n.* a car seatbelt designed to fit children.

chill /tʃɪl/ *n.* **1.** coldness, especially a moderate but penetrating coldness. **2.** a sensation of cold, usually with shivering. **3.** a cold stage, as a first symptom of illness. **4.** a depressing influence or sensation. **5.** a coldness of manner, lack of friendliness. – *adj.* **6.** cold; tending to cause shivering. **7.** shivering with cold. **8.** depressing or discouraging. – *v.i.* **9.** to become cold. – *v.t.* **10.** to affect with cold; make chilly. **11.** to make cool, but not freeze. – **chilly**, *n.*

chilli /ˈtʃɪli/ *n., pl.* **-ies**. the pungent fruit of some species of capsicum, usually small but hot to the taste.

chilo- a word element meaning 'lip', 'labial'.

chime /tʃaɪm/ *n., v.,* **chimed**, **chiming**. – *n.* **1.** an arrangement for striking a bell or bells so as to produce a musical sound. **2.** a set of vertical metal tubes struck with a hammer, as used in the modern orchestra. **3.** harmonious relation; accord. – *v.i.* **4.** to sound harmoniously or in chimes, as a set of bells. **5.** to harmonise; agree. – *v.t.* **6.** to give forth (music, etc.), as a bell or bells.

chimney /ˈtʃɪmni/ *n., pl.* **-neys**. a structure, usually vertical, containing a passage or flue by which the smoke, gases, etc., of a fire or furnace are carried off .

chimpanzee /tʃɪmpænˈzi/ *n.* an anthropoid ape, smaller, with larger ears, and more arboreal than the gorilla.

chin /tʃɪn/ *n.* the lower extremity of the face, below the mouth.

china /ˈtʃaɪnə/ *n.* **1.** a vitreous, translucent earthenware, originally produced in China. **2.** plates, cups, etc., collectively.

Chinese gooseberry /tʃaɪˌnɪz ˈguzbəri/ *n.* → **kiwifruit**.

chink[1] /tʃɪŋk/ *n.* a crack, cleft, or fissure.

chink[2] /tʃɪŋk/ *v.i.* to make a short, sharp, ringing sound, as of coins or glasses striking together.

chintz /tʃɪnts/ *n., pl.* **chintzes**. a printed cotton fabric, glazed or unglazed, used especially for draperies.

chip /tʃɪp/ *n., v.,* **chipped**, **chipping**. – *n.* **1.** a small piece, as of wood, separated by chopping, cutting, or breaking. **2.** a very thin slice or piece of food, etc. **3. a.** a deep-fried finger of potato. **b.** → **crisp** (def. 3). **4.** *Games* a counter, as of ivory or bone, used in certain card games, etc. **5.** *Electronics* a minute square of semi-conductor material, processed in various ways to have certain electrical characteristics. **6. chip on the shoulder,** *Colloquial* a long-standing resentment; grievance. – *v.t.* **7.** to hew or cut with an axe, chisel, etc. – *v.i.* **8.** to break off in small pieces; to become chipped. **9. chip in,** *Colloquial* to contribute money, help, etc.

chipboard /ˈtʃɪpbɔd/ *n.* a resin-bonded artificial wood made from wood chips, sawdust, etc., used in sheets for light structural work.

chipmunk /ˈtʃɪpmʌŋk/ *n.* any of various small striped terrestrial squirrels.

chiro- a word element meaning 'hand', as in *chiropractic.*

chiropody /kəˈrɒpədi/ *n.* the treatment of minor foot ailments, such as corns, bunions, etc. – **chiropodist**, *n.*

chiropractic /kaɪrəˈpræktɪk/ *n.* a therapeutic system based upon the premise that disease is caused by interference with nerve function, the method being to restore normal condition by adjusting the segments of the spinal column. – **chiropractor**, *n.*

chirp /tʃɜp/ *v.i.* to make a short, sharp sound, as small birds and certain insects.

chirpy /ˈtʃɜpi/ *adj. Colloquial* cheerful.

chirrup /ˈtʃɪrəp/ *v.i.,* **-ruped**, **-ruping**. to chirp.

chisel /ˈtʃɪzəl/ *n., v.,* **-elled**, **-elling**. – *n.* **1.** a tool, as of steel, with a cutting edge for cutting or shaping wood, stone, etc. – *v.i.* **2.** to work with a chisel.

chit[1] /tʃɪt/ *n.* a voucher.

chit[2] /tʃɪt/ *n.* a young person, especially a pert girl.

chivalry /ˈʃɪvəlri/ *n.* **1.** the rules and customs of medieval knighthood. **2.** good manners. – **chivalrous**, *adj.*

chives /tʃaɪvz/ *pl. n.* a small bulbous plant related to the leek and onion.

chlor-[1] a word element meaning 'green'.

chlor-[2] a combining form denoting 'chlorine'.

chloride /ˈklɔraɪd/ *n.* **1.** a compound usually of two elements only, one of which is chlorine. **2.** a salt of hydrochloric acid.

chlorine /ˈklɔrin/ *n.* a greenish yellow gaseous element used as a powerful bleaching agent and in various industrial processes. *Symbol*: Cl

chloro-[1] variant of **chlor-**[1], used before consonants, as in *chlorophyll.*

chloro-[2] variant of **chlor-**[2], used before consonants, as in *chloroform.*

chloroform /ˈklɒrəfɔm/ *n.* a colourless volatile liquid, $CHCl_3$, used as an anaesthetic and solvent.

chlorophyll /ˈklɒrəfɪl/ *n.* the green colouring substances of leaves and plants, associated with the production of carbohydrates by photosynthesis.

chock /tʃɒk/ *n.* **1.** a block or wedge of wood, etc., for filling in a space, especially for preventing movement, as of a wheel or a cask. – *adv.* **2.** as close or tight as possible; quite.

chocolate /ˈtʃɒklət, ˈtʃɒkələt/ *n.* a preparation of the seeds of cacao, often sweetened and flavoured, as with vanilla.

choice /tʃɔɪs/ *n., adj.,* **choicer**, **choicest**. – *n.* **1.** the act of choosing; selection. **2.** power of choosing; option. **3.** the person or thing chosen. **4.** an abundance and variety from which to choose. – *adj.* **5.** worthy of being chosen; excellent; superior. **6.** carefully selected.

choir /ˈkwaɪə/ *n.* a company of singers.

choke /tʃoʊk/ *v.,* **choked**, **choking**, *n.* – *v.t.* **1.** to stop the breath of, by squeezing or obstructing the windpipe; strangle; stifle; suffocate. **2.** to obstruct; clog; congest. – *v.i.* **3.** to suffer strangling or suffocation. **4.** to be obstructed or clogged. **5.** to be temporarily overcome, as with emotion. – *n.* **6.** the act or sound of choking. **7.** (in internal-combustion engines) the mechanism by which the air supply to a carburettor is diminished or stopped.

choko /ˈtʃoʊkoʊ/ *n.* a pear-shaped green fruit used as a vegetable. Also, **chayote**.

chol- a word element meaning 'gall' or 'bile'. Also, **chole-**, **cholo-**.

choler /ˈkɒlə/ *n.* anger; wrath; irritability.

cholera /ˈkɒlərə/ *n. Pathology* an acute, infectious disease marked by diarrhoea, vomiting, cramp, etc.

cholesterol /kə'lɛstərɒl/ *n.* a sterol, widely distributed in higher organisms, found in bile and gallstones, and in the blood and brain, the yolk of eggs, etc. Also, **cholesterin** /kɒ'lɛstərən/.

cholo- variant of **chol-** before consonants.

chook /tʃʊk/ *n.* a domestic fowl.

choose /tʃuz/ *v.t.,* **chose**, **chosen**. **1.** to select from a number, or in preference to another or other things or persons. **2.** to prefer and decide (to do something).

choosy /tʃuzi/ *adj. Colloquial* hard to please. Also, **choosey**.

chop[1] /tʃɒp/ *v.,* **chopped**, **chopping**, *n.* – *v.t.* **1.** to cut with a quick, heavy blow or series of blows, using an axe, etc. – *v.i.* **2.** to make a quick heavy stroke or a series of strokes, as with an axe. **3.** to go, come, or move suddenly or violently. – *n.* **4.** the act of chopping. **5.** a cutting blow. **6.** a slice of mutton, lamb, veal, pork, etc. containing some bone. **7.** *Colloquial* the sack; dismissal.

chop[2] /tʃɒp/ *v.i.,* **chopped**, **chopping**. to turn, shift, or change suddenly, as the wind.

chopper /'tʃɒpə/ *n.* **1.** *Colloquial* a helicopter. **2.** a bike with wide, high handlebars.

choppy /'tʃɒpi/ *adj.,* **-pier**, **-piest**. (of the sea, etc.) forming short, irregular, broken waves.

chopstick /'tʃɒpstɪk/ *n.* one of a pair of thin sticks used to raise food to the mouth.

chord[1] /kɔd/ *n.* **1.** a string of a musical instrument. **2.** a feeling or emotion. **3.** *Geometry* that part of a straight line between two of its intersections with a curve.

chord[2] /kɔd/ *n. Music* a combination of three or more tones, mostly in harmonic relation, sounded either simultaneously or in quick succession.

chore /tʃɔ/ *n.* a small or odd job; a piece of minor domestic work.

choreography /kɒri'ɒgrəfi/ *n.* the art of composing ballets, etc., and arranging separate dances. – **choreographer**, *n.* – **choreographic**, *adj.* – **choreograph**, *v.t.*

chortle /'tʃɔtl/ *v.i.* to chuckle with glee.

chorus /'kɔrəs/ *n., pl.* **-ruses**. **1. a.** a group of persons singing in concert. **b.** a part of a song in which others join the principal singer or singers. **c.** any recurring refrain. **2.** simultaneous utterance in singing, speaking, etc. **3.** (in musical shows) the company of dancers and singers. – **choral**, *adj.*

chose /tʃoʊz/ *v.* past tense and obsolete past participle of **choose**.

chowder /'tʃaʊdə/ *n.* a kind of soup or stew made of clams, fish, or vegetables.

christen /'krɪsən/ *v.t.* to give a name to, especially at baptism.

Christian name /'krɪstʃən/ *n.* a first or given name, as distinguished from the family name.

-chroic an adjectival word element indicating colour (of skin, plants, etc.).

chrom- **1.** a word element referring to colour. **2.** a word element referring to chromium.

-chrom- a word element synonymous with **chrom-**, as in *monochromatic.*

chromatic /krə'mætɪk/ *adj.* **1.** relating to colour or colours. **2.** *Music* involving a modification of the diatonic scale by the use of accidentals.

chromato- a word element referring to colour.

chrome /kroʊm/ *n.* chromium, especially as a source of various pigments.

-chrome a word element meaning 'colour', as in *monochrome.*

chromium /'kroʊmiəm/ *n.* a lustrous, hard, brittle metallic element used for making pigments in photography, to harden gelatine, as a mordant, etc.; also used in corrosion-resisting chromium plating. *Symbol*: Cr

chromosome /'kroʊməsoʊm/ *n.* any of several threadlike, rodlike, or beadlike bodies in the cell nucleus which carry the genes.

chron- a word element meaning 'time'.

chronic /'krɒnɪk/ *adj.* **1.** inveterate; constant. **2.** continuing a long time.

chronic fatigue syndrome *n.* a condition of incapacitating fatigue and depression lasting months or years following an apparently mild viral infection.

chronicle /'krɒnɪkəl/ *n., v.,* **-cled**, **-cling**. – *n.* **1.** a record or account of events in the order of time; a history. – *v.t.* **2.** to record in or as in a chronicle.

chrono- variant of **chron-**.

chronograph /'krɒnəgræf/ *n.* a clock-driven instrument for recording the exact instant of occurrences, or for measuring small intervals of time.

chronological /krɒnə'lɒdʒɪkəl/ *adj.* arranged in the order of time.

chronology /krə'nɒlədʒi/ *n., pl.* **-gies**. a particular statement of the supposed or accepted order of past events.

chronometer /krə'nɒmətə/ *n.* a timekeeper with special mechanism for ensuring accuracy.

-chroous → **-chroic**.

chrysalis /'krɪsələs/ *n., pl.* **chrysalises**, **chrysalids**, **chrysalides** /krə'sælədiz/. the hard-shelled pupa of a moth or butterfly.

chrysanthemum /krə'sænθəməm, krə'zænθ-/ *n.* a garden plant with flowers notable for the diversity of colour and size.

chubby /'tʃʌbi/ *adj.,* **-bier**, **-biest**. round and plump.

chuck /tʃʌk/ *v.t.* **1.** to pat or tap lightly, as under the chin. **2.** to throw with a quick motion, usually a short distance. **3.** *Colloquial* to vomit.

chuckle /'tʃʌkəl/ *v.,* **chuckled**, **chuckling**, *n.* – *v.i.* **1.** to laugh in a soft, amused manner, usually with satisfaction. – *n.* **2.** a soft, amused laugh.

chum /tʃʌm/ *n., v.,* **chummed**, **chumming**. – *n.* **1.** an intimate friend or companion. – *v.i.* **2. chum up with,** to become friendly with.

chump /tʃʌmp/ *n.* **1.** *Colloquial* a blockhead or dolt. **2.** the thick blunt end of anything.

chunder /'tʃʌndə/ *v.i., v.t. Colloquial* to vomit.

chunk /tʃʌŋk/ *n.* a thick mass or lump of anything.

church /tʃɜtʃ/ *n.* **1.** an edifice for public worship, especially Christian worship. **2.** (*cap.*) the whole body of Christian believers. **3.** (*cap.*) any division of this body professing the same creed and acknowledging the same ecclesiastical authority; a Christian denomination.

churl /tʃɜl/ *n.* a rude, boorish, or surly person. – **churlish**, *adj.*

churn /tʃɜn/ *n.* **1.** a vessel or machine in which cream or milk is agitated to make butter. – *v.t.* **2.** to shake or agitate with violence or continued motion.

chute /ʃut/ *n.* a channel, trough, tube, shaft, etc., for conveying water, grain, coal, etc., to a lower level.

chutney /'tʃʌtni/ *n., pl.* **-neys**. a fruit or vegetable relish.

cicada /sə'kadə, -'keɪdə/ *n., pl.* **-das**, **-dae** /-di/. any of several large insects noted for the shrill sound produced by the male by means of vibrating membranes or drums on the underside of the abdomen.

-cidal adjective form of **-cide**.

-cide a word element meaning 'killer' or 'act of killing'.

cider /'saɪdə/ *n.* the expressed juice of apples.

cigar /sə'ga/ *n.* a small, shaped roll of tobacco leaves prepared for smoking.

cigarette /sɪgə'rɛt/ *n.* a roll of finely cut tobacco for smoking, usually enclosed in thin paper.

cinch /sɪntʃ/ *n. Colloquial* something certain or easy.

cinders /'sɪndəz/ *pl. n.* any residue of combustion; ashes.

cine- a word element meaning 'motion', used of films, etc.

cinema /'sɪnəmə/ *n.* **1.** a theatre where films are shown. **2. the cinema,** films collectively. – **cinematic**, *adj.* – **cinematically**, *adv.*

cinnamon /'sɪnəmən/ *n.* a spice from the inner bark of certain trees.

-cion a suffix having the same function as **-tion**, as in *suspicion*.

cipher /'saɪfə/ *n.* **1.** an arithmetical symbol (0) which denotes nought, or no quantity or magnitude. **2.** any of the Arabic numerals or figures. **3.** something of no value or importance. **4.** a secret method of writing, as by a specially formed code of symbols. **5.** the key to a secret method of writing. Also, **cypher**.

circa /'sɜkə, 'sɜsə/ *prep., adv.* about (used especially in approximate dates). *Abbrev.*: *c., c,* or *ca.*

circle /'sɜkəl/ *n., v.,* **-cled**, **-cling**. – *n.* **1.** a closed plane curve which is at all points equidistant from a fixed point within it, called the centre. **2.** any circular object, formation, or arrangement. **3.** an upper section of seats in a theatre. **4.** the area within which something acts, exerts influence, etc. **5.** a complete series forming a connected whole; cycle. **6.** a number of persons bound by a common tie; a coterie. – *v.t.* **7.** to enclose in a circle; surround. **8.** to move in a circle or circuit round. – *v.i.* **9.** to move in a circle.

circuit /'sɜkət/ *n.* **1.** the act of going or moving round. **2.** any circular or roundabout journey; a round. **3.** a number of theatres, cinemas, etc., under common control or visited in turn by the same actors, etc. **4.** *Electricity* the complete path of an electric current.

circuit-breaker /'sɜkət-breɪkə/ *n.* a device for interrupting an electric circuit.

circuitous /sə'kjuətəs/ *adj.* roundabout; not direct.

circular /'sɜkjələ/ *adj.* **1.** having the form of a circle. – *n.* **2.** a letter, notice, advertisement, or statement for circulation among the general public or within an organisation. – **circularise = circularize**, *v.*

circulate /'sɜkjəleɪt/ *v.i.,* **-lated**, **-lating**. **1.** to move in a circle or circuit. **2.** *Colloquial* to move amongst the guests at a social function.

circulating capital *n. Finance* capital which has been used to acquire assets intended to be sold or resold at a profit (opposed to *fixed capital*).

circulation /sɜkjə'leɪʃən/ *n.* **1.** the act of circulating. **2.** *Physiology* the recurrent movement of the blood through the various vessels of the body. **3.** the distribution of copies of a publication among readers. **4.** coin, notes, bills, etc., in use as currency; currency.

circum- a prefix referring to movement round or about motion on all sides, as in *circumvent, circumnavigate, circumference*.

circumcise /'sɜkəmsaɪz/ *v.t.,* **-cised**, **-cising**. to remove the foreskin of (males) sometimes as a religious rite. – **circumcision**, *n.*

circumference /sə'kʌmfərəns/ *n.* the outer boundary, especially of a circular area.

circumlocution /sɜkəmlə'kjuʃən/ *n.* a roundabout way of speaking.

circumnavigate /sɜkəm'nævəgeɪt/ *v.t.,* **-gated**, **-gating**. to sail round.

circumscribe /'sɜkəmskraɪb, sɜkəm'skraɪb/ *v.t.,* **-scribed**, **-scribing**. **1.** to draw a line round; encircle. **2.** to enclose within bounds; limit or confine, especially narrowly.

circumspect /'sɜkəmspɛkt/ *adj.* watchful on all sides; cautious; prudent.

circumstance /'sɜkəmstæns/ *n.* **1.** a condition, with respect to time, place, manner, agent, etc., which accompanies, determines, or modifies a fact or event. **2.** ceremonious accompaniment or display. – **circumstantial**, *adj.*

circumstantiate /sɜkəm'stænʃieɪt/ *v.t.,* **-ated**, **-ating**. to set forth or support with circumstances or particulars.

circumvent /sɜkəm'vɛnt, 'sɜkəmvɛnt/ *v.t.* to gain advantage over by artfulness or deception; outwit; overreach.

circus /'sɜkəs/ *n.* a company of performers, animals, etc., especially a travelling company.

cirrhosis /sɪ'roʊsəs, sə-/ *n.* a disease of the liver.

cirro- a combining form of **cirrus**.

cirrus /'sɪrəs/ *n. Meteorology* a high, thin, threadlike cloud.

cistern /'sɪstən/ *n.* a reservoir, tank, or vessel for holding water or other liquid.

citadel /ˈsɪtədɛl/ *n.* any strongly fortified place; a stronghold.

cite /saɪt/ *v.t.,* **cited**, **citing**. **1.** to quote (a passage, book, author, etc.), especially as an authority. **2.** to mention in support, proof, or confirmation; refer to as an example. – **citation**, *n.*

citizen /ˈsɪtəzən/ *n.* **1.** a member, native or naturalised, of a state or nation (as distinguished from *alien*). **2.** an inhabitant of a city or town, especially one entitled to its privileges or franchises. – **citizenry**, *n.*

citizen band radio *n.* point-to-point broadcasting on an assigned frequency band, with transmitters and receivers appropriate to individual use, as by truck drivers, etc.

citrus /ˈsɪtrəs/ *n.* any tree or shrub of the genus *Citrus*, which includes the lemon, lime, orange, grapefruit, etc.

city /ˈsɪti/ *n., pl.* **cities**. **1.** a large or important town; a town so nominated. **2.** the central business area of a city.

civic /ˈsɪvɪk/ *adj.* **1.** of or relating to a city; municipal. **2.** of or relating to citizenship; civil. **3.** of citizens.

civil /ˈsɪvəl/ *adj.* **1.** of or consisting of citizens. **2.** of a commonwealth or state. **3.** of the ordinary life and affairs of citizens (distinguished from *military*, *ecclesiastical*, etc.). **4.** polite; courteous.

civilian /səˈvɪljən/ *n.* someone engaged in civil pursuits, distinguished from a soldier, etc.

civilisation = civilization /sɪvəlaɪˈzeɪʃən/ *n.* **1.** an advanced state of human society, in which a high level of art, science, religion, and government has been reached. **2.** those people or nations that have reached such a state. **3.** the type of culture, society, etc., of a specific group. **4.** the act or process of civilising.

civilise = civilize /ˈsɪvəlaɪz/ *v.t.,* **-lised**, **-lising**. to make civilised.

civilised = civilized /ˈsɪvəlaɪzd/ *adj.* **1.** having an advanced culture, society, etc. **2.** polite; well-bred; refined.

civility /səˈvɪləti/ *n., pl.* **-ties**. courtesy; politeness.

civil marriage *n.* a marriage performed by a government official rather than a member of the clergy.

civil war *n.* a war between parties, regions, etc., within their own country.

CJD /si dʒeɪ ˈdi/ *n.* → **Creutzfeldt-Jakob disease**.

clack /klæk/ *v.i.* to make a quick, sharp sound, or a succession of such sounds, as by striking or cracking.

clad /klæd/ *v.* a past tense and past participle of **clothe**.

clado- a word element meaning 'sprout', 'branch'. Also (*before vowels*), **clad-**.

claim /kleɪm/ *v.t.* **1.** to demand as a right or as due. **2.** to assert or maintain as a fact. – *n.* **3.** a demand for something as due. **4.** a just title to something. **5.** that which is claimed; a piece of public land to which formal claim is made for mining or other purposes. **6.** a payment demanded in accordance with an insurance policy, etc.

claimant /ˈkleɪmənt/ *n.* someone who makes a claim.

clairvoyant /klɛəˈvɔɪənt/ *adj.* **1.** having the power of seeing objects or actions beyond the natural range of the senses. – *n.* **2.** a clairvoyant person.

clam /klæm/ *n., v.,* **clammed**, **clamming**. – *n.* **1.** a type of mollusc. – *v.i.* **2. clam up,** *Colloquial* to be silent.

clamber /ˈklæmbə/ *v.i.* to climb, using both feet and hands.

clammy /ˈklæmi/ *adj.,* **-mier**, **-miest**. covered with a cold, sticky moisture.

clamour = clamor /ˈklæmə/ *n.* **1.** a loud outcry. **2.** popular outcry. – *v.i.* **3.** to make a clamour; raise an outcry.

clamp /klæmp/ *n.* **1.** a device, usually of some rigid material, for strengthening or supporting objects or fastening them together. – *v.t.* **2.** to fasten with or fix in a clamp. – *v.i.* **3. clamp down,** *Colloquial* to become more strict.

clan /klæn/ *n.* a group of people of common descent. – **clannish**, *adj.*

clandestine /klænˈdɛstən/ *adj.* secret; private.

clang /klæŋ/ *v.i.* to give out a loud, resonant sound, as metal when struck.

clangour = clangor /ˈklæŋə, ˈklæŋgə/ *n.* a loud, resonant sound, as of pieces of metal struck together or of a trumpet.

clap[1] /klæp/ *v.,* **clapped**, **clapping**. – *n., v.t.* **1.** to strike with a quick, smart blow, producing an abrupt, sharp sound; slap; pat. **2.** to strike together resoundingly, as the hands to express applause. – *v.i.* **3.** to make an abrupt, sharp sound, as of bodies in collision. **4.** to move or strike with such a sound. **5.** to clap the hands, as in applause. – *n.* **6.** the act or sound of clapping. **7.** a resounding blow; a slap. **8.** a loud and abrupt or explosive noise, as of thunder.

clap[2] /klæp/ *n. Colloquial* gonorrhoea, or any other venereal disease (usually preceded by *the*).

claret /ˈklærət/ *n.* a red (originally light red or yellowish) table wine.

clarify /ˈklærəfaɪ/ *v.t., v.i.,* **-fied**, **-fying**. **1.** to make or become clear, pure, or intelligible. **2.** to make (a liquid) clear by removing sediment, often by heating gently. – **clarification**, *n.* – **clarifier**, *n.*

clarinet /klærəˈnɛt/ *n.* a wind instrument in the form of a cylindrical tube with a single reed attached to its mouthpiece.

clarion /ˈklæriən/ *adj.* **1.** clear and shrill. **2.** inspiring; rousing.

clarity /ˈklærəti/ *n.* clearness.

clash /klæʃ/ *v.i.* **1.** to make a loud, harsh noise. **2.** to collide, especially noisily. **3.** to conflict; disagree, as of temperaments, colours, etc. **4.** to coincide unfortunately (especially of events). – *n.* **5.** the noise of, or as of, a collision. **6.** a collision, especially a noisy one.

clasp /klæsp, klasp/ *n.* **1.** a device, usually of metal, for fastening things or parts together. **2.** a grasp; an embrace. – *v.t.* **3.** to take hold of with an enfolding grasp.

class /klas/ *n.* **1.** a number of persons, things, animals, etc., regarded as forming one group through the possession of similar qualities; a kind; sort. **2.** any division of persons or things according to rank or grade. **3. a.** a group of pupils taught together. **b.** a period during which they are taught. **4.** a social stratum sharing essential economic, political or cultural characteristics, and having the same social position. **5.** *Colloquial* acceptable style in dress or manner. **6.** a grade of accommodation in railway carriages, ships, aeroplanes, etc. – *v.t.* **7.** to arrange, place, or rate as to class.

class action *n.* a legal proceeding brought on by a group of people all with the same grievance or claim.

classic /'klæsɪk/ *adj.* **1.** of the first or highest class or rank. **2.** serving as a standard, model, or guide. **3.** of literary or historical renown. – *n.* **4.** an author or a literary production of the first rank, especially in Greek or Latin. **5.** (*pl.*) the literature of ancient Greece and Rome; the Greek and Latin languages. **6.** something considered to be a perfect example of its type. – **classical**, *adj.*

classified ad /'klæsəfaɪd/ *n.* *Colloquial* a newspaper advertisement, usually single-column, placed in an appropriately headed set, as for job vacancies, objects for sale, etc.

classify /'klæsəfaɪ/ *v.t.*, **-fied**, **-fying**. **1.** to arrange or distribute in classes; place according to class. **2.** to mark or otherwise declare (a document, paper, etc.) of value to an enemy, and limit and safeguard its handling and use. – **classification**, *n.*

clatter /'klætə/ *v.i.* **1.** to make a rattling sound, as of hard bodies striking rapidly together. – *n.* **2.** a clattering noise; disturbance.

clause /klɔz/ *n.* **1.** *Grammar* a group of words containing a subject and a predicate. **2.** part of a written composition containing complete sense in itself, as a sentence or paragraph (in modern use commonly limited to such parts of legal documents, as of statutes, contracts, wills, etc.).

claustrophobia /klɒstrə'foʊbiə, klɔs-/ *n.* a morbid dread of confined places. – **claustrophobic**, *adj.*

clavicle /'klævɪkəl/ *n.* the collarbone.

claw /klɔ/ *n.* **1.** a sharp, usually curved, nail on the foot of an animal. **2.** any part or thing resembling a claw. – *v.t.* **3.** to tear, scratch, seize, pull, etc., with or as with claws.

clay /kleɪ/ *n.* **1.** a natural earthy material used for making bricks, pottery, etc. **2.** earth; mud.

-cle variant of **-cule**.

clean /klin/ *adj.* **1.** free from dirt or filth; unsoiled; unstained. **2.** free from defect or blemish. **3.** free from disease. **4.** free from encumbrances or obstructions. **5.** free from any form of defilement. **6.** neatly or evenly made or proportioned; shapely; trim. – *adv.* **7.** in a clean manner. **8.** wholly; completely; quite. **9. come clean,** to make a full confession. – *v.t.* **10.** to make clean.

clean-cut /'klin-kʌt/ *adj.* **1.** distinctly outlined. **2.** definite. **3.** neatly dressed, wholesome.

clean float *n.* a shift in the currency value of a country in direct response to changes in the international money market.

cleanse /klɛnz/ *v.t.*, **cleansed**, **cleansing**. to make clean.

clear /klɪə/ *adj.* **1.** free from darkness, obscurity, or cloudiness; light. **2.** bright; shining. **3.** transparent; pellucid. **4.** distinctly perceptible to the eye, ear, or mind. **5.** free from guilt or blame; innocent. **6.** free from obstructions or obstacles; open. **7.** unentangled or disengaged; free; quit or rid (fol. by *of*). **8.** without limitation or qualification. **9.** without obligation or liability; free from debt. **10.** without deduction or diminution. – *v.t.* **11.** to make clear. **12.** to pass or get over without entanglement or collision. **13.** to pass (cheques, etc.) through a clearing house. **14.** to gain as clear profit. **15.** to approve or authorise, or to obtain approval or authorisation for, a thing or person. **16.** to remove trees, undergrowth, etc., from (an area of land). – *v.i.* **17.** to become clear.

clearance /'klɪərəns/ *n.* **1.** the act of clearing. **2.** a clear space; a clearing. **3.** distance or extent of an object to be passed over or under. **4.** official approval or consent.

clearing house /'klɪərɪŋ/ *n.* a central office for receiving and distributing information.

clearway /'klɪəweɪ/ *n.* a stretch of road, especially in a built-up area, on which, between stated times, motorists may stop only in emergencies.

cleat /klit/ *n.* a small wedge-shaped block.

cleavage /'klivɪdʒ/ *n.* **1.** the state of being cleft or split; division. **2.** *Colloquial* the cleft between a woman's breasts.

cleave[1] /kliv/ *v.i.*, **cleaved**, **cleaving**. to stick or adhere; cling or hold fast (fol. by *to*).

cleave[2] /kliv/ *v.i.*, **cleft** *or* **cleaved** *or* **clove**, **cleft** *or* **cleaved** *or* **cloven**, **cleaving**. to part or split, especially along a natural line of division.

cleaver /'klivə/ *n.* a heavy knife or long-bladed hatchet used by butchers for cutting up carcasses.

clef /klɛf/ *n.* a symbol in music notation placed upon a stave to indicate the name and pitch of the notes corresponding to its lines and spaces.

cleft[1] /klɛft/ *n.* a space or opening made by cleavage; a split.

cleft[2] /klɛft/ *adj.* cloven; split; divided.

cleft palate *n.* a congenital defect of the palate in which a longitudinal fissure exists in the roof of the mouth.

clement /'klɛmənt/ *adj.* **1.** lenient; compassionate. **2.** (of the weather, etc.) mild or pleasant.

clench /klɛntʃ/ *v.t.* to close (the hands, teeth, etc.) tightly.

clergy /'klɜdʒi/ *n., pl.* **-gies**. – *n.* the body of ministers of religion in the Christian Church, as distinct from the laity.

cleric /'klɛrɪk/ *n.* a member of the clergy.

clerical /'klɛrɪkəl/ *adj.* **1.** relating to a clerk or to clerks. **2.** of, relating to, or characteristic of the clergy.

clerk /klak/ *n.* **1.** one employed in an office, shop, etc., to keep records or accounts, attend to correspondence, etc. **2.** the administrative officer, and chief executive of a town or borough council.

clerk of the peace *n.* an officer of a court

who acts both as a clerk and as the attorney of the crown.

clerk of works *n.* the representative of the owner of the building during day to day supervision of construction works.

clever /'klɛvə/ *adj.* **1.** bright mentally; having quick intelligence; able. **2.** dexterous or nimble with the hands or body.

cliché /'kliʃeɪ/ *n., pl.* **-chés** /-ʃeɪz/. a trite, stereotyped expression, idea, practice, etc.

click /klɪk/ *n.* **1.** a slight, sharp sound. – *v.i.* **2.** to emit or make a click or clicks. **3.** to fall into place or be understood.

client /'klaɪənt/ *n.* **1.** someone who employs or seeks advice from a professional adviser. **2.** a customer.

clientele /kliən'tɛl/ *n.* the customers, clients, etc. (of a solicitor, businessman, etc.) as a whole.

cliff /klɪf/ *n.* the high, steep face of a rocky mass; precipice.

climate /'klaɪmət/ *n.* the composite or generalisation of weather conditions of a region.

climax /'klaɪmæks/ *n.* **1.** the highest point of anything; the culmination. – *v.i.* **2.** to reach the climax. – **climactic**, *adj.*

climb /klaɪm/ *v.i.* **1.** to mount or ascend, especially by using both hands and feet. **2.** to rise slowly by, or as by, continued effort. **3.** to slope upward.

clinch /klɪntʃ/ *v.t.* **1.** to secure (a driven nail, etc.) by beating down the point. **2.** to settle (a matter) decisively. – *n.* **3.** *Boxing, etc.* the act or an instance of one or both contestants holding the other in such a way as to hinder the other's punches.

cling /klɪŋ/ *v.i.,* **clung**, **clinging**. to adhere closely; stick.

clinic /'klɪnɪk/ *n.* any medical centre used for such treatments as X-rays, child care, vaccinations, etc.

clinical /'klɪnɪkəl/ *adj.* **1.** relating to a clinic. **2.** scientific; involving professional knowledge and not affected by the emotions.

clink /klɪŋk/ *v.i.* to make a light, sharp, ringing sound.

clip[1] /klɪp/ *v.,* **clipped**, **clipping**, *n.* – *v.t.* **1.** to cut, or cut off or out, as with shears; trim by cutting. **2.** to punch a hole in (a ticket). **3.** to omit sounds of (a word) in pronouncing. **4.** *Colloquial* to hit with a quick, sharp blow. **5.** *Colloquial* to defraud. – *v.i.* **6.** to clip or cut something; make the motion of clipping something. **7.** to move swiftly. – *n.* **8.** the act of clipping. **9.** anything clipped off. **10.** a short video recording or extract.

clip[2] /klɪp/ *n.* a device for gripping and holding tightly; a metal clasp, especially one for papers, letters, etc.

clipper /'klɪpə/ *n.* **1.** (*often pl.*) a cutting tool, especially shears. **2.** a sailing vessel built and rigged for speed.

clique /klik/ *n.* a small set or coterie, especially one that is snobbishly exclusive.

clitoris /'klɪtərəs, 'klaɪ-/ *n.* the erectile organ of the vulva.

cloak /kloʊk/ *n.* a loose outer garment.

clobber[1] /'klɒbə/ *v.t. Colloquial* to batter severely; maul.

clobber[2] /'klɒbə/ *n. Colloquial* clothes or gear.

clock /klɒk/ *n.* **1.** an instrument for measuring and indicating time. **2.** *Colloquial* a piece of measuring equipment having a dial, as an odometer, taxi-meter, etc. – *v.t.* **3.** to time, test, or ascertain by the clock.

clockwise /'klɒkwaɪz/ *adv., adj.* in the direction of rotation of the hands of a clock.

clockwork /'klɒkwɜk/ *n.* **1.** the mechanism of a clock. **2. like clockwork,** with perfect regularity or precision.

clod /klɒd/ *n.* **1.** a lump or mass, especially of earth or clay. **2.** a stupid person; dolt.

clodhoppers /'klɒdhɒpəz/ *pl. n.* strong, heavy shoes.

clog /klɒg/ *v.,* **clogged**, **clogging**, *n.* – *v.t.* **1.** to hinder or obstruct, especially by sticky matter; choke up. – *n.* **2.** a kind of shoe with a thick sole usually of wood.

cloister /'klɔɪstə/ *n.* **1.** a covered walk. **2.** any quiet, secluded place. – *v.t.* **3.** to confine in retirement; seclude.

clone /kloʊn/ *v.,* **cloned**, **cloning**, *n.* – *v.t.* **1.** to bring about the asexual reproduction of (an individual), the resulting individual being identical with the donor. – *n.* **2.** an asexually produced descendant.

clop /klɒp/ *n.* the sound made by a horse's hoofs.

close /kloʊz/ *v.,* **closed**, **closing**; /kloʊs/ *adj.,* **closer**, **closest**; /kloʊz/ *for defs 21 and 22,* /kloʊs/ *for def. 23 n.* – *v.t.* **1.** to stop or obstruct (a gap, entrance, aperture, etc.). **2.** to stop or obstruct the entrances, apertures, or gaps in. **3.** to refuse access to or passage across. **4.** to bring together the parts of; join; unite. **5.** to bring to an end; to shut down, either temporarily or permanently. – *v.i.* **6.** to become closed; shut. **7.** to come together; unite. **8.** to come close. **9.** to come to an end; terminate. **10.** *Stock Exchange* to be worth at the end of a trading period. – *adj.* **11.** shut; shut tight; not open. **12.** shut in; enclosed. **13.** confined; narrow. **14.** lacking fresh or freely circulating air. **15.** practising secrecy; reticent. **16.** stingy. **17.** near, or near together, in space, time, or relation. **18.** intimate; confidential. **19.** not deviating from a model or original. **20.** nearly even or equal. – *n.* **21.** the act of closing. **22.** the end or conclusion. **23.** a narrow entry or alley, or a courtyard to which it leads; a cul-de-sac.

closed-circuit television *n.* a television system in which cameras and receivers are linked by wire, used to watch what is happening in another part of a building for security, monitoring production operations, etc.

closed shop *n.* a workshop, factory, or the like, in which employees must belong to a particular trade union.

closet /'klɒzət/ *n.* **1.** a small room, enclosed recess, or cabinet for clothing, food, utensils, etc. – *adj.* **2.** secret.

closure /'kloʊʒə/ *n.* the act of closing or shutting.

clot /klɒt/ *n.* **1.** a mass or lump. **2.** a semisolid mass, as of coagulated blood. **3.** *Colloquial* a stupid person.

cloth /klɒθ/ *n., pl.* **cloths** /klɒθs/. **1.** a fabric formed by weaving, felting, etc., used for garments, upholstery, and many other purposes. **2.** a particular profession, especially that of the clergy.

clothe /klouð/ *v.t.*, **clothed** *or* **clad**, **clothing**. to dress; attire.

clothes /klouðz/ *pl. n.* garments for the body; articles of dress; wearing apparel.

cloud /klaʊd/ *n.* **1.** a visible collection of particles of water or ice suspended in the air. **2.** any similar mass, especially of smoke or dust. **3.** anything that obscures, darkens, or causes gloom, trouble, etc. – *v.t.* **4.** to overspread or cover with, or as with, a cloud or clouds. – **cloudy**, *adj.*

clout /klaʊt/ *n.* **1.** *Colloquial* a blow, especially with the hand; a cuff. **2.** effectiveness; force.

clove[1] /klouv/ *n.* the dried flower bud of a tropical tree used whole or ground as a spice.

clove[2] /klouv/ *n.* one of the small bulbs formed in the axils of the scales of a mother bulb, as in garlic.

clove[3] /klouv/ *v.* past tense of **cleave**[2].

cloven /ˈklouvən/ *adj.* divided.

clover /ˈklouvə/ *n.* any of various herbs with trifoliolate leaves and dense flower heads.

clown /klaʊn/ *n.* **1.** a jester or buffoon in a circus, pantomime, etc. – *v.i.* **2.** to act like a clown.

cloy /klɔɪ/ *v.t.* to weary by an excess of food, sweetness, pleasure, etc.

club /klʌb/ *n.*, *v.*, **clubbed**, **clubbing**. – *n.* **1.** a heavy stick, usually thicker at one end than at the other, suitable for a weapon; a cudgel. **2.** a stick or bat used to drive a ball, etc., in various games. **3.** a group of persons organised for a social, literary, sporting, political, or other purpose, regulated by rules agreed by its members. **4.** the building or rooms owned by or associated with such a group. **5.** a black trifoliate figure on a playing card. – *v.t.* **6.** to beat with, or as with, a club. **7.** to unite; combine; join together.

club foot *n.* a deformed or distorted foot.

cluck /klʌk/ *v.i.* to utter the cry of a hen brooding or calling her chicks.

clucky /ˈklʌki/ *adj.* (of a hen) broody.

clue /klu/ *n.* anything that serves to guide or direct in the solution of a problem, mystery, etc.

clump /klʌmp/ *n.* **1.** a cluster, especially of trees, or other plants. – *v.i.* **2.** to walk heavily and clumsily.

clumsy /ˈklʌmzi/ *adj.*, **-sier**, **-siest**. awkward in movement or action.

clung /klʌŋ/ *v.* past tense and past participle of **cling**.

cluster /ˈklʌstə/ *n.* a number of things of the same kind, growing or held together; a bunch.

clutch[1] /klʌtʃ/ *v.t.* **1.** to seize with, or as with, the hands or claws; snatch. **2.** to grip or hold tightly or firmly. – *n.* **3.** (*usu. pl.*) power of disposal or control; mastery: *in the clutches of an enemy.* **4.** a device for gripping something. **5.** (especially in a motor vehicle) the device which engages and disengages the engine from the transmission, or the pedal, etc., which operates the device.

clutch[2] /klʌtʃ/ *n.* a hatch of eggs.

clutter /ˈklʌtə/ *v.t.* **1.** to heap, litter, or strew in a disorderly manner. – *n.* **2.** a disorderly heap or assemblage; litter.

co- **1.** a prefix signifying association and accompanying action. **2.** a prefix signifying partnership, joint responsibility or ownership, as in *co-producer*, *co-writer*.

coach /koutʃ/ *n.* **1.** a large, enclosed, four-wheeled carriage. **2.** a bus, especially a single-decker, used for long distances or for sightseeing. **3.** a person who trains athletes for games, a contest, etc. **4.** a private tutor who prepares a student for an examination. – *v.t.* **5.** to give instruction or advice to in the capacity of a coach.

coagulate /kouˈægjəleɪt/ *v.t.*, *v.i.*, **-lated**, **-lating**. to change from a fluid into a thickened mass; curdle; congeal.

coal /koul/ *n.* a black or brown coloured compact and earthy organic rock formed by the accumulation and decomposition of plant material and used as a fuel.

coalesce /kouəˈlɛs/ *v.i.*, **-lesced**, **-lescing**. to unite so as to form one mass, community, etc.

coalface /ˈkoulfeɪs/ *n.* **1.** the part of the coal seam from which coal is cut. **2. at the coalface,** at the place where the real work is done, as opposed to administration, theorising, etc.

coalition /kouəˈlɪʃən/ *n.* a combination or alliance between persons, political parties, states, etc.

coarse /kɔs/ *adj.*, **coarser**, **coarsest**. **1.** of inferior or faulty quality. **2.** composed of relatively large parts or particles. **3.** lacking in fineness or delicacy of texture, structure, etc.

coast /koust/ *n.* **1.** the land next to the sea; the seashore. – *v.i.* **2.** to move along after effort has ceased; keep going on acquired momentum. – **coastal**, *adj.*

coastguard /ˈkoustgad/ *n.* a coastal police force responsible for preventing smuggling, watching for ships in distress or danger, etc.

coat /kout/ *n.* **1.** an outer garment with sleeves. **2.** a natural covering, as the hair of an animal, the bark of a tree, or the skin of a fruit. **3.** anything that covers or conceals. – *v.t.* **4.** to cover with a layer or coating.

coat of arms *n.* the heraldic bearings of a person, corporation, city, etc.

coax /kouks/ *v.t.* **1.** to influence by gentle persuasion, flattery, etc. **2.** to get or win by coaxing. – *v.i.* **3.** to use gentle persuasion, etc.

cob /kɒb/ *n.* **1.** a corncob. **2.** a short-legged, thickset horse.

cobalt /ˈkoubɔlt, -bɒlt/ *n.* **1.** *Chemistry* a silver-white metallic element which, when occurring as the silicate, gives important blue colouring substances for ceramics; also used in alloys, particularly in cobalt steel. *Symbol*: Co **2.** a blue pigment containing cobalt.

cobber /ˈkɒbə/ *n.* *Colloquial* mate; friend.

cobbler /ˈkɒblə/ *n.* **1.** someone who mends shoes. **2.** a clumsy worker.

COBOL /ˈkoubɒl/ *n.* a language for writing computer programs for general commercial use, as opposed to the more complex languages used in the sciences. Also, **Cobol**.

cobra /ˈkɒbrə, ˈkoʊbrə/ *n.* any of several extremely venomous snakes with the ability to dilate the neck to a hoodlike form.

cobweb /ˈkɒbwɛb/ *n.* a web or net spun by a spider to catch its prey.

cocaine /koʊˈkeɪn/ *n.* a bitter crystalline alkaloid, obtained from coca leaves, used as a local anaesthetic and abused as a narcotic. Also, **cocain**.

coccyx /ˈkɒksɪks, ˈkɒkɪks/ *n., pl.* **coccyges** /kɒkˈsaɪdʒiz/. a small triangular bone forming the lower extremity of the human spinal column. – **coccygeal**, *adj.*

cochineal /kɒtʃəˈnil, ˈkɒtʃənil/ *n.* a red dye.

cock[1] /kɒk/ *n.* **1.** the male of any bird, especially of the gallinaceous kind. **2.** a device for permitting or arresting the flow of a liquid or gas from a receptacle or through a pipe. – *v.t.* **3.** to pull back and set the hammer of (a firearm) preparatory to firing.

cock[2] /kɒk/ *v.t.* to set or turn up or to one side, often in an assertive, jaunty, or significant manner.

cockatoo /kɒkəˈtu/ *n.* any of several crested parrots often white, or white and yellow, pink, or red.

cockerel /ˈkɒkərəl, ˈkɒkrəl/ *n.* a young domestic cock.

cocker spaniel /kɒkə ˈspænjəl/ *n.* one of a breed of small spaniels trained for use in hunting or kept as pets.

cockeyed /ˈkɒkaɪd/ *adj.* having a squinting eye; cross-eyed.

cockle /ˈkɒkəl/ *n.* a type of mollusc.

cockpit /ˈkɒkpɪt/ *n.* **1.** (in some aeroplanes) an enclosed space containing seats for the pilot and copilot. **2.** the driver's seat in a racing car.

cockroach /ˈkɒkroʊtʃ/ *n.* any of various insects of the order Blattodea, usually nocturnal, and having a flattened body.

cockscomb /ˈkɒkskoʊm/ *n.* the comb of a cock.

cocksure /ˈkɒkʃɔ/ *adj.* overconfident.

cocktail /ˈkɒkteɪl/ *n.* **1.** any of various short mixed drinks. **2.** a small piece of chicken, fish, etc., served as a savoury.

cocky[1] /ˈkɒki/ *adj.,* **cockier**, **cockiest**. *Colloquial* arrogantly smart; conceited.

cocky[2] /ˈkɒki/ *n. Colloquial* **1.** a cockatoo, or other parrot. **2.** a farmer, especially one who farms in a small way.

cocoa /ˈkoʊkoʊ/ *n.* **1.** the roasted, husked, and ground seeds of the cacao. **2.** a beverage made from cocoa powder.

coconut /ˈkoʊkənʌt/ *n.* the seed of the coconut palm, large, hard-shelled, lined with a white edible meat, and containing a milky liquid.

cocoon /kəˈkun/ *n.* the silky envelope spun by the larvae of many insects, as silkworms, serving as a covering while they are in the chrysalis or pupal state.

cod /kɒd/ *n.* any of a number of often unrelated fishes both freshwater and marine.

coda /ˈkoʊdə/ *n.* a more or less independent passage, at the end of a musical composition, introduced to bring it to a satisfactory close.

coddle /ˈkɒdl/ *v.t.,* **-dled**, **-dling**. to cook (eggs, fruit, etc.) slowly in water just below boiling point.

code /koʊd/ *n.* **1.** any system or collection of rules and regulations. **2.** a system of symbols for use in communication by telegraph, heliograph, etc., as morse code. **3.** a system of arbitrarily chosen symbols, words etc. used for secrecy.

codger /ˈkɒdʒə/ *n. Colloquial* an odd or peculiar (old) person.

codicil /ˈkɒdəsɪl/ *n.* **1.** a supplement to a will, containing an addition, explanation, modification, etc., of something in the will. **2.** some similar supplement.

codify /ˈkoʊdəfaɪ, ˈkɒdə-/ *v.t.,* **-fied**, **-fying**. **1.** to reduce (laws, etc.) to a code. **2.** to digest; arrange in a systematic collection.

cod-liver oil *n.* a fixed oil, extracted from the liver of the common cod or of allied species, extensively used in medicine as a source of vitamins A and D.

coeducation /ˌkoʊɛdʒəˈkeɪʃən/ *n.* joint education, especially of both sexes in the same institution and classes.

coefficient /koʊəˈfɪʃənt/ *n. Mathematics* a number or quantity placed (generally) before and multiplying another quantity.

-coele a word element referring to some small cavity of the body. Also, **-cele**, **-coel**.

coelenterate /səˈlɛntəreɪt, -tərət/ *n.* one of the phylum of invertebrate animals that includes the jellyfishes, corals, etc.

coemption /koʊˈɛmpʃən, -ˈɛmʃən/ *n.* the buying up of the whole of a particular commodity, especially in order to acquire a monopoly.

coeno- a word element meaning 'common'. Also, **ceno-**; (*before a vowel*), **coen-**.

coerce /koʊˈɜs/ *v.t.,* **-erced**, **-ercing**. to compel by forcible action. – **coercion**, *n.* – **coercive**, *adj.*

coffee /ˈkɒfi/ *n.* a beverage made from the roasted and ground **coffee beans** of various tropical trees and shrubs.

coffer /ˈkɒfə/ *n.* **1.** a box or chest, especially one for valuables. **2.** (*pl.*) a treasury; funds.

coffin /ˈkɒfən/ *n.* the box or case in which a corpse is placed for burial.

cog /kɒg/ *n.* a tooth or projection (usually one of a series) on a wheel, etc., for transmitting motion to, or receiving motion from, a corresponding tooth or part with which it engages.

cogent /ˈkoʊdʒənt/ *adj.* compelling assent or belief; convincing. – **cogency**, *n.*

cogitate /ˈkɒdʒəteɪt/ *v.i.,* **-tated**, **-tating**. to think hard; ponder; meditate.

cognac /ˈkɒnjæk/ *n.* French brandy.

cognate /ˈkɒgneɪt/ *adj.* related by birth or origin.

cognisance = cognizance /ˈkɒgnəzəns, ˈkɒnə-/ *n.* **1.** knowledge; notice; perception. **2.** the right of taking judicial notice, as possessed by a court. – **cognisable**, *adj.*

cognition /kɒgˈnɪʃən/ *n.* the act or process of knowing; perception.

cohabit /koʊˈhæbət/ *v.i.* to live together in a sexual relationship.

cohere /koʊˈhɪə/ *v.i.,* **-hered**, **-hering**. **1.** to hold fast, as parts of the same mass. **2.** to agree; be congruous. – **coherent**, *adj.*

cohesion /koʊ'hiʒən/ *n.* the act or state of cohering, uniting, or sticking together. – **cohesive**, *adj.*

cohort /'koʊhɔt/ *n.* **1.** any group or company. **2.** a crony; ally; supporter: *the union leader and his cohorts.*

coiffure /kwʌ'fjʊə/ *n.* a style of arranging or combing the hair.

coil /kɔɪl/ *v.t.* **1.** to wind into rings one above another; twist or wind spirally. – *n.* **2.** a connected series of spirals or rings. **3.** a single such ring.

coin /kɔɪn/ *n.* **1.** a piece of metal stamped and issued by the authority of the government for use as money. **2.** such pieces collectively. – *v.t.* **3.** to make; invent; fabricate.

coincide /koʊən'saɪd/ *v.i.*, **-cided**, **-ciding**. to occupy the same place in space, the same point or period in time, or the same relative position.

coincidence /koʊ'ɪnsədəns/ *n.* **1.** the condition or fact of coinciding. **2.** a striking occurrence of two or more events at one time apparently by mere chance. **3.** exact agreement in nature, character, etc. – **coincidental**, *adj.*

coinsurance /koʊɪn'ʃɔrəns/ *n.* **1.** insurance jointly with another or others. **2.** a form of fire and various other forms of property insurance in which a person taking out insurance on property for less than its full value is regarded as a joint insurer and becomes jointly and proportionately responsible for losses. **3.** the method of distributing liability, in case of loss, among several insurers whose policies attach to the same risk.

coitus /'koʊətəs/ *n.* sexual intercourse. Also, **coition** /koʊ'ɪʃən/.

coke[1] /koʊk/ *n.* the solid product resulting from imperfect combustion, used as a fuel, in metallurgy, etc.

coke[2] /koʊk/ *n. Colloquial* cocaine.

col-[1] variant of **com-**, by assimilation before *l*, as in *collateral.*

col-[2] variant of **colo-** before vowels.

cola /'koʊlə/ *n.* **1.** the cola nut. **2.** an extract prepared from it. **3.** a carbonated soft drink containing such an extract. **4.** the tree producing it. Also, **kola**.

colander /'kʌləndə, 'kɒl-/ *n.* a strainer for draining off liquids, especially in cookery. Also, **cullender**.

cold /koʊld/ *n.* **1.** having a relatively low temperature; having little or no warmth. **2.** producing or feeling, especially in a high degree, a lack of warmth. **3.** *Colloquial* unconscious because of a severe blow, shock, etc. **4.** not affectionate, cordial, or friendly; unresponsive. – *n.* **5.** the relative absence of heat. **6.** the sensation produced by loss of heat from the body. **7.** Also, **the common cold**. an indisposition caused by a virus, characterised by catarrh, hoarseness, coughing, etc.

cold-blooded *adj.* **1.** without feeling; unsympathetic; cruel. **2.** designating or relating to animals, as fishes and reptiles, whose body temperature approximates to that of the surrounding medium.

cold front *n.* the contact surface between two air-masses where the cooler mass is advancing against and under the warmer mass.

cold-shoulder *v.t.* to ignore; show indifference to.

cold sore *n.* a vesicular eruption on the face often accompanying a cold or a febrile condition; herpes simplex.

cold war *n.* intense economic and political rivalry just short of military conflict.

coleslaw /'koʊlslɔ/ *n.* a dressed salad of finely sliced white cabbage. Also, **slaw**.

colic /'kɒlɪk/ *n.* paroxysmal pain in the abdomen or bowels. – **colicky**, *adj.*

collaborate /kə'læbəreɪt/ *v.i.*, **-rated**, **-rating**. **1.** to work, one with another. **2.** to cooperate treacherously.

collage /kə'laʒ, kɒ'laʒ/ *n.* a pictorial composition made from any or a combination of various materials.

collapse /kə'læps/ *v.*, **-lapsed**, **-lapsing**, *n.* – *v.i.* **1.** to fall or cave in; crumble suddenly. **2.** to break down; come to nothing; fail. – *n.* **3.** a sudden, complete failure; a breakdown.

collapsible /kə'læpsəbəl/ *adj.* designed to fold into a more compact or manageable size, as a pram, bicycle, etc.

collar /'kɒlə/ *n.* **1.** anything worn or placed round the neck. **2.** the part of a shirt, blouse, coat, etc., round the neck, usually folded over. **3.** *Machinery* an enlargement encircling a rod or shaft, and serving usually as a holding or bearing piece. – *v.t.* **4.** to put a collar on; furnish with a collar. **5.** to seize by the collar or neck.

collarbone /'kɒləboʊn/ *n.* either of two slender bones each connecting the breastbone with the shoulder blade, and forming the front part of the shoulder.

collate /kə'leɪt, kɒ-/ *v.t.*, **-lated**, **-lating**. to put together (a document) by sorting its pages into the correct order.

collateral /kə'lætərəl/ *adj.* **1.** situated at the side. **2.** accompanying; attendant; auxiliary. – *n.* **3.** security pledged for the payment of a loan.

colleague /'kɒlig/ *n.* an associate in office, professional work, etc.

collect /kə'lɛkt/ *v.t.* **1.** to gather together; assemble. **2.** to accumulate; make a collection of. **3.** to regain control of (one's thoughts, faculties, etc., or oneself). **4.** to fetch; call for and remove. **5.** to run into or collide with, especially in a motor vehicle. – *v.i.* **6.** to gather together; assemble. **7.** to accumulate. – *adj., adv.* **8.** to be paid for by the receiver. – **collection**, *n.*

collectable = collectible /kə'lɛktəbəl/ *n.* **1.** an object of great antiquarian value, such as a rare coin, often collected as an investment. **2.** an object of no intrinsic value, such as a matchbox or beer can, collected as a hobby or as a memento.

collective /kə'lɛktɪv/ **1.** forming a collection or aggregate; aggregate; combined. **2.** relating to a group of individuals taken together. *n.* **3.** a collective body; aggregate. **4.** a communal enterprise or system.

collective bargaining *n.* a non-institutionalised system of reaching agreement on a matter of industrial disputation between employers and employees through discussions held by their representatives.

collective noun *n.* a noun that under the singular form expresses a grouping of individual objects or persons, as *herd, jury,* and *clergy.*

college /'kɒlɪdʒ/ *n.* **1.** a (usually) post-secondary, diploma-awarding, technical or professional school, as a teachers' college or technical college. **2.** an institution for special or professional instruction, as in medicine, pharmacy, agriculture, music, etc., often part of a university. **3.** an endowed, self-governing association of scholars incorporated within a university, as the church colleges within the University of Sydney. **4.** any of certain large private schools, or sometimes public schools. **5.** an organised association of persons having certain powers and rights, and performing certain duties or engaged in a particular pursuit. – **collegian,** *n.* – **collegiate,** *adj.*

collide /kə'laɪd/ *v.i.,* **-lided, -liding**. to come together with force; come into violent contact; crash. – **collision,** *n.*

collie /'kɒli/ *n.* a dog of any of certain intelligent varieties much used for tending sheep. Also, **colly**.

colliery /'kɒljəri/ *n., pl.* **-ries**. a coal mine, including all buildings and equipment.

collocate /'kɒləkeɪt/ *v.t.,* **-cated, -cating**. to set or place together. – **collocation,** *n.*

colloquial /kə'loʊkwiəl/ *adj.* appropriate to or characteristic of conversational or informal speech or writing.

colloquium /kə'loʊkwiəm/ *n., pl.* **-quia, -quiums**. an informal conference or group discussion.

collusion /kə'luʒən/ *n.* secret agreement for a fraudulent purpose; conspiracy.

colo- a combining form of **colon**[2].

cologne /kə'loʊn/ *n.* a perfumed toilet water.

colon[1] /'koʊlən/ *n.* a point of punctuation (:) marking off a main portion of a sentence (intermediate in force between the semicolon and the period).

colon[2] /'koʊlən/ *n., pl.* **-lons, -la** /-lə/. that portion of the large intestine which extends from the caecum to the rectum.

colonnade /'kɒləneɪd, kɒlə'neɪd/ *n.* **1.** a series of columns set at regular intervals. **2.** a long row of trees.

colony /'kɒləni/ *n., pl.* **-nies**. **1.** a group of people who leave their native country to form in a new land a settlement subject to, or connected with, the parent state. **2.** the country or district settled or colonised. **3.** any people or territory separated from but subject to a ruling power. – **colonial,** *adj.* – **colonise = colonize,** *v.* – **colonist,** *n.*

colophon /'kɒləfɒn, -fən/ *n.* a publisher's distinctive emblem.

colossal /kə'lɒsəl/ *adj.* gigantic; vast.

colostomy /kə'lɒstəmi/ *n.* the surgical formation of an artificial anus.

colour = color /'kʌlə/ *n.* **1.** that quality of light (reflected or transmitted by a substance) which is basically determined by its spectral composition. **2.** racial complexion other than white, especially Negro. **3.** vivid or distinctive quality, as of literary work. **4.** that which is used for colouring; pigment; paint; dye. **5.** (*pl.*) a flag, ensign, etc., as of a military body or ship. **6.** outward appearance or aspect; guise or show. **7.** an apparent or prima-facie right or ground (especially in legal sense). – *v.t.* **8.** to give or apply colour to; tinge; paint; dye. **9.** to cause to appear different from the reality. – *v.i.* **10.** to take on or change colour. **11.** to flush; blush.

colourblind = colorblind /'kʌləblaɪnd/ *adj.* having a congenital inability to detect or distinguish between certain colours (usually red and green). – **colour blindness,** *n.*

colour fast = color fast *adj.* (of fabric dyes) lasting.

-colous a word element indicating habitat.

colt /koʊlt/ *n.* a male horse not past its fourth birthday.

column /'kɒləm/ *n.* **1.** *Architecture* an upright shaft or body of greater length than thickness, usually serving as a support; a pillar. **2.** any column-like object, mass, or formation. **3.** one of the two or more vertical rows of lines of type or printed matter of a page. **4.** a regular contribution to a newspaper, usually signed, and consisting of comment, news, etc.

com- a prefix meaning 'with', 'jointly', 'in combination' and (with intensive force) 'completely'.

coma /'koʊmə/ *n., pl.* **-mas**. a state of prolonged unconsciousness. – **comatose,** *adj.*

comb /koʊm/ *n.* **1.** a toothed piece of bone, metal, etc., for arranging or cleaning the hair, or for keeping it in place. **2.** any comblike instrument, object, or formation. **3.** the fleshy, more or less serrated excrescence or growth on the head of the domestic fowl. – *v.t.* **4.** to dress (the hair, etc.) with, or as with, a comb. **5.** to search everywhere and with great thoroughness.

combat /'kɒmbæt, kəm'bæt/ *v.,* **-bated, -bating,** /'kɒmbæt/ *n.* – *v.t., v.i.* **1.** to fight or contend against; oppose vigorously. – *n.* **2.** a fight between two people, armies, etc.

combine /kəm'baɪn/ *v.,* **-bined, -bining,** /'kɒmbaɪn/ *n.* – *v.t.* **1.** to bring or join into a close union or whole; unite; associate; coalesce. – *n.* **2.** a combination of persons or groups for the furtherance of their political, commercial, or other interests. – **combination,** *n.*

combustible /kəm'bʌstəbəl/ *adj.* capable of catching fire and burning.

combustion /kəm'bʌstʃən/ *n.* the act or process of burning.

come /kʌm/ *v.,* **came, come, coming,** *n.* – *v.i.* **1.** to move towards the speaker or towards a particular place; approach. **2.** to arrive by movement or in course of progress. **3.** to extend; reach. **4.** to issue; emanate; be derived. **5.** to be born in or live in (fol. by *from*). **6.** to arrive or appear as a result. **7.** to turn out to be. **8.** *Colloquial* to have an orgasm. **9. come about,** to arrive in due course; come to pass. **10. come across,** to meet with, especially by chance. **11. come down with,** to become afflicted with, especially with a disease. **12. come good,** *Colloquial* to improve after an unpromising beginning. **13. come in, a.** to enter. **b.** to become useful, fashionable, etc. **14. come into, a.** to get. **b.** to inherit. **15. come out, a.**

to appear; be published. **b.** to be revealed; show itself. **16. come round, a.** to relent. **b.** to recover consciousness; revive. **c.** to change (an opinion, direction, etc.). **17. come the raw prawn,** *Colloquial* to try to deceive (fol. by *with*). **18. come to, a.** to recover consciousness. **b.** to amount to; equal.

comedian /kə'midiən/ *n.* an actor or writer of comedy. – **comedienne**, *fem. n.*

comedy /'kɒmədi/ *n., pl.* **-dies**. **1.** a play, film, etc., of light and humorous character. **2.** the comic element of drama, of literature generally, or of life.

comely /kʌmli/ *adj.,* **-lier**, **-liest**. pleasing in appearance; fair.

comet /'kɒmət/ *n.* a celestial body moving about the sun in an elongated orbit.

comeuppance /kʌm'ʌpəns/ *n. Colloquial* a well-deserved punishment or retribution. Also, **comeupance**.

comfort /'kʌmfət/ *v.t.* **1.** to soothe when in grief; console; cheer. – *n.* **2.** relief in affliction; consolation; solace. **3.** a person or thing that affords consolation. **4.** a state of ease, with freedom from pain and anxiety, and satisfaction of bodily wants.

comfortable /'kʌmftəbəl, 'kʌmfətəbəl/ *adj.* **1.** producing or attended with comfort or ease of mind or body. **2.** being in a state of comfort or ease; easy and undisturbed. **3.** adequate.

comic /'kɒmɪk/ *adj.* **1.** of, relating to, or of the nature of comedy, as distinct from tragedy. **2.** provoking laughter; humorous. – *n.* **3.** *Colloquial* a comic actor. **4.** a magazine containing one or more stories in comic strip form. **5.** (*pl.*) *Colloquial* comic strips.

comical /'kɒmɪkəl/ *adj.* provoking laughter, or amusing; funny.

comic strip *n.* a series of cartoon drawings, relating a comic incident, an adventure story, etc.

comma /'kɒmə/ *n.* a mark of punctuation (,) used to indicate the smallest interruptions in continuity of thought or grammatical construction.

command /kə'mænd, -'mand/ *v.t.* **1.** to order or direct with authority. **2.** to require with authority; demand. **3.** to have or exercise authority over. – *n.* **4.** the act of commanding or ordering. **5.** control; mastery; disposal.

commandant /'kɒməndænt, -dant/ *n.* the commanding officer of a place, group, etc.; a commander.

command-driven *adj.* (of a computer) operated by specific commands entered via a keyboard rather than by selecting options from a menu (opposed to *menu-driven*).

commandeer /kɒmən'dɪə/ *v.t.* to seize (private property) for military or other public use.

commander /kə'mændə, -'mand-/ *n.* someone who exercises authority; a leader; a chief officer.

commandment /kə'mændmənt, kə'mand-/ *n.* a command or edict.

commando /kə'mændoʊ, -'man-/ *n., pl.* **-dos**, **-does**. **1.** a small specially trained fighting force. **2.** a member of such a force.

commemorate /kə'mɛməreɪt/ *v.t.,* **-rated**, **-rating**. **1.** to serve as a memento of. **2.** to honour the memory of by some solemnity or celebration.

commence /kə'mɛns/ *v.t.,* **-menced**, **-mencing**. to begin; start.

commend /kə'mɛnd/ *v.t.* **1.** to present or mention as worthy of confidence, notice, kindness, etc.; recommend. **2.** to entrust; give in charge; deliver with confidence. – **commendation**, *n.*

commensurate /kə'mɛnʃərət/ *adj.* **1.** of equal extent or duration. **2.** proportionate.

comment /'kɒmɛnt/ *n.* a remark, observation, or criticism.

commentary /'kɒməntəri, -tri/ *n., pl.* **-taries**. **1.** a series of comments or annotations. **2.** a description of a public event as a cricket match, official opening of parliament, etc., broadcast or televised as it happens.

commentator /'kɒmənteɪtə/ *n.* a writer or broadcaster who makes critical or explanatory remarks about news, events, or describes sporting events, etc.

commerce /'kɒmɜs/ *n.* **1.** interchange of goods or commodities, especially on a large scale between different countries (**foreign commerce**) or between different parts of the same country (**domestic commerce** or **internal commerce**); trade; business. **2.** social relations.

commercial /kə'mɜʃəl/ *adj.* **1.** of, or of the nature of, commerce. **2.** engaged in commerce. **3.** capable of being sold in great numbers. **4.** setting possible commercial return above artistic considerations. **5.** not entirely or chemically pure. **6.** *Radio, TV* financially dependent on revenue from advertising. – *n.* **7.** *Radio, TV* an advertisement.

commercial bill *n.* a security acknowledging a debt, signed by both the borrower (the drawer) and the lender (the acceptor) and stating the date on which repayment is due.

commercial bill market *n.* the market in which commercial bills are sold or discounted.

commercialese /kəmɜʃə'liz/ *n.* the jargon used by those engaged in commercial activities.

commercial law *n.* the principles and rules drawn chiefly from custom, determining the rights and obligations of commercial transactions.

commercial traveller *n.* a travelling agent, especially for a wholesale business house, who solicits orders for goods.

commiserate /kə'mɪzəreɪt/ *v.i.,* **-rated**, **-rating**. to sympathise (fol. by *with*)

commission /kə'mɪʃən/ *n.* **1.** the act of committing or giving in charge. **2.** an authoritative order, charge, or direction. **3.** a body of persons authoritatively charged with particular functions. **4.** the condition of anything in active service or use. **5.** a task or matter committed to one's charge. **6.** authority to act as agent for another or others in commercial transactions. **7.** a sum or percentage allowed to an agent, salesman, etc., for services. **8.** the position or rank of an officer in the army or navy. – *v.t.* **9.** to give a commission to. **10.** to authorise; send on a mission.

commissionaire /kəmɪʃə'nɛə/ *n.* a uniformed messenger or doorkeeper at a hotel, office, theatre, etc.

commissioner /kə'mɪʃənə/ *n.* **1.** one commissioned to act officially; a member of a commission. **2.** a government official in charge of a department.

commit /kə'mɪt/ *v.t.*, **-mitted**, **-mitting**. **1.** to give in trust or charge; entrust; consign. **2.** to consign to custody in an institution, as a jail, mental hospital, etc. **3.** to hand over for treatment, disposal, etc. **4.** to do; perform; perpetrate. **5.** to bind by pledge or assurance; pledge. – **commitment**, *n.*

committee /kə'mɪti/ *n.* a person or a group of persons elected or appointed from a larger body to investigate, report, or act in special cases.

commode /kə'moʊd/ *n.* **1.** a piece of furniture containing drawers or shelves. **2.** a stand or cupboard containing a chamber-pot or washbasin.

commodious /kə'moʊdiəs/ *adj.* convenient and roomy; spacious.

commodities market /kə'mɒdətiz makət/ *n.* a market in which commodities are bought and sold, either immediately (the **spot market**) or more commonly for delivery at a future date (the **futures market**).

commodity /kə'mɒdəti/ *n.*, *pl.* **-ties**. an article of trade or commerce.

commodore /'kɒmədɔ/ *n.* the senior captain of a line of merchant vessels.

common /'kɒmən/ *adj.* **1.** belonging equally to, or shared alike by, two or more or all in question. **2.** of frequent occurrence; familiar; usual. **3.** of mediocre or inferior quality; mean; low.

commoner /'kɒmənə/ *n.* one of the common people.

common law *n.* **1.** the system of law originating in England, as distinct from the civil or Roman law and the canon or ecclesiastical law. **2.** the unwritten law, especially of England, Australia, and other countries with a similar legal system, based on custom or court decision, as distinct from statute law. **3.** the law administered through the system of writs, as distinct from equity, etc.

common market *n.* a group of countries which agree to trade with one another without tariffs, and to impose common tariffs as countries outside the group.

common noun *n.* *Grammar* a noun that can be preceded by an article or other limiting modifier, in meaning applicable to any one or all the members of a class, as *man*, *men*, *city*, *cities*, in contrast to *Shakespeare*, *Hobart*. Cf. **proper noun**.

commonplace /'kɒmənpleɪs/ *adj.* ordinary; without individuality.

common room *n.* (in schools, universities, etc.) a sitting room for the use of the teaching staff, or, in some cases, of the students.

common rule *n.* a provision of an award of an industrial tribunal which has general application throughout the whole of the industry in which the award is operative.

commons /'kɒmənz/ *pl. n.* the body of people not of noble birth.

commonsense /kɒmən'sɛns/ *n.* sound, practical perception or understanding.

common shares *pl. n.* stock which ordinarily has no preference in the matter of dividends or assets and represents the residual ownership of a corporate business. Also, *US*, **common stock**.

commonwealth /'kɒmənwɛlθ/ *n.* **1.** the whole body of people of a nation or state; the body politic. **2.** (*cap.*) a federation of states and territories with powers and responsibilities divided between a central government and a number of smaller governments, each controlling certain responsibilities in a defined area, as *the Commonwealth of Australia*.

commotion /kə'moʊʃən/ *n.* violent or tumultuous motion; agitation.

communal /kə'mjunəl, 'kɒmjənəl/ *adj.* relating to a commune or a community.

commune[1] /kə'mjun/ *v.i.*, **-muned**, **-muning**. to converse; talk together; interchange thoughts or feelings.

commune[2] /'kɒmjun/ *n.* any community of like-minded people choosing to live independently of the state.

communicate /kə'mjunəkeɪt/ *v.*, **-cated**, **-cating**. – *v.t.* **1.** to give to another as a partaker; impart; transmit. **2.** to impart knowledge of; make known. – *v.i.* **3.** to have interchange of thoughts.

communication /kəmjunə'keɪʃən/ *n.* **1.** the act or fact of communicating; transmission. **2.** a document or message imparting views, information, etc. **3.** (*pl.*) the means of transmitting information by telephone, radio, television, etc.

communicative /kə'mjunəkətɪv/ *adj.* inclined to communicate or impart.

communion /kə'mjunjən/ *n.* **1.** the act of sharing, or holding in common; participation. **2.** interchange of thoughts or interests; communication; intimate talk. **3.** *Ecclesiastical* (*sometimes cap.*) the celebration of the Lord's Supper; the Eucharist.

communiqué /kə'mjunəkeɪ/ *n.* an official bulletin or communication as of war news, events at a conference etc., usually to the press or public.

communism /'kɒmjənɪzəm/ *n.* a theory or system of social organisation based on the holding of all property in common. – **communist**, *n.* – **communistic**, *adj.*

community /kə'mjunəti/ *n.*, *pl.* **-ties**. a social group of any size whose members reside in a specific locality, share government, and have a cultural and historical heritage.

community title *n.* *Law* a form of title which allows for common areas in the subdivision of land, as for community groups, retirement villages, etc.

commute /kə'mjut/ *v.*, **-muted**, **-muting**. **1.** to change (a penalty, etc.) for one less burdensome or severe. **2.** to serve as a substitute. **3.** to make a collective payment, especially of a reduced amount, as an equivalent for a number of payments. **4.** to travel regularly between home (usually distant) and work, generally using a season ticket.

compact[1] /kɒm'pækt, 'kɒmpækt/ *adj.*, /kɒm-

'pækt/ *v.*, /'kɒmpækt/ *n.* – *adj.* **1.** joined or packed together; closely and firmly united; dense; solid. **2.** arranged within a relatively small space. **3.** expressed concisely. – *v.t.* **4.** to join or pack closely together; consolidate; condense. – *n.* **5.** a small case containing a mirror, face powder, a puff, and (sometimes) rouge.

compact² /'kɒmpækt/ *n.* an agreement between parties; covenant; contract.

compact disc *n.* a digitally-encoded disc, used for the reproduction of high-fidelity sound and low-resolution video information, and decoded by a laser beam. Also, **CD**.

companion /kəm'pænjən/ *n.* **1.** someone who accompanies or associates with another. **2.** a handbook; guide.

companionable /kəm'pænjənəbəl/ *adj.* fitted to be a companion; sociable.

company /'kʌmpəni/ *n.* **1.** a number of individuals assembled or associated together; a group of people. **2.** a guest or guests. **3.** a number of persons united or incorporated for joint action, especially for business. **4.** the member or members of a firm not specifically named in the firm's title.

company tax *n.* a tax imposed on the profits of limited companies, intended to separate the taxation of companies from that of individuals.

company title *n.* *Law* a form of interest in property, particularly multi-storey buildings, where the whole of the building is owned by a company, shares in which are held by tenants.

comparative *adj.* **1.** of or relating to comparison. **2.** estimated by comparison; not positive or absolute; relative. **3.** *Grammar* denoting the intermediate degree of the comparison of adjectives and adverbs.

compare /kəm'pɛə/ *v.*, **-pared**, **-paring**. – *v.t.* **1.** to represent as similar or analogous; liken (fol. by *to*). **2.** to note the similarities and differences of (fol. by *with*). – *v.i.* **3.** to bear comparison; be held equal. – **comparable**, *adj.*

comparison /kəm'pærəsən/ *n.* **1.** the act of comparing. **2.** the state of being compared. **3.** a likening; an illustration by similitude; a comparative estimate or statement.

compartment /kəm'patmənt/ *n.* **1.** a part or space marked or partitioned off. **2.** a separate room, section, etc.

compass /'kʌmpəs/ *n.* **1.** an instrument for determining directions. **2.** space within limits; area; extent; range; scope. **3.** (*usu. pl.*) an instrument for describing circles, measuring distances, etc., consisting generally of two movable legs hinged at one end. – *v.t.* **4.** to extend or stretch around; hem in; encircle.

compassion /kəm'pæʃən/ *n.* a feeling of sorrow or pity for the sufferings or misfortunes of another; sympathy. – **compassionate**, *adj.*

compatible /kəm'pætəbəl/ *adj.* **1.** capable of existing together in harmony. **2.** (of a computer device) able to work in conjunction with another specified device.

compatriot /kəm'peɪtriət/ *n.* a fellow countryman or fellow countrywoman.

compel /kəm'pɛl/ *v.t.*, **-pelled**, **-pelling**. to force or drive, especially to a course of action.

compelling /kəm'pɛlɪŋ/ *adj.* (of a person, writer, actor, etc.) demanding attention, respect.

compendium /kəm'pɛndiəm/ *n.*, *pl.* **-diums**, **-dia** /-diə/. a comprehensive summary of a subject.

compensate /'kɒmpənseɪt/ *v.*, **-sated**, **-sating**. – *v.t.* **1.** to counterbalance; offset; make up for. – *v.i.* **2.** to provide or be an equivalent. **3.** make up; make amends (fol. by *for*). – **compensation**, *n.*

compere /'kɒmpɛə/ *n.* someone who introduces and links the acts in an entertainment.

compete /kəm'pit/ *v.i.*, **-peted**, **-peting**. to contend with another for a prize, profit, etc.; engage in a contest; vie.

competent /'kɒmpətənt/ *adj.* **1.** properly qualified, capable. **2.** fitting, suitable, or sufficient for the purpose; adequate. – **competence**, *n.*

competition /kɒmpə'tɪʃən/ *n.* **1.** a contest for some prize or advantage. **2.** the rivalry between two or more business enterprises to secure the patronage of prospective buyers. **3.** a competitor or competitors.

competitive /kəm'pɛtətɪv/ *adj.* of, relating to, involving, or decided by competition.

competitor /kəm'pɛtətə/ *n.* someone who competes; a rival.

compile /kəm'paɪl/ *v.t.*, **-piled**, **-piling**. to put together (literary materials) in one book or work. – **compilation**, *n.*

compiler /kəm'paɪlə/ *n.* *Computers* a computer program which translates programming languages such as FORTRAN and ALGOL into the basic commands which activate the computer.

complacent /kəm'pleɪsənt/ *adj.* pleased, especially with oneself or one's own merits, advantages, etc. – **complacency**, *n.*

complain /kəm'pleɪn/ *v.i.* to express grief, pain, uneasiness, censure, resentment, or dissatisfaction; find fault. – **complaint**, *n.*

complainant /kəm'pleɪnənt/ *n.* someone who makes a complaint, as in a legal action.

complement /'kɒmpləmənt/ *n.*, /'kɒmplə,mɛnt/ *v.* – *n.* **1.** that which completes or makes perfect. **2.** either of two parts or things needed to complete the whole. **3.** full quantity or amount; complete allowance. – *v.t.* **4.** to complete; form a complement to. – **complementary**, *n.*

complete /kəm'plit/ *adj.*, *v.*, **-pleted**, **-pleting**. – *adj.* **1.** having all its parts or elements; whole; entire; full. **2.** finished; ended; concluded. – *v.t.* **3.** to make complete. – **completion**, *n.*

complex /'kɒmplɛks/ *adj.* **1.** composed of interconnected parts; compound; composite. **2.** complicated; intricate. – *n.* **3.** a complex whole or system; a complicated assembly of particulars. – **complexity**, *n.*

complexion /kəm'plɛkʃən/ *n.* **1.** the natural colour and appearance of the skin, especially of the face. **2.** appearance; aspect; character.

compliance /kəm'plaɪəns/ *n.* the act of complying; an acquiescing or yielding.

complicate /'kɒmpləkeɪt/ *v.t.*, **-cated**,

-cating. to make complex, intricate, or involved. – **complication**, *n.*

complicity /kəm'plɪsəti/ *n., pl.* **-ties**. the state of being an accomplice; partnership in wrongdoing.

compliment /'kɒmpləmənt/ *n.,* /'kɒmplə-ˌmɛnt/ *v.* – *n.* **1.** an expression of praise, commendation, or admiration. **2.** a formal act or expression of civility, respect, or regard. – *v.t.* **3.** to pay a compliment to. – **complimentary**, *adj.*

comply /kəm'plaɪ/ *v.i.*, **-plied, -plying**. to act in accordance with wishes, requests, commands, requirements, conditions, etc. (fol. by *with*).

compo /'kɒmpoʊ/ *n. Colloquial* compensation for injury at or in connection with a person's work; workers' compensation.

component /kəm'poʊnənt/ *adj.* **1.** composing; constituent. – *n.* **2.** a constituent part.

comport /kəm'pɔt/ *v.t.* **1.** to bear or conduct (oneself); behave. – *v.i.* **2.** to agree or accord; suit (fol. by *with*).

compose /kəm'poʊz/ *v.t.*, **-posed, -posing**. **1.** to make or form by uniting parts or elements. **2.** to devise and make (a literary or musical production). **3.** to bring (the body or mind) to a condition of repose, calmness, etc.; calm; quiet. – **composer**, *n.*

composite /'kɒmpəzət/ *adj.* made up of various parts or elements; compound.

composite rating *n.* a property rating system based on both unimproved capital value and the commercial value.

composition /kɒmpə'zɪʃən/ *n.* **1.** the act of combining parts or elements to form a whole. **2.** the resulting state or product. **3.** a compound or composite substance. **4.** a short essay written as a school exercise. **5.** an agreement or compromise, especially one by which a creditor (or group of creditors) accepts partial payment from a debtor. **6.** a sum of money so paid.

compositor /kəm'pɒzətə/ *n. Printing* a person who assembles the type for a printed page.

compos mentis /kɒmpəs 'mɛntəs/ *adj.* sane.

compost /'kɒmpɒst/ *n.* a mixture of various kinds of organic matter used for fertilising land.

composure /kəm'poʊʒə/ *n.* serene state of mind; calmness; tranquillity.

compound[1] /'kɒmpaʊnd/ *adj., n.*; /kəm-'paʊnd/ *v.* – *adj.* **1.** composed of two or more parts, elements, or ingredients, or involving two or more actions, functions, etc.; composite. – *n.* **2.** something formed by compounding or combining parts, elements, etc. – *v.t.* **3.** to put together into a whole; combine. **4.** to settle or adjust by agreement, especially for a reduced amount, as a debt. **5.** to pay (interest) on the accrued interest as well as the principal. – *v.i.* **6.** to make a bargain; come to terms; compromise.

compound[2] /'kɒmpaʊnd/ *n.* an enclosure in which people of the same race, occupation, religion, etc., live, sometimes against their will.

compound interest *n.* interest paid, not only on the principal, but on the interest after it has periodically come due and, remaining unpaid, been added to the principal.

comprehend /kɒmprə'hɛnd/ *v.t.* **1.** to understand the meaning or nature of; conceive; know. **2.** to take in or embrace; include; comprise. – **comprehension**, *n.*

comprehensive /kɒmprə'hɛnsɪv/ *adj.* comprehending; inclusive; comprehending much; of large scope.

comprehensive insurance *n.* a form of insurance covering a wide range of instances in which the insured asset or property may be lost or damaged.

compress /kəm'prɛs/ *v.,* /'kɒmprɛs/ *n.* – *v.t.* **1.** to press together; force into less space. – *n.* **2.** *Medicine* a soft pad held in place by a bandage, used as a means of pressure or to supply moisture, cold, heat, or medication. – **compression**, *n.*

comprise /kəm'praɪz/ *v.t.*, **-prised, -prising**. **1.** to comprehend; include; contain. **2.** to consist of; be composed of. **3.** to combine to make up.

compromise /'kɒmprəmaɪz/ *n., v.*, **-mised, -mising**. – *n.* **1.** a settlement of differences by mutual concessions. **2.** something intermediate between different things. **3.** an endangering, especially of reputation; exposure to danger, suspicion, etc. – *v.t.* **4.** to settle by a compromise. **5.** to make liable to danger, suspicion, scandal, etc.; endanger the reputation.

compulsion /kəm'pʌlʃən/ *n.* **1.** the act of compelling; coercion. **2.** *Psychology* a strong irrational impulse to carry out a given act. – **compulsive**, *adj.*

compulsory /kəm'pʌlsəri/ *adj.* **1.** using compulsion; compelling. **2.** compelled; forced; obligatory.

compulsory conference *n.* a meeting to which parties to an industrial dispute and, on occasion, other interested parties, are summoned by an industrial tribunal.

compulsory unionism *n.* the requirement that people become and remain financial members of the union covering their calling as a pre-condition of employment.

compunction /kəm'pʌŋkʃən, -'pʌŋʃən/ *n.* regret for wrongdoing or giving pain to another.

compute /kəm'pjut/ *v.t., v.i.*, **-puted, -puting**. to determine by calculation; reckon; calculate. – **computation**, *n.*

computer /kəm'pjutə/ *n.* an apparatus for performing mathematical computations electronically according to a series of stored instructions called a program; an **analog computer** represents information in the form of continuously varying voltages; a **digital computer** represents information by patterns of on-off states of voltages.

computer-aided design *n.* the use of computers in design allowing the designer greater flexibility in formulating projects on screen. Also, **CAD**.

computer-aided manufacturing *n.* the use of computers in the manufacturing process for networking machines and computerised devices such as robots. Also, **CAM**.

computer crime *n.* crime, usually fraud, involving the illegal subverting of a computer system for personal gain, as in transferring funds or gaining unauthorised access to data.

computerise = computerize /kəm'pjutəraɪz/ *v.t.*, **-ised**, **-ising**. **1.** to process or store (data) in a computer. **2.** to furnish or provide with a computer system. – **computerisation**, *n.*

computer program *n.* a sequence of commands in a machine language which will cause a computer to perform a desired calculation. Also, **computer programme**.

computer terminal *n.* an input or output device connected to a computer but at a distance from it.

comrade /'kɒmreɪd, 'kɒmrəd/ *n.* an associate in occupation or friendship.

con[1] /kɒn/ *adv.* **1.** against a proposition, opinion, etc.; not pro (for). – *n.* **2.** the argument, arguer, or voter against (something).

con[2] /kɒn/ *n.*, *v.*, **conned**, **conning**. – *n.* **1.** a confidence trick; swindle. – *v.t.* **2.** to swindle; defraud.

con- variant of **com-**.

concave /'kɒnkeɪv/ *adj.* curved like the interior of a circle or hollow sphere.

conceal /kən'sil/ *v.t.* to hide.

concede /kən'sid/ *v.t.*, **-ceded**, **-ceding**. **1.** to admit as true, just, or proper; admit. **2.** to grant as a right or privilege; yield. **3.** to admit defeat in an election.

conceit /kən'sit/ *n.* **1.** an exaggerated estimate of one's own ability, importance, wit, etc. **2.** a fanciful thought, idea, or expression, especially of a strained or far-fetched nature.

conceivable /kən'sivəbəl/ *adj.* imaginable.

conceive /kən'siv/ *v.*, **-ceived**, **-ceiving**. – *v.t.* **1.** to form (a notion, opinion, purpose, etc.). **2.** to apprehend in the mind; understand. **3.** to become pregnant with. – *v.i.* **4.** to form an idea; think (fol. by *of*). **5.** to become pregnant.

concentrate /'kɒnsəntreɪt/ *v.*, **-trated**, **-trating**, *n.* – *v.t.* **1.** to bring or draw to a common centre or point of union. **2.** make more intense, stronger, or purer by removing or reducing the proportion of what is foreign or inessential. – *v.i.* **3.** to converge to a centre. **4.** to become more intense, stronger, or purer. **5.** to direct one's thoughts or actions towards one subject. – *n.* **6.** a concentrated form of something; a product of concentration. – **concentration**, *n.*

concentrated /'kɒnsəntreɪtəd/ *adj.* **1.** applied with great energy and intensity; focussed: *concentrated attention.* **2.** reduced to the essential ingredient, as by removing water: *concentrated juice.* **3.** clustered densely together: *concentrated population.*

concentric /kən'sɛntrɪk/ *adj.* having a common centre, as circles or spheres. Also, **concentrical**.

concept /'kɒnsɛpt/ *n.* **1.** a thought, idea, or notion, often one deriving from a generalising mental operation. **2.** an idea that includes all that is associated with a word or other symbol. – **conceptual**, *adj.*

conception /kən'sɛpʃən/ *n.* **1.** the act of conceiving. **2.** the state of being conceived. **3.** fertilisation; inception of pregnancy. **4.** that which is conceived. **5.** beginning; origin.

concern /kən'sɜn/ *v.t.* **1.** to relate to; be connected with; be of interest or importance to; affect. **2.** to interest, engage, or involve. **3.** to disquiet or trouble. – *n.* **4.** that which relates or pertains to one; business; affair. **5.** a matter that engages one's attention, interest, or care, or that affects one's welfare or happiness. **6.** solicitude or anxiety. **7.** important relation or bearing. **8.** a commercial or manufacturing firm or establishment.

concert /'kɒnsət/ *for def. 1*, /kən'sɜt/ *for def. 2* – *n.* **1.** a public performance, usually by two or more musicians. **2.** agreement of two or more in a design or plan.

concerted /kən'sɜtəd/ *adj.* contrived or arranged by agreement.

concession /kən'sɛʃən/ *n.* **1.** the act of conceding or yielding, as a right or privilege, or as a point or fact in an argument. **2.** the thing or point yielded. **3.** something conceded by a government or a controlling authority, as a grant of land, a privilege, or a franchise.

conch /kɒntʃ, kɒŋk/ *n.*, *pl.* **conches** /'kɒntʃəz/, **conchs** /kɒŋks/. the spiral shell of a gastropod.

conciliate /kən'sɪliˌeɪt/ *v.t.*, **-ated**, **-ating**. **1.** to overcome the distrust or hostility of, by soothing or pacifying means; placate; win over. **2.** to render compatible; reconcile.

conciliation /kənsɪli'eɪʃən/ *n.* **1.** the act of conciliating. **2.** a procedure for the resolution of a dispute. **3.** a system of resolving industrial disputes between employees and employers by official talks in the presence of a government-appointed third party. See **arbitration** (def. 2).

concise /kən'saɪs/ *adj.* expressing much in few words.

conclave /'kɒnkleɪv, 'kɒŋ-/ *n.* any private meeting.

conclude /kən'klud, kəŋ-/ *v.*, **-cluded**, **-cluding**. – *v.t.* **1.** to bring to an end; finish; terminate. **2.** to determine by reasoning; deduce; infer. – *v.i.* **3.** to come to an end; finish. **4.** to arrive at an opinion or judgment; come to a decision; decide. – **conclusion**, *n.*

conclusive /kən'klusɪv, kəŋ-/ *adj.* serving to settle or decide a question; decisive; convincing.

concoct /kən'kɒkt, kəŋ-/ *v.t.* to prepare; make up; contrive. – **concoction**, *n.*

concomitant /kən'kɒmətənt, kəŋ-/ *adj.* accompanying; concurrent.

concord /'kɒnkɔd, 'kɒŋ-/ *n.* agreement.

concourse /'kɒnkɔs, 'kɒŋ-/ *n.* **1.** an assembly. **2.** an open space or main hall in a public building, especially a railway station.

concrete /'kɒnkrit, 'kɒŋ-/ *adj.*, *n.*, *v.*, **-creted**, **-creting**. – *adj.* **1.** constituting an actual thing or instance; real. **2.** representing or applied to an actual substance or thing as opposed to an abstract quality. – *n.* **3.** a concrete idea or term; a concrete object or thing. **4.** an artificial stone-like material used for foundations, etc. – *v.t.* **5.** to treat or lay with concrete. – *v.i.* **6.** to coalesce into a mass; become solid; harden. – **concretion**, *n.*

concubine /'kɒŋkjubaɪn/ *n.* (among polygamous peoples) a secondary wife.

concur /kən'kɜ, kəŋ-/ *v.i.*, **-curred**, **-curring**. **1.** to accord in opinion; agree. **2.** to cooperate; combine; be associated. **3.** to coincide. **4.** to come together, as lines; unite. – **concurrent**, *adj.*, *n.*

concussion /kən'kʌʃən, kəŋ-/ *n.* **1.** the act of shaking or shocking, as by a blow. **2.** shock occasioned by a blow or collision.

condemn /kən'dɛm/ *v.t.* **1.** to pronounce adverse judgment on; express strong disapproval of. **2.** to pronounce to be guilty. **3.** to judge or pronounce to be unfit for use or service. – **condemnation**, *n.* – **condemnatory**, *adj.*

condense /kən'dɛns/ *v.t.*, **-densed**, **-densing**. **1.** to make more dense or compact; reduce the volume or compass of. **2.** to reduce to another and denser form, as a gas or vapour to a liquid or solid state. **3.** to compress into fewer words; abridge. – **condensation**, *n.*

condescend /kɒndə'sɛnd/ *v.i.* **1.** to stoop or deign (to do something). **2.** to behave as if one is conscious of descending from a superior position, rank, or dignity.

condiment /'kɒndəmənt/ *n.* something used to give a special or additional flavour to food, as a sauce or seasoning.

condition /kən'dɪʃən/ *n.* **1.** particular mode of being of a person or thing; situation with respect to circumstances; existing state or case. **2.** fit or requisite state. **3.** a circumstance indispensable to some result; a prerequisite; that on which something else is contingent. **4.** something demanded as an essential part of an agreement. – *v.t.* **5.** to put in fit or proper state. **6.** to subject to particular conditions or circumstances.

conditional /kən'dɪʃənəl/ *adj.* **1.** imposing, containing, or depending on a condition or conditions. – *n.* **2.** *Computers* an instruction which is acted upon only when a certain condition pertains.

condole /kən'doʊl/ *v.i.*, **-doled**, **-doling**. to express sympathy with one in affliction. – **condolence**, *n.*

condom /'kɒndɒm/ *n.* a contraceptive device worn over the penis during intercourse.

condominium /kɒndə'mɪniəm/ *n.* **1.** joint or concurrent dominion. **2.** a unit (def. 3).

condone /kən'doʊn/ *v.t.*, **-doned**, **-doning**. **1.** to pardon or overlook (an offence). **2.** to atone for; make up for.

conduce /kən'djus/ *v.i.*, **-duced**, **-ducing**. to lead or contribute to a result (fol. by *to*). – **conducive**, *adj.*

conduct /'kɒndʌkt/ *n.*, /kən'dʌkt/ *v.* – *n.* **1.** personal behaviour; way of acting; deportment. **2.** direction or management; execution. – *v.t.* **3.** to behave (oneself). **4.** to direct in action or course; manage; carry on. **5.** to lead or guide; escort. **6.** to serve as a channel or medium for (heat, electricity, sound, etc.). – **conduction**, *n.*

conductivity /ˌkɒndʌk'tɪvəti/ *n.*, *pl.* **-ties**. the property or power of conducting heat, electricity, or sound.

conductor /kən'dʌktə/ *n.* **1.** someone who conducts; a leader, guide, director, or manager. **2.** the person on a public transport vehicle, who collects fares, issues tickets, etc. **3.** a substance, body, or device that readily conducts heat, electricity, sound, etc.

conduit /'kɒndjuət, 'kɒndɪt/ *n.* a pipe, tube, or the like, for conveying water or other fluid.

cone /koʊn/ *n.* **1.** *Geometry* a solid which tapers to a point from a circular base. **2.** *Botany* the more or less conical multiple fruit of the pine, fir, etc. **3.** anything cone-shaped.

confabulate /kən'fæbjuleɪt/ *v.i.*, **-lated**, **-lating**. to talk together; converse.

confection /kən'fɛkʃən/ *n.* a sweet or bonbon.

confectionery /kən'fɛkʃənri/ *n.*, *pl.* **-ries**. confections or sweets collectively.

confederacy /kən'fɛdərəsi, -'fɛdrəsi/ *n.*, *pl.* **-cies**. an alliance of persons, parties, or states for some common purpose.

confederate /kən'fɛdərət/ *adj.*, *n.*; /kən'fɛdəreɪt/ *v.*, **-rated**, **-rating**. – *adj.* **1.** united in a league or alliance, or a conspiracy. – *n.* **2.** an accomplice. – *v.i.* **3.** to unite in a league or alliance, or a conspiracy. – **confederation**, *n.*

confer /kən'fɜ/ *v.t.*, **-ferred**, **-ferring**. to bestow as a gift, favour, honour, etc. (fol. by *on* or *upon*).

conference /'kɒnfərəns/ *n.* **1.** a meeting for consultation or discussion. **2.** a cartel of shipping interests.

confess /kən'fɛs/ *v.t.* **1.** to acknowledge or avow. **2.** to own or admit; admit the truth or validity of. **3.** to acknowledge one's belief in; declare adherence to. – **confession**, *n.*

confessor /kən'fɛsə/ *n.* a priest authorised to hear confessions.

confetti /kən'fɛti/ *pl. n.*, *sing.* **-fetto** /-'fɛtoʊ/. small bits of coloured paper, thrown at carnivals, weddings, etc.

confidant /kɒnfə'dænt, 'kɒnfədənt/ *n.* one to whom secrets are confided. – **confidante**, *fem. n.*

confide /kən'faɪd/ *v.*, **-fided**, **-fiding**. – *v.i.* **1.** to show trust by imparting secrets (fol. by *in*). – *v.t.* **2.** to tell in assurance of secrecy.

confidence /'kɒnfədəns/ *n.* **1.** full trust; belief in the trustworthiness or reliability of a person or thing. **2.** *Politics* the wish to retain the incumbent government in office, as shown by a vote on a particular issue. **3.** self-reliance, assurance, or boldness. **4.** certitude or assured expectation. **5.** a confidential communication; a secret. **6. in confidence,** as a secret or private matter, not to be divulged to others.

confidence trick *n.* a swindle in which the victim's confidence is gained in order to induce them to part with money or property. Also, *US*, **confidence game**.

confident /'kɒnfədənt/ *adj.* **1.** having strong belief or full assurance; sure. **2.** sure of oneself; bold.

confidential /kɒnfə'dɛnʃəl/ *adj.* **1.** spoken or written in confidence; secret. **2.** enjoying another's confidence.

configuration /kənfɪgə'reɪʃən, -fɪgju-/ *n.* the relative disposition of the parts or elements of a thing.

confine /kən'faɪn/ *v.*, **-fined**, **-fining** /'kɒnfaɪn/. *n.* – *v.t.* **1.** to enclose within bounds; limit or restrict. – *n.* **2.** (*usu. pl.*) a boundary or bound; a border or frontier. – **confiner**, *n.* – **confinement**, *n.*

confirm /kən'fɜm/ *v.t.* **1.** to make certain or sure; corroborate; verify. **2.** to make valid or binding by some formal or legal act; sanction; ratify. **3.** to reaffirm (a booking, ticket reservation, appointment, etc). **4.** to strengthen (a person) in habit, resolution, opinion, etc. – **confirmation**, *n.*

confiscate /'kɒnfəskeɪt/ *v.t.*, **-cated**, **-cating**. **1.** to seize as forfeited to the public treasury; appropriate, by way of penalty, to public use. **2.** to seize as if by authority; appropriate summarily.

conflagration /kɒnflə'greɪʃən/ *n.* a large and destructive fire.

conflict /kən'flɪkt/ *v.*, /'kɒnflɪkt/ *n.* – *v.i.* **1.** to come into collision; clash, or be in opposition or at variance; disagree. – *n.* **2.** a battle or struggle, especially a prolonged struggle; strife.

conform /kən'fɔm/ *v.i.* to act in accord or harmony; comply (fol. by *to*). – **conformist**, *n.* – **conformity**, *n.*

confound /kən'faʊnd/ *v.t.* **1.** to throw into confusion or disorder. **2.** to refute in argument; contradict.

confront /kən'frʌnt/ *v.t.* stand or meet facing.

confuse /kən'fjuz/ *v.t.*, **-fused**, **-fusing**. **1.** to combine without order or clearness; jumble; render indistinct. **2.** to throw into disorder. **3.** to fail to distinguish between; associate by mistake; confound. **4.** to perplex or bewilder. – **confusion**, *n.*

confute /kən'fjut/ *v.t.*, **-futed**, **-futing**. to prove to be false or defective.

congeal /kən'dʒil/ *v.i.* to change from a fluid or soft to a solid or rigid state.

congenial /kən'dʒiniəl/ *adj.* agreeing or suited in nature or character.

congenital /kən'dʒɛnətl/ *adj.* existing at or from one's birth.

congest /kən'dʒɛst/ *v.t.* to fill to excess. – **congestion**, *n.*

conglomerate /kən'glɒmərət, 'kəŋ-/ *n.*, *adj.*; /kən'glɒməreɪt/ *v.*, **-rated**, **-rating**. – *n.* **1.** anything composed of heterogeneous materials or elements. **2.** a company which controls or undertakes a widely diversified range of activities. – *adj.* **3.** gathered into a rounded mass. – *v.i.* **4.** to collect or cluster together.

congratulate /kən'grætʃəleɪt, kəŋ-/ *v.t.*, **-lated**, **-lating**. to express sympathetic joy to (a person), as on a happy occasion. – **congratulation**, *n.* – **congratulatory**, *adj.*

congregate /'kɒŋgrəgeɪt/ *v.i.*, *v.t.*, **-gated**, **-gating**. to come or bring together; assemble, especially in large numbers. – **congregation**, *n.*

congress /'kɒŋgrɛs/ *n.* a formal meeting or assembly of representatives for the discussion, arrangements, or promotion of some matter of common interest. – **congressional**, *adj.*

congruent /'kɒŋgruənt/ *adj.* agreeing; corresponding; congruous.

congruous /'kɒŋgruəs/ *adj.* agreeing or harmonious in character. – **congruity**, *n.*

conifer /'kɒnəfə, 'koʊ-/ *n.* any of the cone-bearing (mostly evergreen) trees and shrubs, such as pine, fir, and spruce. – **coniferous**, *adj.*

conjecture /kən'dʒɛktʃə/ *n.*, *v.*, **-tured**, **-turing**. – *n.* **1.** the formation or expression of an opinion without sufficient evidence for proof. – *v.t.* **2.** to conclude or suppose from grounds or evidence insufficient to ensure reliability.

conjugal /'kɒndʒəgəl, -dʒu-/ *adj.* marital.

conjugate /'kɒndʒəgeɪt/ *v.t.*, **-gated**, **-gating**. *Grammar* to inflect (a verb). – **conjugation**, *n.*

conjunction /kən'dʒʌŋkʃən/ *n.* **1.** the act or result of joining together; combination; union. **2.** *Grammar* something that joins, especially a word joining sentences, clauses, etc.

conjunctiva /ˌkɒndʒʌŋk'taɪvə/ *n.*, *pl.* **-vas**, **-vae** /-vi/. the mucous membrane which lines the inner surface of the eyelids.

conjure /'kʌndʒə/ *v.*, **-jured**, **-juring**. – *v.t.* **1.** to effect, produce, bring, etc., by, or as by, magic. – *v.i.* **2.** to practise conjuring or magic. – **conjuration**, *n.*

conk /kɒŋk/ *Colloquial* – *v.t.* **1.** to hit or strike, especially on the head. **2.** to faint; collapse.

connect /kə'nɛkt/ *v.t.* **1.** to bind or fasten together. **2.** to establish communication between. **3.** to associate or attach. – *v.i.* **4.** to become connected; join or unite. – **connective**, *adj.*

connection /kə'nɛkʃən/ *n.* **1.** the act of connecting. **2.** the state of being connected. **3.** anything that connects; a connecting part. **4.** (*usu. pl.*) influential friends, associates, relatives, etc.

connive /kə'naɪv/ *v.i.*, **-nived**, **-niving**. **1.** to give aid to wrongdoing, etc., by forbearing to act or speak. **2.** to cooperate secretly (fol. by *with*).

connoisseur /kɒnə'sɜ/ *n.* one competent to pass critical judgments in an art, especially one of the fine arts, or in matters of taste.

connote /kə'noʊt/ *v.t.*, **-noted**, **-noting**. to denote secondarily; signify in addition to the primary meaning; imply. – **connotation**, *n.*

conquer /'kɒŋkə/ *v.t.* **1.** to overcome by force; subdue. **2.** to gain the victory over; surmount. – **conqueror**, *n.* – **conquest**, *n.*

consanguineous /kɒnsæŋ'gwɪniəs/ *adj.* related by birth. – **consanguinity**, *n.*

conscience /'kɒnʃəns/ *n.* the internal recognition of right and wrong as regards one's actions and motives.

conscience clause *n.* a clause or article in an act or law or the like, which relieves persons whose conscientious or religious scruples forbid their compliance with it.

conscientious /kɒnʃi'ɛnʃəs/ *adj.* controlled by or done according to conscience; scrupulous.

conscionable /'kɒnʃənəbəl/ *adj.* conformable to conscience; just.

conscious /'kɒnʃəs/ *adj.* **1.** aware of one's own existence, sensations, cognitions, etc.; endowed with consciousness. **2.** having the mental faculties awake.

conscript /ˈkɒnskrɪpt/ *n.*, /kənˈskrɪpt/ *v.* – *n.* **1.** a recruit obtained by conscription. – *v.t.* **2.** to enrol compulsorily for service in the armed forces. – **conscription**, *n.*

consecrate /ˈkɒnsəkreɪt/ *v.t.*, **-crated**, **-crating**. to make or declare sacred. – **consecration**, *n.*

consecutive /kənˈsɛkjətɪv/ *adj.* following one another in uninterrupted succession.

consensus /kənˈsɛnsəs/ *n.* general agreement or concord.

consent /kənˈsɛnt/ *v.i.* **1.** to give assent; agree; comply or yield (fol. by *to* or infinitive). – *n.* **2.** assent; acquiescence; permission; compliance. – **consenting**, *adj.*

consent award *n.* an award made by an industrial tribunal where the parties have already reached agreement on the terms of a settlement but want it to have the force of an arbitrated award and hence submit it to a tribunal for ratification. Also, **consent agreement**.

consequence /ˈkɒnsəkwəns/ *n.* **1.** the act or fact of following as an effect or result upon something antecedent. **2.** that which so follows; an effect or result. **3.** importance or significance. – **consequent**, *n.* – **consequential**, *adj.*

conservation /kɒnsəˈveɪʃən/ *n.* the preservation or conserving of natural resources or areas or objects of cultural significance. – **conservationist**, *n.*

conservative /kənˈsɜvətɪv/ *adj.* **1.** disposed to preserve existing conditions, institutions, etc. **2.** having the power or tendency to conserve; preservative. – *n.* **3.** a person of conservative principles. – **conservatism**, *n.*

conservatorium /kənsɜvəˈtɔriəm/ *n.* a school of music. Also, **conservatoire**.

conservatory /kənˈsɜvətri/ *n.*, *pl.* **-ries**. a glass-covered house or room into which plants in bloom are brought from the greenhouse.

conserve /kənˈsɜv/ *v.*, **served**, **-serving**, /ˈkɒnsɜv, kənˈsɜv/ *n.* – *v.t.* **1.** to keep in a safe or sound state. – *n.* **2.** (*often pl.*) a mixture of several fruits, cooked, with sugar, to a jamlike consistency. – **conserver**, *n.*

consider /kənˈsɪdə/ *v.t.* **1.** to contemplate mentally; meditate or reflect on. **2.** to regard as or deem to be. **3.** to make allowance for. **4.** to regard with consideration or respect; hold in honour; respect.

considerable /kənˈsɪdrəbəl/ *adj.* worthy of consideration.

considerate /kənˈsɪdərət/ *adj.* showing consideration or regard for another's circumstances, feelings, etc.

consideration /kənˈsɪdəreɪʃən/ *n.* **1.** the act of considering; meditation or deliberation. **2.** regard or account; something taken, or to be taken, into account. **3.** a recompense for service rendered, etc.; a compensation. **4.** thoughtful or sympathetic regard or respect; thoughtfulness for others. **5.** estimation; esteem.

consign /kənˈsaɪn/ *v.t.* **1.** to hand over or deliver formally; commit (fol. by *to*). **2.** to transfer to another's custody or charge; entrust. – **consignor**, *n.* – **consignee**, *n.*

consignment /kɒnˈsaɪnmənt/ *n.* property sent to an agent for sale, storage, or shipment.

consist /kənˈsɪst/ *v.i.* **1.** to be made up or composed (fol. by *of*). **2.** to be included or contained (fol. by *in*).

consistency /kənˈsɪstənsi/ *n.*, *pl.* **-cies**. **1.** agreement among themselves of the parts of a complex thing. **2.** degree of density or viscosity. **3.** constant adherence to the same principles, course, etc. Also, **consistence**. – **consistent**, *adj.*

console[1] /kənˈsoʊl/ *v.t.*, **-soled**, **-soling**. to alleviate the grief or sorrow of; comfort; solace; cheer. – **consolation**, *n.*

console[2] /ˈkɒnsoʊl/ *n.* **1.** a desk on which are mounted the controls of an electrical or electronic system. **2.** *Computers* a computer operator's control panel or terminal.

consolidate /kənˈsɒlədeɪt/ *v.t.*, **-dated**, **-dating**. to bring together compactly in one mass or connected whole; unite; combine. – **consolidation**, *n.*

consolidated revenue *n.* the funds which a government treasury receives by way of taxes, duties, etc.

consonant /ˈkɒnsənənt/ *n.* **1.** a sound made with more or less obstruction of the breath stream in its passage outwards, as the *l*, *s*, and *t* of *list*. – *adj.* **2.** in agreement; agreeable or accordant; consistent (fol. by *to* or *with*).

consort /ˈkɒnsɔt/ *n.*, /kənˈsɔt/ *v.* – *n.* **1.** a spouse, especially of a reigning monarch. **2.** one vessel or ship accompanying another. – *v.i.* **3.** to associate; keep company.

consortium /kənˈsɔtiəm, -ʃiəm/ *n.*, *pl.* **-tia** /-tiə, -ʃə/. a combination of financial institutions, capitalists, etc., for carrying into effect some financial operation requiring large resources of capital.

conspicuous /kənˈspɪkjuəs/ *adj.* **1.** easy to be seen. **2.** readily attracting the attention.

conspire /kənˈspaɪə/ *v.i.*, **-spired**, **-spiring**. to agree together, especially secretly, to do something reprehensible or illegal; combine for an evil or unlawful purpose. – **conspiracy**, *n.* – **conspirator**, *n.*

constable /ˈkʌnstəbəl/ *n.* a police officer ranking below sergeant, the lowest in rank in a police force.

constant /ˈkɒnstənt/ *adj.* **1.** invariable; uniform; always present. **2.** continuing without intermission. **3.** standing firm in mind or purpose; resolute. – *n.* **4.** something constant, invariable, or unchanging.

constellation /kɒnstəˈleɪʃən/ *n.* *Astronomy* any of various groups of stars to which definite names have been given.

consternation /kɒnstəˈneɪʃən/ *n.* amazement and dread tending to confound the faculties.

constipation /kɒnstəˈpeɪʃən/ *n.* a condition of the bowels marked by defective or difficult evacuation.

constituency /kɒnˈstɪtʃuənsi/ *n.*, *pl.* **-cies**. any body of supporters; a clientele.

constituent /kɒnˈstɪtʃuənt/ *adj.* **1.** serving to make up a thing; component; elementary. **2.** having power to frame or alter a political constitution or fundamental law (as distinguished from law-making power). – *n.* **3.** a constituent element, material, etc.; a component. **4.** a voter, or (loosely) a resident, in a district represented by an elected official.

constitute /'kɒnstətjut/ *v.t.*, **-tuted, -tuting.** **1.** (of elements, etc.) to compose; form. **2.** to appoint to an office or function; make or create. **3.** to give legal form to (an assembly, court, etc.).

constitution /kɒnstə'tjuʃən/ *n.* **1.** the way in which anything is constituted; make-up or composition. **2.** the physical character of the body as to strength, health, etc. **3.** the act of constituting; establishment. **4.** any established arrangement or custom. **5.** the system of fundamental principles according to which a nation, state or body politic is governed. – **constitutional**, *adj.*

constrain /kən'streɪn/ *v.t.* **1.** to force, compel, or oblige; bring about by compulsion. **2.** to confine forcibly, as by bonds. **3.** to repress or restrain. – **constraint**, *n.*

constrict /kən'strɪkt/ *v.t.* **1.** to draw together; compress. **2.** to restrict. – **constriction**, *n.* – **constrictive**, *adj.*

construct /kən'strʌkt/ *v.*, /'kɒnstrʌkt/ *n.* – *v.t.* **1.** to form by putting together parts; build; frame; devise. – *n.* **2.** a complex image or idea resulting from a synthesis by the mind.

construction /kən'strʌkʃən/ *n.* **1.** the act or art of constructing. **2.** the way in which a thing is constructed; structure. **3.** that which is constructed; a structure. **4.** explanation or interpretation, as of a law or a text, or of conduct or the like.

constructive /kən'strʌktɪv/ *adj.* constructing, or tending to construct.

construe /kən'stru/ *v.t.*, **-strued, -struing.** **1.** to show the meaning or intention of. **2.** to deduce by construction or interpretation; infer.

consul /'kɒnsəl/ *n.* an agent appointed by an independent state to reside in a foreign state and discharge certain administrative duties. – **consular**, *adj.* – **consulate**, *n.*

consult /kən'sʌlt/ *v.t.* **1.** to refer to for information or advice. – *v.i.* **2.** to consider or deliberate.

consultant /kən'sʌltənt/ *n.* someone who gives professional or expert advice.

consultation /ˌkɒnsəl'teɪʃən/ *n.* **1.** the act of consulting; conference. **2.** a meeting for deliberation. **3.** an application for advice to one engaged in a profession, especially to a medical practitioner, etc.

consume /kən'sjum/ *v.t.*, **-sumed, -suming.** **1.** to destroy or expend by use; use up. **2.** to eat or drink up; devour. **3.** to absorb; engross.

consumer /kən'sjumə/ *n.* someone who uses a commodity or service (opposed to *producer*).

consumer goods *pl. n.* goods ready for consumption in satisfaction of human wants, as clothing, food, etc., and which are not utilised in any further production.

consumerism /kən'sjumərɪzəm/ *n.* **1.** a movement which aims at educating consumers to an awareness of their rights and at protecting their interests, as from illegal or dishonest trading practices. **2.** a theory that the economy of a western capitalist society requires an ever increasing consumption of goods.

consumer price index *n.* an index which provides a measure of the change in the average cost of a standard basket of retail goods by relating the cost in the current period to that of a base period; used as a measure of inflation.

consummate /'kɒnsəmeɪt, 'kɒnsjumeɪt/ *v.*, **-mated, -mating,** /'kɒnsjumət, 'kɒnsəmət/ *adj.* – *v.t.* **1.** to bring to completion or perfection. – *adj.* **2.** complete or perfect.

consumption /kən'sʌmpʃən/ *n.* **1.** the act of consuming; destruction or decay. **2.** the amount consumed. **3.** *Economics* the using up of goods and services having an exchangeable value. **4.** *Pathology* a wasting disease, especially tuberculosis of the lungs. – **consumptive**, *adj.*, *n.*

contact /'kɒntækt/ *n.*, /'kɒntækt, kən'tækt/ *v.* – *n.* **1.** the state or fact of touching; a touching or meeting of bodies. **2.** immediate proximity or association. **3.** a person through whom contact is established, often a business acquaintance. – *v.t.* **4.** to put or bring into contact. **5.** to get in touch with (a person).

contact lenses *pl. n.* devices to aid defective vision inconspicuously, consisting of small lenses, usually of plastic, which cover the irises and are held in place by eye fluid.

contact sport *n.* a sport, such as Rugby football, in which bodies regularly come into contact, creating the possibility of injury.

contagious /kən'teɪdʒəs/ *adj.* communicable to other individuals, as a disease.

contain /kən'teɪn/ *v.t.* **1.** to have within itself; hold within fixed limits. **2.** to have as contents or constituent parts; comprise; include. **3.** to keep within proper bounds; restrain.

container /kən'teɪnə/ *n.* **1.** anything that contains or can contain, as a carton, box, crate, tin, etc. **2.** a box-shaped unit for carrying goods; its standardised size facilitates easy transference from one form of transport to another.

contaminate /kən'tæməneɪt/ *v.t.*, **-nated, -nating.** to render impure by contact or mixture. – **contamination**, *n.*

contango /kən'tæŋgoʊ/ *n.* the position in a futures market where the more distantly traded contracts are selling at a premium over the nearer dated contracts.

contemplate /'kɒntəmpleɪt/ *v.*, **-plated, -plating.** – *v.t.* **1.** to look at or view with continued attention; observe thoughtfully. **2.** to have as a purpose; intend. – *v.i.* **3.** to think studiously; meditate; consider deliberately. – **contemplation**, *n.*

contemplative /'kɒntəmˌpleɪtɪv, kən'tɛmplətɪv/ *adj.* given to or characterised by contemplation.

contemporaneous /kəntɛmpə'reɪniəs/ *adj.* contemporary.

contemporary /kən'təmpəri, -pri/ *adj.*, *n.*, *pl.* **-raries.** – *adj.* **1.** belonging to the same time; existing or occurring at the same time. **2.** of the present time. – *n.* **3.** one belonging to the same time or period with another or others.

contempt /kən'tɛmpt/ *n.* **1.** the feeling with which one regards anything considered mean, vile, or worthless. **2.** the state of being despised; dishonour; disgrace. **3.** *Law* disobedience to, or open disrespect of, the rules or orders of a court or legislature.

contemptible /kən'tɛmptəbəl/ *adj.* deserving of or held in contempt; despicable.

contemptuous /kən'tɛmptʃuəs/ *adj.* manifesting or expressing contempt or disdain.

contend /kən'tɛnd/ *v.i.* **1.** to struggle in opposition. – *v.t.* **2.** to assert or maintain earnestly.

content[1] /'kɒntɛnt/ *n.* **1.** (*usu. pl.*) that which is contained. **2.** (*usu. pl.*) the chapters or chief topics of a book or document; a list of such chapters or topics. **3.** substance or purport, as of a document.

content[2] /kən'tɛnt/ *adj.* **1.** having the desires limited to what one has; satisfied. **2.** willing or resigned; assenting.

contention /kən'tɛnʃən/ *n.* **1.** a struggling together in opposition; strife. **2.** strife in debate; a dispute; a controversy. – **contentious**, *adj.*

conterminous /kɒn'tɜmənəs/ *adj.* having a common boundary.

contest /'kɒntɛst/ *n.*, /kən'tɛst/ *v.* – *n.* **1.** struggle for victory or superiority. – *v.t.* **2.** to struggle or fight for, as in battle. **3.** to argue against; dispute.

contestant /kən'tɛstənt/ *n.* someone who takes part in a contest or competition.

context /'kɒntɛkst/ *n.* **1.** the parts of a discourse or writing which precede or follow, and are directly connected with, a given passage or word. **2.** the circumstances or facts that surround a particular situation, event, etc. – **contextual**, *adj.*

contiguous /kən'tɪgjuəs/ *adj.* **1.** touching; in contact. **2.** in close proximity without actually touching; near.

continence /'kɒntənəns/ *n.* **1.** self-restraint, especially in regard to sexual activity; moderation; chastity. **2.** ability to exercise voluntary control over natural functions. Also, **continency**.

continent /'kɒntənənt/ *n.* **1.** one of the main land masses of the globe. – *adj.* **2.** characterised by the ability to exercise control over natural impulses or functions; chaste.

contingent /kən'tɪndʒənt/ *adj.* **1.** dependent for existence, occurrence, character, etc., on something not yet certain; conditional (often fol. by *on* or *upon*). **2.** liable to happen or not; uncertain; possible. – *n.* **3.** the proportion that falls to one as a share to be contributed or furnished. **4.** any one of the representative groups composing an assemblage. – **contingency**, *n.*

continual /kən'tɪnjuəl/ *adj.* **1.** proceeding without interruption or cessation; continuous in time. **2.** of regular or frequent recurrence; often repeated; very frequent.

continue /kən'tɪnju/ *v.*, **-ued**, **-uing**. – *v.i.* **1.** to go forwards or onwards in any course or action; keep on. **2.** to go on after suspension or interruption. **3.** to remain in a particular state or capacity. – *v.t.* **4.** to go on with or persist in. **5.** to extend from one point to another in space; prolong. **6.** to carry on from the point of suspension or interruption. – **continuation**, *n.*

continuity /kɒntə'njuəti/ *n.*, *pl.* **-ties**. the state or quality of being continuous.

continuous /kən'tɪnjuəs/ *adj.* **1.** having the parts in immediate connection, unbroken. **2.** uninterrupted in time; without cessation.

continuum /kən'tɪnjuəm/ *n.*, *pl.* **-tinuums**, **-tinua** /-'tɪnjuə/. a continuous extent, series, or whole.

contort /kən'tɔt/ *v.t.* to twist; bend or draw out of shape; distort. – **contortion**, *n.*

contortionist /kən'tɔʃənəst/ *n.* someone who performs gymnastic feats involving contorted postures.

contour /'kɒntɔ, -tʊə/ *n.* the outline of a figure or body; the line that defines or bounds anything.

contour line *n.* a line joining points of equal elevation on a surface.

contra- a prefix meaning 'against', 'opposite', or 'opposing'.

contraband /'kɒntrəbænd/ *n.* anything prohibited by law from being imported or exported.

contraception /kɒntrə'sɛpʃən/ *n.* the prevention of conception by deliberate measures; birth control. – **contraceptive**, *adj.*, *n.*

contract /'kɒntrækt/ *n.*, /'kɒntrækt, kən'trækt/ *v.* – *n.* **1.** an agreement between two or more parties for the doing or not doing of some definite thing. **2.** an agreement enforceable by law. – *v.t.* **3.** to draw together or into smaller compass; draw the parts of together. **4.** to shorten (a word, etc.) by combining or omitting some of its elements. **5.** to acquire, as by habit or contagion; incur, as a liability or obligation. **6.** to settle or establish by agreement. – **contraction**, *n.* – **contractor**, *n.* – **contractual**, *adj.* – **contractile**, *adj.*

contract note *n.* *Stock Exchange* a note issued by a broker to a client following the carrying out of the client's instructions, giving details of a purchase or sale of shares.

contradict /kɒntrə'dɪkt/ *v.t.* to assert the contrary or opposite of. – **contradiction**, *n.* – **contradictory**, *adj.*

contralto /kən'træltoʊ, -'tral-/ *n.*, *pl.* **-ti**. the lowest female voice.

contraption /kən'træpʃən/ *n.* a contrivance; a device.

contrary /'kɒntrəri/ *for def. 3 also* /kən'trɛəri/ *adj.*, *n.*, *pl.* **-ries**. – *adj.* **1.** opposite in nature or character. **2.** opposite in direction or position. **3.** perverse; self-willed. – *n.* **4.** that which is contrary or opposite. – **contrariety**, *n.*

contrast /kən'trast/ *v.*, /'kɒntrast/ *n.* – *v.t.* **1.** to compare by observing differences. **2.** to afford or form a contrast to; set off. – *v.i.* **3.** to exhibit unlikeness on comparison; form a contrast. **4.** the state of being contrasted. – *n.* **5.** something strikingly unlike. **6.** opposition or juxtaposition of different forms, lines, or colours in a work of art to intensify each other's properties and produce a more dynamic expression.

contravene /kɒntrə'vin/ *v.t.*, **-vened**, **-vening**. to violate, infringe, or transgress. – **contravention**, *n.*

contribute /kən'trɪbjut/ *v.t.*, **-uted**, **-uting**. to give to a common stock or for a common purpose. – **contribution**, *n.* – **contributor**, *n.* – **contributory**, *adj.*

contributing share /kən'trɪbjətɪŋ ʃɛə/ *n. Stock Exchange* an ordinary share which has some part of its capital unpaid.

contrite /kən'traɪt, 'kɒntraɪt/ *adj.* feeling a strong sense of guilt; penitent. – **contrition** /kən'trɪʃən/, **contriteness**, *n.*

contrive /kən'traɪv/ *v.t.*, **-trived**, **-triving**. **1.** to plan with ingenuity; devise; invent. **2.** to bring about or effect by a device, stratagem, plan, or scheme; manage (to do something). – **contrivance**, *n.*

control /kən'troʊl/ *v.*, **-trolled**, **-trolling**, *n.* – *v.t.* **1.** to exercise restraint or direction over; dominate; command. – *n.* **2.** the act or power of controlling; regulation; domination or command. **3.** check or restraint. **4.** something that serves to control; a check; a standard of comparison in scientific experimentation. **5.** (*pl.*) a coordinated arrangement of devices for regulating and guiding a machine.

control computer *n.* a computer, usually of small memory but considerable logical complexity, which controls some industrial or other process, as controlling the size of ingots in a steel mill.

control key *n.* a key on a computer keyboard, which performs certain functions when pressed in combination with other keys.

controversy /'kɒntrəvɜsi, kən'trɒvəsi/ *n., pl.* **-sies**. dispute, debate, or contention; disputation concerning a matter of opinion. – **controversial**, *adj.*

contumely /'kɒntʃuməli, kən'tjuməli/ *n., pl.* **-lies**. contemptuous or humiliating treatment. – **contumelious**, *adj.*

contuse /kən'tjuz/ *v.t.*, **-tused**, **-tusing**. to bruise. – **contusion**, *n.* – **contusive**, *adj.*

conundrum /kə'nʌndrəm/ *n.* a riddle.

convalesce /kɒnvə'lɛs/ *v.i.*, **-lesced**, **-lescing**. to grow stronger after illness. – **convalescence**, *n.* – **convalescent**, *adj., n.*

convection /kən'vɛkʃən/ *n. Physics* the transference of heat by the circulation or movement of the heated parts of a liquid or gas.

convene /kən'vin/ *v.*, **-vened**, **-vening**. – *v.i.* **1.** to come together; assemble, usually for some public purpose. – *v.t.* **2.** to cause to assemble; convoke. – **convener**, *n.*

convenient /kən'viniənt/ *adj.* **1.** agreeable to the needs or purpose. **2.** at hand; easily accessible. – **convenience**, *n.*

convent /'kɒnvənt/ *n.* **1.** a community of persons, especially nuns, devoted to religious life under a superior. **2.** a Roman Catholic or other school where children are taught by nuns.

convention /kən'vɛnʃən/ *n.* **1.** a meeting or assembly, especially a formal assembly. **2.** general agreement or consent; accepted usage, especially as a standard of procedure. – **conventional**, *adj.*

converge /kən'vɜdʒ/ *v.i.*, **-verged**, **-verging**. **1.** to tend to meet in a point or line; incline towards each other, as lines which are not parallel. **2.** to tend to a common result, conclusion, etc. – **convergence**, *n.* – **convergent**, *adj.*

conversant /kən'vɜsənt, 'kɒnvəsənt/ *adj.* familiar by use or study (fol. by *with*).

conversation /kɒnvə'seɪʃən/ *n.* informal interchange of thoughts by spoken words; a talk or colloquy.

converse[1] /kən'vɜs/ *v.i.*, **-versed**, **-versing**. to talk informally with another.

converse[2] /'kɒnvɜs/ *adj.* **1.** turned about; opposite or contrary in direction or action. – *n.* **2.** a thing which is the opposite or contrary of another.

convert /kən'vɜt/ *v.*, /'kɒnvɜt/ *n.* – *v.t.* **1.** to change into something of different form or properties; transmute; transform. **2.** to cause to adopt a different religion, party, opinion, etc., especially one regarded as better. – *n.* **3.** someone who has been converted, as to a religion or an opinion. – **conversion**, *n.*

convertible /kən'vɜtəbəl/ *adj.* **1.** capable of being converted. **2.** (of a motor car) having a removable top.

convex /'kɒnvɛks/ *adj.* bulging and curved.

convey /kən'veɪ/ *v.t.* **1.** to carry or transport from one place to another. **2.** to communicate; impart; make known. **3.** *Law* to transfer; pass the title to.

conveyance /kən'veɪəns/ *n.* **1.** the act of conveying; transmission; communication. **2.** a means of conveyance, especially a vehicle. **3.** *Law* **a.** the transfer of property from one person to another. **b.** the instrument or document by which this is effected.

conveyancing /kən'veɪənsɪŋ/ *n.* that branch of legal practice consisting of examining titles, giving opinions as to their validity, and preparing of deeds, etc., for the conveyance of property from one person to another.

conveyor belt = conveyer belt /kən'veɪə/ *n.* a flexible band passing about two or more wheels, etc., used to transport objects from one place to another, especially in a factory.

convict /kən'vɪkt/ *v.*, /'kɒnvɪkt/ *n.* – *v.t.* **1.** to prove or declare guilty of an offence, especially after a legal trial. – *n.* **2.** a person proved or declared guilty of an offence. **3.** a person serving a prison sentence.

conviction /kən'vɪkʃən/ *n.* **1.** the fact or state of being convicted. **2.** the state of being convinced. **3.** a fixed or firm belief.

convince /kən'vɪns/ *v.t.*, **-vinced**, **-vincing**. to persuade by argument or proof.

convivial /kən'vɪviəl/ *adj.* agreeable; sociable; merry.

convoke /kən'voʊk/ *v.t.*, **-voked**, **-voking**. to call together. – **convocation**, *n.*

convolution /kɒnvə'luʃən/ *n.* a rolled up or coiled condition.

convoy /'kɒnvɔɪ/ *n.* any group of vehicles travelling together.

convulse /kən'vʌls/ *v.t.*, **-vulsed**, **-vulsing**. **1.** to shake violently; agitate. **2.** to cause to laugh violently. **3.** to cause to suffer violent muscular spasms. – **convulsion**, *n.* – **convulsive**, *adj.*

coo /ku/ *v.i.* to utter the soft, murmuring sound characteristic of pigeons or doves, or a similar sound.

cooee /'kui, ku'i/ *n.* a prolonged clear call, the second syllable of which rises rapidly in pitch, used most frequently in the bush as a signal to attract attention.

cook /kʊk/ *v.t.* **1.** to prepare (food) by the action of heat, as by boiling, baking, roasting, etc. – *v.i.* **2.** (of food) to undergo cooking. – *n.* **3.** someone who cooks. – **cookery**, *n.*

cool /kul/ *adj.* **1.** moderately cold; neither warm nor very cold. **2.** imparting or permitting a sensation of moderate coldness. **3.** not excited; calm; unmoved; not hasty; deliberate; aloof. **4.** deficient in ardour or enthusiasm. **5.** *Colloquial* attractive; excellent. – *n.* **6.** that which is cool; the cool part, place, time, etc. – *v.t.*, *v.i.* **7.** to make cool; impart a sensation of coolness to.

coolibah /'kuləba/ *n.* a species of eucalypt common in the Australian inland. Also, **coolabah**.

cooling-off period *n.* a period in which a person may legally back out of a financial agreement.

co-op /'koʊ-ɒp/ *n.* a cooperative shop, store, or society.

coop /kup/ *n.* **1.** an enclosure, cage, or pen, usually with bars or wires on one side or more, in which fowls, etc., are confined. – *v.t.* **2.** to place in, or as in, a coop; confine narrowly (often fol. by *up* or *in*).

cooperate /koʊ'ɒpəreɪt/ *v.i.*, **-rated**, **-rating**. to work or act together or jointly. Also, **co-operate**. – **cooperation**, *n.*

cooperative /koʊ'ɒpərətɪv, -'ɒprətɪv/ *adj.* **1.** cooperating. **2.** showing a willingness to cooperate; helpful. – *n.* **3.** a cooperative society or shop. Also, **co-operative**.

cooperative society *n.* a business undertaking owned and controlled by its members, and formed to provide them with work or with goods at advantageous prices.

coopt /koʊ'ɒpt/ *v.t.* to elect into a body by the votes of the existing members. Also, **co-opt**.

coordinate /koʊ'ɔdənət, -neɪt/ *adj.*, *n.*; /koʊ'ɔdəneɪt/ *v.*, **-nated**, **-nating**. – *adj.* **1.** of the same order or degree; equal in rank or importance. – *n.* **2.** someone who or that which is equal in rank or importance; an equal. **3.** *Mathematics* any of the magnitudes which define the position of a point, line, or the like, by reference to a fixed figure, system of lines, etc. – *v.t.* **4.** to place or class in the same order, rank, division, etc. **5.** to place or arrange in due order or proper relative position. – *v.i.* **6.** to become coordinate. **7.** to act in harmonious combination. Also, **co-ordinate**. – **coordination**, *n.*

cop /kɒp/ *n.*, *v.*, **copped copping**. *Colloquial* – *n.* **1.** a police officer. – *v.t.* **2.** to accept resignedly; put up with.

cope /koʊp/ *v.i.*, **coped**, **coping**. to struggle or contend, especially on fairly even terms or with a degree of success (fol. by *with*).

copha /'koʊfə/ *n.* a white waxy solid derived from coconut flesh used as shortening. Also, **copha butter**.

copious /'koʊpiəs/ *adj.* large in quantity or number; abundant.

cop-out /'kɒp-aʊt/ *n.* *Colloquial* an easy way out of a situation of embarrassment or responsibility.

copper[1] /'kɒpə/ *n.* **1.** *Chemistry* a malleable, ductile metallic element having a characteristic reddish brown colour. *Symbol*: Cu **2.** a large vessel (formerly of copper) for boiling clothes.

copper[2] /'kɒpə/ *n.* *Colloquial* a police officer.

copperplate /'kɒpəpleɪt/ *n.* an ornate, rounded style of handwriting, formerly much used in engravings.

coppice /'kɒpəs/ *n.* a wood, thicket, or plantation of small trees or bushes. Also, **copse**.

copra /'kɒprə/ *n.* the dried kernel or meat of the coconut, from which coconut oil is pressed.

copro- a prefix meaning 'dung'.

copula /'kɒpjələ/ *n.*, *pl.* **-lae** /-li/. **1.** something that connects or links together. **2.** *Grammar* a word, as the verb *be*, which acts as a connecting link between subject and predicate.

copulate /'kɒpjuleɪt/ *v.i.*, **-lated**, **-lating**. to unite in sexual intercourse.

copy /'kɒpi/ *n.*, *pl.* **copies**, *v.*, **copied**, **copying**. – *n.* **1.** a transcript, reproduction, or imitation of an original. **2.** written, typed, or printed matter, or artwork, intended to be reproduced in print. – *v.t.* **3.** to make a copy of; transcribe; reproduce. **4.** to follow as a pattern or model; imitate.

copyedit /'kɒpi,ɛdət/ *v.t.* to correct, style and mark up copy (def. 2) to make it ready for printing.

copyright /'kɒpiraɪt/ *n.* the exclusive right, granted by law for a certain term of years, to make and dispose of copies of, and otherwise to control, a literary, musical, dramatic, or artistic work.

cor- variant of **com-** before *r*, as in *corrupt*.

coral /'kɒrəl/ *n.* **1.** the hard, chalky skeleton of any of various marine animals. **2.** such skeletons collectively, as forming reefs, islands, etc.

cord /kɔd/ *n.* **1.** a string or small rope composed of several strands twisted or woven together. **2.** a ribbed fabric, especially corduroy.

cordial /'kɔdiəl/ *adj.* **1.** hearty; warmly friendly. – *n.* **2.** a sweet, flavoured, concentrated syrup to be mixed with water as a drink.

corduroy /'kɔdʒərɔɪ, 'kɔdərɔɪ/ *n.* a cotton pile fabric with lengthwise cords or ridges.

core /kɔ/ *n.*, *v.*, **cored**, **coring**. – *n.* **1.** the central part of a fleshy fruit, containing the seeds. **2.** the central, innermost, or most essential part of anything. – *v.t.* **3.** to remove the core of (fruit).

core cycle *n.* the time to access and restore the contents of a memory location in a computer.

core memory *n.* a read-write random access memory in a computer which retains data in storage on cores.

co-respondent /koʊ-rə'spɒndənt/ *n.* the person alleged to have committed adultery with the respondent in a suit for divorce (no longer legally relevant in Australia).

core time *n.* that part of the working day during which one must be at one's place of work. See **flexitime**.

corgi /'kɔgi/ *n.* a short-legged Welsh dog with

a squat body, and erect ears.

cork /kɔk/ *n.* **1.** the outer bark of the cork oak, used for making stoppers of bottles, floats, etc. **2.** a piece of cork, or other material (as rubber), used as a stopper for a bottle, etc.

corkage /'kɔkɪdʒ/ *n.* a charge made by a restaurant, etc., for serving liquor brought in by the customers.

corkscrew /'kɔkskru/ *n.* an instrument used to draw corks from bottles.

cormorant /'kɔmərənt/ *n.* any of several large, voracious, waterbirds with a long neck and a pouch under the beak in which captured fish are held.

corn[1] /kɔn/ *n.* **1.** collectively, any edible grain, especially maize in North America and Australia, wheat in England, and oats in Scotland and Ireland . – *v.t.* **2.** to lay down in brine, as meat.

corn[2] /kɔn/ *n.* a horny induration or callosity of the epidermis, usually with a central core, caused by undue pressure or friction, especially on the toes or feet.

cornea /'kɔniə/ *n., pl.* **-neas** /-niəz/, **-neae** /-nii/. the transparent anterior part of the external coat of the eye, covering the iris and the pupil.

corner /'kɔnə/ *n.* **1.** the meeting place of two converging lines or surfaces. **2.** the space between two converging lines or surfaces near their intersection; angle. **3.** the place where two streets meet. **4.** an end; margin; edge. **5.** any situation from which escape is impossible. **6.** *Finance* a monopolising or a monopoly of the available supply of a stock or commodity, to a point permitting control of price. **7.** a region; quarter. **8. cut corners, a.** to take short cuts habitually. **b.** to bypass an official procedure, or the like. – *v.t.* **9.** to place in or drive into a corner. **10.** to form a corner in (a stock, etc.). – *v.i.* **11.** to form a corner in a stock or commodity. **12.** in a motor vehicle, to turn a corner, especially at speed. – *adj.* **13.** situated at a junction of two roads. **14.** made to be fitted or used in a corner.

cornet /'kɔnət/ *n.* a wind instrument of the trumpet class, with valves or pistons.

cornflour /'kɔnflauə/ *n.* a starchy flour made from maize, rice, or other grain, used as a thickening agent in cookery.

cornice /'kɔnəs/ *n.* the moulding or mouldings between the walls and ceiling of a room.

corny /'kɔni/ *adj.*, **-nier**, **-niest**. **1.** *Colloquial* old-fashioned; lacking subtlety. **2.** *Colloquial* sentimental; mawkish and of poor quality.

corollary /kə'rɒləri/ *n., pl.* **-ries**. a natural consequence or result.

corona /kə'rounə/ *n., pl.* **-nas**, **-nae** /-ni/. a white or coloured circle of light seen round a luminous body. – **coronal**, *adj.*

coronary /'kɒrənri/ *adj.* **1.** relating to the arteries which supply the heart tissues. – *n.* **2.** a heart attack.

coronation /kɒrə'neɪʃən/ *n.* the act or ceremony of investing a king, etc., with a crown.

coroner /'kɒrənə/ *n.* an officer, as of a county or municipality, whose chief function is to investigate by inquest (often before a **coroner's jury**) any death not clearly due to natural causes. – **coronial**, *adj.*

coronet /'kɒrənət/ *n.* a small or inferior crown.

corpora /'kɔpərə/ *n.* plural of **corpus**.

corporal /'kɔpərəl/ *adj.* of the human body; bodily; physical.

corporate /'kɔpərət, -prət/ *adj.* **1.** forming a corporation. **2.** of a corporation. **3.** relating to a united body, as of persons.

corporate raider *n.* someone who purchases large blocks of a company's shares, hoping to profit by their increase in value when the company reacts by attempting to secure control.

corporation /kɔpə'reɪʃən/ *n.* an association of individuals, created by law or under authority of law, having a continuous existence irrespective of that of its members, and powers and liabilities distinct from those of its members.

corporeal /kɔ'pɔriəl/ *adj.* of the nature of the physical body; bodily.

corps /kɔ/ *n., pl.* **corps** /kɔz/. a group of persons associated or acting together.

corpse /'kɔps/ *n.* a dead body, usually of a human being.

corpulent /'kɔpjələnt/ *adj.* stout; fat.

corpus /'kɔpəs/ *n., pl.* **-puses**, **-pora** /-pərə/. **1.** the body of a human or animal. **2.** a large or complete collection of writings, laws, etc.

corpuscle /'kɔpəsəl/ *n. Physiology* one of the minute bodies which form a constituent of the blood.

corpus delicti /ˌkɔpəs də'lɪktaɪ/ *n.* the body of essential facts constituting a criminal offence.

correct /kə'rɛkt/ *v.t.* **1.** to set right; remove the errors or faults of. **2.** to point out or mark the errors in. **3.** to counteract the operation or effect of (something hurtful). – *adj.* **4.** conforming to fact or truth; free from error; accurate. **5.** in accordance with an acknowledged or accepted standard; proper. – **correction**, *n.* – **corrective**, *adj.*

correlation /kɒrə'leɪʃən/ *n.* **1.** mutual relation of two or more things, parts, etc. **2.** *Statistics* the degree of relationship of two attributes or measurements on the same group of elements. – **correlate**, *v.* – **correlative**, *adj.*

correspond /kɒrə'spɒnd/ *v.i.* **1.** to be in agreement or conformity (often fol. by *with* or *to*). **2.** to be similar or analogous. **3.** to communicate by exchange of letters.

correspondence /kɒrə'spɒndəns/ *n.* **1.** the act or fact of corresponding. **2.** letters that pass between correspondents.

correspondent /kɒrə'spɒndənt/ *n.* **1.** someone who communicates by letters. **2.** someone employed to contribute news, etc., regularly from a distant place. **3.** a thing that corresponds to something else. – *adj.* **4.** corresponding; having a relation of correspondence.

corridor /'kɒrədɔ/ *n.* a gallery or passage connecting parts of a building.

corrigendum /kɒrə'dʒɛndəm/ *n., pl.* **-da** /-də/. an error to be corrected, especially an error in print.

corroborate /kəˈrɒbəreɪt/ *v.t.*, **-rated -rating**. to make more certain; confirm. – **corroboration**, *n.* – **corroborative**, *adj.*

corroboree /kəˈrɒbəri/ *n.* an Aboriginal assembly of sacred, festive, or warlike character.

corrode /kəˈroʊd/ *v.t.*, **-roded**, **-roding**. to eat away gradually as by chemical action. – **corrosion**, *n.* – **corrosive**, *n.*, *adj.*

corrugate /ˈkɒrəgeɪt/ *v.t.*, **-gated**, **-gating**. to draw or bend into folds or alternate furrows and ridges. – **corrugation**, *n.*

corrupt /kəˈrʌpt/ *adj.* **1.** guilty of dishonesty, especially involving bribery. **2.** made bad by errors or alterations, as a text. **3.** *Computers* (of data or programs) damaged by errors or electrical interference. – *v.t.* **4.** to destroy the integrity of. **5.** to lower morally; pervert; deprave. – **corruption**, *n.*

corsage /kɔˈsaʒ/ *n.* a small bouquet worn on the clothes.

corset /ˈkɔsət/ *n.* (*often pl.*) a shaped, close-fitting undergarment worn to give shape and support to the body; stays.

cortege /kɔˈtɛəʒ, -ˈteɪʒ/ *n.* a train of attendants; retinue.

cortex /ˈkɔtɛks/ *n.*, *pl.* **-tices** /-təsiz/. – *n.* the layer of grey matter around the brain. – **cortical**, *adj.*

corvette /kɔˈvɛt/ *n.* a small, lightly armed, fast ship.

cosh /kɒʃ/ *n.* any instrument, usually flexible, used as a bludgeon.

cosmetic /kɒzˈmɛtɪk/ *n.* **1.** a preparation for beautifying the complexion, skin, etc. – *adj.* **2.** serving to beautify. **3.** designed to effect a superficial alteration while keeping the basis unchanged.

cosmo- a word element representing **cosmos**.

cosmopolitan /kɒzməˈpɒlətn/ *adj.* **1.** belonging to all parts of the world. **2.** free from local, provincial, or national ideas, prejudices, or attachments.

cosmos /ˈkɒzmɒs/ *n.* **1.** the physical universe. **2.** a complete and harmonious system. – **cosmic**, *adj.*

cosset /ˈkɒsət/ *v.t.* to pamper; coddle.

cossie /ˈkɒzi/ *n.* *Colloquial* swimming costume. Also, **cozzie**.

cost /kɒst/ *n.*, *v.*, **cost** *for def. 5* **costed**, **costing**. – *n.* **1.** the price paid to acquire, produce, accomplish, or maintain anything. **2.** outlay or expenditure of money, time, labour, trouble, etc. **3.** (*pl.*) *Law* the sums which the successful party is usually entitled to recover for reimbursement of particular expenses incurred in the litigation. – *v.t.* **4.** to require the expenditure of (money, time, labour, etc.). **5.** to estimate or determine the cost of.

cost accounting *n.* an accounting system indicating the cost items involved in production.

costal /ˈkɒstl/ *adj.* relating to the ribs or the side of the body.

cost-benefit analysis *n.* the study of a project's financial viability by comparing its cost to its actual or expected returns or benefits.

cost-effective /ˈkɒst-əˌfɛktɪv/ *adj.* offering profits deemed to be satisfactory in view of the costs involved.

costly /ˈkɒstli/ *adj.*, **-lier**, **-liest**. costing much; of great price or value.

costo- a word element meaning 'rib'.

cost of living *n.* the average retail prices of food, clothing, and other necessities paid by a person, family, etc., in order to live at their usual standard.

cost-of-living bonus *n.* a bonus, paid to some workers, the sum of which depends on the rise in the cost of living as shown in the cost-of-living index.

cost-of-living index *n.* an index compiled from official statistics which represents the monthly rise or fall in the cost of living in terms of points as compared with a selected earlier year.

cost-plus /kɒst-ˈplʌs/ *n.* the cost of production plus an agreed rate of profit (often used as a basis of payment in government contracts).

cost price *n.* **1.** the price at which a merchant buys goods for resale. **2.** the cost of production.

cost-push inflation *n.* an economic situation in which prices are forced higher as a result of higher costs, such as wage rises or tax increases. Cf. **demand-pull inflation**.

costume /ˈkɒstʃum/ *n.* the style of dress, especially that peculiar to a nation, class, or period.

cosy /ˈkoʊzi/ *adj.*, **-sier**, **-siest**. snug; comfortable.

cot /kɒt/ *n.* a child's bed with enclosed sides.

cote /koʊt/ *n.* a shelter for doves, pigeons, sheep, etc.

coterie /ˈkoʊtəri/ *n.* a clique.

cottage /ˈkɒtɪdʒ/ *n.* a small bungalow.

cottage cheese *n.* a kind of soft unripened white cheese.

cotton /ˈkɒtn/ *n.* **1.** the soft, white, downy fibres of a certain plant, used in making fabrics, thread, etc. **2.** a plant yielding cotton. **3.** cloth, thread, etc., made of cotton. – *v.t.* **4.** *Colloquial* to understand (often fol. by *on*).

cottonwool /kɒtnˈwʊl/ *n.* raw cotton for surgical dressings and toilet purposes.

couch[1] /kaʊtʃ/ *n.* **1.** a seat for two to four people, with a back and sometimes armrests. **2.** a similar piece of upholstered furniture, without a back but with a headrest, as used by doctors for their patients. – *v.t.* **3.** to arrange or frame (words, a sentence, etc.); put into words; express.

couch[2] /kutʃ/ *n.* any of various grasses popular as lawn grass.

cougar /ˈkugə/ *n.* → **puma**.

cough /kɒf/ *v.i.* **1.** to expel the air from the lungs suddenly and with a characteristic noise. – *n.* **2.** the act or sound of coughing.

could /kʊd/ *v.* past tense of **can**[1].

coulomb /ˈkulɒm/ *n.* the derived SI unit of electric charge. *Symbol*: C

council /ˈkaʊnsəl/ *n.* **1.** an assembly of persons summoned or convened for consultation, deliberation, or advice. **2.** a body of persons specially designated or selected to act in an advisory, administrative, or legislative capacity. **3.** the local administrative body of a city, municipality, or shire.

– **councillor**, *n.*

counsel /ˈkaʊnsəl/ *n., v.,* **-selled**, **-selling**. – *n.* **1.** advice. **2.** interchange of opinions as to future procedure; consultation; deliberation. **3.** the barrister or barristers engaged in the direction of a cause in court; a legal adviser. – *v.t.* **4.** to give counsel to; advise. – **counsellor**, *n.*

count[1] /kaʊnt/ *v.t.* **1.** to check over one by one (the individuals of a collection) in order to ascertain their total number; enumerate. **2.** to include in a reckoning; take into account. **3.** to reckon to the credit of another; ascribe; impute. **4.** to esteem; consider. – *v.i.* **5.** to count the items of a collection one by one in order to know the total. **6.** to depend or rely (fol. by *on* or *upon*). **7.** to be accounted or worth. **8.** to enter into consideration. – *n.* **9.** the act of counting. **10.** the number representing the result of a process of counting; the total number. **11.** *Law* a distinct charge or cause of action in a declaration or indictment. **12.** regard; notice.

count[2] /kaʊnt/ *n.* (in some European countries) a nobleman corresponding in rank to the English earl. – **countess**, *fem. n.*

countenance /ˈkaʊntənəns/ *n., v.,* **-nanced**, **-nancing**. – *n.* **1.** aspect; appearance, especially the look or expression of the face. **2.** appearance of favour; encouragement; moral support. – *v.t.* **3.** to give countenance or show favour to; encourage; support. **4.** to tolerate; permit.

counter[1] /ˈkaʊntə/ *n.* **1.** a table or board on which money is counted, business is transacted, or goods are laid for examination. **2.** (in a cafe, restaurant or hotel) a long, narrow table, shelf, bar, etc., at which customers eat. **3.** anything used in keeping account.

counter[2] /ˈkaʊntə/ *adv.* **1.** in the wrong way; contrary to the right course; in the reverse direction. – *adj.* **2.** opposite; opposed; contrary. – *n.* **3.** that which is opposite or contrary to something else. – *v.t.* **4.** to go counter to; oppose. **5.** to meet or answer (a move, blow, etc.) by another in return. – *v.i.* **6.** to make a counter or opposing move.

counteract /kaʊntərˈækt/ *v.t.* to act in opposition to.

counter cheque *n.* a cheque available in a bank for the use of a customer in making a withdrawal from that bank.

counterclaim /ˈkaʊntəkleɪm/ *n.* a claim set up against another claim.

counterfeit /ˈkaʊntəfət, -fit/ *adj.* **1.** not genuine. – *n.* **2.** an imitation designed to pass as an original; a forgery.

counterfoil /ˈkaʊntəfɔɪl/ *n.* a complementary part of a bank cheque, etc., which is retained by the issuer, and on which particulars are noted.

countermand /ˌkaʊntəˈmænd, -ˈmand/ *v.t.* to revoke (a command, order, etc.).

counterpart /ˈkaʊntəpat/ *n.* **1.** a copy; duplicate. **2.** a part that answers to another, as each part of a document executed in duplicate. **3.** one of two parts which fit each other; a thing that complements something else.

countersign /ˈkaʊntəsaɪn/ *v.t.* to sign (a document) in addition to another signature, especially in confirmation or authentication.

country /ˈkʌntri/ *n., pl.* **-tries**. **1.** a tract of land considered apart from geographical or political limits; region; district. **2.** any considerable territory demarcated by geographical conditions or by a distinctive population. **3.** the territory of a nation. **4.** the public. **5.** the rural districts (as opposed to towns or cities).

country and western *n.* a type of music consisting mainly of rural songs accompanied by a stringed instrument. Also, **country music**.

county /ˈkaʊnti/ *n.* **1.** (in NSW) an area of land delineated for administrative convenience or some specific purpose such as development planning or the supply of electricity. **2.** (in some countries) a larger division, as for purposes of local administration.

coup /ku/ *n., pl.* **coups** /kuz/. an unexpected and successfully executed strategem; masterstroke.

coup d'état /ku deɪˈta/ *n.* a sudden and decisive measure in politics, especially one effecting a change of government illegally or by force.

coupé /ˈkupeɪ/ *n.* an enclosed two-door motor car.

couple /ˈkʌpəl/ *n.* **1.** a combination of two; a pair. **2.** two of the same sort connected or considered together.

coupon /ˈkupɒn/ *n.* **1.** a separable part of a certificate, ticket, advertisement, etc., entitling the holder to something. **2.** one of a number of such parts calling for periodical payments on a bond. **3.** a separate ticket or the like, for a similar purpose. **4.** a printed entry form for football pools, newspaper competitions, etc.

courage /ˈkʌrɪdʒ/ *n.* bravery. – **courageous**, *adj.*

courgette /kɔˈʒɛt/ *n.* → **zucchini**.

courier /ˈkʊriə/ *n.* a messenger.

course /kɔs/ *n., v.,* **coursed**, **coursing**. – *n.* **1.** onward movement. **2.** the path, route or channel along which anything moves. **3.** customary manner of procedure. **4.** a particular manner of proceeding. **5.** a systematised or prescribed series. **6.** a part of a meal served at one time. **7. of course, a.** certainly; obviously. **b.** in the natural order. – *v.i.* **8.** to run; move swiftly; race.

court /kɔt/ *n.* **1.** an open space wholly or partly enclosed by a wall, buildings, etc. **2.** a smooth, level area on which to play tennis, netball, etc. **3.** the residence of a sovereign or other high dignitary; palace. **4.** the collective body of persons forming a sovereign's retinue. **5.** assiduous attention directed to gain favour, affection, etc. **6.** *Law* **a.** a place where justice is administered. **b.** a judicial tribunal duly constituted for the hearing and determination of cases. **c.** the judge or judges who sit in a court. **7.** the body of qualified members of a corporation, council, board, etc. – *v.t.* **8.** to endeavour to win the favour of.

courteous /ˈkɜtiəs/ *adj.* having or showing good manners; polite.

courtesan /ˈkɔtəzæn/ *n.* **1.** a court mistress. **2.** any prostitute.

courtesy /ˈkɜtəsi/ *n., pl.* **-sies**. **1.** excellence of manners or behaviour; politeness. **2.** a courteous act or expression.

court martial *n., pl.* **court martials, courts martial**. a court consisting of naval, army, or air force officers appointed by a commander to try charges of offence against martial law.

Court of Appeal *n.* **1.** (in NSW) a court exercising the Supreme Court's appellate jurisdiction in civil matters. **2.** *NZ* a court to which appeals can be made from the High Court and from jury trials in the District Court.

courtship /ˈkɔtʃɪp/ *n.* **1.** the act or period of courting. **2.** solicitation, especially of favours. **3.** distinctive animal behaviour seen before and during mating.

courtyard /ˈkɔtjad/ *n.* a space enclosed by walls.

cousin /ˈkʌzən/ *n.* **1.** the son or daughter of an uncle or aunt. **2.** a kinsman or kinswoman.

couturier /kuˈturiə/ *n.* a person who designs, makes, and sells fashionable clothes for women.

cove /koʊv/ *n.* a small indentation or recess in the shoreline of a sea, lake, or river.

coven /ˈkʌvən/ *n.* a gathering of witches.

covenant /ˈkʌvənənt/ *n.* **1.** an agreement; a contract. – *v.i.* **2.** to enter into a covenant.

cover /ˈkʌvə/ *v.t.* **1.** to put something over or upon as for protection or concealment. **2.** to extend over; occupy the surface of. **3.** to shelter; protect; serve as a defence to. **4.** to hide from view; screen. **5.** to spread thickly the surface of. **6.** to include; comprise; provide for; take in. **7.** to suffice to meet (a charge, expense, etc.). **8.** to act as reporter of (occurrences, performances, etc.), as for a newspaper, etc. **9.** to pass or travel over. – *v.i.* **10.** to serve as substitute for someone who is absent. – *n.* **11.** that which covers. **12.** protection; shelter; concealment. **13.** adequate insurance against risk as loss, damage, etc. **14.** *Finance* funds to cover liability or secure against risk of loss.

cover charge *n.* a fixed amount added to the bill by a restaurant, nightclub, etc., for service or entertainment.

covering /ˈkʌvərɪŋ/ *n.* *Commerce* the operation of buying securities, etc., that one has sold short, in order to return them to the person from whom they were borrowed.

cover note *n.* a document given by an insurance company or agent to the insured to provide temporary cover until a policy is issued.

covert /ˈkʌvət, ˈkoʊvɜt/ *adj.* **1.** covered; sheltered. **2.** concealed; secret; disguised.

covet /ˈkʌvət/ *v.t.* to desire (another's possessions) inordinately.

cow[1] /kaʊ/ *n.* **1.** the female of a bovine animal. **2.** the female of various other large animals, as the elephant, whale, etc. **3.** *Colloquial* an ugly or bad-tempered woman.

cow[2] /kaʊ/ *v.t.* to intimidate.

coward /ˈkaʊəd/ *n.* someone who lacks courage to meet danger or difficulty. – **cowardice**, *n.*

cower /ˈkaʊə/ *v.i.* to crouch in fear or shame.

cowry /ˈkaʊri/ *n., pl.* **-ries**. a glossy, tropical shell. Also, **cowrie**.

coxcomb /ˈkɒkskoʊm/ *n.* a conceited dandy.

coxswain /ˈkɒksən, -sweɪn/ *n.* the person at the helm who steers a boat. Also, **cox**.

coy /kɔɪ/ *adj.* affectedly shy or reserved.

coyote /kɔɪˈoʊti/ *n.* a wild, wolf-like animal.

cozen /ˈkʌzən/ *v.t.* to cheat; deceive.

CPR /si pi ˈa/ cardiopulmonary resuscitation.

CPU /si pi ˈju/ *n.* that section of a computer which controls arithmetic, logical and control functions. Also, **central processor unit**.

crab[1] /kræb/ *n.* a crustacean having a short, broad, more or less flattened body.

crab[2] /kræb/ *n.* an ill-tempered or grouchy person.

crack /kræk/ *v.i.* **1.** to make a sudden, sharp sound in, or as in, breaking; snap, as a whip. **2.** to break with a sudden, sharp sound. **3.** to break without complete separation of parts; become fissured. – *v.t.* **4.** to break with a sudden sharp sound. **5.** *Colloquial* to break into (a safe, vault, etc.). **6.** to utter or tell, as a joke. **7. crack down on,** *Colloquial* to take severe measures, especially in enforcing discipline. **8. crack up,** to suffer a physical, mental or moral breakdown. – *n.* **9.** a sudden, sharp noise, as of something breaking. **10.** a break without complete separation of parts; a fissure; a flaw. **11.** a slight opening, as one between door and doorpost. **12.** *Colloquial* a try; an opportunity or chance.

cracker /ˈkrækə/ *n.* **1.** a thin, crisp biscuit. **2.** a kind of firework which explodes with a loud report.

crackle /ˈkrækəl/ *v.*, **-led**, **-ling**, *n.* – *v.i.* **1.** to make slight, sudden, sharp noises, rapidly repeated. – *v.t.* **2.** to cause to crackle. – *n.* **3.** a crackling noise.

crackling /ˈkræklɪŋ/ *n.* **1.** the making of slight cracking sounds rapidly repeated. **2.** the crisp browned skin or rind of roast pork.

-cracy a noun termination meaning 'rule', 'government', 'governing body'.

cradle /ˈkreɪdl/ *n., v.,* **-dled**, **-dling**. – *n.* **1.** a little bed or cot for an infant, usually built on rockers. **2.** the place where anything is nurtured during its early existence. **3.** any of various contrivances similar to a child's cradle. – *v.t.* **4.** to place or rock in or as in a cradle; hold tenderly.

craft /kraft/ *n.* **1.** skill; ingenuity; dexterity. **2.** cunning; deceit; guile. **3.** an art, trade, or occupation requiring special skill, especially manual skill; a handicraft. **4.** (*construed as pl.*) boats, ships, and vessels collectively.

crafty /ˈkrafti/ *adj.*, **-tier**, **-tiest**. cunning, deceitful; sly.

crag /kræg/ *n.* a steep, rugged rock.

craggy /ˈkrægi/ *adj.*, **-gier**, **-giest**. rugged; rough.

cram /kræm/ *v.t.*, **crammed**, **cramming**. **1.** to fill (something) by force with more than it can conveniently hold. **2.** *Colloquial* to get a knowledge of (a subject) by memorising information quickly.

cramp[1] /kræmp/ *n.* **1.** a sudden involuntary, persistent contraction of a muscle. – *v.t.*

2. to affect with, or as with, a cramp.

cramp² /kræmp/ *n.* **1.** a small metal bar with bent ends, for holding together planks, masonry, etc. – *v.t.* **2.** to confine narrowly; restrict; restrain; hamper.

crane /kreɪn/ *n., v.,* **craned**, **craning**. – *n.* **1.** any of a group of large wading birds. **2.** a device with a hoisting tackle, for lifting and moving heavy weights. – *v.t.* **3.** to hoist, lower, or move by or as by a crane. **4.** to stretch (the neck) as a crane does.

cranio- a combining form of **cranium**. Also, **crani-**.

cranium /ˈkreɪniəm/ *n., pl.* **-nia** /-niə/. the skull of a vertebrate.

crank /kræŋk/ *n.* **1.** *Machinery* a device for communicating motion, or for changing rotary motion into reciprocating motion, or vice versa. **2.** *Colloquial* an eccentric person. – *v.t.* **3.** to cause (a shaft) to revolve by applying force to a crank. – *adj.* **4.** *Colloquial* odd, false or phoney.

crankshaft /ˈkræŋkʃaft/ *n.* a shaft driving or driven by a crank.

cranky /ˈkræŋki/ *adj.,* **-kier**, **-kiest**. **1.** ill-tempered; cross. **2.** eccentric; queer.

cranny /ˈkræni/ *n., pl.* **-nies**. a small, narrow opening (in a wall, rock, etc.).

crap /kræp/ *n.* *Colloquial* **1.** excrement. **2.** nonsense; rubbish.

craps /kræps/ *n.* a gambling game played with two dice.

crash /kræʃ/ *v.t.* **1.** to break in pieces violently and noisily; shatter. **2.** to force or drive with violence and noise. **3.** to damage a car, aircraft, etc., in a collision. – *v.i.* **4.** to break or fall to pieces with noise. **5.** to make a loud, clattering noise as of something dashed to pieces. **6.** to collapse or fail suddenly, as a financial enterprise. **7.** of an aircraft, to fall to the ground. **8.** of a computer system, to shut down because of a fault. – *n.* **9.** a breaking or falling to pieces with loud noise. **10.** the shock of collision and breaking. **11.** the shutting down of a computer system because of a fault. **12.** a sudden collapse of a financial enterprise or the like. **13.** a sudden loud noise. **14.** the act of crashing.

crass /kræs/ *adj.* gross; stupid.

-crat a noun termination meaning 'ruler', 'member of a ruling body', 'advocate of a particular form of rule'. Cf. **-cracy**.

crate /kreɪt/ *n.* a box or framework, usually of wooden slats, for packing and transporting fruit, furniture, etc.

crater /ˈkreɪtə/ *n.* the cup-shaped depression or cavity marking the orifice of a volcano.

cravat /krəˈvæt/ *n.* a scarf worn round the neck.

crave /kreɪv/ *v.t.,* **craved**, **craving**. **1.** to long for or desire eagerly. **2.** to need greatly; require. **3.** to ask earnestly for (something); beg for.

craven /ˈkreɪvən/ *adj.* cowardly.

craw /krɔ/ *n.* **1.** the crop of a bird or insect. **2.** the stomach of an animal.

crawl /krɔl/ *v.i.* **1.** to move by dragging the body along the ground, as a worm, or on the hands and knees, as a young child. **2.** to progress slowly, laboriously, or timorously. **3.** to behave abjectly and obsequiously. **4.** to be, or feel as if, overrun with crawling things. – *n.* **5.** the act of crawling; a slow, crawling motion. **6.** Also, **Australian crawl**. a swimming stroke in prone position characterised by alternate overarm movements and a continuous up and down kick.

crayfish /ˈkreɪfɪʃ/ *n., pl.* **-fishes**, (*esp. collectively*) **-fish**. any of various freshwater decapod crustaceans.

crayon /ˈkreɪɒn/ *n.* **1.** a pointed stick or pencil of coloured wax, chalk, etc., used for drawing. **2.** a drawing in crayons.

craze /kreɪz/ *v.,* **crazed**, **crazing**, *n.* – *v.t.* **1.** to make small cracks on the surface of (pottery, etc.). – *n.* **2.** a mania; a popular fashion, etc., usually short-lived; a rage. **3.** insanity; an insane condition.

crazy /ˈkreɪzi/ *adj.,* **-zier**, **-ziest**. **1.** demented; mad. **2.** eccentric; bizarre; unusual. **3.** unrealistic; impractical.

creak /krik/ *v.i.* **1.** to make a sharp, harsh, grating, or squeaking sound. **2.** to move with creaking. – *n.* **3.** a creaking sound.

cream /krim/ *n.* **1.** the fatty part of milk, which rises to the surface when the liquid is allowed to stand. **2.** any creamlike substance, especially various cosmetics. **3.** the best part of anything. **4.** yellowish white; light tint of yellow or buff. – *v.t.* **5.** to work (butter and sugar, etc.) to a smooth, creamy mass. **6.** to add cream to (coffee, or the like).

crease /kris/ *n., v.,* **creased**, **creasing**. – *n.* **1.** a line or mark produced in anything by folding. – *v.t.* **2.** to make a crease or creases in or on; wrinkle.

create /kriˈeɪt/ *v.t.,* **-ated**, **-ating**. **1.** to bring into being; cause to exist; produce. **2.** to evolve from one's own thought or imagination. **3.** to make by investing with new character or functions; constitute; appoint. – **creator**, *n.*

creation /kriˈeɪʃən/ *n.* **1.** the act of creating. **2.** that which is created. **3.** the world; universe. **4.** an original work, especially of the imaginative faculty.

creative /kriˈeɪtɪv/ *adj.* **1.** having the quality or power of creating. **2.** resulting from originality of thought or expression.

creature /ˈkritʃə/ *n.* anything created, especially an animate being.

creche /kreɪʃ, krɛʃ/ *n.* a nursery where children are cared for while their parents work.

credence /ˈkridns/ *n.* **1.** belief. **2.** something giving a claim to belief or confidence.

credential /krəˈdɛnʃəl/ *n.* **1.** anything which is the basis for the belief or trust of others in a person's abilities, authority, etc. **2.** (*usu. pl.*) a letter or other testimonial attesting the bearer's right to confidence or authority.

credible /ˈkrɛdəbəl/ *adj.* **1.** capable of being believed; believable. **2.** worthy of belief or confidence; trustworthy.

credit /ˈkrɛdət/ *n.* **1.** influence or authority resulting from the confidence of others or from one's reputation. **2.** trustworthiness; credibility. **3.** commendation or honour given for some action, quality, etc. **4.** (*pl.*) a list, appearing at the beginning or end of a film, which shows the names of those who have been associated with its production.

5. time allowed for payment for goods, etc., obtained on trust. **6.** confidence in a purchaser's ability and intention to pay, displayed by entrusting them with goods, etc., without immediate payment. **7.** anything valuable standing on the credit side of an account. **8.** the balance in one's favour in an account. **9.** *Bookkeeping* **a.** the acknowledgment or an entry of payment or value received, in an account. **b.** the side (right-hand) of an account on which such entries are made (opposed to *debit*). **c.** an entry, or the total shown, on the credit side. **10.** any deposit or sum against which one may draw. **11. on credit,** by deferred payment. – *v.t.* **12.** to believe; put confidence in. **13.** to give reputation or honour to. **14.** to ascribe (something) to a person, etc. **15. a.** *Bookkeeping* to enter upon the credit side of an account; give credit for or to. **b.** to give the benefit of such an entry to (a person, etc.).

creditable /ˈkrɛdətəbəl/ *adj.* bringing credit, honour, reputation, or esteem.

credit agency *n.* an organisation that investigates on behalf of a client the credit worthiness of the client's prospective customers.

credit card *n.* a card which identifies the holder as entitled to obtain without payment of cash, goods, food, services, etc., which are then charged to the holder's account.

credit foncier /ˈfɒnsɪə/ *n.* a method of repayment of a long-term housing loan which is repaid by equal monthly instalments comprising principal and interest.

credit insurance *n.* insurance coverage designed to minimise loss to creditors when a debtor defaults.

credit life insurance *n.* insurance guaranteeing payment of the unpaid portion of a loan in the event of a debtor's death.

credit note *n.* a note issued by a trader showing the amount of credit due to a customer, usually for goods to be taken in lieu of those returned.

creditor /ˈkrɛdətə/ *n.* one to whom money is due (opposed to *debtor*).

credit rating *n.* an estimation of the extent to which a customer can be granted credit.

credit squeeze *n.* **1.** restriction by a government of the amount of credit available to borrowers. **2.** the period during which the restrictions are in operation.

credit transfer *n.* a system by which a sum of money due to another person is paid into a bank for transfer to that person's account at another bank or branch.

credit union *n.* a financial organisation for receiving and lending money, usually formed by workers in some industry or at some place of employment.

credulous /ˈkrɛdʒələs/ *adj.* ready or disposed to believe, especially on weak or insufficient evidence. – **credulity**, *n.*

creed /krid/ *n.* **1.** any system of belief or of opinion. **2.** any formula of religious belief, as of a denomination.

creek /krik/ *n.* **1.** a small stream. **2. up the creek (without a paddle)**, *Colloquial* in a predicament; in trouble.

creep /krip/ *v.*, **crept**, **creeping**, *n.* – *v.i.* **1.** to move with the body close to the ground, as a reptile or an insect. **2.** to move slowly, imperceptibly, or stealthily. **3.** to have a sensation as of something creeping over the skin. – *n.* **4.** the act of creeping. **5.** (*usu. pl.*) a sensation as of something creeping over the skin. **6.** *Colloquial* an unpleasant, obnoxious, or insignificant person.

creeper /ˈkripə/ *n.* *Botany* a plant which grows upon or just beneath the surface of the ground, or other surface.

cremate /krəˈmeɪt/ *v.t.*, **-mated**, **-mating**. to reduce (a corpse) to ashes by fire. – **cremation**, *n.*

crematorium /krɛməˈtɔriəm/ *n.* an establishment for cremating dead bodies.

crenellated /ˈkrɛnəleɪtəd/ *adj.* having battlements. – **crenellation**, *n.*

creole /ˈkrioʊl/ *n.* a language which has changed from a pidgin to a community's first language.

crepe /kreɪp/ *n.* **1.** a thin, light fabric with a finely crinkled or ridged surface. **2.** Also, **crepe paper**. thin paper wrinkled to resemble crepe. **3.** a thin pancake.

crept /krɛpt/ *v.* past tense and past participle of **creep**.

crescendo /krəˈʃɛndoʊ/ *n.*, *pl.* **-dos** /ˈdoʊz/. a gradual increase in force or loudness.

crescent /ˈkrɛsənt, ˈkrɛzənt/ *n.* the biconvex figure of the moon in its first or last quarter.

cress /krɛs/ *n.* any of various plants used for salad and as a garnish.

crest /krɛst/ *n.* **1.** a tuft or other natural growth of the top of an animal's head, as the comb of a cock. **2.** anything resembling or suggesting such a tuft. **3.** the head or top of anything. **4.** *Heraldry* a figure or design used as a family emblem.

crestfallen /ˈkrɛstfɔlən/ *adj.* dejected; depressed.

cretin /ˈkrɛtn/ *n.* *Colloquial* a fool; a stupid person. – **cretinous**, *adj.*

Creutzfeldt-Jakob disease /ˌkrɔɪtsfɛlt-ˈjakɒp dəziz/ *n.* a rare, fatal brain disease caused by a slow-acting virus. *Abbrev.*: CJD

crevasse /krəˈvæs/ *n.* a fissure or deep cleft in the ice of a glacier.

crevice /ˈkrɛvəs/ *n.* a crack forming an opening.

crew[1] /kru/ *n.* a group of persons engaged upon a particular work; a gang.

crew[2] /kru/ *v.* past tense of **crow**[2].

crew cut *n.* a very closely cropped haircut.

crib /krɪb/ *n.*, *v.*, **cribbed**, **cribbing**. – *n.* **1.** a child's bed, usually decorated. **2.** *Colloquial* a translation or other illicit aid used by students. – *v.t.* **3.** to confine in, or as in, a crib. **4.** *Colloquial* to pilfer or steal, as a passage from an author.

cribbage /ˈkrɪbɪdʒ/ *n.* a card game.

crick /krɪk/ *n.* a sharp, painful spasm of the muscles, as of the neck or back, making it difficult to move the part.

cricket[1] /ˈkrɪkət/ *n.* any of the insects noted for the ability of the males to produce shrill sounds by friction of their leathery forewings.

cricket[2] /ˈkrɪkət/ *n.* **1.** an outdoor game

played with ball, bats, and wickets, by two sides of eleven players each. **2.** *Colloquial* fair play.

crime /kraɪm/ *n.* an act committed or an omission of duty, injurious to the public welfare, for which punishment is prescribed by law.

criminal /ˈkrɪmənəl/ *adj.* **1.** of or relating to crime or its punishment. **2.** of the nature of or involving crime. – *n.* **3.** a person guilty or convicted of a crime.

criminology /ˌkrɪməˈnɒlədʒi/ *n.* the science dealing with the causes and treatment of crimes and criminals.

crimp /krɪmp/ *v.t.* to press into small regular folds.

crimson /ˈkrɪmzən/ *adj.* deep purplish red.

cringe /krɪndʒ/ *v.i.*, **cringed**, **cringing**. to shrink, bend, or crouch, especially from fear or servility; cower.

crinkle /ˈkrɪŋkəl/ *v.i.*, **-kled**, **-kling**. to wrinkle; ripple.

crinoline /ˈkrɪnələn/ *n.* a hooped skirt.

cripple /ˈkrɪpəl/ *n.*, *v.*, **-pled**, **-pling**. – *n.* **1.** someone who is partially or wholly deprived of the use of one or more limbs; a lame person. – *v.t.* **2.** to disable; impair.

crisis /ˈkraɪsəs/ *n.*, *pl.* **crises** /ˈkraɪsiz/. a critical time or occasion.

crisp /krɪsp/ *adj.* **1.** hard but easily breakable; brittle. **2.** firm and fresh. – *n.* **3.** a wafer of potato fried, dried, and usually served cold.

criterion /kraɪˈtɪəriən/ *n.*, *pl.* **-teria** /-ˈtɪəriə/, **-terions**. an established rule or principle for testing something.

critic /ˈkrɪtɪk/ *n.* **1.** a person skilled in judging the qualities or merits of some class of things, especially of literary or artistic work. **2.** someone who censures or finds fault.

critical /ˈkrɪtɪkəl/ *adj.* **1.** of or relating to critics or criticism. **2.** relating to, or of the nature of, a crisis; crucial.

criticise = criticize /ˈkrɪtəsaɪz/ *v.*, **-cised**, **-cising**. – *v.i.* **1.** to make judgments as to merits and faults. **2.** to find fault. – *v.t.* **3.** to judge or discuss the merits and faults of. **4.** to find fault with. – **criticism**, *n.*

critique /krəˈtik, krɪ-/ *n.*, *v.*, **-tiqued**, **-tiquing**. – *n.* **1.** an article or essay criticising a literary or other work; a review. – *v.t.* **2.** to review critically; evaluate.

croak /kroʊk/ *v.i.* **1.** to utter a low, hoarse, dismal cry, as a frog or a raven. **2.** to speak with a low, hollow voice. **3.** *Colloquial* to die.

crochet /ˈkroʊʃə, ˈkroʊʃeɪ/ *n.*, *v.*, **-cheted** /-ʃəd, -ʃeɪd/ **-cheting** /-ʃərɪŋ, -ʃeɪɪŋ/ – *n.* **1.** a kind of needlework done with a needle having at one end a small hook for drawing the thread or yarn into intertwined loops. – *v.t.*, *v.i.* **2.** to form by crochet.

crock /krɒk/ *n.* an earthen pot, jar, or other vessel.

crockery /ˈkrɒkəri/ *n.* china in general, especially as for domestic use.

crocodile /ˈkrɒkədaɪl/ *n.* any of several large, thick-skinned, lizard-like reptiles.

crocodile tears *pl. n.* a hypocritical show of sorrow.

croissant /ˈkrwʌsɒ̃/ *n.* a roll of leavened dough or puff pastry, shaped into a crescent and baked.

crone /kroʊn/ *n.* an old woman.

crony /ˈkroʊni/ *n.*, *pl.* **-nies**. an intimate friend or companion.

crook /krʊk/ *n.* **1.** a bent or curved implement, piece, appendage, etc. **2.** any bend, turn, or curve. **3.** a dishonest person, especially a swindler, or thief. – *adj.* *Colloquial* **4.** sick; disabled. **5.** bad; inferior.

crooked /ˈkrʊkəd/ *adj.* bent; not straight; curved.

croon /krun/ *v.i.* to sing softly, especially with exaggerated feeling.

crop /krɒp/ *n.*, *v.*, **cropped**, **cropping**. – *n.* **1.** the cultivated produce of the ground, as grain or fruit, while growing or when gathered. **2.** the stock or handle of a whip. **3.** a style of wearing the hair cut short. **4.** a special pouchlike enlargement of the gullet of many birds. **5.** to cut off the ends or a part of. **6.** to cut short. – *v.i.* **7.** to bear or yield a crop or crops. **8.** to appear unintentionally or unexpectedly (fol. by *up* or *out*).

cropper /ˈkrɒpə/ *n.* **1.** a fall. **2. come a cropper,** *Colloquial* to fall heavily.

croquet /ˈkroʊkeɪ, -ki/ *n.* an outdoor game played by knocking wooden balls through a series of iron arches by means of mallets.

croquette /kroʊˈkɛt/ *n.* a small mass of minced meat, fish, etc., fried in deep fat.

cross /krɒs/ *n.* **1.** a structure consisting essentially of an upright and a transverse piece, upon which persons were formerly put to death. **2.** the cross as the symbol of Christianity. **3.** any burden, affliction, responsibility, etc., that one has to bear. **4.** any object, figure, or mark resembling a cross, as two intersecting lines. **5.** an opposing; thwarting. **6.** a mixing of breeds. **7.** something intermediate in character between two things. – *v.t.* **8.** to make the sign of the cross upon or over, as in devotion. **9.** to mark with a cross. **10.** to put or draw (a line, etc.) across. **11.** to mark (the face of a cheque) with two vertical parallel lines with or without the words *not negotiable* written between them. **12.** to lie or pass across; intersect. **13.** to move, pass, or extend from one side to the other side of (a street, river, etc.). **14.** to meet and pass. **15.** to oppose; thwart. **16. cross the floor,** in parliament, to vote with an opposing party. – *v.i.* **17.** to lie or be athwart; intersect. **18.** to move, pass, extend from one side or place to another. **19.** to meet and pass. **20.** to interbreed. – *adj.* **21.** lying or passing crosswise or across each other; transverse. **22.** involving interchange; reciprocal. **23.** contrary; opposite. **24.** adverse; unfavourable. **25.** ill-humoured.

cross- a first element of compounds, modifying the second part, meaning: **1.** going across. **2.** counter. **3.** cross-shaped.

cross-examine /krɒs-əgˈzæmən/ *v.t.*, **-ined**, **-ining**. to examine by questions intended to check a previous examination; examine closely or minutely.

cross-eye /ˈkrɒs-aɪ/ *n.* a disorder in which both eyes turn towards the nose. – **cross-eyed**, *adj.*

crossholding /ˈkrɒshoʊldɪŋ/ *n.* (among a

group of allied commercial companies) the holding of shares in companies within the group, as a mutually protective device.

crossing /ˈkrɒsɪŋ/ *n.* **1.** the act of someone who or that which crosses. **2.** a place where lines, tracks, etc., cross each other. **3.** a place at which a road, river, etc., may be crossed.

cross-reference /krɒs-ˈrɛfrəns/ *n.* a reference from one part of a book, etc., to a word, item, etc., in another part.

cross-section /ˈkrɒs-sɛkʃən/ *n.* **1.** a section made by a plane cutting anything transversely, especially at right angles to the longest axis. **2.** a typical selection.

crossword puzzle /ˈkrɒswɜd pʌzəl/ *n.* a puzzle in which the answers to various clues must be fitted into a grid-like figure.

crotch /krɒtʃ/ *n.* **1.** a forked piece, part, support, etc. **2.** a forking or place of forking, as of the human body between the legs.

crotchet /ˈkrɒtʃət/ *n. Music* a note having half the value of a minim.

crotchety /ˈkrɒtʃəti/ *adj. Colloquial* irritable, difficult, or cross.

crouch /kraʊtʃ/ *v.i.* **1.** (of people) to lower the body with one or both knees bent, in any position which inclines the trunk forward. **2.** (of animals) to lie close to or on the ground with legs bent as in the position taken when about to spring.

croupier /ˈkrupiə/ *n.* an attendant who collects and pays the money at a gaming table.

crow[1] /kroʊ/ *n.* **1.** either of two large, lustrous black, Australian birds having a characteristic harsh call. **2. as the crow flies,** in a straight line.

crow[2] /kroʊ/ *v.i.*, **crowed** *or for def. 1* **crew, crowed, crowing**. **1.** to utter the characteristic cry of a cock. **2.** to utter an inarticulate cry of pleasure, as an infant does. **3.** to exult loudly; boast.

crowbar /ˈkroʊba/ *n.* a bar of iron, for use as a lever, etc.

crowd /kraʊd/ *n.* **1.** a large number of persons gathered closely together; a throng. **2.** a large number of things gathered or considered together. – *v.i.* **3.** to gather in large numbers; throng; swarm. **4.** to press forward; advance by pushing. – *v.t.* **5.** to press closely together; force into a confined space. **6.** to fill to excess; fill by crowding or pressing into.

crown /kraʊn/ *n.* **1.** a decorative covering for the head, worn as a symbol of sovereignty. **2. the crown,** (*often cap.*) **a.** the sovereign as head of the state. **b.** the imperial or regal power; sovereignty. **c.** the government, or governments above local government level, of a country with a constitutional monarch. **3.** the top or highest part of anything. – *adj.* **4.** of or relating to that which belongs to the crown (def. 2) or acts on its behalf: *crown lease*; *crown prosecutor*. – *v.t.* **5.** to invest with a regal crown, or with regal dignity and power. **6.** to honour as with a crown. **7.** to surmount as with a crown; surmount as a crown does.

crown land *n.* land belonging to the government.

crown witness *n.* a witness for the crown in a criminal prosecution.

crow's-foot /ˈkroʊz-fʊt/ *n., pl.* **-feet**. (*usu. pl.*) a wrinkle at the outer corner of the eye.

crucial /ˈkruʃəl/ *adj.* involving a final and supreme decision; decisive; critical.

crucible /ˈkrusəbəl/ *n.* a vessel for heating substances to high temperatures.

crucifix /ˈkrusəfɪks/ *n.* a cross, especially one with the figure of Jesus crucified upon it.

crucify /ˈkrusəfaɪ/ *v.t.*, **-fied**, **-fying**. to put to death by nailing or binding the body to a cross. – **crucifixion**, *n.*

crude /krud/ *adj.*, **cruder**, **crudest**. **1.** in a raw or unprepared state; unrefined. **2.** lacking culture, refinement, tact, etc. – **crudity**, *n.*

cruel /ˈkruəl/ *adj.* **1.** disposed to inflict suffering; hard-hearted; pitiless. **2.** causing, or marked by, great pain or distress. – **cruelty**, *n.*

cruet /ˈkruət/ *n.* a set, on a stand, of containers for salt, pepper, etc.

cruise /kruz/ *v.*, **cruised**, **cruising**, *n.* – *v.i.* **1.** to sail to and fro, or from place to place. **2.** (of a car, aeroplane, etc.) to move along easily at a moderate speed. – *v.t.* **3.** to cruise over. – *n.* **4.** a voyage made by cruising.

cruise missile *n.* a self-propelled, air-breathing guided missile which carries a conventional or a nuclear warhead.

crumb /krʌm/ *n.* **1.** a small particle of bread, cake, etc. **2.** a small particle or portion of anything. – *v.t.* **3.** to dress or prepare with breadcrumbs. **4.** to break into crumbs or small fragments.

crumble /ˈkrʌmbəl/ *v.t., v.i.*, **-bled**, **-bling**. to break into small fragments or crumbs.

crummy /ˈkrʌmi/ *adj.*, **-mier**, **-miest**. *Colloquial* very inferior, mean, or shabby.

crumpet /ˈkrʌmpət/ *n.* a kind of light, soft bread served toasted and buttered.

crumple /ˈkrʌmpəl/ *v.*, **-pled**, **-pling**. – *v.t.* **1.** to draw or press into irregular folds; rumple; wrinkle. – *v.i.* **2.** to collapse; give way.

crunch /krʌntʃ/ *v.t.* **1.** to crush with the teeth; chew with a crushing noise. – *n.* **2.** *Colloquial* a moment of crisis.

crusade /kruˈseɪd/ *n.* any vigorous, aggressive movement for the defence or advancement of an idea, cause, etc.

crush /krʌʃ/ *v.t.* **1.** to press and bruise between two hard bodies. **2.** to break into small fragments or particles, as ore, stone, etc. **3.** to force out by pressing or squeezing. **4.** to put down, overpower, or subdue completely; overwhelm. **5.** to oppress harshly. – *v.i.* **6.** to become crushed. **7.** to advance with crushing; press or crowd forcibly. – *n.* **8.** the act of crushing. **9.** the state of being crushed. **10.** *Colloquial* a great crowd. **11.** *Colloquial* an infatuation.

crust /krʌst/ *n.* **1.** the hard outer portion of a loaf of bread, a pie, etc. **2.** any more or less hard external covering or coating.

crustacean /krʌsˈteɪʃən/ *n.* any of a class of (chiefly marine) animals with a hard shell, as the lobsters, crabs, barnacles, etc.

crusty /ˈkrʌsti/ *adj.*, **crustier**, **crustiest**. **1.** of the nature of or resembling a crust; having a crust. **2.** harsh; surly.

crutch /krʌtʃ/ *n.* **1.** a staff or support to assist a lame or infirm person in walking.

2. the crotch of the human body. **3.** *Colloquial* anything relied on or trusted.

crux /krʌks/ *n., pl.* **cruxes**, **cruces** /ˈkrusiz/. a vital, basic, or decisive point.

cry /kraɪ/ *v.,* **cried**, **crying**, *n., pl.* **cries**. – *v.i.* **1.** to utter inarticulate sounds, especially of lamentation, grief, or suffering, usually with tears. **2.** to weep; shed tears, with or without sound. **3.** to call loudly; shout. **4. cry off,** to break a promise, agreement, etc. – *v.t.* **5.** to utter or pronounce loudly; call out. **6. cry down,** to disparage; belittle. **7. cry up,** to praise; extol. – *n.* **8.** the act or sound of crying. **9.** a political or party slogan. **10.** the utterance or call of an animal.

cryo- a word element meaning 'icy cold', 'frost', 'low temperature'.

cryogenics /kraɪəˈdʒɛnɪks/ *n.* that branch of physics concerned with the properties of materials at very low temperatures.

crypt /krɪpt/ *n.* a subterranean chamber or vault used as a burial place, etc.

cryptic /ˈkrɪptɪk/ *adj.* hidden; secret.

crypto- a word element meaning 'hidden'.

crystal /ˈkrɪstl/ *n.* **1.** a clear, transparent mineral or glass resembling ice. **2.** *Chemistry, Mineralogy* a solid body having a characteristic internal structure.

crystallise = crystallize /ˈkrɪstəlaɪz/ *v.t., v.i.,* **-lised**, **-lising**. **1.** to form into crystals. **2.** to assume or cause to assume definite or concrete form.

crystallo- a word element meaning 'crystal'.

cub /kʌb/ *n.* **1.** the young of certain animals, as the fox, bear, etc. **2.** a novice or apprentice, especially a reporter.

cubbyhouse /ˈkʌbihaʊs/ *n.* a children's playhouse.

cube /kjub/ *n., v.,* **cubed**, **cubing**. – *n.* **1.** solid bounded by six equal squares, the angle between any two adjacent faces being a right angle. **2.** the third power of a quantity. – *v.t.* **3.** to make into a cube or cubes. **4.** to raise to the third power; find the cube of. – **cubic**, *adj.*

cube root *n.* the quantity of which a given quantity is the cube.

cubicle /ˈkjubɪkəl/ *n.* any small space or compartment partitioned off.

cuckold /ˈkʌkəld/ *n.* the husband of an unfaithful wife.

cuckoo /ˈkʊku/ *n.* **1.** any of a number of birds noted for their habit of laying eggs in the nests of other birds. **2.** a fool; simpleton.

cucumber /ˈkjukʌmbə/ *n.* a long fleshy fruit which is commonly eaten green as a salad and used for pickling.

cud /kʌd/ *n.* the portion of food which a ruminating animal returns from the first stomach to the mouth to chew a second time.

cuddle /ˈkʌdl/ *v.,* **-dled**, **-dling**, *n.* – *v.t.* **1.** to draw or hold close in an affectionate manner. – *n.* **2.** the act of cuddling; a hug; an embrace.

cudgel /ˈkʌdʒəl/ *n.* a short, thick stick used as a weapon; a club.

cue[1] /kju/ *n.* **1.** anything said or done on or behind the stage that is followed by a specific line or action. **2.** a hint; an intimation; a guiding suggestion.

cue[2] /kju/ *n.* a long tapering rod, tipped with a soft leather pad, used to strike the ball in billiards, etc.

cuff[1] /kʌf/ *n.* **1.** a fold, band, or variously shaped piece serving as a trimming or finish for the bottom of a sleeve or trouser leg. **2. off the cuff,** impromptu.

cuff[2] /kʌf/ *v.t.* to strike with the open hand.

cufflink /ˈkʌflɪŋk/ *n.* a link which fastens a shirt cuff.

cul-de-sac /ˈkʌl-də-sæk/ *n.* a street, lane, etc., closed at one end; blind alley.

-cule a diminutive suffix of nouns. Also, **-cle**.

culinary /ˈkʌlənri, -ənəri/ *adj.* relating to the kitchen or to cookery.

cull /kʌl/ *v.t.* to choose; select; pick.

culminate /ˈkʌlməneɪt/ *v.i.,* **-nated**, **-nating**. to reach the highest point.

culpable /ˈkʌlpəbəl/ *adj.* deserving blame or censure; blameworthy.

culprit /ˈkʌlprət/ *n.* one guilty of or responsible for a specified offence or fault.

cult /kʌlt/ *n.* **1.** a particular system of religious worship, especially with reference to its rites and ceremonies. **2.** an instance of an almost religious veneration for a person or thing.

cultivate /ˈkʌltəveɪt/ *v.t.,* **-vated**, **-vating**. **1.** to bestow labour upon (land) in raising crops. **2.** to develop or improve by education or training; train; refine. **3.** to promote the growth or development of. **4.** to seek the acquaintance or friendship of (a person).

cultural /ˈkʌltʃərəl/ *adj.* of or relating to culture or cultivation.

culture /ˈkʌltʃə/ *n.* **1.** skills, arts, customs, etc., of a people passed from generation to generation. **2.** development or improvement by education or training. **3.** the action or practice of cultivating the soil.

cum /kʌm, kʊm/ *prep.* **1.** with; together with; including (used sometimes in financial phrases as *cum dividend, cum rights,* etc., which are often abbreviated simply *cum*). **2.** (in combination) serving a dual function as, the functions being indicated by the preceding and following elements.

cumbersome /ˈkʌmbəsəm/ *adj.* burdensome; troublesome.

cumulative /ˈkjumjələtɪv/ *adj.* increasing or growing by accumulation or successive additions.

cumulative preference share *n.* a share issued on terms such that should the dividend in any year or years be not paid in whole or in part, the right to receive the unpaid monies remains.

cumulus /ˈkjumjələs/ *n., pl.* **-li** /-li/. *Meteorology* a cloud made up of rounded heaps, and with flat base.

cunnilingus /kʌnəˈlɪŋgəs/ *n.* oral stimulation of the female genitals.

cunning /ˈkʌnɪŋ/ *n.* **1.** skill employed in a crafty manner; guile. – *adj.* **2.** exhibiting or wrought with ingenuity.

cup /kʌp/ *n., v.,* **cupped**, **cupping**. – *n.* **1.** a small, open container, especially of porcelain or metal, used mainly to drink from. **2.** (*often cap.*) an ornamental cup or other article, especially of precious metal, offered as a prize for a contest: *Melbourne Cup, Davis Cup.* **3.** a unit of capacity formerly equal to 8 fluid ounces, now 250 millilitres. **4.** any of various beverages, as a mixture of wine and various ingredients. **5.** any cuplike utensil, organ, part, cavity, etc. – *v.t.* **6.** to take or place in or as in a cup.

cupboard /ˈkʌbəd/ *n.* a place or article of furniture used for storage.

cupr- a word element referring to copper. Also (*before consonants*), **cupri-**, **cupro-**.

cur /kɜ/ *n.* **1.** a snarling, worthless, or outcast dog. **2.** a low, despicable person.

curate /ˈkjurət/ *n.* a member of the clergy employed as assistant or deputy of a rector or vicar.

curator /kjuˈreɪtə/ *n.* the person in charge of a museum, art collection, etc.

curb /kɜb/ *n.* **1.** anything that restrains or controls; a restraint; a check. – *v.t.* **2.** to control as with a curb; restrain; check.

curd /kɜd/ *n.* (*often pl.*) a substance obtained from milk by coagulation, used for making into cheese or eaten as food.

curdle /ˈkɜdl/ *v.t., v.i.,* **-dled**, **-dling**. to change into curd.

cure /ˈkjuə, ˈkjʊə/ *n., v.,* **cured**, **curing**. – *n.* **1.** a method or course of remedial treatment, as for disease. **2.** successful remedial treatment; restoration to health. – *v.t.* **3.** to relieve or rid of something troublesome or detrimental, as an illness, a bad habit, etc. **4.** to prepare (meat, fish, etc.) for preservation, by salting, drying, etc. – **curable**, *adj.* – **curative**, *n., adj.*

curfew /ˈkɜfju/ *n.* a regulation, as enforced during civil disturbances, which establishes strict controls on movement after nightfall.

curious /ˈkjuriəs/ *adj.* **1.** desirous of learning or knowing; inquisitive. **2.** exciting attention or interest because of strangeness or novelty. **3.** odd; eccentric. – **curiosity**, *n.*

curl /kɜl/ *v.t.* **1.** to form into ringlets, as the hair. **2.** to form into a spiral or curved shape; coil. – *n.* **3.** a ringlet of hair. **4.** anything of a spiral or curved shape.

curlicue /ˈkɜlikju/ *n.* a fantastic curl or twist.

currajong /ˈkʌrədʒɒŋ/ *n.* → **kurrajong**.

currant /ˈkʌrənt/ *n.* a small seedless raisin.

currawong /ˈkʌrəwɒŋ/ *n.* **1.** any of several large black and white or greyish birds. **2.** a small tree.

currency /ˈkʌrənsi/ *n., pl.* **-cies**. **1.** that which is current as a medium of exchange; the money in actual use. **2.** the fact or quality of being passed on, as from person to person. **3.** general acceptance; prevalence; vogue.

current /ˈkʌrənt/ *adj.* **1.** passing in time, or belonging to the time actually passing. **2.** passing from one to another; circulating, as coin. **3.** prevalent. – *n.* **4.** a flowing; flow, as of a river. **5.** a movement or flow of electric charges.

current account *n.* **1.** that part of a country's balance of payments that records transactions in goods, services, income, and transfers between it and the rest of the world. **2.** → **cheque account**.

current assets *pl. n.* cash, together with loans and other assets which can be readily converted to cash within a year.

current expenses *pl. n.* regularly continuing expenditures for the maintenance and carrying on of business.

current liabilities *pl. n.* indebtedness within one year.

curriculum /kəˈrɪkjələm/ *n., pl.* **-lums**, **-la** /-lə/. the aggregate of courses of study given in a school, college, university, etc. – **curricular**, *adj.*

curriculum vitae /kəˌrɪkjələm ˈvitaɪ/ *n., pl.* **curricula vitae**, **curriculum vitaes**. a brief account of one's career to date. Also, **CV**.

curry[1] /ˈkʌri/ *n.* any of several hot sauces or dishes originating in India.

curry[2] /ˈkʌri/ *v.t.,* **-ried**, **-rying**. to rub and clean (a horse, etc.) with a comb.

curse /kɜs/ *n., v.,* **cursed** *or* **curst**, **cursing**. – *n.* **1.** the expression of a wish that evil, etc., befall another. **2.** a profane oath. – *v.t.* **3.** to wish or invoke evil, calamity, injury, or destruction upon. – *v.i.* **4.** to utter curses; swear profanely.

cursive /ˈkɜsɪv/ *adj.* (of writing or printing type) in flowing strokes, with the letters joined together.

cursor /ˈkɜsə/ *n.* an indicator on a video display unit screen, usually a small rectangle of light, which shows where the next character will form.

cursory /ˈkɜsəri/ *adj.* going rapidly over something, without noticing details; hasty; superficial.

curt /kɜt/ *adj.* rudely brief in speech, manner, etc.

curtail /kɜˈteɪl/ *v.t.* to cut short.

curtain /ˈkɜtn/ *n.* **1.** a hanging piece of fabric used to shut out the light from a window, adorn a room, etc. **2.** anything that shuts off, covers, or conceals.

curtsy = curtsey /ˈkɜtsi/ *n., pl.* **-sies**, *v.,* **-sied**, **-sying**. – *n.* **1.** a bow by women in recognition or respect, consisting of bending the knees and lowering the body. – *v.i.* **2.** to make a curtsy.

curvature /ˈkɜvətʃə/ *n.* curved condition, often abnormal.

curve /kɜv/ *n., v.,* **curved**, **curving**. – *n.* **1.** a continuously bending line, usually without angles. **2.** a line on a graph, diagram, etc. representing a continuous variation in force, quantity, etc. – *v.i.* **3.** to bend in a curve.

curvi- a combining form of **curve**.

cushion /ˈkʊʃən/ *n.* **1.** a soft bag filled with feathers, air, etc., used to sit, kneel, or lie on. **2.** anything similar in appearance or use. **3.** something to absorb or counteract a shock, jar, or jolt, as a body of air or steam. – *v.t.* **4.** to lessen or soften the effects of.

cusp /kʌsp/ *n.* **1.** a point; pointed end. **2.** *Astrology* the transitional first or last part of a sign or house.

custard /ˈkʌstəd/ *n.* a sauce made from milk, eggs and sugar.

custard apple /ˈkʌstəd ˈæpəl/ *n.* a tropical fruit with a soft pulp.

custody /ˈkʌstədi/ *n., pl.* **-dies**. **1.** keeping; guardianship; care. **2.** the keeping or charge of officers of the law. – **custodian**, *n.* – **custodial**, *adj.*

custom /'kʌstəm/ *n.* **1.** a habitual practice; the usual way of acting in given circumstances. **2.** habits or usages collectively; convention. **3.** (*pl.*) customs duties. **4.** habitual patronage of a particular shop, etc.; business patronage.

customary /'kʌstəməri, -təmri/ *adj.* according to or depending on custom; usual; habitual.

customer /'kʌstəmə/ *n.* someone who purchases goods from another; buyer; patron.

custom-made /'kʌstəm-meɪd/ *adj.* made to individual order.

customs duties *pl. n.* duties imposed by law on imported or, less commonly, exported goods.

cut /kʌt/ *v.*, **cut**, **cutting**, *n.* – *v.t.* **1.** to penetrate, with or as with a sharp-edged instrument. **2.** to divide, with or as with a sharp-edged instrument; sever; carve. **3.** to reap; mow; harvest. **4.** to stop; halt the running of. **5.** to reduce. **6.** to make or fashion by cutting. **7.** *Colloquial* to absent oneself from. – *v.i.* **8.** to penetrate or divide something as with a sharp-edged instrument; make an incision. **9.** to allow incision or severing. **10.** to pass, go, or come, especially in the most direct way. **11.** *Radio, TV* to stop filming or recording. **12. cut one's losses,** to abandon a project in which one has already invested some part of one's capital, so as not to incur more losses. – *n.* **13.** the act of cutting. **14.** *Colloquial* share. **15.** the result of cutting. **16.** manner or fashion in which anything is cut. **17.** style; manner, kind. **18.** a passage or course straight across: *a short cut.* **19.** a reduction in price, salary, etc.

cute /kjut/ *adj.*, **cuter**, **cutest**. *Colloquial* appealing in manner or appearance.

cuticle /'kjutɪkəl/ *n.* the non-living epidermis which surrounds the edges of the fingernail or toenail.

cutlass /'kʌtləs/ *n.* a short, heavy, slightly curved sword.

cutlery /'kʌtləri/ *n.* cutting instruments collectively, especially those for dinner-table use.

cutlet /'kʌtlət/ *n.* a cut of meat, usually lamb or veal, containing a rib.

cuttlefish /'kʌtlfɪʃ/ *n., pl.* **-fishes**, (*esp. collectively*) **-fish**. any of various marine animals which eject a black, inklike fluid when pursued.

CV /si 'vi/ *n.* → **curriculum vitae**.

-cy a suffix of abstract nouns, as in *accuracy, lunacy, magistracy.*

cyanide /'saɪənaɪd/ *n.* a highly poisonous chemical.

cyber- a prefix popularly used to indicate a connection with computers or the world of computing: *cybertech.*

cybernetics /saɪbə'nɛtɪks/ *n.* the scientific study of those methods of control and communication which are common to living organisms and machines, especially as applied to the analysis of the operations of machines such as computers.

cyberspace /'saɪbəspeɪs/ *n.* **1.** the Internet. **2.** a world created in virtual reality.

cycl- a word element meaning 'cycle'. Also, **cyclo-**.

cycle /'saɪkəl/ *n., v.,* **-cled**, **-cling**. – *n.* **1.** a recurring period of time, especially one in which certain events or phenomena repeat themselves in the same order and at the same intervals. **2.** any round of operations or events. **3.** a bicycle, tricycle, etc. – *v.i.* **4.** to ride or travel by a bicycle, etc. **5.** to move or revolve in cycles; pass through cycles. – **cyclic**, *adj.*

cyclone /'saɪkloʊn/ *n.* a tropical hurricane, especially in the Indian Ocean.

cyder /'saɪdə/ *n.* → **cider**.

cygnet /'sɪgnət/ *n.* a young swan.

cylinder /'sɪləndə/ *n.* **1.** *Geometry* a tube-like figure. **2.** any cylinderlike object or part, whether solid or hollow. – **cylindrical**, *adj.*

cymbal /'sɪmbəl/ *n.* a brass or bronze concave plate giving a metallic sound when struck.

cymo- a word element meaning 'wave'.

cynic /'sɪnɪk/ *n.* someone who doubts or denies the goodness of human motives, and who often displays this attitude by sneers, sarcasm, etc. – **cynical**, *adj.*

cypher /'saɪfə/ *n., v.i., v.t.* → **cipher**.

cypress /'saɪprəs/ *n.* any of several coniferous evergreen trees.

cyrto- a word element meaning 'curved.'

cyst /sɪst/ *n. Pathology* a closed bladder-like sac formed in animal tissues, containing fluid or semifluid morbid matter.

cyst- a combining form representing **cyst**. Also, **cysti-**, **cysto-**.

cystitis /sɪs'taɪtəs/ *n.* inflammation of the urinary bladder.

-cyte a word element referring to cells or corpuscles.

czar /za/ *n.* → **tsar**. – **czardom**, *n.*

D d

D, d *n., pl.* **D's** *or* **Ds**, **d's** *or* **ds**. the fourth letter of the English alphabet.

'd contraction of: **1.** had. **2.** would.

dab /dæb/ *v.t.,* **dabbed**, **dabbing**. to tap lightly, as with the hand.

dabble /'dæbəl/ *v.i.,* **-bled**, **-bling**. **1.** to play in water, as with the hands or feet. **2.** to do anything in a slight or superficial manner.

dachshund /'dæksənd, 'dæʃhənd/ *n.* one of a German breed of small dogs with a long body and very short legs.

D-A converter /ˌdi-eɪ kən'vɜtə/ *n.* digital to analog converter. Also, **D to A converter**.

dad /dæd/ *n. Colloquial* father.

daddy /'dædi/ *n., pl.* **-dies**. (*with children*) dad; father.

daddy-long-legs /ˌdædi-'lɒŋ-lɛgz/ *n.* (*sing. and pl.*) a small web-spinning spider with long, thin legs, frequently found indoors.

dado /'deɪdoʊ/ *n., pl.* **-dos**, **-does**. the part of a pedestal between the base and the cornice or cap.

daffodil /'dæfədɪl/ *n.* a plant with single or double yellow nodding flowers.

daft /daft/ *adj.* simple or foolish.

dag[1] /dæg/ *n.* wool on a sheep's rear quarters, often dirty with mud and excreta.

dag[2] /dæg/ *n. Colloquial* **1.** an untidy, slovenly person. **2.** a person who lacks style or panache.

dagger /'dægə/ *n.* a short-edged and pointed weapon, like a small sword, used for thrusting and stabbing.

dago /'deɪgoʊ/ *n., pl.* **-gos**, **-goes**. *Colloquial* (*derogatory*) a person of Latin race. Also, **Dago**.

dahlia /'deɪljə/ *n.* a plant native to Mexico and Central America, widely cultivated for its showy, variously coloured flowers.

daily /'deɪli/ *adj.* **1.** of, done, occurring, or issued each day or each weekday. – *adv.* **2.** every day.

dainty /'deɪnti/ *adj.,* **-tier**, **-tiest**. of delicate beauty or charm; exquisite.

dairy /'dɛəri/ *n., pl.* **dairies**. a place where milk and cream are kept and made into butter and cheese.

dais /'deɪəs/ *n.* a raised platform, as at the end of a room, for a throne, seats of honour, a lecturer's desk, etc.

daisy /'deɪzi/ *n., pl.* **-sies**. a plant whose flower heads have a yellow disc and white rays.

daks /dæks/ *pl. n. Colloquial* trousers.

dale /deɪl/ *n.* a vale; valley.

dally /'dæli/ *v.i.,* **-lied**, **-lying**. to waste time; loiter; delay. – **dalliance**, *n.*

Dalmatian /dæl'meɪʃən/ *n.* one of a breed of dogs of a white colour profusely marked with small black or liver-coloured spots.

dam[1] /dæm/ *n., v.,* **dammed**, **damming**. – *n.* **1.** a barrier to obstruct the flow of water, especially one of earth, masonry, etc., built across a stream. **2.** a body of water confined by such a barrier. – *v.t.* **3.** to stop up; block up.

dam[2] /dæm/ *n.* a female parent (used especially of quadrupeds).

damage /'dæmɪdʒ/ *n., v.,* **-aged**, **-aging**. – *n.* **1.** injury or harm that impairs value or usefulness. **2.** (*pl.*) *Law* the estimated money equivalent for detriment or injury sustained. – *v.t.* **3.** to cause damage to; injure or harm; impair the usefulness of.

damask /'dæməsk/ *n.* a reversible fabric of linen, silk, cotton, or wool, woven with patterns.

dame /deɪm/ *n.* **1.** a form of address to any woman of rank or authority. **2.** *Colloquial* a woman.

damn /dæm/ *v.t.* **1.** to declare (something) to be bad, unfit, invalid, or illegal. **2.** to bring condemnation upon; ruin. – *n.* **3.** a negligible amount. – *interj.* **4.** (an expression of anger, annoyance, or emphasis.) – **damnation**, *n.* – **damnable**, *adj.*

damp /dæmp/ *adj.* **1.** moderately wet; moist. – *v.t.* **2.** to stifle or suffocate; extinguish.

dampen /'dæmpən/ *v.t.* **1.** to make damp; moisten. **2.** to dull or deaden; depress.

damper /'dæmpə/ *n.* a bush bread made from a simple flour and water dough with or without a raising agent, cooked in the coals or in a camp oven.

dance /dæns, dans/ *v.,* **danced**, **dancing**, *n.* – *v.i.* **1.** to move with the feet or body rhythmically, especially to music. **2.** to bob up and down. – *n.* **3.** a successive group of rhythmical steps, generally executed to music. **4.** an act or round of dancing. **5.** a social gathering for dancing; ball. – **dancer**, *n.*

dandelion /'dændilaɪən, -də-/ *n.* a common weed, with golden yellow flowers.

dandruff /'dændrəf, -rʌf/ *n.* a scurf which forms on the scalp and comes off in small scales.

dandy /'dændi/ *n., pl.* **-dies**. **1.** a man who is excessively concerned about clothes and appearance; a fop. **2.** *Colloquial* something very fine or first rate.

danger /'deɪndʒə/ *n.* liability or exposure to harm or injury; risk; peril. – **dangerous**, *adj.*

dangle /'dæŋgəl/ *v.i.,* **-gled**, **-gling**. to hang loosely with a swaying motion.

dank /dæŋk/ *adj.* unpleasantly moist or humid; damp.

dapper /'dæpə/ *adj.* neat; trim; smart.

dapple /'dæpəl/ *n.* mottled marking, as of an animal's skin or coat.

dare /dɛə/ *v.,* **dared** *or* **durst**, **dared**, **daring**. – *v.i.* **1.** to have the necessary courage or boldness for something; be bold enough. **2.** **dare say,** to assume as probable; have no doubt. – *v.t.* **3.** to meet defiantly. **4.** to challenge or provoke to action, especially by doubting one's courage; defy.

daredevil /'dɛədɛvəl/ *n.* **1.** a recklessly daring person. – *adj.* **2.** recklessly daring.

dark /dak/ *adj.* **1.** without light; with very little light. **2.** not pale or fair. **3.** gloomy; cheerless; dismal. **4.** evil; wicked. – *n.* **5.** absence of light; darkness. **6.** ignorance.

darkroom /'dakrum/ *n.* a room from which the actinic rays of light have been excluded, used in making, handling, and developing photographic film, etc.

darling /ˈdalɪŋ/ *n.* a person very dear to another; person dearly loved.

darn[1] /dan/ *v.t.* to mend (clothes, etc., or a rent or hole) with rows of stitches, sometimes with crossing and interwoven rows to fill up a gap.

darn[2] /dan/ *v.t. Colloquial* to curse.

dart /dat/ *n.* **1.** a long, slender, pointed, missile weapon propelled by the hand or otherwise. – *v.i.* **2.** to move swiftly; spring or start suddenly and run swiftly.

dash[1] /dæʃ/ *v.t.* **1.** to strike violently, especially so as to break to pieces. **2.** to throw or thrust violently or suddenly. **3.** to ruin or frustrate (hopes, plans, etc.). **4.** to write, make, sketch, etc., hastily (usually fol. by *off* or *down*). – *v.i.* **5.** to strike with violence. **6.** to move with violence; rush. – *n.* **7.** a violent and rapid blow or stroke. **8.** a small quantity of anything thrown into or mixed with something else. **9.** a hasty stroke, especially of a pen. **10.** a horizontal line (–) used in writing and printing as a mark of punctuation to indicate an abrupt break or pause in a sentence, to begin and end a parenthetic clause, etc. **11.** an impetuous movement; a rush; a sudden onset. **12.** *Athletics* a short race or sprint decided in one attempt, not in heats. **13. do one's dash,** to exhaust one's energies or opportunities.

dash[2] /dæʃ/ *v.t.* **1.** to confound. – *interj.* **2.** (a mild expletive).

dashboard /ˈdæʃbɔd/ *n.* the instrument board of a motor car or an aeroplane.

dashing /ˈdæʃɪŋ/ *adj.* **1.** impetuous; spirited; lively. **2.** brilliant; showy; stylish.

dastardly /ˈdæstədli/ *adj.* cowardly; meanly base; sneaking.

data /ˈdeɪtə, ˈdatə/ *n.* **1.** plural of **datum**. **2.** (*construed as sing. or pl.*) figures, etc., known or available; information.

database /ˈdeɪtəbeɪs, ˈdatə-/ *n.* **1.** a large volume of information stored in a computer and organised in categories to facilitate retrieval. **2.** any large collection of information or reference material. Also, **databank**.

data bus *n.* a main connecting channel or path for transferring data between sections of a computer system.

data processing *n.* → **automatic data processing**.

date[1] /deɪt/ *n., v.,* **dated**, **dating**. – *n.* **1.** a particular point or period of time when something happens or happened. **2.** *Colloquial* an appointment made for a particular time. **3.** *Colloquial* a person, usually of the opposite sex, with whom one has a social appointment. **4. to date,** to the present time. – *v.i.* **5.** to have a date. **6.** to belong to a particular period; have its origin. – *v.t.* **7.** to mark or furnish with a date. **8.** to ascertain or fix the date or time of; assign a date or time to. **9.** to show to be of a certain age, old-fashioned, or out of date.

date[2] /deɪt/ *n.* the oblong, fleshy fruit of the date palm, a staple food in northern Africa, Arabia, etc.

dative /ˈdeɪtɪv/ *adj. Grammar* denoting a case, in some inflected languages, having as one function indication of the indirect object of a verb.

datum /ˈdeɪtəm, ˈdatəm/ *n., pl.* **-ta** /-tə/. **1.** any proposition assumed or given, from which conclusions may be drawn. **2.** (*often pl.*) any fact assumed to be a matter of direct observation.

daub /dɔb/ *v.t.* to cover or coat with soft, adhesive matter, such as plaster, mud, etc.

daughter /ˈdɔtə/ *n.* **1.** a female child or person in relation to her parents. **2.** any female descendant. **3.** one related as if by the ties binding daughter to parent. – **daughterly**, *adj.*

daughter-in-law /ˈdɔtər-ɪn-lɔ/ *n., pl.* **daughters-in-law**. the wife of one's son.

daunt /dɔnt/ *v.t.* **1.** to overcome with fear; intimidate. **2.** to lessen the courage of; dishearten.

dauntless /ˈdɔntləs/ *adj.* not to be daunted; fearless; intrepid; bold.

dawdle /ˈdɔdəl/ *v.i.,* **-dled**, **-dling**. **1.** to waste time; idle. **2.** to walk slowly or lag behind others.

dawn /dɔn/ *n.* **1.** the first appearance of daylight in the morning. **2.** the beginning or rise of anything; advent. – *v.i.* **3.** to begin to open or develop. **4.** to begin to be perceived (fol. by *on* or *upon*).

day /deɪ/ *n.* **1.** the interval of light between two successive nights; the time between sunrise and sunset. **2.** the light of day. **3.** a day as a point or unit of time, or on which something occurs. **4.** a day of contest, or the contest itself. **5.** (*often pl.*) a particular time or period. **6.** period of power or influence. **7. call it a day,** to bring an activity to a close, either temporarily or permanently. **8. that'll be the day,** *Colloquial* (an expression indicating disbelief, cynicism, etc.).

daybook /ˈdeɪbʊk/ *n.* **1.** *Bookkeeping* a book in which the transactions of the day are entered in the order of their occurrence. **2.** → **log** (def. 2). **3.** a diary.

day care *n.* care and supervision of young children or elderly people given daily by trained staff.

daydream /ˈdeɪdrim/ *n.* **1.** a visionary fancy indulged in while awake; reverie. – *v.i.* **2.** to indulge in daydreams.

daylight robbery *n.* a shameless attempt to rob, overcharge or cheat someone.

daylight saving *n.* a system of reckoning time one or more hours later than the standard time for a country or community, usually used during summer months to give more hours of daylight to the working day.

daze /deɪz/ *v.t.,* **dazed**, **dazing**. **1.** to stun or stupefy with a blow, a shock, etc. **2.** to confuse; bewilder; dazzle.

dazzle /ˈdæzəl/ *v.t.,* **-zled**, **-zling**. **1.** to overpower or dim (the vision) by intense light. **2.** to bewilder by brilliancy or display of any kind.

D-day /ˈdi-deɪ/ *n.* the day, usually unspecified, set for the beginning of a previously planned undertaking.

DDT /di di ˈti/ *n.* a very powerful insecticide, dichlorodiphenyltrichloroethane. Also, **D.D.T**.

de- a prefix meaning: **1.** privation and separation, as in *debar*. **2.** negation, as in *demerit, deranged*. **3.** descent, as in *degrade, deduce*. **4.** reversal, as in *decontaminate*.

deacon /'dikən/ *n.* **1.** (in the Roman Catholic and Anglican Churches) a member of the clergy, ranked below a priest. **2.** a church official with variously defined duties. – **deaconess**, *fem. n.*

dead /dɛd/ *adj.* **1.** no longer living; deprived of life. **2.** not endowed with life; inanimate. **3. a.** bereft of sensation; insensible; numb. **b.** asleep. **4.** no longer in existence or use. **5.** *Law* deprived of civil rights so that one is in the state of civil death, especially deprived of the rights of property. **6.** *Colloquial* very tired; exhausted. **7. a.** without resonance. **b.** without resilience or bounce. **8.** not glossy, bright, or brilliant. **9.** complete; absolute. **10.** *Sport* out of play. – *adv.* **11.** absolutely; completely. **12.** with abrupt and complete stoppage of motion, etc.

deaden /'dɛdən/ *v.t.* **1.** to make less sensitive, active, energetic, or forcible; dull; weaken. **2.** to make impervious to sound, as a floor.

dead letter *n.* **1.** a law, ordinance, etc., which has lost its force, though not formally repealed or abolished. **2.** a letter which lies unclaimed for a certain time at a post office, or which, because of faulty address, etc., cannot be delivered.

deadline /'dɛdlaɪn/ *n.* the latest time for finishing something.

deadlock[1] /'dɛdlɒk/ *n.* **1.** a state of affairs in which progress is impossible; complete standstill. **2.** *Parliamentary Procedure* **a.** a situation in which both houses of parliament are in disagreement. **b.** a tied vote on a motion with no chance or opportunity for a change in the allocation of votes that would break the tie.

deadlock[2] /'dɛdlɒk/ *n.* a type of lock which can only be opened from inside and outside with a key. Also, **dead latch**.

deadly /'dɛdli/ *adj.*, **-lier**, **-liest**. **1.** causing or tending to cause death; fatal. **2.** excessive.

deadpan /'dɛdpæn/ *adj. Colloquial* (of a person or their face) completely lacking expression or reaction.

deadweight tonnage *n.* the mass of the cargo, fuel, ballast, stores, crew, gear, etc., on a ship.

deaf /dɛf/ *adj.* lacking or deprived of the sense of hearing, wholly or partially; unable to hear. – **deafen**, *v.* – **deafness**, *n.*

deal /dil/ *v.*, **dealt**, **dealing**, *n.* – *v.i.* **1.** to occupy oneself or itself (fol. by *with* or *in*). **2.** to take action with respect to a thing or person (usually fol. by *with*). **3.** to trade or do business. **4.** to distribute, especially the cards required in a game. – *v.t.* **5.** to give to someone as their share; apportion (often fol. by *out*). **6.** to distribute among a number of recipients, as the cards required in a game. **7.** to deliver (blows, etc.). – *n.* **8.** *Colloquial* a business transaction. **9.** an indefinite but large amount or extent. **10.** *Cards* **a.** the distribution to the players of the cards in a game. **b.** the turn of a player to deal. **11.** any undertaking, organisation, etc.; affair.

dealer /'dilə/ *n.* **1.** someone who buys and sells articles without altering their condition; trader or merchant. **2.** someone who buys and sells drugs, as marijuana, heroin, etc., in large quantities. **3.** *Cards* the player distributing the cards.

dealt /dɛlt/ *v.* past tense and past participle of **deal**.

dean /din/ *n.* **1.** *Education* the head of a medical school, university faculty, or the like. **2.** any of various ecclesiastical dignitaries, as the head of a division of a diocese.

dear /dɪə/ *adj.* **1.** beloved or loved. **2.** (in the salutation of a letter) highly esteemed. **3.** precious in one's regard. **4.** high-priced; expensive.

dearth /dɜθ/ *n.* scarcity or scanty supply; lack.

death /dɛθ/ *n.* **1.** the act of dying; the end of life; the total and permanent cessation of the vital functions of an animal or plant. **2.** the state of being dead. **3.** extinction; destruction. **4. like grim death,** tenaciously, firmly. **5. put to death,** to kill; execute.

death duty *n.* (*usu. pl.*) a tax paid upon the inheritance of property.

debacle /deɪ'bakəl, də-/ *n.* a general break-up or rout; sudden overthrow or collapse; overwhelming disaster.

debar /di'ba, də-/ *v.t.*, **-barred**, **-barring**. **1.** to bar out or exclude from a place or condition. **2.** to prevent or prohibit (an action, etc.).

debase /də'beɪs/ *v.t.*, **-based**, **-basing**. **1.** to reduce in quality or value; adulterate. **2.** to lower in rank or dignity.

debate /də'beɪt/ *n.*, *v.*, **-bated**, **-bating**. – *n.* **1.** a discussion, especially of a public question in an assembly. **2.** deliberation; consideration. **3.** a systematic contest of speakers in which two opposing points of view of a proposition are advanced. – *v.i.* **4.** to engage in discussion, especially in a legislative or public assembly. – *v.t.* **5.** to dispute about. – **debater**, *n.* – **debatable**, *adj.*

debauch /də'bɔtʃ/ *v.t.* to corrupt by sensuality, intemperance, etc.; seduce. – **debauchery**, *n.*

debenture /də'bɛntʃə/ *n.* **1.** a note or certificate acknowledging a debt, as given by an incorporated company; a bond or one of a series of bonds. **2.** a deed containing a charge or mortgage on a company's assets; a mortgage debenture. **3.** a certificate of drawback issued at a customs house.

debenture stock *n.* a series or group of debentures for a single debt.

debilitate /də'bɪləteɪt/ *v.t.*, **-tated**, **-tating**. to make weak or feeble; weaken. – **debility**, *n.*

debit /'dɛbət/ *n.* **1.** the recording of an entry of debt in an account. **2.** the side (left side) of an account on which such entries are made (opposed to *credit*). – *v.t.* **3.** to charge with a debt. **4.** to charge as a debt. **5.** to enter upon the debit side of an account.

debit card *n.* a plastic card, issued by a bank or other financial institution, which allows the holder to draw funds from their account without a passbook, etc.

debonair /dɛbə'nɛə/ *adj.* **1.** suave; stylish. **2.** of pleasant manners; courteous.

debouch /də'buʃ/ *v.i.* to issue or emerge

from a narrow opening.

debris /ˈdɛbri, ˈdeɪbri, dəˈbri/ *n.* the remains of anything broken down or destroyed; ruins; fragments; rubbish.

debt /dɛt/ *n.* **1.** that which is owed; that which one person is bound to pay to or perform for another. **2.** the condition of being under such an obligation. **3. bad debt,** a debt of which there is no prospect of payment.

debtor /ˈdɛtə/ *n.* someone who is in debt or under obligations to another (opposed to *creditor*).

debug /diˈbʌg/ *v.t.*, **-bugged**, **-bugging**. *Computers* to remove errors or incompatible logical conditions from a program.

debunk /diˈbʌŋk/ *v.t. Colloquial* to strip of false sentiment, etc.; to make fun of.

debut /ˈdeɪbju, -bu, dəˈbu/ *n.* a first public appearance.

debutante /ˈdɛbjətɒnt/ *n.* a girl making a debut, especially into society.

dec- /dɛk-/ → **deka-**.

deca- /ˈdɛkə-/ a prefix denoting 10 times a given unit, as in *decametre. Symbol*: da Also, **deka-**; (*before vowels*), **dec-**, **dek-**.

decade /ˈdɛkeɪd/ *n.* **1.** a period of ten years. **2.** a group, set, or series of ten.

decadence /ˈdɛkədəns/ *n.* the act or process of falling into an inferior condition or state, especially moral; decay; deterioration. – **decadent**, *adj.*

decaffeinated /diˈkæfəneɪtəd/ *adj.* having had the caffeine removed.

decagon /ˈdɛkəgɒn, -gən/ *n.* a polygon having ten angles and ten sides.

decahedron /dɛkəˈhidrən/ *n.*, *pl.* **-drons**, **-dra** /-drə/. a solid figure having ten faces.

decant /dəˈkænt/ *v.t.* **1.** to pour off gently, as liquor, without disturbing the sediment. **2.** to pour from one container into another.

decanter /dəˈkæntə/ *n.* **1.** a bottle used for decanting. **2.** a vessel, usually an ornamental bottle, from which wine, water, etc., are served at table.

decapitate /dəˈkæpəteɪt, di-/ *v.t.*, **-tated**, **-tating**. to cut off the head of; behead; kill by beheading.

decathlon /dəˈkæθlɒn, -lən/ *n.* an athletic contest comprising ten different events, and won by the contestant having the highest total score. – **decathlete**, *n.*

decay /diˈkeɪ, də-/ *v.i.* **1.** to fall away from a state of excellence, prosperity, health, etc.; deteriorate; decline. **2.** to become decomposed; rot. – *n.* **3.** a gradual falling into an inferior condition; progressive decline. **4.** decomposition; rotting.

decease /dəˈsis/ *n.*, *v.*, **-ceased**, **-ceasing**. – *n.* **1.** departure from life; death. – *v.i.* **2.** to depart from life; die.

deceased /dəˈsist/ *adj.* **1.** dead. – *phr.* **2. the deceased,** the dead person or persons.

deceive /dəˈsiv/ *v.t.*, **-ceived**, **-ceiving**. **1.** to mislead by a false appearance or statement; delude. **2.** to be unfaithful to; commit adultery against. – **deceit**, *n.* – **deceitful**, *adj.*

decent /ˈdisənt/ *adj.* **1.** fitting; appropriate. **2.** conforming to recognised standards of propriety, good taste, modesty, etc. **3.** *Colloquial* kind; obliging. – **decency**, *n.*

decentralise = decentralize /diˈsɛntrəlaɪz/ *v.t.*, **-lised**, **-lising**. **1.** to disperse (industry, population, etc.) from an area of concentration or density, especially from large cities to relatively undeveloped rural areas. **2.** to undo the centralisation of administrative powers (of an organisation, government, etc.). – **decentralisation**, *n.*

deception /dəˈsɛpʃən/ *n.* **1.** the act of deceiving. **2.** the state of being deceived. **3.** something that deceives or is intended to deceive; an artifice; a sham; a cheat. – **deceptive**, *adj.*

deci- /ˈdɛsi-/ a prefix denoting 10^{-1} of a given unit, as in *decibel. Symbol*: d

decibel /ˈdɛsəbɛl/ *n.* a unit expressing difference in power, usually between electric or acoustic signals, or between some particular signal and a reference level understood; equal to one tenth of a bel. *Symbol*: dB

decide /dəˈsaɪd/ *v.*, **-cided**, **-ciding**. – *v.t.* **1.** to determine or settle (a question, controversy, struggle, etc.) by giving victory to one side. **2.** to bring (a person) to a decision. – *v.i.* **3.** to settle something in dispute or doubt. **4.** to pronounce a judgment; come to a conclusion.

decided /dəˈsaɪdəd/ *adj.* resolute; determined.

deciduous /dəˈsɪdʒuəs/ *adj.* shedding the leaves annually, as trees, shrubs, etc.

decile /ˈdɛsaɪl/ *n. Statistics* one of the values of a variable which divides its distribution into ten groups having equal frequencies.

decimal /ˈdɛsəməl/ *adj.* **1.** relating to tenths, or to the number ten. **2.** proceeding by tens. – *n.* **3.** a decimal fraction. **4.** a decimal number.

decimal currency *n.* currency in which units are graded in multiples of ten.

decimal fraction *n.* a fraction whose denominator is some power of ten, usually indicated by a dot (the **decimal point**) written before the numerator, as $0.4 = ^4/_{10}$.

decimal number *n. Mathematics* any finite or infinite string of digits containing a decimal point. 1.0, 5.23, 3.14159 ... are decimal numbers.

decimal place *n.* **1.** the position of a digit to the right of a decimal point. In 9.623, 3 is in the third decimal place. **2.** the number of digits to the right of a decimal point. 9.623 is a number in three decimal places.

decimal point *n.* (in the decimal system) a dot preceding the fractional part of a number.

decimate /ˈdɛsəmeɪt/ *v.t.*, **-mated**, **-mating**. to destroy a great number or proportion of.

decipher /dəˈsaɪfə/ *v.t.* **1.** to make out or discover the meaning of. **2.** to interpret by the use of a key, as something written in cipher. – **decipherable**, *adj.*

decision /dəˈsɪʒən/ *n.* **1.** the act of deciding; determination (of a question or doubt). **2.** a judgment, as one formally pronounced by a court.

decisive /dəˈsaɪsɪv/ *adj.* **1.** having the power or quality of determining; putting an end to controversy. **2.** decided; determined.

deck /dɛk/ *n.* **1.** a horizontal platform

extending from side to side of a ship or of part of a ship, forming a covering for the space below and itself serving as a floor. **2.** a floor, platform or tier. **3.** a pack of playing cards. – *v.t.* **4.** to clothe or attire in something ornamental; array.

declaim /də'kleɪm/ *v.i.* **1.** to speak aloud rhetorically; make a formal speech. **2.** to inveigh (fol. by *against*). – **declamatory**, *adj.*

declare /də'klɛə/ *v.t.*, **-clared**, **-claring**. **1.** to make known, especially in explicit or formal terms. **2.** to state emphatically; affirm. **3.** to manifest; reveal. **4.** to make due statement of (dutiable goods, etc.). **5.** to make (a dividend) payable. – **declaration**, *n.* – **declaratory**, *adj.*

declension /də'klɛnʃən/ *n.* **1.** *Grammar* the inflection of nouns, etc., for categories such as case and number. **2.** a bending, sloping, or moving downward.

decline /də'klaɪn/ *v.*, **-clined**, **-clining** /də'klaɪn, 'diklaɪn/ *n.* – *v.t.* **1.** to withhold consent to do, enter upon, or accept; refuse. **2.** to cause to slope or incline downward. **3.** *Grammar* to inflect (a noun, pronoun, or adjective). – *v.i.* **4.** to express courteous refusal; refuse. **5.** to bend or slant down; slope or trend downward; descend. **6.** to fail in strength, vigour, character, value, etc.; deteriorate. – *n.* **7.** a downward incline or slope. **8.** a failing or gradual loss, as in strength, character, value, etc.; deterioration.

decoction /də'kɒkʃən/ *n.* the act of boiling in water, in order to extract the peculiar properties or virtues.

decode /di'koʊd/ *v.t.*, **-coded**, **-coding**. to translate from code into the original language or form.

decompose /dikəm'poʊz/ *v.*, **-posed**, **-posing**. – *v.t.* **1.** to separate or resolve into constituent parts or elements. – *v.i.* **2.** to rot; putrefy. – **decomposition**, *n.*

decompression /dikəm'prɛʃən/ *n.* **1.** the act or process of relieving pressure. **2.** the gradual return of persons, as divers or construction workers, to normal atmospheric pressure after working in deep water or in air under compression.

decongestant /dikən'dʒɛstənt/ *n.* a substance used to relieve congestion especially in the upper respiratory tract.

deconsolidate /dikən'sɒlədeɪt/ *v.t.* to remove goods from a shipping container and place in a store awaiting acceptance or delivery.

decontaminate /dikən'tæməneɪt/ *v.t.*, **-nated**, **-nating**. to make (any object or area) safe for unprotected personnel by absorbing, making harmless, or destroying chemicals with which they have been in contact.

decor /'deɪkɔ, 'dɛkɔ/ *n.* **1.** the interior decoration, especially of a home or office. **2.** a style of decoration.

decorate /'dɛkəreɪt/ *v.t.*, **-rated**, **-rating**. **1.** to furnish or deck with something becoming or ornamental; embellish. **2.** to plan and execute the design, wallpaper, etc., and sometimes the furnishings of (a house, room, or the like). **3.** to confer distinction upon by a badge, a medal of honour, etc. – **decoration**, *n.* – **decorator**, *n.* – **decorative**, *adj.*

decorum /də'kɔrəm/ *n.* propriety of behaviour, speech, dress, etc. – **decorous**, *adj.*

decoy /də'kɔɪ, 'dikɔɪ/ *n.* someone who entices or allures, as into a trap, danger, etc.

decrease /də'kris/ *v.*, **-creased**, **-creasing** /'dikris, də'kris/ *n.* – *v.i.* **1.** to diminish gradually in extent, quantity, strength, power, etc. – *v.t.* **2.** to make less; cause to diminish. – *n.* **3.** a process of growing less, or the resulting condition; gradual diminution. **4.** the amount by which a thing is lessened.

decree /də'kri/ *n.*, *v.*, **-creed**, **-creeing**. – *n.* **1.** an ordinance or edict promulgated by civil or other authority. **2.** *Law* a judicial decision or order. – *v.t.* **3.** to ordain or decide by decree.

decree nisi /dəˌkri 'naɪsaɪ/ *n.* *Law* See **nisi**.

decrement /'dɛkrəmənt/ *n.* **1.** the process or fact of decreasing; gradual diminution. **2.** the amount lost by diminution. – *v.t.* **3.** *Computers* to reduce the numerical contents of (a counter).

decrepit /də'krɛpət/ *adj.* broken down or weakened by old age; feeble; infirm. – **decrepitude**, *n.*

decriminalise = decriminalize /di'krɪmənəlaɪz/ *v.t.* to remove legal restrictions against (an activity, such as smoking marijuana), and thus eliminate the legal penalties previously associated with it.

decry /də'kraɪ/ *v.t.*, **-cried**, **-crying**. to speak disparagingly of; censure as faulty or worthless.

dedicate /'dɛdəkeɪt/ *v.t.*, **-cated**, **-cating**. **1.** to set apart and consecrate to a deity or to a sacred purpose. **2.** to give up wholly or earnestly, as to some person or end; set apart or appropriate. – **dedication**, *n.* – **dedicatory**, *adj.*

dedicated /'dɛdəkeɪtəd/ *adj.* **1.** wholly committed to something. **2.** (of a computer) limited to one purpose or set of operations.

deduce /də'djus/ *v.t.*, **-duced**, **-ducing**. to derive as a conclusion from something known or assumed; infer.

deduct /də'dʌkt/ *v.t.* to take away, as from a sum or amount.

deduction /də'dʌkʃən/ *n.* **1.** the act of deducting; subtraction; abatement. **2.** that which is deducted. **3.** the process of drawing a conclusion from something known or assumed. – **deductive**, *adj.*

deed /did/ *n.* that which is done, performed, or accomplished; an act.

deed poll *n.* a deed in the form of a declaration to all the world of the grantor's act and intention, as, for example, to change his or her name.

deem /dim/ *v.i.* to form or have an opinion; judge; think.

deep /dip/ *adj.* **1.** extending far downwards, inwards, or backwards. **2.** having a specified dimension downwards, inwards, or backwards. **3.** situated far or a certain distance down, in, or back. **4.** difficult to penetrate or understand; abstruse. **5.** not superficial; profound. **6.** great in measure; intense. **7.** (of colours) intense; dark and vivid. **8.** low in pitch, as sound. **9.** absorbed. – *n.* **10.** the deep part of the sea, a river, etc. – *adv.* **11.** to or at a considerable or specified depth.

deep freeze *n.* a locker or compartment in a refrigerator in which food can be quickly frozen and stored at a very low temperature.

deer /dɪə/ *n., pl.* **deer**. a type of ruminant with solid antlers (usually the male only).

deface /də'feɪs/ *v.t.,* **-faced**, **-facing**. **1.** to mar the face or appearance of; disfigure. **2.** to blot out; obliterate; efface.

de facto /di 'fæktoʊ, də, deɪ/ *adj.* **1.** in fact; in reality. **2.** actually existing, whether with or without right. **3.** living with, but not married to, one's partner.

defalcation /difæl'keɪʃən/ *n. Law* **1.** misappropriation of money, etc., held by a trustee or other fiduciary. **2.** the sum misappropriated.

defame /di'feɪm, də-/ *v.t.,* **-famed**, **-faming**. to attack the good name or reputation of, as by uttering or publishing maliciously anything injurious; slander; libel. – **defamation**, *n.* – **defamatory**, *adj.*

default /də'fɔlt/ *n.* **1.** failure to act; neglect. **2.** *Law* failure to perform an act or obligation legally required, especially to appear in court or to plead at a time assigned. **3.** failure to participate in or complete anything, as a scheduled match. – *v.t.* **4.** to fail to perform or pay.

defeasance /də'fizəns/ *n. Law* a rendering null and void.

defeat /də'fit/ *v.t.* **1.** to overcome in a contest, battle, etc.; vanquish; win or achieve victory over. **2.** to frustrate; thwart. – *n.* **3.** the act or result of defeating.

defeatism /də'fitɪzəm/ *n.* the attitude, policy, or conduct of those who admit or expect defeat, usually resulting from a premature decision that further struggle or effort is futile.

defecate /'dɛfəkeɪt/ *v.i.,* **-cated**, **-cating**. to void excrement. – **defecation**, *n.*

defect /'difɛkt, də'fɛkt/ *n.,* /də'fɛkt/ *v.* – *n.* **1.** a falling short; a fault or imperfection. – *v.i.* **2.** to desert a country, cause, etc. – **defection**, *n.* – **defector**, *n.* – **defective**, *adj.*

defence /də'fɛns/ *n.* **1.** resistance against attack; protection. **2.** the defending of a cause or the like by speech, argument, etc. **3.** *Law* the denial or pleading of the defendant in answer to the claim or charge against him or her.

defend /də'fɛnd/ *v.t.* **1.** to ward off attack from; guard against assault or injury (often fol. by *from* or *against*). **2.** to maintain by argument, evidence, etc.; uphold. **3.** to contest (a legal charge, claim, etc.). **4.** to act as counsel for (an accused person).

defendant /də'fɛndənt/ *n. Law* the party against whom a claim or charge is brought in a proceeding.

defensible /də'fɛnsəbəl/ *adj.* capable of being defended.

defensive /də'fɛnsɪv/ *adj.* **1.** serving to defend; protective. **2.** made or carried on for the purpose of resisting attack.

defer[1] /də'fɜ/ *v.t.,* **-ferred**, **-ferring**. to put off (action, etc.) to a future time. – **deferment**, **deferral**, *n.*

defer[2] /də'fɜ/ *v.i.,* **-ferred**, **-ferring**. to yield in judgment or opinion (fol. by *to*).

deference /'dɛfərəns/ *n.* **1.** submission or yielding to the judgment, opinion, will, etc., of another. **2.** respectful or courteous regard. – **deferential**, *adj.*

deferred delivery share *n.* a share which can be sold only on the understanding that buyers must accept a delay in the delivery of scrip, due to reconstruction of the company's share capital. *Abbrev.*: d.d. Also, **deferred share**.

deferred dividend *n.* a dividend to which the holder of a company share is not entitled before a certain lapse of time, unless ordinary shareholders receive more than the stated rate of dividend.

deferred share *n.* **1.** → **deferred delivery share**. **2.** a share which entitles the holder to a deferred dividend.

defiance /də'faɪəns/ *n.* **1.** a daring or bold resistance to authority or to any opposing force. **2.** open disregard. **3.** a challenge to meet in combat or contest. – **defiant**, *adj.*

deficient /də'fɪʃənt/ *adj.* **1.** lacking some element or characteristic; defective. **2.** insufficient; inadequate. – **deficiency**, *n.*

deficit /'dɛfəsət/ *n.* the amount by which a sum of money falls short of the required amount.

defile /də'faɪl/ *v.t.,* **-filed**, **-filing**. **1.** to make foul, dirty, or unclean; pollute; taint. **2.** to violate the chastity of.

define /də'faɪn/ *v.t.,* **-fined**, **-fining**. **1.** to state or set forth the meaning of (a word, phrase, etc.). **2.** to explain the nature or essential qualities of; describe. **3.** to fix or lay down definitely; specify distinctly. – **definition**, *n.*

definite /'dɛfənət/ *adj.* **1.** clearly defined or determined; not vague or general; fixed; precise; exact. **2.** *Colloquial* certain; sure.

definitive /də'fɪnətɪv/ *adj.* **1.** having the function of deciding or settling; determining; conclusive; final. **2.** having its fixed and final form.

deflate /də'fleɪt/ *v.t.,* **-flated**, **-flating**. **1.** to release the air or gas from (something inflated, as a tyre). **2.** to reduce (currency, prices, etc.) from an inflated condition. **3.** to reduce in esteem, especially self-esteem (a person or a person's ego).

deflation /də'fleɪʃən/ *n.* **1.** the act of deflating. **2.** an abnormal decline in the level of commodity prices, especially one not accompanied by an equal reduction in the costs of production.

deflect /də'flɛkt/ *v.i.* **1.** to bend or turn aside; swerve. – *v.t.* **2.** to cause to turn from a true course or right line. – **deflection**, *n.*

defoliate /də'foʊlieɪt/ *v.t.,* **-ated**, **-ating**. to strip or deprive (a tree, etc.) of leaves. – **defoliant**, *n.*

deform /də'fɔm/ *v.t.* **1.** to mar the natural form or shape of; put out of shape; disfigure. **2.** to make ugly, ungraceful, or displeasing; mar the beauty of; spoil. – **deformity**, *n.* – **deformed**, *adj.*

defraud /də'frɔd/ *v.t.* to deprive of a right or property by fraud; cheat.

defray /də'freɪ/ *v.t.* to bear or pay (the costs, expenses, etc.).

defrost /di'frɒst, də-/ *v.t.* **1.** to remove the frost or ice from. **2.** to cause (food, etc.) to thaw, as by removing from a refrigerator.

deft /dɛft/ *adj.* dexterous; nimble; skilful; clever.

defunct /də'fʌŋkt/ *adj.* **1.** deceased; dead; extinct. **2.** no longer operative; not in use.

defuse /di'fjuz/ *v.t.,* **-fused, -fusing**. **1.** to remove the fuse from (a bomb). **2.** to calm (a situation or action).

defy /də'faɪ/ *v.t.,* **-fied, -fying**. **1.** to challenge the power of; resist boldly or openly. **2.** to challenge (one) to do something deemed impossible.

degenerate /də'dʒɛnəreɪt/ *v.,* **-rated, -rating,** /də'dʒɛnərət/ *adj., n.* – *v.i.* **1.** to decline in physical, mental, or moral qualities; deteriorate. – *adj.* **2.** having declined in physical or moral qualities; degraded. – *n.* **3.** someone who has retrogressed from a normal type or standard, as in morals, or character. – **degenerative**, *adj.* – **degeneracy**, *n.* – **degeneration**, *n.*

degrade /də'greɪd/ *v.t.,* **-graded, -grading**. **1.** to reduce from a higher to a lower rank, degree, etc.; deprive of office, rank, degree, or title as a punishment. **2.** to lower in character or quality; debase; deprave. **3.** to lower in dignity or estimation; bring into contempt. – **degradation**, *n.*

degree /də'gri/ *n.* **1.** a step or stage in an ascending or descending scale, or in a course or process. **2.** the angle between two radii of a circle which cut off on the circumference an arc equal to 1/360 of that circumference (often indicated by the sign °). **3.** a unit in the measurement of temperature. **4.** *Geography* the unit of measurement of latitude or longitude, usually employed to indicate position on the earth's surface. **5.** a qualification conferred by a university for successful work, as judged by examination, or as an honorary recognition of achievement.

dehydrate /'dihaɪdreɪt/ *v.,* **-drated, -drating**. – *v.t.* **1.** to deprive of water. **2.** to free (vegetables, etc.) of moisture, for preservation. – *v.i.* **3.** to lose water or moisture. – **dehydration**, *n.*

deify /'diəfaɪ, 'deɪə-/ *v.t.,* **-fied, -fying**. **1.** to make a god of; exalt to the rank of a deity. **2.** to adore or regard as a deity.

deign /deɪn/ *v.i.* to think fit or in accordance with one's dignity; condescend.

deity /'diəti, 'deɪ-/ *n., pl.* **-ties**. **1.** a god or goddess. **2.** divine character or nature.

dejected /də'dʒɛktəd/ *adj.* depressed in spirits; disheartened; low-spirited.

deka- /'dɛkə-/ → **deca-**.

delay /də'leɪ, di-/ *v.t.* **1.** to put off to a later time; defer; postpone. **2.** to impede the progress of; retard; hinder. – *v.i.* **3.** to put off action; linger; loiter. – *n.* **4.** the act of delaying; procrastination; loitering. **5.** an instance of being delayed.

delectable /də'lɛktəbəl/ *adj.* delightful; highly pleasing; enjoyable.

delectation /ˌdilɛk'teɪʃən/ *n.* a high degree of enjoyment or pleasure; delight.

delegate /'dɛləgət, -geɪt/ *n.,* /'dɛləgeɪt/ *v.,* **-gated, -gating**. – *n.* **1.** one delegated to act for or represent another or others; a deputy; a representative, as at a conference, or the like. – *v.t.* **2.** to send or appoint (a person) as deputy or representative. **3.** to commit (powers, functions, etc.) to another as agent or deputy.

delegation /dɛlə'geɪʃən/ *n.* a group of delegates.

delete /də'lit/ *v.t.,* **-leted, -leting**. to strike out or take out (anything written or printed). – **deletion**, *n.*

deleterious /dɛlə'tɪəriəs/ *adj.* **1.** injurious to health. **2.** hurtful; harmful; injurious.

deliberate /də'lɪbərət/ *adj.,* /də'lɪbəreɪt/ *v.,* **-rated, -rating**. – *adj.* **1.** carefully weighed or considered; intentional. **2.** characterised by deliberation; careful or slow in deciding. – *v.i.* **3.** to think carefully or attentively; reflect. – **deliberation**, *n.*

deliberative /də'lɪbərətɪv, -lɪbrə-/ *adj.* **1.** having the function of deliberating, as a legislative assembly. **2.** having to do with policy; dealing with the wisdom and expediency of a proposal.

delicacy /'dɛləkəsi/ *n., pl.* **-cies**. **1.** quality of being delicate. **2.** something delightful or pleasing, especially to the palate.

delicate /'dɛləkət/ *adj.* **1.** fine in texture, quality, construction, etc. **2.** so fine or slight as to be scarcely perceptible; subtle. **3.** easily damaged; fragile. **4.** requiring great care, caution, or tact. **5.** distinguishing subtle differences. **6.** fastidious.

delicatessen /dɛləkə'tɛsən/ *n.* a shop selling cooked or prepared foods ready for serving, such as cold meats.

delicious /də'lɪʃəs/ *adj.* highly pleasing to the senses, especially to taste or smell.

delight /də'laɪt/ *n.* a high degree of pleasure or enjoyment; joy; rapture.

delightful /də'laɪtfəl/ *adj.* affording delight; highly pleasing.

delineate /də'lɪnieɪt/ *v.t.,* **-ated, -ating**. to trace the outline of; sketch or trace in outline; represent pictorially.

delinquent /də'lɪŋkwənt/ *adj.* **1.** guilty of a misdeed or offence. – *n.* **2.** someone who is delinquent, especially a young person. – **delinquency**, *n.*

delirious /də'lɪəriəs/ *adj.* **1.** affected with delirium. **2.** characteristic of delirium. **3.** wild with excitement, enthusiasm, etc.

delirium /də'lɪəriəm/ *n., pl.* **-liriums, -liria** /-'lɪəriə/. a temporary mental disorder marked by excitement, hallucinations, etc.

deliver /də'lɪvə/ *v.t.* **1.** to give up or surrender; give into another's possession or keeping. **2.** to strike (a blow). **3.** to assist (a female) in giving birth. **4.** to set free; liberate. – **deliverance**, *n.*

delivery /də'lɪvəri/ *n., pl.* **-ries**. **1.** the act of delivering. **2.** something delivered. **3.** *Commerce* a shipment of goods from the seller to the buyer.

delta /'dɛltə/ *n.* a nearly flat plain of alluvial deposit between diverging branches of the mouth of a river.

delude /də'lud, -'ljud/ *v.t.,* **-luded, -luding**. to mislead the mind or judgment of; deceive. – **delusion**, *n.*

deluge /'dɛljudʒ/ *n.* a flood.

deluxe /də'lʌks/ *adj.* of special elegance, sumptuousness, or fineness. Also, **de luxe**.

delve /dɛlv/ *v.i.,* **delved**, **delving**. to carry on intensive or thorough research for information, etc.

demagogue /'dɛməgɒg/ *n.* an unprincipled popular orator or agitator.

demand /də'mænd, -'mand/ *v.t.* **1.** to ask for with authority; claim as a right. – *n.* **2.** the act of demanding. **3.** an urgent or pressing requirement. **4.** the state of being in request for purchase or use. **5.** *Economics* **a.** the desire to purchase and possess, coupled with the power of purchasing. **b.** the quantity of any goods which buyers will take at a particular price. See **supply**. **6. on demand,** subject to payment upon presentation and demand.

demand bill *n.* a bill of exchange, note, etc., payable on demand or presentation.

demand economy *n.* an economy in which a seller's market prevails.

demand-pull inflation *n. Economics* a situation where prices are forced higher because a demand for a product greatly exceeds the manufacturer's ability to supply it. Cf. **cost-push inflation**.

demand-side economics *n.* management of the national economy which seeks to overcome recession by stimulating demand for goods and services.

demarcation /dima'keɪʃən/ *n.* **1.** the marking off of the boundaries of something. **2.** a division between things, especially the division between types of work carried out by members of different trade unions.

demean /də'min/ *v.t.* to lower in dignity or standing; debase.

demeanour = demeanor /də'minə/ *n.* conduct; behaviour; bearing.

demented /də'mɛntəd/ *adj.* out of one's mind; insane.

demerit /di'mɛrət/ *n.* **1.** censurable or punishable quality; fault. **2.** a mark against a person for misconduct or deficiency.

demesne /də'meɪn/ *n.* **1.** possession (of land) as one's own. **2.** an estate possessed, or in the actual possession or use of the owner. **3.** a district; region.

demi- a prefix meaning: **1.** half. **2.** inferior.

demise /də'maɪz/ *n., v.,* **-mised**, **-mising**. *-n.* **1.** death or decease. – *v.t.* **2.** *Law* to transfer (an estate, etc.) for a limited time. **3.** *Government* to transfer (sovereignty), as by the death or abdication of the sovereign.

demo- a word element meaning 'people', 'population', 'common people'.

democracy /də'mɒkrəsi/ *n., pl.* **-cies**. government by the people; a form of government in which the supreme power is vested in the people and exercised by them or by their elected agents under a free electoral system. – **democrat**, *n.* – **democratic**, *adj.*

demolish /də'mɒlɪʃ/ *v.t.* to throw or pull down (a building, etc.); reduce to ruins. – **demolition**, *n.*

demon /'dimən/ *n.* an evil spirit; a devil. – **demonic**, **demoniac**, *adj.*

demonetise = demonetize /di'mʌnətaɪz/ *v.t.,* **-tised**, **-tising**. to withdraw from use as money.

demonstrate /'dɛmənstreɪt/ *v.t.,* **-strated**, **-strating**. **1.** to make evident by arguments or reasoning; prove. **2.** to describe and explain with the help of specimens or by experiment. **3.** to manifest or exhibit. – **demonstrative**, *adj.*

demonstration /dɛmən'streɪʃən/ *n.* **1.** the act or result of demonstrating. **2.** a public exhibition of sympathy, opposition, etc., as a parade or mass meeting.

demoralise = demoralize /di'mɒrəlaɪz/ *v.t.,* **-lised**, **-lising**. to deprive of spirit, courage, etc.

demote /də'moʊt, di-/ *v.t.,* **-moted**, **-moting**. to reduce to a lower grade or class (opposed to *promote*). – **demotion**, *n.*

demur /də'mɜ/ *v.,* **-murred**, **-murring**, *n.* – *v.i.* **1.** to make objection; take exception; object. **2.** *Law* to interpose a demurrer. – *n.* **3.** an objection raised. – **demurral**, *n.*

demure /də'mjuə, -'mjʊə/ *adj.,* **-murer**, **-murest**. affectedly or unnaturally modest, decorous, or prim.

demurrage /də'mʌrɪdʒ/ *n. Commerce* **1.** the detention of a vessel, as in loading or unloading, beyond the time agreed upon. **2.** a charge for this.

demurrer /də'mɜrə/ *for def. 1,* /di'mʌrə/ *for def. 2 n.* **1.** someone who demurs; an objector. **2.** *Law* a pleading in effect that even if the facts are as alleged by the opposite party, they do not sustain the contention based on them.

den /dɛn/ *n.* **1.** a secluded place, as a cave, serving as the habitation of a wild beast. **2.** a cosy or secluded room for personal use.

denature /di'neɪtʃə/ *v.t.,* **-tured**, **-turing**. to alter the natural state of.

dendro- a word element meaning 'tree'. Also (*before vowels*), **dendr-**.

-dendron a word element meaning 'tree'.

denial /də'naɪəl/ *n.* **1.** a contradiction of a statement, etc. **2.** refusal.

denigrate /'dɛnəgreɪt/ *v.t.,* **-grated**, **-grating**. **1.** to sully; defame. **2.** to blacken.

denim /'dɛnəm/ *n.* a heavy twilled cotton for overalls, trousers, etc.

denizen /'dɛnəzən/ *n.* an inhabitant.

denomination /dənɒmə'neɪʃən/ *n.* **1.** a class or kind of persons or things distinguished by a specific name. **2.** a religious group.

denominator /də'nɒməneɪtə/ *n. Mathematics* that term of a fraction (usually under the line) which shows the number of equal parts into which the unit is divided. Cf. **numerator**.

denotation /dinoʊ'teɪʃən/ *n.* the meaning of a term when it identifies something by naming it (distinguished from *connotation*).

denote /də'noʊt/ *v.t.,* **-noted**, **-noting**. to be a mark or sign of; indicate.

denounce /də'naʊns/ *v.t.,* **-nounced**, **-nouncing**. to condemn openly; assail with censure.

dense /dɛns/ *adj.,* **denser**, **densest**. **1.** having the component parts closely compacted together; compact. **2.** thick-headed; obtuse; stupid. – **density**, *n.*

dent /dɛnt/ *n.* a hollow or depression in a surface, as from a blow.

dental /ˈdɛntl/ *adj.* **1.** of or relating to the teeth. **2.** of or relating to dentistry.

denti- a word element meaning 'tooth'. Also (*before vowels*), **dent-**.

dentistry /ˈdɛntəstri/ *n.* the science or art dealing with the prevention and treatment of oral disease. – **dentist**, *n.*

dentition /dɛnˈtɪʃən/ *n.* the arrangement of teeth.

denture /ˈdɛntʃə/ *n.* an artificial restoration of teeth.

denude /dəˈnjud/ *v.t.*, **-nuded**, **-nuding**. to make naked or bare; strip.

denunciation /dənʌnsiˈeɪʃən/ *n.* a denouncing.

deny /dəˈnaɪ/ *v.t.*, **-nied**, **-nying**. **1.** to assert the negative of; declare not to be true. **2.** to refuse to grant (a claim, request, etc.). **3.** to refuse to recognise or acknowledge; repudiate.

deodorant /diˈoʊdərənt/ *n.* an agent for destroying odours.

depart /dəˈpat/ *v.i.* **1.** to go away. **2.** to turn aside (fol. by *from*). – **departure**, *n.*

department /dəˈpatmənt/ *n.* a distinct part of anything arranged in divisions; a division of a complex whole or organised system.

depend /dəˈpɛnd/ *v.i.* **1.** to rely; trust. **2.** to be conditioned or contingent. – **dependable**, *adj.*

dependant /dəˈpɛndənt/ *n.* someone who depends on or looks to another for support, favour, etc.

dependent /dəˈpɛndənt/ *adj.* depending on something else. – **dependence**, *n.*

depict /dəˈpɪkt/ *v.t.* to represent by or as by painting; portray; delineate.

depilatory /dəˈpɪlətri/ *adj.*, *n.*, *pl.* **-ries**. – *adj.* **1.** capable of removing hair. – *n.* **2.** a depilatory agent.

deplete /dəˈplit/ *v.t.*, **-pleted**, **-pleting**. to deprive of that which fills; decrease the fullness of; reduce the stock or amount of.

deplorable /dəˈplɔrəbəl/ *adj.* **1.** causing grief; lamentable. **2.** causing censure; bad; wretched. – **deplore**, *v.*

deport /dəˈpɔt/ *v.t.* to expel (an undesirable alien) from a country; banish.

deportment /dəˈpɔtmənt/ *n.* manner of bearing; carriage.

depose /dəˈpoʊz/ *v.*, **-posed**, **-posing**. – *v.t.* **1.** to remove from office or position. – *v.i.* **2.** to bear witness. – **deposal**, *n.*

deposit /dəˈpɒzət/ *v.t.* **1.** to put or lay down. **2.** to place for safekeeping or in trust. – *n.* **3.** anything laid or thrown down, as matter precipitated from a fluid; sediment. **4.** an accumulation. **5.** money placed in a bank. **6.** anything given as security or in part payment.

depot /ˈdɛpoʊ/ *n.* a storehouse.

deprave /dəˈpreɪv/ *v.t.*, **-praved**, **-praving**. to make bad or worse; vitiate; corrupt. – **depravity**, *n.*

deprecate /ˈdɛprəkeɪt/ *v.t.*, **-cated**, **-cating**. to express earnest disapproval of. – **deprecatory**, *adj.*

depreciation /dəpriʃiˈeɪʃən, -prisi-/ *n.* **1.** a decrease in value due to wear and tear, decay, decline in price, etc. **2.** a decrease in the purchasing or exchange value of money. – **depreciate**, *v.*

depredate /ˈdɛprədeɪt/ *v.t.*, **-dated**, **-dating**. to prey upon; plunder.

depress /dəˈprɛs/ *v.t.* **1.** to lower in spirits. **2.** to press down. – **depression**, *n.*

depressed area *n.* a region where unemployment and a low standard of living prevail.

deprive /dəˈpraɪv/ *v.t.*, **-prived**, **-priving**. to divest of something; dispossess. – **deprivation**, *n.*

depth /dɛpθ/ *n.* **1.** measure or distance downwards, inwards, or backwards. **2.** intensity, as of silence, colour, etc. **3.** lowness of pitch. **4.** extent of intellectual penetration, sagacity, or profundity.

deputation /dɛpjuˈteɪʃən/ *n.* **1.** appointment to represent or act for another or others. **2.** the person(s) so appointed.

deputy /ˈdɛpjəti/ *n.*, *pl.* **-ties**. **1.** a person appointed or authorised to act for another or others. **2.** a person appointed or elected as assistant to a public official.

deranged /dəˈreɪndʒd/ *adj.* insane.

derelict /ˈdɛrəlɪkt/ *adj.* **1.** left or abandoned, as by the owner or guardian (said especially of a ship abandoned at sea). – *n.* **2.** a person forsaken or abandoned, especially by society.

dereliction /dɛrəˈlɪkʃən/ *n.* culpable neglect, as of duty; delinquency; fault.

deride /dəˈraɪd/ *v.t.*, **-rided**, **-riding**. to laugh at in contempt; scoff or jeer. – **derision**, *n.* – **derisive**, *adj.*

derivative /dəˈrɪvətɪv/ *adj.* **1.** imitative of others. **2.** derived. **3.** not original or primitive; secondary. – *n.* **4.** *Stock Exchange* a financial instrument or asset, the value of which is derived from a link to some other investment or asset, such as a future contract, option contract, etc.

derive /dəˈraɪv/ *v.*, **-rived**, **-riving**. – *v.t.* **1.** to receive or obtain from a source or origin (fol. by *from*). **2.** to trace, as from a source or origin. **3.** to obtain by reasoning; deduce. – *v.i.* **4.** to come from a source; originate. – **derivation**, *n.*

dermatitis /dɜməˈtaɪtəs/ *n.* inflammation of the skin.

dermatology /dɜməˈtɒlədʒi/ *n.* the science of the skin and its diseases.

derogatory /dəˈrɒgətri, -ətəri/ *adj.* disparaging.

descant /ˈdɛskænt/ *n.* *Music* a melody accompanying a simple theme and usually written above it.

descend /dəˈsɛnd/ *v.i.* **1.** to move or pass from a higher to a lower place; go or come down; fall; sink. **2.** to be derived by birth or extraction. **3.** to come down in a hostile manner, as an army. – **descent**, *n.* – **descendent**, *adj.*

descendant /dəˈsɛndənt/ *n.* one descended from an ancestor; offspring, near or remote.

describe /dəˈskraɪb/ *v.t.*, **-scribed**, **-scribing**. **1.** to set forth in written or spoken words; give an account of. **2.** *Geometry* to draw or trace, as an arc. – **description**, *n.* – **descriptive**, *adj.*

desecrate /ˈdɛsəkreɪt/ *v.t.*, **-crated**, **-crating**. to divest of sacred or hallowed character.

desert[1] /'dɛzət/ *n.* an area so deficient in moisture as to support only a sparse, widely spaced vegetation, or none at all.

desert[2] /də'zɜt/ *v.t.* **1.** to abandon. – *v.i.* **2.** (especially of a soldier or sailor) to forsake one's duty, etc. – **desertion**, *n.*

desert[3] /də'zɜt/ *n.* that which is deserved; a due reward or punishment.

deserve /də'zɜv/ *v.t.*, **-served**, **-serving**. to merit (reward, punishment, esteem, etc.) in return for actions, qualities, etc.

desiccate /'dɛsəkeɪt/ *v.t.*, **-cated**, **-cating**. to dry thoroughly; dry up.

design /də'zaɪn/ *v.t.* **1.** to prepare the preliminary sketch or the plans for (a work to be executed). **2.** to plan or fashion artistically or skilfully. **3.** to intend for a definite purpose. **4.** to form or conceive in the mind; contrive; plan. – *n.* **5.** an outline, sketch, or plan. **6.** the combination of details or features of a picture, building, etc.; the pattern or device of artistic work. **7.** the end in view; intention; purpose. – **designer**, *n.*

designate /'dɛzɪgneɪt/ *v.*, **-nated**, **-nating**, /'dɛzɪgnət, -neɪt/ *adj.* – *v.t.* **1.** to nominate or select for a duty, office, purpose, etc.; appoint; assign. – *adj.* **2.** appointed to an office but not yet in possession of it.

designer drug *n.* a synthetically-produced drug, designed to imitate an illegal drug (especially cocaine or heroin), the new substance being not specifically proscribed by law.

desirable /də'zaɪrəbəl/ *adj.* **1.** worthy to be desired; pleasing, excellent, or fine. **2.** advisable.

desire /də'zaɪə/ *v.*, **-sired**, **-siring**, *n.* – *v.t.* **1.** to wish or long for; crave; want. – *n.* **2.** a longing or craving. **3.** an expressed wish; request.

desirous /də'zaɪrəs/ *adj.* having or characterised by desire; desiring.

desist /də'zɪst/ *v.i.* to cease, as from some action or proceeding; stop.

desk /dɛsk/ *n.* a table specially adapted for convenience in writing or reading.

de-skilling /di-'skɪlɪŋ/ *n.* the process whereby an individual is left without appropriate skills and therefore made unemployable because of changes in work practices, such as the introduction of new technology. Also, **deskilling**.

desktop publishing *n.* the production of printed material by means of a computer system comprising a personal computer, software, and a laser printer.

desolate /'dɛsələt, 'dɛz-/ *adj.*, /'dɛsəleɪt, 'dɛz-/ *v.*, **-lated**, **-lating**. – *adj.* **1.** devastated. **2.** deserted. **3.** left alone; lonely. – *v.t.* **4.** to devastate. **5.** to depopulate. – **desolation**, *n.*

despair /də'spɛə/ *n.* hopelessness.

desperate /'dɛsprət, -pərət/ *adj.* **1.** reckless from despair. **2.** very serious or dangerous. – **desperation**, *n.*

despicable /də'spɪkəbəl/ *adj.* that is to be despised; contemptible.

despise /də'spaɪz/ *v.t.*, **-spised**, **-spising**. to look down upon, as in contempt.

despite /də'spaɪt/ *prep.* in spite of.

despondent /də'spɒndənt/ *adj.* depressed or dejected. – **despondency**, *n.*

despot /'dɛspɒt/ *n.* an absolute ruler; tyrant.

dessert /də'zɜt/ *n.* the final course of a meal including puddings, etc.

destabilise /di'steɪbəlaɪz/ *v.t.* **1.** to make unstable. **2.** *Politics* to deliberately create uncertainty about: *to destabilise the leadership.* – **destabilising**, *adj.* – **destabilisation**, *n.*

destination /dɛstə'neɪʃən/ *n.* the predetermined end of a journey or voyage.

destined /'dɛstənd/ *adj.* **1.** bound for a certain destination. **2.** predetermined.

destiny /'dɛstəni/ *n.*, *pl.* **-nies**. **1.** a predetermined course of events. **2.** the power or agency which determines the course of events.

destitute /'dɛstətjut, -tʃut/ *adj.* bereft of means or resources.

destroy /də'strɔɪ/ *v.t.* **1.** to ruin; spoil; demolish. **2.** to put an end to. – **destruction**, *n.* – **destructive**, *adj.*

desultory /'dɛsəltri, -təri, 'dɛz-/ *adj.* disconnected, unmethodical, or fitful.

detach /də'tætʃ/ *v.t.* to unfasten and separate; disengage; disunite.

detail /'diteɪl/ *n.* **1.** an individual or minute part; an item or particular. **2.** fine, intricate decoration.

detain /də'teɪn/ *v.t.* **1.** to keep from proceeding; keep waiting; delay. **2.** to keep under restraint or in custody. – **detention**, *n.*

detect /də'tɛkt/ *v.t.* to discover or notice a fact, a process, or an action. – **detection**, *n.*

detective /də'tɛktɪv/ *n.* a person, usually a member of the police force, who investigates crimes.

deter /də'tɜ/ *v.t.*, **-terred**, **-terring**. to discourage or restrain (one) from acting or proceeding, through fear, doubt, etc. – **deterrent**, *adj.*, *n.*

detergent /də'tɜdʒənt/ *n.* any cleaning agent, including soap.

deteriorate /də'tɪəriəreɪt/ *v.i.*, **-rated**, **-rating**. to become worse.

determinate /də'tɜmənət/ *adj.* fixed.

determination /dətɜmə'neɪʃən/ *n.* **1.** the act or result of determining. **2.** the quality of being determined or resolute.

determine /də'tɜmən/ *v.t.*, **-mined**, **-mining**. **1.** to settle or decide (a dispute, question, etc.) by an authoritative decision. **2.** to conclude or ascertain, as after reasoning, observation, etc. **3.** to fix or decide causally; condition.

determined /də'tɜmənd/ *adj.* resolute; unflinching; firm.

detest /də'tɛst/ *v.t.* to feel abhorrence of; hate; dislike intensely.

detonate /'dɛtəneɪt/ *v.t.*, **-nated**, **-nating**. to cause to explode. – **detonator**, *n.*

detour /'ditʊə, -tuə, -tɔ/ *n.* a roundabout or circuitous way or course, especially one used temporarily instead of the main route.

detract /də'trækt/ *v.i.* to take away a part, as from quality, value, or reputation.

detriment /'dɛtrəmənt/ *n.* loss, damage, or injury. – **detrimental**, *adj.*

detritus /də'traɪtəs/ *n.* any disintegrated

material; debris.

deuce /djus/ *n.* **1.** a card, or the side of a dice, having two pips. **2.** *Tennis, etc.* a juncture in a game at which the scores are level at forty all.

devaluate /di'væljueɪt/ *v.t.,* **-ated**, **-ating**. to devalue.

devalue /di'vælju/ *v.t.,* **-valued**, **-valuing**. **1.** to lower the legal value of (a currency); devaluate. **2.** to diminish the worth or value of.

devastate /'dɛvəsteɪt/ *v.t.,* **-stated**, **-stating**. to lay waste; ravage; render desolate.

devastavit /dɛvə'steɪvət/ *n.* any violation or neglect of duty by a personal representative which makes them personally responsible to persons having claims on the assets, as creditors and beneficiaries.

develop /də'vɛləp/ *v.t.* **1.** to bring out the capabilities or possibilities of; bring to a more advanced or effective state. **2.** to cause to grow or expand. **3.** to bring into being or activity; generate; evolve. **4.** to build on (land). **5.** to treat (a photographic plate, etc.) with chemical agents so as to bring out the latent image. – *v.i.* **6.** to grow into a more mature or advanced state; advance; expand. **7.** to come gradually into existence or operation; be evolved. – **development**, *n.*

deviant /'diviənt/ *adj.* **1.** deviating from an accepted norm, especially in sexual behaviour. – *n.* **2.** a person or thing that is deviant.

deviate /'divieɪt/ *v.i.,* **-ated**, **-ating**. **1.** to turn aside (from a way or course). **2.** to depart or swerve, as from a procedure, course of action, or acceptable standard.

deviation /divi'eɪʃən/ *n.* **1.** the act of deviating; divergence. **2.** *Statistics* the difference between one of a set of values and the mean of the set.

device /də'vaɪs/ *n.* **1.** an invention or contrivance. **2.** a plan or scheme for effecting a purpose. **3.** (*pl.*) will; desire; ingenuity; inclination. **4.** a figure or design used as an emblem, badge, trademark, etc.

devil /'dɛvəl/ *n.* **1.** *Theology* (*sometimes cap.*) the supreme spirit of evil; Satan. **2.** an atrociously wicked, cruel, or ill-tempered person.

devious /'diviəs/ *adj.* **1.** departing from the accepted way; roundabout. **2.** not straightforward; tricky; deceptive; deceitful.

devise /də'vaɪz/ *v.t.,* **-vised**, **-vising**. **1.** to order or arrange the plan of; think out; plan; contrive; invent. **2.** *Law* to assign or transmit (property, especially real property) by will.

devoid /də'vɔɪd/ *adj.* empty, not possessing, free from, void, or destitute (fol. by *of*).

devolve /də'vɒlv/ *v.,* **-volved**, **-volving**. – *v.t.* **1.** to transfer or delegate (a duty, responsibility, etc.) to or upon another; pass on. – *v.i.* **2.** to fall as a duty or responsibility on a person.

devote /də'voʊt/ *v.t.,* **-voted**, **-voting**. to give up or appropriate to or concentrate on a particular pursuit, occupation, purpose, cause, person, etc. – **devotion**, *n.* – **devotee**, *n.*

devour /də'vaʊə/ *v.t.* to swallow or eat up voraciously or ravenously.

devout /də'vaʊt/ *adj.* devoted to divine worship or service; pious; religious.

dew /dju/ *n.* moisture condensed from the atmosphere, especially at night, and deposited in the form of small drops upon any cool surface.

dexterity /dɛks'tɛrəti/ *n.* adroitness or skill in using the hands or the mind. – **dexterous**, *adj.*

di-[1] a prefix meaning 'twice', 'doubly', 'two'.

di-[2] variant of **dis-**[1], before *b, d, l, m, n, r, s,* and *v,* and sometimes *g* and *j,* as in *divide.*

diabetes /daɪə'bitiz/ *n.* a disease in which the ability of the body to use sugar is impaired. – **diabetic**, *n., adj.*

diabolic /daɪə'bɒlɪk/ *adj.* having the qualities of a devil; fiendish; outrageously wicked. Also, **diabolical**.

diagnosis /daɪəg'noʊsəs/ *n., pl.* **-noses** /-noʊsiz/. *Medicine* the process of determining by examination the nature and circumstances of a diseased condition. – **diagnose**, *v.* – **diagnostic**, *adj.*

diagonal /daɪ'ægənəl/ *adj. Mathematics* connecting, as a straight line, two non-adjacent angles, as between opposite corners of a square.

diagram /'daɪəgræm/ *n.* a drawing or plan that outlines and explains, the parts, operation, etc., of something.

dial /'daɪəl/ *n.* **1.** a face upon which time is indicated by hands, pointers, or shadows. **2.** a plate or disc with graduations or figures, as for measuring, or on a telephone, etc.

dialect /'daɪəlɛkt/ *n.* the language of a particular district or class. – **dialectal**, *adj.*

dialogue /'daɪəlɒg/ *n.* **1.** conversation between two or more persons. **2.** an exchange of ideas or opinions on a particular issue.

diameter /daɪ'æmətə/ *n. Geometry* a straight line passing through the centre of a circle or sphere and terminated at each end by the circumference or surface.

diametrical /daɪə'mɛtrɪkəl/ *adj.* **1.** relating to a diameter; along a diameter. **2.** direct; complete; absolute. Also, **diametric**.

diamond /'daɪəmənd, 'daɪmənd/ *n.* **1.** an extremely hard, pure or nearly pure form of carbon, which, when used as a precious stone, has great brilliancy. **2.** an equilateral quadrilateral, especially as placed with its diagonals vertical and horizontal.

diaphanous /daɪ'æfənəs/ *adj.* transparent; translucent.

diaphragm /'daɪəfræm/ *n.* **1.** *Anatomy* the partition separating the thoracic cavity from the abdominal cavity in mammals. **2.** a contraceptive membrane covering the cervix.

diarrhoea /daɪə'riə/ *n.* an intestinal disorder characterised by morbid frequency and fluidity of faecal evacuations.

diary /'daɪəri/ *n., pl.* **-ries**. a daily record, especially of the writer's own experiences or observations. – **diarist**, *n.* – **diarise = diarize**, *v.*

diatribe /'daɪətraɪb/ *n.* a bitter and violent denunciation, attack, or criticism.

dice /daɪs/ *n., pl. sing.* **die**, *v.,* **diced**, **dicing**. – *n.* **1.** small cubes of plastic, ivory, bone, or wood, marked on each side with a different number of spots (1 to 6), usually used in pairs in games of chance or in gambling. – *v.t.* **2.** to cut into small cubes.

dicey /'daɪsi/ *adj. Colloquial* dangerous; risky; tricky.

dichotomy /daɪ'kɒtəmi/ *n., pl.* **-mies**. division into two parts or into twos; subdivision into halves or pairs.

dick /dɪk/ *n. Colloquial* the penis.

dicky = dickey /'dɪki/ *n., pl.* **-kies**. a detachable shirt front, or blouse front.

dictaphone /'dɪktəfoʊn/ *n.* an instrument that records and reproduces dictation.

dictate /dɪk'teɪt/ *v.t.,* **-tated**, **-tating**. **1.** to say or read aloud (something) to be taken down in writing or recorded mechanically. **2.** to prescribe positively; command with authority. – **dictation**, *n.*

dictator /dɪk'teɪtə, 'dɪkteɪtə/ *n.* a person exercising absolute power. – **dictatorial**, *adj.*

diction /'dɪkʃən/ *n.* style of speaking or writing as dependent upon choice of words.

dictionary /'dɪkʃənri, 'dɪkʃənəri/ *n., pl.* **-ries**. a book containing a selection of the words of a language, usually arranged alphabetically, with explanations of their meanings, pronunciations, and other information concerning them.

did /dɪd/ *v.* past tense of **do**.

didactic /daɪ'dæktɪk, də-/ *adj.* **1.** intended for instruction; instructive. **2.** inclined to teach or lecture others too much.

diddle /'dɪdl/ *v.t.,* **-dled**, **-dling**. *Colloquial* to cheat; swindle; victimise. – **diddler**, *n.*

didgeridoo /ˌdɪdʒəri'du/ *n.* an Aboriginal wind instrument. Also, **didjeridu**.

didn't /'dɪdnt, 'dɪdn/ *v.* contraction of *did not*.

die[1] /daɪ/ *v.i.,* **died**, **dying**. **1.** to cease to live; undergo the complete and permanent cessation of all vital functions. **2.** to pass gradually; fade or subside gradually (usually fol. by *away*, *out*, or *down*).

die[2] /daɪ/ *n., pl.* **dies** *for def. 1* **dice** *for def. 2* – **1.** any of various devices for cutting or forming material in a press or a stamping or forging machine. **2.** singular of **dice**.

diehard /'daɪhad/ *n.* someone who resists vigorously to the last.

diesel engine /'dizəl/ *n.* a type of internal-combustion engine in which an oil is used as fuel.

diet /'daɪət/ *n., v.,* **-eted**, **-eting**. – *n.* **1.** a particular selection of food, especially as prescribed to improve the physical condition, regulate weight, or cure a disease. **2.** the usual or regular food or foods a person eats most frequently. – *v.i.* **3.** to select or limit the food one eats to improve one's physical condition or lose weight. – **dietitian**, *n.* – **dietary**, *adj.*

differ /'dɪfə/ *v.i.* **1.** to be unlike, dissimilar, or distinct in nature or qualities (often fol. by *from*). **2.** to disagree in opinion, belief, etc.; be at variance (often fol. by *with* or *from*).

difference /'dɪfrəns/ *n.* **1.** the state or relation of being different; dissimilarity. **2.** a significant change in or effect upon a situation. **3.** a disagreement in opinion; dispute; quarrel. **4.** *Mathematics* the amount by which one quantity is greater or less than another.

different /'dɪfrənt/ *adj.* **1.** differing in character; having unlike qualities; dissimilar. **2.** various; several. **3.** unusual; not ordinary; striking.

differential /dɪfə'rɛnʃəl/ *adj.* **1.** constituting a difference; distinctive. – *n.* **2.** *Machinery* a set of gears in a motor car which permit the driving wheels to revolve at different speeds when the car is turning.

differential rate *n.* a special lower rate, as one charged by one of two or more competing businesses.

differentiate /dɪfə'rɛnʃieɪt/ *v.,* **-ated**, **-ating**. – *v.t.* **1.** to mark off by differences; distinguish; alter; change. **2.** *Mathematics* to obtain the derivative of. – *v.i.* **3.** to make a distinction; discriminate.

difficult /'dɪfəkəlt/ *adj.* **1.** hard to do, perform, or accomplish; not easy; requiring much effort. **2.** hard to deal with or get on with. – **difficulty**, *n.*

diffident /'dɪfədənt/ *adj.* lacking confidence; timid. – **diffidence**, *n.*

diffraction /də'frækʃən/ *n.* the breaking up of light. – **diffract**, *v.*

diffuse /də'fjuz/ *v.,* **-fused**, **-fusing**, /də'fjus/ *adj.* – *v.t.* **1.** to spread or scatter widely or thinly; disseminate. – *adj.* **2.** widely spread or scattered; dispersed. – **diffusion**, *n.*

dig /dɪg/ *v.,* **dug**, **digging**, *n.* – *v.i.* **1.** to break up, turn over, or remove earth, etc. – *v.t.* **2.** to break up and turn over, or penetrate and loosen (the ground). **3.** to make (a hole, tunnel, etc.) by removing material. **4.** to obtain or remove by digging (often fol. by *up* or *out*). – *n.* **5.** thrust; poke. **6.** a cutting, sarcastic remark. **7.** an archaeological site undergoing excavation. **8.** (*pl.*) lodgings.

digest /də'dʒɛst, daɪ-/ *v.,* /'daɪdʒɛst/ *n.* – *v.t.* **1.** to prepare (food) in the alimentary canal for assimilation into the system. **2.** to assimilate mentally. – *n.* **3.** a collection or summary, especially of literary, historical, legal, or scientific matter, often classified or condensed. – **digestion**, *n.*

digger /'dɪgə/ *n.* **1.** a miner, especially a gold-miner. **2.** *Colloquial* an Australian soldier.

diggings /'dɪgɪŋz/ *pl. n.* a mining operation or locality.

digit /'dɪdʒət/ *n.* **1.** a finger or toe. **2.** any of the figures 0, 1, ... 9.

digital /'dɪdʒətl/ *adj.* **1.** of or relating to a digit. **2.** *Electronics* of or relating to information represented by patterns made up from qualities existing in two states only, on and off, as pulses (opposed to *analog*).

digital display *n.* a display in which information is represented in digital rather than analog form; readout.

digital-to-analog converter *n.* an electronic device for converting digital signals to analog signals.

dignitary /'dɪgnətri, -nətəri/ *n., pl.* **-ries**. someone who holds a high rank or office, especially in government or the church.

dignity /'dɪgnəti/ *n., pl.* **-ties**. **1.** nobility of manner or style; stateliness; gravity. **2.** nobleness or elevation of mind. – **dignify**, *v.*

digress /daɪ'grɛs/ *v.i.* to deviate or wander away from the main purpose. – **digression**, *n.*

dilapidated /də'læpədeɪtəd/ *adj.* reduced to, or fallen into, ruin or decay.

dilate /daɪ'leɪt, də-/ *v.*, **-lated**, **-lating**. – *v.t.* **1.** to make wider or larger; cause to expand. – *v.i.* **2.** to speak at length. – **dilation**, *n.*

dilatory /'dɪlətri, -təri/ *adj.* inclined to delay or procrastinate; slow; tardy.

dilemma /də'lɛmə, daɪ-/ *n.* a situation requiring a choice between equally undesirable alternatives.

diligent /'dɪlədʒənt/ *adj.* constant and persistent in an effort to accomplish something. – **diligence**, *n.*

dill[1] /dɪl/ *n.* a plant bearing a seedlike fruit used in medicine and for flavouring pickles, etc.

dill[2] /dɪl/ *n.* *Colloquial* a fool.

dillybag /'dɪlibæg/ *n.* a small bag.

dillydally /'dɪlidæli/ *v.i.*, **-dallied**, **-dallying**. to waste time, especially by indecision.

dilute /daɪ'lut, -'ljut/ *v.*, **-luted**, **-luting**, *adj.* – *v.t.* **1.** to make thinner or weaker by the addition of water or the like. **2.** to reduce the strength of. **3.** to increase the proportion (in a labour force) of unskilled to skilled. – *adj.* **4.** reduced in strength. – **dilution**, *n.*

dim /dɪm/ *adj.*, **dimmer**, **dimmest**, *v.*, **dimmed**, **dimming**. – *adj.* **1.** not bright or strong. – *v.t.*, *v.i.* **2.** to make or become dim.

dimension /də'mɛnʃən/ *n.* **1.** magnitude measured in a particular direction, or along a diameter or principal axis. **2.** an aspect; appearance.

diminish /də'mɪnɪʃ/ *v.t.* **1.** to make, or cause to seem, smaller; lessen; reduce. – *v.i.* **2.** to lessen; decrease. – **diminution**, *n.*

diminishing returns *pl. n.* the fact, often stated as a law or principle, that as any factor in production (as labour, capital, etc.) is increased, the output per unit factor will eventually decrease.

diminutive /də'mɪnjətɪv/ *adj.* small; little; tiny.

dimple /'dɪmpəl/ *n.* a small natural hollow, especially in the cheek.

din /dɪn/ *n.* a loud, confused noise.

dine /daɪn/ *v.i.*, **dined**, **dining**. to eat the principal meal of the day; have dinner.

ding /dɪŋ/ *v.i.* **1.** to sound, as a bell; ring, especially with wearisome continuance. – *n.* **2.** a blow or stroke. **3.** the sound of a bell or the like. **4.** *Colloquial* a minor accident involving a car, bike, surfboard, etc.

dinghy /'dɪŋgi/ *n.*, *pl.* **-ghies**. a small rowing or sailing boat.

dingo /'dɪŋgoʊ/ *n.*, *pl.* **-goes, gos**. the Australian wild dog, often tawny-yellow in colour, with erect ears, a bushy tail and distinctive gait, and with a call resembling a howl or yelp rather than a bark.

dingy /'dɪndʒi/ *adj.*, **-gier**, **-giest**. of a dark, dull, or dirty colour or aspect; lacking brightness or freshness; shabby.

dinkum /'dɪŋkəm/ *Colloquial* – *adj.* **1.** Also, **dinky-di**. true; honest; genuine. – *adv.* **2.** truly. See **fair dinkum**.

dinky-di /'dɪŋki-daɪ/ *adj.* → **dinkum**.

dinner /'dɪnə/ *n.* the main meal, taken either about noon or in the evening.

dinosaur /'daɪnəsɔ/ *n.* an extinct reptile of gigantic size.

dint /dɪnt/ *n.* force; power.

diocese /'daɪəsəs/ *n.*, *pl.* **dioceses** /'daɪəsəsəz, 'daɪəsiz/ the district, with its population, falling under the care of a bishop.

dioxin /daɪ'ɒksən/ *n.* any of a group of chemical compounds present as contaminants in certain herbicides, especially that found in 2, 4, 5-T.

dip /dɪp/ *v.*, **dipped**, **dipping**, *n.* – *v.t.* **1.** to plunge temporarily into a liquid, as to wet or to take up some of the liquid. **2.** to lower and raise. – *v.i.* **3.** to plunge into water or other liquid and emerge quickly. **4.** to sink or drop down, as if plunging into water. **5.** to incline or slope downwards. – *n.* **6.** the act of dipping; a plunge into water, etc. **7.** a liquid into which something is dipped. **8.** a lowering momentarily; a sinking down. **9.** a soft savoury mixture into which biscuits, etc., are dipped before being eaten. **10.** downward extension, inclination, or slope. **11.** a hollow or depression in the land.

diphtheria /dɪf'θɪəriə/ *n.* an infectious disease marked by the growth of a false membrane in the air passages.

diphthong /'dɪfθɒŋ/ *n.* a combination of two vowel sounds with only one syllabic peak, as *ei* in *vein*.

diploma /də'ploʊmə/ *n.*, *pl.* **-mas**. a document stating one's success in an examination, etc.

diplomacy /də'ploʊməsi/ *n.*, *pl.* **-cies**. **1.** the conduct by government officials of negotiations and other relations between states. **2.** skill in managing any negotiations; artful management. – **diplomat**, *n.* – **diplomatic**, *adj.*

dipsomaniac /dɪpsə'meɪniæk/ *n.* someone who suffers from an irresistible and insatiable craving for intoxicants.

dire /'daɪə/ *adj.*, **direr**, **direst**. causing or attended with great fear or suffering; dreadful; awful.

direct /də'rɛkt, daɪ-/ *v.t.* **1.** to guide. **2.** to give authoritative instructions to; command. **3.** to organise and supervise the artistic production of (a play or film). – *adj.* **4.** proceeding in a straight line or by the shortest course. **5.** without intervening agency; immediate; personal. **6.** going straight to the point; straightforward; downright. – *adv.* **7.** in a direct manner; directly; straight. – **director**, *n.*

direct current *n.* (in electronics) a relatively steady current in one direction in a circuit; a continuous stream of electrons through a conductor. Cf. **alternating current**.

direction /də'rɛkʃən, daɪ-/ *n.* **1.** the act of directing, pointing, aiming, etc. **2.** the line along which anything lies, faces, moves, etc., with reference to the point or region towards which it is directed. **3.** management; control.

directive /də'rɛktɪv, daɪ-/ *n.* an authoritative

instruction or direction.

directly /də'rɛktli, daɪ-/ *adv.* **1.** in a direct line, way, or manner; straight. **2.** without delay; immediately. **3.** presently.

direct marketing *n.* a marketing technique in which the producer sells directly to the customer by such means as door-to-door selling, home parties, etc. Also, **direct selling**.

direct memory access *n.* a data path to a computer memory in which the central processing unit does not intervene.

directory /də'rɛktəri, -tri/ *n., pl.* **-ries**. a book or the like containing names, addresses, telephone numbers, etc.

direct tax *n.* a compulsory monetary contribution such as income tax, demanded by a government for its support and levied directly on the persons who will bear the burden of it.

dirge /dɜdʒ/ *n.* a funeral song or tune.

dirigible /'dɪrɪdʒəbəl, də'rɪdʒəbəl/ *n.* an early airship.

dirt /dɜt/ *n.* **1.** earth or soil, especially when loose. **2.** any foul or filthy substance, as excrement, mud, etc. **3.** unsavoury or malicious gossip.

dirty /'dɜti/ *adj.,* **dirtier**, **dirtiest**, *v.,* **dirtied**, **dirtying**. – *adj.* **1.** soiled with dirt; foul; unclean. **2.** morally unclean; indecent. **3.** stormy; squally, as the weather. **4.** *Colloquial* angry. – *v.t., v.i.* **5.** to make or become dirty.

dis-[1] a prefix meaning 'apart', 'asunder', 'away', 'utterly', or having a privative, negative, or reversing force (see **de-** and **un-**[2]). Also, **di-**.

dis-[2] variant of **di-**[1].

disability /dɪsə'bɪləti/ *n., pl.* **-ties**. lack of competent power, strength, or physical or mental ability; incapacity.

disable /dɪs'eɪbəl/ *v.t.,* **-bled**, **-bling**. **1.** to make unable; weaken or destroy the capability of; cripple; incapacitate. **2.** to make legally incapable; disqualify.

disadvantage /dɪsəd'væntɪdʒ/ *n., v.,* **-taged**, **-taging**. – *n.* **1.** an unfavourable circumstance or condition. – *v.t.* **2.** to subject to disadvantage.

disagree /dɪsə'gri/ *v.i.,* **-greed**, **-greeing**. **1.** to fail to agree; differ (fol. by *with*). **2.** to differ in opinion; dissent.

disagreeable /dɪsə'griəbəl/ *adj.* unpleasant.

disallow /dɪsə'laʊ/ *v.t.* to refuse to admit the truth or validity of.

disappear /dɪsə'pɪə/ *v.i.* **1.** to cease to appear or be seen; vanish from sight. **2.** to cease to exist or be known; pass away; end gradually. – **disappearance**, *n.*

disappoint /dɪsə'pɔɪnt/ *v.t.* **1.** to fail to fulfil the expectations or wishes of (a person). **2.** to defeat the fulfilment of (hopes, plans, etc.); thwart; frustrate. – **disappointment**, *n.*

disapprove /dɪsə'pruv/ *v.i.,* **-proved**, **-proving**. to have an unfavourable opinion (fol. by *of*). – **disapproval**, *n.*

disarm /dɪs'am/ *v.t.* **1.** to deprive of means of attack or defence. **2.** to divest of hostility, suspicion, etc.; make friendly.

disarray /dɪsə'reɪ/ *n.* disorder; confusion.

disaster /də'zastə/ *n.* any unfortunate event, especially a sudden or great misfortune. – **disastrous**, *adj.*

disavow /dɪsə'vaʊ/ *v.t.* to disclaim knowledge of, connection with, or responsibility for; disown; repudiate.

disband /dɪs'bænd/ *v.t.* to break up or disorganise (a band or company).

disbelieve /dɪsbə'liv/ *v.,* **-lieved**, **-lieving**. – *v.t.* **1.** to reject as false. – *v.i.* **2.** to have no faith in (fol. by *in*). – **disbelief**, *n.*

disburse /dɪs'bɜs/ *v.t.,* **-bursed**, **-bursing**. to pay out (money); expend.

disc /dɪsk/ *n.* **1.** any thin, flat, circular plate or object. **2.** a round, flat area. **3.** *Computers* → **disk**. **4. a.** a gramophone record. **b.** → **compact disc**.

discard /dɪs'kad/ *v.,* /'dɪskad/ *n.* – *v.t.* **1.** to cast aside; reject; dismiss, especially from use. **2.** *Cards* to throw out (a card or cards) from one's hand. – *n.* **3.** someone who or that which is cast out or rejected.

discern /də'sɜn/ *v.t.* to perceive by the sight or some other sense or by the intellect; see, recognise, or apprehend clearly.

discernment /də'sɜnmənt/ *n.* faculty of discerning; discrimination.

discharge /dɪs'tʃadʒ/ *v.,* **-charged**, **-charging**, /'dɪstʃadʒ/ *n.* – *v.t.* **1.** to relieve of a charge or load. **2.** to fulfil or perform. **3.** to dismiss from service. – *n.* **4.** the act of discharging a ship, load, etc. **5.** a sending or coming forth; ejection; emission. **6.** a relieving or ridding, or a getting rid, of something of the nature of a charge.

disciple /də'saɪpəl/ *n.* an adherent of the doctrines of another; a follower.

discipline /'dɪsəplən/ *n., v.,* **-plined**, **-plining**. – *n.* **1.** training to act in accordance with rules; drill. **2.** punishment inflicted by way of correction and training. **3.** the training effect of experience, adversity, etc. **4.** a branch of instruction or learning. – *v.t.* **5.** to bring to a state of order and obedience by training and control.

disc jockey *n.* → **DJ**.

disclaim /dɪs'kleɪm/ *v.t.* to repudiate or deny interest in or connection with; disavow; disown.

disclose /dəs'kloʊz/ *v.t.,* **-closed**, **-closing**. **1.** to cause to appear; allow to be seen; make known; reveal. **2.** to uncover; lay open to view.

disco /'dɪskoʊ/ *n.* a place of public entertainment or a club in which patrons may dance, especially to recorded music.

discolour = discolor /dɪs'kʌlə/ *v.t.* to change the colour of; spoil the colour of; stain.

discomfiture /dɪs'kʌmfətʃə/ *n.* **1.** frustration of hopes or plans. **2.** confusion.

discomfort /dɪs'kʌmfət/ *n.* absence of comfort or pleasure; uneasiness; disturbance of peace; pain.

disconcert /dɪskən'sɜt/ *v.t.* to disturb the self-possession of; confuse; perturb.

disconsolate /dɪs'kɒnsələt/ *adj.* without consolation or solace; unhappy.

discord /'dɪskɔd/ *n.* lack of harmony. – **discordant**, *adj.*

discotheque /'dɪskətɛk/ *n.* → **disco**.

discount /'dɪskaʊnt/ *for defs 1-3*, /dɪs'kaʊnt/ *for def. 4 v.*, /'dɪskaʊnt/ *n.* – *v.t.* **1.** to deduct. **2.** to advance money with deduction of interest on (not immediately payable). **3.** to purchase or sell (a bill or note) before maturity at a reduction based on the interest for the time it still has to run. **4.** to leave out of account; disregard. – *n.* **5.** the act of discounting. **6.** amount deducted. **7. at a discount, a.** *Commerce* below par. **b.** not in demand.

discounted cash flow *n.* the current value of all the future cash to be generated by a development project.

discourage /dɪs'kʌrɪdʒ/ *v.t.*, **-raged**, **-raging**. **1.** to deprive of courage; dishearten. **2.** to dissuade (fol. by *from*).

discourse /'dɪskɔs/ *n.* communication of thought by words; talk; conversation.

discover /dəs'kʌvə/ *v.t.* to get knowledge of, learn of, or find out; gain sight or knowledge of (something previously unseen or unknown). – **discovery**, *n.*

discredit /dɪs'krɛdət/ *v.t.* to injure the credit or reputation of.

discreet /dəs'krit/ *adj.* wise or judicious in avoiding mistakes or faults; prudent; circumspect; cautious; not rash.

discrepancy /dɪs'krɛpənsi/ *n.*, *pl.* **-cies**. an instance of difference or inconsistency.

discrete /dɪs'krit/ *adj.* detached from others; separate; distinct.

discretion /dɪs'krɛʃən/ *n.* **1.** freedom of judgment or choice. **2.** the quality of being discreet. – **discretionary**, *adj.*

discretionary income *n.* income which is above that needed for subsistence and which may be spent at the earner's discretion.

discriminate /dəs'krɪmənеɪt/ *v.*, **-nated**, **-nating**. – *v.i.* **1.** to make a distinction, as in favour of or against a person or thing. **2.** to note or observe a difference; distinguish accurately. – *v.t.* **3.** to differentiate. – **discrimination**, *n.*

discursive /dɪs'kɜsɪv/ *adj.* passing irregularly from one subject to another; rambling.

discus /'dɪskəs/ *n.*, *pl.* **discuses**, **disci** /'dɪsaɪ/. a disc, usually made of wood rimmed with metal, thrown by athletes.

discuss /dəs'kʌs/ *v.t.* to examine by argument; sift the considerations for and against; debate; talk over. – **discussion**, *n.*

disdain /dɪs'deɪn/ *n.* a feeling of contempt for anything regarded as unworthy; haughty contempt; scorn.

disease /də'ziz/ *n.* a morbid condition of the body, or of some organ or part; illness; sickness; ailment.

diseconomy /dɪsə'kɒnəmi/ *n.* **1.** the lack of economy; a faulty economy. **2. diseconomies of scale,** a situation where a manufacturer finds that any increase in capital outlay in plant and machinery results in higher costs per unit of production.

disembark /dɪsəm'bak/ *v.i.* to go on shore; land.

disembowel /dɪsəm'baʊəl/ *v.t.*, **-elled**, **-elling**. to remove the bowels or entrails from.

disequilibrium /ˌdɪsikwə'lɪbriəm/ *n.*, *pl.* **-libria**. lack of absence of equilibrium or stability, especially in an economy.

disfavour = disfavor /dɪs'feɪvə/ *n.* lack of favour; state of being regarded unfavourably.

disfigure /dɪs'fɪgə/ *v.t.*, **-ured**, **-uring**. to mar the figure, appearance, or beauty of.

disgrace /dəs'greɪs/ *n.*, *v.*, **-graced**, **-gracing**. – *n.* **1.** the state of being in dishonour; ignominy; shame. **2.** the state of being out of favour. – *v.t.* **3.** to bring or reflect shame or reproach upon. – **disgraceful**, *adj.*

disgruntled /dɪs'grʌntld/ *adj.* mildly upset; discontented.

disguise /dəs'gaɪz/ *v.*, **-guised**, **-guising**, *n.* – *v.t.* **1.** to conceal the identity of. – *n.* **2.** that which disguises. **3.** the make-up, mask or costume of an entertainer.

disgust /dəs'gʌst/ *v.t.* **1.** to cause nausea or loathing in. – *n.* **2.** strong distaste; loathing.

dish /dɪʃ/ *n.* **1.** an open more or less shallow container of pottery, glass, metal, wood, etc., used for various purposes, especially for holding or serving food. **2.** a particular article or preparation of food.

dishevelled /dɪ'ʃɛvəld/ *adj.* untidy.

dishonest /dɪs'ɒnəst/ *adj.* not honest; disposed to lie, cheat, or steal. – **dishonesty**, *n.*

dishonour = dishonor /dɪs'ɒnə/ *n.* **1.** lack of honour; dishonourable character or conduct. **2.** disgrace; ignominy; shame. **3.** failure or refusal of the drawee or acceptor of a bill of exchange or cheque to accept it, or, if it is accepted, to pay it. – *v.t.* **4.** to deprive of honour; disgrace; bring reproach or shame on. – **dishonourable**, *adj.*

disillusion /dɪsə'luʒən/ *v.t.* to free from illusion.

disinfectant /dɪsən'fɛktənt/ *n.* any chemical agent that destroys bacteria. – **disinfect**, *v.*

disinflation /ˌdɪsɪn'fleɪʃən/ *n.* a reduction of prices generally with attendant increase in the purchasing power of money.

disinformation /dɪsɪnfə'meɪʃən/ *n.* misleading information supplied intentionally.

disinherit /ˌdɪsɪn'hɛrət/ *v.t.* to deprive of the right to inherit.

disintegrate /dɪs'ɪntəgreɪt/ *v.i.*, **-grated**, **-grating**. to fall apart; break up.

disinterested /dɪs'ɪntrəstəd/ *adj.* unbiased by personal involvement or advantage.

disjointed /dɪs'dʒɔɪntəd/ *adj.* disconnected; incoherent.

disk /dɪsk/ *n.* a memory unit for computers consisting of a rapidly spinning magnetic disc on which information is recorded by magnetising the surface. Also, **disc**. [var. of DISC]

disk drive *n.* *Computers* a device that enables data to be read from or recorded onto a disk, using an access mechanism.

diskette /dɪs'kɛt/ *n.* → **floppy disk**.

disk file *n.* (in computers) a set of circular disks with magnetic coating, which revolve at high speed and act as a memory unit providing large storage and fast access.

disk storage *n.* a method of high-speed bulk storage of computer programs and data, whereby they are stored on a rotating circular plate coated with a magnetic material, as iron oxide.

dislike /dɪs'laɪk/ *v.t.*, **-liked**, **-liking**. to regard with displeasure or aversion.

dislocate /'dɪsləkeɪt/ *v.t.*, **-cated**, **-cating**. **1.** to displace. **2.** to put out of joint.

dislodge /dɪs'lɒdʒ/ *v.t.*, **-lodged**, **-lodging**. to remove or drive from a place of rest or lodgment.

disloyal /dɪs'lɔɪəl/ *adj.* not loyal.

dismal /'dɪzməl/ *adj.* **1.** gloomy; dreary. **2.** terrible; dreadful.

dismantle /dɪs'mæntl/ *v.t.*, **-tled**, **-tling**. to pull down; take apart; take to pieces.

dismay /dɪs'meɪ/ *v.t.* **1.** to dishearten utterly; daunt. – *n.* **2.** consternation.

dismember /dɪs'mɛmbə/ *v.t.* **1.** to deprive of members or limbs; divide limb from limb. **2.** to separate into parts; divide and distribute the parts of (a kingdom, etc.).

dismiss /dɪs'mɪs/ *v.t.* **1.** to bid or allow (a person) to go; give permission to depart. **2.** to discharge or remove, as from office or service. **3.** to put off or away; lay aside, especially to put aside from consideration. **4.** *Law* to put out of court, as a complaint or appeal. – **dismissal**, *n.*

disobedient /dɪsə'bidiənt/ *adj.* neglecting or refusing to obey; refractory. – **disobedience**, *n.*

disobey /dɪsə'beɪ/ *v.t.* to neglect or refuse to obey (an order, person, etc.).

disorder /dɪs'ɔdə/ *n.* **1.** lack of order or regular arrangement; confusion. **2.** a derangement of physical or mental health or functions. – **disorderly**, *adj.*

disorganise = disorganize /dɪs'ɔgənaɪz/ *v.t.*, **-nised**, **-nising**. to destroy the organisation of.

disorientate /dɪs'ɒriənteɪt/ *v.t.*, **-tated**, **-tating**. **1.** to confuse as to direction. **2.** to perplex; to confuse. Also, **disorient**.

disown /dɪs'oʊn/ *v.t.* to deny the ownership of or responsibility for; renounce.

disparage /dəs'pærɪdʒ/ *v.t.*, **-raged**, **-raging**. to speak of or treat slightingly; belittle.

disparate /'dɪspərət/ *adj.* essentially different; dissimilar. – **disparity**, *n.*

dispassionate /dɪs'pæʃənət/ *adj.* free from or unaffected by passion; devoid of personal feeling or bias; impartial; calm.

dispatch /dəs'pætʃ/ *v.t.* **1.** to send off; put under way. – *n.* **2.** the sending off of a messenger, letter, etc., to a destination. **3.** prompt or speedy transaction, as of business. **4.** a written message sent in haste.

dispel /dɪs'pɛl/ *v.t.*, **-pelled**, **-pelling**. to drive off in various directions; scatter; disperse; dissipate.

dispensable /dɪs'pɛnsəbəl/ *adj.* that may be dispensed with or done without.

dispensary /dɪs'pɛnsəri, -sri/ *n.*, *pl.* **-ries**. a place where something is dispensed, especially medicines.

dispensation /ˌdɪspɛn'seɪʃən/ *n.* **1.** the act of dispensing. **2.** *Roman Catholic Church* the relaxation of a law in a specific case.

dispense /dɪs'pɛns/ *v.*, **-pensed**, **-pensing**. – *v.t.* **1.** to deal out; distribute. **2.** to administer (laws, etc.). – *v.i.* **3. dispense with, a.** to do without; forgo. **b.** to grant exemption from (a law, promise, etc.).

disperse /dəs'pɜs/ *v.t.*, **-persed**, **-persing**. to scatter.

displace /dɪs'pleɪs/ *v.t.*, **-placed**, **-placing**. to put out of the usual or proper place.

display /dɪs'pleɪ/ *v.t.* **1.** to show; exhibit; make visible. **2.** to reveal; betray. **3.** to show ostentatiously. – *n.* **4.** the act of displaying; exhibition; show. **5.** an electronic system capable of representing information visibly, as on a cathode ray tube.

displease /dɪs'pliz/ *v.t.*, **-pleased**, **-pleasing**. to annoy.

disposable income /də'spoʊzəbəl/ *n.* that part of a person's income which remains after the deduction of income tax, etc.

dispose /dəs'poʊz/ *v.*, **-posed**, **-posing**. – *v.t.* **1.** to put in a particular or the proper order or arrangement. **2.** to incline. – *v.i.* **3. dispose of,** to deal with definitely; get rid of.

disposition /dɪspə'zɪʃən/ *n.* mental or moral constitution; turn of mind.

dispossess /dɪspə'zɛs/ *v.t.* to put (a person) out of possession, especially of real property; oust.

dispute /dəs'pjut/ *v.*, **-puted**, **-puting**, *n.* – *v.i.* **1.** to engage in argument or discussion. – *v.t.* **2.** to argue or debate about; discuss. – *n.* **3.** argumentation; a debate or controversy; a quarrel.

disqualify /dɪs'kwɒləfaɪ/ *v.t.*, **-fied**, **-fying**. to deprive of qualification or fitness; render unfit or ineligible.

disquiet /dɪs'kwaɪət/ *v.t.* **1.** to disturb; make uneasy. – *n.* **2.** unrest; uneasiness.

disregard /dɪsrə'gad/ *v.t.* **1.** to pay no attention to; leave out of consideration. – *n.* **2.** lack of regard or attention; neglect.

disrepair /dɪsrə'pɛə/ *n.* the state of being out of repair; impaired condition.

disrepute /dɪsrə'pjut/ *n.* ill repute.

disrespect /dɪsrə'spɛkt/ *n.* lack of respect.

disrupt /dɪs'rʌpt/ *v.t.* to break or rend asunder. – **disruption**, *n.* – **disruptive**, *adj.*

dissect /də'sɛkt, daɪ-/ *v.t.* **1.** to cut apart (an animal body, plant, etc.) to examine it. **2.** to examine minutely part by part.

dissemble /də'sɛmbəl/ *v.*, **-bled**, **-bling**. – *v.t.* **1.** to conceal the real nature of. **2.** to feign. – *v.i.* **3.** to speak or act hypocritically.

disseminate /də'sɛməneɪt/ *v.t.*, **-nated**, **-nating**. to scatter, as seed in sowing.

dissent /də'sɛnt/ *v.i.* **1.** to disagree. – *n.* **2.** difference in sentiment or opinion. – **dissension**, *n.*

dissertation /dɪsə'teɪʃən/ *n.* a written essay, treatise, or thesis.

disservice /dɪs'sɜvəs/ *n.* harm; injury; an ill turn.

dissident /'dɪsədənt/ *n.* someone who differs; a dissenter, especially against a particular political system.

dissipate /'dɪsəpeɪt/ *v.t.*, **-pated**, **-pating**. **1.** to scatter in various directions; disperse; dispel; disintegrate. **2.** to scatter wastefully or extravagantly; squander.

dissociate /dɪ'soʊʃieɪt, -'soʊsieɪt/ *v.t.*, **-ated**, **-ating**. to sever the association of; separate. – **dissociation**, *n.*

dissolute /'dɪsəlut/ *adj.* licentious.

dissolution /dɪsə'luʃən/ *n.* **1.** the undoing or breaking up of a tie, bond, union, etc. **2.** *Government.* an order issued by the head of the state terminating a parliament and necessitating a new election. **3.** death or destruction. **4.** the legal termination of business activity, including the distribution of assets and the fixing of liabilities.

dissolve /də'zɒlv/ *v.*, **-solved**, **-solving**. – *v.t.* **1.** to make a solution of in a solvent. **2.** to break up (an assembly or organisation); dismiss; disperse. **3.** to bring to an end; destroy; dispel. **4.** *Law* to deprive of force; annul. – *v.i.* **5.** to become dissolved, as in a solvent. **6.** to break up or disperse. **7.** to disappear gradually; fade from sight or apprehension.

dissonance /'dɪsənəns/ *n.* **1.** discord. **2.** disagreement.

dissuade /dɪ'sweɪd/ *v.t.*, **-suaded**, **-suading**. to persuade not to do something.

distance /'dɪstns, 'dɪstəns/ *n.* **1.** the extent of space intervening between things or points. **2.** remoteness. **3.** reserve or aloofness.

distant /'dɪstənt/ *adj.* **1.** far off or apart in space; not near at hand; remote (fol. by *from*). **2.** far apart in any respect. **3.** reserved; not familiar or cordial.

distaste /dɪs'teɪst/ *n.* dislike.

distemper[1] /dɪs'tɛmpə/ *n.* an infectious disease of young dogs.

distemper[2] /dɪs'tɛmpə/ *n.* a water paint used for the decoration of interior walls and ceilings.

distend /dəs'tɛnd/ *v.i.* to swell.

distil = distill /dəs'tɪl/ *v.*, **-tilled**, **-tilling**. – *v.t.* **1.** to subject to a process of vaporisation and subsequent condensation, as for purification or concentration. – *v.i.* **2.** to fall in drops; trickle; exude. – **distillery**, *n.* – **distillation**, *n.*

distinct /dəs'tɪŋkt/ *adj.* **1.** distinguished as not being the same; not identical; separate (fol. by *from* or used absolutely). **2.** clear to the senses or intellect; plain; definite; unmistakable.

distinction /dəs'tɪŋkʃən/ *n.* **1.** a marking off or distinguishing as different. **2.** a discrimination made between things as different. **3.** a distinguishing characteristic. **4.** a mark of special favour. **5.** marked superiority; note; eminence. – **distinctive**, *adj.*

distinguish /dəs'tɪŋgwɪʃ/ *v.t.* **1.** to mark off as different (fol. by *from*). **2.** to recognise as distinct or different; discriminate. **3.** to perceive clearly by sight or other sense; discern; recognise. **4.** to serve to separate as different; be a distinctive characteristic of; characterise. **5.** to make prominent, conspicuous, or eminent. – *v.i.* **6.** to indicate or show a difference (fol. by *between*). **7.** to recognise or note differences; discriminate.

distort /dəs'tɔt/ *v.t.* **1.** to twist awry or out of shape; make crooked or deformed. **2.** to pervert; misrepresent. – **distortion**, *n.*

distract /dəs'trækt/ *v.t.* **1.** to draw away or divert, as the mind or attention. **2.** to entertain; amuse; divert. – **distraction**, *n.*

distraught /dəs'trɔt/ *adj.* **1.** distracted; bewildered; deeply agitated. **2.** crazed.

distress /dəs'trɛs/ *n.* great pain, anxiety, or sorrow; acute suffering; affliction; trouble.

distribute /dəs'trɪbjut/ *v.t.*, **-uted**, **-uting**. to divide and bestow in shares; deal out; allot. – **distribution**, *n.* – **distributor**, *n.*

district /'dɪstrɪkt/ *n.* a region or locality.

District Court /dɪstrɪkt 'kɔt/ *n.* **1.** (in NSW, Qld, and WA) an intermediate court. **2.** (in NZ) a court with jurisdiction over limited civil matters and less serious criminal offences, as well as summary and committal proceedings.

disturb /də'stɜb/ *v.t.* **1.** to interfere with; interrupt; hinder. **2.** to throw into commotion or disorder; agitate; disorder; disarrange; unsettle. **3.** to perplex; trouble. – **disturbance**, *n.*

disuse /dɪs'jus/ *n.* discontinuance of use.

ditch /dɪtʃ/ *n.* **1.** a long, narrow hollow made in the earth by digging, as one for draining or irrigating land; a trench. **2.** any open passage or trench, as a natural channel or waterway. – *v.t.* **3.** *Colloquial* to get rid of; get away from.

dither /'dɪðə/ *v.i.* to be vacillating; uncertain.

ditto /'dɪtoʊ/ *n.*, *pl.* **-tos**. the aforesaid; the same (used in accounts, lists, etc., to avoid repetition). *Symbol*: " *Abbrev.*: do.

ditty /'dɪti/ *n.*, *pl.* **-ties**. a simple song.

diurnal /daɪ'ɜnəl/ *adj.* **1.** daily. **2.** of or belonging to the daytime.

divan /də'væn/ *n.* a low bed.

dive /daɪv/ *v.*, **dived**, **diving**, *n.* – *v.i.* **1.** to plunge, especially head first, as into water. **2.** to dart. – *n.* **3.** the act of diving. **4.** *Colloquial* a disreputable place, as for drinking, gambling, etc., especially a cellar or basement.

diverge /daɪ'vɜdʒ/ *v.i.*, **-verged**, **-verging**. to move or lie in different directions from a common point; branch off. – **divergence**, *n.* – **divergent**, *adj.*

diverse /daɪ'vɜs, 'daɪvɜs/ *adj.* different; varied. – **diversity**, *n.*

diversify /daɪ'vɜsəfaɪ, də-/ *v.*, **-fied**, **-fying**. – *v.t.* **1.** to make diverse. **2.** to vary (investments). – *v.i.* **3.** to extend one's activities, especially in business, over more than one field. – **diversification**, *n.*

divert /də'vɜt, daɪ-/ *v.t.* **1.** to turn aside or from a path or course; deflect. **2.** to draw off to a different object, purpose, etc. **3.** to distract from serious occupation; entertain or amuse. – **diversion**, *n.*

divest /daɪ'vɛst/ *v.t.* **1.** to strip of clothing, etc. **2.** to strip or deprive of anything; dispossess.

divide /də'vaɪd/ *v.*, **-vided**, **-viding**. – *v.t.* **1.** to separate. **2.** to deal out in parts; apportion; share. **3.** *Mathematics* to separate into equal parts by the process of division. – *v.i.* **4.** to become divided or separated. **5.** to share something with others. – **divisible**, *adj.*

dividend /'dɪvədɛnd/ *n.* **1.** *Mathematics* a number to be divided by another number (the divisor). **2.** *Finance* **a.** a pro-rata share in an amount to be distributed. **b.** a sum of money paid to shareholders of a company or trading concern out of earnings. **c.** interest payable on public funds. **3.** a payment to creditors and shareholders in a liquidated company. **4.** a share of anything divided.

dividend cover *n.* the number of times that the declared dividend is covered by a company's net profit.

dividend rate *n. Stock Exchange* the dividend shown as a percentage of the par value.

dividend warrant *n.* an order issued by a company in favour of a shareholder for payment of the dividend due.

dividend yield *n. Stock Exchange* the dividend shown as a percentage of the last sale price.

divine /də'vaɪn/ *adj., v.,* **-vined**, **-vining**. – *adj.* **1.** of or relating to a god. – *v.t.* **2.** to discover (water, metal, etc.), by a divining rod. **3.** to prophesy.

divining rod /də'vaɪnɪŋ/ *n.* a rod used in divining, especially a forked stick, said to tremble or move when held over a spot where water, metal, etc., is underground.

divinity /də'vɪnəti/ *n., pl.* **-ties**. **1.** the quality of being divine; divine nature. **2.** the science of divine things; theology.

division /də'vɪʒən/ *n.* **1.** the act of dividing; partition. **2.** the state of being divided. **3.** *Mathematics* the operation inverse to multiplication; the finding of a quantity (the quotient) which, when multiplied by a given quantity (the divisor), gives another given quantity (the dividend). *Symbol: divide* **4.** one of the parts into which a thing is divided; a section.

divisive /də'vɪzɪv, -'vaɪsɪv/ *adj.* creating division or discord.

divisor /də'vaɪzə/ *n. Mathematics* a number by which another number (the dividend) is divided.

divorce /də'vɔs/ *n.* the dissolution of the marriage contract.

divulge /də'vʌldʒ, daɪ-/ *v.t.,* **-vulged**, **-vulging**. to disclose or reveal.

dizzy /'dɪzi/ *adj.,* **-zier**, **-ziest**. **1.** affected with a sensation of whirling, with tendency to fall; giddy. **2.** *Colloquial* foolish or stupid.

DJ /'didʒeɪ, di'dʒeɪ/ *n.* a person who plays and announces recorded music, as on a radio program, at a disco, etc. Also, **disc jockey**, **deejay**.

do /du/ *v., present sing. 1* **do**, *2* **do**, *3* **does**, *pl.* **do**, *past* **did**, *past participle* **done**, *present participle*. **doing**, *n.* – *v.t.* **1.** to perform (acts, duty, penance, a part, etc.). **2.** to be the cause of (good, harm, credit, etc.); bring about; effect. **3.** to render (homage, justice, etc.). **4.** to solve or find the answer to: *to do a maths problem.* **5.** to serve (a period of time) in a prison. **6.** to make; create; form. **7.** to study. **8.** *Colloquial* to serve; suffice for. **9.** *Colloquial* to cheat or swindle. **10.** *Colloquial* to use up; expend. – *v.i.* **11.** to act, especially effectively; be in action. **12.** to get along or fare (well or ill); manage (with; without, etc.). **13.** to serve or be satisfactory, as for the purpose; suffice; be enough. **14.** to deal; treat (fol. by *by*). – *v. (aux)* **15.** (used without special meaning in interrogative, negative, and inverted constructions). **16.** (used to lend emphasis to a principal verb). – *n.* **17.** *Colloquial* a festivity or treat. **18.** (*pl.*) rules; customs, etc.

dob /dɒb/ *v.t.,* **dobbed**, **dobbing**. *Colloquial* to betray, report (someone), as for a misdemeanour (fol. by *in*).

docile /'doʊsaɪl/ *adj.* easily managed or handled; tractable.

dock[1] /dɒk/ *n.* **1.** a wharf. **2.** the space or waterway between two piers or wharves, as for receiving a ship while in port. **3.** a semi-enclosed structure which a plane, truck, etc., can enter for the purpose of loading, repair, maintenance, etc.

dock[2] /dɒk/ *n.* **1.** the solid or fleshy part of an animal's tail. **2.** the part of a tail left after cutting or clipping. – *v.t.* **3.** to cut off the end of (a tail, etc.). **4.** to deduct a part from (wages, etc.).

dock[3] /dɒk/ *n.* an enclosed place in a courtroom where the accused is placed during trial.

docket /'dɒkət/ *n.* a receipt.

doctor /'dɒktə/ *n.* **1.** a person licensed to practise medicine. **2.** a person who has received the highest degree conferred by a faculty of a university. – **doctoral**, *adj.* – **doctorate**, *n.*

doctrine /'dɒktrən/ *n.* a body or system of teachings relating to a particular subject.

document /'dɒkjəmənt/ *n.,* /'dɒkju,mɛnt/ *v.* – *n.* **1.** a written or printed paper furnishing information or evidence; a legal or official paper. – *v.t.* **2.** to furnish with documents, evidence, or the like. – **documentation**, *n.*

documentary /dɒkju'mɛntəri, -tri/ *adj., n., pl.* **-ries**. – *adj.* **1.** relating to, consisting of, or derived from documents. – *n.* **2.** a factual television or radio program, film, etc.

documentary bill *n.* a bill of exchange to which are attached various documents, as a policy of insurance, invoice, etc.

dodder /'dɒdə/ *v.i.* to shake; tremble.

dodge /dɒdʒ/ *v.,* **dodged**, **dodging**. – *v.i.* **1.** to move aside or change position suddenly, as to avoid a blow or to get behind something. **2.** to use evasive methods; prevaricate. – *v.t.* **3.** to elude by a sudden shift of position or by strategy.

doe /doʊ/ *n.* the female of the deer, antelope, and certain other animals.

does /dʌz/, *weak form* /dəz/ – *v.* 3rd person singular present indicative of **do**.

doesn't /'dʌzənt/ *v.* contraction of *does not.*

doff /dɒf/ *v.t.* to remove (the hat) in salutation.

dog /dɒg/ *n., v.,* **dogged**, **dogging**. – *n.* **1.** a domesticated carnivore, bred in a great many varieties. **2.** any animal belonging to the same family, including the wolves, jackals, foxes, etc. – *v.t.* **3.** to follow or track constantly like a dog; hound; worry; plague.

dogbox /'dɒgbɒks/ *n.* a compartment in a passenger train or tram to which there is no access by corridor from other compartments within the carriage.

dog-ear /'dɒg-ɪə/ *n.* the corner of a page in a book folded over like a dog's ear, as by careless use or to mark a place.

dogma /'dɒgmə/ *n., pl.* **-mas**, **-mata** /-mətə/. **1.** a system of principles or tenets, as of a church. **2.** prescribed doctrine.

dogmatic /dɒg'mætɪk/ *adj.* **1.** of, relating to, or of the nature of a dogma or dogmas. **2.** asserting opinions in an authoritative, positive, or arrogant manner; positive; opinionated. Also, **dogmatical**.

doily /'dɔɪli/ *n., pl.* **-lies**. a small ornamental mat, as of embroidery or lace.

doldrums /'dɒldrəmz/ *pl. n.* **1.** the region of relatively calm winds near the equator. **2.** **in the doldrums,** a period of dullness, depression, etc.

dole /doʊl/ *n., v.,* **doled**, **doling**. *– n.* **1.** a payment by a government to an unemployed person. *– v.t.* **2.** to give out sparingly or in small quantities (fol. by *out*).

doleful /'doʊlfəl/ *adj.* full of grief; sorrowful; gloomy.

doll /dɒl/ *n.* **1.** a toy puppet representing a child or other human being. *– v.t.* **2.** to dress (oneself) up rather too smartly or too much (fol. by *up*).

dollar /'dɒlə/ *n.* **1.** the monetary unit of Australia, equal to 100 cents. *Symbol*: $ **2.** any of various units elsewhere, as in the US, Hong Kong, etc.

dollop /'dɒləp/ *n. Colloquial* a lump; a mass.

dolly /'dɒli/ *n., pl.* **-lies**. **1.** a child's name for a doll. **2.** a low truck with small wheels for moving loads too heavy to be carried by hand. **3.** any of a number of devices thought to resemble a doll or which derives from one.

dolorous /'dɒlərəs/ *adj.* expressing pain or sorrow.

dolphin /'dɒlfən/ *n.* any of various cetaceans, some of which are commonly called porpoises.

dolt /doʊlt/ *n.* a dull, stupid fellow.

-dom a noun suffix meaning: **1.** domain, as in *kingdom*. **2.** collection of persons, as in *officialdom*. **3.** rank or station, as in *earldom*. **4.** general condition, as in *freedom*.

domain /də'meɪn/ *n.* **1.** an estate; any land held in possession. **2.** a field of action, thought, etc. **3.** a region with specific characteristics, types of growth, animal life, etc.

dome /doʊm/ *n. Architecture* a large, hemispherical or spheroidal vault, its form produced by rotating an arch on its vertical radius.

domestic /də'mɛstɪk/ *adj.* **1.** of or relating to the home, the household, or household affairs. **2.** living with humans; tame. **3.** of or relating to one's own or a particular country as apart from other countries. – **domesticate**, *v.* – **domesticity**, *n.*

domicile /'dɒməsaɪl/ *n.* **1.** a place of residence; an abode; a house or home. **2.** *Commerce* a place at which a bill of exchange is made payable other than the acceptor's private or business address.

dominate /'dɒməneɪt/ *v.,* **-nated**, **-nating**. *– v.t.* **1.** to rule over; govern; control. **2.** to tower above; overshadow. *– v.i.* **3.** to rule; exercise control; predominate. – **dominant**, *adj.* – **domination**, *n.*

domineer /dɒmə'nɪə/ *v.i.* to govern arbitrarily; tyrannise.

dominion /də'mɪnjən/ *n.* **1.** the power or right of governing and controlling; sovereign authority. **2.** a territory, usually of considerable size, in which a single rulership holds sway.

domino /'dɒmənoʊ/ *n., pl.* **-noes**. **1.** (*pl. construed as sing.*) any of various games played with flat, oblong pieces, the face of which is divided into two parts, each left blank or marked with pips, usually from one to six. **2.** one of these pieces.

don /dɒn/ *v.t.,* **donned**, **donning**. to put on (clothing, etc.).

donate /doʊ'neɪt/ *v.t.,* **-nated**, **-nating**. to present as a gift to a fund or cause. – **donation**, *n.* – **donor**, *n.*

done /dʌn/ *v.* past participle of **do**.

donkey /'dɒŋki/ *n., pl.* **-keys**. a domesticated ass used as a beast of burden.

donkey vote *n.* (in a compulsory preferential system of voting) a vote in which the voter's preferences are marked in the order in which the candidates appear on the ballot paper.

don't /doʊnt/ *v.* contraction of *do not*.

doodle /'dudl/ *v.i.,* **-dled**, **-dling**. to scribble idly.

doom /dum/ *n.* **1.** fate or destiny, especially adverse fate. *– v.t.* **2.** to destine, especially to an adverse fate. **3.** to pronounce judgment against; condemn.

door /dɔ/ *n.* a movable barrier of wood or other material, commonly turning on hinges or sliding in a groove, for closing and opening a passage or opening into a building, room, cupboard, etc.

dope /doʊp/ *n., v.,* **doped**, **doping**. *– n.* **1.** any thick liquid or pasty preparation, as a sauce, lubricant, etc. **2.** *Colloquial* any drug, especially a narcotic. **3.** *Colloquial* information or data. **4.** *Colloquial* a stupid person. *– v.t.* **5.** *Colloquial* to affect with dope or drugs.

dormant /'dɔmənt/ *adj.* lying asleep or as if asleep; inactive as in sleep; torpid.

dormitory /'dɔmətri/ *n., pl.* **-tories**. a room for sleeping, usually large, for the inmates of a school or other institution.

dorsal /'dɔsəl/ *adj. Zoology* of, relating to, or situated on the back.

dosage /'doʊsɪdʒ/ *n.* **1.** the administration of medicine in doses. **2.** the amount of a medicine to be given.

dose /doʊs/ *n.* a quantity of medicine prescribed to be taken at one time.

doss /dɒs/ *v.i. Colloquial* to make a temporary sleeping place for oneself (often fol. by *down*).

dossier /'dɒsiə/ *n.* a bundle of documents on the same subject, especially information about a particular person.

dot /dɒt/ *n., v.,* **dotted**, **dotting**. *– n.* **1.** a minute or small spot on a surface; a speck. **2.** a small, roundish mark made with or as with a pen. **3.** anything relatively small or specklike. **4.** a full stop; a decimal point. *– v.t.* **5.** to mark with or as with a dot or dots.

dote /doʊt/ *v.i.,* **doted**, **doting**. **1.** to bestow excessive love or fondness (fol. by *on* or *upon*). **2.** to be weak-minded, especially from old age. – **dotage**, *n.*

dot-matrix printer /dɒt-'meɪtrɪks/ *n.* a

printer which composes each character out of a series of dots produced by a stylus which moves across the paper.

dotty /'dɒti/ *adj.*, **-tier**, **-tiest**. *Colloquial* crazy; eccentric.

double /'dʌbəl/ *adj.*, *n.*, *v.*, **-led**, **-ling**, *adv.* – *adj.* **1.** twice as great, heavy, strong, etc. **2.** twofold in form, size, amount, extent, etc. **3.** composed of two like parts or members; paired. **4.** twofold in character, meaning, or conduct; ambiguous. – *n.* **5.** a twofold size or amount; twice as much. **6.** a duplicate; a counterpart. **7.** *Film, etc.* a substitute actor who takes another's place, as in difficult or dangerous scenes. **8.** (*pl.*) a game in which there are two players on each side. – *v.t.* **9.** to make double or twice as great. **10.** to bend or fold with one part upon another (often fol. by *over*, *up*, *back*, etc.) **11.** to convey as a second person on a horse, bicycle or motorcycle. – *v.i.* **12.** to become double. **13.** to turn back on a course (often fol. by *back*). **14.** to share quarters, etc. (fol. by *up*). **15.** to serve in two capacities. – *adv.* **16.** twofold; doubly.

double bass *n.* the largest instrument of the violin family.

doublecross /dʌbəl'krɒs/ *v.t.* *Colloquial* to prove treacherous to; betray.

double dipping *n.* the practice whereby a retired person, especially a public servant, draws income from two types of public funds.

double dissolution *n.* *Australian Government* the simultaneous dissolving by the governor or governor-general of both houses of parliament prior to the calling of a general election, used as a means of solving the deadlock situation when the upper house consistently rejects legislation passed by the lower house.

double entry *n.* a bookkeeping method in which each transaction is entered twice in the ledger, once to the debit of one account, and once to the credit of another. Cf. **single entry**.

doubt /daʊt/ *v.t.* **1.** to be uncertain in opinion about; hold questionable. **2.** to distrust. – *v.i.* **3.** to feel uncertainty as to something; be undecided in opinion or belief. – *n.* **4.** undecidedness of opinion or belief; a feeling of uncertainty. **5.** distrust; suspicion.

doubtful /'daʊtfəl/ *adj.* **1.** admitting of or causing doubt; uncertain; ambiguous. **2.** undecided in opinion or belief; hesitating.

douche /duʃ/ *n.* a jet or current of water applied to a body part, organ, or cavity for medicinal, hygienic, or contraceptive purposes.

dough /doʊ/ *n.* **1.** flour or meal combined with water, milk, etc., in a mass for baking into bread, cake, etc. **2.** *Colloquial* money.

doughnut /'doʊnʌt/ *n.* a small ring-shaped cake.

doughty /'daʊti/ *adj.*, **-tier**, **-tiest**. strong; hardy; valiant.

dour /'daʊə, dʊə/ *adj.* hard; severe; stern.

douse /daʊs/ *v.t.*, **doused**, **dousing**. **1.** to plunge into water or the like; drench. **2.** *Colloquial* to put out or extinguish (a light).

dove /dʌv/ *n.* a bird of the pigeon family, as the native peaceful dove.

dowager /'daʊədʒə/ *n.* a woman who holds some title or property from her deceased husband, especially the widow of a king, duke, or the like.

dowdy /'daʊdi/ *adj.*, **-dier**, **-diest**. ill-dressed; not smart, or stylish.

dowel /'daʊəl/ *n.* *Carpentry* a pin, usually round, fitting into corresponding holes in two adjacent pieces to prevent slipping or to align the two pieces.

Dow-Jones index /daʊ-'dʒoʊnz/ *n.* an index of ordinary share prices on the US share market, based on the daily average price of selected lists of industrial, railroad and utility companies in the US.

down[1] /daʊn/ *adv.* **1.** from higher to lower; in descending direction or order; into or in a lower position or condition. **2.** on or to the ground. **3.** to a point of submission, inactivity, etc. **4.** to or in a position spoken of as lower, as the south, the country, a business district, etc. **5.** from a greater to a less bulk, degree of consistency, strength, etc. **6.** in due position or state. **7.** on paper or in a book. **8.** in cash; at once. **9. down to earth,** practical; realistic. – *prep.* **10.** to, towards, or at a lower place on or in. **11.** to, towards, near, or at a lower station, condition, or rank in. – *adj.* **12.** downwards; going or directed downwards. **13.** (especially of a computer) not operational. **14.** *Games* losing or behind an opponent by a specified number of points, holes, etc. **15.** depressed; unhappy. – *n.* **16.** a downward movement; a descent. **17.** *Colloquial* a grudge; a feeling of hostility. – *v.t.* **18.** to put or throw down; subdue. **19.** to drink down.

down[2] /daʊn/ *n.* **1.** the first feathering of young birds. **2.** a soft hairy growth.

down[3] /daʊn/ *n.* (*usu. pl.*) open, rolling, upland country with fairly smooth slopes.

downfall /'daʊnfɔl/ *n.* **1.** descent to a lower position or standing; overthrow; ruin. **2.** a fall, as of rain or snow.

download /daʊn'loʊd/ *v.t.* *Computers* to transfer (data or programs) from one computer to another, typically from a host computer to another computer.

down-market /'daʊn-makət/ *adj.* inferior in style or production. Cf. **up-market**.

down payment *n.* the initial deposit on a purchase made on an instalment plan or mortgage.

downpour /'daʊnpɔ/ *n.* a heavy, continuous fall of water, rain, etc.

downright /'daʊnraɪt/ *adj.* **1.** thorough; absolute; out-and-out. **2.** direct; straightforward.

downwind /daʊn'wɪnd/ *adv.* in the direction of the wind; with the wind.

dowry /'daʊəri, 'daʊri/ *n.*, *pl.* **-ries**. the money, goods, or estate which a woman brings to her husband at marriage.

doze /doʊz/ *v.i.*, **dozed**, **dozing**. to sleep lightly or fitfully.

dozen /'dʌzən/ *n.*, *pl.* **dozen**, **dozens**. a group of twelve units or things.

drab /dræb/ *adj.*, **drabber**, **drabbest**. **1.** having a dull grey colour. **2.** dull.

draft /draft/ *n.* **1.** a drawing, sketch, or design. **2.** a first or preliminary form of any writing, subject to revision and copying. **3.** conscription. **4.** a drain or demand made on anything. **5.** an animal or animals selected and separated from the herd or flock. – *v.t.* **6.** to draw the outlines or plan of, or sketch. **7.** to draw up in written form, as a first draft.

drag /dræg/ *v.*, **dragged**, **dragging**, *n.* – *v.t.* **1.** to draw with force, effort, or difficulty; pull heavily or slowly along; haul; trail. **2.** to introduce, as an irrelevant matter (fol. by *in*). **3.** to protract or pass tediously (often fol. by *out* or *on*). – *v.i.* **4.** to be drawn or hauled along. **5.** to trail on the ground. **6.** to proceed or pass with tedious slowness. – *n.* **7.** something used by or for dragging. **8.** the force due to the relative airflow exerted on an aeroplane or other body tending to reduce its forward motion. **9.** *Colloquial* somebody or something that is extremely boring. **10.** *Colloquial* a puff or a pull on a cigarette. **11.** *Colloquial* women's clothes, worn by men; transvestite costume.

draggle /drægəl/ *v.*, **-gled**, **-gling**. – *v.t.* **1.** to soil by dragging over damp ground or in the mud. – *v.i.* **2.** to hang trailing; become draggled. **3.** to follow slowly; straggle.

dragnet /'drægnɛt/ *n.* a net to be drawn along the bottom of a river, pond, etc., or along the ground, to catch something.

dragon /'drægən/ *n.* **1.** a mythical monster variously represented, generally as a huge winged reptile with crested head and terrible claws, and often spouting fire. **2.** a fierce, violent person. **3.** any of various lizards, as the frill-necked lizard of Australia.

dragonfly /'drægənflaɪ/ *n., pl.* **-flies**. a large, harmless insect which feeds on mosquitoes and other insects.

drain /dreɪn/ *v.t.* **1.** to draw off gradually, as a liquid; remove by degrees, as by filtration. **2.** to draw off or take away completely. – *n.* **3.** that by which anything is drained, as a pipe or conduit. **4.** gradual or continuous outflow, withdrawal, or expenditure.

drainage /'dreɪnɪdʒ/ *n.* **1.** the act or process of draining. **2.** a system of drains, artificial or natural.

drake /dreɪk/ *n.* a male duck.

dram /dræm/ *n.* **1.** a unit of measurement in the imperial system. **2.** a small quantity of anything.

DRAM /'di ræm/ *n.* → **dynamic random access memory**. Also, **Dram**.

drama /'dramə/ *n.* **1.** a composition in prose or verse presenting in dialogue or pantomime a story involving conflict or contrast of character, especially one intended to be acted on the stage; a play. **2.** any series of events having dramatic interest or results.

dramatic /drə'mætɪk/ *adj.* **1.** of or relating to the drama. **2.** characteristic of or appropriate to the drama; involving conflict or contrast.

drank /dræŋk/ *v.* past tense and former past participle of **drink**.

drape /dreɪp/ *v.t.*, **draped**, **draping**. to cover or hang with cloth or some fabric.

draper /'dreɪpə/ *n.* a dealer in textiles and cloth goods, etc. – **drapery**, *n.*

drastic /'dræstɪk/ *adj.* acting with force or violence; violent.

draught /draft/ *n.* **1.** a current of air, especially in a room, chimney, stove, or any enclosed space. **2.** an act of drawing or pulling, or that which is drawn; a pull; haul. **3.** the drawing of a liquid from its receptacle, as of ale from a cask. **4.** an amount drunk as a continuous act. **5.** (*pl. construed as sing.*) a game played by two people each with twelve pieces on a chequered board. – *adj.* **6.** being on draught; drawn as required. **7.** used or suited for drawing loads.

draughtsman /'draftsmən/ *n., pl.* **-men**. someone who draws sketches, plans, or designs.

draw /drɔ/ *v.*, **drew** /dru/, **drawn**, **drawing**, *n.* – *v.t.* **1.** to cause to come in a particular direction as by a pulling force; pull; drag; lead (often fol. by *along*, *away*, *in*, *out*, *off*, etc.). **2.** to bring towards oneself or itself, as by inherent force or influence; attract. **3.** to pick or choose at random. **4.** to sketch in lines or words; delineate; depict. **5.** to frame or formulate as a distinction. **6.** to pull out to full or greater length; stretch; make by attenuating, as wire. **7.** to wrinkle or shrink by contraction. **8.** to write or sign (an order, draft, or bill of exchange). – *v.i.* **9.** to exert a pulling, moving, or attracting force. **10.** to use or practise the art of tracing figures; practise drawing. **11.** *Games* to leave a contest undecided. – *n.* **12.** the act of drawing. **13.** that which is drawn, as a lot. **14.** *Sport* a drawn or undecided contest.

drawback /'drɔbæk/ *n.* **1.** a hindrance or disadvantage. **2.** *Commerce* an amount paid back from a charge made. **3.** *Government* refund of excise or import duty, as when imported goods are re-exported. See **rebate**.

drawbridge /'drɔbrɪdʒ/ *n.* a bridge of which the whole or a part may be drawn up or aside to prevent access or to leave a passage open for boats, etc.

drawee /drɔ'i/ *n.* one on whom an order, draft, or bill of exchange is drawn.

drawer /drɔ/ *for defs 1 and 2*, /'drɔə/ *for def. 3* – *n.* **1.** a sliding compartment, as in a piece of furniture, that may be drawn out in order to get access to it. **2.** (*pl.*) a garment for the lower part of the body, with a separate portion for each leg; underpants. **3.** *Finance* someone who draws an order, draft, or bill of exchange.

drawing-pin /'drɔɪŋ-pɪn/ *n.* a short broad-headed tack designed to be pushed in by the thumb. Also, **thumbtack**.

drawing room *n.* a room for the reception and entertainment of visitors; a living room.

drawl /drɔl/ *v.t., v.i.* **1.** to say or speak with slow, lingering utterance. – *n.* **2.** the act or utterance of someone who drawls.

drawn /drɔn/ *v.* **1.** past participle of **draw**. – *adj.* **2.** haggard; tired; tense.

dray /dreɪ/ *n.* a low, strong cart.

dread /drɛd/ *v.t.* **1.** to fear greatly. – *n.* **2.** terror or apprehension. **3.** deep awe.

– *adj.* **4.** greatly feared.

dreadful /ˈdrɛdfəl/ *adj.* **1.** causing great dread, fear, or terror; terrible. **2.** *Colloquial* extremely bad, unpleasant, ugly, etc.

dream /drim/ *n., v.,* **dreamed** *or* **dreamt**, **dreaming**. – *n.* **1.** a succession of images or ideas present in the mind during sleep. **2.** a vision voluntarily indulged in while awake; daydream. **3.** something or somebody of an unreal beauty or charm. **4.** a hope; an inspiration; an aim. – *v.i.* **5.** to have a dream or dreams. – *v.t.* **6.** to see or imagine in sleep or in a vision.

dreary /ˈdrɪəri/ *adj.,* **drearier**, **dreariest**. **1.** causing sadness or gloom. **2.** dull.

dredge[1] /drɛdʒ/ *n., v.,* **dredged**, **dredging**. – *n.* **1.** a contrivance for gathering material or objects from the bed of a river, etc. – *v.t.* **2.** to clear out with a dredge; remove sand, silt, mud, etc., from the bottom of. – *v.i.* **3.** to use a dredge. **4.** to find, usually with some difficulty (fol. by *up*).

dredge[2] /drɛdʒ/ *v.t.,* **dredged**, **dredging**. to sprinkle or coat with flour, etc.

dreg /drɛg/ *n.* a small remnant or quantity.

dregs /drɛgz/ *pl. n.* **1.** sediment of wine or other drink; lees; grounds. **2.** any waste or worthless residue. – *phr.* **3. the dregs (of society)**, a person or a class of people considered to be worthless, especially irretrievably immoral.

drench /drɛntʃ/ *v.t.* **1.** to wet thoroughly; steep; soak. **2.** *Veterinary Science* to administer medicine to (an animal), especially by force.

dress /drɛs/ *n., adj., v.,* **dressed** *or* **drest**, **dressing**. – *n.* **1.** the chief outer garment worn by women, consisting of a skirt and a bodice, made either separately or together. **2.** clothing; apparel; garb. – *adj.* **3.** of or for a dress or dresses. **4.** of or for a formal occasion. – *v.t.* **5.** to equip with clothing, ornaments, etc.; deck; attire. **6.** to arrange a display in; ornament or adorn. **7.** to prepare (fowl, game, skins, fabrics, timber, stone, ore, etc.) by special processes. **8.** to treat (wounds or sores). **9.** *Colloquial* to scold severely; upbraid and rebuke (fol. by *down*). – *v.i.* **10.** to clothe or attire oneself, especially in formal or evening clothes.

dress circle *n.* the first gallery above the floor in a theatre, etc.

dresser /ˈdrɛsə/ *n.* a kitchen sideboard.

dressing-gown /ˈdrɛsɪŋ-gaʊn/ *n.* a loose gown or robe generally worn over night attire.

dressing-table /ˈdrɛsɪŋ-teɪbəl/ *n.* a table or stand, usually surmounted by a mirror.

drew /dru/ *v.* past tense of **draw**.

dribble /ˈdrɪbəl/ *v.,* **-bled**, **-bling**. – *v.i.* **1.** to fall or flow in drops or small quantities; trickle. **2.** to drivel; slaver. **3.** *Soccer, Hockey, etc.* to advance a ball by a series of short kicks or pushes. – *v.t.* **4.** to let fall in drops.

dried /draɪd/ *v.* past tense and past participle of **dry**.

drift /drɪft/ *n.* **1.** a driving movement or force; impulse; impetus; pressure. **2.** *Navigation* movement or course under the impulse of water currents, wind, etc. **3.** *Physical Geography* a broad and shallow current. **4.** the course of anything; tendency; aim. **5.** something driven, or formed by driving. – *v.i.* **6.** to be carried along by currents of water or air, or by the force of circumstances. **7.** to wander aimlessly.

driftwood /ˈdrɪftwʊd/ *n.* wood floating on, or cast ashore by, the water.

drill[1] /drɪl/ *n.* **1.** a tool or machine for making cylindrical holes, especially by rotation. **2.** *Military* training in formal marching or other precise military or naval movements. **3.** any strict, methodical training, instrument, or exercise. – *v.t.* **4.** to pierce or bore a hole in (anything). **5.** to impart (knowledge) by strict training or discipline.

drill[2] /drɪl/ *n.* strong twilled cotton.

drink /drɪŋk/ *v.,* **drank**, **drunk**, **drinking**, *n.* – *v.i.* **1.** to swallow water or other liquid; imbibe. **2.** to imbibe alcoholic beverages, especially habitually or to excess; tipple. -*v.t.* **3.** to take in (a liquid) in any manner; absorb. **4.** to take in through the senses, especially with eagerness and pleasure. – *n.* **5.** any liquid which is swallowed to quench thirst, for nourishment, etc.; a beverage.

drip /drɪp/ *v.,* **dripped** *or* **dript**, **dripping**, *n.* – *v.i.* **1.** to fall in drops, as a liquid. – *n.* **2.** the liquid that drips. **3.** *Medicine* the continuous slow infusion of fluid containing nutrients or drugs to a patient, especially after surgery. **4.** *Colloquial* an insipid or colourless person; a fool.

dripping /ˈdrɪpɪŋ/ *n.* fat exuded from meat in cooking.

drive /draɪv/ *v.,* **drove**, **driven**, **driving**, *n.* – *v.t.* **1.** to send along, away, off, in, out, back, etc., by compulsion; force along. **2.** to overwork. **3.** to cause and guide the movement of (an animal, vehicle, etc.). **4.** to convey in a vehicle. – *v.i.* **5.** to go along before an impelling force; be impelled. **6.** to rush or dash violently. **7.** to make an effort to reach or obtain; aim (fol. by *at*). **8.** to go or travel in a driven vehicle. – *n.* **9.** the act of driving. **10.** an impelling along, as of game, cattle, or floating logs, in a particular direction. **11.** *Psychology* a source of motivation. **12.** a vigorous onset or onward course. **13.** a united effort to accomplish some purpose, especially to raise money for a government loan or for some charity. **14.** energy and initiative. **15.** a trip in a driven vehicle. **16.** *Computers* a controlling mechanism for moving magnetic tapes, floppy disks, etc., thus enabling data to be accessed.

drive-in /ˈdraɪv-ɪn/ *n.* **1.** a cinema so designed that patrons drive in to a large area in front of an outdoor screen and view the film while seated in their cars. – *adj.* **2.** (of any shop, food outlet, etc.) catering for customers in cars.

drivel /ˈdrɪvəl/ *v.,* **-elled**, **-elling**, *n.* – *v.i.* **1.** to let saliva flow from the mouth or mucus from the nose; slaver. – *n.* **2.** childish, idiotic, or silly talk.

drizzle /ˈdrɪzəl/ *v.,* **-zled**, **-zling**, *n.* – *v.i.* **1.** to rain gently and steadily in fine drops. -*n.* **2.** a very light rain; mist.

droit /drɔɪt/ *n.* **1.** a legal right or claim. **2.** *Finance* duty; custom.

droll /droʊl/ *adj.* amusingly queer.

-drome 1. a word element meaning 'running', 'course', 'racecourse'. **2.** a word element referring to a large structure or area for a specific use, as in *aerodrome.*

drone[1] /droʊn/ *n.* the male of the honey bee and other bees, stingless and making no honey.

drone[2] /droʊn/ *v.i.,* **droned**, **droning**. **1.** to make a dull, continued, monotonous sound; hum; buzz. **2.** to speak in a monotonous tone.

drool /drul/ *v.i. Colloquial* → **drivel** (def. 1).

droop /drup/ *v.i.* to sink, bend, or hang down, as from weakness or exhaustion.

drop /drɒp/ *n., v.,* **dropped**, **dropping**. – *n.* **1.** a small quantity of liquid which falls or is produced in a more or less spherical mass; a liquid globule. **2.** a minute quantity of anything. **3.** something like or likened to a drip. **4.** the distance or depth to which anything drips or falls. **5.** a steep slope. **6.** a fall in degree, amount, value, etc. – *v.i.* **7.** to fall in globules or small portions, as water or other liquid. **8.** to fall vertically like a drop; have an abrupt descent. **9.** to withdraw; disappear (fol. by *out*). **10.** to fall lower in condition, degree, etc.; sink. **11.** to fall or move (back, behind, to the rear, etc.). **12.** to come or go casually or unexpectedly into a place; to visit informally (fol. by *in*, *by*, *across*, etc.). – *v.t.* **13.** to let fall in drops or small portions. **14.** to let fall; allow to sink to a lower position; lower. **15.** to utter or express casually or incidentally, as a hint. **16.** to send or post (a note, etc.). **17.** to set down, as from a ship, car, etc. (fol. by *off*). **18.** to omit (a letter or syllable) in pronunciation or writing. **19.** to cease to keep up or have to do with.

drop-out /ˈdrɒp-aʊt/ *n.* someone who decides to opt out of conventional society, a given social group or an educational institution.

droppings /ˈdrɒpɪŋz/ *pl. n.* animal dung.

drop shipment *n.* an order shipped by a seller to the customer or a distributor, as a shipment by a manufacturer to a retailer that is invoiced to a wholesaler.

drought /draʊt/ *n.* **1.** dry weather; lack of rain. **2.** scarcity.

drove[1] /droʊv/ *v.* past tense of **drive**.

drove[2] /droʊv/ *n., v.,* **droved**, **droving**. – *n.* **1.** a number of oxen, sheep, or swine driven in a group; herd; flock. **2.** a large crowd of human beings, especially in motion. – *v.t.* **3.** to drive herds of cattle or flocks of sheep, usually over long distances, to market. – **drover**, *n.* – **droving**, *n.*

drown /draʊn/ *v.i.* **1.** to be suffocated by immersion in water or other liquid. – *v.t.* **2.** to suffocate (a person, etc.) by immersion in water or other liquid. **3.** to make inaudible; muffle; obscure.

drowse /draʊz/ *v.i.,* **drowsed**, **drowsing**. to be sleepy; be half asleep. – **drowsy**, *adj.*

drudge /drʌdʒ/ *n.* someone who labours at servile or uninteresting tasks; a hard toiler. – **drudgery**, *n.*

drug /drʌg/ *n., v.,* **drugged**, **drugging**. – *n.* **1.** a chemical substance given with the intention of preventing or curing disease or otherwise enhancing the physical or mental welfare of humans or animals. **2.** a habit-forming medicinal substance; a narcotic. – *v.t.* **3.** to stupefy or poison with a drug.

drum /drʌm/ *n., v.,* **drummed**, **drumming**. – *n.* **1.** a musical instrument consisting of a hollow body covered at one or both ends with a tightly stretched membrane, or head, which is struck with the hand, a stick, or a pair of sticks. **2.** a natural organ by which an animal produces a loud or bass sound. **3.** something resembling a drum in shape or structure, or in the noise it produces. **4.** *Computers* a magnetically coated drum revolving at high speed, and similar in function to a disk file. – *v.i.* **5.** to beat or play a drum. **6.** to beat on anything rhythmically. – *v.t.* **7.** to beat rhythmically; perform (a tune) by drumming. **8.** to drive or force by persistent repetition. **9.** to solicit or obtain (trade, customers, etc.) (often fol. by *up*).

drunk /drʌŋk/ *v.* **1.** past participle of **drink**. – *adj.* **2.** (*used predicatively*) intoxicated with, or as with, strong drink. – *n. Colloquial* **3.** a drunken person. – **drunkard**, *n.*

drupe /drup/ *n.* a fruit, as the peach, cherry, plum, etc., with soft, pulpy flesh and a single stone. – **drupaceous**, *adj.*

dry /draɪ/ *adj.,* **drier**, **driest**, *v.,* **dried**, **drying**, *n., pl.* **dries**. – *adj.* **1.** free from moisture; not moist; not wet. **2.** having little or no rain. **3.** not under, in, or on water. **4.** not yielding water or other liquid. **5.** desiring drink; thirsty. **6.** dull; uninteresting. **7.** humorous or sarcastic in an unemotional or impersonal way. **8.** (of wines) not sweet. – *v.t.* **9.** to make dry; to free from moisture. – *v.i.* **10.** to become dry; lose moisture. – *n.* **11.** a dry state, condition, or place. **12.** *Colloquial* dry ginger ale: *brandy and dry.*

dry-clean /draɪ-ˈklin/ *v.t.* to clean (garments, etc.) with chemical solvents, etc., rather than water.

dry dock *n.* a basin-like structure from which the water can be removed after the entrance of a ship, used when making repairs on a ship's bottom, etc.

dry ice *n.* solid carbon dioxide.

dry measure *n.* the system of units of capacity formerly used in Britain, Australia and the US for measuring dry commodities, as grain, fruit, etc.

dual /ˈdjuəl/ *adj.* **1.** of or relating to two. **2.** composed or consisting of two parts; double.

dub[1] /dʌb/ *v.t.,* **dubbed**, **dubbing**. **1.** to strike lightly with a sword in the ceremony of conferring knighthood; make, or designate as, a knight. **2.** to invest with any title; name; call.

dub[2] /dʌb/ *v.t.,* **dubbed**, **dubbing**. to change the soundtrack (of a film or videotape), as in substituting a dialogue in another language.

dubious /ˈdjubiəs/ *adj.* **1.** doubtful; marked by or occasioning doubt. **2.** wavering or hesitating in opinion; inclined to doubt.

duchess /ˈdʌtʃɛs, ˈdʌtʃəs/ *n.* the wife or widow of a duke.

duck[1] /dʌk/ *n.* any of numerous wild or domesticated web-footed swimming birds.

duck[2] /dʌk/ *v.i.* **1.** to plunge the whole body or the head momentarily under water. **2.** to avoid a blow, unpleasant task, etc.

duck[3] /dʌk/ *n. Cricket* an individual score of nought made when batting.

duckbill /ˈdʌkbɪl/ *n.* → **platypus**.

duckling /ˈdʌklɪŋ/ *n.* a young duck.

duct /dʌkt/ *n.* **1.** any tube, canal, or conduit by which fluid or other substances are conducted or conveyed. – *v.t.* **2.** to convey by means of a duct or ducts.

ductile /ˈdʌktaɪl/ *adj.* **1.** capable of being hammered out thin, as certain metals; malleable. **2.** capable of being moulded or shaped; plastic.

dud /dʌd/ *Colloquial* – *n.* **1.** any thing or person that proves a failure. – *adj.* **2.** useless; defective.

dudgeon /ˈdʌdʒən/ *n.* a feeling of offence or resentment; anger.

due /dju/ *adj.* **1.** immediately payable. **2.** owing, irrespective of whether the time of payment has arrived. **3.** rightful; proper; fitting. **4.** attributable, as to a cause. **5.** under engagement as to time; expected to be ready, be present, or arrive. – *n.* **6.** (*usu. pl.*) a payment due, as a charge, a fee, a membership subscription, etc.

duel /ˈdjuəl/ *n.* a prearranged combat between two persons, fought with deadly weapons according to an accepted code of procedure, especially to settle a private quarrel.

duet /djuˈɛt/ *n.* a musical composition for two voices or performers.

duffer /ˈdʌfə/ *n.* a plodding, stupid, or incompetent person.

dug /dʌg/ *v.* past tense and past participle of **dig**.

duke /djuk/ *n.* **1.** a sovereign prince, the ruler of a small state. **2.** (in Britain) a nobleman of the highest rank after that of a prince.

dulcet /ˈdʌlsət/ *adj.* agreeable to the feelings, the eye, or, especially, the ear; soothing.

dull /dʌl/ *adj.* **1.** slow of understanding; obtuse; stupid. **2.** not intense or acute. **3.** listless; spiritless. **4.** tedious; uninteresting. **5.** not bright, intense, or clear; dim. – *v.t., v.i.* **6.** to make or become dull.

duly /ˈdjuli/ *adv.* **1.** in a due manner; properly. **2.** in due season; punctually. **3.** adequately.

dumb /dʌm/ *adj.* **1.** without the power of speech. **2.** made, done, etc., without speech. **3.** stupid; dull-witted.

dumbfound /ˈdʌmfaʊnd/ *v.t.* to strike dumb with amazement.

dummy /ˈdʌmi/ *n., pl.* **-mies**, *adj.* – *n.* **1.** an imitation or copy of something, as for display, to indicate appearance, exhibit clothing, etc. **2.** *Colloquial* a stupid person; dolt. **3.** (at an auction, etc.) someone ostensibly acting on their own behalf while actually acting as an agent for others. **4.** *Cards* **a.** (in bridge) the dealer's partner whose hand is exposed and played by the dealer. **b.** the cards so exposed. **5.** a rubber teat, etc., given to a baby to suck. – *adj.* **6.** counterfeit; sham; imitation.

dump /dʌmp/ *v.t.* **1.** to throw down in a mass; fling down or drop heavily. **2.** to get rid of; hand over to somebody else. **3.** *Computers* to print out, with minimal editing, the content of computer memory, usually for diagnostic purposes in debugging. **4.** *Commerce* **a.** to put (goods) on the market in large quantities and at a low price, especially to a large or favoured buyer. **b.** to market (goods) thus in a foreign country, as at a price below that charged in the home country. – *n.* **5.** a place where rubbish is deposited. **6.** *Military* a collection of ammunition, stores, etc., to be distributed for use. **7.** *Colloquial* a place, house, or town that is poorly kept up, and generally of wretched appearance.

dumping cash security *n.* a cash deposit required to be placed with customs by an Australian importer when it is considered likely that the goods are being dumped in Australia.

dumpling /ˈdʌmplɪŋ/ *n.* a rounded mass of steamed dough.

dumps /dʌmps/ *pl. n. Colloquial* a dull, gloomy state of mind.

dumpy /ˈdʌmpi/ *adj.,* **dumpier**, **dumpiest**. short and stout; squat.

dun[1] /dʌn/ *v.t.,* **dunned**, **dunning**. to make repeated and insistent demands upon, especially for the payment of a debt.

dun[2] /dʌn/ *adj.* **1.** dull or greyish brown. **2.** dark; gloomy.

dunce /dʌns/ *n.* a dull-witted or stupid person.

dune /djun/ *n.* a sand hill or sand ridge formed by the wind, usually in desert regions or near lakes and oceans.

dung /dʌŋ/ *n.* manure; excrement, especially of animals.

dungeon /ˈdʌndʒən/ *n.* any strong, close cell, especially underground.

dunk /dʌŋk/ *v.t.* **1.** to immerse in water. **2.** to dip (biscuits, etc.) into coffee, milk, etc.

dunnart /ˈdʌnat/ *n.* any of various narrow-footed marsupial mice.

dunny /ˈdʌni/ *n. Colloquial* a toilet.

duo /ˈdjuoʊ/ *n., pl.* **duos**, **dui** /ˈdjui/. a pair of singers, entertainers, etc.

duo- a word element meaning 'two'.

duodenum /djuəˈdinəm/ *n.* the first portion of the small intestine. – **duodenal**, *adj.*

duopoly /djuˈɒpəli/ *n.* a market situation where two competing sellers hold control over a product or service.

duopsony /djuˈɒpsəni/ *n.* a market situation where two rival buyers control the demand for a product or service.

dupe /djup/ *n.* a person who is imposed upon or deceived.

duple /ˈdjupəl/ *adj.* double.

duplex /ˈdjuplɛks/ *adj.* **1.** twofold; double. -*n.* **2.** a two-storey block of flats or home units, one flat occupying each floor.

duplicate /ˈdjupləkət/ *adj., n.*; /ˈdjupləkeɪt/ *v.,* **-cated**, **-cating**. – *adj.* **1.** exactly like or corresponding to something else. **2.** double; consisting of or existing in two corresponding parts. – *n.* **3.** a copy exactly like an original. – *v.t.* **4.** to make an exact copy of; repeat. – **duplication**, *n.* – **duplicator**, *n.*

duplicity /djuˈplɪsəti/ *n., pl.* **-ties**. deceitfulness in speech or conduct. – **duplicitous**, *adj.*

durable /ˈdjurəbəl/ *adj.* having the quality of

lasting or enduring; not easily worn out, decayed, etc. – **durability**, *n.*

duration /dju'reɪʃən/ *n.* **1.** continuance in time. **2.** the length of time anything continues.

duress /dju'rɛs/ *n.* **1.** constraint; compulsion. **2.** forcible restraint of liberty; imprisonment.

during /'djurɪŋ/ *prep.* **1.** throughout the continuance of. **2.** in the course of.

durst /dɜst/ *v.* a past tense of **dare**.

dusk /dʌsk/ *n.* partial darkness; a state between light and darkness; twilight.

dusky /'dʌski/ *adj.*, **duskier**, **duskiest**. somewhat dark; dark-coloured.

dust /dʌst/ *n.* **1.** earth or other matter in fine, dry particles. **2.** any finely powdered substance, as sawdust. – *v.t.* **3.** to free from dust; wipe the dust from. **4.** to sprinkle with dust or powder. – **dusty**, *adj.*

dust jacket *n.* a jacket for a book. Also, **dust cover**.

duty /'djuti/ *n.*, *pl.* **-ties**. **1.** that which one is bound to do by moral or legal obligation. **2.** action required by one's position or occupation; office; function. **3.** a levy imposed by law on the import, export, sale, or manufacture of goods, the legal recognition of deeds and documents, etc. – **dutiful**, *adj.* – **dutiable**, *adj.*

duty solicitor *n.* a solicitor who is rostered to appear at a court to advise or represent, subject to a means test, anyone who is appearing in court that day and who does not have legal representation.

dux /dʌks/ *n.* the top pupil academically.

dwarf /dwɔf/ *n.* **1.** an unusually small person or thing. – *adj.* **2.** of unusually small stature or size; diminutive. – *v.t.* **3.** to cause to appear or seem small in size, extent, character, etc.

dwell /dwɛl/ *v.i.*, **dwelt** *or* **dwelled**, **dwelling**. **1.** to abide as a permanent resident. **2.** to continue for a time. **3.** to linger over in thought, speech, or writing; to emphasise (often fol. by *on* or *upon*).

dwindle /'dwɪndl/ *v.i.*, **-dled**, **-dling**. to become smaller and smaller; shrink.

dye /daɪ/ *n.*, *v.*, **dyed**, **dyeing**. – *n.* **1.** a colouring material or matter. – *v.t.* **2.** to colour or stain.

dying /'daɪɪŋ/ *adj.* **1.** ceasing to live; approaching death. **2.** given, uttered, or manifested just before death. **3.** drawing to a close.

dyke = dike /daɪk/ *n.* an embankment for restraining the waters of the sea or a river.

dynamic /daɪ'næmɪk/ *adj.* **1.** of or relating to force not in equilibrium (opposed to *static*) or to force in any state. **2.** relating to or characterised by energy or effective action; active; forceful. Also, **dynamical**.

dynamic random access memory *n.* a computer memory in which the information gradually decays, the cells needing to be topped up at frequent intervals, but the overall system being faster and cheaper than SRAM. Also, **DRAM**.

dynamics /daɪ'næmɪks/ *n.* **1.** *Physics* the branch of mechanics concerned with those forces which cause or affect the motion of bodies. **2.** the science or principles of forces acting in any field.

dynamite /'daɪnəmaɪt/ *n.* **1.** a high explosive. **2.** *Colloquial* anything or anyone potentially dangerous and liable to cause trouble. **3.** *Colloquial* anything or anyone exceptional.

dynamo /'daɪnəmoʊ/ *n.*, *pl.* **-mos**. **1.** any rotating machine in which mechanical energy is converted into electrical energy. **2.** *Colloquial* a forceful, energetic person.

dynasty /'dɪnəsti/ *n.*, *pl.* **-ties**. a sequence of rulers from the same family or stock. – **dynastic**, *adj.*

dyne /daɪn/ *n.* the unit of force in the centimetre-gram-second system, equal to 10×10^{-6} newtons. *Symbol*: dyn

dys- a prefix, especially medical, indicating difficulty, poor condition.

dysentery /'dɪsəntri/ *n.* an infectious disease marked by inflammation and ulceration of the lower part of the bowels, with diarrhoea.

dyslexia /dɪs'lɛksiə/ *n.* impairment in reading ability, often associated with other disorders especially in writing and coordination. – **dyslectic**, *n.*, *adj.*

E e

E, e *n., pl.* **E's** *or* **Es, e's** *or* **es**. the fifth letter of the English alphabet.

e- variant of **ex-**[1].

each /itʃ/ *adj.* **1.** every, of two or more considered individually or one by one. – *pron.* **2.** each one. – *adv.* **3.** apiece.

eager /'igə/ *adj.* keen or ardent in desire or feeling.

eagle /'igəl/ *n.* any of certain large birds of prey.

ear[1] /ɪə/ *n.* **1.** the organ of hearing. **2.** attention, especially favourable.

ear[2] /ɪə/ *n.* that part of a cereal plant which contains the grains or kernels.

earl /ɜl/ *n.* a British nobleman ranked immediately below a marquess.

early /'ɜli/ *adv.,* **-lier**, **-liest**, *adj.* – *adv.* **1.** in or during the first part of some division of time, or of some course or series. **2.** before the usual or appointed time; in good time. – *adj.* **3.** occurring in the first part of some division of time, or of some course or series. **4.** occurring before the usual or appointed time. **5.** belonging to a period far back in time.

earmark /'ɪəmak/ *v.t.* to set aside for a specific purpose or use.

earn /ɜn/ *v.t.* to gain by labour or service. – **earnings**, *pl. n.*

earnest /'ɜnəst/ *adj.* serious in intention, purpose, or effort.

earnings per share *n.* a company's net profit divided by the total number of shares in the company, usually expressed as cents per share. *Abbrev.*: e.p.s.

earnings yield *n.* the fraction calculated by dividing a company's earnings per share by its share price, expressed as a percentage.

earphone /'ɪəfoʊn/ *n.* a small device for converting electric signals into soundwaves, so designed that it is meant to fit into the ear or to be held close to it.

earring /'ɪəˌrɪŋ/ *n.* a ring or other ornament worn in or on the lobe of the ear.

earshot /'ɪəʃɒt/ *n.* range of hearing.

earth /ɜθ/ *n.* **1.** (*often cap.*) the planet which we inhabit. **2.** the softer part of the land, as distinguished from rock; soil. **3.** *Electricity* a conducting connection between an electric circuit or equipment and the ground. **4.** any of several metallic oxides.

earthen /'ɜθən/ *adj.* made of baked clay.

earthquake /'ɜθkweɪk/ *n.* tremors or earth movements in the earth's crust.

earthy /'ɜθi/ *adj.,* **earthier**, **earthiest**. **1.** of the nature of soil. **2.** coarse or unrefined. **3.** direct; unaffected.

ease /iz/ *n., v.,* **eased**, **easing**. – *n.* **1.** freedom from labour, pain, or annoyance of any kind. **2.** freedom from stiffness, constraint, or formality. – *v.t.* **3.** to give rest or relief to. **4.** to mitigate, lighten, or lessen. **5.** to facilitate. **6.** to move slowly and with great care. – *v.i.* **7.** to reduce severity, pressure, pain, tension, etc. (often fol. by *off* or *up*). **8.** to move with great care.

easel /'izəl/ *n.* a frame for supporting an artist's canvas, etc.

easement /'izmənt/ *n. Law* a right held by one person to make use of the land of another.

east /ist/ *n.* **1.** a cardinal point of the compass (90° to the right of north) corresponding to the point where the sun is seen to rise. – *adj.* **2.** lying or proceeding towards the east. **3.** coming from the east. – *adv.* **4.** in the direction of the sunrise; towards or in the east. **5.** from the east. – **easterly**, *adj., n.* – **eastern**, *adj.*

easy /'izi/ *adj.,* **easier**, **easiest**, *adv.* – *adj.* **1.** not difficult; requiring no great labour or effort. **2.** free from pain, discomfort, worry, or care. **3.** *Colloquial* having no firm preferences in a particular matter. **4.** free from formality, constraint, or embarrassment. **5.** *Commerce* **a.** (of a commodity) not difficult to obtain; in plentiful supply and (often) weak in price. **b.** (of the market) not characterised by eager demand. – *adv.* **6.** *Colloquial* in an easy manner; comfortably.

easygoing /'izigoʊɪŋ/ *adj.* taking matters in an easy way.

eat /it/ *v.,* **ate** /eɪt, ɛt/ **eaten**, **eating**. – *v.t.* **1.** to take into the mouth and swallow for nourishment, especially to masticate and swallow, as solid food. **2.** to consume by or as by devouring. – *v.i.* **3.** to consume food; take a meal. **4.** to make a way as by gnawing or corrosion.

eaves /ivz/ *pl. n.* the overhanging lower edge of a roof.

eavesdrop /'ivzdrɒp/ *v.i.,* **-dropped**, **-dropping**. to listen secretly.

ebb /ɛb/ *n.* **1.** the falling of the tide (opposed to *flow*). – *v.i.* **2.** to flow back or away, as the water of a tide. **3.** to decline or decay.

ebony /'ɛbəni/ *n.* a hard, durable wood, usually black, from various tropical trees.

ebullient /ə'bʊljənt, ə'bʌl-, ə'bjul-/ *adj.* **1.** seething or overflowing with fervour, enthusiasm, excitement, etc. **2.** bubbling like a boiling liquid.

ec- variant of **ex-**[3], before consonants.

eccentric /ək'sɛntrɪk/ *adj.* **1.** not conventional; odd. **2.** not concentric, as two circles or spheres. – *n.* **3.** an eccentric person. – **eccentricity**, *n.*

ecclesiastic /əklizi'æstɪk/ *n.* a member of the clergy, or person in orders.

echelon /'ɛʃəlɒn/ *n.* a level of command.

echidna /ə'kɪdnə/ *n., pl.* **-nas**, **-nae** /-ni/. a spine-covered insectivorous monotreme; spiny anteater.

echo /'ɛkoʊ/ *n., pl.* **echoes**, *v.,* **echoed**, **echoing**. – *n.* **1.** a repetition of sound, produced by the reflection of soundwaves from an obstructing surface. – *v.i.* **2.** to emit an echo; resound with an echo. – *v.t.* **3.** to repeat by or as by an echo. – **echoic**, *adj.*

eclectic /ɛ'klɛktɪk/ *adj.* selecting; choosing from various sources.

eclipse /ə'klɪps, i-/ *n., v.,* **eclipsed**, **eclipsing**. – *n.* **1.** *Astronomy* the obscuration of the light of a satellite by the intervention of its primary planet between it and the sun. – *v.t.* **2.** to make dim by comparison; surpass.

ecology /ə'kɒlədʒi/ *n.* the branch of biology that deals with the relations between organisms and their environment.

econometrics /əkɒnə'mɛtrɪks, ikɒn-/ *n.* the analysis by statistical and mathematical methods of economic data theories, etc. – **econometric**, **econometrical**, *adj.* – **econometrician**, **econometrist**, *n.*

economic /ɛkə'nɒmɪk, ikə-/ *adj.* **1.** having to do with the production, distribution, and use of income and wealth. **2.** having to do with the science of economics. **3.** having to do with an economy, or system of organisation or operation, especially of the process of production.

economical /ɛkə'nɒmɪkəl, ikə-/ *adj.* **1.** avoiding waste or extravagance; thrifty. **2.** economic.

economic rationalism *n.* a theory of economics which opposes government intervention and which maintains that the economy of a country works better when it responds to marketplace forces.

economics /ɛkə'nɒmɪks, ikə-/ *n.* the science that deals with the production, distribution, and consumption of goods and services, or the material welfare of humankind. – **economist**, *n.*

economise = economize /ə'kɒnəmaɪz/ *v.i.*, **-mised**, **-mising**. to practise economy; avoid waste.

economy /ə'kɒnəmi/ *n., pl.* **-mies**. **1.** thrifty management; frugality. **2.** *Economics* the interrelationship between the factors of production and the means of production, distribution, and exchange. **3.** the management, or science of management, of the resources of a community, etc., with a view to productiveness and avoidance of waste.

ecotourism /ikoʊ'tʊərɪzəm/ *n.* **1.** tourism so arranged that it involves no degradation of the environment. **2.** tourism which takes in places of ecological interest.

ecstasy /'ɛkstəsi/ *n., pl.* **-sies**. **1.** overpowering emotion, especially delight. **2.** an instance of this. **3.** Also, **MDMA**. a synthetic drug, 3, 4 methylenedioxymethamphetamine, which is used as a stimulant. – **ecstatic**, *adj.*

ecto- a prefix meaning 'outside', 'external'.

-ectomy a combining form attached to the name of a part of the body and producing a word meaning an operation for the excision of that part.

ecumenical /ɛkjə'mɛnəkəl, ik-/ *adj.* general; universal.

eczema /'ɛksəmə/ *n.* an inflammatory disease of the skin.

-ed[1] a suffix forming the past tense, as in *she crossed the river.*

-ed[2] a suffix forming: **1.** the past participle, as in *he had crossed the river.* **2.** participial adjectives indicating a condition or quality resulting from the action of the verb, as *inflated balloons.*

-ed[3] a suffix serving to form adjectives from nouns, as *bearded, moneyed.*

eddy /'ɛdi/ *n., pl.* **eddies**. a current at variance with the main current in a stream of liquid or gas, especially one having a rotary or whirling motion.

edge /ɛdʒ/ *n., v.,* **edged**, **edging**. – *n.* **1.** a brim or margin. **2.** a brink or verge. **3.** one of the narrow surfaces of a thin, flat object. **4.** the line in which two surfaces of a solid object meet. **5.** sharpness or keenness. – *v.t.* **6.** to put an edge on; sharpen. **7.** to move edgeways; move or force gradually. – *v.i.* **8.** to move edgeways; advance gradually.

edgy /'ɛdʒi/ *adj.*, **-ier**, **-iest**. impatient; irritable.

edible /'ɛdəbəl/ *adj.* fit to be eaten.

edict /'idɪkt/ *n.* an authoritative proclamation or command.

edifice /'ɛdəfəs/ *n.* a building, especially large.

edify /'ɛdəfaɪ/ *v.t.*, **-fied**, **-fying**. to instruct or benefit, especially morally. – **edification**, *n.*

edit /'ɛdət/ *v.t.* **1.** to supervise or direct the preparation of (a newspaper, magazine, etc.). **2.** to make (a film, sound recording, etc.) by cutting and arranging, etc. – **editor**, *n.*

edition /ə'dɪʃən/ *n.* one of a number of printings of the same book, newspaper, etc.

editorial /ɛdə'tɔriəl/ *n.* **1.** an article, in a newspaper or the like, presenting the opinion or comment of an editor. – *adj.* **2.** of or relating to an editor.

educate /'ɛdʒəkeɪt/ *v.t.*, **-cated**, **-cating**. to develop the faculties and powers of by teaching, instruction, or schooling. – **education**, *n.*

-ee a suffix of nouns denoting someone who is the object of some action, or undergoes or receives something, as in *employee.*

eel /il/ *n.* a snakelike fish.

EEO /i i 'oʊ/ Equal Employment Opportunity.

-eer a suffix of nouns denoting someone who is concerned with, or employed in connection with, something, as in *auctioneer, engineer, profiteer.* Also, **-ier**.

eerie /'ɪəri/ *adj.*, **eerier**, **eeriest**. weird, strange, or uncanny. Also, **eery**.

ef- variant of **ex-** before *f.*

efface /ə'feɪs/ *v.t.*, **effaced**, **effacing**. to wipe out; destroy; do away with.

effect /ə'fɛkt, i-/ *n.* **1.** a result; a consequence. **2.** power to produce results; efficacy. **3.** the state of being operative. **4.** a mental impression produced, as by a painting, speech, etc. **5.** (of stage properties) a sight, sound, etc., simulated by artificial means to give a particular impression. **6.** a scientific phenomenon: *the Doppler effect.* **7.** (*pl.*) personal property. – *v.t.* **8.** to produce as an effect.

effective /ə'fɛktɪv, i-/ *adj.* **1.** producing the intended or expected result. **2.** actually in effect. **3.** producing a striking impression.

effectual /ə'fɛktʃuəl, i-/ *adj.* producing, or capable of producing, an intended effect.

effeminate /ə'fɛmənət, i-/ *adj.* (of a man) soft or delicate to an unmanly degree.

effervesce /ɛfə'vɛs/ *v.i.*, **-vesced**, **-vescing**. to give off bubbles of gas, as fermenting liquors. – **effervescence**, *n.*

effete /ə'fit/ *adj.* that has lost its vigour or energy.

efficacy /'ɛfəkəsi/ *n.* capacity to produce

effects; effectiveness. – **efficacious**, *adj.*

efficient /ə'fɪʃənt, i-/ *adj.* competent; capable. – **efficiency**, *n.*

effigy /'ɛfədʒi/ *n., pl.* **-gies**. a representation or image.

efflorescence /ɛflə'rɛsəns/ *n. Pathology* a rash or eruption.

effluent /'ɛfluənt/ *adj.* **1.** flowing out. – *n.* **2.** that which flows out, such as outflow from sewage during purification. – **effluence**, *n.*

effort /'ɛfət/ *n.* **1.** exertion of power, physical or mental. **2.** an attempt.

effrontery /ə'frʌntəri, i-/ *n.* shameless or impudent boldness.

effusion /ə'fjuʒən, i-/ *n.* **1.** a pouring forth. **2.** unrestrained expression of feeling.

effusive /ə'fjusɪv, -zɪv, i-/ *adj.* unduly demonstrative; without reserve.

EFT electronic funds transfer.

EFTPOS /'ɛftpɒs/ *n.* a system of electronic funds transfer from a customer's account to a merchant's account, operated by the customer by means of a coded plastic card inserted into a special-purpose terminal and a PIN number by which the transaction is authorised.

egalitarian /əgælə'tɛəriən, i-/ *adj.* asserting the equality of all people.

egg[1] /ɛg/ *n.* **1.** the female reproductive cell and its envelopes. **2.** the egg produced by birds, especially the domestic hen. **3.** the contents of an egg, especially that of a domestic hen, used as food.

egg[2] /ɛg/ *v.t.* to incite or urge; encourage (fol. by *on*).

eggplant /'ɛgplænt/ *n.* a plant with purple egg-shaped fruit; aubergine.

ego /'igoʊ/ *n.* the 'I' or self of any person.

egotism /'ɛgətɪzəm, 'igə-/ *n.* self-conceit.

egress /'igrɛs/ *n.* a means or place of going out.

egret /'igrət/ *n.* any of various herons.

eiderdown /'aɪdədaʊn/ *n.* **1.** down or soft feathers from the eider duck. **2.** a quilt.

eight /eɪt/ *n.* a cardinal number, seven plus one. – **eighth**, *adj., n.*

eighteen /eɪ'tin/ *n.* a cardinal number, ten plus eight. – **eighteenth**, *adj., n.*

eighty /'eɪti/ *n., pl.* **eighties**. a cardinal number, ten times eight. – **eightieth**, *adj., n.*

EIS /i aɪ 'ɛs/ environmental impact statement.

either /'aɪðə, 'iðə/ *adj.* **1.** one or the other of two. **2.** each of the two; the one and the other. – *pron.* **3.** one or the other but not both. – *conj.* **4.** (used as one of two coordinate alternatives). – *adv.* **5.** (used after negative sentences coordinated by *and*, *or*, *nor*).

ejaculate /ə'dʒækjəleɪt, i-/ *v.,* **-lated**, **-lating**. – *v.t.* **1.** to utter suddenly and briefly; exclaim. – *v.i.* **2.** to discharge seminal fluid. – **ejaculation**, *n.*

eject /ə'dʒɛkt, i-/ *v.t.* **1.** to drive or force out. – *v.i.* **2.** to propel oneself out of an aeroplane, etc., by means of a mechanical device. – **ejection**, *n.*

eke /ik/ *v.t.,* **eked**, **eking**. **1.** to use (resources) frugally (fol. by *out*). **2.** to contrive to make (a living).

elaborate /ə'læbərət/ *adj.,* /ə'læbəreɪt, i-/ *v.,* **-rated**, **-rating**. – *adj.* **1.** worked out with great care and nicety of detail; complicated. – *v.i.* **2.** to give additional or fuller treatment (fol. by *on* or *upon*). – **elaboration**, *n.*

elapse /ə'læps, i-/ *v.i.,* **elapsed**, **elapsing**. (of time) to slip by or pass away.

elastic /ə'læstɪk, i-/ *adj.* **1.** springing back or rebounding. **2.** flexible; yielding. – *n.* **3.** elastic material.

elate /ə'leɪt, i-/ *v.t.,* **elated**, **elating**. to put in high spirits. – **elation**, *n.*

elbow /'ɛlboʊ/ *n.* **1.** the bend or joint of the arm between upper arm and forearm. – *v.t.* **2.** to push with or as with the elbow; jostle.

elder[1] /'ɛldə/ *adj.* **1.** older. – *n.* **2.** a person who is older than oneself. **3.** one of the older and more influential people of a tribe or community.

elder[2] /'ɛldə/ *n.* any of several flowering shrubs or trees.

elderly /'ɛldəli/ *adj.* approaching old age.

eldest /'ɛldəst/ *adj.* oldest.

elect /ə'lɛkt, i-/ *v.t.* **1.** to select by vote, as for an office. **2.** to determine in favour of (a course of action, etc.). – *adj.* **3.** selected for an office, but not yet inducted (usually after the noun). – **elector**, *n.*

election /ə'lɛkʃən, i-/ *n.* the selection by vote of a person or persons for office.

elective /ə'lɛktɪv, i-/ *adj.* **1.** (of an office) filled by election. – *n.* **2.** an option.

electoral /ə'lɛktərəl, -trəl, i-/ *adj.* relating to electors or election.

electorate /ə'lɛktərət, -trət, i-/ *n.* **1.** the body of voters represented by an elected member. **2.** such a body, especially as represented by a member of parliament.

electric /ə'lɛktrɪk, -i/ *adj.* relating to, derived from, produced by, or involving electricity. Also, **electrical**.

electrician /əlɛk'trɪʃən, ɛlɛk-, ilɛk-/ *n.* someone who installs, operates, maintains, or repairs electrical devices.

electricity /əlɛk'trɪsəti, ɛlɛk-, ilɛk-/ *n.* an agency producing various physical phenomena, due to the presence and movements of electrons, protons, and other electrically charged particles.

electrify /ə'lɛktrəfaɪ, i-/ *v.t.,* **-fied**, **-fying**. to charge with or subject to electricity.

electro- a word element meaning 'pertaining to or caused by electricity'.

electrocardiograph /əˌlɛktroʊ'kadiəgræf, i-/ *n.* a device which detects and records electrical activity of the heart. *Abbrev.*: ECG

electrocute /ə'lɛktrəkjut, i-/ *v.t.,* **-cuted**, **-cuting**. to kill by electricity. – **electrocution**, *n.*

electrode /ə'lɛktroʊd, i-/ *n.* a conductor of electricity through which a current enters or leaves an electrolytic cell, etc.

electroencephalograph /əˌlɛktroʊɛn'sɛfələgræf, i-/ *n.* a device which detects and records the electrical activity of the brain. *Abbrev.*: EEG

electrolysis /əlɛk'trɒləsəs, i-, ˌɛlək'trɒləsəs/ *n.* **1.** the decomposition of a chemical compound by an electric current. **2.** *Surgery* the destruction of tumours, hair roots, etc., by an electric current. – **electrolytic**, *adj.*

electron /ə'lɛktrɒn, i-/ *n.* a negatively charged elementary particle which is a constituent of all atoms.

electronic /ɛlək'trɒnɪk, əlɛk-, i-/ *adj.* of, relating to, or concerned with, electronics or any devices or systems based on electronics.

electronic banking *n.* banking transactions conducted by means of electronic systems or networks, as by EFTPOS.

electronic data processing *n.* the use of digital computers to handle information. *Abbrev.*: EDP

electronic funds transfer *n.* a computerised banking system for the transfer of funds from one account to another. *Abbrev.*: EFT

electronics /əlɛk'trɒnɪks, i-, ɛlək-/ *n.* the investigation and application of phenomena involving the movement of electrons in valves and semiconductors. – **electronic**, *adj.*

elegant /'ɛləgənt, 'ɛlɪ-/ *adj.* tastefully fine or luxurious in dress, manner, etc. – **elegance**, *n.*

elegy /'ɛlədʒi/ *n., pl.* **-gies**. a mournful or plaintive poem, especially a lament for the dead. – **elegiac**, *adj.*

element /'ɛləmənt/ *n.* **1.** a component or constituent part of a whole. **2.** (*pl.*) the rudimentary principles of an art, science, etc. **3.** (*pl.*) atmospheric agencies or forces. **4.** *Chemistry* one of a class of substances which consist entirely of atoms of the same atomic number. **5.** *Electricity* the heating unit of an electric domestic appliance. – **elemental**, *adj.*

elementary /ɛlə'mɛntri, -təri/ *adj.* relating to or dealing with elements, rudiments, or first principles.

elephant /'ɛləfənt/ *n.* a very large, herbivorous mammal, having a long, prehensile trunk and curved tusks. – **elephantine**, *adj.*

elevate /'ɛləveɪt/ *v.t.*, **-vated**, **-vating**. to move or raise to a higher place or position; lift up.

elevation /ɛlə'veɪʃən/ *n.* **1.** altitude above sea or ground level. **2.** the act of elevating. **3.** the state of being elevated. **4.** *Architecture* a drawing or design of a face of a building.

elevator /'ɛləveɪtə/ *n.* → **lift** (def. 7).

eleven /ə'lɛvən/ *n.* a cardinal number, ten plus one. – **eleventh**, *adj., n.*

elf /ɛlf/ *n., pl.* **elves** /ɛlvz/. one of a class of imaginary beings, usually a diminutive human. – **elfin**, **elfish**, **elvish**, *adj.*

elicit /ə'lɪsət/ *v.t.* to draw or bring out or forth; evoke.

eligible /'ɛlədʒəbəl/ *adj.* fit or proper to be chosen; worthy of choice.

eliminate /ə'lɪməneɪt, i-/ *v.t.*, **-nated**, **-nating**. to get rid of; expel; remove. – **elimination**, *n.*

elite /ə'lit, eɪ-, i-/ *n.* (*construed as pl.*) persons of the highest class.

elixir /ə'lɪksə, ɛ-, i-/ *n.* a preparation formerly believed to prolong life.

elk /ɛlk/ *n., pl.* **elks** *or* **elk**. the largest existing European and Asiatic deer.

ellipse /ə'lɪps, i-/ *n.* a plane figure, oval in shape or outline. – **elliptical**, *adj.*

ellipsis /ə'lɪpsɪs, i-/ *n., pl.* **-lipses** /-lɪpsiz/. *Grammar* the omission from a sentence or argument, of something which would complete or clarify the construction. – **elliptical**, *adj.*

elm /ɛlm/ *n.* any of several large, deciduous trees.

elocution /ɛlə'kjuʃən/ *n.* manner of speaking or reading in public.

elongate /'ilɒŋgeɪt/ *v.t.*, **-gated**, **-gating**. to draw out to greater length. – **elongation**, *n.*

elope /ə'loʊp, i-/ *v.i.*, **eloped**, **eloping**. to run away with a lover, usually in order to marry without parental consent.

eloquent /'ɛləkwənt/ *adj.* characterised by fluent, persuasive expression.

else /ɛls/ *adv.* other than the person or the thing mentioned.

elsewhere /'ɛlswɛə, ɛls'wɛə/ *adv.* somewhere else.

elucidate /ə'lusədeɪt, i-/ *v.t.*, **-dated**, **-dating**. to make lucid or clear; explain.

elude /ə'lud, i-/ *v.t.*, **eluded**, **eluding**. to avoid or escape by dexterity or artifice.

em /ɛm/ *n., pl.* **ems**. *Printing* the square of the body size of any type.

em- variant of **en-**.

emaciated /ə'meɪsieɪtəd, i-/ *adj.* lean; wasted, as by disease.

email /'imeɪl/ *n.* **1.** Also, **electronic mail**. messages sent on a telecommunications system linking computers or terminals. – *v.t.* **2.** to send (a message) by email. **3.** to send such messages to (someone). Also, **e-mail**.

emanate /'ɛməneɪt/ *v.i.*, **-nated**, **-nating**. to flow out, issue, or proceed as from a source or origin. – **emanation**, *n.*

emancipate /ə'mænsəpeɪt, i-/ *v.t.*, **-pated**, **-pating**. to free from restraint.

emasculate /ə'mæskjəleɪt, i-/ *v.t.*, **-lated**, **-lating**. **1.** to castrate. **2.** to deprive of strength or vigour.

embalm /ɛm'bam/ *v.t.* to treat (a dead body) in order to preserve from decay.

embankment /ɛm'bæŋkmənt, ə-/ *n.* a bank, mound, dyke, or the like, raised to hold back water, carry a road, etc.

embargo /ɛm'bagoʊ/ *n., pl.* **-goes**. **1.** an order of a government prohibiting the movement of merchant vessels from or into its ports. **2.** any restriction imposed upon commerce by law.

embark /ɛm'bak/ *v.i.* to board a ship, plane, etc., as for a voyage.

embarrass /ɛm'bærəs/ *v.t.* **1.** to disconcert; make uncomfortable, self-conscious, etc. **2.** to beset with financial difficulties.

embassy /'ɛmbəsi/ *n., pl.* **-sies**. the official headquarters of an ambassador.

embellish /ɛm'bɛlɪʃ/ *v.t.* to beautify by or as by ornamentation; enhance.

ember /'ɛmbə/ *n.* a small live coal.

embezzle /ɛm'bɛzəl/ *v.t.*, **-zled**, **-zling**. to appropriate fraudulently to one's own use.

emblazon /ɛm'bleɪzən/ *v.t.* to portray or inscribe on or as on a heraldic shield.

emblem /'ɛmbləm/ *n.* a symbol.

embody /ɛm'bɒdi/ *v.t.*, **-bodied**, **-bodying**. to give a concrete form to.

emboss /ɛm'bɒs/ *v.t.* to raise designs on the surface of (leather, etc.).

embrace /ɛm'breɪs/ *v.*, **-braced**, **-bracing**, *n.* – *v.t.* **1.** to hug. **2.** to accept (an idea, etc.) willingly. **3.** to include or contain. – *n.* **4.** a hug.

embroider /ɛm'brɔɪdə/ *v.t.* **1.** to decorate with ornamental needlework. **2.** to adorn or embellish rhetorically, especially with fictitious additions. – **embroidery**, *n.*

embroil /ɛm'brɔɪl, əm-/ *v.t.* **1.** to involve in contention or strife. **2.** to throw into confusion; complicate.

embryo /'ɛmbriou/ *n.*, *pl.* **-os**. an organism in the earlier stages of its development, as a mammal still in its mother's body.

emend /ə'mɛnd, i-/ *v.t.* to free from faults or errors; correct. – **emendation**, *n.*

emerald /'ɛmrəld, 'ɛmərəld/ *n.* a green gemstone.

emerge /ə'mɜdʒ, i-/ *v.i.*, **emerged**, **emerging**. to rise or come forth, as from concealment or obscurity.

emergency /ə'mɜdʒənsi, i-/ *n.*, *pl.* **-cies**. a sudden and urgent occasion for action.

emergent /ə'mɜdʒənt, i-/ *adj.* **1.** (of a nation) recently independent or newly formed as a political entity. **2.** emerging. – **emergence**, *n.*

emery /'ɛməri/ *n.* a granular mineral substance used for grinding and polishing.

emetic /ə'mɛtɪk/ *adj.* inducing vomiting, as a medicinal substance.

-emia variant of **-aemia**.

emigrate /'ɛməgreɪt/ *v.i.*, **-grated**, **-grating**. to leave one country or region to settle in another. – **emigration**, *n.* – **emigrant**, *n.*

eminent /'ɛmənənt/ *adj.* **1.** high-ranking; distinguished. **2.** conspicuous. – **eminence**, *n.*

eminent domain *n.* the power of the state to acquire land for works of public utility without the consent of its owner.

emissary /'ɛməsəri, -əsri/ *n.*, *pl.* **-saries**. an agent sent on a mission.

emission control *n.* the control of polluting gases released into the atmosphere by motor vehicles, factories, etc.

emit /ə'mɪt, i-/ *v.t.*, **emitted**, **emitting**. to give out or forth; discharge. – **emission**, *n.*

emollient /ə'mɒliənt, -'mou-/ *adj.* soothing.

emolument /ə'mɒljəmənt/ *n.* profit arising from office or employment; salary or fees.

emotion /ə'mouʃən, i-/ *n.* **1.** any of the feelings of joy, sorrow, fear, hate, love, etc. **2.** a state of agitation of the feelings actuated by experiencing fear, joy, etc.

emotional /ə'mouʃənəl, i-/ *adj.* **1.** easily affected by emotion. **2.** appealing to the emotions.

emotive /ə'moutɪv, i-/ *adj.* exciting emotion.

empathy /'ɛmpəθi/ *n.* an entering into the feeling or spirit of another; appreciative perception or understanding. – **empathetic**, *adj.* – **empathise = empathize**, *v.*

emperor /'ɛmpərə/ *n.* the sovereign or supreme ruler of an empire. – **empress**, *fem. n.*

emphasis /'ɛmfəsəs/ *n.*, *pl.* **-phases** /-fəsiz/. **1.** stress laid upon, or importance or significance attached to anything. **2.** intensity or force of expression, action, etc. **3.** prominence, as of outline. – **emphasise = emphasize**, *v.* – **emphatic**, *adj.*

empire /'ɛmpaɪə/ *n.* an aggregate of nations or peoples ruled over by an emperor or other powerful sovereign or government.

empirical /ɛm'pɪrɪkəl/ *adj.* derived from or guided by experience or experiment.

employ /ɛm'plɔɪ/ *v.t.* **1.** to use the services of (a person). **2.** to make use of (an instrument, means, etc.). **3.** to occupy or devote (time, energies, etc.). – *n.* **4.** employment; service. – **employment**, *n.* – **employer**, *n.* – **employee**, *n.*

emporium /ɛm'pɔriəm/ *n.*, *pl.* **-poriums**, **-poria** /-'pɔriə/. a large store selling a great variety of articles.

empower /ɛm'pauə/ *v.t.* to give power or authority to; authorise.

empty /'ɛmpti, 'ɛmti/ *adj.*, **-tier**, **-tiest**, *v.*, **-tied**, **-tying**. – *adj.* **1.** containing nothing. **2.** vacant; unoccupied. – *v.t.* **3.** to make empty.

emu /'imju/ *n.* a large, flightless, Australian bird.

emulate /'ɛmjuleɪt, -je-/ *v.t.*, **-lated**, **-lating**. to imitate with intent to equal or excel.

emulsion /ə'mʌlʃən/ *n.* a suspension of a liquid in another liquid.

en /ɛn/ *n. Printing* half the width of an em.

en- a prefix meaning primarily 'in', 'into', often with the force of bringing the object into the specified condition, as in *endear*. Cf. **in-**[2], **im-**[1]. Also, **em-**.

-en[1] a suffix forming verbs from adjectives, as in *fasten*, or from nouns, as in *heighten*.

-en[2] a suffix of adjectives indicating 'material', 'appearance', as in *ashen*, *golden*.

-en[3] a suffix used to mark the past participle in some verbs, as in *taken*, *proven*.

-en[4] a suffix forming the plural of some nouns, as in *children*, *oxen*.

-en[5] a diminutive suffix, as in *maiden*, *kitten*, etc.

enable /ɛn'eɪbəl, ən-/ *v.t.*, **-bled**, **-bling**. to make able; give power, means, or ability to.

enabling /ɛn'eɪblɪŋ, ən-/ *adj.* (of an act, statute, or bill) enabling a person or a company to do something otherwise illegal.

enact /ɛn'ækt, ən-/ *v.t.* **1.** to make into an act or statute. **2.** to act the part of.

enamel /ə'næməl/ *n.* **1.** a glassy substance, usually opaque, applied by fusion to the surface of metal, pottery, etc., as an ornament or for protection. **2.** any of various enamel-like varnishes, paints, etc. **3.** *Anatomy*, *Zoology* the hard, glossy, calcareous outer structure of the crowns of the teeth.

enamoured = enamored /ɛn'æməd, ən-/ *adj.* filled with love; charmed; delighted (usually fol. by *of*): *to be enamoured of a lady.*

encapsulate /ɛn'kæpsjəleɪt, ən-, -ʃə-/ *v.t.*, **-lated**, **-lating**. to enclose in or as in a capsule. – **encapsulation**, *n.*

-ence a noun suffix equivalent to **-ance**, and

corresponding to **-ent** in adjectives.

encephalo- a word element meaning 'brain'.

encephalogram /ɛn'sɛfələgræm, ɛnkɛf-/ *n.* an X-ray photograph of the brain.

enchant /ɛn'tʃænt, ən-, -'tʃant/ *v.t.* **1.** to cast a spell over; bewitch. **2.** to delight; charm.

encircle /ɛn'sɜkəl, ən-/ *v.t.*, **-cled**, **-cling**. to form a circle round; surround.

enclave /'ɛnkleɪv, 'ɒnkleɪv/ *n.* a portion of a country surrounded by the territory of another country.

enclose /ɛn'kloʊz, ən-/ *v.t.*, **-closed**, **-closing**. **1.** to shut in; close in on all sides. **2.** to insert in the same envelope, etc., with the main letter, etc. – **enclosure**, *n.*

encompass /ɛn'kʌmpəs, ən-/ *v.t.* **1.** to encircle; surround. **2.** to enclose; contain.

encounter /ɛn'kaʊntə, ən-/ *v.t.* **1.** to come upon; meet with, especially unexpectedly. **2.** to meet (a person, military force, etc.) in conflict. – *n.* **3.** a meeting with a person or thing, especially casually or unexpectedly. **4.** a meeting in conflict or opposition; a battle; a combat.

encourage /ɛn'kʌrɪdʒ, ən-/ *v.t.*, **-raged**, **-raging**. **1.** to inspire with courage, spirit, or confidence. **2.** to stimulate by assistance, approval, etc. – **encouragement**, *n.*

encroach /ɛn'kroʊtʃ, ən-/ *v.i.* to trespass upon the property or rights of another.

encrust /ɛn'krʌst, ən-/ *v.t.* to cover or line with a crust or hard coating.

encumber /ɛn'kʌmbə, ən-/ *v.t.* to impede or hamper. – **encumbrance**, *n.*

encyclopedia = **encyclopaedia** /ɛn,saɪklə'pidiə, ən-/ *n.* a work treating separately various topics from all branches of knowledge, usually in alphabetical arrangement.

end /ɛnd/ *n.* **1.** an extreme or farthermost part of anything extended in space. **2.** anything that bounds an object at one of its extremities; a limit. **3.** the act of coming to an end; termination. **4.** a purpose or aim. **5.** a remnant or fragment. – *v.t.* **6.** to bring to an end or natural conclusion. **7.** to form the end of. – *v.i.* **8.** to come to an end; terminate; cease. **9.** to issue or result. **10.** *Colloquial* to reach a final condition, circumstance, goal (often fol. by *up*).

endanger /ɛn'deɪndʒə, ən-/ *v.t.* to expose to danger.

endear /ɛn'dɪə, ən-/ *v.t.* to make dear, esteemed, or beloved.

endearment /ɛn'dɪəmənt, ən-/ *n.* a caress or an affectionate term.

endeavour = **endeavor** /ɛn'dɛvə, ən-/ *v.i.* **1.** to make an effort; strive. – *n.* **2.** an attempt.

endemic /ɛn'dɛmɪk/ *adj.* peculiar to a particular people or locality, as a disease.

endive /'ɛndaɪv/ *n.* a herb, used in salads and as a cooked vegetable.

endo- a word element meaning 'internal'.

endocrine gland /'ɛndəkrən/ *n.* a gland (as the thyroid gland) which secretes hormones directly to the blood or lymph.

endorse /ɛn'dɔs, ən-/ *v.t.*, **-dorsed**, **-dorsing**. **1.** to write (something) on the back of a document, etc. **2.** to sign one's name on (a commercial document or other instrument). **3.** to designate (another) as payee by one's endorsement. **4.** to acknowledge (payment) by placing one's signature on a bill, draft, etc. **5.** to add a modifying statement to (a document). **6.** (of a branch of a political party) to select as a candidate for an election. Also, **indorse**. – **endorsement**, *n.*

endow /ɛn'daʊ, ən-/ *v.t.* **1.** to provide with a permanent fund or source of income. **2.** to furnish as with some gift, faculty, or quality; equip. – **endowment**, *n.*

endue /ɛn'dju, ən-/ *v.t.*, **-dued**, **-duing**. to invest or endow with some gift, quality, or faculty.

endure /ɛn'djuə/ *v.t.*, **-dured**, **-during**. **1.** to sustain without impairment or yielding; undergo. **2.** to bear without resistance or with patience; tolerate. – **endurance**, *n.*

-ene **1.** a noun suffix used in chemistry, in names of hydrocarbons. **2.** a generalised suffix used in trademarks for substances, often implying synthetic manufacture.

enema /'ɛnəmə/ *n.*, *pl.* **enemas**, **enemata** /ə'nɛmətə, i-/ a fluid injected into the rectum, as to evacuate the bowels.

enemy /'ɛnəmi/ *n.*, *pl.* **-mies**. **1.** someone who cherishes hatred or harmful designs against another; an adversary or opponent. **2.** a hostile nation or state. **3.** a subject of such a state. **4.** something harmful or prejudicial.

energetic /ɛnə'dʒɛtɪk/ *adj.* possessing or exhibiting energy; forcible; vigorous.

energy /'ɛnədʒi/ *n.*, *pl.* **-gies**. **1.** capacity or habit of vigorous activity. **2.** ability to produce action or effect.

enervate /'ɛnəveɪt/ *v.t.*, **-vated**, **-vating**. to deprive of nerve, force, or strength; weaken.

enforce /ɛn'fɔs, ən-/ *v.t.*, **-forced**, **-forcing**. **1.** to put or keep in force; compel obedience to. **2.** to obtain (payment, obedience, etc.) by force or compulsion.

enfranchise /ɛn'fræntʃaɪz, ən-/ *v.t.*, **-chised**, **-chising**. **1.** to admit to citizenship, especially to the right of voting. **2.** *Law* to invest with the right of being represented in Parliament. **3.** to set free; liberate, as from slavery.

engage /ɛn'geɪdʒ, ən-/ *v.t.*, **-gaged**, **-gaging**. **1.** to occupy the attention or efforts of (a person, etc.). **2.** to secure for aid, employment, use, etc.; hire. **3.** to reserve or secure. **4.** to attract or please. **5.** to bind as by pledge, promise, contract, or oath; make liable. **6.** to betroth (usually used in the passive). **7.** to bring (troops) into conflict; enter into conflict with. **8.** *Mechanics* to cause to become interlocked; interlock with.

engender /ɛn'dʒɛndə, ən-/ *v.t.* to produce, cause, or give rise to.

engine /'ɛndʒən/ *n.* **1.** any mechanism or machine designed to convert energy into mechanical work. **2.** any mechanical contrivance.

engineer /ɛndʒə'nɪə/ *n.* **1.** one versed in the design, construction, and use of engines or machines. – *v.t.* **2.** to plan, construct, or manage as an engineer. **3.** to arrange, manage or carry through by skilful or artful contrivance.

engrave /ɛn'greɪv, ən-/ *v.t.*, **-graved**, **-graving**. to cut (letters, designs, etc.) on a hard surface.

engross /ɛn'groʊs, ən-/ *v.t.* to occupy wholly, as the mind or attention; absorb.

engulf /ɛn'gʌlf, ən-/ *v.t.* to swallow up in or as in a chasm.

enhance /ɛn'hæns, -'hans, ən-/ *v.t.*, **-hanced**, **-hancing**. to raise to a higher degree.

enigma /ə'nɪgmə/ *n.* somebody or something puzzling or inexplicable. – **enigmatic**, *adj.*

enjoin /ɛn'dʒɔɪn, ən-/ *v.t.* to order or direct.

enjoy /ɛn'dʒɔɪ, ən-/ *v.t.* **1.** to experience with joy; take pleasure in. **2.** to have the benefit of. **3.** to find or experience pleasure for (oneself). – **enjoyment**, *n.*

enlarge /ɛn'ladʒ, ən-/ *v.t.*, **-larged**, **-larging**. **1.** to make larger. **2.** to speak or write at large. – **enlargement**, *n.*

enlighten /ɛn'laɪtn, ən-/ *v.t.* to give intellectual or spiritual light to; instruct.

enlist /ɛn'lɪst, ən-/ *v.t.* **1.** to secure (a person, services, etc.) for some cause, enterprise, etc. – *v.i.* **2.** to enter into some cause, enterprise, etc.

enliven /ɛn'laɪvən, ən-/ *v.t.* to make vigorous or active; invigorate.

enmity /'ɛnməti/ *n., pl.* **-ties**. a feeling or condition of hostility.

enormous /ə'nɔməs, i-/ *adj.* **1.** greatly exceeding the common size, extent, etc.; huge; immense. **2.** outrageous or atrocious. – **enormity**, *n.*

enough /ə'nʌf, i-/ *adj.* **1.** adequate for the want or need; sufficient. – *n.* **2.** an adequate quantity or number. – *adv.* **3.** sufficiently.

enquire /ɪn'kwaɪə, ən-, ɛn-/ *v.i.*, **-quired**, **-quiring**. → **inquire**.

enrage /ɛn'reɪdʒ, ən-/ *v.t.*, **-raged**, **-raging**. to put into a rage; infuriate.

enrapture /ɛn'ræptʃə, ən-/ *v.t.*, **-tured**, **-turing**. to delight beyond measure.

enrich /ɛn'rɪtʃ, ən-/ *v.t.* **1.** to supply with riches. **2.** to enhance; make finer.

enrol /ɛn'roʊl, ən-/ *v.t.*, **-rolled**, **-rolling**. to insert the name of (a person) in a roll or register. – **enrolment**, *n.*

ensconce /ɛn'skɒns, ən-/ *v.t.*, **-sconced**, **-sconcing**. to settle securely or snugly.

ensemble /ɒn'sɒmbəl/ *n.* **1.** all the parts of a thing taken together. **2.** the entire costume of an individual, especially when all the parts are in harmony.

enshrine /ɛn'ʃraɪn, ən-/ *v.t.*, **-shrined**, **-shrining**. to enclose in or as in a shrine.

ensign /'ɛnsaɪn, 'ɛnsən/ *n.* **1.** a flag or banner, as of a nation. **2.** any sign, token, or emblem.

enslave /ɛn'sleɪv, ən-/ *v.t.*, **-slaved**, **-slaving**. to make a slave of.

ensnare /ɛn'snɛə, ən-/ *v.t.*, **-snared**, **-snaring**. to trap.

ensue /ɛn'sju, ən-/ *v.i.*, **-sued**, **-suing**. to follow, especially in immediate succession.

ensure /ɛn'ʃɔ, ən-/ *v.t.*, **-sured**, **-suring**. to make sure or certain to come, occur, etc.

-ent a suffix equivalent to **-ant**.

entail /ɛn'teɪl, ən-/ *v.t.* **1.** to bring on or involve by necessity or consequences. **2.** to cause (anything) to descend to a fixed series of possessors.

entangle /ɛn'tæŋgəl, ən-/ *v.t.*, **-gled**, **-gling**. to involve in difficulties, etc.

entente /ɒn'tɒnt/ *n.* an understanding or agreement between parties.

enter /'ɛntə/ *v.i.* **1.** to come or go in. **2.** to be admitted. **3.** to make a beginning (often fol. by *on* or *upon*). – *v.t.* **4.** to come or go into. **5.** to become a member of, or join. **6.** to make a record of, as in a register. **7.** *Law* to place in regular form before a court, as a writ.

entero- a word element meaning 'intestine'.

enterprise /'ɛntəpraɪz/ *n.* **1.** a project, especially one that requires boldness or energy. **2.** boldness or readiness in undertaking. **3.** a company organised for commercial purposes.

enterprise agreement *n.* an agreement between the employees and employers of an enterprise regarding pay and working conditions, which results from enterprise bargaining.

enterprise bargaining *n.* bargaining on wages and conditions conducted between the employer and employees of an enterprise.

entertain /ɛntə'teɪn/ *v.t.* **1.** to hold the attention of agreeably; divert; amuse. **2.** to receive as a guest. **3.** to admit into the mind; consider. – **entertainment**, *n.*

enthral /ɛn'θrɔl, ən-/ *v.t.*, **-thralled**, **-thralling**. to captivate; charm.

enthusiasm /ɛn'θuziæzəm, -'θjuz-, ən-/ *n.* absorbing or controlling possession of the mind by any interest or pursuit; lively interest. – **enthusiast**, *n.* – **enthusiastic**, *adj.* – **enthuse**, *v.*

entice /ɛn'taɪs, ən-/ *v.t.*, **-ticed**, **-ticing**. to draw on by exciting hope or desire.

entire /ɛn'taɪə, ən-/ *adj.* **1.** whole; complete. **2.** full or thorough. – **entirety**, *n.*

entitle /ɛn'taɪtl, ən-/ *v.t.*, **-tled**, **-tling**. to give (a person or thing) a title, right, or claim to something. – **entitlement**, *n.*

entitlement issue *n.* a method of raising capital, whereby existing shareholders may buy new shares, usually below market price, which are usually issued in a predetermined ratio to current shareholdings, and cannot be sold or transferred; non-renounceable issue.

entity /'ɛntəti/ *n., pl.* **-ties**. something that has a real existence; a thing.

ento- variant of **endo-**.

entomology /ɛntə'mɒlədʒi/ *n.* the branch of zoology that deals with insects.

entourage /ɒntu'radʒ, -raʒ/ *n.* any group of people accompanying or assisting someone.

entrails /'ɛntreɪlz/ *pl. n.* the internal parts of the trunk of an animal body.

entrance[1] /'ɛntrəns/ *n.* **1.** the act of entering. **2.** a point or place of entering.

entrance[2] /ɛn'træns, -'trans, ən-/ *v.t.*, **-tranced**, **-trancing**. to fill with delight.

entrant /'ɛntrənt/ *n.* a competitor in a contest.

entreat /ɛn'trit, ən-/ *v.t.* to make supplication to; beseech; implore. – **entreaty**, *n.*

entrench /ɛn'trɛntʃ, ən-/ *v.t.* **1.** to dig trenches for defensive purposes around (oneself, a military position, etc.). **2.** to establish so strongly or securely as to make any change very difficult.

entrepreneur /ɒntrəprə'nɜ/ *n.* someone who organises and manages any enterprise.

entrust /ɛn'trʌst, ən-/ *v.t.* **1.** to invest with a trust or responsibility. **2.** to commit (something) in trust (*to*).

entry /'ɛntri/ *n., pl.* **-tries**. **1.** an act of entering. **2.** a place of entrance.

entwine /ɛn'twaɪn, ən-/ *v.t., v.i.,* **-twined**, **-twining**. to twine with, about, or around.

enumerate /ə'njuməreɪt, i-/ *v.t.,* **-rated**, **-rating**. to name one by one.

enunciate /ə'nʌnsieɪt, i-/ *v.t.,* **-ated**, **-ating**. to utter or pronounce (words, etc.), especially in a particular manner.

envelop /ɛn'vɛləp, ən-/ *v.t.* to wrap up in or as in a covering.

envelope /'ɛnvəloʊp, 'ɒn-/ *n.* a cover for a letter, etc., usually sealable.

enviable /'ɛnviəbəl/ *adj.* that is to be envied; highly desirable.

envious /'ɛnviəs/ *adj.* full of envy.

environment /ɛn'vaɪrənmənt, ən-/ *n.* the aggregate of surrounding things, conditions, or influences. – **environmental**, *adj.*

environs /ɛn'vaɪrənz, ən-/ *pl. n.* surrounding parts or districts.

envisage /ɛn'vɪzədʒ, -zɪdʒ, ən-/ *v.t.,* **-aged**, **-aging**. to contemplate.

envoy /'ɛnvɔɪ/ *n.* a diplomatic agent.

envy /'ɛnvi/ *n., pl.* **-vies**, *v.,* **-vied**, **-vying**. – *n.* **1.** a feeling of discontent at seeing another's superiority, advantages, or success. **2.** desire for some advantage possessed by another. – *v.t.* **3.** to regard with envy.

enzyme /'ɛnzaɪm/ *n.* any protein capable of catalysing a chemical reaction necessary to the cell.

eo- a word element meaning 'early'.

eon /'iɒn/ *n.* → **aeon**.

-eous variant of **-ous**.

epaulet /'ɛpəlɛt, -lət/ *n.* an ornamental shoulder piece worn on uniforms. Also, **epaulette**.

ephemeral /ə'fɛmərəl, i-/ *adj.* short-lived; transitory.

epi- a prefix meaning 'on', 'to', 'against', 'above', 'near', 'after', 'in addition to'. Also, **ep-**, **eph-**.

epic /'ɛpɪk/ *adj.* **1.** of or relating to poetry dealing with a series of heroic achievements or events, in a long narrative with elevated style. – *n.* **2.** an epic poem. **3.** any novel or film resembling an epic.

epicure /'ɛpikjuə, 'ɛpə-/ *n.* someone who cultivates a refined taste, as in food, drink, art, music, etc. – **epicurean**, *adj, n.*

epidemic /ɛpə'dɛmɪk/ *adj.* **1.** affecting at the same time a large number of people in a locality, as a disease. – *n.* **2.** a temporary prevalence of a disease.

epidermis /ɛpi'dɜməs, ɛpə-, 'ɛpidɜməs/ *n.* *Anatomy* the outer layer of the skin. – **epidermal**, *adj.*

epigram /'ɛpigræm, 'ɛpə-/ *n.* any witty or pointed saying tersely expressed.

epigraph /'ɛpigræf, -graf, 'ɛpə-/ *n.* an inscription, especially on a building, statue, etc.

epilepsy /'ɛpəlɛpsi/ *n.* a nervous disease usually characterised by convulsions. – **epileptic**, *adj., n.*

epilogue /'ɛpilɒg, 'ɛpə-/ *n.* a speech, usually in verse, by one of the actors after the conclusion of a play.

episcopal /ə'pɪskəpəl/ *adj.* relating to a bishop.

episode /'ɛpəsoʊd/ *n.* **1.** an incident in the course of a series of events. **2.** (in radio, television, etc.) any of the separate programs constituting a serial. – **episodic**, *adj.*

epistemology /əpɪstə'mɒlədʒi/ *n.* the branch of philosophy which investigates the origin, nature, methods, and limits of human knowledge.

epistle /ə'pɪsəl/ *n.* a letter, especially one of formal or didactic character.

epitaph /'ɛpitaf, 'ɛpə-/ *n.* a commemorative inscription on a tomb, etc.

epithet /'ɛpəθɛt, ɛpi-, -θət/ *n.* a term applied to a person or thing to express an attribute.

epitome /ə'pɪtəmi/ *n.* **1.** a summary or condensed account. **2.** a condensed representation or typical characteristic of something. – **epitomise = epitomize**, *v.*

epoch /'ipɒk, 'ɛpɒk/ *n.* a particular period of time as marked by distinctive character, events, etc.

EPROM /'iprɒm/ *n.* a computer memory chip whose contents can be erased and reprogrammed for other purposes.

equable /'ɛkwəbəl/ *adj.* **1.** uniform, as motion or temperature. **2.** tranquil, as the mind.

equal /'ikwəl/ *adj., n., v.,* **equalled**, **equalling**. – *adj.* **1.** like or alike in quantity, degree, value, etc. **2.** evenly proportioned or balanced. **3.** having adequate powers, ability, or means. – *n.* **4.** someone who or that which is equal. – *v.t.* **5.** to be or become equal to. – **equalise = equalize**, *v.* – **equality**, *n.*

equalisation reserve *n.* a reserve held by an insurer to cover an underwriting loss in whole or in part.

equanimity /ikwə'nɪməti, ɛkwə-/ *n.* evenness of mind or temper.

equate /i'kweɪt, ə-/ *v.t.,* **equated**, **equating**. **1.** to state the equality of or between. **2.** to make such correction or allowance in as will reduce to a common standard of comparison. **3.** to regard, treat, or represent as equivalent.

equation /i'kweɪʒən, ə-, -ʃən/ *n.* *Mathematics* an expression of, or a proposition asserting, the equality of two quantities, employing the sign = between them.

equator /ə'kweɪtə, i-/ *n.* the great circle of the earth, equidistant from the North and South Poles. – **equatorial**, *adj.*

equerry /'ɛkwəri/ *n.* **1.** formerly, an officer of a royal or similar household, charged with the care of the horses. **2.** an officer who attends on the British sovereign or on a representative of the sovereign, such as an Australian state governor.

equestrian /ə'kwɛstriən, i-/ *adj.* of or relating to horsemen or horsemanship.

equi- a word element meaning 'equal'.

equilateral /ikwə'lætərəl/ *adj.* having all the sides equal.

equilibrium /ikwə'lɪbriəm, ɛ-/ *n.* a state of rest due to the action of forces that counteract each other.

equine /'ɛkwaɪn, i-/ *adj.* **1.** of or resembling a horse. – *n.* **2.** a horse.

equinox /'ikwənɒks, ɛ-/ *n.* the time when the sun crosses the plane of the earth's equator, making night and day all over the earth of equal length. – **equinoctial**, *adj.*.

equip /ə'kwɪp, i-/ *v.t.*, **equipped**, **equipping**. to furnish or provide with whatever is needed. – **equipment**, *n.*

equity /'ɛkwəti/ *n.*, *pl.* **-ties**. **1.** fairness; impartiality. **2.** the interest of a shareholder, of common stock in a company. **3.** (*pl.*) stocks and shares not bearing fixed interest. **4.** the amount by which the market value of a debtor's securities exceeds his or her indebtedness. – **equitable**, *adj.*

equity of redemption *n.* the right of a mortgagor to redeem the mortgaged property by repaying the debt, within a certain time after the due date.

equivalent /ə'kwɪvələnt, i-/ *adj.* **1.** equal in value, measure, force, effect, significance, etc. **2.** corresponding in position, function, etc. – *n.* **3.** that which is equivalent.

equivocal /ə'kwɪvəkəl, i-/ *adj.* questionable; dubious; suspicious.

equivocate /ə'kwɪvəkeɪt, i-/ *v.i.*, **-cated**, **-cating**. to use equivocal or ambiguous expressions, especially in order to mislead.

-er[1] a suffix serving as the regular English formative of agent nouns, as in *bearer, creeper, employer, harvester, teacher, theoriser.*

-er[2] a suffix of nouns denoting persons or things concerned or connected with something, as in *grocer, officer.*

-er[3] a suffix forming the comparative degree of adjectives and adverbs, as in *harder, smaller, faster.*

-er[4] a termination of certain nouns denoting action or process, as in *dinner, rejoinder, remainder.*

era /'ɪərə/ *n.* **1.** a period of time marked by distinctive character, events, etc. **2.** a system of chronological notation reckoned from a given date.

eradicate /ə'rædəkeɪt, i-/ *v.t.*, **-cated**, **-cating**. to remove or destroy utterly.

erase /ə'reɪz, i-/ *v.t.*, **erased**, **erasing**. to rub or scrape out, as written letters, etc.

erect /ə'rɛkt, i-/ *adj.* **1.** upright in position or posture. – *v.t.* **2.** to build; construct; raise. **3.** to raise and set in an upright or perpendicular position. – **erection**, *n.*

erg /ɜg/ *n.* a unit of work or energy in the centimetre-gram-second system.

ergo /'ɜgoʊ/ *conj.*, *adv.* therefore.

ergonomics /ɜgə'nɒmɪks, ɜgoʊ-/ *n.* the study of the relationship between workers and their working environment.

ermine /'ɜmən/ *n.*, *pl.* **-mines**, (*esp. collectively*) **-mine**. a weasel of northern regions, which turns white in winter. See **stoat**.

-ern *n.* an adjectival suffix occurring in *northern*, etc.

erode /ə'roʊd, i-/ *v.t.*, **eroded**, **eroding**. to wear away. – **erosion**, *n.* – **erosive**, *adj.*

erogenous /ə'rɒdʒənəs, ɛ-, i-/ *adj.* arousing or tending to arouse sexual desire. – **erogeneity**, *n.*

erotic /ə'rɒtɪk, ɛ-, i-/ *adj.* **1.** of or relating to sexual love. **2.** arousing or satisfying sexual desire.

err /ɜ/ *v.i.* to be mistaken or incorrect.

errand /'ɛrənd/ *n.* a short journey for a specific purpose.

errant /'ɛrənt/ *adj.* journeying or travelling. – **errantry**, *n.*

erratic /ə'rætɪk, i-/ *adj.* **1.** irregular in conduct or opinion. **2.** having no certain course; wandering.

erroneous /ə'roʊniəs/ *adj.* containing error; mistaken; incorrect.

error /'ɛrə/ *n.* **1.** deviation from accuracy or correctness. **2.** a mistake.

ersatz /'ɜzæts, 'ɛəz-, -zats/ *adj.* serving as a substitute.

erstwhile /'ɜstwaɪl/ *adj.* former.

erudition /ɛrə'dɪʃən/ *n.* learning; scholarship. – **erudite**, *adj.*

erupt /ə'rʌpt, i-/ *v.i.* **1.** (of a volcano, geyser, etc.) to eject matter. **2.** to break out suddenly or violently, as if from restraint. – **eruption**, *n.*

-ery a suffix of nouns denoting occupation, business, calling, or condition, place or establishment, goods or products, things collectively, qualities, actions, etc., as in *archery, bakery, cutlery, fishery, grocery.*

erythro- a word element meaning 'red'.

erythrocyte /ə'rɪθrəsaɪt, ə'rɪθroʊ-/ *n.* one of the red corpuscles of the blood.

-es a variant of **-s**[2] and **-s**[3] after *s, z, ch, sh,* and in those nouns ending in *-f* which have *-v-* in the plural. Cf. **-ies**.

escalate /'ɛskəleɪt/ *v.t.*, *v.i.*, **-lated**, **-lating**. to intensify. – **escalation**, *n.*

escalation clause *n.* a provision in a contract allowing for adjustments up or down under specific economic conditions, as in the cost of living in a wage agreement. Also, **escalator clause**.

escalator /'ɛskəleɪtə/ *n.* a continuously moving staircase.

escapade /'ɛskəpeɪd, ɛskə'peɪd/ *n.* a reckless proceeding; a wild prank.

escape /əs'keɪp/ *v.*, **-caped**, **-caping**, *n.* – *v.i.* **1.** to slip or get away, as from confinement or restraint. – *v.t.* **2.** to slip away from or elude (pursuers, captors, etc.). **3.** to fail to be noticed or recollected by (a person). – *n.* **4.** an act or instance of escaping. – **escapee**, **escaper**, *n.*

escarpment /əs'kapmənt/ *n.* a long, cliff-like ridge of rock, or the like.

-esce a suffix of verbs meaning to begin to be or do something, as in *convalesce.*

-escence a suffix of nouns denoting action or process, change, state, or condition, etc., and corresponding to verbs ending in *-esce* or adjectives ending in *-escent*, as in *convalescence.*

escheat /əs'tʃit/ *n.* the reversion of property to the owner or to the crown when there is a failure of persons legally qualified to inherit or to claim.

eschew /əs'tʃu, ɛs-/ *v.t.* to abstain from.

escort /'ɛskɔt/ *n.*, /əs'kɔt, ɛs-/ *v.* – *n.* **1.** one or more people or things accompanying another or others for protection, guidance, or courtesy. – *v.t.* **2.** to attend or accompany as an escort.

escrow /'ɛskroʊ, əs'kroʊ, ɛs-/ *n.* a contract, deed, bond, or other written agreement deposited with a third person, by whom it is to be delivered to the grantee or promisee on the fulfilment of some condition.

escutcheon /əs'kʌtʃən/ *n.* an armorial shield.

-ese a noun and adjective suffix referring to locality, nationality, language, literary style, etc., as in *Japanese*, *journalese*.

esky /'ɛski/ *n.*, *pl.* **eskies**. a portable icebox. Also, **Esky**.

ESL /i ɛs 'ɛl/ English as a second language.

esoteric /ɛsə'tɛrɪk, ɛsoʊ-/ *adj.* understood by or meant for a select few.

ESP /i ɛs 'pi/ *n.* extrasensory perception; perception or communication outside of normal sensory activity, as in telepathy and clairvoyance. Also, **e.s.p**.

especial /əs'pɛʃəl/ *adj.* **1.** special; exceptional. **2.** of a particular kind. – **especially**, *adv.*

espionage /'ɛspiənaʒ, -nadʒ/ *n.* the practice of spying on others.

esplanade /'ɛsplənеɪd, -nad/ *n.* any open level space serving for public walks, etc.

espouse /əs'paʊz, ɛs-/ *v.t.*, **-poused**, **-pousing**. to make one's own, adopt, or embrace, as a cause. – **espousal**, *n.*

espy /əs'paɪ, ɛs-/ *v.t.*, **-pied**, **-pying**. to see at a distance; catch sight of; detect.

-esque an adjective suffix indicating style, manner, or distinctive character.

Esquire /əs'kwaɪə, 'ɛs-/ *n.* (a polite title, usually abbreviated to *Esq.*, after a man's last name. *Mr* or *Dr* is omitted when it is used).

-ess a suffix forming distinctively feminine nouns, as *countess*, *hostess*, *lioness*.

essay /'ɛseɪ/ *for def. 1*, /'ɛseɪ, ɛ'seɪ/ *for def. 2* *n.*, /ɛ'seɪ/ *v.* – *n.* **1.** a short literary composition on a particular subject. **2.** an attempt. – *v.t.* **3.** to try; attempt. **4.** to put to the test; make trial of.

essence /'ɛsəns/ *n.* **1.** intrinsic nature; important elements or features of a thing. **2.** a concentrated extract.

essential /ə'sɛnʃəl/ *adj.* **1.** absolutely necessary. **2.** relating to or constituting the essence of a thing. – *n.* **3.** an indispensable element.

-est a suffix forming the superlative degree of adjectives and adverbs, as in *warmest*, *fastest*, *soonest*.

establish /əs'tæblɪʃ/ *v.t.* **1.** to set up on a firm or permanent basis; institute; found. **2.** to settle or install in a position, business, etc. **3.** to show to be valid or well grounded; prove.

establishment /əs'tæblɪʃmənt, ɛs-/ *n.* **1.** a place of business or residence. **2.** an institution.

establishment award *n.* an industrial award covering all employees, whatever their classification, in a particular establishment, and generally designed to provide for a degree of uniformity in conditions throughout that establishment.

estate /ə'steɪt, ɛs-/ *n.* **1.** a piece of landed property, especially one of large extent. **2.** *Law* **a.** property or possessions. **b.** the property of a deceased person, a bankrupt, etc., viewed as an aggregate. **3.** a housing development. **4.** condition or circumstances with reference to worldly prosperity, estimation, etc.; social status or rank.

estate agent *n.* → **real estate agent**.

esteem /əs'tim/ *v.t.* **1.** to regard highly or favourably. **2.** to set a value on; value. – *n.* **3.** favourable opinion or judgment; respect or regard.

ester /'ɛstə/ *n.* a compound formed by the reaction between an acid and an alcohol.

estimable /'ɛstəməbəl/ *adj.* **1.** worthy of esteem. **2.** capable of being estimated.

estimate /'ɛstəmeɪt/ *v.*, **-mated**, **-mating** /'ɛstəmət/. *n.* – *v.t.* **1.** to form an approximate judgment or opinion regarding the value, amount, size, weight, etc., of; calculate approximately. – *n.* **2.** an approximate judgment or calculation. – **estimation**, *n.*

estrange /ə'streɪndʒ/ *v.t.*, **estranged**, **estranging**. to alienate the affections of.

estuary /'ɛstʃuəri, 'ɛstʃəri/ *n.*, *pl.* **-aries**. **1.** that part of the mouth of a river in which its current meets the sea's tides. **2.** an arm or inlet of the sea.

et cetera /ət 'sɛtrə, ɛt-, -ərə/ and others; and so forth; and so on. *Abbrev.*: etc.

etch /ɛtʃ/ *v.t.* **1.** to engrave (metals, etc.) with an acid or the like. **2.** to fix in the memory.

eternity /ə'tɜnəti, i-/ *n.*, *pl.* **-ties**. infinite time; duration without beginning or end. – **eternal**, *adj.*

-eth variant of **-th**[2] after a vowel.

ether /'iθə/ *n.* **1.** *Chemistry* a volatile, flammable, colourless liquid used as an anaesthetic. **2.** the upper regions of space; the clear sky; the heavens.

ethereal /ə'θɪəriəl, i-/ *adj.* **1.** light, airy or tenuous. **2.** heavenly or celestial.

ethical /'ɛθɪkəl/ *adj.* relating to or dealing with morals or the principles of morality.

ethics /'ɛθɪks/ *pl. n.* a system of moral principles, by which human actions and proposals may be judged good or bad or right or wrong.

ethnic /'ɛθnɪk/ *adj.* **1.** relating to or peculiar to a population, especially to a speech group, loosely also to a race. **2.** of or relating to members of the community who are migrants or the descendants of migrants and whose native language is not English.

ethno- a word element meaning 'race', 'nation'.

ethnography /ɛθ'nɒgrəfi/ *n.* the scientific description and classification of the various cultural and racial groups of humankind.

ethnology /ɛθ'nɒlədʒi/ *n.* the science that deals with the distinctive subdivisions of humankind, their origin, relations, speech, institutions, etc.

ethos /'iθɒs/ *n.* *Sociology* the fundamental spiritual characteristics of a culture.

etiquette /'ɛtikət/ *n.* conventional requirements as to social behaviour.

-ette a noun suffix, occurring especially: **1.** with the original diminutive force, as in *cigarette.* **2.** as a distinctively feminine ending, as in *coquette, usherette.* **3.** in trademarks of imitations or substitutes, as in *leatherette.*

etymology /ɛtə'mɒlədʒi/ *n., pl.* **-gies**. **1.** the study of historical linguistic change, especially as applied to individual words. **2.** the derivation of a word.

eu- a prefix meaning 'good', 'well'.

eucalypt /'jukəlɪpt/ *n.* any eucalyptus.

eucalyptus /jukə'lɪptəs/ *n., pl.* **-tuses**, **-ti** /-taɪ/. any of many tall trees native to the Australian region.

Eucharist /'jukərəst/ *n.* (in Christianity) the celebration of the Lord's Supper.

eugenic /ju'dʒinɪk, -'dʒɛn-/ *adj.* of or bringing about improvement in the type of offspring produced.

eulogy /'julədʒi/ *n., pl.* **-gies**. a speech or writing in praise of a person or thing. – **eulogise = eulogize**, *v.* – **eulogistic**, *adj.*

eunuch /'junək/ *n.* a castrated man.

euphemism /'jufəmɪzəm/ *n.* **1.** the substitution of a mild, indirect, or vague expression for a harsh or blunt one. **2.** the expression so substituted. – **euphemistic**, *adj.*

euphony /'jufəni/ *n., pl.* **-nies**. agreeableness of sound. – **euphonic**, **euphonious**, *adj.*

euphoria /ju'fɔriə/ *n.* a feeling or state of well-being, especially one of unnatural elation. – **euphoric**, *adj.*

eureka /ju'rikə/ *interj.* (an exclamation of triumph at a discovery).

eury- a word element meaning 'broad'.

euthanasia /juθə'neɪʒə/ *n.* **1.** painless death. **2.** the putting to death of a person suffering from an incurable and painful disease.

eutrophic /ju'troʊfɪk/ *adj.* (of rivers or lakes) having high levels of nutrients, as nitrogen and phosphorus, encouraging the growth of algae, etc. – **eutrophication**, *n.*

evacuate /ə'vækjueɪt/ *v.t.,* **-ated**, **-ating**. **1.** to leave empty; vacate. **2.** to move (persons or things) from a threatened place, disaster area, etc.

evade /ə'veɪd, i-/ *v.t.,* **evaded**, **evading**. **1.** to escape from by trickery or cleverness. **2.** to avoid answering directly. **3.** to elude.

evaluate /ə'væljueɪt, i-/ *v.t.,* **-ated**, **-ating**. to ascertain the value of.

evangelist /i'vændʒələst/ *n.* someone who spreads the Christian gospel. – **evangelical**, *adj.*

evaporate /ə'væpəreɪt, i-/ *v.i.,* **-rated**, **-rating**. to turn to vapour; pass off in vapour. – **evaporation**, *n.*

evasion /ə'veɪʒən, i-/ *n.* the act of escaping something by trickery or cleverness. – **evasive**, *adj.*

eve /iv/ *n.* the evening, or often the day, before a particular date or event.

even /'ivən/ *adj.* **1.** level; flat; without irregularities; smooth. **2.** on the same level; in the same plane or line; parallel. **3.** uniform in action, character, or quality. **4.** equal in measure or quantity. **5.** divisible by 2 (opposed to *odd*). **6.** leaving no balance of debt on either side. **7.** equitable, impartial, or fair. – *adv.* **8.** evenly. **9.** still; yet (used to emphasise a comparative). **10.** indeed (used for stressing identity or truth of something). – *v.t.* **11.** to make even; level; smooth.

evening /'ivnɪŋ/ *n.* the latter part of the day and the early part of the night.

event /ə'vɛnt, i-/ *n.* anything that happens; an occurrence, especially one of some importance.

eventful /ə'vɛntfəl, i-/ *adj.* full of events or incidents, especially striking ones.

eventual /ə'vɛntʃəl, -tʃuəl/ *adj.* consequent; ultimate.

eventuality /əvɛntʃu'æləti/ *n., pl.* **-ties**. a contingent event; a possible occurrence or circumstance.

eventuate /ə'vɛntʃueɪt/ *v.i.,* **-ated**, **-ating**. to come about.

ever /'ɛvə/ *adv.* **1.** at all times. **2.** continuously. **3.** at any time.

every /'ɛvri/ *adj.* **1.** each (referring one by one to all the members of an aggregate). **2.** all possible.

everybody /'ɛvribɒdi/ *pron.* every person.

everyday /'ɛvrideɪ/ *adj.* **1.** daily. **2.** ordinary; commonplace.

everyone /'ɛvriwʌn/ *pron.* every person.

everything /'ɛvriθɪŋ/ *pron.* every thing or particular of an aggregate or total; all.

everywhere /'ɛvriwɛə/ *adv.* in every place.

evict /ə'vɪkt, i-/ *v.t.* to expel (a person, especially a tenant) from land, a building, etc., by legal process. – **eviction**, *n.*

evidence /'ɛvədəns/ *n.* **1.** that which tends to prove or disprove something. **2.** something that makes evident; an indication or sign.

evident /'ɛvədənt/ *adj.* plain or clear to the sight or understanding.

evil /'ivəl/ *adj.* **1.** violating or inconsistent with the moral law; wicked. **2.** harmful; injurious. **3.** characterised by anger, irascibility, etc. – *n.* **4.** that which is evil.

evince /ə'vɪns, i-/ *v.t.,* **evinced**, **evincing**. to show clearly; make evident.

evoke /ə'voʊk, i-/ *v.t.,* **evoked**, **evoking**. **1.** to call up, or produce (memories, feelings, etc.). **2.** to provoke, or elicit. – **evocation**, *n.* – **evocative**, *adj.*

evolution /ɛvə'luʃən, ivə-/ *n.* **1.** any process of formation or growth; development. **2.** *Biology* the continuous genetic adaptation of organisms or species to the environment.

evolve /ə'vɒlv, i-/ *v.t., v.i.,* **evolved**, **evolving**. to develop gradually.

ewe /ju/ *n.* a female sheep.

ewer /'juə/ *n.* a pitcher with a wide spout.

ex /ɛks/ *prep.* **1.** *Finance* without, not including, or without the right to have. **2.** *Commerce* out of; free out of (free of charges until the time of removal out of the warehouse, ship, etc.).

ex-[1] a prefix meaning 'out of', 'from', and hence 'utterly', 'thoroughly', and sometimes serving to impart a negative force or to indicate a former title, status, etc.

ex-[2] variant of **exo-**.

exacerbate /ɛk'sæsəbeɪt/ *v.t.*, **-bated**, **-bating**. to increase the bitterness or violence of (disease, ill feeling, etc.).

exact /əg'zækt, ɛg-/ *adj.* **1.** strictly accurate or correct. **2.** admitting of no deviation, as laws, discipline, etc.; strict or rigorous. – *v.t.* **3.** to call for, demand, or require. **4.** to force or compel the payment, yielding, or performance of. – **exactitude**, **exactness**, *n.*

exaggerate /əg'zædʒəreɪt, ɛg-/ *v.*, **-rated**, **-rating**. – *v.t.* **1.** to magnify beyond the limits of truth. – *v.i.* **2.** to employ exaggeration, as in speech or writing. – **exaggeration**, *n.*

exalt /əg'zɔlt, ɛg-/ *v.t.* **1.** to elevate in rank, honour, power, character, quality, etc. **2.** to praise; extol. – **exaltation**, *n.*

exam /əg'zæm, ɛg-/ *n.* an examination.

examine /əg'zæmən, ɛg-/ *v.t.*, **-ined**, **-ining**. **1.** to inspect or scrutinise carefully; inquire into or investigate. **2.** to test the knowledge, etc., of, as by questions. **3.** to interrogate. – **examination**, *n.*

example /əg'zæmpəl, ɛg-/ *n.* **1.** one of a number of things, or a part of something, taken to show the character of the whole. **2.** something to be imitated; a pattern or model. **3.** an instance serving for illustration; a specimen.

exasperate /əg'zæspəreɪt, ɛg-/ *v.t.*, **-rated**, **-rating**. to irritate to a high degree. – **exasperation**, *n.*

excavate /'ɛkskəveɪt/ *v.t.*, **-vated**, **-vating**. to make a hole or cavity in, as by digging. – **excavation**, *n.*

exceed /ək'sid, ɛk-/ *v.t.* to go beyond in quantity, degree, rate, etc.

excel /ək'sɛl, ɛk-/ *v.t.*, *v.i.*, **-celled**, **-celling**. to surpass others.

excellence /'ɛksələns/ *n.* the fact or state of excelling; superiority; eminence. – **excellent**, *adj.*

excellency /'ɛksələnsi/ *n.*, *pl.* **-cies**. (*usu. cap.*) a title of honour given to certain high officials, as governors, etc.

except[1] /ək'sɛpt, ɛk-/ *prep.* **1.** with the exclusion of; excluding. – *conj.* **2.** with the exception (that).

except[2] /ək'sɛpt, ɛk-/ *v.t.* to exclude.

exception /ək'sɛpʃən, ɛk-/ *n.* **1.** something excepted; an instance or case not conforming to the general rule. **2.** opposition of opinion; objection; demurral.

exceptional /ək'sɛpʃənəl, ɛk-/ *adj.* **1.** unusual; extraordinary. **2.** extraordinarily good or clever.

excerpt *n.* a passage taken out of a book or the like.

excess /ək'sɛs, 'ɛk-/ *n.* **1.** the amount or degree by which one thing exceeds another. **2.** an extreme or excessive amount or degree. **3.** immoderate indulgence. – **excessive**, *adj.*

exchange /əks'tʃeɪndʒ, ɛk-/ *v.*, **-changed**, **-changing**, *n.* – *v.t.* **1.** to replace by another or something else; change for another. – *n.* **2.** the act or process of exchanging. **3.** a place for buying and selling commodities, securities, etc., typically open only to members. **4.** a central office or central station. **5.** the method or system by which debits and credits in different places are settled without the actual transference of money, by means of documents representing money values. **6.** the discharge of obligations in different places by the transfer of credits. **7.** the reciprocal transference of equivalent sums of money, as in the currencies of two different countries. **8.** the giving or receiving of a sum of money in one place for a bill ordering the payment of an equivalent sum in another. **9.** the varying rate or sum, in one currency, given for a fixed sum in another currency; rate of exchange. **10.** the amount of the difference in value between two or more currencies, or between the values of the same currency at two or more places. **11.** the cheques, drafts, etc., exchanged at a clearing house. **12.** → **stock exchange**.

exchange rate *n.* in international money markets, the rate of exchange of one currency for another.

exchequer /əks'tʃɛkə/ *n.* a treasury, as of a state or nation.

excise[1] /'ɛksaɪz/ *n.* **1.** an inland tax or duty on certain commodities, as spirits, tobacco, etc., levied on their manufacture, sale, or consumption within the country. **2.** a tax levied for a licence to carry on certain employments, pursue certain sports, etc. **3.** that branch of the civil service which collects excise duties. – **excisable**, *adj.*

excise[2] /ɛk'saɪz/ *v.t.*, **-cised**, **-cising**. to cut out or off. – **excision**, *n.*

excite /ək'saɪt, ɛk-/ *v.t.*, **-cited**, **-citing**. **1.** to arouse or stir up the feelings of. **2.** to stir to action; stir up. **3.** *Physiology* to stimulate. – **excitement**, *n.* – **excitation**, *n.*

exclaim /əks'kleɪm, ɛks-/ *v.i.* to cry out or speak suddenly and vehemently, as in surprise, strong emotion, protest, etc. – **exclamation**, *n.*

exclude /əks'klud, ɛks-/ *v.t.*, **-cluded**, **-cluding**. to shut or keep out; prevent the entrance of. – **exclusion**, *n.*

exclusive /əks'klusɪv, ɛks-/ *adj.* **1.** excluding from consideration or account. **2.** shutting out all other activities. **3.** single or sole. **4.** available through only one channel of marketing. **5.** disposed to resist the admission of outsiders to association, intimacy, etc. **6.** *Colloquial* fashionable.

excommunicate /ɛkskə'mjunəkeɪt/ *v.t.*, **-cated**, **-cating**. to cut off from communion or membership, especially from the church.

excrement /'ɛkskrəmənt/ *n.* waste matter discharged from the body, especially the faeces.

excrescence /ɛks'krɛsəns/ *n.* abnormal growth or increase.

excrete /əks'krit, ɛks-/ *v.t.*, **-creted**, **-creting**. to separate and eliminate from the blood or tissues, as waste matter. – **excreta**, *pl. n.* – **excretion**, *n.* – **excretory**, *adj.*

excruciating /əks'kruʃieɪtɪŋ, ɛks-/ *adj.* extremely painful; causing extreme suffering; torturing.

exculpate /'ɛkskʌlpeɪt, ɛks'kʌlpeɪt/ *v.t.*, **-pated**, **-pating**. to free from blame.

excursion /ək'skɜʃən, ɛk-, -ʒən/ *n.* **1.** a short journey or trip for a special purpose.

2. deviation or digression.

excuse /ək'skjuz, ɛk-/ *v.*, **-cused**, **-cusing** /ək'skjus/. *n.* – *v.t.* **1.** to pardon or forgive. **2.** to apologise for; seek to remove the blame of. **3.** to serve as an apology or justification for; justify. **4.** to release from an obligation or duty. – *n.* **5.** that which is offered as a reason for being excused. **6.** an inferior or inadequate example of something specified.

ex date *n. Stock Exchange* the date on which shares change from being quoted *cum* (*dividend*) to *ex* (*dividend*).

ex dividend *adj. Stock Exchange* without dividend, the buyer of the stock being not entitled to the dividend.

execrable /'ɛksəkrəbəl/ *adj.* abominable.

execute /'ɛksəkjut/ *v.t.*, **-cuted**, **-cuting**. **1.** to carry out; accomplish. **2.** to put to death according to law. – **execution**, *n.*

executive /əg'zɛkjətɪv, ɛg-/ *adj.* **1.** of the kind requisite for practical performance or direction. **2.** charged with or relating to execution of laws, or administration of affairs. – *n.* **3.** a person or body having administrative authority, as in a company. **4.** the body of people, members of the governing party or parties, drawn from both houses of parliament, who form policy and control the appropriate government departments and instrumentalities, and who are responsible to parliament for such administration. Cf. **legislature**, **judiciary**.

executor /əg'zɛkjətə, ɛg-/ *n. Law* a person named by a testator in his or her will to carry out the provisions of the will. – **executrix**, *fem. n.*

exemplary /əg'zɛmpləri, ɛg-/ *adj.* **1.** worthy of imitation; commendable. **2.** serving as a model or pattern. **3.** serving as an example; typical.

exemplify /əg'zɛmpləfaɪ, ɛg-/ *v.t.*, **-fied**, **-fying**. **1.** to show or illustrate by example. **2.** to furnish, or serve as, an example of.

exempt /əg'zɛmpt, ɛg-/ *v.t.* to free from an obligation or liability to which others are subject; release. – **exemptible**, *adj.* – **exemption**, *n.*

exercise /'ɛksəsaɪz/ *n.*, *v.*, **-cised**, **-cising**. – *n.* **1.** bodily or mental exertion, especially for the sake of training or improvement. **2.** something done or performed as a means of practice or training. **3.** a putting into action, use, operation, or effect. – *v.t.* **4.** to put through exercises, or forms of practice or exertion, designed to train, develop, condition, etc. **5.** to put (faculties, rights, etc.) into action, practice, or use. **6.** to discharge (a function); perform. – *v.i.* **7.** to go through exercises; take bodily exercise.

exert /əg'zɜt, ɛg-/ *v.t.* to put forth, as power; exercise, as ability or influence.

exertion /əg'zɜʃən, ɛg-/ *n.* vigorous action or effort.

exhale /ɛks'heɪl/ *v.i.*, **-haled**, **-haling**. to emit breath or vapour.

exhaust /əg'zɔst, ɛg-/ *v.t.* **1.** to empty by drawing out the contents. **2.** to use up or consume completely; expend the whole of. **3.** to drain of strength or energy. – *n.* **4.** *Machinery* the escape of gases from the cylinder of an engine. – **exhaustion**, *n.* – **exhaustive**, *adj.*

exhibit /əg'zɪbət, ɛg-/ *v.t.* **1.** to offer or expose to view; present for inspection. **2.** to manifest or display. **3.** to place on show. – *n.* **4.** that which is exhibited. – **exhibition**, *n.*

exhibitionism /ɛksə'bɪʃənɪzəm/ *n.* a tendency to behave in such a way as to attract attention. – **exhibitionist**, *n.*

exhilarate /əg'zɪləreɪt, ɛg-/ *v.t.*, **-rated**, **-rating**. to enliven; stimulate; invigorate.

exhort /əg'zɔt, ɛg-/ *v.t.* to urge, advise, or caution earnestly; admonish urgently. – **exhortation**, *n.*

exhume /ɛks'hjum/ *v.t.*, **-humed**, **-huming**. to dig (something buried, especially a dead body) out of the earth.

exigent /'ɛksədʒənt/ *adj.* requiring immediate action or aid; urgent; pressing. – **exigency**, **exigence**, *n.*

exile /'ɛgzaɪl, 'ɛksaɪl/ *n.*, *v.*, **-iled**, **-iling**. – *n.* **1.** prolonged separation from one's country or home, as by stress of circumstances. **2.** expulsion from one's native land by authoritative decree. – *v.t.* **3.** to separate from country, home, etc.

exist /əg'zɪst, ɛg-, ɪg-/ *v.i.* **1.** to have actual being; be. **2.** to have life or animation; live.

existentialism /ɛgzɪs'tɛnʃəlɪzəm/ *n.* a modern philosophical doctrine which stresses the importance of existence, as such, and of the freedom and responsibility of the human individual. – **existentialist**, *adj.*, *n.*

exit /'ɛgzət, -zɪt, 'ɛksət, -sɪt/ *n.* **1.** a way or passage out. **2.** a going out or away; a departure. – *v.i.* **3.** to depart; go away.

exo- a prefix meaning 'external'. Also, **ex-**[2].

exodus /'ɛksədəs/ *n.* a going out; a departure or emigration, usually of a large number of people.

exonerate /əg'zɒnəreɪt, ɛg-/ *v.t.*, **-rated**, **-rating**. to clear, as of a charge; free from blame; exculpate.

exorbitant /əg'zɔbətənt, ɛg-/ *adj.* exceeding the bounds of custom, propriety, or reason, especially in amount or extent.

exorcise = exorcize /'ɛksɔsaɪz/ *v.t.*, **-cised**, **-cising**. to seek to expel (an evil spirit) by religious or solemn ceremonies. – **exorcism**, *n.*

exoteric /ɛksoʊ'tɛrɪk/ *adj.* suitable for or communicated to the general public.

exotic /əg'zɒtɪk, ɛg-/ *adj.* **1.** of foreign origin or character. **2.** strikingly unusual or colourful in appearance or effect. – **exotically**, *adv.*

expand /ək'spænd, ɛk-/ *v.t.* **1.** to increase in extent, size, volume, scope, etc. **2.** to express in fuller form or greater detail; develop. – *v.i.* **3.** to increase or grow in extent, bulk, scope, etc. – **expansion**, *n.*

expanse /ək'spæns, ɛk-/ *n.* an uninterrupted space or area; a wide extent of anything.

expatiate /əks'peɪʃieɪt, ɛk-/ *v.i.*, **-ated**, **-ating**. to enlarge in discourse or writing.

expatriate /ɛks'pætrieɪt/ *v.*, **-ated**, **-ating** /ɛks'pætriət, -rieɪt/ *adj.*, *n.* – *v.t.* **1.** to banish (a person) from their native country. **2.** to withdraw (oneself) from residence in and/or allegiance to one's native country. – *adj.* **3.** expatriated; exiled. – *n.*

4. an expatriated person.

expect /ək'spɛkt, ɛk-/ *v.t.* **1.** to regard as likely to happen. **2.** to look for with reason or justification. – **expectation**, *n.* – **expectancy**, *n.* – **expectant**, *adj.*

expectorate /ək'spɛktəreɪt, ɛk-/ *v.t.*, **-rated**, **-rating**. to eject or expel (phlegm, etc.). – **expectorant**, *n.*

expedient /ək'spidiənt, ɛk-/ *adj.* **1.** tending to promote some proposed or desired object. **2.** conducive to advantage or interest, as opposed to right. – *n.* **3.** a means to an end. – **expediency**, *n.*

expedite /'ɛkspədaɪt/ *v.t.*, **-dited**, **-diting**. to speed up the progress of; hasten.

expedition /ɛkspə'dɪʃən/ *n.* **1.** an excursion, journey, or voyage made for some specific purpose. **2.** promptness or speed in accomplishing something.

expel /ək'spɛl, ɛk-/ *v.t.*, **-pelled**, **-pelling**. **1.** to drive or force out or away; discharge or eject. **2.** to cut off from membership or relations.

expend /ək'spɛnd, ɛk-/ *v.t.* to use up.

expendable /ək'spɛndəbəl, ɛk-/ *adj.* (of personnel, equipment, etc.) capable of being sacrificed to achieve an objective.

expenditure /ək'spɛndətʃə, ɛk-/ *n.* **1.** the act of expending. **2.** that which is expended; expense.

expense /ək'spɛns, ɛk-/ *n.* **1.** cost or charge. **2.** a cause or occasion of spending.

expense account *n.* a record of expenditure incurred by an employee in the course of business to be refunded by the employer or claimed against tax.

expensive /ək'spɛnsɪv, ɛk-/ *adj.* costly.

experience /ək'spɪəriəns, ɛk-/ *n.*, *v.*, **-enced**, **-encing**. – *n.* **1.** a particular instance of personally encountering or undergoing something. **2.** the process or fact of personally observing, encountering, or undergoing something. **3.** knowledge or practical wisdom gained from what one has observed, encountered, or undergone. – *v.t.* **4.** to have experience of; meet with; undergo; feel. – **experienced**, *adj.* – **experiential**, *adj.*

experience table *n.* a table compiled from statistical information, on the basis of which expectation of life, etc., can be predicted.

experiment /ək'spɛrəmənt, ɛk-/ *n.*, /ək'spɛrəmɛnt, ɛk-/ – *v.*, *n.* **1.** an act or operation for the purpose of discovering something unknown or testing a principle, supposition, etc. – *v.i.* **2.** to try or test in order to find something out. – **experimental**, *adj.* – **experimentation**, *n.*

expert /'ɛkspɜt/ *n.* a person who has special skill or knowledge in some particular field.

expertise /ɛkspɜ'tiz/ *n.* expert skill or knowledge; expertness.

expiate /'ɛkspieɪt/ *v.t.*, **-ated**, **-ating**. to atone for; make amends or reparation for.

expire /ək'spaɪə, ɛk-/ *v.i.*, **-pired**, **-piring**. **1.** to come to an end; terminate. **2.** to emit the last breath; die. – **expiration**, **expiry**, *n.*

explain /ək'spleɪn, ɛk-/ *v.t.* **1.** to make plain or clear; render intelligible. **2.** to make known in detail. **3.** to assign a meaning to; interpret. – **explanation**, *n.* – **explanatory**, *adj.*

expletive /ək'splitɪv, ɛk-/ *n.* an interjectory word or expression, frequently profane; an exclamatory oath.

explicate /'ɛkspləkeɪt/ *v.t.*, **-cated**, **-cating**. **1.** to develop (a principle, etc.). **2.** to make plain or clear; explain; interpret. – **explication**, *n.*

explicit /ək'splɪsət, ɛk-/ *adj.* leaving nothing merely implied; clearly expressed; unequivocal.

explode /ək'sploʊd, ɛk-/ *v.i.*, **-ploded**, **-ploding**. to expand with force and noise because of rapid chemical change or decomposition, as gunpowder, nitroglycerine, etc. – **explosion**, *n.* – **explosive**, *adj*, *n.*

exploit[1] /'ɛksplɔɪt/ *n.* a striking or notable deed.

exploit[2] /ək'splɔɪt, ɛk-/ *v.t.* **1.** to turn to practical account; utilise for profit. **2.** to use selfishly for one's own ends. – **exploitation**, *n.*

explore /ək'splɔ, ɛk-/ *v.t.*, **-plored**, **-ploring**. **1.** to traverse or range over (a region, etc.) for the purpose of discovery. **2.** to look into closely; scrutinise; examine. – **exploration**, *n.* – **exploratory**, *adj.*

expo /'ɛkspoʊ/ *n.* a large exhibition of technology, arts and crafts, industrial products, etc.

exponent /ək'spoʊnənt, ɛk / *n.* **1.** someone who or that which expounds, explains, or interprets. **2.** *Mathematics* a symbol placed above and at the right of another symbol (the base), to denote to what power the latter is to be raised, as in x^3. – **exponential**, *adj.*

export /ək'spɔt, ɛk-, 'ɛkspɔt/ *v.*, /'ɛkspɔt/ *n.* – *v.t.* **1.** to send (commodities) to other countries or places for sale, exchange, etc. – *n.* **2.** the act of exporting; exportation. **3.** that which is exported; an article exported. – **exportation**, *n.*

expose /ək'spoʊz, ɛk-/ *v.t.*, **-posed**, **-posing**. **1.** to lay open. **2.** to uncover. **3.** to display. **4.** to hold up to public reprehension or ridicule. **5.** *Photography* to subject (a plate, film or paper) to the action of light. – **exposure**, *n.*

exposé /ɛkspoʊ'zeɪ/ *n.* an exposing.

exposition /ɛkspə'zɪʃən/ *n.* **1.** an exhibition or show. **2.** an act of expounding, setting forth, or explaining.

expostulate /ək'spɒstʃuleɪt, ɛk-/ *v.i.*, **-lated**, **-lating**. to reason earnestly.

expound /ək'spaʊnd, ɛk-/ *v.t.* **1.** to set forth or state in detail. **2.** to explain; interpret.

express /ək'sprɛs, ɛk-/ *v.t.* **1.** to put (thought) into words. **2.** to show, manifest, or reveal. **3.** to press or squeeze out. – *adj.* **4.** clearly indicated; distinctly stated. **5.** special; particular; definite. **6.** specially direct or fast, as a train, etc. – *n.* **7.** an express train, bus or coach. – **expressive**, *adj.*

expression /ək'sprɛʃən, ɛk-/ *n.* **1.** the act of expressing or setting forth in words. **2.** a particular word, phrase, or form of words. **3.** indication of feeling, spirit, character, etc.

expropriate /ɛks'proʊprieɪt/ *v.t.*, **-ated**,

-ating. to take, especially for public use.

expulsion /ək'spʌlʃən, ɛk-/ *n.* the act of driving out or expelling.

expunge /ək'spʌndʒ, ɛk-/ *v.t.*, **-punged**, **-punging**. to erase; obliterate. – **expunction**, *n.*

expurgate /'ɛkspɜgeɪt, -pəgeɪt/ *v.t.*, **-gated**, **-gating**. to amend by removing offensive or objectionable matter.

exquisite /'ɛkskwəzət, ək'skwɪzət, ɛk-/ *adj.* **1.** of peculiar beauty or charm, or rare and appealing excellence. **2.** intense or keen, as pleasure, pain, etc.

extant /ɛk'stænt, 'ɛkstənt/ *adj.* in existence; still existing.

extempore /ək'stɛmpəri, ɛk-/ *adv.* without premeditation or preparation.

extend /ək'stɛnd, ɛk-/ *v.t.* **1.** to stretch out. **2.** to increase the length or duration of. **3.** to stretch out in various or all directions; expand. **4.** to hold forth as an offer or grant. **5.** *Commerce* to transfer (figures) from one column to another in bookkeeping, invoices, etc. – *v.i.* **6.** to be or become extended.

extension /ək'stɛnʃən, ɛk-/ *n.* **1.** the act of extending. **2.** that by which something is extended, as an addition to a house. **3.** an extra telephone connected to the same line as a main telephone. **4.** *Commerce* a written engagement on the part of a creditor, allowing a debtor further time to pay a debt.

extensive /ək'stɛnsɪv, ɛk-/ *adj.* of great extent.

extent /ək'stɛnt, ɛk-/ *n.* **1.** the space or degree to which something extends; length, area or volume. **2.** a particular extent.

extenuate /ək'stɛnjueɪt, ɛk-/ *v.t.*, **-ated**, **-ating**. to represent (a fault, offence, etc.) as less serious.

exterior /ək'stɪəriə, ɛk-/ *adj.* **1.** outer; being on the outer side. – *n.* **2.** the outer surface or part; the outside; outward form or appearance.

exterminate /ək'stɜməneɪt, ɛk-/ *v.t.*, **-ated**, **-ating**. to get rid of by destroying; destroy totally; extirpate.

external /ək'stɜnəl, ɛk-/ *adj.* **1.** of or relating to the outside or outer part; outer. **2.** relating to the outward or visible appearance or show. **3.** *Education* studying or studied outside the campus of a university or similar institution.

extinct /əks'tɪŋkt, ɛk-/ *adj.* **1.** extinguished; quenched; having ceased eruption, as a volcano. **2.** having come to an end; without a living representative, as a species. – **extinction**, *n.*

extinguish /ək'stɪŋgwɪʃ, ɛk-/ *v.t.* **1.** to put out (a fire, light, etc.). **2.** to put an end to or bring to an end.

extirpate /'ɛkstɜpeɪt, -stə-/ *v.t.*, **-pated**, **-pating**. to remove utterly; destroy totally.

extol /ək'stoʊl, ɛk-/ *v.t.*, **-tolled**, **-tolling**. to praise highly.

extort /ək'stɔt, ɛk-/ *v.t.* to obtain (money, information, etc.) by force, torture, threat, or the like. – **extortion**, *n.* – **extortionate**, *adj.*

extra /'ɛkstrə/ *adj.* **1.** beyond or more than what is usual, expected, or necessary; additional. – *n.* **2.** something extra or additional. – *adv.* **3.** in excess of the usual or specified amount.

extra- a prefix meaning 'outside', 'beyond', 'besides'. Also, **extro-**.

extract /ək'strækt, ɛk-/ *v.*, /'ɛkstrækt/ *n.* – *v.t.* **1.** to draw forth or get out by force. **2.** to derive or obtain from a particular source. **3.** to take or copy out (matter from a book, etc.). **4.** to separate or obtain (a juice, ingredient, principle, etc.) from a mixture by pressure, distillation, treatment with solvents, or the like. – *n.* **5.** something extracted.

extraction /ək'strækʃən, ɛk-/ *n.* **1.** the act of extracting. **2.** the state or fact of being extracted. **3.** descent or lineage.

extradite /'ɛkstrədaɪt/ *v.t.*, **-dited**, **-diting**. to give up (a fugitive or prisoner) to another nation, state, or authority. – **extradition**, *n.*

extraneous /ək'streɪniəs, ɛk-/ *adj.* not belonging or proper to a thing; foreign; not essential.

extraordinary /ək'strɔdənri, ɛk-/ *adj.* **1.** beyond what is ordinary. **2.** exceptional; unusual; remarkable.

extrapolate /ɛk'stræpəleɪt/ *v.t.*, **-lated**, **-lating**. to infer (what is not known) from that which is known; conjecture.

extrasensory /ɛkstrə'sɛnsəri/ *adj.* outside the normal sense perception. See **ESP**.

extravagant /ək'strævəgənt, ɛk-/ *adj.* **1.** wasteful. **2.** exceeding the bounds of reason. – **extravagance**, *n.*

extravaganza /əkstrævə'gænzə, ɛk-/ *n.* a lavish, elaborate opera or other entertainment.

extreme /ək'strim, ɛk-/ *adj.*, **-tremer**, **-tremist**, *n.* – *adj.* **1.** of a character or kind farthest removed from the ordinary or average. **2.** utmost or exceedingly great in degree. **3.** last or final. – *n.* **4.** the utmost or highest degree, or a very high degree. **5.** one of two things as remote or different from each other as possible. – **extremity**, *n.*

extremity /ək'strɛməti, ɛk-/ *n.* **1.** the extreme or terminal point, limit, or part. **2.** the utmost, or an extreme degree. **3.** an extreme measure. **4.** extreme adversity.

extricate /'ɛkstrəkeɪt/ *v.t.*, **-cated**, **-cating**. to disentangle; disengage; free.

extrinsic /ɛks'trɪnzɪk/ *adj.* extraneous.

extro- variant of **extra-**.

extroversion /ɛkstrə'vɜʒən/ *n.* *Psychology* interest directed outwards or to things outside the self (opposed to *introversion*). Also, **extraversion**. – **extrovert**, *n.*

extrude /ɛk'strud/ *v.t.*, **-truded**, **-truding**. to force or press out.

exuberant /əg'zjubərənt, ɛg-/ *adj.* **1.** lavish; effusive. **2.** full of vigour; abounding in high spirits.

exude /əg'zjud, ɛg-/ *v.i.*, **-uded**, **-uding**. to come out gradually in drops like sweat through pores or small openings; ooze out. – **exudation**, *n.*

exult /əg'zʌlt, ɛg-/ *v.i.* to show or feel a lively or triumphant joy.

-ey[1] variant of **-y**[1].

-ey[2] variant of **-y**[2], used especially after *y*.

eye /aɪ/ *n.*, *pl.* **eyes**, *v.*, **eyed**, **eyeing** *or*

eying. – *n.* **1.** the organ of sight or vision. **2.** this organ with respect to the colour of the iris. **3.** the region surrounding the eye. **4.** sight; vision. **5.** power of seeing; appreciative or discriminating visual perception. **6.** (*often pl.*) look, glance, or gaze. **7.** regard, respect, view, aim, or intention. **8.** (*often pl.*) estimation, or opinion. **9.** mental view. **10.** something resembling or suggesting the eye in appearance, shape, etc. **11.** *Meteorology* the central region of low pressure in a tropical hurricane, where calm conditions prevail. **12. catch someone's eye,** to attract someone's attention. **13. keep an eye on,** to watch attentively; mind. **14. see eye to eye,** to have the same opinion; agree. – *v.t.* **15.** to fix the eyes upon; view. **16.** to observe or watch narrowly.

eyeball /'aɪbɔl/ *n.* the ball or globe of the eye.

eyebrow /'aɪbraʊ/ *n.* **1.** the arch or ridge forming the upper part of the orbit of the eye. **2.** the fringe of hair growing upon it.

eyelash /'aɪlæʃ/ *n.* one of the short, thick, curved hairs growing as a fringe on the edge of an eyelid.

eyelet /'aɪlət/ *n.* **1.** a small, typically round hole, especially one finished at the edge, as in cloth or leather. **2.** a metal ring for lining a small hole.

eyelid /'aɪlɪd/ *n.* the movable lid of skin which serves to cover and uncover the eyeball.

eyesore /'aɪsɔ/ *n.* something unpleasant to look at.

eyetooth /'aɪtuθ/ *n., pl.* **-teeth** /-tiθ/. a canine tooth, especially of the upper jaw.

eyewitness /'aɪwɪtnəs/ *n.* someone who actually beholds some act or occurrence.

eyrie /'ɪəri, 'ɛəri/ *n.* **1.** the nest of a bird of prey. **2.** an elevated habitation or situation. Also, **aerie**, **aery**, **eyry**.

F f

F, f /ɛf/ *n., pl.* **F's** *or* **Fs**, **f's** *or* **fs**. the sixth letter of the English alphabet.

fable /'feɪbəl/ *n.* a short tale to teach a moral.

fabric /'fæbrɪk/ *n.* **1.** cloth, especially woven. **2.** framework; structure.

fabricate /'fæbrəkeɪt/ *v.t.,* **-cated**, **-cating**. **1.** to construct. **2.** to assemble. **3.** to devise or invent (a legend, lie, etc.). **4.** to forge. – **fabrication**, *n.*

fabulous /'fæbjuləs/ *adj.* **1.** *Colloquial* wonderful; exceptionally pleasing. **2.** told about in fables; not true or real.

facade /fə'sad, fæ-/ *n.* **1.** *Architecture* a face or front of a building. **2.** an appearance, especially a misleading one.

face /feɪs/ *n., v.,* **faced**, **facing**. – *n.* **1.** the front part of the head, from the forehead to the chin. **2.** a look or expression on the face, especially showing ridicule, disgust, etc. **3.** *Colloquial* boldness; impudence. **4.** outward appearance. **5.** the surface. **6.** any one of the surfaces of a solid figure. **7.** *Printing* the style or appearance of type; typeface. **8. on the face of it,** to all appearances; seemingly. – *v.t.* **9.** to have the front towards or in the direction of. **10.** to meet face to face; confront. **11.** to cover or partly cover with a different material. – *v.i.* **12.** to be turned (often fol. by *to*, *towards*).

facelift /'feɪslɪft/ *n.* plastic surgery to eliminate wrinkles, etc.

facet /'fæsət/ *n.* **1.** one of the polished surfaces of a cut gem. **2.** aspect; phase.

facetious /fə'siʃəs/ *adj.* **1.** intended to be amusing. **2.** trying to be amusing.

face value *n.* **1.** par value; the value stated on the face of a financial instrument or document. **2.** apparent value.

facial /'feɪʃəl/ *adj.* **1.** of the face. – *n.* **2.** *Colloquial* a massage or treatment for the face.

-facient a suffix forming adjectives meaning 'that makes or causes (something)' and nouns meaning 'one that makes or causes (something)'.

facile /'fæsaɪl/ *adj.* **1.** moving, acting, working, proceeding, etc., with ease. **2.** agreeable or easily influenced. **3.** glib.

facilitate /fə'sɪləteɪt/ *v.t.,* **-tated**, **-tating**. to make easier or less difficult.

facility /fə'sɪləti/ *n., pl.* **-ties**. **1.** freedom from difficulty; ease. **2.** a building or complex of buildings, designed for a specific purpose.

facsimile /fæk'sɪməli/ *n.* **1.** an exact copy. **2.** → **fax** (defs 1–3).

fact /fækt/ *n.* **1.** what has really happened; truth; reality. **2.** something known to have happened. – **factual**, *adj.*

faction /'fækʃən/ *n.* a smaller group of people within a larger group.

factitious /fæk'tɪʃəs/ *adj.* artificial.

factor /'fæktə/ *n.* **1.** one of the elements that contribute to bringing about any given result. **2.** *Mathematics* one of two or more numbers, algebraic expressions, or the like, which when multiplied together produce a given product; a divisor.

factorial /fæk'tɔriəl/ *n.* *Mathematics* the product of an integer multiplied by all the lower integers.

factoring /'fæktərɪŋ/ *n.* the business of purchasing and collecting accounts receivable.

factory /'fæktri, -təri/ *n., pl.* **-ries**. a building or group of buildings, usually with equipment, where goods are manufactured.

faculty /'fækəlti/ *n., pl.* **-ties**. **1.** one of the powers of the mind, as memory, reason, speech, etc. **2.** *Education* one of the branches of learning in a university.

fad /fæd/ *n.* a temporary, usually irrational, pursuit, fashion, etc.

fade /feɪd/ *v.i.,* **faded**, **fading**. **1.** to lose freshness, vigour, strength, or health. **2.** to disappear or die gradually (often fol. by *away* or *out*).

faeces = feces /'fisiz/ *pl. n.* excrement.

fag[1] /fæg/ *v.,* **fagged**, **fagging**, *n.* – *v.t.* **1.** to tire (often fol. by *out*). – *n.* **2.** *Colloquial* a cigarette.

fag[2] /fæg/ *n. Colloquial* (*derogatory*) a homosexual.

faggot /'fægət/ *n.* a bundle of sticks.

Fahrenheit /'færənhaɪt/ *adj.* denoting or relating to a thermometric scale in which the melting point of ice is 32 degrees above zero (32°F) and the boiling point of water is 212 degrees above zero (212°F).

fail /feɪl/ *v.i.* **1.** to come short or be wanting in action, detail, or result. **2.** to fall off; dwindle. – *v.t.* **3.** to neglect to perform or observe. **4.** to prove of no use or help to. **5.** to take (an examination, etc.) without passing. **6.** to declare (a person) unsuccessful in a test, course of study, etc. – **failure**, *n.*

faint /feɪnt/ *adj.* **1.** lacking brightness, loudness, strength, etc. **2.** feeling weak, dizzy, or exhausted. – *v.i.* **3.** to lose consciousness temporarily.

fair[1] /fɛə/ *adj.* **1.** free from bias, dishonesty, or injustice. **2.** proper under the rules. **3.** moderately good, large, or satisfactory. **4.** (of the weather) fine. **5.** free from imperfection. **6.** of a light hue; not dark. **7.** beautiful. – *adv.* **8.** in a fair manner.

fair[2] /fɛə/ *n.* **1.** an amusement show. **2.** an exhibition or display.

fair dinkum *Colloquial* – *adj.* **1.** true; genuine; dinkum. – *interj.* **2.** Also, **fair dink**. (an assertion of truth or genuineness).

fair rent *n.* a periodical payment from a tenant to his or her landlord, held by a tribunal to be the just rental for the premises.

fairway /'fɛəweɪ/ *n.* **1.** an unobstructed passage or way. **2.** *Golf* that part of the links between tees and putting greens where the grass is kept short.

fairy /'fɛəri/ *n., pl.* **-ries**. **1.** a small magical being. **2.** a male homosexual.

fairytale /'fɛəriteɪl/ *n.* **1.** a tale, usually involving fairies and folklore, as told to children. – *adj.* **2.** unreal.

faith /feɪθ/ *n.* **1.** confidence or trust in a person or thing. **2.** belief which is not based on proof. **3.** belief in the doctrines or teachings of religion. **4.** a system of religious belief.

faithful /ˈfeɪθfəl/ *adj.* **1.** strict or thorough in the performance of duty. **2.** full of or showing loyalty or fidelity. **3.** that may be relied upon, trusted, or believed. **4.** adhering or true to fact or an original.

fake /feɪk/ *v.,* **faked**, **faking**, *n., adj. Colloquial – v.t., v.i.* **1.** to pretend. *– n.* **2.** something faked. **3.** someone who fakes. *– adj.* **4.** designed to deceive or cheat.

falcon /ˈfælkən, ˈfɔlkən, ˈfɔkən/ *n.* any of various birds of prey.

fall /fɔl/ *v.,* **fell**, **fallen**, **falling**, *n. – v.i.* **1.** to descend from a higher to a lower place or position through loss or lack of support; drop. **2.** to come down suddenly from a standing or erect position. **3.** to become less or lower. **4.** to hang down; extend downwards. **5.** to succumb to temptation. **6.** to succumb to attack. **7.** to come to pass; occur; happen. **8.** to be naturally divisible (fol. by *into*). **9.** to lose animation, as the face. **10.** to slope, as land. **11. fall for,** *Colloquial* **a.** to be deceived by. **b.** to fall in love with. **12. fall through,** to come to naught; fail; miscarry. *– n.* **13.** the act of falling. **14.** (*usu. pl.*) a cataract or waterfall. **15.** *Chiefly US* autumn.

fallacy /ˈfæləsi/ *n., pl.* **-cies**. a deceptive, misleading, or false notion, belief, etc. – **fallacious**, *adj.*

fallible /ˈfæləbəl/ *adj.* liable to be deceived or mistaken; liable to err.

fallout /ˈfɔlaʊt/ *n.* the descent of airborne particles of radioactive materials resulting from a nuclear explosion.

fallow[1] /ˈfæloʊ/ *adj.* ploughed and left unseeded for a season or more; uncultivated.

fallow[2] /ˈfæloʊ/ *adj.* pale yellow; light brown.

false /fɔls, fɒls/ *adj.,* **falser**, **falsest**. **1.** not true or correct; erroneous. **2.** deceptive; used to deceive or mislead. **3.** not genuine.

falsehood /ˈfɔlshʊd/ *n.* a lie.

false pretences *pl. n.* the obtaining of money or property by the use of false representations, forged documents, or similar illegal device.

falsetto /fɔlˈsɛtoʊ/ *n., pl.* **-tos**. an unnaturally or artificially high-pitched voice or register, especially in a man.

falsify /ˈfɔlsəfaɪ/ *v.t.,* **-fied**, **-fying**. **1.** to make false or incorrect, especially so as to deceive. **2.** to alter fraudulently.

falter /ˈfɔltə/ *v.i.* to hesitate or waver.

fame /feɪm/ *n.* widespread reputation.

familiar /fəˈmɪljə/ *adj.* **1.** commonly or generally known or seen. **2.** well-acquainted; thoroughly conversant. **3.** easy; informal; unceremonious; unconstrained. – **familiarity**, *n.* – **familiarise = familiarize**, *v.*

family /ˈfæməli, ˈfæmli/ *n., pl.* **-lies**. **1.** parents and their children, whether dwelling together or not. **2.** all those persons descended from a common progenitor. **3.** *Biology* the usual major subdivision of an order or suborder. **4.** any group of related things. – **familial**, *adj.*

family tree *n.* a genealogical chart.

famine /ˈfæmən/ *n.* extreme and general scarcity of food.

famished /ˈfæmɪʃt/ *adj. Colloquial* very hungry.

famous /ˈfeɪməs/ *adj.* celebrated in fame or public report; renowned; well-known.

fan[1] /fæn/ *n., v.,* **fanned**, **fanning**. *– n.* **1.** any device for causing a current of air. *– v.t.* **2.** to move or agitate (the air) with, or as with, a fan. **3.** to stir to activity with, or as with, a fan. **4.** to spread out like a fan. *– v.i.* **5.** to spread out like a fan (fol. by *out*).

fan[2] /fæn/ *n. Colloquial* an enthusiastic devotee or follower.

fanatic /fəˈnætɪk/ *n.* a person with an extreme and unreasoning enthusiasm or zeal, especially in religious matters. – **fanatical**, *adj.* – **fanaticism**, *n.*

fanbelt /ˈfænbɛlt/ *n.* the belt which drives the cooling fan of a motor, especially a car motor.

fancy /ˈfænsi/ *n., pl.* **-cies**, *adj.,* **-cier**, **-ciest**, *v.,* **-cied**, **-cying**. *– n.* **1.** imagination. **2.** a mental image or conception. **3.** a caprice; whim; vagary. *– adj.* **4.** adapted to please the taste or fancy; of delicate or refined quality. *– v.t.* **5.** to form a conception of; picture to oneself. **6.** to take a liking to; like. **7.** to place one's hopes or expectations on. – **fanciful**, *adj.*

fanfare /ˈfænfɛə/ *n.* a flourish or short air played on trumpets or the like.

fang /fæŋ/ *n.* **1.** one of the long, sharp, hollow or grooved teeth of a snake, by which venom is injected. **2.** a canine tooth.

fanlight /ˈfænlaɪt/ *n.* a fan-shaped or other window above a door or other opening.

fantastic /fænˈtæstɪk/ *adj.* **1.** odd, quaint, eccentric, or grotesque. **2.** extravagantly fanciful; irrational. **3.** *Colloquial* very good; fine; wonderful. Also (for defs 1 and 2), **fantastical**.

fantasy /ˈfæntəsi, -zi/ *n., pl.* **-sies**. imagination, especially when unrestrained. – **fantasise = fantasize**, *v.*

far /fa/ *adv.,* **further** *or especially for def. 1* **farther**, **furthest** *or especially for def. 1* **farthest**, *adj.,* **further** *or* **farther**, **furthest** *or* **farthest**. *– adv.* **1.** at or to a great distance; a long way off; to a remote point. **2.** to or at a remote time, etc. **3.** to a great degree; very much. *– adj.* **4.** distant. **5.** more distant of the two.

farad /ˈfærəd/ *n.* the derived SI unit of electric capacitance. *Symbol*: F

faraway /ˈfarəweɪ/ *adj.* **1.** distant; remote. **2.** abstracted or dreamy, as a look.

farce /fas/ *n.* **1.** a light, humorous play. **2.** foolish show; mockery; a ridiculous sham. – **farcical**, *adj.*

fare /fɛə/ *n., v.,* **fared**, **faring**. *– n.* **1.** the price of conveyance or passage. **2.** the person or persons who pay to be conveyed in a vehicle. **3.** food. *– v.i.* **4.** to experience good or bad fortune, treatment, etc.; get on. **5.** to go; turn out; happen (used impersonally).

farewell /fɛəˈwɛl/ *interj.* goodbye; may you fare well.

farinaceous /ærəˈneɪʃəs/ *adj.* of or relating to flour.

farm /fam/ *n.* **1.** a tract of land devoted to agriculture or some other industry. *– v.t.*

2. to cultivate (land). 3. to raise (livestock, fish, etc.) on a farm. 4. to distribute (responsibilities, duties, etc.) (usually fol. by *out*). – **farmer**, *n.* – **farming**, *n.*

fart /fat/ *Colloquial* – *n.* 1. an emission of wind from the anus, especially an audible one. – *v.i.* 2. to emit wind from the anus.

farther /'faðə/ *adj., adv.* comparative of **far**.

farthest /'faðəst/ *adj., adv.* superlative of **far**.

farthing /'faðɪŋ/ *n.* a former British coin.

fascinate /'fæsəneɪt/ *v.t.*, **-nated**, **-nating**. to attract and hold irresistibly by delightful qualities. – **fascination**, *n.*

fascism /'fæʃɪzəm, 'fæsɪzəm/ *n.* (*often cap.*) a governmental system with strong centralised power, permitting no opposition or criticism, controlling all affairs of the nation (industrial, commercial, etc.), and emphasising an aggressive nationalism.

fashion /'fæʃən/ *n.* 1. a prevailing custom or style of dress, etiquette, procedure, etc. 2. manner; way; mode. 3. the make or form of anything. 4. a kind; sort. – *v.t.* 5. to give a particular shape or form to; make. – **fashionable**, *adj.*

fast[1] /fast/ *adj.* 1. moving or able to move quickly; quick; swift; rapid. 2. done in comparatively little time. 3. indicating a time in advance of the correct time, as a clock. 4. resistant. 5. firmly fixed in place; not easily moved; securely attached. 6. deep or sound, as sleep. 7. deceptive, insincere, inconstant, or unreliable. – *adv.* 8. tightly. 9. soundly. 10. quickly, swiftly, or rapidly. – **fasten**, *v.*

fast[2] /fast/ *v.i.* 1. to abstain from all food. 2. to eat only sparingly or of certain kinds of food, especially as a religious observance. – *n.* 3. a fasting.

fast forward *n.* the mode on a video or audio tape recorder which runs the tape forward quickly. – **fast-forward**, *v.*

fastidious /fæs'tɪdiəs/ *adj.* 1. hard to please; excessively critical. 2. anxious to achieve the best result; particular.

fast-track /'fast-træk/ *v.t.* 1. to move (people, oneself, etc.) into or through a system with unusual speed. 2. to bring (something) about with unusual speed.

fat /fæt/ *adj.*, **fatter**, **fattest**, *n.* – *adj.* 1. having much flesh other than muscle; fleshy; corpulent; obese. – *n.* 2. any of several white or yellowish substances, greasy to the touch, forming the chief part of the adipose tissue of animals and also found in plants. 3. the richest or best part of anything. – **fatty**, *adj.*

fatal /'feɪtl/ *adj.* 1. causing death. 2. causing destruction or ruin.

fatalism /'feɪtəlɪzəm/ *n.* 1. the doctrine that all events are subject to fate. 2. the acceptance of all things and events as inevitable. – **fatalist**, *n.* – **fatalistic**, *adj.*

fatality /fə'tæləti/ *n., pl.* **-ties**. 1. a disaster resulting in death; a calamity or misfortune. 2. someone who is killed in an accident or disaster.

fate /feɪt/ *n., v.*, **fated**, **fating**. – *n.* 1. fortune; lot; destiny. – *v.t.* 2. to predetermine.

fateful /'feɪtfəl/ *adj.* decisively important.

father /'faðə/ *n.* 1. a male parent. 2. any male ancestor, especially the founder of a race, family, or line. 3. *Ecclesiastical* (*often cap.*) a title of reverence. – *v.t.* 4. to beget. – **fatherly**, *adj.*

father-in-law /'faðər-ɪn-lɔ/ *n., pl.* **fathers-in-law**. the father of one's husband or wife.

fathom /'fæðəm/ *n., pl.* **fathoms**, (*esp. collectively*) **fathom**, *v.* – *n.* 1. a unit of depth in the imperial system. *Symbol*: fm – *v.t.* 2. to penetrate to or find the bottom or extent of.

fatigue /fə'tig/ *n., v.*, **-tigued**, **-tiguing**. – *n.* 1. weariness from bodily or mental exertion. 2. *Mechanics* the weakening of material subjected to stress. – *v.t.* 3. to weary with bodily or mental exertion. – *v.i.* 4. to grow weary as a result of exertion.

fatuous /'fætʃuəs/ *adj.* foolish, especially in an unconscious, complacent manner; silly.

fault /fɔlt, fɒlt/ *n.* 1. a defect or imperfection; a flaw; a failing. 2. an error or mistake. 3. culpability. 4. *Geology*, *Mining* a break in the continuity of a body of rock. 5. **to a fault,** excessively. – *v.t.* 6. to find fault with, blame, or censure.

fauna /'fɔnə/ *n., pl.* **-nas**, **-nae**. the animals of a given region or period.

favour = favor /'feɪvə/ *n.* 1. a kind act; something done or granted out of goodwill, rather than from justice or for remuneration. 2. a state of being approved, or held in regard. 3. **in favour of, a.** in support of; on the side of. **b.** to the advantage of. **c.** (of a cheque, etc.) payable to. – *v.t.* 4. to regard with favour. 5. to have a preference for; treat with partiality. 6. to aid or support. – **favourable**, *adj.*

favourite = favorite /'feɪvərət, -vrət/ *n.* 1. a person or thing regarded with special favour or preference. 2. *Sport* a competitor considered likely to win. – *adj.* 3. regarded with particular favour or preference.

favouritism = favoritism /'feɪvərətɪzəm, -vrə-/ *n.* the favouring of one person or group over others having equal claims.

fawn[1] /fɔn/ *n.* 1. a young deer. – *adj.* 2. light yellowish brown.

fawn[2] /fɔn/ *v.i.* to seek notice or favour by servile demeanour.

fax /fæks/ *n.* Also, **facsimile**. 1. a method of transmission of documents, pictures, etc., by wire or radio. 2. a document, picture, etc., so transmitted. 3. a machine which transmits and receives graphic data by wire or radio. – *v.t.* 4. to send (a document, picture, etc.) by fax.

FBT /ɛf bi 'ti/ fringe benefits tax.

fear /fɪə/ *n.* 1. a painful feeling of impending danger, evil, trouble, etc.; the feeling or condition of being afraid. 2. reverential awe, as towards a god. – *v.t.* 3. to regard with fear; be afraid of.

fearsome /'fɪəsəm/ *adj.* causing fear.

feasible /'fizəbəl/ *adj.* 1. capable of being done, effected, or accomplished. 2. likely; probable. – **feasibility**, **feasibleness**, *n.* – **feasibly**, *adv.*

feast /fist/ *n.* 1. a periodical celebration of religious or other character. 2. a sumptuous entertainment or meal for many guests. 3. any rich or abundant meal. – *v.i.* 4. to have, or partake of, a feast; eat sumptuously.

feat /fit/ *n.* a noteworthy or extraordinary act

or achievement, usually displaying boldness, skill, etc.

feather /'fɛðə/ *n.* **1.** one of the epidermal appendages which together constitute the plumage of birds. **2.** something like a feather. – *v.t.* **3.** to provide with feathers, as an arrow.

featherbedding /'fɛðəbɛdɪŋ/ *n.* the employment of more workers than are necessary.

feature /'fitʃə/ *n., v.,* **-tured**, **-turing**. – *n.* **1.** any part of the face, as the nose, chin, etc. **2.** a prominent or conspicuous part or characteristic. **3.** a special article, column, cartoon, etc., in a newspaper or magazine. – *v.t.* **4.** to be a feature or distinctive mark of. **5.** to make a feature of, or give prominence to.

febri- a word element meaning 'fever'.

febrile /'fɛbraɪl, 'fi-/ *adj.* relating to, or marked by fevers.

feces /'fisiz/ *pl. n.* → **faeces**.

feckless /'fɛkləs/ *adj.* **1.** ineffective; feeble. **2.** spiritless; worthless.

fed /fɛd/ *v.* past tense and past participle of **feed**.

federacy /'fɛdərəsi/ *n.* → **confederacy**.

federal /'fɛdərəl, 'fɛdrəl/ *adj.* of or relating to a compact or a league, especially a league between nations or states.

federate /'fɛdəreɪt/ *v.t., v.i.,* **-rated**, **-rating**. to unite in a federation.

federation /fɛdə'reɪʃən/ *n.* **1.** the formation of a political unity, with a central government, out of a number of separate states, etc., each of which retains control of its own internal affairs. **2.** the unity so formed.

fee /fi/ *n.* a payment for services.

feeble /'fibəl/ *adj.,* **-bler**, **-blest**. **1.** physically weak, as from age, sickness, etc. **2.** weak intellectually or morally.

feed /fid/ *v.,* **fed**, **feeding**, *n.* – *v.t.* **1.** to give food to; supply with nourishment. **2.** to yield, or serve as, food for. **3.** to satisfy; minister to; gratify. – *v.i.* **4.** to take food; eat. – *n.* **5.** food, especially for cattle, etc.

feedback /'fidbæk/ *n.* the returning of a part of the output of any system as input, especially for correction or control purposes.

feel /fil/ *v.,* **felt**, **feeling**, *n.* – *v.t.* **1.** to perceive or examine by touch. **2.** to have a sensation (other than sight, hearing, taste, and smell) of. **3.** to be emotionally affected by. **4.** to experience the effects of. – *v.i.* **5.** to have perception by touch or by any nerves of sensation other than those of sight, hearing, taste, and smell. **6.** to be consciously, in emotion, opinion, etc. **7.** to have sympathy or compassion (fol. by *with* or *for*). **8. feel like,** to have a desire or inclination for. – *n.* **9.** a quality of an object that is perceived by feeling or touching.

feeler /'filə/ *n. Zoology* an organ of touch, as an antenna or a tentacle.

feelgood /'filgʊd/ *adj.* (of a film, play, etc.) heart-warming.

feeling /'filɪŋ/ *n.* **1.** the function or the power of perceiving by touch. **2.** a consciousness or impression. **3.** an intuition or premonition. **4.** capacity for emotion; pity. **5.** (*pl.*) sensibilities; susceptibilities.

feet /fit/ *n.* plural of **foot**.

feign /feɪn/ *v.t., v.i.* to pretend.

feint[1] /feɪnt/ *n.* a movement made with the object of deceiving an adversary.

feint[2] /feɪnt/ *n.* the lightest weight of line used in printing ruled paper.

feldspar /'fɛldspa, 'fɛlspa/ *n.* → **felspar**.

felicitate /fə'lɪsəteɪt/ *v.t.,* **-tated**, **-tating**. to compliment upon a happy event; congratulate. – **felicitation**, *n.*

felicity /fə'lɪsəti/ *n., pl.* **-ties**. **1.** the state of being happy, especially in a high degree. **2.** a source of happiness. – **felicitous**, *adj.*

feline /'filaɪn/ *adj.* **1.** belonging or relating to the cat family. – *n.* **2.** a feline animal.

fell[1] /fɛl/ *v.* past tense of **fall**.

fell[2] /fɛl/ *v.t.* to cause to fall; knock, strike, or cut down.

fell[3] /fɛl/ *adj.* fierce; cruel; dreadful.

fellatio /fə'leɪʃioʊ/ *n.* oral stimulation of the male genitals.

fellow /'fɛloʊ, 'fɛlə/ *n.* **1.** *Colloquial* a man; boy. **2.** one belonging to the same class; an equal; peer. **3.** one of a pair; a mate or match. **4.** (*usu. cap.*) a member of any of certain learned or professional societies. – *adj.* **5.** belonging to the same class or group. – **fellowship**, *n.*

felony /'fɛləni/ *n., pl.* **-nies**. *Law* any of various indictable offences, as murder, burglary, etc., of graver character than those called misdemeanours. – **felon**, *n.* – **felonious**, *adj.*

felspar /'fɛlspa/ *n.* any of a group of minerals, characterised by two cleavages at nearly right angles. Also, **feldspar**.

felt[1] /fɛlt/ *v.* past tense and past participle of **feel**.

felt[2] /fɛlt/ *n.* a non woven fabric.

female /'fimeɪl/ *n.* **1.** a human being of the sex which conceives and brings forth young; a woman or girl. **2.** any animal of corresponding sex. – *adj.* **3.** relating to or characteristic of this sex. **4.** *Machinery* designating some part, etc., into which a corresponding part fits.

feminine /'fɛmənən/ *adj.* relating to a woman. – **femininity**, *n.*

feminism /'fɛmənɪzəm/ *n.* advocacy of equal rights and opportunities for women. – **feminist**, *n.*

femur /'fimə/ *n., pl.* **femurs**, **femora** /'fɛmərə/. *Anatomy* the thighbone.

fence /fɛns/ *n., v.,* **fenced**, **fencing**. – *n.* **1.** an enclosure or barrier. **2.** *Colloquial* a person who receives and disposes of stolen goods. – *v.t.* **3.** to enclose by some barrier. – *v.i.* **4.** to take part in fencing.

fencing /'fɛnsɪŋ/ *n.* the act, practice, or art of using a sword, foil, etc., for defence and attack.

fend /fɛnd/ *v.t.* **1.** to ward (often fol. by *off*). – *v.i.* **2.** *Colloquial* to provide (fol. by *for*).

fender /'fɛndə/ *n.* a metal guard.

fender case *n. Law Colloquial* any litigation arising from a motor accident.

fennel /'fɛnəl/ *n.* a plant bearing aromatic fruits used in cookery and medicine.

-fer a noun suffix meaning 'bearing', 'producing', 'yielding'.

feral /'fɛrəl, 'fiərəl/ *adj.* wild, or existing in a

state of nature.

ferment /ˈfɜmɛnt/ *n.*, /fəˈmɛnt, fɜ-/ *v.* – *n.* **1.** any of various agents or substances which cause fermentation. – *v.t.* **2.** to act upon as a ferment. – *v.i.* **3.** to seethe with agitation or excitement.

fermentation /fɜmɛnˈteɪʃən/ *n.* **1.** *Biochemistry* the breakdown of complex molecules brought about by a ferment, as in the changing of grape sugar into ethyl alcohol by yeast enzymes. **2.** the act or process of undergoing such a change. **3.** agitation; excitement. – **fermentative**, *adj.*

fern /fɜn/ *n.* a leafy plant bearing spores.

ferocious /fəˈroʊʃəs/ *adj.* savagely fierce; violently cruel. – **ferocity**, *n.*

-ferous an adjective suffix meaning 'bearing', 'producing', 'yielding'.

ferret /ˈfɛrət/ *n.* a domesticated form of the polecat, used for hunting rabbits and rats in their burrows.

ferri- a word element meaning 'iron'.

ferric /ˈfɛrɪk/ *adj.* of or containing iron, especially in the trivalent state.

ferro- a word element meaning 'iron'.

ferrous /ˈfɛrəs/ *adj.* of or containing iron, especially in the divalent state.

ferrule /ˈfɛrul, -rəl/ *n.* a metal ring or cap put round the end of a post, stick, handle, etc., for strength or protection.

ferry /ˈfɛri/ *n., pl.* **-ries**, *v.,* **-ried**, **-rying**. – *n.* **1.** (a vessel used in) a service for transport across a body of water. – *v.t.* **2.** to carry or convey over water in a boat or plane.

fertile /ˈfɜtaɪl/ *adj.* **1.** bearing or capable of bearing vegetation, crops, etc., abundantly, as land or soil. **2.** abundantly productive or inventive. **3.** able to produce offspring. – **fertility**, *n.*

fertilise = fertilize /ˈfɜtəlaɪz/ *v.t.,* **-lised**, **-lising**. **1.** *Biology* to render (an egg, ovum, or female cell) capable of development by union with the male element, or sperm. **2.** to make fertile; enrich (soil, etc.) for crops, etc. – **fertilisation**, *n.*

fervour = fervor /ˈfɜvə/ *n.* great warmth and earnestness of feeling. – **fervent**, *adj.*

fester /ˈfɛstə/ *v.i.* **1.** to generate purulent matter; suppurate. **2.** to rankle, as a feeling of resentment.

festival /ˈfɛstəvəl/ *n.* a public festivity, with performances of music, processions, exhibitions, etc.

festive /ˈfɛstɪv/ *adj.* joyful; merry.

festivity /fɛsˈtɪvəti/ *n., pl.* **-ties**. a festive celebration or occasion.

festoon /fɛsˈtun/ *v.t.* to adorn with, or as with, a string or chain of flowers, foliage, ribbon, etc., suspended in a curve between two points.

fetch /fɛtʃ/ *v.t.* **1.** to go and return with, or bring to or from a particular place. **2.** to realise or bring in (a price, etc.).

fetching /ˈfɛtʃɪŋ/ *adj.* charming; captivating.

fete /feɪt/ *n., v.,* **feted**, **feting**. – *n.* **1.** a function to raise money for charity, church, school, etc., frequently outdoor and combining the activities of bazaar and fair. – *v.t.* **2.** to give a hospitable public reception to (someone).

fetid /ˈfɛtəd, ˈfitəd/ *adj.* having a strong, offensive smell; stinking. Also, **foetid**.

fetish /ˈfɛtɪʃ, ˈfit-/ *n.* an obsession or fixation.

fetlock /ˈfɛtlɒk/ *n.* a part of a horse's leg bearing a tuft of hair.

fetter /ˈfɛtə/ *n.* (*usu. pl.*) anything that confines or restrains.

fettle /ˈfɛtl/ *n.* state; condition.

feud /fjud/ *n.* **1.** a bitter, continuous hostility, especially between two families, clans, etc. – *v.i.* **2.** to conduct a feud.

feudal /ˈfjudl/ *adj.* of or relating to a medieval system of holding land in return for service.

fever /ˈfivə/ *n.* a morbid condition of the body characterised by undue rise of temperature.

few /fju/ *adj.* **1.** not many; a small number (of). – *n.* **2. a few,** a small number.

fey /feɪ/ *adj.* aware of supernatural influences.

fiancée /fiˈɒnseɪ/ *n.* a woman engaged to be married. – **fiancé**, *masc. n.*

fiasco /fiˈæskoʊ/ *n., pl.* **-cos**. an ignominious failure.

fiat /ˈfiæt, ˈfiət/ *n.* an authoritative decree, sanction, or order.

fib /fɪb/ *n., v.,* **fibbed**, **fibbing**. – *n.* **1.** a trivial falsehood. – *v.i.* **2.** to tell a fib.

fibr- a word element meaning 'fibre'.

fibre /ˈfaɪbə/ *n.* **1.** a fine threadlike piece, as of cotton, jute, or asbestos. **2.** character. **3.** cellulose and other undigested material which add bulk to the contents of the large intestine. – **fibrous**, *adj.*

fibreglass /ˈfaɪbəglas/ *n.* a material consisting of extremely fine filaments of glass.

fibro /ˈfaɪbroʊ/ *n.* compressed asbestos and cement used for building materials.

fibula /ˈfɪbjələ/ *n., pl.* **-las**, **-lae** /-li/. *Anatomy* the outer and thinner of the two bones of the lower leg, extending from the knee to the ankle. – **fibular**, *adj.*

-fic an adjective suffix meaning 'making', 'producing', 'causing'.

-fication a suffix of nouns of action or state corresponding to verbs ending in *-fy*.

fickle /ˈfɪkəl/ *adj.* likely to change, from caprice, irresolution, or instability.

fiction /ˈfɪkʃən/ *n.* the branch of literature comprising works of imaginative narration, especially in prose form.

fictitious /fɪkˈtɪʃəs/ *adj.* counterfeit; false; not genuine.

-fid an adjective suffix meaning 'divided'.

FID /ɛf aɪ ˈdi/ financial institutions duty.

fiddle /ˈfɪdl/ *n., v.,* **-dled**, **-dling**. – *n.* **1.** a violin. **2.** *Colloquial* an illegal or underhand transaction or contrivance. – *v.i.* **3.** *Colloquial* to play on the fiddle. **4.** to make aimless movements, as with the hands.

fiddly /ˈfɪdli/ *adj.* *Colloquial* difficult or exacting, as something small done with the hands.

fidelity /fəˈdɛləti/ *n., pl.* **-ties**. **1.** loyalty; faithfulness. **2.** quality of sound reproduction.

fidget /ˈfɪdʒət/ *v.i.* to move about restlessly or impatiently; be uneasy.

fiduciary /fɪˈdjuʃəri/ *adj., n., pl.* **-ries**. – *adj.*

1. *Law* of or relating to the relation between a fiduciary and his or her principal. **2.** depending on public confidence for value or currency. – *n.* **3.** *Law* a trustee.

field /fild/ *n.* **1.** a piece of open or cleared ground, especially one suitable for pasture or tillage. **2.** a piece of ground devoted to sports or contests. **3.** a sphere, or range of activity, interest, opportunity, study, etc. **4.** a place of investigation, work, etc., away from one's office, laboratory, study, etc., especially one where basic data and original material are gathered for later analysis. **5.** *Computers* a specified area of a record, considered as a unit of information. – *v.t., v.i.* **6.** *Cricket, etc.* to stop, or catch, and throw (the ball).

field-glasses /'fild-glasəz/ *pl. n.* a compact binocular telescope for use out of doors.

fiend /find/ *n.* **1.** any evil spirit. **2.** a diabolically cruel or wicked person. **3.** *Colloquial* someone who is devoted or addicted to some game, sport, etc.

fierce /fɪəs/ *adj.,* **fiercer**, **fiercest**. **1.** wild or vehement in temper, appearance, or action. **2.** violent in force, intensity, etc.

fiery /'faɪəri/ *adj.,* **fierier**, **fieriest**. **1.** consisting of, attended with, characterised by, or containing fire. **2.** flashing or glowing, as the eye. **3.** easily angered; irritable.

fiesta /fi'ɛstə/ *n.* a festival.

fife /faɪf/ *n.* a high-pitched flute.

FIFO /'faɪfoʊ/ *n.* first in first out; a method of storing and retrieving items from a stack, table or list on the principle that first in is first out. Cf. **LIFO**.

fifteen /fɪf'tin/ *n.* a cardinal number, ten plus five. – **fifteenth**, *n., adj.*

fifty /'fɪfti/ *n., pl.* **-ties**. a cardinal number, ten times five. – **fiftieth**, *adj., n.*

fig /fɪg/ *n.* any of several trees or shrubs bearing a pear-shaped fruit.

fight /faɪt/ *n., v.,* **fought**, **fighting**. – *n.* **1.** a battle or combat. **2.** any quarrel, contest, or struggle. **3.** ability or inclination to fight. – *v.i.* **4.** to engage in battle or in single combat. **5.** to contend in any manner. – *v.t.* **6.** to contend with. **7.** to carry on (a battle, duel, etc.).

figment /'fɪgmənt/ *n.* a mere product of the imagination; a pure invention.

figurative /'fɪgjərətɪv, 'fɪgə-/ *adj.* of the nature of or involving a figure of speech, especially a metaphor; metaphorical; not literal.

figure /'fɪgə/ *n., v.,* **-ured**, **-uring**. – *n.* **1.** a written symbol other than a letter. **2.** an amount or value expressed in numbers. **3.** form or shape. **4.** appearance or impression. **5.** a representation, pictorial or sculptured, of something, especially of the human form. **6.** a movement, pattern, or series of movements in skating. – *v.t.* **7.** to conclude, judge, reason, reflect. **8.** to solve; understand; make out; (often fol. by *out*). – *v.i.* **9.** to compute or work with numerical figures. **10.** to make a figure or appearance; be conspicuous.

figurehead /'fɪgəhɛd/ *n.* a person who is nominally the head of a society, community, etc., but has no real authority or responsibility.

figure of speech *n.* a literary mode of expression, as a metaphor, simile, personification, antithesis, etc., in which words are used out of their literal sense.

figurine /'fɪgjurin/ *n.* a small ornamental figure of pottery, metalwork, etc.

filament /'fɪləmənt/ *n.* a very fine thread or threadlike structure.

filch /fɪltʃ/ *v.t.* to steal (especially something of small value).

file[1] /faɪl/ *n., v.,* **filed**, **filing**. – *n.* **1.** any device, as a cabinet, in which papers, etc., are arranged or classified for convenient reference. **2.** *Computers* a memory storage device other than a core store. **3.** a line of persons or things arranged one behind another. – *v.t.* **4.** to place in a file. **5.** *Law* to bring (a suit) before a court of law.

file[2] /faɪl/ *n., v.,* **filed**, **filing**. – *n.* **1.** a tool for smoothing or cutting. – *v.t.* **2.** to reduce, smooth, cut, or remove with or as with a file.

filial /'fɪljəl, -iəl/ *adj.* relating to or befitting a son or daughter.

filibuster /'fɪləbʌstə/ *n.* the use of obstructive tactics to delay legislative action.

filigree /'fɪləgri/ *n.* ornamental work of fine wires.

fill /fɪl/ *v.t.* **1.** to make full; put as much as can be held into. **2.** to supply to fullness or plentifully. **3.** to extend throughout; pervade completely. **4.** to occupy and perform the duties of (a position, post, etc.). **5.** to execute (a business order). – *v.i.* **6.** to become full. **7. fill in, a.** to complete (a document, design, etc.) by filling blank spaces. **b.** to act as a substitute, replace. **8. fill out,** to complete the details of (a plan, form, etc.). – *n.* **9.** a full supply; enough to satisfy want or desire. **10.** a mass of earth, stones, etc., used to fill a hollow, etc.

fillet /'fɪlət/ *n.* **1.** a narrow band. **2.** *Cookery* **a.** a boneless piece of fish. **b.** a cut of beef or pork.

filly /'fɪli/ *n., pl.* **-lies**. a young mare.

film /fɪlm/ *n.* **1.** a thin layer or coating. **2.** a strip or roll of cellulose coated with a light-sensitive emulsion, used in photography. **3.** a series of pictures or photographs on a strip of film, which, when projected, give the illusion of movement. – *v.t.* **4.** to reproduce in the form of a film or films.

filmy /'fɪlmi/ *adj.,* **filmier**, **filmiest**. of the nature of, resembling, or covered with a thin layer or film.

filter /'fɪltə/ *n.* **1.** any device through which liquid is passed to remove suspended impurities or to recover solids. – *v.t.* **2.** to remove by the action of a filter.

filth /fɪlθ/ *n.* **1.** foul matter; offensive or disgusting dirt. **2.** foul condition. **3.** moral impurity, corruption, or obscenity. **4.** foul language.

fin /fɪn/ *n.* **1.** an organ of fishes and certain other aquatic animals, used for propulsion, steering, or balancing. **2.** any part, as of a mechanism, resembling a fin.

final /'faɪnəl/ *adj.* **1.** relating to or coming at the end; last in place, order, or time. **2.** conclusive or decisive. – *n.* **3.** that which is last; that which forms an end or termination of a series. – **finalise = finalize**, *v.* – **finality**, *n.*

finance /ˈfaɪnæns, fəˈnæns/ *n., v.,* **-nanced, -nancing**. – *n.* **1.** the conduct or transaction of money matters. **2.** (*pl.*) pecuniary resources. – *v.t.* **3.** to supply with means of payment; provide capital for. – **financial**, *adj.* – **financier**, *n.*

finance lease *n.* a lease in which most of the benefits and risks involved in ownership are transferred to the lessee.

financial institutions duty *n.* a tax on receipts by banks, credit unions, etc. *Abbrev.*: FID

financial year *n.* any twelve-monthly period at the end of which a government, company, etc., balances its accounts and determines its financial condition. Also, **fiscal year**.

finch /fɪntʃ/ *n.* any of numerous small birds.

find /faɪnd/ *v.,* **found, finding,** *n.* – *v.t.* **1.** to come upon by chance; meet. **2.** to discover. **3.** to recover (something lost). **4.** *Law* to pronounce as an official act (an indictment, verdict, or judgment). – *n.* **5.** the act of finding; a discovery.

fine[1] /faɪn/ *adj.,* **finer, finest**. **1.** of very high grade or quality. **2.** consisting of minute particles. **3.** very thin or slender. **4.** polished or refined. **5.** in good health; well.

fine[2] /faɪn/ *n., v.,* **fined, fining**. – *n.* **1.** a sum of money exacted as a penalty for an offence. – *v.t.* **2.** to punish by a fine.

fine arts *pl. n.* those arts which seek expression through beautiful or significant modes, as architecture, sculpture, painting, music, and engraving.

finery /ˈfaɪnəri/ *n., pl.* **-ries**. fine or showy dress, ornaments, etc.

finesse /fəˈnɛs/ *n.* delicacy of execution.

finger /ˈfɪŋgə/ *n.* **1.** any of the terminal members of the hand, especially one other than the thumb. **2.** something like or likened to a finger. – *v.t.* **3.** to touch with the fingers; handle; toy or meddle with.

fingerprint /ˈfɪŋgəprɪnt/ *n.* an impression of the markings of the inner surface of the last joint of the thumb or a finger.

finicky /ˈfɪnɪki/ *adj.* fastidious; fussy.

finish /ˈfɪnɪʃ/ *v.t.* **1.** to bring to an end or to completion. **2.** to come to the end of (a course, period of time, etc.). **3.** to use up completely (often fol. by *up* or *off*). **4.** to complete and perfect in detail; put the final touches on. – *v.i.* **5.** to come to an end. **6.** to complete a course, etc. – *n.* **7.** the end or conclusion; the last stage. **8.** the quality of being finished or completed with smoothness, elegance, etc. **9.** the surface coating or texture of wood, metal, etc.

finite /ˈfaɪnaɪt/ *adj.* **1.** having bounds or limits. **2.** *Grammar* (of a verb) limited by person, number, tense, etc.

fink /fɪŋk/ *n.* a contemptible or undesirable person.

fiord /ˈfiɔd/ *n.* a long, relatively narrow arm of the sea, bordered by steep cliffs, as on the coast of Norway. Also, **fjord**.

fir /fɜ/ *n.* a pyramidal coniferous tree.

fire /ˈfaɪə/ *n., v.,* **fired, firing**. – *n.* **1.** the active principle of burning or combustion, manifested by the evolution of light and heat. **2.** a burning mass of material, as on a hearth or in a furnace. **3.** the destructive burning of a building, town, forest, etc.; a conflagration. **4.** flashing light; luminous appearance. **5.** burning passion; ardour; enthusiasm. **6.** the discharge of firearms. – *v.t.* **7.** to set on fire. **8.** to apply heat to in a kiln, for glazing, etc. **9.** to discharge, as a gun. **10.** to project (a missile) by discharging from a gun, etc. **11.** to dismiss from a job. – *v.i.* **12.** to take fire; be kindled. **13.** to discharge a gun, etc. **14.** (of an internal-combustion engine) to cause ignition of the air-fuel mixture in the cylinder or cylinders.

firearm /ˈfaɪəram/ *n.* a small arms weapon from which a projectile is discharged by an explosion.

firebreak /ˈfaɪəbreɪk/ *n.* a strip of ploughed or cleared land made to check the spread of fire.

fire-engine /ˈfaɪər-ɛndʒən/ *n.* a motor vehicle equipped for fire fighting.

firefighter /ˈfaɪəfaɪtə/ *n.* a person employed to extinguish or prevent fires.

firefly /ˈfaɪəflaɪ/ *n., pl.* **-flies**. a beetle with abdominal light-producing organs.

fireplace /ˈfaɪəpleɪs/ *n.* that part of a chimney which opens into a room and in which fuel is burnt.

fireworks /ˈfaɪəwɜks/ *pl. n.* combustible or explosive devices for producing a striking display of light, etc.

firing squad *n.* a military detachment assigned to execute a condemned person by shooting.

firm[1] /fɜm/ *adj.* **1.** comparatively solid, hard, stiff or rigid. **2.** securely fixed in place. **3.** steady; not shaking or trembling.

firm[2] /fɜm/ *n.* **1.** a business organisation or partnership. **2.** the name or title under which associated parties transact business.

firmament /ˈfɜməmənt/ *n.* the vault of heaven; the sky.

firmware /ˈfɜmwɛə/ *n.* programs fixed into a computer's memory, which cannot be altered without changing the hardware, especially subroutines which are to last for the life of the computer.

first /fɜst/ *adj.* **1.** being before all others. – *adv.* **2.** before all others. **3.** for the first time. – *n.* **4.** that which is first in time, order, rank, etc.

first aid *n.* emergency aid or treatment given to persons suffering from accident, etc., until the services of a doctor can be obtained.

first-class /ˈfɜst-klas/ *adj.,* /fɜst-ˈklas/ *adv.* – *adj.* **1.** of the highest or best class or quality. – *adv.* **2.** by first-class conveyance.

first cost *n.* cost not including profit.

first-hand /ˈfɜst-hænd/ *adj.* direct from the original source.

first mortgage *n.* a mortgage having priority over all other mortgages on property.

first-past-the-post /ˌfɜst-past-ðə-ˈpoʊst/ *adj.* of or relating to an electoral system in which the candidate who gains the largest number of votes wins. Cf. **proportional representation, preferential voting**.

first person *n.* the class of a pronoun or verb in which the speaker is the subject. See **person** (def. 3).

first refusal *n.* the right of a customer to

buy or refuse goods before they can be sold to anyone else.

fiscal /ˈfɪskəl/ *adj.* **1.** of or relating to the public treasury or revenues. **2.** relating to financial matters in general.

fiscal year *n.* → **financial year**.

fish /fɪʃ/ *n., pl.* **fishes**, (*esp. collectively*) **fish**, *v.* – *n.* **1.** any of various cold-blooded, completely aquatic vertebrates, having gills, fins, and typically an elongated body usually covered with scales. **2.** any of various other aquatic animals. – *v.t.* **3.** to draw as by fishing (fol. by *up*, *out*, etc.). – *v.i.* **4.** to catch or attempt to catch fish, as by angling or drawing a net. **5.** to seek to obtain something by artifice or indirectly.

fisherman /ˈfɪʃəmən/ *n., pl.* **-men**. someone engaged in fishing.

fishwife /ˈfɪʃwaɪf/ *n., pl.* **-wives**. **1.** a woman who sells fish. **2.** a woman who has coarse manners and uses abusive language.

fishy /ˈfɪʃi/ *adj.*, **fishier**, **fishiest**. **1.** fishlike. **2.** *Colloquial* of questionable character.

fissi- a word element meaning 'cleft'.

fissile /ˈfɪsaɪl/ *adj.* capable of being split or divided; cleavable.

fission /ˈfɪʃən/ *n.* the act of cleaving or splitting into parts.

fissure /ˈfɪʃə/ *n.* a narrow opening produced by cleavage or separation of parts; a cleft.

fist /fɪst/ *n.* the hand closed tightly, with the fingers doubled into the palm.

fisticuffs /ˈfɪstɪkʌfs/ *pl. n.* combat with the fists.

fit[1] /fɪt/ *adj.*, **fitter**, **fittest**, *v.*, **fitted**, **fitting**, *n.* – *adj.* **1.** well adapted or suited. **2.** proper or becoming. **3.** in good health. – *v.t.* **4.** to be adapted to or suitable for (a purpose, object, occasion, etc.). **5.** to conform or adjust to something. **6.** to put with precise adjustment (fol. by *in*, *into*, *on*, *over*, *together*, etc.). **7.** to provide; furnish; equip. – *v.i.* **8.** to be suitable or proper. **9.** to be of the right size or shape. – *n.* **10.** the manner in which a thing fits.

fit[2] /fɪt/ *n.* **1.** a sudden, acute attack or manifestation of a disease. **2.** an access, spell or period of emotion or feeling, inclination, activity, idleness, etc. **3.** a convulsion.

fitful /ˈfɪtfəl/ *adj.* irregularly intermittent.

five /faɪv/ *n.* a cardinal number, four plus one. – **fifth**, *n., adj.*

fix /fɪks/ *v.*, **fixed**, **fixing**, *n.* – *v.t.* **1.** to make fast, firm, or stable. **2.** to settle definitely; determine. **3.** to direct (the eyes, the attention, etc.) steadily. **4.** to put or place (responsibility, blame, etc.) on a person. **5.** to repair. **6.** to settle down. – *n.* **7.** *Colloquial* a predicament. **8.** *Colloquial* the determining of a position, as of an aeroplane by mathematical, electronic, or other means.

fixation /fɪkˈseɪʃən/ *n.* **1.** the state of being fixed. **2.** *Psychology* an obsession.

fixed assets *pl. n.* any long-term assets which are held solely for use and not for conversion into cash, as land, buildings, machinery, etc. Also, **capital assets**.

fixed capital *n.* capital which has been used to acquire property, execute permanent constructions, or erect plant and machinery intended for retention and employment with a view to making profits (as opposed to *circulating capital*).

fixed charge *n.* a legal charge on specific property, as contrasted with a floating charge, both of which are usually contained in a debenture.

fixed deposit *n.* a deposit with an institution for a fixed term and receiving a fixed rate of interest, typically a debenture with a finance company or an interest-bearing deposit with a bank, building society, or credit union.

fixed interest *n.* an interest rate which is payable on a loan and which is fixed for the entire period of the loan.

fixed liability *n.* a long-term liability, as a mortgage, debenture, etc.

fixed trust *n.* a unit trust whose trust deed provides for a fixed portfolio of investments during the lifetime of the trust, save in exceptional circumstances (opposed to *flexible trust*).

fixture /ˈfɪkstʃə/ *n.* **1.** something securely fixed in position. **2.** a sporting event.

fizz /fɪz/ *v.i.* **1.** to make a hissing or sputtering sound. – *n.* **2.** a hissing sound; effervescence.

fizzle /ˈfɪzəl/ *v.*, **-zled**, **-zling**. – *v.t.* **1.** to make a hissing or sputtering sound, especially one that dies out weakly. – *v.i.* **2.** *Colloquial* to fail ignominiously after a good start (often fol. by *out*).

fjord /ˈfiɔd/ *n.* → **fiord**.

flab /flæb/ *n.* *Colloquial* bodily fat.

flabbergast /ˈflæbəgæst, -gast/ *v.t.* to overcome with surprise and bewilderment; astound.

flaccid /ˈflæsəd/ *adj.* soft and drooping.

flag[1] /flæg/ *n.*, *v.*, **flagged**, **flagging**. *n.* **1.** a piece of cloth of varying size, shape, colour, and device, used as an ensign, standard, symbol, signal, decoration, display, etc. – *v.t.* **2.** to signal or warn (a person, motor vehicle, etc.) with, or as with a flag (sometimes fol. by *down*).

flag[2] /flæg/ *v.i.*, **flagged**, **flagging**. to fall off in vigour, energy, activity, interest, etc.

flag[3] /ˈflæg/ *n.* a flat slab of stone used for paving, etc.

flagellate /ˈflædʒəleɪt/ *v.t.*, **-lated**, **-lating**. to whip; scourge; flog; lash.

flag fall *n.* an initial fee for hiring a taxi.

flag of convenience *n.* the flag of a country in which a ship has been registered only to gain some financial or legal advantage.

flagon /ˈflægən/ *n.* a large bottle.

flagrant /ˈfleɪgrənt/ *adj.* glaring; notorious; scandalous.

flagship /ˈflægʃɪp/ *n.* **1.** a ship which carries the admiral of a fleet, etc. **2.** the best example of a commercial item or enterprise. – *adj.* **3.** relating to the finest example of some commercial item or enterprise.

flail /fleɪl/ *v.t.*, *v.i.* to strike out wildly (at).

flair /flɛə/ *n.* talent; aptitude; keen perception.

flak /flæk/ *n.* anti-aircraft fire.

flake[1] /fleɪk/ *n.*, *v.*, **flaked**, **flaking**. – *n.* **1.** a small, flat, thin piece of anything. – *v.i.* **2.** to peel off or separate in flakes. **3.** Also, **flake out**. *Colloquial* to collapse, faint, or fall asleep.

flake[2] /fleɪk/ *n.* the flesh of various sharks.

flamboyant /flæm'bɔɪənt/ *adj.* **1.** extroverted and consciously theatrical. **2.** flaming; gorgeous. **3.** florid; ornate; showy.

flame /fleɪm/ *n., v.,* **flamed**, **flaming**. – *n.* **1.** burning gas or vapour, as from wood, etc., undergoing combustion. **2.** heat or ardour. **3.** *Colloquial* a sweetheart. – *v.i.* **4.** to burn with a flame or flames; burst into flames; blaze.

flamingo /flə'mɪŋgoʊ/ *n., pl.* **-gos**, **-goes**. an aquatic bird with very long neck and legs and pinkish plumage.

flammable /'flæməbəl/ *adj.* easily set on fire; combustible; inflammable. – **flammability**, *n.*

flan /flæn/ *n.* an open tart.

flange /flændʒ/ *n.* a projecting rim.

flank /flæŋk/ *n.* **1.** the side of an animal or a human being between the ribs and hip. **2.** the side of anything, as of a building. – *v.t.* **3.** to stand or be placed or posted at the flank or side of.

flannel /'flænəl/ *n.* **1.** a warm, soft fabric. **2.** → **washer** (def. 2).

flannelette /flænə'lɛt/ *n.* a cotton fabric made to imitate flannel.

flap /flæp/ *v.,* **flapped**, **flapping**, *n.* – *v.i.* **1.** to swing or sway about loosely, especially with noise. **2.** to move up and down, as wings. **3.** to flap the wings, or make similar movements. – *v.t.* **4.** to move (arms, wings, etc.) up and down. – *n.* **5.** a flapping motion. **6.** something broad and flexible, or flat and thin, that hangs loosely, attached at one side only. **7.** *Colloquial* a state of panic or nervous excitement.

flare /flɛə/ *v.,* **flared**, **flaring**, *n.* – *v.i.* **1.** to burn with an unsteady, swaying flame. **2.** to blaze with a sudden burst of flame (often fol. by *up*). **3.** to start up or burst out in sudden fierce activity. **4.** to spread gradually outwards as the end of a trumpet. – *n.* **5.** a sudden blaze of fire or light used as a signal or for illumination or guidance, etc. **6.** a sudden burst, as of zeal or of temper. **7.** a gradual spread outwards in form; outward curvature.

flash /flæʃ/ *n.* **1.** a sudden, transitory outburst of flame or light. **2.** a sudden, brief outburst or display of joy, wit, etc. **3.** the time occupied by a flash of light; an instant. **4.** ostentatious display. – *v.i.* **5.** to break forth into sudden flame or light, especially transiently or intermittently; to gleam. **6.** to move like a flash. – *v.t.* **7.** to emit or send forth (fire or light) in sudden flashes. – *adj.* **8.** showy or ostentatious.

flashback /'flæʃbæk/ *n.* a representation, during the course of a novel, film, etc., of some event or scene which occurred at a previous time.

flask /flask/ *n.* a bottle-shaped container.

flat[1] /flæt/ *adj.,* **flatter**, **flattest**, *adv., n.* – *adj.* **1.** level, even, or without inequalities of surface, as land, etc. **2.** lying at full length, as a person. **3.** low and broad. **4.** (of feet) having little or no arch. **5.** spread out. **6.** collapsed; deflated. **7.** unqualified, downright, or positive. **8.** uninteresting, dull, or tedious. **9.** (of beer, etc.) having lost its effervescence. – *adv.* **10.** in a flat position; horizontally; levelly. **11.** *Music* below the true pitch. **12. flat out**, *Colloquial* **a.** as fast as possible. **b.** very busy. – *n.* **13.** something flat. **14.** a flat surface, side or part of anything.

flat[2] /flæt/ *n., v.,* **flatted**, **flatting**. – *n.* **1.** a suite of rooms, usually on one floor only, forming a complete residence, and usually rented. – *v.i.* **2.** to live in a flat.

flathead /'flæthɛd/ *n.* a food fish with a depressed, ridged head.

flatter /'flætə/ *v.t.* **1.** to seek to please by complimentary speech or attentions; compliment or praise, especially insincerely. **2.** to show to advantage. – **flattery**, *n.*

flatulent /'flætʃələnt/ *adj.* **1.** generating gas in the alimentary canal. **2.** pretentious; empty. – **flatulence**, *n.*

flaunt /flɔnt/ *v.i.* to parade or display oneself conspicuously or boldly.

flautist /'flɔtəst/ *n.* a flute player.

flavour = flavor /'fleɪvə/ *n.* **1.** taste, especially a characteristic taste, or a noticeable element in the taste, of a thing. **2.** the characteristic quality of a thing.

flaw /flɔ/ *n.* a defect.

flax /flæks/ *n.* **1.** a plant cultivated for its fibre and seeds. **2.** the fibre of this plant, manufactured into linen yarn for thread or woven fabrics.

flaxen /'flæksən/ *adj.* **1.** made of flax. **2.** of a pale yellowish colour.

flay /fleɪ/ *v.t.* **1.** to strip off the skin or outer covering of. **2.** to criticise or reprove with scathing severity.

flea /fli/ *n.* any of numerous small, wingless, blood-sucking insects.

fleck /flɛk/ *n.* **1.** any spot or patch of colour, light, etc. – *v.t.* **2.** to mark with a fleck or flecks; spot; dapple.

fled /flɛd/ *v.* past tense and past participle of **flee**.

fledge /flɛdʒ/ *v.t.,* **fledged**, **fledging**. to bring up (a young bird) until it is able to fly.

fledgling /'flɛdʒlɪŋ/ *n.* **1.** a young bird just fledged. **2.** an inexperienced person. Also, **fledgeling**.

flee /fli/ *v.t., v.i.,* **fled**, **fleeing**. to run away (from).

fleece /flis/ *n., v.,* **fleeced**, **fleecing**. – *n.* **1.** the coat of wool that covers a sheep or some similar animal. – *v.t.* **2.** to strip of money or belongings; plunder; swindle.

fleet[1] /flit/ *n.* **1.** the largest organised unit of naval ships. **2.** the vessels, aeroplanes or vehicles collectively of a single transport company or undertaking.

fleet[2] /flit/ *adj.* swift; rapid.

fleeting /'flitɪŋ/ *adj.* passing swiftly; transient; transitory.

flesh /flɛʃ/ *n.* **1.** the soft substance of an animal body, consisting of muscle and fat. **2.** the body, especially as distinguished from the spirit or soul. **3.** the soft pulpy portion of a fruit, vegetable, etc.

flew /flu/ *v.* past tense of **fly**[1].

flex /flɛks/ *v.t.* **1.** to bend (something pliant or jointed). – *n.* **2.** a small, flexible insulated electric cable or wire.

flexible /'flɛksəbəl/ *adj.* **1.** easily bent.

2. adaptable. – **flexibility**, *n.*

flexible trust *n.* a unit trust whose trust deed provides for changes being made in the portfolio of investments at the discretion of the management company, usually after approval by the trustee company (opposed to *fixed trust*).

flexiday /ˈflɛksideɪ/ *n.* a day taken off from work under a flexitime scheme.

flexitime /ˈflɛksitaɪm/ *n.* an arrangement of ordinary hours of work in which employees may elect to vary their commencing, ceasing, and meal-break times while still maintaining the total number of hours worked.

flick[1] /flɪk/ *n.* **1.** a sudden light blow or stroke, as with a whip or the finger. – *v.t.* **2.** to remove with a flick.

flick[2] /flɪk/ *n.* *Colloquial* **1.** a cinema film. **2.** (*pl.*) the cinema.

flicker /ˈflɪkə/ *v.i.* **1.** to burn unsteadily; shine with a wavering light. – *n.* **2.** an unsteady flame or light. **3.** a brief spark.

flight[1] /flaɪt/ *n.* **1.** the act, manner, or power of flying. **2.** the distance covered or the course pursued by a flying object. **3.** a journey by air, especially by aeroplane. **4.** swift movement in general. **5.** a soaring above or transcending ordinary bounds. **6.** *Architecture* the series of steps or stairs between two adjacent landings.

flight[2] /flaɪt/ *n.* the act of fleeing.

flighty /ˈflaɪti/ *adj.*, **-tier**, **-tiest**. given to flights or sallies of fancy, caprice, etc.

flimsy /ˈflɪmzi/ *adj.*, **-sier**, **-siest**. without material strength or solidity.

flinch /flɪntʃ/ *v.i.* to draw back or shrink from what is dangerous, difficult, or unpleasant.

fling /flɪŋ/ *v.*, **flung**, **flinging**, *n.* – *v.t.* **1.** to throw, cast, or hurl, especially with violence. **2.** to put suddenly or violently. – *n.* **3.** a spell of unrestrained indulgence of one's impulses.

flint /flɪnt/ *n.* a hard kind of stone.

flip /flɪp/ *v.*, **flipped**, **flipping**, *n.* – *v.t.* **1.** to toss or put in motion with a snap of a finger and thumb; flick. – *n.* **2.** a smart tap or strike. **3.** a somersault.

flip-flop /ˈflɪp-flɒp/ *n.* **1.** an electronic circuit which alternates polarity. **2.** *Computers* an electronic device used to store a binary digit.

flippant /ˈflɪpənt/ *adj.* **1.** clever or pert in speech. **2.** characterised by a shallow or disrespectful levity.

flipper /ˈflɪpə/ *n.* **1.** a broad, flat limb, as of a seal, whale, etc., especially adapted for swimming. **2.** a device resembling in form an animal's flipper, usually made of rubber, used as an aid in swimming.

flirt /flɜt/ *v.i.* **1.** to trifle in love. – *n.* **2.** a person given to flirting.

flit /flɪt/ *v.i.*, **flitted**, **flitting**. to move lightly and swiftly.

float /floʊt/ *v.i.* **1.** to rest on the surface of a liquid; be buoyant. **2.** to move or drift about free from attachment. **3.** *Commerce* to be in circulation, as an acceptance; be awaiting maturity. – *v.t.* **4.** to cause to float. **5.** to launch (a company, scheme, etc.). **6.** to allow the rate of exchange of (a currency) to find its own level in a foreign exchange market. – *n.* **7.** something that floats, as a raft. **8.** a platform on wheels, bearing a display and drawn in a procession. **9.** an inflated bag to sustain a person in water; a life jacket. **10.** a quantity of money used by shopkeepers and others to provide change. **11.** the total value of cheques written but still not presented at one's bank.

floating assets *pl. n.* assets which are continually changing, as cash, stock in trade, bills of exchange, etc.

floating charge *n.* an equitable charge on the assets of a going concern, which does not become fixed and remains dormant until the company is wound up or breaks some condition, thus permitting the person(s) in whose favour the charge is created to intervene to protect their interests.

flocculent /ˈflɒkjələnt/ *adj.* consisting of or containing loose woolly masses.

flock[1] /flɒk/ *n.* **1.** a number of animals of one kind now especially of sheep or goats, or of birds. – *v.i.* **2.** to gather or go in a flock, company, or crowd.

flock[2] /flɒk/ *n.* a lock or tuft of wool, hair, etc.

floe /floʊ/ *n.* a field of floating ice formed on the surface of the sea, etc.

flog /flɒg/ *v.t.*, **flogged**, **flogging**. **1.** to beat hard with a whip, stick, etc.; whip. **2.** *Colloquial* to sell or attempt to sell. **3.** to steal.

flood √/flʌd/ *n.* **1.** a great flowing or overflowing of water, especially over land not usually submerged. **2.** any great outpouring or stream. – *v.t.* **3.** to overflow in or cover with a flood; fill to overflowing. **4.** to overwhelm with an abundance of something. – *v.i.* **5.** to flow or pour in or as in a flood.

floodlight /ˈflʌdlaɪt/ *n.*, *v.*, **-lighted** *or* **-lit**, **-lighting**. – *n.* **1.** an artificial light so directed or diffused as to give a comparatively uniform illumination over a given area. – *v.t.* **2.** to illuminate with or as with a floodlight.

floor /flɔ/ *n.* **1.** that part of a room or the like which forms its lower enclosing surface, and upon which one walks. **2.** a storey of a building. **3.** the flat bottom of any more or less hollow place. **4.** any more or less flat extent or surface. **5.** the part of a legislative chamber, etc., where the members sit, and from which they speak. **6.** the right of one member to speak from such a place in preference to other members. **7.** the main part of a stock exchange or the like, as distinct from galleries, etc. **8.** the bottom, base, or minimum charged or paid. – *v.t.* **9.** to cover or furnish with a floor. **10.** *Colloquial* to confound or nonplus.

flop /flɒp/ *v.*, **flopped**, **flopping**, *n.* – *v.i.* **1.** to drop or turn with a sudden bump or thud. **2.** *Colloquial* to yield or break down suddenly; fail. – *n.* *Colloquial* **3.** a failure.

floppy disk /flɒpi ˈdɪsk/ *n.* a flexible magnetically coated disk used for storing data; diskette.

flora /ˈflɔrə/ *n.*, *pl.* **floras**, **florae** /ˈflɔri/. the plants of a particular region.

floral /ˈflɒrəl, ˈflɔrəl/ *adj.* relating to or consisting of flowers.

florid /ˈflɒrəd/ *adj.* highly coloured or ruddy, as complexion, cheeks, etc.

florin /ˈflɒrən/ *n.* a silver coin worth two shillings.

florist /ˈflɒrəst/ *n.* a retailer of flowers.

-florous an adjectival suffix meaning ‘flower’.

floss /flɒs/ *n.* **1.** silky filamentous matter. **2.** Also, **dental floss**. soft, waxed thread used for cleaning between the teeth.

flotation /floʊˈteɪʃən/ *n.* **1.** the act or state of floating. **2.** the floating or launching of a commercial venture, a loan, etc.

flotilla /fləˈtɪlə/ *n.* a number of small naval vessels.

flotsam /ˈflɒtsəm/ *n.* such part of the wreckage of a ship and its cargo as is found floating on the water. Cf. **jetsam**.

flotsam and jetsam *n.* the wreckage of a ship and its cargo found either floating upon the sea or washed ashore.

flounce[1] /flaʊns/ *v.i.*, **flounced**, **flouncing**. to go with an impatient or angry fling of the body.

flounce[2] /flaʊns/ *n.* a gathered strip of material on a skirt, etc.

flounder[1] /ˈflaʊndə/ *v.i.* **1.** to struggle with stumbling or plunging movements. **2.** to struggle clumsily or helplessly in embarrassment or confusion.

flounder[2] /ˈflaʊndə/ *n.*, *pl.* **-der**. any of numerous species of flatfishes.

flour /ˈflaʊə/ *n.* the finely ground meal of wheat or other grain.

flourish /ˈflʌrɪʃ/ *v.i.* **1.** to be in a vigorous state; thrive; prosper; be successful. – *v.t.* **2.** to brandish or wave (a sword, a stick, the limbs, etc.) about in the air. – *n.* **3.** a brandishing or waving, as of a sword, a stick, or the like. **4.** a parade or ostentatious display. **5.** a decoration or embellishment in writing. **6.** *Music* a trumpet call or fanfare.

flout /flaʊt/ *v.t.* to mock; scoff at.

flow /floʊ/ *v.i.* **1.** to move along in a stream, as a liquid; circulate, as the blood. **2.** to proceed continuously and smoothly, like a stream, as thought, speech, or verse. **3.** to fall or hang loosely at full length, as hair. – *n.* **4.** the act of flowing. **5.** movement in or as in a stream; any continuous movement, as of thought, speech, trade, etc., like that of a stream of water. **6.** the rise of the tide (opposed to *ebb*).

flow chart *n.* a diagram showing the step-by-step operation of a system. Also, **flow diagram**, **flow sheet**.

flower /ˈflaʊə/ *n.* **1.** the blossom of a plant. **2.** the best or finest member or part of a number, body, or whole. – *v.i.* **3.** to produce flowers, or blossom, as a plant; to come to full bloom. **4.** to reach the stage of full development.

flower girl *n.* a very young girl attending a bride.

flowery /ˈflaʊəri/ *adj.*, **-rier**, **-riest**. **1.** abounding in or covered with flowers. **2.** containing highly ornate language.

flown /floʊn/ *v.* past participle of **fly**[1].

flow-on /ˈfloʊ-ɒn/ *n.* the wider application of changes in wages, costs, etc., which have arisen in one part of the community.

flu /flu/ *n.* *Colloquial* → **influenza**.

fluctuate /ˈflʌktʃueɪt/ *v.i.*, **-ated**, **-ating**. to change continually, as by turns, from one course, position, condition, amount, etc., to another.

flue /flu/ *n.* any duct or passage for air, gases, or the like.

fluent /ˈfluənt/ *adj.* **1.** flowing smoothly and easily. **2.** able to speak or write readily. **3.** easy; graceful.

fluff /flʌf/ *n.* **1.** light, downy particles, as of cotton. **2.** *Colloquial* a blunder or error.

fluid /ˈfluəd/ *n.* a substance which is capable of flowing; a liquid or a gas.

fluidics /fluˈɪdɪks/ *n.* the branch of computing which uses hydraulic systems to simulate problems and manipulate data. Fluidic systems are slow in operation compared with electronic circuits but are suitable for specialised applications. – **fluidic**, *adj.*

fluke[1] /fluk/ *n.* any accidental advantage; a lucky chance.

fluke[2] /fluk/ *n.* **1.** a type of flounder. **2.** a flatworm.

flummox /ˈflʌməks/ *v.t.* *Colloquial* to bewilder; confuse.

flung /flʌŋ/ *v.* past tense and past participle of **fling**.

flunk /flʌŋk/ *v.t.*, *v.i.* *Colloquial* to fail, as a student in an examination.

flunkey /ˈflʌŋki/ *n.*, *pl.* **-keys**. **1.** a male servant in livery; a lackey. **2.** a servile follower; a toady.

fluorescence /fluəˈrɛsəns, flə-/ *n.* the property possessed by certain substances of emitting light upon exposure to external radiation or bombardment by a stream of particles. – **fluorescent**, *adj.*

fluoride /ˈfluəraɪd, ˈflu-/ *n.* an organic compound used to prevent tooth decay.

fluorine /ˈfluərin, ˈflu-/ *n.* a pale yellow corrosive gas. *Symbol*: F

fluorspar /ˈfluəspa/ *n.* a common mineral, calcium fluoride.

flurry /ˈflʌri/ *n.* **1.** a sudden gust of wind. **2.** commotion.

flush[1] /flʌʃ/ *n.* **1.** a blush; a rosy glow. **2.** a rushing or overspreading flow, as of water. **3.** a rush of emotion; elation. **4.** waves of heat, as during fever, menopause, etc.

flush[2] /flʌʃ/ *adj.* **1.** even or level, as with a surface; in one plane. **2.** well-supplied, as with money; affluent; prosperous.

flush[3] /flʌʃ/ *v.t.* to cause (others) to reveal themselves (often fol. by *out*).

flush[4] /flʌʃ/ *n.* *Cards* a hand consisting entirely of cards of one suit.

fluster /ˈflʌstə/ *v.t.* to confuse; make nervous.

flute /flut/ *n.* **1.** a musical wind instrument consisting of a tube with a series of finger holes or keys. **2.** a channel or furrow.

flutter /ˈflʌtə/ *v.i.* **1.** to flap or wave lightly in air, as a flag. **2.** to beat fast and irregularly, as the heart. – *n.* **3.** a fluttering movement. **4.** a state of nervous excitement or mental agitation. **5.** *Colloquial* a small wager or bet.

fluvial /ˈfluviəl/ *adj.* of, relating to, or produced by a river.

flux /flʌks/ *n.* a flowing or flow.

fly[1] /flaɪ/ *v.*, **flew**, **flown**, **flying**, *n.*, *pl.* **flies**. – *v.i.* **1.** to move through the air on wings, as a bird. **2.** to be borne through the air. **3.** to move or pass swiftly; move with a start or rush. **4.** to flee. – *v.t.* **5.** to cause to fly. **6.** to avoid; flee from. – *n.* **7.** a strip sewn along one edge of a garment, to aid in concealing the buttons or other fasteners. **8.** a flap forming the door of a tent. **9.** a piece of canvas extending over the ridgepole of a tent and forming an outer roof. **10.** a light tent. **11.** (*pl.*) *Theatre* the space and apparatus above the stage. **12.** *Colloquial* an attempt: *give it a fly*.

fly[2] /flaɪ/ *n.*, *pl.* **flies**. **1.** any of various two-winged insects, especially the common housefly. **2.** *Angling* a fishhook dressed with silk, tinsel, etc., to resemble an insect.

flying fox /'flaɪɪŋ/ *n.* **1.** any of various large bats having a foxlike head. **2.** a cable-operated carrier over watercourses or difficult terrain.

flying saucer *n.* any of various disc-shaped objects allegedly seen flying at high speeds and altitudes.

flyleaf /'flaɪlif/ *n.*, *pl.* **-leaves** /-livz/. a blank leaf in the front or at the back of a book.

foal /foʊl/ *n.* **1.** the young of a horse. – *v.i.* **2.** to bring forth a foal.

foam /foʊm/ *n.* **1.** an aggregation of minute bubbles formed on the surface of a liquid by agitation, fermentation, etc. **2.** the froth of perspiration or saliva. **3.** a light material, in either spongy or rigid form, used for packing, etc.

fob[1] /fɒb/ *n.* **1.** Also, **fob pocket**. a small pocket just below the waistline in trousers, to hold a watch, etc. **2.** a short chain for a watch.

fob[2] /fɒb/ *v.t.*, **fobbed**, **fobbing**. **1.** to palm off (fol. by *off*). **2.** to put off (fol. by *off*).

focaccia /fə'katʃiə/ *n.* flat Italian bread which can be eaten with various fillings or toppings.

focus /'foʊkəs/ *n.*, *pl.* **-ci** /-saɪ, -kaɪ/ **-cuses**, *v.*, **-cused**, **-cusing** *or* **-cussed**, **-cussing**. – *n.* **1.** *Physics* a point at which rays of light, heat, or other radiation, meet after being refracted or reflected. **2.** clear and sharply defined condition of an image. **3.** a central point, as of attraction, attention, or activity. – *v.t.* **4.** to bring to a focus or into focus. **5.** to concentrate. – **focal**, *adj.*

fodder /'fɒdə/ *n.* food for livestock.

foe /foʊ/ *n.* an enemy or opponent.

foetus = fetus /'fitəs/ *n.* the young of a mammal in the womb or in the egg, especially in its later stages. – **foetal**, *adj.*

fog /fɒg/ *n.* **1.** a cloudlike mass or layer of minute globules of water in the air near the earth's surface; thick mist. **2.** a state of mental confusion or obscurity.

foghorn /'fɒghɔn/ *n.* *Nautical* a horn for sounding warning signals, as to vessels, in foggy weather.

fogy = fogey /'foʊgi/ *n.*, *pl.* **-gies**. an old-fashioned or excessively conservative person.

foible /'fɔɪbəl/ *n.* a weakness or failing of character.

foil[1] /fɔɪl/ *v.t.* to frustrate (a person, an attempt, a purpose); baffle; baulk.

foil[2] /fɔɪl/ *n.* **1.** a metallic substance formed into very thin sheets by rolling and hammering. **2.** anything that serves to set off another thing distinctly or to advantage by contrast.

foil[3] /fɔɪl/ *n.* a flexible, thin sword with a button at the point, for use in fencing.

foist /fɔɪst/ *v.t.* to palm off or impose fraudulently or unwarrantably (fol. by *on* or *upon*).

fold[1] /foʊld/ *v.t.* **1.** to double or bend (cloth, paper, etc.) over upon itself. **2.** to bring into a compact form, or shut, by bending and laying parts together (often fol. by *up*). **3.** *Cookery* to mix (*in*) gently. – *v.i.* **4.** to be folded or be capable of folding. **5.** to be closed or brought to an end, usually with financial loss, as a business enterprise or theatrical production. – *n.* **6.** a part that is folded; pleat; layer. **7.** a hollow place in undulating ground.

fold[2] /foʊld/ *n.* **1.** an enclosure for domestic animals, especially sheep. **2.** a church or congregation.

-fold a suffix denoting multiplication by or division into a certain number, as in *twofold*, *manifold*.

folder /'foʊldə/ *n.* an outer cover, usually a folded sheet of light cardboard, for papers.

foliage /'foʊliɪdʒ/ *n.* the leaves of a plant, collectively.

folio /'foʊlioʊ/ *n.* **1.** a sheet of paper folded once to make two leaves (four pages) of a book. **2.** a paper size. **3.** *Printing* the page number of a book. **4.** *Bookkeeping* a page of an account book, or a left-hand page and a right-hand page facing each other and having the same serial number. **5.** *Law* a certain number of words, usually 72, taken as a unit for computing the length of a document. – *v.t.* **6.** to number the leaves of (a book) on one side only.

folk /foʊk/ *n.*, *pl.* **folk**, **folks**. people in general, especially the common people.

folk dance *n.* a dance which originated among, and has been transmitted through, the common people.

folklore /'foʊklɔ/ *n.* the traditional beliefs, legends, customs, etc., of a people.

folk music *n.* **1.** music, usually of simple character, originating and handed down among the common people. **2.** music originating in the urban American beat generation of the 1940s and 1950s which concentrates on lyrics of social comment. Also, **folk**.

follicle /'fɒlɪkəl/ *n.* **1.** *Botany* a seed vessel. **2.** *Anatomy* a small cavity, sac, or gland.

follow /'fɒloʊ/ *v.t.* **1.** to come after in natural sequence, order of time, etc.; succeed. **2.** to go or come after; move behind in the same direction. **3.** to accept as a guide or leader. **4.** to move forward along (a path, etc.). **5.** to watch the movements, progress, or course of. **6.** **follow through,** to carry out completely. **7.** **follow suit, a.** *Cards* to play a card of the same suit as that first played. **b.** to follow the example of another. **8.** **follow up, a.** to pursue closely, or to a conclusion. **b.** to take further action, investigation, etc., after the elapse of an interval of time; reopen. – *v.i.* **9.** to come next after something else in natural sequence, order of time, etc. **10.** to result as an effect; occur as a consequence.

folly /ˈfɒli/ *n., pl.* **-lies**. **1.** the state or quality of being foolish. **2.** a foolish action, practice, idea, etc.

foment /fəˈmɛnt/ *v.t.* **1.** to promote the growth or development of; instigate or foster (discord, rebellion, etc.). **2.** to apply warm water or medicated liquid to (the surface of the body).

fond /fɒnd/ *adj.* **1.** liking (fol. by *of*). **2.** loving. **3.** foolishly tender; over-affectionate; doting. **4.** cherished with strong or unreasoning affection.

fondle /ˈfɒndl/ *v.t.*, **-dled**, **-dling**. to show fondness to, as by manner, words, or caresses.

fondue /ˈfɒndju/ *n.* a dish of melted cheese or other sauce into which pieces of bread, meat, etc., are dipped.

font[1] /fɒnt/ *n.* a receptacle for the water used in baptism.

font[2] /fɒnt/ *n.* a complete assortment of printing type of one style and size. Also, **fount**.

food /fud/ *n.* **1.** what is eaten, or taken into the body, for nourishment. **2.** more or less solid nourishment (as opposed to *drink*).

fool /ful/ *n.* **1.** someone who lacks sense; a silly or stupid person. **2.** a professional jester. **3.** someone who is made to appear a fool; someone who has been imposed on by others. – *v.t.* **4.** to make a fool of; impose on; trick; deceive. – *v.i.* **5.** to act like a fool; joke; play.

foolhardy /ˈfulhadi/ *adj.*, **-dier**, **-diest**. bold without judgment.

foolish /ˈfulɪʃ/ *adj.* silly; without sense.

foolscap /ˈfulzkæp/ *n.* a printing paper size.

foot /fʊt/ *n., pl.* **feet**, *v.* – *n.* **1.** (in vertebrates) the terminal part of the leg, below the ankle joint, on which the body stands and moves. **2.** (in invertebrates) any part similar in position or function. **3.** a unit of length in the imperial system, equal to 0.3048 m. **4.** any thing or part resembling a foot, as in function. **5.** the part of a stocking, etc., covering the foot. **6.** the part of anything opposite the top or head. – *v.i.* **7.** to walk; go on foot (often followed by indefinite *it*). – *v.t.* **8.** *Colloquial* to pay or settle (a bill).

footage /ˈfʊtɪdʒ/ *n.* **1.** length or extent in feet. **2.** a length of film; the film used for a scene or scenes.

foot-and-mouth disease *n.* a contagious virus disease of cattle, etc.

football /ˈfʊtbɔl/ *n.* **1.** any game in which the kicking of a ball has a large part, as Australian Rules, Rugby Union, Rugby League, soccer, American football, etc. **2.** the ball used in such games.

foothill /ˈfʊthɪl/ *n.* a minor elevation at the base of a mountain or mountain range.

footing /ˈfʊtɪŋ/ *n.* **1.** a secure position. **2.** the basis or foundation on which anything is established. **3.** position or status assigned to a person, etc., in estimation or treatment.

footlights /ˈfʊtlaɪts/ *pl. n. Theatre* a row of lights at the front of the stage.

footloose /ˈfʊtlus/ *adj.* free to go or travel about; not confined by responsibilities, etc.

footman /ˈfʊtmən/ *n., pl.* **-men**. a male servant, especially in livery.

footnote /ˈfʊtnoʊt/ *n.* a note or comment at the foot of a page, referring to a specific part of the text on the page.

footstep /ˈfʊtstɛp/ *n.* a step or tread of the foot, or the sound produced by it.

fop /fɒp/ *n.* a man who is excessively concerned about his manners and appearance.

for /fɔ/, *weak forms* /fə, f/ – *prep.* **1.** with the object or purpose of. **2.** intended to belong to, suit the purposes or needs of, or be used in connection with. **3.** in order to obtain. **4.** in consideration of, or in return for. **5.** appropriate or adapted to. **6.** with regard or respect to. **7.** during the continuance of. **8.** in favour of, or on the side of. **9.** in place of, or instead of. **10.** by reason of, or because of. – *conj.* **11.** seeing that; since. **12.** because.

for- a prefix meaning 'away', 'off', 'extremely', 'wrongly', or imparting a negative force.

forage /ˈfɒrɪdʒ/ *n., v.*, **-raged**, **-raging**. – *n.* **1.** food for horses and cattle. – *v.i.* **2.** to hunt or search about.

forasmuch /fɔrəzˈmʌtʃ/ *conj.* in view of the fact that; seeing that; since (fol. by *as*).

foray /ˈfɒreɪ, ˈfɔ-/ *n.* a raid for the purpose of taking plunder.

forbade /fəˈbeɪd/ *v.* past tense of **forbid**. Also, **forbad** /fəˈbæd/.

forbear /fɔˈbɛə/ *v.t.*, **-bore**, **-borne**, **-bearing**. to refrain from; desist from; cease.

forbearance /fɔˈbɛərəns/ *n.* **1.** patience. **2.** an abstaining from the enforcement of a right.

forbid /fəˈbɪd/ *v.t.*, **-bade** *or* **-bad**, **-bidden** *or* **-bid**, **-bidding**. **1.** to command (a person, etc.) not to do, have, use, etc., something, or not to enter some place. **2.** to prohibit (something).

force /fɔs/ *n., v.*, **forced**, **forcing**. – *n.* **1.** strength; power. **2.** *Law* violence offered to persons or things. **3.** (*often pl.*) a large body of armed personnel; an army. **4.** any body of persons combined for joint action. **5.** operation. **6.** *Physics* an influence which produces or tends to produce motion or change of motion. **7.** value; significance; meaning. – *v.t.* **8.** to compel to do something. **9.** to drive or propel against resistance. **10.** to break open (a door, lock, etc.).

forceps /ˈfɔsəps/ *n., pl.* **-ceps**, **-cipes** /-səpiz/. an instrument, as pincers or tongs, for seizing and holding objects, as in surgical operations.

forcible /ˈfɔsəbəl/ *adj.* **1.** effected by force. **2.** having force; producing a powerful effect; effective.

ford /fɔd/ *n.* **1.** a place where a river or other body of water may be crossed by wading. – *v.t.* **2.** to cross (a river, etc.) by a ford.

fore /fɔ/ *adj.* **1.** situated at or towards the front, as compared with something else. **2.** first in place, time, order, rank, etc.; forward; earlier. – *n.* **3.** the forepart of anything; the front.

fore- a prefix form of **before** meaning 'front' (*forehead*), 'ahead of time' (*forecast*), 'superior' (*foreman*), etc.

forearm /'fɔram/ *n.* the part of the arm between the elbow and the wrist.

forebear /'fɔbɛə/ *n.* (*usu. pl.*) an ancestor; forefather.

forebode /fɔ'boʊd/ *v.t.*, **-boded**, **-boding**. to foretell or predict; portend. – **foreboding**, *n.*

forecast /'fɔkast/ *v.*, **-cast** *or* **-casted**, **-casting**, *n.* – *v.t.* **1.** to conjecture beforehand; predict. – *n.* **2.** a prediction, especially as to the weather.

foreclose /fɔ'kloʊz/ *v.*, **-closed**, **-closing**. – *v.t.* **1.** *Law* **a.** to deprive (a mortgagor or pledgor) of the right to redeem his or her property. **b.** to take away the right to redeem (a mortgage or pledge). – *v.i.* **2.** to foreclose a mortgage or pledge.

forefather /'fɔfaðə/ *n.* an ancestor.

forefinger /'fɔfɪŋgə/ *n.* the first finger, next to the thumb; the index finger.

foregift /'fɔgɪft/ *n.* a premium sometimes paid in consideration of the granting of a lease.

forego /fɔ'goʊ/ *v.t.*, *v.i.*, **-went**, **-gone**, **-going**. to go before.

foreground /'fɔgraʊnd/ *n.* the ground or parts situated, or represented as situated, in the front.

forehand /'fɔhænd/ *adj. Sport* (of a stroke, etc.) made to the right side of the body (when the player is right-handed).

forehead /'fɒrəd/ *n.* the part of the face above the eyes; the brow.

foreign /'fɒrən/ *adj.* **1.** relating to, characteristic of, or derived from another country or nation; not native or domestic. **2.** not related to or connected with the thing under consideration. – **foreigner**, *n.*

foreign exchange *n.* **1.** the buying and selling of the money of other countries. **2.** the money of other countries.

foreign exchange rate *n.* the rate at which the money of one country is exchanged for that of another.

forelock /'fɔlɒk/ *n.* the lock of hair that grows from the front part of the head.

foreman /'fɔmən/ *n.*, *pl.* **-men**. **1.** the supervisor of a group of workers. **2.** the spokesperson of a jury.

foremost /'fɔmoʊst/ *adj.*, *adv.* first in place, order, rank, etc.

forename /'fɔneɪm/ *n.* a name that precedes the family name or surname; a first name.

forensic /fə'rɛnsɪk, -zɪk/ *adj.* **1.** relating to, connected with, or used in courts of law or public discussion and debate. **2.** adapted or suited to argumentation; argumentative.

foreplay /'fɔpleɪ/ *n.* stimulation preceding sexual intercourse.

forerunner /'fɔrʌnə/ *n.* **1.** a predecessor; ancestor. **2.** a herald. **3.** a portent.

foresee /fɔ'si/ *v.t.*, **-saw**, **-seen**, **-seeing**. to see beforehand.

foreshore /'fɔʃɔ/ *n.* the part of the shore between the ordinary high-water mark and low-water mark.

foresight /'fɔsaɪt/ *n.* care or provision for the future; provident care.

foreskin /'fɔskɪn/ *n.* → **prepuce**.

forest /'fɒrəst/ *n.* a large tract of land covered with trees. – **forestry**, *n.*

forestall /fɔ'stɔl/ *v.t.* to take measures concerning or deal with (a thing) in advance.

forever /fər'ɛvə/ *adv.* **1.** eternally; without ever ending. **2.** continually.

foreword /'fɔwɜd/ *n.* a preface or introductory statement in a book, etc.

forex /'fɒrɛks/ *n.* **1.** foreign exchange. – *adj.* **2.** having to do with foreign exchange.

forfeit /'fɔfət/ *n.* **1.** a fine; a penalty. **2.** the act of forfeiting. – *v.t.* **3.** to lose as a forfeit. **4.** to lose, or become liable to lose, in consequence of crime, fault, breach of engagement, etc.

forgave /fə'geɪv/ *v.* past tense of **forgive**.

forge[1] /fɔdʒ/ *n.*, *v.*, **forged**, **forging**. – *n.* **1.** the special fireplace, hearth, or furnace in which metal is heated before shaping. – *v.t.* **2.** to form by heating and hammering. **3.** to form or make in any way. **4.** to imitate (a signature, etc.) fraudulently. – **forgery**, *n.*

forge[2] /fɔdʒ/ *v.i.*, **forged**, **forging**. to move ahead slowly.

forget /fə'gɛt/ *v.*, **-got**, **-gotten**, **-getting**. -*v.t.* **1.** to cease to remember; fail to remember; be unable to recall. **2.** to neglect or omit; overlook. – *v.i.* **3.** to cease or omit to think of something.

forgetful /fə'gɛtfəl/ *adj.* apt to forget.

forgive /fə'gɪv/ *v.*, **-gave**, **-given**, **-giving**. – *v.t.* **1.** to grant free pardon for. **2.** to cease to feel resentment against. – *v.i.* **3.** to pardon an offence or an offender.

forgo /fɔ'goʊ/ *v.t.*, **-went**, **-gone**, **-going**. to abstain or refrain from; do without.

fork /fɔk/ *n.* **1.** an instrument having two or more prongs for holding, lifting, etc. **2.** something resembling or suggesting this in form.

forlorn /fə'lɔn/ *adj.* **1.** unhappy or miserable, as in feeling, condition, or appearance. **2.** desperate or hopeless.

form /fɔm/ *n.* **1.** external shape or appearance considered apart from colour or material. **2.** a particular structural condition, character, or mode of being exhibited by a thing. **3.** any assemblage of similar things constituting a component of a group, especially of a zoological group. **4.** a document with blank spaces to be filled in with particulars before it is executed. **5.** procedure or conduct, as judged by social standards: *good form*; *bad form*. **6.** condition, especially good condition, with reference to fitness for performing. **7.** a single division of a school containing pupils of about the same age or of the same level of scholastic progress. **8.** a bench or long seat. **9.** *Horseracing, etc.* the record of an entrant's past performance by which chances of success in a race are assessed. – *v.t.* **10.** to construct or frame. **11.** to make or produce; to serve to make up, or compose. **12.** to contract (habits, friendships, etc.). **13.** to give form or shape to; shape; fashion. – *v.i.* **14.** to take or assume form.

-form a suffix meaning 'having the form of'.

formal /'fɔməl/ *adj.* **1.** being in accordance with conventional requirements; conventional. **2.** marked by form or ceremony. **3.** made or done in accordance with forms ensuring validity. – **formalise = formalize**, *v.* – **formality**, *n.*

formaldehyde /fɔ'mældəhaɪd/ *n.* a disinfectant and preservative gas.

format /'fɔmæt/ *n.* **1.** the general physical appearance of a book, newspaper, or magazine, etc., such as the typeface, binding, quality of paper, margins, etc. **2.** the plan or style of something. **3.** *Computers* an orderly arrangement of data elements to form a larger entity, as a list, table, file, etc.

formation /fɔ'meɪʃən/ *n.* **1.** the manner in which a thing is formed; disposition of parts. **2.** a group of things arranged according to a fixed plan.

formative /'fɔmətɪv/ *adj.* **1.** giving form or shape. – *n.* **2.** *Grammar* an affix, especially one which changes the part of speech of a word.

formidable /'fɔmədəbəl, fɔ'mɪdəbəl/ *adj.* that is to be feared or dreaded.

formula /'fɔmjələ/ *n., pl.* **-las**, **-lae** /-li/. **1.** a set form of words. **2.** *Mathematics* a rule or principle, frequently expressed in algebraic symbols. **3.** a fixed and successful method of doing something. **4.** a recipe or prescription. – **formulaic**, *adj.*

formulate /'fɔmjəleɪt/ *v.t.*, **-lated**, **-lating**. to express in precise form; state definitely or systematically.

fornication /fɔnə'keɪʃən/ *n.* voluntary sexual intercourse between unmarried persons. – **fornicate**, *v.*

forsake /fə'seɪk/ *v.t.*, **-sook**, **-saken**, **-saking**. **1.** to desert or abandon. **2.** to give up or renounce (a habit, way of life, etc.).

forswear /fɔ'swɛə/ *v.t.*, **-swore**, **-sworn**, **-swearing**. **1.** to reject or renounce upon oath or with protestations. **2.** to perjure (oneself).

fort /fɔt/ *n.* a strong or fortified place.

forth /fɔθ/ *adv.* **1.** forwards; onwards or outwards. **2.** out, as from concealment or inaction; into view or consideration.

forthcoming /'fɔθkʌmɪŋ/ *adj.* **1.** about to appear; approaching in time. **2.** ready or available when required or expected. **3.** ready to provide information; open.

forthright /'fɔθraɪt/ *adj.* going straight to the point; outspoken.

forthwith /fɔθ'wɪθ, -'wɪð/ *adv.* immediately; at once; without delay.

fortify /'fɔtəfaɪ/ *v.t.*, **-fied**, **-fying**. **1.** to strengthen against attack. **2.** to furnish with a means of resisting force or standing strain, wear, etc. – **fortification**, *n.*

fortitude /'fɔtətʃud/ *n.* moral strength or endurance.

fortnight /'fɔtnaɪt/ *n.* the space of fourteen nights and days; two weeks.

FORTRAN /'fɔtræn/ *n.* a computer language for scientific calculations in which instructions are expressed in an algebraic notation. Also, **Fortran**.

fortress /'fɔtrəs/ *n.* a large fortified place.

fortuitous /fɔ'tjuətəs/ *adj.* happening or produced by chance; accidental.

fortunate /'fɔtʃənət/ *adj.* **1.** having good fortune; receiving good from uncertain or unexpected sources; lucky. **2.** bringing or presaging good fortune.

fortune /'fɔtʃən/ *n.* **1.** position in life as determined by wealth. **2.** great wealth; ample stock of wealth. **3.** chance; luck. **4.** lot; destiny.

fortune-teller /'fɔtʃən-tɛlə/ *n.* someone who professes to tell people what will happen in the future. – **fortune-telling**, *adj., n.*

forty /'fɔti/ *n., pl.* **-ties**, *adj.* a cardinal number, ten times four. – **fortieth**, *adj., n.*

forum /'fɔrəm/ *n., pl.* **forums, fora** /'fɔrə/. an assembly for the discussion of questions of public interest.

forward /'fɔwəd/ *adj.* **1.** directed towards a point in advance; moving ahead; onward. **2.** being in a condition of advancement; well-advanced. **3.** presumptuous, pert, or bold. **4.** situated in the front or forepart. **5.** of or relating to the future. – *n.* **6.** *Australian Rules, etc.* a player placed in front of the rest of the team. – *adv.* **7.** forwards. – *v.t.* **8.** to send forward; transmit, especially to a new address. **9.** to advance or help onwards; hasten; promote.

forward exchange *n.* foreign currency bought or sold for future delivery.

fossick /'fɒsɪk/ *v.i.* to search unsystematically or in a small way.

fossil /'fɒsəl/ *n.* any remains, impression, or trace of an animal or plant of a former geological age, as a skeleton or a footprint.

foster /'fɒstə/ *v.t.* **1.** to promote the growth or development of; further; encourage. **2.** to bring up or rear, as a foster-child.

foster-child /'fɒstə-tʃaɪld/ *n., pl.* **-children**. a child brought up by someone not its own mother or father.

fought /fɔt/ *v.* past tense and past participle of **fight**.

foul /faʊl/ *adj.* **1.** grossly offensive to the senses; disgustingly loathsome; noisome. **2.** filthy or dirty, as places, vessels, or clothes. **3.** unfavourable or stormy, as weather. **4.** abominable, wicked, or vile, as deeds, crime, slander, etc. **5.** contrary to the rules or established usages, as of a sport or game; unfair. **6.** abounding in errors or in marks of correction, as a printer's proof. – *adv.* **7.** in a foul manner; foully; unfairly. – *n.* **8.** that which is foul. **9.** a violation of the rules of a sport or game. – *v.t.* **10.** to make foul; defile; soil. **11.** to defile; dishonour; disgrace.

found[1] /faʊnd/ *v.* past tense and past participle of **find**.

found[2] /faʊnd/ *v.t.* **1.** to set up or establish on a firm basis or for enduring existence. **2.** to lay the lowest part of, fix, or build (a structure) on a firm base or ground. **3.** to base or ground (fol. by *on* or *upon*).

found[3] /faʊnd/ *v.t.* to melt and pour (metal, glass, etc.) into a mould. – **foundry**, *n.*

foundation /faʊn'deɪʃən/ *n.* **1.** that on which something is founded. **2.** the natural or prepared ground or base on which some structure rests. **3.** the act of founding, setting up, establishing, etc. **4.** an endowed institution.

founder /'faʊndə/ *v.i.* to fill with water and sink, as a ship.

founders' shares *pl. n.* shares created in order to remunerate the founder or promoter of a company, often receiving a large share of the net profit after certain fixed dividends have been paid on the ordinary and other classes of stock.

foundling /'faʊndlɪŋ/ *n.* an infant found abandoned.

fount /faʊnt/ *n.* **1.** a spring of water; fountain. **2.** a source or origin.

fountain /'faʊntn/ *n.* **1.** a spring or source of water. **2.** the source or origin of anything. **3.** a jet or stream of water (or other liquid) made by mechanical means to spout or rise from an opening or structure.

fountain pen *n.* a pen with a reservoir for supplying ink to the point of the nib.

four /fɔ/ *n.* a cardinal number, three plus one. – **fourth**, *n., adj.*

4GL /fɔ dʒi 'ɛl/ *n.* → **fourth-generation language**.

fourteen /fɔ'tin/ *n.* a cardinal number, ten plus four. – **fourteenth**, *n., adj.*

fourth-generation language *n.* a computer language in which the instructions are made in simple English statements by the user and interpreted by the computer into lower level languages. *Abbrev.*: 4GL

fowl /faʊl/ *n., pl.* **fowls**, (*esp. collectively*) **fowl**. **1.** the domestic or barnyard hen or cock. **2.** any bird (now chiefly in combination).

fox /fɒks/ *n.* **1.** any of certain carnivores of the dog family. **2.** a cunning or crafty person. – *v.t.* **3.** *Colloquial* to deceive or trick.

foyer /'fɔɪə, 'fɔɪjə/ *n.* **1.** (in theatres and cinemas) the area between the outer lobby and the auditorium. **2.** a hall or anteroom, especially in a hotel.

fracas /'frækα, -kəs/ *n.* an uproar.

fractal /'fræktəl/ *n.* a geometric structure having an irregular or fragmented appearance which is of a similar character at all magnifications.

fraction /'frækʃən/ *n.* **1.** *Mathematics* one or more parts of a unit or whole number. **2.** a part as distinct from the whole of anything. – **fractional**, *adj.*

fractious /'frækʃəs/ *adj.* **1.** cross, fretful, or peevish. **2.** refractory or unruly.

fracto- a word element meaning 'broken'.

fracture /'fræktʃə/ *n., v.,* **-tured**, **-turing**. – *n.* **1.** a break, breach, or split, especially in a bone. – *v.t.* **2.** to break or crack. **3.** to cause or to suffer a fracture in (a bone, etc.). – *v.i.* **4.** to undergo fracture; break.

fragile /'frædʒaɪl/ *adj.* easily broken, shattered, or damaged. – **fragility**, *n.*

fragment /'frægmənt/ *n.* **1.** a part broken off or detached. **2.** an odd piece, bit, or scrap. – **fragmentary**, *adj.*

fragrant /'freɪgrənt/ *adj.* having a pleasant odour. – **fragrance**, *n.*

frail /freɪl/ *adj.* **1.** weak; not robust; having delicate health. **2.** easily broken or destroyed; fragile. – **frailty**, *n.*

frame /freɪm/ *n., v.,* **framed**, **framing**. – *n.* **1.** an enclosing border or case, as for a picture. **2.** anything composed of parts fitted and joined together; a structure. **3.** the body, especially the human body, with reference to its make or build. **4.** a particular state, as of the mind. **5.** one of the successive small pictures on a strip of film. – *v.t.* **6.** to form or make, as by fitting and uniting parts together; construct. **7.** *Colloquial* to incriminate unjustly by a plot, as a person.

framework /'freɪmwɜk/ *n.* **1.** a structure composed of parts fitted and united together. **2.** a structure designed to support or enclose something.

franchise /'fræntʃaɪz/ *n.* **1.** the rights of a citizen, especially the right to vote. **2.** permission granted by a manufacturer to a distributor or retailer to sell the manufacturer's products. – **franchisor**, *n.* – **franchising**, *n.*

frangible /'frændʒəbəl/ *adj.* capable of being broken; breakable.

frangipani /frændʒə'pæni/ *n., pl.* **-nies**. a shrub or tree cultivated for its strongly scented yellow and white, occasionally pink, flowers.

frank /fræŋk/ *adj.* **1.** open or unreserved in speech; candid or outspoken; sincere. **2.** undisguised; avowed; downright. – *v.t.* **3.** to mark (a letter, parcel, etc.) for transmission free of the usual charge.

frankfurt /'fræŋkfət/ *n.* a reddish variety of sausage. Also, **frankfurter**, **frank**.

frantic /'fræntɪk/ *adj.* wild with excitement, passion, fear, pain, etc.

fraternal /frə'tɜnəl/ *adj.* of or befitting a brother or brothers; brotherly.

fraternise = fraternize /'frætənaɪz/ *v.i.,* **-nised**, **-nising**. to associate in a fraternal or friendly way.

fraternity /frə'tɜnəti/ *n., pl.* **-ties**. a body of persons associated as by ties of brotherhood.

fraud /frɔd/ *n.* **1.** deceit, trickery, sharp practice, or breach of confidence, by which it is sought to gain some unfair or dishonest advantage. **2.** someone who makes deceitful pretences; impostor. – **fraudulent**, *adj.*

fraught /frɔt/ *adj.* involving; attended (with); full (of).

fray[1] /freɪ/ *n.* a fight, skirmish, or battle.

fray[2] /freɪ/ *v.t.* **1.** to wear (cloth, rope, etc.) to loose, ravelled threads or fibres at the edge or end; cause to unravel. **2.** to strain (a person's temper); exasperate; upset. – *v.i.* **3.** to become frayed, as cloth, etc.; ravel out.

frazzled /'fræzəld/ *adj.* weary; tired out.

freak /frik/ *n.* **1.** a sudden and apparently causeless change or turn of events, the mind, etc. **2.** any abnormal product or curiously unusual object. – *adj.* **3.** unusual; odd; irregular.

freckle /'frɛkəl/ *n.* a small brownish spot in the skin.

free /fri/ *adj.,* **freer**, **freest**, *v.,* **freed**, **freeing**. – *adj.* **1.** enjoying personal rights or liberty, as one not in slavery. **2.** not literal, as a translation. **3.** clear of obstructions or obstacles, as a corridor. **4.** available; unoccupied; not in use. **5.** exempt or released from something specified. **6.** that may be used by or open to all. **7.** unimpeded, as motion or movements; easy, firm, or swift in movement. **8.** loose, or not held fast or attached. **9.** ready in giving, liberal, or lavish. **10.** provided without, or not subject to, a charge or payment. – *v.t.* **11.** make free; set at liberty. **12.** to disengage (fol. by *from* or *of*).

free alongside ship *adj.* (a term of sale meaning that the seller agrees to deliver the merchandise alongside ship without extra charge to the buyer).

freedom /'fridəm/ *n.* **1.** civil liberty, as opposed to subjection to an arbitrary or despotic government. **2.** exemption from external control, interference, regulation, etc. **3.** absence of or release from ties, obligations, etc. **4.** ease or facility of movement or action.

free enterprise *n.* the doctrine or practice of a minimum amount of government control of private business and industry.

freehand /'frihænd/ *adj.* done by the hand without guiding instruments, measurements, or other aids.

freehold /'frihoʊld/ *n.* **1.** a tenure of real property by which an estate of inheritance is held. **2.** an estate held by such tenure. Cf. **leasehold**.

freelance /'frilæns/ *n.* a journalist, commercial artist, editor, etc., who does not work on a regular salaried basis for any one employer.

freeload /'friloʊd/ *v.i.* to contrive to take food, benefits, etc., without paying or contributing; cadge.

free on board *adj.* (a term of sale meaning that the seller agrees to deliver the merchandise aboard the carrier without extra charge to the buyer).

free port *n.* a port open under equal conditions to all traders.

free-range /'fri-reɪndʒ/ *adj.* of, relating to, or denoting chickens reared in an open or free environment rather than in a battery.

freesia /'friʒə/ *n.* a type of plant cultivated for its fragrant tubular flowers.

freestyle /'fristaɪl/ *n.* → **crawl** (def. 6).

free-to-air /fri-tu-'ɛə/ *adj.* (of television programs) supplied at no cost to the consumer.

free vote *n.* in a house of parliament, a vote on a motion in which members are free to vote according to their own judgment without being bound by any party policy or decision; conscience vote.

freeway /'friweɪ/ *n.* a road designed for high speed traffic. Also, **expressway**.

freeze /friz/ *v.*, **froze**, **frozen**, **freezing**, *n.* – *v.i.* **1.** to change from the liquid to the solid state by loss of heat. **2.** to be extremely cold. **3.** to suffer the effects of intense cold; have the sensation of extreme cold. **4.** to stop suddenly; become immobilised, as through fear, shock, etc. – *v.t.* **5.** to congeal by loss of heat. **6.** to subject (something) to a freezing temperature, as in a refrigerator. **7.** to exclude, or compel to withdraw, from society, business, etc., as by chilling behaviour, severe competition, etc. (fol. by *out*). **8.** *Finance* to render impossible of liquidation or collection. **9.** to fix (wages, prices, etc.) at a specific level, usually by government order. – *n.* **10.** the act of freezing. **11.** the state of being frozen. **12.** legislative action by a government to fix wages, prices, etc., at a specific level.

freight /freɪt/ *n.* **1.** cargo or lading carried for pay either by land, water, or air. **2.** the charge made for transporting goods. – *v.t.* **3.** to transport as freight; send by freight.

French fries *pl. n.* thin strips of potatoes fried in deep fat; chips. Also, **French fried potatoes**.

French horn *n.* a mellow-toned brass wind instrument.

frenetic /frə'nɛtɪk/ *adj.* frantic.

frenzy /'frɛnzi/ *n., pl.* **-zies**. **1.** violent mental agitation; wild excitement or enthusiasm. **2.** mental derangement; delirium. – **frenzied**, *adj.*

frequency /'frikwənsi/ *n., pl.* **-cies**. **1.** the state or fact of being frequent; frequent occurrence. **2.** rate of recurrence. **3.** *Physics* the number of cycles, oscillations, or vibrations of a wave motion or oscillation in unit time. **4.** *Statistics* the number of items occurring in a given category.

frequent /'frikwənt/ *adj.*, /frə'kwɛnt/ *v.* – *adj.* **1.** happening or occurring at short intervals. **2.** constant, habitual, or regular. – *v.t.* **3.** to visit often; go often to; be often in.

frequent flyer /frikwənt 'flaɪə/ *n.* a person who is part of a scheme in which discounted or free flights are awarded by an airline after a certain number of kilometres have been flown with that airline or associated airlines.

fresco /'frɛskoʊ/ *n., pl.* **-coes**, **-cos**. the art of painting on fresh lime plaster, as on a wall or ceiling.

fresh /frɛʃ/ *adj.* **1.** newly made or obtained, etc. **2.** newly arrived. **3.** new; not previously known, met with, etc.; novel. **4.** (of water) not salt. **5.** retaining the original properties unimpaired; not deteriorated. **6.** looking youthful and healthy. **7.** pure, cool, or refreshing, as air. **8.** forward or presumptuous; cheeky.

fret[1] /frɛt/ *v.i.*, **fretted**, **fretting**. to give oneself up to feelings of irritation, resentful discontent, regret, worry, or the like. – **fretful**, *adj.*

fret[2] /frɛt/ *n.* an interlaced, angular design; fretwork.

fret[3] /frɛt/ *n.* any of the ridges set across the fingerboard of a guitar, etc., which help the fingers to stop the strings at the correct points.

fretwork /'frɛtwɜk/ *n.* ornamental work consisting of interlacing parts.

friable /'fraɪəbəl/ *adj.* easily crumbled.

friar /'fraɪə/ *n.* a brother or member of one of certain Christian religious orders.

friction /'frɪkʃən/ *n.* **1.** clashing or conflict, as of opinions, etc. **2.** *Mechanics*, *Physics* the resistance to the relative motion (sliding or rolling) of surfaces of bodies in contact. **3.** the rubbing of the surface of one body against that of another.

fridge /frɪdʒ/ *n. Colloquial* → **refrigerator**.

fried /fraɪd/ *v.* past tense and past participle of **fry**[1].

friend /frɛnd/ *n.* **1.** one attached to another by feelings of affection or personal regard. **2.** (*cap.*) someone who supports an institution, charity, etc., with money or honorary services. – **friendly**, *adj.*

fries /fraɪz/ *pl. n.* → **French fries**.

frieze /friz/ *n.* any decorative band or feature, as on a wall.

frigate /'frɪgət/ *n.* a general-purpose warship.

fright /fraɪt/ *n.* **1.** sudden and extreme fear; a sudden terror. **2.** a person or thing of shocking, grotesque, or ridiculous appearance. – **frighten**, *v.*

frightful /ˈfraɪtfəl/ *adj.* such as to cause fright; dreadful, terrible, or alarming.

frigid /ˈfrɪdʒəd/ *adj.* **1.** very cold in temperature. **2.** without warmth of feeling; without ardour or enthusiasm.

frill /frɪl/ *n.* a trimming consisting of a strip of material or lace, gathered at one edge and left loose at the other; a ruffle.

frill-necked lizard *n.* a lizard of northern Australia possessing a large, ruff-like, erectable frill behind the head and using hind legs for propulsion.

fringe /frɪndʒ/ *n.* **1.** an ornamental bordering having projecting lengths of thread, cord, etc. **2.** anything resembling or suggesting this. **3.** hair falling over the brow. **4.** border; margin; outer part or extremity. – *adj.* **5.** accessory; supplementary. **6.** of or relating to a person or group living on the outskirts of social acceptability.

fringe benefit *n.* any remuneration received in addition to one's wage, as a pension, travel allowance, etc.

frisk /frɪsk/ *v.i.* **1.** to dance, leap, skip, or gambol, as in frolic. – *v.t.* **2.** *Colloquial* to search (a person) for concealed weapons, etc., by feeling their clothing. – **frisky**, *adj.*

fritter[1] /ˈfrɪtə/ *v.t.* to waste little by little (usually fol. by *away*).

fritter[2] /ˈfrɪtə/ *n.* a small cake of batter, sometimes containing fruit, etc.

frivolous /ˈfrɪvələs/ *adj.* **1.** not worthy of serious notice. **2.** given to trifling or levity, as persons.

frizz /frɪz/ *v.*, **frizzed**, **frizzing**, *n.*, *pl.* **frizzes**. – *v.t.* **1.** to make into small, crisp curls or little tufts. – *n.* **2.** something frizzed; frizzed hair. Also, **friz**. – **frizzy**, *adj.*

frizzle /ˈfrɪzəl/ *v.i.*, **-zled**, **-zling**. to make a sizzling or sputtering noise in frying or the like.

fro /froʊ/ *adv. in the phr.* **to and fro,** back and forth.

frock /frɒk/ *n.* a dress.

frog /frɒg/ *n.* **1.** a tailless amphibian having a smooth skin and long hind legs adapted for leaping. **2.** a slight hoarseness due to mucus on the vocal cords.

frogman /ˈfrɒgmən/ *n.*, *pl.* **-men**. a swimmer specially equipped for swimming underwater.

frolic /ˈfrɒlɪk/ *n.*, *v.*, **-icked**, **-icking**. – *n.* **1.** merry play; gaiety; fun. – *v.i.* **2.** to play merrily; have fun.

from /frɒm/, *weak form* /frəm/ – *prep.* a particle specifying a starting point, and hence used to express removal or separation in space, time, order, etc., discrimination or distinction, source or origin, instrumentality, and cause or reason.

frond /frɒnd/ *n.* a finely divided leaf, often large.

front /frʌnt/ *n.* **1.** the foremost part or surface of anything. **2.** someone or something which serves as a cover for another activity, especially an illegal or disreputable one. **3.** outward impression of rank, position, or wealth. **4.** *Meteorology* a surface of discontinuity separating two dissimilar air masses. – *adj.* **5.** of or relating to the front. – *v.t.* **6.** to have the front towards; face. – *v.i.* **7.** to have or turn the front in some specified direction. **8.** Also, **front up**. *Colloquial* to arrive; turn up. – **frontal**, *adj.*, *n.*

frontbencher /ˈfrʌntbɛntʃə, frʌntˈbɛntʃə/ *n.* a member of parliament who is a government minister or opposition spokesperson. – **frontbench**, *adj.*

frontier /frʌnˈtɪə, ˈfrʌntɪə/ *n.* that part of a country which borders another country; boundary; border; extreme limit.

frontispiece /ˈfrʌntəspis/ *n.* an illustrated leaf preceding the titlepage of a book.

frost /frɒst/ *n.* **1.** a covering of minute ice needles, formed from the atmosphere at night on cold surfaces. – *v.t.* **2.** to cover with frost. **3.** to give a frostlike surface to (glass, etc.). **4.** to ice (a cake, etc.).

frostbite /ˈfrɒstbaɪt/ *n.* the inflamed, sometimes gangrenous effect on a part of the body, especially the extremities, due to excessive exposure to extreme cold.

frosting /ˈfrɒstɪŋ/ *n.* a fluffy cake icing.

froth /frɒθ/ *n.* an aggregation of bubbles; foam.

frown /fraʊn/ *v.i.* to contract the brow as in displeasure or deep thought; scowl.

frowzy /ˈfraʊzi/ *adj.*, **-zier**, **-ziest**. dirty and untidy; slovenly.

frozen /ˈfroʊzən/ *v.* past participle of **freeze**.

fructify /ˈfrʌktəfaɪ, frʊk-/ *v.*, **-fied**, **-fying**. – *v.i.* **1.** to bear fruit. – *v.t.* **2.** to make fruitful or productive; fertilise.

frugal /ˈfrugəl/ *adj.* economical in use or expenditure; prudently saving or sparing.

fruit /frut/ *n.* **1.** any product of vegetable growth useful to humans or animals. **2.** anything produced or accruing; product, result or effect; return or profit.

fruition /fruˈɪʃən/ *n.* attainment of anything desired; attainment of maturity; realisation of results.

fruity /ˈfruti/ *adj.*, **-tier**, **-tiest**. **1.** resembling fruit; having the taste or flavour of fruit. **2.** (of wine) having body and fullness of flavour. **3.** sexually suggestive; salacious.

frump /frʌmp/ *n.* a dowdy, drably dressed woman.

frustrate /frʌsˈtreɪt/ *v.t.*, **-trated**, **-trating**. **1.** to make (plans, efforts, etc.) of no avail; defeat; baffle; nullify. **2.** to disappoint or thwart (a person). – **frustration**, *n.*

fry[1] /fraɪ/ *v.*, **fried**, **frying**, *n.*, *pl.* **fries**. – *v.t.* **1.** to cook in fat, oil, etc., usually over direct heat. – *n.* **2.** a dish of something fried.

fry[2] /fraɪ/ *n.*, *pl.* **fry**. **1.** the young of fishes, or of some other animals, as frogs. **2. small fry,** unimportant or insignificant people; young children.

fuchsia /ˈfjuʃə/ *n.* any of several plants cultivated for their handsome drooping flowers.

fuddle /ˈfʌdl/ *v.t.*, **-dled**, **-dling**. **1.** to intoxicate. **2.** to muddle or confuse.

fuddy-duddy /ˈfʌdi-dʌdi/ *n.* a fussy, stuffy, or old-fashioned person.

fudge[1] /fʌdʒ/ *n.* a kind of soft sweet composed of sugar, butter, milk, chocolate, or the like.

fudge[2] /fʌdʒ/ *v.*, **fudged**, **fudging**. – *v.t.* **1.** to put together in a makeshift, clumsy, or dishonest way; fake. – *v.i.* **2.** (in games and contests) to gain advantage improperly.

fuel /ˈfjuəl, fjul/ *n.* **1.** combustible matter used to maintain fire, as coal, wood, oil etc. **2.** something which nourishes or sustains.

-fuge a word element referring to 'flight'.

fugitive /ˈfjudʒətəv, -ɪv/ *n.* a person who is fleeing; a runaway.

fugue /fjug/ *n.* *Music* a composition based upon one, two, or even more themes, which are enunciated by the several voices or parts in turn.

-ful a suffix meaning: **1.** full of or characterised by. **2.** tending or able to. **3.** as much as will fill.

fulcrum /ˈfʊlkrəm/ *n.*, *pl.* **-crums**, **-cra** /-krə/. the support, or point of rest, on which a lever turns in moving a body.

fulfil /fʊlˈfɪl/ *v.t.*, **-filled**, **-filling**. **1.** to carry out, or bring to consummation, as a prophecy, promise, etc. **2.** to satisfy (requirements, etc.)

full /fʊl/ *adj.* **1.** filled; containing all that can be held; filled to utmost capacity. **2.** complete; entire; maximum. **3.** (of garments, etc.) wide, ample, or having ample folds. **4.** *Colloquial* intoxicated. – *adv.* **5.** completely or entirely. **6.** exactly or directly.

full blood *n.* **1.** an individual of unmixed ancestry, especially for dark-skinned peoples. **2.** (especially of horses) purebred.

full stop *n.* the point or character (.) used to mark the end of a complete declarative sentence, indicate an abbreviation, etc.; a period. Also, **full point**.

full-time /ˈfʊl-taɪm/ *adj.* of, or relating to, or taking all the normal working hours (opposed to *part-time*).

fully-paid /ˈfʊli-peɪd/ *adj.* of or relating to shares or stock on which the face value of the capital represented has been paid in full.

fulminate /ˈfʊlməneɪt, ˈfʌl-/ *v.*, **-nated**, **-nating**, *n.* – *v.i.* **1.** to issue denunciations or the like (often fol. by *against*). – *n.* **2.** *Chemistry* an unstable explosive compound.

fulsome /ˈfʊlsəm/ *adj.* offensive to good taste, especially as being excessive.

fumble /ˈfʌmbəl/ *v.i.*, **-bled**, **-bling**. to feel or grope about clumsily.

fume /fjum/ *n.*, *v.*, **fumed**, **fuming**. – *n.* **1.** (*often pl.*) any smokelike or vaporous exhalation from matter or substances. – *v.i.* **2.** to show irritation or anger.

fumigate /ˈfjuməgeɪt/ *v.t.*, **-gated**, **-gating**. to expose to smoke or fumes, as in disinfecting.

fun /fʌn/ *n.* mirthful sport or diversion; merry amusement; joking; playfulness.

function /ˈfʌŋkʃən, ˈfʌŋʃən/ *n.* **1.** the kind of action or activity proper to a person, thing, or institution. **2.** any ceremonious public or social gathering or occasion. **3.** any basic computer operation. – *v.i.* **4.** to perform a function; act; serve; operate. **5.** to carry out normal work, activity, or processes. – **functional**, *adj.*

function key *n.* any of a numbered set of keys (usually 10 or 12) on a computer keyboard, which can be programmed to perform certain functions.

fund /fʌnd/ *n.* **1.** a stock of money or pecuniary resources. **2.** a store or stock of something, now often of something immaterial. – *v.t.* **3.** to raise or provide money for: *to fund a child's education* **4.** to convert (a floating debt or debts) into a more or less permanent debt or loan, represented by interest-bearing bonds. **5.** to arrange for (a debt or debts) to be on a long-term basis. **6.** to provide a fund to pay the interest or principle of (a debt).

fundamental /fʌndəˈmɛntl/ *adj.* serving as, or being a component part of, a foundation or basis; basic; underlying.

funded debt *n.* a government debt, not repayable before twelve months, for the repayment of which a sinking fund has been established.

funeral /ˈfjunrəl, ˈfjunərəl/ *n.* the ceremonies connected with the disposal of the body of a dead person. – **funereal**, *adj.*

fungus /ˈfʌŋgəs/ *n.*, *pl.* **fungi** /ˈfʌŋgi/, **funguses**. **1.** a plant without chlorophyll, as mushrooms, moulds, or mildews. **2.** *Pathology* a spongy morbid growth.

funicular railway /fəˈnɪkjələ/ *n.* a railway system operating up steep gradients, in which cable-linked cars or trains move up and down simultaneously.

funk /fʌŋk/ *n.* *Colloquial* cowering fear; state of fright or terror.

funky /ˈfʌŋki/ *adj.* exciting, satisfying, or pleasurable.

funnel /ˈfʌnəl/ *n.* **1.** a cone-shaped utensil with a tube at the apex, for conducting liquid, etc., through a small opening, as into a bottle. **2.** a metal chimney, especially of a ship or a steam-engine.

funnel-web /ˈfʌnəl-wɛb/ *n.* either of two species of large, aggressive, venomous, eastern Australian spiders.

funny /ˈfʌni/ *adj.*, **-nier**, **-niest**. **1.** affording fun; amusing; comical. **2.** curious; strange; queer; odd.

funny money *n.* *Colloquial* **1.** money which is nominally exchanged between different sections of the one organisation for bookkeeping purposes. **2.** foreign currency. **3.** counterfeit money.

fur /fɜ/ *n.* **1.** the skin of certain animals, covered with a thick, hairy coating. **2.** the cured and treated skin of some of these animals, used in garments, etc.

furbish /ˈfɜbɪʃ/ *v.t.* to restore to freshness of appearance or condition (often fol. by *up*).

furcate /ˈfɜkeɪt, -kət/ *adj.* forked.

furious /ˈfjuriəs/ *adj.* **1.** full of fury, violent passion, or rage. **2.** intensely violent, as wind, storms, etc.

furl /fɜl/ *v.t.* to draw into a compact roll, as a sail, etc.

furlong /ˈfɜlɒŋ/ *n.* a unit of distance in the imperial system, equal to 201.168 m. *Symbol*: fur

furlough /ˈfɜloʊ/ *n.* leave of absence from official duty usually for a longish period.

furnace /ˈfɜnəs/ *n.* **1.** a structure or apparatus in which to generate heat, as for heating buildings, smelting ores, producing steam, etc. **2.** a place of burning heat.

furnish /ˈfɜnɪʃ/ *v.t.* **1.** to provide or supply. **2.** to fit up (a house, room, etc.) with necessary appliances, especially furniture.

furniture /ˈfɜnətʃə/ *n.* the movable articles, as tables, chairs, bedsteads, desks, cabinets, etc., required for use or ornament in a house, office, or the like.

furore = furor /ˈfjurɔ/ *n.* a general outburst of enthusiasm or excited disorder.

furphy /ˈfɜfi/ *n., pl.* **-phies**. a rumour; a false story.

furrow /ˈfʌroʊ/ *n.* a narrow trench or groove.

further /ˈfɜðə/ *adv.* (*comparative of far*) **1.** at or to a greater distance; farther. **2.** at or to a more advanced point; to a greater extent; farther. **3.** in addition; moreover. – *adj.* (*comparative of far*) **4.** more distant or remote; farther. **5.** more extended. **6.** additional; more. – *v.t.* **7.** to help forward (a work, undertaking, cause, etc.); promote; advance; forward.

furthermore /fɜðəˈmɔ/ *adv.* moreover; in addition.

furtive /ˈfɜtɪv/ *adj.* **1.** taken, done, used, etc., by stealth; secret. **2.** sly; shifty.

fury /ˈfjuri/ *n., pl.* **-ries**. frenzied or unrestrained violent passion, especially anger.

fuse[1] /fjuz/ *n.* **1.** *Electricity* a device for preventing an excessive current from passing through a circuit. **2.** a tube, ribbon, or the like, filled or saturated with combustible matter, for igniting an explosive.

fuse[2] /fjuz/ *v.t.,* **fused**, **fusing**. to combine or blend by melting together; melt.

fuselage /ˈfjuzəlaʒ, -lɪdʒ/ *n.* the body of an aircraft.

fusion /ˈfjuʒən/ *n.* **1.** the act or process of fusing. **2.** that which is fused. **3.** *Physics* a thermonuclear reaction in which nuclei of light atoms join to form nuclei of heavier atoms, usually with the release of large amounts of energy.

fuss /fʌs/ *n.* **1.** an excessive display of anxious activity; needless or useless bustle. **2.** a commotion, argument, or dispute. – *v.i.* **3.** to make a fuss; make much ado about trifles; to move fussily about. – **fussy**, *adj.*

fusty /ˈfʌsti/ *adj.,* **-tier**, **-tiest**. **1.** mouldy; musty; having a stale smell; stuffy. **2.** old-fashioned; fogyish.

futile /ˈfjutaɪl/ *adj.* incapable of producing any result; ineffective; useless; not successful. – **futility**, *n.*

future /ˈfjutʃə/ *n.* **1.** time that is to be or come hereafter. **2.** what will exist or happen in future time. **3.** (*pl.*) *Stock Exchange* futures contracts. – *adj.* **4.** relating to or connected with time to come.

futures contract *n.* a purchase or sale of commodities for future receipt or delivery.

futures exchange *n.* a market place where futures contracts are traded. Also, **futures market**.

futuristic /fjutʃəˈrɪstɪk/ *adj.* (of design in clothes, furniture, etc.) anticipating the space age.

fuzz /fʌz/ *n.* **1.** loose, light, fibrous, or fluffy matter. **2.** *Colloquial* a blur. **3.** *Colloquial* the police. – **fuzzy**, *adj.*

-fy a suffix meaning: **1.** to make; cause to be; render. **2.** to become; be made. Also, **-ify**

G g

G, g /dʒi/ *n., pl.* **G's** *or* **Gs**, **g's** *or* **gs**. the seventh letter of the English alphabet.

gabble /ˈgæbəl/ *v.i.*, **-bled**, **-bling**. to talk rapidly and unintelligibly; jabber.

gaberdine = gabardine /gæbəˈdin, ˈgæbədin/ *n.* a closely woven twill fabric of worsted, cotton or spun rayon.

gable /ˈgeɪbəl/ *n.* the triangular wall enclosed by the two slopes of a roof and a horizontal line across the eaves.

gad /gæd/ *v.i.*, **gadded**, **gadding**. to move restlessly or idly from place to place, especially in search of pleasure (fol. by *about*).

gadget /ˈgædʒət/ *n.* a mechanical contrivance or device; any ingenious article.

gaff /gæf/ *n.* a strong hook with a handle, used for landing large fish.

gaffe /gæf/ *n.* a social blunder.

gag¹ /gæg/ *v.*, **gagged**, **gagging**, *n.* – *v.t.* **1.** to stop up the mouth so as to prevent sound or speech. **2.** to restrain by force or authority from freedom of speech or expression. – *v.i.* **3.** to retch, as with nausea. – *n.* **4.** something thrust into or bound around the mouth to prevent speech.

gag² /gæg/ *v.*, **gagged**, **gagging**, *n.* – *v.i.* **1.** to make jokes. – *n.* **2.** a joke.

gaga /ˈgaga/ *adj.* *Colloquial* **1.** senile. **2.** eccentric.

gage¹ /geɪdʒ/ *n.* a pledge or pawn.

gage² /geɪdʒ/ *n., v.t.,* **gaged**, **gaging**. → **gauge**.

gaggle /ˈgægəl/ *n.* a flock of geese.

gaiety /ˈgeɪəti/ *n., pl.* **-ties**. the state of being gay or cheerful.

gain /geɪn/ *v.t.* **1.** to obtain; secure (something desired); acquire. **2.** to acquire as an increase or addition. **3.** to reach by effort; get to; arrive at. – *v.i.* **4.** to improve; make progress; advance. – *n.* **5.** profit; advantage. **6.** an increase or advance.

gainsay /geɪnˈseɪ/ *v.t.*, **-said**, **-saying**. **1.** to deny. **2.** to speak or act against.

'gainst /gɛnst, geɪnst/ *prep., conj.* → **against**. Also, **gainst**.

gait /geɪt/ *n.* **1.** a particular manner of walking. **2.** the pace of a horse.

gaiter /ˈgeɪtə/ *n.* a covering for the ankle and instep.

gala /ˈgalə/ *n.* a festive occasion.

galah /gəˈla/ *n.* **1.** a common small cockatoo, pale grey above and deep pink below. **2.** *Colloquial* a fool.

galaxy /ˈgæləksi/ *n., pl.* **-axies**. *Astronomy* any large system of stars held together by mutual gravitation. – **galactic**, *adj.*

gale /geɪl/ *n.* a strong wind.

gall /gɔl/ *n.* **1.** bile. **2.** something very bitter or severe. **3.** bitterness of spirit. **4.** impudence; effrontery.

gallant /ˈgælənt, gəˈlænt/ *adj.* **1.** brave and dashing. **2.** noticeably polite and attentive to women. **3.** generous or sporting.

gall bladder *n.* a vesicle attached to the liver containing bile.

galleon /ˈgæliən, ˈgæljən/ *n.* a kind of large sailing vessel.

gallery /ˈgæləri/ *n., pl.* **-leries**. **1.** a long, narrow, covered walk, open at one or both sides. **2.** a platform projecting from the interior walls of a church, theatre, etc., to provide seats or room for a part of the audience. **3.** any audience. **4.** a room, series of rooms, or building devoted to the exhibition of works of art.

galley /ˈgæli/ *n., pl.* **-leys**. **1.** an early seagoing vessel propelled by oars or by oars and sails. **2.** the kitchen of a ship or airliner.

gallinaceous /gæləˈneɪʃəs/ *adj.* relating to or resembling the domestic fowls.

gallivant /ˈgæləvænt/ *v.i.* to go from place to place in a rollicking, frivolous or flirtatious manner. Also, **galavant**.

gallon /ˈgælən/ *n.* a unit of capacity in the imperial system, for the measurement of liquids and dry goods.

gallop /ˈgæləp/ *v.i.* **1.** to ride a horse at a gallop; ride at full speed. **2.** to go fast, race, or hurry.

gallows /ˈgæloʊz/ *n., pl.* **-lows**, **-lowses**. a wooden frame used for the hanging of condemned persons.

gallstone /ˈgɔlstoʊn/ *n.* a stone formed in the bile ducts or gall bladder.

gallup poll /ˈgæləp/ *n.* the questioning of a representative cross-section of the population in order to assess public opinion, as of voting intentions.

galore /gəˈlɔ/ *adj.* (*used only after nouns*) in abundance.

galoshes /gəˈlɒʃəz/ *pl. n.* a pair of overshoes of rubber.

galvanise = galvanize /ˈgælvənaɪz/ *v.t.*, **-nised**, **-nising**. **1.** to startle into sudden activity. **2.** to coat (iron or steel) with zinc.

gambit /ˈgæmbət/ *n.* an opening in chess, in which the player seeks by sacrificing a pawn or other piece to obtain some advantage.

gamble /ˈgæmbəl/ *v.*, **-bled**, **-bling**, *n.* – *v.i.* **1.** to play at any game of chance for stakes. **2.** to act on favourable hopes or assessment. – *n.* **3.** any matter or thing involving risk or uncertainty.

gambol /ˈgæmbəl/ *v.i.*, **-bolled**, **-bolling**. to frolic.

game /geɪm/ *n., adj.*, **gamer**, **gamest**. – *n.* **1.** an amusement or pastime. **2.** a contest for amusement according to set rules; a match. **3.** sport of any kind; joke. **4.** wild animals, including birds and fishes, such as are hunted or taken for sport, food, or profit. – *adj.* **5.** relating to animals hunted or taken as game. **6.** with fighting spirit; plucky.

gamete /ˈgæmit, gəˈmit/ *n.* either of the two germ cells which unite to form a new organism; a mature reproductive cell.

gamin /ˈgæmən/ *adj.* (of a person's appearance, or hairstyle) elfin.

gammon /ˈgæmən/ *n.* a smoked or cured ham.

gamo- a word element meaning 'sexual union'.

-gamous an adjectival word element corresponding to the noun element **-gamy**, as in *polygamous.*

gamut /'gæmət/ *n.* the whole scale or range.

-gamy 1. a word element meaning 'marriage', as in *polygamy.* **2.** *Biology* a word element meaning 'sexual union'.

gander /'gændə/ *n.* **1.** the male of the goose. **2.** *Colloquial* a look at something.

gang /gæŋ/ *n.* **1.** a band or group. **2.** a group of persons, usually considered disreputable, violent or criminal, associated for a particular purpose. – **gangster**, *n.*

gangling /'gæŋglɪŋ/ *adj.* awkwardly tall and spindly. Also, **gangly** /'gæŋgli/.

gangplank /'gæŋplæŋk/ *n.* a plank used as a temporary bridge in passing into and out of a ship, etc.

gangrene /'gæŋgrin/ *n.* the dying of tissue, as from interruption of circulation. – **gangrenous**, *adj.*

gangway /'gæŋweɪ/ *n.* a passageway.

gannet /'gænət/ *n.* a large seabird.

gantry /'gæntri/ *n., pl.* **-tries**. a spanning framework.

gaol /dʒeɪl/ *n.* → **jail**.

gap /gæp/ *n.* **1.** a break or opening. **2.** a vacant space or interval.

gape /geɪp/ *v.i.,* **gaped**, **gaping**. **1.** to stare with open mouth, as in wonder. **2.** to open as a gap; split or become open wide.

garage /'gæraʒ, -radʒ, gə'raʒ, -'radʒ/ *n.* **1.** a building for sheltering a motor vehicle or vehicles. **2.** an establishment where motor vehicles are repaired, petrol is sold, etc.

garb /gab/ *n.* fashion or mode of dress.

garbage /'gabɪdʒ/ *n.* rubbish.

garble /'gabəl/ *v.t.,* **-bled**, **-bling**. to make unfair or misleading selections from (facts, statements, writings, etc.).

garden /'gadn/ *n.* **1.** a plot of ground devoted to the cultivation of useful or ornamental plants. – *v.i.* **2.** to lay out or cultivate a garden. – **gardener**, *n.*

gardenia /ga'dinjə, -niə/ *n.* a plant cultivated for its fragrant, waxlike, white flowers.

garfish /'gafɪʃ/ *n., pl.* **-fishes**, (*esp. collectively*) **-fish**. a fish having a slender body and the lower jaw produced as a needle-like point.

gargantuan /ga'gæntʃuən/ *adj.* gigantic; prodigious.

gargle /'gagəl/ *v.t.,* **-gled**, **-gling**. to wash or rinse (the throat or mouth) with a liquid held in the throat and kept in motion by a stream of air from the lungs.

gargoyle /'gagɔɪl/ *n.* a spout, often terminating in a grotesque head.

garish /'gɛərɪʃ, 'gar-/ *adj.* glaring, or excessively bright.

garland /'galənd/ *n.* a wreath or string of flowers, leaves, or other material.

garlic /'galɪk/ *n.* a hardy plant, with a strong-scented pungent bulb used in cookery and medicine.

garment /'gamənt/ *n.* any article of clothing.

garnet /'ganət/ *n.* a deep red gemstone.

garnish /'ganɪʃ/ *v.t.* **1.** to fit out with something that adorns or decorates. **2.** *Law* to warn; give notice.

garnishee /ganə'ʃi/ *v.,* **-sheed**, **-sheeing**, *n.* – *v.t.* **1.** to attach (money or property) by garnishment. **2.** to make (a person) a garnishee. – *n.* **3.** a person served with a garnishment.

garnishment /'ganɪʃmənt/ *n.* a warning served on a person, at the suit of a creditor plaintiff, to hold, subject to the court's direction, money or property of the defendant in his or her possession.

garret /'gærət/ *n.* → **attic**.

garrison /'gærəsən/ *n.* a body of troops stationed in a fortified place.

garrotte /gə'rɒt/ *n.* a Spanish mode of capital punishment, originally by means of an instrument causing death by strangulation.

garrulous /'gærələs/ *adj.* given to much talking, especially about trifles.

garter /'gatə/ *n.* a fastening to keep up stockings or long socks.

gas[1] /gæs/ *n., pl.* **gases**, *v.,* **gassed**, **gassing**. – *n.* **1.** *Physics* a substance consisting of atoms or molecules which are sufficiently mobile for it to occupy the whole of the space in which it is contained. – *v.t.* **2.** to affect, overcome, or asphyxiate with gas or fumes.

gas[2] /gæs/ *n. Chiefly US Colloquial* **1.** petrol. **2. step on the gas,** to hurry.

gash /gæʃ/ *n.* a long, deep wound or cut.

gasket /'gæskət/ *n.* anything used as a packing or jointing material for making joints fluid-tight.

gasp /gæsp, gasp/ *n.* **1.** a sudden, short breath. **2.** a short, convulsive utterance, especially as a result of fear or surprise. -*v.i.* **3.** to catch the breath, or struggle for breath, with open mouth, as from exhaustion; breathe convulsively.

gastric /'gæstrɪk/ *adj.* relating to the stomach.

gastro- a word element meaning 'stomach', as in *gastropod, gastronome.* Also, **gastero-**, **gastr-**.

gastronome /'gæstrənoum/ *n.* a gourmet.

gastropod /'gæstrəpɒd/ *n.* any of a class of molluscs including the snails.

gate /geɪt/ *n.* **1.** a movable barrier, as a swinging frame, in a fence or wall, or across a passageway. **2.** a device for regulating the passage of water, steam, or the like, as in a dam, pipe, etc.; valve. **3.** *Electricity* an electronic circuit which controls the passage of information signals.

gatecrash /'geɪtkræʃ/ *v.t.* to attend (a party) uninvited.

gather /'gæðə/ *v.t.* **1.** to bring (persons, animals, or things) together into one company or aggregate. **2.** to learn or infer from observation. **3.** to wrap or draw around or close to someone or something. **4.** to draw up (cloth) on a thread in fine folds or puckers by running a thread through. **5.** to increase (speed, etc.). – *v.i.* **6.** to come together or assemble.

gauche /gouʃ/ *adj.* awkward; clumsy. – **gaucheness**, **gaucherie**, *n.*

gaudy /'gɔdi/ *adj.,* **-dier**, **-diest**. brilliant; excessively showy.

gauge /geɪdʒ/ *v.,* **gauged**, **gauging**, *n.* – *v.t.* **1.** to appraise, estimate, or judge. **2.** to determine the dimensions, capacity, quantity, or force of. – *n.* **3.** a standard of measure; standard dimension or quantity. **4.** a means of estimating or judging; criterion; test. **5.** any instrument for measuring pressure, volume, or dimensions, as a pressure gauge, micrometer gauge, etc.

gaunt /gɔnt/ *adj.* abnormally thin; emaciated; haggard.

gauntlet /'gɔntlət/ *n.* **1.** a medieval glove. **2. throw down the gauntlet,** to extend a challenge, originally to a duel. Also, **gantlet**.

gauss /gaʊs/ *n. Electricity* a unit of magnetic induction in the centimetre-gram-second system, equal to 0.1×10^{-3} teslas.

gauze /gɔz/ *n.* any thin transparent fabric.

gave /geɪv/ *v.* past tense of **give**.

gavel /'gævəl/ *n.* a small mallet used by a presiding officer to signal for attention or order.

gawk /gɔk/ *v.i. Colloquial* to stare stupidly.

gay /geɪ/ *adj.*, **gayer**, **gayest**, *n.* – *adj.* **1.** having or showing a joyous mood. **2.** bright or showy. **3.** (especially of a male) homosexual. – *n.* **4.** a homosexual, especially a male.

gaze /geɪz/ *v.*, **gazed**, **gazing**, *n.* – *v.i.* **1.** to look steadily or intently. – *n.* **2.** a steady or intent look.

gazebo /gə'zibou/ *n., pl.* **-bos**, **-boes**. a structure commanding an extensive prospect, especially a turret, pavilion, or summerhouse.

gazelle /gə'zɛl/ *n.* any of various small antelopes.

gazette /gə'zɛt/ *n., v.*, **-zetted**, **-zetting**. – *n.* **1.** a newspaper (now common only in newspaper titles). **2.** an official government journal, containing lists of government appointments and promotions, bankruptcies, etc. – *v.t.* **3.** to publish, announce, or list in a gazette.

gazump /gə'zʌmp/ *v.t.* **1.** (of a vendor before entering upon a binding contract) to force a buyer to accept a price higher than that previously agreed upon. **2.** (of a buyer) to conclude a deal with a seller while another buyer is raising finance, etc.

GDP /dʒi di 'pi/ gross domestic product.

gear /gɪə/ *n.* **1.** *Machinery* **a.** a mechanism for transmitting or changing motion, as by toothed wheels. **b.** a toothed wheel which engages with another wheel or part. **2.** implements, tools, or apparatus, especially as used for a particular operation; harness; tackle.

gearing /'girɪŋ/ *n. Stock Exchange* the relationship of total invested capital to equity capital. A company with high gearing has a high amount of fixed capital compared with ordinary capital.

geese /gis/ *n.* plural of **goose**.

geezer /'gizə/ *n. Colloquial* an odd character. Also, **geeser**.

Geiger counter /'gaɪgə/ *n.* an instrument for detecting radioactivity.

gel /dʒɛl/ *n.* a jellylike substance.

gelatine /'dʒɛlətin, dʒɛlə'tin/ *n.* a brittle, nearly transparent organic substance, the basis of jellies, glues, and the like. – **gelatinous**, *adj.*

geld /gɛld/ *v.t.*, **gelded** *or* **gelt**, **gelding**. to castrate (especially animals).

gelding /'gɛldɪŋ/ *n.* a castrated animal, especially a horse.

gelignite /'dʒɛləgnaɪt/ *n.* an explosive.

gem /dʒɛm/ *n.* **1.** a stone used in jewellery, fashioned to bring out its beauty. **2.** something likened to, or prized as, a gem because of its beauty or worth, especially something small.

-gen a suffix meaning: **1.** something produced, or growing. **2.** something that produces.

gender /'dʒɛndə/ *n.* **1.** *Grammar* (in many languages) a set of classes, such as masculine, feminine and neuter, which together include all nouns. **2.** sex (def. 1).

gender-neutral /'dʒɛndə-njutrəl/ *adj.* (of a term, word, etc.) designed so as not to give any indication of the gender of the person to whom it refers.

gene /dʒin/ *n. Biology* the unit of inheritance, situated on and transmitted by the chromosome, which develops into a hereditary character as it reacts with the environment and with the other genes.

genealogy /dʒini'ælədʒi/ *n., pl.* **-gies**. an account of the descent of a person or family through an ancestral line.

genera /'dʒɛnərə/ *n.* plural of **genus**.

general /'dʒɛnrəl/ *adj.* **1.** relating to, affecting, including, or participated in by all members of a class or group; not partial or particular. **2.** not specific or special.

general election *n.* a parliamentary election in which all seats in the house are thrown open, as a federal or state election for the lower house.

generalise = generalize /'dʒɛnrəlaɪz/ *v.*, **-lised**, **-lising**. – *v.t.* **1.** to give a general (rather than specific or special) character to. **2.** to infer (a general principle, etc.) from facts, etc. – *v.i.* **3.** to form general notions.

generality /dʒɛnə'rælәti/ *n., pl.* **-ties**. **1.** a general or vague statement. **2.** general principle; general rule or law.

general practitioner *n.* a doctor who does not specialise in any particular branch of medicine. *Abbrev.*: GP

general register *n.* one of a specified number of internal addressable registers in a CPU which can be used for temporary storage, as an accumulator, or for any other general purpose.

generate /'dʒɛnəreɪt/ *v.t.*, **-rated**, **-rating**. to bring into existence; give rise to; produce; cause to be.

generation /dʒɛnə'reɪʃən/ *n.* **1.** the whole body of individuals born about the same time. **2.** production by natural or artificial processes; evolution, as of heat or sound.

generation X *n.* the generation following the baby boomers, characterised as not being vocal on social issues but rather concerned with individual gain. Also, **X generation**.

generator /'dʒɛnəreɪtə/ *n.* a machine which converts mechanical energy into electrical energy.

generic /dʒə'nɛrɪk/ *adj.* **1.** relating to a genus. **2.** applicable or referring to all the members of a genus or class. **3.** of or relating to a class of commodities marketed under the brand name of a retailing chain with the implication of greater cheapness than if they appeared under the brand name of the producer. **4.** identified by the name of the product itself, not by a particular brand name. – *n.* **5.** a generic commodity. Also, **generical**.

generous /ˈdʒɛnərəs, ˈdʒɛnrəs/ *adj.* **1.** munificent or bountiful; unselfish. **2.** free from meanness or smallness of mind or character. – **generosity**, *n.*

genesis /ˈdʒɛnəsəs/ *n., pl.* **-neses** /-nəsiz/. origin; production; creation.

gene therapy *n. Medicine* a procedure in which defective genes are replaced or mutated in order to correct a genetic defect.

genetics /dʒəˈnɛtɪks/ *n.* the science of heredity, dealing with resemblances and differences of related organisms flowing from the interaction of their genes and the environment. – **geneticist**, *n.* – **genetic**, *adj.*

genial /ˈdʒiniəl/ *adj.* sympathetically cheerful.

genie /ˈdʒini/ *n.* a spirit in Arabian mythology.

genital /ˈdʒɛnətl/ *adj.* relating to reproduction or the organs of reproduction.

genital herpes *n.* a sexually transmitted form of herpes.

genitalia /dʒɛnəˈteɪliə/ *pl. n.* the genitals.

genitals /ˈdʒɛnətlz/ *pl. n.* the reproductive organs, especially the external organs.

genitive /ˈdʒɛnətɪv/ *adj. Grammar* (of a case) possessive.

genius /ˈdʒinɪəs/ *n.* **1.** exceptional natural capacity for creative and original conceptions, the highest level of mental ability. **2.** a person having such capacity.

genocide /ˈdʒɛnəsaɪd/ *n.* extermination of a national or racial group as a planned move. – **genocidal**, *adj.*

-genous an adjective suffix derived from nouns in **-gen** and **-geny**.

genre /ˈʒɒnrə/ *n.* genus; kind; sort; style.

genteel /dʒɛnˈtil/ *adj.* belonging or suited to polite society.

gentile /ˈdʒɛntaɪl/ *adj.* of or relating to any people not Jewish.

gentility /dʒɛnˈtɪləti/ *n., pl.* **-ties**. **1.** superior refinement or elegance, possessed or affected. **2.** gentle or noble birth.

gentle /ˈdʒɛntl/ *adj.,* **-tler**, **-tlest**. **1.** mild, kindly, or amiable. **2.** not severe, rough, or violent. **3.** moderate; gradual. **4.** of good birth or family; well-born.

gentleman /ˈdʒɛntlmən/ *n., pl.* **-men**. **1.** a man of good breeding, education, and manners. **2.** (as a polite form of speech) any man.

gentry /ˈdʒɛntri/ *n.* the class below the nobility.

genuflect /ˈdʒɛnjəflɛkt/ *v.i.* to bend the knee or knees, especially in reverence.

genuine /ˈdʒɛnjuən/ *adj.* **1.** being truly such; real; authentic. **2.** sincere; free from pretence or affectation.

genus /ˈdʒinəs/ *n., pl.* **genera** /ˈdʒɛnərə/. **1.** a kind; sort; class. **2.** *Biology* the usual major subdivision of a family or subfamily.

-geny a suffix meaning 'origin'.

geo- a word element meaning 'the earth'.

geography /dʒiˈɒgrəfi/ *n., pl.* **-phies**. the study of the earth's surface, climate, vegetation, population, etc. – **geographer**, *n.* – **geographical**, *adj.*

geology /dʒiˈɒlədʒi/ *n., pl.* **-gies**. the science that deals with the earth, the rocks of which it is composed, and the changes which it has undergone or is undergoing. – **geological**, *adj.* – **geologist**, *n.*

geometry /dʒiˈɒmətri/ *n.* that branch of mathematics which deduces the properties of figures in space. – **geometric**, *adj.*

geophysics /dʒioʊˈfɪzɪks/ *n.* the physics of the earth, dealing especially with the study of inaccessible portions of the earth.

geranium /dʒəˈreɪniəm/ *n.* a plant cultivated for its showy flowers.

geriatric /dʒɛriˈætrɪk/ *n.* an aged person, especially one incapacitated or invalided by old age.

germ /dʒɜm/ *n.* **1.** a micro-organism, especially when disease-producing. **2.** that from which anything springs as if from a seed.

german /ˈdʒɜmən/ *adj.* **1.** sprung from the same father and mother (always placed after the noun). **2.** sprung from the brother or sister of one's father or mother, or from brothers or sisters.

germane /dʒɜˈmeɪn/ *adj.* closely related; pertinent.

German measles *n.* → **rubella**.

German shepherd *n.* a highly intelligent wolflike breed of dog; Alsatian.

germinate /ˈdʒɜməneɪt/ *v.i.,* **-nated**, **-nating**. to begin to grow or develop.

gerrymander /ˈdʒɛrimændə/ *n. Politics* an arbitrary arrangement of the political divisions of an electorate, etc., made so as to give one party an unfair advantage in elections.

gerund /ˈdʒɛrənd/ *n. Grammar* the *-ing* form of a verb when in nominal function, as *walking* in the sentence 'walking is good exercise'.

gestate /ˈdʒɛsteɪt/ *v.t.,* **-tated**, **-tating**. to carry in the womb during the period from conception to delivery. – **gestation**, *n.*

gesticulate /dʒɛsˈtɪkjəleɪt/ *v.i.,* **-lated**, **-lating**. to make or use gestures, especially in an animated or excited manner with or instead of speech.

gesture /ˈdʒɛstʃə/ *n., v.,* **-tured**, **-turing**. – *n.* **1.** movement of the body, head, arms, hands, or face expressive of an idea or an emotion. **2.** any action or proceeding intended for effect or as a formality; demonstration. – *v.i.* **3.** to make or use gestures.

get /gɛt/ *v.,* **got**, **getting**. – *v.t.* **1.** to obtain, gain, or acquire by any means. **2.** to fetch or bring. **3.** to hear or understand. **4.** to be afflicted with (an illness, etc.). **5.** *Colloquial* to hit. – *v.i.* **6.** to come to or arrive. **7.** to become; grow. **8.** to succeed in coming or going (fol. by *away*, *in*, *into*, *out*, *over*, *through*, etc.). – *v.* **9. get across,** to make understood. **10. get at, a.** to reach; make contact with. **b.** *Colloquial* to hint at or imply. **c.** *Colloquial* to tamper with, as by corruption or bribery. **11. get away**

with, to avoid punishment or blame for. **12. get by,** to manage; carry on in spite of difficulties. **13. get down,** to depress; discourage. **14. get even with,** to square accounts with. **15. get his, hers, etc.,** to get a just reward. **16. get on, a.** to age. **b.** to make progress; proceed; advance. **c.** to agree or be friendly (with). **17. get one's own back,** to be revenged. **18. get round, a.** to outwit. **b.** to cajole or ingratiate oneself with. **c.** to overcome (difficulties, etc.). **19. get (stuck) into,** *Colloquial* **a.** to attack (someone) vigorously either physically or verbally. **b.** to set about (a task) vigorously. **20. get to, a.** to arouse deep feeling in. **b.** to annoy or irritate. **21. get up, a.** to arise. **b.** to dress elaborately. **c.** to prepare, arrange, or organise. **d.** to win (an election, court case, contest, etc.) **22. get up to,** to be involved in (mischief, etc.). **23. get with child,** to make pregnant.

geyser /'gizə, 'gaɪzə/ *n.* a hot spring which intermittently sends up fountain-like jets of water and steam into the air.

ghastly /'gastli/ *adj.,* **-lier**, **-liest**. frightful; dreadful; horrible.

ghee /gi/ *n.* a kind of liquid butter, clarified by boiling.

gherkin /'gɜkən/ *n.* the small, immature fruit of cucumber, used in pickling.

ghetto /'gɛtoʊ/ *n., pl.* **-tos**, **-toes**. a quarter in a city in which any minority group lives.

ghost /goʊst/ *n.* **1.** the disembodied spirit of a dead person imagined as wandering among or haunting living persons. **2.** *Optics, Television* a bright spot or secondary image, from a defect of the instrument. – *v.t.* **3.** to write for someone else who is publicly known as the author.

ghoul /gul/ *n.* **1.** an evil demon. **2.** a grave robber. **3.** someone who revels in what is revolting. – **ghoulish**, *adj.*

giant /'dʒaɪənt/ *n.* **1.** an imaginary being of human form but superhuman size, strength, etc. **2.** a person or thing of unusually great size, endowments, importance, etc. – *adj.* **3.** gigantic; huge.

gibber[1] /'dʒɪbə/ *v.i.* to speak inarticulately; chatter. – **gibberish**, *n.*

gibber[2] /'gɪbə/ *n.* a stone; boulder.

gibbon /'gɪbən/ *n.* a small ape.

gibe /dʒaɪb/ *v.,* **gibed**, **gibing**, *n.* – *v.i.* **1.** to utter mocking words; scoff; jeer. – *n.* **2.** a taunting or sarcastic remark. Also, **jibe**.

giblet /'dʒɪblət/ *n.* (*usu. pl.*) the heart, liver, or gizzard from a fowl.

giddy /'gɪdi/ *adj.,* **-dier**, **-diest**. **1.** frivolously light; impulsive; flighty. **2.** affected with vertigo; dizzy.

gift /gɪft/ *n.* **1.** something given; a present. **2.** a quality, or special ability; natural endowment; talent.

gig[1] /gɪg/ *n.* a light, two-wheeled one-horse carriage.

gig[2] /gɪg/ *n.* *Colloquial* a booking for an entertainer or band to perform.

gig[3] /gɪg/ *v.,* **gigged**, **gigging**, *n.* *Colloquial* – *v.i.* **1.** to watch; stare. – *n.* **2.** an observer; eye witness.

gigantic /dʒaɪ'gæntɪk/ *adj.* **1.** of, like, or befitting a giant. **2.** huge.

giggle /'gɪgəl/ *v.,* **-gled**, **-gling**, *n.* – *v.i.* **1.** to laugh in a silly, undignified way, as from youthful spirits or ill-controlled amusement; titter. – *n.* **2.** a silly, spasmodic laugh; a titter. **3.** *Colloquial* an amusing occasion.

gigolo /'ʒɪgəloʊ/ *n., pl.* **-los**. a man supported by a woman, especially a young man supported by an older woman in return for companionship.

gild /gɪld/ *v.t.,* **gilded** *or* **gilt**, **gilding**. to coat with gold, gold leaf, or gold-coloured substance.

gill[1] /gɪl/ *n.* an aquatic respiratory organ.

gill[2] /dʒɪl, gɪl/ *n.* a unit of liquid measure in the imperial system, equal to¼ pint.

gilt /gɪlt/ *v.* a past tense and past participle of **gild**.

gilt-edged /'gɪlt-ɛdʒd/ *adj.* of the highest order or quality.

gimlet /'gɪmlət/ *n.* a small tool for boring holes, consisting of a shaft with a pointed screw at one end and a handle at the other.

gimmick /'gɪmɪk/ *n.* *Colloquial* a pronounced eccentricity of dress, manner, voice, etc., or an eccentric action or device, especially one exploited to gain publicity.

gin[1] /dʒɪn/ *n.* an alcoholic beverage obtained by redistilling spirits with flavouring agents, especially juniper berries, orange peel, etc.

gin[2] /dʒɪn/ *n.* **1.** a machine for separating cotton from its seeds, as a cotton gin. **2.** a trap or snare for game, etc.

gin[3] /dʒɪn/ *n.* a card game similar to rummy. Also, **gin rummy**.

ginger /'dʒɪndʒə/ *n.* **1.** the pungent, spicy rhizome of any of a reedlike plant, variously used in cookery and medicine. **2.** (of hair) red. – *v.t.* **3.** *Colloquial* to impart spiciness or piquancy to; make lively.

gingerly /'dʒɪndʒəli/ *adv.* with extreme care or caution; warily. – **gingerliness**, *n.*

gingham /'gɪŋəm/ *n.* yarn-dyed, plain-weave cotton fabric.

gingival /dʒɪn'dʒaɪvəl, 'dʒɪndʒəvəl/ *adj.* of or relating to the gums.

gipsy = gypsy /'dʒɪpsi/ *n., pl.* **-sies**. **1.** (*often cap.*) one of a nomadic Caucasian minority race thought to be of Hindu origin. **2.** a person who resembles or lives like a gipsy.

giraffe /dʒə'raf/ *n.* a tall, long-necked, spotted ruminant of Africa.

gird /gɜd/ *v.t.,* **girt** *or* **girded**, **girding**. **1.** to encircle with a belt or girdle. **2.** to prepare (oneself) mentally for action (often fol. by *up*).

girder /'gɜdə/ *n.* (in structural work) any main horizontal supporting member or beam.

girdle /'gɜdl/ *n., v.,* **-dled**, **-dling**. – *n.* **1.** a belt, cord, or the like, worn about the waist. **2.** a lightweight undergarment which supports the abdominal region of the body. -*v.t.* **3.** to encompass; enclose; encircle.

girl /gɜl/ *n.* a female child or young person.

girth /gɜθ/ *n.* **1.** the measure around anything; circumference. **2.** a band passed under the belly of a horse, etc., to secure a saddle or pack on its back.

gist /dʒɪst/ *n.* the substance or pith of a

matter; essential part.

give /gɪv/ *v.*, **gave**, **given**, **giving**, *n.* – *v.t.* **1.** to deliver freely; bestow; hand over. **2.** to deliver to another in exchange for something; pay. **3.** to grant permission or opportunity to; enable; assign; award. **4.** to present. **5.** to assign as a basis of calculation or reasoning; suppose; assume. **6.** to assign to someone as their right, lot, etc. **7.** *Originally US Colloquial* to tell; offer as explanation. **8.** to furnish or provide. **9.** to produce; present. – *v.i.* **10.** to make a gift or gifts. **11.** to yield, as to pressure or strain; draw back; relax. – *v.* **12. give in, a.** to yield; acknowledge defeat. **b.** to hand in. **13. give up, a.** to lose all hope. **b.** to abandon as hopeless. **c.** to desist from; forsake. **d.** to surrender. **e.** to devote entirely. **f.** to inform against. – *n.* **14.** the act or fact of yielding to pressure; elasticity.

gizzard /'gɪzəd/ *n.* the grinding or muscular stomach of birds.

glacier /'gleɪsiə, 'glæsiə/ *n.* an extended mass of ice formed from falling snow and moving very slowly. – **glacial**, *adj*

glad /glæd/ *adj.* delighted or pleased (fol. by *of*, *at*, etc., or an infinitive or clause).

glade /gleɪd/ *n.* an open space in a forest.

gladiator /'glædieɪtə/ *n.* *Roman History* a person, often a slave or captive, who fought in public with a sword or other weapon to entertain the people.

gladiolus /glædi'oʊləs/ *n.*, *pl.* **-lus**, **-li** /laɪ/, **-luses**. a plant with erect leaves, and spikes of variously coloured flowers.

glair /glɛə/ *n.* the white of an egg.

glamour = glamor /'glæmə/ *n.* alluring and often illusory charm; fascination. – **glamorous**, *adj.*

glance /glæns, glans/ *v.*, **glanced**, **glancing**, *n.* – *v.i.* **1.** to look quickly or briefly. **2.** to gleam or flash. **3.** to go off in an oblique direction from an object struck. – *n.* **4.** a quick or brief look.

gland /glænd/ *n.* *Anatomy* an organ or tissue which elaborates and discharges a substance which is used elsewhere in the body (*secretion*), or eliminated (*excretion*). – **glandular**, *adj.*

glare /glɛə/ *n.*, *v.*, **glared**, **glaring**. – *n.* **1.** a strong, dazzling light; brilliant lustre. – *v.i.* **2.** to shine with a strong, dazzling light. **3.** to be conspicuous. **4.** to look with a fierce or piercing stare.

glass /glas/ *n.* **1.** a hard, brittle, more or less transparent substance produced by fusion. **2.** (*pl.*) a device to aid defective vision, consisting usually of two glass lenses set in a frame which rests on the nose and is held in place by pieces passing over the ears. **3.** a glass container for drinking water, beer, etc.

glaze /gleɪz/ *v.*, **glazed**, **glazing**, *n.* – *v.t.* **1.** to furnish or fit with glass; cover with glass. **2.** to produce a vitreous or glossy surface on (pottery, pastry, etc.). – *n.* **3.** a smooth, glossy surface or coating.

gleam /glim/ *n.* **1.** a flash or beam of light. **2.** dim or subdued light. – *v.i.* **3.** to send forth a gleam or gleams. **4.** to appear suddenly and clearly, like a flash of light.

glean /glin/ *v.t.* **1.** to gather slowly and laboriously in bits. **2.** to gather (grain, etc.) after the reapers or regular gatherers. **3.** to discover or find out.

glee /gli/ *n.* demonstrative joy.

glen /glɛn/ *n.* a small, narrow, secluded valley.

glib /glɪb/ *adj.*, **glibber**, **glibbest**. ready and fluent, often thoughtlessly or insincerely so.

glide /glaɪd/ *v.*, **glided**, **gliding**, *n.* – *v.i.* **1.** to move smoothly along, as if without effort or difficulty, as a flying bird. **2.** *Aeronautics* to move in the air, especially at an easy angle downwards, by the action of gravity or by virtue of momentum already acquired. – *n.* **3.** a gliding movement, as in dancing.

glider /'glaɪdə/ *n.* *Aeronautics* a motorless aeroplane for gliding from a higher to a lower level by the action of gravity, or from a lower to a higher level by the action of air currents.

glimmer /'glɪmə/ *n.* a faint or unsteady light; gleam.

glimpse /glɪmps/ *n.*, *v.*, **glimpsed**, **glimpsing**. – *n.* **1.** a momentary sight or view. -*v.t.* **2.** to catch a glimpse of.

glint /glɪnt/ *n.* **1.** a gleam or glimmer; flash. **2.** gleaming brightness; lustre. – *v.i.* **3.** to gleam or flash.

glisten /'glɪsən/ *v.i.* **1.** to shine with a sparkling light, especially as a result of being wet. – *n.* **2.** a glistening; sparkle.

glitch /glɪtʃ/ *n.* *Colloquial* a hitch; snag; malfunction.

glitter /'glɪtə/ *v.i.* to shine with a brilliant, sparkling light or lustre.

gloat /gloʊt/ *v.i.* to smile smugly or scornfully.

global /'gloʊbəl/ *adj.* **1.** relating to or covering the whole world. **2.** all-embracing; comprehensive. **3.** *Computers* operating over an entire database, set of records, etc.

global warming *n.* the significant rise in temperature of the whole of the earth's atmosphere.

globe /gloʊb/ *n.* **1.** the earth (usually preceded by *the*). **2.** a sphere on which is depicted a map of the earth. **3.** anything more or less spherical. – **globular**, *adj.*

globule /'glɒbjul/ *n.* a small spherical body.

glockenspiel /'glɒkənspil, -kənʃpil/ *n.* a set of steel bars mounted in a frame and struck with hammers.

gloom /glum/ *n.* a state of melancholy or depression; low spirits.

glorious /'glɔriəs/ *adj.* **1.** full of glory. **2.** brilliantly beautiful.

glory /'glɔri/ *n.*, *pl.* **glories**, *v.*, **gloried**, **glorying**. – *n.* **1.** exalted praise, honour, or distinction, accorded by common consent. **2.** resplendent beauty or magnificence. **3.** the splendour and bliss of heaven; heaven. – *v.i.* **4.** to be boastful; exult arrogantly (fol. by *in*).

glory box *n.* a chest in which young women store clothes, linen, etc., in expectation of being married.

gloss[1] /glɒs/ *n.* a superficial lustre. – **glossy**, *adj.*

gloss[2] /glɒs/ *n.* **1.** an explanation by means of a marginal or interlinear note, of a technical or unusual expression in a manuscript text. **2.** to give a specious interpretation of; explain away (often fol. by *over*).

glossary /ˈglɒsəri/ *n., pl.* **-ries**. a list of technical, dialectal, and difficult terms in a subject or field, with definitions.

-glot a suffix indicating proficiency in language, as in *polyglot*.

glottis /ˈglɒtəs/ *n.* the opening at the upper part of the larynx, between the vocal cords. – **glottal**, *adj.*

glove /glʌv/ *n.* a covering for the hand.

glow /gloʊ/ *n.* **1.** light emitted by a substance heated to luminosity; incandescence. **2.** warmth of emotion or passion; ardour. – *v.i.* **3.** to emit bright light and heat without flame; be incandescent. **4.** to be animated with emotion.

glower /ˈgloʊə, ˈglaʊə/ *v.i.* to stare with sullen dislike or discontent.

glow-worm /ˈgloʊ-wɜm/ *n.* a firefly.

glucose /ˈglukoʊz, -oʊs/ *n. Chemistry* a sugar occurring in many fruits, animal tissues and fluids, etc.

glue /glu/ *n., v.,* **glued**, **gluing**. – *n.* **1.** any adhesive substance made from any natural or synthetic resin or material. – *v.t.* **2.** to join or fasten with glue.

gluggy /ˈglʌgi/ *adj. Colloquial* sticky.

glum /glʌm/ *adj.,* **glummer**, **glummest**. gloomily sullen or silent; dejected.

glut /glʌt/ *v.,* **glutted**, **glutting**, *n.* – *v.t.* **1.** to feed or fill to satiety; sate. **2. glut the market,** to overstock the market. – *n.* **3.** a full supply. **4.** a surfeit.

gluten /ˈglutn/ *n.* the tough, viscid nitrogenous substance remaining when the flour of wheat or other grain is washed to remove the starch.

glutinous /ˈglutənəs/ *adj.* of the nature of glue; gluey; viscid; sticky.

glutton /ˈglʌtn/ *n.* **1.** someone who eats to excess. **2.** someone who accepts an inordinate amount of unpleasantness or difficulty (fol. by *for*). – **gluttonous**, *adj.* – **gluttony**, *n.*

glycerine /glɪsəˈrin, ˈglɪsərən/ *n. Chemistry* → **glycerol**. Also, **glycerin** /ˈglɪsərən/.

glycerol /ˈglɪsərɒl/ *n.* a colourless, odourless, liquid alcohol, of syrupy consistency and sweet taste, used as a solvent, plasticiser, or sweetener.

gnarled /nald/ *adj.* **1.** (of trees) knotty. **2.** (of persons) having a rugged, weather-beaten appearance.

gnash /næʃ/ *v.t.* to grind (the teeth).

gnat /næt/ *n.* any of various small dipterous insects.

gnaw /nɔ/ *v.,* **gnawed**, **gnawed** *or* **gnawn**, **gnawing**. – *v.t.* **1.** to wear away or remove by persistent biting. **2.** to consume with passion; torment. – *v.i.* **3.** to bite persistently.

gneiss /ˈnaɪs/ *n.* a metamorphic rock. – **gneissic**, *adj.*

gnome /noʊm/ *n.* **1.** one of a species of diminutive beings. **2.** a banker, involved in international currency and loan dealings, thought to exercise a mysterious and sinister effect on world economic affairs.

gnomic /ˈnoʊmɪk, ˈnɒm-/ *adj.* like or containing aphorisms.

GNP /dʒi ɛn ˈpi/ gross national product.

gnu /nu/ *n., pl.* **gnus**, (*esp. collectively*) **gnu**. → **wildebeest**.

go /goʊ/ *v.,* **went**, **gone**, **going**, *n., pl.* **goes**. – *v.i.* **1.** to move or pass along; proceed. **2.** to move away or out; depart (opposed to *come* or *arrive*). **3.** to keep or be in motion; act, work, or run. **4.** to become; assume another state or condition. **5.** to belong; have a place. **6.** (of colours, etc.) to harmonise; be compatible; be suited. **7.** to develop, especially with reference to success, or failure. **8.** to fail; give way. **9.** to carry final authority. **10.** to be contained (fol. by *into*): *4 goes into 12.* **11.** to be about, intending, or destined (used in the present participle followed by an infinitive). – *v.t.* **12.** to proceed on. **13. go at, a.** to undertake with vigour. **b.** to attack. **14. go down, a.** to descend; slope down. **b.** to be defeated. **c.** to be remembered by posterity. **15. go into,** to investigate or study thoroughly. **16. go off, a.** to discharge; explode. **b.** (of food, etc.) to become bad; deteriorate. **c.** to take place (in a specified manner). **d.** *Colloquial* to come to dislike. **17. go over, a.** to read or reread. **b.** to repeat. **c.** to examine. **d.** to have an effect (as specified). – *n.* **18.** the act of going. **19.** *Colloquial* energy, spirit, or animation. **20.** one's turn to play or to make an attempt at something. **21.** *Colloquial* something that goes well; a success. **22. fair go,** *Colloquial* adequate opportunity. **23. have a go,** *Colloquial* to make an attempt; try. **24. on the go,** *Colloquial* constantly going; very active.

goad /goʊd/ *n.* **1.** a stick with a pointed end, for driving cattle, etc. – *v.t.* **2.** to prick or drive with or as with a goad; incite.

goal /ˈgoʊl/ *n.* **1.** that towards which effort is directed; aim or end. **2.** (in ball games) an area, basket, cage, object or structure towards which the players strive to advance the ball, etc.

goanna /goʊˈænə/ *n.* any of various large Australian lizards.

goat /ˈgoʊt/ *n.* **1.** an agile hollow-horned ruminant closely related to the sheep. **2.** *Colloquial* a fool.

goatee /goʊˈti/ *n.* a man's beard trimmed to a tuft or a point on the chin.

gob[1] /gɒb/ *n.* a mass or lump.

gob[2] /gɒb/ *n. Colloquial* the mouth.

gobble[1] /ˈgɒbəl/ *v.t.,* **-bled**, **-bling**. to swallow hastily in large pieces; gulp.

gobble[2] /ˈgɒbəl/ *v.i.,* **-bled**, **-bling**. to make the characteristic throaty cry of a turkey cock.

gobbledegook = gobbledygook /ˈgɒbldiˌgʊk, -ˌguk/ *n. Colloquial* language characterised by circumlocution and jargon. Also, **gobbledy-gook**.

goblet /ˈgɒblət/ *n.* a drinking glass with a foot and stem.

goblin /ˈgɒblən/ *n.* a grotesque mischievous sprite or elf.

gobsmacked /ˈgɒbsmækt/ *adj. Colloquial* astonished; flabbergasted.

go-cart /ˈgoʊ-kat/ *n.* a small, wheeled vehicle for small children to ride in.

god /gɒd/ *n.* **1.** a deity, especially a male deity, presiding over some portion of worldly affairs. **2.** (*pl.*) the highest gallery in a theatre.

godchild /'gɒdtʃaɪld/ *n., pl.* **-children**. one for whom a person (godparent) stands sponsor at baptism.

goddess /'gɒdəs, 'gɒdɛs/ *n.* a female god or deity.

godforsaken /'gɒdfəseɪkən/ *adj. Colloquial* desolate; remote.

godly /'gɒdli/ *adj.,* **-lier**, **-liest**. pious.

godsend /'gɒdsɛnd/ *n.* something unexpected but particularly welcome and timely.

godspeed /gɒd'spid/ *interj.* **1.** God speed you. – *n.* **2.** a wish of success to one setting out on a journey or undertaking.

goggle /'gɒgəl/ *n., v.,* **-gled**, **-gling**. – *n.* **1.** (*pl.*) spectacles often with special rims, lenses, or sidepieces, so devised as to protect the eyes from wind, dust, water, or glare. – *v.i.* **2.** to stare with bulging eyes. **3.** to roll the eyes.

goitre /'gɔɪtə/ *n.* an enlargement of the thyroid gland, on the front and sides of the neck.

go-kart /'goʊ-kat/ *n.* a small light vehicle, especially one without bodywork, having a low-powered engine, used for relatively safe racing. Also, **go-cart**, **kart**.

gold /goʊld/ *n.* **1.** a precious yellow metal, highly malleable and ductile, and free from liability to rust. *Symbol*: Au **2.** something likened to this metal in brightness, preciousness, etc. **3.** bright metallic yellow, sometimes tending towards brown. – **golden**, *adj.*

gold bullion standard *n.* a monetary system permitting the movement of gold bullion into and out of the country for international payments, in which the central authority buys and sells gold at the current market rate, and token money (not gold coins) forms the money in circulation.

golden handshake *n. Colloquial* a gratuity or benefit given to employees in recognition of their services on the occasion of their retirement.

golden mean /goʊldən 'min/ *n.* the happy medium between extremes.

gold exchange standard *n.* a monetary system whose monetary unit is kept at a fixed relation with that of a country on the gold standard by dealings in foreign exchange by the central authority, the money in circulation being token money.

goldfish /'goʊldfɪʃ/ *n., pl.* **-fishes**, (*esp. collectively*) **-fish**. a small fish of the carp family.

gold leaf *n.* gold beaten into a very thin sheet, used for gilding, etc.

goldmine /'goʊldmaɪn/ *n.* **1.** a mine yielding gold. **2.** a source of great wealth. **3.** a source of anything required.

gold point *n.* the point at which it is equally expensive to buy (or sell), exchange, or export (or import) gold in adjustment of foreign claims (or counterclaims).

gold standard *n.* a monetary system in which there is a free mintage of gold into standard legal coins, free movement of gold into and out of the country, and in which the currency unit is based on gold of a fixed weight and fineness.

golf /gɒlf/ *n.* an outdoor game, in which a small resilient ball is driven with special clubs into a series of holes, distributed at various distances over a course. – **golfer**, *n.*

-gon a suffix denoting geometrical figures having a certain number or kind of angles, as in *polygon, pentagon.*

gonad /'goʊnæd/ *n.* the sex gland, male or female, in which gametes develop and appropriate sex hormones are produced.

gondola /'gɒndələ/ *n.* a long, narrow boat used on the Venetian canals.

gone /gɒn/ *adj.* departed; left.

gong /gɒŋ/ *n. Music* an oriental bronze disc with the rim turned up, to be struck with a soft-headed stick.

gonorrhoea /gɒnə'riə/ *n.* a sexually transmitted disease causing purulent inflammation mainly of the urethra and cervix.

-gony a word element meaning 'production', 'genesis', 'origination'.

good /gʊd/ *adj.,* **better**, **best**, *n., interj.* – *adj.* **1.** morally excellent; righteous; pious. **2.** satisfactory in quality, quantity, or degree; excellent. **3.** right; proper; qualified; fit. **4.** fresh and palatable; not tainted. **5.** reliable; safe. **6.** agreeable; pleasant. **7.** (of clothes) best or newest. **8.** competent or skilful; clever. **9.** **a.** valid (often fol. by *for*). **b.** entitling (a person) to (fol. by *for*). **c.** (of a person) willing to provide (fol. by *for*). **10. feel good,** *Colloquial* to be happy or in good health. **11. good luck,** *Colloquial* (an expression wishing a person well). **12. make good, a.** to make recompense for; pay for. **b.** to keep to an agreement; fulfil. **c.** to be successful. **d.** to prove the truth of; substantiate. – *n.* **13.** profit; worth; advantage; benefit. **14.** excellence or merit; righteousness; kindness; virtue. **15.** (*pl.*) possessions, especially movable effects or personal chattels. **16.** (*pl.*) articles of trade; wares; merchandise, especially that which is transported by land. **17. all to the good,** *Colloquial* generally advantageous, often used to justify an unpleasant event. **18. be up to no good,** *Colloquial* to do wrong; break the law in some undisclosed way; behave in a suspicious manner. **19. for good (and all),** finally and permanently; forever. – *interj.* **20.** (an expression of approval or satisfaction). **21. good on** (or **for**) **you,** *Colloquial* (an expression of approval, encouragement, etc.).

goodbye /gʊd'baɪ/ *interj.* farewell (a conventional expression used at parting).

goodwill /gʊd'wɪl/ *n.* **1.** friendly disposition; benevolence; favour. **2.** *Commerce* an intangible, saleable asset arising from the reputation of a business and its relations with its customers.

goog /gʊg/ *n. Colloquial* an egg.

goose /gus/ *n., pl.* **geese**. **1.** any of numerous wild or domesticated web-footed birds, most of them larger and with a longer neck than the ducks. **2.** the female of this bird, as distinguished from the male (or gander). **3.** a silly or foolish person; simpleton.

gooseberry /'gʊzbəri, -bri/ *n., pl.* **-ries**. the small fruit or berry of certain prevailingly prickly shrubs.

goose pimples *pl. n.* a rough condition of the skin induced by cold or fear. Also, **goose bumps**, **goose flesh**.

gopher /'goʊfə/ *n.* a rodent of North America.

gore[1] /gɔ/ *n.* blood that is shed, especially when clotted.

gore[2] /gɔ/ *v.t.*, **gored**, **goring**. (of an animal) to pierce with the horns or tusks.

gorge /gɔdʒ/ *n.*, *v.*, **gorged**, **gorging**. – *n.* **1.** a narrow cleft with steep, rocky walls, especially one through which a stream runs. **2.** the throat; gullet. – *v.t.* **3.** to stuff with food (mainly reflexive and passive).

gorgeous /'gɔdʒəs/ *adj.* sumptuous; magnificent; splendid in appearance or colouring.

gorilla /gə'rɪlə/ *n.* the largest of the anthropoid apes.

gormless /'gɔmləs/ *adj. Colloquial* (of a person) dull; stupid; senseless.

gory /'gɔri/ *adj.*, **gorier**, **goriest**. **1.** covered or stained with gore; bloody. **2.** *Colloquial* distasteful or unpleasant.

goshawk /'gɒshɔk/ *n.* any of various powerful, short-winged hawks.

gosling /'gɒzlɪŋ/ *n.* a young goose.

go-slow /'goʊ-sloʊ/ *n. Colloquial* a deliberate curtailment of output by workers as an industrial sanction; work-to-rule.

gospel /'gɒspəl/ *n.* **1.** (*often cap.*) (in Christianity) the body of doctrine taught by Christ and the apostles. **2.** something regarded as true and implicitly believed.

gossamer /'gɒsəmə/ *n.* a fine filmy cobweb.

gossip /'gɒsəp/ *n.*, *v.*, **-siped** *or* **-sipped**, **-siping** *or* **-sipping**. – *n.* **1.** idle talk, especially about the affairs of others. **2.** a person given to tattling or idle talk. – *v.i.* **3.** to talk idly, especially about the affairs of others; go about tattling.

got /gɒt/ *v.* past tense and past participle of **get**.

gouge /gaʊdʒ/ *n.*, *v.*, **gouged**, **gouging**. – *n.* **1.** a chisel whose blade is curved. – *v.t.* **2.** to dig or force out with or as with a gouge.

gourd /gʊəd, gɔd/ *n.* a fruit whose dried shell is used for bottles, bowls, etc.

gourmand /gɔ'mɒnd, 'gɔmənd/ *n.* someone fond of good eating. Also, **gormand**.

gourmet /'gʊəmeɪ, 'gɔ-/ *n.* a connoisseur in the delicacies of the table; an epicure.

gout /gaʊt/ *n.* a constitutional disease characterised by painful inflammation of the joints.

govern /'gʌvən/ *v.t.* **1.** to rule by right of authority, as a sovereign does. **2.** to exercise a directing or restraining influence over; guide. **3.** *Grammar* to be accompanied by (a particular form) as in *'they helped us'*, not *'they helped we'*; the verb *'helped'* is said to govern the objective case of the pronoun.

governess /'gʌvənɛs/ *n.* a woman who directs the education of children, generally in their own homes.

government /'gʌvənmənt/ *n.* **1.** the authoritative direction and restraint exercised over the actions of people in communities, societies, and states. **2.** (*sometimes construed as pl.*) the governing body of persons in a state, community, etc.; the executive power; the administration.

governor /'gʌvənə, 'gʌvnə/ *n.* **1.** one charged with the direction or control of an institution, society, etc. **2.** the principal representative of the sovereign in a state of the Commonwealth of Australia.

governor-general /gʌvənə-'dʒɛnrəl/ *n.*, *pl.* **governor-generals**, **governors-general**. the principal representative of the sovereign in certain independent Commonwealth countries.

gown /gaʊn/ *n.* **1.** a woman's dress. **2.** a loose, flowing, outer garment.

grab /græb/ *v.t.* **1.** to seize suddenly and eagerly; snatch. **2.** *Colloquial* to affect; impress.

grace /greɪs/ *n.*, *v.*, **graced**, **gracing**. – *n.* **1.** elegance or beauty of form, manner, motion, or act. **2.** mercy; clemency; pardon. **3.** (*pl.*) affected manner; manifestation of pride or vanity. **4.** *Law* an allowance of time to a debtor before suit can be brought against him or her after the debt has by its terms become payable. **5.** a short prayer before or after a meal, in which a blessing is asked and thanks are given. **6.** (*usu. cap.*) a formal title used in addressing or mentioning a duke, duchess, or archbishop, and formerly also a sovereign (preceded by *your*, *her*, etc.). – *v.t.* **7.** to lend or add grace to; adorn. **8.** to favour or honour. – **graceful**, *adj.*

gracious /'greɪʃəs/ *adj.* disposed to show grace or favour; kind; benevolent; courteous.

gradation /grə'deɪʃən/ *n.* any process or change taking place through a series of stages, by degrees, or gradually.

grade /greɪd/ *n.*, *v.*, **graded**, **grading**. – *n.* **1.** a degree in a scale, as of rank, advancement, quality, value, intensity, etc. **2.** a step or stage in a course or process. **3.** inclination with the horizontal of a road, railway, etc. – *v.t.* **4.** to arrange in a series of grades; class; sort. **5.** to determine the grade of. **6.** to reduce to a level.

-grade a word element meaning 'walking', 'moving', 'going', as in *retrograde.*

grader /'greɪdə/ *n.* a motor-driven vehicle, with a blade for pushing earth, used for grading roads and for shallow excavation.

gradient /'greɪdiənt/ *n.* **1.** the degree of inclination, or the rate of ascent or descent, in a railway, etc. **2.** an inclined surface; grade; ramp.

gradual /'grædʒuəl/ *adj.* **1.** taking place, changing, moving, etc., by degrees or little by little. **2.** rising or descending at an even, moderate inclination.

graduate /'grædʒuət/ *n.*, *v.*, **-ated**, **-ating**. *-n.* **1.** someone who has received a degree on completing a course of study, as at a university or college. – *v.i.* **2.** to receive a degree or diploma on completing a course of study. – *v.t.* **3.** to divide into or mark with degrees or other divisions, as the scale of a thermometer. – **graduation**, *n.*

graffiti /grə'fiti/ *pl. n.*, *sing.* **graffito** /grə'fitoʊ/. (*usu. construed as sing.*) drawings or words, sometimes obscene, sometimes political, etc., written on public walls.

graft[1] /graft/ *n.* **1.** *Horticulture* a shoot or part of a plant (the scion) inserted in a groove, slit, or the like in another plant or tree (the stock) so as to become nourished by and united with it. **2.** *Surgery* a portion of living tissue surgically transplanted. – *v.t.* **3.** to cause (a plant) to reproduce through grafting. **4.** *Surgery* to transplant (a portion of living tissue) as a graft.

graft[2] /graft/ *n.* **1.** work, especially hard work. **2.** the acquisition of gain or advantage by dishonest, unfair, or shady means, especially through the abuse of one's position or influence in politics, business, etc.

grail /greɪl/ *n.* a cup (also taken as a chalice) which according to medieval legend was used by Jesus at the Last Supper.

grain /greɪn/ *n.* **1.** a small hard seed. **2.** any small, hard particle, as of sand, gold, pepper, gunpowder, etc. **3.** the arrangement or direction of fibres in wood. **4.** temper or natural character.

gram /græm/ *n.* a metric unit of mass, one thousandth of a kilogram. *Symbol*: g

-gram[1] a word element meaning something drawn or written, as in *diagram.*

-gram[2] a word element meaning grams; of or relating to a gram, as in *kilogram.*

gramma /'græmə/ *n.* a type of pumpkin.

grammar /'græmə/ *n.* the features of a language (sounds, words, formation and arrangement of words, etc.) considered systematically as a whole, especially with reference to their mutual contrasts and relations. – **grammarian**, *n.* – **grammatical**, *adj.*

gramophone /'græməfoun/ *n.* a record-player.

grampus /'græmpəs/ *n.* a cetacean of the dolphin family.

granary /'grænəri/ *n., pl.* **-ries**. a storehouse or repository for grain.

grand /grænd/ *adj.* **1.** imposing in size or appearance or general effect. **2.** magnificent or splendid. **3.** of great importance, distinction, or pretension. **4.** one degree more remote in ascent or descent (used in compounds), as in *grand-aunt, grandchild,* etc. – **grandeur**, *n.*

grandchild /'græntʃaɪld/ *n., pl.* **-children**. a child of one's son or daughter.

grandiloquent /græn'dɪləkwənt/ *adj.* speaking or expressed in a lofty or pompous style; bombastic.

grandiose /'grændious/ *adj.* grand in an imposing or impressive way.

grandparent /'grænpɛərənt/ *n.* a parent of a parent.

grandstand /'grænstænd, 'grænd-/ *n.* **1.** the principal stand for spectators at a racecourse, athletic field, etc. – *v.i.* **2.** to behave ostentatiously in order to impress or win approval.

granite /'grænət/ *n.* a granular igneous rock composed chiefly of felspar (orthoclase) and quartz.

grant /grænt, grant/ *v.t.* **1.** to bestow or confer, especially by a formal act. **2.** to give or accord. **3.** to admit or concede; accept for the sake of argument. **4. take for granted,** to accept without appreciation. – *n.* **5.** that which is granted, as a privilege or right, a sum of money, as for a student's maintenance, or a tract of land. – **grantor**, *n.* – **grantee**, *n.*

granular /'grænjələ/ *adj.* **1.** of the nature of granules. **2.** composed of or bearing granules or grains. **3.** showing a granulated structure.

granulate /'grænjəleɪt/ *v.,* **-lated**, **-lating**. – *v.t.* **1.** to form into granules or grains. – *v.i.* **2.** to become granular. – **granulator**, *n.* – **granulation**, *n.*

granule /'grænjul/ *n.* a little grain, pellet, or particle.

grape /greɪp/ *n.* the edible, pulpy, smooth-skinned berry or fruit which grows in clusters on vines of the genus *Vitis.*

grapefruit /'greɪpfrut/ *n.* a large roundish, yellow-skinned edible citrus fruit.

graph /græf, graf/ *n.* **1.** a diagram representing a system of connections or interrelations among two or more things by a number of distinctive dots, lines, bars, etc. – *v.t.* **2.** to draw a graph of.

graph- variant of **grapho-** before vowels.

-graph a word element meaning: **1.** drawn or written, as in *autograph.* **2.** something drawn or written, as in *lithograph, monograph.* **3.** an apparatus for drawing, writing, recording, etc., as in *barograph.*

graphic /'græfɪk/ *adj.* **1.** life-like; vivid. **2.** relating to the use of diagrams, graphs, mathematical curves, or the like; diagrammatic. **3.** relating to writing.

graphite /'græfaɪt/ *n.* a very common mineral, soft native carbon.

grapho- a word element meaning 'writing'. Also, **graph-**.

-graphy a combining form denoting some process or form of drawing, representing, writing, recording, describing, etc.

grapnel /'græpnəl/ *n.* a device consisting essentially of one or more hooks or clamps, for grasping or holding something.

grapple /'græpəl/ *n., v.,* **-pled**, **-pling**. – *n.* **1.** a hook or an iron instrument by which one thing, as a ship, fastens on another; a grapnel. – *v.i.* **2.** to hold or make fast to something as with a grapple. **3.** to seize another, or each other, in a firm grip, as in wrestling; clinch. **4.** to try to overcome or deal (fol. by *with*).

grasp /græsp, grasp/ *v.t.* **1.** to seize and hold by or as by clasping with the fingers. **2.** to lay hold of with the mind; comprehend; understand. – *v.i.* **3.** to make the motion of seizing; seize something firmly or eagerly. – *n.* **4.** a grasping or gripping; grip of the hand. **5.** hold, possession, or mastery. **6.** broad or thorough comprehension.

grass /gras/ *n.* **1.** a plant with jointed stems, sheathing leaves, flower spikelets, and fruit consisting of a seed-like grain. **2.** *Colloquial* → **marijuana**.

grasshopper /'grashɒpə/ *n.* a terrestrial, herbivorous insect with hind legs for leaping.

grate[1] /greɪt/ *n.* a frame of metal bars for holding fuel when burning, as in a fireplace or furnace.

grate[2] /greɪt/ *v.,* **grated**, **grating**. – *v.i.* **1.** to have an irritating or unpleasant effect on the feelings. **2.** to make a sound as of rough scraping. – *v.t.* **3.** to rub together with a harsh, jarring sound. **4.** to reduce to small particles by rubbing against a rough surface or a surface with many sharp-edged openings.

grateful /'greɪtfəl/ *adj.* warmly or deeply appreciative of kindness or benefits received; thankful. – **gratitude**, *n.*

gratify /'grætəfaɪ/ *v.t.*, **-fied**, **-fying**. **1.** to give pleasure to (persons) by satisfying desires or humouring inclinations or feelings. **2.** to satisfy; indulge; humour. – **gratifier**, *n.* – **gratification**, *n.*

gratuitous /grə'tjuətəs/ *adj.* **1.** freely bestowed or obtained; free. **2.** being without reason, cause, or justification.

gratuity /grə'tjuəti/ *n.*, *pl.* **-ties**. a gift, usually of money, over and above payment due for service; tip.

grave[1] /greɪv/ *n.* an excavation made in the earth to receive a dead body in burial.

grave[2] /greɪv/ *adj.* **1.** dignified; sedate; serious; earnest; solemn. **2.** important or critical; involving serious issues.

grave[3] /greɪv/ *v.t.*, **graved**, **graved** *or* **graven**, **graving**. to impress deeply.

gravel /'grævəl/ *n.* small stones and pebbles, or a mixture of these with sand.

gravitate /'grævəteɪt/ *v.i.*, **-tated**, **-tating**. **1.** to move or tend to move under the influence of gravitational force. **2.** to have a natural tendency or be strongly attracted (fol. by *to* or *towards*).

gravitation /grævə'teɪʃən/ *n.* *Physics* that force of attraction between all particles or bodies, or that acceleration of one towards another, of which the fall of bodies to the earth is an instance. – **gravitational**, *adj.* – **gravitationally**, *adv.*

gravity /'grævəti/ *n.*, *pl.* **-ties**. **1.** *Physics* the force of attraction by which terrestrial bodies tend to fall towards the centre of the earth. **2.** seriousness; dignity; solemnity. **3.** serious or critical character.

gravy /'greɪvi/ *n.*, *pl.* **-vies**. the fat and juices that drip from meat during cooking, often made into a dressing for meat, etc.

graze[1] /greɪz/ *v.i.*, **grazed**, **grazing**. to feed on growing herbage, as cattle, sheep etc.

graze[2] /greɪz/ *v.*, **grazed**, **grazing**, *n.* – *v.t.* **1.** to touch or rub lightly in passing. **2.** to scrape the skin from (the leg, arm, etc.); abrade. – *n.* **3.** a slight scratch in passing; abrasion.

grazier /'greɪziə/ *n.* the owner of a rural property on which sheep or cattle are grazed.

grease /gris/ *n.*, /griz, gris/ *v.*, **greased**, **greasing**. – *n.* **1.** the melted or rendered fat of animals, especially when in a soft state. **2.** fatty or oily matter in general; lubricant. – *v.t.* **3.** to smear with grease.

great /greɪt/ *adj.* **1.** unusually or comparatively large in size or dimensions. **2.** notable or remarkable. **3.** of much consequence; important. **4.** being such in an extreme degree. **5.** *Colloquial* first-rate; very good; fine. **6.** one degree more remote in direct ascent or descent than a specified relationship.

greed /grid/ *n.* inordinate or rapacious desire, especially for food or wealth. – **greedy**, *adj.*

green /grin/ *adj.* **1.** of the colour of growing foliage, between yellow and blue in the spectrum. **2.** covered with herbage or foliage; verdant. **3.** characterised by a concern for environmental issues. **4.** not fully developed or perfected in growth or condition; unripe; not properly aged. **5.** immature in age or judgment; untrained; inexperienced. **6.** uncooked, raw. – *n.* **7.** green colour. **8.** *Golf* the whole course or links on which golf is played. **9.** a bowling green.

green ban *n.* **1.** a refusal by employees to work or to allow work to proceed on a building site that is situated in a green belt. **2.** a similar refusal with respect to any construction work which would necessitate destroying something of natural, historical or social significance.

green belt *n.* an area of parkland, rural or uncultivated land, or native bush, near a town or a city on which building is either strictly controlled or not permitted.

green-eyed /'grin-aɪd/ *adj.* jealous.

greengrocer /'gringrousə/ *n.* a retailer of fresh vegetables and fruit.

greenhouse /'grinhaus/ *n.* a building, chiefly of glass, for the cultivation or protection of plants.

greenhouse effect *n.* the increase in the temperature of the earth caused by its atmosphere acting as the glass of a greenhouse does, possibly to be increased as pollution adds more and more carbon dioxide to the atmosphere.

greet /grit/ *v.t.* to address with some form of salutation; welcome.

greeting /'gritɪŋ/ *n.* **1.** the act or words of someone who greets. **2.** (*usu. pl.*) a friendly message.

gregarious /grə'gɛəriəs/ *adj.* **1.** living in flocks or herds, as animals. **2.** *Botany* growing in open clusters; not matted together. **3.** fond of company; sociable.

gremlin /'grɛmlən/ *n.* a mischievous invisible being, said by airmen to cause engine trouble and mechanical difficulties.

grenade /grə'neɪd/ *n.* a small explosive shell thrown by hand or fired from a rifle.

grevillea /grə'vɪliə/ *n.* any shrub or tree of a very large, mainly Australian, genus.

grew /gru/ *v.* past tense of **grow**.

grey /greɪ/ *adj.* **1.** of a colour between white and black, having no definite hue; ash-coloured; technically of an achromatic colour. **2.** dark, overcast, dismal, gloomy. **3.** grey-haired. – *n.* **4.** any achromatic colour; any colour with zero chroma from white to black. **5.** a grey horse.

greyhound /'greɪhaund/ *n.* one of a breed of tall, slender dogs, notable for keen sight and for fleetness.

grey market *n.* the non-official section of the money market which includes the buy-back market, the inter-company market and the commercial bill market.

grey nurse shark *n.* a common shark of Australian waters with long, thin, ripping teeth.

grid /grɪd/ *n.* **1.** a grating of crossed bars. **2.** a network of cables, pipes, etc., for the distribution and supply of electricity, gas, water, etc. **3.** a network of horizontal and vertical lines designed to give fixed points of reference, as those superimposed on a map, etc.

griddle /ˈgrɪdl/ *n.* a flat, heated surface on top of a stove.

grief /grif/ *n.* **1.** keen mental suffering or distress over affliction or loss; sharp sorrow; painful regret. **2. come to grief,** to come to a bad end; turn out badly.

grievance /ˈgrivəns/ *n.* a wrong, real or fancied, considered as grounds for complaint.

grieve /griv/ *v.,* **grieved**, **grieving**. – *v.i.* **1.** to feel grief; sorrow. – *v.t.* **2.** to distress mentally; cause to feel grief or sorrow.

grievous /ˈgrivəs/ *adj.* **1.** causing grief or sorrow. **2.** flagrant; atrocious.

grill[1] /grɪl/ *n.* **1.** a griller. **2.** a meal in which the meat component is grilled. – *v.t.* **3.** to cook under a griller.

grill[2] /grɪl/ *n.* → **grille**.

grille /grɪl/ *n.* **1.** a lattice or openwork screen, as a window or gate, usually of metal and often of decorative design. **2.** an ornamental metal screen at the front of a motor car. – **grilled**, *adj.*

griller /ˈgrɪlə/ *n.* a cooking device, or that part of a stove, in which meat, etc., is cooked by exposure to direct radiant heat.

grim /grɪm/ *adj.,* **grimmer**, **grimmest**. **1.** stern; unrelenting; uncompromising. **2.** of a fierce or forbidding aspect.

grimace /ˈgrɪməs, grəˈmeɪs/ *n., v.,* **-maced**, **-macing**. – *n.* **1.** a wry face; facial contortion; ugly facial expression. – *v.i.* **2.** to make grimaces. – **grimacer**, *n.*

grime /graɪm/ *n.* dirt or foul matter, especially on or ingrained in a surface.

grin /grɪn/ *v.,* **grinned**, **grinning**, *n.* – *v.i.* **1.** to smile broadly, or with a wide distension of the mouth. – *n.* **2.** a broad smile.

grind /graɪnd/ *v.,* **ground**, **grinding**, *n.* – *v.t.* **1.** to wear, smooth, or sharpen by friction; whet. **2.** to reduce to fine particles as by pounding or crushing. – *n.* **3.** the act of grinding. **4.** *Colloquial* laborious or monotonous work; close or laborious study.

grip /grɪp/ *n., v.,* **gripped** *or* **gript**, **gripping**. – *n.* **1.** the act of grasping; a seizing and holding fast; firm grasp. **2.** mental or intellectual hold; competence. **3.** a special mode of clasping hands. **4.** something which seizes and holds, as a clutching device on a cable car. **5.** a sudden, sharp pain; spasm of pain. – *v.t.* **6.** to grasp or seize firmly; hold fast. **7.** to take hold on; hold the interest of.

gripe /graɪp/ *v.,* **griped**, **griping**, *n.* – *v.i.* **1.** *Colloquial* to complain constantly; grumble. – *n.* **2.** an objection; complaint.

grisly /ˈgrɪzli/ *adj.,* **-lier**, **-liest**. such as to cause a shuddering horror; gruesome.

grist /grɪst/ *n.* corn to be ground.

gristle /ˈgrɪsəl/ *n.* → **cartilage**.

grit /grɪt/ *n., v.,* **gritted**, **gritting**. – *n.* **1.** fine, stony, or hard particles such as are deposited like dust from the air or occur as impurities in food, etc. **2.** firmness of character; indomitable spirit; pluck. – *v.t.* **3.** to clench or grind.

grizzle[1] /ˈgrɪzəl/ *v.i.,* **-zled**, **-zling**. to become grey.

grizzle[2] /ˈgrɪzəl/ *v.i.,* **-zled**, **-zling**. to whimper; whine; complain fretfully.

groan /groʊn/ *n.* **1.** a low, mournful sound uttered in pain or grief. **2.** a deep murmur uttered in derision, disapproval, etc. – *v.i.* **3.** to utter a moan.

grocer /ˈgroʊsə/ *n.* a dealer in general supplies for the table, as flour, sugar, coffee, etc. – **grocery**, *n.*

grog /grɒg/ *n.* *Colloquial* alcohol.

groggy /ˈgrɒgi/ *adj.,* **-gier**, **-giest**. *Colloquial* **1.** staggering, as from exhaustion or blows. **2.** drunk; intoxicated.

groin /grɔɪn/ *n.* *Anatomy* the fold or hollow on either side of the body where the thigh joins the abdomen.

grommet /ˈgrɒmət/ *n.* a ring or eyelet of metal, rubber, etc. Also, **grummet**.

groom /grum/ *n.* **1.** a man or boy in charge of horses or the stable. **2.** a man newly married, or about to be married; bridegroom. – *v.t.* **3.** to tend carefully as to person and dress; make neat or tidy. **4.** to prepare for a position, election, etc.

groomsman /ˈgrumzmən/ *n., pl.* **-men**. a man who attends the bridegroom at a wedding.

groove /gruv/ *n.* **1.** a furrow or channel cut by a tool. **2.** a fixed routine.

groovy /ˈgruvi/ *adj.* *Colloquial* **1.** exciting, satisfying, or pleasurable. **2.** appreciative.

grope /groʊp/ *v.i.,* **groped**, **groping**. **1.** to feel about with the hands; feel one's way. **2.** to search blindly or uncertainly.

groper /ˈgroʊpə/ *n., pl.* **-pers**, (*esp. collectively*) **-per**. any of several species of large Australian or New Zealand marine fish, typically with enormous gape.

gross /groʊs/ *adj.* **1.** whole, entire, or total, especially without having been subjected to deduction, as for charges, loss, etc. **2.** glaring or flagrant. **3.** morally coarse; lacking refinement; indelicate or indecent. **4.** large, big, or bulky. – *n.* **5.** a unit consisting of twelve dozen, or 144. – *v.t.* **6.** to make a gross profit of; earn a total of.

gross domestic product *n.* an estimate of the total value of all legal goods and services produced in a country in a specified time, usually a year. Also, **GDP**.

gross national product *n.* gross domestic product plus income earned by domestic residents from overseas investments, minus income earned in the domestic market accruing to overseas (foreign) residents. Also, **GNP**.

gross tonnage *n.* a measure of the enclosed internal volume of a ship and its superstructure, with certain spaces exempted.

grotesque /groʊˈtɛsk/ *adj.* odd or unnatural in shape, appearance, or character; fantastically ugly or absurd; bizarre.

grotto /ˈgrɒtoʊ/ *n., pl.* **-toes**, **-tos**. a cave or cavern.

grotty /ˈgrɒti/ *adj.* *Colloquial* **1.** dirty; filthy. **2.** useless; rubbishy.

grouch /graʊtʃ/ *Colloquial* – *v.i.* **1.** to be sulky or morose; show discontent; complain. – *n.* **2.** a sulky or morose person.

ground[1] /graʊnd/ *n.* **1.** the earth's solid surface; firm or dry land. **2.** earth or soil. **3.** (*often pl.*) a tract of land occupied, or appropriated to a special use. **4.** (*often pl.*)

the foundation or basis on which a theory or action rests; motive; reason. **5.** the underlying or main surface or background, in painting, decorative work, lace, etc. **6. common ground,** matters on which agreement exists. **7. gain ground,** to advance; make progress. **8. hold** (or **stand**) **one's ground,** to maintain one's position. **9. lose ground,** to lose what one has gained; retreat; give way. **10. run to ground,** to hunt down; track down. – *adj.* **11.** situated on or at, or adjacent to, the surface of the earth. **12.** relating to the ground. – *v.t.* **13.** to lay or set on the ground. **14.** to place on a foundation; found; fix firmly; settle or establish. **15.** *Electricity* to establish an earth for (a circuit, device, etc.). **16.** to prevent (an aircraft or a pilot) from flying. **17.** to restrict, or withdraw privileges from.

ground[2] /graʊnd/ *v.* past tense and past participle of **grind**.

ground plan *n.* the plan of a ground floor of a building.

ground rent *n.* the rent at which land is leased to a tenant for a specified term, usually ninety-nine years.

ground rule *n.* (*usu. pl.*) a basic rule of a game, meeting, procedure, etc.

groundsheet /'graʊndʃit/ *n.* a waterproof sheet spread on the ground to give protection against dampness.

groundswell *n.* **1.** a broad, deep swell or rolling of the sea, due to a distant storm or gale. **2.** a strong movement of public opinion.

groundwork /'graʊndwɜk/ *n.* the foundation, base, or basis of anything.

group /grup/ *n.* **1.** any assemblage of persons or things; cluster. **2.** a number of persons or things ranged or considered together as being related in some way. – *v.t.* **3.** to place in a group, as with others.

group certificate *n.* a certificate issued by an employer to an employee at the end of a financial year or on termination of employment, detailing gross income, tax paid, etc.

grouper /'grupə/ *n., pl.* **-pers**, (*esp. collectively*) **-per**. any of various often large fishes found in warm seas.

grouse[1] /graʊs/ *n., pl.* **grouse**. a game bird of the Northern Hemisphere.

grouse[2] /graʊs/ *v.i.,* **groused**, **grousing**. *Colloquial* to grumble; complain.

grouse[3] /graʊs/ *adj. Colloquial* **1.** very good. **2. extra grouse,** excellent.

grout /graʊt/ *n.* a thin coarse mortar poured into the joints of masonry and brickwork.

grove /groʊv/ *n.* a small wood or plantation of trees.

grovel /'grɒvəl/ *v.i.,* **-elled**, **-elling**. to humble oneself or act in an abject manner, as in fear or in mean servility. – **groveller**, *n.*

grow /groʊ/ *v.,* **grew**, **grown**, **growing**. – *v.i.* **1.** to increase by natural development, as any living organism or part by assimilation of nutriment; increase in size or substance. **2.** to increase gradually; become greater. **3.** to come to be, or become, by degrees. **4. grow up,** to increase in growth; attain maturity. – *v.t.* **5.** to cause to grow.

growl /graʊl/ *v.i.* **1.** to utter a deep guttural sound of anger or hostility. – *n.* **2.** the act or sound of growling.

grown-up /'groʊn-ʌp/ *adj.* **1.** adult. – *n.* **2.** a grown-up person; an adult.

growth /groʊθ/ *n.* **1.** the act, process, or manner of growing; development; gradual increase. **2.** *Pathology* a morbid mass of tissue, as a tumour.

grub /grʌb/ *n.* **1.** the bulky larva of certain insects, especially of scarabaeid and other beetles. **2.** *Colloquial* food or victuals.

grubby /'grʌbi/ *adj.,* **-bier**, **-biest**. dirty; slovenly.

grudge /grʌdʒ/ *n.* a feeling of ill will or resentment excited by some special cause, as a personal injury or insult, etc.

gruel /'gruəl/ *n.* a light, usually thin, cooked cereal made by boiling meal, especially oatmeal, in water or milk.

gruelling /'gruəlɪŋ/ *adj.* exhausting; very tiring; severe.

gruesome /'grusəm/ *adj.* inspiring horror; revolting.

gruff /grʌf/ *adj.* **1.** low and harsh; hoarse. **2.** rough; surly.

grumble /'grʌmbəl/ *v.,* **-bled**, **-bling**, *n.* – *v.i.* **1.** to murmur in discontent; complain ill-humouredly. – *n.* **2.** an ill-humoured complaining; murmur; growl.

grumpy /'grʌmpi/ *adj.,* **-pier**, **-piest**. surly; ill-tempered. – **grump**, *n.*

grunt /grʌnt/ *v.i.* to utter the deep guttural sound characteristic of a pig.

GST /dʒi ɛs 'ti/ *n.* goods and services tax.

guarantee /gærən'ti/ *n., v.,* **-teed**, **-teeing**. – *n.* **1.** a warrant, pledge, or promise accepting responsibility for the discharging of another's liabilities, as the payment of a debt. **2.** a promise or assurance, especially one given in writing by a manufacturer, that something is of a specified quality, and generally including an undertaking to make good any defects under certain conditions. **3.** someone who gives a guarantee; guarantor. **4.** something that has the force or effect of a guarantee. – *v.t.* **5.** to secure, as by giving or taking security. **6.** to make oneself answerable for on behalf of one primarily responsible. **7.** to undertake to secure to another, as rights or possessions. **8.** to serve as a warrant or guarantee for. **9.** to engage to protect or indemnify (fol. by *from*, *against*, or *in*). **10.** to promise.

guarantor /gærən'tɔ/ *n.* someone who makes or gives a guarantee.

guaranty /'gærənti/ *n., pl.* **-ties**, *v.,* **-tied**, **-tying**. → **guarantee**.

guard /gad/ *v.t.* **1.** to keep safe from harm; protect; watch over. **2.** to keep under close watch in order to prevent escape, outbreaks, etc. – *v.i.* **3.** to take precautions (fol. by *against*). – *n.* **4.** someone who guards, protects, or keeps a protecting or restraining watch. **5.** something intended or serving to guard or protect; a safeguard. **6.** an official in general charge of a railway train.

guardian /'gadiən/ *n.* **1.** someone who guards, protects, or preserves. **2.** *Law* someone who is entrusted by law with the care of the person or property, or both, of another. – *adj.* **3.** guarding; protecting.

guava /ˈgwavə/ *n.* any of various trees and shrubs with a fruit used for jelly, etc.

guerilla = guerrilla /gəˈrɪlə/ *n.* a member of a small, independent band of soldiers which harasses the enemy by surprise raids, attacks on communication and supply lines, etc.

guess /gɛs/ *v.t.* to form an opinion of at random or from evidence admittedly uncertain.

guest /gɛst/ *n.* a person entertained at the house or table of another.

guff /gʌf/ *n. Colloquial* empty or foolish talk.

guffaw /gʌˈfɔ, gə-/ *n.* **1.** a loud, coarse burst of laughter. – *v.i.* **2.** to laugh loudly.

guidance /ˈgaɪdns/ *n.* advice; instruction.

guide /gaɪd/ *v.,* **guided**, **guiding**, *n.* – *v.t.* **1.** to lead or conduct on the way, as to a place or through a region; show the way to. **2.** to direct the movement or course of. – *n.* **3.** someone who guides.

guild /gɪld/ *n.* an organisation of persons with common professional or cultural interests formed for mutual aid and protection. Also, **gild**.

guile /gaɪl/ *n.* insidious cunning.

guillotine /ˈgɪlətin/ *n.* **1.** a machine for beheading persons by means of a heavy blade falling in two grooved posts. **2.** a device incorporating a long blade for trimming paper. **3.** a time restriction imposed by resolution on a parliamentary debate.

guilt /gɪlt/ *n.* **1.** the fact or state of having committed an offence or crime. **2.** a feeling of responsibility or remorse for some crime, wrong, etc., either real or imagined. – **guilty**, *adj.*

guinea pig /ˈgɪni pɪg/ *n.* a short-eared, short-tailed rodent much used in scientific experiments.

guise /gaɪz/ *n.* **1.** external appearance in general; aspect or semblance. **2.** assumed appearance or mere semblance.

guitar /gəˈta/ *n.* a musical stringed instrument with a long fretted neck and a flat, somewhat violin-like body.

gulf /gʌlf/ *n.* **1.** a portion of an ocean or sea partly enclosed by land. **2.** a deep hollow; chasm or abyss.

gull /gʌl/ *n.* a web-footed, aquatic bird.

gullet /ˈgʌlət/ *n.* the oesophagus, or tube by which food and drink swallowed pass to the stomach.

gullible /ˈgʌləbəl/ *adj.* easily deceived or cheated. – **gullibility**, *n.* – **gullibly**, *adv.*

gully /ˈgʌli/ *n.* a small valley cut by running water.

gulp /gʌlp/ *v.i.* **1.** to gasp or choke as when taking large draughts of liquids. – *n.* **2.** the act of gulping.

gum[1] /gʌm/ *n., v.,* **gummed**, **gumming**. – *n.* **1.** any of various viscid, amorphous exudations from plants. **2.** a preparation of such a substance, as for use in the arts, etc. **3.** Also, **gum tree**, **gumtree**. any tree or shrub of the myrtaceous genus *Eucalyptus*. – *v.t.* **4.** to smear, stiffen, or stick together with gum. **5.** to clog with or as with some gummy substance (often fol. by *up*).

gum[2] /gʌm/ *n.* (*often pl.*) the firm, fleshy tissue covering the alveolar parts of either jaw and enveloping the bases of the teeth.

gumboot /ˈgʌmbut/ *n.* a rubber boot reaching to the knee or thigh.

gumption /ˈgʌmpʃən/ *n. Colloquial* **1.** initiative; resourcefulness. **2.** shrewd, practical common sense.

gum tree *n.* **1.** → **gum**[1] (def. 3). **2. up a gum tree**, *Colloquial* **a.** in difficulties; in a predicament. **b.** completely baffled. Also, **gumtree**.

gun /gʌn/ *n., v.,* **gunned**, **gunning**, *adj.* – *n.* **1.** a metallic tube, with its stock or carriage and attachments, from which heavy missiles are thrown by the force of an explosive; a piece of ordnance. **2.** any similar device for projecting something. **3.** *Colloquial* a champion, especially in shearing. – *v.t.* **4.** to shoot with a gun (often fol. by *down*). – *adj.* **5.** *Colloquial* of or relating to someone who is expert, especially in shearing.

gunboat diplomacy *n.* diplomacy or foreign affairs in conjunction with the use or threat of military force.

gunnery /ˈgʌnəri/ *n.* **1.** the art and science of constructing and managing guns, especially large guns. **2.** the firing of guns. **3.** guns collectively.

gunny /ˈgʌni/ *n., pl.* **-nies**. a strong, coarse material made commonly from jute, used for sacking, etc.

gunpowder /ˈgʌnpaʊdə/ *n.* an explosive mixture of saltpetre (potassium nitrate), sulfur, and charcoal, used especially in gunnery.

gunwale /ˈgʌnəl/ *n.* the upper edge of a vessel's or boat's side.

gunyah /ˈgʌnjə/ *n.* an Aborigine's hut made of boughs and bark; humpy; mia-mia; wurley. Also, **gunya**.

gurgle /ˈgɜgəl/ *v.i.,* **-gled**, **-gling**. **1.** to flow in a broken, irregular, noisy current. **2.** to make a sound as of water doing this (often used of birds or of human beings).

guru /ˈgʊru, ˈguru/ *n.* (in Hinduism) a preceptor and spiritual guide.

gush /gʌʃ/ *v.i.* **1.** to issue with force, as a fluid escaping from confinement; flow suddenly and copiously. **2.** *Colloquial* to express oneself extravagantly or emotionally; talk effusively.

gusset /ˈgʌsət/ *n.* an angular piece of material inserted in a garment to strengthen, enlarge or give freedom of movement to some part of it.

gust /gʌst/ *n.* a sudden, strong blast, as of wind. – **gusty**, *adj.*

gusto /ˈgʌstoʊ/ *n.* keen relish or hearty enjoyment, as in eating, drinking, or in action or speech generally.

gut /gʌt/ *n., v.,* **gutted**, **gutting**. – *n.* **1.** the alimentary canal between the stomach and the anus, or some portion of it. **2.** (*pl.*) the bowels or entrails. **3.** (*pl.*) *Colloquial* courage; stamina; endurance. **4.** (*pl.*) *Colloquial* essential information. **5.** a preparation of the intestines of an animal used for various purposes, as for violin strings, tennis rackets, fishing lines, etc. – *v.t.* **6.** to take out the guts or entrails of; disembowel. **7.** to destroy the interior of. – *adj.* **8.** of or relating to feelings, emotion, intuition. – **gutsy**, *adj.*

gutter /ˈgʌtə/ *n.* **1.** a channel at the side (or in the middle) of a road or street, for leading off surface water. **2.** Also, **guttering**. a channel at the eaves or on the roof of a building, for carrying off rainwater.

guttural /ˈgʌtərəl/ *adj.* **1.** relating to the throat. **2.** harsh; throaty.

guy[1] /gaɪ/ *n. Colloquial* a fellow or man.

guy[2] /gaɪ/ *n.* a rope or appliance used to guide and steady a thing being hoisted or lowered.

guzzle /ˈgʌzəl/ *v.t.*, **-zled**, **-zling**. to drink (or sometimes eat) frequently and greedily.

gym /dʒɪm/ *n.* **1.** a gymnasium. **2.** gymnastics.

gymkhana /dʒɪmˈkanə/ *n.* a horseriding event featuring games and novelty contests.

gymnasium /dʒɪmˈneɪziəm/ *n., pl.* **-siums**, **-sia** /-ziə/. a building or room equipped with facilities for gymnastics and sport.

gymnastic /dʒɪmˈnæstɪk/ *adj.* relating to exercises which develop flexibility, strength, and agility. – **gymnastics**, *n.*

gyn- variant of **gyno-**.

gynaecology = gynecology /gaɪnəˈkɒlədʒi/ *n.* the department of medical science which deals with the functions and diseases peculiar to women. – **gynaecologist**, *n.*

gyno- a word element meaning 'woman', 'female'. Also, **gyn-**.

-gynous 1. an adjective combining form referring to the female sex, as in *androgynous*. **2.** a suffix meaning 'woman'.

gyp /dʒɪp/ *v.*, **gypped**, **gypping**, *n. Colloquial* – *v.t.* **1.** to swindle; cheat; defraud or rob by some sharp practice. – *n.* **2.** a swindle.

gyprock /ˈdʒɪprɒk/ *n.* → **plasterboard**.

gypsum /ˈdʒɪpsəm/ *n.* a very common mineral, used to make plaster as an ornamental material, as a fertiliser, etc.

gypsy /ˈdʒɪpsi/ *n., pl.* **-sies**, *adj.* → **gipsy**.

gyrate /dʒaɪˈreɪt/ *v.i.*, **-rated**, **-rating**. to move in a circle or spiral, or round a fixed point; whirl. – **gyration**, *n.* – **gyratory**, *adj.*

gyre /ˈdʒaɪə/ *n.* a ring or circle.

gyro- a word element meaning: **1.** 'ring'; 'circle'. **2.** 'spiral'.

gyroscope /ˈdʒaɪrəskoʊp/ *n.* an apparatus consisting of a rotating wheel so mounted that its axis can turn freely in certain or all directions, and capable of maintaining the same absolute direction in space in spite of movements of the mountings and surroundings parts. – **gyroscopic**, *adj.*

H h

H, h /eɪtʃ/, *non-standard* /heɪtʃ/ *n., pl.* **H's** *or* **Hs, h's** *or* **hs**. the 8th letter of the English alphabet.

habeas corpus /ˌheɪbiəs 'kɔpəs/ *n.* a writ commanding that a prisoner appear in court.

haberdashery /hæbə'dæʃəri/ *n., pl.* **-ries**. **1.** a shop where goods such as buttons, needles, etc., are sold. **2.** the goods themselves. – **haberdasher**, *n.*

habit /'hæbət/ *n.* **1.** a disposition or tendency, constantly shown, to act in a certain way. **2.** garb of a particular rank, profession, religious order, etc. – **habitual**, *adj.*

habitable /'hæbɪtəbəl/ *adj.* capable of being inhabited.

habitat /'hæbətæt/ *n.* the native environment of an animal or plant.

habitation /hæbə'teɪʃən/ *n.* a place of abode; dwelling.

habituate /hə'bɪtʃueɪt/ *v.t.*, **-ated**, **-ating**. **1.** to accustom. **2.** *Colloquial* to frequent.

hack[1] /hæk/ *v.t.* **1.** to cut, notch, or chop irregularly, as with heavy blows. **2.** to damage by cutting harshly or ruthlessly. **3. hack into,** to gain unauthorised access, as to the information stored on an organisation's computer. – *n.* **4.** a short, broken cough.

hack[2] /hæk/ *n.* **1.** a horse kept for common hire, or adapted for general work, especially ordinary riding. **2.** a person who for a living undertakes literary or other work of little or no originality. – *v.t.* **3.** *Colloquial* to put up with; endure.

hacker /'hækə/ *n. Computers Colloquial* **1.** a computer enthusiast who studies computers and writes programs as a hobby. **2.** someone who gains unauthorised access to a computer system and makes amendments. Also, **hack**.

hackle /'hækəl/ *n.* **1.** a neck feather of certain birds, as the domestic cock. **2.** (*pl.*) the hair on a dog's neck.

hackneyed /'hæknid/ *adj.* trite.

hackwork /'hækwɜk/ *n.* the routine aspects of a creative or artistic occupation, considered as mundane, or of an inferior quality, especially in the literary field.

had /hæd/, *weak forms* /həd, əd, d/ – *v.* past tense and past participle of **have**.

haddock /'hædək/ *n., pl.* **-docks**, (*esp. collectively*) **-dock**. a food fish related to the cod.

hades /'heɪdiz/ *n. Colloquial* hell.

haemo- = hemo- a word element meaning 'blood'. Also, **haem-**, **haema-**, **haemat-**, **haemato-**.

haemoglobin /himə'gloʊbən/ *n.* a protein responsible for the red colour of blood which carries oxygen to the tissues.

haemophilia /himə'fɪliə/ *n.* a hereditary disease in which blood fails to coagulate. – **haemophiliac**, *n.*

haemorrhage /'hɛmərɪdʒ/ *n.* a discharge of blood, as from a ruptured blood vessel.

haemorrhoid /'hɛmərɔɪd/ *n.* a swelling of a vein of the anus; pile.

haft /'haft/ *n.* a handle, as of a knife.

hag /hæg/ *n.* a repulsive old woman.

haggard /'hægəd/ *adj.* careworn; gaunt, as from prolonged suffering, anxiety, etc.

haggis /'hægəs/ *n.* a dish made of the heart, liver, etc., of a sheep, etc.

haggle /'hægəl/ *v.i.*, **-gled**, **-gling**. to bargain in a petty and tedious manner.

hagiology /hægi'ɒlədʒi, heɪdʒi-/ *n., pl.* **-gies**. that branch of literature which deals with the lives and legends of the saints.

hail[1] /heɪl/ *v.t.* **1.** to salute or greet; welcome. **2.** to acclaim; to approve with enthusiasm. **3.** to call out to, in order to attract attention. – *v.i.* **4. hail from,** to belong to as the place of residence, point of departure, etc.

hail[2] /heɪl/ *n.* **1.** pellets of ice falling from the clouds in a shower. – *v.i.* **2.** to pour down hail.

hair /hɛə/ *n.* **1.** the natural covering of the human head. **2.** the aggregate of hairs which grow on an animal. **3.** one of the numerous fine, usually cylindrical filaments growing from the skin and forming the coat of most mammals.

hairdo /'hɛədu/ *n., pl.* **-dos**. the style in which a person's hair is arranged, etc.

hairdresser /'hɛədrɛsə/ *n.* someone who arranges or cuts hair.

hair-raising /'hɛə-reɪzɪŋ/ *adj.* terrifying.

hair-trigger /'hɛə-trɪgə/ *n.* a trigger that allows the firing mechanism of a firearm to be operated by very slight pressure.

haka /'hakə/ *n.* a Maori ceremonial posture dance with vocal accompaniment.

hake /heɪk/ *n., pl.* **hakes**, (*esp. collectively*) **hake**. a fish related to the cod.

hakea /'heɪkiə/ *n.* any shrub or tree of the Australian genus *Hakea*, family Proteaceae, characterised by hard woody fruit with winged seeds.

halal /hæ'læl/ *adj.* of meat from animals slaughtered in accordance with Muslim rites.

halcyon /'hælsiən/ *adj.* **1.** calm, tranquil, or peaceful. **2.** carefree; joyous.

hale /heɪl/ *adj.*, **haler**, **halest**. free from disease or infirmity; robust; vigorous.

half /haf/ *n., pl.* **halves** /havz/. *adj., adv.* – *n.* **1.** one of the two equal parts into which anything is or may be divided. **2.** *Sport* either of the two periods of a game. **3.** one of a pair. – *adj.* **4.** being one of the two equal parts into which anything is or may be divided. **5.** being equal to only about half of the full measure. – *adv.* **6.** to the extent or measure of half. **7.** to some extent.

half-adder *n.* a circuit in a computer which performs part of the function of adding two numbers.

half-back /'haf-bæk/ *n.* **1.** *Rugby Football* the player who puts the ball in the scrum, and tries to catch it as it emerges. **2.** *Australian Rules* any of the three positions on the line between the centre-line and the full-back line. **3.** *Soccer* one of the three players in the next line behind the forward line.

half-brother /'haf-brʌðə/ *n.* a brother by one parent only.

half-caste /ˈhaf-kast/ *n.* a person of mixed race, especially where the races are of different colours.

half-hearted /ˈhaf-hatəd/ *adj.* having or showing little enthusiasm.

half-life /ˈhaf-laɪf/ *n.* the time required for one half of a sample of unstable material to undergo chemical change, as the disintegration of radioactive material, etc.

half-sister /ˈhaf-sɪstə/ *n.* a sister by one parent only.

halfway /hafˈweɪ/ *adv.*, /ˈhafweɪ/ *adj.* – *adv.* **1.** to or at half the distance. – *adj.* **2.** midway, as between two places or points.

halibut /ˈhæləbət/ *n., pl.* **-buts**, (*esp. collectively*) **-but**. a large food fish of northern seas.

halitosis /hæləˈtoʊsəs/ *n.* bad breath.

hall /hɔl/ *n.* **1.** the entrance room or vestibule of a house or building. **2.** a corridor or passageway in a building. **3.** a large building or room for public assembly and other community uses.

hallelujah /hæləˈlujə/ *interj.* Praise ye the Lord!

hallmark /ˈhɔlmak/ *n.* **1.** an official mark or stamp indicating a standard of purity, used in marking gold and silver articles. **2.** any outstanding feature or characteristic.

hallow /ˈhæloʊ/ *v.t.* to make holy.

hallucination /həlusəˈneɪʃən/ *n.* subjective sense perceptions for which there is no appropriate external source, as 'hearing voices'. – **hallucinate**, *v.*

halo /ˈheɪloʊ/ *n., pl.* **-loes**, **-los**. **1.** a radiance surrounding the head in the representation of a sacred personage. **2.** a circle of light, appearing round the sun or moon.

halt[1] /hɔlt, hɒlt/ *v.i.* **1.** to make a temporary or permanent stop. – *n.* **2.** a temporary stop.

halt[2] /hɔlt, hɒlt/ *v.i.* to falter as in speech, reasoning, etc.

halter /ˈhɔltə, ˈhɒltə/ *n.* a rope or strap for leading or fastening horses or cattle.

halve /hav/ *v.t.*, **halved**, **halving**. **1.** to divide in halves; share equally. **2.** to reduce to half.

halves /havz/ *n.* plural of **half**.

halyard /ˈhæljəd/ *n.* a rope or tackle used to hoist or lower a sail, yard, flag, etc. Also, **halliard**.

ham[1] /hæm/ *n.* **1.** one of the rear quarters of a pig. **2.** the meat of this part.

ham[2] /hæm/ *n.* *Colloquial* **1.** an actor who overacts. **2.** an amateur.

hamburger /ˈhæmbɜgə/ *n.* a cooked cake of minced beef, especially as in a bread roll with salad, etc.

hamlet /ˈhæmlət/ *n.* a small village.

hammer /ˈhæmə/ *n.* **1.** an instrument consisting of a solid head, usually of metal, set crosswise on a handle, used for beating metals, driving in nails, etc. **2.** any of various instruments or devices resembling a hammer in form, action, or use. – *v.t.* **3.** to beat or drive with or as with a hammer. **4.** to hit with some force; pound. **5.** *Stock Exchange* **a.** to announce a defaulter on the Stock Exchange. **b.** to depress or beat down (the price of a stock).

hammerhead /ˈhæməhɛd/ *n.* a shark with a head resembling a double-headed hammer.

hammock /ˈhæmək/ *n.* a kind of hanging bed or couch made of canvas, etc.

hamper[1] /ˈhæmpə/ *v.t.* to impede; hinder.

hamper[2] /ˈhæmpə/ *n.* **1.** a large basket. **2.** a package of foods.

hamster /ˈhæmstə/ *n.* a short-tailed, stout-bodied, burrowing rodent.

hamstring /ˈhæmstrɪŋ/ *n., v.*, **-strung**, **-stringing**. – *n.* **1.** one of the tendons bounding the hollow of the knee. – *v.t.* **2.** to cripple; render useless; thwart.

hand /hænd/ *n.* **1.** the terminal, prehensile part of the arm, consisting of the palm and five digits. **2.** something resembling a hand in shape or function. **3.** a person employed in manual labour. **4.** (*often pl.*) possession or power; control, custody, or care. **5.** a side of a subject, question, etc. **6.** style of handwriting. **7.** a person, with reference to action, ability, or skill. **8.** a pledge of marriage. **9.** a linear measure in the imperial system, used in giving the height of horses, etc., equal to four inches or approx. 10 cm. **10.** *Cards* **a.** the cards dealt to or held by each player at one time. **b.** a single part of a game, in which all the cards dealt at one time are played. **11.** a bundle or bunch of various fruit, leaves, etc. **12.** a round or outburst of applause for a performer. **13. at hand, a.** within reach. **b.** near in time. **c.** ready for use. **14. free hand,** freedom to act as desired. **15. give a hand,** to help; assist. **16. in hand, a.** under control. **b.** in immediate possession. **c.** in process. **d.** See **pay in hand**. **17. on hand, a.** in immediate possession. **b.** before one for attention. **c.** present. – *v.t.* **18.** to deliver or pass with the hand. **19.** to pass on; transmit (fol. by *on*). **20. hand it to,** to give due credit to.

handbag /ˈhændbæg/ *n.* a small bag used for carrying money, personal articles, etc., held in the hand or worn over the shoulder by means of a strap.

handbill /ˈhændbɪl/ *n.* a small printed bill or announcement, usually for distribution by hand.

handbook /ˈhændbʊk/ *n.* a small book or treatise serving for guidance, as in an occupation or study.

handcuff /ˈhændkʌf/ *n.* a ring-shaped shackle for the wrist, usually one of a pair connected by a short chain or linked bar.

handicap /ˈhændikæp/ *n., v.*, **-capped**, **-capping**. – *n.* **1.** a race or other contest in which certain disadvantages or advantages of weight, distance, time, past records, etc., are placed upon competitors to equalise their chances of winning. **2.** the disadvantage or advantage itself. **3.** any encumbrance or disadvantage that makes success more difficult. **4.** a physical disability. – *v.t.* **5.** to serve as a handicap or disadvantage to.

handicraft /ˈhændikraft/ *n.* **1.** manual skill. **2.** a manual art or occupation.

handiwork /ˈhændiwɜk/ *n.* work done or a thing or things made by the hands.

handkerchief /ˈhæŋkətʃif/ *n.* a small square piece of fabric, usually cotton, carried about the person for wiping the face, nose, etc.

handle /ˈhændl/ *n., v.,* **-dled**, **-dling**. – *n.* **1.** a part of a thing which is intended to be grasped by the hand in using or moving it. – *v.t.* **2.** to touch or feel with the hand; use the hands on, as in picking up. **3.** to manage, direct, or control. **4.** to deal with or treat in a particular way. **5.** to deal or trade in (goods, etc.). – *v.i.* **6.** to respond to handling.

handlebar /ˈhændlba/ *n.* (*usu. pl.*) the curved steering bar of a bicycle, motorcycle, etc., in front of the rider.

handshake /ˈhænʃeɪk, ˈhænd-/ *n.* **1.** a clasping of another's right hand as in salutation, congratulation, agreement, etc. **2.** *Computers* a signal sent from one device to another, indicating readiness to receive transferred information.

handsome /ˈhænsəm/ *adj.,* **-somer**, **-somest**. **1.** of fine or admirable appearance; comely; tastefully or elegantly fine. **2.** considerable, ample, or liberal in amount.

handstand /ˈhænstænd, ˈhænd-/ *n.* the act, or an instance of balancing upside down on one's hands.

handwriting /ˈhændˌraɪtɪŋ/ *n.* **1.** writing done with the hand. **2.** a kind or style of writing.

handy /ˈhændi/ *adj.,* **-dier**, **-diest** **1.** ready to hand; conveniently accessible. **2.** ready or skilful with the hands; deft; dexterous. **3.** convenient or useful.

hang /hæŋ/ *v.,* **hung** *or* (*esp. for capital punishment and suicide*) **hanged**, **hanging**, *n.* – *v.t.* **1.** to fasten or attach (a thing) so that it is supported only from above; suspend. **2.** to suspend by the neck until dead. **3.** to let droop or bend downwards. **4.** to fasten into position; fix at a proper angle. **5.** to attach (paper, etc.) to walls. – *v.i.* **6.** to be suspended; dangle. **7.** to be suspended from a cross or gallows. **8.** to bend forwards or downwards; lean over. **9.** to be conditioned or contingent; be dependent. **10.** to hold fast, cling, or adhere; rest for support (fol. by *on* or *upon*). **11.** to be doubtful or undecided; remain unfinished. **12. hang about** (or **around**), to loiter. **13. hang on, a.** to persevere. **b.** to linger. **c.** to wait. **14. hang out,** *Colloquial* to live at or frequent a particular place. **15. hang up, a.** to suspend on a hook or peg. **b.** to break off a telephone call by putting down the receiver. – *n.* **16.** the way in which a thing hangs.

hangar /ˈhæŋə/ *n.* **1.** a shed or shelter. **2.** a shed for aeroplanes or airships.

hang-glider /ˈhæŋ-glaɪdə/ *n.* a simple kite-like glider without a fuselage but with a framework from which a person hangs feet downwards.

hangover /ˈhæŋoʊvə/ *n. Colloquial* the after-effects of excessive indulgence in alcoholic drink.

hang-up /ˈhæŋ-ʌp/ *n. Colloquial* something which occasions unease, inhibition, or conflict in an individual.

hank /hæŋk/ *n.* a skein.

hanker /ˈhæŋkə/ *v.i.* to have a restless or incessant longing (often fol. by *after*, *for*, or an infinitive).

hanky /ˈhæŋki/ *n. Colloquial* → **handkerchief**. Also, **hankie**.

hanky-panky /ˌhæŋki-ˈpæŋki/ *n. Colloquial* **1.** trickery; subterfuge or the like. **2.** sexual play.

Hansard /ˈhænsad/ *n.* the official printed reports of the debates and proceedings of parliament.

haphazard /hæpˈhæzəd/ *adj.* determined by or dependent on mere chance.

hapless /ˈhæpləs/ *adj.* luckless.

happen /ˈhæpən/ *v.i.* **1.** to come to pass, take place, or occur. **2.** to befall, as to a person or thing. **3.** to come by chance (fol. by *on* or *upon*).

happy /ˈhæpi/ *adj.,* **-pier**, **-piest**. **1.** characterised by or indicative of pleasure, content, or gladness. **2.** delighted, pleased, or glad, as over a particular thing. **3.** favoured by fortune; fortunate or lucky.

harakiri /hærəˈkɪri/ *n.* suicide by ripping open the abdomen with a dagger or knife.

harangue /həˈræŋ/ *n., v.,* **-rangued**, **-ranguing**. – *n.* **1.** a passionate, vehement speech; noisy and intemperate address. – *v.t.* **2.** to address in a harangue.

harass /həˈræs, ˈhærəs/ *v.t.* to disturb persistently.

harbinger /ˈhabɪŋə, -bɪndʒə/ *n.* **1.** someone who goes before and makes known the approach of another. **2.** something that foreshadows a future event; an omen.

harbour = harbor /ˈhabə/ *n.* **1.** a portion of a body of water along the shore deep enough for ships to anchor and offering either natural or artificial shelter. **2.** any place of shelter or refuge. – *v.t.* **3.** to conceal; give a place to hide. **4.** to entertain in the mind; indulge (usually unfavourable or evil feelings).

hard /had/ *adj.* **1.** solid and firm to the touch; not soft. **2.** firmly formed; tight. **3.** difficult to do or accomplish; troublesome. **4.** involving or performed with great exertion, energy, or persistence. **5.** carrying on work in this manner. **6.** vigorous or violent; harsh; severe. **7.** unfeeling; callous. **8.** harsh or unpleasant to the eye, ear, or aesthetic sense. **9.** severe or rigorous in terms. **10. a.** alcoholic or intoxicating. **b.** dangerously addictive. **11.** (of water) containing mineral salts which interfere with the action of the soap. – *adv.* **12.** with great exertion; with vigour or violence. **13.** harshly or severely; badly.

hardback /ˈhadbæk/ *n.* a book bound in stiff covers, usually of boards covered with cloth, leather, laminated paper, etc.

hard disk *n.* a rigid magnetic storage disk, usually built into the computer, with a higher recording density than a floppy disk, providing fast access to a greater amount of stored data.

harden /ˈhadn/ *v.t.* **1.** to make hard or harder. – *v.i.* **2.** to become hard or harder. **3.** *Commerce* (of prices, the market, etc.) **a.** to become higher; rise. **b.** to cease to fluctuate.

hard-headed /ˈhad-hɛdəd/ *adj.* not easily moved or deceived; practical; shrewd.

hardline /ˈhadlaɪn/ *adj.* not deviating from a set doctrine, policy, etc.

hardly /'hadli/ *adv.* **1.** barely; almost not at all. **2.** not quite.

hard-nosed /'had-noʊzd/ *adj.* ruthless.

hard sell *n.* a method of selling or advertising which is direct, forceful, and insistent. Cf. **soft sell**. – **hard-sell**, *v.*

hardship /'hadʃɪp/ *n.* **1.** a condition that bears hard upon one; severe toil, trial, oppression, or need. **2.** an instance of this; something hard to bear.

hard-up /'had-ʌp/ *adj.* in financial difficulties; poor.

hardware /'hadwɛə/ *n.* **1.** building materials, tools, etc. **2.** the physical components of a computer system, as the circuitry, magnetic tape units, etc. (opposed to *software*).

hardy /'hadi/ *adj.*, **-dier**, **-diest**. **1.** capable of enduring fatigue, hardship, exposure, etc. **2.** (of plants) able to withstand the cold of winter in the open air.

hare /hɛə/ *n.*, *pl.* **hares**, (*esp. collectively*) **hare**. a rabbit-like mammal.

harebrained = hairbrained /'hɛəbreɪnd/ *adj.* irrational; reckless.

harelip /'hɛəlɪp/ *n.* a congenitally deformed lip.

harem /'hɛərəm, ha'rim/ *n.* the wives and concubines in an oriental household.

hark /hak/ *v.i.* **1.** (*used chiefly in the imperative*) to listen. **2. hark back,** to return to a previous point or subject.

harlot /'halət/ *n.* a promiscuous woman; prostitute.

harm /ham/ *n.* **1.** injury; damage; hurt. – *v.t.* **2.** to do harm to; injure; damage; hurt.

harmonica /ha'mɒnɪkə/ *n.* a musical instrument having a set of small metallic reeds mounted in a case and played by the breath; a mouth organ.

harmony /'haməni/ *n.*, *pl.* **-nies**. **1.** agreement; accord. **2.** a consistent, orderly, or pleasing arrangement of parts; congruity. **3.** *Music* any simultaneous combination of notes. – **harmonise = harmonize**, *v.* – **harmonic**, **harmonious**, *adj.*

harness /'hanəs/ *n.* **1.** the combination of straps, bands, and other parts forming the working gear of a horse or other draught animal (except the ox). **2.** a similar combination worn by persons for safety, protection, restraint, etc. – *v.t.* **3.** to put harness on (a horse, etc.); attach by a harness, as to a vehicle. **4.** to bring under conditions for working.

harp /hap/ *n.* **1.** a triangular stringed instrument, played with the hands. – *v.i.* **2.** to dwell persistently or tediously in speaking or writing (fol. by *on* or *upon*).

harpoon /ha'pun/ *n.* a spear attached to a rope.

harpsichord /'hapsəkɔd/ *n.* a keyboard instrument, precursor of the piano.

harridan /'hærədən/ *n.* a disreputable violent woman.

harrow /'hæroʊ/ *n.* **1.** an implement for levelling soil, etc. – *v.t.* **2.** to disturb keenly or painfully; distress the mind, feelings, etc.

harry /'hæri/ *v.t.*, **-ried**, **-rying**. **1.** to harass by forced exactions, rapacious demands, etc.; torment; worry. **2.** to ravage, as in war; devastate.

harsh /haʃ/ *adj.* **1.** ungentle and unpleasant in action or effect. **2.** rough to the touch or to any of the senses.

hart /hat/ *n.*, *pl.* **harts**, (*esp. collectively*) **hart**. a male deer.

harvest /'havəst/ *n.* **1.** the gathering of crops. **2.** a crop or yield, as of grain. **3.** the product or result of any labour or process. – *v.t.* **4.** to gather, as a crop.

has /hæz/, *weak forms* /həz, əz/ – *v.* 3rd person singular present indicative of **have**.

hash /hæʃ/ *n.* **1.** a dish of reheated food. **2.** a mess, jumble, or muddle.

hashish /hæ'ʃiʃ, 'hæʃɪʃ/ *n.* the flowering tops, leaves, etc., of Indian hemp, smoked, chewed, or otherwise used as a narcotic and intoxicant.

hasp /hæsp, hasp/ *n.* a clasp for a door, lid, etc.

hassle /'hæsəl/ *n.*, *v.*, **-led**, **-ling**. – *n.* **1.** a quarrel; squabble. **2.** a struggle; period of unease. – *v.t.* **3.** worry; harass.

hassock /'hæsək/ *n.* a thick, firm cushion used as a footstool or for kneeling.

haste /heɪst/ *n.* **1.** energetic speed in motion or action. **2.** quickness without due reflection; thoughtless or rash speed. – **hasty**, *adj.*

hasten /'heɪsən/ *v.i.* to move or act with haste; proceed with haste; hurry.

hat /hæt/ *n.* a shaped covering for the head, usually with a crown and a brim, worn outdoors.

hatch¹ /hætʃ/ *v.t.* **1.** to bring forth (young) from the egg. **2.** to contrive; devise; concoct.

hatch² /hætʃ/ *n.* a cover for an opening in a ship's deck, a floor, a roof, or the like.

hatch³ /hætʃ/ *v.t.* to mark with lines, especially closely set parallel lines, as for shading in drawing or engraving.

hatchet /'hætʃət/ *n.* a small, short-handled axe for use with one hand.

hatchet man *n.* someone employed or delegated to perform unpleasant tasks, such as cutting costs, firing personnel, etc., for an employer.

hate /heɪt/ *v.t.*, **hated**, **hating**. to regard with a strong or passionate dislike; detest.

hateful /'heɪtfəl/ *adj.* odious.

hatred /'heɪtrəd/ *n.* intense dislike.

haughty /'hɔti/ *adj.*, **-tier**, **-tiest**. disdainfully proud; arrogant; supercilious.

haul /hɔl/ *v.t.* **1.** to pull or draw with force; move or transport by drawing. – *v.i.* **2.** (of the wind) to change direction, shift, or veer (often fol. by *round* or *to*). – *n.* **3.** the act of hauling; a strong pull or tug. **4.** the distance over which anything is hauled. **5. in** (or **over**) **the long haul,** in the long term; in a long period of time. **6. in** (or **over**) **the short haul,** in the short term; in a short period of time.

haunch /hɔntʃ/ *n.* the hip.

haunt /hɔnt/ *v.t.* **1.** to visit habitually as a supposed spirit or ghost. **2.** to worry or disturb. **3.** to visit frequently. – *n.* **4.** (*often pl.*) a place of frequent resort.

have /hæv/ *v.*, *present 1* **have**, *2* **have**, *3* **has**, *pl.* **have**, *past tense and past participle* **had**, *present participle* **having**. – *v.t.* **1.** to hold or possess. **2.** to get, receive, or take. **3.** to be required, compelled, or under obligation (followed by an infinitive). **4.** to experience, enjoy or suffer. **5.** to require or cause (to do something, to be done, or as specified). **6.** to engage in or perform. **7.** to permit or allow. **8.** to give birth to. **9.** *Colloquial* to outwit, deceive, or cheat. – *v. (aux)* **10.** (used with the past participle of a verb to form a compound or perfect tense).

haven /'heɪvən/ *n.* **1.** a harbour or port. **2.** any place of shelter and safety.

haversack /'hævəsæk/ *n.* a bag carried on the back or shoulders, used for provisions and the like.

havoc /'hævək/ *n.* devastation.

hawk[1] /hɔk/ *n.* any of numerous birds of prey.

hawk[2] /hɔk/ *v.i.* to clear the throat noisily.

hawker /'hɔkə/ *n.* someone who travels from place to place selling goods.

hawthorn /'hɔθɔn/ *n.* a thorny shrub.

hay /heɪ/ *n.* grass cut and dried for use as fodder.

hay fever *n.* inflammation of the mucous membranes of the eyes and respiratory tract, caused by pollen.

haywire /'heɪwaɪə/ *adj.* **1.** in disorder; out of order. **2.** out of control; crazy.

hazard /'hæzəd/ *n.* **1.** a risk; exposure to danger or harm. – *v.t.* **2.** to venture to offer (a statement, conjecture, etc.). **3.** to put to the risk of being lost; to expose to risk. **4.** to take or run the risk of (a misfortune, penalty, etc.). – **hazardous**, *adj.*

haze /heɪz/ *n.* a thin mist, caused by dust, heat, etc. – **hazy**, *adj.*

hazel /'heɪzəl/ *n.* **1.** a type of shrub or small tree which bears edible nuts. **2.** light yellowish-brown.

he /hi/ *pron., possessive* **his**, *objective* **him**, *pl.* **they**. **1.** the male being in question or last mentioned. **2.** anyone; that person.

head /hɛd/ *n., pl.* **heads**, **head** *for def. 6, adj., v.* – *n.* **1.** the upper part of the body, joined to the trunk by the neck. **2.** the head considered as the seat of thought, memory, understanding, etc. **3.** the position of leadership. **4.** that part of anything which forms or is regarded as forming the top, summit, or upper end. **5.** the foremost part or end of anything; a projecting part. **6.** a person or animal considered merely as one of a number. **7.** culmination or crisis; conclusion. **8.** something resembling a head in form. **9.** a projecting point of a coast. **10.** the obverse of a coin, as bearing a head or other principal figure (opposed to *tail*). **11.** the source of a river or stream. **12.** collar, froth or foam, as that formed on beer when poured. – *adj.* **13.** situated at the top or front. **14.** being in the position of leadership or superiority. – *v.t.* **15.** to go at the head of or in front of; lead, precede. **16.** to be the head or chief of. **17. head off,** to intercept (something) and force (it) to change course. – *v.i.* **18.** to move forwards towards a point specified (often fol. by *for*).

headache /'hɛdeɪk/ *n.* **1.** a pain situated in the head. **2.** *Colloquial* a troublesome or worrying problem.

headhunting /hɛdhʌntɪŋ/ *n. Colloquial* **1.** the eliminating of political enemies. **2.** (in a business or other organisation) the seeking of a scapegoat for a misfortune or setback. **3.** the search for new executives, usually senior, through personal contacts rather than advertisements.

heading /'hɛdɪŋ/ *n.* a title or caption of a page, chapter, etc.

headland /'hɛdlənd, -lænd/ *n.* a promontory extending into a large body of water.

headlight /'hɛdlaɪt/ *n.* a light equipped with a reflector, on the front of any vehicle.

headline /'hɛdlaɪn/ *n.* a display line over an article, etc., as in a newspaper.

headmaster /'hɛdmastə, hɛd'mastə/ *n.* the male principal of a school.

headmistress /'hɛdmɪstrəs, hɛd'mɪstrəs/ *n.* the female principal of a school.

headquarters /'hɛdkwɔtəz, hɛd'kwɔtəz/ *pl. n.* any centre of operations.

head start *n.* an initial advantage in a race, competition, etc.

headstone /'hɛdstoun/ *n.* a stone set at the head of a grave.

headstrong /'hɛdstrɒŋ/ *adj.* bent on having one's own way; wilful.

headway /'hɛdweɪ/ *n.* progress.

headwind /'hɛdwɪnd/ *n.* a wind that blows directly against the course of a ship or the like.

heady /'hɛdi/ *adj.,* **-ier**, **-iest**. **1.** rashly impetuous. **2.** intoxicating.

heal /hil/ *v.t.* to make whole or sound; restore to health; free from ailment.

health /hɛlθ/ *n.* **1.** soundness of body; freedom from disease or ailment. **2.** the general condition of the body or mind. – **healthy**, *adj.*

heap /hip/ *n.* **1.** an assemblage of things, lying one on another; a pile. **2.** *Colloquial* a great quantity or number. – *v.t.* **3.** to gather, put, or cast in a heap; pile (often fol. by *up*, *on*, *together*, etc.).

hear /hɪə/ *v.,* **heard** /hɜd/, **hearing**. – *v.t.* **1.** to perceive by the ear. **2.** to listen to. **3.** to give a formal, official, or judicial hearing to, as a sovereign, a teacher, an assembly, or a judge does. – *v.i.* **4.** to have perception of sound by the ear; have the sense of hearing. **5.** to receive information by the ear or otherwise.

hearing /'hɪərɪŋ/ *n.* **1.** the faculty or sense by which sound is perceived. **2.** *Law* the trial of an action. **3.** earshot.

hearsay /'hɪəseɪ/ *n.* gossip; rumour.

hearse /hɜs/ *n.* a funeral vehicle.

heart /hat/ *n.* **1.** a hollow muscular organ which by rhythmic contraction and dilation keeps the blood in circulation throughout the body. **2.** this organ considered as the seat of life, or vital powers, or of thought, feeling, or emotion. **3.** the seat of emotions and affections (often in contrast to the *head* as the seat of the intellect). **4.** feeling; sensibility. **5.** spirit, courage, or enthusiasm. **6.** the innermost or middle part of anything. **7.** a figure or object with rounded sides meeting in an obtuse point at the bottom and curving inwards to a cusp at the top.

heart attack *n.* a sudden, severe heart malfunction.

heartburn /'hatbɜn/ *n.* a burning sensation above the abdomen.

hearten /'hatn/ *v.t.* to give courage to; cheer.

heart failure *n.* inability of the heart to pump adequate blood for maintenance of the circulation leading to congestion of the tissues, shortness of the breath, etc.

hearth /haθ/ *n.* **1.** that part of the floor of a room on which the fire is made. **2.** the fireside; home.

heart-rending /'hat-rɛndɪŋ/ *adj.* causing acute mental anguish.

heart-throb /'hat-θrɒb/ *n.* the object of an infatuation.

hearty /'hati/ *adj.*, **-tier**, **-tiest**. **1.** warm-hearted; affectionate; cordial; friendly. **2.** enthusiastic or zealous; vigorous. **3.** substantial or satisfying.

heat /hit/ *n.* **1.** the quality or condition of being hot. **2.** the sensation of hotness. **3.** hot weather. **4.** warmth or intensity of feeling. **5.** a single course in or division of a race or other contest. **6.** *Zoology* sexual excitement in animals, especially females. – *v.t., v.i.* **7.** to make or become hot or warm.

heated /'hitəd/ *adj.* inflamed; vehement; angry.

heath /hiθ/ *n.* **1.** a tract of open, uncultivated land. **2.** a low, evergreen shrub.

heathen /'hiðən/ *n., pl.* **-thens**, **-then**. an irreligious or unenlightened person.

heather /'hɛðə/ *n.* any of various heaths (def. 2).

heatwave /'hitweɪv/ *n.* a prolonged period of hot weather.

heave /hiv/ *v.*, **heaved** *or Chiefly Nautical* **hove**, **heaving**. – *v.t.* **1.** to raise or lift with effort or force; hoist. – *v.i.* **2.** to rise and fall with or as with a swelling motion. **3.** to vomit; retch.

heaven /'hɛvən/ *n.* **1.** (*also cap.*) (in many religions and mythologies) a place or state of existence where people (often those who have lived righteously or those chosen by a god or gods) live on after death in happiness. **2.** (*chiefly plural*) the sky or firmament. **3.** a place or state of supreme bliss. – **heavenly**, *adj.*

heavy /'hɛvi/ *adj.*, **-vier**, **-viest**, *n., pl.* **-vies**. – *adj.* **1.** of great weight; hard to lift or carry. **2.** bearing hard upon; burdensome. **3.** connected or concerned with the manufacture of goods of more than the usual weight. **4.** serious; grave. **5.** exceptionally dense in substance. **6.** (of music, literature, etc.) intellectual or deep. – *n.* **7.** *Colloquial* a person who is eminent and influential in the sphere of his or her activities, as an important businessperson, etc.

heckle /'hɛkəl/ *v.t.*, **-led**, **-ling**. to badger or torment; harass, especially a public speaker, with questions and gibes. Also, **hatchel**.

hectare /'hɛktɛə/ *n.* a surface measure, the common unit of land measure in the metric system, equal to 100 ares, or 10 000 square metres (approx. 2.47 acres). *Symbol*: ha

hectic /'hɛktɪk/ *adj.* characterised by great excitement, passion, activity, confusion, haste.

hedge /hɛdʒ/ *n., v.*, **hedged**, **hedging**. – *n.* **1.** a row of bushes or small trees planted close together, especially when forming a fence or boundary. – *v.t.* **2.** to enclose with or separate by a hedge (often fol. by *in*, *off*, *about*, etc.). **3.** to protect (a bet, etc.) by taking some offsetting risk. – *v.i.* **4.** to avoid taking an open or decisive course. **5.** *Finance* to enter transactions that will protect against loss through a compensatory price movement.

hedgehog /'hɛdʒhɒg/ *n.* a spiny, nocturnal, insectivorous mammal.

hedonism /'hidənɪzəm, 'hɛ-/ *n.* the doctrine that pleasure or happiness is the highest good. – **hedonist**, *n.*

-hedron a combining form denoting geometrical solid figures having a certain number of faces, as in *polyhedron*.

heed /hid/ *v.t.* to give attention to; regard; notice.

heel[1] /hil/ *n.* **1.** the back part of the foot, below and behind the ankle. **2.** the part of a stocking, shoe, or the like, covering or supporting the heel. **3.** *Colloquial* a despicable person; cad. – *v.t.* **4.** to furnish with heels, as shoes.

heel[2] /hil/ *v.i.* (of a ship, etc.) to lean.

heeler /'hilə/ *n.* a cattle or sheep dog which rounds up stock by following at their heels.

hefty /'hɛfti/ *adj.*, **-tier**, **-tiest**. *Colloquial* **1.** heavy; weighty. **2.** big and strong; powerful; muscular.

hegemony /'hɛgəməni, 'hɛdʒ-, hə'gɛməni/ *n., pl.* **-nies**. leadership; predominance.

heifer /'hɛfə/ *n.* a cow that has not produced a calf and is under three years of age.

height /haɪt/ *n.* **1.** the state of being high. **2.** extent upwards; altitude; stature; distance upwards; elevation. **3.** a high place or level; a hill or mountain. **4.** the highest or culminating point; utmost degree. **5.** high degree, as of a quality.

heinous /'heɪnəs, 'hi-/ *adj.* hateful.

heir /ɛə/ *n.* **1.** *Law* someone who inherits the estate (def. 2b) of a deceased person, normally after it has been reduced by the payment of any debts, liabilities or charges which may pertain to it. **2.** someone to whom something falls or is due. – **heiress**, *fem. n.*

heirloom /'ɛəlum/ *n.* any family possession transmitted from generation to generation.

heist /haɪst/ *n.* a robbery; burglary.

held /hɛld/ *v.* past tense and past participle of **hold**.

helicopter /'hɛlikɒptə, 'hɛlə-/ *n.* a heavier-than-air craft which is lifted and sustained in the air by horizontal rotating blades.

helio- a word element meaning 'sun'.

heliotrope /'hɛliətroup, 'hiliə-, 'hɛljə-, 'hiljə-/ *n.* **1.** *Botany* any plant that turns towards the sun. **2.** light tint of purple; reddish lavender. – **heliotropic**, *adj.*

heliport /'hɛlipɔt/ *n.* a landing place for helicopters, often the roof of a building.

helium /'hiliəm/ *n.* an inert gaseous element present in the sun's atmosphere, certain minerals, natural gas, etc., and also occurring as a radioactive decomposition product. *Symbol*: He

helix /'hilıks, 'hɛl-/ *n., pl.* **helices** /'hɛləsiz, 'hil-/, **helixes**. a spiral. – **helical**, *adj.*

hell /hɛl/ *n.* **1.** (*also cap.*) (in many religions and mythologies) the abode of the spirits of the dead, often, as in Christianity, a place or state of existence where the wicked are punished after death. **2.** any place or state of torment or misery. **3.** the powers of evil. – **hellish**, *adj.*

hello /hʌ'loʊ, hə-/ *interj.* (an exclamation to attract attention, answer a telephone, or express greeting).

helm /hɛlm/ *n.* **1.** the tiller or wheel by which the rudder of a vessel is controlled. **2.** the place or post of control.

helmet /'hɛlmət/ *n.* a defensive covering for the head.

help /hɛlp/ *v.t.* **1.** to cooperate effectively with; aid; assist. **2.** to succour; save; rescue. **3.** to relieve (someone) in need, sickness, pain, or distress. **4.** to refrain from; avoid (with *can* or *cannot*). **5.** to remedy, stop, or prevent. **6. help oneself (to),** to take or appropriate at will. – *n.* **7.** the act of helping; aid or assistance; relief or succour. **8.** a person or thing that helps.

helpless /'hɛlpləs/ *adj.* unable to help oneself; weak or dependent.

helter-skelter /hɛltə-'skɛltə/ *adv.* in headlong, disorderly haste.

hem /hɛm/ *v.,* **hemmed, hemming**, *n.* – *v.t.* **1.** to enclose or confine (fol. by *in, round,* or *about*). **2.** to fold back and sew down the edge of (cloth, a garment, etc.). – *n.* **3.** the edge or border of a garment, etc., especially at the bottom.

hemi- a prefix meaning 'half'.

hemisphere /'hɛməsfıə/ *n.* **1.** half of the terrestrial globe or celestial sphere. **2.** the half of a sphere. – **hemispherical**, *adj.*

hemlock /'hɛmlɒk/ *n.* a poisonous herb.

hemp /hɛmp/ *n.* **1.** a tall, Asian herb yielding hashish, etc. **2.** the tough fibre of this plant used for making coarse fabrics, ropes, etc.

hen /hɛn/ *n.* **1.** the female of the domestic fowl. **2.** the female of any bird.

hence /hɛns/ *adv.* as an inference from this fact; for this reason; therefore.

henceforth /hɛns'fɔθ/ *adv.* from this time forth; from now on. Also, **henceforwards**.

henchman /'hɛntʃmən/ *n., pl.* **-men**. **1.** a trusty attendant or follower. **2.** a ruthless and unscrupulous follower.

henna /'hɛnə/ *n.* (the reddish-orange dye from) a small Asian tree.

hepatic /hə'pætık/ *adj.* of or relating to the liver.

hepatitis /hɛpə'taıtəs/ *n.* a serious viral disease characterised by inflammation or enlargement of the liver, fever or jaundice, some forms of which are transmitted by infected blood and can therefore be contracted through sexual contact or use of contaminated needles.

hepta- a prefix meaning 'seven'. Also (*before vowels*), **hept-**.

her /hɜ/ *pron.* **1.** the objective case of **she**. – *adj.* **2.** the possessive form of **she**, used before a noun (cf. **hers**).

herald /'hɛrəld/ *n.* **1.** a messenger; forerunner or harbinger. **2.** someone who proclaims or announces (often used as the name of a newspaper). – *v.t.* **3.** to give tidings of; proclaim. **4.** to usher in.

heraldic /hə'rældık/ *adj.* of or relating to heralds or heraldry.

heraldry /'hɛrəldri/ *n., pl.* **-dries**. **1.** the science of armorial bearings. **2.** a coat of arms; armorial bearings.

herb /hɜb/ *n.* **1.** a flowering plant whose stem above ground does not become woody and persistent. **2.** such a plant when valued for its medicinal properties, flavour, scent, or the like. – **herbal, herbaceous**, *adj.*

herbivorous /hɜ'bıvərəs/ *adj.* feeding on plants. – **herbivore**, *n.*

herd /hɜd/ *n.* a number of animals, especially cattle, kept, feeding, or travelling together; drove; flock.

here /hıə/ *adv.* **1.** in this place; in this spot or locality (opposed to *there*). **2.** to or towards this place; hither. **3.** at this point; at this juncture.

here- a word element meaning 'this (place)', 'this (time)', etc., used in combination with certain adverbs and prepositions.

hereditary /hə'rɛdətri/ *adj.* **1.** passing, or capable of passing, naturally from parents to offspring. **2.** *Law* descending by inheritance.

heredity /hə'rɛdəti/ *n., pl.* **-ties**. the transmission of genetic characteristics from parents to progeny.

heresy /'hɛrəsi/ *n., pl.* **-sies**. **1.** doctrine contrary to the orthodox or accepted doctrine of a church or religious system. **2.** the maintaining of such an opinion or doctrine. – **heretic**, *n.* – **heretical**, *adj.*

heritage /'hɛrətıdʒ/ *n.* that which comes or belongs to one by reason of birth; an inherited lot or portion.

hermaphrodite /hɜ'mæfrədaıt/ *n.* a person or animal with male and female sexual organs and characteristics.

hermetic /hɜ'mɛtık/ *adj.* made airtight by fusion or sealing. – **hermetically**, *adv.*

hermit /'hɜmət/ *n.* someone who has retired to a solitary place, especially for a life of religious seclusion. – **hermitage**, *n.*

hernia /'hɜniə/ *n., pl.* **-nias**. the protrusion of an organ or tissue through an opening in its surrounding tissues, especially in the abdominal region; a rupture.

hero /'hıəroʊ/ *n., pl.* **-roes**. **1.** a person of distinguished courage or performance. **2.** the principal male character in a story, play, etc. – **heroic**, *adj.*

heroin /'hɛrəwən/ *n.* a derivative of morphine, formerly used as a sedative, etc., and constituting a dangerous addictive drug.

heroine /'hɛrəwən/ *n.* **1.** a woman of heroic character; a female hero. **2.** the principal female character in a story, play, etc.

heron /'hɛrən/ *n.* a wading bird with a long neck, bill, and legs.

herpes /'hɜpiz/ *n.* any of certain inflammatory viral infections of the skin or mucous membrane, characterised by clusters of vesicles which tend to spread.

herring /'hɛrıŋ/ *n., pl.* **-rings**, (*esp. collectively*) **-ring**. a food fish of northern seas.

herringbone /'hɛrıŋboʊn/ *n.* a pattern consisting of adjoining rows of parallel lines so arranged that any two rows have the form of a V or inverted V.

hers /hɜz/ *pron.* **1.** (form of the possessive **her**, used predicatively or without a noun following). **2.** the person(s) or thing(s) belonging to her.

herself /həˈsɛlf/ *pron.* **1.** a reflexive form of **she**. **2.** an emphatic form of **her** or **she** used: **a.** as object. **b.** in apposition to a subject or object. **3.** her proper or normal self; her normal state of mind (used after *be*, *become*, or *come to*).

hertz /hɜts/ *n.* the derived SI unit of frequency. *Symbol*: Hz

hesitate /ˈhɛzəteɪt/ *v.i.*, **-tated**, **-tating**. **1.** to hold back in doubt or indecision. **2.** to pause. – **hesitation**, *n.* – **hesitant**, *adj.*

hessian /ˈhɛʃən/ *n.* a strong fabric made from jute, used for sacks, etc.

hetero- a word element meaning 'other' or 'different'. Also (*before vowels*), **heter-**.

heterodox /ˈhɛtərədɒks, ˈhɛtrə-/ *adj.* not in accordance with established or accepted doctrines or opinions, especially in theology.

heterogeneous /hɛtəroʊˈdʒiniəs/ *adj.* composed of parts of different kinds.

heterosexuality /hɛtəroʊˌsɛkʃuˈæləti/ *n.* sexual feeling for a person (or persons) of opposite sex. – **heterosexual**, *n.*, *adj.*

heuristic /hjuˈrɪstɪk/ *adj.* **1.** serving to find out; furthering investigation. **2.** (of a teaching method) encouraging the student to discover for himself or herself.

hew /hju/ *v.t.*, **hewed**, **hewed** *or* **hewn**, **hewing**. to strike forcibly with an axe, sword, or the like; chop; hack.

hex /hɛks/ *n.* an evil spell or charm.

hexa- a prefix meaning 'six', as in *hexagon*. Also (*before vowels*), **hex-**.

hexagon /ˈhɛksəgɒn, -gən/ *n.* a polygon having six angles and six sides.

hey /heɪ/ *interj.* (an exclamation used to call attention, give encouragement, etc.).

heyday /ˈheɪdeɪ/ *n.* the stage or period of highest vigour or fullest strength.

hi /haɪ/ *interj.* (an exclamation, especially of greeting).

hiatus /haɪˈeɪtəs/ *n.*, *pl.* **-tuses**, **-tus**. **1.** a break, with a part missing; an interruption. **2.** a gap or opening.

Hib /eɪtʃ aɪ ˈbi/ *n.* Hemophilus influenza, type b; a bacterium which causes meningitis, etc.

hibernate /ˈhaɪbəneɪt/ *v.i.*, **-nated**, **-nating**. to spend the winter in close quarters in a dormant condition, as certain animals.

hibiscus /haɪˈbɪskəs/ *n.* a tree with broad, showy, short-lived flowers.

hiccup /ˈhɪkʌp/ *n.* a quick, involuntary inspiration suddenly checked by closure of the glottis, producing a characteristic sound. Also, **hiccough**.

hickory /ˈhɪkəri/ *n.*, *pl.* **-ries**. a North American tree bearing sweet, edible nuts.

hide[1] /haɪd/ *v.*, **hid**, **hidden** *or* **hid**, **hiding**. – *v.t.* **1.** to conceal from sight; prevent from being seen or discovered. **2.** to conceal from knowledge; keep secret. – *v.i.* **3.** to conceal oneself; lie concealed.

hide[2] /haɪd/ *n.* **1.** the skin of an animal. **2.** *Colloquial* impudence.

hideous /ˈhɪdiəs/ *adj.* horrible or frightful to the senses; very ugly.

hiding /ˈhaɪdɪŋ/ *n.* **1.** a beating. **2.** a defeat.

hierarchy /ˈhaɪəraki/ *n.*, *pl.* **-chies**. **1.** any system of persons or things in a graded order, etc. **2.** *Science* a series of successive terms of different rank.

hiero- a word element meaning 'sacred'. Also (*before a vowel*), **hier-**.

hieroglyphic /haɪərəˈglɪfɪk/ *adj.* Also, **hieroglyphical**. **1.** designating or relating to a writing system, particularly that of the ancient Egyptians, in which many of the symbols are conventionalised pictures of the thing named by the words for which the symbols stand. – *n.* **2.** (*usu. pl.*) hieroglyphic writing.

high /haɪ/ *adj.* **1.** having a great or considerable reach or extent upwards; lofty; tall. **2.** having a specified extent upwards. **3.** situated above the ground or some base; elevated. **4.** of more than average or normal height or depth. **5.** intensified; exceeding the common degree or measure; strong; intense; energetic. **6.** produced by relatively rapid vibrations; shrill. **7.** of great amount, degree, force, etc. **8.** chief; principal; main. **9.** of a period of time, at its fullest point of development. **10.** *Colloquial* intoxicated or elated with alcohol or drugs. **11.** smelly; bad. – *adv.* **12.** at or to a high point, place, or level, or a high rank or estimate, a high amount or price, or a high degree. – *n.* **13.** that which is high; a high level. **14.** *Meteorology* a pressure system characterised by relatively high pressure at its centre; an anticyclone.

high-fidelity /haɪ-fəˈdɛləti/ *adj.* (of an amplifier, radio receiver, etc.) reproducing the full audio range of the original sounds with relatively little distortion. Also, **hi-fi**.

high-handed /ˈhaɪ-hændəd/ *adj.* overbearing; arbitrary.

highland /ˈhaɪlənd/ *n.* an elevated region; a plateau.

high-level language *n.* a language used for writing computer programs which is closer to human language or conventional mathematical notation than to machine language. Cf. **low-level language**.

highlight /ˈhaɪlaɪt/ *v.*, **-lighted**, **-lighting**, *n.* – *v.t.* **1.** to emphasise or make prominent. – *n.* **2.** a conspicuous or striking part. **3.** (*pl.*) flecks of colour in hair which gleam in the light.

highness /ˈhaɪnəs/ *n.* **1.** the state of being high; loftiness; dignity. **2.** (*cap.*) a title of honour given to royal or princely personages (preceded by *Her*, *His*, *Your*, etc.).

high-pressure /ˈhaɪ-prɛʃə/ *adj.* **1.** having or involving a pressure above the normal. **2.** vigorous; persistent.

high school *n.* → **secondary school**.

high-tech /ˈhaɪ-tɛk/ *adj.* **1.** of or relating to high technology. **2.** ultra-modern, especially using materials or styles associated with high technology.

high technology *n.* highly-sophisticated, innovative technology, especially electronic.

highway /ˈhaɪweɪ/ *n.* a main road, as one between towns.

highwayman /ˈhaɪweɪmən/ *n.*, *pl.* **-men**. a

robber on the highway, especially one on horseback.

hijack /'haɪdʒæk/ *v.t.* **1.** to steal (something) in transit, as a lorry and the goods it carries. **2.** to seize by force or threat of force (a vehicle, especially a passenger-carrying vehicle, as an aircraft).

hike /haɪk/ *v.*, **hiked**, **hiking**, *n.* – *v.i.* **1.** to walk a long distance, especially through country districts, for pleasure. – *n.* **2.** a long walk, especially in the country. **3.** an increase in wages, fares, prices, etc.

hilarious /hə'lɛəriəs/ *adj.* **1.** very funny. **2.** boisterously merry. – **hilarity**, *n.*

hill /hɪl/ *n.* a conspicuous natural elevation of the earth's surface, smaller than a mountain.

hillbilly /'hɪlbɪli/ *n.*, *pl.* **-lies**. *Originally US* a rustic or yokel living in the backwoods or mountains.

hilt /hɪlt/ *n.* the handle of a sword or dagger.

him /hɪm/ *pron.* objective case of **he**.

himself /hɪm'sɛlf/ *pron.* **1.** a reflexive form of **he**. **2.** an emphatic form of **him** or **he** used: **a.** as object: *he used it for himself.* **b.** in apposition to a subject or object. **3.** his proper or normal self; his usual state of mind (used after such verbs as *be, become*, or *come to*).

hind[1] /haɪnd/ *adj.*, **hinder**, **hindmost** *or* **hindermost**. situated behind or at the back; posterior.

hind[2] /haɪnd/ *n.* the female of the deer.

hinder /'hɪndə/ *v.t.* **1.** to interrupt; check; retard. **2.** to prevent from acting or taking place; stop. – **hindrance**, *n.*

hindsight /'haɪndsaɪt/ *n.* perception of the nature and exigencies of a case after the event.

hinge /hɪndʒ/ *n.*, *v.*, **hinged**, **hinging**. – *n.* **1.** the movable joint or device on which a door, gate, shutter, lid, etc., turns or moves. – *v.i.* **2.** to depend or turn on, or as if on, a hinge.

hint /hɪnt/ *n.* **1.** an indirect or covert suggestion or implication; an intimation. **2.** a very small or barely perceptible amount. – *v.t.* **3.** to give a hint of. – *v.i.* **4.** to make indirect suggestion or allusion (usually fol. by *at*).

hinterland /'hɪntəlænd/ *n.* the land lying behind a coastal district.

hip[1] /hɪp/ *n.* the projecting part of each side of the body formed by the side of the pelvis and the upper part of the femur.

hip[2] /hɪp/ *n.* the ripe fruit of a rose.

hippopotamus /hɪpə'pɒtəməs/ *n.*, *pl.* **-muses, -mi**. a large herbivorous mammal having a thick hairless body, short legs and large head and muzzle.

hire /'haɪə/ *v.t.*, **hired**, **hiring**. **1.** to engage the services of for payment. **2.** to engage the temporary use of for payment. **3.** to grant the temporary use of, or the services of, for a payment (often fol. by *out*).

hire-purchase /haɪə-'pɜtʃəs/ *n.* a system whereby a person pays for a commodity by regular instalments, while having full use of it after the first payment.

hirsute /'hɜsjut/ *adj.* hairy.

his /hɪz/ *pron.* **1.** the possessive form of **he**. **2.** the person(s) or thing(s) belonging to him. – *adj.* **3.** belonging to, relating to, or owned by him; made, done, experienced, etc., by him.

hiss /hɪs/ *v.i.* **1.** to make or emit a sharp sound like that of the letter *s* prolonged. **2.** to express disapproval or contempt by making this sound. – *n.* **3.** a hissing sound, especially in disapproval.

histamine /'hɪstəmin/ *n.* a substance released by the tissues in allergic reactions.

histology /hɪs'tɒlədʒi/ *n.* the study of the structure, especially the microscopic structure, of organic tissues.

history /'hɪstri, 'hɪstəri/ *n.*, *pl.* **-ries**. **1.** the branch of knowledge dealing with past events. **2.** the record of past events, especially in connection with the human race. **3.** a continuous, systematic written narrative, in order of time, of past events as relating to a particular people, country, period, person, etc. **4.** the aggregate of past events. – **historian**, *n.* – **historic**, **historical**, *adj.*

histrionics /hɪstri'ɒnɪks/ *pl. n.* artificial or melodramatic behaviour, speech, etc., for effect. – **histrionic**, *adj.*

hit /hɪt/ *v.*, **hit**, **hitting**, *n.*, *adj.* – *v.t.* **1.** to come against with an impact or collision. **2.** to succeed in striking with a missile, a weapon, a blow, or the like (intentionally or otherwise). **3.** to have a marked effect on; affect severely. **4.** to reach. – *v.i.* **5.** to strike with a missile, weapon, or the like; deal a blow or blows (often fol. by *out*). -*n.* **6.** an impact or collision, as of one thing against another. **7.** a successful stroke, performance, or production; success. **8.** *Colloquial* a shot of heroin or any drug; a fix. – *adj.* **9.** successful; achieving popularity.

hitch /hɪtʃ/ *v.t.* **1.** to make fast, especially temporarily, by means of a hook, rope, strap, etc.; tether. **2.** to raise with jerks (usually fol. by *up*). **3.** *Colloquial* to obtain or seek to obtain (a ride) from a passing vehicle. – *n.* **4.** a halt; an obstruction.

hitchhike /'hɪtʃhaɪk/ *v.i.*, **-hiked**, **-hiking**. *Colloquial* to travel by obtaining rides in passing vehicles.

hither /'hɪðə/ *adv.* to or towards this place; here.

hitherto /hɪðə'tu/ *adv.* up to this time; until now.

HIV /eɪtʃ aɪ 'vi/ *n.* human immunodeficiency virus; the virus which causes AIDS.

hive /haɪv/ *n.* **1.** an artificial shelter for honeybees; a beehive. **2.** a place swarming with busy occupants.

hives /haɪvz/ *n.* (*construed as sing.*) any of various eruptive diseases of the skin.

hoard /hɔd/ *n.* **1.** an accumulation of something for preservation or future use. – *v.t.* **2.** to accumulate for preservation or future use, especially in a secluded place.

hoarding /'hɔdɪŋ/ *n.* **1.** a temporary fence enclosing a building during erection. **2.** a large billboard on which advertisements or notices are displayed.

hoarfrost /'hɔfrɒst/ *n.* → **frost** (def. 1).

hoarse /hɔs/ *adj.*, **hoarser**, **hoarsest**. **1.** having a raucous voice. **2.** husky.

hoary /'hɔri/ *adj.*, **hoarier**, **hoariest**. grey or white with age.

hoax /houks/ *n.* a humorous or mischievous deception, especially a practical joke.

hobble /'hɒbəl/ *v.*, **-bled**, **-bling**. – *v.i.* **1.** to walk lamely; limp. – *v.t.* **2.** to fasten together the legs of (a horse, etc.) so as to prevent free motion.

hobby /'hɒbi/ *n.*, *pl.* **-bies**. a spare-time activity or pastime, etc.

hobgoblin /'hɒbgɒblən/ *n.* anything causing superstitious fear.

hobnob /'hɒbnɒb/ *v.i.*, **-nobbed**, **-nobbing**. to associate on very friendly terms.

hobo /'houbou/ *n.*, *pl.* **-bos**, **-boes**. a tramp or vagrant.

hock[1] /hɒk/ *n.* the joint in the hind leg of the horse, etc., above the fetlock joint.

hock[2] /hɒk/ *n.* a dry white wine.

hock[3] /hɒk/ *v.i.* *Colloquial* → **pawn**[1].

hockey /'hɒki/ *n.* a ball game in which curved sticks are used to drive the ball.

hod /hɒd/ *n.* a portable trough for carrying mortar, bricks, etc.

hoe /hou/ *n.*, *v.*, **hoed**, **hoeing**. – *n.* **1.** a long-handled implement with a thin, flat blade usually set transversely, used to break up the surface of the ground, destroy weeds, etc. – *v.t.* **2.** to dig, scrape, weed, cultivate, etc., with a hoe.

hog /hɒg/ *n.*, *v.*, **hogged**, **hogging**. – *n.* **1.** a domesticated swine, especially a castrated boar, bred for slaughter. **2.** *Colloquial* a selfish, gluttonous, or filthy person. – *v.t.* **3.** *Colloquial* to appropriate selfishly; take more than one's share of.

hogget /'hɒgət/ *n.* a young sheep of either sex, from the age of ten months to the cutting of its first two adult teeth.

hoick /hɔɪk/ *v.t.* to hoist abruptly.

hoist /hɔɪst/ *v.t.* **1.** to raise or lift, especially by some mechanical appliance. – *n.* **2.** an apparatus for hoisting, as a lift.

hold[1] /hould/ *v.*, **held**, **holding**, *n.* – *v.t.* **1.** to have or keep in the hand; keep fast; grasp. **2.** to reserve; retain; set aside. **3.** to bear, sustain, or support with the hand, arms, etc., or by any means. **4.** to keep in a specified state, relation, etc. **5.** to contain or be capable of containing. **6.** to regard or consider. **7. hold up, a.** to delay. **b.** to stop by force in order to rob. – *v.i.* **8.** to remain or continue in a specified state, relation, etc. **9.** to remain valid; be in force. – *n.* **10.** the act of holding fast by a grasp of the hand or by some other physical means; grasp; grip. **11.** a controlling force, or dominating influence.

hold[2] /hould/ *n.* *Nautical* the interior of a ship below the deck.

holder /'houldə/ *n.* **1.** something to hold a thing with. **2.** someone who has the ownership, possession, or use of something. **3.** the payee or endorsee in possession of a bill of exchange or promissory note. **4.** shareholder.

holder for value *n.* a holder of a bill of exchange or promissory note for which valuable consideration has been given.

holder in due course *n.* a holder who has taken a bill of exchange, cheque, or note, which is complete and regular on the face of it under certain conditions, namely that the bill is not overdue, that it is without notice of previous dishonour, and it is taken in good faith and for value without notice of any defect.

holding /'houldɪŋ/ *n.* **1.** (*often pl.*) property owned, especially stocks and shares, and land. – *adj.* **2.** used as an interim measure: *a holding yard.*

holding company *n.* **1.** a company controlling, or able to control, other companies by virtue of share ownership in these companies. **2.** a company which owns stocks or securities of other companies, deriving income from them.

hold-up /'hould-ʌp/ *n.* *Colloquial* **1.** a forcible stopping and robbing of a person, bank, etc. **2.** a delay; stoppage.

hole /houl/ *n.* **1.** an opening through anything; an aperture. **2.** a hollow place in a solid body or mass; a cavity. **3.** a small, mean abode or town.

holiday /'hɒlədeɪ/ *n.* **1.** a day fixed by law or custom on which ordinary business is suspended in commemoration of some event or in honour of some person, etc. **2.** (*often pl.*) a period of cessation from work, or of recreation; a vacation. – *v.i.* **3.** to take a holiday.

hollow /'hɒlou/ *adj.* **1.** having a hole or cavity within; not solid; empty. **2.** sunken, as the cheeks or eyes. – *v.t.* **3.** to make hollow.

holly /'hɒli/ *n.*, *pl.* **-lies**. a plant with glossy, spiny-edged leaves and red berries.

holocaust /'hɒləkɒst, -kɔst/ *n.* great or wholesale destruction of life, especially by fire.

holster /'houlstə/ *n.* a leather case for a pistol, attached to a belt or a saddle.

holy /'houli/ *adj.*, **-lier**, **-liest**. **1.** specially recognised as or declared sacred by religious use or authority; consecrated. **2.** dedicated or devoted to the service of God or religion; saintly. – **holiness**, *n.*

homage /'hɒmɪdʒ/ *n.* respect or reverence paid or rendered.

home /houm/ *n.* **1.** a house, or other shelter that is the fixed residence of a person, a family, or a household. **2.** (*often cap.*) an institution for the homeless, sick, etc. **3.** the place or region where something is native or most common. **4.** one's native place or own country. – *adv.* **5.** to, towards, or at home.

home invasion *n.* the holding up of a family in their home.

homely /'houmli/ *adj.*, **-lier**, **-liest**. not good-looking; plain.

home page *n.* the introductory page for a site on the Internet.

home rule *n.* self-government in internal affairs by the inhabitants of a dependent country.

homesick /'houmsɪk/ *adj.* ill or depressed from a longing for home.

homespun /'houmspʌn/ *adj.* plain; unpolished; simple.

homestead /'houmstɛd/ *n.* the main residence on a sheep or cattle station or large farm.

home truth *n.* a disagreeable statement of fact that hurts the sensibilities.

home unit *n.* one of a number of dwelling

apartments in the same building, each owned under separate title, frequently by the occupier.

homicide /'hɒməsaɪd/ *n.* **1.** the killing of one human being by another. **2.** a murderer. – **homicidal**, *adj.*

homily /'hɒməli/ *n., pl.* **-lies**. a religious discourse addressed to a congregation; a sermon.

homo- a combining form meaning 'the same' (opposed to *hetero-*).

homoeo- a word element meaning 'similar' or 'like'. Also, **homeo-**, **homoio-**.

homoeopathy /hoʊmi'ɒpəθi/ *n.* a method of treating disease by drugs, given in minute doses, which produce in a healthy person symptoms similar to those of the disease. Also, **homeopathy**. – **homoeopathic**, *adj.* – **homoeopath**, *n.*

homogeneous /hoʊmə'dʒiniəs, hɒmə-/ *adj.* **1.** composed of parts all of the same kind; not heterogeneous. **2.** of the same kind or nature; essentially alike. – **homogeneity**, *n.*

homogenise = homogenize /hə'mɒdʒənaɪz/ *v.t.,* **-nised**, **-nising**. to make homogeneous; form by mixing and emulsifying.

homogenous /hə'mɒdʒənəs/ *adj.* **1.** *Biology* corresponding in structure because of a common origin. **2.** → **homogeneous**.

homologous /hə'mɒləgəs/ *adj.* having the same or a similar relation; corresponding, as in relative position, structure, etc.

homonym /'hɒmənɪm/ *n.* a word like another in sound and perhaps in spelling, but different in meaning, as *meat* and *meet*.

homophobia /hoʊmə'foʊbiə/ *n.* fear of homosexuals, usually linked with hostility towards them. – **homophobic**, *adj.*

homosexuality /ˌhoʊmoʊsɛkʃu'æləti, ˌhɒmə-/ *n.* sexual feeling for a person of the same sex. – **homosexual**, *n., adj.*

hone /hoʊn/ *n., v.,* **honed**, **honing**. – *n.* **1.** a whetstone of fine, compact texture, especially one for sharpening razors. – *v.t.* **2.** to sharpen on or as on a hone. **3.** to improve by careful attention or practice: *to hone one's skills.*

honest /'ɒnəst/ *adj.* **1.** honourable in principles, intentions, and actions; upright. **2.** open; sincere. **3.** genuine or unadulterated. – **honesty**, *n.*

honey /'hʌni/ *n.* a sweet, viscid fluid produced by bees from the nectar collected from flowers.

honeycomb /'hʌnikoʊm/ *n.* **1.** a structure of wax containing rows of hexagonal cells, formed by bees for the reception of honey and pollen and of their eggs. – *v.t.* **2.** to pierce with many holes or cavities.

honeyeater /'hʌniˌitə/ *n.* a bird with a bill and tongue adapted for extracting the nectar from flowers.

honeymoon /'hʌnimun/ *n.* a holiday spent by a newly married couple before settling down to normal domesticity.

honeysuckle /'hʌnisʌkəl/ *n.* a fragrant, climbing plant.

honk /hɒŋk/ *n.* **1.** the cry of the goose. **2.** any similar sound, as a motor-car horn. – *v.i.* **3.** to emit a honk.

honorarium /ɒnə'rɛəriəm/ *n., pl.* **-riums**, **-ria**. an honorary reward, as in recognition of professional services on which no price may be set.

honorary /'ɒnərəri/ *adj.* **1.** given for honour only, without the usual duties, privileges, emoluments, etc. **2.** holding a title or position conferred for honour only. **3.** (of a position, job, etc.) unpaid. **4.** (of an obligation) depending on one's honour for fulfilment. – *n.* **5.** a specialist working in a public hospital.

honorific /ɒnə'rɪfɪk/ *adj.* doing or conferring honour.

honour = honor /'ɒnə/ *n.* **1.** high public esteem; fame; glory. **2.** credit or reputation for behaviour that is becoming or worthy. **3.** a source of credit or distinction. **4.** a special privilege or favour. **5.** high-minded character or principles; fine sense of one's obligations. **6.** (*pl.*) (in universities) scholastic or academic achievement in a degree examination higher than that required for a pass degree. – *v.t.* **7.** to hold in honour or high respect; revere. **8.** to confer honour or distinction upon. **9.** to accept and pay (a cheque, etc.) when due. **10.** to accept the validity of (a document, etc.). – **honourable**, *adj.*

hood /hʊd/ *n.* **1.** a soft or flexible covering for the head and neck, either separate or attached to a cloak or the like. **2.** something resembling or suggesting this. **3.** a motor-car bonnet. **4.** *Colloquial* a hoodlum.

-hood a suffix denoting state, condition, character, nature, etc., or a body of persons of a particular character or class.

hoodlum /'hudləm/ *n.* a petty gangster.

hoodwink /'hʊdwɪŋk/ *v.t.* to deceive.

hoof /hʊf/ *n., pl.* **hoofs**, **hooves**. the horny covering protecting the ends of the digits or encasing the foot in certain animals, as the ox, horse, etc.

hook /hʊk/ *n.* **1.** a curved or angular piece of metal or other firm substance catching, pulling, or sustaining something. **2.** that which catches; a snare; a trap. **3.** something curved or bent like a hook. **4.** *Boxing* a curving blow made with the arm bent, and coming in to the opponent from the side. – *v.t.* **5.** to seize, fasten, or catch hold of and draw in with or as with a hook. – *v.i.* **6.** to become attached or fastened by or as by a hook; join on.

hookah /'hʊkə/ *n.* a pipe with a long, flexible tube by which the smoke of tobacco, marijuana, etc., is drawn through a vessel of water and thus cooled. Also, **hooka**.

hooked /hʊkt/ *adj.* **1.** bent like a hook; hookshaped. **2.** made with a hook. **3.** caught, as a fish. **4.** *Colloquial* addicted; obsessed (usually fol. by *on*).

hooker /'hʊkə/ *n.* *Colloquial* a prostitute.

hooligan /'huləgən/ *n.* *Colloquial* a hoodlum; young street rough.

hoop /hup/ *n.* **1.** a circular band or ring of metal, wood, or other stiff material. **2.** something resembling a hoop.

hooray /hə'reɪ, 'hureɪ/ *interj.* (an exclamation of joy, applause, or the like).

hoot /hut/ *v.i.* **1.** to cry out or shout, especially in disapproval or derision. **2.** (of an owl) to utter its cry. **3.** to blow a horn or factory hooter; honk. – *n.* **4.** the cry of an owl. **5.** any similar sound.

hooves /huvz/ *n.* a plural of **hoof**.

hop[1] /hɒp/ *v.*, **hopped**, **hopping**, *n.* – *v.i.* **1.** to spring or leap on one foot. **2.** *Colloquial* to board or alight from a car, train, etc. (fol. by *in*, *on* or *off*). – *v.t.* **3.** *Colloquial* to jump off (something elevated), or over (a fence, ditch, etc.). – *n.* **4.** a leap on one foot. **5.** *Colloquial* a dance, or dancing party.

hop[2] /hɒp/ *n.* a twining plant whose dried ripe cones are used in brewing, etc.

hope /hoʊp/ *n.*, *v.*, **hoped**, **hoping**. – *n.* **1.** expectation of something desired; desire accompanied by expectation. **2.** confidence in a future event; ground for expecting something. – *v.t.* **3.** to look forward to with desire and more or less confidence. **4.** to trust in the truth of a matter (with a clause). – *v.i.* **5.** to have an expectation of something desired. – **hopeful**, **hopeless**, *adj.*

hopefully /ˈhoʊpfəli/ *adv.* **1.** in a hopeful fashion. **2.** *Colloquial* it is hoped.

hopsack /ˈhɒpsæk/ *n.* a coarse, jute sacking material.

horde /hɔd/ *n.* a great company or multitude.

horizon /həˈraɪzən/ *n.* the line or circle which forms the apparent boundary between earth and sky.

horizontal /hɒrəˈzɒntl/ *adj.* **1.** at right-angles to the vertical; in a horizontal position. **2.** near, on, or parallel to the horizon.

hormone /ˈhɔmoʊn/ *n.* **1.** any of various substances which are formed in endocrine glands and which activate specifically receptive organs when transported to them by the body fluids. **2.** a synthetic substance having the same effect.

hormone replacement therapy *n.* the administration of oestrogen and progesterone to women to reduce the risk of osteoporosis and reduce menopausal symptoms.

horn /hɔn/ *n.* **1.** a hard, projected, often curved and pointed, hollow and permanent growth (usually one of a pair) on the head of certain mammals. **2.** any hornlike projection or extremity. **3.** *Music* a wind instrument. **4.** an instrument for sounding a warning signal.

hornblende /ˈhɔnblɛnd/ *n.* a common black or dark-coloured mineral.

hornet /ˈhɔnət/ *n.* a large, strong, social wasp.

horology /həˈrɒlədʒi/ *n.* the art or science of making timepieces or of measuring time.

horoscope /ˈhɒrəskoʊp/ *n.* a forecast of a person's future derived from a study of the relative positions of the sun, moon, planets, etc., at the time of the person's birth.

horrendous /hɒˈrɛndəs, hə-/ *adj.* dreadful; horrible.

horrible /ˈhɒrəbəl/ *adj.* **1.** causing or tending to cause horror; dreadful. **2.** extremely unpleasant; deplorable.

horrid /ˈhɒrəd/ *adj.* **1.** such as to cause horror; dreadful; abominable. **2.** *Colloquial* extremely unpleasant or disagreeable.

horrific /hɒˈrɪfɪk, hə-/ *adj.* causing horror.

horrify /ˈhɒrəfaɪ/ *v.t.*, **-fied**, **-fying**. to strike with horror; shock intensely.

horror /ˈhɒrə/ *n.* **1.** a shuddering fear or abhorrence. **2.** *Colloquial* something considered atrocious or bad. **3.** a painful or intense aversion or repugnance.

horse /hɔs/ *n.*, *pl.* **horses**, (*esp. collectively*) **horse**. **1.** a large, solid-hoofed quadruped, often used for carrying a rider. **2.** a leather-covered vaulting block, used for gymnastics.

horse float *n.* a van or trailer for conveying horses by road, rail, etc.

horseplay /ˈhɔspleɪ/ *n.* rough or boisterous play.

horsepower /ˈhɔspaʊə/ *n.* a unit of measurement of power, or rate of doing work, in the imperial system, defined as 550 foot-pounds per second (equal to 745.7 watts).

horseradish /ˈhɔsrædɪʃ/ *n.* a cultivated plant with a pungent root, which is ground and used as a condiment.

horseshoe /ˈhɔsʃu/ *n.* **1.** a U-shaped iron plate nailed to a horse's hoof to protect it. **2.** a symbol of good luck.

hortatory /hɔˈteɪtəri, ˈhɔtətri/ *adj.* encouraging; inciting, exhorting.

horticulture /ˈhɔtəkʌltʃə/ *n.* the science or art of growing fruit, vegetables, flowers or ornamental plants.

hose /hoʊz/ *n.*, *pl.* **hose**, *v.*, **hosed**, **hosing**. – *n.* **1.** an article of clothing for the foot and lower part of the leg; stockings, tights, pantihose, etc. **2.** a flexible tube for conveying water, etc., to a desired point. – *v.t.* **3.** to water, wash, or drench by means of a hose.

hosiery /ˈhoʊzəri/ *n.* hose or stockings of any kind.

hospice /ˈhɒspəs/ *n.* **1.** (formerly) a house of shelter or rest for pilgrims, strangers, etc., especially one kept by a religious order. **2.** a hospital for terminally ill patients.

hospital /ˈhɒspɪtl/ *n.* an institution in which sick or injured persons are given medical or surgical treatment.

hospitalise = hospitalize /ˈhɒspətəlaɪz/ *v.t.*, **-lised**, **-lising**. to place in a hospital.

hospitality /hɒspəˈtæləti/ *n.*, *pl.* **-ties**. the reception and entertainment of guests or strangers with liberality and kindness. – **hospitable**, *adj.*

host[1] /hoʊst/ *n.* **1.** someone who entertains guests in his or her own home or elsewhere. **2.** the landlord of an inn. **3.** an animal or plant from which a parasite obtains nutrition.

host[2] /hoʊst/ *n.* a multitude or great number of persons or things.

hostage /ˈhɒstɪdʒ/ *n.* **1.** a person given or held as a security for the performance of certain actions as the payment of ransom, etc. **2.** a security or pledge.

hostel /ˈhɒstəl, hɒsˈtɛl/ *n.* a supervised place of accommodation, usually supplying board and lodging, provided at a comparatively low cost, as one for students, nurses, or the like.

hostess /ˈhoʊstɛs/ *n.* a female host; a woman who entertains guests.

hostile /ˈhɒstaɪl/ *adj.* opposed in feeling, action, or character; unfriendly; antagonistic. – **hostility**, *n.*

hot /hɒt/ *adj.*, **hotter**, **hottest**. **1.** having or communicating heat; having a high temperature. **2.** having a sensation of great bodily heat; attended with or producing such a sensation. **3.** new; recent; fresh. **4.** following very closely; close. **5.** (of motor cars) tuned or modified for high speeds. **6.** *Colloquial* recently stolen or otherwise illegally obtained; wanted by the police.

hotbed /'hɒtbɛd/ *n.* a place favouring rapid growth, especially of something bad.

hotchpotch /'hɒtʃpɒtʃ/ *n.* a heterogeneous mixture; a jumble.

hot dog *n.* a hot frankfurter or sausage, especially as served in a split roll.

hotel /hoʊ'tɛl/ *n.* a building in which accommodation and food, and usually alcoholic drinks are available; public house.

hothouse /'hɒthaʊs/ *n.* an artificially heated greenhouse for the cultivation of tender plants.

hot money *n. Colloquial* money in a money market or foreign exchange market which is likely to be withdrawn hastily following small changes in market conditions.

hotplate /'hɒtpleɪt/ *n.* **1.** a portable appliance for cooking or keeping food warm. **2.** a solid, electrically heated metal plate, usually on top of an electric stove, upon which food, etc., may be heated or cooked.

hound /haʊnd/ *n.* **1.** a dog of any of various breeds used in the chase and commonly hunting by scent. **2.** any dog. – *v.t.* **3.** to hunt or track with hounds, or as a hound does; pursue. **4.** to harass unceasingly.

hound's-tooth /'haʊndz-tuθ/ *n.* a pattern of contrasting jagged checks.

hour /'aʊə/ *n.* **1.** a space of time equal to one 24th part of a mean solar day or civil day; 60 minutes. **2.** a particular or appointed time. **3.** distance normally covered in an hour's travelling.

hourly /'aʊəli/ *adj.* of, relating to, occurring, or done each successive hour.

house /haʊs/ *n., pl.* **houses** /haʊzəz, haʊz/ *v.,* **housed**, **housing**. – *n.* **1.** a building for human habitation. **2.** a household. **3.** the audience of a theatre, etc. **4.** the building in which a legislative or deliberative body meets. **5.** the body itself. **6.** a firm or commercial establishment. **7.** a subdivision of a school, comprising children of all ages and classes. – *v.t.* **8.** to put or receive into a house; provide with a house.

household /'haʊshoʊld/ *n.* **1.** the people of a house collectively; a family, including servants, etc.; a domestic establishment. – *adj.* **2.** of or relating to a household; domestic. **3.** very common.

house journal *n.* an internal journal of a company, presenting its news to its employees.

housekeeper /'haʊskipə/ *n.* **1.** a paid employee who is hired to run a house, direct the domestic work, catering, etc. **2.** an employee of a hotel responsible for the cleaning staff.

house-train /'haʊs-treɪn/ *v.t.* to train (an animal) so that it may be kept inside a house without inconvenience to other occupants; especially to train it to control its natural excretory functions.

house union *n.* a union to which all employees, regardless of profession or trade, may belong by virtue of working for the one employer.

house-warming /'haʊs-wɔmɪŋ/ *n.* a party to celebrate beginning one's occupancy of a new house.

housewife /'haʊswaɪf/ *n., pl.* **-wives**. the woman in charge of a household, especially a wife who does no other job.

housework /'haʊswɜk/ *n.* the work of cleaning, cooking, etc.

housing /'haʊzɪŋ/ *n.* **1.** something serving as a shelter, covering, or the like; a shelter; lodging. **2.** the providing of houses for the community. **3.** *Machinery* a frame, plate or the like, that supports a part of a machine, etc.

hove /hoʊv/ *v.* a past tense and past participle of **heave**.

hovel /'hɒvəl/ *n.* a small, mean dwelling house; a wretched hut.

hover /'hɒvə/ *v.i.* **1.** to hang fluttering or suspended in the air. **2.** to keep lingering about; wait near at hand.

hovercraft /'hɒvəkraft/ *n.* a vehicle able to travel in close proximity to the ground or water, on a cushion of air.

how /haʊ/ *adv.* **1.** in what way or manner; by what means. **2.** to what extent, degree, etc. **3.** in what state or condition. – *conj.* **4.** concerning the condition or state in which. **5.** concerning the extent or degree to which. **6.** concerning the means or way in which.

however /haʊ'ɛvə/ *conj.* **1.** nevertheless; yet; in spite of that. – *adv.* **2.** to whatever extent or degree; no matter how (far, much, etc.). **3.** in whatever condition, state, or manner. **4.** Also, **how ever**. (interrogatively) how in any circumstances.

howl /haʊl/ *v.i.* **1.** to utter a loud, prolonged, mournful cry, as that of a dog or wolf. – *n.* **2.** the cry of a dog, wolf, etc. **3.** a cry or wail, as of pain or rage.

HR /eɪtʃ 'a/ human resources.

HRT /eɪtʃ a 'ti/ hormone replacement therapy.

HTML /eɪtʃ ti ɛm 'ɛl/ *n.* hypertext markup language; a computer markup language, similar to SGML, used primarily to create documents for the World Wide Web.

hub /hʌb/ *n.* **1.** the central part of a wheel, as that part into which the spokes are inserted. **2.** the part in central position around which all else revolves.

huddle /'hʌdl/ *v.,* **-dled**, **-dling**, *n.* – *v.t.* **1.** to heap or crowd together confusedly. – *v.i.* **2.** to gather or crowd together in a confused mass. – *n.* **3.** a confused heap, mass, or crowd; a jumble.

hue[1] /hju/ *n.* **1.** that property of colour by which the various regions of the spectrum are distinguished, as red, blue, etc. **2.** variety of a colour; a tint.

hue[2] /hju/ *n.* outcry.

huff /hʌf/ *n.* **1.** a sudden swell of anger; a fit of resentment. – *v.i.* **2.** to puff or blow.

hug /hʌg/ *v.,* **hugged**, **hugging**, *n.* – *v.t.* **1.** to clasp tightly in the arms, especially with affection; embrace. – *n.* **2.** a tight clasp with the arms; a warm embrace.

huge /hjudʒ/ *adj.,* **huger**, **hugest**. extraordinarily large.

hulk /hʌlk/ *n.* **1.** the body of an old or dismantled ship. **2.** a bulky or unwieldy person or mass of anything.

hull[1] /hʌl/ *n.* **1.** the husk, shell, or outer covering of a seed or fruit. **2.** the calyx of certain fruits, as the strawberry and raspberry. – *v.t.* **3.** to remove the hull of.

hull[2] /hʌl/ *n.* the frame or body of a ship.

hullabaloo /hʌləbə'lu/ *n.* a clamorous noise or disturbance; an uproar.

hum /hʌm/ *v.i.*, **hummed**, **humming**. **1.** to make a low, continuous, droning sound. **2.** *Colloquial* to be in a state of busy activity.

human /'hjumən/ *adj.* **1.** of, relating to, or characteristic of people. – *n.* **2.** a human being.

humane /hju'meɪn/ *adj.* characterised by tenderness and compassion for the suffering or distressed.

human immunodeficiency virus *n.* → **HIV**.

humanitarian /hjumænə'tɛəriən/ *adj.* **1.** having regard to the interests of all humankind; broadly philanthropic. – *n.* **2.** a philanthropist.

humanity /hju'mænəti/ *n.*, *pl.* **-ties**. **1.** the human race; humankind. **2.** the quality of being humane; kindness; benevolence.

humankind /hjumən'kaɪnd/ *n.* the human race.

human resources *pl. n.* the human component of an organisation, country, etc., seen as one of the elements requiring skilled management to achieve a productive output. *Abbrev*: HR

humble /'hʌmbəl/ *adj.*, **-bler**, **-blest**, *v.*, **-bled**, **-bling**. – *adj.* **1.** low in station, grade of importance, etc.; lowly. **2.** modest; meek; without pride. – *v.t.* **3.** to lower in condition, importance, or dignity; abase.

humbug /'hʌmbʌg/ *n.* *Colloquial* a quality of falseness or deception.

humdrum /'hʌmdrʌm/ *adj.* lacking variety; dull.

humerus /'hjumərəs/ *n.*, *pl.* **-meri** /-məraɪ/. (in humans) the single long bone in the arm which extends from the shoulder to the elbow.

humid /'hjuməd/ *adj.* moist or damp, with liquid or vapour.

humidicrib /hju'mɪdikrɪb/ *n.* *Medicine* an enclosed crib with controlled temperature and humidity.

humidity /hju'mɪdəti/ *n.* **1.** humid condition; dampness. **2.** *Meteorology* the condition of the atmosphere with regard to its water-vapour content.

humiliate /hju'mɪlieɪt/ *v.t.*, **-ated**, **-ating**. to lower the pride or self-respect of; cause a painful loss of dignity to; mortify.

humility /hju'mɪləti/ *n.*, *pl.* **-ties**. the quality of being humble; modest sense of one's own significance.

hummingbird /'hʌmɪŋbɜd/ *n.* a small bird whose narrow wings vibrate very rapidly, producing a humming sound.

hummock /'hʌmək/ *n.* a hillock.

humorous /'hjumərəs/ *adj.* **1.** characterised by humour; amusing; funny. **2.** having or showing the faculty of humour; droll; facetious.

humour = humor /'hjumə/ *n.* **1.** the quality of being funny. **2.** the faculty of perceiving what is amusing or comical. **3.** speech or writing showing this faculty. **4.** mental disposition or tendency; frame of mind. **5.** *Physiology Obsolete* one of the four chief bodily fluids, blood, choler or yellow bile, phlegm, and melancholy or black bile. – *v.t.* **6.** to comply with the wishes of; indulge.

hump /hʌmp/ *n.* **1.** a rounded protuberance, especially on the back. **2.** a low, rounded rise of ground; hummock.

humpy /'hʌmpi/ *n.* a temporary bush shelter used by Aborigines; gunyah.

humus /'hjuməs/ *n.* the dark organic material in soils, produced by the decomposition of vegetable or animal matter.

hunch /hʌntʃ/ *v.t.* **1.** to thrust out or up in a hump. – *v.i.* **2.** to walk, sit, or stand in a bent position (usually fol. by *up*). – *n.* **3.** a hump. **4.** *Colloquial* a premonition or suspicion.

hundred /'hʌndrəd/ *n.*, *pl.* **-dreds**, (*as after a numeral*) **-dred**. a cardinal number, ten times ten.

hundredweight /'hʌndrədweɪt/ *n.*, *pl.* **-weights**, (*as after a numeral*) **-weight**. a unit of weight in the imperial system, equal to 112 lb. (approx. 50.8 kg) and, in the US, to 100 lb. (approx. 45.36 kg). *Symbol*: cwt

hung /hʌŋ/ *v.* past tense and past participle of **hang**.

hunger /'hʌŋgə/ *n.* **1.** the painful sensation or state of exhaustion caused by need of food. **2.** strong or eager desire. – **hungry**, *adj.*

hunk /hʌŋk/ *n.* a large piece or lump; a chunk.

hunt /hʌnt/ *v.t.* **1.** to chase (game or other wild animals) for the purpose of catching or killing. **2.** to search for; seek; endeavour to obtain or find. – *v.i.* **3.** to engage in the chase. **4.** to make a search or quest (often fol. by *for* or *after*). – *n.* **5.** the act of hunting game or other wild animals; the chase. **6.** pursuit; a search.

hurdle /'hɜdl/ *n.*, *v.*, **-dled**, **-dling**. – *n.* **1.** a barrier in a racetrack, to be leapt by the contestants. **2.** a difficult problem to be overcome; obstacle. – *v.t.* **3.** to leap over (a hurdle, etc.) as in a race. **4.** to master (a difficulty, problem, etc.).

hurl /hɜl/ *v.t.* to drive or throw with great force.

hurricane /'hʌrəkən, -ɪkən/ *n.* a violent tropical cyclonic storm.

hurry /'hʌri/ *v.*, **-ried**, **-rying**, *n.*, *pl.* **-ries**. – *v.i.* **1.** to move, proceed, or act with haste, often undue haste. – *v.t.* **2.** to drive or move (someone or something) with speed, often with confused haste. – *n.* **3.** need or desire for haste.

hurt /hɜt/ *v.*, **hurt**, **hurting**, *n.* – *v.t.* **1.** to cause injury or pain to. **2.** to affect adversely; harm. – *v.i.* **3.** to cause pain (bodily or mental). – *n.* **4.** a blow that inflicts a wound; bodily injury. **5.** injury; damage or harm.

hurtle /hɜtl/ *v.i.*, **-tled**, **-tling**. to rush violently and noisily.

husband /'hʌzbənd/ *n.* the man of a married pair (correlative of *wife*).

husbandry /'hʌzbəndri/ *n.* the business of a farmer; agriculture; farming.

hush /hʌʃ/ *v.t.* **1.** to make silent; silence. **2.** to suppress mention of; keep concealed.

husk /hʌsk/ *n.* the dry external covering of certain fruits or seeds, especially of an ear of maize.

husky[1] /'hʌski/ *adj.*, **-kier**, **-kiest**. **1.** *Colloquial* burly; big and strong. **2.** having a semi-whispered vocal tone; somewhat hoarse.

husky[2] /'hʌski/ *n., pl.* **-kies**. a strong dog used in a team to pull sledges over snow.

hussy /'hʌsi, 'hʌzi/ *n., pl.* **-sies**. **1.** an ill-behaved girl. **2.** a lewd woman.

hustings /'hʌstɪŋz/ *pl. n.* an electioneering platform.

hustle /'hʌsəl/ *v.*, **-tled**, **-tling**, *n.* – *v.i.* **1.** to proceed or work rapidly or energetically. – *v.t.* **2.** to force roughly or hurriedly. – *n.* **3.** energetic activity.

hut /hʌt/ *n.* a simple, small house as a beach hut, bushwalker's hut, etc.

hutch /hʌtʃ/ *n.* a coop for confining small animals.

hyacinth /'haɪəsənθ/ *n.* a bulbous plant with spikes of fragrant, bell-shaped flowers.

hybrid /'haɪbrɪd, -brəd/ *n.* **1.** the offspring of two animals or plants of different races, breeds, varieties, species, or genera. **2.** anything derived from heterogeneous sources, or composed of elements of different or incongruous kind.

hydatid /haɪ'dætəd/ *n.* a cyst with watery contents, produced in humans and animals by a tapeworm in the larval state.

hydrangea /haɪ'dreɪndʒə/ *n.* a shrub with large showy flower clusters.

hydrant /'haɪdrənt/ *n.* an upright pipe with a spout, nozzle, or other outlet, usually in the street, for drawing water from a main or service pipe.

hydraulic /haɪ'drɒlɪk/ *adj.* operated by or employing water or other liquid.

hydraulics /haɪ'drɒlɪks/ *n.* the science that deals with the laws governing water or other liquids in motion and their applications in engineering.

hydro-[1] a word element meaning 'water', as in *hydrogen.* Also, **hydr-**.

hydro-[2] *Chemistry* a word element often indicating combination of hydrogen with a negative element or radical. Also, **hydr-**.

hydrocarbon /haɪdroʊ'kabən/ *n.* any of a class of compounds containing only hydrogen and carbon.

hydro-electric /ˌhaɪdroʊ-ə'lɛktrɪk/ *adj.* relating to the generation and distribution of electric energy derived from the energy of falling water or other hydraulic source.

hydrofoil /'haɪdrəfɔɪl/ *n.* a boat which, at speed, lifts above the surface of the water on two or more ski-like members.

hydrogen /'haɪdrədʒən/ *n.* a colourless, odourless, flammable gas, which combines chemically with oxygen to form water; the lightest of the known elements. *Symbol*: H

hydroplane /'haɪdrəpleɪn/ *n.* **1.** a plane surface designed to control or facilitate the movement of an aeroplane or boat on or in the water. **2.** a motorboat, with hydrofoils or a shaped bottom, designed to plane along the surface of the water at high speeds.

hydroponics /haɪdrə'pɒnɪks/ *n.* the cultivation of plants by placing the roots in liquid nutrient solutions rather than in soil; soilless growth of plants.

hyena = hyaena /haɪ'inə/ *n.* any of various doglike nocturnal carnivores, feeding chiefly on carrion.

hyeto- a word element meaning 'rain'.

hygiene /'haɪdʒin/ *n.* **1.** the science which deals with the preservation of health. **2.** the practices, such as keeping oneself clean, which maintain good health.

hygienic /haɪ'dʒinɪk/ *adj.* **1.** sanitary; clean. **2.** relating to hygiene.

hygro- a word element meaning 'wet', 'moist'. Also *(before vowels)*, **hygr-**.

hygrometer /haɪ'grɒmətə/ *n.* an instrument for determining the humidity of the atmosphere.

hymen /'haɪmən/ *n.* a fold of mucous membrane partially closing the external orifice of the vagina.

hymn /hɪm/ *n.* a song or ode in praise or honour of God, a deity, a nation, etc.

hymnal /'hɪmnəl/ *n.* **1.** Also, **hymnbook**. a book of hymns. – *adj.* **2.** of or relating to hymns.

hype /haɪp/ *n.* **1.** hypocrisy; pretentiousness. **2.** *Colloquial* an atmosphere of deliberately stimulated excitement and enthusiasm.

hyper- a prefix meaning 'over', and usually implying excess or exaggeration.

hyperbola /haɪ'pɜbələ/ *n., pl.* **-las**. a curve consisting of two distinct and similar branches, formed by the intersection of a plane with a right circular cone when the plane makes a greater angle with the base than does the generator of the cone.

hyperbole /haɪ'pɜbəli/ *n.* obvious exaggeration, for effect; an extravagant statement not intended to be taken literally.

hyperbolic /haɪpə'bɒlɪk/ *adj.* **1.** having the nature of hyperbole; exaggerated. **2.** of or relating to the hyperbola.

hypertext /'haɪpətɛkst/ *n.* *Computers* the facility for creating a text which is drawn from a number of different computer packages, such as a word processor, spreadsheet, graphics, etc., each of which can be accessed from within any other.

hyphen /'haɪfən/ *n.* a short stroke (-) used to connect the parts of a compound word or the parts of a word divided for any purpose. – **hyphenate**, *v.*

hypno- a word element meaning 'sleep' or 'hypnosis'.

hypnosis /hɪp'noʊsəs/ *n., pl.* **-noses** /-noʊsiz/. **1.** *Psychology* a trance-like mental state induced in a cooperative subject by suggestion. **2.** → **hypnotism**.

hypnotic /hɪp'nɒtɪk/ *adj.* **1.** relating to hypnosis or hypnotism. – *n.* **2.** an agent or drug that produces sleep; a sedative.

hypnotise = hypnotize /'hɪpnətaɪz/ *v.t.*, **-tised**, **-tising**. to put in the hypnotic state.

hypnotism /'hɪpnətɪzəm/ *n.* **1.** the science dealing with the induction of hypnosis. **2.** the induction of hypnosis. – **hypnotist**, *n.*

hypo /'haɪpoʊ/ *n. Colloquial* a hypodermic needle or injection.

hypo- a prefix meaning 'under', either in place or in degree ('less', 'less than').

hypochondria /haɪpə'kɒndriə/ *n. Psychology* a morbid condition characterised by depressed spirits and fancies of ill health, referable to the physical condition of the body or one of its parts. – **hypochondriac**, *n., adj.* – **hypochondriacal**, *adj.*

hypocrisy /hɪ'pɒkrəsi/ *n., pl.* **-sies**. **1.** the act of pretending to have a character or beliefs, principles, etc., that one does not possess. **2.** pretence of virtue or piety; false goodness.

hypocrite /'hɪpəkrɪt/ *n.* someone given to hypocrisy; someone who feigns virtue or piety; a pretender. – **hypocritical**, *adj.*

hypodermic /haɪpə'dɜmɪk/ *adj.* **1.** characterised by the introduction of medical remedies under the skin. **2.** lying under the skin, as tissue. – *n.* **3.** a hypodermic needle.

hypotenuse /haɪ'pɒtənjuz/ *n.* the side of a right-angled triangle opposite the right angle.

hypothesis /haɪ'pɒθəsəs/ *n., pl.* **-theses** /-θəsiz/. **1.** a proposition (or set of propositions) proposed as an explanation for the occurrence of some specified group of phenomena. **2.** a proposition assumed as a premise in an argument.

hypothetical /haɪpə'θɛtɪkəl/ *adj.* assumed by hypothesis; supposed.

hyster- variant of **hystero-**, before vowels; as in *hysterectomy.*

hysterectomy /hɪstə'rɛktəmi/ *n., pl.* **-mies**. the surgical excision of the uterus.

hysteria /his'tɪəriə/ *n.* morbid or senseless emotionalism; emotional frenzy.

hysterical /his'tɛrɪkəl/ *adj.* **1.** resembling or suggesting hysteria; emotionally disordered. **2.** of, relating to, or characteristic of hysteria.

hystero- a word element meaning 'uterus'. Also, **hyster-**.

I i

I, i /aɪ/ *n., pl.* **I's** *or* **Is**, **i's** *or* **is**. the ninth letter of the English alphabet.

-i- an ending for the first element in many compounds, as in *Frenchify*, etc.

I /ai/ *pron., sing. nominative* **I**, *possessive* **my** *or* **mine**, *objective* **me**; *pl. nominative* **we**, *possessive* **our** *or* **ours**, *objective* **us**. the subject form of the singular pronoun of the first person used by a speaker of himself or herself.

-ia a suffix of nouns, especially having restricted application in various fields, as in medicine, geography, botany, etc.

-ial variant of **-al**[1], as in *judicial*, *imperial*.

iamb /'aɪæmb, 'aɪæm/ *n.* a metrical foot of two syllables, a short followed by a long. – **iambic**, *adj.*

-ian variant of **-an**, as in *amphibian*.

-iasis a word element forming names of diseases.

-iatry a combining form meaning 'medical care', as in *psychiatry*.

ibidem /'ɪbədɛm, ɪ'baɪdəm/ *adv.* in the same book, chapter, page, etc.

ibis /'aɪbəs/ *n.* a wading bird with a long, thin, down-curved bill.

-ible variant of **-able**, as in *credible*.

-ic a suffix forming adjectives from nouns or stems not used as words themselves, meaning 'pertaining or belonging to'.

-ical a compound suffix forming adjectives from nouns (*rhetorical*), providing synonyms to words ending in *-ic* (*poetical*), and providing an adjective with additional meanings to those in the *-ic* form (*economical*).

ice /aɪs/ *n., v.,* **iced**, **icing**. – *n.* **1.** the solid form of water, produced by freezing; frozen water. – *v.t.* **2.** to cover with ice. **3.** to cool with ice, as a drink. **4.** to cover (cakes, etc.) with icing. – **icy**, *adj.*

-ice a suffix used in many nouns to indicate state or quality, as in *service*, *justice*.

iceberg /'aɪsbɜg/ *n.* **1.** a large floating mass of ice, detached from a glacier and carried out to sea. **2.** *Colloquial* a regular winter swimmer.

ice-cream /'aɪs-krim/ *n.* a frozen food made of cream, rich milk, or evaporated milk, sweetened and variously flavoured.

ichthyo- a word element meaning 'fish'.

ichthyology /ɪkθi'ɒlədʒi/ *n.* the branch of zoology that deals with fishes.

-ician a compound suffix especially applied to an expert in a field, as in *geometrician*.

icicle /'aɪsɪkəl/ *n.* a pendent tapering mass of ice formed by the freezing of dripping water. – **icicled**, *adj.*

icing /'aɪsɪŋ/ *n.* a preparation of sugar, often made with egg whites, for covering cakes, etc.

icon /'aɪkɒn/ *n.* **1.** a representation in painting, enamel, etc., of some sacred personage, itself venerated as sacred. **2.** a sign or representation which stands for its object by virtue of a resemblance or analogy to it. **3.** *Computers* a picture on a video display unit screen representing an instruction or menu option.

icono- a word element meaning 'likeness' or 'image'.

iconoclast /aɪ'kɒnəklæst/ *n.* **1.** a breaker or destroyer of images, especially those set up for religious veneration. **2.** someone who attacks cherished beliefs as based on error or superstition.

-ics a suffix of nouns, as in *ethics*, *physics*, *politics*, *tactics*.

id /ɪd/ *n.* (in psychoanalysis) the part of the psyche residing in the unconscious which is the source of instinctive energy.

-id[1] a suffix of nouns and adjectives indicating members of a zoological family.

-id[2] variant of **-ide**.

-id[3] a quasi-suffix common in adjectives, especially of states which appeal to the senses, as in *torrid*, *acid*.

I'd /aɪd/ contraction of *I would*, or *I had*.

-idae a suffix of the taxonomic names of families in zoology.

-ide a noun suffix in names of chemical compounds. Also, **-id**[2].

idea /aɪ'dɪə/ *n.* any conception existing in the mind as the result of mental apprehension or activity.

ideal /aɪ'dɪəl/ *n.* **1.** a conception of something in its highest perfection. **2.** that which exists only in idea. – *adj.* **3.** conceived as constituting a standard of perfection or excellence. **4.** not real or practical.

idealise = idealize /aɪ'dɪəlaɪz/ *v.t.,* **-lised**, **-lising**. to make ideal; represent in an ideal form or character.

idealism /aɪ'dɪəlɪzəm/ *n.* the cherishing or pursuit of ideals, as for attainment. – **idealist**, *n.* – **idealistic**, *adj.*

ideate /aɪ'dieɪt/ *v.t.,* **-ated**, **-ating**. to form in idea, thought, or imagination.

idem /'ɪdɛm, 'aɪdɛm/ *pron., adj.* the same as previously given or mentioned.

identical /aɪ'dɛntɪkəl/ *adj.* **1.** agreeing exactly. **2.** same, or being the same one.

identify /aɪ'dɛntəfaɪ/ *v.t.,* **-fied**, **-fying**. **1.** to recognise or establish as being a particular person or thing. **2.** to associate in feeling, interest, action, etc. (fol. by *with*). **3.** to serve as a means of identification for. – **identification**, *n.*

identity /aɪ'dɛntəti/ *n., pl.* **-ties**. **1.** the state or fact of remaining the same one, as under varying aspects or conditions. **2.** the condition of being oneself or itself, and not another.

ideo- a word element meaning 'idea'.

ideology /aɪdi'ɒlədʒi/ *n., pl.* **-gies**. the body of doctrine, myth, and symbols of a social movement, institution, class, or large group. – **ideological**, *adj.* – **ideologist**, *n.*

id est /ɪd 'ɛst/ that is.

idio- a word element meaning 'peculiar' or 'proper to one', as in *idiosyncrasy*.

idiom /'ɪdiəm/ *n.* **1.** a form of expression peculiar to a language, especially one having a significance other than its literal one. **2.** a distinct style or character, as in music, art, etc. – **idiomatic**, *adj.*

idiosyncrasy /,ɪdiou'sɪŋkrəsi/ *n., pl.* **-sies**.

any tendency, characteristic, mode of expression, or the like, peculiar to an individual. – **idiosyncratic**, *adj.*

idiot /'ɪdiət/ *n.* an utterly foolish or senseless person. – **idiotic**, *adj.* – **idiocy**, *n.*

idiot tape *n.* an unjustified tape used for computer typesetting.

-idium a diminutive suffix used in scientific terms.

idle /'aɪdl/ *adj.*, **idler**, **idlest**, *v.*, **idled**, **idling**. – *adj.* **1.** unemployed, or doing nothing. **2.** habitually doing nothing or avoiding work. – *v.i.* **3.** to pass time in idleness. **4.** *Machinery* to operate, usually at minimum speed, while the transmission is disengaged.

idol /'aɪdl/ *n.* **1.** an image or other material object representing a deity to which religious worship is addressed. **2.** any person or thing blindly adored or revered. – **idolatry**, *n.* – **idolise = idolize**, *v.*

idyll /'aɪdəl, 'ɪdəl/ *n.* **1.** a poem or prose composition consisting of a 'little picture', usually describing pastoral scenes or events. **2.** an episode or scene of simple or poetic charm. – **idyllic**, *adj.*

-ie a suffix of nouns, the same as **-y**², used colloquially: **1.** as an endearment, or affectionately, especially with and among children. **2.** as a familiar abbreviation. **3.** as a nominalisation.

i.e. id est.

-ier variant of **-eer**, as in *brigadier.*

-ies a word element representing the plural formation of nouns and third person singular of verbs for words ending in *-y*, *-ie*, and sometimes *-ey*. See **-s**², **-s**³, **-es**.

if /ɪf/ *conj.* **1.** in case that; granting or supposing that; on condition that. **2.** whether.

-ify variant of **-fy**, used when the preceding stem or word element ends in a consonant, as in *intensify.*

igloo /'ɪglu/ *n.*, *pl.* **-loos**. a dome-shaped Inuit hut, built of blocks of hard snow.

igneous rock /'ɪgniəs/ *n.* rock formed from magma.

ignite /ɪg'naɪt/ *v.*, **-nited**, **-niting**. – *v.t.* **1.** to set on fire; kindle. – *v.i.* **2.** to begin to burn.

ignition /ɪg'nɪʃən/ *n.* **1.** the act of igniting. **2.** the state of being ignited. **3.** (in an internal-combustion engine) the process which ignites the fuel in the cylinder.

ignoble /ɪg'noʊbəl/ *adj.* of low character, aims, etc.; mean; base.

ignominy /'ɪgnəməni/ *n.*, *pl.* **-minies**. disgrace; dishonour. – **ignominious**, *adj.*

ignoramus /ɪgnə'reɪməs/ *n.*, *pl.* **-muses**. an ignorant person.

ignorant /'ɪgnərənt/ *adj.* destitute of knowledge. – **ignorance**, *n.*

ignore /ɪg'nɔ/ *v.t.*, **-nored**, **-noring**. to refrain from noticing or recognising.

iguana /ɪ'gwanə/ *n.* a large tropical American lizard.

il-¹ variant of **in-**¹, (by assimilation) before *l.*

il-² variant of **in-**², (by assimilation) before *l.*

-ile a suffix of adjectives expressing capability, susceptibility, liability, aptitude, etc., as in *agile, docile, ductile, fragile, prehensile, tensile, volatile.* Also, **-il**.

-ility a compound suffix making abstract nouns from adjectives by replacing the adjective suffixes as in *civility, ability*, etc.

ilk /ɪlk/ *n.* family, class, or kind.

ill /ɪl/ *adj.*, **worse**, **worst**, *n.*, *adv.* – *adj.* **1.** unwell, sick, or indisposed. **2.** evil, wicked, or bad. – *n.* **3.** evil. **4.** harm or injury. **5.** a disease or ailment. – *adv.* **6.** unsatisfactorily or poorly. **7.** with displeasure or offence. **8.** faultily or improperly. – **illness**, *n.*

I'll /aɪl/ contraction of *I will* or *I shall.*

illegal /ɪ'ligəl/ *adj.* not legal. – **illegality**, *n.*

illegible /ɪ'lɛdʒəbəl/ *adj.* not legible; impossible or hard to read or decipher.

illegitimate /ɪlə'dʒɪtəmət/ *adj.* **1.** not legitimate. **2.** born out of wedlock.

ill-fated /'ɪl-feɪtəd/ *adj.* **1.** destined to an unhappy fate. **2.** bringing bad fortune.

ill-gotten /'ɪl-gɒtn/ *adj.* acquired by evil means, as *ill-gotten gains.*

illicit /ɪ'lɪsət/ *adj.* not permitted or authorised; unlicensed; unlawful.

illiquid /ɪ'lɪkwəd/ *adj.* (of a business concern, etc.) without liquidity.

illiterate /ɪ'lɪtərət, ɪ'lɪtrət/ *adj.* **1.** unable to read and write. – *n.* **2.** an illiterate person.

ill-mannered /'ɪl-mænəd/ *adj.* having bad manners; impolite; rude.

illuminate /ɪ'ljuməneɪt/ *v.t.*, **-nated**, **-nating**. **1.** to supply with light; light up. **2.** to enlighten, as with knowledge. **3.** to decorate (a letter, a page, a manuscript, etc.) with colour, gold, or the like.

illusion /ɪ'luʒən/ *n.* something that deceives by producing a false impression. – **illusory**, *n.*

illustrate /'ɪləstreɪt/ *v.t.*, **-strated**, **-strating**. **1.** to make clear or intelligible, as by examples. **2.** to furnish (a book, etc.) with drawings or pictorial representations intended for elucidation or adornment. – **illustration**, *n.*

illustrious /ɪ'lʌstriəs/ *adj.* **1.** highly distinguished; renowned; famous. **2.** glorious, as deeds, etc.

im-¹ variant of **in-**² used before *b*, *m*, and *p*, as in *immoral.*

im-² variant of **in-**¹ used before *b*, *m*, and *p*. Also, **em-**.

I'm /aɪm/ contraction of *I am.*

image /'ɪmɪdʒ/ *n.* **1.** a likeness or similitude of a person, animal, or thing. **2.** an optical counterpart or appearance of an object. **3.** a mental picture or representation; an idea or conception. **4.** the impression a public figure, especially a politician, strives to create for the public. **5.** Also, **spitting image**. a counterpart or copy. **6.** *Rhetoric* a figure of speech, especially a metaphor or a simile. – **imagery**, *n.*

imaginary /ɪ'mædʒənəri, -ənri/ *adj.* existing only in the imagination or fancy; not real.

imagination /ɪmædʒə'neɪʃən/ *n.* the action of imagining, or of forming mental images or concepts of what is not actually present to the senses. – **imaginative**, *adj.*

imagine /ɪ'mædʒən/ *v.t.*, **-ined**, **-ining**. **1.** to form a mental image of (something not actually present to the senses). **2.** to think, believe, or fancy. **3.** to assume or suppose.

imago /ɪ'meɪgoʊ/ *n., pl.* **imagos, imagines** /ɪ'meɪdʒəniz/. **1.** *Entomology* an adult insect. **2.** *Psychoanalysis* an idealised concept of a loved one, formed in childhood and retained uncorrected in adult life.

imbecile /'ɪmbəsil, -saɪl/ *n.* **1.** a person of defective mentality. **2.** *Colloquial* a silly person; fool.

imbibe /ɪm'baɪb/ *v.,* **-bibed, -bibing**. – *v.t.* **1.** to drink in, or drink. – *v.i.* **2.** to drink; absorb liquid or moisture.

imbroglio /ɪm'broʊlioʊ/ *n., pl.* **-lios**. an intricate and perplexing state of affairs.

imbue /ɪm'bju/ *v.t.,* **-bued, -buing**. to impregnate or inspire, as with feelings, opinions, etc.

imitate /'ɪmәteɪt/ *v.t.,* **-tated, -tating**. **1.** to follow or endeavour to follow in action or manner. **2.** to mimic or counterfeit. **3.** to make a copy of; reproduce closely. – **imitation**, *n.*

immaculate /ɪ'mækjulәt, -kjә-/ *adj.* free from spot or stain; spotlessly clean, as linen.

immanent /'ɪmәnәnt/ *adj.* remaining within; indwelling; inherent.

immaterial /ɪmә'tɪәriәl/ *adj.* **1.** of no essential consequence; unimportant. **2.** not material; spiritual.

immediate /ɪ'midiәt/ *adj.* **1.** occurring or accomplished without delay; instant. **2.** having no object or space intervening; nearest or next. – **immediacy**, *n.*

immemorial /ɪmә'mɔriәl/ *adj.* extending back beyond memory, record, or knowledge.

immense /ɪ'mɛns/ *adj.* **1.** vast; huge; very great. **2.** immeasurable; boundless.

immerse /ɪ'mɜs/ *v.t.,* **-mersed, -mersing**. to plunge into or place under a liquid; dip; sink. – **immersion**, *n.*

immigrate /'ɪmәgreɪt/ *v.i.,* **-grated, -grating**. to come into a country of which one is not a native for the purpose of permanent residence. – **immigration**, *n.* – **immigrant**, *n., adj.*

imminent /'ɪmәnәnt/ *adj.* likely to occur at any moment.

immolate /'ɪmәleɪt/ *v.t.,* **-lated, -lating**. to sacrifice.

immoral /ɪ'mɒrәl/ *adj.* not moral; not conforming to the moral law; not conforming to accepted patterns of conduct. – **immorality**, *n.*

immortal /ɪ'mɔtl/ *adj.* **1.** not mortal; not liable or subject to death; undying. **2.** remembered or celebrated through all time. – **immortality**, *n.* – **immortalise = immortalize**, *v.*

immune /ә'mjun, ɪ-/ *adj.* **1.** protected from a disease or the like, as by inoculation. **2.** exempt. – **immunise = immunize**, *v.* – **immunisation**, *n.* – **immunity**, *n.*

immunology /ɪmju'nɒlәdʒi/ *n.* that branch of medical science which deals with immunity from disease and the production of such immunity.

immure /ɪ'mjuә/ *v.t.,* **-mured, -muring**. **1.** to enclose within walls. **2.** to imprison.

imp /ɪmp/ *n.* **1.** a little devil or demon; an evil spirit. **2.** a mischievous child.

impact /'ɪmpækt/ *n.,* /ɪm'pækt/ *v.* – *n.* **1.** the striking of one body against another. **2.** influence or effect exerted by a new idea, concept, ideology, etc. – *v.t.* **3.** to drive or press closely or firmly into something; pack in. **4.** **impact on,** to have an affect on: *this law impacts on all of us.*

impair /ɪm'pɛә/ *v.t.* to make worse; diminish in value, excellence, etc.

impala /ɪm'palә/ *n.* an African antelope.

impale /ɪm'peɪl/ *v.t.,* **-paled, -paling**. to fix upon a sharpened stake or the like.

impart /ɪm'pat/ *v.t.* to give or bestow.

impartial /ɪm'paʃәl/ *adj.* unbiased.

impasse /'ɪmpas/ *n.* a position from which there is no escape.

impassive /ɪm'pæsɪv/ *adj.* without emotion; apathetic; unmoved.

impatient /ɪm'peɪʃәnt/ *adj.* not patient; not bearing pain, opposition, etc., with composure. – **impatience**, *n.*

impeach /ɪm'pitʃ/ *v.t.* **1.** to challenge the credibility of. **2.** to accuse of a grave criminal offence.

impeccable /ɪm'pɛkәbәl/ *adj.* faultless or irreproachable.

impecunious /ɪmpә'kjuniәs/ *adj.* poor; penniless.

impede /ɪm'pid/ *v.t.,* **-peded, -peding**. to obstruct; hinder.

impediment /ɪm'pɛdәmәnt/ *n.* **1.** some physical defect, especially a speech disorder. **2.** obstruction or hindrance; obstacle.

impel /ɪm'pɛl/ *v.t.,* **-pelled, -pelling**. to drive or urge forward.

impend /ɪm'pɛnd/ *v.i.* to be imminent.

imperative /ɪm'pɛrәtɪv/ *adj.* **1.** not to be avoided or evaded. **2.** of the nature of or expressing a command; commanding.

imperfect /ɪm'pɜfәkt/ *adj.* **1.** characterised by or subject to defects. **2.** *Grammar* designating a tense which denotes action going on but not completed, especially in the past.

imperial /ɪm'pɪәriәl/ *adj.* **1.** of or relating to an empire. **2.** of a commanding quality, manner, or aspect. **3.** (of weights and measures) conforming to the standards legally established in Britain.

imperious /ɪm'pɪәriәs/ *adj.* domineering, dictatorial, or overbearing.

impersonal /ɪm'pɜsәnәl/ *adj.* **1.** not personal; without personal reference or connection. **2.** *Grammar* (of a verb) having only third person singular forms, rarely if ever accompanied by an expressed subject.

impersonate /ɪm'pɜsәneɪt/ *v.t.,* **-nated, -nating**. to assume the character of; pretend to be.

impertinent /ɪm'pɜtәnәnt/ *adj.* intrusive or presumptuous.

impervious /ɪm'pɜviәs/ *adj.* **1.** not penetrable. **2.** not disposed to be influenced or affected. Also, **imperviable**.

impetigo /ɪmpә'taɪgoʊ/ *n.* a contagious skin disease, especially of children.

impetuous /ɪm'pɛtʃuәs/ *adj.* acting with or characterised by a sudden or rash energy.

impetus /'ɪmpәtәs/ *n., pl.* **-tuses**. moving force; impulse; stimulus.

impinge /ɪm'pɪndʒ/ *v.i.,* **-pinged, -pinging**.

1. to collide. 2. to encroach or infringe (fol. by *on* or *upon*).

implacable /ɪm'plækəbəl/ *adj.* not placable; not to be appeased or pacified.

implant /ɪm'plænt, -'plant/ *v.t.* to instil or inculcate.

implement /'ɪmpləmənt/ *n.*, /'ɪmpləmɛnt/ *v.* – *n.* **1.** an instrument, tool, or utensil. – *v.t.* **2.** to put (a plan, proposal, etc.) into effect.

implicate /'ɪmpləkeɪt/ *v.t.*, **-cated**, **-cating**. **1.** to involve as being concerned in a matter, affair, condition, etc. **2.** to imply. – **implication**, *n.*

implicit /ɪm'plɪsət/ *adj.* **1.** (of belief, confidence, obedience, etc.) unquestioning, unreserved, or absolute. **2.** implied, rather than expressly stated.

implied contract *n.* a contract not based on express words but arising from other circumstances. Also, **implied promise**, **implied term**.

implore /ɪm'plɔ/ *v.t.*, **-plored**, **-ploring**. to call upon in urgent or piteous supplication, as for aid or mercy; beseech.

imply /ɪm'plaɪ/ *v.t.*, **-plied**, **-plying**. **1.** to involve as a necessary circumstance. **2.** to indicate or suggest.

import /ɪm'pɔt, 'ɪmpɔt/ *v.*, /'ɪmpɔt/ *n.* – *v.t.* **1.** to bring in from another country, as merchandise or commodities, for sale, use, processing, or re-export. **2.** to convey as a meaning or implication. – *n.* **3.** that which is imported from abroad. **4.** meaning; implication; purport. **5.** consequence or importance.

important /ɪm'pɔtnt/ *adj.* **1.** of much significance or consequence. **2.** mattering much (fol. by *to*). **3.** of considerable influence or authority, as a person, position, etc. – **importance**, *n.*

importune /ɪm'pɔtʃun, ɪmpɔ'tjun/ *v.t.*, **-tuned**, **-tuning**. to beg urgently or persistently. – **importunate**, *adj.*

impose /ɪm'poʊz/ *v.*, **-posed**, **-posing**. – *v.t.* **1.** to lay on or set as something to be borne, endured, obeyed, fulfilled, etc. **2.** to subject to some penalty, etc. – *v.i.* **3.** to obtrude oneself or one's requirements. – **imposition**, *n.*

imposing /ɪm'poʊzɪŋ/ *adj.* making an impression on the mind, as by great size, stately appearance, etc.

impossible /ɪm'pɒsəbəl/ *adj.* **1.** not possible; that cannot be, exist, or happen. **2.** that cannot be done or effected. – **impossibly**, *adv.* – **impossibility**, *n.*

impost /'ɪmpɒst/ *n.* a tax.

impostor /ɪm'pɒstə/ *n.* someone who practises deception under an assumed character or name. – **imposture**, *n.*

impotent /'ɪmpətənt/ *adj.* **1.** not potent; lacking power or ability. **2.** (of a male) unable to perform sexual intercourse. – **impotence**, *n.*

impound /ɪm'paʊnd/ *v.t.* **1.** to shut up in a pound, as a stray animal. **2.** to seize, take, or appropriate summarily.

impoverish /ɪm'pɒvərɪʃ, -vrɪʃ/ *v.t.* to reduce to poverty.

imprecate /'ɪmprəkeɪt/ *v.t.*, **-cated**, **-cating**. to call down or invoke (especially evil or curses), as upon a person. – **imprecation**, *n.*

impregnable /ɪm'prɛgnəbəl/ *adj.* strong enough to resist attack.

impregnate /'ɪmprɛgneɪt/ *v.t.*, **-nated**, **-nating**. **1.** to make pregnant; get with child or young. **2.** to charge with something infused or permeating throughout; saturate.

impresario /ɪmprə'sarioʊ/ *n.*, *pl.* **-rios**. the organiser or manager of an opera, ballet, or theatre company or orchestra.

impress /ɪm'prɛs/ *v.t.*, **-pressed** *or Archaic* **-prest**, **-pressing**. **1.** to affect deeply or strongly in mind or feelings, especially favourably; influence in opinion. **2.** to urge, as something to be remembered or done. **3.** to produce (a mark, figure, etc.) by pressure; stamp; imprint. – **impressive**, *adj.*

impression /ɪm'prɛʃən/ *n.* **1.** a strong effect produced on the intellect, feelings, or conscience. **2.** a notion, remembrance, or belief. **3.** a mark, indentation, figure, etc., produced by pressure. **4.** an imitation, especially one given for entertainment, of the idiosyncrasies of some well-known person or type.

impressionable /ɪm'prɛʃənəbəl, -prɛʃnəbəl/ *adj.* easily impressed or influenced.

imprest /'ɪmprɛst/ *n.* an advance of money, especially for some public business.

imprint /'ɪmprɪnt/ *n.*, /ɪm'prɪnt/ *v.* – *n.* **1.** a mark made by pressure; a figure impressed or printed on something. – *v.t.* **2.** to impress (a quality, character, or distinguishing mark). **3.** to fix firmly on the mind, memory, etc.

imprison /ɪm'prɪzən/ *v.t.* to put into or confine in a prison; detain in custody.

impromptu /ɪm'prɒmptju/ *adj.* made or done without previous preparation.

improve /ɪm'pruv/ *v.*, **-proved**, **-proving**. – *v.t.* **1.** to bring into a more desirable or excellent condition. – *v.i.* **2.** to increase in value, excellence, etc.; become better. – **improvement**, *n.*

improvise /'ɪmprəvaɪz/ *v.t.*, **-vised**, **-vising**. to prepare or provide offhand or hastily. – **improvisation**, *n.*

impudent /'ɪmpjudənt, -pjə-/ *adj.* characterised by a shameless boldness.

impugn /ɪm'pjun/ *v.t.* to call in question; challenge as false.

impulse /'ɪmpʌls/ *n.* **1.** sudden, involuntary inclination prompting to action, or a particular instance of it. **2.** an impelling action or force. – **impulsive**, *adj.*

impunity /ɪm'pjunəti/ *n.* exemption from punishment or ill consequences.

impute /ɪm'pjut/ *v.t.*, **-puted**, **-puting**. **1.** to attribute or ascribe. **2.** *Law* to charge. – **imputation**, *n.*

in /ɪn/ *prep.* **1.** a particle expressing inclusion within space, limits, a whole, material or immaterial surroundings, etc. – *adv.* **2.** in or into some place, position, state, relation, etc. – *adj.* **3.** that is or gets in; internal; inward; incoming.

in-[1] a prefix representing *in*, as in *income*, *inland*, but used also as a verb-formative with transitive, intensive, or sometimes little apparent force. Also, **il-**[1], **im-**[1], **ir-**[1].

in-[2] a prefix corresponding to *un-*, having a negative or privative force, freely used as an English formative, especially of adjectives and their derivatives and of nouns, as in *inattention, indefensible, inexpensive, inorganic.*

inadvertent /ɪnəd'vɜtnt/ *adj.* **1.** not attentive; heedless. **2.** characterised by lack of attention, as actions, etc. **3.** unintentional.

inane /ɪn'eɪn/ *adj.* lacking sense or ideas; silly. – **inanity**, *n.*

inanimate /ɪn'ænəmət/ *adj.* **1.** not animate; lifeless. **2.** spiritless; sluggish; dull.

inasmuch as /ɪnəz'mʌtʃ əz/ *conj.* in view of the fact that; seeing that; since.

inaugurate /ɪn'ɔgjəreɪt/ *v.t.*, **-rated**, **-rating**. **1.** to make a formal beginning of; initiate; commence; begin. **2.** to induct into office with formal ceremonies; install. – **inaugural**, *adj.* – **inauguration**, *n.*

inborn /'ɪnbɔn/ *adj.* implanted by nature; innate.

inbreed /ɪn'brid/ *v.t.*, **-bred**, **-breeding**. to breed (animals) repeatedly within the same strain. – **inbred**, *adj.*

incalculable /ɪn'kælkjuləbəl, -kjə-/ *adj.* that cannot be calculated; beyond calculation.

in camera /ɪn 'kæmərə/ *adj.* → **camera** (def. 2).

incandescence /ɪnkæn'dɛsəns/ *n.* the state of a body caused by approximately white heat, when it may be used as a source of artificial light. – **incandesce**, *v.* – **incandescent**, *adj.*

incantation /ɪnkæn'teɪʃən/ *n.* a magic spell; charm.

incapacitate /ɪnkə'pæsəteɪt/ *v.t.*, **-tated**, **-tating**. to make incapable or unfit.

incarcerate /ɪn'kasəreɪt/ *v.t.*, **-rated**, **-rating**. to imprison; confine.

incarnate /ɪn'kanət, -neɪt/ *adj.*, /'ɪnkaneɪt/ *v.*, **-nated**, **-nating**. – *adj.* **1.** embodied in flesh; invested with a bodily, especially a human, form. **2.** personified or typified, as a quality or idea. – *v.t.* **3.** to be the embodiment or type of. – **incarnation**, *n.*

incendiary /ɪn'sɛndʒəri/ *adj.* used or adapted for setting property on fire.

incense[1] /'ɪnsɛns/ *n.* an aromatic gum or other substance producing a sweet smell when burnt, used especially in religious ceremonies.

incense[2] /ɪn'sɛns/ *v.t.*, **-censed**, **-censing**. to inflame with wrath; make angry; enrage.

incentive /ɪn'sɛntɪv/ *n.* **1.** that which encourages action, greater effort, etc. **2.** an inducement such as extra money, better conditions, etc., offered to employees to encourage better work.

inception /ɪn'sɛpʃən/ *n.* beginning; start.

incessant /ɪn'sɛsənt/ *adj.* continuing without interruption.

incest /'ɪnsɛst/ *n.* sexual intercourse between persons closely related by blood. – **incestuous**, *adj.*

inch /ɪntʃ/ *n.* **1.** a unit of length in the imperial system, $\frac{1}{12}$ foot or 25.4×10^{-3} m (25.4 mm). – *v.t.*, *v.i.* **2.** to move by inches or small degrees.

inchoate /'ɪnkoʊeɪt/ *adj.* just begun.

incidence /'ɪnsədəns/ *n.* **1.** the range of occurrence or influence of a thing, or the extent of its effects. **2.** the falling of a ray of light, etc., on a surface.

incident /'ɪnsədənt/ *n.* **1.** an occurrence or event. – *adj.* **2.** naturally appertaining. **3.** falling or striking on something.

incidental /ɪnsə'dɛntl/ *adj.* **1.** happening or likely to happen in fortuitous or subordinate conjunction with something else. **2.** incurred casually and in addition to the regular or main amount.

incinerate /ɪn'sɪnəreɪt/ *v.t.*, **-rated**, **-rating**. to reduce to ashes. – **incinerator**, *n.*

incipient /ɪn'sɪpiənt/ *adj.* beginning.

incise /ɪn'saɪz/ *v.t.*, **-cised**, **-cising**. to cut into. – **incision**, *n.*

incisive /ɪn'saɪsɪv/ *adj.* penetrating, trenchant, or biting.

incisor /ɪn'saɪzə/ *n.* a tooth in the anterior part of the jaw adapted for cutting.

incite /ɪn'saɪt/ *v.t.*, **-cited**, **-citing**. to urge on; stimulate or prompt to action.

in-clearing /'ɪn-klɪərɪŋ/ *n.* the total of cheques, etc., drawn on a member bank of a clearing house, and received by that bank for settlement from the clearing house.

incline /ɪn'klaɪn/ *v.*, **-clined**, **-clining** /'ɪnklaɪn, ɪn'klaɪn/ *n.* – *v.i.* **1.** to have a mental tendency; be disposed. **2.** to deviate from the vertical or horizontal; slant. **3.** to tend, in a physical sense; approximate. – *v.t.* **4.** to dispose (a person) in mind, habit, etc. (fol. by *to*). **5.** to bow (the head, etc.). **6.** to cause to lean or bend in a particular direction. – *n.* **7.** an inclined surface; a slope. – **inclination**, *n.*

include /ɪn'klud/ *v.t.*, **-cluded**, **-cluding**. **1.** to contain, embrace, or comprise, as a whole does parts or any part or element. **2.** to place in an aggregate, class, category, or the like. – **inclusive**, *adj.*

inclusive language *n.* non-sexist language.

incognito /ɪnkɒg'nitoʊ/ *adv.* with the real identity concealed.

income /'ɪnkʌm, 'ɪŋ-/ *n.* the returns that come in periodically, especially annually, from one's work, property, business, etc.; revenue; receipts.

income group *n.* a group of people having similar incomes.

income tax /'ɪnkʌm tæks/ *n.* an annual government tax on personal incomes, usually graduated and with certain deductions and exemptions.

incommodious /ɪnkə'moʊdiəs/ *adj.* **1.** not affording sufficient room. **2.** inconvenient.

incommunicado /ˌɪnkəmjunə'kadoʊ/ *adj.* (especially of a prisoner) deprived of communication with others.

incomputerate /ɪnkəm'pjutərət/ *adj.* without a working knowledge of computers or their technology.

incongruous /ɪn'kɒŋgruəs/ *adj.* **1.** out of keeping or place; inappropriate; unbecoming; absurd. **2.** not harmonious in character; lacking harmony of parts. – **incongruity**, *n.*

inconsequential /ˌɪnkɒnsə'kwɛnʃəl/ *adj.* **1.** of no consequence; trivial. **2.** illogical.

inconvenient /ɪnkən'viniənt/ *adj.* arranged or happening in such a way as to be awkward, inopportune, disadvantageous, or troublesome. – **inconvenience**, *n.*

inconvertible /ɪnkən'vɜtəbəl/ *adj.* **1.** (of paper money) not capable of being converted into specie. **2.** not interchangeable.

incorporate /ɪn'kɔpəreɪt/ *v.t.*, **-rated**, **-rating**. **1.** to create or form a legal corporation. **2.** to form into a society or organisation. **3.** to put or introduce into a body or mass as an integral part or parts.

incorrigible /ɪn'kɒrədʒəbəl/ *adj.* **1.** bad beyond correction or reform. **2.** firmly fixed; not easily changed.

increase /ɪn'kris/ *v.*, **-creased**, **-creasing**, /'ɪnkris/ *n.* – *v.t.* **1.** to make greater in any respect; augment; add to. – *v.i.* **2.** to become greater or more numerous. – *n.* **3.** growth or augmentation in numbers. **4.** that by which something is increased.

incredible /ɪn'krɛdəbəl/ *adj.* **1.** seeming too extraordinary to be possible. **2.** not credible; that cannot be believed.

incredulous /ɪn'krɛdʒələs/ *adj.* **1.** not credulous; indisposed to believe; sceptical. **2.** indicating unbelief.

increment /'ɪnkrəmənt, 'ɪŋ-/ *n.* **1.** something added or gained; an addition or increase. **2.** an increase in salary resulting from progression within a graduated scale of salaries, designed to reward an employee for increases in skill or experience. – *v.t.* **3.** *Computers* to increase the numerical contents of (a counter).

incriminate /ɪn'krɪməneɪt/ *v.t.*, **-nated**, **-nating**. **1.** to imply or provide evidence of the fault of (someone). **2.** to involve in an accusation. **3.** to charge with a crime or fault.

incubate /'ɪnkjubeɪt, 'ɪŋ-/ *v.t.*, **-bated**, **-bating**. **1.** to sit upon (eggs) for the purpose of hatching. **2.** to maintain (bacterial cultures, etc.) at the most favourable temperature for development. **3.** to keep at even temperature, as prematurely born infants. – **incubator**, *n.*

inculcate /'ɪnkʌlkeɪt/ *v.t.*, **-cated**, **-cating**. to impress by repeated statement or admonition; teach persistently and earnestly; instil (usually fol. by *upon* or *in*).

incumbent /ɪn'kʌmbənt/ *adj.* resting on one; obligatory.

incur /ɪn'kɜ/ *v.t.*, **-curred**, **-curring**. to run or fall into (some consequence, usually undesirable or injurious).

incursion /ɪn'kɜʒən/ *n.* an invasion.

ind- variant of **indo-** before vowels.

indebted /ɪn'dɛtəd/ *adj.* **1.** owing money. **2.** being under an obligation for benefits, favours, assistance etc., received.

indecent /ɪn'disənt/ *adj.* offending against recognised standards of propriety or good taste; vulgar.

indeed /ɪn'did/ *adv.* in fact; in reality; in truth; truly (used for emphasis, to confirm and amplify a previous statement, to intensify, to indicate a concession or admission, or, interrogatively, to obtain confirmation).

indefatigable /ɪndə'fætɪgəbəl/ *adj.* incapable of being tired out.

indefeasible /ɪndə'fizəbəl/ *adj.* not to be annulled or made void.

indefensible /ɪndə'fɛnsəbəl/ *adj.* that cannot be justified; inexcusable.

indelible /ɪn'dɛləbəl/ *adj.* incapable of being deleted or obliterated.

indelicate /ɪn'dɛləkət/ *adj.* offensive to a sense of propriety, or modesty; unrefined.

indemnity /ɪn'dɛmnəti/ *n.*, *pl.* **-ties**. **1.** protection or security against damage or loss. **2.** compensation for damage or loss sustained. **3.** legal protection, as by insurance, from liabilities or penalties incurred by one's actions.

indent /ɪn'dɛnt/ *v.*, /'ɪndɛnt/ *n.* – *v.t.* **1.** to form deep recesses in. **2.** to set in or back from the margin, as the first line of a paragraph. **3.** to sever (a document drawn up in duplicate) along an irregular line as a means of identification. **4.** to order, as commodities. – *v.i.* **5.** to form a recess. – *n.* **6.** a toothlike notch or deep recess; an indentation. **7.** an order for goods.

indentation /ɪndɛn'teɪʃən/ *n.* **1.** a cut, notch, or deep recess. **2.** a series of incisions or notches.

indenture /ɪn'dɛntʃə/ *n.* **1.** an indented document. **2.** a contract by which a person, as an apprentice, is bound to service. **3.** the formal agreement between a group of bondholders and the debtor as to the terms of the debt.

independent /ɪndə'pɛndənt/ *adj.* **1.** not influenced by others. **2.** not subject to another's authority or jurisdiction; autonomous; free. **3.** not dependent; not depending or contingent on something or someone else for existence, operation, etc. **4.** (of a school) non-government. – *n.* **5.** *Politics* a politician who is not formally affiliated with a political party. – **independence**, *n.*

indeterminate /ɪndə'tɜmənət/ *adj.* not determinate; not fixed in extent; indefinite; uncertain.

index /'ɪndɛks/ *n.*, *pl.* **-dexes**, **-dices** /-dəsɪz/ *v.* – *n.* **1.** a detailed alphabetical key to names, places, and topics in a book with reference to their page number, etc., in the book. **2.** something used or serving to point out; a sign, token, or indication. – *v.t.* **3.** to provide with an index, as a book.

indexation /ɪndɛk'seɪʃən/ *n.* the adjustment of one variable in the light of changes in another variable, especially the adjustment of wages to compensate for rises in the cost of living.

index finger /'ɪndɛks fɪŋgə/ *n.* → **forefinger**.

index number *n.* a number indicating change in magnitude, as of price, wage, employment, or production shifts, relative to the magnitude at some specified point usually taken to be 100.

indicate /'ɪndəkeɪt, -dɪkeɪt/ *v.t.*, **-cated**, **-cating**. **1.** to be a sign of; imply. **2.** to point out or point to; direct attention to. – **indication**, *n.*

indicative /ɪn'dɪkətɪv/ *adj.* **1.** that indicates; pointing out; suggestive (fol. by *of*). **2.** *Grammar* mood used in ordinary statements, questions, etc.

indicator /'ɪndəkeɪtə/ *n.* **1.** something that indicates. **2.** a pointing or directing instrument, as a pointer on an instrument or a flashing light on a car. **3.** a statistic or set of statistics which suggest the state of some aspect of society: *a market indicator.*

indices /ˈɪndəsiz/ *n.* a plural of **index**.

indict /ɪnˈdaɪt/ *v.t.* to charge with an offence or crime. – **indictment**, *n.*

indifference curve *n.* a graph whose coordinates represent the quantities of alternative goods and services that tend to leave the consumer indifferent in making a choice because he or she judges them of equal value.

indifferent /ɪnˈdɪfrənt/ *adj.* **1.** without interest or concern; not caring; apathetic. **2.** neutral in character or quality; neither good nor bad. **3.** not very good. **4.** immaterial or unimportant.

indigenous /ɪnˈdɪdʒənəs/ *adj.* originating in and characterising a particular region or country; native (usually fol. by *to*).

indigent /ˈɪndədʒənt/ *adj.* poor.

indigestion /ɪndəˈdʒɛstʃən, ɪndaɪ-/ *n.* incapability of, or difficulty in, digesting food. – **indigestive**, *adj.*

indignation /ɪndɪgˈneɪʃən/ *n.* strong displeasure at something deemed unworthy, unjust, or base. – **indignant**, *adj.*

indignity /ɪnˈdɪgnəti/ *n., pl.* **-ties**. injury to dignity.

indigo /ˈɪndɪgoʊ/ *n., pl.* **-gos**. a deep violet blue.

indirect tax /ɪndəˈrɛkt/ *n.* a tax levied on persons who reimburse themselves by passing the cost on to others, as sales tax which is levied on commodities before they reach the consumer, and ultimately paid as part of their market price.

indiscriminate /ɪndəsˈkrɪmənət/ *adj.* not discriminating; making no distinction.

indispensable /ɪndəsˈpɛnsəbəl/ *adj.* absolutely necessary.

indisposed /ɪndəsˈpoʊzd/ *adj.* **1.** sick or ill, especially slightly. **2.** disinclined or unwilling. – **indisposition**, *n.*

individual /ɪndəˈvɪdʒuəl/ *adj.* **1.** single; particular; separate. **2.** relating or peculiar to a single person or thing. **3.** distinguished by peculiar and marked characteristics. – *n.* **4.** a single human being or thing, as distinguished from a group. – **individuality**, *n.* – **individualise = individualize**, *v.* – **individualist**, *n.*

indoctrinate /ɪnˈdɒktrəneɪt/ *v.t.,* **-nated**, **-nating**. **1.** to instruct (someone) in some particular teaching or doctrine. **2.** to so instruct (someone) in a manner which leads to their total and uncritical acceptance of the teaching; brainwash.

indolent /ˈɪndələnt/ *adj.* having or showing a disposition to avoid exertion. – **indolence**, *n.*

indomitable /ɪnˈdɒmətəbəl/ *adj.* that cannot be subdued or overcome, as persons, pride, courage, etc.

indoor /ˈɪndɔ/ *adj.* occurring, used, etc., in a house or building, rather than out of doors. – **indoors**, *adv.*

indubitable /ɪnˈdjubətəbəl/ *adj.* that cannot be doubted; unquestionable; certain. – **indubitably**, *adv.*

induce /ɪnˈdjus/ *v.t.,* **-duced**, **-ducing**. **1.** to lead or move by persuasion or influence, as to some action, state of mind, etc. **2.** to bring about, produce, or cause. **3.** to initiate (labour) artificially in pregnancy.

induct /ɪnˈdʌkt/ *v.t.* to lead or bring in; introduce, especially formally, as into a place, office, etc.

induction /ɪnˈdʌkʃən/ *n.* **1.** a bringing forward or adducing, as of facts, evidence, etc. **2.** the act of inducing. **3.** the act of inducting.

indulge /ɪnˈdʌldʒ/ *v.,* **-dulged**, **-dulging**. – *v.i.* **1.** to indulge oneself; yield to an inclination (often fol. by *in*). – *v.t.* **2.** to yield to, satisfy, or gratify (desires, feelings, etc.). **3.** to yield to the wishes or whims of. **4.** *Commerce* to grant an extension of time, for payment or performance, to (a person, etc.) or on (a bill, etc.) – **indulgence**, *n.* – **indulgent**, *adj.*

industrial /ɪnˈdʌstriəl/ *adj.* **1.** of or relating to, of the nature of, or resulting from industry or productive labour. **2.** having highly developed industries. **3.** relating to the workers in industries.

industrial action *n.* organised disruptive action, as a strike or go-slow, taken by a group of workers.

industrial arts *pl. n.* the skills and techniques required in industry, as technical drawing, metalwork, etc.

industrial court *n.* a court set up to hear trade and industrial disputes.

industrial design *n.* the designing of objects for manufacture.

industrialise = industrialize /ɪnˈdʌstriəlaɪz/ *v.t.,* **-lised**, **-lising**. to introduce industry into (an area) on a large scale. – **industrialisation**, *n.*

industrialist /ɪnˈdʌstriələst/ *n.* someone who conducts or owns an industrial enterprise.

industrial park *n.* an area of land planned for industry and business. Also, **industrial estate**.

industrial relations *pl. n.* **1.** the management or study of the relations between employers and employees. **2.** the relationship itself usually in a given industry, locality, etc.

industrial union *n.* **1.** a union having the right to enrol as members all of the people employed in a particular industry. **2.** a trade union, or organisation of employers, registered under the appropriate industrial legislation to give it access to industrial tribunals, etc.

industrious /ɪnˈdʌstriəs/ *adj.* hard-working; diligent.

industry /ˈɪndəstri/ *n., pl.* **-tries**. **1.** a particular branch of trade or manufacture. **2.** any large-scale business activity. **3.** manufacture or trade as a whole. **4.** assiduous activity at any work or task.

industry allowance *n.* an allowance paid to employees in a particular industry or section of a industry, to compensate them for the existence of certain unfavourable features (as intermittency of work) characteristic of the industry.

industry award *n.* an award covering all employees, whatever their classification, in a particular industry or branch of industry.

industry standard *n.* a standard which everyone involved in a particular industry agrees to adopt.

-ine[1] an adjective suffix meaning 'of or relating to', 'of the nature of', 'made of', 'like'.

-ine[2] **1.** a noun suffix denoting some action, procedure, art, place, etc., as in *discipline, doctrine, medicine, latrine*. **2.** a suffix occurring in many nouns of later formation and various meanings, as in *famine, routine*.

inebriate /ɪn'ibrieɪt/ *v.,* **-ated**, **-ating**, *adj.* – *v.t.* **1.** to make drunk; intoxicate. – *adj.* **2.** Also, **inebriated**. drunk. – **inebriety**, *n.*

ineffable /ɪn'ɛfəbəl/ *adj.* that cannot be uttered or expressed; inexpressible.

inept /ɪn'ɛpt/ *adj.* **1.** not apt, fitted, or suitable; unsuitable. **2.** absurd or foolish, as a proceeding, remark, etc. **3.** (of a person) ineffectual; useless.

inert /ɪn'ɜt/ *adj.* having no inherent power of action, motion, or resistance.

inertia /ɪn'ɜʃə/ *n.* **1.** inert condition; inactivity; sluggishness. **2.** *Physics* that tendency of matter to retain its state of rest or of uniform motion in a straight line.

inertia selling *n.* the provision of articles to people who have not asked for them, in the hope that these people, rather than refusing or returning them, will accept and pay for them.

inestimable /ɪn'ɛstəməbəl/ *adj.* that cannot be estimated, or too great to be estimated. – **inestimably**, *adv.*

inevitable /ɪn'ɛvətəbəl/ *adj.* that cannot be avoided, evaded, or escaped; certain or necessary.

inexorable /ɪn'ɛksərəbəl, ɪn'ɛgz-/ *adj.* unyielding or unalterable.

in extremis /ɪn ɛk'strimәs/ *adv.* **1.** in extremity. **2.** near death.

infallible /ɪn'fæləbəl/ *adj.* not fallible; exempt from liability to error, as persons, their judgment, pronouncements, etc.

infamous /'ɪnfəməs/ *adj.* of ill fame; having an extremely bad reputation. – **infamy**, *n.*

infant /'ɪnfənt/ *n.* **1.** a child during the earliest period of its life, or a baby. **2.** *Law* a person who is not of full age, especially someone who has not attained the age of eighteen years. **3.** anything in the first period of existence or the first stage of progress. – **infancy**, *n.*

infantile /'ɪnfəntaɪl/ *adj.* characteristic of or befitting an infant; babyish; childish.

infantry /'ɪnfəntri/ *n.* soldiers or military units that fight on foot.

infatuate /ɪn'fætʃueɪt/ *v.t.,* **-ated**, **-ating**. **1.** to affect with folly; make fatuous. **2.** to inspire or possess with a foolish or unreasoning passion, as of love. – **infatuation**, *n.*

infect /ɪn'fɛkt/ *v.t.* **1.** to impregnate (a person, organ, wound, etc.) with disease-producing germs. **2.** to taint, contaminate, or affect morally. – **infection**, *n.*

infectious /ɪn'fɛkʃəs/ *adj.* tending to spread from one to another.

infer /ɪn'fɜ/ *v.t.,* **-ferred**, **-ferring**. to derive by reasoning; conclude or judge from premises or evidence. – **inference**, *n.*

inferior /ɪn'fɪəriə/ *adj.* **1.** lower in station, rank, or degree (fol. by *to*). **2.** of comparatively low grade; poor in quality. **3.** lower in place or position. – *n.* **4.** one inferior to another or others, as in rank or merit. – **inferiority**, *n.*

inferno /ɪn'fɜnoʊ/ *n., pl.* **-nos**. hell. – **infernal**, *adj.*

infest /ɪn'fɛst/ *v.t.* to haunt or overrun in a troublesome manner. – **infestation**, *n.*

infidel /'ɪnfədɛl/ *n.* an unbeliever.

infidelity /ɪnfə'dɛləti/ *n., pl.* **-ties**. **1.** unfaithfulness. **2.** a breach of trust.

infiltrate /'ɪnfəltreɪt/ *v.,* **-trated**, **-trating**. **1.** to cause to pass in by, or as by, filtering. **2.** to join (an organisation) for the unstated purpose of influencing it; subvert.

infinite /'ɪnfənət/ *adj.* **1.** immeasurably great. **2.** unbounded or unlimited; perfect. – **infinity**, *n.*

infinitesimal /ˌɪnfɪnə'tɛzməl, -'tɛsəməl/ *adj.* indefinitely or exceedingly small.

infinitive /ɪn'fɪnətɪv/ *n. Grammar* the simple form of the verb (*come, take, eat*) used after certain other verbs (I didn't *eat*), or this simple form preceded by *to* (the **marked infinitive**) (I wanted *to come*).

infirm /ɪn'fɜm/ *adj.* **1.** feeble in body or health. **2.** not steadfast, unfaltering, or resolute, as persons, the mind, etc. – **infirmity**, *n.*

infirmary /ɪn'fɜməri/ *n., pl.* **-ries**. a place for the care of the infirm, sick, or injured.

inflame /ɪn'fleɪm/ *v.t.,* **-flamed**, **-flaming**. **1.** to set aflame or afire. **2.** to kindle or excite (passions, anger, etc.). **3.** to excite inflammation in. – **inflammatory**, *adj.*

inflammable /ɪn'flæməbəl/ *adj.* capable of being set on fire; combustible.

inflammation /ɪnflə'meɪʃən/ *n. Pathology* a reaction of the body to injurious agents, commonly characterised by heat, redness, swelling, pain, etc., and disturbed function.

inflate /ɪn'fleɪt/ *v.,* **-flated**, **-flating**. – *v.t.* **1.** to distend; swell or puff out. **2.** to distend with gas. **3.** to puff up with pride, satisfaction, etc. **4.** to expand (currency, prices, etc.) unduly; raise above the previous or proper amount or value. – *v.i.* **5.** to cause inflation. **6.** to become inflated.

inflation /ɪn'fleɪʃən/ *n.* **1.** undue expansion or increase of the currency of a country, especially by the issuing of paper money not redeemable in specie. **2.** a substantial rise of prices caused by an undue expansion in paper money or bank credit, or because demand exceeds supply. **3.** the act of inflating. **4.** the state of being inflated. – **inflationary**, *adj.*

inflationary spiral *n.* the situation in which increasing prices lead to increasing wages which lead to increasing prices, and so on.

inflationism /ɪn'fleɪʃənɪzəm/ *n.* the policy or practice of inflation through expansion of currency or bank deposits.

inflection = inflexion /ɪn'flɛkʃən/ *n.* **1.** modulation of the voice; change in pitch or tone of voice. **2.** *Grammar* a change in the form of a word, generally by affixation, by means of which a change of meaning or relationship to some other word or group of words is indicated. **3.** a bend or angle. – **inflect**, *v.*

inflict /ɪn'flɪkt/ *v.t.* **1.** to impose as something that must be borne or suffered. **2.** to impose (anything unwelcome). – **infliction**, *n.*

inflorescence /inflə'rɛsəns/ *n.* **1.** a flowering or blossoming. **2.** the arrangement of flowers on the axis.

influence /'ɪnfluəns/ *n., v.,* **-enced**, **-encing**. – *n.* **1.** invisible or insensible action exerted by one thing or person on another. **2.** power of producing effects by invisible or insensible means. **3.** a thing or person that exerts action by invisible or insensible means. – *v.t.* **4.** to exercise influence on; modify, affect, or sway. – **influential**, *adj.*

influenza /ɪnflu'ɛnzə/ *n. Pathology* an acute, contagious, viral disease marked usually by nasal catarrh and bronchial inflammation.

influx /'ɪnflʌks/ *n.* the act of flowing in; an inflow.

inform /ɪn'fɔm/ *v.t.* **1.** to impart knowledge of a fact or circumstance to. **2.** to animate or inspire. – *v.i.* **3.** to give information, especially to furnish incriminating evidence to a prosecuting officer. – **informant**, *n.*

informal /ɪn'fɔməl/ *adj.* **1.** not according to prescribed or customary forms; irregular. **2.** without formality; unceremonious. **3.** (of a vote) invalid because not correctly marked on the ballot paper, etc. – **informality**, *n.*

information /ɪnfə'meɪʃən/ *n.* knowledge communicated or received concerning some fact or circumstance; news. – **informative**, *adj.*

information retrieval *n.* the recovering of specific information from data stored in a computer.

information science *n.* the study of the collection, organisation, and communication of data, usually with computers.

information superhighway /'supəhaɪweɪ/ *n.* the system of information exchange via computer expected to revolutionise learning, commerce, and entertainment.

information theory *n.* the theory of coding and transmitting messages over communication channels subject to interference.

infotainment /ɪnfoʊ'teɪnmənt/ *n.* a program on television, etc., which presents factual information in a format designed primarily to entertain.

infra /'ɪnfrə/ *adv.* (in a text) below. Cf. **supra**.

infra- a prefix meaning 'below' or 'beneath'.

infract /ɪn'frækt/ *v.t.* to infringe.

infra-red /ɪnfrə-'rɛd/ *n.* the part of the invisible spectrum contiguous to the red end of the visible spectrum, comprising radiation of greater wavelength than that of red light.

infrastructure /'ɪnfrəstrʌktʃə/ *n.* **1.** the basic framework or underlying foundation (as of an organisation or a system). **2.** the buildings or permanent installations associated with an organisation, operation, etc.

infringe /ɪn'frɪndʒ/ *v.,* **-fringed**, **-fringing**. – *v.t.* **1.** to violate or transgress. – *v.i.* **2.** to encroach or trespass (fol. by *on* or *upon*). – **infringement**, *n.*

infuriate /ɪn'fjurieɪt/ *v.t.,* **-ated**, **-ating**. to make furious; enrage.

infuse /ɪn'fjuz/ *v.t.,* **-fused**, **-fusing**. **1.** to introduce as by pouring; cause to penetrate; instil (fol. by *into*). **2.** to steep or soak in a liquid to extract soluble properties or ingredients. – **infusion**, *n.*

-ing[1] a suffix of nouns formed from verbs, expressing the action of the verb or its result, product, material, etc., as in *the art of building, a new building*. It is also used to form nouns from words other than verbs, as in *offing*.

-ing[2] a suffix forming the present participle of verbs, such participles often being used as adjectives (participial adjectives), as in *warring factions*. Cf. **-ing**[1].

ingenious /ɪn'dʒiniəs/ *adj.* **1.** (of things, actions, etc.) showing cleverness of invention or construction. **2.** having inventive faculty; skilful in contriving or constructing. – **ingenious**, *n.*

ingenuous /ɪn'dʒɛnjuəs/ *adj.* artless; innocent.

ingest /ɪn'dʒɛst/ *v.t. Physiology* to put or take (food, etc.) into the body. – **ingestion**, *n.* – **ingestive**, *adj.*

ingot /'ɪŋgət/ *n.* the casting obtained when melted metal is poured into a mould.

ingrain /ɪn'greɪn/ *v.t.* to fix deeply and firmly, as in the nature or mind.

ingrate /'ɪngreɪt/ *n.* **1.** an ungrateful person. – *adj.* **2.** ungrateful.

ingratiate /ɪn'greɪʃieɪt/ *v.t.,* **-ated**, **-ating**. to establish (oneself) in the favour or good graces of others.

ingratitude /ɪn'grætətʃud/ *n.* the state of being ungrateful; unthankfulness.

ingredient /ɪn'gridiənt/ *n.* something that enters as an element into a mixture.

ingress /'ɪngrɛs/ *n.* **1.** the act of going in or entering. **2.** the right of going in. **3.** a means or place of going in.

inhabit /ɪn'hæbət/ *v.t.* to live or dwell in (a place), as persons or animals. – **inhabitant**, *n.*

inhale /ɪn'heɪl/ *v.t., v.i.,* **-haled**, **-haling**. to breathe in. – **inhalation**, *n.*

inherent /ɪn'hɛrənt, ɪn'hɪərənt/ *adj.* existing in something as a permanent and inseparable element, quality, or attribute. – **inhere**, *v.* – **inherence**, *n.*

inherit /ɪn'hɛrət/ *v.t.* **1.** to take or receive (property, a right, a title, etc.) as the heir of the former owner. **2.** to possess as a hereditary characteristic. – *v.i.* **3.** to have succession as heir. – **inheritance**, *n.* – **inheritor**, *n.* – **inheritress**, **inheritrix**, *fem. n.*

inhesion /ɪn'hiʒən/ *n.* inherence.

inhibit /ɪn'hɪbət/ *v.t.* to restrain, hinder, arrest, or check (an action, impulse, etc.). – **inhibition**, *n.*

inhume /ɪn'hjum/ *v.t.,* **-humed**, **-huming**. to bury; inter. – **inhumation**, *n.*

inimical /ɪ'nɪmɪkəl/ *adj.* **1.** adverse in tendency or effect. **2.** unfriendly or hostile. – **inimicality**, *n.*

inimitable /ɪ'nɪmɪtəbəl/ *adj.* incapable of being imitated; surpassing imitation.

iniquity /ɪ'nɪkwəti/ *n., pl.* **-ties**. gross injustice; wickedness. – **iniquitous**, *adj.*

initial /ɪ'nɪʃəl/ *adj., n., v.,* **-ialled**, **-ialling**. – *adj.* **1.** of or relating to the beginning; incipient. – *n.* **2.** an initial letter, as of a word. – *v.t.* **3.** to mark or sign with an initial or initials, especially as an indication of responsibility for or approval of the contents.

initiate /ɪ'nɪʃieɪt/ *v.t.*, **-ated**, **-ating**. **1.** to begin, set going, or originate. **2.** to introduce into the knowledge of some art or subject. **3.** to admit with formal rites into secret knowledge, a society, etc. – **initiation**, *n.*

initiative /ɪ'nɪʃiətɪv/ *n.* **1.** an introductory act or step; leading action. **2.** readiness and ability in initiating action; enterprise.

inject /ɪn'dʒɛkt/ *v.t.* **1.** to force (a fluid) into a passage, cavity, or tissue. **2.** to introduce (something new or different) into a thing. – **injection**, *n.*

injunction /ɪn'dʒʌŋkʃən/ *n. Law* a judicial process or order requiring the person or persons to whom it is directed to do or (more commonly) not to do a particular thing.

injure /'ɪndʒə/ *v.t.*, **-jured**, **-juring**. **1.** to do or cause harm of any kind to; damage; hurt; impair. **2.** to do wrong or injustice to. – **injurious**, *adj.* – **injury**, *n.*

injustice /ɪn'dʒʌstəs/ *n.* **1.** the quality or fact of being unjust. **2.** unjust action or treatment; violation of another's rights.

ink /ɪŋk/ *n.* a fluid or viscous substance used for writing or printing.

inkling /'ɪŋklɪŋ/ *n.* a hint, intimation, or slight suggestion.

inland /'ɪnlænd/ *adj.* **1.** relating to or situated in the interior part of a country or region. – *adv.* **2.** in or towards the interior of a country. – *n.* **3.** the interior part of a country, away from the border.

in-law /'ɪn-lɔ/ *n.* a relative by marriage.

inlay /ɪn'leɪ/ *v.t.*, **-laid**, **-laying**. to decorate (an object) with veneers of fine materials set in its surface.

inlet /'ɪnlət/ *n.*, **-let**, **-letting**. an indentation of a shore line, usually long and narrow, or a narrow passage between islands.

inmate /'ɪnmeɪt/ *n.* one of those confined in a hospital, prison, etc.

inn /ɪn/ *n.* a small hotel that provides lodging, food, etc., for travellers and others.

innards /'ɪnədz/ *pl. n.* the inward parts of the body; entrails; viscera.

innate /ɪn'eɪt/ *adj.* **1.** inborn; existing or as if existing in one from birth. **2.** inherent.

inner /'ɪnə/ *adj.* **1.** situated farther within; interior. **2.** mental or spiritual.

innings /'ɪnɪŋz/ *pl. n.* **1.** (*construed as sing.*) *Cricket* **a.** the turn of any one member of the batting team to bat. **b.** one of the major divisions of a match. **2.** any opportunity for some activity; a turn.

innocent /'ɪnəsənt/ *adj.* **1.** free from any moral wrong; not tainted with sin; pure. **2.** free from legal or specific wrong; guiltless. **3.** free from any quality that can cause physical or moral injury; harmless. – *n.* **4.** an innocent person. – **innocence**, *n.*

innocuous /ɪn'ɒkjuəs/ *adj.* harmless.

innovate /'ɪnəveɪt/ *v.t.*, **-vated**, **-vating**. to bring in (something new) for the first time. – **innovative**, *adj.* – **innovation**, *n.* – **innovator**, *n.*

innuendo /ɪnju'ɛndoʊ/ *n.*, *pl.* **-dos**, **-does**. an indirect intimation about a person or thing, especially of a derogatory nature.

innumerable /ɪ'njumərəbəl, ɪ'njumrəbəl/ *adj.* **1.** very numerous. **2.** incapable of being numbered or definitely counted.

inoculate /ɪ'nɒkjuleɪt/ *v.t.*, **-lated**, **-lating**. to implant (a disease) in a person or animal by the introduction of germs or virus, as through a puncture, in order to produce a mild form of the disease and thus secure immunity. – **inoculation**, *n.*

inopportune /ɪn'ɒpətʃun/ *adj.* not opportune; inappropriate; untimely.

inordinate /ɪn'ɔdənət/ *adj.* not within proper limits; excessive.

inorganic /'ɪnɔgænɪk/ *adj.* **1.** not having the organisation which characterises living bodies. **2.** *Chemistry* denoting or relating to compounds not containing carbon, excepting cyanides and carbonates. Cf. **organic** (def. 1).

in-patient /'ɪn-peɪʃənt/ *n.* a patient who is staying in a hospital.

input /'ɪnpʊt/ *n.* **1.** that which is put in. **2.** *Computers* information which is fed into a computer before computation.

inquest /'ɪnkwɛst/ *n.* **1.** a legal or judicial inquiry, especially before a jury. **2.** such an inquiry made by a coroner (**coroner's inquest**).

inquire /ɪn'kwaɪə/ *v.i.*, **-quired**, **-quiring**. to seek information by questioning; ask. Also, **enquire**. – **inquiry**, *n.*

inquisition /ɪnkwə'zɪʃən/ *n.* **1.** the act of inquiring; inquiry; research. **2.** an investigation, or process of inquiry. – **inquisator**, *n.* – **inquisatorial**, *adj.*

inquisitive /ɪn'kwɪzətɪv/ *adj.* **1.** unduly curious; prying. **2.** inquiring; desirous of or eager for knowledge.

inroad /'ɪnroʊd/ *n.* forcible or serious encroachment.

insane /ɪn'seɪn/ *adj.* **1.** not sane; not of sound mind; mentally deranged. **2.** set apart for the care and confinement of mentally deranged persons. **3.** utterly senseless. **4.** *Colloquial* fantastic; wonderful. – **insanity**, *n.*

insatiable /ɪn'seɪʃəbəl/ *adj.* not satiable; incapable of being satisfied.

inscribe /ɪn'skraɪb/ *v.t.*, **-scribed**, **-scribing**. **1.** to write or engrave (words, characters, etc.). **2.** to mark (a surface) with words, characters, etc., especially in a durable or conspicuous way. **3.** to address or dedicate (a book, photograph, etc.) informally, especially by a handwritten note. **4.** to enrol, as on an official list. – **inscription**, *n.*

inscrutable /in'skrutəbəl/ *adj.* not easily understood; mysterious.

insect /'ɪnsɛkt/ *n. Zoology* a small, air-breathing arthropod with a body clearly divided into three parts, and with three pairs of legs, and usually two pairs of wings.

insecticide /ɪn'sɛktəsaɪd/ *n.* a substance or preparation used for killing insects.

insectivorous /ɪnsɛk'tɪvərəs/ *adj.* adapted to feeding on insects.

insecure /ɪnsə'kjuə/ *adj.* **1.** exposed to danger; unsafe. **2.** not firm or safe. **3.** not free from fear, doubt, etc. – **insecurity**, *n.*

inseminate /ɪn'sɛməneɪt/ *v.t.*, **-nated**, **-nating**. to introduce semen into (a female) to cause fertilisation; impregnate. – **insem-**

ination, *n.*

insensible /ɪn'sɛnsəbəl/ *adj.* incapable of feeling or perceiving; deprived of sensation; unconscious, as a person after a violent blow.

insert /ɪn'sɜt/ *v.*, /'ɪnsɜt/ *n.* – *v.t.* **1.** to put or set in. **2.** to introduce into the body of something. – *n.* **3.** something inserted, or to be inserted. – **insertion**, *n.*

inset /'ɪnsɛt/ *n.*, /ɪn'sɛt/ *v.*, **-set**, **-setting**. – *n.* **1.** something inserted; an insert. – *v.t.* **2.** to set in; insert.

inside /ɪn'saɪd/ *prep., adv.*; /'ɪnsaɪd/ *n., adj.* – *prep.* **1.** on the inner side of; within. **2.** before the elapse of. – *adv.* **3.** in or into the inner part. **4.** indoors. **5.** by nature; fundamentally. – *n.* **6.** the inner part; interior. – *adj.* **7.** situated or being on or in the inside; interior.

insider /ɪn'saɪdə/ *n.* **1.** one who is inside some place, society, etc. **2.** *Colloquial* one who is within a limited circle of persons who understand the actual facts of a case.

insider trading *n.* the statutory offence of dealing in a company's securities by someone who through some connection has special information which would materially affect the price of the securities if it were generally known.

insidious /ɪn'sɪdiəs/ *adj.* stealthily treacherous or deceitful.

insight /'ɪnsaɪt/ *n.* **1.** an understanding gained or given of something. **2.** penetrating mental vision or discernment; faculty of seeing into inner character or underlying truth.

insignia /ɪn'sɪgniə/ *n., pl.* **insignia**, **insignias**. a badge or distinguishing mark of office or honour.

insinuate /ɪn'sɪnjueɪt/ *v.t.*, **-ated**, **-ating**. **1.** to suggest or hint slyly. **2.** instil or infuse subtly or artfully into the mind. **3.** to bring or introduce into a position or relation by indirect or artful methods. – **insinuation**, *n.*

insipid /ɪn'sɪpəd/ *adj.* without distinctive, interesting, or attractive qualities.

insist /ɪn'sɪst/ *v.i.* **1.** to be emphatic, firm, or pertinacious on some matter of desire, demand, intention, etc. **2.** to lay emphasis in assertion (fol. by *on*). **3.** to assert or maintain positively (fol. by *on*). – **insistent**, *adj.*

in situ /ɪn 'sɪtʃu/ *adv.* in the original, actual or appropriate place.

insolent /'ɪnsələnt/ *adj.* boldly rude or disrespectful; contemptuously impertinent; insulting. – **insolence**, *n.*

insomnia /ɪn'sɒmniə/ *n.* inability to sleep, especially when chronic. – **insomniac**, *n.* – **insomnious**, *adj.*

inspect /ɪn'spɛkt/ *v.t.* **1.** to look carefully at or over. **2.** to examine officially. – **inspection**, *n.* – **inspector**, *n.*

inspire /ɪn'spaɪə/ *v.t.*, **-spired**, **-spiring**. **1.** to infuse an animating, quickening, or exalting influence into. **2.** to produce or arouse (a feeling, thought, etc.). **3.** to give rise to, occasion, or cause. **4.** to take (air, gases, etc.) into the lungs in breathing; inhale. – **inspiration**, *n.*

inspirit /ɪn'spɪrət/ *v.t.* to infuse (new) spirit or life into.

install /ɪn'stɔl/ *v.t.* **1.** to place in position for service or use, as a system of electric lighting, etc. **2.** to establish in any office, position, or place. – **installation**, *n.*

instalment /ɪn'stɔlmənt/ *n.* **1.** any of several parts into which a debt is divided for payment. **2.** a single portion of something furnished or issued by parts at successive times.

instance /'ɪnstəns/ *n., v.*, **-stanced**, **-stancing**. – *n.* **1.** a case of anything. **2.** an example put forth in proof or illustration. – *v.t.* **3.** to cite as an instance or example.

instant /'ɪnstənt/ *n.* **1.** an infinitesimal or very short space of time; a moment. **2.** a particular moment. – *adj.* **3.** succeeding without any interval of time; immediate. **4.** (of a foodstuff) processed for immediate and simple preparation, as by adding water. – **instancy**, *n.*

instantaneous /ɪnstən'teɪniəs/ *adj.* occurring, done, or completed in an instant.

instead /ɪn'stɛd/ *adv.* **1.** in the stead or place; in lieu (fol. by *of*). **2.** in one's (its, their, etc.) stead.

instep /'ɪnstɛp/ *n.* the arched upper surface of the human foot between the toes and the ankle.

instigate /'ɪnstəgeɪt/ *v.t.*, **-gated**, **-gating**. to spur on, set on, or incite to some action or course. – **instigation**, *n.*

instil /ɪn'stɪl/ *v.t.*, **-stilled**, **-stilling**. to infuse slowly or by degrees into the mind or feelings; insinuate; inject.

instinct /'ɪnstɪŋkt/ *n.* **1.** innate impulse or natural inclination, or a particular natural inclination or tendency. **2.** a natural aptitude or gift for something. **3.** natural intuitive power. – **instinctive**, *adj.*

institute /'ɪnstətʃut/ *v.*, **-tuted**, **-tuting**, *n.* – *v.t.* **1.** to set up or establish. **2.** to set in operation. **3.** to establish in an office or position. – *n.* **4.** a society or organisation for carrying on a particular work, as of literary, scientific, or educational character.

institution /ɪnstə'tjuʃən/ *n.* **1.** an organisation or establishment for the promotion of a particular object, usually one for some public, educational, charitable, or similar purpose. **2.** any established law, custom, etc. **3.** the act of instituting or setting up; establishment.

institutional /ɪnstə'tjuʃənəl/ *adj.* **1.** of, relating to, or established by institution. **2.** of the nature of an institution. **3.** characterised by uniformity and dullness.

institutionalise = institutionalize /ɪnstə'tjuʃənəlaɪz/ *v.t.*, **-lised**, **-lising**. to make (a person) dependent on an institution, as a prison, mental hospital, etc., to the point where he or she cannot live successfully outside it.

instruct /ɪn'strʌkt/ *v.t.* **1.** to direct or command; furnish with orders or directions. **2.** to furnish with knowledge, especially by a systematic method; teach; train; educate. **3.** to furnish with information; inform or apprise. – **instructive**, *adj.* – **instructor**, *n.*

instruction /ɪn'strʌkʃən/ *n.* **1.** the act or practice of instructing or teaching; education. **2.** (*usu. pl.*) an order or direction. **3.** *Computers* a number or symbol which causes a computer to perform some specified action.

instrument /'ɪnstrəmənt/ *n.* **1.** a tool or implement. **2.** a contrivance for producing musical sounds. **3.** a thing with or by which something is effected; a means; an agency. **4.** a legal document. **5.** a device for measuring the present value of a quantity under observation. – **instrumental**, *adj.*

insubordinate /ɪnsə'bɔdənət/ *adj.* disobedient; rebellious. – **insubordination**, *n.*

insufferable /ɪn'sʌfərəbəl, -frəbəl/ *adj.* not to be endured; intolerable; unbearable.

insular /'ɪnsjulə, 'ɪnʃulə/ *adj.* **1.** of or relating to an island or islands. **2.** detached; standing alone. **3.** narrow or illiberal. – **insularity**, *n.*

insulate /'ɪnʃuleɪt/ *v.t.*, **-lated**, **-lating**. **1.** to cover or surround (an electric wire, etc.) with non-conducting material. **2.** to place in an isolated situation or condition; segregate. **3.** to install an insulating material in the roof of (a house), to retain warmth in winter and keep out heat in summer. – **insulation**, *n.* – **insulator**, *n.*

insulin /'ɪnʃələn, -sjələn, -sələn/ *n.* a hormone produced in the pancreas, a deficiency of which produces diabetes.

insult /ɪn'sʌlt/ *v.*, /'ɪnsʌlt/ *n.* – *v.t.* **1.** to treat insolently or with contemptuous rudeness; affront. – *n.* **2.** an insolent or contemptuously rude action or speech; affront.

insuperable /ɪn'supərəbəl, -prəbəl, -'sju-/ *adj.* incapable of being passed over, overcome, or surmounted.

insurance /ɪn'ʃɔrəns, -'ʃʊə-/ *n.* the act, system, or business of insuring property, life, the person, etc., against loss or harm arising in specified contingencies, as fire, accident, death, disablement, or the like, in consideration of a payment proportionate to the risk involved.

insure /ɪn'ʃɔ, '-ʃʊə/ *v.t.*, **-sured**, **-suring**. **1.** to guarantee against risk of loss or harm. **2.** to secure indemnity to or on, in case of loss, damage, or death. **3.** to issue or procure an insurance policy on.

insured /ɪn'ʃɔd, ɪn'ʃʊəd/ *n.* a person covered by an insurance policy.

insurer /ɪn'ʃɔrə, -'ʃʊə-/ *n.* **1.** one who or that which contracts to indemnify against losses, etc., such as an insurance company. **2.** a person who seeks some sort of protection by taking out insurance.

insurgent /ɪn'sɜdʒənt/ *n.* **1.** someone who rises in forcible opposition to lawful authority. – *adj.* **2.** rising in revolt; rebellious.

insurrection /ɪnsə'rɛkʃən/ *n.* the act of rising in arms or open resistance against civil or established authority.

intact /ɪn'tækt/ *adj.* remaining uninjured, unaltered, sound, or whole; unimpaired.

intake /'ɪnteɪk/ *n.* **1.** the act of taking in. **2.** that which is taken in.

integer /'ɪntədʒə/ *n.* **1.** Also, **positive integer**. a whole number. **2.** a complete entity.

integral /'ɪntəgrəl/ *adj.* of or relating to a whole; belonging as a part of the whole; constituent or component.

integrate /'ɪntəgreɪt/ *v.t.*, **-grated**, **-grating**. **1.** to bring together (parts) into a whole. **2.** to amalgamate (a racial or religious minority group) with the rest of the community. – **integration**, *n.*

integrated circuit *n.* an array of interconnected circuit elements integrated with or deposited on a single semiconductor base.

integrity /ɪn'tɛgrəti/ *n.* **1.** soundness of moral principle and character; uprightness; honesty. **2.** sound, unimpaired, or perfect condition.

integument /ɪn'tɛgjumənt/ *n.* **1.** a skin, shell, rind, or the like. **2.** a covering.

intellect /'ɪntəlɛkt/ *n.* the power or faculty of the mind by which one knows, understands, or reasons.

intellectual /ɪntə'lɛktʃuəl/ *adj.* **1.** of, appealing to or engaging the intellect. **2.** possessing or showing intellect or mental capacity, especially to a high degree. – *n.* **3.** an intellectual being or person.

intelligence /ɪn'tɛlədʒəns/ *n.* **1.** aptitude in grasping truths, facts, meaning, etc. **2.** good mental capacity. **3.** knowledge of an event, circumstance, etc., received or imparted; news; information. **4.** the gathering or distribution of information, especially secret information which might prove detrimental to an enemy. **5.** the capacity which a computerised machine derives from programs built into it to recognise specified conditions and perform nonconstant functions independently of an operator. – **intelligent**, *adj.*

intelligentsia /ɪn,tɛlə'dʒɛntsiə/ *pl. n.* a class or group of persons having or claiming special enlightenment in views or principles; the intellectuals.

intelligible /ɪn'tɛlədʒəbəl/ *adj.* capable of being understood; comprehensible.

intemperate /ɪn'tɛmpərət, -prət/ *adj.* **1.** given to or characterised by immoderate indulgence in intoxicating drink. **2.** not temperate; unrestrained or unbridled. – **intemperance**, *n.*

intend /ɪn'tɛnd/ *v.t.* to have in mind as something to be done or brought about.

intense /ɪn'tɛns/ *adj.* **1.** of an extreme kind; very great, strong, keen, severe, etc. **2.** having or showing great strength or vehemence of feeling, as a person, the face, language, etc. – **intensify**, *v.*

intensifier /ɪn'tɛnsəfaɪə/ *n. Grammar* a linguistic element or word which increases the semantic effect of a word or phrase but has itself minimal semantic content, as *very*.

intensity /ɪn'tɛnsəti/ *n., pl.* **-ties**. **1.** the quality or condition of being intense. **2.** the degree or extent to which something is intense.

intensive /ɪn'tɛnsɪv/ *adj.* **1.** of, relating to, or characterised by intensity. **2.** *Economics* of or denoting methods designed to increase effectiveness, as, in agriculture.

intensive care *n.* medical therapy for the critically ill, usually given under hospital supervision and for a short period of time.

intent[1] /ɪn'tɛnt/ *n.* that which is intended; purpose; aim; design; intention.

intent[2] /ɪn'tɛnt/ *adj.* firmly or steadfastly fixed or directed (upon something).

intention /ɪn'tɛnʃən/ *n.* the act of determining mentally upon some action or result; a purpose or design. – **intentional**, *adj.*

inter /ɪn'tɜ/ *v.t.*, **-terred**, **-terring**. to deposit (a dead body, etc.) in a grave or tomb; bury, especially with ceremonies.

inter- a prefix meaning 'between', 'among', 'mutually', 'reciprocally', 'together', as in *interlope*, *intermarry*.

interact /ɪntər'ækt/ *v.i.* to act on each other. – **interaction**, *n.*

interactive /ɪntər'æktɪv/ *adj.* **1.** of or relating to things or persons which act on each other. **2.** *Computers* (of systems, etc.) immediately responsive to commands, data, etc., as opposed to systems arranged for batch processing.

inter alia /ɪntər 'eɪliə/ *adv.* among other things.

intercede /ɪntə'sid/ *v.i.*, **-ceded**, **-ceding**. to interpose on behalf of one in difficulty or trouble, as by pleading or petition. – **intercession**, *n.*

intercept /ɪntə'sɛpt/ *v.t.* **1.** to take or seize on the way from one place to another; cut off from the intended destination. **2.** to stop or check (passage, etc.).

interchange /ɪntə'tʃeɪndʒ/ *v.*, **-changed**, **-changing**, /'ɪntətʃeɪndʒ/ *n.* – *v.t.* **1.** to put each of (two things) in the place of the other. – *v.i.* **2.** to change places, as two persons or things, or as one with another. – *n.* **3.** the act of interchanging; reciprocal exchange.

intercom /'ɪntəkɒm/ *n.* an intercommunication system.

intercommunication system *n.* an internal or closed audio system, as within an office complex, school, ship, etc.

inter-company market *n.* the section of the money market which deals with loans between companies.

intercourse /'ɪntəkɔs/ *n.* **1.** dealings or communication between individuals. **2.** interchange of thoughts, feelings, etc. **3.** sexual intercourse.

interdict /'ɪntədɪkt, -daɪt/ *n.*, /ɪntə'dɪkt, -'daɪt/ *v.* – *n.* **1.** *Civil Law* any prohibitory act or decree of a court or an administrative officer. – *v.t.* **2.** to forbid; prohibit. – **interdictory**, *adj.* – **interdiction**, *n.*

interest /'ɪntrəst, -tərəst/ *n.* **1.** the feeling of one whose attention or curiosity is particularly engaged by something. **2.** the power of exciting such feeling; interesting quality. **3.** a share in the ownership of property, in a commercial or financial undertaking, or the like. **4.** any right of ownership in property, commercial undertakings, etc. **5.** something in which one has an interest, as of ownership, advantage, attention, etc. **6.** benefit or advantage. **7.** *Commerce* **a.** payment, or a sum paid, for the use of money borrowed (the principal), or for the forbearance of a debt. **b.** the rate per cent per unit of time represented by such payments. – *v.t.* **8.** to engage or excite the attention or curiosity of.

interface /'ɪntəfeɪs/ *n.* **1.** a surface regarded as the common boundary to two bodies or spaces. **2.** the point or area at which any two systems or disciplines interact.

interfere /ɪntə'fɪə/ *v.i.*, **-fered**, **-fering**. **1.** to clash; come into collision; be in opposition. **2.** to interpose or intervene for a particular purpose. **3.** to take a part in the affairs of others; meddle.

interference /ɪntə'fɪərəns/ *n.* **1.** the act or fact of interfering. **2.** *Radio* the jumbling of radio signals by receiving signals other than the desired ones.

interim /'ɪntərəm/ *n.* **1.** an intervening time; the meantime. – *adj.* **2.** belonging to or connected with an intervening period of time.

interior /ɪn'tɪəriə/ *adj.* **1.** being within; inside of anything; internal; farther towards a centre. **2.** relating to the inland. **3.** inner, private, or secret. – *n.* **4.** the internal part; the inside. **5.** the inland parts of a region, country, etc.

interject /ɪntə'dʒɛkt/ *v.t.* to interpolate; interpose.

interjection /ɪntə'dʒɛkʃən/ *n.* **1.** the utterance of ejaculations expressive of emotion; an ejaculation or exclamation. **2.** something, as a remark, interjected. **3.** *Grammar* **a.** (in many languages) a form class, or 'part of speech', comprising words which constitute utterances or clauses in themselves, without grammatical connection. **b.** such a word, as English *ouch!*, *never!*

interlace /ɪntə'leɪs/ *v.t.*, **-laced**, **-lacing**. **1.** to dispose (threads, strips, parts, branches, etc.) so as to intercross one another, passing alternately over and under. **2.** to mingle; blend.

interlock /ɪntə'lɒk/ *v.*, /'ɪntəlɒk/ *n.* – *v.i.* **1.** to engage with each other. **2.** to fit into each other, as parts of machinery, so that all action is simultaneous. – *v.t.* **3.** to lock one with another. **4.** to fit the parts of (something) together so that all must move together, or in the same way. – *n.* **5.** *Textiles* a smooth knitted fabric, especially one made of cotton yarn. – **interlocker**, *n.*

interlocutor /ɪntə'lɒkjətə/ *n.* someone who takes part in a conversation or dialogue. – **interlocutory**, *adj.* – **interlocution**, *n.*

interlope /'ɪntəloʊp/ *v.i.*, **-loped**, **-loping**. to intrude into the affairs of others.

interlude /'ɪntəlud/ *n.* **1.** an intervening episode, period, space, etc. **2.** a period of inactivity; lull.

intermarry /ɪntə'mæri/ *v.i.*, **-ried**, **-rying**. **1.** to become connected by marriage, as two families, tribes, castes, or races. **2.** to marry within the limits of the family or of near relationship.

intermediate[1] /ɪntə'midiət, -dʒət/ *adj.* being, situated, or acting between two points, stages, things, persons, etc. – **intermediary**, *n.*

intermediate[2] /ɪntə'midieɪt/ *v.i.*, **-ated**, **-ating**. to act as an intermediary; intervene; mediate. – **intermediation**, *n.* – **intermediator**, *n.*

interminable /ɪn'tɜmənəbəl/ *adj.* that cannot be terminated; unending.

interminable debt *n.* a debt without maturity date.

intermission /ɪntə'mɪʃən/ *n.* an interval, especially in the cinema.

intermit /ɪntə'mɪt/ *v.t.*, **-mitted**, **-mitting**. to discontinue temporarily; suspend.

intermittent /ɪntə'mɪtənt/ *adj.* alternately ceasing and beginning again.

intern[1] /ɪn'tɜn/ *v.t.* to oblige to reside within

prescribed limits under prohibition to leave them.

intern[2] /ˈɪntɜn/ *n.* a resident member of the medical staff of a hospital, usually a recent graduate still in partial training.

internal /ɪnˈtɜnəl/ *adj.* **1.** situated or existing in the interior of something; interior. **2.** of or relating to the inside or inner part. **3.** existing or occurring within a country; domestic.

internal-combustion engine *n.* an engine of one or more working cylinders in which the process of combustion takes place within the cylinder.

international /ɪntəˈnæʃnəl/ *adj.* **1.** between or among nations. **2.** of or relating to different nations or their citizens.

International Phonetic Alphabet *n.* an alphabet designed to provide a consistent and universally understood system of letters and other symbols for writing the speech sounds of all languages. *Abbrev.*: IPA

International System of Units *n.* an internationally recognised system of metric units, now adopted as the basis of Australia's metric system, in which the seven base units are the metre, kilogram, second, ampere, kelvin, mole and candela. *Abbrev.*: SI Also, **Système Internationale d'Unités**. See **metric system**.

internecine /ɪntəˈnisaɪn/ *adj.* mutually destructive.

Internet /ˈɪntənɛt/ *n.* **the,** the communications system created by the interconnecting networks of computers around the world. Also, **the Net**.

interpellation /ɪnˌtɜpəˈleɪʃən, ɪntəpəˈleɪʃən/ *n.* a procedure in some legislative bodies of asking a government official to explain an act or policy. – **interpellate**, *v.*

interplay /ˈɪntəpleɪ/ *n.* reciprocal play, action, or influence.

interpolate /ɪnˈtɜpəleɪt/ *v.t.*, **-lated**, **-lating**. **1.** to alter (a text, etc.) by the insertion of new matter, especially deceptively or without authorisation. **2.** to introduce (something additional or extraneous) between other things or parts. **3.** *Mathematics* to insert or find intermediate terms in (a sequence). – **interpolation**, *n.*

interpose /ɪntəˈpoʊz/ *v.*, **-posed**, **-posing**. – *v.t.* **1.** to place between; cause to intervene. **2.** to put in (a remark, etc.) in the midst of a conversation, discourse, or the like. – *v.i.* **3.** to come between other things; assume an intervening position or relation. **4.** to put in or make a remark by way of interruption.

interpret /ɪnˈtɜprət/ *v.t.* **1.** to set forth the meaning of; explain or elucidate. **2.** to explain, construe, or understand in a particular way. **3.** to translate. – **interpretation**, *n.* – **interpreter**, *n.*

interpretation section *n.* a section in a legal statute or clause in a deed setting out the meanings attached to particular words used in the instrument.

interregnum /ɪntəˈrɛgnəm/ *n.*, *pl.* **-nums**, **-na** /nə/. **1.** an interval of time between the close of a sovereign's reign and the accession of his or her normal or legitimate successor. **2.** any pause or interruption in continuity.

interrogate /ɪnˈtɛrəgeɪt/ *v.t.*, **-gated**, **-gating**. to ask a question or a series of questions of (a person), especially closely or formally. – **interrogation**, *n.*

interrogative /ɪntəˈrɒgətɪv/ *adj.* **1.** relating to or conveying a question. – *n.* **2.** *Grammar* an interrogative word, element, or construction, as *'who?'* and *'what?'*

interrogatory /ɪntəˈrɒgətri/ *adj.*, *n.*, *pl.* **-tories**. – *adj.* **1.** interrogative; questioning. – *n.* **2.** *Law* a formal or written question.

interrupt /ɪntəˈrʌpt/ *v.*, /ˈɪntərʌpt/ *n.* – *v.t.* **1.** to make a break in (an otherwise continuous extent, course, process, condition, etc.). **2.** to stop (a person) in the midst of doing or saying something, especially as by an interjected remark. – *n.* **3.** *Computers* a command causing the computer to transfer from one program to another; break-in. **4.** *Computers* such a suspension of program. – **interruption**, *n.* – **interruptive**, *adj.*

intersect /ɪntəˈsɛkt/ *v.t.* to cut or divide by passing through or lying across.

intersection /ɪntəˈsɛkʃən, ˈɪntəsɛkʃən/ *n.* **1.** the act, fact, or place of intersecting. **2.** a place where two or more roads meet.

intersperse /ɪntəˈspɜs/ *v.t.*, **-spersed**, **-spersing**. **1.** to scatter here and there among other things. **2.** to diversify with something scattered or introduced here and there. – **interspersion**, *n.*

interstate /ˈɪntəsteɪt/ *adj.*, /ɪntəˈsteɪt/ *adv.* – *adj.* **1.** between or jointly involving states. – *adv.* **2.** to or in another state. **3.** from another state. Cf. **intrastate**.

interstice /ɪnˈtɜstəs/ *n.* a small or narrow space between things or parts; small chink, crevice, or opening.

interval /ˈɪntəvəl/ *n.* **1.** an intervening period of time. **2.** a period of cessation; a pause. **3.** a space intervening between things, points, limits, qualities, etc. **4.** *Music* the difference in pitch between two notes.

intervene /ɪntəˈvin/ *v.i.*, **-vened**, **-vening**. **1.** to come between in action; intercede. **2.** to fall or happen between other events or periods. **3.** *Law* to interpose and become a party to a suit pending between other parties. – **intervention**, *n.*

interview /ˈɪntəvju/ *n.* **1.** a meeting of persons face to face, especially for formal conference in business, etc., or for radio and television entertainment, etc. – *v.t.* **2.** to have an interview with. – **interviewer**, *n.*

intestate /ɪnˈtɛsteɪt, -tət/ *adj.* (of a person) dying without having made a will. – **intestacy**, *n.*

intestine /ɪnˈtɛstən/ *n.* (*often pl.*) the lower part of the alimentary canal. – **intestinal**, *adj.*

intimate[1] /ˈɪntəmət/ *adj.* **1.** associated in close personal relations. **2.** private; closely personal. **3.** maintaining sexual relations. **4.** (of acquaintance, knowledge, etc.) arising from close personal connection or familiar experience. **5.** detailed; deep. – *n.* **6.** an intimate friend or associate. – **intimacy**, *n.*

intimate[2] /ˈɪntəmeɪt/ *v.t.*, **-mated**, **-mating**. **1.** to make known indirectly; hint. **2.** to make known, especially formally; announce. – **intimation**, *n.*

intimidate /ɪn'tɪmədeɪt/ *v.t.*, **-dated**, **-dating**. **1.** to make timid, or inspire with fear; overawe. **2.** to force into or deter from some action by inducing fear. – **intimidation**, *n.* – **intimidator**, *n.*

into /'ɪntu/, *before consonants* /'ɪntə/ – *prep.* **1.** in to; in and to (expressing motion or direction towards the inner part of a place or thing). **2.** *Mathematics* being the divisor of.

intolerable /ɪn'tɒlərəbəl/ *adj.* not tolerable, unable to be endured.

intonation /ɪntə'neɪʃən/ *n.* the pattern or melody of pitch changes revealed in connected speech.

intone /ɪn'toʊn/ *v.*, **-toned**, **-toning**. – *v.t.* **1.** to utter with a particular tone. – *v.i.* **2.** to speak or recite in a singing voice, especially in monotone.

intoxicate /ɪn'tɒksəkeɪt/ *v.*, **-cated**, **-cating**. – *v.t.* **1.** to affect temporarily with loss of control over the physical and mental powers, by means of alcoholic liquor, a drug, or other substance. **2.** to excite mentally beyond self-control or reason. – **intoxication**, *n.* – **intoxicant**, *n.*

intra- a prefix meaning 'within'.

intractable /ɪn'træktəbəl/ *adj.* not docile; stubborn.

intransigent /ɪn'trænsədʒənt/ *adj.* uncompromising, especially in politics.

intransitive verb *n.* **1.** a verb that is never accompanied by a direct object, as *come, sit, lie,* etc. **2.** a verb occurring without a direct object, as *drinks* in the sentence *he drinks only when thirsty.* Cf. **transitive verb**.

intrastate /'ɪntrəsteɪt/ *adj.* within a state.

intravenous /ɪntrə'vinəs/ *adj.* within a vein or the veins.

intrepid /ɪn'trɛpəd/ *adj.* fearless.

intricate /'ɪntrəkət/ *adj.* perplexingly entangled or involved. – **intricacy**, *n.*

intrigue /ɪn'trig/ *v.*, **-trigued**, **-triguing**, /ɪn'trig, 'ɪntrig/ *n.* – *v.t.* **1.** to excite the curiosity or interest of by puzzling, novel, or otherwise arresting qualities. – *v.i.* **2.** to use underhand machinations; plot craftily. – *n.* **3.** the use of underhand machinations to accomplish designs. **4.** a clandestine or illicit love affair.

intrinsic /ɪn'trɪnzɪk, -sɪk/ *adj.* belonging to a thing by its very nature.

intro- a prefix meaning 'inwardly', 'within'.

introduce /ɪntrə'djus/ *v.t.*, **-duced**, **-ducing**. **1.** to bring into notice, knowledge, use, vogue, etc. **2.** to bring forward with preliminary or preparatory matter. **3.** to bring (a person) to the knowledge or experience of something (fol. by *to*). **4.** to bring (a person) into the acquaintance of another. – **introductory**, *adj.*

introduction /ɪntrə'dʌkʃən/ *n.* **1.** the act of introducing. **2.** something introduced. **3.** a preliminary part, as of a book.

introspection /ɪntrə'spɛkʃən/ *n.* observation or examination of one's own mental states or processes. – **introspective**, *adj.*

introvert /'ɪntrəvɜt/ *n.*, /ɪntrə'vɜt/ *v.* – *n.* **1.** *Psychology* a person concerned chiefly with his or her own self and thoughts. – *v.t.* **2.** to turn inwards. – **introversion**, *n.*

intrude /ɪn'trud/ *v.*, **-truded**, **-truding**. – *v.t.* **1.** to thrust or bring in without reason, permission, or welcome. – *v.i.* **2.** to thrust oneself in; come uninvited. – **intrusion**, *n.* – **intrusive**, *adj.*

intuition /ɪntʃu'ɪʃən/ *n.* direct perception of truths, facts, etc., independently of any reasoning process. – **intuitive**, *adj.*

inundate /'ɪnʌndeɪt/ *v.t.*, **-dated**, **-dating**. to overspread with or as with a flood. – **inundation**, *n.*

inure /ən'juə, ɪn-/ *v.*, **inured**, **inuring**. to toughen or harden by exercise; accustom; habituate (fol. by *to*).

invade /ɪn'veɪd/ *v.t.*, **-vaded**, **-vading**. **1.** to enter as an enemy; go into with hostile intent. **2.** to intrude upon.

invalid[1] /'ɪnvəlɪd, -lid/ *n.* **1.** an infirm or sickly person. – *adj.* **2.** deficient in health; weak; sick. **3.** of or for invalids. – *v.t.* **4.** to affect with disease; make an invalid. – *v.i.* **5.** to become an invalid.

invalid[2] /ɪn'væləd/ *adj.* not valid. – **invalidity**, *n.* – **invalidate**, *v.*

invaluable /ɪn'væljəbəl/ *adj.* that cannot be valued or appraised; of inestimable value.

invasion /ɪn'veɪʒən/ *n.* **1.** the act of invading or entering as an enemy. **2.** infringement by intrusion. – **invasive**, *adj.*

invective /ɪn'vɛktɪv/ *n.* vehement denunciation; an utterance of violent censure or reproach.

inveigh /ɪn'veɪ/ *v.i.* to attack vehemently in words; rail.

inveigle /ɪn'veɪgəl/ *v.t.*, **-gled**, **-gling**. to draw by beguiling or artful inducements (fol. by *into*, sometimes *from, away,* etc.).

invent /ɪn'vɛnt/ *v.t.* to originate as a product of one's own contrivance. – **inventive**, *adj.* – **inventor**, *n.*

invention /ɪn'vɛnʃən/ *n.* **1.** the act of inventing. **2.** *Patent Law* the conception of an idea and the means or apparatus by which the result is obtained. **3.** anything invented or devised. **4.** the act of producing or creating by exercise of the imagination.

inventory /'ɪnvəntri, ɪn'vɛntəri/ *n.* **1.** a detailed descriptive list of articles, with number, quantity, and value of each. **2.** the value of a stock of goods.

inverse /ɪn'vɜs, 'ɪnvɜs/ *adj.* **1.** reversed in position, direction, or tendency. – *n.* **2.** an inverted state or condition. **3.** that which is inverse; the direct opposite.

invert /ɪn'vɜt/ *v.t.* **1.** to turn upside down, inside out, or inwards. **2.** to reverse in position, direction, or order. **3.** to turn or change to the opposite or contrary, as in nature, bearing, or effect. – **inversion**, *n.*

invertebrate /ɪn'vɜtəbrət, -breɪt/ *adj.* **1.** *Zoology* not vertebrate; without a backbone. – *n.* **2.** an invertebrate animal.

invest /ɪn'vɛst/ *v.t.* **1.** to put (money) to use, by purchase or expenditure, in something offering profitable returns, especially interest or income. **2.** to endue or endow. **3.** to install in an office or position; furnish with power, authority, rank, etc. – **investor**, *n.*

investigate /ɪn'vɛstəgeɪt/ *v.t.*, **-gated**, **-gating**. to search or inquire into; search or examine into the particulars of; examine in detail. – **investigation**, *n.* – **investiga-**

tive, *adj.*

investiture /ɪn'vɛstɪtʃə/ *n.* the formal bestowal of an office or rank, usually involving the giving of insignia.

investment /ɪn'vɛstmənt/ *n.* **1.** the investing of money or capital in order to secure profitable returns, especially interest or income. **2.** a thing invested in. **3.** that which is invested.

investment bank *n.* a private banking firm which moves or issues securities; an underwriter.

investment trust *n.* a trust whose function is the judicious buying and selling of shares of companies at the discretion of its board of management.

inveterate /ɪn'vɛtərət/ *adj.* **1.** confirmed in a habit, practice, feeling, or the like. **2.** firmly established by long continuance.

invidious /ɪn'vɪdiəs/ *adj.* such as to bring odium.

invigorate /ɪn'vɪgəreɪt/ *v.t.*, **-rated**, **-rating**. to give vigour to; fill with life and energy.

invincible /ɪn'vɪnsəbəl/ *adj.* that cannot be conquered or vanquished.

inviolable /ɪn'vaɪələbəl/ *adj.* that must not be violated; that is to be kept free from violence or violation of any kind.

inviolate /ɪn'vaɪələt, -leɪt/ *adj.* free from violation, injury, desecration, or outrage.

invisible /ɪn'vɪzəbəl/ *adj.* not visible.

invisible exports *pl. n.* services, as banking commissions, insurance premiums, freight charges, etc., which earn foreign currency for the country providing them.

invisible imports *pl. n.* activities, services incurred, etc., as holidays abroad, which spend currency in foreign countries.

invite /ɪn'vaɪt/ *v.t.*, **-vited**, **-viting**. **1.** to ask in a kindly, courteous, or complimentary way, to come or go to some place, gathering, entertainment, etc., or to do something. **2.** to act so as to bring on or render probable. – **invitation**, *n.*

in vitro /ɪn 'vɪtroʊ/ *adv., adj.* in an artificial environment, as a test tube.

in-vitro fertilisation /ɪn-'vɪtroʊ/ *n.* the fertilisation of an ovum by a sperm in a test tube, the resulting embryo to be implanted in a uterus. *Abbrev.*: IVF

invoice /'ɪnvɔɪs/ *n., v.*, **-voiced**, **-voicing**. – *n.* **1.** a written list of merchandise, with prices, delivered or sent to a buyer. **2.** an itemised bill containing the prices which comprise the total charge. – *v.t.* **3.** to present an invoice to (a customer, etc.).

invoke /ɪn'voʊk/ *v.t.*, **-voked**, **-voking**. **1.** to call for with earnest desire; make supplication or prayer for. **2.** to call on (a divine being, etc.), as in prayer. – **invocation**, *n.*

involuntary /ɪn'vɒləntri/ *adj.* acting, done or made without one's own volition or choice.

involve /ɪn'vɒlv/ *v.t.*, **-volved**, **-volving**. **1.** to include as a necessary circumstance, condition, or consequence; imply; entail. **2.** to include, contain, or comprehend within itself or its scope. **3.** to bring into an intricate or complicated form or condition. **4.** to implicate, as in guilt or crime, or in any matter or affair. **5.** (usually in passive) to concern or interest, especially excessively.

inward /'ɪnwəd/ *adj.* **1.** proceeding or directed towards the inside or interior. **2.** situated within; interior, internal. **3.** relating to the inside or inner part. – *adv.* **4.** inwards.

inwards /'ɪnwədz/ *adv.* towards the inside or interior, as of a place, a space, or a body.

iodine /'aɪədin, 'aɪədaɪn/ *n.* a non-metallic element used in medicine as an antiseptic. *Symbol*: I

iodo- a word element meaning 'iodine'.

ion /'aɪən/ *n.* *Chemistry* an electrically charged atom, radical, or molecule, formed by the loss or gain of one or more electrons. **Positive ions**, created by electron loss, are called *cations* and are attracted to the cathode in electrolysis. **Negative ions**, created by electron gain, are called *anions* and are attracted to the anode.

-ion a suffix of nouns denoting action or process, state or condition, or sometimes things or persons. Cf. **-cion**, **-xion**. Also, **-tion** and **-ation**.

iota /aɪ'oʊtə/ *n.* a very small quantity; a tittle; a jot.

IOU /aɪ oʊ 'ju/ *n.* a written acknowledgment of a debt, containing the expression IOU (I owe you). Also, **I.O.U**.

-ious a termination consisting of the suffix **-ous** with a preceding original or euphonic vowel **i**. Cf. **-eous**.

ipso facto /ɪpsoʊ 'fæktoʊ/ *adv.* by the fact itself; by that very fact.

ir-[1] variant of **in-**[1], before *r*, as in *irradiate*.

ir-[2] variant of **in-**[2], before *r*, as in *irrevocable*.

irascible /ɪ'ræsəbəl/ *adj.* easily provoked to anger.

irate /aɪ'reɪt/ *adj.* angry; enraged.

ire /'aɪə/ *n.* anger; wrath.

iridescent /ɪrə'dɛsənt/ *adj.* displaying colours like those of the rainbow.

iridology /ɪrə'dɒlədʒi/ *n.* the diagnosis of the iris to detect pathological changes in the body. – **iridologist**, *n.*

irk /ɜk/ *v.t.* to weary, annoy, or trouble.

iron /'aɪən/ *n.* **1.** *Chemistry* a ductile, malleable, silver-white metallic element, scarcely known in a pure condition, but abundantly used in its crude or impure forms for making tools, implements, machinery, etc. *Symbol*: Fe **2.** an iron or steel implement used heated for smoothing or pressing cloth, etc. **3.** a metal-headed golf club. **4.** (*pl.*) an iron shackle or fetter. – *adj.* **5.** made of iron. **6.** resembling iron in colour, firmness, etc. – *v.t.* **7.** to smooth or press with a heated iron, as clothes, etc. **8.** to shackle or fetter with irons.

ironbark /'aɪənbak/ *n.* any of a group of eucalypts with a characteristic dark deeply fissured bark.

ironic /aɪ'rɒnɪk/ *adj.* relating to, of the nature of, or characterised by irony. Also, **ironical**.

iron lung *n.* a chamber in which alternate pulsations of high and low pressure can be used to force normal lung movements, used especially in some cases of poliomyelitis.

irony /'aɪrəni/ *n., pl.* **-nies**. **1.** a figure of speech or literary device in which the literal meaning is the opposite of that intended. **2.** an outcome of events contrary to what was, or might have been, expected. **3.** an ironical quality.

irradiate /ɪ'reɪdieɪt/ *v.*, **-ated**, **-ating**. – *v.t.* **1.** to shed rays of light upon; illuminate. **2.** to illumine intellectually or spiritually. **3.** to radiate (light, etc.). **4.** to heat with radiant energy. **5.** to cure or treat by exposure to radiation, as of ultraviolet light. **6.** to expose to radiation. – *v.i.* **7.** to emit rays; shine. **8.** to become radiant. – **irradiation**, *n.* – **irradiant**, *adj.*

irrational /ɪ'ræʃənəl/ *adj.* **1.** without the faculty of, or not endowed with, reason. **2.** without, or deprived of, sound judgment. **3.** not rational.

irrefrangible /ɪrə'frændʒəbəl/ *adj.* not to be broken or violated; inviolable.

irrespective /ɪrə'spɛktɪv/ *adj.* without regard to something else, especially something specified; independent (fol. by *of*).

irrevocable /ɪ'rɛvəkəbəl/ *adj.* not to be revoked or recalled; that cannot be repealed or annulled.

irrigate /'ɪrəgeɪt/ *v.t.*, **-gated**, **-gating**. **1.** to supply (land) with water and thereby promote vegetation. **2.** *Medicine* to supply (a wound, etc.) with a constant flow of some liquid. – **irrigation**, *n.*

irritable /'ɪrətəbəl/ *adj.* easily irritated; readily excited to impatience or anger.

irritate /'ɪrəteɪt/ *v.t.*, **-tated**, **-tating**. **1.** to excite to impatience or anger. **2.** *Physiology*, *Biology* to excite (a living system) to some characteristic action or function. **3.** *Pathology* to bring (a bodily part, etc.) to an abnormally excited or sensitive condition. – **irritation**, *n.* – **irritant**, *n.*, *adj.*

irrupt /ɪ'rʌpt/ *v.i.* to burst or intrude suddenly. – **irruption**, *n.*

is /ɪz/, *weak forms* /z, s/ – *v.* 3rd person singular present indicative of **be**.

is- variant of **iso-**, before some vowels.

-isation = -ization a noun suffix, combination of **-ise/-ize** with **-ation**.

-ise[1] = -ize a suffix forming intransitive and transitive verbs.

-ise[2] a noun suffix indicating quality, condition, or function, as in *merchandise.*

-ish[1] **1.** a suffix used to form adjectives from nouns, with the sense of: **a.** 'belonging to' (a people, country, etc.), as in *British, Danish, English, Spanish.* **b.** 'after the manner of', 'having the characteristics of', 'like', as in *babyish, girlish, mulish.* **c.** 'addicted to', 'inclined or tending to', as in *bookish, freakish.* **2.** a suffix used to form adjectives from other adjectives, with the sense of 'somewhat', 'rather', as in *oldish, reddish, sweetish.*

-ish[2] a suffix forming simple verbs.

island /'aɪlənd/ *n.* **1.** a tract of land completely surrounded by water, and not large enough to be called a continent. **2.** something resembling an island. **3.** a platform in the middle of a street, at a crossing, for the safety of pedestrians.

isle /aɪl/ *n.* a small island.

-ism a suffix of nouns denoting action or practice, state or condition, principles, doctrines, a usage or characteristic, etc., as in *Australianism, baptism, barbarism, criticism, plagiarism, realism.* Cf. **-ist**, **-ise[1]**.

isn't /'ɪzənt/ *v.* contraction of *is not.*

iso- a prefix meaning 'equal'.

isobar /'aɪsəba/ *n. Meteorology, etc.* a line drawn on a weather map, etc., connecting all points having the same barometric pressure at a specified time or over a certain period. – **isobaric**, *adj.*

isolate /'aɪsəleɪt/ *v.t.*, **-lated**, **-lating**. to set or place apart; detach or separate so as to be alone. – **isolation**, *n.*

isomeric /aɪsoʊ'mɛrɪk/ *adj. Chemistry* (of compounds) composed of the same kinds and numbers of atoms which differ from each other in the arrangement of the atoms and, therefore, in one or more properties. – **isomerism**, *n.* – **isomer**, *n.*

isometric /aɪsə'mɛtrɪk/ *adj.* **1.** relating to or having equality of measure. – *n.* **2.** (*pl.*) a system of physical exercises in which muscles are pitted against each other or against a fixed object.

isosceles /aɪ'sɒsəliz/ *adj.* (of a triangle) having two sides equal.

isotope /'aɪsətoʊp/ *n.* any of two or more forms of a chemical element, having the same number of protons but different numbers of neutrons in the nucleus. – **isotopic**, *adj.* – **isotopy**, *n.*

issue /'ɪʃu, 'ɪʃju, 'ɪsju/ *n.*, *v.*, **issued**, **issuing**. – *n.* **1.** the act of sending, or promulgation; delivery; emission. **2.** that which is issued. **3.** a point in question or dispute, as between contending parties in an action at law. **4.** a point or matter the decision of which is of special or public importance. **5.** a distribution of food (rations), clothing, equipment, or ammunition to servicemen, or to a military unit. **6.** offspring or progeny. **7.** *Chiefly Law* the yield or profit from land or other property. – *v.t.* **8.** to put out; deliver for use, sale, etc.; put into circulation. **9.** to send out; discharge; emit. – *v.i.* **10.** to go, pass, or flow out; come forth; emerge. **11.** to come or proceed from any source. **12.** to arise as a result or consequence; result. **13.** *Chiefly Law* to proceed as offspring, or be born or descended. **14.** *Chiefly Law* to come as a yield or profit, as from land.

issued capital *n.* → **paid-up capital**.

-ist a suffix of nouns, often accompanying verbs ending in *-ise* or nouns ending in *-ism*, denoting someone who does, practises, or is concerned with something, or holds certain principles, doctrines, etc.

isthmus /'ɪsməs/ *n.*, *pl.* **-muses**. a narrow strip of land, bordered on both sides by water, connecting two larger bodies of land.

-istic a suffix of adjectives (and in the plural of nouns from adjectives) formed from nouns in *-ist*, and having reference to such nouns, or to associated nouns in *-ism.*

-istical See **-istic**, **-al[1]**.

-istics See **-istic**, **-ics**.

it /ɪt/, *weak form* /ət/ *pron.*, *possessive* **its**, *objective* **it**, *pl.* **they**. a personal pronoun of the third person and neuter gender, which corresponds to *he* and *she*, and which is used: **1.** as a substitute for a neuter noun or a noun representing something possessing sex when sex is not particularised or considered: *the baby lost its rattle.* **2.** to refer to some matter expressed or understood, or some thing or notion not definitely conceived. **3.** as the grammatical subject of a clause of which the logical subject is a phrase or clause. **4.** in impersonal constructions. **5.** without definite force after an intransitive verb.

italic /ɪ'tælɪk, aɪ-/ *adj.* **1.** designating or relating to a style of printing types in which the letters usually slope to the right (thus, *italic*), patterned upon a compact manuscript hand, and used for emphasis, etc. – *n.* **2.** (*often pl.*) italic type. – **italicise = italicize**, *v.*

itch /ɪtʃ/ *v.i.* **1.** to have or feel a peculiar irritation of the skin which causes a desire to scratch the part affected. – *n.* **2.** the sensation of itching. – **itchy**, *adj.*

-ite[1] a suffix of nouns denoting especially **1.** persons associated with a place, tribe, leader, doctrine, system, etc. **2.** minerals and fossils. **3.** chemical compounds, especially salts of acids whose names end in *-ous.* **4.** a member or component of a part of the body.

-ite[2] a suffix forming adjectives and nouns from adjectives, and some verbs, as in *composite*, *opposite*, *requisite*, *erudite*, etc.

item /'aɪtəm/ *n.* **1.** a separate article or particular. **2.** a separate piece of information or news, as in a newspaper.

itemise = itemize /'aɪtəmaɪz/ *v.t.*, **-mised**, **-mising**. to state by items; give the particulars of.

iterate /'ɪtəreɪt/ *v.t.*, **-rated**, **-rating**. to utter again or repeatedly. – **iteration**, *n.*

itinerant /aɪ'tɪnərənt/ *adj.* **1.** travelling from place to place. **2.** moving on a circuit, as a preacher, judge, or pedlar. – **itinerancy**, **itineracy**, *n.* – **itinerate**, *v.*

itinerary /aɪ'tɪnəri/ *n., pl.* **-ries**. an account of a journey; a record of travel.

-ition a noun suffix, **-ite**[1] + **-ion**.

-itious an adjective suffix occurring in adjectives associated with nouns in *-ition.*

-itis a noun suffix used in pathological terms denoting inflammation of some part or organ, as in *bronchitis.*

-itive a suffix of adjectives and nouns of adjectival origin, as in *definitive*, *fugitive.*

it'll /'ɪtl/ contraction of *it will* or *it shall.*

its /ɪts/ *adj., pron.* possessive form of **it**.

it's /ɪts/ contraction of *it is.*

itself /ɪt'sɛlf/ *pron.* **1.** the reflexive form of **it**: *a thermostatically controlled electric fire switches itself off.* **2.** an emphatic form of **it** used: **a.** as object: *the earth gathers its fruits to itself.* **b.** in opposition to a subject or object. **3.** in its normal or usual state.

-ity a suffix forming abstract nouns of condition, characteristics, etc., as in *civility.*

-ium a suffix representing Latin neuter suffix, used especially to form names of metallic elements.

-ive a suffix of adjectives (and nouns of adjectival origin) expressing tendency, disposition, function, connection, etc., as in *active*, *corrective*, *destructive.* Cf. **-ative**.

I've /aɪv/ contraction of *I have.*

IVF /aɪ vi 'ɛf/ in-vitro fertilisation.

ivory /'aɪvəri, 'aɪvri/ *n., pl.* **-ries**. **1.** the hard white substance composing the main part of the tusks of the elephant, walrus, etc. **2.** (*pl.*) *Colloquial* **a.** the keys of a piano, accordion, etc. **b.** dice. **3.** creamy white.

J j

J, j /dʒeɪ/ *n., pl.* **J's** *or* **Js**, **j's** *or* **js**. the 10th letter of the English alphabet.

jab /dʒæb/ *v.,* **jabbed**, **jabbing**, *n.* – *v.i.* **1.** to thrust smartly or sharply, as with the end or point of something. – *v.t.* **2.** to poke (something) smartly or sharply. – *n.* **3.** a poke with the end or point of something.

jabber /'dʒæbə/ *v.i.* to utter rapidly, indistinctly, imperfectly, or nonsensically; chatter.

jabiru /dʒæbə'ru/ *n.* Australia's only stork.

jacaranda /dʒækə'rændə/ *n.* a tall tropical tree with lavender-blue flowers.

jack /dʒæk/ *n.* **1.** a man or fellow. **2.** a contrivance for raising heavy weights short distances. **3.** any of the four knaves in playing cards. **4.** a knucklebone or plastic imitation used in a children's game. **5.** *Colloquial* venereal disease. – *v.t.* **6.** to lift or raise with or as with a jack. – *v.i.* **7.** **jack up,** *Colloquial* to refuse; be obstinate; resist.

jackal /'dʒækəl/ *n.* any of several kinds of wild dog.

jackaroo = jackeroo /dʒækə'ru/ *n.* **1.** a young man gaining practical experience on a sheep or cattle station. – *v.i.* **2.** to work as a trainee on such a station.

jackass /'dʒækæs/ *n.* **1.** a male donkey. **2.** a very stupid or foolish person. **3.** a kookaburra.

jacket /'dʒækət/ *n.* **1.** a short coat. **2.** Also, **dust jacket**. a detachable paper cover, usually illustrated in colour, for protecting the binding of a book; dustcover. **3.** the outer casing or covering of a boiler, pipe, tank, etc.

jackhammer /'dʒækhæmə/ *n.* a hand-held drill operated by compressed air, used for drilling rocks.

jack-in-the-box /'dʒæk-ɪn-ðə-bɒks/ *n.* a toy consisting of a figure, enclosed in a box, which springs out when the lid is unfastened.

jackknife /'dʒæknaɪf/ *n., pl.* **-knives**, *v.,* **-knifed**, **-knifing**. – *n.* **1.** a large knife with a blade that folds into the handle. – *v.i.* **2.** to bend or fold up, like a jackknife.

jackpot /'dʒækpɒt/ *n.* the chief prize to be won in a lottery, a game or contest.

jade /dʒeɪd/ *n.* a mineral, sometimes green, highly esteemed as an ornamental stone.

jaded /'dʒeɪdəd/ *adj.* **1.** worn out. **2.** sated.

jaffle /'dʒæfəl/ *n.* a sealed toasted sandwich with a savoury or sweet filling.

jagged /'dʒægəd/ *adj.* having notches, teeth, or ragged edges.

jaguar /'dʒægjuə/ *n.* a large, ferocious, spotted feline.

jail /dʒeɪl/ *n.* a prison. Also, **gaol**.

jalopy /dʒə'lɒpi/ *n., pl.* **-lopies**. *Colloquial* an old, decrepit, or unpretentious motor car.

jam[1] /dʒæm/ *v.,* **jammed**, **jamming**, *n.* – *v.t.* **1.** to press or squeeze tightly between bodies or surfaces, so that motion or extrication is made difficult or impossible. **2.** to fill or block up by crowding. **3.** to cause to become wedged, caught, or displaced, so that it cannot work, as a machine, part, etc. **4.** *Radio* to interfere with (signals, etc.) by sending out others of approximately the same frequency. **5.** to apply (brakes) forcibly (fol. by *on*). – *v.i.* **6.** to become wedged or fixed; stick fast. **7.** to press or push violently, as into a confined space or against one another. **8.** (of a machine, etc.) to become unworkable as through the wedging or displacement of a part. – *n.* **9.** the act of jamming. **10.** the state of being jammed. **11.** a mass of vehicles, people, or objects jammed together. **12.** *Colloquial* a difficult or awkward situation; a fix.

jam[2] *n.* a preserve of boiled and crushed fruit.

jam[3] /dʒæm/ *n.* a meeting of musicians for the spontaneous and improvisatory performance of music. Also, **jam session**.

jamb /dʒæm/ *n.* a vertical piece forming the side of a doorway, window, or the like.

jangle /'dʒæŋgəl/ *v.,* **-gled**, **-gling**, *n.* – *v.i.* **1.** to sound harshly or discordantly. – *n.* **2.** a harsh or discordant sound.

janitor /'dʒænətə/ *n.* **1.** a caretaker. **2.** a doorkeeper or porter.

jape /dʒeɪp/ *n.* a joke; jest; gibe.

japonica /dʒə'pɒnɪkə/ *n.* any of several garden shrubs with white, pink or red flowers.

jar[1] /dʒa/ *n.* a broad-mouthed earthen or glass vessel.

jar[2] /dʒa/ *v.i.,* **jarred**, **jarring**. **1.** to produce a harsh, grating sound; sound discordantly. **2.** to have a harshly unpleasant effect upon the nerves, feelings, etc. **3.** to be at variance; conflict; clash.

jargon /'dʒagən/ *n* the language peculiar to a trade, profession, or other group.

jarrah /'dʒærə/ *n.* a large tree of western Australia.

jasmine /'dʒæzmən/ *n.* any of several shrubs or climbing plants with fragrant flowers.

jasper /'dʒæspə/ *n.* a coloured variety of quartz.

jaundice /'dʒɔndəs/ *n., v.,* **-diced**, **-dicing**. – *n.* **1.** *Pathology* a disease characterised by yellowness of the skin, etc. – *v.t.* **2.** to distort or prejudice, as with pessimism, jealousy, resentment, etc.

jaunt /dʒɔnt/ *v.i.* **1.** to make a short journey, especially for pleasure. – *n.* **2.** such a journey.

jaunty /'dʒɔnti/ *adj.,* **-tier**, **-tiest**. easy and sprightly in manner or bearing.

javelin /'dʒævələn/ *n.* a spear to be thrown by hand.

jaw /dʒɔ/ *n.* one of the two bones or structures (upper and lower) which form the framework of the mouth.

jay /dʒeɪ/ *n.* any of a number of Australian birds.

jaywalk /'dʒeɪwɔk/ *v.i.* *Colloquial* to cross a street otherwise than by a pedestrian crossing.

jazz /dʒæz/ *n.* **1.** a type of popular music marked by frequent improvisation and syncopated rhythms. – *v.t.* **2.** *Colloquial* to put vigour or liveliness into (often fol. by *up*).

jealous /'dʒɛləs/ *adj.* **1.** inclined to or troubled by suspicions or fears of rivalry, as in love or aims. **2.** solicitous or vigilant in maintaining or guarding something. – **jealousy**, *n.*

jeans /dʒinz/ *pl. n.* trousers made of denim or other sturdy fabric.

jeep /dʒip/ *n.* a small military motor vehicle.

jeer /dʒɪə/ *v.i.* to speak or shout derisively; gibe or scoff rudely.

jelly /'dʒɛli/ *n., pl.* **-lies**, *v.,* **-lied**, **-lying**. – *n.* **1.** a food preparation of a soft, elastic consistency. – *v.t., v.i.* **2.** to bring or come to the consistency of jelly.

jellyfish /'dʒɛlifɪʃ/ *n., pl.* **-fishes**, (*esp. collectively*) **-fish**. any of various marine coelenterates of a soft, gelatinous structure.

jemmy /'dʒɛmi/ *n., pl.* **-mies**. a short crowbar.

jeopardy /'dʒɛpədi/ *n.* hazard or risk of loss or harm. – **jeopardise = jeopardize**, *v.*

jerk /dʒɜk/ *n.* **1.** a quick, sharp thrust, pull, throw, or the like. **2.** *Colloquial* a stupid or naive person. – *v.t.* **3.** to move or throw with a quick, suddenly arrested motion.

jersey /'dʒɜzi/ *n.* **1.** a close-fitting, usually woollen, outer garment for the upper part of the body; jumper. **2.** a machine-knitted fabric.

jest /dʒɛst/ *n.* **1.** a witticism, joke, or pleasantry. **2.** sport or fun. – *v.i.* **3.** to speak in a playful, humorous, or facetious way; joke.

jet[1] /dʒɛt/ *n., v.,* **jetted**, **jetting**. – *n.* **1.** a stream of fluid from a nozzle, orifice, etc. **2.** a jet plane. – *v.i.* **3.** to spout. **4.** to fly in a jet plane.

jet[2] /dʒɛt/ *n.* a compact black coal, susceptible of a high polish, used for making beads, jewellery, buttons, etc.

jet plane *n.* an aeroplane operated by jet propulsion.

jet propulsion *n.* a method of producing a propelling force upon an air or water craft through the reaction of a high-velocity jet, usually of heated gases, discharged towards the rear. – **jet-propelled**, *adj.*

jetsam /'dʒɛtsəm/ *n.* goods thrown overboard to lighten a vessel in distress, which sink or are washed ashore. Cf. **flotsam**.

jettison /'dʒɛtəsən, -zən/ *v.t.* to throw (cargo, etc.) overboard, especially to lighten a vessel or aircraft in distress.

jetty /'dʒɛti/ *n., pl.* **-ties**. a small wharf.

jewel /'dʒuəl/ *n.* a cut and polished precious or semiprecious stone; a gem. – **jeweller**, *n.*

jewellery /'dʒuəlri/ *n.* jewels for personal adornment.

jewfish /'dʒufɪʃ/ *n., pl.* **-fishes**, (*esp. collectively*) **-fish**. (in Australia) any of several species of large food fishes.

jib /dʒɪb/ *v.i.,* **jibbed**, **jibbing**. to hold back or baulk at doing something.

jiffy /'dʒɪfi/ *n., pl.* **-fies**. *Colloquial* a very short time. Also, **jiff**.

jig[1] /dʒɪg/ *n.* a device for holding the work in a machine tool.

jig[2] /dʒɪg/ *n., v.,* **jigged**, **jigging**. – *n.* **1.** a rapid, lively dance. – *v.t.* **2.** to move with a jerky or bobbing motion.

jigger[1] /'dʒɪgə/ *n.* a measure for alcohol used in cocktails.

jigger[2] /'dʒɪgə/ *v.t.* to break or destroy.

jiggle /'dʒɪgəl/ *v.t., v.i.,* **-gled**, **-gling**. to move up and down or to and fro with short, quick jerks.

jigsaw puzzle /'dʒɪgsɔ/ *n.* small, irregularly shaped pieces of wood or cardboard, which, when correctly fitted together, form a picture.

jillaroo = jilleroo /dʒɪlə'ru/ *n.* a female jackaroo.

jilt /dʒɪlt/ *v.t.* to cast off (a lover or sweetheart) after encouragement or engagement.

jingle /'dʒɪŋgəl/ *v.,* **-gled**, **-gling**, *n.* – *v.i.* **1.** to make clinking or tinkling sounds, as coins, keys, etc., when struck together repeatedly. – *n.* **2.** a clinking or tinkling sound. **3.** a simple, repetitious, catchy rhyme set to music, used especially for advertising.

jingoism /'dʒɪŋgoʊɪzəm/ *n.* fervent and excessive patriotism.

jinx /dʒɪŋks/ *Colloquial n.* **1.** a person, thing, or influence supposed to bring bad luck. – *v.t.* **2.** to bring bad luck to someone; hex.

jitters /'dʒɪtəz/ *pl. n. Colloquial* nervousness; nerves (usually preceded by *the*).

jive /dʒaɪv/ *n.* **1.** jargon used by jazz musicians. **2.** a dance performed to beat music.

job[1] /dʒɒb/ *n., v.,* **jobbed**, **jobbing**, *adj.* – *n.* **1.** an individual piece of work done in the routine of one's occupation or trade. **2.** a post of employment. – *v.i.* **3.** to work at jobs, or odd pieces of work. **4.** to do business as a jobber (def. 2). – *adj.* **5.** of or for a particular job or transaction. **6.** bought or sold together; lumped together.

job[2] /dʒɒb/ *n. Colloquial* a jab; hit; punch.

jobber /'dʒɒbə/ *n.* **1.** a wholesale merchant, especially one selling to retailers. **2.** a dealer in stock exchange securities. Cf. **broker**.

job costing *n.* a type of costing in which costs are recorded against each individual job or order.

job share *n.* an arrangement whereby one job is shared between two or more employees.

jockey /'dʒɒki/ *n.* someone who professionally rides horses in races.

jockstrap /'dʒɒkstræp/ *n. Colloquial* a support for the genitals worn by male athletes, dancers, etc.

jocose /dʒə'koʊs/ *adj.* given to or characterised by joking; jesting; humorous.

jocular /'dʒɒkjələ/ *adj.* given to, characterised by, intended for, or suited to joking or jesting.

jocund /'dʒɒkənd/ *adj.* cheerful; merry.

jodhpurs /'dʒɒdpəz/ *pl. n.* riding breeches reaching to the ankle, and fitting closely from the knee down.

joey /'dʒoʊi/ *n., pl.* **joeys**. any young animal, especially a kangaroo.

jog /dʒɒg/ *v.,* **jogged**, **jogging**. – *v.t.* **1.** to move or shake with a push or jerk. **2.** to stir up by hint or reminder. – *v.i.* **3.** to move with a jolt or jerk. **4.** to run at a slow, regular pace.

joggle /'dʒɒgəl/ *v.t.,* **-gled**, **-gling**. to shake slightly; move to and fro as by repeated jerks.

john /dʒɒn/ *n. Colloquial* a toilet.

John Dory *n.* a thin, deep-bodied, highly esteemed food fish.

join /dʒɔɪn/ *v.t.* **1.** to bring or put together, in contact or connection (sometimes fol. by *up*). **2.** to become a member of. **3.** to come into the company of. – *v.i.* **4.** to come into or be in contact or connection, or form a junction. **5.** to take part with others (often fol. by *in*). – *n.* **6.** a place or line of joining; a seam.

joiner /ˈdʒɔɪnə/ *n.* a worker in wood who constructs the fittings of a house, furniture, etc. – **joinery**, *n.*

joint /dʒɔɪnt/ *n.* **1.** the place or part in which two things, or parts of one thing, are joined or united. **2.** one of the portions into which a carcass is divided by a butcher, especially one ready for cooking. **3.** *Colloquial* the house, unit, office, etc., regarded as in some sense one's own. **4.** *Colloquial* a marijuana cigarette. – *adj.* **5.** shared by or common to two or more. **6.** sharing or acting in common. – *v.t.* **7.** to unite by a joint or joints. **8.** to form or provide with a joint or joints. **9.** to divide at a joint, or separate into pieces.

joint-stock company *n.* a company whose ownership is divided into transferable shares, the object usually being the division of profits among the members in proportion to the number of shares held by each.

joist /dʒɔɪst/ *n.* any of the parallel lengths of timber, steel, etc., used for supporting floors, ceilings, etc.

jojoba /həˈhoʊbə/ *n.* an evergreen shrub having edible seeds containing a liquid wax with many uses.

joke /dʒoʊk/ *n., v.,* **joked**, **joking**. – *n.* **1.** something said or done to excite laughter or amusement. **2.** an amusing or ridiculous circumstance. – *v.i.* **3.** to speak or act in a playful or merry way. **4.** to say something in mere sport, rather than in earnest.

joker /ˈdʒoʊkə/ *n.* an extra playing card in a pack, used in some games.

jolly /ˈdʒɒli/ *adj.,* **-lier**, **-liest**, *adv.* – *adj.* **1.** in good spirits; cheerful. – *adv.* **2.** *Colloquial* extremely; very.

jolt /dʒoʊlt/ *v.t.* **1.** to jar or shake as by a sudden rough thrust. – *n.* **2.** a jolting shock or movement.

jonquil /ˈdʒɒŋkwɪl/ *n.* a species of narcissus.

jostle /ˈdʒɒsəl/ *v.,* **-tled**, **-tling**. – *v.t.* **1.** to strike or push roughly or rudely against; elbow roughly; hustle. – *v.i.* **2.** to collide (fol. by *with*) or strike or push (fol. by *against*) as in passing or in a crowd.

jot /dʒɒt/ *n., v.,* **jotted**, **jotting**. – *n.* **1.** the least part of something; a little bit. – *v.t.* **2.** to write or mark down briefly (usually fol. by *down*).

joule /dʒul/ *n.* the derived SI unit of work or energy. *Symbol*: J

journal /ˈdʒɜnəl/ *n.* **1.** a daily record, as of occurrences, experiences, or observations; diary. **2.** a newspaper, especially a daily one. **3.** any periodical or magazine, especially one published by a learned society. **4.** *Bookkeeping* **a.** a daybook. **b.** (in double entry) a book in which all transactions are entered (from the daybook or blotter) in systematic form, to facilitate posting into the ledger.

journalise = journalize /ˈdʒɜnəlaɪz/ *v.t.,* **-lised**, **lising**. **1.** to enter or record in a journal. **2.** (in double-entry bookkeeping) to systematise and enter in a journal, preparatory to posting to the ledger.

journalism /ˈdʒɜnəlɪzəm/ *n.* the occupation of writing for, editing, and producing newspapers and other periodicals, and television and radio shows. – **journalist**, *n.*

journey /ˈdʒɜni/ *n., pl.* **-neys**, *v.,* **-neyed**, **-neying**. – *n.* **1.** a course of travel from one place to another, especially by land. – *v.i.* **2.** to make a journey; travel.

joust /dʒaʊst/ *n.* a combat in which two armoured knights or men-at-arms on horseback opposed each other with lances.

jovial /ˈdʒoʊviəl/ *adj.* endowed with or characterised by a hearty, joyous humour or a spirit of good fellowship.

jowl[1] /dʒaʊl/ *n.* **1.** a jaw, especially the underjaw. **2.** the cheek.

jowl[2] /dʒaʊl/ *n.* a fold of flesh hanging from the jaw, as of a fat person.

joy /dʒɔɪ/ *n.* an emotion of keen or lively pleasure; great gladness; delight.

jube /dʒub/ *n.* a chewy lolly. Also, **jujube**.

jubilate /ˈdʒubəleɪt/ *v.i.,* **-lated**, **-lating**. to manifest or feel great joy; rejoice; exult. – **jubilation**, *n.* – **jubilant**, *adj.*

jubilee /dʒubəˈli/ *n.* the celebration of any of certain anniversaries.

judder /ˈdʒʌdə/ *v.i.* to vibrate; shake.

judge /dʒʌdʒ/ *n., v.,* **judged**, **judging**. – *n.* **1.** a public officer authorised to hear and determine causes in a court of law. **2.** a person appointed to decide in any competition or contest. – *v.t.* **3.** to try (a person or a case) as a judge does; pass sentence on or in. **4.** to form a judgment or opinion of or upon. – *v.i.* **5.** to act as a judge; pass judgment. **6.** to make a mental judgment.

judgment = judgement /ˈdʒʌdʒmənt/ *n.* **1.** the act of judging. **2.** *Law* the judicial decision of a cause in court. **3.** ability to judge justly or wisely. **4.** the forming of an opinion, estimate, notion, or conclusion, as from circumstances presented to the mind.

judicature /ˈdʒudəkətʃə/ *n.* **1.** the administration of justice, as by judges or courts. **2.** a body of judges.

judicial /dʒuˈdɪʃəl/ *adj.* **1.** relating to judgment in courts of justice or to the administration of justice. **2.** relating to courts of law or to judges. **3.** of or relating to a judge; proper to the character of a judge; judgelike.

judiciary /dʒuˈdɪʃəri/ *n., pl.* **-ries**. the system of courts of justice in a country.

judicious /dʒuˈdɪʃəs/ *adj.* **1.** using or showing judgment as to action or practical expediency. **2.** having, exercising, or showing good judgment; wise, sensible, or well-advised.

judo /ˈdʒudoʊ/ *n.* a style of self-defence derived from jujitsu, employing less violent methods and emphasising the sporting element.

jug /dʒʌg/ *n.* a vessel in various forms for holding liquids, commonly having a handle.

juggernaut /ˈdʒʌgənɔt/ *n.* **1.** anything

requiring blind devotion or extreme sacrifice. **2.** any large, relentless, destructive force.

juggle /'dʒʌgəl/ *v.t.*, **-gled**, **-gling**. **1.** to keep (several objects) in continuous motion in the air at the same time by tossing and catching. **2.** to manipulate or alter by artifice or trickery.

jugular /'dʒʌgjulə/ *adj. Anatomy* **1.** of or relating to the throat or neck. – *n.* **2.** one of the large veins in the neck.

juice /dʒus/ *n.* **1.** the liquid part of plant or animal substance. **2.** any extracted liquid, especially from a fruit. – **juicy**, *adj.*

jujitsu /dʒu'dʒɪtsu/ *n.* a Japanese method of defending oneself without weapons. Also, **jiujitsu**, **jiujutsu**, **jujutsu**.

jukebox /'dʒukbɒks/ *n.* a coin-operated machine which plays a select musical item or items.

jumble /'dʒʌmbəl/ *v.*, **-bled**, **-bling**, *n.* – *v.t.* **1.** to mix in a confused mass; put or throw together without order. – *n.* **2.** a confused mixture.

jumbuck /'dʒʌmbʌk/ *n. Colloquial* a sheep.

jump /dʒʌmp/ *v.i.* **1.** to spring clear of the ground or other support by a sudden muscular effort; leap. **2.** to move suddenly or abruptly, as from surprise or shock; start. **3.** to pass abruptly, ignoring intervening stages. – *v.t.* **4.** to leap or spring over. **5.** to skip or pass over; bypass. – *n.* **6.** the act of jumping; a leap. **7.** a space or obstacle or apparatus cleared in a leap. **8.** a sudden rise in amount, price, etc. **9.** an abrupt transition from one point or thing to another, with omission of what intervenes.

jumper /'dʒʌmpə/ *n.* an outer garment, usually of wool, for the upper part of the body; pullover; sweater; jersey.

jumper leads *pl. n.* a pair of heavy leads used in starting a motor vehicle with a flat battery, by connecting this battery to a charged one.

jumpsuit /'dʒʌmpsut/ *n.* a close-fitting outer garment covering all of the body and the legs.

jumpy /'dʒʌmpi/ *adj.*, **jumpier**, **jumpiest**. characterised by or inclined to sudden, involuntary starts, especially from nervousness, fear, excitement, etc.

junction /'dʒʌŋkʃən/ *n.* **1.** the act of joining; combination. **2.** a place of joining or meeting.

juncture /'dʒʌŋktʃə/ *n.* **1.** a point of time, especially one made critical or important by a concurrence of circumstances. **2.** the line or point at which two bodies are joined.

jungle /'dʒʌŋgəl/ *n.* a tropical rainforest with thick, impenetrable undergrowth.

junior /'dʒunjə/ *adj.* **1.** younger. **2.** of lower rank or standing. – *n.* **3.** a person who is younger than another. **4.** any minor or child, especially a male. **5.** one employed as the subordinate of another.

juniper /'dʒunəpə/ *n.* any of several coniferous evergreen shrubs or trees.

junk[1] /dʒʌŋk/ *n.* **1.** any old or discarded material. **2.** *Colloquial* anything regarded as worthless.

junk[2] /dʒʌŋk/ *n.* a kind of seagoing ship used in Chinese and other waters.

junk bond *n.* a high-yield security, especially one issued to finance a takeover, and often involving high risk.

junket /'dʒʌŋkət/ *n.* **1.** a sweet custard-like food. **2.** a feast or merrymaking; a picnic; a pleasure excursion.

junkie /'dʒʌŋki/ *n. Colloquial* a drug addict. Also, **junky**.

junk mail *n.* unsolicited mail, usually advertisements or prospectuses.

junta /'dʒʌntə/ *n.* a small ruling group in a country, either elected or self-chosen, especially one which has come to power after a revolution.

jurisdiction /dʒurəs'dɪkʃən/ *n.* **1.** the right, power, or authority to administer justice by hearing and determining controversies. **2.** power; authority; control.

jurisprudence /dʒurəs'prudns/ *n.* **1.** the science or philosophy of law. **2.** a body or system of laws. – **jurisprudent**, *n.*, *adj.* – **jurisprudential**, *adj.*

jurist /'dʒurəst, 'dʒʊə-/ *n.* one versed in the law.

juror /'dʒʊərə, 'dʒurə/ *n.* a member of any jury.

jury /'dʒʊəri, 'dʒuri/ *n.*, *pl.* **-ries**. **1.** a body of people selected according to law and sworn to inquire into or determine the facts concerning a cause or an accusation submitted to them and to render a verdict. **2.** a body of persons chosen to adjudge prizes, etc., as in a competition.

just /dʒʌst/ *adj.* **1.** actuated by truth, justice, and lack of bias. **2.** based on right; rightful; lawful. **3.** true; correct. **4.** given or awarded rightly, or deserved, as a sentence, punishment, reward, etc. **5.** in accordance with standards, or requirements. – *adv.* **6.** within a brief preceding time, or but a moment before. **7.** exactly or precisely. **8.** by a narrow margin; barely. **9.** only or merely. **10.** *Colloquial* actually; truly; positively.

justice /'dʒʌstəs/ *n.* **1.** the quality of being just. **2.** that which is just. **3.** the requital of desert as by punishment or reward. **4.** the maintenance or administration of law, as by judicial or other proceedings. **5.** a judicial officer; a judge or magistrate.

justify /'dʒʌstəfaɪ/ *v.t.*, **-fied**, **-fying**. **1.** to show (an act, claim, etc.) to be just, right, or warranted. **2.** declare guiltless; absolve; acquit. **3.** *Printing* to adjust exactly; make (lines) of the proper length by spacing. – **justification**, *n.*

jut /dʒʌt/ *v.i.*, **jutted**, **jutting**. to extend beyond the main body or line; project; protrude (often fol. by *out*).

jute /dʒut/ *n.* a strong fibre used for making fabrics, cordage, etc.

juvenile /'dʒuvənaɪl/ *adj.* **1.** relating to, suitable for, characteristic of, or intended for young persons. **2.** young. **3.** inappropriately suggestive of the behaviour or sentiments of a young person. – *n.* **4.** a young person; a youth.

juxta- a word element meaning 'near', 'close to', 'beside'.

juxtapose /dʒʌkstə'poʊz, 'dʒʌkstəpoʊz/ *v.t.*, **-posed**, **-posing**. to place in close proximity or side by side. – **juxtaposition**, *n.*

K k

K, k /keɪ/ *n., pl.* **K's** *or* **Ks**, **k's** *or* **ks**. the 11th letter of the English alphabet.

kafuffle /kə'fʌfəl, -'fʊfəl/ *n. Colloquial* argument; commotion; rumpus. Also, **kafoofle**, **kerfuffle**, **kerfoofle**.

kale /keɪl/ *n.* a kind of cabbage with leaves not forming a head. Also, **kail**.

kaleidoscope /kə'laɪdəskoʊp/ *n.* an optical instrument in which pieces of coloured glass, etc., in a rotating tube are shown by reflection in continually changing symmetrical forms. – **kaleidoscopic**, *adj.*

kangaroo /kæŋgə'ru/ *n.* any of several herbivorous marsupials of the Australian region, with powerful hind legs developed for leaping, and very short forelimbs.

kaput /kæ'pʊt, kə-/ *adj. Colloquial* **1.** smashed; ruined. **2.** broken; not working.

karate /kə'rati/ *n.* a method of defensive fighting in which hands, elbows, feet, and knees are the only weapons used.

karma /'kamə/ *n.* fate; destiny.

karri /'kæri/ *n., pl.* **-ris**. a tree valuable for its hard, durable timber.

kata- variant of **cata-**. Also, **kat-**, **kath-**.

kauri /'kaʊri/ *n., pl.* **-ris**. a tall coniferous tree of New Zealand, yielding a valuable timber and a resin.

kava /'kavə/ *n.* an intoxicating beverage made from the roots of a Polynesian shrub.

kayak /'kaɪæk/ *n.* an Inuit hunting canoe.

kazoo /kə'zu/ *n.* a short plastic or metal tube with a membrane-covered side hole, into which a person sings or hums. Also, **gazoo**.

keel /kil/ *n.* **1.** a longitudinal timber, or combination of timbers, iron plates, or the like supporting the whole frame of a ship. – *v.i.* **2. keel over,** *Colloquial* to collapse suddenly.

keen[1] /kin/ *adj.* **1.** sharp. **2.** characterised by strength and distinctness of perception, as the ear or hearing, the eye, sight, etc. **3.** having or showing great mental penetration or acumen. **4.** intense, as feeling, desire, etc. **5.** having a fondness or devotion (for) (fol. by *on*).

keen[2] /kin/ *v.i.* to wail in lamentation for the dead.

keep /kip/ *v.,* **kept**, **keeping**, *n.* – *v.t.* **1.** to maintain in one's action or conduct. **2.** to cause to continue in some place, position, state, course, or action specified. **3.** to have habitually in stock or for sale. **4.** to withhold from use; reserve. **5.** to maintain or carry on, as an establishment, business, etc.; manage. **6.** to maintain or support (a person, etc.). **7.** to save, hold, or retain in possession. – *v.i.* **8.** to continue in an action, course, position, state, etc. **9.** to continue unimpaired or without spoiling. **10.** to remain; stay (fol. by *away*, *back*, *off*, *out*, etc.). – *n.* **11.** subsistence; board and lodging. **12.** the innermost and strongest structure or central tower of a medieval castle. **13. for keeps,** *Colloquial* permanently.

keeping /'kipɪŋ/ *n.* just conformity in things or elements associated together.

keepsake /'kipseɪk/ *n.* anything kept as a token of remembrance, friendship, etc.

keg /kɛg/ *n.* a barrel, especially of beer.

kelp /kɛlp/ *n.* any of the large brown seaweeds.

kelpie /'kɛlpi/ *n.* one of a breed of Australian sheepdogs.

kelvin /'kɛlvən/ *n.* a unit of temperature, equal to one degree Celsius.

Kelvin scale *n.* a scale of temperature (**Kelvin temperature**), based on thermodynamic principles, in which zero is equivalent to -273.16°C.

ken /kɛn/ *n.* knowledge.

kennel /'kɛnəl/ *n.* **1.** a house for a dog or dogs. **2.** (*usu. pl., construed as sing.*) an establishment where dogs are bred or boarded.

kept /kɛpt/ *v.* past tense and past participle of **keep**.

kerb /kɜb/ *n.* a line of joined stones, concrete, or the like at the edge of a street, wall, etc.

kerchief /'kɜtʃəf, kə'tʃif/ *n.* a cloth worn as a head covering.

kernel /'kɜnəl/ *n.* **1.** the softer, usually edible, part contained in the shell of a nut or the stone of a fruit. **2.** the central part of anything; the nucleus; the core.

kero /'kɛroʊ/ *n. Colloquial* → **kerosene**.

kerosene = kerosine /kɛrə'sin, 'kɛrəsin/ *n.* a mixture of liquid hydrocarbons, obtained in the distillation of petroleum, used for lamps, engines, heaters.

ketchup /'kɛtʃəp/ *n.* any of several sauces or condiments for meat, fish, etc.

kettle /'kɛtl/ *n.* a portable container in which to boil water.

kettledrum /'kɛtldrʌm/ *n.* a hollow metal drum which can be tuned.

key /ki/ *n., pl.* **keys**, *adj., v.,* **keyed**, **keying**. – *n.* **1.** an instrument for fastening or opening a lock by moving its bolt. **2.** a means of attaining, understanding, solving, etc. **3.** a systematic explanation of abbreviations, symbols, etc. **4.** something that secures or controls entrance to a place. **5.** a pin, bolt, wedge, or other piece inserted in a hole or space to lock or hold parts of a mechanism or structure together. **6.** one of a set of levers or parts pressed in operating a telegraph, typewriter, musical instrument, etc. **7.** *Music* the keynote or tonic of a scale. – *adj.* **8.** chief; indispensable. **9.** identifying. – *v.t.* **10.** to bring to a particular degree of intensity of feeling (often fol. by *up*). **11.** to adjust (one's speech, actions, etc.) to external factors, as the level of understanding of one's hearers. **12.** to fasten, secure, or adjust with a key, wedge, or the like, as parts of a mechanism. **13.** to provide with a key or keys. **14.** to give (an advertisement) a letter or number to enable replies to it to be identified.

keyboard /'kibɔd/ *n.* the row or set of keys on a piano, typewriter, computer, etc.

keynote /'kinoʊt/ *n.* **1.** *Music* the note on which a system of notes is founded; the tonic. **2.** the main interest or determining principle of a conference, political campaign, advertising campaign, etc.

keystone /'kistoʊn/ *n.* something on which associated things depend.

keystroke /'kistroʊk/ *n.* an instance of pressing down a key on a typewriter or computer keyboard.

khaki /ka'ki, 'kaki/ *n., pl.* **-kis**. **1. a.** dull yellowish brown. **b.** a dull green with a yellowish or brownish tinge. **2.** stout twilled cotton uniform cloth of this colour, worn especially by soldiers.

kibble /'kɪbəl/ *v.t.,* **-bled**, **-bling**. to grind into small particles.

kibbutz /kɪ'bʊts/ *n., pl.* **kibbutzim** /kɪ'bʊtsɪm, kɪbʊt'sim/ (in Israel) a communal agricultural settlement.

kick /kɪk/ *v.t.* **1.** to strike with the foot. **2.** to drive, force, make, etc., by or as by kicks. **3.** to strike in recoiling. **4.** *Football* to score (a goal) by a kick. **5. kick out,** *Colloquial* to dismiss; get rid of. – *v.i.* **6.** to strike out with the foot. **7.** *Colloquial* to resist, object, or complain. **8.** to recoil, as a firearm when fired. – *n.* **9.** the act of kicking; a blow or thrust with the foot. **10.** power or disposition to kick. **11.** the right of or a turn at kicking. **12.** a recoil, as of a gun. **13.** *Colloquial* any thrill or excitement that gives pleasure. **14.** *Colloquial* vigour, energy, or vim.

kickback /'kɪkbæk/ *n. Colloquial* **1.** a response, usually vigorous. **2.** any sum paid for favours received or hoped for.

kid¹ /kɪd/ *n.* **1.** a young goat. **2.** leather made from the skin of a young goat. **3.** *Colloquial* a child or young person.

kid² /kɪd/ *v.,* **kidded**, **kidding**. *Colloquial* to tease; banter; jest with.

kidnap /'kɪdnæp/ *v.t.,* **-napped**, **-napping**. to carry off (a person) against their will by unlawful force or by fraud, often with a demand for ransom. – **kidnapper**, *n.*

kidney /'kɪdni/ *n., pl.* **-neys**. either of a pair of bean-shaped glandular organs which excrete urine.

kidney bean *n.* a kind of bean with a somewhat kidney-shaped seed.

kikuyu /kaɪ'kuju/ *n.* a perennial grass widely used as a lawn grass.

kill /kɪl/ *v.t.* **1.** to deprive (any living creature or thing) of life. **2.** to destroy. **3.** to defeat or veto (a legislative bill, etc.). – *v.i.* **4.** to inflict or cause death. – *n.* **5.** the act of killing (game, etc.). **6.** an animal or animals killed.

killing /'kɪlɪŋ/ *n. Colloquial* a stroke of extraordinary success, as in a successful speculation in stocks.

kiln /kɪln/ *n.* a furnace or oven for burning, baking, or drying something, especially one for baking bricks.

kilo /'kiloʊ/ *n. Colloquial* → **kilogram**.

kilo- a prefix denoting 10^3 of a given unit, as in *kilogram*. *Symbol*: k

kilogram /'kɪləgræm/ *n.* a unit of mass equal to 1000 grams. *Symbol*: kg

kilohertz /'kɪləhɜts/ *n.* a unit of frequency equal to 1000 hertz; commonly used to express radiofrequency. *Symbol*: kHz

kilojoule /'kɪlədʒul/ *n.* one thousand joules. *Symbol*: kJ

kilometre /'kɪləmitə, kə'lɒmətə/ *n.* a unit of length, the common measure of distances; equal to 1000 metres. *Symbol*: km

kilopascal /'kɪləpæskəl/ *n.* a unit of pressure equal to 1000 pascals; used to express the amount of pressure in tyres, pumps, etc. *Symbol*: kPa

kilowatt /'kɪləwɒt/ *n.* a unit of power equal to 1000 watts. *Symbol*: kW

kilowatt-hour /kɪləwɒt-'aʊə/ *n.* a unit of energy equivalent to that transferred or expended in one hour by one kilowatt of power, 3.6 × 10^6 joules. *Symbol*: Kw.h

kilt /kɪlt/ *n.* any short, pleated skirt, especially one worn by men in the Scottish Highlands.

kilter /'kɪltə/ *n.* good condition; order.

kimono /'kɪmənoʊ, kə'moʊnoʊ/ *n., pl.* **-nos**. a wide-sleeved robe characteristic of Japanese costume.

kin /kɪn/ *n.* relatives collectively.

-kin a diminutive suffix, attached to nouns to signify a little object of the kind mentioned.

kind¹ /kaɪnd/ *adj.* of a good or benevolent nature or disposition, as a person. – **kindness**, **kindliness**, *n.* – **kindly**, *adj., adv.*

kind² /kaɪnd/ *n.* **1.** a class or group of individuals of the same nature or character. **2.** nature or character as determining likeness or difference between things. **3. in kind,** in something of the same kind in the same way. **4. kind of,** (*used adverbially*) *Colloquial* after a fashion; to some extent.

kindergarten /'kɪndəgatn/ *n.* a school for young children, usually under the age of five.

kindle /'kɪndəl/ *v.t.,* **-dled**, **-dling**. **1.** to set (a fire, flame, etc.) burning or blazing. **2.** to excite; animate, rouse, or inflame.

kindred /'kɪndrəd/ *n.* **1.** a body of persons related to one another, or a family, tribe, or race. – *adj.* **2.** associated by origin, nature, qualities, etc.

kinetic /kə'nɛtɪk, kaɪ-/ *adj.* **1.** relating to motion. **2.** caused by motion.

kinetics /kə'nɛtɪks, kaɪ-/ *n.* the branch of mechanics which treats of the action of forces in producing or changing the motion of masses.

king /kɪŋ/ *n.* a male sovereign or monarch.

kingdom /'kɪŋdəm/ *n.* **1.** a state or government having a king or queen as its head. **2.** a realm or province of nature.

kingfisher /'kɪŋfɪʃə/ *n.* any of numerous fish- or insect-eating birds.

kingpin /'kɪŋpɪn/ *n. Colloquial* the principal person or element in a company or system, etc.

king prawn *n.* a large, edible prawn of eastern Australian waters.

kink /kɪŋk/ *n.* **1.** a twist or curl, as in a thread, rope, or hair, caused by its doubling or bending upon itself. **2.** a deviation, especially sexual. – **kinky**, *adj.*

kinship /'kɪnʃɪp/ *n.* **1.** the state or fact of being of kin; family relationship. **2.** relationship by nature, qualities, etc.; affinity.

kiosk /'kiɒsk/ *n.* a small, light structure for the sale of newspapers, cigarettes, etc.

kip /kɪp/ *n. Colloquial* sleep.

kipper /'kɪpə/ *n.* a smoked fish, especially a herring.

kirk /kɜk/ *n. Scot* a church.

kismet /ˈkɪzmət, ˈkɪs-/ *n.* fate; destiny.

kiss /kɪs/ *v.t.* **1.** to touch or press with the lips, while compressing and then separating them, in token of greeting, affection, etc. – *n.* **2.** the act of kissing.

kit /kɪt/ *n.* **1.** a set or collection of tools, supplies, etc., for a specific purpose. **2.** a set or collection of parts to be assembled.

kitchen /ˈkɪtʃən/ *n.* a room or place equipped for or appropriated to cooking.

kitchen tea *n.* a party for a bride-to-be to which the guests, usually other women, bring a present for her home; shower tea.

kite /kaɪt/ *n.* **1.** a light frame covered with some thin material, to be flown in the wind at the end of a long string. **2.** any of various medium-sized hawks. **3.** *Commerce* a fictitious negotiable instrument, not representing any actual transaction, used for raising money or sustaining credit.

kith /kɪθ/ *n. in the phr.* **kith and kin,** friends and relatives.

kitsch /kɪtʃ/ *n.* pretentious or worthless art, literature, etc.

kitten /ˈkɪtn/ *n.* a young cat.

kitty /ˈkɪti/ *n., pl.* **-ties**. a jointly held fund or collection, usually of small amounts of money.

kiwi /ˈkiwi/ *n.* any of several flightless birds of New Zealand.

kiwifruit *n.* an oval-shaped, hairy fruit about 7 cm long with a somewhat gooseberry-like flavour; Chinese gooseberry. Also, **Kiwi fruit**.

klaxon /ˈklæksən/ *n.* a type of warning hooter with a strident tone, originally used in motor vehicles.

kleptomania /klɛptəˈmeɪniə/ *n. Psychology* an irresistible desire to steal, without regard to personal needs. – **kleptomaniac**, *n.*

knack /næk/ *n.* a faculty or power of doing something with ease as from special skill; aptitude.

knacker /ˈnækə/ *n.* someone who buys old or useless horses for slaughter. – **knackery**, *n.*

knapsack /ˈnæpsæk/ *n.* a backpack, originally one of leather or canvas.

knave /neɪv/ *n.* **1.** an unprincipled or dishonest fellow. **2.** *Cards* a playing card bearing the formalised picture of a prince; jack. – **knavery**, *n.* – **knavish**, *adj.*

knead /nid/ *v.t.* to work (dough, etc.) into a uniform mixture by pressing, folding and stretching.

knee /ni/ *n., v.,* **kneed**, **kneeing**. – *n.* **1.** the joint or region in humans between the thigh and the lower part of the leg. – *v.t.* **2.** to strike or touch with the knee.

kneecap /ˈnikæp/ *n.* the flat, movable bone at the front of the knee.

kneel /nil/ *v.i.,* **knelt** *or* **kneeled**, **kneeling**. to fall or rest on the knees or a knee.

knell /nɛl/ *n.* the sound made by a bell rung slowly for a death or a funeral.

knew /nju/ *v.* past tense of **know**.

knickerbockers /ˈnɪkəbɒkəz/ *pl. n.* loosely fitting short breeches gathered in at the knee.

knickers /ˈnɪkəz/ *pl. n.* **1.** women's underpants. **2.** → **knickerbockers**.

knick-knack /ˈnɪk-næk/ *n.* **1.** a pleasing trifle; a trinket. **2.** a bit of bric-a-brac. Also, **nick-nack**.

knife /naɪf/ *n., pl.* **knives**, *v.,* **knifed**, **knifing**. – *n.* **1.** a cutting instrument consisting essentially of a thin blade (usually of steel and with a sharp edge) attached to a handle. – *v.t.* **2.** to apply a knife to; cut, stab, etc., with a knife.

knight /naɪt/ *n.* **1.** *History* a man, usually of noble birth, bound to chivalrous conduct. **2.** a man upon whom a certain dignity, and with it the honorific *Sir*, is conferred by a sovereign for life, because of personal merit or for services rendered to the country. – *v.t.* **3.** to dub or create (a person) a knight.

knit /nɪt/ *v.,* **knitted** *or* **knit**, **knitting**, *n.* – *v.t.* **1.** to make (a garment, fabric, etc.) by interlacing loops of yarn either by hand with knitting needles or by machine. **2.** to join closely and firmly together, as members or parts. – *v.i.* **3.** to perform the action of knitting, especially by hand: *can you knit?* **4.** to become closely and firmly joined together; grow together, as broken bones do. **5.** to contract, as the brow does. – *n.* **6.** fabric produced by interlooping of a yarn or yarns.

knives /naɪvz/ *n.* plural of **knife**.

knob /nɒb/ *n.* **1.** a projecting part, usually rounded, forming the handle of a door, drawer, or the like. **2.** a rounded lump or protuberance.

knock /nɒk/ *v.i.* **1.** to strike a sounding blow with the fist, knuckles, or anything hard, especially on a door, as in seeking admittance, giving a signal, etc. **2.** (of an internal-combustion engine) to make a metallic noise as a result of faulty combustion. **3.** to collide (usually fol. by *against* or *into*). **4. knock off,** *Colloquial* to stop an activity, especially work. – *v.t.* **5.** to give a sounding or forcible blow to. **6.** to drive, force or render by a blow or blows. **7.** to strike (a thing) against something else. **8.** *Colloquial* to criticise; find fault with. **9. knock out,** to render senseless. – *n.* **10.** the act or sound of knocking.

knock-back /ˈnɒk-bæk/ *n. Colloquial* a refusal; rejection.

knock-for-knock agreement *n.* an agreement between insurance companies, whereby each company bears the loss to its own policy holder without requiring the policy holder to bring an action against the other party involved, as in a motor car collision.

knockout /ˈnɒkaʊt/ *n.* **1.** the act of knocking out. **2.** *Colloquial* a person or thing of overwhelming success or attractiveness.

knoll /nɒl/ *n.* a small, rounded hill or eminence; a hillock.

knot /nɒt/ *n., v.,* **knotted**, **knotting**. – *n.* **1.** an interlacement of a cord, rope, or the like, drawn tight into a lump or knob, as for fastening two cords, etc., together or to something else. **2.** the hard, cross-grained mass of wood at the place where a branch joins the trunk of a tree. **3.** a unit of speed, used in marine and aerial navigation, and in meteorology. – *v.t.* **4.** to tie in a knot or knots; form a knot or knots in. – *v.i.* **5.** to become tied or tangled in a knot or knots.

know /noʊ/ *v.*, **knew**, **known**, **knowing**. – *v.t.* **1.** to perceive or understand as fact or truth, or apprehend with clearness and certainty. **2.** to have fixed in the mind or memory. **3.** to be cognisant or aware of; to be acquainted with (a thing, place, person, etc.), as by sight, experience, or report. **4.** to understand from experience or attainment (fol. by *how* before an infinitive). – *v.i.* **5.** to have knowledge, or clear and certain perception, as of fact or truth. **6.** to be cognisant or aware, as of some fact, circumstances, or occurrence; have information, as about something. – **knowledge**, *n.*

knuckle /ˈnʌkəl/ *n.*, *v.*, **-led**, **-ling**. – *n.* **1.** a joint of a finger. – *v.i.* **2.** to apply oneself vigorously or earnestly, as to a task (fol. by *down*). **3.** to yield or submit (often fol. by *down* or *under*).

knurl /nɜl/ *n.* **1.** a small ridge or the like, especially one of a series. – *v.t.* **2.** to make knurls or ridges on.

koala /koʊˈalə/ *n.* a tailless, grey, furry, arboreal marsupial. Also, **koala bear**.

kook /kuk/ *n.* *Colloquial* a strange or eccentric person. – **kooky**, *adj.*

kookaburra /ˈkʊkəbʌrə/ *n.* either of two Australian kingfishers renowned for their call resembling human laughter.

kosher /ˈkɒʃə, ˈkoʊʃə/ *adj.* fit, lawful, or ritually permitted, according to the Jewish law.

kowtow /kaʊˈtaʊ/ *v.i.* to act in an obsequious manner; show servile deference.

krypton /ˈkrɪptɒn/ *n.* an inert gaseous element. *Symbol*: Kr

kudos /ˈkjudɒs/ *n.* glory; renown.

kumquat /ˈkʌmkwɒt/ *n.* a small, round, or oblong citrus fruit with a sweet rind and acid pulp.

kung-fu /kʊŋ-ˈfu, kʌŋ-ˈfu/ *n.* an ancient Chinese martial art with fluid hand and leg movements used for self-defence and resembling karate.

kurrajong /ˈkʌrədʒɒŋ/ *n.* a tree of eastern Australia, valued as fodder.

L l

L, l /ɛl/ *n., pl.* **L's** *or* **Ls**, **l's** *or* **ls**. the 12th letter of the English alphabet.

label /'leɪbəl/ *n., v.,* **-belled**, **-belling**. – *n.* **1.** a slip of paper or other material for affixing to something to indicate its nature, ownership, destination, etc. **2.** *Colloquial* the trade name, especially of a gramophone record company. – *v.t.* **3.** to affix a label to; mark with a label.

laboratory /lə'bɒrətri/ *n., pl.* **-ries**. a building or part of a building fitted with apparatus for conducting scientific investigations, experiments, tests, etc., or for manufacturing chemicals, medicines, etc.

laborious /lə'bɔriəs/ *adj.* requiring much labour, exertion, or perseverance.

labour = labor /'leɪbə/ *n.* **1.** bodily toil for the sake of gain or economic production. **2.** Also, **labour force**. the workers engaged in this. **3.** work, especially of a hard or fatiguing kind. **4.** the time during which the uterine contractions of childbirth occur. – *v.i.* **5.** to perform labour; exert one's powers of body or mind; work; toil.

labour-intensive = labor-intensive /'leɪbər-ɪn,tɛnsɪv/ *adj.* of or relating to an industry which, while not needing a very large capital investment in plant, etc., requires a comparatively large labour force (opposed to *capital-intensive*).

labour market = labor market *n.* the available supply of labour considered with reference to the demand for it.

labrador /'læbrədɔ/ *n.* one of a breed of dogs with black or golden coats.

labyrinth /'læbərɪnθ/ *n.* an intricate combination of passages in which it is difficult to find one's way or to reach the exit.

lace /leɪs/ *n., v.,* **laced**, **lacing**. – *n.* **1.** a netlike ornamental fabric made of threads by hand or machine. **2.** a cord or string for holding or drawing together, as when passed through holes in opposite edges. – *v.t.* **3.** to fasten, draw together, or compress by means of a lace. **4.** to intermix, as coffee with spirits.

lacerate /'læsəreɪt/ *v.t.,* **-rated**, **-rating**. **1.** to tear roughly; mangle. **2.** to hurt.

lack /læk/ *n.* **1.** deficiency or absence of something requisite, desirable, or customary. – *v.t.* **2.** to be deficient in, destitute of, or without.

lackadaisical /lækə'deɪzɪkəl/ *adj.* sentimentally or affectedly languishing; weakly sentimental; listless.

lacklustre /'læklʌstə, læk'lʌstə/ *adj.* lacking lustre or brightness; dull.

laconic /lə'kɒnɪk/ *adj.* using few words.

lacquer /'lækə/ *n.* a resinous varnish.

lactate /læk'teɪt/ *v.i.,* **-tated**, **-tating**. (of mammals) to produce milk.

lad /læd/ *n.* a boy or youth.

ladder /'lædə/ *n.* **1.** a structure of wood, metal, or rope, commonly consisting of two sidepieces between which a series of bars or rungs are set at suitable distances, forming a means of ascent or descent. **2.** a line or a place in a stocking, etc., where a series of stitches have slipped out or come undone.

lade /leɪd/ *v.t.,* **laded**, **laden** *or* **laded**, **lading**. to put (something) on or in as a burden, load, or cargo; load.

lading /'leɪdɪŋ/ *n.* load; freight; cargo.

ladle /'leɪdl/ *n., v.,* **-dled**, **-dling**. – *n.* **1.** a long-handled utensil with a dish-shaped or cup-shaped bowl for dipping or conveying liquids. – *v.t.* **2.** to dip or convey with or as with a ladle.

lady /'leɪdi/ *n., pl.* **-dies**. **1.** a woman of good family or social position, or of good breeding, refinement, etc. (correlative of *gentleman*). **2.** (a polite term for any woman). **3.** a prefix to a title of honour or respect.

ladybird /'leɪdibɜd/ *n.* a beetle of graceful form and delicate colouration. Also, **lady beetle**, **ladybug**.

lady-in-waiting /,leɪdi-ɪn-'weɪtɪŋ/ *n., pl.* **ladies-in-waiting**. a lady who is in attendance upon a queen or princess.

lag /læg/ *v.i.,* **lagged**, **lagging**. to move slowly; fall behind; hang back (often fol. by *behind*).

lager /'lagə/ *n.* a German type of beer.

laggard /'lægəd/ *adj.* **1.** lagging; backward; slow. – *n.* **2.** someone who lags; lingerer.

lagoon /lə'gun/ *n.* any small, pondlike body of water.

laid /leɪd/ *v.* past tense and past participle of **lay**[1].

lain /leɪn/ *v.* past participle of **lie**[2].

lair[1] /lɛə/ *n.* the den or resting place of a wild beast.

lair[2] /lɛə/ *n.* *Colloquial* a flashily dressed young man of brash and vulgar behaviour.

laird /lɛəd/ *n.* in Scotland, a landed proprietor.

laissez faire /,leɪseɪ 'fɛə/ *n.* **1.** the theory or system of government that upholds the autonomous character of the economic order, believing that government should intervene as little as possible in the direction of economic affairs. **2.** the doctrine of non-interference, especially in the conduct of others. Also, **laisser faire**.

laity /'leɪəti/ *n.* laypeople, as distinguished from members of the clergy.

lake[1] /leɪk/ *n.* a body of water (fresh or salt) of considerable size, surrounded by land.

lake[2] /leɪk/ *n.* a red pigment.

lama /'lamə/ *n.* a priest or monk of the form of Buddhism prevailing in Tibet, Mongolia, etc.

lamb /læm/ *n.* a young sheep.

lame /leɪm/ *adj.,* **lamer**, **lamest**. crippled or physically disabled, as a person or animal, especially in the foot or leg so as to limp or walk with difficulty.

lamé /'lameɪ/ *n.* an ornamental fabric in which metallic threads are woven with silk, wool, artificial fibres, or cotton.

lament /lə'mɛnt/ *v.t.* **1.** to feel or express sorrow or regret for; mourn for or over. – *n.* **2.** an expression of grief or sorrow. – **lamentable**, *adj.*

lamina /'læmənə/ *n., pl.* **-nae** /-ni/, **-nas**. a thin plate, scale, or layer.

laminate /ˈlæmәneɪt/ *v.t.*, **-nated**, **-nating**. **1.** to separate or split into thin layers. **2.** to construct by placing layer upon layer.

lamington /ˈlæmɪŋtәn/ *n.* a cake confection made by covering a cube of sponge cake in chocolate icing and shredded coconut.

lamp /læmp/ *n.* any of various devices for using an illuminant, as gas or electricity, or for heating, as by burning alcohol.

lampoon /læmˈpun/ *n.* a malicious or virulent satire upon a person, institution, government, etc., in either prose or verse.

lamprey /ˈlæmpri/ *n., pl.* **-preys**. an eel-like fish.

LAN /læn/ local area network.

lance /læns, lans/ *n., v.,* **lanced**, **lancing**. – *n.* **1.** a long, shafted weapon with a metal head, used by mounted soldiers in charging. – *v.t.* **2.** to pierce with or as with a lance.

land /lænd/ *n.* **1.** the solid substance of the earth's surface. **2.** agricultural areas as opposed to urban. **3.** *Economics* natural resources as a factor of production. – *v.t.* **4.** to bring to or put on land or shore. **5.** to give (someone) a task which they may be unwilling to perform (fol. by *with*). – *v.i.* **6.** to alight upon the ground as from an aeroplane, a train, or after a jump or the like.

land certificate *n.* a certificate under the seal of a land registry, containing a copy of the registered particulars of a piece of land.

landing /ˈlændɪŋ/ *n.* **1.** the act of arriving on land as by a plane, etc. **2.** the floor at the head or foot of a flight of stairs.

landlady /ˈlændleɪdi/ *n., pl.* **-dies**. **1.** a woman who owns and leases land, buildings, etc. **2.** a woman who owns or runs an inn, lodging house, or boarding house.

landlord /ˈlændlɔd/ *n.* **1.** someone who owns and leases land, buildings, etc., to another. **2.** the master of an inn, lodging house, etc.

landlubber /ˈlændlʌbә/ *n. Nautical* someone who lives on land.

landmark /ˈlændmak/ *n.* **1.** a conspicuous object on land that serves as a guide, as to vessels at sea. **2.** a prominent or distinguishing feature, part, event, etc.

land rights *pl. n.* the rights of the original inhabitants of a country to possess land, especially sacred tribal grounds.

landscape /ˈlændskeɪp/ *n.* a view or prospect of rural scenery, more or less extensive, such as is comprehended within the scope or range of vision from a single point of view.

landslide /ˈlændslaɪd/ *n.* **1.** the sliding down of a mass of soil, detritus, or rock on a steep slope. **2.** any overwhelming victory.

land tax *n.* a tax on land the unimproved value of which exceeds a certain sum.

lane /leɪn/ *n.* **1.** a narrow way or passage between fences, walls, or houses. **2.** any narrow or well-defined passage, track, channel, or course.

language /ˈlæŋgwɪdʒ, ˈlæŋwɪdʒ/ *n.* **1.** communication by voice in the distinctively human manner, using arbitrary auditory symbols in conventional ways with conventional meanings. **2.** any set or system of such symbols as used in a more or less uniform fashion by a number of people, who are thus enabled to communicate intelligibly with one another.

languid /ˈɪæŋgwәd/ *adj.* **1.** lacking in spirit or interest; indifferent. **2.** lacking in vigour or activity; slack; dull. – **languor**, *n.*

languish /ˈlæŋgwɪʃ/ *v.i.* **1.** to become or be weak or feeble; droop or fade. **2.** to lose activity and vigour. **3.** to pine with desire or longing for.

lank /læŋk/ *adj.* **1.** meagrely slim; lean; gaunt. **2.** (of hair) straight and limp; not resilient or wiry. – **lanky**, *adj.*

lanolin /ˈlænәlәn/ *n.* a fatty substance, extracted from wool, used in ointments. Also, **lanoline**.

lantana /lænˈtanә/ *n.* a tropical plant which has become a troublesome weed in some areas.

lantern /ˈlæntәn/ *n.* a transparent or translucent case for enclosing a light and protecting it from the wind, rain, etc.

lap[1] /læp/ *n.* (the part of the clothing that lies on) the front portion of the body from the waist to the knees when one sits.

lap[2] /læp/ *v.,* **lapped**, **lapping**, *n.* – *v.t.* **1.** to fold over or about something; wrap or wind round something. **2.** to get a lap or more ahead of (a competitor) in racing. – *n.* **3.** a single round or circuit of the course in racing.

lap[3] /læp/ *v.t.,* **lapped**, **lapping**. **1.** to take up (liquid) with the tongue; lick up (often fol. by *up*). **2.** to receive and accept avidly (fol. by *up*).

lapel /lәˈpɛl/ *n.* part of a garment folded back on the breast, especially a continuation of a coat collar.

lapidary /ˈlæpәdәri/ *n., pl.* **-ries**. someone who cuts, polishes, and engraves stones, especially precious stones.

lapis lazuli /læpәs ˈlæzjәli, -laɪ/ *n.* a deep blue stone.

lapse /læps/ *n., v.,* **lapsed**, **lapsing**. – *n.* **1.** a slip or slight error. **2.** a gliding or passing away, as of time. **3.** a falling, or sinking to a lower grade, condition, or degree. – *v.i.* **4.** to pass slowly, silently, or by degrees. **5.** to cease to be in force or use.

laptop /ˈlæptɒp/ *adj.* **1.** (of a computer) portable and small enough to be operated while held on one's knees. – *n.* **2.** a laptop computer.

larceny /ˈlasәni/ *n., pl.* **-nies**. *Law* the wrongful taking and carrying away of the personal goods of another.

lard /lad/ *n.* rendered pig fat.

larder /ˈladә/ *n.* a room or place where food is kept; pantry.

large /ladʒ/ *adj.,* **larger**, **largest**. being of more than common size, amount, or number.

large-scale integration *n.* an electronic manufacturing process which creates memories and complex circuits for computers with storage densities of millions of words per cubic centimetre.

largess /laˈdʒɛs/ *n.* generous bestowal of gifts. Also, **largesse**.

lark[1] /lak/ *n.* a singing bird.

lark[2] /lak/ *n. Colloquial* a merry or hilarious

adventure; prank.

larrikin /'lærəkən/ *n. Colloquial* a hoodlum.

larva /'lavə/ *n.* (*plural* **larvae** /'lavi/, **larvas**) *Entomology* the young of any insect which undergoes metamorphosis.

larynx /'lærıŋks/ *n., pl.* **larynges** /lə'rındʒiz/, **larynxes**. *Anatomy, Zoology* the cavity at the upper end of the trachea or windpipe containing the vocal cords.

lascivious /lə'sıviəs/ *adj.* inclined to lust; wanton or lewd.

laser /'leızə/ *n.* a device for producing a coherent, monochromatic, high-intensity beam of radiation of a frequency within, or near to, the range of visible light.

laser disc *n.* a grooveless disc on which digitally-encoded data, as music, text, or pictures, is stored as tiny pits in the surface, and is read or played by a laser beam which scans the surface of the disc. Also, **laser disk**.

laser printer *n.* a high-speed sophisticated printer that uses a laser to form dot-matrix patterns on paper which are then covered with fused metallic particles by an electronic process.

lash[1] /læʃ/ *n.* **1.** the flexible part of a whip. **2.** a swift stroke or blow, with a whip, etc., as a punishment. **3.** an eyelash. – *v.t.* **4.** to strike or beat, now usually with a whip or something slender and flexible. – *v.i.* **5.** to strike vigorously at, as with a weapon, whip, or the like (often fol. by *out*).

lash[2] /læʃ/ *v.t.* to bind or fasten with a rope, cord, or the like.

lass /læs/ *n.* a girl or young woman.

lassitude /'læsətʃud/ *n.* weariness.

lasso /læ'su/ *n., pl.* **-sos, -soes**. a long rope with a running noose at one end, used for catching horses, cattle, etc.

last[1] /last/ *adj.* **1.** occurring or coming latest, or after all others, as in time, order, or place. **2.** latest; next before the present; most recent. **3.** being the only remaining. **4.** conclusive. – *adv.* **5.** after all others. **6.** on the most recent occasion. – *n.* **7.** that which is last.

last[2] /last/ *v.i.* to go on, or continue in progress, existence or life; endure.

last[3] /last/ *n.* a model of the human foot, used in shoemaking.

latch /lætʃ/ *n.* a device for holding a door, gate, or the like closed, consisting basically of a bar falling or sliding into a catch, groove, hole, etc.

late /leıt/ *adj.* **1.** occurring, coming, or being after the usual or proper time. **2.** far advanced in time. **3.** recently deceased. – *adv.* **4.** after the usual or proper time, or after delay. **5.** until after the usual time or hour; until a late hour at night.

lately /'leıtli/ *adv.* recently.

latency /'leıtnsi/ *n.* **1.** the state of being latent or concealed. **2.** *Computers* a delay encountered when waiting for a specific response, often caused by queueing of discs or tapes.

latent /'leıtnt/ *adj.* hidden; concealed; present, but not visible or apparent.

lateral /'lætərəl, 'lætrəl/ *adj.* of or relating to the side; situated at, proceeding from, or directed to a side.

latex /'leıtɛks/ *n., pl.* **latices** /'lætəsiz/, **latexes** /'leıtɛksəz/. *Botany* a milky liquid in certain plants, as those yielding rubber.

lath /laθ/ *n., pl.* **laths** /laðz, laθs/ a thin, narrow strip of wood.

lathe /leıð/ *n.* a machine for use in working metal, wood, etc.

lather /'læðə/ *n.* foam or froth made from soap moistened with water, as by a brush for shaving.

latitude /'lætətjud/ *n.* **1.** *Geography* the angular distance north or south from the equator of a point on the earth's surface, measured on the meridian of the point. **2.** freedom from narrow restrictions; permitted freedom of action, opinion, etc.

latrine /lə'trin/ *n.* a toilet.

latter /'lætə/ *adj.* **1.** being the second mentioned of two (opposed to *former*). **2.** more advanced in time; later. **3.** nearer, or comparatively near, to the end or close. – *n.* **4. the latter,** the item or person (out of two) last mentioned.

lattice /'lætəs/ *n.* a structure of crossed wooden or metal strips with open spaces between, used as a screen, etc.

laud /lɔd/ *v.t.* to praise; extol.

laugh /laf/ *v.i.* **1.** to express mirth, amusement, derision, etc., by an explosive, inarticulate sound of the voice, facial expressions, etc. – *n.* **2.** the act or sound of laughing, or laughter. **3.** (*often ironic*) a cause for laughter. – **laughter**, *n.*

launch[1] /lɔntʃ/ *n.* a heavy open or half-decked boat.

launch[2] /lɔntʃ/ *v.t.* **1.** to set (a boat) afloat; lower into the water. **2.** to set going.

launder /'lɔndə/ *v.t.* **1.** to wash and iron (clothes, etc.). **2.** to transfer (funds of suspect or illegal origin) usually to a foreign country, and then later to recover them from sources which give them the appearance of being legitimate.

laundry /'lɔndri/ *n., pl.* **-dries**. **1.** articles of clothing, etc., to be washed. **2.** the room in a house set aside for the washing of clothes. **3.** the act of laundering.

laurel /'lɒrəl/ *n.* **1.** a small evergreen tree. **2.** (*usu. pl.*) honour won, as by achievement.

laurel wreath /lɒrəl 'riθ/ *n.* a wreath made from the foliage of the laurel or bay tree, seen as an emblem of distinction.

lava /'lavə/ *n.* the molten or fluid rock (magma), which issues from a volcanic vent.

lavatory /'lævətri/ *n., pl.* **-ries**. (a room with) a toilet.

lavender /'lævəndə/ *n.* a plant with fragrant, pale purple flowers.

lavish /'lævıʃ/ *adj.* **1.** using or bestowing in great abundance or without stint (often fol. by *of*). – *v.t.* **2.** to expend or bestow in great abundance or without stint.

law /lɔ/ *n.* **1.** the principles and regulations emanating from a government and applicable to a people. **2.** the profession which deals with law and legal procedure. **3.** (in philosophical and scientific use) a statement of a relation or sequence of phenomena invariable under the same conditions. – **lawful**, *adj.*

lawn[1] /lɔn/ *n.* a stretch of grass-covered land, especially one closely mowed.

lawn[2] /lɔn/ *n.* a thin or sheer linen or cotton fabric, either plain or printed.

lawn bowls *n.* a game in which the players roll biased or weighted balls along a green in an effort to bring them as near as possible to a stationary ball called the jack.

law of diminishing returns *n.* the theory or principle that constant increases in input or production will eventually result in progressively smaller increases in output or profit.

law of increasing returns *n.* the observed fact that in some industries expenditure of labour or capital up to a certain point has the capacity to decrease the cost per unit of a commodity and thereby increase the corresponding returns.

lawyer /ˈlɔɪjə/ *n.* one whose profession it is to conduct suits in court or to give legal advice and aid.

lax /læks/ *adj.* **1.** lacking in strictness or severity; careless or negligent. **2.** loose or slack; not tense, rigid, or firm.

laxative /ˈlæksətɪv/ *adj. Medicine* mildly purgative.

lay[1] /leɪ/ *v.*, **laid**, **laying**, *n.* – *v.t.* **1.** to put or place in a position of rest or recumbency. **2.** to bring forth and deposit. **3.** to put away for future use (fol. by *by*). **4.** to set. **5.** to present, bring forward, or prefer, as a claim, charge, etc. **6.** to place on or over a surface, as paint; cover or spread with something else. **7. lay off, a.** to put aside. **b.** to dismiss, especially temporarily, as an employee. **c.** *Colloquial* to desist. **8. lay on,** to provide or supply. – *v.i.* **9.** to lay eggs. **10.** to apply oneself vigorously. – *n.* **11.** the way or position in which a thing is laid or lies.

lay[2] /leɪ/ *v.* past tense of **lie**[2].

lay[3] /leɪ/ *adj.* belonging to, relating to, or performed by the people or laity, as distinguished from the clergy.

lay-by /ˈleɪ-baɪ/ *n.* the reservation of an article by payment of a cash deposit.

layer /ˈleɪə/ *n.* a thickness of some material laid on or spread over a surface; a stratum.

layman /ˈleɪmən/ *n., pl.* **-men**. a male layperson.

layout /ˈleɪaʊt/ *n.* an arrangement or plan.

layperson /ˈleɪpɜsən/ *n.* **1.** one of the laity; someone who is not a member of the clergy. **2.** someone who is not a member of a particular profession. Also, **lay person**.

laze /leɪz/ *v.i.*, **lazed**, **lazing**. to be lazy; idle or lounge lazily.

lazy /ˈleɪzi/ *adj.*, **-zier**, **-ziest**. disinclined to exertion or work; idle.

leach /litʃ/ *v.t.* to cause (water, etc.) to percolate through something.

lead[1] /lid/ *v.*, **led**, **leading**, *n., adj.* – *v.t.* **1.** to take or conduct on the way; go before or with to show the way. **2.** to guide in direction, course, action, opinion, etc.; to influence or induce. **3.** to conduct or bring (water, wire, etc.) in a particular course. **4.** to be at the head of, command, or direct (an army, organisation, etc.). **5.** to go through or pass (life, etc.). – *v.i.* **6.** to act as a guide; show the way. **7.** to afford passage to a place, etc., as a road, stairway, or the like. **8.** to go first; be in advance. – *n.* **9.** the first or foremost place; position in advance of others. **10.** the extent of advance. **11.** a thong or line for holding a dog or other animal in check. **12.** a guiding indication; clue. **13.** *Electricity* a single conductor, often flexible and insulated, used in connections between pieces of electrical apparatus. – *adj.* **14.** solo or dominating as in a musical structure.

lead[2] /lɛd/ *n.* **1.** *Chemistry* a heavy, comparatively soft, malleable bluish-grey metal. *Symbol*: Pb **2.** a plummet or mass of lead suspended by a line, as for taking soundings.

leaden /ˈlɛdn/ *adj.* **1.** consisting or made of lead. **2.** inertly heavy, or hard to lift or move, as weight, the limbs, etc.

leader /ˈlidə/ *n.* **1.** someone who or that which leads. **2.** a principal or important editorial article, as in a newspaper.

leadlight window *n.* a window made from various pieces of glass, sometimes coloured or frosted, set in a lead frame.

leaf /lif/ *n., pl.* **leaves**, *v.* – *n.* **1.** one of the expanded, usually green, organs borne by the stem of a plant. **2.** *Bibliography* a unit generally comprising two printed pages of a book. **3.** a thin sheet of metal, etc. **4.** a sliding, hinged, or detachable flat part, as of a door, tabletop, etc. – *v.t.* **5. leaf through,** to turn the pages of quickly.

leaflet /ˈliflət/ *n.* a small flat or folded sheet of printed matter, as for distribution.

league[1] /lig/ *n.* **1.** a covenant or compact made between persons, parties, states, etc., for the maintenance or promotion of common interests or for mutual assistance or service. **2.** the aggregation of persons, parties, states, etc., associated in such a covenant; a confederacy.

league[2] /lig/ *n.* a former unit of distance.

leak /lik/ *n.* **1.** an unintended hole, crack, or the like by which fluid, gas, etc., enters or escapes. **2.** an accidental or apparently accidental disclosure of information, etc. – *v.i.* **3.** to let fluid, gas, etc., enter or escape, as through an unintended hole, crack, permeable material, or the like. **4.** to pass in or out in this manner, as water, etc. **5.** to transpire or become known undesignedly (fol. by *out*). – *v.t.* **6.** to disclose (information, especially of a confidential nature), especially to the media. – **leakage**, *n.*

lean[1] /lin/ *v.i.*, **leant** *or* **leaned**, **leaning**. **1.** to incline or bend from a vertical position or in a particular direction. **2.** to rest against or on something for support. **3.** to depend or rely.

lean[2] /lin/ *adj.* **1.** (of persons or animals) scant of flesh; thin; not plump or fat. **2.** (of meat) containing little or no fat.

leap /lip/ *v.*, **leapt** *or* **leaped**, **leaping**, *n.* – *v.i.* **1.** to spring through the air from one point or position to another. **2.** to pass, come, rise, etc., as if with a bound. – *v.t.* **3.** to jump over. – *n.* **4.** a spring, jump, or bound; a light springing movement.

leap year *n.* a year containing 366 days, or one day (29 February) more than the ordinary year.

learn /lɜn/ *v.t.,* **learnt** *or* **learned** /lɜnd/, **learning**. to acquire knowledge of or skill in by study, instruction, or experience.

learned /ˈlɜnəd/ *adj.* having much knowledge gained by study; scholarly.

lease /lis/ *n., v.,* **leased**, **leasing**. – *n.* **1.** an instrument conveying property to another for a definite period, or at will, usually in consideration of rent or other periodical compensation. – *v.t.* **2.** to grant the temporary possession or use of (lands, etc.) to another, usually for compensation at a fixed rate; let. **3.** to take or to hold by a lease, as a flat, house, etc.

lease-back /ˈlis-bæk/ *n.* a financial arrangement in which the owner of a property sells it to an investor who at the same time grants the seller a long-term lease of the property.

leasehold /ˈlishould/ *n.* **1.** a land interest acquired under a lease. – *adj.* **2.** having to do with land owned by the crown and which is leased out, usually for a specified time period. Cf. **freehold**.

leash /liʃ/ *n.* a lead for a dog.

least /list/ *adj.* **1.** little beyond all others in size, amount, degree, etc.; smallest; slightest. – *n.* **2.** that which is least; the least amount, quantity, degree, etc.

leather /ˈlɛðə/ *n.* the skin of animals prepared for use by tanning or a similar process.

leave[1] /liv/ *v.,* **left**, **leaving**. – *v.t.* **1.** to go away from, depart from, or quit, as a place, a person, or a thing. **2.** to let stay or be as specified. **3.** to omit or exclude (fol. by *out*). **4.** to give in charge; give for use after one's death or departure. **5.** to have as a remainder after subtraction. – *v.i.* **6.** to go away, depart, or set out.

leave[2] /liv/ *n.* **1.** permission to do something. **2.** permission to be absent, as from duty. **3.** a farewell.

leaven /ˈlɛvən/ *n.* a mass of fermenting dough reserved for producing fermentation in a new batch of dough.

lecher /ˈlɛtʃə/ *n.* a man immoderately given to sexual indulgence; a lewd man. – **lechery**, *n.* – **lecherous**, *adj.*

lectern /ˈlɛktən/ *n.* a reading desk in a church, especially that from which the lessons are read.

lecture /ˈlɛktʃə/ *n., v.,* **-tured**, **-turing**. – *n.* **1.** a discourse read or delivered before an audience, especially for instruction or to set forth some subject. – *v.i.* **2.** to give a lecture. – *v.t.* **3.** to deliver a lecture to or before.

led /lɛd/ *v.* past tense and past participle of **lead**[1].

ledge /lɛdʒ/ *n.* any relatively narrow, horizontal projecting part, or any part affording a horizontal shelf-like surface.

ledger /ˈlɛdʒə/ *n.* *Bookkeeping* an account book of final entry, containing all the accounts.

lee[1] /li/ *n.* the side or part that is sheltered or turned away from the wind.

lee[2] /li/ *n.* (*usu. pl.*) that which settles from a liquid, especially from wine.

leech /litʃ/ *n.* a bloodsucking or carnivorous, usually aquatic, worm.

leek /lik/ *n.* a plant allied to the onion but having a cylindrical bulb.

leer /lɪə/ *n.* a side glance, especially of sly or insulting suggestion or significance.

leeway /ˈliweɪ/ *n.* *Colloquial* extra space, time, money, etc.

left[1] /lɛft/ *adj.* belonging or relating to the side of a person or thing which is turned towards the west when facing north (opposed to *right*).

left[2] /lɛft/ *v.* past tense and past participle of **leave**[1].

left-handed /ˈlɛft-hændəd/ *adj.* having the left hand more serviceable than the right; preferring to use the left hand.

leftover /ˈlɛftouvə/ *n.* something left over or remaining.

left wing *n.* members of a socialist, progressive, or radical political party or section of a party, generally those favouring extensive political reform.

leg /lɛg/ *n.* **1.** one of the members or limbs which support and move the human or animal body. **2.** something resembling or suggesting a leg in use, position, or appearance. **3.** one of the distinct portions of any course.

legacy /ˈlɛgəsi/ *n., pl.* **-cies**. **1.** *Law* a gift of property, especially personal property, as money, by will; a bequest. **2.** a consequence.

legal /ˈligəl/ *adj.* **1.** appointed, established, or authorised by law; deriving authority from law. **2.** of or relating to law. **3.** connected with the law or its administration.

legal tender *n.* currency which may be lawfully tendered or offered in payment of money debts and which may not be refused by creditors.

legate /ˈlɛgət/ *n.* an ecclesiastic delegated by the pope as his representative.

legatee /lɛgəˈti/ *n.* one to whom a legacy is bequeathed.

legation /ləˈgeɪʃən/ *n.* (formerly) a diplomatic mission of lesser rank than an embassy.

legend /ˈlɛdʒənd/ *n.* **1.** a non-historical or unverifiable story handed down by tradition from earlier times and popularly accepted as historical. **2.** an inscription. – **legendary**, *adj.*

legging /ˈlɛgɪŋ/ *n.* (*usu. pl.*) an extra outer covering for the leg, usually extending from the ankle to the knee, but sometimes higher.

legible /ˈlɛdʒəbəl/ *adj.* that may be read or deciphered, especially with ease, as writing or printing. – **legibility**, *n.*

legion /ˈlidʒən/ *n.* **1.** an infantry brigade in the army of ancient Rome. **2.** one of certain military bodies of modern times, as the Foreign Legion. **3.** any great host or multitude, whether of persons or of things.

legislation /lɛdʒəsˈleɪʃən/ *n.* **1.** the act of making or enacting laws. **2.** a law or a body of laws enacted. – **legislate**, *v.* – **legislative**, *adj.*

Legislative Assembly *n.* the lower chamber of certain bicameral parliaments.

Legislative Council *n.* the upper chamber of certain bicameral parliaments.

legislature /ˈlɛdʒəsleɪtʃə, -lətʃə/ *n.* the arm

of government whose function is to make, amend and repeal laws, as a parliament.

legitimate /lə'dʒɪtəmət/ *adj.* **1.** according to law; lawful. **2.** born in wedlock, or of parents legally married. **3.** genuine; not spurious. – **legitimacy**, *n.*

legume /'lɛgjum/ *n.* **1.** a pod-bearing plant. **2.** the pod. – **leguminous**, *adj.*

leisure /'lɛʒə/ *n.* **1.** the condition of having one's time free from the demands of work or duty; ease. **2.** free or unoccupied time.

leisurely /'lɛʒəli/ *adj.* unhurried.

lemming /'lɛmɪŋ/ *n.* a small rodent noted for its mass migrations in periods of population increase.

lemon /'lɛmən/ *n.* **1.** a yellowish acid fruit. **2.** clear, light yellow. **3.** *Colloquial* something distasteful, disappointing, or unpleasant.

lemonade /lɛmə'neɪd/ *n.* a lemon-flavoured carbonated soft drink.

lend /lɛnd/ *v.t.*, **lent**, **lending**. **1.** to give the temporary use of (money, etc.) for a consideration. **2.** to grant the use of (something) with the understanding that it (or its equivalent in kind) shall be returned. **3.** to furnish or impart. **4.** to adapt (oneself or itself) to something.

length /lɛŋθ/ *n.* **1.** the linear magnitude of anything as measured from end to end. **2.** extent from beginning to end of a series, enumeration, account, book, etc. **3.** a piece or portion of a certain or a known length.

lenient /'liniənt/ *adj.* mild, clement, or merciful, as in treatment, spirit, or tendency; gentle.

lenitive /'lɛnətɪv/ *adj.* softening, soothing, or mitigating, as medicines.

lens /lɛnz/ *n.*, *pl.* **lenses**. a piece of transparent substance, usually glass, having two (or two main) opposite surfaces, either both curved or one curved and one plane, used for changing the convergence of light rays, as in magnifying, or in correcting errors of vision.

lentil /'lɛntəl/ *n.* an annual plant with flattened, biconvex seeds.

leonine /'liənaɪn/ *adj.* lionlike.

leopard /'lɛpəd/ *n.* a large, ferocious, spotted carnivore of the cat family.

leotard /'liətad/ *n.* a close-fitting one-piece garment worn by acrobats, dancers, etc.

leper /'lɛpə/ *n.* a person affected with leprosy.

leprechaun /'lɛprəkɔn/ *n.* (in Irish folklore) a little sprite, or goblin.

leprosy /'lɛprəsi/ *n.* a mildly infectious disease marked by ulcerations, loss of fingers and toes, etc.

lesbian /'lɛzbiən/ *n.* a female homosexual.

lesion /'liʒən/ *n.* an injury; a hurt; a wound.

less /lɛs/ *adv.* **1.** to a smaller extent, amount, or degree. – *adj.* **2.** smaller in size, amount, degree, etc.; not so large, great, or much. – *prep.* **3.** minus; without.

-less a suffix of adjectives meaning 'without'.

lessee /lɛ'si/ *n.* one to whom a lease is granted.

lessen /'lɛsən/ *v.i.* to become less.

lesser /'lɛsə/ *adj.* **1.** less; smaller, as in size, amount, importance, etc. **2.** being the smaller or less important of two.

lesson /'lɛsən/ *n.* **1.** something to be learned or studied. **2.** a length of time during which a pupil or class studies one subject.

lessor /lɛ'sɔ, 'lɛsɔ/ *n.* someone who grants a lease.

lest /lɛst/ *conj.* **1.** for fear that; that ... not; so that ... not. **2.** (after words expressing fear, danger, etc.) that.

let[1] /lɛt/ *v.*, **let**, **letting**. – *v.t.* **1.** to allow or permit. **2.** to grant the occupancy or use of (land, buildings, rooms, space, etc., or movable property) for rent or hire (occasionally fol. by *out*). **3.** to cause or make. **4.** (as an auxiliary used to propose or order): *let me see.* – *v.i.* **5.** to be rented or leased.

let[2] /lɛt/ *n.* *Tennis, etc.* an interference with the course of the ball (of some kind specified in the rules) on account of which the stroke or point must be played over again.

-let a diminutive suffix, used often for little objects, as in *frontlet, bracelet, kinglet.*

lethal /'liθəl/ *adj.* of, relating to, or such as to cause death; deadly.

lethargy /'lɛθədʒi/ *n.*, *pl.* **-gies**. a state of drowsy dullness or suspension of the faculties and energies; apathetic or sluggish inactivity. – **lethargic**, *adj.*

letter /'lɛtə/ *n.* **1.** a communication in writing or printing addressed to a person or a number of persons. **2.** one of the marks or signs conventionally used in writing and printing to represent speech sounds; an alphabetic character.

letter of advice *n.* **1.** a document, especially in commercial shipments, giving specific information as to the consignor's agent, bank, warehouse, etc. **2.** *Commerce* a drawer's document, usually forwarded ahead of the bill of lading and other papers giving title to goods shipped by the drawer, stating that a bill has been issued against the drawee.

letter of credit *n.* an order issued by a banker, allowing a person named to draw money to a specified amount from correspondents of the issuer.

letter of identification *n.* a letter signed by a banker issued together with a letter of credit, also signed by the person in whose favour the credit is issued, thus enabling identification to the paying agent when cashing drafts drawn under the letter of credit.

letters patent *pl. n.* a written or printed instrument issued by the sovereign power, conferring upon a patentee for a limited time the exclusive right to make, use, and sell his or her invention.

lettuce /'lɛtəs/ *n.* a leafy plant, much used in salads.

levee /'lɛvi/ *n.* a raised riverside.

level /'lɛvəl/ *adj.*, *n.*, *v.*, **-elled**, **-elling**. – *adj.* **1.** having no part higher than another; having an even surface. **2.** being in a plane parallel to the plane of the horizon; horizontal. **3.** even, equable, or uniform. – *n.* **4.** a device used for determining, or adjusting something to, a horizontal surface. **5.** a position or plane, high or low. – *v.t.* **6.** to make level. **7.** to bring (something) to the level of the ground. **8.** to bring (two or more things) to an equality of status, condition, etc. **9.** to aim or point at a mark, as a weapon, criticism, etc. – *v.i.* **10.** to arrive at a common level; stabilise (often fol. by *out*).

lever /'livə/ *n.* a bar or rigid piece acted upon at different points by two forces, as a voluntarily applied force (the *power*) and a resisting force (the *weight*), which generally tend to rotate it in opposite directions about a fixed axis or support (the *fulcrum*).

leverage /'livərɪdʒ/ *n.* **1.** the action of a lever. **2.** power of action; means of influence.

leveraged lease /'lɛvərɪdʒd/ *n.* a complex form of lease which, apart from the lessor and lessee, involves one or more long-term lenders of funds.

levitate /'lɛvəteɪt/ *v.i.*, **-tated**, **-tating**. to rise or float in the air, especially through some allegedly supernatural power that overcomes gravity.

levity /'lɛvəti/ *n., pl.* **-ties**. lightness of mind, character, or behaviour; lack of proper seriousness or earnestness.

levy /'lɛvi/ *n., pl.* **-vies**, *v.*, **-vied**, **-vying**. – *n.* **1.** a raising or collecting, as of money or troops, by authority or force. – *v.t.* **2.** to impose (a tax).

lewd /lud, ljud/ *adj.* inclined to, characterised by, or inciting to lust or lechery.

lexicon /'lɛksəkən/ *n.* **1.** a wordbook or dictionary, especially of Greek, Latin, or Hebrew. **2.** the total stock of words in a given language. – **lexical**, *adj.*

LGS ratio /ɛl dʒi ɛs 'reɪʃiou/ *n.* the ratio of a trading bank's liquid assets and government securities to its deposits.

liability /laɪə'bɪləti/ *n., pl.* **-ties**. **1.** an obligation, especially for payment (opposed to *asset*). **2.** something disadvantageous.

liable /'laɪəbəl/ *adj.* **1.** subject, exposed, or open to something possible or likely, especially something undesirable. **2.** under legal obligation; responsible or answerable.

liaison /li'eɪzən/ *n.* a connection or relationship.

liana /li'anə/ *n.* a climbing plant or vine.

liar /'laɪə/ *n.* someone who tells lies.

libel /'laɪbəl/ *n. Law* defamation by written or printed words, pictures, or in any form other than by spoken words or gestures.

liberal /'lɪbrəl, 'lɪbərəl/ *adj.* **1.** favourable to progress or reform, as in religious or political affairs. **2.** favourable to or in accord with the policy of leaving the individual as unrestricted as possible in the opportunities for self-expression or self-fulfilment. **3.** giving freely or in ample measure. **4.** not strict or rigorous. – *n.* **5.** a person of liberal principles or views, especially in religion or politics.

liberate /'lɪbəreɪt/ *v.t.*, **-rated**, **-rating**. **1.** to set free; release. **2.** to disengage; set free from combination, as a gas. – **liberation**, *n.* – **liberator**, *n.*

libertine /'lɪbətin/ *n.* one free from restraint or control, especially in moral or sexual matters; a dissolute or licentious person.

liberty /'lɪbəti/ *n., pl.* **-ties**. **1.** freedom from control, interference, obligation, restriction, etc. **2.** freedom from captivity, confinement, or physical restraint. **3.** unwarranted or impertinent freedom in action or speech, or a form or instance of it.

libidinous /lə'bɪdənəs/ *adj.* full of lust.

libido /lə'bidou/ *n.* the innate actuating or impelling force in living beings; the vital impulse or urge.

library /'laɪbri, -brəri/ *n., pl.* **-ries**. a place set apart to contain books and other literary material for reading, study, or reference, as a room, set of rooms, or building where books may be read or borrowed. – **librarian**, *n.*

lice /laɪs/ *n.* plural of **louse**.

licence /'laɪsəns/ *n.* **1.** formal permission or leave to do or not to do something. **2.** a certificate of such permission; an official permit. **3.** excessive or undue freedom or liberty.

license /'laɪsəns/ *v.t.*, **-censed**, **-censing**. to grant authoritative permission or licence to; authorise. – **licensor**, **licenser**, *n.* – **licensee**, *n.*

licentious /laɪ'sɛnʃəs/ *adj.* sensually unbridled; libertine; lewd.

lichen /'laɪkən/ *n.* a type of plant growing in crustlike patches on rocks, trees, etc.

lick /lɪk/ *v.t.* **1.** to pass the tongue over the surface of (often fol. by *off*, *from*, etc.) **2.** *Colloquial* to overcome; defeat; outdo; surpass. – *n.* **3.** a stroke of the tongue over something. **4.** a place to which wild animals resort to lick salt occurring naturally there.

licorice = liquorice /'lɪkərɪʃ, 'lɪkrɪʃ, -rəs/ *n.* the sweet-tasting dried root of a certain plant, or an extract made from it, used in medicine, confectionery, etc.

lid /lɪd/ *n.* a movable piece, whether separate or hinged, for closing the opening of a vessel, box, etc.; a movable cover.

lie[1] /laɪ/ *n., v.,* **lied**, **lying**. – *n.* **1.** a false statement made with intent to deceive; an intentional untruth; a falsehood. – *v.i.* **2.** to speak falsely or utter untruth knowingly.

lie[2] /laɪ/ *v.i.*, **lay**, **lain**, **lying**. **1.** to be in a recumbent or prostrate position, as on a bed or the ground; recline. **2.** to assume such a position (fol. by *down*). **3.** to rest in a horizontal position; be stretched out or extended. **4.** to be placed or situated.

liege /lidʒ, liʒ/ *n.* a lord entitled to allegiance and service.

lien /'liən/ *n.* (in law) the right to hold property or to have it sold or applied for payment of a claim.

lieu /lu, lju/ *n.* **1.** place; stead. **2. in lieu of**, instead of.

lieutenant /lɛf'tɛnənt/, *US* /lu'tɛnənt/ – *n.* someone who holds an office, civil or military, in subordination to a superior, for whom he or she acts.

life /laɪf/ *n., pl.* **lives**. **1.** the condition which distinguishes animals and plants from inorganic objects and dead organisms. **2.** the animate existence, or the term of animate existence, of an individual. **3.** the term of existence, activity, or effectiveness of something inanimate, as a machine or a lease. **4.** a living being. **5.** course or mode of existence. **6.** animation, liveliness. **7. a.** a prison sentence covering the rest of the convicted person's natural life. **b.** the maximum possible term of imprisonment that can be awarded by the laws of a state.

life insurance *n.* insurance providing payment of a specific sum of money to a named beneficiary upon the death of the insured, or to the insured or to a named beneficiary should the insured reach a specified age. Also, **life assurance**.

life interest *n.* an entitlement, lasting for one's life time only, to benefits, dividends or interest from an investment, property, etc.

lifeline /'laɪflaɪn/ *n.* **1.** a line or rope for saving life, as one attached to a lifeboat. **2.** any vital line of communication.

lifesaver /'laɪfseɪvə/ *n.* one of a group of volunteers who patrol surfing beaches, etc., making sure that bathers swim in designated safe areas, and who are trained in rescue and resuscitation methods.

LIFO /'laɪfoʊ/ *n.* last in first out; a method of storing and retrieving items from a stack table, or list, on the principle that last in is first out. Cf. **FIFO**.

lift /lɪft/ *v.t.* **1.** to move or bring (something) upwards from the ground or other support to some higher position; hoist. **2.** to raise in rank, condition, estimation, etc.; elevate or exalt. **3.** *Colloquial* to steal or plagiarise. – *v.i.* **4.** to go up; give to upward pressure. **5.** to move upwards or rise; rise and disperse, as clouds, fog, etc. – *n.* **6.** the act of lifting, raising, or rising. **7.** a moving platform or cage for conveying goods, people, etc., from one level to another, as in a building. **8.** a ride in a vehicle, especially one given free of charge to a traveller on foot. **9.** exaltation or uplift, as in feeling.

ligament /'lɪgəmənt/ *n., pl.* **ligaments**, **ligamenta**. *Anatomy* a band of tissue, usually white and fibrous, serving to connect bones, hold organs in place, etc.

ligature /'lɪgətʃə/ *n.* a tie or bond.

light[1] /laɪt/ *n., adj., v.,* **lit** *or* **lighted**, **lighting**. – *n.* **1.** that which makes things visible, or affords illumination. **2.** an illuminating agent or source, as the sun, a lamp, or a beacon. **3.** the illumination from the sun, or daylight. **4.** the aspect in which a thing appears or is regarded. **5.** a traffic light. – *adj.* **6.** having light or illumination, rather than dark. – *v.t.* **7.** to set burning (a candle, lamp, pipe for smoking, etc.); kindle (a fire); ignite (fuel, a match, etc.). – *v.i.* **8.** to take fire or become kindled. **9.** to brighten with animation or joy, as the face, eyes, etc., (often fol. by *up*).

light[2] /laɪt/ *adj.* **1.** of little weight; not heavy. **2.** gentle; delicate; exerting only slight pressure. **3.** easy to endure, deal with, or perform. **4.** free from any burden of sorrow or care. **5.** characterised by lack of proper seriousness; frivolous.

light[3] /laɪt/ *v.i.,* **lighted** *or* **lit**, **lighting**. **1.** to get down or descend, as from a horse or a vehicle. **2.** to come by chance, happen, or hit (fol. by *on* or *upon*).

lighthouse /'laɪthaʊs/ *n.* a tower or other structure displaying a light or lights for the guidance of vessels at sea.

lightning /'laɪtnɪŋ/ *n.* a flashing of light, or a sudden illumination of the sky, caused by the discharge of atmospheric electricity.

lightning strike *n.* a stoppage of work by employees with little or no warning to employers.

light-pen /'laɪt-pɛn/ *n.* a light sensitive device, made to look like a pen, which by moving the position of a point of light on a display screen, can interact with a computer.

light-year /'laɪt-jɪə/ *n.* the distance traversed by light in one year ($9.460\,55\times 10^{15}$ metres), used as a unit in measuring stellar distances. *Symbol*: l.y.

ligneous /'lɪgniəs/ *adj.* of the nature of or resembling wood; woody.

like[1] /laɪk/ *prep.* **1.** similarly to; in a manner characteristic of. **2.** bearing resemblance to. **3.** for example; as; such as. **4.** indicating a probability of. **5.** desirous of; disposed to (after *feel*). – *adj.* **6.** of the same or similar form, appearance, kind, character, amount, etc. – *n.* **7.** something of a similar nature (preceded by *the*).

like[2] /laɪk/ *v.t.,* **liked**, **liking**. to find agreeable.

-like a suffix of adjectives, use of **like**[1], as in *childlike*, *lifelike*, *horselike*, sometimes hyphenated.

likely /'laɪkli/ *adj.,* **-lier**, **-liest**. **1.** probably or apparently going or destined (to do, be, etc.). **2.** seeming like truth, fact, or certainty, or reasonably to be believed or expected; probable. – **likelihood**, *n.*

liken /'laɪkən/ *v.t.* to compare.

likewise /'laɪkwaɪz/ *adv.* in like manner.

lilac /'laɪlək/ *n.* a shrub with large clusters of fragrant purple or white flowers.

lilt /lɪlt/ *n.* rhythmic swing or cadence.

lily /'lɪli/ *n., pl.* **lilies**. a scaly-bulbed herb with showy funnel-shaped or bell-shaped flowers.

lima bean /laɪmə/ *n.* a kind of bean with a broad, flat, edible seed.

limb /lɪm/ *n.* **1.** a part or member of an animal body distinct from the head and trunk, as a leg, arm, or wing. **2.** a large or main branch of a tree.

limber /'lɪmbə/ *adj.* **1.** bending readily; flexible; pliant. **2.** characterised by ease in bending the body; supple; lithe. – *v.i.* **3.** to make oneself limber (fol. by *up*).

limbo /'lɪmboʊ/ *n.* (*often cap.*) a supposed region on the border of hell or heaven.

lime[1] /laɪm/ *n.* the oxide of calcium, CaO, used in making mortar and cement.

lime[2] /laɪm/ *n.* a small, greenish yellow, acid fruit allied to the lemon.

limelight /'laɪmlaɪt/ *n.* **1.** (formerly) a strong light, made by heating a cylinder of lime. **2.** the glare of public interest or notoriety.

limerick /'lɪmərɪk/ *n.* a type of humorous verse of five lines.

limestone /'laɪmstoʊn/ *n.* a rock consisting wholly or chiefly of calcium carbonate.

limit /'lɪmət/ *n.* **1.** the final or furthest bound or point as to extent, amount, continuance, procedure, etc. – *v.t.* **2.** to restrict by or as by fixing limits (fol. by *to*). – **limitation**, *n.*

limited company *n.* a company which can issue subscription and which may be listed on the stock exchange; there is a minimum number of shareholders but no maximum;

on liquidation the liability of the shareholders for the companies debts is limited to any amounts unpaid on their shares. Also, **limited-liability company**.

limited liability *n.* the liability, either by law or contract, only to a limited amount for debts of a trading company or limited partnership.

limited partnership *n.* a partnership in which at least one partner must be a general or unlimited partner liable for all the debts and obligations of the partnership, the others being liable only to the extent of the amount of capital each has put into the partnership.

limousine /'lɪməzin, lɪmə'zin/ *n.* any large, luxurious car.

limp[1] /lɪmp/ *v.i.* **1.** to walk with a laboured, jerky movement, as when lame. – *n.* **2.** a lame movement or gait.

limp[2] /lɪmp/ *adj.* lacking stiffness or firmness.

limpet /'lɪmpət/ *n. Zoology* a marine gastropod mollusc found adhering to rocks.

limpid /'lɪmpəd/ *adj.* clear.

line[1] /laɪn/ *n., v.,* **lined, lining**. – *n.* **1.** a mark or stroke long in proportion to its breadth, made with a pen, pencil, tool, etc., on a surface. **2.** something resembling a traced line, as a band of colour, a seam, a furrow, etc. **3.** a row of written or printed letters, words, etc. **4.** a verse of poetry. **5.** a course of action, procedure, thought, etc. **6.** a continuous series of persons or animals in chronological succession, especially in family descent. **7.** a department of activity; a kind of occupation or business. **8.** any transport company or system. **9.** a strip of railway track, a railway, or a railway system. **10.** *Mathematics* a continuous extent of length, straight or curved, without breadth or thickness; the trace of a moving point. **11.** a supply of commercial goods of the same general class. **12.** the line of arrangement of an army or of the ships of a fleet as drawn up ready for battle. **13.** a thread, string, or the like. **14.** a telephonic channel. – *v.i.* **15.** to take a position in a line; range or queue (often fol. by *up*). – *v.t.* **16.** to bring into a line, or into line with others (often fol. by *up*). **17.** to mark with a line or lines.

line[2] /laɪn/ *v.t.,* **lined, lining**. to provide with a layer of material applied to the inner side.

lineage /'lɪniɪdʒ/ *n.* lineal descent from an ancestor; ancestry or extraction.

lineal /'lɪniəl/ *adj.* being in the direct line, as a descendant, ancestor, etc., or descent, etc.

linear /'lɪniə/ *adj.* **1.** extended in a line. **2.** involving measurement in one dimension only; relating to length. **3.** of or relating to a line or lines. **4.** *Mathematics* of the first degree, as an equation.

linedance /'laɪndæns, 'laɪndans/ *n.* a dance, performed to country music, which consists of a repeated sequence of steps performed by a group of dancers facing the same direction in a line. – **linedancing**, *n.* – **linedancer**, *n.*

linen /'lɪnən/ *n.* **1.** fabric woven from flax yarns. **2.** clothes or other articles made of linen cloth or some substitute, as cotton.

liner /'laɪnə/ *n.* one of a commercial line of steamships or aeroplanes.

linesman /'laɪnzmən/ *n., pl.* **-men**. **1.** *Sport* an official on the sidelines who assists the referee or umpire in determining whether the ball is still in play. **2.** the member of a surf-lifesaving team who handles the surf-line. Also, **lineman**.

-ling a suffix found in some nouns, often pejorative, denoting one concerned with (*hireling, underling*); also diminutive (*princeling, duckling*).

linger /'lɪŋgə/ *v.i.* **1.** to remain or stay on in a place longer than is usual or expected, as if from reluctance to leave it. **2.** to dwell in contemplation, thought, or enjoyment.

lingerie /'lɒnʒəreɪ/ *n.* women's underwear.

lingo /'lɪŋgoʊ/ *n., pl.* **-goes**. *Colloquial* **1.** language. **2.** language or terminology peculiar to a particular field, group, etc.; jargon.

linguist /'lɪŋgwəst/ *n.* **1.** a person who is skilled in foreign languages. **2.** a person who specialises in linguistics.

linguistics /lɪŋ'gwɪstɪks/ *n.* the science of language. – **linguistic**, *adj.*

liniment /'lɪnəmənt/ *n.* a liquid preparation, usually oily, for rubbing on or applying to the skin, as for sprains, bruises, etc.

link /lɪŋk/ *n.* **1.** one of the rings or separate pieces of which a chain is composed. **2.** anything serving to connect one part or thing with another; a bond or tie. **3.** one of the 100 wire rods forming the divisions of a surveyor's chain of 66 ft (20.12 m). – *v.t.* **4.** to join by or as by a link or links.

links /lɪŋks/ *pl. n.* a golf course.

linoleum /laɪ'noʊliəm/ *n.* a floor covering formed by coating hessian or canvas with linseed oil, powdered cork, and rosin, and adding pigments of the desired colour. Also, **lino**.

linseed /'lɪnsid/ *n.* the seed of flax.

lint /lɪnt/ *n.* a soft material for dressing wounds, etc.

lintel /'lɪntl/ *n.* a horizontal supporting member above an opening such as a window or a door. Also, **lintol**.

lion /'laɪən/ *n.* a large, greyish tan cat native to Africa and southern Asia, the male of which usually has a mane. – **lioness**, *fem. n.*

lip /lɪp/ *n.* **1.** either of the two fleshy parts or folds forming the margins of the mouth and performing an important function in speech. **2.** a liplike part or structure. **3.** any edge or rim.

lip-read /'lɪp-rid/ *v.t., v.i.,* **-read** /-rɛd/, **-reading**. to understand spoken words by watching the movement of a speaker's lips.

lip-service /'lɪp-sɜvəs/ *n.* insincere profession of devotion or goodwill.

lipstick /'lɪpstɪk/ *n.* a stick or elongated piece of cosmetic preparation for colouring the lips.

liquefy = liquify /'lɪkwəfaɪ/ *v.t., v.i.,* **-fied, -fying**. to make or become liquid.

liqueur /lə'kjuə, lə'kɜ/ *n.* any of a class of alcoholic liquors, usually strong, sweet, and highly flavoured.

liquid /'lɪkwəd/ *adj.* **1.** such as to flow like water; fluid. **2.** in cash or readily convertible into cash. **3. go liquid,** to realise assets for cash. – *n.* **4.** a liquid substance. – **liq-**

uidity, *n.*

liquidate /ˈlɪkwədeɪt/ *v.*, **-dated**, **-dating**. – *v.t.* **1.** to settle or pay (a debt, etc.). **2.** to reduce (accounts) to order; determine the amount of (indebtedness or damages). **3.** to convert into cash. **4.** to get rid of, especially by killing or other violent means. – *v.i.* **5.** to liquidate debts or accounts; go into liquidation.

liquidation /lɪkwəˈdeɪʃən/ *n.* **1.** the process of realising upon assets and of discharging liabilities in winding up the affairs of a business, estate, etc. **2.** the process of converting securities or commodities into cash for the purpose of taking profits or preventing losses.

liquidator /ˈlɪkwədeɪtə/ *n.* a person appointed to carry out the winding up of a company.

liquidity preference *n.* the choice between holding wealth as idle money or in the form of income-earning assets.

liquid ratio *n.* the ratio of a company's liquid assets to its current liabilities. Also, **liquidity ratio**.

liquor /ˈlɪkə/ *n.* spirits (as brandy or whisky) as distinguished from fermented beverages (as wine or beer).

liquorice /ˈlɪkərɪʃ, ˈlɪkrɪʃ, -rəs/ *n.* → **licorice**.

lisp /lɪsp/ *n.* **1.** a speech defect consisting in pronouncing *s* and *z* like or nearly like the *th* sounds of *thin* and *this*, respectively. – *v.i.* **2.** to speak with a lisp.

lissom /ˈlɪsəm/ *adj.* lithe; limber.

list[1] /lɪst/ *n.* **1.** a record consisting of a series of names, words, or the like. – *v.t.* **2.** to set down together in a list. **3.** to register a security on a stock exchange so that it may be traded there.

list[2] /lɪst/ *v.i.* (of a ship) to careen; incline to one side.

listen /ˈlɪsən/ *v.i.* to give attention with the ear; attend closely for the purpose of hearing; give ear.

listless /ˈlɪstləs/ *adj.* feeling no inclination towards or interest in anything.

lit /lɪt/ *v.* past tense and past participle of **light**[1] and **light**[3].

litany /ˈlɪtəni/ *n., pl.* **-nies**. a ceremonial or liturgical form of prayer consisting of a series of invocations or supplications with responses which are the same for a number in succession.

-lite a word element used in names of minerals, or fossils. Cf. **-lith**.

literal /ˈlɪtrəl, ˈlɪtərəl/ *adj.* **1.** following the letter, or exact words, of the original, as a translation. **2.** in accordance with, involving, or being the natural or strict meaning of the words or word; not figurative or metaphorical.

literary /ˈlɪtərəri, ˈlɪtrəri/ *adj.* relating to or of the nature of books and writings, especially those classed as literature.

literate /ˈlɪtərət/ *adj.* **1.** able to read and write. **2.** having an education; educated. – **literacy**, *n.*

literature /ˈlɪtrətʃə, ˈlɪtərətʃə/ *n.* **1.** writings in which expression and form, in connection with ideas of permanent and universal interest, are characteristic or essential features, as poetry, romance, history, biography, essays, etc. **2.** *Colloquial* printed matter of any kind, as circulars or advertising matter.

lith- a combining form meaning 'stone'. Also, **litho-**.

-lith a noun termination meaning 'stone'.

lithe /laɪð/ *adj.* pliant; supple.

lithium /ˈlɪθiəm/ *n.* a soft silver-white metallic element (the lightest of all metals) occurring combined in certain minerals. *Symbol*: Li

lithography /lɪˈθɒgrəfi/ *n.* the art or process of printing a picture, writing, or the like, from a flat surface of aluminium, zinc or stone, with some greasy or oily substance. – **lithograph**, *n.*

litigant /ˈlɪtəgənt/ *n.* **1.** one engaged in a lawsuit. – *adj.* **2.** litigating; engaged in a lawsuit.

litigate /ˈlɪtəgeɪt/ *v.*, **-gated**, **-gating**. – *v.t.* **1.** to contest at law. **2.** to dispute (a point, etc). – *v.i.* **3.** to carry on a lawsuit. – **litigable**, *adj.* – **litigator**, *n.* – **litigation**, *n.*

litmus /ˈlɪtməs/ *n.* a blue colouring matter which is turned red by acid solutions and blue by alkaline solutions.

litre /ˈlitə/ *n.* a unit of capacity in the metric system equal to $10^{-3}m^3$. *Symbol*: L

-litre a word element meaning litres.

litter /ˈlɪtə/ *n.* **1.** things scattered about; scattered rubbish. **2.** a condition of disorder or untidiness. **3.** a number of young brought forth at one birth. **4.** a vehicle carried by people or animals, consisting of a bed or couch, often covered and curtained, suspended between shafts. – *v.t.* **5.** to strew (a place) with scattered objects. **6.** to scatter (objects) in disorder.

litterbug /ˈlɪtəbʌg/ *n.* someone who drops rubbish, especially in public places.

little /ˈlɪtl/ *adj.*, **less** *or* **lesser**, **least**; *or* **littler**, **littlest**, *adv.*, **less**, **least**, *n.* – *adj.* **1.** small in size; not big or large. **2.** small in extent or duration; short; brief. **3.** small in number. **4.** small in amount or degree; not much. – *adv.* **5.** not at all (before a verb). **6.** rarely; infrequently. – *n.* **7.** that which is little; a small amount, quantity, or degree.

liturgy /ˈlɪtədʒi/ *n., pl.* **-gies**. a form of public worship; a ritual. – **liturgical**, *adj.*

live[1] /lɪv/ *v.*, **lived** /lɪvd/, **living**. – *v.i.* **1.** to have life, as an animal or plant; be alive. **2.** to continue in existence, operation, memory, etc.; last. **3.** to feed or subsist (fol. by *on* or *upon*). **4.** to dwell or reside. **5.** to pass life (as specified). – *v.t.* **6.** to pass (life).

live[2] /laɪv/ *adj.* **1.** being in life; living, or alive. **2.** characterised by or indicating the presence of living creatures. **3.** burning or glowing, as a coal. **4.** loaded or unexploded, as a cartridge or shell. **5.** *Electricity* electrically charged. **6.** (of a radio or television program) broadcast or televised at the moment it is being presented at the studio.

livelihood /ˈlaɪvlihʊd/ *n.* means of maintaining life; maintenance.

lively /ˈlaɪvli/ *adj.*, **-lier**, **-liest**. **1.** full or suggestive of life or vital energy; active, vigorous, or brisk. **2.** animated, spirited, vivacious, or sprightly. **3.** eventful, stirring, or exciting.

liven /ˈlaɪvən/ *v.t.* to put life into; rouse; cheer (often fol. by *up*).

liver /ˈlɪvə/ *n.* (in humans) a large, reddish brown glandular organ secreting bile and performing various metabolic functions.

livery /ˈlɪvəri/ *n., pl.* **-ries**. **1.** a kind of uniform worn by menservants. **2.** a distinctive dress worn by an official, a member of a company or guild, etc.

livery stable *n.* a stable where horses and vehicles are cared for or let out for hire.

lives /laɪvz/ *n.* plural of **life**.

livestock /ˈlaɪvstɒk/ *n.* the horses, cattle, sheep, and other useful animals kept or bred on a farm or ranch.

liveware /ˈlaɪvwɛə/ *n.* the personnel involved with the use of a computer, as programmers, key punch operators, etc. See **software**, **hardware**.

livid /ˈlɪvəd/ *adj.* **1.** having a discoloured bluish appearance due to a bruise, etc. **2.** angry; enraged.

living /ˈlɪvɪŋ/ *adj.* **1.** that lives; alive, or not dead. – *n.* **2.** the act or condition of someone who or that which lives. **3.** means of maintaining life; livelihood.

lizard /ˈlɪzəd/ *n.* any of various long-bodied reptiles with tails.

'll a shortening of *will* or *shall*.

llama /ˈlamə/ *n.* a woolly-haired South American ruminant.

lo /loʊ/ *interj.* look! see! behold!

load /loʊd/ *n.* **1.** that which is laid on or placed in anything for conveyance. **2.** anything borne or sustained. **3.** something that weighs down or oppresses like a burden. **4.** the amount of work required of a person, machine, organisation, etc. **5.** the weight supported by a structure or part. – *v.t.* **6.** to put a load on or in. **7.** to supply abundantly or excessively with something. **8.** to give bias to, especially by fraudulent means. **9.** *Insurance* to increase (a net premium, etc.). See **loading** (def. 2). **10.** to charge (a firearm, camera, etc.)

loading /ˈloʊdɪŋ/ *n.* **1.** an extra rate paid to employees in recognition of a particular aspect of their employment, as shift work. **2.** *Insurance* an addition to the normal premium on the policy of a person whose life expectancy is considered to be less than the mortality tables would indicate.

load shedding *n.* a temporary reduction in the supply of electricity to a particular area in order to reduce overloading.

loaf[1] /loʊf/ *n., pl.* **loaves** /loʊvz/. **1.** a portion of bread or cake baked in a mass of definite form. **2.** a shaped or moulded mass of food, as of sugar, chopped meat, etc.

loaf[2] /loʊf/ *v.i.* to lounge or saunter lazily and idly.

loaf[3] /loʊf/ *n.* *Colloquial* the head.

loafers /ˈloʊfəz/ *pl. n.* casual shoes.

loam /loʊm/ *n.* a loose soil composed of clay and sand.

loan /loʊn/ *n.* **1.** something lent or furnished on condition of being returned, especially a sum of money lent at interest. – *v.t.* **2.** to make a loan of; lend. **3.** to lend (money) at interest.

loath /loʊθ/ *adj.* reluctant, averse, or unwilling.

loathe /loʊð/ *v.t.*, **loathed**, **loathing**. to feel hatred, disgust, or intense aversion for. – **loathing**, *n.* – **loathsome**, *adj.*

loaves /loʊvz/ *n.* plural of **loaf**[1].

lob /lɒb/ *v.t.*, **lobbed**, **lobbing**. **1.** *Tennis* to strike (a ball) high into the air. **2.** to throw (something) up so that it lands after a high curve.

lobby /ˈlɒbi/ *n., pl.* **-bies**, *v.*, **-bied**, **-bying**. – *n.* **1.** a corridor, vestibule, or entrance hall. **2.** a group of persons who attempt to enlist popular and political support for some particular cause. – *v.i.* **3.** to frequent the lobby of a legislative chamber to influence the members.

lobe /loʊb/ *n.* a roundish projection.

lobotomy /ləˈbɒtəmi/ *n.* the cutting into or across a lobe of the brain.

lobster /ˈlɒbstə/ *n.* a large, edible, marine crustacean.

local /ˈloʊkəl/ *adj.* **1.** relating to or characterised by place, or position in space. **2.** relating to, characteristic of, or restricted to a particular place or particular places. **3.** relating to or affecting a particular part or particular parts.

Local Court /ˈloʊkəl kɔt/ *n.* **1.** (in NSW) a magistrate's court with criminal and civil jurisdiction. **2.** (in Tas. and WA) a magistrate's court of limited civil jurisdiction. **3.** (in the NT) a court with jurisdiction equivalent to that of a District or County Court in other states.

local government *n.* the administration of the affairs of some nominated area smaller than that of a State, such as a shire, municipality, town, etc., by officers elected by the residents and ratepayers of that area.

locality /loʊˈkæləti/ *n., pl.* **-ties**. a place, spot, or district, with or without reference to things or persons in it.

locate /loʊˈkeɪt/ *v.t.*, **-cated**, **-cating**. to discover the place or location of.

location /loʊˈkeɪʃən/ *n.* **1.** a place of settlement or residence. **2.** *Film* a place, outside the studio, affording suitable environment for photographing particular plays, incidents, etc. hence, *on location*. **3.** *Computers* a specific register in the high-speed memory of a computer.

loch /lɒk/ *n.* *Scot* a lake.

lock[1] /lɒk/ *n.* **1.** a device for securing a door, gate, lid, drawer, or the like, in position when closed. **2.** an enclosed portion of a canal, river, etc., with gates at each end, for raising or lowering vessels from one level to another. **3.** the radius of turning in the steering mechanism of a vehicle. – *v.t.* **4.** to fasten or secure (a door, building, etc.) by the operation of a lock. **5.** to shut in a place fastened by a lock or locks, as for security or restraining (fol. by *up*, *in*, etc.). **6.** to exclude by or as by a lock (usually fol. by *out*). **7.** to join or unite firmly by interlinking or intertwining. – *v.i.* **8.** to become locked.

lock[2] /lɒk/ *n.* a tress or portion of hair.

locker /ˈlɒkə/ *n.* a chest, drawer, compartment, closet, or the like, that may be locked.

locket /ˈlɒkət/ *n.* a small case for a miniature

portrait, a lock of hair, or other keepsake, usually worn on a chain hung round the neck.

lockjaw /'lɒkdʒɔ/ *n.* tetanus in which the jaws become firmly locked together.

locomotion /loʊkə'moʊʃən/ *n.* the act or power of moving from place to place.

locomotive /loʊkə'moʊtɪv/ *n.* a self-propelled vehicle running on a railway track, designed to pull railway carriages or trucks.

locum /'loʊkəm/ *n.* a temporary substitute for a doctor, lawyer, etc. Also, **locum tenens** /loʊkəm 'tɛnənz/.

locus /'lɒkəs, 'loʊkəs/ *n., pl.* **loci** /'lɒki, 'loʊki/ a place; a locality.

locust /'loʊkəst/ *n.* **1.** a type of grasshopper which swarms in immense numbers and strips vegetation. **2.** *Colloquial* → **cicada**.

lode /loʊd/ *n.* a veinlike deposit, usually metal bearing.

lodge /lɒdʒ/ *n., v.,* **lodged**, **lodging**. – *n.* **1.** a cabin or hut. **2.** a house or cottage, as in a park or on an estate, occupied by a gatekeeper, caretaker, gardener, or the like. **3.** the meeting place of a branch of a secret society. – *v.i.* **4.** to have a habitation or quarters, especially temporarily. **5.** to be fixed or implanted. – *v.t.* **6.** to furnish with a habitation or quarters, especially temporarily. **7.** to lay (information, a complaint, etc.) before a court or the like.

loft /lɒft/ *n.* the space between the underside of a roof and the ceiling of a room beneath it.

lofty /'lɒfti/ *adj.,* **-tier**, **-tiest**. **1.** extending high in the air; of imposing height. **2.** elevated in style or sentiment, as writings, etc. **3.** haughty; proud.

log /lɒg/ *n., v.,* **logged**, **logging**. – *n.* **1.** an unhewn portion or length of wood. **2.** Also, **logbook**. the official record of significant data concerning a ship's journey, a plane's flight, a machine's operation, etc. – *v.t.* **3.** to cut (trees) into logs. **4.** to cut down trees or timber on (land). **5.** to enter in a log. – *v.i.* **6.** to cut down trees and get out logs from the forest for timber. **7. log in** (or **on**), to begin a session on a computer, usually gaining access with a username and password. **8. log off** (or **out**), to end a session on a computer.

loganberry /'loʊgənbəri, -bri/ *n., pl.* **-ries**. a large, dark red, acid berry.

logarithm /'lɒgərɪðəm/ *n.* the exponent of that power to which a fixed number (called the *base*) must be raised in order to produce a given number (called the *antilogarithm*). – **logarithmic**, *adj.*

logic /'lɒdʒɪk/ *n.* **1.** the system or principles of reasoning applicable to any branch of knowledge or study. **2.** reasons or sound sense, as in utterances or actions. – **logical**, *adj.*

logical design *n.* the design of a digital computer or other digital equipment out of logical elements.

logical element *n.* the basic unit from which computers and other digital equipment are built, which operates on signals represented by ones and zeros and acts as a gate, passing or stopping one signal according to whether other signals have certain required values or not.

logistics /lə'dʒɪstɪks/ *n.* the branch of military science concerned with the mathematics of transportation and supply, and the movement of bodies of troops.

logo /'loʊgoʊ/ *n.* a trademark or symbol designed to identify a company, organisation, etc.

logo- a word element denoting speech.

-logy **1.** a combining form naming sciences or bodies of knowledge. **2.** a termination of many nouns referring to writing.

loin /lɔɪn/ *n.* (*usu. pl.*) the part or parts of the body of humans or of quadruped animals on either side of the vertebral column, between the false ribs and hipbone.

loiter /'lɔɪtə/ *v.i.* to linger idly or aimlessly in or about a place.

loll /lɒl/ *v.i.* to recline or lean in a relaxed or indolent manner; lounge.

lollipop /'lɒlipɒp/ *n.* a kind of boiled sweet or toffee, often a piece on the end of a stick.

lollop /'lɒləp/ *v.i.* to move with bounding, ungainly leaps.

lolly /'lɒli/ *n.* any sweet, especially a boiled one.

lone /loʊn/ *adj.* solitary.

lonely /'loʊnli/ *adj.,* **-lier**, **-liest**. **1.** lone; solitary. **2.** destitute of sympathetic or friendly companionship or relationships.

lonesome /'loʊnsəm/ *adj.* depressed by solitude or by a sense of being alone.

long[1] /lɒŋ/ *adj.,* **longer** /'lɒŋgə/, **longest** /'lɒŋgəst/, *n., adv.* – *adj.* **1.** having considerable or great extent from end to end; not short. **2.** having considerable or great extent in duration. **3.** having a specified extension in space, duration, etc. **4.** tall. **5.** *Commerce* **a.** owning some commodity or stock. **b.** depending for profit on a rise in prices. – *n.* **6.** something that is long. – *adv.* **7.** for or through a great extent of space or, especially, time. **8. so long,** *Colloquial* goodbye.

long[2] /lɒŋ/ *v.i.* to have a prolonged or unceasing desire, as for something not immediately (if ever) attainable.

longevity /lɒn'dʒɛvəti/ *n.* long life; great duration of life.

longhand /'lɒŋhænd/ *n.* writing of the ordinary kind, in which the words are written out in full (distinguished from *shorthand*).

longitude /'lɒŋgətjud, 'lɒŋə,tjud/ *n. Geography* angular distance east or west on the earth's surface, measured along the equator.

longitudinal /lɒŋgə'tjudənəl/ *adj.* of or relating to longitude or length.

long service leave *n.* an extended period of leave from employment, earned through long service.

long shot *n.* an attempt which has little hope of success, but which if successful may offer great rewards.

long-term bond *n.* a bond not maturing for many years.

longwinded /'lɒŋwɪndəd/ *adj.* tediously wordy in speech or writing.

loofah /'lufə/ *n.* a bath sponge.

look /lʊk/ *v.i.* **1.** to fix the eyes upon something or in some direction in order to see.

2. to glance or gaze, in a manner specified. **3.** to use the sight in seeking, searching, examining, watching, etc. **4.** to tend, as in bearing or significance. **5.** to appear or seem. **6.** to direct the mental regard or attention. **7.** to have an outlook or afford a view. **8.** to face or front. **9. look after,** to take care of. **10. look forward to,** to anticipate with pleasure. **11. look out,** to be on guard. – *v.t.* **12.** to try to find; seek (fol. by *up*, *out*, etc.). **13.** to view, inspect or examine (fol. by *over*). **14.** to have the aspect or appearance appropriate to. – *n.* **15.** the act of looking. **16.** a visual search or examination. **17.** way of looking or appearing to the eye or mind; aspect. **18.** (*pl.*) general aspect; appearance.

lookout /'lʊkaʊt/ *n.* **1.** a watch kept, as for something that may come or happen. **2.** a person or group stationed or employed to keep such a watch. **3.** a place on a high vantage point, especially a mountain, from which one can admire the view.

loom[1] /lum/ *n.* a machine or apparatus for weaving yarn or thread into a fabric.

loom[2] /lum/ *v.i.* to appear indistinctly, or come into view in indistinct and enlarged form.

loop /lup/ *n.* **1.** a folding or doubling of a portion of a cord, lace, ribbon, etc., upon itself, so as to leave an opening between the parts. **2.** anything shaped more or less like a loop. – *v.t.* **3.** to form into a loop or loops.

loophole /'luphoʊl/ *n.* an outlet, or means of escape or evasion.

loose /lus/ *adj.*, **looser**, **loosest**, *v.*, **loosed**, **loosing**. – *adj.* **1.** free from bonds, fetters, or restraint. **2.** free or released from fastening or attachment. **3.** not bound together, as papers or flowers. **4.** not put in a package or other container. **5.** lax, as the bowels. **6.** not fitting closely, as garments. **7.** not close or compact in structure or arrangement. **8.** not strict, exact, or precise. – *v.t.* **9.** to let loose, or free from bonds or restraint. **10.** to unfasten, undo, or untie. **11.** to make less tight; slacken or relax. **12.** to render less firmly fixed, or loosen.

loose end *n.* **1.** something left unsettled or incomplete. **2. at a loose end,** without a specific task.

loot /lut/ *n.* **1.** spoils or plunder taken by pillaging, as in war. **2.** *Colloquial* money. – *v.t.* **3.** to plunder or pillage (a city, house, etc.), as in war.

lop /lɒp/ *v.t.*, **lopped**, **lopping**. to cut off (protruding parts) of a tree, etc.

lope /loʊp/ *v.i.*, **loped**, **loping**. to move or run with a long, easy stride.

lopsided /'lɒpsaɪdəd/ *adj.* heavier, larger, or more developed on one side than on the other; asymmetrical.

loquacious /lə'kweɪʃəs/ *adj.* talkative. – **loquacity**, *n.*

loquat /'loʊkwɒt, -kwət/ *n.* a small, evergreen tree bearing a yellow plumlike fruit.

lord /lɔd/ *n.* **1.** someone who has dominion over others; a master, chief, or ruler. **2.** a titled nobleman, or peer. – *v.i.* **3.** to play the lord; behave in a lordly manner; domineer (often with indefinite *it*).

lore /lɔ/ *n.* the body of knowledge, especially of a traditional, anecdotal, or popular nature, on a particular subject.

lorikeet /'lɒrəkit, lɒrə'kit/ *n.* any of various small, brightly-coloured, arboreal parrots.

lorry /'lɒri/ *n.* → **truck**[1] (def. 2).

lose /luz/ *v.*, **lost**, **losing**. – *v.t.* **1.** to come to be without, by some chance, and not know the whereabouts of. **2.** to suffer the loss or deprivation of. **3.** to become separated from and ignorant of (the way, etc.). **4.** to leave far behind in a pursuit, race, etc. **5.** to fail to win (a prize, stake, etc.). **6.** to absorb or engross (oneself) in something. – *v.i.* **7.** to suffer loss.

loss /lɒs/ *n.* **1.** detriment or disadvantage from failure to keep, have, or get. **2.** that which is lost. **3.** amount or number lost. **4.** a being deprived of or coming to be without something that one has had. **5.** a losing by defeat, or failure to win. **6.** *Commerce* failure to recover the costs of a transaction or the like, in the form of benefits derived. **7.** *Insurance* **a.** occurrence of a risk covered by a contract of insurance so as to result in insurer liability. **b.** that which causes such a loss. **c.** an example of such a loss.

loss ratio *n.* the ratio of paid-in premiums to losses sustained during a certain period.

lost /lɒst/ *v.* past tense of **lose**.

lost time allowance *n.* an allowance paid to casual employees to compensate them for time lost in finding new employment.

lot /lɒt/ *n.* **1.** one of a set of objects drawn from a receptacle, etc., to decide a question or choice by chance. **2.** the decision or choice so made. **3.** one's fate, fortune, or destiny. **4.** a distinct portion or parcel of anything, as land, merchandise, etc. **5.** *Colloquial* a great many or a great deal. **6. the lot,** the entire amount or quantity.

lotion /'loʊʃən/ *n.* a liquid containing oils or medicines, to be applied externally to the skin for soothing, healing or cleansing.

lottery /'lɒtəri, 'lɒtri/ *n.*, *pl.* **-ries**. any scheme for the distribution of prizes by chance.

lotus /'loʊtəs/ *n.* **1.** a plant referred to in Greek legend as yielding a fruit which induced a state of dreamy and contented forgetfulness in those who ate it. **2.** any of various waterlilies.

loud /laʊd/ *adj.* **1.** striking strongly upon the organs of hearing, as sound, noise, the voice, etc.; strongly audible. **2.** excessively striking to the eye, or offensively showy, as colours, dress or the wearer, etc.; garish.

loudspeaker /laʊd'spikə, 'laʊdspikə/ *n.* any of various devices by which speech, music, etc., can be made audible throughout a room, hall, or the like.

lounge /laʊndʒ/ *v.*, **lounged**, **lounging**, *n.* – *v.i.* **1.** to pass time idly and indolently. **2.** to recline indolently; loll. – *n.* **3.** a living room. **4.** a large room in a hotel, etc., used by guests for relaxation purposes.

lour /'laʊə/ *v.i.* **1.** to be dark and threatening, as the sky or the weather. **2.** to frown, scowl, or look sullen.

louse /laʊs/ *n.*, *pl.* **lice** /laɪs/ *or for def. 2* **louses**, *v.*, **loused**, **lousing**. – *n.* **1.** a small, wingless, blood-sucking insect. **2.** *Colloquial* a despicable person. – *v.t.*

3. *Colloquial* to spoil (fol. by *up*).

lousy /ˈlaʊzi/ *adj.*, **lousier**, **lousiest**. **1.** infested with lice. **2.** *Colloquial* mean, contemptible or unpleasant. **3.** *Colloquial* inferior; no good.

lout /laʊt/ *n. Colloquial* a rough, uncouth and sometimes violent young man.

louvre /ˈluvə/ *n.* an arrangement of slats closing a window or other opening.

lovable = loveable /ˈlʌvəbəl/ *adj.* of such a nature as to attract love.

love /lʌv/ *n., v.,* **loved**, **loving**. – *n.* **1.** a strong or passionate affection for another person. **2.** a feeling of warm personal attachment or deep affection. **3.** strong predilection or liking for anything. **4.** *Tennis, etc.* nothing; no score. – *v.t.* **5.** to have love or affection for.

lovebird /ˈlʌvbɜd/ *n.* any of various small parrots.

lovelorn /ˈlʌvlɔn/ *adj.* forlorn or pining from love.

lovely /ˈlʌvli/ *adj.*, **-lier**, **-liest**. charmingly or exquisitely beautiful.

lover /ˈlʌvə/ *n.* **1.** someone who loves another. **2.** a sexual partner.

low[1] /loʊ/ *adj.* **1.** situated or occurring not far above the ground, floor, or base. **2.** lying or being below the general level. **3.** designating or relating to regions near the sea level or sea as opposed to highland or inland regions. **4.** rising but slightly from a surface. **5.** lacking in strength or vigour; feeble; weak. **6.** small in amount, degree, force, etc. **7.** assigning or attributing no great amount, value, or excellence. **8.** depressed or dejected. **9.** far down in the scale of rank or estimation; humble. **10.** lacking in dignity or elevation, as of thought or expression. **11.** *Biology* having a relatively simple structure; not complex in organisation. **12.** produced by relatively slow vibrations, as sounds. **13.** not loud. – *adv.* **14.** in or to a low position, point, degree, etc. – *n.* **15.** that which is low; a low level. **16.** *Meteorology* a pressure system characterised by relatively low pressure at the centre. **17.** a point of least value, amount, etc.

low[2] /loʊ/ *v.i.* to utter the sound characteristic of cattle.

lowboy /ˈloʊbɔɪ/ *n.* a piece of furniture for holding clothes, similar to a wardrobe, but not so tall.

lowdown /ˈloʊdaʊn/ *n. Colloquial* the actual unadorned facts or truth on some subject.

lower /ˈloʊə/ *adj.* **1.** comparative of **low**[1]. – *v.t.* **2.** to reduce in amount, price, degree, force, etc. **3.** to cause to descend, or let down.

lower case *n.* the small letters of the alphabet. *Abbrev.*: l.c.

lower house *n.* in a bicameral parliament, the lower legislative body, usually more numerous and more directly representative of the electorate than the upper house. Also, **lower chamber**.

low-key /ˈloʊ-ki/ *adj.* underplayed; restrained.

lowland /ˈloʊlənd/ *n.* land low with respect to neighbouring country.

low-level language *n.* a language used for writing computer programs which is closer to machine language than human language. Cf. **high-level language**.

lowly /ˈloʊli/ *adj.*, **-lier**, **-liest**. humble in station, condition, or nature.

low profile *n.* a low-keyed, uncommitted policy or reticent style of behaviour.

lowry /ˈlaʊri/ *n.* any of various rosellas.

loyal /ˈlɔɪəl/ *adj.* **1.** faithful to one's allegiance. **2.** faithful to one's oath, engagements or obligations.

lozenge /ˈlɒzəndʒ/ *n.* a small flavoured confection, often medicated.

LSD /ɛl ɛs ˈdi/ *n.* a hallucinogenic drug.

lubricate /ˈlubrəkeɪt/ *v.t.*, **-cated**, **-cating**. to apply some oily, greasy, or other substance to, in order to diminish friction. – **lubricant**, *n.* – **lubrication**, *n.* – **lubricity**, *n.*

lucerne /ˈlusən/ *n.* a forage plant.

lucid /ˈlusəd/ *adj.* **1.** shining or bright. **2.** clear.

luck /lʌk/ *n.* **1.** that which happens to a person, either good or bad, as if by chance, in the course of events. **2.** good fortune; advantage or success considered as the result of chance. – **lucky**, *adj.*

lucrative /ˈlukrətɪv/ *adj.* profitable; remunerative.

lucre /ˈlukə/ *n.* gain or money as the object of sordid desire.

ludicrous /ˈludəkrəs/ *adj.* such as to cause laughter or derision; ridiculous; amusingly absurd.

lug /lʌg/ *v.t.*, **lugged**, **lugging**. to pull along or carry with force or effort.

luggage /ˈlʌgɪdʒ/ *n.* trunks, suitcases, etc., used in travelling; baggage.

lugubrious /ləˈgubriəs/ *adj.* mournful; doleful; dismal.

lukewarm /ˈlukwɔm/ *adj.* **1.** moderately warm; tepid. **2.** having or showing little ardour or zeal; indifferent.

lull /lʌl/ *v.t.* **1.** to put to sleep or rest by soothing means. **2.** to soothe or quiet. – *n.* **3.** a temporary quiet or stillness.

lullaby /ˈlʌləbaɪ/ *n.* a song intended to put a baby to sleep.

lumbar /ˈlʌmbə/ *adj.* of or relating to the loin or loins.

lumber[1] /ˈlʌmbə/ *n.* **1.** timber sawn or split into planks, boards, etc. – *v.i.* **2.** to cut timber and prepare it for market. – *v.t.* **3.** *Colloquial* to foist off on or leave with, as with something or someone unwelcome or unpleasant.

lumber[2] /ˈlʌmbə/ *v.i.* to move clumsily or heavily, especially from great or ponderous bulk.

lumberjack /ˈlʌmbədʒæk/ *n. Chiefly US and Canada* someone who works at lumbering.

luminary /ˈlumənəri, -mənri/ *n., pl.* **-ries**. **1.** a celestial body, as the sun or moon. **2.** a person who enlightens humankind or makes some subject clear.

luminescence /luməˈnɛsəns/ *n.* an emission of light not due directly to incandescence. – **luminescent**, *adj.*

luminous /ˈlumənəs/ *adj.* **1.** radiating or reflecting light; shining. **2.** lighted up or illuminated; well lighted. **3.** clear; readily intelligible. – **luminosity**, *n.*

lump[1] /lʌmp/ *n.* **1.** a piece or mass of solid matter without regular shape. – *v.t.* **2.** to unite into one aggregation, collection, or mass.

lump[2] /lʌmp/ *v.t. Colloquial* to endure or put up with (a disagreeable necessity).

lunacy /ˈlunəsi/ *n., pl.* **-cies**. insanity. – **lunatic**, *n., adj.*

lunar /ˈlunə/ *adj.* of or relating to the moon.

lunch /lʌntʃ/ *n.* **1.** a meal taken in the middle of the day. – *v.i.* **2.** to eat lunch.

luncheon /ˈlʌntʃən/ *n.* lunch.

lung /lʌŋ/ *n.* either of the two saclike respiratory organs in the thorax of humans and the higher vertebrates.

lunge[1] /lʌndʒ/ *n., v.,* **lunged**, **lunging**. – *n.* **1.** a thrust, as in fencing. – *v.i.* **2.** to make a lunge.

lunge[2] /lʌndʒ/ *n.* a long rope used to guide a horse during training or exercise.

luni- a word element meaning 'moon'.

lupine /ˈlupaɪn/ *adj.* relating to or resembling the wolf.

lurch[1] /lɜtʃ/ *n.* **1.** a sudden leaning or roll to one side, as of a ship or a staggering person. – *v.i.* **2.** to make a lurch; move with lurches; stagger.

lurch[2] /lɜtʃ/ *n.* the position of one discomfited or in a helpless plight.

lure /ˈluə, ˈljuə/ *n., v.,* **lured**, **luring**. – *n.* **1.** anything that attracts, entices, or allures. – *v.t.* **2.** to decoy; entice; allure.

lurid /ˈlurəd/ *adj.* **1.** glaringly vivid or sensational. **2.** wan, pallid, or ghastly in hue.

lurk /lɜk/ *v.i.* **1.** to remain in or about a place secretly or furtively. – *n. Colloquial* **2.** a convenient, often unethical, method of performing a task, earning a living, etc.

luscious /ˈlʌʃəs/ *adj.* **1.** highly pleasing to the taste or smell. **2.** very luxurious; extremely attractive.

lush[1] /lʌʃ/ *adj.* **1.** tender and juicy, as plants or vegetation; succulent; luxuriant. **2.** *Colloquial* characterised by luxury and comfort.

lush[2] /lʌʃ/ *n.* a drunken person or someone given to excessive drinking of alcohol.

lust /lʌst/ *n.* **1.** passionate or overmastering desire. **2.** sexual desire or appetite. – *v.i.* **3.** to have strong or inordinate desire, especially sexual desire (often fol. by *for* or *after*).

lustre /ˈlʌstə/ *n.* the state or quality of shining by reflecting light; glitter, glisten, sheen, or gloss. – **lustrous**, *adj.*

lusty /ˈlʌsti/ *adj.,* **-tier**, **-tiest**. full of or characterised by healthy vigour.

lute /lut/ *n.* a stringed musical instrument. – **lutenist**, *n.*

luxuriant /lʌgˈʒuriənt/ *adj.* abundant or exuberant in growth, as vegetation.

luxuriate /lʌgˈʒurieɪt/ *v.t.,* **-ated**, **-ating**. **1.** to indulge in luxury; revel. **2.** to take great delight.

luxury /ˈlʌkʃəri/ *n.* anything conducive to sumptuous living, usually a delicacy, elegance, or refinement of living rather than a necessity. – **luxurious**, *adj.*

-ly **1.** the normal adverbial suffix, added to almost any descriptive adjective, as in *gladly, gradually.* **2.** the adverbial suffix applied to units of time, meaning 'per', as in *hourly.* **3.** adjective suffix meaning 'like', as in *saintly, manly.*

lye /laɪ/ *n.* any solution resulting from leaching, percolation, or the like.

lymph /lɪmf/ *n.* a clear, yellowish, slightly alkaline fluid derived from the tissues of the body and conveyed to the bloodstream by the lymphatic vessels. – **lymphatic**, *adj.*

lynch /lɪntʃ/ *v.t.* to put (a person) to death without authority or process of law. – **lynching**, *n.*

lynx /lɪŋks/ *n., pl.* **lynxes**, (*esp. collectively*) **lynx**. any of various wildcats having long limbs and short tails.

lyre /ˈlaɪə/ *n.* a musical instrument of ancient Greece.

lyrebird /ˈlaɪəbɜd/ *n.* either of two ground-dwelling birds of south-eastern Australia, the males of which have long, lyre-shaped tails.

lyric /ˈlɪrɪk/ *adj.* Also, **lyrical**. **1.** (of poetry) having the form and musical quality of a song. **2.** relating to, rendered by, or employing singing. – *n.* **3.** a lyric poem. **4.** (*often pl.*) the words of a song.

lyricist /ˈlɪrəsəst/ *n.* someone who writes the words for songs.

-lyse a word element making verbs of processes represented by nouns in *-lysis.*

-lysis a word element, especially in scientific terminology, meaning 'breaking down', 'decomposition'.

-lyte a word element denoting something subjected to a certain process (indicated by a noun ending in *-lysis*).

-lytic a termination of adjectives corresponding to nouns in *-lysis.*

M m

M, m /ɛm/ *n., pl.* **M's** *or* **Ms**, **m's** *or* **ms**. the 13th letter of the English alphabet.

ma'am /mæm, mam/, *if unstressed* /məm/ – *n.* madam.

macabre /mə'kab, mə'kabə, -brə/ *adj.* gruesome; horrible; grim; ghastly.

macadamia /mækə'deɪmiə/ *n.* an ornamental tree which bears edible, hard-shelled nuts.

macadamise = macadamize /mə'kædəmaɪz/ *v.t.*, **-mised**, **-mising**. to construct (a road) by laying and rolling successive layers of broken stone.

macaroni /mækə'rouni/ *n.* a kind of pasta.

macaroon /mækə'run/ *n.* a sweet cake or biscuit, usually with coconut.

macaw /mə'kɔ/ *n.* a large, brightly-coloured parrot with a harsh voice.

mace[1] /meɪs/ *n.* **1.** *History* a clublike weapon of war. **2.** a staff borne as a symbol of office.

mace[2] /meɪs/ *n.* a spice resembling nutmeg in flavour.

macerate /'mæsəreɪt/ *v.t.*, **-rated**, **-rating**. **1.** to soften by steeping in a liquid. **2.** to cause to grow thin.

mach /mæk/ *n.* the ratio of the speed of an object to the speed of sound in the medium, usually air.

machete /mə'ʃɛti/ *n.* a large, heavy knife.

machinate /'mæʃəneɪt, 'mækəneɪt/ *v.t.*, **-nated**, **-nating**. to contrive or devise, especially artfully or with evil purpose.

machine /mə'ʃin/ *n., v.*, **-chined**, **-chining**. – *n.* **1.** an apparatus consisting of interrelated parts with separate functions, which is used in the performance of some kind of work. **2.** *Mechanics* a device which transmits and modifies force or motion. – *v.t.* **3.** to make, prepare, or finish with a machine.

machine gun *n.* a small arm able to fire rapidly and continuously.

machine language *n.* a low-level and therefore complex binary code which is a precise set of operating instructions for a computer.

machinery /mə'ʃinəri/ *n., pl.* **-ries**. **1.** machines or mechanical apparatus. **2.** the parts of a machine, collectively.

machismo /mə'tʃɪzmou, mə'kɪzmou/ *n.* masculine display emphasising strength.

macho /'mætʃou, 'mækou/ *n.* **1.** a man who displays machismo. – *adj.* **2.** showily virile.

-machy a combining form meaning 'combat'.

mackerel /'mækərəl/ *n.* a common iridescent greenish fish with irregular darker markings on the back.

mackintosh /'mækəntɒʃ/ *n.* a raincoat.

macramé /mə'krami/ *n.* a kind of lace or ornamental work made by knotting thread or cord in patterns.

macro[1] /'mækrou/ *adj.* having to do with macro-economics.

macro[2] /'mækrou/ *n.* a single-word computer command which sets in train a number of other commands.

macro- a prefix meaning 'long', 'large', 'great', 'excessive'. Also (*before vowels*), **macr-**.

macrobiotic /ˌmækroubaɪ'ɒtɪk/ *adj.* of or relating to a largely vegetarian dietary system intended to prolong life.

macro-economics /ˌmækrou-ɛkə'nɒmɪks, -ikə-/ *n.* (*construed as sing.*) study of the economic system as a whole. Cf. **micro-economics**.

macroscopic /mækrə'skɒpɪk/ *adj.* **1.** visible to the naked eye (opposed to *microscopic*). **2.** comprehensive; concerned with large units or issues.

mad /mæd/ *adj.*, **madder**, **maddest**. disordered in intellect; insane.

madam /'mædəm/ *n., pl.* **madams** /'mædəmz/, **mesdames** /meɪ'dæm, -'dam/. **1.** a polite term of address to a woman. **2.** the woman in charge of a brothel.

made /meɪd/ *v.* **1.** past tense and past participle of **make**. – *adj.* **2.** assured of success or fortune.

madeira /mə'dɪərə/ *n.* a rich, strong, white wine resembling sherry.

made-money /'meɪd-mʌni/ *adj.* of or relating to a money-market borrow-and-lend operation which results in a sure profit.

madrigal /'mædrɪgəl/ *n.* a song with parts for several voices, performed without instrumental accompaniment.

maelstrom /'meɪlstrəm/ *n.* a restless confusion of affairs, influence, etc.

maestro /'maɪstrou/ *n., pl.* **-tros**, **-tri** /-tri/. an eminent musical composer, teacher, or conductor.

magazine /mægə'zin/ *n.* **1.** a periodical publication, usually bound and with a paper cover. **2.** a room or place for keeping gunpowder and other explosives. **3.** a metal receptacle for a number of cartridges which is inserted into certain types of automatic weapons. **4.** *Photography* a light-proof enclosure containing film.

magenta /mə'dʒɛntə/ *n., adj.* reddish purple.

maggot /'mægət/ *n.* the legless larva of a fly.

magic /'mædʒɪk/ *n.* **1.** the art of producing effects claimed to be beyond the natural human power. **2.** any extraordinary or irresistible influence. **3.** conjuring. – *adj.* **4.** of, relating to, or due to magic.

magisterial /mædʒəs'tɪəriəl/ *adj.* **1.** of or befitting a magistrate or a magistrate's office. **2.** of the rank of a magistrate.

magistrate /'mædʒəstreɪt, -trət/ *n.* a justice of the peace, paid or unpaid, who officiates in a magistrate's court. – **magistracy**, *n.*

magistrate's court *n.* a court used to try less serious criminal offences or to hear certain civil matters, presided over by a magistrate.

magma /'mægmə/ *n.* *Geology* molten material at great heat and pressure, occurring beneath the crust of the earth.

magnanimous /mæg'nænəməs/ *adj.* generous in forgiving an insult or injury. – **magnanimity**, *n.*

magnate /'mægneɪt, 'mægnət/ *n.* a person of

eminence or distinction in any field.

magnesium /mæg'niziəm/ *n.* a light, ductile, silver-white metallic element which burns with a dazzling white light, used in lightweight alloys. *Symbol*: Mg

magnet /'mægnət/ *n.* **1.** a body (as a piece of iron or steel) which possesses the property of attracting certain substances. **2.** a thing or person that attracts, as by some inherent power or charm. – **magnetic,** *adj.*

magnetic disk /mæg'nɛtɪk/ *n.* → **disk**.

magnetic north *n.* the direction in which the needle of a compass points, differing in most places from true north.

magnetic tape *n.* a plastic tape coated with a ferromagnetic powder, especially iron oxide, used to record sound, video signals, digital information, etc.

magneto /mæg'nitoʊ/ *n., pl.* **-tos**. a small electric generator, the poles of which are permanent magnets.

magneto- a combining form of **magnet** or **magnetic**.

magni- a word element meaning 'large', 'great'.

magnification /mægnəfə'keɪʃən/ *n.* **1.** a magnified copy or reproduction. **2.** (of an optical instrument) the ratio of the linear dimensions of the final image to that of the object.

magnificent /mæg'nɪfəsənt/ *adj.* extraordinarily fine.

magnify /'mægnəfaɪ/ *v.,* **-fied**, **-fying**. – *v.t.* **1.** to increase the apparent size of, as a lens does. **2.** to make greater in size; enlarge. – *v.i.* **3.** to increase or be able to increase the apparent size of an object, as a lens does.

magnitude /'mægnətʃud/ *n.* **1.** size; extent. **2.** great amount, importance, etc.

magnolia /mæg'noʊliə/ *n.* any of several shrubs and trees, usually with fragrant flowers.

magnum /'mægnəm/ *n., pl.* **-nums**. a bottle for wine or spirits, holding about 2 normal bottles, or 1.5 litres.

magpie /'mægpaɪ/ *n.* any of several common black and white birds.

mag wheel *n. Colloquial* a magnesium alloy wheel.

mah-jong /'ma-dʒɒŋ/ *n.* a game of Chinese origin, usually for four persons, with 136 (or sometimes 144) domino-like pieces or tiles. Also, **mah-jongg**.

mahogany /mə'hɒgəni/ *n., pl.* **-nies**. **1.** any of certain tropical American trees yielding a hard, reddish brown wood highly esteemed for making fine furniture, etc. **2.** a reddish brown colour.

maid /meɪd/ *n.* **1.** a girl; unmarried woman. **2.** a woman employed for various light domestic duties in houses, hotels, etc.; housemaid.

maiden /'meɪdn/ *n.* **1.** a maid; girl; young unmarried woman; virgin. **2.** made, tried, appearing, etc., for the first time.

maiden name *n.* a woman's surname before marriage.

maiden over *n.* (in cricket) an over in which no runs are made.

mail[1] /meɪl/ *n.* **1.** letters, packages, etc., arriving or sent by post. **2.** the system of transmission of letters, etc., by post. – *adj.* **3.** of or relating to mail. – *v.t.* **4.** to send by mail; place in a post office or post-box for transmission.

mail[2] /meɪl/ *n.* flexible armour of interlinked rings.

mail order *n.* an order for goods, etc., received and transmitted by post.

maim /meɪm/ *v.t.* **1.** to deprive of the use of some bodily member; mutilate; cripple. **2.** to impair; make essentially defective.

main /meɪn/ *adj.* **1.** chief; principal; leading. – *n.* **2.** a principal pipe or duct in a system used to distribute water, gas, etc. **3.** strength; force; violent effort. **4.** the chief or principal part or point.

mainframe computer /'meɪnfreɪm/ *n.* a powerful computer with a large storage capacity.

mainland /'meɪnlænd, -lənd/ *n.* the principal land mass as distinguished from nearby islands and peninsulas.

mainline /'meɪnlaɪn/ *v.i.,* **-lined**, **-lining**. *Colloquial* to inject a narcotic drug directly into the vein.

mainstream /'meɪnstrim/ *n.* the dominant trend; chief tendency.

maintain /meɪn'teɪn, mən-/ *v.t.* **1.** to keep in existence or continuance; preserve; retain. **2.** to affirm; assert.

maintenance /'meɪntənəns/ *n.* **1.** the act of maintaining. **2.** *Law* the money paid for the support of the other spouse or infant children, usually after divorce.

maize /meɪz/ *n.* a widely cultivated cereal plant bearing grain in large ears or spikes.

majesty /'mædʒəsti/ *n., pl.* **-ties**. **1.** supreme greatness or authority; sovereignty. **2.** (*usu. cap.*) a title used when speaking of or to a sovereign (preceded by *his*, *her*, *your*, etc.).

major /'meɪdʒə/ *adj.* **1.** greater, as in size, amount, extent, importance, rank, etc. **2.** of full legal age. – *n.* **3.** a field of study chosen by a student to represent their principal interest.

majority /mə'dʒɒrəti/ *n., pl.* **-ties**. **1.** the greater part or number. **2.** the state or time of being of full legal age.

Major Mitchell /meɪdʒə 'mɪtʃəl/ *n.* a white cockatoo with a scarlet crest.

make /meɪk/ *v.,* **made**, **making**, *n.* – *v.t.* **1.** to produce by any action or causative agency. **2.** to cause to be or become; render. **3.** to put into proper condition for use. **4.** to cause, induce, or compel (to do something). **5.** to do; effect. **6.** to become by development; prove to be. **7.** to estimate; reckon. **8.** to arrive at or reach. **9.** to arrive in time for. **10.** *Colloquial* to seduce or have sexual intercourse with. – *v.i.* **11.** to cause oneself, or something understood, to be as specified. **12.** to show oneself in action or behaviour. **13.** to direct or pursue the course; go. – *v.* **14. make a face,** to grimace. **15. make believe,** to pretend. **16. make do,** to operate or carry on using minimal or improvised resources. **17. make love,** *Colloquial* to have sexual intercourse. **18. make out, a.** to discern; decipher. **b.** to present as; impute to be. **19. make tracks,** *Colloquial* to depart. **20. make up, a.** to put together; construct; compile. **b.** to compensate for; make good. **c.** to bring to a definite conclusion, as one's mind. **d.** Also, **make it up**. to become reconciled after a quarrel. **e.** to apply cosmetics to, as the face. – *n.* **21.** style or manner of being made; form; build.

makeshift /ˈmeɪkʃɪft/ *n.* a temporary expedient; substitute.

make-up /ˈmeɪk-ʌp/ *n.* **1.** cosmetics, as those used by a woman to enhance her features. **2.** the manner of being made up or put together; composition. **3.** physical or mental constitution.

makings /ˈmeɪkɪŋz/ *pl. n.* material of which something may be made.

mal- a prefix meaning 'bad', 'wrongful', 'ill'.

maladjustment /mæləˈdʒʌstmənt/ *n.* **1.** a faulty adjustment. **2.** *Psychology* a failure to function successfully with regard to personal relationships and environment, often a symptom of mental disturbance.

malady /ˈmælədi/ *n., pl.* **-dies**. any bodily disorder or disease, especially one that is chronic or deep-seated.

malapropism /ˈmæləprɒpˌɪzəm/ *n.* a word ridiculously misused.

malaria /məˈlɛəriə/ *n.* any of a group of diseases characterised by attacks of chills, fever, and sweating.

malcontent /ˈmælkəntɛnt/ *adj.* **1.** dissatisfied, especially with the existing administration; inclined to rebellion. – *n.* **2.** a malcontent person.

male /meɪl/ *adj.* **1.** belonging to the sex which begets young, or any division or group corresponding to it. **2.** relating to or characteristic of this sex; masculine. **3.** *Machinery* designating some part, etc., which fits into a corresponding part. – *n.* **4.** a male person or animal.

male chauvinist /ˈʃoʊvənəst/ *n.* a man who discriminates against women.

malevolent /məˈlɛvələnt/ *adj.* wishing evil to another or others; showing ill will.

malformation /mælfɔˈmeɪʃən, -fə-/ *n.* faulty or anomalous formation or structure, especially in a living body. – **malformed**, *adj.*

malfunction /mælˈfʌŋkʃən/ *v.i.* **1.** to fail to function properly. – *n.* **2.** failure to function properly.

malice /ˈmæləs/ *n.* **1.** desire to inflict injury or suffering on another. **2.** *Law* evil intent on the part of someone who commits a wrongful act injurious to others.

malign /məˈlaɪn/ *v.t.* **1.** to speak ill of; slander. – *adj.* **2.** having or showing an evil disposition; malevolent.

malignant /məˈlɪgnənt/ *adj.* very dangerous; harmful in influence or effect.

malinger /məˈlɪŋgə/ *v.i.* to feign sickness or injury, especially in order to avoid work, etc.

mall /mɔl, mæl/ *n.* **1.** a shaded walk, usually public. **2.** a shopping complex.

malleable /ˈmæliəbəl/ *adj.* **1.** capable of being extended or shaped by hammering or by pressure with rollers. **2.** adaptable or tractable.

mallee /ˈmæli/ *n.* **1.** any of various eucalypts having a number of almost unbranched stems arising from a large underground woody tuber. **2. the mallee,** any remote, isolated or unsettled area.

mallet /ˈmælət/ *n.* a hammer-like tool.

malnutrition /mælnjuˈtrɪʃən/ *n.* lack of proper nutrition resulting from deficiencies in the diet or the process of assimilation.

malpractice /mælˈpræktəs/ *n.* improper professional action.

malt /mɔlt, mɒlt/ *n.* germinated grain (usually barley), used in brewing and distilling.

maltreat /mælˈtrit/ *v.t.* to treat badly; handle roughly or cruelly; abuse.

mama /məˈma/ *n.* mother; mummy.

mamilla /mæˈmɪlə/ *n., pl.* **-millae** /-ˈmɪli/. the nipple of the breast.

mammal /ˈmæməl/ *n.* a member of the class of vertebrates whose young feed upon milk from the mother's breast.

mammary /ˈmæməri/ *adj.* of or relating to the breast.

mammoth /ˈmæməθ/ *n.* **1.** a large, extinct species of elephant. – *adj.* **2.** huge; gigantic.

man /mæn/ *n., pl.* **men**, *v.,* **manned**, **manning**. **1.** the human creature or being as representing the species or as distinguished from other beings, animals, or things; the human race; humankind. **2.** a human being; a person. **3.** a male human being, as distinguished from woman. **4.** an adult male person. **5.** a male servant; a valet. **6.** one of the pieces used in playing certain games, as chess or draughts. – *v.t.* **7.** to furnish with personnel, as for service or defence. **8.** to take one's place for service, as at a gun, post, etc.

manacle /ˈmænəkəl/ *n., v.,* **-cled**, **-cling**. – *n.* (*usu. pl.*) **1.** a shackle for the hand; handcuff. **2.** a restraint. – *v.t.* **3.** to handcuff; fetter.

manage /ˈmænɪdʒ/ *v.,* **-aged**, **-aging**. – *v.t.* **1.** to bring about; succeed in accomplishing. **2.** to take charge or care of. **3.** to contrive to get along. – *v.i.* **4.** to conduct affairs.

managed currency *n.* a form of money management where the purchasing power of a nation's currency is adjusted by the monetary authorities to influence business activities and prices (contrasted with the *gold standard*).

management /ˈmænɪdʒmənt/ *n.* **1.** the act or manner of managing. **2.** the person or persons managing an institution, business, etc.

management buyout *n.* the purchase of a company by its own company managers. Also, **management buy-out**, **MBO**.

management information system *n.* *Computers* a software package which is designed to provide information for decision-making, usually intended for senior management.

manager /ˈmænədʒə/ *n.* **1.** one charged with the management or direction of an institution, a business or the like. **2.** a person in charge of the business affairs of an entertainer, etc. – **managerial**, *adj.*

manchester /ˈmæntʃəstə/ *n.* household linen.

-mancy a word element meaning 'divination'.

mandarin /'mændərən, mændə'rɪn/ *n.* **1.** (formerly) a public official in the Chinese Empire. **2.** a small, roundish citrus fruit. Also, **mandarine**.

mandate /'mændeɪt/ *n.* **1.** a commission given to one nation (the mandatary) by an associated group of nations (such as the League of Nations) to administer the government and affairs of a people in a backward territory. **2.** *Politics* the instruction as to policy given or supposed to be given by electors to a legislative body or to one or more of its members.

mandatory /'mændətri, -təri/ *adj.* obligatory.

mandible /'mændəbəl/ *n.* the bone of the lower jaw.

mandolin /mændə'lɪn/ *n.* a musical instrument with a pear-shaped wooden body and metal strings.

mane /meɪn/ *n.* the long hair growing on the back of or about the neck of some animals.

manganese /mæŋgə'niz/ *n.* a hard, brittle, greyish white metallic element used in alloys. *Symbol*: Mn

mange /meɪndʒ/ *n.* any of various skin diseases characterised by loss of hair and scabby eruptions. – **mangy**, *adj.*

manger /'meɪndʒə/ *n.* a box or trough, as in a stable, from which horses or cattle eat.

mangle[1] /'mæŋgəl/ *v.t.*, **-gled**, **-gling**. to cut, slash, or crush so as to disfigure.

mangle[2] /'mæŋgəl/ *n.* a machine for pressing water out of cloth by means of rollers.

mango /'mæŋgoʊ/ *n., pl.* **-goes**, **-gos**. the ovoid fruit of a tropical tree.

mangrove /'mæŋgroʊv, 'mæn-/ *n.* a tree found in subtropical and tropical countries on salt or brackish mudflats.

manhandle /'mænhændl/ *v.t.*, **-dled**, **-dling**. to handle roughly.

manhole /'mænhoʊl/ *n.* a hole, usually with a cover, through which a person may enter a sewer, drain, steam boiler, etc.

man-hour /'mæn-aʊə/ *n.* an hour of work by one person, used as an industrial time unit.

mania /'meɪniə/ *n.* great excitement or enthusiasm; craze.

-mania a combining form of **mania**.

maniac /'meɪniæk/ *n.* a raving lunatic.

manic /'mænɪk/ *adj.* **1.** relating to mania. **2.** *Colloquial* experiencing manic depression.

manic depression *n.* → **bipolar affective disorder**. Also, **manic-depression**. – **manic depressive**, *n.* – **manic-depressive**, *adj.*

manicure /'mænəkjuə/ *n.* professional care of the hands and fingernails.

manifest /'mænəfəst, -fɛst/ *adj.* **1.** readily perceived by the eye or the understanding. – *v.t.* **2.** to make manifest. – *n.* **3.** a list of goods or cargo carried, as by a ship, truck, etc. – **manifestation**, *n.*

manifesto /mænə'fɛstoʊ/ *n., pl.* **-tos**, **-toes**. a public declaration, making known intentions, objects, motives, etc.

manifold /'mænəfoʊld/ *adj.* **1.** of many kinds; numerous and varied. **2.** having many different parts, elements, features, forms, etc. **3.** a pipe or chamber with a number of inlets or outlets. – *v.t.* **4.** to make copies of, as with carbon paper.

Manila paper /mə'nɪlə/ *n.* strong light brown paper.

manipulate /mə'nɪpjəleɪt/ *v.t.*, **-lated**, **-lating**. **1.** to handle, manage, or use, especially with skill. **2.** to adapt or change (accounts, figures, etc.) to suit one's purpose or advantage.

mankind /mæn'kaɪnd/ *n.* **1.** → **humankind**. **2.** men, as distinguished from women; the male sex.

mannequin /'mænəkən, -kwən/ *n.* **1.** a model of the human figure for displaying or fitting clothes. **2.** → **model** (def. 4).

manner /'mænə/ *n.* **1.** way of doing, being done, or happening. **2.** (*pl.*) ways of behaving, especially with reference to polite standards. **3.** kind; sort. **4. to the manner born,** accustomed or destined by birth (to a high position, etc.).

mannerism /'mænərɪzəm/ *n.* a habitual peculiarity of manner.

manoeuvre /mə'nuvə/ *n., v.*, **-vred**, **-vring**. – *n.* **1.** a planned and regulated movement of troops, war vessels, etc. **2.** an adroit move; skilful measure. – *v.t.* **3.** to manipulate with skill or adroitness. – *v.i.* **4.** to perform a manoeuvre or manoeuvres. **5.** to scheme; intrigue.

manor /'mænə/ *n.* the main house or mansion on an estate.

manse /mæns/ *n.* the house and land occupied by a minister or parson.

-manship a suffix signifying proficiency in an activity, as *gamesmanship*.

mansion /'mænʃən/ *n.* an imposing residence.

manslaughter /'mænslɔtə/ *n.* *Law* the killing of a human being unlawfully but without malice aforethought.

mantelpiece /'mæntlpis/ *n.* the structure around a fireplace.

mantelshelf /'mæntlʃɛlf/ *n.* the projecting part of a mantelpiece.

mantis /'mæntəs/ *n., pl.* **-tises**, **-tes** /-tiz/. any of various insects which hold the forelegs doubled up as if in prayer. Also, **praying mantis**.

mantle /'mæntl/ *n.* **1.** Also, **mantua**. a loose, sleeveless cloak. **2.** something that covers, envelops, or conceals. **3.** *Geology* a layer of the earth between crust and core, consisting of solid rock.

mantra /'mæntrə/ *n.* a word, phrase or verse intoned, often repetitively, as a sacred formula in Hinduism and Mahayana Buddhism. Also, **mantram**. – **mantric**, *adj.*

manual /'mænjuəl/ *adj.* **1.** of or relating to the hand or hands. **2.** using or involving human energy, power, etc. – *n.* **3.** a book, giving information or instructions.

manufacture /mænjə'fæktʃə, 'mænjəfæktʃə/ *n., v.*, **-tured**, **-turing**. – *n.* **1.** the making of goods or wares by manufacturing. – *v.t.* **2.** to make or produce by hand or machinery, especially on a large scale. **3.** to invent fictitiously; concoct; devise.

manure /mə'njuə/ *n.* excrement, especially of animals, used as fertiliser.

manuscript /'mænjəskrɪpt/ *n.* **1.** a book, document, letter, musical score, etc., written by hand. **2.** an author's copy of a work, written by hand or typewriter, which is used as the basis for typesetting. **3.** writing, as distinguished from print.

many /'mɛni/ *adj.*, **more**, **most**. **1.** constituting or forming a large number. **2.** relatively numerous (after *as*, *so*, *too*, or *how*). **3.** being one of a large number (fol. by *a* or *an*). – *n.* **4.** a great or considerable number (often followed by a noun with *of* expressed or understood). **5.** (as a collective plural) many persons or things.

map /mæp/ *n.* a representation, on a flat surface, of a part or the whole of the earth's surface, the heavens, or a heavenly body.

maple /'meɪpəl/ *n.* a tree of the north temperate zone from the sap of which maple syrup is made.

mar /ma/ *v.t.*, **marred**, **marring**. to damage; impair; ruin.

marathon /'mærəθɒn, -θən/ *n.* a long-distance race.

maraud /mə'rɔd/ *v.i.* to rove in quest of plunder.

marble /'mabəl/ *n.* **1.** limestone in a more or less crystalline state and capable of taking a polish, occurring in a wide range of colours and markings, and much used in sculpture and architecture. **2.** something resembling marble in hardness, coldness, smoothness, etc. **3.** *Games* **a.** a little ball of stone, baked clay, glass, etc., used in a children's game. **b.** (*pl. construed as sing.*) the game itself. – *adj.* **4.** consisting of marble. **5.** like marble, as being hard, cold, unfeeling, etc. **6.** of variegated or mottled colour. – *v.t.* **7.** to colour or stain like variegated marble.

march /matʃ/ *v.i.* **1.** to walk with regular and measured tread, as soldiers; advance in step in an organised body. **2.** to proceed; advance. – *v.t.* **3.** to cause to march. – *n.* **4.** the act or course of marching. **5.** a piece of music with a rhythm suited to accompany marching.

marching orders *pl. n. Colloquial* orders to leave; dismissal.

mare /mɛə/ *n.* a female horse.

margarine /madʒə'rin, mag-, 'madʒərən/ *n.* a butter-like product made from refined vegetable or animal oils.

margin /'madʒən/ *n.* **1.** a border or edge. **2.** *Finance* a security, as a percentage in money, deposited with a broker as a provision against loss on transactions on behalf of the investor. **3.** *Commerce* the difference between the cost and the selling price. **4.** *Economics* the point at which the return from economic activity barely covers the cost of production, and below which production is unprofitable. **5.** *Banking* the excess value of the relative security over the loan for which it is collateral. **6.** that part of a wage, additional to the basic wage, which is offered to account for the employee's particular skills; secondary wage. – **marginal**, *adj.*

marginalism /'madʒənəlɪzəm/ *n.* a type of economic analysis which places stress on marginal factors in the economy.

marigold /'mærigoʊld/ *n.* any of various golden-flowered plants.

marijuana = marihuana /mærə'wanə/ *n.* the dried leaves and flowers of Indian hemp, used in cigarettes as a narcotic and intoxicant.

marinade /mærə'neɪd/ *n.*, /'mærəneɪd/ *v.*, **-naded**, **-nading**. – *n.* **1.** a liquid, especially wine or vinegar with oil and seasonings, in which meat, fish, vegetables, etc., may be steeped before cooking. – *v.t.* **2.** → **marinate**.

marinate /'mærəneɪt/ *v.t.*, **-nated**, **-nating**. to let stand in a liquid before cooking or serving in order to impart flavour.

marine /mə'rin/ *adj.* **1.** of or relating to the sea. **2.** relating to navigation or shipping.

mariner /'mærənə/ *n.* someone who directs or assists in the navigation of a ship; sailor.

marital /'mærətəl/ *adj.* of or relating to marriage.

maritime /'mærətaɪm/ *adj.* of or relating to the sea.

mark /mak/ *n.* **1.** a visible trace or impression upon anything. **2.** a sign, token, or indication. **3.** a symbol used in rating conduct, proficiency, attainment, etc., as of pupils in a school. **4.** a recognised or required standard. **5.** something aimed at, as a target. – *v.t.* **6.** to be a distinguishing feature of. **7.** to put a mark or marks on. **8.** to castrate (a lamb, calf, etc.). **9.** to indicate or designate by or as by marks. **10.** to notice or observe. **11. mark down/up,** to reduce/increase the price of. – *v.i.* **12.** to take notice; give attention; consider.

market /'makət/ *n.* **1.** a meeting of people for selling and buying. **2.** a place where such meetings are held, especially for the sale of food, etc. **3.** a body of persons carrying on extensive transactions in a specified commodity. **4.** **a.** trade or traffic, particularly as regards a particular commodity. **b.** demand for a particular commodity. **5.** current price or value. – *v.i.* **6.** to deal (buy or sell) in a market. **7.** to dispose of in a market; sell.

marketable /'makətəbəl/ *adj.* readily saleable.

marketable parcel *n.* the minimum number of shares necessary for a normal market transaction.

market economy *n.* an economic structure in which the allocation of resources is achieved by the interdependent decisions of persons supplying and demanding those resources rather than by the decisions of a centralised planning agency such as a bureaucracy.

market garden *n.* a garden or smallholding where vegetables and fruit are grown for sale.

marketing /'makətɪŋ/ *n.* **1.** the total process whereby goods are put onto the market. **2.** the act of buying or selling in a market.

market order *n.* an order to purchase or sell at the current market price.

market overt /'oʊvɜt/ *n.* the tenet that all sales are binding, not only on parties to a sale but on all other persons; thus a purchaser acting in good faith acquires a valid title to goods even if they are stolen unless the true owner has prosecuted the thief to conviction.

market price *n.* the price at which a commodity, security, or service is selling in the open market. Also, **market value**.

market research *n.* the gathering of information by a firm about the preferences, purchasing power, etc., of consumers, especially as a preliminary to putting a product on the market.

markup language /'makʌp læŋgwɪdʒ/ *n.* a computer language in which various elements of a document, database, etc., are marked with tags, providing a flexible means of arranging and retrieving data. See **HTML**, **SGML**.

marlin /'malən/ *n.* any of various species of large, powerful, game-fishes.

marmalade /'maməleɪd/ *n.* a jelly-like preserve with fruit (usually citrus) suspended in small pieces.

marmot /'mamət/ *n.* a bushy-tailed, thickset rodent.

maroon[1] /mə'roʊn, mə'run/ *n.* **1.** dark brownish red. – *adj.* **2.** of a dark brownish red colour.

maroon[2] /mə'run/ *v.t.* to put ashore and leave on a desolate island or coast.

marquee /ma'ki/ *n.* a large tent or tentlike shelter, sometimes with open sides.

marriage /'mærɪdʒ/ *n.* **1.** the legal union of a man with a woman for life. **2.** any intimate union. **3.** *Economics* the offsetting of a buying order and a selling order in a broker's office, both orders having been placed by the broker's clients.

marriage celebrant /'sɛləbrənt/ *n.* someone who performs a marriage, especially in a civil service.

married /'mærid/ *adj.* united in wedlock; wedded.

marron[1] /'mærən/ *n.* a chestnut.

marron[2] /'mærən/ *n.* a large freshwater crayfish of western Australia.

marrow /'mæroʊ/ *n.* **1.** a soft, fatty vascular tissue in the interior cavities of bones. **2.** an elongated fruit widely used as a cooked vegetable.

marry /'mæri/ *v.*, **-ried**, **-rying**. – *v.t.* **1.** to take in marriage. **2.** to unite in wedlock. – *v.i.* **3.** to take a husband or wife; wed.

marsala /mə'salə, ma-/ *n.* a sweet, dark, fortified wine.

marsh /maʃ/ *n.* a tract of low, wet land.

marshal /'maʃəl/ *n.*, *v.*, **-shalled**, **-shalling**. – *n.* **1.** the title of various officials having certain police duties. – *v.t.* **2.** to arrange in due or proper order; set out in an orderly manner.

marshmallow /'maʃmæloʊ, -mɛl-/ *n.* confection with an elastic, spongy texture.

marsupial /ma'supiəl, -'sjup-/ *n.* any member of the order which includes all of the viviparous but non-placental mammals such as kangaroos, wombats, possums, etc. Most marsupials carry their young in a pouch.

mart /mat/ *n.* market.

martial /'maʃəl/ *adj.* relating to or appropriate for war.

martial arts *pl. n.* the several methods of unarmed self-defence originating in China, Korea and Japan, as judo, kung-fu, etc.

martial law *n.* the law imposed upon an area by military forces when civil authority has broken down.

martinet /matə'nɛt/ *n.* a rigid disciplinarian, especially a military one.

martyr /'matə/ *n.* someone who is put to death or endures great suffering on behalf of any belief, principle, or cause, especially religious.

marvel /'mavəl/ *n.*, *v.*, **-velled**, **-velling**. – *n.* **1.** something that arouses wonder or admiration. – *v.t.* **2.** to wonder at (usually followed by a clause as object).

marvellous /'mavələs/ *adj.* **1.** such as to excite wonder; surprising; extraordinary. **2.** excellent; superb. **3.** improbable or incredible.

marzipan /'mazəpæn/ *n.* a confection made of almond paste.

-mas a final element in certain names of holidays and Christian feasts.

mascara /mæs'karə/ *n.* a substance used as a cosmetic to colour the eyelashes.

mascot /'mæskɒt/ *n.* a person, animal, or thing supposed to bring good luck.

masculine /'mæskjələn/ *adj.* relating to or characteristic of a man or men.

mash /mæʃ/ *n.* **1.** a soft, pulpy mass. **2.** mashed potatoes. – *v.t.* **3.** to reduce to a soft, pulpy mass, as by heating or pressure.

mask /mask/ *n.* **1.** a covering for the face, especially one worn for disguise or protection. **2.** anything that disguises or conceals; a disguise; a pretence. – *v.t.* **3.** to disguise or conceal.

masking tape *n.* an adhesive tape used for defining edges and protecting surfaces not to be painted.

masochism /'mæsəkɪzəm/ *n.* a condition in which one compulsively seeks, and sometimes derives pleasure from, suffering, as humiliation, pain, etc.

mason /'meɪsən/ *n.* someone who builds or works with stone.

masonite /'meɪsənaɪt/ *n.* a kind of woodfibre material, pressed in sheets and used for partitions, insulation, etc.

masquerade /mæskə'reɪd, mas-/ *n.*, *v.*, **-raded**, **-rading**. – *n.* **1.** a party at which everyone wears a mask. **2.** disguise, or false outward show. – *v.i.* **3.** to disguise oneself.

mass[1] /mæs/ *n.* **1.** a body of coherent matter, usually of indefinite shape and often of considerable size. **2.** an aggregation of incoherent particles, parts, or objects regarded as forming one body. **3. the masses,** the great body of the common people. – *adj.* **4.** relating to or involving a large number of people. **5.** large-scale or wide-reaching. – *v.i.* **6.** to come together in or form a mass or masses. – *v.t.* **7.** to gather into or dispose in a mass or masses; assemble.

mass[2] /mæs/ *n.* the celebration of the Eucharist.

massacre /'mæsəkə/ *n.*, *v.*, **-cred**, **-cring**. – *n.* **1.** the unnecessary, indiscriminate slaughter of human beings. – *v.t.* **2.** to kill indiscriminately or in a massacre.

massage /'mæsaʒ, 'mæsadʒ/ *n.*, *v.*, **-saged**, **-saging**. – *n.* **1.** the act or art of treating the body by rubbing, kneading, etc. – *v.t.* **2.** to treat by massage.

masseur /mæ'sɜ/ *n.* a man who practises massage. – **masseuse**, *fem. n.*

massive /'mæsɪv/ *adj.* consisting of or forming a large mass; bulky and heavy.

mass media *n.* the means of communication, as radio, television, newspapers, magazines, etc., that reach large numbers of people. Also, **the media**.

mass-produce /mæs-prə'djus/ *v.t.*, **-duced**, **-ducing**. to manufacture in large quantities by standardised mechanical processes.

mast /mast/ *n.* a tall spar which supports the yards, sails, etc., of a ship.

mast- variant of **masto-** before vowels.

mastectomy /mæs'tɛktəmi/ *n., pl.* **-mies**. the operation of removing the breast.

master /'mastə/ *n.* **1.** someone who has the power of controlling, using, or disposing of something. **2.** the male head of a household. **3.** a tradesperson qualified to carry on their trade independently and to teach apprentices. **4.** *Law* an officer of the Supreme Court of Judicature whose main function is to decide preliminary issues in High Court cases. **5.** the head teacher in a particular subject department in a secondary school. – *adj.* **6.** being master. **7.** chief or principal. – *v.t.* **8.** to conquer or subdue; reduce to subjection. **9.** to rule or direct as master. **10.** to make oneself master of. – **mastery**, *n.*

master key *n.* a key that will open a number of locks whose proper keys are not interchangeable. Also, **pass key**.

master of ceremonies *n.* a person who directs the entertainment at a party, dinner, etc.

masterpiece /'mastəpis/ *n.* **1.** one's most excellent production, as in an art. **2.** any production of masterly skill. **3.** a consummate example of skill or excellence of any kind.

masterstroke /'mastəstroʊk/ *n.* a masterly action or achievement.

masticate /'mæstəkeɪt/ *v.t., v.i.*, **-cated**, **-cating**. to chew.

masto- a word element meaning the breast. Also, **mast-**.

masturbation /mæstə'beɪʃən/ *n.* sexual stimulation not involving intercourse. – **masturbate**, *v.*

mat /mæt/ *n., v.*, **matted**, **matting**. – *n.* **1.** a piece of fabric made of plaited or woven rushes, straw, hemp, or other fibre, used to cover a floor, to wipe the shoes on, etc. **2.** a small piece of material, often ornamental, set under a dish of food, a lamp, vase, etc. – *v.t.* **3.** to form into a mat, as by interweaving. – *v.i.* **4.** to become entangled; form tangled masses.

matador /'mætədɔ/ *n.* the bullfighter who kills the bull in a bullfight.

match[1] /mætʃ/ *n.* a short, slender piece of wood or other material tipped with a chemical substance which produces fire when rubbed on a rough or chemically prepared surface.

match[2] /mætʃ/ *n.* **1.** a person or thing that equals or resembles another in some respect. **2.** a contest or game. **3.** a matrimonial compact or alliance. – *v.t.* **4.** to equal, or be equal to. **5.** to adapt; make to correspond. **6.** to fit together, as two things. – *v.i.* **7.** to be equal or suitable. **8.** to correspond.

match point *n.* the final point needed to win a contest.

mate /meɪt/ *n., v.*, **mated**, **mating**. – *n.* **1.** one joined with another in any pair. **2.** one of a pair of mated animals. **3. a.** a friend. **b.** (a form of address): *How are you going mate?* **4.** an assistant to a tradesman. – *v.t.* **5.** to join as a mate or as mates. **6.** (of animals) to copulate.

material /mə'tɪəriəl/ *n.* **1.** the substance or substances of which a thing is made or composed. **2.** information, ideas, or the like on which a report, thesis, etc., is based. **3.** a textile fabric. – *adj.* **4.** formed or consisting of matter; physical; corporeal. **5.** relating to the physical rather than the spiritual or intellectual aspect of things. **6.** pertinent or essential (fol. by *to*).

materialise = materialize /mə'tɪəriəlaɪz/ *v.i.*, **-lised**, **-lising**. **1.** to assume material or bodily form. **2.** to come into perceptible existence; appear.

materialist /mə'tɪəriələst/ *n.* one absorbed in material interests. – **materialistic**, *adj.*

maternal /mə'tɜnəl/ *adj.* **1.** of or relating to, befitting, having the qualities of, or being a mother. **2.** related through a mother.

maternity /mə'tɜnəti/ *n.* the state of being a mother; motherhood.

mathematics /mæθə'mætɪks/ *n.* the science that deals with the measurement, properties, and relations of quantities, including arithmetic, geometry, algebra, etc. – **mathematician**, *n.* – **mathematical**, *adj.*

maths /mæθs/ *n.* → **mathematics**.

matinee /'mætəneɪ/ *n.* an entertainment, as a dramatic or musical performance, film, etc., held in the daytime.

matri- a word element meaning 'mother'.

matriarch /'meɪtriak, 'mæt-/ *n.* a woman holding a position of leadership in a family or tribe.

matrices /'meɪtrəsiz/ *n.* a plural form of **matrix**.

matriculate /mə'trɪkjəleɪt/ *v.i.*, **-lated**, **-lating**. to pass matriculation.

matriculation /mətrɪkjə'leɪʃən/ *n.* a secondary-school examination in which a required level must be reached before qualification for admission to a tertiary education institution.

matrimony /'mætrəməni/ *n., pl.* **-nies**. the rite, ceremony, or sacrament of marriage. – **matrimonial**, *adj.*

matrix /'meɪtrɪks/ *n., pl.* **matrices** /'meɪtrəsiz/, **matrixes**. **1.** that which gives origin or form to a thing, or which serves to enclose it. **2.** *Mathematics, Computers* a rectangular array of numbers.

matron /'meɪtrən/ *n.* **1.** a married woman. **2.** a woman in charge of the sick bay, as in a school or workplace, on board a ship, etc.

matt /mæt/ *adj.* lustreless and dull in surface.

matter /'mætə/ *n.* **1.** the substance or substances of which physical objects consist or are composed. **2.** importance or significance. **3.** the trouble or difficulty (preceded by *the*). **4.** *Law* statement or allegation. – *v.i.* **5.** to be of importance; signify.

matter-of-fact /mætər-əv-'fækt/ *adj.* adhering to actual facts; not imaginative; prosaic; commonplace.

mattock /'mætək/ *n.* an instrument for loosening soil.

mattress /'mætrəs/ *n.* a case filled with soft material, often reinforced with springs, used as or on a bed.

mature /mə'tjuə/ *adj., v.,* **-tured**, **-turing**. – *adj.* **1.** complete in natural growth or development. **2.** *Commerce* having reached the limit of its time; having become payable or due, as a note, insurance policy, etc. – *v.t.* **3.** to make mature; ripen. – *v.i.* **4.** to become mature.

maturity /mə'tjurəti/ *n.* **1.** the state of being mature; ripeness. **2.** the time when a note or bill of exchange becomes due.

maudlin /'mɔdlən/ *adj.* tearfully or weakly emotional or sentimental.

maul /mɔl/ *v.t.* to handle roughly; to injure by rough treatment.

mausoleum /mɔsə'liəm, mɔz-/ *n., pl.* **-leums**, **-lea** /-'liə/. **1.** a stately and magnificent tomb. **2.** *Colloquial* a large, old, gloomy building.

mauve /moʊv/ *n.* **1.** pale bluish purple. – *adj.* **2.** of the colour of mauve.

maw /mɔ/ *n.* the mouth, throat, or gullet, especially of an animal.

mawkish /'mɔkɪʃ/ *adj.* sickly or slightly nauseating.

maxim /'mæksəm/ *n.* an expression, especially an aphoristic or sententious one, of a general truth, especially as to conduct.

maxima /'mæksəmə/ *n.* a plural form of **maximum**.

maximise = maximize /'mæksəmaɪz/ *v.t.,* **-mised**, **-mising**. to increase to the greatest possible amount or degree.

maximum /'mæksəməm/ *n., pl.* **-mums**, **-ma** /-mə/. the greatest quantity or amount possible, assignable, allowable, etc.

may /meɪ/ *v., past tense* **might**. used as an auxiliary to express **1.** possibility, opportunity, or permission. **2.** wish or prayer. **3.** contingency, especially in clauses expressing condition, concession, purpose, result, etc.

maybe /'meɪbi, meɪ'bi/ *adv.* perhaps.

mayhem /'meɪhɛm/ *n.* **1.** *Law* the crime of violently inflicting a bodily injury. **2.** any tumult, fracas, or fight. Also, **maihem**.

mayonnaise /meɪə'neɪz/ *n.* a thick dressing used for salads or vegetables.

mayor /mɛə/ *n.* the principal officer of a municipality; the chief magistrate of a city or borough. – **mayoress**, *fem. n.*

maze /meɪz/ *n.* a confusing network of intercommunicating paths or passages; a labyrinth.

me /mi/ *personal pron.* objective case of the pronoun **I**.

mead /mid/ *n.* an alcoholic liquor made by fermenting honey and water.

meadow /'mɛdoʊ/ *n.* *Chiefly Brit* a piece of grassland.

meagre /'migə/ *adj.* deficient in quantity or quality.

meal[1] /mil/ *n.* one of the regular repasts of the day, as breakfast, lunch, or dinner.

meal[2] /mil/ *n.* the edible part of a grain ground to a (coarse) powder.

mealy-mouthed /'mili-maʊðd/ *adj.* avoiding the use of plain terms, as from timidity, excessive delicacy, or hypocrisy.

mean[1] /min/ *v.,* **meant**, **meaning**. – *v.t.* **1.** to have in the mind as in intention or purpose. **2.** to intend for a particular purpose, destination, etc. **3.** (of words, things, etc.) to have as the signification; signify. – *v.i.* **4.** to be minded or disposed; have intentions. – **meaning**, *n.*

mean[2] /min/ *adj.* **1.** inferior in grade, quality or character. **2.** penurious, stingy, or miserly. **3.** *Colloquial* powerful, effective.

mean[3] /min/ *n.* **1.** something intermediate; that which is midway between two extremes. **2.** *Mathematics* a quantity having a value intermediate between the values of other quantities; an average. – *adj.* **3.** occupying a middle position.

meander /mi'ændə/ *v.i.* to proceed by a winding course.

means /minz/ *pl. n.* **1.** (*often construed as sing.*) an agency, instrumentality, method, etc., used to attain an end. **2.** disposable resources, especially pecuniary resources.

means test *n.* an evaluation of the income and resources of a person, in order to determine eligibility for part or all of a pension, grant, allowance, etc.

meantime /'mintaɪm/ *n.* **1.** the intervening time. – *adv.* **2.** meanwhile.

meanwhile /'minwaɪl, min'waɪl/ *adv.* in the intervening time; at the same time.

measles /'mizəlz/ *n.* an acute infectious disease occurring mostly in children.

measly /'mizli/ *adj.,* **-lier**, **-liest**. *Colloquial* wretchedly poor or unsatisfactory.

measure /'mɛʒə/ *n., v.,* **-ured**, **-uring**. **1.** size, dimensions, quantity, etc. **2.** a unit or standard of measurement. **3.** a system of measurement. **4.** any standard of comparison, estimation, or judgment. **5.** an action or procedure intended as a means to an end. **6. for good measure,** as an extra and probably unnecessary act, precaution, etc. – *v.t.* **7.** to ascertain the extent, dimensions, quantity, capacity, etc., of, especially by comparison with a standard. **8.** to mark or lay off or out, or deal out, with reference to measure (often fol. by *off* or *out*). – *v.i.* **9.** to take measurements. **10.** to be of a specified measure.

meat /mit/ *n.* **1.** the flesh of animals as used for food. **2.** the edible part of anything, as a fruit, nut, etc. **3.** the main substance of something, as an argument.

mechanic /mə'kænɪk/ *n.* a skilled worker with tools or machines.

mechanical /mə'kænɪkəl/ *adj.* **1.** having to do with machinery. **2.** relating to, or controlled or effected by, physical forces.

mechanics /mə'kænɪks/ *n.* **1.** the branch of knowledge concerned (both theoretically and practically) with machinery or mechanical appliances. **2.** the science dealing with the action of forces on bodies and with motion.

mechanise = mechanize /'mɛkənaɪz/ *v.t.,*

-nised, **-nising**. to introduce machinery into (an industry, etc.).

mechanism /'mɛkənɪzəm/ *n.* **1.** the machinery, or the agencies or means, by which a particular effect is produced or a purpose is accomplished. **2.** the way in which a thing works or operates.

medal /'mɛdl/ *n.* a flat piece of inscribed metal, given as a reward for bravery, merit, etc.

medallion /mə'dæljən/ *n.* a large medal.

meddle /'mɛdl/ *v.i.*, **-dled**, **-dling**. to concern oneself with or in something without warrant or necessity; interfere.

media /'midiə/ *n.* **1.** a plural of **medium**. **2.** → **mass media**.

medial /'midiəl/ *adj.* situated in or relating to the middle; median; intermediate.

median /'midiən/ *adj.* **1.** situated in or relating to the middle; medial. – *n.* **2.** the middle number in a given sequence of numbers.

median strip *n.* a dividing area, often raised or landscaped, between opposing traffic lanes on a highway.

mediate /'midieɪt/ *v.i.*, **-ated**, **-ating**. to act between parties to effect an agreement, compromise, or reconciliation. – **mediator**, *n.*

medical /'mɛdɪkəl/ *adj.* **1.** of or relating to the science or practice of medicine. – *n.* **2.** a medical examination.

medical certificate *n.* a certificate made out by a doctor testifying to the state of a person's health.

medicament /mə'dɪkəmənt/ *n.* a curative or healing substance.

medicate /'mɛdəkeɪt/ *v.t.*, **-cated**, **-cating**. to treat with medicine or medicaments. – **medication**, *n.*

medicine /'mɛdəsən, 'mɛdsən/ *n.* **1.** any substance or substances used in treating disease. **2.** the art or science of restoring or preserving health. **3.** the medical profession.

medieval = mediaeval /mɛdi'ivəl/ *adj.* of or relating to, characteristic of, or in the style of the Middle Ages.

medifraud /'mɛdifrɔd/ *n.* the obtaining of money from a health insurance service on the basis of fraudulent claims.

mediocre /midi'oʊkə, 'midioʊkə/ *adj.* of middling quality; indifferent; ordinary.

meditate /'mɛdəteɪt/ *v.i.*, **-tated**, **-tating**. to engage in thought or contemplation; reflect.

medium /'midiəm/ *n., pl.* **-dia** /-diə/, **-diums**, *adj.* – *n.* **1.** a middle state or condition; a mean. **2.** an intervening substance, as air, etc., through which a force acts or an effect is produced. **3.** the element in which an organism has its natural habitat. **4.** an agency means, or instrument. – *adj.* **5.** intermediate in degree, quality, etc.

medley /'mɛdli/ *n.* a mixture, especially of heterogeneous elements.

meek /mik/ *adj.* humbly patient or submissive.

meet /mit/ *v.*, **met**, **meeting**, *n.* – *v.t.* **1.** to come into contact, junction, or connection with. **2.** to go to the place of arrival of, as to welcome. **3.** to come into personal acquaintance with. **4.** to cope or deal effectively with. – *v.i.* **5.** to come together, face to face, or into company. **6.** to come into contact or form a junction, as lines, planes, areas, etc. **7.** to come together in opposition or conflict. – *n.* **8.** a meeting, as of huntsmen for a hunt, or cyclists for a ride, etc.

meeting /'mitɪŋ/ *n.* an assembly or gathering held.

mega- /'mɛgə-/ **1.** a prefix denoting 10^6 of a given unit, as in *megawatt*. *Symbol*: M **2.** a prefix meaning 'great', 'huge'.

megabyte /'mɛgəbaɪt/ *n.* a unit of measurement of computer memory size equal to 2^{20} or 1 048 576 bytes. Also, **meg**.

megahertz /'mɛgəhɜts/ *n.* a unit of radiofrequency equal to 1×10^6 hertz. *Symbol*: MHz

megalo- a word element denoting bigness or exaggeration.

megalomania /mɛgəloʊ'meɪniə/ *n.* a form of mental alienation marked by delusions of greatness, wealth, etc.

megaphone /'mɛgəfoʊn/ *n.* a device for magnifying sound.

megaton /'mɛgətʌn/ *n.* **1.** one million tons. **2.** an explosive force equal to that of one million tons of TNT.

meiosis /maɪ'oʊsəs/ *n.* the maturation process of gametes, consisting of chromosome conjugation and two cell divisions, in the course of which the diploid chromosome number becomes reduced to the haploid. – **meiotic**, *adj.*

melancholia /mɛlən'koʊliə/ *n.* mental disease characterised by great depression of spirits and gloomy forebodings.

melancholy /'mɛlənkɒli/ *n., pl.* **-cholies**, *adj.* – *n.* **1.** a gloomy state of mind, especially when habitual or prolonged; depression. – *adj.* **2.** affected with, characterised by, or showing melancholy.

melanin /'mɛlənən/ *n.* the dark pigment in the body of humans and certain animals.

melano- a word element meaning 'black'.

Melba toast /'mɛlbə/ *n.* very thinly sliced bread, baked in the oven until crisp.

meld /mɛld/ *v.t.* **1.** to cause to merge or blend. – *v.i.* **2.** to blend or combine.

melee /mɛ'leɪ, -'li/ *n.* **1.** a confused general hand-to-hand fight. **2.** any noisy or confused situation.

mellifluous /mə'lɪfluəs/ *adj.* sweetly or smoothly flowing.

mellow /'mɛloʊ/ *adj.* **1.** soft and full-flavoured from ripeness, as fruit. **2.** soft and rich, as sound, tones, colour, light, etc. **3.** genial; jovial. – *v.t., v.i.* **4.** to make or become mellow.

melodic /mə'lɒdɪk/ *adj.* **1.** melodious. **2.** relating to melody as distinguished from harmony and rhythm.

melodrama /'mɛlədramə/ *n.* a play in which the drama is exaggerated.

melody /'mɛlədi/ *n., pl.* **-dies**. musical sounds in agreeable succession or arrangement. – **melodious**, *adj.*

melon /'mɛlən/ *n.* any of several large, juicy fruits.

melt /mɛlt/ *v.*, **melted**, **melted** *or* **molten**, **melting**. – *v.i.* **1.** to become liquefied by heat. **2.** to pass, change, or blend gradually (often fol. by *into*). – *v.t.* **3.** to reduce to a liquid state by heat. **4.** to soften in feeling, as a person, the heart, etc.

member /'mɛmbə/ *n.* a constituent part of any structural or composite whole.

membrane /'mɛmbreɪn/ *n.* any thin connecting layer.

memento /mə'mɛntoʊ/ *n., pl.* **-tos**, **-toes**. something that serves as a reminder of what is past or gone.

memo /'mɛmoʊ, 'mi-/ *n., pl.* **memos**. → **memorandum**.

memoirs /'mɛmwaz/ *pl. n.* records of one's own life and experiences.

memorable /'mɛmrəbəl, -ərəbəl/ *adj.* **1.** worthy of being remembered; notable. **2.** easy to remember.

memorandum /mɛmə'rændəm/ *n., pl.* **-dums**, **-da** /-də/. **1.** a note made of something to be remembered. **2.** a document which includes the main terms of a shipment of unsold goods and authorises their return within a specified time.

memorial /mə'mɔriəl/ *n.* something designed to preserve the memory of a person, event, etc.

memorise = memorize /'mɛməraɪz/ *v.t.*, **-rised**, **-rising**. to commit to memory, or learn by heart.

memory /'mɛməri/ *n., pl.* **-ries**. **1.** the mental capacity or faculty of retaining and reviving impressions, or of recalling or recognising previous experiences. **2.** a mental impression retained; a recollection. **3.** the state or fact of being remembered. **4.** *Computers* the part of a digital computer in which data and instructions are held until they are required.

memory bank *n.* the primary storage inside the main part of a computer to which fast random access is available.

memory cycle *n.* the process of replacing one unit of data in the memory bank of a computer by another.

memory snatch *n.* the accessing of a computer memory in the interval between two computer instructions.

men /mɛn/ *n.* plural of **man**.

menace /'mɛnəs/ *n., v.*, **-aced**, **-acing**. – *n.* **1.** a threat. **2.** *Colloquial* → **nuisance**. – *v.t.* **3.** to serve as a probable cause of evil, etc., to.

menagerie /mə'nædʒəri/ *n.* a collection of wild or strange animals, especially for exhibition.

mend /mɛnd/ *v.t.* **1.** to make whole or sound by repairing. **2.** to set right; make better; improve.

menial /'miniəl/ *adj.* **1.** relating or proper to domestic servants. **2.** → **servile**.

meno- a word element meaning 'month'.

menopause /'mɛnəpɔz/ *n.* the period of the cessation of menstruation.

menses /'mɛnsiz/ *pl. n.* the (approximately) monthly discharge of blood and mucosal tissue from the uterus.

menstruate /'mɛnstrueɪt/ *v.i.*, **-ated**, **-ating**. to discharge the menses. – **menstruation**, *n.* – **menstrual**, *adj.*

mensuration /mɛnʃə'reɪʃən/ *n.* the act, art, or process of measuring.

-ment a suffix of nouns, often concrete, denoting an action or state resulting (*abridgment, refreshment*), a product (*fragment*), or means (*ornament*).

mental /'mɛntl/ *adj.* **1.** of or relating to the mind. **2.** designated for or relating to the care of those with disordered minds. **3.** *Colloquial* foolish or mad.

mentality /mɛn'tæləti/ *n., pl.* **-ties**. mental capacity or endowment.

mention /'mɛnʃən/ *v.t.* **1.** to refer to briefly or incidentally. – *n.* **2.** a referring or reference.

mentor /'mɛntɔ/ *n.* **1.** a wise and trusted counsellor. **2.** (especially in an organisation) a person who is considered to have sufficient experience or expertise to be able to assist others less experienced.

menu /'mɛnju, 'minju/ *n.* **1.** a list of the dishes served at a meal. **2.** *Computers* a range of optional procedures presented to an operator by a computer.

menu-driven *adj.* of or relating to a computer or computerised device which the user operates by selection, one option at a time, from a limited set of options presented (opposed to *command-driven*).

mercantile /'mɜkəntaɪl/ *adj.* of or relating to merchants or to trade; commercial.

mercantile agency *n.* a concern which obtains information concerning the financial standing, business reputation, and credit ratings of individuals, firms and companies for the benefit of its subscribers.

mercenary /'mɜsənri, -sənəri/ *adj., n., pl.* **-ries**. – *adj.* **1.** working or acting merely for gain. – *n.* **2.** a professional soldier serving in a foreign army.

merchandise /'mɜtʃəndaɪs/ *n.*, /'mɜtʃəndaɪz/ *v.*, **-dised**, **-dising**. – *n.* **1.** the stock of a store. – *v.i.* **2.** to trade. – *v.t.* **3.** to trade in; buy and sell.

merchandising /'mɜtʃəndaɪzɪŋ/ *n.* the promotion and planning of the sales of a product.

merchant /'mɜtʃənt/ *n.* **1.** someone who buys and sells commodities for profit; a wholesaler. – *adj.* **2.** relating to trade or commerce.

merchant bank *n.* a private banking firm engaged chiefly in accepting and endorsing bills of exchange, underwriting new issues of securities and advising on corporate strategy.

merchant navy *n.* the vessels of a nation engaged in commerce.

mercury /'mɜkjəri/ *n.* *Chemistry* a heavy, silver-white metallic element, remarkable for its fluidity at ordinary temperatures; quicksilver. *Symbol*: Hg

mercy /'mɜsi/ *n., pl.* **-cies**. **1.** compassionate or kindly forbearance shown towards an offender, an enemy, or other person in one's power. **2. at the mercy of,** defenceless or unprotected against. – **merciful**, *adj.*

mere /mɪə/ *adj., superlative* **merest**. being nothing more or better than what is specified.

merely /'mɪəli/ *adv.* only as specified, and nothing more; simply.

merge /mɜdʒ/ *v.*, **merged**, **merging**. – *v.t.* **1.** to unite or combine. – *v.i.* **2.** to become swallowed up or absorbed (often fol. by *in* or *into*).

merger /ˈmɜdʒə/ *n.* a statutory combination of two or more companies by the transfer of the properties to one surviving company.

meridian /məˈrɪdiən/ *n. Geography* a line of longitude.

meringue /məˈræŋ/ *n.* a mixture of sugar and beaten eggwhites, baked.

Merino /məˈrinoʊ/ *n., pl.* **-nos**. one of a variety of sheep valued for its fine wool.

merit /ˈmɛrət/ *n.* **1.** claim to commendation; excellence; worth. **2.** (*pl.*) the substantial right and wrong of a matter unobscured by technicalities. – *v.t.* **3.** to be worthy of; deserve.

meritorious /mɛrəˈtɔriəs/ *adj.* deserving of reward or commendation.

mermaid /ˈmɜmeɪd/ *n.* an imaginary creature with the torso of a woman and the tail of a fish.

merry /ˈmɛri/ *adj.,* **-rier**, **-riest**. full of cheer or gaiety.

merry-go-round /ˈmɛri-goʊ-ˌraʊnd/ *n.* a machine on which children ride for amusement.

mesh /mɛʃ/ *n.* **1.** a network or net. **2.** light woven or welded interlocking links or wires, as used for reinforcement, for sieves, etc. – *v.t.* **3.** to catch or entangle in or as in a mesh. **4.** *Machinery* to engage, as gear teeth. – *v.i.* **5.** to become meshed.

mesmerise = mesmerize /ˈmɛzməraɪz/ *v.t.,* **-rised**, **-rising**. to hypnotise. – **mesmeric**, *adj.*

mesne /min/ *adj. Law* intermediate or intervening.

meso- a word element meaning 'middle'. Also, **mes-**.

mess /mɛs/ *n.* **1.** a dirty or untidy condition. **2.** excrement, especially of an animal. **3.** a place used by service personnel, etc., for eating, recreation, etc. – *v.t.* **4.** to make dirty or untidy (often fol. by *up*). – *v.i.* **5.** to eat in company, especially as a member of a mess. **6. mess around** (or **about**), to waste time.

message /ˈmɛsɪdʒ/ *n.* a communication, as of information, advice, direction, or the like, transmitted through a messenger or other agency.

messenger /ˈmɛsəndʒə/ *n.* someone who bears a message or goes on an errand, especially as a matter of duty or business.

met /mɛt/ *v.* past tense and past participle of **meet**.

meta- a prefix meaning 'among', 'together with', 'after'.

metabolism /məˈtæbəlɪzəm/ *n.* the sum of the processes in an organism by which food is built up into living protoplasm and protoplasm is broken down into simpler compounds, with the exchange of energy.

metal /ˈmɛtl/ *n.* **1.** any of a class of opaque, ductile, conductive, elementary substances, as silver, copper, etc. **2.** an alloy or mixture composed wholly or partly of such substances. **3.** Also, **road metal**. broken stone used for ballast on railway tracks or for surfacing roads; blue metal. – **metallic**, *adj.*

metalanguage /ˈmɛtəlæŋgwɪdʒ/ *n.* a language or code used to discuss a given object language or some aspect of it.

metallurgy /ˈmɛtəlɜdʒi, məˈtælədʒi/ *n.* **1.** the science of metals and their structures and properties. **2.** the art or science of separating metals from their ores, compounding alloys or working metals.

metalwork /ˈmɛtlwɜk/ *n.* **1.** the art or craft of working with metal. **2.** objects produced by metalwork.

metamorphosis /mɛtəˈmɔfəsəs/ *n., pl.* **-phoses** /-fəsiz/. **1.** any complete change in appearance, character, circumstances, etc. **2.** a form resulting from any such change. – **metamorphic**, *adj.* – **metamorphose**, *v.*

metaphor /ˈmɛtəfə, -fɔ/ *n.* a figure of speech in which a term is applied to something to which it is not literally applicable, in order to suggest a resemblance. – **metaphorical**, *adj.*

metaphysical /mɛtəˈfɪzɪkəl/ *adj. Philosophy* concerned with abstract thought or subjects.

metaphysics /mɛtəˈfɪzɪks/ *n.* philosophy, especially in its more abstruse branches.

mete /mit/ *v.t.,* **meted**, **meting**. to distribute or apportion by measure; allot (usually fol. by *out*).

meteor /ˈmitiə, -ɔ/ *n.* a transient fiery streak in the sky produced by a comet, etc., passing through the earth's atmosphere. – **meteoric**, *adj.*

meteorite /ˈmitiəraɪt/ *n.* a mass of stone or metal that has reached the earth from outer space.

meteorology /mitiəˈrɒlədʒi/ *n.* the science dealing with the atmosphere and its phenomena, especially as relating to weather.

meter /ˈmitə/ *n.* an instrument that measures.

-meter[1] a word element used in names of measuring instruments.

-meter[2] a word element denoting a certain poetic measure or rhythmic pattern.

methadone /ˈmɛθədoʊn/ *n.* a powerful analgesic drug used for the treatment of drug withdrawal symptoms.

methane /ˈmiθeɪn/ *n.* a colourless, odourless, flammable gas.

methinks /miˈθɪŋks/ *v., past tense* **methought**. *Archaic and Poetic* it seems to me.

metho /ˈmɛθoʊ/ *n. Colloquial* **1.** methylated spirits. **2.** one addicted to drinking methylated spirits.

method /ˈmɛθəd/ *n.* a way of doing something, especially in accordance with a definite plan.

methodical /məˈθɒdɪkəl/ *adj.* performed, disposed, or acting in a systematic way.

methyl alcohol /mɛθəl/ *n.* a colourless, flammable, poisonous liquid used as a fuel, solvent, etc.

methylated spirits /mɛθəleɪtəd/ *n.* a denatured alcohol, used for burning, cleaning, etc.

meticulous /məˈtɪkjələs/ *adj.* solicitous about minute details; minutely careful.

metre[1] /ˈmitə/ *n.* the base SI unit of measurement of length approximately equal to 1.094 yards. *Symbol*: m

metre[2] /ˈmitə/ *n.* arrangement of words in

rhythmic lines or verses.

-metre a word element meaning metres; of or relating to a metre, as in *kilometre*.

metric /'mɛtrɪk/ *adj.* relating to the metre or to the system of measures and weights originally based upon it.

metrication /mɛtrə'keɪʃən/ *n.* the process of conversion from British or imperial units to the metric system. – **metricate**, *v.*

metric system *n.* a decimal system of measurement. The modern metric system, known as the International System of Units (SI), comprises seven *base units*, the metre (m), kilogram (kg), second (s), ampere (A), kelvin (k), mole (mol), and candela (cd).

metric ton *n.* → **tonne**.

metronome /'mɛtrənoʊm/ *n.* a mechanical contrivance for marking time, as for music.

metropolis /mə'trɒpələs/ *n., pl.* **-lises**. the chief city (not necessarily the capital) of a country, state, or region. – **metropolitan**, *adj.*

-metry a word element denoting the process of measuring.

mettle /'mɛtl/ *n.* **1.** the characteristic disposition or temper. **2.** spirit; courage.

mew /mju/ *n.* **1.** the sound a cat makes. – *v.i.* **2.** to make this sound.

mews /mjuz/ *pl. n.* (*usu. construed as sing.*) a set of stables or garages.

mezzanine /'mɛzənin, mɛzə'nin/ *n.* a low storey between two other storeys.

mica /'maɪkə/ *n.* any member of a group of minerals that separate readily (by cleavage) into thin, tough, often transparent laminae.

mice /maɪs/ *n.* plural of **mouse**.

Mickey Mouse money *n.* → **funny money** (def. 1).

micra /'maɪkrə/ *n.* a plural of **micron**.

MICR encoding /'maɪkə/ *n.* a machine-reading system by which characters encoded on documents, as cheques, are read by a magnetically-sensitive device.

micro- /'maɪkroʊ-/ **1.** a prefix meaning **a.** 'very small'. **b.** 'enlarging' or 'amplifying'. **2.** a prefix denoting 10^{-6} of a given unit. *Symbol*: µ

microbe /'maɪkroʊb/ *n.* a micro-organism, usually one of vegetable nature; a germ.

microcomputer /'maɪkroʊkəm,pjutə/ *n.* a computer which has its central processor functions contained on a single printed circuit board constituting a stand-alone module, usually small in size and cost.

microcopy /'maɪkroʊ,kɒpi/ *n., pl.* **-pies**. a greatly reduced photographic copy of a book, page, etc.

microcosm /'maɪkrəkɒzəm/ *n.* anything regarded as a world in miniature.

microdot /'maɪkroʊ,dɒt/ *n.* a photograph reduced to the size of a printed or typed dot.

micro-economics /,maɪkroʊ-ɛkə'nɒmɪks/ *n.* (*construed as sing.*) study of the economic system in terms of its different sectors. Cf. **macro-economics**.

microfiche /'maɪkroʊfiʃ/ *n.* a microfilmed transparency about the size and shape of a filing card which may have on it many pages of print.

microfilm /'maɪkroʊfɪlm/ *n.* **1.** a narrow film, especially of motion-picture stock, on which microcopies are made. **2.** a film reproduction of a large or bulky publication, as a file of newspapers, in miniature form.

micron /'maɪkrɒn/ *n., pl.* **-cra**, **-crons**. *Obsolete* the millionth part of a metre. *Symbol*: µ

microphone /'maɪkrəfoʊn/ *n.* an instrument which is capable of transforming the air-pressure waves of sound into changes in electric currents or voltages.

microprocessor /maɪkroʊ'proʊsɛsə/ *n.* a small stand-alone computer, often dedicated to specific functions.

microscope /'maɪkrəskoʊp/ *n.* an optical instrument for inspecting objects too small to be seen, or to be seen distinctly and in detail, by the naked eye.

microscopic /maɪkrə'skɒpɪk/ *adj.* **1.** so small as to be invisible or indistinct without the use of the microscope. **2.** of or relating to the microscope or its use.

microwave /'maɪkrəweɪv/ *n.* **1.** an electromagnetic wave of extremely high frequency, approximately comprising the wavelength range from 50 cm to 1 mm. **2.** Also, **microwave oven**. an oven which cooks with unusual rapidity, by passing microwaves through food and generating heat inside it. – *v.t.* **3.** to cook (food) by using a microwave oven.

mid[1] /mɪd/ *adj.* central; at or near the middle point.

mid[2] /mɪd/ *prep.* → **amid**. Also, **'mid**.

mid- a combining form of **middle**.

midair /mɪd'ɛə/ *n.* any elevated position above the ground.

midday /'mɪddeɪ/ *n.* the middle of the day; noon.

middle /'mɪdl/ *adj., n., v.,* **-dled**, **-dling**. – *adj.* **1.** equally distant from extremes or limits. **2.** medium. – *n.* **3.** the point, part, etc., equidistant from extremes or limits. – *v.t.* **4.** to place in the middle.

middle-aged /'mɪdl-eɪdʒd/ *adj.* **1.** intermediate in age between youth and old age. **2.** characteristic of or suitable for middle-aged people.

middle class *n.* a social class comprising especially business and professional people and public servants of middle income.

middleman /'mɪdlmæn/ *n., pl.* **-men**. a trader who makes a profit by buying from producers and selling to retailers or consumers. Also, **middle man**.

middling /'mɪdlɪŋ/ *adj.* medium in size, quality, grade, rank, etc.

middy /'mɪdi/ *n., pl.* **-dies**. a medium size beer glass; pot.

midge /mɪdʒ/ *n.* any of various small flying insects.

midget /'mɪdʒət/ *n.* something very small of its kind.

midnight /'mɪdnaɪt/ *n.* **1.** the middle of the night; 12 o'clock at night. **2.** resembling midnight, as in darkness. **3. burn the midnight oil,** to study or work far into the night.

midnight sun *n.* the sun visible at midnight in midsummer in arctic and antarctic regions.

midriff /'mɪdrɪf/ *n.* **1.** the middle part of the body, between the chest and the waist. – *adj.* **2.** of a dress, blouse, etc., which exposes this part of the body.

midshipman /'mɪdʃɪpmən/ *n., pl.* **-men**. a probationary rank held by naval cadets before qualifying as officers.

midst /mɪdst/ *n.* the middle point, part, or stage.

midstream /mɪd'strim/ *n.* **1.** the middle of the stream. **2. in midstream,** *Colloquial* in the middle; at a critical point.

midway /mɪd'weɪ/ *adv.,* /'mɪdweɪ/ *adj.* – *adv.* **1.** to the middle of the way or distance; halfway. – *adj.* **2.** in the middle.

midwifery /'mɪdwɪfəri/ *n.* the art or practice of assisting women in childbirth. – **midwife**, *n.*

mien /min/ *n.* air, bearing, or aspect, as showing character, feeling, etc.

miffed /mɪft/ *adj. Colloquial* annoyed; displeased.

might[1] /maɪt/ *v.* past tense of **may**.

might[2] /maɪt/ *n.* effective power or force of any kind. – **mighty**, *adj.*

migraine /'maɪgreɪn, 'migreɪn/ *n.* a severe headache often confined to one side of the head and usually associated with nausea.

migrant /'maɪgrənt/ *n.* **1.** someone who migrates. **2.** an immigrant. – *adj.* **3.** of or relating to migration or migrants.

migrate /maɪ'greɪt/ *v.i.,* **-grated**, **-grating**. to pass periodically from one region to another, as certain birds, fishes, and animals. – **migration**, *n.*

mike /maɪk/ *n. Colloquial* → **microphone**.

mild /maɪld/ *adj.* **1.** amiably gentle or temperate in feeling or behaviour towards others. **2.** gentle or moderate in force or effect. **3.** moderate in intensity, degree, or character.

mildew /'mɪldju/ *n.* a plant disease usually characterised by a whitish coating.

mile /maɪl/ *n.* **1.** a unit of measurement of length in the imperial system, equal to 5280 feet (1609.34 m). **2.** (*often pl.*) a large distance or quantity.

mileage /'maɪlɪdʒ/ *n.* **1.** the total length or distance expressed in miles. **2.** the number of miles travelled by a motor vehicle on a specified quantity of fuel.

milestone /'maɪlstoʊn/ *n.* **1.** a stone set up to mark the distance to or from a town, as along a highway. **2.** a significant point in one's life or career.

milieu /mi'ljɜ/ *n.* medium or environment.

militant /'mɪlətənt/ *adj.* engaged in warfare; warring.

military /'mɪlətri, -təri/ *adj.* **1.** of or relating to the army, armed forces, affairs of war, or a state of war. – *n.* **2.** soldiers generally; the armed forces.

militate /'mɪləteɪt/ *v.i.,* **-tated**, **-tating**. to operate (*against* or *in favour of*); have effect or influence.

militia /mə'lɪʃə/ *n.* a body of citizen soldiers as distinguished from professional soldiers.

milk /mɪlk/ *n.* **1.** an opaque white liquid secreted by the mammary glands of female mammals, serving for the nourishment of their young, and, in the case of the cow and some other animals, used for food or as a source of dairy products. – *v.t.* **2.** to press or draw milk by hand or machine from the udder of (a cow or other animal). **3.** to extract (something) as if by milking; draw. – *v.i.* **4.** to milk a cow or other animal.

milk bar *n.* a shop where milk drinks, ice-cream, sandwiches, etc., are sold.

milk of magnesia *n.* a liquid suspension of magnesium hydroxide used medicinally as an antacid or laxative.

milkshake /'mɪlkʃeɪk/ *n.* a frothy drink made of milk, flavouring, and sometimes ice-cream, shaken together. Also, **milk shake**.

milk tooth *n.* one of the temporary teeth of a mammal which are replaced by the permanent teeth. Also, **baby tooth**.

mill /mɪl/ *n.* **1.** a building or establishment fitted with machinery, in which any of various mechanical operations or forms of manufacture is carried on. **2.** a machine which does its work by rotary motion. **3. run of the mill,** conventional; commonplace. – *v.t.* **4.** to grind, work, treat, or shape in or with a mill. – *v.i.* **5.** to move confusedly in a circle (often fol. by *about*).

millennium /mə'lɛniəm/ *n., pl.* **-niums**, **-nia** /-niə/. **1.** a period of a thousand years. **2.** a thousandth anniversary.

millet /'mɪlət/ *n.* a cereal grass.

milli- /'mɪli-/ a prefix denoting 10^{-3} of a given unit. *Symbol*: m

millibar /'mɪliba/ *n.* a widely used unit of atmospheric pressure.

milligram /'mɪligræm/ *n.* a unit of mass equal to 0.001 gram. *Symbol*: mg

millilitre /'mɪlilitə/ *n.* a unit of capacity equal to 0.001 litre. *Symbol*: ml

millimetre /'mɪlimitə/ *n.* a unit of length equal to 0.001 metre. *Symbol*: mm

milliner /'mɪlənə/ *n.* someone who makes or sells hats for women. – **millinery**, *n.*

million /'mɪljən/ *n.* **1.** a cardinal number, one thousand times one thousand, or 10^6. **2.** a very great number. – *adj.* **3.** amounting to one million in numbers. – **millionth**, *adj., n.*

millionaire /mɪljə'nɛə/ *n.* a person worth a million or millions, as of pounds, dollars, or francs.

millipede /'mɪləpid/ *n.* any of several kinds of arthropods with segmented bodies and many legs. Also, **millepede**.

millstone /'mɪlstoʊn/ *n.* **1.** either of a pair of circular stones used for grinding. **2.** a heavy burden.

mime /maɪm/ *n., v.,* **mimed**, **miming**. – *n.* **1.** the art or technique of expressing emotion, character, action, etc., by mute gestures and bodily movements. **2.** a play or performance in mime. **3.** one skilled in mime.

mimeograph /'mɪmiəgræf, -graf/ *n.* **1.** a stencil device for duplicating letters, drawings, etc. – *v.t.* **2.** to make copies of, using a mimeograph.

mimic /'mɪmɪk/ *v.,* **-icked**, **-icking**, *n.* – *v.t.* **1.** to imitate or copy. – *n.* **2.** one clever at imitating or mimicking the characteristic voice or gesture of others. – **mimicry**, *n.*

minaret /mɪnə'rɛt, 'mɪnərɛt/ *n.* a tall, thin tower attached to a mosque.

mince /mɪns/ *v.*, **minced**, **mincing**, *n.* – *v.t.* **1.** to cut or chop into very small pieces. **2.** to perform or utter with affected elegance. – *v.i.* **3.** to act, behave, or speak with affected elegance. – *n.* **4.** minced meat.

mincemeat /'mɪnsmit/ *n.* **1.** a mixture composed of minced apples, suet, candied peel, etc., with raisins, currants, etc., for filling a pie (**mince pie**). **2.** minced meat. **3.** anything cut up very small.

mind /maɪnd/ *n.* **1.** that which thinks, feels, and wills, exercises perception, judgment, reflection, etc., as in a human or other conscious being. **2.** intellectual power or ability. **3.** purpose, intention, or will. **4. make up one's mind,** to come to a decision. **5. out of one's mind,** demented; delirious. **6. to one's mind,** in one's opinion or judgment. – *v.t.* **7.** to apply oneself or attend to. **8.** to be careful, cautious, or wary concerning. **9.** to perceive or notice. **10.** to be careful or wary. **11.** to regard a thing as concerning oneself or as mattering.

minded /'maɪndəd/ *adj.* inclined or disposed.

mindful /'maɪndfəl/ *adj.* attentive; careful (usually fol. by *of*).

mine[1] /maɪn/ *pron.* possessive form of **I**, used without a noun following.

mine[2] /maɪn/ *n.*, *v.*, **mined**, **mining**. – *n.* **1.** an excavation made in the earth for the purpose of getting out ores, precious stones, coal, etc. **2.** an abounding source or store of anything. **3.** an explosive device. – *v.i.* **4.** to dig a mine. – *v.t.* **5.** to dig in (earth, etc.) in order to obtain ores, coal, etc. **6.** to extract (ores, coal, etc.) from a mine. **7.** to dig or lay military mines under.

miner /'maɪnə/ *n.* **1.** someone who works in a mine, especially a coalmine. **2.** *Stock Exchange* a mining company, or the shares in that company.

mineral /'mɪnərəl, 'mɪnrəl/ *n.* **1.** a substance obtained by mining; ore. **2.** any of a class of inorganic substances occurring in nature, having a definite chemical composition and crystal structure.

mineral water *n.* **1.** water containing dissolved mineral salts or gases. **2.** carbonated water.

mingle /'mɪŋgəl/ *v.*, **-gled**, **-gling**. – *v.i.* **1.** to become mixed, blended, or united. **2.** to associate or mix in company. – *v.t.* **3.** to mix or combine; put together in a mixture; blend.

mini /'mɪni/ *n.* something small in size or dimension, as a skirt or motor vehicle.

mini- a word element meaning 'small' or 'miniature'.

miniature /'mɪnətʃə/ *n.* **1.** a representation or image of anything on a very small scale. – *adj.* **2.** on a very small scale; reduced.

mini-budget /'mɪni-bʌdʒət/ *n.* a budget which seeks to implement government fiscal policies decided upon after the normal budget session.

minimise = minimize /'mɪnəmaɪz/ *v.t.*, **-mised**, **-mising**. to reduce to the smallest possible amount or degree.

minimum /'mɪnəməm/ *n.*, *pl.* **-mums**, **-ma** /-mə/. *adj.* – *n.* **1.** the least quantity or amount possible, assignable, allowable, etc. **2.** the lowest amount, value, or degree attained or recorded (opposed to *maximum*). – *adj.* **3.** relating to a minimum or minimums. – **minimal**, *adj.*

minion /'mɪnjən/ *n.* a subordinate or employee, usually seen as favoured or servile.

minister /'mɪnəstə/ *n.* **1.** one authorised to conduct religious worship; a member of the clergy; a pastor. **2.** a diplomatic representative accredited by one government to another ranking below an ambassador, especially an envoy. – *v.i.* **3.** to give service, care, or aid. – **ministerial**, *adj.* – **ministry**, *n.*

mink /mɪŋk/ *n.*, *pl.* **minks**, (*esp. collectively*) **mink**. **1.** a semi-aquatic weasel-like animal. **2.** its valuable fur.

minor /'maɪnə/ *adj.* **1.** lesser, as in size, extent, or importance, or being the lesser of two. **2.** under legal age. – *n.* **3.** a person under legal age.

minority /maɪ'nɒrəti, mə-/ *n.*, *pl.* **-ties**, *adj.* – *n.* **1.** the smaller part or number. **2.** the state or period of being a minor. – *adj.* **3.** of or relating to a minority.

minstrel /'mɪnstrəl/ *n.* one of a class of medieval musicians who sang or recited to the accompaniment of instruments.

mint[1] /mɪnt/ *n.* **1.** any of several aromatic herbs. **2.** a mint-flavoured sweet.

mint[2] /mɪnt/ *n.* **1.** a place where money is coined by public authority. – *v.t.* **2.** to coin (money). – **mintage**, *n.*

minuet /mɪnju'ɛt/ *n.* a slow stately dance of French origin.

minus /'maɪnəs/ *prep.* **1.** less by the subtraction of; decreased by. – *adj.* **2.** algebraically negative. – *n.* **3.** a deficiency or loss.

minuscule /'mɪnəskjul/ *adj.* very small; tiny.

minute[1] /'mɪnət/ *n.* **1.** the sixtieth part of an hour; sixty seconds. **2.** a point of time; an instant or moment. **3.** (*pl.*) the official record of the proceedings at a meeting. **4.** *Geometry, etc.* the sixtieth part of a degree, or sixty seconds.

minute[2] /maɪ'njut/ *adj.*, **-nuter**, **-nutest**. **1.** extremely small. **2.** attentive to or concerned with even very small details or particulars.

minutia /maɪ'njuʃə, -tiə/ *n.*, *pl.* **-tiae** /-ʃii, -tii/ (*usu. pl.*) a small or trivial detail.

minx /mɪŋks/ *n.* a pert, impudent, or flirtatious young woman.

miracle /'mɪrəkəl/ *n.* a wonderful thing; a marvel. – **miraculous**, *adj.*

mirage /mə'raʒ/ *n.* an optical illusion by which reflected images of distant objects are seen, often inverted.

mire /'maɪə/ *n.*, *v.*, **mired**, **miring**. – *n.* **1.** a piece of wet, swampy ground. – *v.t.* **2.** to cause to stick fast in mire.

mirror /'mɪrə/ *n.* **1.** a reflecting surface, usually glass with a metallic backing; a looking glass. – *v.t.* **2.** to reflect in or as in a mirror, or as a mirror does.

mirth /mɜθ/ *n.* rejoicing; joyous gaiety.

mis-[1] a prefix meaning 'ill', 'mistaken', 'wrong', or simply negating.

mis-[2] variant of **miso-**.

misadventure /mɪsəd'vɛntʃə/ *n.* an accident.

misanthropy /mə'zænθrəpi/ *n.* hatred, dislike, or distrust of humankind.

misappropriate /mɪsə'proʊprieɪt/ *v.t.*, **-ated**, **-ating**. to apply wrongfully or dishonestly to one's own use. – **misappropriation**, *n.*

miscarriage /mɪs'kærɪdʒ, 'mɪskærɪdʒ/ *n.* **1.** failure to attain the right or desired result. **2.** premature expulsion of a foetus from the uterus, especially before it is viable. **3.** a transmission of goods not in accordance with the contract of shipment. – **miscarry**, *v.*

miscellaneous /mɪsə'leɪniəs/ *adj.* consisting of members or elements of different kinds.

miscellany /mə'sɛləni/ *n., pl.* **-nies**. a miscellaneous collection.

mischief /'mɪstʃəf/ *n.* **1.** conduct such as to tease or cause playfully petty annoyance. **2.** an injury due to some cause. – **mischievous**, *adj.*

misdemeanour = misdemeanor /mɪsdə'minə/ *n.* *Law* a less serious crime. Cf. **felony**.

miser /'maɪzə/ *n.* a niggardly, avaricious person.

miserable /'mɪzrəbəl, -zərəbəl/ *adj.* **1.** wretchedly unhappy, uneasy, or uncomfortable. **2.** attended with or causing misery.

misère /mə'zɛə/ *n.* *Cards* a hand which contains no winning card.

misery /'mɪzəri/ *n., pl.* **-ries**. **1.** great distress of mind; extreme unhappiness. **2.** wretchedness of condition or circumstances.

misfire /mɪs'faɪə/ *v.i.*, **-fired**, **-firing**. **1.** to fail to fire or explode. **2.** to fail to have a desired effect; be unsuccessful.

misfit /'mɪsfɪt/ *n.* someone who feels ill at ease or out of place in a given environment.

misgiving /mɪs'gɪvɪŋ/ *n.* a feeling of doubt, distrust, or apprehension.

mishap /'mɪshæp/ *n.* an unfortunate accident.

mishmash /'mɪʃmæʃ/ *n.* a hotchpotch; jumble.

mislay /mɪs'leɪ/ *v.t.*, **-laid**, **-laying**. to put in a place afterwards forgotten.

mislead /mɪs'lid/ *v.t.*, **-led**, **-leading**. **1.** to lead or guide wrongly; lead astray. **2.** to lead into error of conduct, thought, or judgment.

misnomer /mɪs'noʊmə/ *n.* a misapplied name or designation.

miso- a word element referring to hate.

misogamy /mə'sɒgəmi/ *n.* hatred of marriage. – **misogamist**, *n.*

misogyny /mə'sɒdʒəni/ *n.* hatred of women.

misprint /'mɪsprɪnt/ *n.* a mistake in printing.

miss[1] /mɪs/ *v.t.* **1.** to fail to hit, light upon, meet, catch, receive, obtain, attain, accomplish, see, hear, etc. **2.** to perceive the absence or loss of, often with regret. – *v.i.* **3.** to fail to hit, light upon, receive, or attain something. **4.** to fail of effect or success; be unsuccessful. **5. miss out,** to fail to receive, especially something desired. **6.** *Colloquial* (of an internal combustion engine) to fail to fire in one or more cylinders. – *n.* **7.** a failure to hit, meet, obtain, or accomplish something.

miss[2] /mɪs/ *n., pl.* **misses**. (*cap.*) the conventional title of respect for an unmarried woman, prefixed to the name.

misshapen /mɪs'ʃeɪpən/ *adj.* badly shaped; deformed.

missile /'mɪsaɪl/ *n.* an object or weapon that can be thrown, hurled, or shot.

missing /'mɪsɪŋ/ *adj.* lacking; absent; not found.

mission /'mɪʃən/ *n.* **1.** a body of persons sent to a foreign country to conduct negotiations, establish relations, or the like. **2.** the business with which an agent, envoy, etc., is charged. **3.** a missionary post or station. **4.** a self-imposed or assigned duty. **5.** the goals of an organisation.

missionary /'mɪʃənri/ *n.* a person sent to work for the propagation of their religious faith in a heathen land or a newly settled district.

missive /'mɪsɪv/ *n.* **1.** a written message; a letter. – *adj.* **2.** sent, especially from an official source.

mist /mɪst/ *n.* a cloudlike aggregation of minute globules of water suspended in the atmosphere at or near the earth's surface.

mistake /mə'steɪk/ *n., v.*, **-took**, **-taken**, **-taking**. – *n.* **1.** an error in action, opinion or judgment. – *v.t.* **2.** to conceive of or understand wrongly.

mister /'mɪstə/ *n.* (*cap.*) the conventional title of respect for a man, prefixed to the name (usually written *Mr*).

mistletoe /'mɪsəltoʊ/ *n.* any of various plants much used in Christmas decorations.

mistress /'mɪstrəs/ *n.* **1.** a woman who has authority or control. **2.** a female head teacher in a particular subject department in a secondary school. **3.** a woman who has a continuing sexual relationship with one man outside marriage.

mistrust /mɪs'trʌst/ *n.* **1.** lack of trust or confidence; distrust. – *v.t.* **2.** to regard with mistrust; distrust.

misunderstanding /ˌmɪsʌndə'stændɪŋ, mɪsˌʌn-/ *n.* disagreement or dissension.

misuse /mɪs'jus/ *n.*, /mɪs'juz/ *v.*, **-used**, **-using**. – *n.* **1.** wrong or improper use; misapplication. – *v.t.* **2.** to ill-use; maltreat.

mite /maɪt/ *n.* any of various small arachnids, many being parasitic on plants and animals.

mitigate /'mɪtəgeɪt/ *v.*, **-gated**, **-gating**. – *v.t.* **1.** to moderate the severity of (anything distressing). – *v.i.* **2.** to become milder; moderate in severity. – **mitigation**, *n.*

mitre /'maɪtə/ *n.* **1.** the ceremonial headdress of a bishop. **2.** a right-angled joint, as of a picture frame.

mitten /'mɪtn/ *n.* a kind of hand-covering enclosing the four fingers together and the thumb separately.

mix /mɪks/ *v.*, **mixed, mixing,** *n.* – *v.t.* **1.** to put together in one mass or assemblage with more or less thorough diffusion of the constituent elements among one another. – *v.i.* **2.** to become mixed. **3.** to associate, as in company. – *n.* **4.** a mixing, or a mixed condition; a mixture.

mixed /mɪkst/ *adj.* **1.** composed of different constituents or elements. **2.** comprising persons of different sexes, or of different classes, status, character, opinions, race, etc.

mixed business *n.* a small grocery shop which also sells a selection of other types of merchandise.

mixed industry *n.* an industry in which employees are engaged under a number of separate awards and/or agreements, the particular provisions of which may not be uniform in regard to conditions of employment.

mixer /ˈmɪksə/ *n.* **1.** *Colloquial* a person with reference to their sociability. **2.** a kitchen utensil or electrical appliance used for beating.

mixture /ˈmɪkstʃə/ *n.* any combination of differing elements, kinds, qualities, etc.

mix-up /ˈmɪks-ʌp/ *n.* a confused state of things; a muddle; a tangle.

mnemonic /nəˈmɒnɪk/ *adj.* **1.** assisting, or intended to assist, the memory. – *n.* **2.** a verse or the like intended to assist the memory.

moa /ˈmoʊə/ *n.* any of various extinct, flightless birds of New Zealand.

moan /moʊn/ *n.* **1.** a prolonged, low, inarticulate sound uttered from or as if from physical or mental suffering. – *v.i.* **2.** to utter moans, as of pain or grief.

moat /moʊt/ *n.* a deep, wide trench surrounding a fortified place, as a town or a castle, usually filled with water.

mob /mɒb/ *n., v.,* **mobbed**, **mobbing**. – *n.* **1.** a large number, especially of people. **2.** a disorderly, riotous or destructive group of people. – *v.t.* **3.** to surround and attack with riotous violence.

mobile /ˈmoʊbaɪl/ *adj.* **1.** movable; moving readily. – *n.* **2.** a construction or sculpture of delicately balanced movable parts. – **mobility**, *n.*

mobile phone *n.* a portable cellular telephone.

mobilise = mobilize /ˈmoʊbəlaɪz/ *v.t.,* **-lised**, **-lising**. to put (armed forces) into readiness for active service.

moccasin /ˈmɒkəsən/ *n.* a shoe made entirely of soft leather.

mocha /ˈmɒkə/ *n.* **1.** a choice variety of coffee. **2.** a flavouring obtained from coffee infusion or combined chocolate and coffee infusion.

mock /mɒk/ *v.t.* **1.** to assail or treat with ridicule or derision. **2.** to mimic, imitate, or counterfeit. – *v.i.* **3.** to use ridicule or derision; scoff; jeer (often fol. by *at*). – *adj.* **4.** imitation.

mockery /ˈmɒkəri/ *n., pl.* **-ries**. **1.** ridicule or derision. **2.** a mere travesty, or mocking pretence.

mockingbird /ˈmɒkɪŋbɜd/ *n.* any of various scrub birds noted for their ability as mimics.

mock-up /ˈmɒk ʌp/ *n.* a model, built to scale, of a machine, apparatus, or weapon, used in testing, teaching, etc.

mod cons *pl. n. Colloquial* modern conveniences.

mode[1] /moʊd/ *n.* **1.** manner of acting or doing; a method; a way. **2.** the manner of existence or action of anything; a form. **3.** *Statistics* (in a statistical population) the category, value, or interval of the variable having the greatest frequency.

mode[2] /moʊd/ *n.* a prevailing style or fashion.

model /ˈmɒdl/ *n., adj., v.,* **-elled**, **-elling**. – *n.* **1.** a standard or example for imitation or comparison. **2.** a representation, generally in miniature, to show the construction or serve as a copy of something. **3.** a person who poses for a painter, etc. **4.** one employed in the fashion industry to put on articles of apparel to display them to customers; mannequin. **5.** a typical or specific form or style. – *adj.* **6.** worthy to serve as a model; exemplary. – *v.t.* **7.** to form or plan according to a model. **8.** to display, especially by wearing. – *v.i.* **9.** to serve or be employed as a model.

modem /ˈmoʊdəm/ *n.* an electronic device that facilitates the linking of one computer to another via the telephone system.

moderate /ˈmɒdrət, -ərət/ *adj., n.*; /ˈmɒdəreɪt/ *v.,* **-rated**, **-rating**. – *adj.* **1.** not extreme, excessive, or intense. – *n.* **2.** someone who is moderate in opinion or action, especially in politics or religion. – *v.t.* **3.** to reduce the excessiveness of; make less violent, severe, intense, or rigorous. – *v.i.* **4.** to become less violent, severe, intense, or rigorous.

moderation /mɒdəˈreɪʃən/ *n.* **1.** the quality of being moderate. **2.** the act of moderating.

modern /ˈmɒdn/ *adj.* **1.** of or relating to present and recent time; not ancient or remote. – *n.* **2.** one whose views and tastes are modern.

modest /ˈmɒdəst/ *adj.* **1.** having or showing a moderate or humble estimate of one's merits, importance, etc. **2.** moderate. **3.** having or showing regard for the decencies of behaviour, speech, dress, etc. – **modesty**, *n.*

modicum /ˈmɒdəkəm/ *n.* a moderate or small quantity.

modify /ˈmɒdəfaɪ/ *v.,* **-fied**, **-fying**. – *v.t.* **1.** to change somewhat the form or qualities of; alter somewhat. **2.** to reduce in degree; moderate; qualify. – *v.i.* **3.** to change; to become changed. – **modification**, *n.*

modular /ˈmɒdʒələ/ *adj.* **1.** of or relating to a module. **2.** composed of standardised units or sections for easy construction or flexible arrangement.

modulate /ˈmɒdʒəleɪt/ *v.t.,* **-lated**, **-lating**. to regulate by or adjust to a certain measure or proportion; soften; tone down. – **modulation**, *n.*

module /ˈmɒdʒul/ *n.* **1.** a selected unit of measure used as a basis for planning and standardisation of building materials. **2.** a structural component. **3.** *Astronautics* a detachable section of a space vehicle.

mogul /ˈmoʊgəl/ *n.* an important person.

mohair /ˈmoʊheə/ *n.* a fabric made from the hair of the Angora goat.

moiety /ˈmɔɪəti/ *n., pl.* **-ties**. a half.

moist /mɔɪst/ *adj.* moderately or slightly wet; damp; humid.

moisture /ˈmɔɪstʃə/ *n.* water or other liquid

rendering anything moist.

molar /'moʊlə/ *n.* a tooth adapted for grinding.

molasses /mə'læsəz/ *n.* the thick brown bitter uncrystallised syrup drained from raw sugar.

mole[1] /moʊl/ *n.* a small congenital spot or blemish on the human skin.

mole[2] /moʊl/ *n.* any of various small insectivorous mammals living chiefly underground.

mole[3] /moʊl/ *n.* the SI base unit of measurement of amount of substance. *Symbol*: mol

molecule /'mɒləkjul/ *n. Chemistry, Physics* the smallest physical unit of an element or compound. – **molecular**, *adj.*

molest /mə'lɛst/ *v.t.* to interfere with annoyingly, injuriously, or with hostile intent.

mollify /'mɒləfaɪ/ *v.t.*, **-fied**, **-fying**. to soften in feeling or temper.

mollusc /'mɒləsk/ *n.* any of a phylum of (usually shelled) invertebrates including the snails, bivalves, squids, octopuses, etc.

mollycoddle /'mɒlikɒdl/ *v.t.*, **-dled**, **-dling**. to coddle; pamper.

mollydooker /mɒli'dukə/ *n. Colloquial* a left-handed person.

Molotov cocktail /'mɒlətɒv/ *n.* a home-made bomb, usually a bottle filled with petrol, with a wick which is ignited before the bottle is thrown.

molten /'moʊltn/ *adj.* liquefied by heat; in a state of fusion.

molybdenum /mə'lɪbdənəm/ *n.* a silver-white high-melting element. *Symbol*: Mo

moment /'moʊmənt/ *n.* **1.** an indefinitely short space of time; an instant. **2.** importance or consequence.

momentary /'moʊməntri/ *adj.* lasting but a moment; very brief.

momentous /moʊ'mɛntəs, mə-/ *adj.* of great importance or consequence.

momentum /mə'mɛntəm/ *n.*, *pl.* **ta** /-tə/. **1.** the quantity of motion of a moving body, equal to the product of its mass and velocity. **2.** impetus, as of a moving body.

mon- variant of **mono-**, before vowels.

monarch /'mɒnək, -ak/ *n.* a hereditary sovereign with more or less limited powers, as a king, queen, emperor, etc.

monarchy /'mɒnəki/ *n.*, *pl.* **-chies**. a government or state in which the supreme power is actually or nominally lodged in a monarch.

monastery /'mɒnəstri, -təri/ *n.*, *pl.* **-teries**. a place occupied by a community of monks living in seclusion from the world under religious vows. – **monastic**, *adj.*

monetarism /'mʌnətərɪzəm/ *n.* an economic theory which holds that a nation's economy is governed by changes in the money supply. – **monetarist**, *adj.*, *n.*

monetarist /'mʌnətərəst/ *n.* someone who seeks to control the economy of a country by adjustments to the money supply. – **monetarism**, *n.*

monetary /'mʌnətri, -təri/ *adj.* of or relating to money, or pecuniary matters.

monetary unit *n.* the standard unit of value of the currency of a country.

money /'mʌni/ *n.*, *pl.* **-neys**, **-nies**. **1.** coin or certificate (as banknotes, etc.) generally accepted in payment of debts and current transactions. **2.** a particular form or denomination of currency. **3.** wealth viewed in terms of money.

money bill *n.* a bill imposing taxation or appropriating public moneys for expenditure.

moneychanger /'mʌnitʃeɪndʒə/ *n.* one whose business it is to change money at a fixed or official rate.

moneyed /'mʌnid/ *adj.* having money; wealthy.

money market *n.* a market in which large amounts of money are borrowed and lent for short periods of time (usually less than a month).

money order *n.* an order for the payment of money, as one issued by one post office and payable at another, and requiring proof of ownership before being cashed. Cf. **postal note**.

money wages *pl. n.* the actual amount of money paid out as wages for work done (opposed to *real wages*).

monger /'mʌŋgə/ *n.* (*usu. in compounds*) **1.** a dealer in some commodity: *fishmonger*. **2.** someone who busies himself or herself with something in a sordid or petty way: *scandalmonger*.

mongrel /'mʌŋgrəl/ *n.* **1.** any animal or plant resulting from the crossing of different breeds or varieties. – *adj.* **2.** inferior.

monilia /mə'nɪliə/ *n.* a yeast-like fungus which can cause infection.

monition /mə'nɪʃən/ *n.* **1.** admonition; warning; caution. **2.** an official or legal notice.

monitor /'mɒnətə/ *n.* **1.** a device used to check, observe, or record the operation of a machine or system. **2.** any of several large lizards. – *v.t.* **3.** to check, observe, or record the operation of (a machine, etc.), without interfering with the operation.

monk /mʌŋk/ *n.* a man who has withdrawn from the world from religious motives and lives under vows of poverty, chastity, and obedience.

monkey /'mʌŋki/ *n.*, *pl.* **-keys**, *v.*, **-keyed**, **-keying**. – *n.* **1.** any member of the mammalian order Primates, excluding humans, the anthropoid apes, and the lemurs. **2.** any of various mechanical devices. – *v.i.* **3.** *Colloquial* to play or trifle idly.

monkey wrench *n.* a spanner or wrench with an adjustable jaw, for turning nuts of different sizes, etc.

mono- a word element: meaning 'alone', 'single', 'one'.

monochromatic /mɒnəkroʊ'mætɪk/ *adj.* of, producing, or relating to one colour or one wavelength.

monocle /'mɒnəkəl/ *n.* an eyeglass for one eye.

monogamy /mə'nɒgəmi/ *n.* marriage of one woman with one man.

monogram /'mɒnəgræm/ *n.* a character consisting of two or more letters combined or interlaced.

monograph /'mɒnəgræf, -graf/ *n.* a treatise on a particular subject.

monolith /'mɒnəlɪθ/ *n.* **1.** a single block or piece of stone of considerable size. **2.** something resembling a large block of stone, especially in having a massive, uniform, or unyielding quality or character. – **monolithic**, *adj.*

monologue /'mɒnəlɒg/ *n.* a prolonged talk or discourse by a single speaker.

monophonic /mɒnə'fɒnɪk/ *adj.* of or denoting a system of sound reproduction through only one loudspeaker. Cf. **stereophonic**.

monoplane /'mɒnəpleɪn/ *n.* an aeroplane with only one pair of wings.

monopolise = monopolize /mə'nɒpəlaɪz/ *v.t.*, **-lised**, **-lising**. **1.** to acquire, have, or exercise a monopoly of (a market, commodity, etc.). **2.** to keep entirely to oneself.

monopoly /mə'nɒpəli/ *n., pl.* **-lies**. exclusive control of a commodity or service in a particular market, or a control that makes possible the manipulation of prices.

monopsony /mɒn'ɒpsəni/ *n., pl.* **-nies**. a market situation where there is a single buyer of a product or service from a large number of sellers.

monorail /'mɒnəreɪl/ *n.* a railway with coaches running on a single (usually overhead) rail.

monosaccharide /mɒnoʊ'sækəraɪd, -rəd/ *n.* a simple sugar, such as glucose.

monosodium glutamate /mɒnə,soʊdiəm 'glutəmeɪt/ *n.* a sodium salt used in cookery to enhance the natural flavour of a dish. Also, **MSG**.

monosyllabic /mɒnəsə'læbɪk/ *adj.* **1.** having only one syllable, as a word. **2.** having a vocabulary composed exclusively of monosyllables.

monotheism /'mɒnoʊθi,ɪzəm, mɒnoʊ'θiɪzəm/ *n.* the doctrine or belief that there is only one God.

monotone /'mɒnətoʊn/ *n.* a single tone without harmony or variation in pitch.

monotony /mə'nɒtəni/ *n.* **1.** lack of variety, or wearisome uniformity, as in occupation, scenery, etc. **2.** sameness of tone or pitch, as in utterance. – **monotonous**, *adj.*

monotreme /'mɒnətrim/ *n.* a mammal which both lays eggs and suckles its young, as the platypus and echidna.

monsoon /mɒn'sun/ *n.* the rainy season.

monster /'mɒnstə/ *n.* **1.** a legendary animal compounded of brute and human shape. – *adj.* **2.** huge; enormous; monstrous.

monstrosity /mɒn'strɒsəti/ *n., pl.* **-ties**. something monstrous.

monstrous /'mɒnstrəs/ *adj.* **1.** huge; extremely great. **2.** revolting; outrageous; shocking. **3.** deviating greatly from the natural or normal form or type.

montage /mɒn'taʒ/ *n.* the combination in one picture, etc., of composition elements from several sources.

Monte Carlo method /mɒnti 'kaloʊ/ *n.* a method of computer simulation in which probabilistic methods are employed to estimate a solution to problems too complex or ill-defined to program directly.

month /mʌnθ/ *n.* **1.** approximately one twelfth of a tropical or solar year. **2.** a period of four weeks or of thirty days. **3.** the period (**lunar month**) of a complete revolution of the moon. – **monthly**, *adj., n.*

monument /'mɒnjəmənt/ *n.* something erected in memory of a person, event, etc.

monumental /mɒnjə'mentl/ *adj.* **1.** resembling a monument; massive or imposing. **2.** of lasting significance.

-mony a noun suffix indicating result or condition, as in *parsimony*; but sometimes having the same function as **-ment**.

mooch /mutʃ/ *v.i.* **1.** to hang or loiter about. – *v.t.* **2.** to get without paying or at another's expense; cadge.

mood[1] /mud/ *n.* frame of mind, or state of feeling, as at a particular time.

mood[2] /mud/ *n. Grammar* a set of categories of verb inflection which show the syntactic relation of the verb to other verbs in the sentence, or the speaker's attitude towards the action expressed by the verb.

moody /'mudi/ *adj.*, **-dier**, **-diest**. **1.** given to gloomy or sullen moods; ill-humoured. **2.** exhibiting sharply varied moods; temperamental.

moon /mun/ *n.* **1.** the body which revolves around the earth monthly. **2.** a month. **3.** any planetary satellite. – *v.i.* **4.** *Colloquial* to wander about or gaze idly, dreamily, or listlessly.

moonlight /'munlaɪt/ *n.* **1.** the light of the moon. – *adj.* **2.** relating to moonlight. **3.** illuminated by moonlight. – *v.i.* **4.** to work at a second job, often at night, in addition to one's regular employment.

moonshine /'munʃaɪn/ *n.* **1.** the light of the moon. **2.** empty or foolish talk, ideas, etc.; nonsense. **3.** *Colloquial* smuggled or illicitly distilled liquor.

moonstone /'munstoʊn/ *n.* a white translucent variety of felspar with a bluish pearly lustre, used as a gem.

moor[1] /mɔ/ *n.* a tract of open, waste land; a heath.

moor[2] /mɔ/ *v.t.* to secure (a ship, etc.) in a particular place. – **moorage**, *n.*

moorings /'mɔrɪŋz/ *pl. n.* the place where a vessel is or may be moored.

moose /mus/ *n., pl.* **moose**. a large animal of the deer family.

moot /mut/ *adj.* subject to argument or discussion; debatable; doubtful.

moot court *n.* a mock court for the conduct of hypothetical legal cases, as for practice for students of law.

mop /mɒp/ *n., v.,* **mopped**, **mopping**. – *n.* **1.** a bundle of coarse yarn, a piece of cloth, or the like, fastened at the end of a stick or handle, used for washing floors, dishes, etc. **2.** a thick mass, as of hair. – *v.t.* **3.** to rub, wipe, clean, or remove with a mop. **4. mop up,** to clean up.

mope /moʊp/ *v.i.,* **moped**, **moping**. to be sunk in listless apathy or dull dejection.

moral /'mɒrəl/ *adj.* **1.** relating to or concerned with right conduct or the distinction between right or wrong. **2.** conforming to the rules of right conduct (opposed to *immoral*). – *n.* **3.** the moral teaching or practical lesson contained in a fable, tale, experience, etc. **4.** (*pl.*) principles or habits with respect to right or wrong conduct; ethics.

morale /mə'ral/ *n.* mental condition with respect to cheerfulness, confidence, zeal, etc.

moralise = moralize /'mɒrəlaɪz/ *v.i.*, **-lised**, **-lising**. to make moral reflections.

morality /mə'rælǝti/ *n., pl.* **-ties**. conformity to the rules of right conduct.

morass /mə'ræs/ *n.* a tract of low, soft, wet ground.

moratorium /mɒrə'tɔriəm/ *n., pl.* **-toria** /-'tɔriə/, **-toriums**. a general suspension of some type of legal obligation. – **moratory**, *adj.*

morbid /'mɔbəd/ *adj.* affected by, proceeding from, or characteristic of, disease.

mordant /'mɔdnt/ *adj.* caustic or sarcastic, as wit, a speaker, etc.

more /mɔ/ *adj., superlative* **most**, *n., adv.* – *adj.* **1.** in greater quantity, amount, measure, degree, or number (as the comparative of *much* and *many*). **2.** additional or further. – *n.* **3.** an additional quantity, amount, or number. **4.** a greater quantity, amount, or degree. – *adv.* **5.** in or to a greater extent or degree. **6. more or less,** to a certain extent; approximately.

more-ish /'mɔr-ɪʃ/ *adj.* of or relating to something of which one would like more.

moreover /mɔr'oʊvə/ *adv.* beyond what has been said; further; besides.

mores /'mɔreɪz/ *pl. n.* customs or conventions accepted without question and embodying the fundamental moral views of a group.

morgue /mɔg/ *n.* a place in which the bodies of persons found dead are exposed for identification.

moribund /'mɒrəbʌnd/ *adj.* dying.

mornay /'mɔneɪ/ *adj.* covered with a thick white sauce which has grated cheese added to it.

morning /'mɔnɪŋ/ *n.* the first part or period of the day.

morocco /mə'rɒkoʊ/ *n.* a fine leather made from goatskins.

moron /'mɔrɒn/ *n.* a person of rather low intelligence.

morose /mə'roʊs/ *adj.* gloomily or sullenly ill-humoured as a person, mood, etc.

-morph a word element meaning 'form', 'shape' or 'structure'.

morpheme /'mɔfim/ *n.* any of the minimum meaningful elements in a language.

-morphic a word element used as adjective termination corresponding to **-morph**.

morphine /'mɔfin/ *n.* a drug used to dull pain, induce sleep, etc. Also, **morphia** /'mɔfiə/.

morpho- initial word element corresponding to **-morph**.

morphology /mɔ'fɒlədʒi/ *n.* the study of form, structure, and the like.

-morphous a word element used as adjective termination corresponding to **-morph**, as in *amorphous*.

morrow /'mɒroʊ/ *n.* the day next after this or after some other particular day or night.

morse code /mɔs/ *n.* a system of dots, dashes, and spaces used to represent the letters of the alphabet, numerals, etc.

morsel /'mɔsəl/ *n.* a small piece, quantity, or amount of anything; a scrap; a bit.

mortal /'mɔtl/ *adj.* **1.** liable or subject to death. **2.** of or relating to human beings as subject to death; human. **3.** causing death; fatal. – *n.* **4.** a being subject to death.

mortality /mɔ'tæləti/ *n., pl.* **-ties**. **1.** the condition of being mortal. **2.** relative frequency of death, or death rate, as in a district or community.

mortality table *n.* an actuarial table compiled by an insurance company from statistics on the life spans of an arbitrarily selected population group or of former policyholders.

mortar[1] /'mɔtə/ *n.* **1.** a bowl in which drugs, etc., are reduced to powder with a pestle. **2.** a type of cannon.

mortar[2] /'mɔtə/ *n.* a material which binds bricks, stones, etc., into a compact mass.

mortarboard /'mɔtəbɔd/ *n.* a kind of cap with a stiff, square top, worn by university graduates, etc.

mortgage /'mɔgɪdʒ/ *n., v.,* **-gaged**, **-gaging**. *Law* – *n.* **1.** a security by way of conveyance or assignment of property securing the payment of a debt or the performance of an obligation where the property is redeemable upon payment or performance. – *v.t.* **2.** to put (property, especially houses or land) under a mortgage.

mortice = mortise /'mɔtəs/ *n.* a rectangular cavity in a piece of wood, etc., for receiving a corresponding projection (tenon) on another piece, so as to form a joint.

mortify /'mɔtəfaɪ/ *v.t.*, **-fied**, **-fying**. to humiliate. – **mortification**, *n.*

mortuary /'mɔtʃəri/ *n., pl.* **-ries**. a place where dead bodies are temporarily kept.

mosaic /moʊ'zeɪɪk, mə'zeɪɪk/ *n.* a picture or decoration made of small pieces of stone, glass, etc., of different colours, inlaid to form a design.

moselle /moʊ'zɛl/ *n.* a light white wine.

mosque /mɒsk/ *n.* a Muslim temple.

mosquito /məs'kitoʊ/ *n., pl.* **-toes**, **-tos**. any of various insects the females of which suck the blood of animals.

moss /mɒs/ *n.* any of various small leafy-stemmed plants growing in tufts in moist places.

most /moʊst/ *adj.* (*superlative of* **more**) *n., adv.* – *adj.* **1.** in the greatest quantity, amount, measure, degree, or number. – *n.* **2.** the greatest quantity, amount, or degree. **3.** (*construed as pl.*) the majority of persons. – *adv.* **4.** in or to the greatest extent or degree.

-most a suffixal use of **most** found in a series of superlatives, as in *utmost*, *foremost*.

most favoured nation *n.* a country with which trade is carried on under conditions which are no less favourable than those relating to trade with any other country. *Abbrev.*: MFN

mostly /'moʊstli/ *adv.* for the most part; in the main.

mote /moʊt/ *n.* a particle or speck, especially of dust.

motel /moʊ'tɛl/ *n.* a roadside hotel with self-contained units.

moth /mɒθ/ *n., pl.* **moths**. any of a large group of insects similar to the butterflies.

mothball /ˈmɒθbɔl/ *n.* a small ball of naphthalene or (sometimes) camphor, stored with clothes, etc., to repel moths.

mother /ˈmʌðə/ *n.* **1.** a female parent. **2.** the head or superior of a female religious community. *– adj.* **3.** relating to or characteristic of a mother. *– v.t.* **4.** to be the mother of; give origin or rise to. **5.** to care for or protect as a mother does.

motherboard /ˈmʌðəbɔd/ *n.* a printed circuit board plugged into the back of a computer into which other boards (**daughter boards**) can be slotted so that the computer can operate an optional range of peripheral devices. Also, **mother board**.

mother-in-law /ˈmʌðər-ən-lɔ/ *n., pl.* **mothers-in-law**. the mother of one's spouse.

mother-of-pearl /mʌðər-əv-ˈpɜl/ *n.* a hard, iridescent substance which forms the inner layer of certain shells, as that of the pearl oyster.

mother tongue *n.* the language first learned by a person; native language.

motif /moʊˈtif, ˈmoʊtəf/ *n.* a recurring subject or theme as in art, literature, or music.

motion /ˈmoʊʃən/ *n.* **1.** the process of moving, or changing place or position. **2.** a bodily movement or gesture. **3.** a proposal formally made to a deliberative assembly. **4.** → **faeces**. *– v.t.* **5.** to direct by a significant motion or gesture, as with the hand. *– v.i.* **6.** to make a significant motion; gesture.

motivated /ˈmoʊtəveɪtəd/ *adj.* ambitious; determined; energetic.

motive /ˈmoʊtɪv/ *n.* **1.** something that prompts a person to act in a certain way. *– adj.* **2.** causing, or tending to cause, motion.

motley /ˈmɒtli/ *adj.* exhibiting great diversity of elements.

motocross /ˈmoʊtəkrɒs/ *n.* a short distance motorcycle race on rough terrain.

motor /ˈmoʊtə/ *n.* **1.** a comparatively small and powerful engine, especially an internal-combustion engine. **2.** any self-powered vehicle. *– adj.* **3.** causing or imparting motion.

motorcade /ˈmoʊtəkeɪd/ *n.* a procession or parade of motor cars.

motorcycle /ˈmoʊtəsaɪkəl/ *n.* a motor vehicle resembling a bicycle.

motorist /ˈmoʊtərəst/ *n.* someone who drives a car.

motor vehicle *n.* a road vehicle driven by a motor.

motorway /ˈmoʊtəweɪ/ *n.* an expressway; freeway.

mottled /ˈmɒtld/ *adj.* spotted or blotched in colouring.

motto /ˈmɒtoʊ/ *n., pl.* **-tos, -toes**. a maxim adopted as expressing one's guiding principle.

mould[1] /moʊld/ *n.* **1.** a hollow form or matrix for giving a particular shape to something in a molten or plastic state. **2.** something formed in or on a mould. *– v.t.* **3.** to work into a required shape or form; shape.

mould[2] /moʊld/ *n.* a growth of minute fungi forming on vegetable or animal matter.

moulder /ˈmoʊldə/ *v.i.* to turn to dust by natural decay.

moult = molt /moʊlt/ *v.i.* to cast or shed the feathers, skin, or the like, to be succeeded by a new growth.

mound /maʊnd/ *n.* **1.** an elevation of earth; a hillock or knoll. **2.** a heap or raised mass.

mount[1] /maʊnt/ *v.t.* **1.** to go up or ascend. **2.** to get up on (a platform, a horse, etc.) **3.** to go or put on (guard), as a sentry or watch. **4.** to fix on or in a support, backing, setting, etc. **5.** to get up on something, as a platform, horse, etc. **6.** a horse, bicycle, etc., used for riding. **7.** a support, backing, setting, or the like, on or in which something is, or is to be, mounted or fixed.

mount[2] /maʊnt/ *n.* a mountain or hill.

mountain /ˈmaʊntən/ *n.* a natural elevation of the earth's surface, higher than a hill.

mountaineer /maʊntəˈnɪə/ *n.* **1.** a climber of mountains. *– v.i.* **2.** to climb mountains. *–* **mountaineering**, *n.*

mountainous /ˈmaʊntənəs/ *adj.* **1.** abounding in mountains. **2.** of the nature of a mountain.

mountebank /ˈmaʊntəbæŋk/ *n.* a charlatan or quack.

mourn /mɔn/ *v.i.* **1.** to feel or express sorrow or grief. *– v.t.* **2.** to grieve or lament over (the dead).

mournful /ˈmɔnfəl/ *adj.* **1.** full of, expressing, or showing sorrow or grief. **2.** gloomy, sombre or dreary.

mourning /ˈmɔnɪŋ/ *n.* the conventional manifestation of sorrow for a person's death, especially by the wearing of black, the hanging of flags at half-mast, etc.

mouse /maʊs/ *n., pl.* **mice** /maɪs/, *also, for def. 3* **mouses** /maʊsəz/; /maʊz/ *v.,* **moused, mousing**. *– n.* **1.** any of various small rodents. **2.** *Colloquial* a quiet, shy person. **3.** *Computers* a hand-held device for positioning the cursor on a VDU. *– v.i.* **4.** to hunt for or catch mice.

mousse /mus/ *n.* any of various preparations of whipped cream, beaten eggs, gelatine, etc., flavoured (sweet or savoury) and usually chilled.

moustache /məˈstaʃ/ *n.* the hair growing on the upper lip.

mouth /maʊθ/ *n., pl.* **mouths** /maʊðz/, /maʊð/ *v.* *– n.* **1.** the opening through which an animal takes in food. **2.** a person or other animal as requiring food. **3.** utterance or expression. **4.** a part of a river or the like where its waters are discharged into some other body of water. *– v.t.* **5.** to utter with unnecessarily noticeable use of the mouth or lips. **6.** to form (words) with the lips, uttering no sound.

mouthful /ˈmaʊθfʊl/ *n., pl.* **-fuls**. as much as a mouth can hold.

mouth organ *n.* → **harmonica**.

mouthpiece /ˈmaʊθpis/ *n.* **1.** a piece placed at or forming the mouth, as of a receptacle, tube, or the like. **2.** a piece or part, as of an instrument, to which the mouth is applied or which is held in the mouth. **3.** a person, a newspaper, or the like that voices or communicates the sentiments, decisions, etc., of another or others; a spokesperson.

move /muv/ *v.*, **moved**, **moving**, *n.* – *v.i.* **1.** to change place or position. **2.** *Commerce* to be disposed of by sale, as goods in stock. **3.** (of the bowels) to operate. **4.** to make a formal request, application, or proposal. – *v.t.* **5.** to change the place or position of. **6.** to prompt, actuate, or impel to some action. **7.** to affect with tender or compassionate emotion; touch. **8.** to propose formally for consideration by a deliberative assembly. – *n.* **9.** the act of moving; a movement. **10.** a change of abode or residence. – **movable = moveable**, *adj.*, *n.*

movement /'muvmənt/ *n.* **1.** the act or process or result of moving. **2.** (*chiefly plural*) an action or activity, as of a person or a body of persons. **3.** the price change in the market of some commodity or security. **4.** the works of a mechanism, as a watch. **5.** *Music* a principal division or section of a sonata, symphony, or the like.

movie /'muvi/ *n.* → **film** (def. 3).

mow /moʊ/ *v.t.*, **mowed**, **mown** *or* **mowed**, **mowing**. **1.** to cut down (grass, grain, etc.) with a scythe or a machine. **2.** to cut down, destroy, or kill indiscriminately.

MSG /ɛm ɛs 'dʒi/ *n.* → **monosodium glutamate**.

much /mʌtʃ/ *adj.*, **more**, **most**, *n.*, *adv.* – *adj.* **1.** in great quantity, amount, measure, or degree. – *n.* **2.** a great quantity or amount; a great deal. **3. make much of,** to treat (a person) with great, flattering, or fond consideration. – *adv.* **4.** to a great extent or degree; greatly; far.

muck /mʌk/ *n.* **1.** farmyard dung, decaying vegetable matter, etc., in a moist state; manure. **2.** filth; dirt. – *v.t.* **3.** to remove muck from (often fol. by *out*). **4.** *Colloquial* to spoil; make a mess of. – *v.i.* **5. muck about** (or **around**), *Colloquial* to idle; potter; fool about. **6. muck up,** *Colloquial* to misbehave.

muck-up /'mʌk-ʌp/ *n.* *Colloquial* fiasco; muddle.

mucous /'mjukəs/ *adj.* **1.** relating to, consisting of, or resembling mucus. **2.** containing or secreting mucus.

mucus /'mjukəs/ *n.* a viscid secretion of the mucous membranes.

mud /mʌd/ *n.* **1.** wet, soft earth or earthy matter. **2. one's name is mud,** *Colloquial* one is in disgrace. **3. throw** (or **sling**) **mud at,** *Colloquial* speak ill of; abuse. – **muddy**, *adj.*

muddle /'mʌdl/ *v.*, **-dled**, **-dling**, *n.* – *v.t.* **1.** to mix up or jumble together in a confused or bungling way. – *v.i.* **2. muddle through,** to come to a satisfactory conclusion without planned direction. – *n.* **3.** a muddled condition; a confused mental state.

mudflat /'mʌdflæt/ *n.* an area of muddy ground covered by water at high tide.

mudguard /'mʌdgad/ *n.* a guard or shield shaped to fit over the wheels of a vehicle to prevent splashing of water, mud, etc.

muesli /'mjuzli/ *n.* a breakfast cereal of oats, wheatgerm, chopped fruit and nuts, etc.

muff /mʌf/ *n.* **1.** a case covered with fur or other material, in which the hands are placed for warmth. **2.** *Colloquial* a failure. – *v.t.*, *v.i.* **3.** to bungle (something).

muffin /'mʌfən/ *n.* a thick, flat yeast cake, grilled and served with butter.

muffle /'mʌfəl/ *v.t.*, **-fled**, **-fling**. **1.** to wrap or envelop in a cloak, shawl, scarf, etc. **2.** to wrap with something to deaden or prevent sound. **3.** to deaden (sound) by wrappings or other means.

muffler /'mʌflə/ *n.* **1.** a heavy neck scarf used for warmth. **2.** any device that reduces noise, especially that on the exhaust of an internal combustion engine.

mug /mʌg/ *n.*, *v.*, **mugged**, **mugging**. – *n.* **1.** a drinking cup, usually cylindrical and commonly with a handle. **2.** *Colloquial* the face. **3.** *Colloquial* a fool; someone who is easily duped. – *v.t.* **4.** *Colloquial* to assault and rob.

muggy /'mʌgi/ *adj.*, **-gier**, **-giest**. (of the atmosphere, weather, etc.) damp and close; humid and oppressive.

mulatto /mju'lætoʊ, mə-/ *n.*, *pl.* **-tos**, **-toes**. the offspring of a Negro and a white person.

mulberry /'mʌlbəri, -bri/ *n.*, *pl.* **-ries**. **1.** a type of berry. **2.** a dull, dark, reddish purple colour.

mulch /mʌltʃ/ *n.* straw, leaves, loose earth, etc., spread on the ground.

mule[1] /mjul/ *n.* **1.** the sterile offspring of a male donkey and a mare, used especially as a beast of burden. **2.** *Colloquial* a stupid or stubborn person.

mule[2] /mjul/ *n.* a kind of slipper which leaves the heel exposed.

mulga /'mʌlgə/ *n.* **1.** any of several species of Acacia found in drier parts of Australia. **2.** the bush; back country. **3.** an Aborigine's shield.

mull[1] /mʌl/ *v.t.* to study or ruminate (*over*).

mull[2] /mʌl/ *v.t.* to heat, sweeten, and spice for drinking, as ale, wine, etc.

mullet /'mʌlət/ *n.*, *pl.* **-lets**, (*esp. collectively*) **-let**. a type of freshwater fish.

multi- a word element meaning 'many'.

multicoloured = multicolored /'mʌltikʌləd/ *adj.* of many colours.

multicultural /mʌlti'kʌltʃərəl/ *adj.* of or relating to a society which embraces a number of minority cultures.

multifarious /mʌltə'fɛəriəs/ *adj.* **1.** having many different parts, elements, forms, etc. **2.** of many kinds, or numerous and varied.

multigrade /'mʌltigreɪd/ *adj.* denoting a motor oil with a stable viscosity level over a wide range of temperatures.

multilateral /mʌlti'lætərəl, -'lætrəl/ *adj.* **1.** having many sides; many-sided. **2.** *Government* denoting an agreement, etc., in which three or more nations participate; multipartite.

multilingual /mʌlti'lɪŋgwəl/ *adj.* able to speak three or more languages.

multimeter /'mʌltimitə/ *n.* a meter for measuring voltages, currents and resistances.

multinational /mʌlti'næʃənəl/ *adj.* **1.** of, relating to, or spreading across many nations. – *n.* **2.** a large, usually powerful, company with members from several nations.

multipartite /mʌlti'pataɪt/ *adj.* **1.** divided into many parts; having many divisions. **2.** *Government* → **multilateral** (def. 2).

multiple /'mʌltəpəl/ *adj.* **1.** consisting of, having, or involving many individuals, parts, elements, relations, etc.; manifold. – *n.* **2.** *Mathematics* a number which contains another number some number of times without a remainder.

multiple-choice /'mʌltəpəl-tʃɔɪs/ *adj.* offering a number of choices.

multiple sclerosis /sklə'rousəs/ *n.* a disease of the nervous system caused by loss of part of the myelin sheath around certain nerve fibres. *Abbrev.*: MS

multiplicity /mʌltə'plɪsəti/ *n., pl.* **-ties**. a multitude or great number.

multiplier /'mʌltəplaɪə/ *n.* an indicator of the relative sizes of a given initial increase in investment and the total ultimate increase in income.

multiply /'mʌltəplaɪ/ *v.,* **-plied**, **-plying**. – *v.t.* **1.** to make many or manifold; increase the number, quantity, etc., of. **2.** *Mathematics* to take by addition a given number of times. **3.** to produce (animals or plants) by propagation. – *v.i.* **4.** to grow in number, quantity, etc.; increase. – **multiplication**, *n.*

multiracial /mʌlti'reɪʃəl/ *adj.* of or relating to more than one race or extraction.

multiskilling /'mʌltiskɪlɪŋ/ *n.* the development of a number of skills from which workers may earn a livelihood.

multitude /'mʌltətjud/ *n.* **1.** a great number; host. **2.** a great number of persons gathered together; a crowd or throng. – **multitudinous**, *adj.*

mum[1] /mʌm/ *adj.* silent; not saying a word.

mum[2] /mʌm/ *n. Colloquial* mother.

mumble /'mʌmbəl/ *v.,* **-bled**, **-bling**, *n.* – *v.i.* **1.** to speak indistinctly or unintelligibly. – *v.t.* **2.** to utter indistinctly. – *n.* **3.** a low, indistinct utterance or sound.

mumbo jumbo /mʌmbou 'dʒʌmbou/ *n.* meaningless incantation or ritual.

mummy[1] /'mʌmi/ *n., pl.* **-mies**. the dead body of a human being or animal preserved by embalming.

mummy[2] /'mʌmi/ *n. Colloquial* mother.

mumps /mʌmps/ *pl. n.* (*construed as sing.*) an infectious viral disease causing swelling of the glands.

munch /mʌntʃ/ *v.t., v.i.* to chew steadily or vigorously, and often audibly.

munchies /'mʌntʃiz/ *pl. n. Colloquial* **1.** anything to eat, especially snacks between meals. **2. have the munchies,** to experience a craving for food.

mundane /'mʌndeɪn, mʌn'deɪn/ *adj.* ordinary; boring.

mung bean /mʌŋ/ *n.* a bushy annual herb, a chief source of bean sprouts.

municipal /mju'nɪsəpəl, mjunə'sɪpəl/ *adj.* of or relating to a municipality, its government, facilities, etc.

municipality /mjunəsə'pæləti/ *n., pl.* **-ties**. **1.** an area of land delineated for the purposes of local government; borough. **2.** the governing body of such a district or community.

munificent /mju'nɪfəsənt/ *adj.* extremely liberal in giving or bestowing; very generous.

munitions /mju'nɪʃənz/ *pl. n.* materials used in war, especially weapons and ammunition.

mural /'mjurəl/ *adj.* **1.** of or relating to a wall; resembling a wall. – *n.* **2.** a painting on a wall.

murder /'mɜdə/ *n.* **1.** *Law* the unlawful killing of another human being with malice aforethought. **2.** *Colloquial* an uncommonly laborious or difficult task. – *v.t.* **3.** *Law* to kill by an act constituting murder. – **murderous**, *adj.*

murky /'mɜki/ *adj.,* **-kier**, **-kiest**. cloudy and dirty, as water.

murmur /'mɜmə/ *n.* **1.** any low, continuous sound. **2.** a mumbled or private expression of discontent. – *v.i.* **3.** to make a low or indistinct continuous sound. **4.** to speak in a low tone or indistinctly. **5.** to complain in a low tone, or in private.

muscat /'mʌskət/ *n.* a type of sweet wine. Also, **muscatel**.

muscle /'mʌsəl/ *n., v.,* **-cled**, **-cling**. – *n.* **1.** a discrete bundle or sheet of contractile fibres having the function of producing movement in the animal body. **2.** muscular strength; brawn. **3.** political or financial strength, especially when exercised in a ruthless fashion. **4. muscle in (on),** to force one's way in(to).

musclebound /'mʌsəlbaund/ *adj.* having muscles enlarged and inelastic, as from excessive exercise.

muscular /'mʌskjələ/ *adj.* **1.** of or relating to muscle or the muscles. **2.** having well-developed muscles; brawny.

muscular dystrophy /'dɪstrəfi/ *n.* a disease causing muscular deterioration and wastage.

muse[1] /mjuz/ *v.i.,* **mused**, **musing**. to reflect or meditate in silence.

muse[2] /mjuz/ *n.* the goddess or power thought to inspire a poet.

museum /mju'ziəm/ *n.* a building or place for the keeping, exhibition, and study of objects of scientific, artistic, and historical interest.

mush /mʌʃ/ *n.* **1.** any thick, soft mass. **2.** *Colloquial* weak or maudlin sentiment or sentimental language.

mushroom /'mʌʃrum/ *n.* **1.** any of various fleshy edible fungi. **2.** anything of similar shape or correspondingly rapid growth. – *adj.* **3.** of, relating to, or made of mushrooms. **4.** resembling or suggesting a mushroom in shape. **5.** to spread or grow quickly, as mushrooms.

music /'mjuzɪk/ *n.* **1.** an art of organising sound in significant forms to express ideas and emotions through the elements of rhythm, melody, harmony, and colour. **2.** the tones or sounds employed. **3.** musical work or compositions for singing or playing. **4.** the written or printed score of a musical composition. **5.** such scores collectively. **6. face the music,** to face the consequences, usually unpleasant, of one's actions.

musical /'mjuzɪkəl/ *adj.* **1.** of, relating to, or producing music. **2.** fond of or skilled in music.

musician /mju'zɪʃən/ *n.* one skilled in playing a musical instrument.

musk /mʌsk/ *n.* **1.** a substance secreted by certain animals, having a strong smell, and used in perfumery. **2.** a synthetic imitation of this substance.

musket /'mʌskət/ *n.* the predecessor of the modern rifle. – **musketeer**, *n.*

muslin /'mʌzlən/ *n.* a fine cotton fabric.

mussel /'mʌsəl/ *n.* an edible bivalve mollusc.

must /mʌst, mʌs/, *weak forms* /məst, məs/ – *v. (aux)* **1.** to be obliged or compelled to. **2.** may reasonably be supposed to. – *n. Colloquial* **3.** anything necessary or vital.

mustard /'mʌstəd/ *n.* **1.** a pungent powder or paste much used as a food seasoning or condiment. – *adj.* **2.** brownish-yellow in colour.

mustard gas *n.* a chemical-warfare agent.

muster /'mʌstə/ *v.t.* **1.** to gather, summon, or round up (often fol. by *up*). – *v.i.* **2.** to come together, collect, or gather. – *n.* **3.** the act of mustering. **4. pass muster,** to measure up to specified standards.

musty /'mʌsti/ *adj.*, **-tier**, **-tiest**. having a smell or flavour suggestive of mould.

mutant /'mjutnt/ *n.* a new type of organism produced as the result of mutation.

mutate /mju'teɪt/ *v.i.*, **-tated**, **-tating**. to change; undergo mutation.

mutation /mju'teɪʃən/ *n.* **1.** the act or process of changing. **2.** a change or alteration, as in form, qualities, or nature.

mute /mjut/ *adj.*, *n.*, *v.*, **muted**, **muting**. – *adj.* **1.** silent; refraining from speech or utterance. **2.** incapable of speech; dumb. – *n.* **3.** one unable to utter words. **4.** *Law* a person who makes no response when arraigned. **5.** a mechanical device for muffling the tone of a musical instrument. – *v.t.* **6.** to deaden or muffle the sound of (a musical instrument, etc.).

mutilate /'mjutəleɪt/ *v.t.*, **-lated**, **-lating**. to deprive (a person or animal, the body, etc.) of a limb or other important part or parts. – **mutilation**, *n.*

mutiny /'mjutəni/ *n.*, *pl.* **-nies**, *v.*, **-nied**, **-nying**. – *n.* **1.** a revolt or rebellion against constituted authority, especially by soldiers or seamen against their officers. – *v.i.* **2.** to commit mutiny. – **mutinous**, *adj.*

mutt /mʌt/ *n. Colloquial* **1.** a dog, especially a mongrel. **2.** a simpleton; a stupid person.

mutter /'mʌtə/ *v.i.* **1.** to utter words indistinctly or in a low tone; murmur; grumble. **2.** to make a low, rumbling sound. – *v.t.* **3.** to utter indistinctly or in a low tone.

mutton /'mʌtn/ *n.* the flesh of sheep, used as food.

mutton-bird /'mʌtn-bɜd/ *n.* any of various species of petrel.

mutton-chops /'mʌtn-tʃɒps, mʌtn-'tʃɒps/ *pl. n.* side-whiskers narrow at the top, and broad and trimmed short at the bottom.

mutual /'mjutʃuəl/ *adj.* **1.** possessed, experienced, performed, etc., by each of two or more with respect to the other or others; reciprocal. **2.** relating to mutual insurance.

mutual fund *n.* an investment trust which pools the money of a large number of investors and invests on their behalf.

mutual insurance *n.* insurance in which those insured become members of a company who reciprocally engage, by payment of certain amounts into a common fund, to indemnify one another against loss.

mutual savings bank *n.* a non-capitalised savings bank distributing its profits to depositors.

muu-muu /'mu-mu/ *n.* a long, loose dress, usually brightly coloured.

muzak /'mjuzæk/ *n.* recorded background music.

muzzle /'mʌzəl/ *n.*, *v.*, **-zled**, **-zling**. – *n.* **1.** the mouth, or end for discharge, of the barrel of a gun, pistol, etc. **2.** the projecting part of the head of an animal, including jaws, mouth, and nose. **3.** a device placed over an animal's mouth to prevent the animal from biting, eating, etc. – *v.t.* **4.** to put a muzzle on. **5.** to restrain (by physical, legal, or procedural means) from speech or the expression of opinion; gag.

my /maɪ/, *weak forms* /mi, mə/ – *pron.* **1.** the possessive form corresponding to **I** and **me**, used before a noun. – *interj.* **2.** (an exclamation of surprise).

my- a word element meaning 'muscle'. Also, **myo-**.

myall /'maɪɔl/ *n.* **1.** an Aborigine living in a traditional tribal way, outside European civilisation. – *adj.* **2.** wild or uncivilised.

myc- a word element meaning 'fungus'. Also, **myco-**.

-mycetes a word element meaning 'fungus'.

myelin /'maɪələn/ *n.* a soft, white, fatty substance encasing certain nerve fibres.

myna = mynah /'maɪnə/ *n.* **1.** a noisy scavenging bird with yellow legs and beak. **2.** any of various Asian birds known for their ability to talk. Also, **mina**.

myocardiograph /maɪoʊ'kadiəgræf/ *n.* an apparatus which records the movements of the heart muscle.

myopia /maɪ'oʊpiə/ *n.* near-sightedness. – **myopic**, *adj.*

myriad /'mɪriəd/ *n.* **1.** an indefinitely great number. – *adj.* **2.** of an indefinitely great number; innumerable.

myrrh /mɜ/ *n.* an aromatic resinous exudation from certain plants used for incense, perfume, etc.

myrtle /'mɜtl/ *n.* a type of shrub with fragrant white flowers.

myself /maɪ'sɛlf, mə'sɛlf/ *pron.* **1.** a reflexive form of **I**. **2.** an emphatic form of **me** or **I**, used: **a.** as object. **b.** in apposition to a subject or object. – *n.* **3.** one's proper or normal self.

mystery /'mɪstri, -təri/ *n.*, *pl.* **-ries**. **1.** anything that is kept secret or remains unexplained or unknown. **2.** obscure, puzzling, or mysterious quality or character. **3.** any truth unknowable except by divine revelation. – **mysterious**, *adj.*

mystic /'mɪstɪk/ *adj.* **1.** spiritually significant or symbolic. **2.** of occult character, power, or significance. **3.** of or relating to mystics or mysticism. – *n.* **4.** someone who claims to attain insights into mysteries transcending ordinary human knowledge.

mysticism /'mɪstəsɪzəm/ *n.* **1.** the beliefs, ideas, or mode of thought of mystics.

2. obscure thought or speculation.

mystify /ˈmɪstəfaɪ/ *v.t.*, **-fied**, **-fying**. **1.** to involve (a subject, etc.) in mystery or obscurity. **2.** to confuse (someone). – **mystification**, *n.*

mystique /mɪsˈtik/ *n.* an air of mystery or mystical power surrounding a particular person, object, pursuit, belief, etc.

myth /mɪθ/ *n.* **1.** a traditional story which attempts to explain natural phenomena. **2.** any invented story. – **mythical**, *adj.*

mytho- a word element meaning 'myth.'

mythology /məˈθɒlədʒi/ *n.*, *pl.* **-gies**. myths collectively.

myx- a word element meaning 'slimy'.

N n

N, n /ɛn/ *n., pl.* **N's** *or* **Ns**, **n's** *or* **ns**. the 14th letter of the English alphabet.

nab /næb/ *v.t.,* **nabbed**, **nabbing**. *Colloquial* to catch or seize, especially suddenly.

nacre /'neɪkə/ *n.* → **mother-of-pearl**.

nadir /'neɪdɪə/ *n.* the lowest point.

nag[1] /næg/ *v.,* **nagged**, **nagging**. – *v.t.* **1.** to torment by persistent fault-finding, complaints, or importunities. – *v.i.* **2.** to keep up an irritating or wearisome fault-finding, complaining, or the like (often fol. by *at*). **3.** to cause continual pain, discomfort, or depression, as a headache, feeling of guilt, etc.

nag[2] /næg/ *n. Colloquial* a horse.

nail /neɪl/ *n.* **1.** a slender piece of metal, usually with one end pointed and the other enlarged, for driving into or through wood, etc., as to hold separate pieces together. **2.** a thin, horny plate, consisting of modified epidermis, growing on the upper side of the end of a finger or toe. – *v.t.* **3.** to fasten with a nail or nails. **4.** *Colloquial* to secure by prompt action; catch or seize.

naive /naɪ'iv, na-/ *adj.* unsophisticated; ingenuous. Also, **naïve**. – **naivety**, *n.*

naked /'neɪkəd/ *adj.* **1.** without clothing or covering; nude. **2.** (of the eye, sight, etc.) unassisted by a microscope, telescope, or other instrument.

name /neɪm/ *n., v.,* **named**, **naming**. – *n.* **1.** a word or a combination of words by which a person, place, or thing, a body or class, or any object of thought, is designated or known. **2.** an appellation, title, or epithet, applied descriptively, in honour, abuse, etc. **3.** a reputation of a particular kind given by common report. – *v.t.* **4.** to give a name to. **5.** to call by a specified name.

name-day /'neɪm-deɪ/ *n.* the day on which buying stockbrokers pass to selling brokers the names of the purchasers of the stocks since the last settlement. Also, **ticket day**.

namely /'neɪmli/ *adv.* that is to say.

namesake /'neɪmseɪk/ *n.* **1.** one having the same name as another. **2.** one named after another.

nanny /'næni/ *n., pl.* **-nies**. **1.** a nurse for children. **2.** a grandmother.

nanny-goat /'næni-goʊt/ *n.* a female goat.

nap[1] /næp/ *v.,* **napped**, **napping**, *n.* – *v.i.* **1.** to have a short sleep; doze. – *n.* **2.** a short sleep; a doze.

nap[2] /næp/ *n.* the short fuzzy ends of fibres on the surface of cloth.

napalm /'neɪpam, 'næpam/ *n.* an aluminium soap, in the form of a granular powder; mixed with petrol it forms a sticky gel used in flame throwers and fire bombs.

nape /neɪp/ *n.* the back (of the neck).

napery /'neɪpəri/ *n.* table linen.

naphthalene /'næfθəlin/ *n.* a white crystalline hydrocarbon used in dyes and as a moth-repellent, etc.

napkin /'næpkən/ *n.* **1.** → **serviette**. **2.** a square or oblong piece of linen, cotton cloth or paper, as for a towel, or a baby's nappy.

nappy /'næpi/ *n., pl.* **-pies**. a piece of cotton, muslin, or some disposable material, fastened round a baby to absorb and contain its excrement.

narcissism /'nasəsɪzəm/ *n.* extreme admiration for oneself or one's own attributes; egoism; self-love. – **narcissist**, *n.* – **narcissistic**, *adj.*

narcosis /na'koʊsəs/ *n.* a state of sleep or drowsiness.

narcotic /na'kɒtɪk/ *n.* any of a class of substances that blunt the senses, relieving pain, etc., and inducing sleep.

nark /nak/ *n. Colloquial* **1.** an informer. **2.** a scolding, complaining person.

narrate /nə'reɪt/ *v.t.,* **-rated**, **-rating**. to give an account of or tell the story of (events, experiences, etc.). – **narrator**, *n.* – **narration**, *n.*

narrative /'nærətɪv/ *n.* a story of events, experiences, or the like, whether true or fictitious.

narrow /'næroʊ/ *adj.* **1.** of little breadth or width; not broad or wide. **2.** limited in extent or space, or affording little room. **3.** lacking breadth of view or sympathy, as persons, the mind, ideas, etc. – *v.i.* **4.** to become narrower. – *v.t.* **5.** to make narrower. – *n.* **6.** a narrow part, place or thing. **7.** (*pl.*) a narrow part of a strait, river, ocean current, etc.

nasal /'neɪzəl/ *adj.* of or relating to the nose.

nascent /'næsənt/ *adj.* beginning to exist or develop.

nasturtium /nə'stɜʃəm/ *n.* a garden plant with showy flowers.

nasty /'nasti/ *adj.,* **-tier**, **-tiest**. vicious, spiteful, or ugly.

natal /'neɪtl/ *adj.* of or relating to birth.

natant /'neɪtənt/ *adj.* swimming; floating.

nation /'neɪʃən/ *n.* a body of people associated with a particular territory who are sufficiently conscious of their unity to seek or to possess a government peculiarly their own. – **national**, *adj.*

national debt /'næʃənəl/ *n.* the financial indebtedness of a country in respect of money borrowed from individuals for national purposes, as opposed to the personal liabilities of its inhabitants.

national income *n.* the total net value of commodities produced and services rendered by all the people of a nation during a specified period.

nationalise = nationalize /'næʃnəlaɪz/ *v.t.,* **-lised**, **-lising**. to bring under the control or ownership of a government as industries, land, etc.

nationalism /'næʃnəlɪzəm/ *n.* devotion to the interests of one's own nation. – **nationalistic**, *adj.*

nationality /næʃə'næləti, næʃ'næl-/ *n., pl.* **-ties**. the quality of membership in a particular nation (original or acquired).

native /'neɪtɪv/ *adj.* **1.** being the place or environment in which one was born or a thing came into being: *one's native land*; *a native habitat*. **2.** belonging to a person or thing by birth or nature; inborn; inherent;

natural (often fol. by *to*). **3.** of indigenous origin, growth, or production (often fol. by *to*). **4.** belonging or relating to one by reason of one's birthplace or nationality. **5.** born in a particular place or country. **6.** originating naturally in a particular country or region, as animals or plants. – *n.* **7.** one of those descended from the original inhabitants of a place or country, especially as distinguished from strangers, foreigners, colonisers, etc. **8.** one born in a particular place or country. **9.** an animal or plant indigenous to a particular region.

native title *n.* (in Australia) the right to land or water enjoyed by indigenous people who have maintained their connection to the land or water and whose possession under their traditional law or customs is recognised by Australian law.

nativity /nəˈtɪvəti/ *n., pl.* **-ties**. birth.

natural /ˈnætʃərəl, ˈnætʃrəl/ *adj.* **1.** existing in or formed by nature; not artificial. **2.** of or relating to nature or the created universe. **3.** free from affectation or constraint. **4.** in accordance with the nature of things. **5.** being such by nature; born such. **6.** *Music* neither sharp nor flat; without sharps or flats. – *n.* **7.** *Colloquial* a thing or a person that is by nature satisfactory or successful. **8.** *Music* **a.** a white key on the pianoforte, etc. **b.** the sign (♮) placed before a note cancelling the effect of a previous sharp or flat.

naturalise = naturalize /ˈnætʃrəlaɪz/ *v.t.*, **-lised**, **-lising**. **1.** to invest (an alien) with the rights and privileges of a subject or citizen; confer the rights and privileges of citizenship upon. **2.** to introduce (animals or plants) into a region and cause to flourish as if native.

naturalist /ˈnætʃrələst/ *n.* someone who is versed in or devoted to natural history, especially a zoologist or botanist.

nature /ˈneɪtʃə/ *n.* **1.** the particular combination of qualities belonging to a person or thing by birth or constitution; native or inherent character. **2.** character, kind, or sort. **3.** the material world, especially as surrounding humankind and existing independently of their activities. **4.** the sum total of the forces at work throughout the universe. **5.** reality, as distinguished from any effect of art. **6.** a primitive, wild condition; an uncultivated state.

naught /nɔt/ *n.* destruction, ruin, or complete failure.

naughty /ˈnɔti/ *adj.*, **-tier**, **-tiest**. **1.** disobedient; mischievous (especially in speaking to or about children). **2.** improper; obscene.

nausea /ˈnɔsiə, -ziə/ *n.* sickness at the stomach; a sensation of impending vomiting. – **nauseous**, *adj.* – **nauseate**, *v.*

nautical /ˈnɔtɪkəl/ *adj.* of or relating to seamen, ships, or navigation.

nave /neɪv/ *n.* the main body, or middle part, lengthwise, of a church.

navel /ˈneɪvəl/ *n.* a pit or depression in the middle of the surface of the belly.

navigate /ˈnævəgeɪt/ *v.*, **-gated**, **-gating**. – *v.t.* **1.** to traverse (the sea, a river, etc.) in a vessel, or (the air) in an aircraft. – *v.i.* **2.** to travel by using a ship or boat, as over the water; sail. – **navigator**, *n.* – **navigable**, *adj.*

navy /ˈneɪvi/ *n., pl.* **-vies**. **1.** the whole body of warships and auxiliaries belonging to a country or ruler. **2.** Also, **navy blue**. a dark blue, as of a naval uniform. – **naval**, *adj.*

nay /neɪ/ *adv.* **1.** no (used in dissent, denial, or refusal). **2.** also; and not only so but: *many good, nay, noble qualities.*

neap /nip/ *adj.* designating those tides, midway between spring tides, which attain the least height.

near /nɪə/ *adv.* **1.** close. **2.** nigh; at, within, or to a short distance. **3.** close at hand in time. **4.** close in relation; closely with respect to connection, similarity, etc. – *adj.* **5.** being close by; not distant. **6.** closely related or connected. – *prep.* **7.** (*strictly, the adverb with 'to' understood*) at, within, or to a short distance, or no great distance, from. **8.** close upon (a condition, etc.). **9.** close to (doing something). – *v.t.* **10.** to come or draw near (to); approach.

nearby /ˈnɪəbaɪ/ *adj.*, /nɪəˈbaɪ/ *adv.* close at hand; not far off.

nearly /ˈnɪəli/ *adv.* **1.** all but; almost. **2.** with close approximation.

neat /nit/ *adj.* **1.** in a pleasingly orderly condition. **2.** habitually orderly in appearance, etc. **3.** clever, dexterous, or apt. **4.** unadulterated or undiluted, as liquors.

neb /nɛb/ *n.* **1.** a bill or beak, as of a bird. **2.** the nose, especially of an animal.

nebula /ˈnɛbjələ/ *n., pl.* **-lae** /-li/, **-las**. *Astronomy* a diffuse, cloudlike patch of gases, particles, etc.

nebulous /ˈnɛbjələs/ *adj.* hazy, vague, indistinct, or confused.

necessary /ˈnɛsəsɛri, ˈnɛsəsri/ *adj.* **1.** that cannot be dispensed with. **2.** happening or existing by necessity. – **necessarily**, *adv.*

necessitate /nəˈsɛsəteɪt/ *v.t.*, **-tated**, **-tating**. to make necessary.

necessitous /nəˈsɛsətəs/ *adj.* being in or involving necessity; needy; indigent.

necessity /nəˈsɛsəti/ *n., pl.* **-ties**. **1.** something necessary or indispensable. **2.** an imperative requirement or need for something. **3.** a state of being in difficulty or need; poverty.

neck /nɛk/ *n.* **1.** that part of an animal's body which is between the head and the trunk and connects these parts. **2.** the slender part of a bottle or any similar object. **3.** any narrow, connecting, or projecting part suggesting the neck of an animal. – *v.i.* **4.** *Colloquial* to play amorously.

neckerchief /ˈnɛkətʃif/ *n.* a cloth worn round the neck by women or men.

necklace /ˈnɛkləs/ *n.* an ornament of precious stones, beads, or the like, worn especially by women round the neck.

necr- a word element meaning 'dead', 'corpse', 'death'. Also (*before consonants*), **necro-**.

necromancy /ˈnɛkrəˌmænsi/ *n.* magic.

nectar /ˈnɛktə/ *n.* **1.** *Botany* the saccharine secretion of a plant. **2.** any delicious drink.

nectarine /ˈnɛktərən, nɛktəˈrin/ *n.* a form of the common peach, having a skin without down.

nee /neɪ/ *adj.* born (placed after the name of

a married woman to introduce her maiden name). Also, **née** /neɪ/.

need /nid/ *n.* **1.** a case or instance in which some necessity or want exists; a requirement. **2.** urgent want, as of something requisite. **3.** a condition marked by the lack of something requisite. **4.** destitution; extreme poverty. – *v.t.* **5.** to have need of; require. – *v.i.* **6.** to be necessary. **7.** (usually in negatives and questions) to be under a necessity (followed by infinitive, in certain cases without *to*; in the 3rd person singular the form is *need*, not *needs*).

needle /'nidl/ *n., v.,* **-dled**, **-dling**. – *n.* **1.** a small, slender, pointed instrument, now usually of polished steel, with an eye or hole for thread, used in sewing. **2.** a slender, rodlike implement for use in knitting, or one hooked at the end for use in crocheting, etc. **3.** any of various objects resembling or suggesting a needle. **4.** *Botany* a needle-shaped leaf, as of a conifer. – *v.t.* **5.** to sew or pierce with or as with a needle. **6.** to tease or heckle.

needlework /'nidlwɜk/ *n.* the process or the product of working with a needle as in sewing or embroidery.

needy /'nidi/ *adj.,* **-dier**, **-diest**. in, or characterised by, need or want; very poor.

ne'er-do-well /'nɛə-du-wɛl/ *n.* a worthless person.

nefarious /nə'fɛəriəs/ *adj.* wicked.

negate /nə'geɪt/ *v.t.,* **-gated**, **-gating**. to deny; nullify.

negative /'nɛgətɪv/ *adj.* **1.** expressing or containing refusal or denial. **2.** characterised by the absence of distinguishing or marked qualities or features; lacking positive attributes. **3.** not positive. **4.** *Photography* denoting an image in which the gradations of light and shade are represented in reverse. **5.** *Electricity* denoting or relating to the kind of electricity developed on resin, amber, etc., when rubbed with flannel, or that present at the pole from which electrons leave an electric generator or battery, having an excess of electrons. **6.** *Chemistry* (of an element or radical) tending to gain electrons and become negatively charged. – *n.* **7.** something negative. – **negativity**, *n.*

negative gearing *n.* a financial situation where an investor borrows against an investment, and the loan interest payments exceed the income from the investment, resulting in a negative cash flow and thus taxation benefits.

neglect /nə'glɛkt/ *v.t.* **1.** to pay no attention to; disregard. **2.** to be remiss in care for or treatment of. – *n.* **3.** the act or fact of neglecting; disregard. **4.** the fact or state of being neglected; negligence.

negligee /'nɛgləʒeɪ/ *n.* a woman's dressing-gown, especially a very flimsy one, of nylon, or the like.

negligent /'nɛglədʒənt/ *adj.* guilty of or characterised by neglect. – **negligence**, *n.*

negligible /'nɛglədʒəbəl/ *adj.* that may be neglected or disregarded; very little.

negotiate /nə'goʊʃieɪt/ *v.t.,* **-ated**, **-ating**. **1.** to arrange for or bring about by discussion and settlement of terms. **2.** to clear or pass (an obstacle, etc.). **3.** to transfer (a bill of exchange, etc.) by assignment, endorsement, or delivery. **4.** to dispose of by sale or transfer. – **negotiable**, *adj.* – **negotiation**, *n.*

neigh /neɪ/ *n.* the sound a horse makes; a whinny.

neighbour = neighbor /'neɪbə/ *n.* **1.** someone who lives near another. – *v.i.* **2.** to live or be situated nearby.

neighbourhood = neighborhood /'neɪbəhʊd/ *n.* **1.** the region near or about some place or thing. **2.** a district or locality, often with reference to its character or inhabitants.

neither /'naɪðə, 'niðə/ *adj., pron., conj.* not either.

nematode /'nɛmətoʊd/ *n.* an elongated, smooth roundworm.

nemesis /'nɛməsəs/ *n., pl.* **-meses** /-məsiz/. an agent of retribution or punishment.

neo- a word element meaning 'new', 'recent'.

neologism /ni'ɒlədʒɪzəm/ *n.* **1.** a new word or phrase. **2.** a new doctrine.

neon /'niɒn/ *n.* a chemically inert gaseous element occurring in small amounts in the earth's atmosphere, and chiefly used in orange-red tubular electrical discharge lamps. *Symbol*: Ne

neonate /'nioʊneɪt/ *n.* a newborn child.

neophyte /'nioʊfaɪt/ *n.* **1.** a converted heathen, heretic, etc. **2.** a beginner.

nephew /'nɛfju, 'nɛvju/ *n.* **1.** a son of one's brother or sister. **2.** a son of one's husband's or wife's brother or sister.

nephritis /nə'fraɪtəs/ *n.* inflammation of the kidneys.

nephro- a word element referring to the kidneys. Also, **nephr-**.

nepotism /'nɛpətɪzəm/ *n.* patronage bestowed in consideration of family relationship and not of merit.

nerve /nɜv/ *n.* **1.** one or more bundles of fibres, forming part of a system which conveys impulses of sensation, motion, etc., between the brain or spinal cord and other parts of the body. **2.** firmness or courage in trying circumstances. **3.** (*pl.*) nervousness. **4.** *Colloquial* impertinent assurance.

nervous /'nɜvəs/ *adj.* **1.** of or relating to the nerves. **2.** characterised by or attended with acute uneasiness or apprehension.

nervy /'nɜvi/ *adj.,* **-vier**, **-viest**. **1.** nervous. **2.** excitable; irritable.

-ness a suffix used to form, from adjectives and participles, nouns denoting quality or state (also often, by extension, something exemplifying a quality or state), as in *darkness, goodness, kindness*.

nest /nɛst/ *n.* **1.** a structure formed or a place used by a bird for incubation and the rearing of its young. **2.** an assemblage of things lying or set close together, as a series of tables, trays, etc., that fit within each other. – *v.i.* **3.** to build or have a nest.

nest egg *n.* money saved as the basis of a fund or for emergencies.

nestle /'nɛsəl/ *v.i.,* **-tled**, **-tling**. to lie close and snug, like a bird in a nest; snuggle or cuddle.

net[1] /nɛt/ *n.* **1.** a lacelike fabric with a uniform mesh of cotton, silk, etc. **2.** a piece or bag of net for catching fish, butterflies, etc.

net[2] /nɛt/ *adj., n., v.,* **netted, netting**. – *adj.* **1.** exclusive of deductions, as for charges, expenses, loss, discount, etc. **2.** sold at net prices. **3.** ultimate; conclusive. – *n.* **4.** net income, profits, or the like. – *v.t.* **5.** to gain or produce as clear profit. Also, **nett**.

Net /nɛt/ *n.* **the → Internet**.

netball /'nɛtbɔl/ *n.* a game similar to basketball usually played by women.

nether /'nɛðə/ *adj.* **1.** lying, or conceived as lying, beneath the earth's surface; infernal. **2.** lower or under.

nettle /nɛtl/ *n.* a plant with stinging hairs.

network /'nɛtwɜk/ *n.* **1.** a system of interconnected people, companies, television stations, etc. **2.** *Computers* a system of connecting computer systems or peripheral devices, each one remote from the others.

neural /'njurəl/ *adj.* of or relating to a nerve or the nervous system.

neuro- a word element meaning 'tendon', 'nerve'. Also, **neur-**.

neuroscience /'njuroʊ,saɪəns/ *n.* the study of the nervous system. – **neuroscientist**, *n.*

neurosis /nju'roʊsəs/ *n., pl.* **-roses** /-'roʊsiz/. emotional disorder in which feelings of anxiety, obsessional thoughts, compulsive acts, and physical complaints without objective evidence of disease, in various patterns, dominate the personality. – **neurotic**, *adj., n.*

neuter /'njutə/ *adj.* **1.** *Grammar* of a gender which is neither masculine or feminine. **2.** sexless, or of indeterminate sex.

neutral /'njutrəl/ *adj.* **1.** (of a person or state) refraining from taking part in a controversy or war between others. **2.** of no particular kind, colour, characteristics, etc.; indefinite. **3.** *Chemistry* exhibiting neither acid nor alkaline qualities. **4.** *Electricity* neither positive nor negative; not electrified; not magnetised. – *n.* **5.** a person or a state that remains neutral, as in a war. **6.** *Machinery* the position or state of disengaged gears or other interconnecting parts. – **neutralise = neutralize**, *v.* – **neutrality**, *n.*

neutron /'njutrɒn/ *n.* an elementary particle which is a constituent of all atomic nuclei except normal hydrogen. It has zero electric charge and approximately the same mass as the proton.

neutron bomb *n.* a nuclear weapon which releases a shower of neutrons but relatively little blast, thus killing people but causing relatively little damage to property. Also, **clean bomb**.

never /'nɛvə/ *adv.* not ever; at no time.

nevertheless /nɛvəðə'lɛs/ *adv.* nonetheless; notwithstanding; however.

new /nju/ *adj.* **1.** of recent origin or production, or having only lately come or been brought into being. **2.** of a kind now existing or appearing for the first time; novel. **3.** unfamiliar or strange (fol. by *to*). **4.** coming or occurring afresh; further; additional. **5.** fresh or unused. **6.** other than the former or the old. – *adv.* **7.** recently or lately. **8.** freshly; anew or afresh.

New Age *n.* a social revolution which replaces traditional attitudes with a new approach based on a loose mysticism, especially in health and medicine and attitudes to the environment.

newel /'njuəl/ *n.* a central pillar or upright from which the steps of a winding stair radiate.

news /njuz/ *pl. n.* **1.** (*construed as sing.*) a report of any recent event, situation, etc. **2.** the report of events published in a newspaper, journal, radio, television, or any other medium. **3.** information not previously known.

newsgroup /'njuzgrup/ *n.* *Computers* an online discussion forum for a particular topic, in which users can write and post messages, and read messages posted by others.

newspaper /'njuzpeɪpə/ *n.* a printed publication issued at regular intervals, usually daily or weekly, and commonly containing news, comment, features, and advertisements.

newsprint /'njuzprɪnt/ *n.* paper used or made to print newspapers on.

newsreel /'njuzril/ *n.* a short film presenting current news events.

newt /njut/ *n.* any of various small, semiaquatic salamanders.

newton /'njutn/ *n.* the derived SI unit of force. *Symbol*: N

next /nɛkst/ *adj.* (*superlative of* **nigh**) *adv.* – *adj.* **1.** immediately following. **2.** nearest. – *adv.* **3.** in the nearest place, time, importance, etc. **4.** on the first subsequent occasion.

next of kin *n.* a person's nearest relative or relatives.

nexus /'nɛksəs/ *n., pl.* **nexus**. a tie or link; a means of connection.

nib /nɪb/ *n.* the point of a pen, especially a small, tapering metallic device having a split tip for drawing up ink and for writing.

nibble /'nɪbəl/ *v.,* **-bled**, **-bling**, *n.* – *v.i.* **1.** to bite off small bits. **2.** to evince interest (*at*) without actually accepting. – *v.t.* **3.** to bite off small bits of (a thing). – *n.* **4.** a small morsel or bit.

nice /naɪs/ *adj.,* **nicer**, **nicest**. **1.** pleasing; agreeable; delightful. **2.** characterised by or requiring great accuracy, precision, skill, or delicacy. **3.** minute, fine, or subtle, as a distinction. – **nicety**, *n.*

niche /niʃ, nɪtʃ/ *n.* **1.** an ornamental recess in a wall, etc. **2.** a place or position suitable or appropriate for a person or thing.

niche market *n.* a section of a market (def. 4), usually small, which can be highly profitable if the product supplied is specially designed to meet targeted needs.

nick[1] /nɪk/ *n.* **1.** a notch, groove, or the like, cut into or existing in a thing. – *v.t.* **2.** to make a nick or nicks in; notch.

nick[2] /nɪk/ *v.t.* *Colloquial* **1.** to capture or arrest. **2.** to steal.

nickel /'nɪkəl/ *n.* *Chemistry* a hard, silvery white, ductile and malleable metallic element. *Symbol*: Ni

nickname /'nɪkneɪm/ *n.* a name added to or substituted for the proper name of a person, place, etc., as in ridicule or familiarity.

nicotine /nɪkə'tin, 'nɪkətin/ *n.* a poisonous alkaloid, the active principle of tobacco.

niece /nis/ *n.* **1.** a daughter of one's brother or sister. **2.** a daughter of one's husband's or wife's brother or sister.

nifty /'nɪfti/ *adj.,* **-tier**, **-tiest**. *Colloquial* smart; stylish; fine.

niggard /'nɪgəd/ *n. Rare* a parsimonious or stingy person. – **niggardly**, *adj.*

niggle /'nɪgəl/ *v.,* **-gled**, **-gling**. – *v.i.* **1.** to make constant petty criticisms. – *v.t.* **2.** to irritate; annoy.

nigh /naɪ/ *adv., adj.,* **nigher**, **nighest** *or* **next**. – *adv.* **1.** near in space, time, or relation. – *adj.* **2.** being near; not distant; near in relationship. **3.** short or direct.

night /naɪt/ *n.* the interval of darkness between sunset and sunrise.

nightcap /'naɪtkæp/ *n. Colloquial* an alcoholic or other drink, especially a hot one, taken before going to bed.

nightingale /'naɪtɪŋgeɪl/ *n.* a small migratory bird of the thrush family, noted for the melodious song of the male.

nightly /'naɪtli/ *adj.* **1.** coming, occurring, appearing, or active at night. **2.** coming or occurring each night. – *adv.* **3.** at or by night. **4.** on every night.

nightmare /'naɪtmɛə/ *n.* **1.** a condition during sleep, or a dream, marked by a feeling of suffocation or distress, with acute fear, anxiety, or other painful emotion. **2.** a condition, thought, or experience suggestive of a nightmare in sleep.

nihilism /'naɪəlɪzəm, 'ni-/ *n.* total disbelief in religion or moral principles and obligations, or in established laws and institutions.

nil /nɪl/ *n.* nothing.

nimble /'nɪmbəl/ *adj.,* **-bler**, **-blest**. quick and light in movement; moving with ease; agile; active; rapid.

nimbus /'nɪmbəs/ *n., pl.* **-bi** /-baɪ/, **-buses**. a disc or otherwise shaped figure representing a radiance about the head of a divine or sacred personage, etc.; a halo.

nincompoop /'nɪŋkəmpup/ *n.* a fool.

nine /naɪn/ *n.* a cardinal number, eight plus one. – **ninth**, *adj., n.*

nineteen /naɪn'tin, 'naɪntin/ *n.* a cardinal number, ten plus nine. – **nineteenth**, *adj., n.*

ninety /'naɪnti/ *n.* a cardinal number, ten times nine. – **ninetieth**, *adj., n.*

ninny /'nɪni/ *n., pl.* **-nies**. a fool.

nip[1] /nɪp/ *v.,* **nipped**, **nipping**. – *v.t.* **1.** to compress sharply between two surfaces or points; pinch or bite. **2.** to check in growth or development. **3.** to affect sharply and painfully or injuriously, as cold does. – *v.i.* **4.** *Colloquial* to move or go suddenly or quickly, or slip (fol. by *away*, *off*, *up*, etc.).

nip[2] /nɪp/ *n.* **1.** a small drink; a sip. **2.** a small measure of spirits.

nipple /'nɪpəl/ *n.* **1.** a protuberance of the udder or breast where, in the female, the milk ducts discharge; a teat. **2.** something resembling it.

nippy /'nɪpi/ *adj.,* **-pier**, **-piest**. biting, as the cold.

nit /nɪt/ *n.* the egg of a parasitic insect attached to a hair, or fibre of clothing; particularly the egg of a louse.

nitrogen /'naɪtrədʒən/ *n.* a colourless, odourless, gaseous element which forms about four-fifths of the volume of the atmosphere. *Symbol*: N – **nitrogenous**, *adj.*

nitroglycerine /naɪtroʊ'glɪsərin/ *n.* a colourless, highly explosive oil.

nitty-gritty /'nɪti-ˌgrɪti/ *n. Colloquial* the hard core of a matter.

nitwit /'nɪtwɪt/ *n.* a slow-witted or foolish person.

nix /nɪks/ *n. Colloquial* nothing.

no[1] /noʊ/ *adv., n., pl.* **noes**. – *adv.* **1.** a word used: to express dissent, denial, or refusal, as in response (opposed to *yes*). **2.** not in any degree; not at all (used with a comparative). – *n.* **3.** a denial or refusal. **4.** a negative vote or voter.

no[2] /noʊ/ *adj.* **1.** not any. **2.** not at all; very far from being; not at all a.

nobble /'nɒbəl/ *v.t.,* **-bled**, **-bling**. *Colloquial* to disable (a horse), as by drugging it.

noble /'noʊbəl/ *adj.,* **nobler**, **noblest**, *n.* – *adj.* **1.** distinguished by birth, rank, or title. **2.** of an exalted moral character or excellence. **3.** of an admirably high quality; notably superior. **4.** *Chemistry* inert; chemically inactive. – *n.* **5.** a person of noble birth or rank; a nobleman. – **nobility**, *n.*

nobody /'noʊbɒdi, -bədi/ *pron., n., pl.* **-bodies**. – *pron.* **1.** no person. – *n.* **2.** a person of no importance, especially socially.

nocturnal /nɒk'tɜnəl/ *adj.* **1.** of or relating to the night. **2.** active by night.

nod /nɒd/ *v.,* **nodded**, **nodding**, *n.* – *v.i.* **1.** to make a slight, quick inclination of the head, as in assent, greeting, command, etc. **2. nod off,** *Colloquial* to go to sleep. – *v.t.* **3.** to incline (the head) in a short, quick movement, as of assent, greeting, etc. – *n.* **4.** a short, quick inclination of the head, as in assent, greeting, command, or drowsiness.

node /noʊd/ *n.* **1.** a knot, protuberance, or knob. **2.** a centring point of component parts. **3.** *Geometry* a point on a curve or surface, at which there can be more than one tangent line or plane. – **nodal**, *adj.*

no-fault /'noʊ-fɔlt/ *adj.* of or relating to legislation, insurance, etc., which does not depend on the assignation of guilt or blame to any of the parties involved.

noggin /'nɒgən/ *n.* **1.** a small measure of spirits. **2.** *Colloquial* the head.

noise /nɔɪz/ *n.* **1.** sound, especially of a loud, harsh, or confused kind. **2.** loud shouting, outcry, or clamour. – **noisy**, *adj.*

noisome /'nɔɪsəm/ *adj.* offensive.

no-liability company *n.* an exploration company in which the acceptance or purchase of a partly paid share does not legally bind the holder to pay up the uncalled part of the capital.

nomad /'noʊmæd/ *n.* **1.** one of a race or tribe without fixed abode. **2.** any wanderer. – **nomadic**, *adj.*

nomenclature /nə'mɛnklətʃə, 'noʊmənkleɪtʃə/ *n.* **1.** a set or system of names or terms. **2.** the terms forming such a set.

nominal /'nɒmənəl/ *adj.* **1.** being such in name only; so-called. **2.** (of a price, consideration, etc.) named as a mere matter of form, being trifling in comparison with the actual value. **3.** *Grammar* used as or like a noun.

nominal value *n.* face value.

nominal wages *pl. n.* wages measured in terms of money and not by their ability to command goods and services. Cf. **real wages**.

nominate /ˈnɒməneɪt/ *v.t.*, **-nated**, **-nating**. to propose as a proper person for appointment or election to an office. – **nomination**, *n.*

nominee /nɒməˈni/ *n.* one nominated as to fill an office or stand for election.

-nomy a final word element meaning 'distribution', 'arrangement', 'management', or having reference to laws or government, as in *astronomy*, *economy*, *taxonomy*.

non- a prefix indicating: **1.** exclusion from a specified class or group. **2.** objective negation or opposition. **3.** spuriousness or failure to fulfil a claim. **4.** the absence of activity or achievement in the area named.

nonagenarian /nɒnədʒəˈnɛəriən, noʊ-/ *adj.* of the age of 90 years, or between 90 and 100 years old.

nonagon /ˈnɒnəgɒn, -gən/ *n.* a polygon having nine angles and nine sides.

nonce /nɒns/ *n.* the one or particular occasion or purpose.

nonchalant /ˈnɒnʃələnt/ *adj.* coolly unconcerned, indifferent, or unexcited; casual. – **nonchalance**, *n.*

non-committal /ˈnɒn-kəmɪtl/ *adj.* not committing oneself, or not involving committal, to a particular view, course, or the like.

nonconformity /nɒnkənˈfɔməti/ *n.* **1.** lack of conformity or agreement. **2.** failure or refusal to conform, as to an established church. – **nonconformist**, *n.*

nondescript /ˈnɒndəskrɪpt/ *adj.* of no recognised, definite, or particular type or kind.

none /nʌn/ *pron.* **1.** no one; not one. **2.** not any, as of something indicated. **3.** no part; nothing. **4.** (*construed as pl.*) no, or not any, persons or things. – *adv.* **5.** to no extent; in no way; not at all.

nonentity /nɒnˈɛntəti/ *n.*, *pl.* **-ties**. a person or thing of no importance.

nonetheless /nʌnðəˈlɛs/ *adv.* however.

nong /nɒŋ/ *n.* *Colloquial* a fool; an idiot.

nonplus /nɒnˈplʌs/ *v.*, **-plussed**, **-plussing**, *n.* – *v.t.* **1.** to puzzle completely. – *n.* **2.** a state of utter perplexity.

non-productive /ˈnɒn-prədʌktɪv/ *adj.* not producing goods directly, as employees in charge of personnel, inspectors, etc.

non-profit-making /nɒn-ˈprɒfət-meɪkɪŋ/ *adj.* established or entered into for some motive other than the hope of making a profit. Also, **non-profit**.

non-renounceable issue *n.* → **entitlement issue**.

nonsense /ˈnɒnsəns/ *n.* that which makes no sense or is lacking in sense. – **nonsensical**, *adj.*

non sequitur /nɒn ˈsɛkwɪtə/ *n.* an inference or a conclusion which does not follow from the premises.

noodle /ˈnudl/ *n.* a type of pasta, cut into long, narrow, flat strips and served in soups or, with a sauce, as a main dish.

nook /nʊk/ *n.* **1.** a corner, as in a room. **2.** any secluded or obscure corner.

noon /nun/ *n.* midday.

no-one /ˈnoʊ-wʌn/ *pron.* nobody.

noose /nus/ *n.* a loop with a running knot, as in a snare, lasso, hangman's halter, etc., which tightens as the rope is pulled.

no-par /ˈnoʊ-pa/ *adj.* without par, or face, value.

nor /nɔ/ *conj.* a negative conjunction used: **1.** as the correlative to a preceding *neither*: *he could neither read nor write*. **2.** to continue the force of a negative, such as *not*, *no*, *never*, etc., occurring in a preceding clause. **3.** after an affirmative clause, or as a continuative, in the sense of *and ... not*: *they are happy, nor need we mourn*.

nor' /nɔ/ *n.*, *adj.*, *adv.* *Chiefly Nautical* north.

norm /nɔm/ *n.* **1.** a standard, model, or pattern. **2.** a mean or average.

normal /ˈnɔməl/ *adj.* **1.** conforming to the standard or the common type; regular, usual, natural, or not abnormal. **2.** serving to fix a standard. – *n.* **3.** the standard or type. **4.** the normal form or state; the average or mean. – **normality**, *n.*

north /nɔθ/ *n.* **1.** a cardinal point of the compass lying in the plane of the meridian and to the right of a person facing the setting sun or west. – *adj.* **2.** lying or proceeding towards the north. **3.** coming from the north, as a wind. – *adv.* **4.** towards or in the north. **5.** from the north. Also, *especially Nautical*, **nor'**. – **northerly**, *adj.*, *n.* – **northern**, *adj.*

nose /noʊz/ *n.*, *v.*, **nosed**, **nosing**. – *n.* **1.** the part of the face or head which contains the nostrils, affording passage for air in respiration, etc. **2.** this part as the organ of smell. **3.** something regarded as resembling the nose of a person or animal. – *v.t.* **4.** to perceive by or as by the nose or the sense of smell. **5.** to touch or rub with the nose; nuzzle. – *v.i.* **6.** to smell or sniff. **7.** to seek as if by smelling or scent (fol. by *after*, *for*, etc.); pry (fol. by *about*, *into*, etc.).

nosedive /ˈnoʊzdaɪv/ *n.* a plunge of an aeroplane with the fore part of the craft vertically downwards.

nosegay /ˈnoʊzgeɪ/ *n.* a bunch of flowers, or herbs; a bouquet; a posy.

nosh /nɒʃ/ *v.i.* *Colloquial* to eat; have a snack or a meal.

nostalgia /nɒsˈtældʒə/ *n.* a longing and desire for home, family and friends, or the past. – **nostalgic**, *adj.*

nostril /ˈnɒstrəl/ *n.* one of the external openings of the nose.

nostrum /ˈnɒstrəm/ *n.* **1.** a patent medicine. **2.** a quack medicine.

nosy = nosey /ˈnoʊzi/ *adj.*, **-sier**, **-siest**. *Colloquial* prying; inquisitive.

not /nɒt/ *adv.* (a word expressing negation, denial, refusal, or prohibition).

nota bene /noʊtə ˈbɛni, ˈbeɪneɪ/ note well.

notable /ˈnoʊtəbəl/ *adj.* **1.** worthy of note or notice; noteworthy. **2.** prominent, important, or distinguished, as persons.

notary public /'noutəri/ *n., pl.* **notaries public**. an official, usually a solicitor, authorised to certify contracts, acknowledge deeds, take affidavits, protest bills of exchange.

notation /nou'teɪʃən/ *n.* a system of graphic symbols for a specialised use, other than ordinary writing.

notch /nɒtʃ/ *n.* **1.** a more or less angular cut, indentation, or hollow in a narrow object or surface or an edge. – *v.t.* **2.** to cut or make a notch or notches in. **3.** to score, as in a game (fol. by *up*).

note /nout/ *n., v.,* **noted**, **noting**. – *n.* **1.** a brief record of something set down to assist the memory, or for reference or development. **2.** a short informal letter. **3.** a certificate, as of a government or a bank, passing current as money; a banknote. **4.** importance or consequence. **5.** notice, observation, or heed. **6.** *Music* a sign or character used to represent a sound, the position and form of which indicates the pitch and duration of the sound. **7.** way of speaking or thinking. – *v.t.* **8.** to mark down, as in writing; make a memorandum of. **9.** to observe carefully; give attention or heed to.

noteworthy /'noutwɜði/ *adj.* worthy of note or notice; notable.

nothing /'nʌθɪŋ/ *n.* **1.** no thing; not anything; naught. **2.** a cipher or nought. – *adv.* **3.** in no respect or degree; not at all.

notice /'noutəs/ *n., v.,* **-ticed**, **-ticing**. – *n.* **1.** information or intelligence. **2.** an intimation or warning. **3.** a note, placard, or the like conveying information or warning. **4.** a notification of the termination, at a specified time, of an agreement, as for renting or employment, given by one of the parties to the agreement. **5.** observation, perception, attention, or heed. – *v.t.* **6.** to pay attention to or take notice of. **7.** to perceive.

notify /'noutəfaɪ/ *v.t.,* **-fied**, **-fying**. to give notice to, or inform, of something. – **notification**, *n.*

notion /'nouʃən/ *n.* a more or less general, vague or imperfect conception or idea of something.

not negotiable /nə'gouʃəbəl/ *adj.* of or relating to a cheque which is crossed, indicating that the person to whom it is given has no better title to it than the person had from whom it was received; popularly and inaccurately held to mean that the cheque can be paid only into the account, the name of which appears on the cheque.

notorious /nə'tɔriəs/ *adj.* widely but unfavourably known. – **notoriety**, *n.*

notwithstanding /ˌnɒtwɪθ'stændɪŋ/ *prep.* **1.** in spite of. – *adv.* **2.** nevertheless. – *conj.* **3.** although.

nougat /'nuga/ *n.* a hard, pastelike sweet.

nought /nɔt/ *n.* a cipher (0); zero.

noun /naun/ *n.* the part of speech comprising words denoting person, places, things, and such other words as show similar grammatical behaviour, as English *friend, city, desk, whiteness, virtue.*

nourish /'nʌrɪʃ/ *v.t.* **1.** to sustain with food or nutriment; supply with what is necessary for maintaining life. **2.** to foster or promote. – **nourishment**, *n.*

nous /naus/ *n. Colloquial* commonsense.

nouvelle cuisine /ˌnuvɛl kwi'zin/ *n.* a style of cooking emphasising small, simple meals, delicately flavoured and garnished.

novel[1] /'nɒvəl/ *n.* a fictitious prose narrative of considerable length. – **novelist**, *n.*

novel[2] /'nɒvəl/ *adj.* of a new kind, or different from anything seen or known before.

novelty /'nɒvəlti/ *n., pl.* **-ties**. **1.** novel character, newness, or strangeness. **2.** a novel thing, experience, or proceeding.

novice /'nɒvəs/ *n.* someone who is new to the circumstances, work, etc., in which he or she is placed.

novitiate /nou'vɪʃiət, -ieɪt/ *n.* **1.** the state or period of being a novice of a religious order or congregation. **2.** the quarters occupied by religious novices during probation. Also, **noviciate**.

now /nau/ *adv.* **1.** at the present time or moment. **2.** (more emphatically) immediately or at once. **3.** at the time or moment only just past. **4.** in these present times; nowadays. – *conj.* **5.** now that; since, or seeing that.

nowadays /'nauədeɪz/ *adv.* at the present day; in these times.

nowhere /'nouwɛə/ *adv.* in, at, or to no place; not anywhere.

noxious /'nɒkʃəs/ *adj.* **1.** harmful or injurious to health or physical wellbeing. **2.** (of an animal, insect, plant, etc.) declared harmful by statute law for compulsory eradication.

nozzle /'nɒzəl/ *n.* a projecting spout, terminal discharging pipe, or the like, as of a hose or rocket.

-n't a combining form of **not**, as in *didn't, won't, can't.*

nth /ɛnθ/ *adj.* denoting the last in a series of infinitely decreasing or increasing values, amounts, etc.

nuance /'njuɒns, nju'ans/ *n.* a shade of colour, expression, meaning, feeling, etc.

nub /nʌb/ *n.* **1.** a knob or protuberance. **2.** *Colloquial* the point or gist of anything.

nubile /'njubaɪl/ *adj.* (of a girl or young woman) marriageable, especially as to age or physical development.

nuclear /'njukliə/ *adj.* **1.** of, relating to, or forming a nucleus. **2.** relating to, involving, or powered by atomic energy.

nuclei /'njukliaɪ/ *n.* plural of **nucleus**.

nucleonics /njukli'ɒnɪks/ *n.* the techniques of applying nuclear science to industry and to biology, physics, chemistry, and other sciences.

nucleus /'njukliəs/ *n., pl.* **-clei** /-kliaɪ/, **-cleuses**. **1.** a central part or thing about which other parts or things are grouped. **2.** *Biology* a differentiated mass (usually rounded) of protoplasm, encased in a delicate membrane, present in the interior of nearly all living cells and forming an essential element in their growth metabolism and reproduction. **3.** *Physics* the central core of an atom, composed of protons and neutrons. It has a net positive charge equal to the number of protons.

nude /njud/ *adj.* **1.** naked or unclothed, as a person, the body, etc. **2.** without the usual coverings, furnishings, etc.; bare. – **nudity**, *n.*

nudge /nʌdʒ/ *v.*, **nudged**, **nudging**, *n.* – *v.t.* **1.** to push slightly or jog, especially with the elbow, as in calling attention or giving a hint or with sly meaning. – *n.* **2.** a slight push or jog.

nudism /'njudɪzəm/ *n.* the practice of going nude as a means of healthful living. – **nudist**, *n.*

nugatory /'njugətəri, -tri/ *adj.* worthless.

nugget /'nʌgət/ *n.* **1.** a lump of something. **2.** a lump of native gold.

nuggety /'nʌgəti/ *adj.* **1.** of or resembling a nugget. **2.** *Colloquial* (of a person) short and sturdy. Also, **nuggetty**.

nuisance /'njusəns/ *n.* **1.** a highly obnoxious or annoying thing or person. **2.** something offensive or annoying to individuals or to the community, to the prejudice of their legal rights.

null /nʌl/ *adj.* **1.** of no effect, consequence, or significance. **2.** being none, lacking, or non-existent. – **nullify**, *v.*

nulla-nulla /'nʌlə-nʌlə/ *n.* an Aboriginal club or heavy weapon. Also, **nulla**.

numb /nʌm/ *adj.* deprived of or deficient in the power of sensation and movement.

numbat /'nʌmbæt/ *n.* a small, slender, reddish-brown, diurnal marsupial.

number /'nʌmbə/ *n.* **1.** the sum, total, count, or aggregate of a collection of units or any generalisation of this concept. **2.** the particular numeral assigned to anything in order to fix its place in a series. **3.** a word or symbol, or a combination of words or symbols, used in counting or to denote a total. **4.** a quantity (large or small) of individuals. **5.** (*pl.*) numerical strength or superiority, as in a political party, organisation, etc. **6.** an article of merchandise. – *v.t.* **7.** to ascertain the number of. **8.** to mark with or distinguish by a number or numbers. **9.** to amount to in number. – *v.i.* **10.** to be numbered or included.

number crunching *n.* *Colloquial* long, laborious, recursive mathematical computation, especially as done by computers.

numeral /'njumərəl/ *n.* **1.** a word or words expressing a number. **2.** a letter or figure, or a group of letters or figures, denoting a number.

numerate /'njuməreɪt/ *v.t.*, **-rated**, **-rating**. to number; count; enumerate.

numerator /'njuməreɪtə/ *n.* *Mathematics* that term (usually written above the line) of a fraction which shows how many parts of a unit are taken.

numerical /nju'merɪkəl/ *adj.* **1.** of or relating to number; of the nature of number. **2.** denoting number or a number.

numerical analysis *n.* the use of numerical methods for the analysis of problems and the ascertaining of margins of error, usually with the aid of a computer.

numerous /'njumərəs/ *adj.* very many.

numismatics /njuməz'mætɪks/ *n.* the science of coins and medals.

nun /nʌn/ *n.* a woman devoted to a religious life under vows.

nunnery /'nʌnəri/ *n.*, *pl.* **-neries**. a religious house for nuns; a convent.

nuptial /'nʌpʃəl/ *adj.* of or relating to marriage or the marriage ceremony.

nurse /nɜs/ *n.*, *v.*, **nursed**, **nursing**. – *n.* **1.** a person who has the care of the sick or infirm. – *v.t.* **2.** to tend in sickness or infirmity. **3.** to seek to cure (a cold, etc.) by taking care of oneself. **4.** to look after carefully so as to promote growth, development, etc.; foster; cherish (a feeling, etc.). **5.** to hold in the lap while travelling. **6.** to suckle (an infant). – *v.i.* **7.** to act as nurse; tend the sick or infirm. **8.** to suckle a child.

nursery /'nɜsri/ *n.*, *pl.* **-eries**. **1.** a room or place set apart for young children. **2.** a place where young trees or other plants are raised for transplanting or for sale.

nurture /'nɜtʃə/ *v.t.*, **-tured**, **-turing**. to feed, nourish, or support during the stages of growth, as children or young; rear.

nut /nʌt/ *n.* **1.** a dry fruit consisting of an edible kernel or meat enclosed in a woody or leathery shell. **2.** any of various devices or parts supposed in some way to resemble a nut. **3.** *Colloquial* an enthusiast. **4.** *Colloquial* a foolish or eccentric person. **5.** *Colloquial* an insane person. **6.** a perforated block (usually of metal) with an internal thread or female screw, used to screw on the end of a bolt, etc.

nutmeg /'nʌtmeg/ *n.* an aromatic spice.

nutrient /'njutriənt/ *adj.* **1.** nourishing; affording nutriment. – *n.* **2.** a nutrient substance.

nutriment /'njutrəmənt/ *n.* that which nourishes; nourishment; food.

nutrition /nju'trɪʃən/ *n.* **1.** the act or process of nourishing or of being nourished. **2.** the process by which the food material taken into an organism is converted into living tissue, etc.

nutritious /nju'trɪʃəs/ *adj.* nourishing, especially in a high degree.

nutritive /'njutrətɪv/ *adj.* serving to nourish; affording nutriment.

nuzzle /'nʌzəl/ *v.i.*, **-zled**, **-zling**. **1.** to burrow or root with the nose, as an animal does. **2.** to snuggle or cuddle up with someone or something.

nylon /'naɪlɒn/ *n.* a synthetic material used for yarn, bristles, etc.

nymph /nɪmf/ *n.* **1.** one of a numerous class of inferior divinities of mythology, conceived as beautiful maidens inhabiting the sea, rivers, woods, trees, mountains, meadows, etc. **2.** a beautiful or graceful young woman.

nymphomania /nɪmfə'meɪniə/ *n.* uncontrollable sexual desire in women. – **nymphomaniac**, *adj.*, *n.*

O o

O, o /oʊ/ *n., pl.* **O's** *or* **Os**, **o's** *or* **os**. **1.** the 15th letter of the English alphabet. **2.** the Arabic cipher; zero; nought (0).

o' /ə/ *prep.* an abbreviated form of **of**.

o-[1] *Chemistry* an abridgment of **ortho-**.

o-[2] variant of **ob-**, before *m*.

-o- an ending for the first element of many compounds, often used as a connective, as in *Franco-Italian, speedometer,* etc.

-o a suffix used: **1.** in colloquial abbreviations, as *arvo* for *afternoon, combo* for *combination.* **2.** in colloquial responses showing compliance or agreement, as *goodo, righto.*

oaf /oʊf/ *n.* a lout.

oak /oʊk/ *n.* a large tree which bears acorns.

oar /ɔ/ *n.* **1.** a long shaft of wood with a blade at one end, used for propelling a boat. **2. put one's oar in,** to interfere; meddle.

oasis /oʊ'eɪsəs/ *n., pl.* **oases** /oʊ'eɪsiz/. a fertile place in a desert region.

oat /oʊt/ *n.* **1.** (*usu. pl.*) a cereal grass cultivated for its edible seed. **2.** (*pl.*) the seeds. **3. sow one's wild oats,** to indulge in the excesses or follies of youth.

oatcake /'oʊtkeɪk/ *n.* a cake, usually thin and brittle, made of oatmeal.

oath /oʊθ/ *n., pl.* **oaths** /oʊðz/. **1.** a solemn appeal to God, or to some revered person or thing, in attestation of the truth of a statement or the binding character of a promise. **2.** a statement or promise strengthened by such an appeal. **3.** any profane expression; a curse.

ob- a prefix meaning 'towards', 'to', 'on', 'over', 'against', now used also with the sense of 'reversely' or 'inversely'. Also, **o-**, **oc-**, **of-**, **op-**.

obdurate /'ɒbdʒərət/ *adj.* hardened against persuasions or tender feelings.

obedient /ə'bidiənt/ *adj.* obeying, or willing to obey. – **obedience**, *n.*

obeisance /oʊ'beɪsəns/ *n.* deference or homage.

obelisk /'ɒbələsk/ *n.* a tapering, four-sided shaft of stone.

obese /oʊ'bis/ *adj.* excessively fat. – **obesity**, *n.*

obey /oʊ'beɪ/ *v.t.* **1.** to comply with or fulfil the commands or instructions of. **2.** (of things) to respond conformably in action to. – *v.i.* **3.** to be obedient.

obituary /ə'bɪtʃəri/ *n.* a notice of the death of a person, often with a brief biographical sketch, as in a newspaper.

object /'ɒbdʒɛkt/ *n.,* /əb'dʒɛkt/ *v.* – *n.* **1.** a visible or tangible thing. **2.** the end towards which effort is directed. **3.** *Grammar* the noun or its substitute which represents the goal of an action or the ending point of a relation. – *v.i.* **4.** to express or feel disapproval; be averse.

objection /əb'dʒɛkʃən/ *n.* something adduced or said in disagreement or disapproval.

objectionable /əb'dʒɛkʃənəbəl/ *adj.* that may be objected to; unpleasant; offensive.

objective /əb'dʒɛktɪv/ *n.* **1.** an end towards which efforts are directed; something aimed at. – *adj.* **2.** free from personal feelings or prejudice; unbiased. **3.** of or relating to an object or objects. – **objectivity**, *n.*

obligation /ɒblə'geɪʃən/ *n.* **1.** a binding requirement as to action; duty. **2.** *Law* an agreement enforceable by law. **3.** a benefit, favour, or service, for which gratitude is due. **4.** the state or fact of being indebted for a benefit, favour, or service. – **obligate**, *v.*

obligatory /ɒ'blɪgətəri, -tri/ *adj.* required as a matter of obligation.

oblige /ə'blaɪdʒ/ *v.,* **obliged**, **obliging**. – *v.t.* **1.** to require or constrain, as by law, command, conscience, or necessity. **2.** to place under a debt of gratitude for some benefit, favour, or service. **3.** to favour or accommodate (fol. by *with*). – *v.i.* **4.** to do something as a favour.

obliging /ə'blaɪdʒɪŋ/ *adj.* disposed to do favours or services, as a person.

oblique /ə'blik/ *adj.* **1.** neither perpendicular nor parallel to a given line or surface. **2.** not straight or direct.

obliterate /ə'blɪtəreɪt/ *v.t.,* **-rated**, **-rating**. to remove all traces of; do away with; destroy.

oblivion /ə'blɪviən/ *n.* the state of being forgotten.

oblivious /ə'blɪviəs/ *adj.* unmindful; unconscious (fol. by *of* or *to*).

oblong /'ɒblɒŋ/ *adj.* **1.** in the form of a rectangle; of greater length than breadth. – *n.* **2.** an oblong figure.

obnoxious /əb'nɒkʃəs, ɒb-/ *adj.* objectionable; offensive; odious.

oboe /'oʊboʊ/ *n.* a woodwind instrument.

obscene /əb'sin, ɒb-/ *adj.* offensive to modesty or decency. – **obscenity**, *n.*

obscure /əb'skjuə, -'skjʊə/ *adj.,* **-scurer**, **-scurest**, *v.,* **-scured**, **-scuring**. – *adj.* **1.** (of meaning) not clear or plain; uncertain. **2.** inconspicuous or unnoticeable; indistinct. – *v.t.* **3.** to make obscure, dark, dim, indistinct, etc. – **obscurity**, *n.* – **obscuration**, *n.*

obsequious /əb'sikwiəs, ɒb-/ *adj.* servilely compliant or deferential.

observant /əb'zɜvənt/ *adj.* quick to notice or perceive; alert.

observatory /əb'zɜvətri/ *n., pl.* **-tories**. a place in or from which observations, especially astrological or meteorological, are made.

observe /əb'zɜv/ *v.t.,* **-served**, **-serving**. **1.** to see, perceive, or notice. **2.** to regard with attention, so as to see or learn something. **3.** to remark; comment. **4.** to show regard for by some appropriate procedure, ceremonies, etc. – **observation**, *n.*

obsession /əb'sɛʃən/ *n.* a persistent feeling, idea, or the like, which a person cannot escape. – **obsess**, *v.* – **obsessive**, *adj.*

obsolescent /ɒbsə'lɛsənt/ *adj.* becoming obsolete.

obsolete /'ɒbsəlit/ *adj.* fallen into disuse, or no longer in use.

obstacle /'ɒbstəkəl/ *n.* something that stands in the way or obstructs progress.

obstetrics /ɒb'stɛtrɪks, əb-/ *n.* the branch of medicine dealing with childbirth. – **obstetrician**, *n.* – **obstetric**, *adj.*

obstinate /'ɒbstənət/ *adj.* firmly and often perversely adhering to one's purpose, opinion, etc. – **obstinacy**, *n.*

obstreperous /əb'strɛpərəs, ɒb-/ *adj.* resisting control in a noisy manner; unruly.

obstruct /əb'strʌkt/ *v.t.* **1.** to block or close up. **2.** to interrupt, make difficult, or oppose the passage, progress, course, etc., of. – **obstruction**, *n.*

obtain /əb'teɪn/ *v.t.* **1.** to come into possession of; get or acquire. – *v.i.* **2.** to be prevalent, customary, or in vogue.

obtrusive /əb'trusɪv, -zɪv/ *adj.* undesirably obvious.

obtuse /əb'tjus, ɒb-/ *adj.* **1.** blunt in form; not sharp or acute. **2.** not sensitive or observant.

obviate /'ɒbvieɪt/ *v.t.*, **-ated**, **-ating**. to meet and dispose of or prevent (difficulties, etc.).

obvious /'ɒbviəs/ *adj.* clearly perceptible or evident.

oc- variant of **ob-** before *c*.

occasion /ə'keɪʒən/ *n.* **1.** a particular time, especially as marked by certain circumstances or occurrences. **2.** the ground, reason, immediate or incidental cause of some action or result. **3. on occasion,** now and then; occasionally. – *v.t.* **4.** to give occasion or cause for; bring about.

occasional /ə'keɪʒənəl/ *adj.* **1.** occurring or appearing on one occasion or another or now and then. **2.** intended for use whenever needed. – **occasionally**, *adv.*

occlude /ə'klud/ *v.t.*, **-cluded**, **-cluding**. to close, shut, or stop up (a passage, etc.). – **occlusion**, *n.*

occult /'ɒkʌlt, ə'kʌlt/ *adj.* **1.** beyond the bounds of ordinary knowledge. – *n.* **2.** the supernatural.

occupant /'ɒkjəpənt/ *n.* a tenant of a house, estate, office, etc. – **occupancy**, *n.*

occupation /ɒkjə'peɪʃən/ *n.* **1.** one's habitual employment; business, trade, or calling. **2.** the period during which a country is under the control of foreign military forces.

occupational therapy *n.* a method of therapy which uses self-care, work and play activities to increase development and independent function, and to prevent disability.

occupy /'ɒkjəpaɪ/ *v.t.*, **-pied**, **-pying**. **1.** to take up (space, time, etc.). **2.** to engage or employ (the mind, attention, etc., or the person). **3.** to take possession of (a place), as by invasion. **4.** to hold (a position, office, etc.).

occur /ə'kɜ/ *v.i.*, **-curred**, **-curring**. **1.** to come to pass, take place, or happen. **2.** to suggest itself in thought (usually fol. by *to*). – **occurrence**, *n.*

ocean /'oʊʃən/ *n.* the vast body of salt water which covers almost three fourths of the earth's surface.

ochre /'oʊkə/ *n.* **1.** any of a class of natural earths used as pigments. **2.** the colour of ochre, ranging from pale yellow to an orange or reddish yellow.

ocker /'ɒkə/ *n.* *Colloquial* the archetypal uncultivated Australian working man.

ockie strap /'ɒki/ *n.* *Colloquial* → **octopus strap**.

o'clock /ə'klɒk/ *adv.* of or by the clock (used in specifying or inquiring the hour of the day).

OCR /oʊ si 'a, 'oʊkə/ *n.* a system of machine reading by a light-sensitive electrical cell of standard character sets encoded on documents such as gas bills, etc.

octa- a word element meaning 'eight'. Also, **oct-**, **octo-**.

octagon /'ɒktəgɒn, -gən/ *n.* a polygon having eight angles and eight sides.

octave /'ɒktɪv/ *n.* a series or group of eight.

octet /ɒk'tɛt/ *n.* any group of eight. Also, **octette**.

octopus /'ɒktəpəs, -pʊs/ *n.*, *pl.* **-puses**, **-pi** /-paɪ/. a sea animal with eight arms.

octopus strap *n.* a stretchable rope with hooks on either end used for securing luggage to roof-racks, etc.

oculist /'ɒkjələst/ *n.* an ophthalmologist.

OD /oʊ 'di/ *n.*, *v.*, **OD'd**, **OD'ing**. *Colloquial* – *n.* **1.** an overdose, especially of an injected addictive drug. – *v.i.* **2.** to give oneself an overdose.

odd /ɒd/ *adj.* **1.** differing in character from what is ordinary or usual. **2.** (of a number) leaving a remainder of one when divided by two (opposed to *even*). **3.** additional to a whole mentioned in round numbers; more or less. **4.** (of a pair) not matching. **5.** occasional or casual. **6.** not forming part of any particular group, set, or class. – **oddity**, *n.*

oddball /'ɒdbɔl/ *n.* *Colloquial* someone who is unusual or peculiar, an eccentric.

odd lot *n.* a number of shares which is not a marketable parcel.

oddment /'ɒdmənt/ *n.* an odd article, bit, remnant, or the like.

odds /ɒdz/ *pl. n.* **1.** the amount by which the bet of one party to a wager exceeds that of the other. **2.** balance of probability in favour of something occurring or being the case. **3. at odds,** in disagreement; at variance. **4. make no odds,** not to matter; be of no importance. **5. odds and ends,** odd bits; scraps; remnants; fragments.

ode /oʊd/ *n.* a lyric poem.

odium /'oʊdiəm/ *n.* hatred or repulsion. – **odious**, *adj.*

odometer /ɒ'dɒmətə, oʊ-/ *n.* an instrument for measuring distance passed over, as by a motor vehicle.

odonto- a word element meaning 'tooth'. Also, **odont-**.

odour = odor /'oʊdə/ *n.* **1.** that property of a substance which affects the sense of smell. **2.** an agreeable scent; fragrance. **3.** a bad smell.

-odynia a word element meaning 'pain'.

o'er /ɔ/ *prep., adv. Poetic* over.

oesophagus = esophagus /ə'sɒfəgəs/ *n.*, *pl.* **-gi** /-gaɪ/. a tube connecting the mouth or pharynx with the stomach.

oestrogen = estrogen /'ɪstrədʒən, 'ɛs-/ *n.* any one of a group of female sex hormones.

of /ɒv/, *weak form* /əv/ – *prep.* a particle indicating: **1.** distance or direction from, separation, deprivation, riddance, etc.: *within a* *metre of; to cure of.* **2.** derivation, origin, or source. **3.** concerning: *and what of Marie-Louise?* **4.** cause, occasion, or reason. **5.** material, substance, or contents. **6.** a relation of identity. **7.** reference or respect. **8.** the attribution of a quality to.

of- variant of **ob-**, before *f*.

off /ɒf/ *adv.* **1.** away from a position occupied, or from contact, connection, or attachment. **2.** as a deduction. **3.** away; distant (in future time). **4.** out of operation or effective existence; disconnected. **5.** away from employment or service. **6.** to fulfilment, or into execution or effect. **7.** on one's way or journey, as from a place. **8. off and on,** Also, **on and off**. intermittently. – *prep.* **9.** away from; so as no longer to be or rest on. **10.** from by subtraction or deduction. **11.** away or disengaged from (duty, work, etc.). **12.** *Colloquial* refraining from (some food, activity, etc.). – *adj.* **13.** no longer in effect or operation. **14.** below the normal or expected standard; inferior. **15.** in bad taste; deviating from normal or accepted behaviour. **16.** (of food) tainted.

offal /ˈɒfəl/ *n.* **1.** the inedible parts of a meat carcass after slaughter, excluding the skin. **2.** the internal organs of animals used for food, as brains, heart, kidney, liver, etc.

off-beat /ˈɒf-bit/ *adj.* unusual; unconventional.

off-chance /ˈɒf-tʃæns, -tʃans/ *n.* a remote chance or possibility.

off-colour = off-color /ɒf-ˈkʌlə/ *adj. Colloquial* unwell.

off-cut /ˈɒf-kʌt/ *n.* that which is cut off, as from paper which has been reduced to a particular size.

offence /əˈfɛns/ *n.* **1.** a transgression; a wrong; a sin. **2.** a crime which is not indictable, but is punishable summarily (**summary offence**). **3.** a feeling of resentful displeasure. **4.** the act of attacking; attack or assault. – **offensive**, *adj.*

offend /əˈfɛnd/ *v.t.* **1.** to cause resentful displeasure in. **2.** to affect (the sense, taste, etc.) disagreeably. – *v.i.* **3.** to err in conduct; commit a sin, crime, or fault.

offer /ˈɒfə/ *v.t.* **1.** to present for acceptance or rejection; proffer. **2.** to propose or volunteer (to do something). **3.** to tender or bid, as a price. – *v.i.* **4.** to present itself; occur. – *n.* **5.** a proposal to give or accept something as a price or equivalent for something else; a bid. **6.** the condition of being offered. **7.** something offered.

offering /ˈɒfərɪŋ/ *n.* something offered.

offhand /ɒfˈhænd/ *adv.*, /ˈɒfhænd/ *adj.* – *adv.* **1.** without previous thought or preparation; extempore. – *adj.* **2.** informal or casual.

office /ˈɒfəs/ *n.* **1.** a room or place for the transaction of business, the discharge of professional duties, or the like. **2.** a place where tickets, etc., are sold, information given, etc. **3.** official employment or position.

officer /ˈɒfəsə/ *n.* someone who holds a position of rank or authority.

official /əˈfɪʃəl/ *n.* **1.** someone who holds an office or is charged with some form of official duty. – *adj.* **2.** of or relating to an office or position of duty, trust, or authority.

officialese /əfɪʃəˈliz/ *n.* a style of language found in official documents and characterised by pretentiousness, pedantry, obscurity, and the use of jargon.

officiate /əˈfɪʃieɪt/ *v.i.*, **-ated**, **-ating**. to perform the duties of any office or position.

officious /əˈfɪʃəs/ *adj.* forward in tendering or obtruding one's services upon others.

offing /ˈɒfɪŋ/ *n. in the phr.* **in the offing,** not very distant.

off-peak /ˈɒf-pik/ *adj.* of or relating to a period of time of less activity than at the peak time: *off-peak train services.*

off-putting /ɒf-ˈpʊtɪŋ/ *adj. Colloquial* disconcerting; discouraging.

off-season /ˈɒf-sizən/ *adj.* denoting a time of year other than the usual or most popular for a specific activity.

offset /ˈɒfsɛt, ɒfˈsɛt/ *v.*, **-set**, **-setting** /ˈɒfsɛt/. *n.* – *v.t.* **1.** to balance by something else as an equivalent. – *n.* **2.** something that offsets or counterbalances; a compensating equivalent.

offshoot /ˈɒfʃut/ *n.* a shoot from a main stem.

offside /ɒfˈsaɪd, ˈɒfsaɪd/ *adj. Sport* in an illegal position.

offsider /ɒfˈsaɪdə/ *n.* a partner; assistant.

offspring /ˈɒfsprɪŋ/ *n.* children or young of a particular parent.

off-the-record /ˈɒf-ðə-rɛkɔd/ *adj.* unofficial.

off-white /ɒf-ˈwaɪt/ *n.* a white colour with a slight touch of grey in it.

often /ˈɒfən, ˈɒftən/ *adv.* **1.** many times; frequently. **2.** in many cases.

ogle /ˈoʊgəl/ *v.t.*, **ogled**, **ogling**. to eye with amorous or impertinently familiar glances.

ogre /ˈoʊgə/ *n.* a monster, commonly represented as a hideous giant.

oh /oʊ/ *interj.* (an expression denoting surprise, pain, disapprobation, etc., or for attracting attention).

ohm /oʊm/ *n.* the derived SI unit of resistance. *Symbol*: Ω

-oid a suffix used to form adjectives meaning 'like' or 'resembling', and nouns meaning 'something resembling' what is indicated by the preceding part of the word (and often implying an incomplete or imperfect resemblance).

oil /ɔɪl/ *n.* **1.** any of a large class of viscous substances, liquid at ordinary temperatures, and insoluble in water. **2.** *Painting* an oil colour. **3. the good** (or **dinkum**) **oil,** correct (and usually profitable) information. – *v.t.* **4.** to smear, lubricate, or supply with oil. – *adj.* **5.** concerned with the production or use of oil. **6.** using oil, especially as a fuel.

oil colour = oil color *n.* a colour or paint made by grinding a pigment in oil. Also, **oil paint**.

oilskin /ˈɔɪlskɪn/ *n.* a cotton fabric made waterproof by treatment with oil.

ointment /ˈɔɪntmənt/ *n.* medicated cream for application to the skin.

okra /ˈɒkrə, ˈoʊk-/ *n.* the edible pods of a certain plant, used in soups, etc.

-ol[1] *Chemistry* a noun suffix representing

'alcohol'.

-ol[2] variant of **-ole**.

-olatry a word element meaning 'worship of'.

old /oυld/ *adj.*, **older**, **oldest** *or* **elder**, **eldest**, *n.* – *adj.* **1.** far advanced in years or life. **2.** having reached a specified age. **3.** long known or in use; familiar. **4.** belonging to a past time. **5.** formerly in use. **6.** deteriorated through age or long use. – *n.* **7.** (used in combination) a person or animal of a specified age or age-group.

old boy *n.* a former pupil of a specific school.

olden /'oυldən/ *adj.* of old; ancient.

olde-worlde /oυldi-'wɜldi/ *adj.* excessively quaint or old-fashioned.

old-fashioned /'oυld-fæʃənd/ *adj.* out of fashion.

old girl *n.* a former pupil of a specific school.

old guard *n.* the ultra-conservative members of any group, country, etc.

old hand *n.* one experienced in some activity.

old hat *adj.* old-fashioned; out-of-date; outmoded.

old maid *n.* an elderly or confirmed spinster.

old man *n.* *Colloquial* **1.** a father, usually one's own. **2.** a husband, usually one's own.

old school *n.* advocates or supporters of long-established, especially conservative, policies and practices.

old school tie *n.* (*usually derogatory*) the network of influences and associations formed among former students of independent schools.

old-timer /'oυld-taɪmə/ *n.* an old person.

old wives' tale *n.* an erroneous idea, superstitious belief, etc., such as is traditionally ascribed to old women.

old-world /'oυld-wɜld/ *adj.* of or relating to past times.

-ole a noun suffix meaning 'oil'.

oleo- a word element meaning 'oil'.

oligarchy /'ɒləgaki/ *n.*, *pl.* **-chies**. a form of government in which the power is vested in a few, or in a dominant class or clique.

oligopoly /ɒlə'gɒpəli/ *n.* *Economics* a market situation in which a product is supplied by a relatively small number of firms whose actions and policies are constrained by the expected reactions of each other.

oligopsony /ɒlə'gɒpsəni/ *n.*, *pl.* **-nies**. a market situation where a small number of buyers influence the supply of a product or service.

olive /'ɒləv, -lɪv/ *n.* **1.** an evergreen tree cultivated chiefly for its fruit. **2.** the fruit, edible and valuable as a source of oil. **3.** a shade of green or yellowish green. – *adj.* **4.** of the colour olive.

olive branch *n.* a branch of the olive tree (an emblem of peace).

Olympic /ə'lɪmpɪk/ *adj.* relating to the Olympic Games.

-oma *pl.* **-omas**, **-omata**. a suffix of nouns denoting a morbid condition of growth (tumour).

ombudsman /'ɒmbədzmən/ *n.* an official appointed to investigate complaints by citizens against the government or its agencies.

omelette = omelet /'ɒmlət/ *n.* a dish consisting of eggs beaten and fried.

omen /'oυmən/ *n.* a prophetic sign.

ominous /'ɒmənəs/ *adj.* portending evil; inauspicious; threatening.

omit /oυ'mɪt, ə-/ *v.t.*, **omitted**, **omitting**. **1.** to leave out. **2.** to forbear or fail to do, make, use, send, etc. – **omission**, *n.*

omni- a word element meaning 'all'.

omnibus /'ɒmnɪbəs, -bʌs/ *n.*, *pl.* **-buses**. **1.** → **bus**. **2.** a volume of reprinted works by a single author or related in interest or nature.

omnipotent /ɒm'nɪpətənt/ *adj.* almighty, or infinite in power.

omnipresent /ɒmnə'prɛzənt/ *adj.* present everywhere at the same time.

omniscient /ɒm'nɪsiənt, ɒm'nɪʃənt/ *adj.* knowing all things.

on /ɒn/ *prep.* a particle expressing: **1.** position above and in contact with a supporting surface: *on the table*. **2.** contact with any surface: *on the wall*. **3.** support, suspension, dependence, reliance, or means of conveyance: *on foot*. **4.** time or occasion. **5.** with reference to something else: *on the left*. **6.** membership or association. – *adv.* **7.** on oneself or itself: *to put clothes on*. **8.** fast to a thing, as for support: *to hold on*. **9.** forwards, onwards or along, as in any course or process: *to go on*. **10.** with continuous procedure: *to work on*. **11.** into or in active operation or performance: *to turn a machine on*. – *adj.* **12.** operating or in use. **13.** occurring; taking place. **14. be on about,** to be talking about. **15. not on,** *Colloquial* not a possibility; not allowable.

once /wʌns/ *adv.* **1.** at one time in the past; formerly. **2.** a single time. **3. once and for all,** finally and decisively. **4. once upon a time,** long ago. – *conj.* **5.** if or when at any time; if ever. **6.** whenever. – *n.* **7. all at once,** suddenly. **8. at once,** immediately.

once-over /'wʌns-oυvə/ *n.* *Colloquial* a quick or superficial examination.

oncoming /'ɒnkʌmɪŋ/ *adj.* approaching.

one /wʌn/ *adj.* **1.** being a single unit or individual. **2.** some (day, etc., in the future). **3.** single through union, agreement, or harmony. **4.** a certain (often used in naming a person otherwise unknown or undescribed). **5.** a particular (day, night, time, etc. in the past). – *n.* **6.** the first and lowest whole number. **7.** a unit; a single person or thing. **8. one and all,** everybody. – *pron.* **9.** a person or thing of number or kind indicated or understood. **10.** (*in certain pronominal combinations*) a person, unless definitely specified otherwise. **11.** a person indefinitely; anyone. **12.** (to avoid repetition) a person or thing of the kind just mentioned.

one-off /'wʌn-ɒf/ *adj.* individual, unique.

onerous /'oυnərəs/ *adj.* burdensome, oppressive, or troublesome.

oneself /wʌn'sɛlf/ *pron.* **1.** a person's self (often used for emphasis or reflexively). **2.** one's proper or normal self.

one-time /ˈwʌn-taɪm/ *adj.* having been (as specified) at one time; former.

one-upmanship /wʌn-ˈʌpmənʃɪp/ *n.* the art or practice of achieving or demonstrating superiority over others.

onion /ˈʌnjən/ *n.* **1.** a widely cultivated plant with an edible bulb. **2.** the bulb.

on-lending /ˈɒn-lɛndɪŋ/ *n.* the act of lending out, at a slightly higher rate of interest, money which has just been borrowed.

online /ˈɒn-laɪn/ *adj.* **1.** of or relating to a computer-controlled device which is directly linked to a computer (opposed to *stand-alone*). **2.** having direct access to a computer. **3.** (of information, etc.) able to be accessed directly by connection to a computer database, the Internet, etc.

onlooker /ˈɒnlʊkə/ *n.* a spectator.

only /ˈoʊnli/ *adv.* **1.** without others or anything further; alone; solely. **2.** as recently as. **3. only too,** very; extremely. – *adj.* **4.** being the single one or the relatively few of the kind. – *conj.* **5.** but (introducing a single restriction). **6.** except that; but or except for.

onset /ˈɒnsɛt/ *n.* **1.** an assault or attack. **2.** a beginning or start.

onshore /ˈɒnʃɔ, ɒnˈʃɔ/ *adj.,* /ɒnˈʃɔ/ *adv.* – *adj.* **1.** towards or located on the shore. – *adv.* **2.** towards the shore.

onside /ɒnˈsaɪd/ *adj.* in agreement, acting favourably.

onslaught /ˈɒnslɔt/ *n.* an onset, assault, or attack, especially a vigorous or furious one.

onto /ˈɒntu/ *prep.* **1.** to a place or position on; upon; on. **2.** aware of (especially something improper or secret).

onus /ˈoʊnəs/ *n.* a burden; a responsibility.

onward /ˈɒnwəd/ *adj.* directed or moving onwards or forwards.

onwards /ˈɒnwədz/ *adv.* towards a point ahead or in front.

oo- a word element meaning 'egg'.

oodles /ˈudlz/ *pl. n. Colloquial* a large quantity.

oomph /ʊmf/ *n. Colloquial* vitality; energy.

oops /ʊps, ups/ *interj.* (an exclamation of surprise or shock).

ooze[1] /uz/ *v.,* **oozed**, **oozing**. – *v.i.* **1.** (of moisture, etc.) to percolate or exude, as through pores or small openings. – *v.t.* **2.** to exude or radiate abundantly.

ooze[2] /uz/ *n.* soft mud, or slime.

op- variant of **ob-**, before *p*.

opal /ˈoʊpəl/ *n.* a mineral, some varieties of which are valued as gems.

opaque /oʊˈpeɪk/ *adj.* **1.** impenetrable to light. **2.** hard to understand; not clear or lucid; obscure. – **opacity**, *n.*

open /ˈoʊpən/ *adj.* **1.** not shut, as a door, gate, etc. **2.** not closed, covered, or shut up, as a house, box, drawer, etc. **3.** not enclosed as by barriers, as a space. **4.** that may be entered, used, shared, competed for, etc., by all. **5.** (of shops, etc.) ready to do business; ready to admit members of the public. **6.** undecided, as a question. **7.** liable or subject. **8.** unobstructed, as a passage, country, stretch of water, view, etc. **9.** exposed to general view or knowledge; frank or flagrant: *an open face*; *open rebellion*. **10.** expanded, extended, or spread out. **11.** generous, liberal, or bounteous. **12.** not yet balanced or adjusted, as an account. **13.** (of a cheque) uncrossed. – *v.t.* **14.** to make, or cause to be, open. **15.** to give access to; make accessible or available, as for use. **16.** to render accessible to knowledge, enlightenment, sympathy, etc. **17.** to set in action, begin, start, or commence (sometimes fol. by *up*). – *v.i.* **18.** to become open. **19.** to afford access (into, to, etc.). **20.** to become receptive to knowledge, sympathy, etc., as the mind. **21.** to disclose or reveal one's knowledge, thoughts, feelings, etc. **22.** to become less compact, less close together, or the like. **23.** to begin, start, or commence; start operations. – *n.* **24.** an open or clear space. **25.** the open air. **26.** the situation of someone who does not use or seek concealment. **27.** an open competition.

open-and-shut /ˈoʊpən-ən-ʃʌt/ *adj.* obvious; easily decided.

open day *n.* a day on which certain institutions, as schools, are open to members of the public.

open door *n.* admission to all upon equal terms.

open-ended /ˈoʊpən-ɛndəd/ *adj.* organised or arranged so as to allow for various contingencies; without fixed limits.

opening /ˈoʊpnɪŋ, ˈoʊpənɪŋ/ *n.* **1.** the act of someone who or that which opens (in any sense). **2.** an open space in solid matter; a gap, hole, or aperture. **3.** the first part or initial stage of anything. **4.** a vacancy. **5.** an opportunity. **6.** a formal or official beginning.

open letter *n.* a letter made public by radio, newspaper, or such, but written as though to a specific person.

open market *n. Commerce* a market where there is free trade, and prices are determined by supply and demand, not fixed by some outside agency.

open-mouthed /oʊpən-ˈmaʊðd/ *adj.* **1.** having the mouth open. **2.** gaping with surprise or astonishment. **3.** greedy, ravenous, or rapacious.

open order *n.* a voucher, etc., exchangeable for goods up to a specified value from a particular shop.

open-plan /ˈoʊpən-plæn/ *adj.* (of the interior space of a dwelling, office, etc.) not having walls between areas designed for different uses.

open slather *n. Colloquial* a situation in which there are no restraints.

opera[1] /ˈɒprə, ˈɒpərə/ *n.* an extended dramatic composition in which music is an essential and predominant factor.

opera[2] /ˈɒpərə/ *n.* plural form of **opus**.

operable /ˈɒpərəbəl, ˈɒprə-/ *adj.* **1.** that can be put into practice. **2.** admitting of a surgical operation.

operate /ˈɒpəreɪt/ *v.,* **-rated**, **-rating**. – *v.i.* **1.** to work or run, as a machine does. **2.** to act effectively. **3.** to perform some process of work or treatment. **4.** *Surgery* to perform surgery on a patient. **5.** to carry on transactions in securities, or some commodity, especially speculatively or on a large scale. – *v.t.* **6.** to manage or use (a machine, etc.)

at work. – **operation**, *n.*

operating lease *n.* a type of lease under which most of the risks and benefits involved in ownership of the property are retained by the lessor.

operational /ɒpəˈreɪʃənəl/ *adj.* **1.** of or relating to an operation or operations. **2.** ready for use; in working order.

operations research *n.* the analysis, usually involving mathematical treatment, of a process, problem, or operation to determine its purpose and effectiveness and to gain maximum efficacy. Also, **operational research**.

operative /ˈɒpərətɪv, ˈɒprə-/ *adj.* **1.** operating, or exerting force or influence. **2.** engaged in, concerned with, or relating to work or productive activity.

operative date *n.* the date upon which the provisions of a contract, award, or agreement come into force.

operator /ˈɒpəreɪtə/ *n.* **1.** someone who deals in shares, currency, etc., especially speculatively or on a large scale. **2.** *Colloquial* someone who successfully manipulates people or situations.

ophthalmic /ɒfˈθælmɪk/ *adj.* of or relating to the eye.

ophthalmo- a word element meaning 'eye'.

ophthalmology /ɒfθælˈmɒlədʒi/ *n.* the science dealing with the anatomy, functions, and diseases of the eye.

-opia a word element of nouns denoting a condition of sight or of the visual organs.

opiate /ˈoupiət, -eɪt/ *n.* **1.** a medicine that contains opium and hence has the quality of inducing sleep. **2.** anything that causes dullness or inaction, or that soothes the feelings.

opinion /əˈpɪnjən/ *n.* a personal view, attitude, or estimation.

opinionated /əˈpɪnjəneɪtəd/ *adj.* obstinate or conceited with regard to one's opinions.

opinion poll *n.* → **gallup poll**.

opium /ˈoupiəm/ *n.* a narcotic, used in medicine to induce sleep, relieve pain, etc.

opossum /əˈpɒsəm/ *n.* → **possum**.

opponent /əˈpounənt/ *n.* someone who is on the opposite side in a contest, controversy or the like; an adversary.

opportune /ˈɒpətjun/ *adj.* **1.** appropriate or favourable. **2.** occurring or coming at an appropriate time; timely.

opportunism /ɒpəˈtjunɪzəm, ˈɒpətʃunɪzəm/ *n.* the policy or practice of adapting actions, etc., to expediency or circumstances.

opportunity /ɒpəˈtjunəti/ *n., pl.* **-ties**. an appropriate or favourable time or occasion.

opportunity shop *n.* a shop run by a church, charity, etc., for the sale of second hand goods, especially clothes. Also, **op-shop**.

oppose /əˈpouz/ *v.,* **-posed**, **-posing**. – *v.t.* **1.** to act or contend in opposition to. **2.** to stand in the way of; hinder. **3.** to set as an obstacle or hindrance. – *v.i.* **4.** to be or act in opposition.

opposite /ˈɒpəsət/ *adj.* **1.** placed or lying over against something else or each other, or in a corresponding position from an intervening line, space, or thing. **2.** in a complementary role or position. – *n.* **3.** someone who or that which is opposite or contrary. – *adv.* **4.** on opposite sides.

opposition /ɒpəˈzɪʃən/ *n.* **1.** the action of opposing, resisting, or combating. **2.** an opposing group or body.

oppress /əˈprɛs/ *v.t.* **1.** to lie heavily upon, as care, sorrow, etc. **2.** to burden with cruel or unjust impositions or restraints. – **oppression**, *n.* – **oppressive**, *adj.*

opprobrium /əˈproubrɪəm/ *n.* the disgrace incurred by shameful conduct. – **opprobrious**, *adj.*

-opsis a word element indicating apparent likeness.

opt /ɒpt/ *v.i.* **1.** to make a choice; choose. **2. opt out,** to decide not to participate.

optical /ˈɒptɪkəl/ *adj.* **1.** acting by means of sight or light, as instruments. **2.** relating to sight; visual.

optical scanner *n.* a photoelectric cell that scans printed data and converts it into the electric impulses fed into a computer or data-processing machine.

optician /ɒpˈtɪʃən/ *n.* a maker or seller of optical glasses and instruments.

optimism /ˈɒptəmɪzəm/ *n.* disposition to hope for the best. – **optimist**, *n.* – **optimistic**, *adj.*

optimum /ˈɒptəməm/ *n., pl.* **-ima** /-əmə/, **-imums**, *adj.* – *n.* **1.** the best or most favourable point, degree, amount, etc., for the purpose. – *adj.* **2.** best or most favourable.

option /ˈɒpʃən/ *n.* **1.** power or liberty of choosing; right of freedom of choice. **2.** something which may be or is chosen; choice. **3.** the right, conferred by an agreement, to buy (or to decline to buy) a property, etc., within a certain time. – **optional**, *adj.*

optometry /ɒpˈtɒmətri/ *n.* the practice or art of testing the eyes in order to supply suitable glasses. – **optometrist**, *n.*

opulent /ˈɒpjələnt/ *adj.* wealthy, rich, or affluent, as persons or places. – **opulence**, *n.*

opus /ˈoupəs/ *n., pl.* **opera** /ˈɒpərə/. a work or composition. *Abbrev.*: op

or /ɔ/ *conj.* a particle used: **1.** to connect words, phrases, or clauses representing alternatives: *to be or not to be*. **2.** to connect alternative terms. **3.** often in correlation: *either ... or; or ... or; whether ... or.*

-or[1] **1.** a suffix of nouns denoting a state or condition, a quality or property, etc. **2.** an alternative of **-our**, as in *color, odor*, etc.

-or[2] a suffix of nouns denoting someone who or that which does something, or has some particular function or office. In some cases it is used as an alternative or a substitute for **-er**[1], especially in legal terms (often correlative with forms in **-ee**), as in *lessor, lessee.*

oracle /ˈɒrəkəl/ *n.* any person or thing serving as an agency of divine communication.

oral /ˈɒrəl/ *adj.* **1.** uttered by the mouth; spoken. **2.** employing speech, as teachers or methods of teaching. **3.** of or relating to the mouth.

orange /ˈɒrɪndʒ/ *n.* **1.** a common citrus

fruit. **2.** a colour between yellow and red in the spectrum; reddish yellow. – *adj.* **3.** of or relating to the orange. **4.** reddish yellow.

orange pekoe /'pikoʊ/ *n.* a superior black tea.

orange stick *n.* a small stick used in manicure.

orang-outang /ə'ræŋ-ətæŋ/ *n.* a large, long-armed anthropoid ape. Also, **orang, orang-utan**.

oration /ɒ'reɪʃən/ *n.* a formal speech, especially one delivered on a special occasion.

orator /'ɒrətə/ *n.* a public speaker, especially one of great eloquence.

oratory /'ɒrətri/ *n.* the art of an orator.

orb /ɔb/ *n.* a sphere or globe.

orbit /'ɔbət/ *n.* **1.** the elliptical or curved path described by a planet, satellite, etc., about a body, as the earth or sun. – *v.t.* **2.** to move or travel in an orbital path around.

orchard /'ɔtʃəd/ *n.* a place where fruit trees are grown.

orchestra /'ɔkəstrə/ *n.* a group of performers on various musical instruments.

orchestrate /'ɔkəstreɪt/ *v.t.*, **-trated, -trating**. **1.** to compose or arrange (music) for performance by an orchestra. **2.** to put together cohesively. – **orchestration**, *n.*

orchid /'ɔkəd/ *n.* a tropical plant noted for its beautiful flowers.

ordain /ɔ'deɪn/ *v.t.* to appoint authoritatively; decree; enact.

ordeal /ɔ'dil, 'ɔdil/ *n.* any severe test or trial.

order /'ɔdə/ *n.* **1.** an authoritative direction, injunction, command, or mandate. **2.** the disposition of things following one after another. **3.** a condition in which everything is in its proper place. **4.** proper or satisfactory condition. **5.** any class, kind, or sort. **6.** a direction or commission to make, provide or furnish something. **7.** a quantity of goods purchased. **8.** a written direction to pay money or deliver goods. **9. in order that,** to the end that. **10. in order to,** as a means to. **11. in short order,** speedily; promptly. **12. on order** ordered but not yet received. – *v.t.* **13.** to give an order, direction, or command to. **14.** to give an order for. **15.** to regulate, conduct, or manage.

orderly /'ɔdəli/ *adj.*, *n.*, *pl.* **-lies**. – *adj.* **1.** arranged or disposed in order, in regular sequence, or in a tidy manner. **2.** characterised by or observant of order, rule, or discipline. – *n.* **3.** a person employed, as in a hospital, for general duties.

orderly marketing *n.* the maintenance of a level of prices of goods and services by agreement among suppliers.

ordinal number /'ɔdənəl/ *n.* any of the numbers *first, second, third,* etc., which indicate the order in which things occur.

ordinance /'ɔdənəns/ *n.* **1.** an authoritative rule or command. **2.** a public injunction or regulation.

ordinary /'ɔdənəri, 'ɔdənri/ *adj.*, *n.*, *pl.* **-ries**. – *adj.* **1.** such as is commonly met with; of the usual kind. **2.** somewhat inferior. – *n.* **3.** the ordinary condition, degree, run, or the like.

ordinary pay *n.* remuneration for an employee's normal weekly number of hours fixed under the terms of employment but excluding any amount payable for shift work, overtime, or other penalty.

ordinary share *n.* one of the series of shares into which the capital of a company is divided, which rank for dividends after preference shares and before deferred shares, if any such are in issue.

ordure /'ɔdʒʊə/ *n.* filth; dung; excrement.

ore /ɔ/ *n.* a metal-bearing mineral or rock.

oregano /ɒrə'ganoʊ/ *n.* a plant of the mint family, used in cookery.

organ /'ɔgən/ *n.* **1.** a keyboard instrument consisting of one or more sets of pipes sounded by means of compressed air. **2.** (in an animal or a plant) a part or member, as the heart, having some specific function.

organdie /'ɔgəndi/ *n.*, *pl.* **-dies**. a fine, thin stiff cotton fabric.

organic /ɔ'gænɪk/ *adj.* **1.** denoting or relating to a class of chemical compounds derived from living organisms. **2.** characteristic of, relating to, or derived from living organisms. **3.** of or relating to the non-use of chemical fertilisers or pesticides. **4.** of or relating to an organ or the organs of an animal or plant. **5.** characterised by the systematic arrangement of parts.

organically /ɔ'gænɪkli/ *adv.* **1.** in an organic manner. **2.** *Horticulture* without the use of chemical fertilisers or pesticides.

organisation = organization /ɔgənaɪ'zeɪʃən/ *n.* **1.** the act or process or organising. **2.** the state or manner of being organised. **3.** any organised whole. **4.** the administrative personnel or apparatus of a business. – **organisational**, *adj.*

organise = organize /'ɔgənaɪz/ *v.*, **-nised, -nising**. – *v.t.* **1.** to systematise. **2.** to give organic structure or character to. **3.** to build a trade union among. – *v.i.* **4.** to combine in an organised company, party, or the like.

organism /'ɔgənɪzəm/ *n.* any form of animal or plant life.

organo- word element meaning 'organ' or 'organic'.

orgasm /'ɔgæzəm/ *n.* *Physiology* a complex series of responses of the genital organs and skin at the culmination of a sexual act.

orgy /'ɔdʒi/ *n.*, *pl.* **-gies**. wild, drunken, or licentious festivities or revelry.

orient /'ɔriənt, 'ɒ-/ *n.* **1. the Orient,** the East, comprising the countries to the east (and south-east) of the Mediterranean. – *v.t.*, *v.i.* **2.** → **orientate**.

oriental /ɔri'ɛntl, ɒri-/ *adj.* (*sometimes cap.*) of, relating to, or characteristic of the Orient or East.

orientate /'ɒriənteɪt, 'ɔri-/ *v.t.*, **-tated, -tating**. to adjust with relation to, or bring into due relation to, surroundings, circumstances, facts, etc. – **orientation**, *n.*

orienteering /ɒriən'tɪərɪŋ/ *n.* a sport in which competitors race over a course consisting of a number of checkpoints which must be located with the aid of maps, compasses, etc.

orifice /'ɒrəfəs/ *n.* a mouthlike opening or hole.

origami /ɒrə'gami/ *n.* the art of folding paper into shapes of flowers, birds, etc.

origin /'ɒrədʒən/ *n.* **1.** that from which anything arises or is derived; the source. **2.** rise or derivation from a particular source. **3.** birth; parentage; extraction.

original /ə'rɪdʒənəl/ *adj.* **1.** belonging or relating to the origin or beginning of something, or to a thing at its beginning. **2.** new; fresh; novel. **3.** arising or proceeding from a thing itself, or independently of anything else. **4.** being that from which a copy, a translation, or the like is made. – *n.* **5.** a primary form or type from which varieties are derived. – **originality**, *n.*

originate /ə'rɪdʒəneɪt/ *v.*, **-nated**, **-nating**. – *v.i.* **1.** to take its origin or rise; arise; spring. – *v.t.* **2.** to give origin or rise to; initiate; invent.

orlon /'ɔlɒn/ *n.* a synthetic acrylic fabric.

ornament /'ɔnəmənt/ *n.*, /'ɔnəmɛnt/ *v.* – *n.* **1.** an accessory, article, or detail used to beautify the appearance or general effect. – *v.t.* **2.** to furnish with ornaments. **3.** to be an ornament to. – **ornamental**, *adj.* – **ornamentation**, *n.*

ornate /ɔ'neɪt/ *adj.* elaborately adorned.

ornitho- a word element meaning 'bird'. Also, **ornith-**.

ornithology /ɔnə'θɒlədʒi/ *n.* the branch of zoology that deals with birds.

oro- a word element meaning 'mountain'.

orphan /'ɔfən/ *n.* **1.** a child bereaved by death of both parents, or, less commonly, of one parent. – *v.t.* **2.** to bereave of parents or a parent.

orphanage /'ɔfənɪdʒ/ *n.* an institution for orphans.

ortho- a word element meaning 'straight', 'upright', 'right', 'correct'.

orthodontics /ɔθə'dɒntɪks/ *n.* the branch of dentistry that is concerned with the correction of irregularities of the teeth or jaw.

orthodox /'ɔθədɒks/ *adj.* of, relating to, or conforming to the approved or accepted form of any doctrine, philosophy, ideology, etc. – **orthodoxy**, *n.*

orthopaedics = orthopedics /ɔθə'pidɪks/ *n.* the correction or cure of deformities and diseases of the skeletal system.

orthoptics /ɔ'θɒptɪks/ *n.* the study and treatment of abnormality of eye muscle function.

orthosis /ɔ'θoʊsəs/ *n.*, *pl.* **-thoses** /-'θoʊsiz/. a device applied to the body to modify position or motion, as a supporting collar. – **orthotics**, *n.*

-ory[1] a suffix of adjectives meaning 'having the function or effect of'.

-ory[2] a suffix of nouns denoting especially a place or an instrument or thing for some purpose.

oscillate /'ɒsəleɪt/ *v.i.*, **-lated**, **-lating**. **1.** to swing or move to and fro, as a pendulum does; vibrate. **2.** to have, produce, or generate oscillations.

oscillation /ɒsə'leɪʃən/ *n.* **1.** the act or fact of oscillating. **2.** a single swing, or movement in one direction, of an oscillating body, etc.

-ose[1] an adjective suffix meaning 'full of', 'abounding in', 'given to', 'like'.

-ose[2] a noun termination used to form chemical terms, especially names of sugars and other carbohydrates.

-osis *pl.* **-oses**. a noun suffix denoting action, process, state, condition, etc.

-osity a noun suffix equivalent to **-ose**[1] (or **-ous**) plus **-ity**.

osmium /'ɒzmiəm/ *n.* a hard, heavy, metallic element used for electric-light filaments, etc. *Symbol*: Os

osmosis /ɒz'moʊsəs/ *n.* the diffusion of fluids through membranes or porous partitions.

ostensible /ɒs'tɛnsəbəl/ *adj.* professed; pretended.

ostentation /ɒstɛn'teɪʃən/ *n.* pretentious show. – **ostentatious**, *adj.*

osteo- a word element meaning 'bone'. Also (*before vowels*), **oste-**.

osteoarthritis /ˌɒstioʊa'θraɪtəs/ *n.* a degenerative type of chronic arthritis.

osteopathy /ɒsti'ɒpəθi/ *n.* the curing of disease by manipulation of parts of the body.

osteoporosis /ˌɒstioʊpə'roʊsəs/ *n.* a condition in which bones become thin and brittle, common especially in women past the menopause.

ostracise = ostracize /'ɒstrəsaɪz/ *v.t.*, **-cised**, **-cising**. to exclude by general consent from society, privileges, etc.

ostrich /'ɒstrɪtʃ/ *n.* a large flightless bird.

other /'ʌðə/ *adj.* **1.** additional or further. **2.** different in nature or kind. **3.** being the remaining one or ones. **4. every other**, every alternate. **5. the other day** (**night, etc.**), a day (night, etc.) or two ago. – *pron.* **6.** the other one. **7.** another person or thing.

otherwise /'ʌðəwaɪz/ *adv.* **1.** under other circumstances. **2.** in another manner; differently. **3.** in other respects.

-otic an adjectival form for nouns ending in **-osis**, as *hypnotic* from *hypnosis*, *neurotic* from *neurosis*.

oto- a word element meaning 'ear'.

otter /'ɒtə/ *n.*, *pl.* **-ters**, (*esp. collectively*) **-ter**. any of various furred, carnivorous, aquatic mammals with webbed feet.

ottoman /'ɒtəmən/ *n.*, *pl.* **-mans**. a cushioned footstool.

ouch /aʊtʃ/ *interj.* (an exclamation expressing sudden pain).

ought /ɔt/ *v. (aux)* **1.** was (were) or am (is, are) bound in duty or moral obligation. **2.** was (am, etc.) bound or required on any ground, as of justice, probability, expediency, etc. (usually followed by an infinitive with *to*): *he ought to be punished.*

ouija /'widʒə, -dʒi/ *n.* a board or table covering marked with words, letters of the alphabet, etc., used during seances.

ounce /aʊns/ *n.* a unit of mass in the imperial system, equal to $\frac{1}{16}$ lb. avoirdupois or $28.349\,523\,125 \times 10^{-3}$ kg.

our /'aʊə/ *pron., adj.* the possessive form corresponding to **we** and **us**, used before a noun. Cf. **ours**.

-our = -or a suffix of nouns denoting state or condition, a quality or property, etc.

ours /'aʊəz/ *pron.* a form of **our** used with

out a noun following.

ourselves /aʊə'sɛlvz/ *pl. pron.* **1.** a reflexive form of **we**: *we hurt ourselves.* **2.** an emphatic form of **us** or **we** used: **a.** as object: *we used it for ourselves.* **b.** in opposition to a subject or object.

-ous an adjective suffix meaning 'full of', 'characterised by', 'like', etc.

oust /aʊst/ *v.t.* to expel from a place or position occupied.

out /aʊt/ *adv.* **1.** forth from, away from, or not in a place, position, state, etc. **2.** into the open. **3.** to exhaustion, extinction, or conclusion; to the end. – *adj.* **4.** no longer or not burning or furnishing light; extinguished. **5.** not in vogue or fashion. **6.** into or in public notice or knowledge. **7.** on strike. **8.** so as to project or extend. **9.** from a source, ground or cause, material, etc. (with *of*). **10.** in or into a state of dispute. **11.** so as to deprive or be deprived (with *of*). **12.** having used the last (with *of*). **13.** with completeness or effectiveness. **14.** so as to make illegible or indecipherable. **15.** incorrect or inaccurate. **16.** lacking; without. **17.** unconscious; senseless. **18.** not in office or employment; unemployed. **19.** finished; ended. **20.** external; exterior; outer. **21. out of it,** *Colloquial* incapacitated as a result of taking drugs or alcohol. – *prep.* **22.** out or forth from. **23.** outside; on the exterior of; beyond. – *n.* **24.** a means of escaping.

out- (*prefixal use of* **out**, *adv., prep. or adj.*) occurring in various senses in compounds, as in *outcast, outcome, outside,* and serving also to form many transitive verbs denoting a going beyond, surpassing, or outdoing in the particular action indicated.

out-and-out /'aʊt-ən-aʊt/ *adj.* thoroughgoing; thorough; complete; unqualified.

outback /'aʊtbæk/ *n.* (*sometimes cap.*) remote, sparsely inhabited back country.

outbreak /'aʊtbreɪk/ *n.* **1.** a breaking out; an outburst. **2.** a public disturbance; a riot; an insurrection.

outbuilding /'aʊtbɪldɪŋ/ *n.* a detached building subordinate to a main building.

outburst /'aʊtbɜst/ *n.* a sudden and violent outpouring.

outcast /'aʊtkast/ *n.* a person who is cast out, as from home or society.

outcome /'aʊtkʌm/ *n.* that which results from something; the consequence or issue.

outcrop /'aʊtkrɒp/ *n.* an emerging part.

outcry /'aʊtkraɪ/ *n., pl.* **-cries**. loud clamour.

outdated /'aʊtdeɪtəd/ *adj.* old-fashioned.

outdoors /aʊt'dɔz/ *adv.* **1.** out of doors; in the open air. – *n.* **2.** the world outside houses; open air.

outfit /'aʊtfɪt/ *n., v.,* **-fitted**, **-fitting**. – *n.* **1.** a set of articles for any purpose. – *v.t.* **2.** to furnish with an outfit; fit out; equip.

outflow /'aʊtfloʊ/ *n.* **1.** that which flows out. **2.** any outward movement.

outgo /'aʊtgoʊ/ *n., pl.* **-goes**. expenditure.

outgoing /'aʊtgoʊɪŋ/ *adj.* **1.** going out; departing. **2.** interested in and responsive to others. – *n.* **3.** (*usu. pl.*) an amount of money expended; outlay; expenses.

outgrowth /'aʊtgroʊθ/ *n.* **1.** a natural development, product, or result. **2.** an offshoot.

outing /'aʊtɪŋ/ *n.* an excursion.

outlandish /aʊt'lændɪʃ/ *adj.* freakish.

outlaw /'aʊtlɔ/ *n.* **1.** a habitual criminal. – *v.t.* **2.** to deprive of the benefits and protection of the law. **3.** to prohibit.

outlay /'aʊtleɪ/ *n.,* /aʊt'leɪ/ *v.,* **-laid**, **-laying**. – *n.* **1.** an amount expended. – *v.t.* **2.** to expend, as money.

outlet /'aʊtlɛt, -lət/ *n.* **1.** an opening or passage by which anything is let out; a vent or exit. **2.** *Commerce* **a.** a market for goods. **b.** (of a wholesaler or manufacturer) a shop, merchant, or agency selling one's goods.

outline /'aʊtlaɪn/ *n., v.,* **-lined**, **-lining**. – *n.* **1.** the line, real or apparent, by which a figure or object is defined or bounded; the contour. **2.** a general sketch, account or report, indicating only the main features. – *v.t.* **3.** to draw the outline of, or draw in outline, as a figure or object. **4.** to give an outline of (a subject, etc.).

outlook /'aʊtlʊk/ *n.* the view or prospect from a place.

out-of-the-way /'aʊt-əv-ðə-weɪ/ *adj.* unusual.

outpatient /'aʊtpeɪʃənt/ *n.* a patient receiving treatment at a hospital but not being an inmate.

outpost /'aʊtpoʊst/ *n.* any remote settlement.

output /'aʊtpʊt/ *n.* **1.** the quantity or amount produced, as in a given time. **2.** *Computers* information obtained from a computer on the completion of a calculation. – *v.t.* **3.** *Computers* to give out (results).

outrage /'aʊtreɪdʒ/ *n., v.,* **-raged**, **-raging**. – *n.* **1.** any gross violation of law or decency. – *v.t.* **2.** to affect with a sense of offended right or decency; shock. – **outrageous**, *adj.*

outright /'aʊtraɪt/ *adj.* **1.** complete or total. – *adv.* **2.** completely; entirely.

outset /'aʊtsɛt/ *n.* the beginning or start.

outside /'aʊtsaɪd/ *n., adj.*; /aʊt'saɪd/ *adv., prep.* – *n.* **1.** the outer side, surface, or part; the exterior. **2.** the space without or beyond an enclosure, boundary, etc. **3. at the outside,** *Colloquial* at the utmost limit. – *adj.* **4.** being, acting, done, or originating beyond an enclosure, boundary, etc. **5.** situated on or relating to the outside; exterior; external. **6.** not belonging to or connected with an institution, society, etc. **7.** extremely unlikely or remote. – *adv.* **8.** on or to the outside, exterior, or space without. – *prep.* **9.** on or towards the outside of.

outsider /aʊt'saɪdə/ *n.* one not belonging to a particular group, set, party, etc.

outskirts /'aʊtskɜts/ *pl. n.* outer or bordering parts or districts, as of a city.

outsource /'aʊtsɔs/ *v.t.* to contract (work) outside the company rather than employ more in-house staff. – **outsourcing**, *n.*

outspoken /'aʊtspoʊkən/ *adj.* free or unreserved in speech.

outstanding /aʊt'stændɪŋ/ *adj.* prominent; conspicuous; striking.

out-station /'aʊt-steɪʃən/ *n.* any remote post.

outstrip /aʊt'strɪp/ *v.t.,* **-stripped,**

-stripping. to outdo; surpass; excel.

out-tray /ˈaʊt-treɪ/ *n.* a tray or other receptacle for out-going letters, files, job assignments, etc. which have received attention.

outward /ˈaʊtwəd/ *adj.* **1.** proceeding or directed towards the outside or exterior. **2.** of or relating to the outside, outer surface, or exterior. – *adv.* **3.** outwards.

outwardly /ˈaʊtwədli/ *adv.* as regards appearance or outward manifestation.

outwards /ˈaʊtwədz/ *adv.* towards the outside; out. Also, **outward**.

outwit /aʊtˈwɪt/ *v.t.*, **-witted**, **-witting**. to get the better of by superior ingenuity or cleverness.

ouzo /ˈuzoʊ/ *n.* an aniseed-flavoured liqueur of Greece.

ova /ˈoʊvə/ *n.* plural of **ovum**.

oval /ˈoʊvəl/ *adj.* **1.** egg-shaped. – *n.* **2.** any of various oval things. **3.** a flat area (sometimes elliptical) on which sporting activities can take place.

ovary /ˈoʊvəri/ *n., pl.* **-ries**. *Anatomy, Zoology* the female reproductive gland. – **ovarian**, *adj.*

ovate /ˈoʊveɪt/ *adj.* egg-shaped.

ovation /oʊˈveɪʃən/ *n.* enthusiastic applause.

oven /ˈʌvən/ *n.* a chamber or receptacle for baking or heating.

over /ˈoʊvə/ *prep.* **1.** above in place or position; higher up than. **2.** above and to the other side of. **3.** on or upon; so as to rest on or cover. **4.** here and there on or in. **5.** in excess of, or more than. **6.** in preference to. **7.** throughout the duration of. **8.** in reference to, concerning, or about. **9.** by the agency of. **10. over and above,** in addition to; besides. – *adv.* **11.** over the top or upper surface, or edge of something. **12.** so as to cover the surface, or affect the whole surface. **13.** through a region, area, etc. **14.** across any intervening space. **15.** from beginning to end, or all through. **16.** from one person, party, etc., to another. **17.** so as to bring the upper end or side down or under. **18.** in repetition. **19.** in excess or addition. **20. all over, a.** thoroughly; entirely. **b.** done with; finished. **21. all over with,** done with; finished. **22. over against, a.** opposite to; in front of. **b.** as contrasted with or distinguished from. – *adj.* **23.** higher in authority, station, etc. **24.** serving, or intended, as an outer covering. **25.** in excess or addition; surplus; extra. **26.** at an end; done; past. – *n.* **27.** an amount in excess or addition; an extra. **28.** *Cricket* the number of balls delivered between successive changes of bowlers.

over- (*prefixal use of* **over**, *prep., adv. or adj.*) occurring in various senses in compounds, especially employed, with the sense of 'over the limit', 'to excess', 'too much', 'too', to form verbs, adjectives, adverbs, and nouns. A hyphen, commonly absent from old or well-established formations, is often used in new coinages, or in any words whose compound parts it may be desirable to set off distinctly.

overall /ˈoʊvərɔl/ *adj., n.*; /oʊvərˈɔl/ *adv.* – *adj.* **1.** covering or including everything. – *pl. n.* **2.** loose trousers, usually with an attached top or shoulder straps. – *adv.* **3.** covering or including everything.

overarm /ˈoʊvəram/ *adj.* **1.** performed with the arm being raised above the shoulder, as bowling or swimming. – *adv.* **2.** in an overarm manner.

overawe /oʊvərˈɔ/ *v.t.*, **-awed**, **-awing**. to restrain or subdue by inspiring awe.

overbalance /oʊvəˈbæləns/ *v.*, **-anced**, **-ancing**. – *v.t.* **1.** to cause to lose balance or to fall or turn over. – *v.i.* **2.** to lose (one's balance).

overbearing /oʊvəˈbɛərɪŋ/ *adj.* domineering; dictatorial; haughtily or rudely arrogant.

overboard /ˈoʊvəbɔd/ *adv.* over the side of a ship or boat, especially into or in the water.

overcapitalise = overcapitalize /oʊvəˈkæpətəlaɪz/ *v.t.*, **-lised**, **-lising**. **1.** to fix the nominal capital (total amount of securities) of (a company) in excess of the limits set by law or by sound financial policy. **2.** to overestimate the capital value of (a business property or enterprise). **3.** to provide an excessive amount of capital for (a business enterprise).

overcast /ˈoʊvəkast/ *adj., v.*, **-cast**, **-casting**. – *adj.* **1.** overspread with clouds, as the sky; cloudy. **2.** dark; gloomy. – *v.t.* **3.** to overcloud, darken, or make gloomy. – *v.i.* **4.** to become cloudy or dark.

overcharge /oʊvəˈtʃadʒ/ *v.*, **-charged**, **-charging**, /ˈoʊvətʃadʒ/ *n.* – *v.t.* **1.** to charge (a person) too high a price. – *v.i.* **2.** to make an excessive charge. – *n.* **3.** a charge in excess of a just price.

overcome /oʊvəˈkʌm/ *v.*, **-came**, **-come**, **-coming**. – *v.t.* **1.** to get the better of in a struggle or conflict; conquer; defeat. – *v.i.* **2.** to gain the victory; conquer.

overdo /oʊvəˈdu/ *v.t.*, **-did**, **-done**, **-doing**. **1.** to carry to excess or beyond the proper limit. **2.** to cook too much; overcook.

overdose /ˈoʊvədoʊs/ *n.*, /oʊvəˈdoʊs/ *v.*, **-dosed**, **-dosing**. – *n.* **1.** an excessive dose. – *v.i.* **2.** to take an overdose of a drug.

overdraft /ˈoʊvədraft/ *n.* **1.** a draft in excess of one's credit balance. **2.** the amount of the excess. **3.** the act of overdrawing an account, as at a bank.

overdraw /oʊvəˈdrɔ/ *v.t.*, **-drew**, **-drawn**, **-drawing**. to draw upon (an account, allowance, etc.) in excess of the balance standing to one's credit or at one's disposal.

overdue /ˈoʊvədju/ *adj.* past due, as a belated train or a bill not paid by the assigned date.

overflow /oʊvəˈfloʊ/ *v.*, **-flowed**, **-flown**, **-flowing**, /ˈoʊvəfloʊ/ *n.* – *v.i.* **1.** to flow or run over, as rivers, water, etc. **2.** to be filled or supplied in overflowing measure (fol. by *with*). – *v.t.* **3.** to flow over; flood; inundate. – *n.* **4.** that which flows or runs over. **5.** an excess or superabundance. **6.** an outlet for excess liquid.

overgrow /oʊvəˈgroʊ/ *v.*, **-grew**, **-grown**, **-growing**. – *v.t.* **1.** to grow over; cover with a growth of something. – *v.i.* **2.** to grow to excess; grow too large.

overhand /ˈoʊvəhænd/ *adj.* **1.** done or delivered overhand. – *adv.* **2.** with the hand over the object.

overhang /oʊvəˈhæŋ/ *v.*, **-hung**, **-hanging**,

/'ouvəhæŋ/ *n.* – *v.t.* **1.** to hang or be suspended over. **2.** to extend, project, or jut over. – *v.i.* **3.** to hang over; project or jut out over something below. – *n.* **4.** an overhanging; a projection.

overhaul /ouvə'hɔl/ *v.*, /'ouvəhɔl/ *n.* – *v.t.* **1.** to investigate or examine thoroughly, as for repair. – *n.* **2.** a thorough examination.

overhead /ouvə'hɛd/ *adv.*, /'ouvəhɛd/ *adj.*, *n.* – *adv.* **1.** over one's head. – *adj.* **2.** situated, operating, or passing overhead, aloft, or above. – *n.* **3.** (*pl.*) the general cost of running a business. **4.** (*pl.*) the general cost which cannot be assigned to particular products or orders.

overhear /ouvə'hɪə/ *v.t.*, **-heard**, **-hearing**. to hear (speech, etc., or a speaker) without the speaker's intention or knowledge.

overkill /'ouvəkɪl/ *n.* the use of more resources or energy than is necessary to achieve one's aim.

overlap /ouvə'læp/ *v.*, **-lapped**, **-lapping**, /'ouvəlæp/ *n.* – *v.t.* **1.** to cover and extend beyond (something else). **2.** to coincide in part with; correspond partly with. – *v.i.* **3.** to lap over. – *n.* **4.** the extent or amount of overlapping. **5.** an overlapping part.

overleaf /ouvə'lif/ *adv.* on the other side of the page or sheet.

overlook /ouvə'lʊk/ *v.t.* **1.** to fail to notice, perceive, or consider. **2.** to afford a view down over. **3.** to look after, oversee, or supervise.

overnight /ouvə'naɪt/ *adv.*, /'ouvənaɪt/ *adj.* – *adv.* **1.** during the night. **2.** suddenly; very quickly. – *adj.* **3.** done, occurring, or continuing during the night. **4.** staying for one night. **5.** designed to be used one night or very few nights. **6.** occurring suddenly or rapidly.

overpass /'ouvəpas/ *n.* a bridge over a road or railway.

overpower /ouvə'pauə/ *v.t.* to overwhelm.

overproof /'ouvəpruf/ *adj.* containing a greater proportion of alcohol than proof spirit does.

overreach /ouvə'ritʃ/ *v.t.* **1.** to reach or extend over or beyond. **2.** to defeat (oneself) by overdoing matters, often by excessive eagerness or cunning. – *v.i.* **3.** to reach too far.

overriding /'ouvəraɪdɪŋ/ *adj.* prevailing over all other considerations.

overrule /ouvə'rul/ *v.t.*, **-ruled**, **-ruling**. to rule against or disallow.

overrun /ouvə'rʌn/ *v.*, **-ran**, **-run**, **-running**, /'ouvərʌn/ *n.* – *v.t.* **1.** to spread over rapidly and occupy. **2.** to exceed. – *v.i.* **3.** to run over; overflow. – *n.* **4.** an amount overrunning or carried over; excess.

overseas /ouvə'siz/ *adv.*, /'ouvəsiz/ *adj.*, *n.* – *adv.* **1.** over, across, or beyond the sea; abroad. – *adj.* **2.** situated beyond the sea. – *n.* **3.** (*construed as sing.*) countries or territories overseas.

oversee /ouvə'si/ *v.t.*, **-saw**, **-seen**, **-seeing**. to direct (work or workers); supervise; manage.

overshadow /ouvə'ʃædou/ *v.t.* to tower over so as to cast a shadow over.

overshoot /ouvə'ʃut/ *v.*, **-shot**, **-shooting**. – *v.t.* **1.** to shoot or go beyond (a point, limit, etc.). – *v.i.* **2.** to shoot over or too far.

oversight /'ouvəsaɪt/ *n.* **1.** failure to notice or take into account. **2.** an omission or mistake. **3.** supervision; watchful care.

oversubscribed /'ouvəsəbskraɪbd/ *adj.* (of share issues) having applications to buy exceeding the number of shares available.

overt /'ouvɜt/ *adj.* open to view or knowledge; not concealed or secret.

overtake /ouvə'teɪk/ *v.*, **-took**, **-taken**, **-taking**. – *v.t.* **1.** to come up with or pass. **2.** to come upon suddenly or unexpectedly. – *v.i.* **3.** to pass another vehicle.

over-the-counter /'ouvə-ðə-kauntə/ *adj.* (especially of securities, etc.) having been sold or purchased at a place of business other than an exchange.

overthrow /ouvə'θrou/ *v.*, **-threw**, **-thrown**, **-throwing**, /'ouvəθrou/ *n.* – *v.t.* **1.** to depose as from a position of power; overcome, defeat, or vanquish. **2.** to throw over; upset; overturn. – *n.* **3.** the act of overthrowing. **4.** the resulting state.

overtime /'ouvətaɪm/ *n.* **1.** time during which one works before or after regularly scheduled working hours; extra time. **2.** pay for such time.

overtone /'ouvətoun/ *n.* (*usu. pl.*) additional meaning or implication.

overtrade /ouvə'treɪd/ *v.i.*, **-traded**, **-trading**. to trade in excess of one's capital or the requirements of the market.

overture /'ouvətʃuə/ *n.* **1.** an introductory part. **2.** an opening of negotiations, or a formal proposal or offer.

overturn /ouvə'tɜn/ *v.t.* **1.** to overthrow. **2.** to turn over on its side, face, or back; upset. – *v.i.* **3.** to turn on its side, face, or back; upset; capsize.

overview /'ouvəvju/ *n.* a comprehensive survey.

overwhelm /ouvə'wɛlm/ *v.t.* **1.** to overcome completely in mind or feeling. **2.** to vanquish; defeat, especially by force of numbers.

overwrought /'ouvərɔt/ *adj.* worked up or excited excessively.

ovi-[1] a word element meaning 'egg'.

ovi-[2] a word element meaning 'sheep'.

ovine /'ouvaɪn/ *adj.* relating to, of the nature of, or like sheep.

oviparous /ou'vɪpərəs/ *adj.* producing eggs which hatch outside the mother's body.

ovoid /'ouvɔɪd/ *adj.* egg-shaped; having the solid form of an egg.

ovulate /'ɒvjəleɪt/ *v.i.*, **-lated**, **-lating**. to shed eggs from an ovary or ovarian follicle.

ovum /'ouvəm/ *n.*, *pl.* **ova** /'ouvə/. the female reproductive cell.

owe /ou/ *v.*, **owed**, **owing**. – *v.t.* **1.** to be indebted or beholden for. **2.** to be in debt to. – *v.i.* **3.** to be in debt.

owing /'ouɪŋ/ *adj.* **1.** owed or due. **2. owing to, a.** on account of; because of. **b.** attributable to.

owl /aul/ *n.* any of numerous nocturnal birds of prey.

own /oun/ *adj.* **1.** belonging or relating to oneself or itself. – *n.* **2. come into one's own, a.** to receive an inheritance. **b.** to be in a situation where particular skills or attributes are evident. **3. get one's own back,** to have revenge. **4. on one's own,** *Colloquial* on one's own account, responsibility, resources, etc. – *v.t.* **5.** to have or hold as one's own; possess. **6.** to acknowledge or admit. – *v.i.* **7.** to confess (often fol. by *up*).

ox /ɒks/ *n., pl.* **oxen**. any member of the bovine family.

oxide /ˈɒksaɪd/ *n.* a compound, usually containing two elements only, one of which is oxygen.

oxidise = oxidize /ˈɒksədaɪz/ *v.,* **-dised, -dising.** – *v.t.* **1.** to convert (an element) into its oxide; to combine with oxygen. **2.** to cover with a coating of oxide, or rust. – *v.i.* **3.** to become oxidised.

oxy- a combining form of **oxygen**.

oxygen /ˈɒksədʒən/ *n.* a colourless, odourless gaseous element, constituting about one fifth of the volume of the atmosphere and present in a combined state throughout nature. It is the supporter of combustion in air and is vital for aerobic respiration. *Symbol*: O

oyez /oʊˈjɛs, oʊˈjɛz/ *interj.* hear! attend!

oyster /ˈɔɪstə/ *n.* any of various edible marine bivalve molluscs.

Oz /ɒz/ *adj. Colloquial* Australian.

ozone /ˈoʊzoʊn/ *n. Chemistry* a form of oxygen, O_3, having three atoms to the molecule.

ozone layer *n.* a region in the outer portion of the stratosphere, where much of the atmospheric ozone (O_3) is concentrated. Also, **ozonosphere**.

P p

P, p /pi/ *n., pl.* **P's** *or* **Ps, p's** *or* **ps**. the 16th letter of the English alphabet.

pace /peɪs/ *n., v.,* **paced, pacing**. – *n.* **1.** rate of stepping, or of movement in general. **2.** rate or style of doing anything. **3.** the distance covered in a single step. **4.** manner of stepping; gait. – *v.t.* **5.** to set the pace for, as in racing. **6.** to traverse with paces or steps. – *v.i.* **7.** to walk, especially in a state of nervous excitement.

pacemaker /'peɪsmeɪkə/ *n. Medicine* an instrument implanted beneath the skin to control the rate of the heartbeat.

pachyderm /'pækidɜm/ *n.* any of the thick-skinned non-ruminant ungulates, as the elephant, hippopotamus, and rhinoceros.

pacific /pə'sɪfɪk/ *adj.* **1.** peaceable; not warlike. **2.** peaceful; at peace.

pacifism /'pæsəfɪzəm/ *n.* opposition to war or violence of any kind. – **pacifist**, *n.*

pacify /'pæsəfaɪ/ *v.t.,* **-fied, -fying**. to bring into a state of peace; quiet; calm.

pack[1] /pæk/ *n.* **1.** a quantity of anything wrapped or tied up; a parcel. **2.** a load or burden, as one carried by a person or animal. **3.** a company of certain animals of the same kind. **4.** a group of things, usually abstract. **5.** a complete set, as of playing cards, usually 52 in number. – *v.t.* **6.** to make into a pack or bundle. **7.** to make into a group or compact mass, as animals, ice, etc. **8.** to press or crowd together within; cram. **9.** to send off summarily (sometimes fol. by *off, away,* etc.). – *v.i.* **10.** to pack goods, etc., in compact form. **11.** to crowd together, as persons, etc.

pack[2] /pæk/ *v.t.* to collect, arrange, or manipulate (cards, persons, facts, etc.) so as to serve one's own purposes.

package /'pækɪdʒ/ *n., v.,* **-aged, -aging**. – *n.* **1.** a bundle or parcel. **2.** a unit, group of parts, or the like, considered as a single entity. – *v.t.* **3.** to put into wrappings or a container. **4.** to combine as a single entity.

packet /'pækət/ *n.* a small pack or package.

pact /pækt/ *n.* an agreement; a compact.

pad[1] /pæd/ *n., v.,* **padded, padding**. – *n.* **1.** a cushion-like mass of some soft material, for comfort, protection, or stuffing. **2.** Also, **writing pad**. a number of sheets of paper held together at the edge. **3.** one of the cushion-like protuberances on the underside of the feet of dogs, foxes, and some other animals. – *v.t.* **4.** to furnish, protect, fill out, or stuff with a pad or padding. **5.** to expand (writing or speech) with unnecessary words or matter.

pad[2] /pæd/ *n., v.,* **padded, padding**. – *n.* **1.** a dull sound, as of footsteps on the ground. **2.** a path worn by animals. – *v.i.* **3.** to travel on foot.

paddle[1] /'pædl/ *n., v.,* **-dled, -dling**. – *n.* **1.** a short oar held in the hands (not resting in the rowlock) and used especially for propelling canoes. – *v.i.* **2.** to propel a canoe or the like by using a paddle. **3.** to row lightly or gently with oars. – *v.t.* **4.** to propel with a paddle.

paddle[2] /'pædl/ *v.i.,* **-dled, -dling**. to dabble or play in or as in shallow water.

paddock /'pædək/ *n.* an enclosed field or piece of land.

paddywhack /'pædiwæk/ *n. Colloquial* **1.** Also, **paddy**. a rage. **2.** a spanking.

padlock /'pædlɒk/ *n.* a portable or detachable lock.

padre /'padreɪ/ *n.* a military or naval chaplain.

paed- a word element meaning 'child'. Also, **paedi-, paedo-**; *US,* **ped-**.

paediatrics = pediatrics /pidi'ætrɪks/ *n.* the study and treatment of the diseases of children. – **paediatrician**, *n.*

paedophile = pedophile /'pɛdəfaɪl, 'pid-/ *n.* a person who engages in sexual activities with children. – **paedophilia**, *n.*

pagan /'peɪgən/ *n.* **1.** an irreligious or heathenish person. – *adj.* **2.** heathen; irreligious.

page[1] /peɪdʒ/ *n.* one side of a leaf of a book, manuscript, letter, or the like.

page[2] /peɪdʒ/ *n., v.,* **paged, paging**. – *n.* **1.** a boy servant or attendant. – *v.t.* **2.** to seek (a person) by calling out their name.

pageant /'pædʒənt/ *n.* an elaborate public spectacle. – **pageantry**, *n.*

pagoda /pə'goʊdə/ *n.* (in India, Burma, China, etc.) a temple or sacred building, usually more or less pyramidal.

paid /peɪd/ *v.* past tense and past participle of **pay**[1].

paid-up capital *n.* the amount of a company's capital which has been issued to shareholders. Also, **issued capital**.

pail /peɪl/ *n.* a bucket.

pain /peɪn/ *n.* **1.** bodily or mental distress. **2.** a distressing sensation in a particular part of the body. **3.** (*pl.*) laborious or careful efforts. – *v.t.* **4.** to inflict pain on; hurt; distress.

painstaking /'peɪnzteɪkɪŋ/ *adj.* assiduously careful.

paint /peɪnt/ *n.* **1.** a substance composed of solid colouring matter mixed with a liquid vehicle or medium, and applied as a coating. – *v.t.* **2.** to execute (a picture, design, etc.) in colours or pigment. **3.** to coat, cover, or decorate (something) with colour or pigment. **4.** to apply like paint, as a liquid medicine, etc. – **painter**, *n.*

painter /'peɪntə/ *n.* a rope, usually at the bow, for fastening a boat to a ship, stake, etc.

painting /'peɪntɪŋ/ *n.* a picture or design executed in paints.

pair /pɛə/ *n., pl.* **pairs, pair**, *v.* – *n.* **1.** two things of a kind, matched for use together. – *v.t.* **2.** to arrange in pairs. **3.** to join in a pair; mate. – *v.i.* **4.** to separate into pairs (often fol. by *off*).

paisley /'peɪzli/ *n., pl.* **-leys**. **1.** a soft fabric made from wool and woven with a colourful and minutely detailed pattern. **2.** any pattern similar to that woven on paisley.

pal /pæl/ *n. Colloquial* a comrade; a chum.

palace /'pæləs/ *n.* the official residence of a sovereign, a bishop, etc. – **palatial**, *adj.*

palaeo- a prefix meaning 'old', 'ancient'. Also, **palae-, paleo-**.

palaeontology = paleontology /ˌpæliɒnˈtɒlədʒi, ˌpeɪ-/ *n.* the science of the forms of life existing in former geological periods, as represented by fossil animals and plants.

palatable /ˈpælətəbəl/ *adj.* agreeable to the taste.

palate /ˈpælət/ *n.* **1.** the roof of the mouth. **2.** the sense of taste. – **palatal**, *adj.*

palatine /ˈpælətaɪn/ *adj.* possessing or characterised by royal privileges.

palaver /pəˈlavə/ *n.* **1.** a conference or discussion. **2.** profuse and idle talk.

pale[1] /peɪl/ *adj.*, **paler**, **palest**, *v.*, **paled**, **paling**. – *adj.* **1.** of a whitish appearance; without intensity of colour. – *v.t.*, *v.i.* **2.** to make or become pale.

pale[2] /peɪl/ *n.* **1.** a stake or picket, as of a fence. **2.** a barrier.

palette /ˈpælət/ *n.* a thin, usually oval or oblong, board or tablet with a thumb hole at one end, used by painters to lay and mix colours on.

palindrome /ˈpæləndroʊm/ *n.* a word, verse, etc., reading the same backwards as forwards, as *madam, I'm Adam.* – **palindromic**, *adj.*

palisade /pæləˈseɪd/ *n.* a fence of pales or stakes set firmly in the ground, as for enclosure or defence.

pall[1] /pɔl/ *n.* **1.** a cloth, often of velvet, for spreading over a coffin, or tomb. **2.** something that covers, shrouds, or overspreads, especially with darkness or gloom.

pall[2] /pɔl/ *v.i.* to have a wearying effect (fol. by *on* or *upon*).

pallbearer /ˈpɔlbɛərə/ *n.* one of those who carry or attend the coffin at a funeral.

pallet /ˈpælət/ *n.* a movable platform on which goods are placed for storage or transportation, especially one designed to be lifted by a forklift truck.

palliate /ˈpælieɪt/ *v.t.*, **-ated**, **-ating**. **1.** to cause (an offence, etc.) to appear less grave or heinous; extenuate; excuse. **2.** to mitigate or alleviate. – **palliative**, *adj.*

palliative care /ˈpæliətɪv/ *n. Medicine* the total care of patients whose disease is not responsive to curative treatment, including attention to the needs of their family, etc.

pallid /ˈpæləd/ *adj.* pale. – **pallor**, *n.*

palm[1] /pam/ *n.* **1.** that part of the inner surface of the hand which extends from the wrist to the bases of the fingers. – *v.t.* **2.** to conceal in the palm, as in cheating at cards.

palm[2] /pam/ *n.* **1.** a tropical tall, unbranched tree surmounted by a crown of large fan-shaped leaves. **2.** a palm leaf as an emblem of victory.

palmistry /ˈpaməstri/ *n.* the art or practice of telling fortunes and interpreting character by the lines and configurations of the palm of the hand. – **palmist**, *n.*

palomino /pæləˈminoʊ/ *n.*, *pl.* **-nos**. a tan or cream-coloured horse with a white mane and tail. Also, **palamino**.

palpable /ˈpælpəbəl/ *adj.* **1.** readily or plainly seen, heard, perceived, etc.; obvious. **2.** that can be touched or felt.

palpate /ˈpælpeɪt/ *v.t.*, **-pated**, **-pating**. to examine by the sense of touch.

palpitate /ˈpælpəteɪt/ *v.i.*, **-tated**, **-tating**. to pulsate with unnatural rapidity, as the heart. – **palpitation**, *n.*

palsy /ˈpɔlzi/ *n.* paralysis.

paltry /ˈpɔltri/ *adj.*, **-trier**, **-triest**. petty.

pamper /ˈpæmpə/ *v.t.* to indulge.

pamphlet /ˈpæmflət/ *n.* a short publication; a booklet.

pan[1] /pæn/ *n.*, *v.*, **panned**, **panning**. – *n.* **1.** a dish commonly of metal, usually broad and shallow. **2.** a depression in the ground, natural or artificial, containing salt water, mineral salts, etc. -*v.t.* **3.** to wash (auriferous gravel, sand, etc.) in a pan, to separate the gold or other heavy valuable metal. **4.** *Colloquial* to criticise or reprimand severely.

pan[2] /pæn/ *v.i.*, **panned**, **panning**. *Film, TV, etc.* (of a camera) to move continuously while shooting.

pan- a word element or prefix meaning 'all'.

panacea /pænəˈsiə/ *n.* a remedy for all diseases; cure-all. – **panacean**, *adj.*

panache /pəˈnæʃ, -ˈnaʃ/ *n.* a grand or flamboyant manner.

pancake /ˈpænkeɪk/ *n.* a thin flat cake made from batter.

pancreas /ˈpæŋkriəs/ *n.* a gland situated near the stomach. – **pancreatic**, *adj.*

panda /ˈpændə/ *n.* a mammal closely related to the bear and largely herbivorous in diet.

pandemic /pænˈdɛmɪk/ *adj.* (of a disease) prevalent throughout an entire country or continent, or the whole world.

pandemonium /pændəˈmoʊniəm/ *n.* a place of riotous uproar or lawless confusion.

pander /ˈpændə/ *v.i.* to indulge (fol. by *to*).

pane /peɪn/ *n.* one of the divisions of a window, etc., consisting of a single plate of glass in a frame.

panegyric /pænəˈdʒɪrɪk/ *n.* an oration, discourse, or writing in praise of a person or thing.

panel /ˈpænəl/ *n.*, *v.*, **-elled**, **-elling**. – *n.* **1.** a distinct portion or division. **2.** a broad strip of the same or another material set vertically, as for ornament, in or on a woman's dress, etc. **3.** a surface or section of a machine on which controls, dials, etc., are mounted. **4.** the body of persons composing a jury. – *v.t.* **5.** to arrange in, or furnish with, panels.

pang /pæŋ/ *n.* a sharp pain.

panic /ˈpænɪk/ *n.*, *v.*, **-icked**, **-icking**. – *n.* **1.** a sudden demoralising terror, with or without clear cause, often as affecting a group of persons or animals. – *v.t.* **2.** to affect with panic. – *v.i.* **3.** to be stricken with panic.

panoply /ˈpænəpli/ *n.*, *pl.* **-plies**. a complete covering or array of something.

panorama /pænəˈramə/ *n.* an unobstructed view or prospect over a wide area. – **panoramic**, *adj.*

pansy /ˈpænzi/ *n.* **1.** any of several species of herbaceous plants of the genus *Viola.* **2.** *Colloquial* **a.** an effeminate man. **b.** a male homosexual.

pant /pænt/ *v.i.* **1.** to breathe hard and quickly, as after exertion. – *n.* **2.** the act of panting. **3.** a short, quick, laboured effort of breathing; a gasp.

pantechnicon /pæn'tɛknɪkən/ *n.* a furniture van.

panther /'pænθə/ *n., pl.* **-thers**, (*esp. collectively*) **-ther**. the leopard, especially in its black form.

pantomime /'pæntəmaɪm/ *n.* a form of theatrical entertainment common during the Christmas season.

pantry /'pæntri/ *n., pl.* **-tries**. a room or cupboard in which bread and other provisions, or silverware, dishes, etc., are kept.

pants /pænts/ *pl. n.* **1.** trousers. **2.** women's underpants.

pap[1] /pæp/ *n.* soft food for infants or invalids.

pap[2] /pæp/ *n.* a teat or nipple.

papa /pə'pa/ *n.* → **father**.

papacy /'peɪpəsi/ *n., pl.* **-cies**. **1.** the office, dignity, or jurisdiction of the pope. **2.** the system of ecclesiastical government in which the pope is recognised as the supreme head.

papal /'peɪpəl/ *adj.* of or relating to the pope, the papacy, or the Roman Catholic Church.

papaya /pə'paɪə/ *n.* → **pawpaw**.

paper /'peɪpə/ *n.* **1.** a substance made from rags, straw, wood, or other fibrous material, usually in thin sheets, for writing or printing on, wrapping things in, etc. **2.** negotiable notes, bills, etc., collectively. **3.** (*pl.*) documents establishing identity, status, etc. **4.** a set of questions for an examination, or an individual set of written answers to them. **5.** an essay, article, etc. on a particular topic. **6.** a newspaper or journal. – *v.t.* **7.** to decorate (a wall, room, etc.) with wallpaper.

paperback /'peɪpəbæk/ *n.* a book bound in a flexible paper cover.

papier-mâché /peɪpə-'mæʃeɪ/ *n.* a substance made of pulped paper and glue which becomes hard and strong when dry.

paprika /'pæprɪkə, pə'prikə/ *n.* the dried fruit of a cultivated form of capsicum, ground as a condiment.

papyrus /pə'paɪrəs/ *n., pl.* **-pyri** /-'paɪraɪ/. **1.** a tall aquatic plant of the Nile valley, Egypt, and elsewhere. **2.** a material for writing on, prepared from the pith of this plant.

par /pa/ *n.* **1.** an equality in value or standing. **2.** an average or normal amount, degree, quality, condition, or the like. **3.** *Commerce* **a.** the legally established value of the monetary unit of one country in terms of that of another using the same metal as a standard of value (**mint par of exchange**). **b.** the state of the shares of any business, undertaking, loan, etc., when they may be purchased at the original price (called **issue par**) or at their face value (called **nominal par**). Shares or bonds sold or acquired at a premium are said to be **above par**, and at a discount **below par**. **4.** *Golf* the number of strokes allowed to a hole or course as representing a target standard.

para-[1] a prefix meaning 'beside', 'near', 'beyond', 'aside', 'amiss', and sometimes implying alteration or modification.

para-[2] a prefix of a few words meaning 'guard against', as in *parachute*.

parable /'pærəbəl/ *n.* a short allegorical story, designed to convey some truth or moral lesson.

parabola /pə'ræbələ/ *n. Geometry* a plane curve formed by the intersection of a right circular cone with a plane parallel to a generator of the cone.

parachute /'pærəʃut/ *n.* an apparatus used in descending safely through the air, especially from an aircraft, being umbrella-like in form and rendered effective by the resistance of the air.

parade /pə'reɪd/ *n., v.,* **-raded**, **-rading**. – *n.* **1.** show, display, or ostentation. **2.** the orderly assembly of troops, etc., for inspection or display. **3.** a public procession. – *v.t.* **4.** to make parade of; display ostentatiously. – *v.i.* **5.** to march or proceed with display. **6.** to promenade in a public place to show oneself.

paradigm /'pærədaɪm/ *n. Grammar* the set of all forms containing a particular element, especially the set of all inflected forms of a single root, stem, or theme.

paradise /'pærədaɪs/ *n.* **1.** heaven, as the final abode of the righteous. **2.** a place of extreme beauty or delight.

paradox /'pærədɒks/ *n.* a statement or proposition seemingly self-contradictory or absurd, and yet explicable as expressing a truth.

paraffin /'pærəfən/ *n. Chemistry* any hydrocarbon of the methane series having general formula C_NH_{2N+2}.

paragon /'pærəgən/ *n.* a model or pattern of excellence, or of a particular excellence.

paragraph /'pærəgræf, -graf/ *n.* a distinct portion of written or printed matter dealing with a particular point, and usually beginning (commonly with indention) on a new line.

parakeet /'pærəkit/ *n.* a small, slender parrot, usually with a long, pointed tail.

parallax /'pærəlæks/ *n.* the apparent displacement of an observed object due to a change or difference in position of the observer.

parallel /'pærəlɛl/ *adj., n., v.,* **-leled**, **-leling** *or* **-lelled**, **-lelling**. – *adj.* **1.** having the same direction, course, or tendency; corresponding; similar; analogous. **2.** *Geometry* (of straight lines) lying in the same plane but never meeting no matter how far extended. **3.** *Computers, etc.* denoting or relating to a system in which several activities are carried on concurrently. – *n.* **4.** anything parallel in direction, course, or tendency. **5.** *Geography* a line of latitude. **6.** *Electricity* a connection of two or more circuits in which all ends having the same instantaneous polarity are electrically connected together and all ends having the opposite polarity are similarly connected. – *v.t.* **7.** to form a parallel to; be equivalent to; equal.

parallelogram /pærə'lɛləgræm/ *n.* a quadrilateral the opposite sides of which are parallel.

paralysis /pə'ræləsəs/ *n., pl.* **-lyses** /-ləsiz/. **1.** *Pathology* **a.** loss of power of a voluntary muscular contraction. **b.** a disease characterised by this; palsy. **2.** a more or less complete crippling, as of powers or activities. – **paralyse**, *v.* – **paralytic**, *n., adj.*

paramedical /pærə'mɛdɪkəl/ *adj.* related to the medical profession in a supplementary capacity.

parameter /pə'ræmətə/ *n.* any constituent variable quality.

paramount /'pærəmaʊnt/ *adj.* chief in importance; supreme; pre-eminent.

paramour /'pærəmɔ/ *n.* an illicit lover.

paranoia /pærə'nɔɪə/ *n.* a psychotic disorder characterised by systematised delusions. – **paranoid**, *adj.* – **paranoiac**, *n., adj.*

parapet /'pærəpət/ *n.* any protective wall or barrier at the edge of a balcony, roof, bridge, or the like.

paraphernalia /pærəfə'neɪliə/ *pl. n.* **1.** personal belongings. **2.** (*sometimes construed as sing.*) any collection of miscellaneous articles.

paraphrase /'pærəfreɪz/ *n., v.,* **-phrased**, **-phrasing**. – *n.* **1.** a restatement of the sense of a text or passage, as for clearness. – *v.t., v.i.* **2.** to restate; render in, or make, a paraphrase. – **paraphrastic**, *adj.*

paraplegia /pærə'plidʒə/ *n.* paralysis of the lower part of the body. – **paraplegic**, *adj., n.*

parasite /'pærəsaɪt/ *n.* an animal or plant which lives on or in an organism of another species (the host), from the body of which it obtains nutriment. – **parasitic**, *adj.*

parasol /'pærəsɒl/ *n.* a woman's small or light sun umbrella; a sunshade.

parataxis /pærə'tæksəs/ *n. Grammar* the placing together of sentences, clauses, or phrases without a conjunctive word.

parboil /'pabɔɪl/ *v.t.* to boil partially, or for a short time.

parcel /'pasəl/ *n., v.,* **-celled**, **-celling**. – *n.* **1.** a quantity of something wrapped or packaged together; a package or bundle. **2.** a quantity of something, as of a commodity for sale. **3.** a part or portion of anything. – *v.t.* **4.** to divide into or distribute in parcels or portions (usually fol. by *out*).

parch /patʃ/ *v.t.* to make dry, especially to excess.

parchment /'patʃmənt/ *n.* the skin of sheep, goats, etc., prepared for use as a writing material, etc.

pardon /'padn/ *n.* **1.** courteous indulgence or allowance, as in excusing fault or seeming rudeness. **2.** *Law* a remission of penalty. – *v.t.* **3.** to remit the penalty of (an offence). **4.** to release (a person) from liability for an offence. **5.** to make courteous allowance for, or excuse (an action or circumstance, or a person).

pare /pɛə/ *v.t.,* **pared**, **paring**. to cut off the outer coating, layer, or part of.

parent /'pɛərənt/ *n.* **1.** a father or a mother. **2.** an author or source. – **parental**, *adj.* – **parentage**, *n.*

parent award *n.* an award which is regarded as setting the minimum standard of payment for employees in a particular calling or classification.

parent company *n.* a company which has subsidiary companies.

parenthesis /pə'rɛnθəsəs/ *n., pl.* **-theses** /-θəsiz/. **1.** the upright brackets (and) collectively, or either of them separately. **2.** *Grammar* a qualifying or explanatory word (as an appositive), phrase, clause (as a descriptive clause), sentence, or other sequence of forms which interrupts the syntactic construction without otherwise affecting it and shown in writing by commas, parentheses, or dashes. **3.** an interval; interlude. – **parenthetic**, **parenthetical**, *adj.*

pariah /pə'raɪə/ *n.* an outcast.

parietal /pə'raɪətl/ *adj. Anatomy* referring to the side of the skull, or to any wall or wall-like structure.

parish /'pærɪʃ/ *n.* an ecclesiastical district having its own church and priest or minister. – **parishioner**, *n.*

parity /'pærəti/ *n.* **1.** equality, as in amount, status, or character. **2.** equivalence; correspondence; similarity or analogy. **3.** *Finance* **a.** equivalence in value in the currency of another country. **b.** equivalence in value at a fixed ratio between moneys of different metals. **4.** *Computers* a method of checking information in a computer, by counting the number of digits present in a binary number.

parity-pricing /pærəti-'praɪsɪŋ/ *n.* the policy of basing the local price of a commodity on an agreed international price where such exists.

park /pak/ *n.* **1.** an area of land within a town, often with recreational and other facilities, which is set aside for public use. – *v.t.* **2.** to put or leave (a car, etc.) for a time in a particular place, as at the side of the road.

parka /'pakə/ *n.* a strong waterproof jacket with a hood.

Parkinson's disease /'pakənsənz dəziz/ *n.* a form of paralysis characterised by tremor, muscular rigidity, and weakness of movement. Also, **Parkinsonism**.

parlance /'paləns/ *n.* way of speaking, or language; idiom; vocabulary.

parley /'pali/ *n.* a discussion.

parliament /'paləmənt/ *n.* (*usu. cap.*) an assembly of elected representatives, often comprising an upper and lower house, which forms the legislature of a nation or constituent state. – **parliamentary**, *n.* – **parliamentarian**, *n.*

parlour = parlor /'palə/ *n.* a room for the reception and entertainment of visitors.

parochial /pə'roʊkiəl/ *adj.* **1.** of or relating to a parish or parishes. **2.** confined to or interested only in some particular narrow district or field.

parody /'pærədi/ *n., pl.* **-dies**, *v.,* **-died**, **-dying**. – *n.* **1.** a humorous or satirical imitation of a serious piece of literature or writing. **2.** a poor imitation; a travesty. – *v.t.* **3.** to imitate (a composition, author, etc.) in such a way as to ridicule.

parole /pə'roʊl/ *n.* the liberation of a person from prison, conditional upon good behaviour, prior to the end of the maximum sentence imposed upon that person.

-parous an adjective termination meaning 'bringing forth', 'bearing', 'producing', as in *oviparous, viviparous.*

paroxysm /'pærəksɪzəm/ *n.* any sudden, violent outburst; a fit of violent action or emotion.

parquetry /ˈpakətri/ *n.* mosaic work of wood used for floors, wainscoting, etc.

parrot /ˈpærət/ *n.* any of numerous hook-billed, fleshy-tongued, often gaily coloured birds.

parry /ˈpæri/ *v.t.*, **-ried**, **-rying**. to ward off (a thrust, stroke, weapon, etc.), as in fencing.

parse /paz/ *v.t.*, **parsed**, **parsing**. to describe (a word or series of words) grammatically, telling the part of speech, inflectional form, syntactic relations, etc.

parsimony /ˈpasəməni/ *n.* extreme or excessive economy or frugality; niggardliness. – **parsimonious**, *adj.*

parsley /ˈpasli/ *n.* a garden herb used to garnish or season food.

parsnip /ˈpasnɪp/ *n.* **1.** a plant with a large, whitish, edible root. **2.** the root.

parson /ˈpasən/ *n.* a member of the clergy.

part /pat/ *n.* **1.** a portion or division of a whole, separate in reality, or in thought only; a piece, fragment, fraction, or section. **2.** (*usu. pl.*) a region, quarter, or district. **3.** one of the sides to a contest, question, agreement, etc. **4.** a character sustained in a play or in real life; a role. **5.** a parting in the hair. – *v.t.* **6.** to divide (a thing) into parts; break; cleave; divide. **7.** to comb (the hair) away from a dividing line. **8.** to put or keep asunder (two or more parts, persons, etc., or one part, person, etc., from another); draw or hold apart; separate. – *v.i.* **9.** to go apart from each other or one another, as persons. – *adj.* **10.** in part; partial.

partake /paˈteɪk/ *v.i.*, **-took**, **-taken**, **-taking**. to take or have a part or share in common with others; participate (fol. by *in*).

partial /ˈpaʃəl/ *adj.* **1.** relating to or affecting a part. **2.** being such in part only; not total or general; incomplete. **3.** biased or prejudiced in favour of a person, group, side, etc., as in a controversy. – **partiality**, *n.*

participate /paˈtɪsəpeɪt/ *v.i.*, **-pated**, **-pating**. to take or have a part or share, as with others; share (fol. by *in*). – **participant**, *n.*, *adj.* – **participation**, *n.*

participle /ˈpatəsɪpəl/ *n.* an adjective form derived from verbs. – **participial**, *adj.*

particle /ˈpatɪkəl/ *n.* **1.** a minute portion, piece, or amount; a very small bit. **2.** a small word of functional or relational use, such as an article, preposition, or conjunction, whether of a separate form class or not.

particular /pəˈtɪkjələ/ *adj.* **1.** relating to some one person, thing, group, class, occasion, etc., rather than to others or all; special, not general. **2.** attentive to or exacting about details or small points.

partisan /ˈpatəzən, patəˈzæn/ *n.* an adherent or supporter of a person, party, or cause.

partition /paˈtɪʃən/ *n.* **1.** division into or distribution in portions or shares. **2.** separation, as of two or more things. **3.** something that separates. – *v.t.* **4.** to divide into parts or portions.

partner /ˈpatnə/ *n.* **1.** a sharer or partaker; an associate. **2.** *Law* one associated with another or others as a principal or a contributor of capital in a business or a joint venture. **3.** See **silent partner**. – *v.t.* **4.** to associate as a partner or partners. **5.** to be, or act as, the partner of. – **partnership**, *n.*

partridge /ˈpatrɪdʒ/ *n.*, *pl.* **-tridges**, (*esp. collectively*) **-tridge**. a game bird.

part-time /ˈpat-taɪm, pat-ˈtaɪm/ *adj.*, /patˈtaɪm/ *adv.* – *adj.* **1.** of, relating to, or occupying less than all normal working hours (opposed to *full-time*). **2.** not being one's chief occupation. – *adv.* **3.** during less than all normal working hours. – **part-timer**, *n.*

parturition /patʃəˈrɪʃən/ *n.* the act of bringing forth young; childbirth.

party /ˈpati/ *n.*, *pl.* **-ties**. **1.** a group gathered together for some purpose, as for amusement or entertainment. **2.** (*often cap.*) a number or body of persons ranged on one side, or united in purpose or opinion, in opposition to others, as in politics, etc. **3.** someone who participates in some action or affair. **4.** a person in general.

parvenu /ˈpavənu, -nju/ *n.* **1.** someone who has risen above their class or to a position above their qualifications. – *adj.* **2.** being, resembling, or characteristic of a parvenu.

pascal /ˈpæskəl/ *n.* the derived SI unit of pressure. *Symbol*: Pa

pass /pas/ *v.t.* **1.** to go by or move past (something). **2.** to go by without acting upon or noticing; leave unmentioned. **3.** to go or get through. **4.** to undergo successfully (an examination, etc.). **5.** to exist through; live during; spend. **6.** to convey, transfer, or transmit; deliver. **7.** to discharge or void, as excrement. **8.** to sanction or approve. **9.** to express or pronounce, as an opinion or judgment. – *v.i.* **10.** to go or move onwards; proceed; make one's, or its, way. **11.** to elapse, as time. **12.** to die. **13.** to go on or take place; happen; occur. **14.** to be interchanged, as between two persons. **15.** to go or get through something, such as a barrier, test, examination, etc. **16.** to go unheeded, uncensured, or unchallenged. – *n.* **17.** a narrow route across a relatively low notch or depression in a mountain barrier. **18.** a permission or licence to pass, go, come, or enter. **19.** the passing of an examination, etc., especially without honours. **20.** the transference of a ball, etc., from one player to another, as in football.

passage /ˈpæsɪdʒ/ *n.* **1.** an indefinite portion of a writing, speech, or the like, usually one of no great length; a paragraph, verse, etc. **2.** the act of passing. **3.** liberty, leave, or right to pass. **4.** that by which a person or thing passes; a means of passing; a way, route, avenue, channel, etc. **5.** a voyage across the sea from one port to another.

passbook /ˈpasbʊk/ *n.* **1.** a bankbook. **2.** a record of payments made to a building society.

passenger /ˈpæsəndʒə/ *n.* someone who travels by some form of conveyance.

passerine /ˈpæsəraɪn/ *adj.* belonging to the order of perching birds.

passion /ˈpæʃən/ *n.* **1.** any kind of feeling or emotion, as hope, fear, joy, grief, anger, love, desire, etc., especially when of compelling force. **2.** a strong or extravagant fondness, enthusiasm, or desire for anything. **3.** the object of such a fondness or desire. – **passionate**, *adj.*

passionfruit /ˈpæʃənfrut/ *n.* (the edible fruit

of) a type of climbing vine.

passive /'pæsɪv, -səv/ *adj.* **1.** not acting, or not attended with or manifested in open or positive action. **2.** suffering action, acted upon, or being the object of action (opposed to *active*). **3.** produced by or due to external agency. **4.** suffering, receiving, or submitting without resistance. **5.** *Grammar* denoting a verb form or voice, in which the subject is represented as being acted on. For example, in the sentence *He was hit, was hit* is in the passive voice. **6.** (of a communications satellite) only able to reflect signals, and not retransmit them.

passive smoker *n.* a non-smoker who inhales the cigarette, etc., smoke produced by others. – **passive smoking**, *n.*

passport /'paspɔt/ *n.* an official document granting permission to the person specified to visit foreign countries, and authenticating the holder's identity, citizenship and right to protection while abroad.

password /'paswɜd/ *n.* a secret word or expression used to obtain access to a restricted area or to a computer system, etc.

past /past/ *adj.* **1.** gone by in time. **2.** belonging to, or having existed or occurred in time previous to this. – *n.* **3.** the time gone by. **4.** the events of that time. – *adv.* **5.** so as to pass by or beyond. **6.** ago. – *prep.* **7.** beyond in time, position or amount.

pasta /'pæstə, 'pas-/ *n.* any of the several preparations made from a dough or paste of wheat flour, salt, water, and sometimes egg, such as spaghetti, macaroni, etc.

paste /peɪst/ *n., v.,* **pasted**, **pasting**. – *n.* **1.** a mixture of flour and water, often with starch, etc., used for causing paper, etc., to adhere. **2.** any material or preparation in a soft or plastic mass. **3.** a brilliant, heavy glass, used for making artificial gems. – *v.t.* **4.** to fasten or stick with paste or the like.

pastel /'pæstl/ *n.* **1.** a soft, subdued shade. **2.** a crayon. **3.** the art of drawing with such crayons.

pasteurise = pasteurize /'pastʃəraɪz/ *v.t.,* **-rised**, **-rising**. to expose (milk, etc.) to a high temperature in order to destroy certain micro-organisms and prevent or arrest fermentation.

pastie /'pæsti, 'pasti/ *n.* a type of pie in which a circular piece of pastry is folded around a filling of vegetables, meat, etc. and baked. Also, **pasty**, **Cornish pastie**.

pastille /pæs'til, 'pæstl/ *n.* a lozenge.

pastime /'pastaɪm/ *n.* that which serves to make time pass agreeably.

pastor /'pastə/ *n.* a minister or member of the clergy with reference to his or her congregation.

pastoral /'pastərəl, -trəl/ *adj.* **1.** of or relating to the raising of stock, especially sheep or cattle, on rural properties. **2.** used for pasture, as land. **3.** relating to the country or life in the country. **4.** relating to the clergy, or to their duties, etc. – *n.* **5.** a poem, play, or the like, dealing with the life of shepherds, commonly in a conventional or artificial manner, or with simple rural life generally.

pastry /'peɪstri/ *n., pl.* **-tries**. food made of paste or dough.

pasture /'pastʃə/ *n.* ground covered with grass or herbage, used or suitable for the grazing of cattle, etc.; grassland.

pasty[1] /'peɪsti/ *adj.* of or like paste in consistency, colour, etc.

pasty[2] /'pæsti, 'pasti/ *n., pl.* **pasties**. → **pastie**.

pat[1] /pæt/ *v.,* **patted**, **patting**, *n.* – *v.t.* **1.** to strike lightly with something flat. – *n.* **2.** a light stroke or blow with something flat. **3.** a small mass of something, as butter, shaped by patting or other manipulation.

pat[2] /pæt/ *adj.* **1.** exactly to the point or purpose. **2.** apt; opportune; ready. – *adv.* **3.** exactly or perfectly.

patch /pætʃ/ *n.* **1.** a piece of material used to mend a hole or break, or strengthen a weak place. **2.** a small piece or scrap of anything. – *v.t.* **3.** to mend or strengthen with or as with a patch or patches. **4.** to repair or restore, especially in a hasty or makeshift way (usually fol. by *up*).

patchwork /'pætʃwɜk/ *n.* work made of pieces of cloth or leather of various colours or shapes sewn together.

pate /peɪt/ *n.* the head.

pâté /'pæteɪ, 'pa-/ *n.* a paste or spread made of finely minced liver, meat, fish, etc.

patella /pə'tɛlə/ *n., pl.* **-las**, **-lae** /-li/. *Anatomy* the kneecap.

patent /'peɪtnt/ *n.* **1.** a government grant to an inventor, for a stated period of time, conferring a monopoly of the exclusive right to make, use, and vend an invention or discovery. – *adj.* **2.** of a kind specially protected by a patent. **3.** open to view or knowledge; manifest; evident; plain. – *v.t.* **4.** to take out a patent on; obtain the exclusive rights to (an invention) by a patent.

patent leather *n.* leather lacquered to produce a hard, glossy, smooth finish.

paternal /pə'tɜnəl/ *adj.* **1.** fatherly. **2.** related on the father's side.

path /paθ/ *n.* **1.** a way beaten or trodden by the feet of humans or animals. **2.** a course of action, conduct, or procedure.

pathetic /pə'θɛtɪk/ *adj.* exciting pity or sympathetic sadness.

pathology /pə'θɒlədʒi/ *n., pl.* **-gies**. the science that deals with the origin, nature, and course of diseases. – **pathologist**, *n.* – **pathological**, *adj.*

pathos /'peɪθɒs/ *n.* the quality or power, as in speech, music, etc., of evoking a feeling of pity or sympathetic sadness.

patient /'peɪʃənt/ *n.* **1.** someone who is under medical or surgical treatment. – *adj.* **2.** quietly persevering or diligent. **3.** quietly enduring strain, annoyance, etc. – **patience**, *n.*

patio /'pætioʊ, 'peɪʃioʊ/ *n., pl.* **-tios**. an area, usually paved, adjoining a house, used for outdoor living.

patri- a word element meaning 'father'.

patriarch /'peɪtriak, 'pæt-/ *n.* **1.** the male head of a family or tribal line. **2.** a person regarded as the father or founder of an order, class, etc.

patriarchy /'peɪtriaki, 'pæt-/ *n., pl.* **-archies**. a form of social organisation in which the father is head of the family, and in which descent is reckoned in the male line, the children belonging to the father's clan.

patrician /pəˈtrɪʃən/ *n.* **1.** a member of the original senatorial aristocracy in ancient Rome. **2.** any noble or aristocrat.

patricide /ˈpætrəsaɪd/ *n.* **1.** someone who kills their father. **2.** the act of killing one's father. – **patricidal**, *adj.*

patriot /ˈpeɪtriət, ˈpæt-/ *n.* a person who loves their country, zealously supporting and defending it and its interests. – **patriotic**, *adj.* – **patriotism**, *n.*

patrol /pəˈtroʊl/ *v.*, **-trolled**, **-trolling**, *n.* – *v.i.* **1.** to go the rounds in a camp or garrison, as a guard. – *n.* **2.** a person or a body of persons charged with patrolling. **3.** the act of patrolling.

patron /ˈpeɪtrən/ *n.* **1.** someone who supports with their patronage a shop, hotel, or the like. **2.** a protector or supporter, as of a person, cause, institution, art, or enterprise. – **patronage**, *n.*

patronise = patronize /ˈpætrənaɪz/ *v.t.*, **-nised**, **-nising**. **1.** to favour (a shop, restaurant, etc.) with one's patronage; to trade with. **2.** to treat in a condescending way.

patter[1] /ˈpætə/ *v.i.* **1.** to strike or move with a succession of slight tapping sounds. **2.** the act of pattering.

patter[2] /ˈpætə/ *n.* the glib and rapid speech used by a salesperson, etc., to attract attention or amuse.

pattern /ˈpætn/ *n.* **1.** a decorative design, as for china, wallpaper, textile fabrics, etc. **2.** style or type in general. **3.** anything fashioned or designed to serve as a model or guide for something to be made. – *v.t.* **4.** to make after a pattern.

patty /ˈpæti/ *n.*, *pl.* **-ties**. a savoury mixture formed into a flattened ball, usually fried.

paucity /ˈpɔsəti/ *n.* smallness of quantity.

paunch /pɔntʃ/ *n.* the belly.

pauper /ˈpɔpə/ *n.* a very poor person.

pause /pɔz/ *n.*, *v.*, **paused**, **pausing**. – *n.* **1.** a temporary stop or rest, especially in speech or action. – *v.i.* **2.** to make a pause; stop; wait; hesitate.

pave /peɪv/ *v.t.*, **paved**, **paving**. **1.** to cover or lay (a road, walk, etc.) with stones, bricks, tiles, wood, concrete, etc., so as to make a firm, level surface. **2.** to prepare (the way) for.

pavement /ˈpeɪvmənt/ *n.* a walk or footway, especially a paved one, at the side of a street or road.

pavilion /pəˈvɪljən/ *n.* a light, more or less open structure for purposes of shelter, pleasure, etc., as in a park.

pavlova /pævˈloʊvə/ *n.* a dessert made of a large soft-centred meringue.

paw /pɔ/ *n.* **1.** the foot of an animal with nails or claws. – *v.t.* **2.** to strike or scrape with the paws or feet. – *n.* **3.** a pivoted bar adapted to engage with the teeth of a ratchet or the like.

pawn[1] /pɔn/ *v.t.* to deposit as security, as for money borrowed.

pawn[2] /pɔn/ *n.* *Chess* one of the 16 pieces of lowest value, usually moving one square straight ahead, but capturing diagonally.

pawnbroker /ˈpɔnbroʊkə/ *n.* someone who lends money at interest on pledged personal property. – **pawnbroking**, *n.*

pawpaw /ˈpɔpɔ/ *n.* a large yellow melon-like fruit. Also, **papaw**, **papaya**.

pay /peɪ/ *v.*, **paid**, **paying**, *n.* – *v.t.* **1.** to discharge (a debt, obligation, etc.), as by giving or doing something. **2.** to give compensation for. **3.** to yield a recompense or return to; be profitable to. **4.** to give or render (attention, regard, court, compliments, etc.) as if due or fitting. **5.** to make (a call, visit, etc.). – *v.i.* **6.** to give money, etc., due. **7.** to yield a return or profit; be advantageous or worthwhile. **8.** to suffer, or be punished, as for something; make amends. – *n.* **9.** payment, as of wages, salary, or stipend. **10.** paid employ.

pay-as-you-earn tax *n.* a system of collection of income tax, whereby an employer makes deductions from the employee's wage before he or she receives it. Also, **PAYE tax**.

pay in hand *n.* the amount of pay which an employer may hold, determined by the number of days allowed to elapse between the end of the pay period and the pay day for it.

paymaster /ˈpeɪmastə/ *n.* an officer or an official responsible for the payment of wages or salaries.

payment /ˈpeɪmənt/ *n.* **1.** the act of paying. **2.** that which is paid.

payment in lieu *n.* payment made to an employee as an alternative to leave or other such entitlements.

payroll /ˈpeɪroʊl/ *n.* **1.** a roll or list of persons to be paid, with the amounts due. **2.** the aggregate of these amounts. **3.** the total number of people employed by a firm.

payroll tax *n.* a tax levied by the government on employers, based on the salaries and wages they pay out.

pay sheet *n.* a chart kept by an employer showing the names and classifications of his or her employees, details of hours worked by them, their rates of pay, the amounts of wages paid them together with any deductions and details of overtime worked, etc.

PC /pi ˈsi/ **1.** personal computer. **2.** politically correct.

PCB /pi si ˈbi/ *n.* polychlorinated biphenyl; one of a group of highly toxic chemicals, used in making plastics and electrical insulators.

pea /pi/ *n.*, *pl.* **peas**, *Archaic* **pease**. the round, highly nutritious seed of a common plant.

peace /pis/ *n.* **1.** freedom from war, hostilities, strife or dissension. **2.** a state of being tranquil or serene. – **peaceful**, *adj.*

peaceable /ˈpisəbəl/ *adj.* **1.** disposed to peace; inclined to avoid strife or dissension. **2.** peaceful.

peach /pitʃ/ *n.* a juicy, drupaceous fruit.

peacock /ˈpikɒk/ *n.* the male of the peafowl distinguished for its long, colourful, erectile tail.

peafowl /ˈpifaʊl/ *n.* a peacock or peahen.

peahen /ˈpihɛn/ *n.* the female peafowl.

peak /pik/ *n.* **1.** the pointed top of a mountain. **2.** the highest point. **3.** the maximum point or degree of anything. **4.** a projecting front piece, or visor, of a cap.

peal /pil/ *n.* **1.** a loud, prolonged sound of

bells. **2.** any other loud, prolonged sound as of cannon, thunder, applause, laughter, etc. *– v.i.* **3.** to sound forth in a peal; resound.

peanut /ˈpinʌt/ *n.* the fruit (pod) or the edible seed of a leguminous plant native to Brazil, the pod of which is forced underground in growing, where it ripens. Also, **groundnut**.

pear /pɛə/ *n.* an edible fruit, typically rounded but elongated and growing smaller towards the stem.

pearl /pɜl/ *n.* **1.** a hard, smooth, often highly lustrous concretion, white or variously coloured, secreted within the shell of various molluscs, and often valuable as a gem. **2.** something precious or choice.

peasant /ˈpɛzənt/ *n.* one of a class of persons, of inferior social rank, living in the country and engaged usually in agricultural labour. – **peasantry**, *n.*

peat /pit/ *n.* a highly organic soil (more than fifty per cent combustible) of partially decomposed vegetable matter, in marshy or damp regions.

pebble /ˈpɛbəl/ *n.* a small, rounded stone, especially one worn by the action of water.

pecan /ˈpikæn, piˈkæn/ *n.* (the oval, smooth-skinned nut of) a type of hickory tree.

peccadillo /pɛkəˈdɪloʊ/ *n., pl.* **-loes**, **-los**. a petty sin or offence; a trifling fault.

peck[1] /pɛk/ *n.* a dry measure in the imperial system, equal to 8 quarts or 9.092 18 × 10^{-3} m^3.

peck[2] /pɛk/ *v.t.* **1.** to strike or indent with the beak, as a bird does, or with some pointed instrument, especially with quick, repeated movements. **2.** to kiss in a hasty dabbing manner. *– v.i.* **3.** to make strokes with the beak or a pointed instrument. *– n.* **4.** a pecking stroke. **5.** a hasty kiss.

peckish /ˈpɛkɪʃ/ *adj. Colloquial* mildly hungry.

pectin /ˈpɛktən/ *n.* an organic acid which occurs in ripe fruits. – **pectic**, *adj.*

pectoral /ˈpɛktərəl/ *adj.* of or relating to the breast or chest; thoracic.

peculate /ˈpɛkjəleɪt/ *v.i., v.t.,* **-lated**, **-lating**. to embezzle (public money).

peculiar /pəˈkjuliə, -ljə/ *adj.* **1.** strange, odd, or queer. **2.** belonging characteristically (fol. by *to*).

peculiarity /pəkjuliˈærəti/ *n., pl.* **-ties**. an odd trait or characteristic.

pecuniary /pəˈkjuniəri, -nəri/ *adj.* **1.** consisting of or given or exacted in money. **2.** of or relating to money.

-ped a word element meaning 'foot', serving to form adjectives and nouns, as *biped, quadruped.* Cf. **-pod**.

pedagogue /ˈpɛdəgɒg/ *n.* a teacher of children; a schoolteacher.

pedal /ˈpɛdl/ *n., v.,* **-alled**, **-alling**. *– n.* **1.** a lever worked by the foot. *– v.t.* **2.** to work or use the pedals of, as in playing an organ or propelling a bicycle. *– v.i.* **3.** to operate the pedals.

pedant /ˈpɛdnt/ *n.* someone who makes an excessive or tedious show of learning or learned precision. – **pedantic**, *adj.*

peddle /ˈpɛdl/ *v.t.,* **-dled**, **-dling**. to carry about for sale, often from door to door.

-pede a word element meaning 'foot', as in *centipede.*

pederasty = paederasty /ˈpɛdəræsti/ *n.* homosexual relations.

pedestal /ˈpɛdəstl/ *n.* a supporting structure or piece; a base.

pedestrian /pəˈdɛstriən/ *n.* **1.** someone who goes or travels on foot. *– adj.* **2.** prosaic; dull.

pedi- a word element meaning 'foot'.

pedicel /ˈpɛdəsɛl/ *n. Botany* a small stalk.

pedicure /ˈpɛdəkjuə/ *n.* professional care or treatment of the feet.

pedigree /ˈpɛdəgri/ *n.* an ancestral line, or line of descent, especially as recorded.

pediment /ˈpɛdəmənt/ *n. Architecture* a low triangular gable.

pedlar /ˈpɛdlə/ *n.* (formerly) one who travelled from place to place selling clothing and other domestic articles.

peduncle /pəˈdʌŋkəl/ *n.* a flower stalk or something similar.

peek /pik/ *v.i.* to peep; peer.

peel /pil/ *v.t.* to strip off the skin, rind, bark, etc.

peep[1] /pip/ *v.i.* **1.** to look through or as through a small aperture. **2.** to peer, as from a hiding place. *– n.* **3.** a peeping look or glance.

peep[2] /pip/ *n.* **1.** a peeping cry or sound. *– v.i.* **2.** to utter a shrill little cry; cheep; squeak. **3.** to speak in a thin, weak voice.

peer[1] /pɪə/ *n.* **1.** a person of the same civil rank or standing; an equal before the law. **2.** someone who ranks with another in respect to endowments or other qualifications; an equal in any respect. **3.** a nobleman. – **peerless**, *adj.*

peer[2] /pɪə/ *v.i.* to look narrowly, as in the effort to discern clearly.

peevish /ˈpivɪʃ/ *adj.* cross, querulous, or fretful.

peg /pɛg/ *n., v.,* **pegged**, **pegging**. *– n.* **1.** a pin of wood or other material driven or fitted into something, as to fasten parts together, to hang things on, or to mark some point, etc. *– v.t.* **2.** to drive or insert a peg into. **3.** to fasten with or as with pegs. **4.** to mark with pegs (often fol. by *out*).

peignoir /ˈpeɪnwa/ *n.* **1.** a dressing-gown. **2.** a negligee.

pejorative /pəˈdʒɒrətɪv/ *adj.* deprecatory.

pelican /ˈpɛlɪkən/ *n.* a bird with a large fish-catching bill.

pellet /ˈpɛlət/ *n.* a round or spherical body, especially one of small size.

pellicle /ˈpɛlɪkəl/ *n.* a thin skin; a film.

pellucid /pəˈlusəd/ *adj.* **1.** allowing the passage of light; translucent. **2.** clear in meaning.

pelmet /ˈpɛlmət/ *n.* a short ornamental drapery or board, placed across the top of a window in order to hide the curtain rail.

pelt[1] /pɛlt/ *v.t.* **1.** to assail with repeated blows or with missiles. *– v.i.* **2.** (of rain) to fall very heavily. *– n.* **3.** the act of pelting. **4. full pelt,** the utmost energy or speed.

pelt[2] /pɛlt/ *n.* the skin of an animal.

pelvis /ˈpɛlvəs/ *n., pl.* **-vises**, **-ves** /-viz/. the basin-like cavity in the lower part of the trunk of many vertebrates.

pen[1] /pɛn/ *n., v.,* **penned**, **penning**. – *n.* **1.** any instrument for writing with ink. **2.** *Ornithology* a large feather of the wing or tail; a quill feather; a quill. – *v.t.* **3.** to write with a pen; set down in writing.

pen[2] /pɛn/ *n.* an enclosure for domestic animals or livestock.

penal /'pinəl/ *adj.* of or relating to punishment, as for offences or crimes.

penalty /'pɛnəlti/ *n., pl.* **-ties**. **1.** a punishment imposed or incurred for a violation of law or rule. **2.** consequence or disadvantage attached to any action, condition, etc. – **penalise = penalize**, *v.*

penalty rate *n.* a rate of pay determined by an award, higher than the usual rate, in compensation for working outside the normal spread of hours.

penance /'pɛnəns/ *n.* punishment undergone in token of penitence for sin.

pence /pɛns/ *n.* plural of **penny**, used especially when value is indicated.

penchant /'pɛnʃənt/ *n.* a strong inclination; a taste or liking for something.

pencil /'pɛnsəl/ *n., v.,* **-cilled**, **-cilling**. – *n.* **1.** a thin tube of wood, etc., with a core of graphite, chalk, the like, for drawing or writing. – *v.t.* **2.** to use a pencil on. **3.** to execute, draw, colour, or write with or as with a pencil.

pendant /'pɛndənt/ *n.* a hanging ornament, as of a necklace or earring.

pendent /'pɛndənt/ *adj.* **1.** hanging or suspended. **2.** overhanging; jutting or leaning over.

pending /'pɛndɪŋ/ *prep.* **1.** until. **2.** during. – *adj.* **3.** remaining undecided.

pendulous /'pɛndʒələs/ *adj.* **1.** hanging. **2.** swinging freely. **3.** vacillating.

pendulum /'pɛndʒələm/ *n.* a body so suspended from a fixed point as to move to and fro by the action of gravity and acquired kinetic energy.

penetrate /'pɛnətreɪt/ *v.t.,* **-trated**, **-trating**. **1.** to pierce into or through. **2.** to enter the interior of. – **penetrable**, *adj.* – **penetrative**, *adj.*

penguin /'pɛŋgwən, 'pɛngwən/ *n.* a flightless aquatic bird of the Southern Hemisphere, with webbed feet, and wings reduced to flippers.

penicillin /pɛnə'sɪlən/ *n.* a powerful antibacterial substance.

peninsula /pə'nɪnʃələ/ *n.* a piece of land almost surrounded by water.

penis /'pinəs/ *n., pl.* **-nises**, **-nes** /-niz/. the male organ of copulation and urination.

penitent /'pɛnətənt/ *adj.* repentant; contrite; sorry for sin or fault and disposed to atonement and amendment. – **penitence**, *n.* – **penitential**, *adj.*

penitentiary /pɛnə'tɛnʃəri/ *n., pl.* **-ries**, *adj.* – *n.* **1.** *US* a prison. – *adj.* **2.** of or relating to penance; penitential.

pen-name /'pɛn-neɪm/ *n.* a name assumed to write under; an author's pseudonym.

pennant /'pɛnənt/ *n.* **1.** Also, **pendant**, **pennon**. a long triangular flag, borne on naval or other vessels or used in signalling, etc. **2.** any flag serving as an emblem, as of success in an athletic contest.

penny /'pɛni/ *n., pl.* **pennies**, (*esp. collectively*) **pence**. a former unit of currency. *Abbrev.*: d. – **penniless**, *adj.*

pension /'pɛnʃən/ *n.* a fixed periodical payment made in consideration of past services, injury or loss sustained, merit, poverty, etc. – **pensioner**, *n.*

pensive /'pɛnsɪv/ *adj.* deeply or sadly thoughtful.

pent /pɛnt/ *adj.* shut in; confined.

pent- a word element meaning 'five'. Also (*before consonants*), **penta-**.

pentagon /'pɛntəgɒn, -gən/ *n.* a polygon having five angles and five sides.

penthouse /'pɛnthaʊs/ *n.* a separate flat on a roof.

penultimate /pə'nʌltəmət/ *adj.* next to the last.

penumbra /pə'nʌmbrə/ *n., pl.* **-bras**, **-brae** /-bri/. the partial or imperfect shadow outside the complete shadow (umbra) of an opaque body.

penury /'pɛnjəri/ *n.* **1.** extreme poverty; destitution. **2.** dearth or insufficiency. – **penurious**, *adj.*

peony /'piəni/ *n., pl.* **-nies**. a garden plant with large showy flowers.

people /'pipəl/ *n., pl.* **-ple**, **-ples** *for def. 1, v.,* **-pled**, **-pling**. – *n.* **1.** the whole body of persons constituting a community, tribe, race, or nation. **2.** the common people; populace. – *v.t.* **3.** to furnish with people; populate.

pep /pɛp/ *n. Colloquial* vigour.

pepper /'pɛpə/ *n.* **1.** a pungent condiment obtained from the dried berries of various plants used either whole or ground. **2.** any species of *Capsicum.* – *v.t.* **3.** to season with or as with pepper. **4.** to sprinkle as with pepper; dot.

peppermint /'pɛpəmənt/ *n.* **1.** a herb cultivated for its aromatic pungent oil. **2.** a lozenge or confection flavoured with peppermint.

peptic /'pɛptɪk/ *adj.* relating to or concerned in digestion; digestive.

per /pɜ/, *weak form* /pə/ – *prep.* through; by; for each.

per- a prefix meaning 'through', 'thoroughly', 'utterly', 'very', as in *pervert, pervade, perfect.*

perambulate /pə'ræmbjəleɪt/ *v.i.,* **-lated**, **-lating**. to walk or travel about.

perambulator /pə'ræmbjəleɪtə/ *n.* → **pram**.

per annum /pər 'ænəm/ *adv.* by the year; yearly.

per capita /pə 'kæpətə/ *adv.* by the individual person.

perceive /pə'siv/ *v.t.,* **-ceived**, **-ceiving**. **1.** to gain knowledge of through one of the senses; discover by seeing, hearing, etc. **2.** to apprehend with the mind; understand. – **perception**, *n.* – **perceptive**, *adj.*

per cent *adv.* **1.** by the hundred; for or in every hundred (used in expressing proportions, rates of interest, etc.). – *n.* **2.** a stock which bears a specified rate of interest. *Symbol*: % Also, **percent**.

percentage /pə'sɛntɪdʒ/ *n.* **1.** a rate or proportion per hundred. **2.** a proportion in general.

percentile /pə'sɛntaɪl/ *n.* one of the values of a variable which divides the distribution of the variable into 100 groups having equal frequencies.

perceptible /pə'sɛptəbəl/ *adj.* capable of being perceived; cognisable; appreciable.

perch[1] /pɜtʃ/ *n.* **1.** a pole or rod usually fixed horizontally to serve as a roost for birds. **2.** a rod, or linear measurement in the imperial system of 5½ yards or 16½ feet, equal to 5.0292 m. – *v.i.* **3.** to alight or rest upon a perch, as a bird. **4.** to settle or rest in some elevated position, as if on a perch.

perch[2] /pɜtʃ/ *n., pl.* **perches**, (*esp. collectively*) **perch**. any of a number of species of Australian food and sport fishes, mainly freshwater but some marine.

percipient /pə'sɪpiənt/ *adj.* **1.** perceiving. **2.** having perception. – *n.* **3.** someone who or that which perceives.

percolate /'pɜkəleɪt/ *v.i.*, **-lated**, **-lating**. **1.** to pass through a porous substance; filter; ooze. **2.** gradually to become known.

percolator /'pɜkəleɪtə/ *n.* a kind of coffeepot in which boiling water is forced up a hollow stem, filters through ground coffee, and returns to the pot below.

percussion /pə'kʌʃən/ *n.* **1.** the striking of one body against another with some violence; impact. **2.** *Music* the instruments in an orchestra which are played by striking.

per diem /pɜ 'diəm/ *adv.* **1.** by the day. – *n.* **2.** a daily allowance, usually for living expenses while travelling in connection with one's work.

perdition /pɜ'dɪʃən/ *n.* a condition of final spiritual ruin or damnation.

peremptory /pə'rɛmptri, -təri/ *adj.* **1.** imperative. **2.** imperious or dictatorial. **3.** *Law* that precludes or does not admit of debate, question, etc.

perennial /pə'rɛniəl/ *adj.* **1.** lasting for an indefinitely long time; enduring. **2.** *Botany* having a life cycle lasting more than two years. – *n.* **3.** a perennial plant.

perfect /'pɜfəkt/ *adj.*, /pɜ'fɛkt/ *v.* – *adj.* **1.** in a state proper to a thing when completed; having all essential elements, characteristics, etc.; lacking in no respect; complete. **2.** in a state of complete excellence; without blemish or defect. **3.** *Grammar* designating a tense denoting an action or state brought to a close prior to some temporal point of reference. – *v.t.* **4.** to bring to completion, complete, or finish. **5.** to make perfect or faultless, bring to perfection. – **perfection**, *n.*

perfidy /'pɜfədi/ *n., pl.* **-dies**. a deliberate breach of faith or trust; faithlessness; treachery. – **perfidious**, *adj.*

perforate /'pɜfəreɪt/ *v.t.*, **-rated**, **rating**. to make a hole or holes through by boring, punching or other process. – **perforation**, *n.*

perforce /pə'fɔs/ *adv.* of necessity.

perform /pə'fɔm/ *v.t.* **1.** to carry out; execute; do. **2.** to act (a play, a part, etc.), as on the stage. **3.** to render (music), as by playing or singing. – *v.i.* **4.** to fulfil a command, promise, or undertaking. **5.** to execute or do something. **6.** to act in a play. **7.** to perform music. **8.** to go through any performance. **9.** to display anger.

performance /pə'fɔməns/ *n.* **1.** a musical, dramatic or other entertainment. **2.** the act of performing. **3.** the way in which something reacts under certain conditions or fulfils the purpose for which it was intended.

perfume /'pɜfjum/ *n.* a substance, extract, or preparation for diffusing or imparting a fragrant or agreeable smell.

perfunctory /pə'fʌŋktəri/ *adj.* performed merely as an uninteresting or routine duty; mechanical; indifferent, careless.

perhaps /pə'hæps, præps/ *adv.* maybe; possibly.

peri- a prefix meaning 'around', 'about', 'beyond'.

peril /'pɛrəl/ *n.* exposure to injury, loss, or destruction; risk; jeopardy; danger. – **perilous**, *adj.*

perimeter /pə'rɪmətə/ *n.* the circumference, border, or outer boundary of a two-dimensional figure.

period /'pɪəriəd/ *n.* **1.** an indefinite portion of time, or of history, life, etc., characterised by certain features or conditions. **2.** any specified division or portion of time. **3.** menstruation. **4.** → **full stop**. – *adj.* **5.** relating to, denoting, characteristic of, imitating, or representing a past period or the fashions current during a specific period of history.

periodic /pɪəri'ɒdɪk/ *adj.* **1.** occurring or appearing at regular intervals. **2.** intermittent.

periodical /pɪəri'ɒdɪkəl/ *n.* a magazine, journal, etc., issued at regularly recurring intervals.

periodising /'piəriədaizɪŋ/ *n.* an accounting procedure by which items of income and expenditure relating to time periods which do not coincide with the financial year, are segregated in the final accounts into one portion which affects the result of the financial year under review, and another portion which is transferred to one or more subsequent financial years.

periphery /pə'rɪfəri/ *n., pl.* **-ries**. **1.** the external boundary of any surface or area. **2.** the external surface, or outside, of a body. – **peripheral**, *adj.*

periphrastic /pɛri'fræstɪk/ *adj.* circumlocutory; roundabout.

periscope /'pɛrəskoʊp/ *n.* an optical instrument by which a view at the surface of water, etc., may be seen from below or behind. – **periscopic**, *adj.*

perish /'pɛrɪʃ/ *v.i.* **1.** to suffer death, or lose life, through violence, privation, etc. **2.** to pass away; decay and disappear. **3.** to rot.

perishable /'pɛrɪʃəbəl/ *adj.* **1.** liable to perish; subject to decay or destruction. – *n.* **2.** (*usu. pl.*) a perishable thing, as food.

perjure /'pɜdʒə/ *v.t.*, **-jured**, **-juring**. to render (oneself) guilty of swearing falsely, or of wilfully making a false statement under oath or solemn affirmation. – **perjury**, *n.*

perk /pɜk/ *v.i.* to become lively or vigorous, as after depression or sickness (fol. by *up*).

permanent /'pɜmənənt/ *adj.* lasting or

intended to last indefinitely; remaining unchanged; not temporary; enduring; abiding. – **permanence**, *n.*

permanent building society *n.* an organisation which accepts money on deposit and channels it into housing loans, the repayments from which constantly renew the society's funds.

permeable /'pɜmiəbəl/ *adj.* capable of being permeated. – **permeability**, *n.*

permeate /'pɜmieɪt/ *v.t.*, **-ated**, **-ating**. **1.** to penetrate through the pores, interstices, etc., of. **2.** to be diffused through; pervade; saturate.

permission /pə'mɪʃən/ *n.* the act of permitting; formal or express allowance or consent.

permissive /pə'mɪsɪv/ *adj.* **1.** tolerant. **2.** sexually and morally tolerant.

permit /pə'mɪt/ *v.*, **-mitted**, **-mitting**, /'pɜmɪt/ *n.* – *v.t.* **1.** to allow (a person, etc.) to do something. **2.** to let (something) be done or occur. – *n.* **3.** a written order granting leave to do something. **4.** an authoritative or official certificate of permission; a licence.

permutation /pɜmjə'teɪʃən/ *n.* *Mathematics* **1.** the act of changing the order of elements arranged in a particular order (as, *abc* into *acb*, *bac*, etc.), or of arranging a number of elements in groups made up of equal numbers of the elements in different orders (as, *a* and *b* in *ab* and *ba*). **2.** any of the resulting arrangements or groups.

pernicious /pə'nɪʃəs/ *adj.* **1.** ruinous; highly hurtful. **2.** deadly; fatal.

peroxide /pə'rɒksaɪd/ *n.* *Chemistry* that oxide of an element or radical which contains an unusually large amount of oxygen.

perpendicular /pɜpən'dɪkjələ/ *adj.* **1.** vertical; upright. **2.** *Geometry* meeting a given line or surface at right angles.

perpetrate /'pɜpətreɪt/ *v.t.*, **-trated**, **-trating**. to perform, execute, or commit (a crime, deception, etc.). – **perpetration**, *n.* – **perpetrator**, *n.*

perpetual /pə'pɛtʃuəl/ *adj.* continuing or enduring forever or indefinitely. – **perpetuate**, *v.* – **perpetuity**, *n.*

perplex /pə'plɛks/ *v.t.* to cause to be puzzled over what is not understood or certain; bewilder; confuse mentally.

perquisite /'pɜkwəzət/ *n.* an incidental emolument, fee, or profit over and above fixed income, salary, or wages.

per se /pɜ 'seɪ/ *adv.* by or in itself; intrinsically.

persecute /'pɜsəkjut/ *v.t.*, **-cuted**, **-cuting**. **1.** to harass persistently. **2.** to oppress with injury or punishment for adherence to principles or religious faith. – **persecution**, *n.*

persevere /pɜsə'vɪə/ *v.i.*, **-vered**, **-vering**. to persist in anything undertaken; maintain a purpose in spite of difficulty or obstacles. – **perseverance**, *n.*

persimmon /'pɜsəmən, pə'sɪmən/ *n.* (a tree bearing) an astringent plumlike fruit.

persist /pə'sɪst/ *v.i.* to continue steadily or firmly in some state, purpose, course of action, or the like, especially in spite of opposition. – **persistent**, *adj.*

person /'pɜsən/ *n.* **1.** a human being, whether man, woman, or child. **2.** the living body of a human being, often including the clothes worn. **3.** *Grammar* (in some languages) a category of verb inflection and of pronoun classification, distinguishing between the speaker (**first person**), the one addressed (**second person**), and anyone or anything else (**third person**). **4. in person,** in one's own bodily presence.

-person a noun suffix used to avoid the specification or implication of sex, as in *chairman, salesman*; hence *chairperson, salesperson.*

personable /'pɜsənəbəl/ *adj.* of pleasing personal appearance and manner; comely; presentable.

personage /'pɜsənɪdʒ/ *n.* **1.** a person of distinction or importance. **2.** any person.

personal /'pɜsənəl/ *adj.* **1.** of or relating to a particular person; individual; private. **2.** relating to, directed to, or aimed at, a particular person. **3.** done, affected, held, etc., in person. **4.** relating to the person, body, or bodily aspect.

personal computer *n.* a microcomputer designed for individual use, for such applications as word processing, accounting, etc.

personal identification number *n.* → **PIN number**.

personality /pɜsə'næləti/ *n.*, *pl.* **-ties**. **1.** distinctive or notable personal character. **2.** a well-known or prominent person; celebrity.

personify /pə'sɒnəfaɪ/ *v.t.*, **-fied**, **-fying**. **1.** to attribute personal nature or character to (an inanimate object or an abstraction), as in speech or writing. **2.** to be an embodiment of; typify. – **personification**, *n.*

personnel /pɜsə'nɛl/ *n.* the body of persons employed in any work, undertaking, or service.

perspective /pə'spɛktɪv/ *n.* **1.** the art of depicting on a flat surface, various objects, architecture, landscape, etc., in such a way as to express dimensions and spatial relations. **2.** a mental view or prospect.

perspex /'pɜspɛks/ *n.* a plastic substitute for glass.

perspicacious /pɜspə'keɪʃəs/ *adj.* having keen mental perception; discerning.

perspire /pə'spaɪə/ *v.i.*, **-spired**, **-spiring**. to excrete watery fluid through the pores; sweat. – **perspiration**, *n.*

persuade /pə'sweɪd/ *v.t.*, **-suaded**, **-suading**. **1.** to prevail on (a person, etc.), by advice, urging, reasons, inducements, etc., to do something. **2.** to induce to believe; convince. – **persuasion**, *n.* – **persuasive**, *adj.*

pert /pɜt/ *adj.* bold; saucy.

pertain /pə'teɪn/ *v.i.* to have reference or relation; relate.

pertinacious /pɜtə'neɪʃəs/ *adj.* extremely persistent.

pertinent /'pɜtənənt/ *adj.* relating or relating to the matter in hand; relevant.

perturb /pə'tɜb/ *v.t.* to disturb or disquiet greatly in mind; agitate.

peruse /pə'ruz/ *v.t.*, **-rused**, **-rusing**. **1.** to read through, as with thoroughness or care. **2.** to read. – **perusal**, *n.*

perv /pɜv/ *Colloquial* – *n.* **1.** a pervert. – *v.i.*

2. to look at lustfully (fol. by *on*).

pervade /pə'veɪd/ *v.t.*, **-vaded**, **-vading**. **1.** to extend its presence, activities, influence, etc., throughout. **2.** to go, pass, or spread through. – **pervasive**, *adj.*

perverse /pə'vɜs/ *adj.* wilfully determined or disposed to go counter to what is expected or desired; contrary.

perversion /pə'vɜʒən/ *n.* **1.** the act of perverting. **2.** a perverted form of something. **3.** *Psychology* unnatural or abnormal condition of the sexual instincts (**sexual perversion**).

pervert /pə'vɜt/ *v.*, /'pɜvɜt/ *n.* – *v.t.* **1.** to turn away from the right course. **2.** to lead astray morally. **3.** to distort. **4.** *Pathology* to change to what is unnatural or abnormal. – *n.* **5.** *Psychology*, *Pathology* one affected with perversion.

pervious /'pɜviəs/ *adj.* **1.** admitting of passage or entrance; permeable. **2.** accessible to reason, feeling, etc.

pessary /'pɛsəri/ *n.*, *pl.* **-ries**. *Medicine* **1.** an instrument worn in the vagina to remedy uterine displacement. **2.** a vaginal suppository.

pessimism /'pɛsəmɪzəm, 'pɛz-/ *n.* disposition to take the gloomiest possible view. – **pessimist**, *n.* – **pessimistic**, *adj.*

pest /pɛst/ *n.* a noxious, destructive, or troublesome thing or person; nuisance.

pester /'pɛstə/ *v.t.* to harass with petty annoyances; torment.

pesticide /'pɛstəsaɪd/ *n.* a chemical substance for destroying pests, such as mosquitoes, flies, etc.

pestilence /'pɛstələns/ *n.* a deadly epidemic disease. – **pestilential**, *adj.*

pestilent /'pɛstələnt/ *adj.* **1.** infectious, as a disease; pestilential. **2.** destructive to life; deadly; poisonous.

pestle /'pɛsəl/ *n.* an instrument for breaking up and grinding substances in a mortar.

pet /pɛt/ *n.*, *adj.*, *v.*, **petted**, **petting**. – *n.* **1.** any domesticated or tamed animal that is cared for affectionately. – *adj.* **2.** treated as a pet, as an animal. **3.** favourite. – *v.t.* **4.** to treat as a pet; fondle; indulge.

petal /'pɛtl/ *n.* one of the floral leaves, usually brightly coloured, of a flower or blossom.

peter /'pitə/ *v.i.* to diminish gradually and then disappear or cease (fol. by *out*).

peter principle *n.* the theory that in a hierarchy every employee tends to rise to a level just beyond his or her level of competence.

petite /pə'tit/ *adj.* (of women) small.

petition /pə'tɪʃən/ *n.* **1.** a formally drawn-up request addressed to a person or a body of persons in authority or power, soliciting some favour, right, mercy, or other benefit. – *v.t.* **2.** to address a formal petition to (a sovereign, a legislative body, etc.).

petrel /'pɛtrəl/ *n.* a seabird.

petrify /'pɛtrəfaɪ/ *v.t.*, **-fied**, **-fying**. **1.** to convert into stone or a stony substance. **2.** to stupefy or paralyse with astonishment, horror, fear, or other strong emotion.

petrol /'pɛtrəl/ *n.* a mixture of volatile liquid hydrocarbons, as hexane, heptane, and octane, used as a solvent and extensively as a fuel in internal-combustion engines. – **petrolic**, *adj.*

petroleum /pə'troʊliəm/ *n.* an oily, usually dark-coloured liquid (a form of bitumen or mixture of various hydrocarbons). Also, **rock-oil**.

petticoat /'pɛtikoʊt/ *n.* a skirt, especially an underskirt, worn by women and girls; a slip.

petty /'pɛti/ *adj.*, **-tier**, **-tiest**. **1.** of small importance; trifling; trivial. **2.** having or showing narrow ideas, interests, etc.

petty cash *n.* a small cash fund set aside to meet incidental expenses, as for office supplies.

petulant /'pɛtʃələnt/ *adj.* moved to or showing sudden, impatient irritation, especially over some trifling annoyance.

petunia /pə'tjunjə/ *n.* a plant with funnel-shaped flowers of various colours.

pew /pju/ *n.* (in a church) one of an assemblage of fixed benchlike seats (with backs), accessible by aisles, for the use of the congregation.

pewter /'pjutə/ *n.* any of various alloys in which tin is the chief constituent, originally one of tin and lead.

-phagous a word element used as an adjective termination meaning 'eating', 'feeding on'.

phallus /'fæləs/ *n.*, *pl.* **phalluses**, **phalli** /'fælaɪ/. **1.** an image of the erect male reproductive organ. **2.** *Anatomy* the penis, clitoris, or the sexually undifferentiated embryonic organ out of which each develops. – **phallic**, *adj.*

phantom /'fæntəm/ *n.* **1.** an image appearing in a dream or formed in the mind. **2.** an apparition or spectre.

pharmaceutical /famə'sjutɪkəl/ *adj.* relating to pharmacy. Also, **pharmaceutic**.

pharmaceutics /famə'sjutɪks/ *n.* → **pharmacy** (def. 1).

pharmacology /famə'kɒlədʒi/ *n.* the science of drugs, their preparation, uses, and effects.

pharmacy /'faməsi/ *n.*, *pl.* **-cies**. **1.** the art or practice of preparing and dispensing drugs and medicines. **2.** a dispensary; chemist's shop. – **pharmacist**, *n.*

pharyngitis /færən'dʒaɪtəs/ *n.* inflammation of the mucous membrane of the pharynx.

pharynx /'færɪŋks/ *n.*, *pl.* **pharynxes**, **pharynges** /fə'rɪndʒiz/. the tube or cavity, with its surrounding membrane and muscles, which connects the mouth with the oesophagus.

phase /feɪz/ *n.*, *v.*, **phased**, **phasing**. – *n.* **1.** a stage of change or development. – *v.t.* **2. phase in,** to introduce gradually and synchronise into a system, or the like. **3. phase out,** to withdraw gradually from a system.

pheasant /'fɛzənt/ *n.* a large, long-tailed, gallinaceous bird.

phenomenon /fə'nɒmənən/ *n.*, *pl.* **-mena** /-mənə/. **1.** a fact, occurrence, or circumstance observed or observable. **2.** something that impresses the observer as extraordinary; a remarkable thing or person. – **phenomenal**, *adj.*

phial /'faɪəl/ *n.* a small bottle.

phil- a word element meaning 'loving', as in

philanthropy. Also, **philo-**.

-phil → **-phile**.

-phile a word element meaning 'loving', 'friendly', or 'lover', 'friend'. Also, **-phil**.

philander /fə'lændə/ *v.i.* (of a man) to make love, especially without serious intentions.

philanthropy /fə'lænθrəpi/ *n., pl.* **-pies**. love of humankind, especially as manifested in deeds of practical beneficence. – **philanthropist**, *n.* – **philanthropic**, *adj.*

philately /fə'lætəli/ *n.* the collecting and study of postage stamps, etc. – **philatelic**, *adj.* – **philatelist**, *n.*

-philia a word element used as a noun termination meaning 'fondness', 'craving' or 'affinity for'.

philistine /'fɪləstaɪn/ *n.* (*sometimes cap.*) someone looked down on as lacking in and indifferent to culture, aesthetic refinement, etc.

philology /fə'lɒlədʒi/ *n.* linguistics.

philosophical /fɪlə'sɒfɪkəl/ *adj.* **1.** of or relating to philosophy. **2.** rationally or sensibly calm in trying circumstances.

philosophy /fə'lɒsəfi/ *n., pl.* **-phies**. **1.** the study or science of the truths or principles underlying all knowledge and being (or reality). **2.** a system of principles for guidance in practical affairs. **3.** philosophical spirit or attitude; wise composure throughout the vicissitudes of life. – **philosopher**, *n.*

-philous a word element used as an adjective termination meaning 'loving'.

philtre /'fɪltə/ *n.* a love potion.

phlegm /flɛm/ *n. Physiology* the thick mucus secreted in the respiratory passages and discharged by coughing, etc.

phlegmatic /flɛg'mætɪk/ *adj.* **1.** not easily excited to action or feeling; sluggish or apathetic. **2.** cool or self-possessed.

-phobe a word element used as a noun termination meaning 'someone who fears or dreads'.

phobia /'foʊbiə/ *n.* any obsessing or morbid fear or dread.

-phobia a word element used as a noun termination meaning 'fear' or 'dread', often morbid, or with implication of aversion or hatred.

phoenix /'finɪks/ *n.* a mythical bird.

phone /foʊn/ *n., v.t., v.i.*, **phoned**, **phoning**. *Colloquial* → **telephone**.

phonetic /fə'nɛtɪk/ *adj.* of or relating to speech sounds and their production.

phonetics /fə'nɛtɪks/ *n.* the science of speech sounds and their production. – **phonetician**, *n.*

phoney = phony /'foʊni/ *adj.*, **-nier**, **-niest**. *Colloquial* not genuine; spurious, counterfeit, or bogus; fraudulent.

phosphorescence /fɒsfə'rɛsəns/ *n.* the property of being luminous at temperatures below incandescence, as from slow oxidation. – **phosphorescent**, *adj.*

phosphorus /'fɒsfərəs/ *n., pl.* **-ri** /-raɪ/. *Chemistry* a solid non-metallic element used in matches and in fertilisers. *Symbol*: P – **phosphoric**, *adj.*

photo /'foʊtoʊ/ *n., pl.* **-tos**. → **photograph**.

photo- 1. a combining form meaning 'light' as in *photosynthesis, photoelectron*. **2.** a word element meaning 'photograph' or 'photographic' as in *photocopy*.

photocopy /'foʊtoʊkɒpi/ *n., pl.* **-copies**, *v.*, **-copied**, **-copying**. – *n.* **1.** a photographic reproduction of written or printed material. – *v.t.* **2.** to make a photocopy of. – **photocopier**, *n.*

photoelectric cell /ˌfoʊtoʊə'lɛktrɪk/ *n.* a device used for the detection of light.

photogenic /foʊtə'dʒɛnɪk, -'dʒinɪk/ *adj. Photography* (of a person) suitable for being photographed for artistic purposes, etc.

photograph /'foʊtəgræf, -graf/ *n.* **1.** a picture produced by photography. – *v.t.* **2.** to take a photograph of.

photography /fə'tɒgrəfi/ *n.* the process or art of producing images of objects on sensitised surfaces by the chemical action of light or of other forms of radiant energy, as X-rays, gamma rays, cosmic rays, etc. – **photographer**, *n.* – **photographic**, *adj.*

photostat /'foʊtəstæt/ *n., v.*, **-statted**, **-statting**. – *n.* **1.** a special camera for making facsimile copies of maps, drawings, pages of books or manuscripts, etc., which photographs directly as a positive on sensitised paper. **2.** a copy so made. – *v.t.* **3.** to make such a copy or copies of.

photosynthesis /foʊtoʊ'sɪnθəsəs/ *n.* the synthesis of complex organic materials by plants from carbon dioxide, water, and inorganic salts using sunlight as the source of energy and with the aid of a catalyst such as chlorophyll.

phrase /freɪz/ *n., v.*, **phrased**, **phrasing**. *-n.* **1.** *Grammar* a sequence of two or more words arranged in a grammatical construction and acting as a unit in the sentence. **2.** a characteristic, current, or proverbial expression. **3.** a group or sequence making up a recognisable entity. – *v.t.* **4.** to express or word in a particular way. – **phrasal**, *adj.*

phraseology /freɪzi'ɒlədʒi/ *n.* manner or style of verbal expression; characteristic language. – **phraseological**, *adj.*

phrenetic /frə'nɛtɪk/ *adj.* delirious; insane; frantic; frenzied.

phrenology /frə'nɒlədʒi/ *n.* the theory that one's mental powers are indicated by the shape of the skull.

-phyll a word element used as a noun termination meaning 'leaf'. Also, **-phyl**.

phyllo- a word element meaning 'leaf'. Also (*before vowels*), **phyll-**.

-phyllous a word element used as an adjective termination meaning 'having leaves', 'leaved', or implying some connection with a leaf, as in *diphyllous*.

phylo- a word element meaning 'tribe'.

phylum /'faɪləm/ *n., pl.* **-la** /-lə/. *Biology* a primary division of the animal or vegetable kingdom.

physical /'fɪzəkəl, 'fɪzɪkəl/ *adj.* **1.** relating to the body; bodily. **2.** of or relating to material nature; material. **3.** of or relating to the physics.

physician /fə'zɪʃən/ *n.* one legally qualified to practise medicine.

physics /'fɪzɪks/ *n.* the science dealing with natural laws and processes, and the states and properties of matter and energy, other than those restricted to living matter and to chemical changes. – **physicist**, *n.*

physiognomy /fɪzi'ɒnəmi/ *n., pl.* **-mies**. the face or countenance, especially as considered as an index to the character.

physiology /fɪzi'ɒlədʒi/ *n.* the science dealing with the functioning of living organisms or their parts. – **physiologist**, *n.* – **physiological**, *adj.*

physiotherapy /ˌfɪzioʊ'θɛrəpi/ *n.* the treatment of disease or bodily weaknesses or defects by physical remedies, such as massage, gymnastics, etc. Also, **physio**. – **physiotherapist**, *n.*

physique /fə'zik/ *n.* human bodily structure or type.

pi /paɪ/ *n., pl.* **pis**. *Mathematics* the ratio (3.141 592) of the circumference of a circle to its diameter.

piano /pi'ænoʊ/ *n.* a musical instrument in which hammers, operated from a keyboard, strike upon metal strings. – **pianist**, *n.* – **pianistic**, *adj.*

piano accordion *n.* an accordion having a piano-like keyboard for the right hand.

pianoforte /piænoʊ'fɔteɪ, pianoʊ-/ *n.* → **piano**.

picador /'pɪkədɔ/ *n.* one of the horsemen who open a bullfight by irritating and enraging the bull by pricking it with lances, without disabling it.

picaresque /pɪkə'rɛsk/ *adj.* of or relating to rogues.

piccolo /'pɪkəloʊ/ *n., pl.* **-los**. a small flute, sounding an octave higher than the ordinary flute.

pick[1] /pɪk/ *v.t.* **1.** to choose or select carefully. **2.** to choose (one's way or steps), as over rough ground or through a crowd. **3.** to steal the contents of (a person's pocket, purse, etc.). **4.** to open (a lock) with a pointed instrument, a wire, or the like, as for robbery. **5.** to pierce, indent, dig into, or break up (something) with a pointed instrument. **6.** to pluck or gather. **7.** *Music* to pluck (the strings of an instrument). – *v.i.* **8.** to strike with or use a pointed instrument or the like on something. **9.** to eat with dainty bites. – *v.* **10. pick on,** *Colloquial* **a.** to annoy; tease; criticise or blame. **b.** to choose (a person) indiscriminately, especially for an unpleasant task. **11. pick out, a.** to choose. **b.** to distinguish (a thing) from surrounding or accompanying things. **c.** to make out (sense or meaning). **d.** to extract by picking. **12. pick someone's brains,** to find out as much as one can, from someone else's knowledge of a subject. **13. pick to pieces,** to criticise, especially in petty detail. **14. pick up, a.** to take up. **b.** to learn by occasional opportunity or without special teaching. **c.** to get casually. **d.** to take (a person or thing) into a car, ship, etc., or along with one. **e.** to bring into the range of reception, observation, etc. **f.** to accelerate, especially in speed. **g.** *Colloquial* to improve. **h.** *Colloquial* to arrest. – *n.* **15.** the choicest or most desirable part, example, or examples. **16.** → **plectrum**. – **picker**, *n.*

pick[2] /pɪk/ *n.* a hand tool for loosening and breaking up soil, etc.

pickaxe /'pɪkæks/ *n.* a pick.

picket /'pɪkət/ *n.* **1.** a pointed post, stake, pale, or peg. **2.** a person or a body of persons stationed by a trade union or the like in front of a place of work and attempting to dissuade or prevent workers from entering the building during a strike. – *v.i.* **3.** to stand or march by a place of employment as a picket.

pickle /'pɪkəl/ *n., v.,* **-led**, **-ling**. – *n.* **1.** (*often pl.*) vegetables, as cucumbers, onions, cauliflowers, etc., preserved in vinegar, brine, etc., and eaten as a relish. **2.** a liquid or marinade prepared with salt or vinegar for the preservation of fish, meat, vegetables, etc., or for the hardening of wood, leather, etc. **3.** *Colloquial* a predicament. – *v.t.* **4.** to preserve or steep in pickle.

pickpocket /'pɪkpɒkət/ *n.* someone who steals from the pockets, handbags, etc., of people in public places.

picnic /'pɪknɪk/ *n., v.,* **-nicked**, **-nicking**. – *n.* **1.** an outing or excursion, typically one in which those taking part carry food with them and share a meal in the open air. **2.** *Colloquial* an enjoyable experience or time. **3.** *Colloquial* an easy undertaking. – *v.i.* **4.** to hold, or take part in, a picnic. – **picnicker**, *n.*

Picnic Day *n.* an extra holiday awarded to a particular union or group of employees.

pictorial /pɪk'tɔriəl/ *adj.* relating to, expressed in, or of the nature of, a picture or pictures.

picture /'pɪktʃə/ *n., v.,* **-tured**, **-turing**. – *n.* **1.** a representation, upon a surface, usually flat, as a painting, drawing or photograph, etc. **2.** any visible image, however produced. **3. the pictures,** a cinema. – *v.t.* **4.** to form a mental image of.

picturesque /pɪktʃə'rɛsk/ *adj.* visually charming or quaint.

piddle /'pɪdl/ *v.i.,* **-dled**, **-dling**. *Colloquial* to urinate.

pidgin /'pɪdʒən/ *n.* a language used for communication between groups having different first languages, and which typically has features deriving from those languages. Also, **pigeon**.

pie /paɪ/ *n.* a baked dish consisting of a sweet (fruit, etc.) or savoury filling (meat, fish, etc.), enclosed in or covered by pastry.

piebald /'paɪbɔld/ *adj.* having patches of black and white or of other colours.

piece /pis/ *n., v.,* **pieced**, **piecing**. – *n.* **1.** a limited portion or quantity, of something. **2.** one of the parts, fragments, or shreds into which something may be divided or broken. **3.** an individual article of a set or collection. **4.** any of the counters, discs, blocks, or the like, of wood, ivory, or other material, used in any of a number of board games, as draughts, backgammon, or chess. **5.** an amount of work forming a single job. **6.** a musical composition, usually a short one. **7.** *Military* a firearm. – *v.t.* **8.** to mend (something broken); reassemble (usually fol. by *together*). **9.** to fit together, as pieces or parts.

piecemeal /'pismil/ *adv.* piece by piece; gradually.

pie-eyed /'paɪ-aɪd/ *adj. Colloquial* drunk.

pier /pɪə/ *n.* **1.** a structure built out into the water to serve as a landing place for ships.

2. one of the supports of a span of a bridge or of two adjacent spans.

pierce /pɪəs/ *v.t.*, **pierced**, **piercing**. **1.** to penetrate or run into or through (something), as a sharp-pointed instrument does; puncture. **2.** to penetrate with the eye or mind; see into or through. **3.** to sound sharply through (the air, stillness, etc.) as a cry. – **piercer**, *n.* – **piercingly**, *adv.*

piety /ˈpaɪəti/ *n., pl.* **-ties**. reverence for God, or regard for religious obligations.

piffle /ˈpɪfəl/ *n. Colloquial* nonsense.

pig /pɪg/ *n.* **1.** an omnivorous non-ruminant mammal; a sow, hog, or boar; a swine. Cf. **hog**. **2.** *Colloquial* a greedy, dirty person. **3.** *Colloquial* (*derogatory*) a police officer. **4.** *Metallurgy* an oblong mass of metal that has been run while still molten into a mould of sand or the like.

pigeon /ˈpɪdʒən/ *n.* a bird with a compact body and short legs, often bred for racing, etc.

pigeonhole /ˈpɪdʒənhoʊl/ *n., v.,* **-holed**, **-holing**. – *n.* **1.** one of a series of small compartments in a desk, cabinet, or the like, used for papers, etc. – *v.t.* **2.** to put away for reference at some indefinite future time. **3.** to assign a definite place in some orderly system.

piggyback /ˈpɪgibæk/ *adv.* sitting on the back or shoulders of another.

pig-headed /ˈpɪg-hɛdəd/ *adj.* stupidly obstinate.

piglet /ˈpɪglət/ *n.* a little pig.

pigment /ˈpɪgmənt/ *n.* a colouring matter or substance.

pigtail /ˈpɪgteɪl/ *n.* a braid of hair hanging down the back of the head.

pike[1] /paɪk/ *n., pl.* **pikes**, (*esp. collectively*) **pike**. any of various elongated fishes.

pike[2] /paɪk/ *n.* a sharp point; a spike.

pike[3] /paɪk/ *n.* a jackknife dive.

pikelet /ˈpaɪklət/ *n.* a small thick, sweet pancake.

piker /ˈpaɪkə/ *n.* someone who, from lack of courage or from diffidence, does anything in a contemptibly small or cheap way.

pilchard /ˈpɪltʃəd/ *n.* a small abundant fish.

pilchers /ˈpɪltʃəz/ *pl. n.* flannel or plastic pants or a plastic wrapper worn by an infant over a nappy.

pile[1] /paɪl/ *n., v.,* **piled**, **piling**. – *n.* **1.** an assemblage of things laid or lying one upon another in a more or less orderly fashion. – *v.t.* **2.** to lay or dispose in a pile (often fol. by *up* or *on*). **3.** to accumulate (fol. by *up*). – *v.i.* **4.** to accumulate, as money, debts, evidence, etc. (fol. by *up*).

pile[2] /paɪl/ *n.* a heavy timber, stake or pole, sometimes pointed at the lower end, driven vertically into the ground or the bed of a river, etc., to support a superstructure or form part of a wall.

pile[3] /paɪl/ *n.* **1.** hair, especially soft, fine hair or down. **2.** a raised surface on cloth.

pile[4] /paɪl/ *n.* (*usu. pl.*) → **haemorrhoid**.

pilfer /ˈpɪlfə/ *v.t.* **1.** to steal (a small amount or object). – *v.i.* **2.** to practise petty theft. – **pilferer**, *n.* – **pilferage**, *n.*

pilgrim /ˈpɪlgrəm/ *n.* someone who journeys, especially a long distance, to some sacred place as an act of devotion. – **pilgrimage**, *n.*

pill /pɪl/ *n.* a small globular or rounded mass of medicinal substance, to be swallowed whole; tablet.

pillage /ˈpɪlɪdʒ/ *v.,* **-laged**, **-laging**, *n.* – *v.t.* **1.** to strip of money or goods by open violence, as in war; plunder. – *n.* **2.** the act of plundering, especially in war.

pillar /ˈpɪlə/ *n.* an upright supporting part.

pillion /ˈpɪljən/ *n.* an extra seat behind the driver's seat on a bicycle, etc.

pillory /ˈpɪləri/ *n., pl.* **-ries**, *v.,* **-ried**, **-rying**. – *n.* **1.** a wooden framework erected on a post, with holes for securing the head and hands, used to expose an offender to public derision. – *v.t.* **2.** to expose to public ridicule or abuse.

pillow /ˈpɪloʊ/ *n.* a bag or case filled with feathers, down, or other soft material, commonly used as a support for the head during sleep or rest.

pilot /paɪlət/ *n.* **1.** one duly qualified to steer ships into or out of a harbour or through certain difficult waters. **2.** someone who controls an aeroplane, balloon, or other aircraft. **3.** a guide or leader. **4.** a sample episode for a television series. – *v.t.* **5.** to steer. **6.** to guide or conduct, as through unknown places, intricate affairs, etc.

pimp /pɪmp/ *n.* someone who solicits for a prostitute or brothel; a procurer.

pimple /ˈpɪmpəl/ *n.* a small, usually inflammatory swelling or elevation of the skin.

pin /pɪn/ *n., v.,* **pinned**, **pinning**. – *n.* **1.** a small, slender, sometimes tapered or pointed piece of wood, metal, etc., used to fasten, or hold things together, etc. **2.** a short, slender piece of wire with a point at one end and a head at the other, for fastening things together, as cloth or paper. – *v.t.* **3.** to fasten or attach with a pin or pins, or as if with a pin. **4.** Also, **pin down**. to hold (a person, etc.) fast in a spot or position.

PIN /pɪn/ *n.* → **PIN number**.

pinafore /ˈpɪnəfɔ/ *n.* an apron. Also, **pinny**.

pinball /ˈpɪnbɔl/ *n.* game played on a sloping board, in which a ball, driven by a spring, hits pins or bumpers which electrically record the score.

pince-nez /ˈpæns-neɪ, ˈpɪns-neɪ/ *n.* a pair of spectacles kept in place by a spring which pinches the nose.

pincers /ˈpɪnsəz/ *n.* (*pl. or sing.*) **1.** a gripping tool consisting of two pivoted limbs forming a pair of jaws and a pair of handles. **2.** *Zoology* a grasping organ or pair of organs resembling this.

pinch /pɪntʃ/ *v.t.* **1.** to compress between the finger and thumb, the jaws of an instrument, or any two opposed surfaces. **2.** to cramp within narrow bounds or quarters. **3.** to stint the supply or amount of (a thing). **4.** *Colloquial* to steal. **5.** *Colloquial* to arrest. – *v.i.* **6.** to exert a sharp or painful compressing force. **7.** to cause sharp discomfort or distress. – *n.* **8.** the act of pinching; nip; squeeze. **9.** a very small quantity of anything. **10.** sharp or painful stress, as of hunger, need, or any trying circumstances.

pincushion /ˈpɪnkʊʃən/ *n.* a small cushion

in which pins are stuck, in readiness for use.

pine[1] /paɪn/ *n.* an evergreen coniferous trees with long needle-shaped leaves.

pine[2] /paɪn/ *v.i.,* **pined, pining**. to suffer with longing, or long painfully (fol. by *for*).

pineapple /'paɪnæpəl/ *n.* an edible juicy tropical fruit being a large collective fruit developed from a spike or head of flowers, and surmounted by a crown of leaves.

pinion[1] /'pɪnjən/ *n. Machinery* a small cogwheel engaging with a larger cogwheel or with a rack.

pinion[2] /'pɪnjən/ *n.* **1.** the end section of a bird's wing. – *v.t.* **2.** to cut off the pinion of (a wing) or bind (the wings), as in order to prevent a bird from flying. **3.** to bind (a person's arms or hands) so as to deprive them of their use.

pink[1] /pɪŋk/ *n.* **1.** a light tint of crimson; pale reddish purple. **2.** the highest form or degree: *in the pink of condition.* – *adj.* **3.** of the colour pink.

pink[2] /pɪŋk/ *v.t.* **1.** to pierce with a rapier or the like; stab. **2.** to finish at the edge with a scalloped, notched, or other ornamental pattern.

pinnacle /'pɪnəkəl/ *n.* **1.** a lofty peak. **2.** the highest or culminating point.

PIN number *n.* personal identification number; a sequence of numbers and/or letters used as part of an identification procedure in electronic banking. Also, **PIN**.

pin-up /'pɪn-ʌp/ *n. Colloquial* **1.** a picture, usually pinned to the wall, of an attractive member of the opposite sex. **2.** the person depicted.

pioneer /paɪə'nɪə/ *n.* **1.** one of those who first enter or settle a region, thus opening it for occupation and development by others. **2.** one of those who are first or earliest in any field of inquiry, enterprise, or progress. – *v.i.* **3.** to act as a pioneer. – *v.t.* **4.** to open or prepare (a way, etc.), as a pioneer does. **5.** to open a way for. **6.** to be a pioneer in.

pious /'paɪəs/ *adj.* **1.** having or displaying religious fervour or conscientiousness in religious observance. **2.** respectful or dutiful. **3.** sanctimonious.

pip[1] /pɪp/ *n.* **1.** one of the spots on dice, playing cards, or dominoes. **2.** *Military Colloquial* a badge of rank worn on the shoulders of certain commissioned officers.

pip[2] /pɪp/ *n.* a small seed, especially of a fleshy fruit, as an apple or orange.

pip[3] /pɪp/ *n.* **1.** a brief high-pitched sound made by a radio receiver, echo-sounder, or the like. **2.** the signal on the screen of a radar set or the like.

pipe[1] /paɪp/ *n.* **1.** a hollow cylinder of metal, wood, or other material, for the conveyance of water, gas, steam, etc., or for some other purpose; a tube. **2.** a tube of wood, clay, hard rubber, or other material, with a small bowl at one end, used for smoking tobacco, opium, etc. **3.** *Music* **a.** a musical wind instrument. **b.** one of the wooden or metal tubes from which the sounds of an organ are produced. – *v.i.* **4.** to play on a pipe. – *v.t.* **5.** to convey by means of pipes. **6.** to utter in a shrill tone. **7.** to trim or finish (a garment, etc.) with piping.

pipe[2] /paɪp/ *n.* a large cask, of varying capacity, for wine, etc.

pipedream /'paɪpdrim/ *n.* a futile hope, far-fetched fancy, or fantastic story.

pipeline /'paɪplaɪn/ *n.* **1.** pipe(s) used for the transmission of petroleum, etc. **2. in the pipeline,** on the way; in preparation.

pipette /pɪ'pɛt/ *n.* a slender graduated tube for measuring and transferring liquids from one vessel to another. Also, **pipet**.

pipi /'pɪpi/ *n.* an edible, smooth-shelled burrowing, bivalve mollusc.

piping /'paɪpɪŋ/ *n.* **1.** the act of someone who or that which pipes. **2.** a cordlike ornamentation made of icing, used on cakes, pastry, etc. **3.** a tubular band of material, sometimes containing a cord, for trimming garments, etc., as along edges and seams.

pipsqueak /'pɪpskwik/ *n. Colloquial* a small or insignificant person or thing.

piquant /'pikənt/ *adj.* **1.** agreeably pungent or sharp in taste or flavour; biting; tart. **2.** agreeably stimulating, interesting, or attractive. – **piquancy**, *n.*

pique /pik/ *v.,* **piqued, piquing**, *n.* – *v.t.* **1.** to affect with sharp irritation and resentment, especially by some wound to pride. **2.** to excite (interest, curiosity, etc.). – *n.* **3.** anger, resentment, or ill feeling, as resulting from a slight or injury, especially to pride or vanity; offence taken.

piranha /pə'ranə/ *n.* a small fish noted for its voracious habits.

pirate /'paɪrət/ *n., v.,* **-rated, -rating**. – *n.* **1.** someone who robs or commits illegal violence at sea or on the shores of the sea. **2.** any plunderer. **3.** someone who appropriates and reproduces without authorisation, as for his or her own profit, the literary, artistic, or other work or any invention of another. **4.** Also, **pirate radio**. a radio station broadcasting on an unauthorised wavelength, and often operating outside territorial waters or in a foreign country so as to avoid payment of copyright fees or other legal restrictions. – *v.t.* **5.** to appropriate and reproduce (literary work, etc.) without authorisation or legal right. – **piracy**, *n.*

pirouette /pɪru'ɛt/ *n.* a whirling about on one foot or on the points of the toes, as in dancing.

piscatorial /pɪskə'tɔriəl/ *adj.* of or relating to fishing.

pisci- a word element meaning 'fish'.

piss /pɪs/ *Colloquial* – *v.i.* **1.** to urinate. **2. piss off,** (*sometimes offensive*) to go away. – *v.t.* **3. piss someone off, a.** to send someone away. **b.** to annoy someone intensely. – *n.* **4.** urine. **5.** an act of passing water; urination.

pistachio /pɪs'taʃioʊ/ *n., pl.* **-chios**. a hard-shelled nut with an edible greenish kernel.

pistil /'pɪstl/ *n. Botany* the ovule-bearing or seed-bearing organ of a flower.

pistol /'pɪstl/ *n.* a short firearm intended to be held and fired with one hand.

piston /'pɪstən/ *n.* a movable disc or cylinder fitting closely within a tube or hollow cylinder, and capable of being driven alternately forwards and backwards in the tube by pressure, as in an internal-combustion engine.

pit[1] /pɪt/ *n., v.,* **pitted**, **pitting**. – *n.* **1.** a hole or cavity in the ground. **2.** *Mining* an excavation made in digging for some mineral deposit. **3.** a natural hollow or depression in the body. **4.** an enclosure for combats, as of dogs or cocks. **5.** any of the stalls beside the motor-racing track in which competing cars undergo running repairs, are refuelled, etc., during a race. – *v.t.* **6.** to mark with pits or depressions. **7.** to set in active opposition, as one against another.

pit[2] /pɪt/ *n.* the stone of a fruit.

pitch[1] /pɪtʃ/ *v.t.* **1.** to set up or erect (a tent, camp, etc.). **2.** *Music* to set at a particular pitch, or determine the key or keynote of (a tune, etc.). **3.** to throw, fling or toss. – *v.i.* **4.** to plunge or fall forward or headlong. **5.** to plunge with alternate fall and rise of bow and stern, as a ship, aeroplane, etc. (opposed to *roll*). **6. pitch in,** *Colloquial* to contribute or join in. – *n.* **7.** relative point, position, or degree. **8.** height (now chiefly in certain specific uses). **9.** *Acoustics*, *Music* the apparent predominant frequency of a sound from an acoustical source, musical instrument, etc. **10.** the act or manner of pitching. **11.** inclination or slope, as of ground or a roof. **12. a.** *Sport* the whole area of play, usually of grass, of cricket, football, hockey, etc. **b.** *Cricket* the area between the wickets. **13.** a sales talk.

pitch[2] /pɪtʃ/ *n.* any of various dark-coloured tenacious or viscous substances used for covering the seams of vessels after caulking, for making pavements, etc.

pitchblende /ˈpɪtʃblɛnd/ *n.* a mineral; the principal ore of uranium and radium.

pitcher /ˈpɪtʃə/ *n.* a container, usually with a handle and spout or lip, for holding and pouring liquids.

pitchfork /ˈpɪtʃfɔk/ *n.* a fork for lifting and pitching hay, etc.

piteous /ˈpɪtiəs/ *adj.* such as to excite or deserve pity.

pitfall /ˈpɪtfɔl/ *n.* any trap or danger for the unwary.

pith /pɪθ/ *n.* **1.** the soft, spongy lining of the rind of oranges and other citrus fruits. **2.** *Botany* the central cylinder of soft tissue in the stems of certain plants. **3.** the important or essential part; essence.

pithy /ˈpɪθi/ *adj.*, **-ier**, **-iest**. full of vigour, substance, or meaning; terse.

pitiable /ˈpɪtiəbəl/ *adj.* **1.** deserving to be pitied; such as justly to excite pity; lamentable; deplorable. **2.** such as to excite a contemptuous pity; miserable; contemptible.

pitiful /ˈpɪtəfəl/ *adj.* **1.** such as to excite or deserve pity. **2.** such as to excite contempt by smallness, poor quality, etc.

pittance /ˈpɪtns/ *n.* **1.** a small allowance or sum for living expenses. **2.** a scanty income or remuneration.

pituitary gland /pəˈtʃuətri/ *n.* a small, oval, endocrine gland attached to the base of the brain.

pity /ˈpɪti/ *n., pl.* **pities**, *v.,* **pitied**, **pitying**. – *n.* **1.** sympathetic or kindly sorrow excited by the suffering or misfortune of another, often leading one to give relief or to show mercy. – *v.t.* **2.** to feel pity or compassion for. – **pitiless**, *adj.*

pivot /ˈpɪvət/ *n.* **1.** a pin or short shaft on the end of which something rests and turns, or upon and about which something rotates or oscillates. **2.** that on which something turns, hinges, or depends. – *v.i.* **3.** to turn on or as on a pivot.

pixel /ˈpɪksəl/ *n. Computers* the smallest element of a graphic image which can be produced in a visual display unit.

pixie /ˈpɪksi/ *n., pl.* **pixies**. a fairy or sprite. Also, **pixy**.

pizza /ˈpitsə, ˈpɪtsə/ *n.* an Italian dish made from yeast dough covered with tomato, grated cheese, anchovies, etc.

placard /ˈplækad/ *n.* a written or printed notice to be posted in a public place; a poster.

placate /pləˈkeɪt/ *v.t.,* **-cated**, **-cating**. to appease; pacify. – **placatory**, *adj.*

place /pleɪs/ *n., v.,* **placed**, **placing**. – *n.* **1.** a particular portion of space, of definite or indefinite extent. **2.** any part or spot. **3.** a space or seat for a person, as in a theatre, train, etc. **4.** position, situation, or circumstances. **5.** a short street, a court, etc. **6.** a job, post, or office. **7.** a function or duty. **8.** a region. **9.** an area, especially one regarded as an entity. **10.** stead or lieu. **11.** *Arithmetic* **a.** the position of a figure in a series, as in decimal notation. **12.** *Sport* **a.** a position among the leading competitors, usually the first three, at the finish of a race. **b.** the position of the second or third (opposed to *win*). – *v.t.* **13.** to put in a particular place; set. **14.** to fix (confidence, esteem, etc.) in a person or thing. **15.** to appoint (a person) to a post or office. **16.** to put or set in a particular place, position, situation, or relation. **17.** to identify by connecting with the proper place, circumstances, etc.

placebo /pləˈsiboʊ/ *n., pl.* **-bos**, **-boes**. *Medicine* a medicine which performs no physiological function but may benefit the patient psychologically.

placenta /pləˈsɛntə/ *n., pl.* **-tas**, **-tae** /-ti/. *Zoology*, *Anatomy* the organ providing for the nourishment of the foetus and the elimination of its waste products.

placid /ˈplæsəd/ *adj.* pleasantly calm.

placket /ˈplækət/ *n.* an opening at the top of a skirt, or in a dress or blouse.

plagiarism /ˈpleɪdʒərɪzəm/ *n.* the appropriation or imitation of another's ideas and manner of expressing them, as in art, literature, etc., to be passed off as one's own. – **plagiarist**, *n.* – **plagiaristic**, *adj.* – **plagiarise = plagiarize**, *v.*

plagioclase /ˈpleɪdʒioʊˌkleɪz, -ˌkleɪs/ *n.* an important constituent of many igneous rocks.

plague /pleɪg/ *n., v.,* **plagued**, **plaguing**. – *n.* **1.** an epidemic disease of high mortality; a pestilence. **2.** any cause of trouble or vexation. – *v.t.* **3.** to trouble or torment in any manner.

plaid /plæd/ *n.* any fabric woven of different coloured yarns in a cross-barred pattern.

plain /pleɪn/ *adj.* **1.** clear or distinct to the eye or ear. **2.** clear to the mind; evident, manifest, or obvious. **3.** conveying the meaning clearly or simply; easily understood. **4.** without special pretensions, superiority, elegance, etc.; ordinary. **5.** not beautiful; unattractive. **6.** without pattern, device, or colouring. **7.** flat or level. – *adv.* **8.** simply; absolutely. **9.** clearly or intelligibly. – *n.* **10.** an area of land not significantly higher than adjacent areas and with relatively minor differences in elevation within the area.

plaint /pleɪnt/ *Law* a statement of grievance made to a court for the purpose of asking redress.

plaintiff /'pleɪntəf/ *n. Law* someone who brings an action in a civil case.

plaintive /'pleɪntɪv/ *adj.* expressing sorrow or melancholy discontent; mournful.

plait /plæt/ *n.* **1.** a braid, as of hair or straw. – *v.t.* **2.** to braid (hair, etc.).

plan /plæn/ *n., v.,* **planned**, **planning**. – *n.* **1.** a scheme of action or procedure. **2.** a design or scheme of arrangement. **3.** a representation of a thing drawn on a plane, as a map or diagram. – *v.t.* **4.** to arrange a plan or scheme for (any work, enterprise, or proceeding). **5.** to form a plan, project, or purpose of.

plane[1] /pleɪn/ *n.* **1.** a flat or level surface. **2.** *Mathematics* a surface such that the straight line joining any two distinct points in it lies entirely within it. **3.** an aeroplane. – *adj.* **4.** flat or level, as a surface.

plane[2] /pleɪn/ *n., v.,* **planed**, **planing**. – *n.* **1.** a tool with an adjustable blade for paring, truing, smoothing, or finishing the surface of wood, etc. – *v.t.* **2.** to smooth or dress with or as with a plane.

planet /'plænət/ *n. Astronomy* a solid body revolving around the sun, or a similar body revolving around a star other than the sun; planets are only visible by reflected light. – **planetary**, *adj.*

plangent /'plændʒənt/ *adj.* **1.** beating or dashing, as waves. **2.** resounding loudly.

plank /plæŋk/ *n.* a long, flat piece of timber thicker than a board.

plankton /'plæŋktən/ *n.* the small animal and plant organisms that float or drift in the water, especially at or near the surface.

plant /plænt, plant/ *n.* **1.** any member of the vegetable group of living organisms. **2.** a herb or other small vegetable growth, in contrast to a tree or a shrub. **3.** the equipment, including the fixtures, machinery, tools, etc., and often the buildings, necessary to carry on any industrial business. **4.** *Colloquial* **a.** something or someone intended to trap, decoy, or lure, as criminals. **b.** a spy. – *v.t.* **5.** to put or set in the ground for growth, as seeds, young trees, etc. **6.** to implant (ideas, sentiments, etc.); introduce and establish (principles, doctrines, etc.) **7.** to insert or set firmly in or on the ground or some other body or surface. **8.** to put or place. **9.** *Colloquial* to hide or conceal, as stolen goods. **10.** to place (evidence) so that it will be discovered and incriminate an innocent person.

plantar /'plæntə/ *adj.* of or relating to the sole of the foot.

plantation /plæn'teɪʃən/ *n.* a farm or estate, especially in a tropical or semitropical country, on which cotton, tobacco, coffee, sugar, or the like is cultivated, usually by resident labourers.

plaque /plak, plæk/ *n.* **1.** a plate or tablet of metal, porcelain, etc., as on a wall or set in a piece of furniture, for ornamentation or, if inscribed, commemoration. **2.** a film on teeth harbouring bacteria.

plasma /'plæzmə/ *n. Anatomy, Physiology* the liquid part of blood or lymph, as distinguished from the corpuscles.

plaster /'plastə/ *n.* **1.** a pasty composition, as of lime, sand, water, and often hair, used for covering walls, ceilings, etc., where it hardens in drying. **2.** an adhesive bandage. – *v.t.* **3.** to cover (walls, etc.) with plaster. **4.** to overspread with anything, especially thickly or to excess.

plasterboard /'plastəbɔd/ *n.* plaster in paper-covered sheets, used for walls.

plastic /'plæstɪk/ *adj.* **1.** capable of being moulded or of receiving form. **2.** produced by moulding. **3.** pliable; impressionable. – *n.* **4.** any of a group of synthetic or natural organic materials which may be shaped when soft and then hardened.

plasticine /'plæstəsin/ *n.* a plastic modelling compound, in various colours.

plastic money *n.* credit cards collectively. Also, **plastic**.

plastic surgery *n.* surgery which attempts to remodel malformed or damaged parts of the body.

plate /pleɪt/ *n., v.,* **plated**, **plating**. – *n.* **1.** a shallow, usually circular dish, now usually of earthenware or porcelain, from which food is eaten. **2.** a plate of sandwiches, cakes, etc., prepared and brought to a social occasion. **3.** domestic dishes, utensils, etc., of gold or silver. **4.** a thin, flat sheet or piece of metal or other material, especially of uniform thickness. **5.** a sheet of metal for printing from, formed by stereotyping or electrotyping a page of type, or metal or plastic formed by moulding, etching, or photographic development. **6.** plated metallic ware. **7.** *Dentistry* a piece of metal, vulcanite, or plastic substance, with artificial teeth attached. – *v.t.* **8.** to coat (metal) with a thin film of gold, silver, nickel, etc., by mechanical or chemical means.

plateau /'plætoʊ/ *n., pl.* **-eaus**, **-eaux** /-oʊz/. **1.** a tabular surface of high elevation, often of considerable extent. **2.** any period of minimal growth or decline.

plateau indexation *n.* a form of indexation in which wages below a certain value are increased on a proportional basis, and wages above that value by a fixed amount.

platform /'plætfɔm/ *n.* **1.** a raised flooring or structure. **2.** a plan or set of principles.

platinum /'plætənəm/ *n. Chemistry* a heavy, greyish white, highly malleable and ductile metallic element. *Symbol*: Pt

platitude /'plætətjud/ *n.* a flat, dull, or trite remark.

platonic /plə'tɒnɪk/ *adj.* purely spiritual; free from sensual desire.

platoon /plə'tun/ *n.* a group of soldiers forming a unit.

platter /'plætə/ *n.* a large, shallow dish.

platypus /'plætəpʊs/ *n., pl.* **-puses**, **-pi** /paɪ/. an amphibious, egg-laying monotreme with webbed feet and a muzzle like the bill of a duck.

plaudit /'plɔdət/ *n.* (*usu. pl.*) a demonstration or round of applause, as for some approved or admired performance.

plausible /'plɔzəbəl/ *adj.* having an appearance of truth or reason.

play /pleɪ/ *n.* **1.** a dramatic composition or piece; a drama. **2.** exercise or action by way of amusement or recreation. **3.** fun, jest, or trifling, as opposed to earnest. **4.** action, activity, or operation. **5.** freedom of movement, as within a space, as of a part of a mechanism. – *v.t.* **6.** to act or sustain (a part) in a dramatic performance or in real life. **7.** to engage in (a game, pastime, etc.). **8.** to contend against in a game. **9.** to perform on (a musical instrument). **10.** to perform (music) on an instrument. **11.** to do, perform, bring about, or execute. – *v.i.* **12.** to exercise or employ oneself in diversion, amusement, or recreation. **13.** to amuse oneself or toy; trifle (fol. by *with*). **14.** to take part or engage in a game. **15.** to perform on a musical instrument. **16.** to work on (the feelings, weaknesses, etc., of another) for one's own purposes (fol. by *on* or *upon*).

playhouse /'pleɪhaʊs/ *n.* a theatre.

playing card *n.* one of the conventional set of 52 cards, in 4 suits (diamonds, hearts, spades, and clubs), used in playing various games of chance and skill.

plaything /'pleɪθɪŋ/ *n.* a thing to play with; a toy.

playwright /'pleɪraɪt/ *n.* a writer of plays.

plaza /'plazə/ *n.* a public square.

plea /pli/ *n.* **1.** an excuse; a pretext. **2.** *Law* an allegation made by, or on behalf of, a party to a legal suit, in support of his or her claim or defence. **3.** an appeal or entreaty.

plead /plid/ *v.,* **pleaded** *or* **plead** /plɛd/, **pleading**. – *v.i.* **1.** to make earnest appeal or entreaty. **2.** *Law* **a.** to make any allegation or plea in an action at law. **b.** to address a court as an advocate. – *v.t.* **3.** to allege or urge in defence, justification, or excuse. **4.** *Law* **a.** to maintain (a cause, etc.) by argument before a court. **b.** to allege or set forth (something) formally in an action at law. **c.** to allege or cite in legal defence.

pleasant /'plɛzənt/ *adj.* **1.** pleasing, agreeable, or affording enjoyment; pleasurable. **2.** (of persons, manners, disposition, etc.) agreeable socially.

pleasantry /'plɛzəntri/ *n., pl.* **-tries**. good-humoured raillery; pleasant humour in conversation.

please /pliz/ *v.t.,* **pleased**, **pleasing**. **1.** to act to the pleasure or satisfaction of. **2.** to be the pleasure or will of; seem good to.

pleasurable /'plɛʒərəbəl/ *adj.* such as to give pleasure; agreeable; pleasant.

pleasure /'plɛʒə/ *n.* **1.** the state or feeling of being pleased. **2.** enjoyment or satisfaction derived from what is to one's liking; gratification; delight.

pleat /plit/ *n.* **1.** a fold made by doubling cloth upon itself. – *v.t.* **2.** to fold or arrange in pleats.

plebeian /plə'biən/ *adj.* **1.** belonging or relating to the common people. – *n.* **2.** a plebeian person.

plebiscite /'plɛbəsaɪt, -sət/ *n.* a direct vote of the qualified electors of a state in regard to some important public question.

plectrum /'plɛktrəm/ *n., pl.* **-trums**, **-tra** /-trə/. a piece of metal, plastic, etc., for plucking strings of a guitar, etc.

pledge /plɛdʒ/ *n., v.,* **pledged**, **pledging**. – *n.* **1.** a solemn promise of something, or to do or refrain from doing something. **2.** anything given or regarded as a security of something. **3.** a toast. – *v.t.* **4.** to bind by or as by a pledge. **5.** to promise solemnly, or engage to give, maintain, etc. **6.** to give or deposit as a pledge; pawn.

plenary /'plinəri/ *adj.* **1.** full; complete; entire; absolute; unqualified. **2.** attended by all qualified members, as a council. **3.** (of a conference session) scheduled without parallel sessions, and so likely to be attended by most of those registered as participants, usually to hear a prominent invited speaker.

plenipotentiary /,plɛnəpə'tɛnʃəri/ *n., pl.* **-ries**, *adj.* – *n.* **1.** a person, especially a diplomatic agent, invested with full power or authority to transact business. – *adj.* **2.** invested with full power or authority.

plenitude /'plɛnətjud/ *n.* abundance.

plenteous /'plɛntiəs/ *adj.* plentiful.

plentiful /'plɛntəfəl/ *adj.* existing in great plenty; abundant.

plenty /'plɛnti/ *n., pl.* **-ties**. **1.** a full or abundant supply. **2.** abundance.

plethora /'plɛθərə/ *n.* overfullness.

pleur- a word element meaning 'side', sometimes 'rib'. Also (*before consonants*), **pleuro-**.

plexus /'plɛksəs/ *n., pl.* **plexuses**, **plexus**. a network, as of nerves.

pliable /'plaɪəbəl/ *adj.* **1.** easily bent; flexible; supple. **2.** easily influenced; yielding; adaptable.

pliant /'plaɪənt/ *adj.* pliable.

pliers /'plaɪəz/ *pl. n.* small pincers with long jaws, for bending wire, etc.

plight[1] /plaɪt/ *n.* condition, state, or situation (usually bad).

plight[2] /plaɪt/ *v.t.* to give in pledge.

plinth /plɪnθ/ *n. Architecture* the lower square part of the base of a column.

plod /plɒd/ *v.t.,* **plodded**, **plodding**. **1.** to walk heavily; trudge; move laboriously. **2.** to work with dull perseverance; drudge.

plonk[1] /plɒŋk/ *v.t.* to place or drop heavily or suddenly (often fol. by *down*).

plonk[2] /plɒŋk/ *n. Colloquial* cheap wine.

plop /plɒp/ *v.i.,* **plopped**, **plopping**. to make a sound like that of a flat object striking water without a splash.

plot[1] /plɒt/ *n., v.,* **plotted**, **plotting**. – *n.* **1.** a secret plan or scheme to accomplish some purpose, especially a hostile, unlawful, or evil purpose. **2.** the plan, scheme, or main story of a play, novel, poem, or the like. – *v.t.* **3.** to plan secretly (something hostile or evil). **4.** to determine and mark (points), as on graph paper, by means of measurements or co-ordinates.

plot[2] /plɒt/ *n.* a small piece or area of ground.

plough /plaʊ/ *n.* **1.** an agricultural implement for cutting and turning over the soil.

– *v.t.* **2.** to furrow, remove, etc., or make (a furrow, groove, etc.) with or as with a plough. – *v.i.* **3.** to till the soil with a plough; work with a plough.

ploy /plɔɪ/ *n.* a manoeuvre or stratagem.

pluck /plʌk/ *v.t.* **1.** to pull off or out from the place of growth, as fruit, flowers, feathers, etc. **2.** to pull with sudden force or with a jerk. **3.** to sound (the strings of a musical instrument) by pulling at them with the fingers or a plectrum. – *n.* **4.** the act of plucking; a pull, tug, or jerk. **5.** the heart, liver, and lungs, especially of an animal used for food. **6.** courage or resolution in the face of difficulties. – **plucky**, *adj.*

plug /plʌg/ *n., v.,* **plugged, plugging**. – *n.* **1.** a piece of rubber or plastic for stopping the flow of water from a basin, bath or sink. **2.** a device, usually with three prongs, which by insertion in a socket establishes contact between an electrical appliance and a power supply. – *v.t.* **3.** to stop or fill with or as with a plug. **4.** *Colloquial* to mention (a publication, product or the like) favourably and, often, repetitively as in a lecture, radio show, etc. **5.** to connect (an electrical device) with an outlet (fol. by *in*).

plum /plʌm/ *n.* **1.** a purplish-coloured stone fruit. **2.** a good or choice thing, as one of the best parts of anything, a fine situation or appointment, etc.

plumage /ˈplumɪdʒ/ *n.* feathers collectively.

plumb /plʌm/ *n.* **1.** a small mass of lead or heavy material, used for various purposes. **2. out of plumb, a.** not perpendicular. **b.** not functioning properly. – *adj.* **3.** true according to a plumbline; perpendicular. – *adv.* **4.** in a perpendicular or vertical direction. **5.** exactly, precisely, or directly. – *v.t.* **6.** to make vertical. **7.** to sound (the ocean, etc.) with, or as with, a plumbline.

plumbing /ˈplʌmɪŋ/ *n.* the system of pipes and other apparatus for conveying water, liquid wastes, etc., as in a building. – **plumber**, *n.*

plumbline /ˈplʌmlaɪn/ *n.* a string to one end of which is attached a metal bob, used to determine perpendicularity, find the depth of water, etc.

plume /plum/ *n., v.,* **plumed, pluming**. – *n.* **1.** a feather. – *v.t.* **2.** to furnish, cover, or adorn with plumes or feathers. **3.** to display or feel satisfaction with or pride in (oneself); pride (oneself) complacently (fol. by *on* or *upon*).

plummet /ˈplʌmət/ *n.* **1.** a plumbline. – *v.i.* **2.** to plunge.

plump[1] /plʌmp/ *adj.* well filled out or rounded in form; somewhat fleshy or fat.

plump[2] /plʌmp/ *v.i.* **1.** to fall heavily or suddenly and directly. **2.** to vote exclusively for or choose one out of a number (often fol. by *for*).

plunder /ˈplʌndə/ *v.t.* **1.** to rob of goods or valuables by open force, as in war, hostile raids, brigandage, etc. – *n.* **2.** plundering, pillage, or spoliation. **3.** that which is taken in plundering; loot.

plunge /plʌndʒ/ *v.,* **plunged, plunging**, *n.* – *v.t.* **1.** to cast or thrust forcibly or suddenly into a liquid, etc. – *v.i.* **2.** to cast oneself, or fall as if cast, into water, a deep place, etc. **3.** to rush or dash with headlong haste. **4.** to throw oneself impetuously or abruptly into some condition, situation, matter, etc. **5.** to descend abruptly or precipitously, as a cliff, a road, etc. – *n.* **6.** the act of plunging.

plunk /plʌŋk/ *v.t.* **1.** to pluck (a stringed instrument or its strings); twang. **2.** to throw, push, put, etc., heavily or suddenly.

pluperfect /pluˈpɜfəkt/ *adj. Grammar* perfect with respect to a temporal point of reference in the past. Cf. **perfect, imperfect**.

plural /ˈplurəl/ *adj.* consisting of, containing, or relating to more than one.

plurality /pluˈræləti/ *n., pl.* **-ties**. more than half of the whole; the majority.

plus /plʌs/ *prep.* **1.** with the addition of; with. – *adj.* **2.** involving or denoting addition. **3.** positive. – *n.* **4.** a plus quantity. **5.** an advantage, asset, or gain.

plush /plʌʃ/ *adj.* denoting something, especially a room, furnishings, or the like, luxurious and costly.

plutocracy /pluˈtɒkrəsi/ *n., pl.* **-cies**. the rule or power of wealth or of the wealthy.

plutonium /pluˈtoʊniəm/ *n. Chemistry* a radioactive element. *Symbol*: Pu

pluvial /ˈpluviəl/ *adj.* **1.** of or relating to rain; rainy. **2.** *Geology* due to rain.

ply[1] /plaɪ/ *v.,* **plied, plying**. – *v.t.* **1.** to use; employ busily, or work with or at. **2.** to carry on, practise, or pursue. **3.** to supply with something pressingly offered. **4.** to address persistently or importunately, as with questions, solicitations, etc.; importune. **5.** to traverse (a river, etc.), especially on regular trips. – *v.i.* **6.** to travel or run regularly over a fixed course or between certain places, as a boat, a stage, etc.

ply[2] /plaɪ/ *n., pl.* **plies**. **1.** a fold; a thickness. **2.** a strand of yarn.

plywood /ˈplaɪwʊd/ *n.* a material consisting of an odd number of thin sheets or strips of wood glued together with the grains (usually) at right angles.

PMT /pi ɛm ˈti/ premenstrual tension.

pneumatic /njuˈmætɪk/ *adj.* **1.** of or relating to air, or gases in general. **2.** operated by air, or by pressure or exhaustion of air. **3.** containing air; filled with compressed air, as a tyre.

pneumonia /njuˈmoʊnjə/ *n.* inflammation of the lungs.

poach[1] /poʊtʃ/ *v.i.* **1.** to take game or fish illegally. **2.** to encroach on another's rights; take something belonging to another.

poach[2] /poʊtʃ/ *v.t.* to simmer in liquid in a shallow pan.

pock /pɒk/ *n.* a pustule on the body in an eruptive disease, as smallpox.

pocket /ˈpɒkət/ *n.* **1.** a small bag inserted in a garment, for carrying a purse or other small articles. **2.** money, means, or financial resources. **3.** a small isolated area. – *adj.* **4.** a small bag or net at the corner or side of a billiard table. **5.** small enough to go in the pocket; diminutive. – *v.t.* **6.** to put into one's pocket. **7.** to take possession of as one's own, often dishonestly.

pocket money *n.* a small weekly allowance of money.

pod /pɒd/ *n.* a more or less elongated, two-valved seed vessel, as that of the pea.

-pod a word element meaning 'footed', as in *cephalopod*.

poddy /ˈpɒdi/ *n.* a handfed calf.

podium /ˈpoʊdiəm/ *n., pl.* **-diums**, **-dia** /-diə/. a small platform for the conductor of an orchestra, for a public speaker, etc.

poem /ˈpoʊəm/ *n.* a composition in verse, especially one characterised by artistic construction and imaginative or elevated thought.

poesy /ˈpoʊəzi/ *n., pl.* **-sies**. *Poetic* poetry in general.

poet /ˈpoʊət/ *n.* **1.** someone who composes poetry. **2.** one having the gift of poetic thought, imagination, and creation, together with eloquence of expression.

poetic /poʊˈɛtɪk/ *adj.* **1.** possessing the qualities or the charm of poetry. **2.** of or relating to poets or poetry. – **poetically**, *adv.*

poetry /ˈpoʊətri/ *n.* the art of rhythmical composition, written or spoken, for exciting pleasure by beautiful, imaginative, or elevated thoughts.

pogrom /ˈpɒgrəm/ *n.* an organised massacre, especially of Jews.

poignant /ˈpɔɪnjənt, ˈpɔɪnənt/ *adj.* keenly distressing to the mental or physical feelings. – **poignancy**, *n.*

poinciana /pɔɪnsiˈanə, -ˈænə/ *n.* a tree or shrub with showy orange or scarlet flowers.

poinsettia /pɔɪnˈsɛtiə/ *n.* a perennial with variously lobed leaves and brilliant usually scarlet bracts.

point /pɔɪnt/ *n.* **1.** a sharp or tapering end, as of a dagger. **2.** a mark made as with a sharp end of something. **3.** a mark of punctuation. **4.** a decimal point, etc. **5.** something that has position but not extension, as the intersection of two lines. **6.** any definite position, as in a scale, course, etc. **7.** each of the 32 positions indicating direction marked at the circumference of the card of a compass. **8.** a degree or stage. **9.** a particular instant of time. **10.** the important or essential thing. **11.** a particular aim, end, or purpose. **12.** a dance shoe with a stiffened toe worn by a ballerina to enable her to dance on the tip of her toes. **13.** a single unit, as in counting, scoring a game, etc. **14.** *Commerce* a unit of price quotation in share transactions on the stock exchange. – *v.t.* **15.** to direct (the finger, a weapon, the attention, etc.) at, to, or upon something. **16.** to direct attention to (fol. by *out*). – *v.i.* **17.** to indicate position or direction, or direct attention, with or as with the finger. **18.** to aim. **19.** to have a tendency, as towards something. **20.** to face in a particular direction, as a building.

point-blank /pɔɪnt-ˈblæŋk/ *adj.* **1.** aimed or fired straight at the mark at close range; direct. **2.** straight-forward, plain, or explicit.

poise /pɔɪz/ *n., v.,* **poised**, **poising**. – *n.* **1.** a state of balance or equilibrium, as from equality or equal distribution of weight. **2.** composure; self-possession. – *v.t.* **3.** to balance evenly; adjust, hold, or carry in equilibrium. **4.** to hold supported or raised, as in position for casting, using, etc. – *v.i.* **5.** to be balanced; rest in equilibrium. **6.** to hang supported or suspended.

poison /ˈpɔɪzən/ *n.* **1.** any substance (liquid, solid, or gaseous) which by reason of an inherent deleterious property tends to destroy life or impair health. – *v.t.* **2.** to administer poison to (a person or animal). – **poisonous**, *adj.*

poke /poʊk/ *v.,* **poked**, **poking**, *n.* – *v.t.* **1.** to thrust against or into (something) with the finger or arm, a stick, etc.; prod. **2.** to thrust obtrusively. – *v.i.* **3.** to make a thrusting or pushing movement with the finger, a stick, etc. **4.** to pry; search curiously (often fol. by *about* or *around*). – *n.* **5.** a thrust or push.

poker[1] /ˈpoʊkə/ *n.* a metal rod for poking or stirring a fire.

poker[2] /ˈpoʊkə/ *n.* a card game, usually involving gambling.

poker machine *n.* a coin-operated gambling machine.

poky /ˈpoʊki/ *adj.,* **-kier**, **-kiest**. (of a place) small and cramped.

polar /ˈpoʊlə/ *adj.* of or relating to a pole, as of the earth, a magnet, an electric cell, etc.

polar bear *n.* a large white bear of the arctic regions.

polarisation = polarization /poʊləraɪˈzeɪʃən/ *n. Optics* a state, or the production of a state, in which rays of light, or similar radiation, exhibit different properties in different directions. – **polarise = polarize**, *v.*

polaroid /ˈpoʊlərɔɪd/ *n.* a material which allows only light polarised in a particular direction to pass.

pole[1] /poʊl/ *n., v.,* **poled**, **poling**. – *n.* **1.** a long, rounded, usually slender piece of wood, metal, etc. – *v.t.* **2.** to push, strike, propel, etc., with a pole.

pole[2] /poʊl/ *n.* **1.** each of the extremities of the axis of the earth or of any more or less spherical body. **2.** each of the two points in which the extended axis of the earth cuts the celestial sphere, about which the stars seem to revolve (**celestial pole**). **3.** *Physics* each of the two regions or parts of a magnet, electric battery, etc., at which certain opposite forces are manifested or appear to be concentrated. **4.** one of two completely opposed or contrasted principles, tendencies, etc.

poleaxe /ˈpoʊlæks/ *n.* an axe, usually with a hammer opposite the cutting edge, used in felling or stunning animals.

polecat /ˈpoʊlkæt/ *n.* a mammal of the weasel family.

polemic /pəˈlɛmɪk/ *n.* **1.** a controversial argument; argumentation against some opinion, doctrine, etc. – *adj.* **2.** Also, **polemical**. of or relating to disputation or controversy; controversial.

police /pəˈlis/ *n., v.,* **-liced**, **-licing**. – *n.* (*construed as pl.*) **1. the police,** an organised civil force for maintaining order, preventing and detecting crime, and enforcing the laws. **2.** the members of such a force. – *v.t.* **3.** to regulate, control, or keep in order by police or as a police force does.

policy[1] /ˈpɒləsi/ *n., pl.* **-cies**. **1.** a definite course of action adopted as expedient or from other considerations. **2.** prudence, practical wisdom, or expediency.

policy[2] /ˈpɒləsi/ *n., pl.* **-cies**. a document

embodying a contract of insurance.

polio /'poʊlioʊ/ *n.* → **poliomyelitis**.

poliomyelitis /ˌpoʊlioʊmaɪə'laɪtəs/ *n.* an acute viral disease resulting in paralysis.

-polis a word element meaning 'city'.

polish /'pɒlɪʃ/ *v.t.* **1.** to make smooth and glossy, especially by friction. **2.** to render finished, refined or elegant. **3.** *Colloquial* to finish, or dispose of quickly (fol. by *off*). – *n.* **4.** a substance used to give smoothness or gloss. **5.** the act of polishing. **6.** smoothness and gloss of surface. **7.** superior or elegant finish imparted; refinement; elegance.

polite /pə'laɪt/ *adj.* showing good manners towards others, as in behaviour, speech, etc.; courteous; civil.

politic /'pɒlətɪk/ *adj.* **1.** sagacious; prudent; judicious. **2.** shrewd; artful; expedient.

political /pə'lɪtɪkəl/ *adj.* **1.** relating to or dealing with the science or art of politics. **2.** relating to or connected with a political party, or its principles, aims, activities, etc. **3.** of or relating to the state or its government. – **politically**, *adv.*

political economy *n.* a social science dealing with the relationship between political and economic policies and their influence on social institutions.

politically correct *adj.* conforming to current beliefs about correctness in language and behaviour with regard to policies on sexism, racism, ageism, etc. – **political correctness**, *n.*

politics /'pɒlətɪks/ *n.* (*construed as sing. or pl.*) **1.** the science or art of political government. **2.** the practice or profession of conducting political affairs. **3.** political affairs. **4.** the use of underhand or unscrupulous methods in obtaining power or advancement within an organisation. – **politician**, *n.*

polity /'pɒləti/ *n., pl.* **-ties**. **1.** a particular form or system of government (civil, ecclesiastical, or other). **2.** government or administrative regulation.

polka /'pɒlkə/ *n.* a lively dance.

poll /poʊl/ *n.* **1.** the registering of votes, as at an election. **2.** the number of votes cast. **3.** an analysis of public opinion on a subject, usually by selective sampling. **4.** the head, especially the part of it on which the hair grows. – *v.t.* **5.** to receive at the polls, as votes. **6.** to take or register the votes of, as persons. **7.** to cut off or cut short the hair, etc., of (a person, etc.); crop; clip; shear. **8.** to cut off or cut short the horns of (cattle).

pollard /'pɒləd/ *n.* **1.** a tree cut back nearly to the trunk, so as to produce a dense mass of branches. **2.** an animal, as a stag, ox, or sheep, without horns.

pollen /'pɒlən/ *n.* the fertilising element of flowering plants, consisting of fine, powdery, yellowish grains or spores.

pollinate /'pɒləneɪt/ *v.t.*, **-nated**, **-nating**. to convey pollen for fertilisation to.

pollute /pə'lut/ *v.t.*, **-luted**, **-luting**. to make foul or unclean. – **pollution**, *n.* – **pollutant**, *n.*

polo /'poʊloʊ/ *n.* a game resembling hockey, played on horseback.

poltergeist /'pɒltəgaɪst/ *n.* a ghost or spirit which manifests its presence by noises, knockings, etc.

poltroon /pɒl'trun/ *n.* a wretched coward.

poly- a word element or prefix, meaning 'much', 'many'. Cf. **mono-**.

polyandry /pɒli'ændri/ *n.* the practice or the condition of having more than one husband at one time.

polyester /'pɒliɛstə/ *n.* a synthetic polymer used in fabrics, etc.

polygamy /pə'lɪgəmi/ *n.* the practice or condition of having many or several spouses, especially wives, at one time.

polyglot /'pɒliglɒt/ *adj.* knowing many or several languages, as a person.

polygon /'pɒligɒn, -gən/ *n.* a figure, especially a closed plane figure, having many (more than four) angles and sides.

polygyny /pə'lɪdʒəni/ *n.* the practice or the condition of having more than one wife at one time.

polyhedron /pɒli'hidrən/ *n., pl.* **-drons**, **-dra** /-drə/. a solid figure having many faces.

polymer /'pɒləmə/ *n.* a compound of high molecular weight derived either by the combination of many smaller molecules or by the condensation of many smaller molecules eliminating water, alcohol, etc. – **polymerise = polymerize**, *v.*

polyp /'pɒləp/ *n.* **1.** *Zoology* an animal form with a more or less fixed base and free end with mouth and tentacles. **2.** *Pathology* a projecting growth from a mucous surface, as of the nose.

polysemy /pə'lɪsəmi/ *n.* the acquisition and retention of many meanings by one word, as in the case of the word *tank* which referred to a receptacle for liquids and then additionally to a military vehicle.

polystyrene /pɒli'staɪrin/ *n.* a clear plastic, easily coloured and moulded and used as an insulating material.

polytheism /'pɒliθiˌɪzəm/ *n.* the doctrine of, or belief in, many gods or more gods than one.

polythene /'pɒləθin/ *n.* a plastic used for containers, electrical insulation, packaging, etc.

polyunsaturated /ˌpɒliʌn'sætʃəreɪtəd/ *adj. Chemistry* **1.** of or relating to a fat or oil based on fatty acids which have two or more double bonds per molecule, such as linoleic acids. **2.** of or relating to foodstuffs based on polyunsaturated fat, oils, and believed not to increase cholesterol levels in the blood.

polyurethane /pɒli'jurəθeɪn/ *n.* a substance used in making foam products for insulation, decoration, etc.

pomander /pə'mændə/ *n.* a mixture of aromatic substances, often in the form of a ball.

pomegranate /'pɒməgrænət/ *n.* a several-chambered, many-seeded fruit.

pommel /'pʌməl, 'pɒməl/ *n.* **1.** a terminating knob, as on the top of a tower, hilt of a sword, etc. **2.** the protuberant part at the front and top of a saddle. Also, **pummel**.

pommy /'pɒmi/ *n., pl.* **-mies**. *Colloquial* a British person.

pomp /pɒmp/ *n.* stately or splendid display.

pompom /'pɒmpɒm/ *n.* an ornamental tuft or ball of feathers, wool, or the like.

pompous /'pɒmpəs/ *adj.* **1.** characterised by an ostentatious parade of dignity or importance. **2.** (of language, style, etc.) ostentatiously lofty.

ponce /pɒns/ *n., v.,* **ponced**, **poncing**. *Colloquial* – *n.* **1.** → **pimp**. – *v.i.* **2.** to flounce; behave in a foolishly effeminate fashion (fol. by *about*). – **poncy**, *adj.*

poncho /'pɒntʃoʊ/ *n., pl.* **-chos**. a blanket-like cloak.

pond /pɒnd/ *n.* a body of water smaller than a lake, often one artificially formed.

ponder /'pɒndə/ *v.i.* **1.** to consider deeply; meditate. – *v.t.* **2.** to weigh carefully in the mind, or consider carefully.

ponderable /'pɒndərəbəl/ *adj.* capable of being weighed; having appreciable weight.

ponderous /'pɒndərəs, -drəs/ *adj.* **1.** of great weight; heavy; massive. **2.** without graceful lightness or ease; dull.

pontiff /'pɒntɪf/ *n.* **1.** a high or chief priest. **2.** *Ecclesiastical* **a.** a bishop. **b.** the bishop of Rome (the pope). – **pontifical**, *adj.*

pontificate /pɒn'tɪfəkeɪt/ *v.i.,* **-cated**, **-cating**. to speak in a pompous manner.

pontoon[1] /pɒn'tun/ *n.* a boat, or some other floating structure, used as one of the supports for a temporary bridge over a river.

pontoon[2] /pɒn'tun/ *n.* a card game.

pony /'poʊni/ *n., pl.* **-nies**. a small horse.

ponytail /'poʊniteɪl/ *n.* a bunch of hair tied at the back of the head.

poo /pu/ *n. Colloquial* (*euphemistic*) → **faeces**.

poodle /'pudl/ *n.* one of a breed of intelligent pet dogs with thick curly hair.

poofter /'pʊftə/ *n. Colloquial* a male homosexual.

pool[1] /pul/ *n.* **1.** a small body of standing water; pond. **2.** a swimming pool.

pool[2] /pul/ *n.* **1.** an association of competitors who agree to control the production, market, and price of a commodity for mutual benefit, although they appear to be rivals. **2.** a combination of interests, funds, etc., for common advantage. **3.** a facility or service that is shared by a number of people. **4.** Also, **pocket billiards**. any of various games played on a billiard table in which the object is to drive all the balls into the pockets with the cue ball. – *v.t.* **5.** to put (interests, money, etc.) into a pool, or common stock or fund, as for a financial venture, according to agreement.

poop[1] /pup/ *n.* the enclosed space in the aftermost part of a ship.

poop[2] /pup/ *v.t. Colloquial* to tire or exhaust.

poop[3] /pʊp/ *n. Colloquial* excrement.

poor /pɔ/ *adj.* **1.** having little or nothing in the way of wealth, goods, or means of subsistence. **2.** of an inferior, inadequate, or unsatisfactory kind; not good. **3.** humble. **4.** unfortunate.

pop[1] /pɒp/ *v.,* **popped**, **popping**, *n.* – *v.i.* **1.** to make a short, quick, explosive sound or report. **2.** to burst open with such a sound. **3.** to come or go quickly, suddenly or unexpectedly (fol. by *in, into, out,* etc.). – *v.t.* **4.** to cause to make a sudden, explosive sound. – *n.* **5.** a short, quick, explosive sound. **6.** **a pop,** *Colloquial* each.

pop[2] /pɒp/ *adj. Colloquial* **1.** popular. **2.** denoting or relating to a type of tune or song having great but ephemeral popularity, especially among the young. **3.** denoting or relating to a singer or player of such music.

pop[3] /pɒp/ *n. Colloquial* father, or grandfather.

popcorn /'pɒpkɔn/ *n.* any of several varieties of maize whose kernels burst open and puff out when subjected to dry heat.

pope /poʊp/ *n.* (*often cap.*) the bishop of Rome as head of the Roman Catholic Church.

poplar /'pɒplə/ *n.* a tall, spire-shaped tree.

poplin /'pɒplən/ *n.* a strong, finely ribbed, mercerised cotton material.

poppet /'pɒpət/ *n.* a term of endearment for a girl or child.

poppy /'pɒpi/ *n., pl.* **-pies**. a plant with showy flowers of various colours.

populace /'pɒpjələs/ *n.* the common people of a community.

popular /'pɒpjələ/ *adj.* **1.** regarded with favour or approval by associates, acquaintances, the general public, etc. **2.** of, relating to, or representing the people, or the common people. – **popularity**, *n.*

populate /'pɒpjəleɪt/ *v.t.,* **-lated**, **-lating**. **1.** to inhabit. **2.** to furnish with inhabitants, as by colonisation; people.

population /pɒpjə'leɪʃən/ *n.* **1.** the total number of persons inhabiting a country, town, or any district or area. **2.** the body of inhabitants of a place. **3.** the act or process of populating.

populous /'pɒpjələs/ *adj.* full of people or inhabitants, as a region; well populated.

porcelain /'pɔsələn, 'pɔslən/ *n.* a vitreous, more or less translucent, ceramic material; china.

porch /pɔtʃ/ *n.* an exterior appendage to a building, forming a covered approach or vestibule to a doorway.

porcine /'pɔsaɪn/ *adj.* **1.** of or resembling swine. **2.** swinish, hoggish, or piggish.

porcupine /'pɔkjəpaɪn/ *n.* any of various rodents covered with stout, erectile spines or quills.

pore[1] /pɔ/ *v.t.,* **pored**, **poring**. to meditate or ponder intently (usually fol. by *over, on,* or *upon*).

pore[2] /pɔ/ *n.* a minute opening or orifice, as in the skin or a leaf, a rock, etc.

pork /pɔk/ *n.* the flesh of pigs.

pork barrel *n. Colloquial* a government appropriation, bill, or policy which supplies funds for local improvements designed to ingratiate legislators with their constituents.

pork-barrelling /'pɔk-bærəlɪŋ/ *n.* the use of patronage for political advantage.

pornography /pɔ'nɒgrəfi/ *n.* obscene literature, art, or photography, designed to excite sexual desire. – **pornographic**, *adj.*

porous /'pɔrəs/ *adj.* **1.** having pores. **2.** permeable by water, air, etc.

porphyry /'pɔfəri/ *n., pl.* **-ries**. an igneous rock.

porpoise /ˈpɔpəs/ *n., pl.* **-poises**, (*esp. collectively*) **-poise**. **1.** any of various cetaceans, usually blackish above and paler underneath, with a blunt, rounded snout. **2.** → **dolphin**.

porridge /ˈpɒrɪdʒ/ *n.* an oatmeal breakfast dish.

port[1] /pɔt/ *n.* **1.** a town or place where ships load or unload. **2.** a place along the coast where ships may take refuge from storms.

port[2] /pɔt/ *n.* the left-hand side of a ship or aircraft facing forward (opposed to *starboard*).

port[3] /pɔt/ *n.* any of a class of very sweet, fortified wines, mostly dark red.

port[4] /pɔt/ *n.* **1.** *Nautical* a porthole. **2.** a steel door in the side of a ship for loading and discharging cargo and baggage.

port[5] /pɔt/ *v.t.* **1.** *Military* to carry (a rifle, etc.) with both hands, in a slanting direction across the front of the body with the barrel or like part near the left shoulder. **2.** to carry (something).

port[6] /pɔt/ *n.* a portmanteau; suitcase.

portable /ˈpɔtəbəl/ *adj.* **1.** capable of being transported or conveyed. **2.** (of benefits, superannuation, etc.) capable of being transferred with a change in job, especially from one department of the public service to another.

portal /ˈpɔtl/ *n.* a door, gate, or entrance.

portend /pɔˈtɛnd/ *v.t.* to indicate beforehand, as an omen does.

porter[1] /ˈpɔtə/ *n.* one employed to carry burdens or luggage, as at a railway station.

porter[2] /ˈpɔtə/ *n.* someone who has charge of a door or gate; a doorkeeper; a janitor.

portfolio /pɔtˈfouliou/ *n., pl.* **-lios**. **1.** a portable case for loose papers, prints, etc. **2.** *Government* **a.** the office or post of a minister of state or member of a cabinet. **b.** the public service department or departments for which a minister is responsible. **3.** an itemised account or list of financial assets, as securities, shares, discount paper, etc., of an investment organisation, bank or other investor.

porthole /ˈpɔthoul/ *n.* an aperture in the side of a ship, for admitting light and air.

portion /ˈpɔʃən/ *n.* **1.** a part of any whole, whether actually separated from it or not. **2.** the part of a whole allotted to or belonging to a person or group; a share. – *v.t.* **3.** to divide into or distribute in portions or shares; parcel (often fol. by *out*).

portly /ˈpɔtli/ *adj.*, **-lier**, **-liest**. stout.

portmanteau /pɔtˈmæntou/ *n., pl.* **-teaus**, **-teaux**. a case or bag. Also, **port**.

portrait /ˈpɔtrət, ˈpɔtreɪt/ *n.* a likeness of a person, especially of the face.

portray /pɔˈtreɪ/ *v.t.* **1.** to represent by a drawing, painting, carving, or the like. **2.** to represent dramatically, as on the stage. – **portrayal**, *n.*

pose /pouz/ *v.*, **posed**, **posing**, *n.* – *v.i.* **1.** to affect a particular character as with a view to the impression made on others. **2.** to assume or hold a position or attitude for some artistic purpose. – *n.* **3.** attitude or posture of body. **4.** a studied attitude or mere affectation, as of some character, quality, sentiment, or course.

posh /pɒʃ/ *adj. Colloquial* elegant; luxurious; smart; first-class.

position /pəˈzɪʃən/ *n.* **1.** condition with reference to place; location. **2.** proper or appropriate place. **3.** a post of employment. **4.** mental attitude; way of viewing a matter; stand. **5.** condition (of affairs, etc.). – *v.t.* **6.** to put in a particular or appropriate position; place.

positive /ˈpɒzətɪv/ *adj.* **1.** explicitly laid down or expressed. **2.** admitting of no question. **3.** confident in opinion or assertion, as a person; fully assured. **4.** absolute. **5.** characterised by optimism or hopefulness. **6.** *Electricity* having a deficiency of electrons. **7.** *Mathematics* denoting a quantity greater than zero.

positive discrimination *n.* discrimination which works actively to favour a previously disadvantaged group in society.

posse comitatus /pɒsi kɒməˈtatəs/ *n.* the body of people that a sheriff is empowered to call to assist in preserving the peace, making arrests, and serving writs.

possess /pəˈzɛs/ *v.t.* **1.** to have as property; to have belonging to one. **2.** to have as a faculty, quality, or the like. **3.** (of a spirit, especially an evil one) to occupy and control, or dominate from within, as a person. – **possessory**, *adj.*

possession /pəˈzɛʃən/ *n.* **1.** the act or fact of possessing. **2.** ownership. **3.** a thing possessed. **4.** control over oneself, one's mind, etc.

possessive /pəˈzɛsɪv/ *adj.* exerting or seeking to exert excessive influence on the affections, behaviour, etc., of others.

possible /ˈpɒsəbəl/ *adj.* that may or can be, exist, happen, be done, be used, etc. – **possibility**, *n.*

possum /ˈpɒsəm/ *n.* a herbivorous, largely arboreal, marsupial.

post[1] /poust/ *n.* **1.** a strong piece of timber, metal, or the like, set upright as a support, a point of attachment, a mark, a place for displaying notices, etc. – *v.t.* **2.** to affix (a notice, etc.) to a post, wall, or the like.

post[2] /poust/ *n.* a position of duty, employment, or trust to which one is assigned or appointed.

post[3] /poust/ *n.* **1.** a single collection or delivery of letters, packages, etc. **2.** the letters, packages, etc., themselves; mail. – *v.t.* **3.** to place (a letter, etc.) in a post-box, post office, etc., for transmission. **4.** *Bookkeeping* **a.** to transfer (an entry or item), as from the journal to the ledger. **b.** to enter (an item) in due place and form. **5.** to supply with up-to-date information; inform. – **postage**, *n.*

post[4] /poust/ *n.* an examination held after the main examination.

post- a prefix meaning 'behind', 'after'.

postal note *n.* an order for the payment of a small amount of money, bought from and generally cashed at a post office. Also, **postal order**.

postcode /ˈpoustkoud/ *n.* a group of numbers or letters added as part of the address and intended to facilitate the delivery of mail.

postdate /poustˈdeɪt/ *v.t.*, **-dated**, **-dating**. **1.** to date (a document, cheque, invoice, etc.) with a date later than the current date. **2.** to follow in time.

poster /ˈpoʊstə/ *n.* a large placard or bill, often incorporating photographs or illustrations, and posted for advertisement or publicity or for decorative purposes.

posterior /pɒsˈtɪəriə/ *adj.* **1.** situated behind, or hinder (opposed to *anterior*). – *n.* **2.** the hinder parts of the body; the buttocks.

posterity /pɒˈstɛrəti/ *n.* succeeding generations collectively.

postgraduate /poʊstˈgrædʒuət/ *n.* one studying at a university for a higher degree.

posthaste /poʊstˈheɪst/ *adv.* with all possible speed or promptness.

posthumous /ˈpɒstʃəməs/ *adj.* **1.** (of books, music, medals, etc.) published or awarded after a person's death. **2.** arising, existing, or continuing after one's death.

postmark /ˈpoʊstmak/ *n.* an official mark stamped on letters or other mail, to cancel the postage stamp, indicate the place and date of sending.

postmodern /poʊstˈmɒdn/ *adj.* of, relating to or in the style of a trend in art or literature which developed in the 1970s as a reaction to the idea of modernism with its emphasis on individual expression. Also, **post-modern**. – **postmodernism**, *n.* – **postmodernist**, *n.*

post-mortem /ˈpoʊst-mɔtəm/ *adj.,* /poʊstˈmɔtəm/ *n.* – *adj.* **1.** subsequent to death, as an examination of the body. – *n.* **2.** a post-mortem examination.

post-obit /poʊst-ˈoʊbət, -ˈɒbət/ *adj.* effective after a particular person's death.

postpone /poʊstˈpoʊn, poʊsˈpoʊn/ *v.t.,* **-poned, -poning**. to put off to a later time; defer.

postscript /ˈpoʊstskrɪpt/ *n.* a paragraph, sentence, etc., added to a letter which has already been concluded and signed by the writer. *Abbrev.*: PS

postulate /ˈpɒstʃəleɪt/ *v.t.,* **-lated, -lating**. **1.** to ask, demand, or claim. **2.** to claim or assume the existence or truth of, especially as a basis for reasoning.

posture /ˈpɒstʃə/ *n., v.,* **-tured, -turing**. – *n.* **1.** the relative disposition of the various parts of anything. **2.** the position of the body and limbs as a whole. – *v.t.* **3.** to place in a particular posture or attitude; dispose in postures.

posy /ˈpoʊzi/ *n., pl.* **-sies**. a bouquet.

pot /pɒt/ *n., v.,* **potted, potting**. – *n.* **1.** an earthen, metallic, or other container, usually round and deep, used for domestic or other purposes. **2.** a wicker vessel for trapping fish or crustaceans. **3.** *Colloquial* → **marijuana**. – *v.t.* **4.** to put into a pot. **5.** to preserve or cook (food) in a pot. **6.** to plant in a pot of soil. **7.** *Colloquial* to capture, secure, or win.

potable /ˈpoʊtəbəl/ *adj.* fit or suitable for drinking.

potash /ˈpɒtæʃ/ *n.* **1.** potassium carbonate, especially the crude impure form obtained from wood ashes. **2.** potassium.

potassium /pəˈtæsiəm/ *n.* a silvery white metallic element whose compounds are used as fertiliser and in special hard glasses. *Symbol*: K – **potassic**, *adj.*

potato /pəˈteɪtoʊ/ *n., pl.* **-toes**. the edible tuber of a cultivated plant.

potch /pɒtʃ/ *n.* an opal which may have colour, but lacks the fine play of colour which distinguishes gem-quality opal.

potent /ˈpoʊtnt/ *adj.* **1.** powerful; mighty. **2.** having sexual power. – **potency**, *n.*

potentate /ˈpoʊtnteɪt/ *n.* someone who possesses great power.

potential /pəˈtɛnʃəl/ *adj.* **1.** possible as opposed to actual. **2.** capable of being or becoming; latent. – *n.* **3.** a possibility or potentiality.

pothole /ˈpɒthoʊl/ *n.* **1.** a deep hole; a pit. **2.** a hole in the surface of a road.

potion /ˈpoʊʃən/ *n.* a drink or draught, especially one of a medicinal, poisonous, or magical kind.

potpourri /pɒtˈpʊəri, poʊpəˈri/ *n., pl.* **-ris**. a mixture of dried petals, spices, etc., kept in a jar for the fragrance.

potter[1] /ˈpɒtə/ *n.* someone who makes earthen pots or other vessels. – **pottery**, *n.*

potter[2] /ˈpɒtə/ *v.i.* to busy or occupy oneself in an ineffective manner.

potty[1] /ˈpɒti/ *adj. Colloquial* foolish; crazy.

potty[2] /ˈpɒti/ *n. Colloquial* a chamber-pot.

pouch /paʊtʃ/ *n.* **1.** a bag, sack, or similar receptacle, especially one for small articles. **2.** something shaped like or resembling a bag or pocket. **3.** *Zoology* a baglike or pocketlike part, as the sac beneath the bill of pelicans, or the receptacle for the young of marsupials.

pouf /puf, pʊf/ *n.* a stuffed cushion of thick material forming a low seat.

poultice /ˈpoʊltəs/ *n.* a soft, moist mass of bread, meal, linseed, etc., applied as a medicament to the body.

poultry /ˈpoʊltri/ *n.* domestic fowls collectively, as chickens, turkeys, etc.

pounce[1] /paʊns/ *v.,* **pounced, pouncing**, *n.* – *v.i.* **1.** to swoop down suddenly and lay hold, as a bird does on its prey. – *n.* **2.** a sudden swoop, as on prey.

pounce[2] /paʊns/ *n.* a fine powder, as of cuttlebone, formerly used to prevent ink from spreading in writing or to prepare parchment for writing.

pound[1] /paʊnd/ *v.t.* **1.** to strike repeatedly and with great force, as with an instrument, the fist, heavy missiles, etc. – *v.i.* **2.** to strike heavy blows repeatedly. **3.** to beat or throb violently, as the heart. – *n.* **4.** the act of pounding.

pound[2] /paʊnd/ *n., pl.* **pounds**, (*collectively*) **pound**. **1.** a unit of mass, varying in different periods and different countries. **2.** a British unit of currency (**pound sterling**) of the value of 100 new pence.

pound[3] /paʊnd/ *n.* **1.** an enclosure maintained by public authorities for confining stray or homeless animals. **2.** a place of confinement or imprisonment.

pour /pɔ/ *v.t.* **1.** to send (a fluid, or anything in loose particles) flowing or falling, as from a container or into, over, or on something. – *v.i.* **2.** to issue, move, or proceed in great quantity or number. **3.** to rain heavily. – *n.* **4.** the act or process of pouring molten metal, concrete, etc., into a mould.

pout /paʊt/ *v.i.* to thrust out or protrude the lips, especially in displeasure or sullenness.

poverty /ˈpɒvəti/ *n.* the condition of being poor with respect to money, goods, or means of subsistence.

poverty line *n.* officially, the level of income below which one cannot afford to obtain the necessities of life.

powder /ˈpaʊdə/ *n.* **1.** any solid substance in the state of fine, loose particles, as produced by crushing, grinding, or disintegration; dust. – *v.t.* **2.** to reduce to powder; pulverise. **3.** to sprinkle or cover with, or as with, powder.

power /ˈpaʊə/ *n.* **1.** ability to do or act; capability of doing or effecting something. **2.** great or marked ability to do or act; strength; might; force. **3.** the possession of control or command over others; dominion; authority; ascendancy or influence. **4.** legal ability, capacity, or authority. **5.** a state or nation having international authority or influence. **6.** mechanical energy as distinguished from hand labour. **7.** *Mathematics* the product obtained by multiplying a quantity by itself one or more times. – **powerful**, *adj.*

power of attorney *n.* a written document given by one person or party to another authorising the latter to act for the former.

powwow /ˈpaʊwaʊ/ *n. Colloquial* any conference or meeting.

pox /pɒks/ *n.* **1.** a disease characterised by multiple skin pustules, as smallpox. **2.** *Colloquial* any venereal disease.

practicable /ˈpræktɪkəbəl/ *adj.* capable of being put into practice, done, or effected, especially with the available means or with reason or prudence; feasible.

practical /ˈpræktɪkəl/ *adj.* **1.** relating or relating to practice or action. **2.** relating to or connected with the ordinary activities, business, or work of the world. **3.** adapted for actual use. **4.** mindful of the results, usefulness, advantages or disadvantages, etc., of action or procedure. **5.** matter-of-fact; prosaic. **6.** being such in practice or effect; virtual. – **practically**, *adv.* – **practicality**, *n.*

practice /ˈpræktəs/ *n.* **1.** habitual or customary performance. **2.** repeated performance or systematic exercise for the purpose of acquiring skill or proficiency. **3.** the action or process of performing or doing something (opposed to *theory* or *speculation*). **4.** the exercise of a profession or occupation, especially law or medicine.

practise /ˈpræktəs/ *v.*, **-tised**, **-tising**. – *v.t.* **1.** to carry out, perform, or do habitually or usually. **2.** to exercise or pursue as a profession, art, or occupation. **3.** to perform or do repeatedly in order to acquire skill or proficiency. – *v.i.* **4.** to pursue a profession, especially law or medicine. **5.** to exercise oneself by performance tending to give proficiency.

practitioner /prækˈtɪʃənə/ *n.* one engaged in the practice of a profession or the like.

pragmatic /prægˈmætɪk/ *adj.* **1.** concerned with practical consequences or values. **2.** relating to the affairs of a state or community. Also, **pragmatical**.

prairie /ˈprɛəri/ *n.* an extensive or slightly undulating treeless tract of land.

praise /preɪz/ *n.*, *v.*, **praised**, **praising**. – *n.* **1.** the act of expressing approval or admiration. – *v.t.* **2.** to express approval or admiration of. – **praiseworthy**, *adj.*

pram /præm/ *n.* a small, four-wheeled vehicle used for carrying a baby.

prance /præns, prans/ *v.i.*, **pranced**, **prancing**. **1.** to spring, or move by springing, from the hind legs, as a horse. **2.** to move or go in an elated manner; swagger.

prang /præŋ/ *v.t. Colloquial* **1.** to crash (a car or the like). – *n.* **2.** a crash, especially a minor one, in a motor vehicle or the like.

prank /præŋk/ *n.* **1.** a trick of a playful nature. **2.** a trick of a malicious nature.

prate /preɪt/ *v.i.*, **prated**, **prating**. to talk too much; talk foolishly or pointlessly; chatter; babble.

prattle /ˈprætl/ *v.i.*, **-tled**, **-tling**. to talk or chatter in a simple-minded or foolish way; babble.

prawn /prɔn/ *n.* a shrimplike crustacean, often used as food.

pray /preɪ/ *v.t.* **1.** to make earnest or devout petition to (a person, God, etc.). – *v.i.* **2.** to make entreaty or supplication, as to a person or for a thing.

prayer /prɛə/ *n.* **1.** a devout petition to, or any form of spiritual communion with, God or an object of worship. **2.** a petition or entreaty.

praying mantis *n.* → **mantis**.

pre- a prefix applied freely to mean 'prior to', 'in advance of' (*prewar*), also 'early', 'beforehand' (*prepay*), 'before', 'in front of' (*preoral, prefrontal*), and in many figurative meanings, often attached to stems not used alone (*prevent, preclude, preference, precedent*).

preach /pritʃ/ *v.t.* **1.** to proclaim or make known by sermon (the gospel, good tidings, etc.). – *v.i.* **2.** to deliver a sermon.

preamble /priˈæmbəl/ *n.* an introductory statement; a preface.

precarious /prəˈkɛəriəs/ *adj.* **1.** uncertain; unstable; insecure. **2.** dangerous; perilous.

precaution /prəˈkɔʃən/ *n.* **1.** a measure taken beforehand to ward off possible evil or secure good results. **2.** caution employed beforehand; prudent foresight.

precede /priˈsid/ *v.t.*, **-ceded**, **-ceding**. to go before, as in place, order, rank, importance, or time.

precedence /ˈprɛsədəns, priˈsidəns/ *n.* **1.** the act or fact of preceding. **2.** priority in order, rank, importance, etc.

precedent /ˈprisədənt, ˈprɛ-/ *n.* a preceding instance or case which may serve as an example for or a justification in subsequent cases.

precentor /prəˈsɛntə/ *n.* someone who leads a church choir or congregation in singing.

precept /ˈprisɛpt/ *n.* a commandment or direction given as a rule of action or conduct.

precession /priˈsɛʃən/ *n.* the act or fact of preceding; precedence.

precinct /ˈprisɪŋkt/ *n.* a place or space of definite or understood limits.

precious /ˈprɛʃəs/ *adj.* **1.** of great price or value; valuable; costly. **2.** dear or beloved.

precipice /ˈprɛsəpəs/ *n.* a steep cliff.

precipitant /prəˈsɪpətənt/ *adj.* **1.** hasty; rash. **2.** unduly sudden or abrupt.

precipitate /prəˈsɪpəteɪt/ *v.*, **-tated**, **-tating**, /prəˈsɪpətət/ *adj.*, *n.* – *v.t.* **1.** to hasten the occurrence of; bring about in haste or suddenly. **2.** *Chemistry* to separate (a substance) in solid form from a solution, as by means of a reagent. **3.** to cast down headlong; fling or hurl down. – *adj.* **4.** proceeding rapidly or with great haste. **5.** exceedingly sudden or abrupt. – *n.* **6.** *Chemistry* a substance precipitated from a solution.

precipitation /prəsɪpəˈteɪʃən/ *n.* **1.** the act of precipitating. **2.** *Meteorology* falling products of condensation in the atmosphere, as rain, snow, hail.

precipitous /prəˈsɪpətəs/ *adj.* **1.** extremely or impassably steep. **2.** precipitate.

precis /ˈpreɪsi/ *n.*, *pl.* **-cis** /-siz/. an abstract or summary.

precise /prəˈsaɪs/ *adj.* **1.** definite or exact; definitely or strictly stated, defined, or fixed. **2.** carefully distinct, as the voice. **3.** exact in measuring, recording, etc., as an instrument. **4.** excessively or rigidly particular; puritanical. – **precision**, *n.*

preclude /priˈklud/ *v.t.*, **-cluded**, **-cluding**. to shut out or exclude.

precocious /prəˈkoʊʃəs/ *adj.* forward in development, especially mental development, as a child.

preconceive /prikənˈsiv/ *v.t.*, **-ceived**, **-ceiving**. to conceive beforehand; form an idea of in advance. – **preconception**, *n.*

precursor /ˌpriˈkɜsə/ *n.* someone who or that which precedes; a predecessor.

predatory /ˈprɛdətəri, -tri/ *adj.* **1.** of, relating to, or characterised by plundering, pillaging, or robbery. **2.** *Zoology* habitually preying upon other animals. – **predator**, *n.*

predecessor /ˈpridəsɛsə/ *n.* someone who precedes another in an office, position, etc.

predestine /priˈdɛstən/ *v.t.*, **-tined**, **-tining**. to destine beforehand; predetermine.

predetermine /pridəˈtɜmən/ *v.t.* to determine or decide beforehand.

predicament /prəˈdɪkəmənt/ *n.* an unpleasant, trying, or dangerous situation.

predicate /ˈprɛdɪkeɪt/ *v.*, **-cated**, **-cating**, /ˈprɛdɪkət/ *n.* – *v.t.* **1.** to proclaim; declare; affirm or assert. – *n.* **2.** *Grammar* (in many languages) the active verb in a sentence or clause together with all the words it governs and those which modify it, as *is here* in *Jack is here*. – **predicative**, *adj.*

predict /prəˈdɪkt/ *v.t.* **1.** to foretell; prophesy. – *v.i.* **2.** to foretell the future.

predilection /pridəˈlɛkʃən/ *n.* a predisposition of the mind in favour of something.

predispose /pridəsˈpoʊz/ *v.t.*, **-posed**, **-posing**. **1.** to give a previous inclination or tendency to. **2.** to render subject, susceptible, or liable.

predominate /prəˈdɒməneɪt/ *v.i.*, **-nated**, **-nating**. **1.** to be the stronger or leading element. **2.** to have or exert controlling power (often fol. by *over*). – **predominant**, *adj.*

pre-eminent /pri-ˈɛmənənt/ *adj.* superior to or surpassing others; distinguished beyond others.

pre-empt /pri-ˈɛmpt/ *v.t.* **1.** to occupy (land) in order to establish a prior right to buy. **2.** to acquire or appropriate beforehand. – **pre-emptive**, *adj.*

preen /prin/ *v.t.* **1.** to trim or dress with the beak, as a bird does its feathers. **2.** to prepare, dress, or array (oneself) carefully in making one's toilet.

preface /ˈprɛfəs/ *n.*, *v.*, **-aced**, **-acing**. – *n.* **1.** a preliminary statement by the author or editor of a book. **2.** something preliminary or introductory. – *v.t.* **3.** to provide with or introduce by a preface. **4.** to serve as a preface to.

prefect /ˈprifɛkt/ *n.* a person appointed to any of various positions of command, authority, or superintendence. – **prefecture**, *n.*

prefer /prəˈfɜ/ *v.t.*, **-ferred**, **-ferring**. **1.** to set or hold before or above other persons or things in estimation; like better; choose rather. **2.** to put forward or present (a statement, suit, charge, etc.) for consideration or sanction. **3.** to put forward or advance, as in rank or office.

preference /ˈprɛfərəns, ˈprɛfrəns/ *n.* **1.** the act of preferring one thing above another. **2.** the state of being preferred. **3.** that which is preferred. **4.** a prior right or claim, as to payment of dividends, or to assets upon dissolution. **5.** a vote, usually specified in rank, given to a candidate in a preferential voting system. – **preferential**, *adj.*

preference share *n.* *Stock Exchange* a share which ranks before ordinary shares in the entitlement to dividends, usually at a fixed rate of interest. Also, *US*, **preferred stock**.

preferential voting /prɛfəˈrɛnʃəl/ *n.* a system of voting which enables the voter to indicate his or her order of preference for candidates in the ballot.

prefix /ˈprifɪks/ *n.*, /priˈfɪks, ˈprifɪks/ *v.* – *n.* **1.** *Grammar* an affix which is put before a word, stem, or word element to add to or qualify its meaning (as *un-* in *unkind*). – *v.t.* **2.** to fix or put before or in front. **3.** *Grammar* to add as a prefix. – **prefixal**, *adj.*

pregnant /ˈprɛgnənt/ *adj.* **1.** being with child or young, as a woman or female mammal; having a foetus in the womb. **2.** full of meaning; highly significant. – **pregnancy**, *n.*

prehensile /priˈhɛnsaɪl/ *adj.* adapted for seizing, grasping, or laying hold of anything.

prehistory /ˌpriˈhɪstəri/ *n.* the history of humanity in the period before recorded events. – **prehistoric**, *adj.*

prejudice /ˈprɛdʒədəs/ *n.*, *v.*, **-diced**, **-dicing**. – *n.* **1.** any preconceived opinion or feeling, favourable or unfavourable. **2.** disadvantage resulting from some judgment or action of another. **3.** resulting injury or detriment. – *v.t.* **4.** to affect with a prejudice, favourable or unfavourable. **5.** to affect disadvantageously or detrimentally. – **prejudicial**, *adj.*

prelate /ˈprɛlət/ *n.* an ecclesiastic of a high

order, as an archbishop, bishop, etc.

preliminary /prəˈlɪmənəri/ *adj., n., pl.* **-naries**. – *adj.* **1.** introductory; preparatory. – *n.* **2.** something preliminary.

prelude /ˈprɛljud/ *n., v.,* **-uded**, **-uding**. – *n.* **1.** a preliminary to an action, event, condition, or work of broader scope and higher importance. **2.** *Music* a piece which precedes a more important movement. – *v.t.* **3.** to serve as a prelude or introduction to.

premarital /ˌpriˈmærətl/ *adj.* before marriage.

premature /ˈprɛmətʃə, prɛməˈtjuə/ *adj.* coming into existence or occurring too soon.

premeditate /priˈmɛdəteɪt/ *v.t., v.i.,* **-tated**, **-tating**. to plan beforehand.

premenstrual tension /priˈmɛnstruəl/ *n.* symptoms of physiological and emotional upset experienced by women in the week prior to menstruation.

premier /ˈprɛmiə/ *n.* **1.** the leader of a state government. – *adj.* **2.** first in rank; chief; leading. **3.** earliest.

premiere /prɛmiˈɛə/ *n.* a first public performance of a play, etc.

premise /ˈprɛməs/ *n., v.,* **-ised**, **-ising**. – *n.* **1.** (*pl.*) **a.** the property forming the subject of a conveyance. **b.** a house or building with the grounds, etc., belonging to it. **2.** Also, **premiss**. *Logic* a proposition (or one of several) from which a conclusion is drawn. – *v.t.* **3.** to set forth beforehand, as by way of introduction or explanation.

premium /ˈprimiəm/ *n.* **1.** a bonus, prize, or the like. **2.** the amount paid or agreed to be paid, in one sum or periodically, as the consideration for a contract of insurance. **3.** a sum above the nominal or par value of a thing. **4.** *Stock Exchange* the amount that a buyer is prepared to pay for the right to subscribe for a new or rights issue of stocks or shares in a company. **5. at a premium, a.** in high esteem; in demand. **b.** at a high price. – *adj.* **6.** of highest quality; best.

premonition /prɛməˈnɪʃən, pri-/ *n.* **1.** a forewarning. **2.** → **presentiment**.

preoccupy /priˈɒkjəpaɪ/ *v.t.,* **-pied**, **-pying**. to absorb or engross to the exclusion of other things.

preparation /prɛpəˈreɪʃən/ *n.* **1.** a proceeding, measure, or provision by which one prepares for something. **2.** homework, or, especially in a boarding school, individual work supervised by a teacher. **3.** the act of preparing. **4.** something prepared, manufactured, or compounded.

prepare /prəˈpɛə/ *v.t.,* **-pared**, **-paring**. **1.** to make ready, or put in due condition, for something. **2.** to get ready for eating, as a meal, by due assembling, dressing, or cooking. **3.** to manufacture, compound, or compose. – **preparatory**, *adj.*

preponderant /prəˈpɒndərənt, pri-, -drənt/ *adj.* superior in weight, force, influence, number, etc.; preponderating; predominant.

preponderate /prəˈpɒndəreɪt, pri-/ *v.i.,* **-rated**, **-rating**. to be superior in power, force, influence, number, amount, etc.; predominate.

preposition /prɛpəˈzɪʃən/ *n.* (in some languages) one of the major form-classes, or parts of speech, comprising words placed before nouns to indicate their relation to other words or their function in the sentence. *By*, *to*, *in*, *from* are prepositions in English.

prepossessing /pripəˈzɛsɪŋ/ *adj.* impressing favourably beforehand or at the outset.

preposterous /prəˈpɒstərəs/ *adj.* directly contrary to nature, reason, or common sense; absurd, senseless, or utterly foolish.

prepuce /ˈpripjus/ *n.* the fold of skin which covers the head of the penis or clitoris; foreskin. – **preputial**, *adj.*

prerogative /prəˈrɒgətɪv/ *n.* an exclusive right or privilege.

presage /ˈprɛsɪdʒ/ *n.,* /ˈprɛsɪdʒ, prəˈseɪdʒ/ *v.,* **-saged**, **-saging**. – *n.* **1.** an omen. – *v.t.* **2.** to forecast; predict.

prescience /ˈprɛsiəns/ *n.* knowledge of things before they exist or happen.

prescribe /prəˈskraɪb/ *v.t.,* **-scribed**, **-scribing**. **1.** to lay down, in writing or otherwise, as a rule or a course to be followed; appoint, ordain, or enjoin. **2.** *Medicine* to designate or order for use, as a remedy or treatment.

prescribed payment *n.* that part of the tax liability of a contractor or subcontractor which is withheld by the person hiring, and remitted to the government.

prescription /prəˈskrɪpʃən/ *n.* **1.** *Medicine* a direction (usually written) by the doctor to the pharmacist for the preparation and use of a medicine or remedy. **2.** *Law* the process of acquiring a right by uninterrupted assertion of the right over a long period of time.

prescriptive /prəˈskrɪptɪv/ *adj.* **1.** that prescribes; giving directions or injunctions. **2.** depending on or arising from effective prescription, as a right or title.

pre-sell /pri-ˈsɛl/ *v.t.,* **-sold**, **-selling**. to sell (a home unit, etc.) before it is built.

presence /ˈprɛzəns/ *n.* **1.** the state or fact of being present, as with others or in a place. **2.** personal appearance or bearing, especially of a dignified or imposing kind. **3.** a divine or spiritual being.

present[1] /ˈprɛzənt/ *adj.* **1.** being, existing, or occurring at this time or now. **2.** being here or there, rather than elsewhere. – *n.* **3.** the present time.

present[2] /prəˈzɛnt/ *v.,* /ˈprɛzənt/ *n.* – *v.t.* **1.** to furnish or endow with a gift or the like, especially by formal act. **2.** afford or furnish (an opportunity, possibility, etc.). **3.** to hand or send in, as a bill or a cheque for payment. **4.** to introduce (a person) to another. **5.** to show or exhibit. **6.** to level or aim (a weapon, especially a firearm). – *n.* **7.** a thing presented as a gift; a gift.

presentable /prəˈzɛntəbəl/ *adj.* of sufficiently good appearance, or fit to be seen.

presentation /prɛzənˈteɪʃən/ *n.* **1.** the act of presenting. **2.** the presentment of a bill, note, or the like.

presentiment /prəˈzɛntəmənt/ *n.* a feeling or impression of something about to happen, especially something evil; a foreboding.

presently /ˈprɛzəntli/ *adv.* **1.** in a little while or soon. **2.** at this time, currently.

presentment /priˈzɛntmənt/ *n.* *Commerce* the

presenting of a bill, note, or the like, as for acceptance or payment.

preservative /prə'zɜvətɪv/ *n.* a chemical substance used to preserve foods, etc., from decomposition or fermentation.

preserve /prə'zɜv/ *v.*, **-served**, **-serving**, *n.* – *v.t.* **1.** to keep safe from harm or injury; save. **2.** to keep up; maintain. **3.** to prepare (food or any perishable substance) so as to resist decomposition or fermentation. – *n.* **4.** something that preserves. **5.** that which is preserved.

preside /prə'zaɪd/ *v.i.*, **-sided**, **-siding**. to occupy the place of authority or control.

president /'prɛzədənt/ *n.* **1.** (*often cap.*) the highest official in a republic. **2.** an officer appointed or elected to preside over an organised body of persons, as a council, society, etc. – **presidency**, *n.* – **presidential**, *adj.*

press[1] /prɛs/ *v.t.* **1.** to act upon with weight or force. **2.** to compress or squeeze, as to alter in shape or size. **3.** to make flat by subjecting to weight. **4.** to iron (clothes, etc.). **5.** to urge (a person, etc.). – *v.i.* **6.** to exert weight, force, or pressure. **7.** to compel haste. **8.** to crowd or throng. – *n.* **9.** printed publications collectively, especially newspapers and periodicals. **10.** *Printing* machine used for printing. **11.** an establishment for printing books, etc. **12.** any of various instruments or machines for exerting pressure. **13.** a crowd, throng, or multitude. **14.** pressure or urgency, as of affairs or business. **15.** an upright case, or piece of furniture, for holding clothes, books, etc.

press[2] /prɛs/ *v.t.* to force into service, especially naval or military service; to impress.

pressure /'prɛʃə/ *n.* **1.** the exertion of force upon a body by another body in contact with it; compression. **2.** *Physics* the force per unit area exerted at a given point. **3.** the act of pressing. **4.** harassment; oppression. **5.** a constraining or compelling force or influence. **6.** urgency, as of affairs or business.

pressurise = pressurize /'prɛʃəraɪz/ *v.t.*, *v.i.*, **-rised**, **-rising**. to maintain normal air pressure in (the cockpit or cabin of) an aeroplane designed to fly at high altitudes.

prestige /prɛs'tiʒ/ *n.* reputation or influence arising from success, achievement, rank, or other circumstances. – **prestigious**, *adj.*

presume /prə'zjum/ *v.*, **-sumed**, **-suming**. – *v.t.* **1.** to take for granted, assume, or suppose. – *v.i.* **2.** to act or proceed with unwarrantable or impertinent boldness. – **presumption**, *n.*

presumptuous /prə'zʌmptʃuəs/ *adj.* unwarrantedly or impertinently bold; forward.

pretence /prə'tɛns/ *n.* **1.** pretending or feigning; make-believe. **2.** a false show of something. **3.** a piece of make-believe. **4.** the act of pretending or alleging, now especially falsely. **5.** an alleged or pretended reason or excuse, or a pretext. **6.** insincere or false profession. **7.** the putting forth of a claim. **8.** the claim itself. **9.** pretension (fol. by *to*).

pretend /prə'tɛnd/ *v.t.* **1.** to put forward a false appearance of; feign. **2.** to allege or profess, especially insincerely or falsely. – *v.i.* **3.** to make believe. **4.** to lay claim (fol. by *to*). – **pretension**, *n.*

pretentious /prə'tɛnʃəs/ *adj.* **1.** characterised by assumption of dignity or importance. **2.** making an exaggerated outward show; ostentatious.

preter- a prefix meaning 'beyond', 'more than'.

preterite /'prɛtərət, 'prɛtrət/ *adj.* *Grammar* designating a tense usually denoting an action or state which was completed in the past.

pretext /'pritɛkst/ *n.* that which is put forward to conceal a true purpose or object; an ostensible reason.

pretty /'prɪti/ *adj.*, **-tier**, **-tiest**, *adv.*, *v.*, **-tied**, **-tying**. – *adj.* **1.** fair or attractive to the eye in a feminine or childish way. **2.** (of things, places, etc.) pleasing to the eye, especially without grandeur. – *adv.* **3.** moderately. **4.** quite; very. – *v.t.* **5.** to make pretty.

pretzel /'prɛtzəl/ *n.* a crisp, dry biscuit.

prevail /prə'veɪl/ *v.i.* **1.** to be widespread or current; to exist everywhere or generally. **2.** to be or prove superior in strength, power, or influence. **3.** to use persuasion or inducement successfully (fol. by *on*, *upon*, or *with*).

prevalent /'prɛvələnt/ *adj.* widespread. – **prevalence**, *n.*

prevaricate /prə'værəkeɪt/ *v.i.*, **-cated**, **-cating**. to act or speak evasively; equivocate; quibble.

prevent /prə'vɛnt/ *v.t.* to keep from doing or occurring; hinder. – **prevention**, *n.*

preventive /prə'vɛntɪv/ *adj.* **1.** *Medicine* warding off disease. **2.** serving to prevent or hinder. Also, **preventative**.

preview /'privju/ *n.* a previous view; a view in advance, as of a film.

previous /'priviəs/ *adj.* coming or occurring before something else; prior.

prey /preɪ/ *n.* **1.** an animal hunted or seized for food, especially by a carnivorous animal. **2.** a person or thing that falls a victim to an enemy, a disease, or any adverse agency. – *v.i.* **3.** to seek for and seize prey, as an animal does.

price /praɪs/ *n.*, *v.*, **priced**, **pricing**. – *n.* **1.** the sum or amount of money or its equivalent for which anything is bought, sold, or offered for sale. **2.** that which must be given, done, or undergone in order to obtain a thing. – *v.t.* **3.** to fix the price of.

price discrimination *n.* the selling of identical goods to different buyers at different prices.

price earnings ratio *n.* a figure calculated by dividing the price of a share by its earnings per share.

price index *n.* an indicator used to show the general level of prices.

priceless /'praɪsləs/ *adj.* valuable.

price ring *n.* an agreement whereby suppliers of goods or services agree to charge uniform prices.

price war *n.* a fiercely competitive price-cutting battle, usually among retailers.

prick /prɪk/ *n.* **1.** a puncture made by a needle, thorn, or the like. **2.** the act of pricking. – *v.t.* **3.** to pierce with a sharp point; puncture. **4.** to cause to stand erect or point upwards. – *v.i.* **5.** to perform the action of piercing or puncturing something. **6.** to rise erect or point upwards, as the ears of an animal (fol. by *up*).

prickle /'prɪkəl/ *n., v.,* **-led**, **-ling**. – *n.* **1.** a sharp point. **2.** a small, pointed process growing from the bark of a plant; a thorn. – *v.t.* **3.** to prick. **4.** to cause a pricking sensation in.

pride /praɪd/ *n., v.,* **prided**, **priding**. – *n.* **1.** high or inordinate opinion of one's own dignity, importance, merit, or superiority. **2.** the state or feeling of being proud. **3.** self respect. **4.** the best or most admired part of anything. **5.** a company of lions. – *v.t.* **6.** to indulge or plume (oneself) in a feeling of pride (usually fol. by *on* or *upon*).

priest /prist/ *n.* one whose office it is to perform religious rites, and especially to make sacrificial offerings.

prig /prɪg/ *n.* someone who is precise to an extreme in attention to principle or duty, especially in a self-righteous way.

prim /prɪm/ *adj.,* **primmer**, **primmest**. affectedly precise or proper.

primacy /'praɪməsi/ *n., pl.* **-cies**. **1.** the state of being first in order, rank, importance, etc. **2.** *Ecclesiastical* the office, rank, or dignity of a primate.

prima-facie evidence /praɪmə-'feɪʃi, praɪmə-'feɪsi/ *n.* (in law) evidence sufficient to establish a fact, or to raise a presumption of fact, unless rebutted.

primage /'praɪmɪdʒ/ *n.* a primary ad valorem revenue placed by the government on imports.

primal /'praɪməl/ *adj.* first; original; primeval.

primary /'praɪməri, 'praɪmri/ *adj.* **1.** first or highest in rank or importance; chief; principal. **2.** constituting, or belonging to, the first stage in any process. **3.** original, not derived or subordinate; fundamental; basic. – **primarily**, *adv.*

primary industry *n.* any industry such as dairy farming, forestry, mining, etc., which is involved in the growing, producing, extracting, etc., of natural resources.

primary school *n.* a school for full-time elementary instruction of children from the age of six to about eleven years.

primary vote *n.* **1.** Also, **primary**. a first preference (def. 5). **2.** the collective vote from such first preferences.

primate /'praɪmət/ *for def. 1*, /'praɪmeɪt/ *for def. 2* – *n.* **1.** *Ecclesiastical* an archbishop. **2.** any mammal of the order Primates, that includes humans, the apes, the monkeys, the lemurs, etc.

prime /praɪm/ *adj., n., v.,* **primed**, **priming**. – *adj.* **1.** first in importance, excellence, or value. **2.** first or highest in rank, dignity, or authority; chief; principal; main. **3.** original; fundamental. – *n.* **4.** the most flourishing stage or state. **5.** the choicest or best part of anything. – *v.t.* **6.** to prepare or make ready for a particular purpose or operation. **7.** to supply (a firearm) with powder for communicating fire to a charge. **8.** to pour water into (a pump) so as to swell the sucker and so act as a seal, making it work effectively. **9.** to cover (a surface) with a preparatory coat or colour, as in painting. **10.** to supply or equip with information, words, etc., for use.

prime minister *n.* (*often cap.*) the first or principal minister of certain governments; the chief of the cabinet or ministry. – **prime ministry**, *n.*

primer /'praɪmə, 'prɪmə/ *n.* **1.** an elementary book for teaching children to read. **2.** any small book of elementary principles.

primeval /praɪ'mivəl/ *adj.* of or relating to the first age or ages, especially of the world. Also, **primaeval**.

primitive /'prɪmətɪv/ *adj.* **1.** early in the history of the world or of humankind. **2.** characteristic of early ages or of an early state of human development. **3.** unaffected or little affected by civilising influences. **4.** being in its or the earliest period; early.

primogeniture /praɪmoʊ'dʒɛnətʃə/ *n. Law* the principle of inheritance or succession by the firstborn, specifically the eldest son.

primordial /praɪ'mɔdiəl/ *adj.* relating to or existing at or from the very beginning.

primrose /'prɪmroʊz/ *n.* a garden plant usually with yellow flowers.

prince /prɪns/ *n.* **1.** a non-reigning male member of a royal family. **2.** a sovereign or monarch; a king. **3.** the ruler of a small state, as one actually or nominally subordinate to a suzerain.

princess /'prɪnsɛs/ *n.* **1.** a non-reigning female member of a royal family. **2.** a female sovereign. **3.** the consort of a prince.

principal /'prɪnsəpəl/ *adj.* **1.** first or highest in rank, importance, value, etc.; chief; foremost. – *n.* **2.** a chief or head. **3.** something of principal or chief importance. **4.** *Law* a person authorising another (an agent) to represent him or her. **5.** a person primarily liable for an obligation (opposed to an *endorser*). **6.** the main body of an estate, etc., as distinguished from income. **7.** *Commerce* a capital sum, as distinguished from interest or profit.

principality /prɪnsə'pæləti/ *n., pl.* **-ties**. a state ruled by a prince.

principle /'prɪnsəpəl/ *n.* **1.** an accepted or professed rule of action or conduct. **2.** a fundamental, primary, or general truth, on which other truths depend. **3.** guiding sense of the requirements and obligations of right conduct. **4.** a rule or law exemplified in natural phenomena, in the construction or operation of a machine, the working of a system, or the like.

print /prɪnt/ *v.t.* **1.** to produce (a text, a picture, etc.) by applying inked types, plates, blocks, or the like, with direct pressure to paper or other material. **2.** to write in letters like those commonly used in print. **3.** to produce or fix (an indentation, mark, etc.) as by pressure. **4.** *Photography* to produce a positive picture from (a negative) by the transmission of light. **5.** *Computers* to produce (a result, data, etc.) in a legible form on paper (often fol. by *out*). – *n.* **6.** the state of being printed. **7.** printed lettering, especially with reference to character, style, or size. **8.** printed matter. **9.** a design, usually in colour, pressed on woven cotton with engraved rollers. **10.** the cloth so treated. **11.** *Photography* a picture made from a negative.

print-out /'prɪnt-aʊt/ *n.* results, data, or the like printed automatically by a computer in legible form.

prior[1] /'praɪə/ *adj.* **1.** preceding in time, or in order; earlier or former; anterior or antecedent. – *adv.* **2.** previously (fol. by *to*).

prior[2] /'praɪə/ *n.* the superior of certain monastic orders and houses.

priority /praɪ'ɒrəti/ *n., pl.* **-ties**. **1.** the state of being earlier in time, or of preceding something else. **2.** precedence in order, rank, etc. **3.** *Computers* the position in rank of an interrupt system in gaining the attention of the computer when there is more than one interrupt system.

prior period adjustment *n. Accounting* a current account adjustment referring to an earlier date.

prise = prize /praɪz/ *v.t.,* **prised**, **prising**. to raise, move, or force with or as with a lever.

prism /'prɪzəm/ *n.* **1.** *Optics* a transparent prismatic body (especially one with triangular bases) used for decomposing light into its spectrum or for reflecting light beams. **2.** *Geometry* a solid whose bases or ends are any congruent and parallel polygons, and whose sides are parallelograms. – **prismatic**, *adj.*

prison /'prɪzən/ *n.* a public building for the confinement or safe custody of criminals and others committed by law.

prisoner /'prɪzənə, 'prɪznə/ *n.* someone who is confined in prison or kept in custody, especially as the result of legal process.

prison officer *n.* an official having charge of prisoners in a jail; warder.

prissy /'prɪsi/ *adj.,* **-sier**, **-siest**. *Colloquial* precise; prim; affectedly nice.

pristine /'prɪstin/ *adj.* **1.** of or relating to the earliest period or state; original; primitive. **2.** having its original purity.

private /'praɪvət/ *adj.* **1.** belonging to some particular person or persons; belonging to oneself; being one's own. **2.** confined to or intended only for the person or persons immediately concerned; confidential. **3.** not holding public office employment, as a person. **4.** (of a company) having the right to transfer its shares restricted, the number of its members limited to 50, and prohibited from using public subscription for its shares or debentures. **5.** removed from or out of public view of knowledge; secret. **6.** without the presence of others; alone; secluded. **7.** (of a member of parliament) not holding a government post. – **privacy**, *n.*

private enterprise *n.* **1.** business or commercial activities independent of state ownership or control. **2.** the principle of free enterprise.

private secretary *n.* someone who handles the individual or confidential correspondence, etc., of a person or business organisation.

private sector *n.* that sector of an economy which is owned and operated by individuals and privately-owned companies (opposed to the *public sector*).

privation /praɪ'veɪʃən/ *n.* lack of the usual comforts or necessaries of life, or an instance of this. – **privative**, *adj.*

privatise = privatize /'praɪvətaɪz/ *v.t.,* **-tised**, **-tising**. to change the status of (land, industries, etc.) from that of state to private ownership. – **privatisation**, *n.*

privative /'prɪvətɪv/ *adj.* **1.** having the quality of depriving. **2.** *Grammar* indicating negation or absence.

privet /'prɪvət/ *n.* one of two shrubs, *Ligustrum sinese* or *L. lucidum*, with evergreen leaves and small, heavily perfumed, white flowers, now considered noxious.

privilege /'prɪvəlɪdʒ/ *n., v.,* **-leged**, **-leging**. – *n.* **1.** a right or immunity enjoyed by a person or persons beyond the common advantages of others. **2.** a prerogative, advantage, or opportunity enjoyed by anyone in a favoured position (as distinct from a right). – *v.t.* **3.** to grant a privilege to.

privy /'prɪvi/ *adj., n., pl.* **privies**. – *adj.* **1.** participating in the knowledge of something private or secret (usually fol. by *to*). – *n.* **2.** an outhouse serving as a toilet. **3.** *Law* one participating directly in a legal transaction, or claiming through or under such a one. – **privity**, *n.*

prize[1] /praɪz/ *n.* **1.** a reward of victory or superiority, as in a contest or competition. **2.** that which is won in a lottery or the like.

prize[2] /praɪz/ *v.t.,* **prized**, **prizing**. to value or esteem highly.

prize[3] /praɪz/ *v.t.,* **prized**, **prizing**. → **prise**.

pro /proʊ/ *adv., n., pl.* **pros**. – *adv.* **1.** in favour of a proposition, opinion, etc. (opposed to *con*). – *n.* **2.** an argument, consideration, vote, etc., for something.

pro- **1.** a prefix indicating favour for some party, system, idea, etc., having *anti-* as its opposite. **2.** a prefix of priority in space or time having especially a meaning of advancing or projecting forwards or outwards, having also extended figurative meanings, including substitution, and attached widely to stems not used as words, as *provision, prologue, proceed, produce, protract.*

proactive /proʊ'æktɪv/ *adj.* taking the initiative, rather than waiting until things happen and then reacting.

probability /prɒbə'bɪləti/ *n., pl.* **-ties**. **1.** the quality or fact of being probable. **2.** a likelihood or chance of something. **3.** a probable event, circumstance, etc. **4.** *Statistics* the relative frequency of the occurrence of an event as measured by the ratio of the number of cases or alternatives favourable to the event to the total number of cases or events. – **probabilistic**, *adj.*

probable /'prɒbəbəl/ *adj.* **1.** likely to occur or prove true. **2.** affording ground for belief. – **probably**, *adv.*

probate /'proʊbeɪt/ *n. Law* the official proving of a will as authentic or valid.

probation /prə'beɪʃən/ *n.* **1.** the act of testing. **2.** *Law* a method of dealing with offenders, especially young persons guilty of minor crimes or first offences, by allowing them to go at large conditionally under supervision.

probe /proʊb/ *v.,* **probed**, **probing**, *n.* – *v.t.* **1.** to search into or examine thoroughly; question closely. **2.** to examine or explore as with a probe. – *n.* **3.** the act of probing. **4.** a slender surgical instrument for exploring the depth or direction of a wound, sinus, or the like.

probity /'proubəti/ *n.* integrity; uprightness; honesty.

problem /'prɒbləm/ *n.* **1.** any question or matter involving doubt, uncertainty, or difficulty. **2.** a question proposed for solution or discussion. – **problematic**, **problematical**, *adj.*

proboscis /prə'bɒskəs, prə'bousəs/ *n., pl.* **-boscises** /-'bɒskəsəz, -'bɒsəsəz/, **-boscides** /-'bɒskədiz, -'bɒsədiz/ **1.** an elephant's trunk. **2.** any long flexible snout.

procedure /prə'sidʒə/ *n.* the act or manner of proceeding in any action or process; conduct.

proceed /prə'sid/ *v.,* /'prousid/ *n.* – *v.i.* **1.** to go on with or carry on any action or process. **2.** to take legal proceedings (fol. by *against*). **3.** to be carried on, as an action, process, etc. **4.** to go or come forth; issue. – *n.* **5.** (*usu. pl.*) the sum derived from a sale or other transaction.

proceeding /prə'sidɪŋ/ *n.* **1.** action, course of action, or conduct. **2.** (*pl.*) records of the doings of a society. **3.** *Law* **a.** the instituting or carrying on of an action at law. **b.** a legal step or measure.

process /'prousɛs/ *n.* **1.** a systematic series of actions directed to some end. **2.** the whole course of the proceedings in an action at law. **3.** a prominence or protuberance. **4.** the action of going forward or on. **5.** the condition of being carried on. **6.** course or lapse, as of time. – *v.t.* **7.** to treat or prepare by some particular process, as in manufacturing. **8.** *Computers* to manipulate data in order to abstract the required information.

process costing *n.* a method of costing used to ascertain the cost of the product at each stage of manufacture.

procession /prə'sɛʃən/ *n.* the proceeding or moving along in orderly succession, in a formal or ceremonious manner, of a line or body of persons, animals, vehicles, etc.

proclaim /prə'kleɪm/ *v.t.* to announce or declare, publicly and officially. – **proclamation**, *n.*

proclivity /prə'klɪvəti/ *n., pl.* **-ties**. natural or habitual inclination or tendency.

procrastinate /prou'kræstəneɪt/ *v.i.,* **-nated**, **-nating**. to defer action; delay. – **procrastinator**, *n.*

procreate /'proukrieɪt/ *v.t.,* **-ated**, **-ating**. **1.** to beget or generate (offspring). **2.** to produce; bring into being.

proctor /'prɒktə/ *n.* (in certain universities) an official charged with various duties, especially with the maintenance of discipline.

procure /prə'kjuə/ *v.t.,* **-cured**, **-curing**. **1.** to obtain or get by care, effort, or the use of special means. **2.** to effect; cause; bring about, especially by unscrupulous or indirect means.

prod /prɒd/ *v.,* **prodded**, **prodding**, *n.* – *v.t.* **1.** to poke or jab with something pointed. – *n.* **2.** the act of prodding; a poke or jab. **3.** any of various pointed instruments, as a goad.

prodigal /'prɒdɪgəl/ *adj.* **1.** wastefully or recklessly extravagant. – *n.* **2.** a spendthrift.

prodigious /prə'dɪdʒəs/ *adj.* **1.** extraordinary in size, amount, extent, degree, force, etc. **2.** wonderful or marvellous.

prodigy /'prɒdədʒi/ *n., pl.* **-gies**. a person, especially a child, endowed with extraordinary gifts or powers.

produce /prə'djus/ *v.,* **-duced**, **-ducing**, /'prɒdʒus/ *n.* – *v.t.* **1.** to bring into existence. **2.** to make; create. **3.** *Economics* to create (something having an exchangeable value). **4.** to yield. **5.** to bring forward. **6.** to bring (a play, film, etc.) before the public. **7.** to extend or prolong (a line, etc.). – *n.* **8.** that which is produced; yield; product. **9.** agricultural or natural products collectively. – **production**, *n.* – **productive**, *adj.*

producer /prə'djusə/ *n.* someone who supervises the production of a film, play, television or radio show, etc., with particular responsibility for administrative and financial aspects.

producer goods *pl. n.* goods that are used in the process of creating final consumer goods, as machinery, raw materials, etc.

product /'prɒdʌkt/ *n.* **1.** a thing produced by any action or operation, or by labour; an effect or result. **2.** something produced; a thing produced by nature or by a natural process. **3.** *Mathematics* the result obtained by multiplying two or more quantities together.

productivity /prɒdʌk'tɪvɪti/ *n.* efficiency of production, as measured by a comparison of product output with input cost.

productivity bargaining *n.* a negotiation between employers and employees in which the employees agree to certain changes in work practices, thus resulting in increased productivity, in exchange for better wages, etc.

profane /prə'feɪn/ *adj.* characterised by irreverence or contempt for God or sacred things; irreligious, especially speaking or spoken in manifest or implied contempt for sacred things. – **profanity**, *n.*

profess /prə'fɛs/ *v.t.* **1.** to lay claim to (a feeling, etc.), often insincerely; pretend to. **2.** to declare openly; announce or affirm; avow or acknowledge.

profession /prə'fɛʃən/ *n.* a vocation requiring knowledge of some department of learning or science.

professional /prə'fɛʃnəl, -ʃənəl/ *adj.* **1.** following an occupation as a means of livelihood or for gain. **2.** relating or appropriate to a profession. **3.** following as a business an occupation ordinarily engaged in as a pastime. – *n.* **4.** someone belonging to one of the learned or skilled professions. **5.** someone who makes a business of an occupation, etc., especially of an art or sport, in which amateurs engage for amusement or recreation.

professor /prə'fɛsə/ *n.* a teacher of the highest rank, usually holding a chair in a particular branch of learning, in a university or college.

proffer /'prɒfə/ *v.t.* to put before a person for acceptance; offer.

proficient /prə'fɪʃənt/ *adj.* well advanced or expert in any art, science, or subject; skilled. – **proficiency**, *n.*

profile /'proʊfaɪl/ *n.* **1.** the outline or contour of the human face, especially as seen from the side. **2.** the outline of something seen against a background. **3.** a vivid and concise sketch of the biography and personality of an individual.

profit /'prɒfət/ *n.* **1.** (*often pl.*) pecuniary gain resulting from the employment of capital in any transaction: **a. gross profit,** gross receipts less the immediate costs of production. **b. net profit,** the amount remaining after deducting all costs from gross receipts. **c.** the ratio of such pecuniary gain to the amount of capital invested. **2.** *Economics* the surplus left to the producer or employer after deducting wages, rent, cost of raw materials, etc. **3.** advantage; benefit; gain. – *v.i.* **4.** to gain advantage or benefit. **5.** to make profit.

profitable /'prɒfətəbəl/ *adj.* **1.** yielding profits; remunerative. **2.** beneficial or useful. – **profitability**, *n.*

profit and loss *n.* the gain and loss arising from commercial or other transactions, applied especially to an account in bookkeeping showing gains and losses in business. – **profit-and-loss**, *adj.*

profit and loss account *n.* the financial statement of an accounting entity disclosing the revenues, expenses, gains, and losses arising in a specific period, and the result of the period expressed as an operating profit or an operating loss.

profiteer /prɒfə'tɪə/ *n.* someone who seeks or exacts exorbitant profits, as by taking advantage of public necessity.

profit sharing *n.* a system whereby an employee receives, in addition to wages, a share in the profits of a business.

profit-taking /'prɒfət-ˌteɪkɪŋ/ *n.* *Stock Exchange* the selling of commodities, securities, etc., especially after a sharp rise in value or in the expectation of a fall in value, so as to maximise profit.

profligate /'prɒfləgət/ *adj.* utterly and shamelessly immoral.

pro forma /proʊ 'fɔmə/ *adv.* according to form; as a matter of form. – **pro-forma**, *adj.*

profound /prə'faʊnd/ *adj.* **1.** penetrating or entering deeply into subjects of thought or knowledge. **2.** deep. – **profundity**, *n.*

profuse /prə'fjus/ *adj.* **1.** extravagant. **2.** abundant; in great amount. – **profusion**, *n.*

progeny /'prɒdʒəni/ *n., pl.* **-nies**. offspring; issue; descendants. – **progenitor**, *n.*

progesterone /prə'dʒɛstəroʊn/ *n.* a hormone which prepares the uterus for the fertilised ovum and helps to maintain pregnancy.

prognosis /prɒg'noʊsəs/ *n., pl.* **-noses** /-'noʊsiz/. **1.** a forecasting of the probable course and termination of a disease. **2.** a particular forecast made. – **prognostic**, *adj.*

prognosticate /prɒg'nɒstəkeɪt/ *v.t.,* **-cated**, **-cating**. to prophesy.

program /'proʊgræm/ *n., v.,* **-grammed**, **-gramming**. – *n.* **1.** a plan or policy to be followed. **2.** a list of items, pieces, performers, etc., in a musical, theatrical, or other entertainment. **3.** an entertainment with reference to its pieces or numbers. **4.** a prospectus or syllabus. **5.** → **computer program**. – *v.t.* **6.** *Computers* to organise and arrange (data, etc.) relevant to a problem so that it can be solved by a computer. – *v.i.* **7.** to plan a program. **8.** to write a computer program. Also, **programme**. – **programmer**, *n.*

progress /'proʊgrɛs/ *n.,* /prə'grɛs/ *v.* – *n.* **1.** advancement in general. **2.** growth or development; continuous improvement. **3.** course of action, of events, of time, etc. – *v.i.* **4.** to advance.

progression /prə'grɛʃən/ *n.* **1.** forward or onward movement. **2.** a passing successively from one member of a series to the next; succession; sequence.

progressive /prə'grɛsɪv/ *adj.* **1.** favouring or advocating progress, improvement, or reform, especially in political matters. **2.** progressing or advancing. **3.** denoting or relating to a form of taxation in which the rate increases with certain increases in the taxable income.

prohibit /prə'hɪbət/ *v.t.* to forbid (an action, a thing) by authority. – **prohibition**, *n.*

prohibitive /prə'hɪbətɪv/ *adj.* **1.** that prohibits or forbids something. **2.** serving to prevent the use, purchase, etc., of something. Also, **prohibitory**.

project /'proʊdʒɛkt, 'prɒ-/ *n.,* /prə'dʒɛkt/ *v.* – *n.* **1.** something that is contemplated, devised, or planned; a plan; a scheme; an undertaking. – *v.t.* **2.** to propose, contemplate, or plan. **3.** to throw, cast, or impel forwards or onwards. **4.** to communicate; convey; make known (an idea, impression, etc.). **5.** to cause (a figure or image) to appear as on a background. **6.** to cause to jut out or protrude. – *v.i.* **7.** to extend or protrude beyond something else.

projectile /prə'dʒɛktaɪl/ *n.* an object set in motion by an exterior force which then continues to move by virtue of its own inertia.

projector /prə'dʒɛktə/ *n.* an apparatus for throwing an image on a screen, as of a slide; a film projector, etc.

prolapse /'proʊlæps/ *n.* *Pathology* a falling down of an organ or part, as the uterus, from its normal position.

prolate /'proʊleɪt/ *adj.* elongated along the polar diameter.

proletariat /proʊlə'tɛəriət/ *n.* **1.** the unpropertied class; that class which is dependent for support on the sale of its labour. **2.** the working class, or wage-earners in general.

proliferate /prə'lɪfəreɪt/ *v.i., v.t.,* **-rated**, **-rating**. to grow or produce by multiplication of parts, as in budding or cell division. – **proliferation**, *n.*

prolific /prə'lɪfɪk/ *adj.* **1.** producing offspring, young, fruit, etc., especially abundantly; fruitful. **2.** abundantly productive of or fruitful in something specified.

prolix /'proʊlɪks/ *adj.* tediously long.

prologue /'proʊlɒg/ *n.* an introductory speech, often in verse, calling attention to the theme of a play.

prolong /prə'lɒŋ/ *v.t.* to make longer.

promenade /prɒmə'nad/ *n., v.,* **-naded**, **-nading**. – *n.* **1.** a walk, especially in a public place, as for pleasure or display.

– *v.i.* **2.** to take a promenade.

prominent /'prɒmənənt/ *adj.* **1.** standing out so as to be easily seen; conspicuous; very noticeable. **2.** important; leading; well-known. – **prominence**, *n.*

promiscuous /prə'mɪskjuəs/ *adj.* characterised by or involving indiscriminate mingling or association, especially indulging in sexual intercourse with a number of partners. – **promiscuity**, *n.*

promise /'prɒməs/ *n., v.,* **-ised**, **-ising**. – *n.* **1.** an express assurance on which expectation is to be based. **2.** indication of future excellence or achievement. – *v.t.* **3.** to engage or undertake by promise (with an infinitive or clause). **4.** to make a promise of. – *v.i.* **5.** to afford ground for expectation (often fol. by *well* or *fair*).

promissory note /'prɒməsəri/ *n.* a written promise to pay a specified sum of money to a person designated or to his or her order, or to the bearer, at a time fixed or on demand.

promontory /'prɒməntri/ *n., pl.* **-ries**. a high point of land or rock projecting into the sea or other water beyond the line of coast; a headland.

promote /prə'moʊt/ *v.t.,* **-moted**, **-moting**. **1.** to advance in rank, dignity, position, etc. **2.** to further the growth, development, progress, etc., of; encourage. – **promotion**, *n.*

prompt /prɒmpt/ *adj.* **1.** done, performed, delivered, etc., at once or without delay. **2.** ready in action; quick to act as occasion demands. – *v.t.* **3.** to move or incite to action. **4.** to assist (a person speaking) by suggesting something to be said. – *v.i.* **5.** *Theatre* to supply offstage cues and effects. – *n.* **6.** *Commerce* a limit of time given for payment for merchandise purchased, the limit being stated on a note of reminder called a **prompt note**. **7.** something that prompts. **8.** *Computers* a message from a computer, appearing as words or symbols on the screen, which indicate to the user that the computer is ready for further instructions.

promulgate /'prɒməlgeɪt/ *v.t.,* **-gated**, **-gating**. **1.** to make known by open declaration. **2.** to set forth or teach publicly (a creed, doctrine, etc.).

prone /proʊn/ *adj.* **1.** having a natural inclination or tendency to something; disposed; liable. **2.** having the front or ventral part downwards; lying face downwards. **3.** lying flat; prostrate.

prong /prɒŋ/ *n.* one of the pointed divisions or tines of a fork.

pronoun /'proʊnaʊn/ *n.* a word used as a substitute for a noun. – **pronominal**, *adj.*

pronounce /prə'naʊns/ *v.,* **-nounced**, **-nouncing**. – *v.t.* **1.** to enunciate or articulate (words, etc.). **2.** to utter or sound in a particular manner in speaking. **3.** to declare (a person or thing) to be as specified. **4.** to utter or deliver formally or solemnly. – *v.i.* **5.** to give an opinion or decision (usually fol. by *on*). – **pronunciation**, *n.*

pronounced /prə'naʊnst/ *adj.* **1.** strongly marked. **2.** clearly indicated.

proof /pruf/ *n.* **1.** evidence sufficient to establish a thing as true, or to produce belief in its truth. **2.** the establishment of the truth of anything; demonstration. **3.** an arithmetical operation serving to check the correctness of a calculation. **4.** the arbitrary standard strength, as of alcoholic liquors. **5.** *Photography* a trial print from a negative. **6.** *Printing* a trial impression as of composed type, taken to correct errors and make alterations. – *adj.* **7.** impenetrable, impervious, or invulnerable. **8.** of tested or proved strength or quality.

-proof a suffix meaning 'insulated from', 'impervious to', 'not affected by', etc., as in *waterproof*.

proofread /'prufrid/ *v.t., v.i.,* **-read**, **-reading**. to read (printers' proofs, etc.) in order to detect and mark errors.

prop /prɒp/ *v.,* **propped**, **propping**, *n.* – *v.t.* **1.** to support, or prevent from falling, with or as with a prop (often fol. by *up*). **2.** to support or sustain. – *n.* **3.** a stick, rod, pole, beam, or other rigid support. **4.** a person or thing serving as a support or stay.

propaganda /prɒpə'gændə/ *n.* dissemination of ideas, information or rumour for the purpose of injuring or helping an institution, a cause or a person.

propagate /'prɒpəgeɪt/ *v.t.,* **-gated**, **-gating**. **1.** to cause (plants, animals, etc.) to multiply by any process of natural reproducing from the parent stock. **2.** to transmit (traits, etc.) in reproduction, or through offspring. **3.** to spread (a report, doctrine, practice, etc.) from person to person; disseminate. **4.** to cause to extend to a greater distance, or transmit through space or a medium.

propane /'proʊpeɪn/ *n.* a gaseous hydrocarbon found in petroleum.

propel /prə'pɛl/ *v.t.,* **-pelled**, **-pelling**. to drive, or cause to move, forwards.

propellant /prə'pɛlənt/ *n.* **1.** a propelling agent. **2.** *Aeronautics* one or more substances used in rocket motors for the chemical generation of gas at the controlled rates required to provide thrust.

propellent /prə'pɛlənt/ *adj.* **1.** propelling; driving forward. – *n.* **2.** a propelling agent.

propeller /prə'pɛlə/ *n.* a device having a revolving hub with radiating blades, for propelling a ship, aircraft, etc.

propensity /prə'pɛnsəti/ *n., pl.* **-ties**. natural or habitual inclination or tendency.

proper /'prɒpə/ *adj.* **1.** adapted or appropriate to the purpose or circumstances; fit; suitable. **2.** conforming to established standards of behaviour or manners; correct or decorous. **3.** belonging or relating exclusively or distinctly to a person or thing. **4.** strict; accurate.

proper noun *n.* a noun that is not usually preceded by an article or other limiting modifier, in meaning applicable only to a single person or thing, or to several persons or things which constitute a unique class only by virtue of having the same name. See **common noun**.

property /'prɒpəti/ *n., pl.* **-ties**. **1.** that which one owns; the possession or possessions of a particular owner. **2.** a piece of land owned. **3.** Also, **country property**. a farm, station, orchard, etc. **4.** an essential or distinctive attribute or quality of a thing. **5.** Also, **prop**. *Theatre* an item of furniture, ornament, or decoration in a stage setting; any object handled or used by an actor in performance.

property trust *n. Law* a unit trust which invests in property (mainly real estate).

prophecy /'prɒfəsi/ *n., pl.* **-cies**. prediction.

prophesy /'prɒfəsaɪ/ *v.,* **-sied**, **-sying**. – *v.t.* **1.** to foretell or predict. – *v.i.* **2.** to make predictions. – **prophetic**, *adj.*

prophet /'prɒfət/ *n.* **1.** someone who speaks for God or a deity, or by divine inspiration. **2.** someone who foretells or predicts what is to come.

prophylactic /prɒfə'læktɪk/ *adj.* **1.** defending or protecting from disease, as a drug. – *n.* **2.** a contraceptive, especially a condom. – **prophylaxis**, *n.*

propinquity /prə'pɪŋkwəti/ *n.* **1.** nearness in place; proximity. **2.** nearness of relation; kinship.

propitiate /prə'pɪʃieɪt/ *v.t.,* **-ated**, **-ating**. to make favourably inclined; appease.

propitious /prə'pɪʃəs/ *adj.* presenting favourable conditions; favourable.

proponent /prə'pounənt/ *n.* **1.** someone who puts forward a proposition or proposal. **2.** someone who supports a cause or doctrine.

proportion /prə'pɔʃən/ *n.* **1.** comparative relation between things or magnitudes as to size, quantity, number, etc.; ratio. **2.** proper relation between things or parts. **3.** (*pl.*) dimensions. **4.** a portion or part, especially in its relation to the whole. **5.** symmetry; harmony; balanced relationship. – **proportional**, *adj.* – **proportionate**, *adj.*

proportional representation *n.* a system of electing representatives to a legislative assembly in which there are a number of members representing any one electorate. The number of successful candidates from each party is directly proportional to the percentage of the total vote won by the party.

propose /prə'pouz/ *v.t.,* **-posed**, **-posing**. **1.** to put forward (a matter, subject, case, etc.) for consideration, acceptance, or action. **2.** to present (a person) for some position, office, membership, etc. **3.** to propound (a question, riddle, etc.). – **proposal**, *n.* – **proposition**, *n.*

propound /prə'paund/ *v.t.* to put forward for consideration, acceptance, or adoption.

proprietary /prə'praɪətri/ *adj.* **1.** belonging to a proprietor or proprietors. **2.** manufactured and sold only by the owner of the patent, formula, brand name, or trademark associated with the product.

proprietary limited company *n.* a company with a limit of 50 shareholders, which cannot issue shares for public conscription and which is not listed on the stock exchange; shareholders enjoy limited liability, on liquidation. Also, **proprietary company**.

proprietor /prə'praɪətə/ *n.* **1.** the owner of a business establishment, a hotel, newspaper, etc. **2.** someone who has the exclusive right or title to something; an owner, as of property. – **proprietorship**, *n.*

propriety /prə'praɪəti/ *n., pl.* **-ties**. **1.** conformity to established standards of behaviour or manners. **2.** appropriateness to the purpose or circumstances; suitability.

propulsion /prə'pʌlʃən/ *n.* the act of propelling or driving forward or onward.

pro rata /prou 'ratə/ *adv.* **1.** in proportion; according to a certain rate. – *adj.* **2.** proportionate.

prorogue /prə'roug/ *v.t.,* **-rogued**, **-roguing**. to discontinue meetings of (parliament or similar legislative body) until the next session.

prosaic /prou'zeɪɪk, prə-/ *adj.* commonplace or dull; matter-of-fact.

proscenium /prə'siniəm/ *n., pl.* **-nia** /-niə/. (in the modern theatre) the decorative arch or opening between the stage and the auditorium.

proscribe /prou'skraɪb/ *v.t.,* **-scribed**, **-scribing**. **1.** to denounce or condemn (a thing) as dangerous; to prohibit. **2.** to banish, exile or outlaw.

prose /prouz/ *n.* the ordinary form of spoken or written language, without metrical structure (as distinguished from poetry or verse).

prosecute /'prɒsəkjut/ *v.t.,* **-cuted**, **-cuting**. *Law* **1.** to institute legal proceedings against (a person, etc.). **2.** to seek to enforce or obtain by legal process. **3.** to conduct criminal proceedings in court against. – **prosecution**, *n.* – **prosecutor**, *n.*

proselyte /'prɒsəlaɪt/ *n.* someone who has come over or changed from one opinion, religious belief, sect, or the like to another; a convert.

prosody /'prɒsədi, 'prɒz-/ *n.* the science or study of poetic metres and versification.

prospect /'prɒspɛkt/ *n.* **1.** (*usu. pl.*) an apparent probability of advancement, success, profit, etc. **2.** the outlook for the future. **3.** something in view as a source of profit. **4.** a view or scene presented to the eye, especially of scenery. – *v.t.* **5.** to search or explore (a region), as for gold. – *v.i.* **6.** to search or explore a region for gold or the like. – **prospector**, *n.*

prospective /prə'spɛktɪv/ *adj.* **1.** of or in the future. **2.** potential; likely; expected.

prospectus /prə'spɛktəs/ *n.* **1.** a circular or advertisement inviting applications from the public to subscribe for securities of a corporation or proposed corporation. **2.** a pamphlet issued by a school or other institution giving details about itself.

prosperous /'prɒspərəs, -prəs/ *adj.* **1.** having or characterised by continued good fortune; flourishing; successful. **2.** well-to-do or well-off. – **prosper**, *v.* – **prosperity**, *n.*

prostate gland /'prɒsteɪt/ *n.* the composite gland which surrounds the urethra of males at the base of the bladder.

prosthesis /prɒs'θisəs, prəs-/ *n., pl.* **-theses** /-'θisiz/. **1.** the addition of an artificial part to supply a defect of the body. **2.** such a part, as an artificial limb. – **prosthetics**, *n.*

prostitute /'prɒstətjut/ *n.* a person, especially a woman, who engages in sexual intercourse for money as a livelihood.

prostrate /prɒs'treɪt/ *v.,* **-trated**, **-trating**, /'prɒstreɪt/ *adj.* – *v.t.* **1.** to throw down level with the ground. – *adj.* **2.** submissive. **3.** *Botany* (of a plant or stem) lying flat on the ground.

protagonist /prə'tægənəst/ *n.* the leading character in a play, novel, etc.

protean /prə'tiən, 'proutiən/ *adj.* readily assuming different forms or characters.

protect /prə'tɛkt/ *v.t.* **1.** to defend or guard from attack, invasion, annoyance, insult, etc.; cover or shield from injury or danger. **2.** *Economics* to guard (a country's industry) from foreign competition by imposing import duties. – **protective**, *adj.* – **protection**, *n.* – **protector**, *n.*

protective trust *n.* a trust for life or any lesser period of the beneficiary, which is to be determined in certain events such as bankruptcy of the beneficiary, whereupon the trust income is to be applied for the maintenance of the beneficiary and his or her family at the absolute discretion of the trustee.

protectorate /prə'tɛktərət, -trət/ *n.* **1.** the relation of a strong state towards a weaker state or territory which it protects and partly controls. **2.** a state or territory so protected.

protégé /'proutəʒeɪ/ *n.* someone who is under the protection or friendly patronage of another.

protein /'proutin/ *n. Biochemistry* any of the polymers formed from amino acids, which are found in all cells and which include enzymes, plasma and proteins.

protest /'proutɛst/ *n.*, /prə'tɛst, prou-/ *v.* – *n.* **1.** an expression or declaration of objection or disapproval. **2.** *Commerce* a formal notarial certificate attesting the fact that a cheque, note, or bill of exchange has been presented for acceptance or payment and that it has been refused. – *v.i.* **3.** to give formal expression to objection or disapproval; remonstrate. – *v.t.* **4.** to declare solemnly or formally; affirm; assert.

protestation /prɒtəs'teɪʃən, prou-/ *n.* a solemn declaration or affirmation.

proto- a word element meaning 'first', 'earliest form of', as *prototype*.

protocol /'proutəkɒl/ *n.* the customs and regulations dealing with the ceremonies and etiquette of the diplomatic corps and others at a court or capital.

proton /'proutɒn/ *n.* a positively-charged elementary particle present in every atomic nucleus.

protoplasm /'proutəplæzəm/ *n.* the living matter of all vegetable and animal cells and tissues.

prototype /'proutətaɪp/ *n.* the original or model after which anything is formed.

protozoan /proutə'zouən/ *adj.* an animal consisting of one cell.

protract /prə'trækt/ *v.t.* **1.** to prolong. **2.** *Surveying, etc.* to plot; to draw by means of a scale and protractor.

protractor /prə'træktə/ *n.* a flat semicircular instrument, graduated around the circular edge, used to measure or mark off angles.

protrude /prə'trud/ *v.i.*, **-truded**, **-truding**. to project.

protuberant /prə'tjubərənt, -brənt/ *adj.* bulging. – **protuberance**, *n.*

proud /praud/ *adj.* **1.** feeling pleasure or satisfaction over something conceived as highly honourable or creditable to oneself (often fol. by *of*, an infinitive, or a clause). **2.** having or showing self-respect or self-esteem. **3.** (of things) stately, majestic, or magnificent. **4.** projecting beyond the surrounding elements or objects.

prove /pruv/ *v.t.*, **proved**, **proved** *or* **proven**, **proving**. **1.** to establish the truth or genuineness of, as by evidence or argument. **2.** to put to the test; try or test. **3.** to determine the characteristics of by scientific analysis. **4.** *Cookery* to cause (dough) to rise in a warm place before baking.

provedore = providore /'prɒvədɔ/ *n.* someone who provides supplies as for a ship, tuckshop, etc. Also, **provedor**, **providor**.

provenance /'prɒvənəns/ *n.* the place of origin, as of a work of art, etc.

provender /'prɒvəndə/ *n.* dry food for livestock, as hay; fodder.

proverb /'prɒvɜb/ *n.* a short popular saying, long current, embodying some familiar truth or useful thought in expressive language. – **proverbial**, *adj.*

provide /prə'vaɪd/ *v.*, **-vided**, **-viding**. – *v.t.* **1.** to furnish or supply. – *v.i.* **2.** to supply means of support, etc. (often fol. by *for*).

provided /prə'vaɪdəd/ *conj.* on the condition or supposition (that).

providence /'prɒvədəns/ *n.* **1.** the foreseeing care and guardianship of God over his creatures. **2.** provident or prudent management of resources; economy.

provident /'prɒvədənt/ *adj.* having or showing foresight; careful in providing for the future.

providing /prə'vaɪdɪŋ/ *conj.* → **provided**.

providore /'prɒvədɔ/ *n.* → **provedore**.

province /'prɒvəns/ *n.* **1.** an administrative division or unit of a country. **2. the provinces**, the parts of a country outside the capital or the largest cities. **3.** the sphere or field of action of a person, etc.; one's office, function, or business. – **provincial**, *adj.*

provision /prə'vɪʒən/ *n.* **1.** a clause in a legal instrument, a law, etc., providing for a particular matter; stipulation; proviso. **2.** arrangement or preparation beforehand, as for the doing of something, the meeting of needs, the supplying of means, etc. **3.** (*pl.*) supplies of food.

provisional /prə'vɪʒənəl/ *adj.* temporary; conditional.

provisional tax *n.* tax paid in advance on income to be earned in the next financial year from sources other than salary and wages.

proviso /prə'vaɪzou/ *n.*, *pl.* **-sos**, **-soes**. a stipulation or condition.

provoke /prə'vouk/ *v.t.*, **-voked**, **-voking**. **1.** to anger, enrage, exasperate, or vex. **2.** to stir up, arouse, or call forth. **3.** to give rise to, induce, or bring about. – **provocation**, *n.* – **provocative**, *adj.*

provost /'prɒvəst/ *n.* a person appointed to superintend or preside. – **provostship**, *n.*

prow /prau/ *n.* the forepart of a ship or boat above the waterline; the bow.

prowess /'prauɛs, prau'ɛs/ *n.* **1.** valour; bravery. **2.** outstanding ability.

prowl /praul/ *v.i.* to rove or go about stealthily in search of prey, plunder, etc.

proximate /'prɒksəmət/ *adj.* next; nearest.

proximity /prɒk'sɪməti/ *n.* nearness.

proximo /'prɒksəmoʊ/ *adv.* in or of the next or coming month. Cf. **ultimo**. *Abbrev.:* prox.

proxy /'prɒksi/ *n., pl.* **proxies**. the agency of a person deputed to act for another.

prude /prud/ *n.* a person who affects extreme modesty or propriety. – **prudery**, *n.*

prudence /'prudns/ *n.* **1.** cautious practical wisdom; good judgment; discretion. **2.** provident care in management; economy or frugality. – **prudential**, *adj.* – **prudent**, *adj.*

prune[1] /prun/ *n.* a purplish black dried fruit.

prune[2] /prun/ *v.t.,* **pruned**, **pruning**. to cut or lop superfluous or undesired twigs, branches, or roots from; to trim.

prurient /'pruriənt/ *adj.* inclined to or characterised by lascivious thought.

pry /praɪ/ *v.i.,* **pried**, **prying**. **1.** to look closely or curiously, peer, or peep. **2.** to search or inquire curiously or inquisitively into something.

psalm /sam/ *n.* a sacred or solemn song, or hymn.

psephology /sə'fɒlədʒi/ *n.* the study of elections by analysing their results, trends, etc.

pseudo- a word element meaning 'false', 'pretended'.

pseudonym /'sjudənɪm/ *n.* an assumed name adopted by an author to conceal his or her identity; pen-name.

psyche /'saɪki/ *n.* the human soul, spirit, or mind.

psychedelic /saɪkə'dɛlɪk/ *adj.* **1.** denoting or relating to a mental state of enlarged consciousness, involving a sense of aesthetic joy and increased perception transcending verbal concepts. **2.** *Colloquial* having bright colours and imaginative patterns, as materials.

psychiatry /sə'kaɪətri, saɪ-/ *n.* the practice or the science of treating mental diseases. – **psychiatric**, *adj.* – **psychiatrist**, *n.*

psychic /'saɪkɪk/ *adj.* Also, **psychical**. **1.** of or relating to the human soul or mind; mental (opposed to *physical*). **2.** *Psychology* relating to super- or extra-sensory mental functioning, such as clairvoyance, telepathy. – *n.* **3.** a person specially susceptible to psychic influences.

psycho- a word element representing 'psyche' (as in *psychology* and *psychoanalysis*). Also, **psych-**.

psychoanalysis /ˌsaɪkoʊə'næləsəs/ *n.* a technical procedure for investigating unconscious mental processes, and for treating neuroses. – **psychoanalyse**, *v.*

psychological /saɪkə'lɒdʒɪkəl/ *adj.* **1.** of or relating to psychology. **2.** relating to the mind or to mental phenomena.

psychology /saɪ'kɒlədʒi/ *n., pl.* **-gies**. **1.** the science of mind, or of mental states and processes; the science of human nature. **2.** the science of human and animal behaviour. – **psychologist**, *n.*

psychopath /'saɪkəpæθ/ *n.* one affected with psychopathy or a psychopathic personality.

psychopathic /saɪkə'pæθɪk/ *adj.* denoting a personality outwardly normal but characterised by a diminished sense of social responsibility, inability to establish deep human relationships, and sometimes, abnormal or dangerous acts.

psychopathy /saɪ'kɒpəθi/ *n.* **1.** mental disease or disorder. **2.** a psychopathic personality.

psychosis /saɪ'koʊsəs/ *n., pl.* **-choses** /-koʊsiz/. *Pathology* any major, severe form of mental affection or disease. – **psychotic**, *adj., n.*

psychosomatic /ˌsaɪkoʊsə'mætɪk/ *adj.* denoting a physical disorder which is caused by or notably influenced by the emotional state of the patient.

ptomaine /tə'meɪn/ *n.* any of a class of basic nitrogenous substances, some of them very poisonous, produced during putrefaction of animal or plant proteins. Also, **ptomain**.

pub /pʌb/ *n. Colloquial* a hotel.

puberty /'pjubəti/ *n.* sexual maturity; the earliest age at which a person is capable of procreating offspring.

pubic /'pjubɪk/ *adj.* relating to the lower part of the abdomen, or groin.

public accountant *n.* an accountant in private practice, a partnership, or in the public service, who provides accounting and auditing services for a fee.

publican /'pʌblɪkən/ *n.* the owner or manager of a hotel.

publication /pʌblə'keɪʃən/ *n.* **1.** the publishing of a book, periodical, map, piece of music, engraving, or the like. **2.** that which is published, as a book or the like.

public company *n.* → **limited company**.

publicity /pʌb'lɪsəti/ *n.* **1.** the measures, process, or business of securing public notice. **2.** advertisement matter, as leaflets, films, etc., intended to attract public notice. – **publicise = publicize**, *v.* – **publicist**, *n.*

public relations *n.* the practice of promoting goodwill among the public for a company, government body, individual or the like; the practice of working to present a favourable image.

public sector *n.* that sector of an economy which is owned and operated by government and government authorities (opposed to the *private sector*).

public service *n.* the structure of departments and personnel responsible for the administration of government policy and legislation. – **public servant**, *n.*

publish /'pʌblɪʃ/ *v.t.* **1.** to issue, or cause to be issued, in copies made by printing or other processes, for sale or distribution to the public, as a book, periodical, map, piece of music, engraving, or the like. **2.** to make publicly or generally known.

puce /pjus/ *n.* dark or purplish brown.

pucker /'pʌkə/ *v.t., v.i.* to draw or gather into wrinkles or irregular folds.

pudding /'pʊdɪŋ/ *n.* **1.** a sweet or savoury dish made in many forms and of various ingredients. **2.** a course in a meal following the main or meat course.

puddle /'pʌdl/ *n.* **1.** a small pool of water, especially dirty water, as in a road after rain. **2.** a small pool of any liquid.

puerile /'pjuəraɪl, 'pjʊəraɪl/ *adj.* **1.** of or relating to a child or boy. **2.** childishly foolish, irrational, or trivial.

puff /pʌf/ *n.* **1.** a short, quick blast, as of wind or breath. **2.** an inflated or distended part of a thing; a swelling; a protuberance. **3.** inflated or exaggerated praise, especially as uttered or written from interested motives. **4. out of puff,** *Colloquial* out of breath. – *v.i.* **5.** to blow with short, quick blasts, as the wind. **6.** to emit puffs or whiffs of vapour or smoke. **7.** to become inflated or distended (usually fol. by *up*). – *v.t.* **8.** to send forth (air, vapour, etc.) in short quick blasts. **9.** to inflate or distend, especially with air.

puffin /'pʌfən/ *n.* a seabird with a brightly coloured bill.

puff pastry *n.* a rich, flaky pastry used for pies, tarts, etc.

puffy /'pʌfi/ *adj.*, **puffier**, **puffiest**. inflated or distended.

pug /pʌg/ *n.* a breed of dog.

pugilist /'pjudʒələst/ *n.* a boxer.

pugnacious /pʌg'neɪʃəs/ *adj.* given to fighting; quarrelsome; aggressive.

pull /pʊl/ *v.t.* **1.** to draw or haul towards oneself or itself, in a particular direction, or into a particular position. **2.** to draw, rend, or tear (apart, to pieces, etc.). **3.** to draw or pluck away from a place of growth, attachment, etc. **4.** to cause to form, as a grimace. **5.** to strain, as a ligament. – *v.i.* **6.** to exert a drawing, tugging, or hauling force (often fol. by *at*). – *v.* **7. pull in,** (of a vehicle, driver, etc.) to move to the side of the road in order to stop. **8. pull out, a.** to leave; depart. **b.** (of a vehicle, driver, etc.) to move out of a lane or stream of traffic, as in preparing to overtake. **c.** *Colloquial* to withdraw, as from an agreement or enterprise. **9. pull through,** *Colloquial* to recover, as from an illness, period of adversity, or the like. **10. pull up, a.** to stop. **b.** to correct or rebuke. – *n.* **11.** the act of pulling or drawing. **12.** force used in pulling; pulling power. **13.** *Colloquial* influence, as with persons able to grant favours.

pull date *n.* the date after which a consumer commodity should no longer be sold.

pullet /'pʊlət/ *n.* a young hen.

pulley /'pʊli/ *n., pl.* **-leys**. a wheel with a grooved rim for carrying a line, turning in a frame or block and serving to change the direction of or transmit power, as in pulling at one end of the line to raise a weight at the other end.

pullover /'pʊloʊvə/ *n.* → **jumper**.

pulmonary /'pʌlmənri, 'pʊl-/ *adj.* of or relating to the lungs.

pulp /pʌlp/ *n.* **1.** the succulent part of a fruit. **2.** any soft, moist, slightly cohering mass, as that into which linen, wood, etc., are converted in the making of paper.

pulpit /'pʊlpət/ *n.* a platform or raised structure in a church, from which the priest or minister delivers a sermon, etc.

pulsate /pʌl'seɪt/ *v.i.*, **-sated**, **-sating**. **1.** to expand and contract rhythmically, as the heart; beat; throb. **2.** to vibrate; quiver.

pulse[1] /pʌls/ *n., v.,* **pulsed**, **pulsing**. – *n.* **1.** the regular throbbing of the arteries caused by the successive contractions of the heart, especially as felt in an artery at the wrist. **2.** a single stroke, vibration, or undulation. **3.** a throb of life, emotion, etc. – *v.i.* **4.** to beat or throb; pulsate.

pulse[2] /pʌls/ *n.* the edible seeds of certain leguminous plants, as peas, beans, etc.

pulverise = pulverize /'pʌlvəraɪz/ *v.t.*, **-rised**, **-rising**. to reduce to dust or powder, as by pounding, grinding, etc.

puma /'pjumə/ *n.* a large tawny feline.

pumice /'pʌməs/ *n.* a porous or spongy form of volcanic glass, used, especially when powdered, as an abrasive, etc. Also, **pumice stone**. – **pumiceous**, *adj.*

pummel /'pʌməl/ *v.t.*, **-melled**, **-melling**. to beat or thrash with rapid blows, as with the fists.

pump[1] /pʌmp/ *n.* **1.** an apparatus or machine for raising, driving, exhausting, or compressing fluids, as by means of a piston, plunger, or rotating vanes. – *v.t.* **2.** to raise, drive, etc., with a pump. **3.** to free from water, etc., by means of a pump (sometimes fol. by *out*). **4.** to seek to elicit information from, as by artful questioning. – *v.i.* **5.** to work a pump; raise or move water, etc., with a pump. **6.** to operate as a pump does.

pump[2] /pʌmp/ *n.* a type of shoe.

pumpkin /'pʌmpkən/ *n.* a large, usually orange, vegetable.

pun /pʌn/ *n.* a play on words.

punch[1] /pʌntʃ/ *n.* **1.** a thrusting blow, especially with the fist. – *v.t.* **2.** to give a sharp thrust or blow to, especially with the fist.

punch[2] /pʌntʃ/ *n.* a tool or apparatus for piercing, or perforating tickets, leather, etc., or stamping materials, impressing a design, forcing nails beneath a surface, driving bolts out of holes, etc.

punch[3] /pʌntʃ/ *n.* a beverage consisting of wine or spirits mixed with water, fruit juice, etc.

punctilious /pʌŋk'tɪliəs/ *adj.* strict in the observance of forms in conduct or actions.

punctual /'pʌŋktʃuəl/ *adj.* strictly observant of an appointed or regular time; not late. – **punctuality**, *n.*

punctuation /pʌŋktʃu'eɪʃən/ *n.* the practice, art, or system of inserting marks or points in writing or printing in order to make the meaning clear. – **punctuate**, *v.*

puncture /'pʌŋktʃə/ *v.t.*, **-tured**, **-turing**. to prick, pierce, or perforate.

pundit /'pʌndət/ *n.* *Colloquial* someone who sets up as an expert.

pungent /'pʌndʒənt/ *adj.* sharply affecting the organs of taste, as if by a penetrating power; biting; acrid.

punish /'pʌnɪʃ/ *v.t.* to subject to a penalty, or to pain, loss, confinement, death, etc., for some offence, transgression, or fault. – **punishment**, *n.* – **punitive**, *adj.*

punk /pʌŋk/ *n.* **1.** *Chiefly US Colloquial* something or someone worthless, degraded, or bad. **2.** a follower of punk rock and an associated style of dress and behaviour.

punk rock *n.* a type of rock music usually associated with aggression and rebelliousness.

punnet /ˈpʌnət/ *n.* a small, shallow container, as for strawberries.

punt[1] /pʌnt/ *n.* **1.** a shallow, flat-bottomed, square-ended boat. **2.** a ferry for carrying vehicles across rivers, etc.

punt[2] /pʌnt/ *v.i.* to gamble; wager.

puny /ˈpjuni/ *adj.*, **-nier**, **-niest**. of less than normal size and strength; weakly.

pup /pʌp/ *n.* **1.** a young dog, under one year; a puppy. **2.** a young seal.

pupa /ˈpjupə/ *n., pl.* **-pae** /-pi/, **-pas**. an insect in the non-feeding, usually immobile, transformation stage between the larva and the imago. – **pupal**, *adj.*

pupil[1] /ˈpjupəl/ *n.* someone who is under an instructor or teacher; a student.

pupil[2] /ˈpjupəl/ *n.* the expanding and contracting opening in the iris of the eye, through which light passes to the retina.

puppet /ˈpʌpət/ *n.* **1.** a doll. **2.** *Theatre* an artificial figure of a person, animal or object, usually in miniature and capable of articulated movement, controlled by a puppeteer. – **puppeteer**, *n.* – **puppetry**, *n.*

purchase /ˈpɜtʃəs/ *v.*, **-chased**, **-chasing**, *n.* – *v.t.* **1.** to acquire by the payment of money or its equivalent; buy. – *n.* **2.** something which is purchased or bought.

pure /ˈpjuə, pjʊə/ *adj.*, **purer**, **purest**. **1.** free from extraneous matter, or from mixture with anything of a different, inferior, or contaminating kind. **2.** abstract or theoretical (opposed to *applied*). **3.** unqualified; absolute; utter; sheer. **4.** being that and nothing else; mere. **5.** clean, spotless, or unsullied. **6.** untainted with evil; innocent. – **purify**, *v.* – **purity**, *n.*

puree /ˈpjureɪ/ *n.* a cooked and sieved vegetable or fruit.

purgative /ˈpɜgətɪv/ *adj.* purging; cleansing; specifically, causing evacuation of the bowels.

purgatory /ˈpɜgətri/ *n., pl.* **-ries**. any condition, situation, or place of temporary suffering, expiation, or the like.

purge /pɜdʒ/ *v.*, **purged**, **purging**, *n.* – *v.t.* **1.** to cleanse; rid of whatever is impure or undesirable; purify. – *n.* **2.** the elimination from political activity, as by killing, of political opponents and others.

purism /ˈpjurɪzəm/ *n.* scrupulous or excessive observance of or insistence on purity in language, style, etc. – **purist**, *n.*

puritan /ˈpjurətən/ *n.* someone who aspires to great purity or strictness of life in moral and religious matters. – **puritanical**, *adj.*

purl /pɜl/ *n.* a stitch used in hand knitting to make a rib effect.

purloin /pɜˈlɔɪn/ *v.t.* to steal.

purple /ˈpɜpəl/ *n.* **1.** any colour having components of both red and blue, especially a dark shade of such a colour. – *adj.* **2.** of the colour of purple. – *v.t.* **3.** to make purple.

purport /pɜˈpɔt, ˈpɜpɔt/ *v.*, /ˈpɜpɔt, -pət/ *n.* – *v.t.* **1.** to profess or claim. **2.** to convey to the mind as the meaning or thing intended; express; imply. – *n.* **3.** tenor, import, or meaning. **4.** purpose or object.

purpose /ˈpɜpəs/ *n.* **1.** the object for which anything exists or is done, made, used, etc. **2.** an intended or desired result; end or aim. **3.** intention or determination. **4. on purpose,** by design; intentionally. – **purposive**, *adj.*

purr /pɜ/ *v.i.* to utter a low, continuous murmuring sound expressive of satisfaction, as a cat does.

purse /pɜs/ *n.* **1.** a small bag, pouch, or case for carrying money on the person. **2.** a sum of money offered as a prize.

purser /ˈpɜsə/ *n.* an officer, especially on board a ship, charged with keeping accounts, etc.

pursuance /pəˈsjuəns/ *n.* the following or carrying out of some plan, course, injunction, or the like.

pursuant /pəˈsjuənt/ *adv.* according (fol. by *to*). Also, **pursuantly**.

pursue /pəˈsju/ *v.t.*, **-sued**, **-suing**. **1.** to follow with the view of overtaking, capturing, killing, etc.; chase. **2.** to strive to gain; seek to attain or accomplish (an end, object, purpose, etc.). **3.** to carry on (a course of action, train of thoughts, etc.). **4.** to continue to discuss (a subject, topic, etc.). – **pursuit**, *n.*

purvey /pəˈveɪ/ *v.t.* to provide, furnish, or supply (especially food or provisions). – **purveyance**, *n.* – **purveyor**, *n.*

purview /ˈpɜvju/ *n.* range of operation, activity, concern, etc.

pus /pʌs/ *n.* a yellow-white, more or less viscid substance, produced by suppuration and found in abscesses, sores, etc.

push /pʊʃ/ *v.t.* **1.** to exert force upon or against (a thing) in order to move it away. **2.** to press or urge (a person, etc.) to some action or course. **3.** to peddle (narcotics). – *v.i.* **4.** to exert a thrusting force upon something. **5.** to use steady force in moving a thing away; shove. – *n.* **6.** the act of pushing; a shove or thrust. **7.** a determined pushing forward or advance. **8.** the pressure of circumstances. **9.** *Colloquial* persevering energy; enterprise.

pushover /ˈpʊʃoʊvə/ *n.* *Colloquial* anything done easily.

pusillanimous /pjusəˈlænəməs/ *adj.* faint-hearted; cowardly.

puss /pʊs/ *n.* a cat.

pussy /ˈpʊsi/ *n., pl.* **pussies**. a cat.

pussyfoot /ˈpʊsifʊt/ *v.i.* **1.** to go with a soft, stealthy tread like that of a cat. **2.** to act cautiously or timidly, as if afraid to commit oneself on a point at issue.

pustule /ˈpʌstjul/ *n.* *Pathology* a small elevation of the skin containing pus.

put /pʊt/ *v.*, **put**, **putting**. – *v.t.* **1.** to move or place (anything) so as to get it into or out of some place or position. **2.** to bring into some relation, state, etc. **3.** to set at a particular place, point, amount, etc., in a scale of estimation. **4.** to express or state. **5.** to set, give, or make. **6.** to throw or cast, especially with a forward motion of the hand when raised close to the shoulder. **7. put across,** to communicate; cause to be understood; explain effectively. **8. put down, a.** to write down. **b.** to repress or suppress. **c.** to ascribe or attribute (usually fol. by *to*). **d.** to pay as a lump sum. **e.** to destroy an animal, for reasons of disease, etc. **f.** to nominate. **9. put in, a.** *Nautical* to enter a port or harbour. **b.** to apply (often fol. by *for*). **c.** to devote, as time, work, etc. **10. put off, a.** to postpone. **b.** to disgust or cause to dislike. **11. put on, a.** to assume sincerely or falsely. **b.** to dress in (clothing). **c.** to produce; stage. **d.** to cause to speak on the telephone. **12. put out, a.** to extinguish (fire, etc.). **b.** to confuse or embarrass. **c.** *Nautical* to go out to sea. **13. put up, a.** to erect. **b.** to provide (money, etc.). **c.** to give lodging to. **d.** to persuade to do (fol. by *to*).

putative /'pjutətɪv/ *adj.* commonly regarded as such; reputed; supposed.

put option *n.* *Stock Exchange* the right to sell a parcel of shares at an agreed price within a specified period.

putrefy /'pjutrəfaɪ/ *v.i.*, **-fied**, **-fying**. to become putrid; rot. – **putrefaction**, *n.*

putrid /'pjutrəd/ *adj.* **1.** in a state of foul decay or decomposition. **2.** offensively or disgustingly objectionable or bad.

putt /pʌt/ *v.t.* *Golf* to strike (the ball) gently and carefully so as to make it roll along the putting green into the hole.

putty /'pʌti/ *n.*, *pl.* **-ties. 1.** a kind of cement, of doughlike consistency, made of with linseed oil and used for securing panes of glass, stopping up holes in woodwork, etc. **2.** any person or thing easily moulded, influenced, etc.

puzzle /'pʌzəl/ *n.*, *v.*, **-zled**, **-zling**. – *n.* **1.** a toy or other contrivance designed to amuse by presenting difficulties to be solved by ingenuity or patient effort. **2.** something puzzling; a puzzling matter or person. – *v.t.* **3.** to cause to be at a loss; bewilder; confuse. **4.** to solve (a problem) or resolve (a difficulty) by careful study and reflection (fol. by *out*).

pygmy = pigmy /'pɪgmi/ *n.*, *pl.* **-mies**. a small or dwarfish person.

pyjamas /pə'dʒaməz/ *n.* (*construed as pl.*) nightclothes consisting of loose trousers and jacket.

pylon /'paɪlɒn/ *n.* **1.** a steel tower or mast carrying high-tension, telephonic or other cables and lines. **2.** a relatively tall structure at either side of a gate, bridge, or avenue, marking an entrance or approach.

pyramid /'pɪrəmɪd/ *n.* **1.** *Architecture* a massive structure built of stone, with square (or polygonal) base, and sloping sides meeting at an apex, such as those built by the ancient Egyptians. **2.** anything of such form. **3.** *Geometry* a solid having a triangular, square, or polygonal base, and triangular sides which meet in a point. **4.** *Economics* a multi-company structure in which one company controls two or more companies, each of which may itself control a number of companies, and so on.

pyre /'paɪə/ *n.* **1.** a pile or heap of wood or other combustible material. **2.** such a pile for burning a dead body.

pyrites /paɪ'raɪtiz/ *n.* any of various sulfides, as of iron, tin, etc.

pyro- a word element meaning 'of, relating to, or concerned with fire'. Also (*before vowels*), **pyr-**.

pyrogenic /paɪroʊ'dʒɛnɪk/ *adj.* **1.** producing heat or fever. **2.** produced by fire, as igneous rocks.

pyromania /paɪrə'meɪniə/ *n.* a mania for setting things on fire. – **pyromaniac**, *n.*

pyrotechnics /paɪroʊ'tɛknɪks/ *n.* **1.** the art of making fireworks. **2.** the making and use of fireworks for display, military purposes, etc. **3.** a brilliant or sensational display, as of rhetoric, etc. Also (for defs 1 and 2), **pyrotechny** /'paɪroʊtɛkni/.

python /'paɪθən/ *n.* any of various non-venomous snakes, generally large and with vestiges of hind limbs, which kill by constriction.

Q q

Q, q /kju/ *n., pl.* **Q's** *or* **Qs**, **q's** *or* **qs**. the 17th letter of the English alphabet.

qua /kweɪ, kwa/ *adv.* as; as being; in the character or capacity of.

quack[1] /kwæk/ *v.i.* to utter the cry of a duck, or a sound resembling it.

quack[2] /kwæk/ *n.* someone who pretends professionally or publicly to skill, knowledge, or qualifications which he or she does not possess; a charlatan. – **quackery**, *n.*

quad /kwɒd/ *n. Colloquial* **1.** → **quadruplet**. **2.** → **quadrangle**.

quadrangle /'kwɒdræŋgəl/ *n.* **1.** a plane figure having four angles and four sides, as a square. **2.** a quadrangular space or court. – **quadrangular**, *adj.*

quadrant /'kwɒdrənt/ *n.* the quarter of a circle; an arc of 90°.

quadraphonic /kwɒdrə'fɒnɪk/ *adj.* of or relating to four-channel sound reproduction. Cf. **stereophonic**. Also, **quadrasonic**.

quadrate /'kwɒdrət/ *adj.* **1.** square; rectangular. – *n.* **2.** a square, or something square or rectangular.

quadratic /kwɒd'rætɪk/ *adj.* **1.** square. **2.** *Algebra* involving the square and no higher power of the unknown quantity.

quadri- a word element meaning 'four'. Also (*before vowels*), **quadr-**.

quadrilateral /kwɒdrə'lætrəl, -'lætərəl/ *adj.* **1.** having four sides. – *n.* **2.** a plane figure having four sides and four angles.

quadrille /kwə'drɪl/ *n.* a square dance for four couples.

quadriplegia /kwɒdrə'plidʒə/ *n.* a condition in which the arms and legs are paralysed. – **quadriplegic**, *n., adj.*

quadrisonic /kwɒdrə'sɒnɪk/ *adj.* → **quadraphonic**.

quadrumanous /kwɒ'drumənəs/ *adj.* four-handed; having all four feet adapted for use as hands.

quadruped /'kwɒdrəpɛd/ *adj.* **1.** four-footed. – *n.* **2.** an animal, especially a mammal, having four feet. – **quadrupedal**, *adj.*

quadruple /kwɒ'drupəl, 'kwɒdrəpəl/ *adj., v.,* **-pled**, **-pling**. – *adj.* **1.** fourfold; consisting of four parts. – *v.t.* **2.** to make four times as great. – *v.i.* **3.** to become four times as great.

quadruplet /kwɒ'druplət/ *n.* **1.** any group or combination of four. **2.** one of four children born at one birth.

quaff /kwɒf/ *v.t.* to drink (a beverage, etc.), copiously and heartily.

quagmire /'kwɒgmaɪə, 'kwæg-/ *n.* a piece of miry or boggy ground.

quail[1] /kweɪl/ *n., pl.* **quails**, (*esp. collectively*) **quail**. a small ground-dwelling bird.

quail[2] /kweɪl/ *v.i.* to lose heart or courage in difficulty or danger; shrink with fear.

quaint /kweɪnt/ *adj.* strange or odd in an interesting, pleasing, or amusing way.

quake /kweɪk/ *v.,* **quaked**, **quaking**, *n.* – *v.i.* **1.** (of persons) to shake from cold, weakness, fear, anger, or the like. – *n.* **2.** an earthquake.

qualify /'kwɒləfaɪ/ *v.,* **-fied**, **-fying**. – *v.t.* **1.** to invest with proper or necessary qualities, skills, etc.; make competent. **2.** to attribute some quality or qualities to; characterise, call, or name. **3.** to modify in some way. – *v.i.* **4.** to make or show oneself competent for something. – **qualification**, *n.*

qualitative /'kwɒlə,teɪtɪv, 'kwɒlətətɪv/ *adj.* relating to or concerned with quality or qualities.

quality /'kwɒləti/ *n., pl.* **-ties**, *adj.* – *n.* **1.** a characteristic, property, or attribute. **2.** high grade; superior excellence. – *adj.* **3.** of fine quality: *a quality wine.*

qualm /kwam/ *n.* an uneasy feeling or a pang of conscience as to conduct.

quandary /'kwɒndri/ *n., pl.* **-ries**. a state of embarrassing perplexity or uncertainty, especially as to what to do; a dilemma.

quantify /'kwɒntəfaɪ/ *v.t.,* **-fied**, **-fying**. to determine the quantity of; measure.

quantitative /'kwɒntə,teɪtɪv, 'kwɒntətətɪvi/ *adj.* of or relating to the describing or measuring of quantity.

quantity /'kwɒntəti/ *n., pl.* **-ties**. **1.** a particular, indefinite, or considerable amount of anything. **2.** amount or measure.

quantum /'kwɒntəm/ *n., pl.* **-ta**. a particular quantity or amount.

quarantine /'kwɒrəntin/ *n., v.,* **-tined**, **-tining**. – *n.* **1.** a strict isolation designed to prevent the spread of disease. – *v.t.* **2.** to put in or subject to quarantine.

quarrel[1] /'kwɒrəl/ *n., v.,* **-relled**, **-relling**. – *n.* **1.** an angry dispute or altercation. – *v.i.* **2.** to disagree angrily, squabble, or fall out. – **quarrelsome**, *adj.*

quarrel[2] /'kwɒrəl/ *n.* **1.** a square-headed bolt or arrow. **2.** a small square or diamond-shaped pane of glass.

quarry[1] /'kwɒri/ *n., pl.* **-ries**, *v.,* **-ried**, **-rying**. – *n.* **1.** an excavation or pit, usually open to the air, from which building stone, slate, or the like is obtained by cutting, blasting, etc. – *v.t.* **2.** to obtain (stone, etc.) from, or as from, a quarry.

quarry[2] /'kwɒri/ *n., pl.* **-ries**. an animal or bird hunted or pursued.

quart /kwɔt/ *n.* a liquid measure of capacity in the imperial system, equal to a quarter of a gallon, or approximately 1.137 litres.

quarter /'kwɔtə/ *n.* **1.** one of the four equal or equivalent parts into which anything is or may be divided. **2.** *Astronomy* a fourth of the moon's period or monthly revolution. **3.** a region, district, or place. **4.** (*usu. pl.*) a place of stay; lodgings; residence. **5.** a part or member of a community, government, etc., which is not specified. – *v.t.* **6.** to divide into four equal or equivalent parts. **7.** to provide with lodgings in a particular place.

quarterdeck /'kwɔtədɛk/ *n.* the upper deck between the mainmast and the stern.

quarterly /'kwɔtəli/ *adj., n., pl.* **-lies**. – *adj.* **1.** occurring, done, etc., at the end of every quarter of a year. – *n.* **2.** a periodical issued every three months.

quartermaster /'kwɔtəmastə/ *n. Military* a regimental officer in charge of quarters, rations, clothing, equipment, and transport.

quarter sessions *n.* a criminal court which tries certain indictable offences and hears appeals from the magistrate's court.

quartet /kwɔ'tɛt/ *n.* a group of four singers or players.

quartile /'kwɔtaɪl/ *n. Statistics* (in a frequency distribution) one of the values of a variable which divides the distribution of the variable into four groups having equal frequencies.

quarto /'kwɔtoʊ/ *n., pl.* **-tos**. **1.** a volume printed from sheets folded twice to form four leaves or eight pages. *Abbrev.*: 4to or 4°. **2.** a paper size.

quartz /kwɔts/ *n.* one of the commonest minerals, having many varieties which differ in colour, lustre, etc.

quartz-crystal /'kwɔts-krɪstəl/ *adj.* (of a watch, clock, etc.) having the function of the hairspring of a traditional clock performed by a specially prepared quartz crystal, which gives great accuracy. Also, **quartz**.

quartzite /'kwɔtsaɪt/ *n.* a granular rock consisting essentially of quartz in interlocking grains.

quasar /'kweɪsa/ *n.* one of many extragalactic, very massive sources of high-energy, radio-frequency, electromagnetic radiation of unknown constitution or structure.

quash[1] /kwɒʃ/ *v.t.* to put down or suppress completely; subdue.

quash[2] /kwɒʃ/ *v.t.* to make void, annul, or set aside (a law, indictment, decision, etc.).

quasi- /'kwazi-/ a prefix meaning 'resembling', 'seeming'.

quaternary /kwɒ'tɜnəri/ *adj.* **1.** consisting of four. **2.** arranged in fours.

quaver /'kweɪvə/ *v.i.* **1.** to shake tremulously, quiver, or tremble (now said usually of the voice). – *n.* **2.** a quavering or tremulous shake, especially in the voice. **3.** *Music* a note equal in length to half a crotchet.

quay /ki/ *n.* an artificial landing place for vessels unloading or loading cargo, etc.

queasy /'kwizi/ *adj.*, **-sier**, **-siest**. inclined to nausea.

queen /kwin/ *n.* **1.** the wife or consort of a king. **2.** a female sovereign or monarch. **3.** a fertile female of ants, bees, wasps, or termites. **4.** *Colloquial* a male homosexual. – *adj.* **5.** (of a bed, mattress, etc.) slightly smaller than king-size.

Queen's Counsel *n.* a senior barrister who has received a commission to act as adviser to the crown, as a form of recognition of his or her eminence. Also, **QC**; (*when the reigning monarch is a man*), **King's Counsel**.

queer /'kwɪə/ *adj.* **1.** strange from a conventional point of view; singular or odd. **2.** out of the normal state of feeling physically. **3.** *Colloquial* mentally unbalanced or deranged. **4.** *Colloquial* (*sometimes derogatory*) homosexual. – *n.* **5.** *Colloquial* (*sometimes derogatory*) a male homosexual.

quell /kwɛl/ *v.t.* **1.** to suppress (disorder, mutiny, etc.); put an end to; extinguish. **2.** to quiet or allay (feelings, etc.).

quench /kwɛntʃ/ *v.t.* **1.** to slake, as thirst; allay; satisfy. **2.** to suppress; stifle; subdue; overcome.

querulous /'kwɛrələs/ *adj.* full of complaints; complaining.

query /'kwɪəri/ *n., pl.* **-ries**, *v.*, **-ried**, **-rying**. – *n.* **1.** a question; an inquiry. **2.** a doubt; uncertainty. – *v.t.* **3.** to ask or inquire about. **4.** to question (a statement, etc.) as doubtful or obscure. **5.** to ask questions of.

quest /kwɛst/ *n.* a search or pursuit made in order to find or obtain something.

question /'kwɛstʃən/ *n.* **1.** a sentence in an interrogative form, addressed to someone in order to elicit information. **2.** a matter for investigation. **3.** a matter or point of uncertainty or difficulty; a case (fol. by *of*). – *v.t.* **4.** to ask a question or questions of; interrogate. **5.** to ask or enquire. **6.** to make a question of; doubt. **7.** to challenge; dispute.

questionable /'kwɛstʃənəbəl/ *adj.* doubtful.

question mark *n.* a mark indicating a question, as (?).

questionnaire /kwɛstʃən'ɛə, kɛs-/ *n.* a list of questions, usually printed on a form, as for statistical purposes, or to obtain opinions on some subject.

queue /kju/ *n., v.*, **queued**, **queuing** *or* **queueing**. – *n.* **1.** a file or line of people, vehicles, etc., waiting in turn. – *v.i.* **2.** to form in a line while waiting.

quibble /'kwɪbəl/ *n., v.*, **-bled**, **-bling**. – *n.* **1.** trivial, petty, or carping criticism. – *v.i.* **2.** to make petty criticisms.

quiche /kiʃ/ *n.* a savoury custard tart.

quick /kwɪk/ *adj.* **1.** done, proceeding, or occurring with promptness or rapidity. **2.** hasty; impatient. **3.** lively or keen, as feelings. **4.** of ready intelligence. **5.** *Finance* readily convertible into cash; liquid, as assets. – *n.* **6.** living persons. **7.** the tender sensitive flesh of the living body, especially that under the nails. – *adv.* **8.** in a quick manner.

quick assets *pl. n.* liquid assets including cash, receivables and marketable securities.

quicksand /'kwɪksænd/ *n.* an area of soft or loose wet sand of considerable depth, apt to engulf persons, animals, etc.

quick shift *n.* a shift which an employee is called upon to work, with less than sixteen hours break since a previous shift.

quicksilver /'kwɪksɪlvə/ *n.* mercury.

quid /kwɪd/ *n., pl.* **quid**, **quids**. *Colloquial* **1.** (formerly) a pound in money. **2.** (*pl.*) money, especially a large amount.

quid pro quo /kwɪd proʊ 'kwoʊ/ *n.* one thing in return for another.

quiescent /kwi'ɛsənt/ *adj.* being at rest, quiet, or still; inactive or motionless.

quiet /'kwaɪət/ *n.* **1.** freedom from disturbance or tumult; tranquillity; rest; repose. – *adj.* **2.** making no disturbance or trouble. **3.** free from disturbing emotions, etc.; mentally peaceful. **4.** refraining or free from activity, especially busy or vigorous activity. **5.** motionless or still; moving gently. **6.** making no noise or sound, especially no disturbing sound. **7.** restrained in speech, manner, etc.; saying little. **8.** *Commerce* commercially inactive. – *v.t.* **9.** to make quiet. – *v.i.* **10.** to become quiet.

quill /kwɪl/ *n.* **1.** one of the large feathers of the wing or tail of a bird. **2.** a feather, as of a goose, formed into a pen for writing. **3.** one of the hollow spines on a porcupine or hedgehog.

quilt /kwɪlt/ *n.* **1.** a coverlet for a bed. – *v.t.* **2.** to stitch together (two pieces of cloth with a soft interlining), usually in an ornamental pattern. **3.** to pad or line with some material.

quin /kwɪn/ *n.* *Colloquial* one of five children born at one birth.

quince /kwɪns/ *n.* a hard, yellowish, acid fruit.

quinine /'kwɪnin, kwə'nin/ *n.* a bitter colourless alkaloid, used in medicine as a stimulant and to treat malaria.

quinque- a word element meaning 'five'.

quintessence /kwɪn'tɛsəns/ *n.* **1.** the pure and concentrated essence of a substance. **2.** the most perfect embodiment of something. – **quintessential**, *adj.*

quintet /kwɪn'tɛt/ *n.* a set of five singers or players.

quintuple /'kwɪntəpəl, kwɪn'tjupəl/ *adj., v.,* **-pled, -pling**. – *adj.* **1.** fivefold; consisting of five parts. – *v.t.* **2.** to make five times as great. – *v.i.* **3.** to become five times as great.

quintuplet /kwɪn'tʌplət/ *n.* **1.** any group or combination of five. **2.** one of five children born at one birth.

quip /kwɪp/ *n., v.,* **quipped**, **quipping**. – *n.* **1.** a clever or witty saying. – *v.i.* **2.** to utter quips.

quire /'kwaɪə/ *n.* **1.** a set of 24 uniform sheets of paper. **2.** *Bookbinding* a section of pages in proper sequence after the printed sheet or sheets have been folded.

quirk /kwɜk/ *n.* **1.** a trick or peculiarity. **2.** a sudden twist, turn, or curve.

quisling /'kwɪzlɪŋ/ *n.* someone who betrays their own country.

quit /kwɪt/ *v.,* **quitted** *or* **quit**, **quitting**, *adj.* – *v.t.* **1.** to stop, cease, or discontinue. **2.** to depart from; leave. **3.** to give up; let go; relinquish. – *v.i.* **4.** to cease from doing something; stop. **5.** to depart or leave. **6.** to give up one's job or position; resign. – *adj.* **7.** released from obligation, penalty, etc.; free, clear, or rid (usually fol. by *of*).

quit claim *n.* a transfer of all one's interest, as in a parcel of real estate.

quite /kwaɪt/ *adv.* **1.** completely, wholly, or entirely. **2.** actually, really, or truly. **3.** *Colloquial* to a considerable extent or degree.

quitrent /'kwɪtrɛnt/ *n.* rent paid by a freeholder or copyholder in lieu of services which might otherwise have been required of him or her. Also, **quit-rent**.

quittance /'kwɪtns/ *n.* recompense or requital.

quiver[1] /'kwɪvə/ *v.i., v.t.* to shake with a slight but rapid motion; vibrate tremulously; tremble.

quiver[2] /'kwɪvə/ *n.* a case for holding arrows.

quixotic /kwɪk'sɒtɪk/ *adj.* extravagantly chivalrous or romantic.

quiz /kwɪz/ *v.,* **quizzed**, **quizzing**, *n., pl.* **quizzes**. – *v.t.* **1.** to question closely. **2.** to examine or test (a student or class) informally by questions. – *n.* **3.** a general knowledge test.

quizzical /'kwɪzɪkəl/ *adj.* odd, queer, or comical.

quoin /kɔɪn/ *n.* an external solid angle of a wall or the like.

quoit /kɔɪt/ *n.* **1.** Also, **deck quoit**. a flattish ring thrown in play to encircle a peg stuck in the ground. **2.** (*pl., construed as sing.*) the game so played.

quorum /'kwɔrəm/ *n.* the number of members of a body required to be present to transact business legally.

quota /'kwoʊtə/ *n.* **1.** a proportional part or share of a fixed total amount or quantity. **2.** the number of persons of a particular group allowed to immigrate to a country, join an institution, etc.

quotation /kwoʊ'teɪʃən/ *n.* **1.** that which is quoted; a passage quoted from a book, speech, etc. **2.** *Commerce* **a.** the statement of the current or market price of a commodity or security. **b.** the price so stated.

quote /kwoʊt/ *v.,* **quoted**, **quoting**, *n.* – *v.t.* **1.** to repeat (a passage, etc.) from a book, speech, etc. **2.** to bring forward, adduce, or cite. **3.** *Commerce* **a.** to state (a price). **b.** to state the current price of. – *n.* **4.** a quotation.

quotient /'kwoʊʃənt/ *n.* (in mathematics) the result of division.

R r

R, r /a/ *n., pl.* **R's** *or* **Rs**, **r's** *or* **rs**. the 18th letter of the English alphabet.

rabbi /'ræbaɪ/ *n., pl.* **-bis**. the spiritual leader of a Jewish community.

rabbit /'ræbət/ *n., v.,* **-bited**, **-biting**. – *n.* **1.** a small, long-eared, burrowing mammal. – *v.i.* **2.** to hunt rabbits.

rabble /'ræbəl/ *n.* **1.** a disorderly crowd; a mob. **2.** (*derogatory*) the lowest class of people (preceded by *the*).

rabid /'ræbəd/ *adj.* **1.** irrationally extreme in opinion or practice. **2.** furious or raging; violently intense. **3.** affected with or relating to rabies; mad.

rabies /'reɪbiz/ *n.* a fatal, infectious disease of the brain, transmitted by the bite of an afflicted animal, generally a dog.

raccoon /rə'kun/ *n.* any of several small nocturnal carnivores with a bushy ringed tail.

race[1] /reɪs/ *n., v.,* **raced**, **racing**. – *n.* **1.** a contest of speed, as in running, riding, driving, sailing, etc. **2.** (*pl.*) a series of races, especially horseraces or greyhound races run at a set time over a regular course. **3.** any contest or competition. **4.** a narrow passageway. – *v.i.* **5.** to engage in a contest of speed; run a race. **6.** to engage in or practise horseracing. **7.** to run, move, or go swiftly. – *v.t.* **8.** to run a race with; try to beat in a contest of speed. **9.** to cause to run in a race or races.

race[2] /reɪs/ *n.* **1.** a group of persons connected by common descent. **2.** *Ethnology* a subdivision of a stock, characterised by a more or less unique combination of physical traits which are transmitted in descent.

racial /'reɪʃəl/ *adj.* **1.** relating to or characteristic of race or extraction, or a race or races. **2.** relating to the relations between people of different races.

racism /'reɪsɪzəm/ *n.* the belief that human races have distinctive characteristics which determine their respective cultures, usually involving the idea that one's own race is superior. – **racist**, *n., adj.*

rack[1] /ræk/ *n.* **1.** a framework of bars, wires, or pegs on which articles are arranged or deposited. **2.** an apparatus or instrument formerly in use for torturing persons by stretching the body. **3.** violent strain. – *v.t.* **4.** to strain in mental effort.

rack[2] /ræk/ *n.* wreck; destruction.

rack[3] /ræk/ *v.i. Colloquial* to leave; go (fol. by *off*).

racket[1] /'rækət/ *n.* **1.** a loud noise. **2.** *Colloquial* an organised illegal activity.

racket[2] /'rækət/ *n.* → **racquet**.

raconteur /rækɒn'tɜ/ *n.* a person skilled in relating stories and anecdotes.

racquet = racket /'rækət/ *n.* a light bat having a network of cord, catgut or nylon, stretched in a more or less elliptical frame, used in tennis, etc.

racy /'reɪsi/ *adj.,* **-cier**, **-ciest**. **1.** vigorous; lively; spirited. **2.** suggestive; risqué.

radar /'reɪda/ *n.* a device to determine the presence and location of an object by measuring the time for the echo of a radio wave to return from it, and the direction from which it returns.

radial /'reɪdiəl/ *adj.* of, like, or relating to a radius or a ray.

radial-ply tyre /ˌreɪdiəl-plaɪ 'taɪə/ *n.* a pneumatic tyre with flexible walls.

radian /'reɪdiən/ *n.* the supplementary SI unit of measurement of plane angle. *Symbol*: rad

radiant /'reɪdiənt/ *adj.* emitting rays of light; shining; bright.

radiate /'reɪdieɪt/ *v.,* **-ated**, **-ating**. – *v.i.* **1.** to spread or move like rays or radii from a centre. **2.** to emit rays, as of light or heat. – *v.t.* **3.** (of persons) to exhibit abundantly (good humour, benevolence, etc.).

radiation /reɪdi'eɪʃən/ *n. Physics* the emission and propagation of particles or waves such as by a radioactive substance.

radiator /'reɪdieɪtə/ *n.* a device which radiates heat.

radical /'rædɪkəl/ *adj.* **1.** going to the root or origin; fundamental. **2.** thoroughgoing or extreme. **3.** (*often cap.*) favouring drastic political, social or other reforms. **4.** *Mathematics* relating to or forming a root. – *n.* **5.** someone who holds or follows extreme principles, especially left-wing political principles; an extremist.

radii /'reɪdiaɪ, -dii/ *n.* plural of **radius**.

radio /'reɪdioʊ/ *n., pl.* **-dios**, *v.,* **-dioed**, **-dioing**. – *n.* **1.** wireless telegraphy or telephony. **2.** an apparatus for receiving radio broadcasts; a wireless. – *v.t.* **3.** to transmit (a message) by radio. **4.** to send a message to (a person) by radio.

radio- a word element meaning: **1.** radio. **2.** radial. **3.** radium, radioactive, or radiant energy.

radioactivity /ˌreɪdioʊæk'tɪvəti/ *n.* the property of spontaneous disintegration possessed by certain elements due to changes in their atomic nuclei. – **radioactive**, *adj.*

radiogram /'reɪdioʊˌgræm/ *n.* **1.** a combined radio and gramophone. **2.** a message transmitted by radiotelegraphy.

radiography /reɪdi'ɒgrəfi/ *n.* the production of images by the action of X-rays on a photographic plate, especially as used in medicine.

radio station *n.* an organisation engaged in broadcasting radio programs on a fixed frequency.

radio telescope *n.* a large parabolic reflector used to gather radio signals emitted by celestial bodies or spacecraft and focus them for reception by a receiver.

radish /'rædɪʃ/ *n.* the crisp, pungent, edible root of a plant.

radium /'reɪdiəm/ *n.* a naturally occurring radioactive metallic element. *Symbol*: Ra

radius /'reɪdiəs/ *n., pl.* **-dii** /-diaɪ/, **-diuses**. **1.** a straight line extending from the centre of a circle or sphere to the circumference or surface. **2.** *Anatomy* that one of the two bones of the forearm which is on the thumb side.

raffia /'ræfiə/ *n.* a fibre used for making matting, baskets, hats, and the like.

raffle /'ræfəl/ *n., v.,* **-fled**, **-fling**. – *n.* **1.** a lottery in which the prizes are usually goods rather than money. – *v.t.* **2.** to dispose of by a raffle (sometimes fol. by *off*).

raft /raft/ *n.* a more or less rigid floating platform made of buoyant materials, assembled for the conveyance of people, goods, etc.

rafter /ˈraftə/ *n.* one of the sloping timbers or members sustaining the outer covering of a roof.

rag[1] /ræg/ *n.* **1.** a comparatively worthless fragment of cloth, especially one resulting from tearing or wear. **2.** a shred, scrap, or fragmentary bit of anything. **3.** *Colloquial* a newspaper or magazine, especially one considered as being of little value.

rag[2] /ræg/ *v.t.*, **ragged**, **ragging**. to tease; torment.

ragamuffin /ˈrægəmʌfən/ *n.* a ragged child.

rage /reɪdʒ/ *n.*, *v.*, **raged**, **raging**. – *n.* **1.** angry fury; violent anger. **2.** the object of widespread enthusiasm. – *v.i.* **3.** to show or feel violent anger.

ragged /ˈrægəd/ *adj.* **1.** clothed in tattered garments. **2.** torn or worn to rags; tattered. **3.** full of rough or sharp projections; jagged.

raglan /ˈræglən/ *adj.* (of a garment or sleeve) having no shoulder seam, the sleeve continuing up to the collar.

raid /reɪd/ *n.* **1.** a sudden onset or attack, as upon something to be seized or suppressed. – *v.t.* **2.** to make a raid on. – **raider**, *n.*

rail[1] /reɪl/ *n.* **1.** a bar of wood or metal fixed more or less horizontally for any of various purposes. **2.** one of a pair of steel bars that provide a guide and running surface for the wheels of vehicles. **3.** the railway, as a means of transportation.

rail[2] /reɪl/ *v.i.* to utter bitter complaint or vehement denunciation (often fol. by *at* or *against*).

raillery /ˈreɪləri/ *n.*, *pl.* **-ries**. good-humoured ridicule; banter.

railway /ˈreɪlweɪ/ *n.* **1.** a permanent road or way, laid or provided with rails on which vehicles run for the transporting of passengers, goods, and mail. **2.** the company owning or operating it.

raiment /ˈreɪmənt/ *n.* *Archaic or Poetic* clothing; apparel; attire.

rain /reɪn/ *n.* **1.** water in drops falling from the sky to the earth. **2.** (*pl.*) the seasonal rainfalls in tropical regions. – *v.i.* **3.** (of rain) to fall. **4.** to fall like rain. – *v.t.* **5.** to offer, bestow, or give abundantly. **6. rain cats and dogs,** to rain heavily.

rainbow /ˈreɪnboʊ/ *n.* **1.** a bow or arc of prismatic colours appearing in the sky opposite the sun, due to the refraction and reflection of the sun's rays in drops of rain. **2.** the spectrum. – *adj.* **3.** multicoloured.

rainfall /ˈreɪnfɔl/ *n.* **1.** a fall or shower of rain. **2.** the amount of water falling as rain, snow, etc., within a given time and area.

rainforest /ˈreɪnfɒrəst/ *n.* dense forest found in tropical and temperate areas.

raise /reɪz/ *v.*, **raised**, **raising**, *n.* – *v.t.* **1.** to move to a higher position; lift up; elevate. **2.** to cause to rise or stand up. **3.** to build; erect. **4.** to cause to be or appear. **5.** to cultivate, produce, breed (crops, plants, animals, etc.). **6.** to bring up; rear (children, etc.). **7.** to give rise to; bring up or about. **8.** to give vigour to; animate (the mind, spirits, hopes). **9.** to gather together; collect. **10.** to increase in degree, intensity, pitch, or force. **11.** to increase in amount, as rent, prices, wages, etc. **12.** to increase the price of (a commodity, stock, etc.). – *n.* **13.** a rise (in wages). **14.** a raising, lifting, etc.

raisin /ˈreɪzən/ *n.* a dried grape.

rake[1] /reɪk/ *n.*, *v.*, **raked**, **raking**. – *n.* **1.** a long-handled tool with teeth, used for various purposes. – *v.t.* **2.** to gather together, draw, or remove with or as with a rake. **3.** to collect, especially with difficulty (often fol. by *up*). – *v.i.* **4.** to use a rake. **5.** to search as with a rake. **6.** to scrape or sweep (fol. by *against*, *over*, etc.).

rake[2] /reɪk/ *n.* a profligate or dissolute man.

rally /ˈræli/ *v.*, **-lied**, **-lying**, *n.*, *pl.* **-lies**. – *v.t.* **1.** to bring together or into order again. **2.** to draw or call (persons) together for common action. – *v.i.* **3.** to come together for common action. **4.** to come to the assistance of a person, party, or cause. **5.** to acquire fresh strength or vigour. – *n.* **6.** a recovery from dispersion or disorder, as of troops. **7.** a renewal or recovery of strength, activity, etc. **8.** a drawing or coming together of persons, as for common action. **9.** *Finance* a sharp rise in price and active trading, after a declining market. **10.** *Tennis, etc.* the return of the ball by both sides a number of times consecutively.

ram /ræm/ *n.*, *v.*, **rammed**, **ramming**. – *n.* **1.** an uncastrated male sheep. **2.** any of various devices for battering, crushing, driving, or forcing something. – *v.t.* **3.** to drive or force by heavy blows. **4.** to push firmly.

RAM /ræm/ *n.* random-access memory; a computer memory which is so structured that each item can be accessed equally quickly.

ramble /ˈræmbəl/ *v.*, **-bled**, **-bling**, *n.* – *v.i.* **1.** to wander about in a leisurely manner. – *n.* **2.** a walk without a definite route, taken for pleasure.

ramification /ræməfəˈkeɪʃən/ *n.* a division or subdivision springing or derived from a main stem or source.

ramp /ræmp/ *n.* **1.** a sloping surface connecting two different levels. **2.** to act violently; rage; storm.

rampage /ˈræmpeɪdʒ/ *n.*, /ræmˈpeɪdʒ/ *v.*, **-paged**, **-paging**. – *n.* **1.** violent or furious behaviour. – *v.i.* **2.** to rush, move, or act furiously or violently.

rampant /ˈræmpənt/ *adj.* in full sway; unchecked.

ramrod /ˈræmrɒd/ *n.* any person or thing considered as exemplifying or exercising stiffness or unyielding rigidity.

ramshackle /ˈræmʃækəl/ *adj.* loosely made or held together; rickety; shaky.

ran /ræn/ *v.* past tense of **run**.

ranch /ræntʃ/ *n.* a farm for cattle, horses, or the like, generally having extensive grazing land.

rancid /ˈrænsəd/ *adj.* having a rank, unpleasant, stale smell or taste.

rancour = rancor /ˈræŋkə/ *n.* bitter, rankling resentment or ill will; hatred; malice.

– **rancorous**, *adj.*

random /'rændəm/ *adj.* **1.** not according to a pattern or method. – *n.* **2. at random,** in a haphazard way; without definite aim, purpose, or method.

random-access memory *n.* → **RAM**.

random breath test *n.* a breath test to detect the presence of alcohol, applied to randomly selected motorists. *Abbrev.*: RBT

random sampling *n.* the drawing of a sample from a statistical population in which all members of the population have equal probabilities of being included in the sample.

randy /'rændi/ *adj.* sexually aroused.

rang /ræŋ/ *v.* past tense of **ring**[2].

range /reɪndʒ/ *n., v.,* **ranged**, **ranging**. – *n.* **1.** the extent or scope of the operation or efficacy of something. **2.** an area in which shooting at targets is practised. **3.** *Statistics* the difference between the smallest and largest varieties in a statistical distribution. **4.** a row or line, as of persons or things. **5.** the region over which something is distributed, is found, or occurs. **6.** a chain of mountains. **7.** a form of large stove for cooking. – *v.t.* **8.** to dispose systematically; set in order; arrange. **9.** to make straight, level, or even, as lines of type. **10.** to pass over or through (an area or region) in all directions, as in exploring or searching. – *v.i.* **11.** to vary within certain limits. **12.** to have range of operation. **13.** to extend, run or go in a certain direction. **14.** to move about or through a region in all directions, as persons, animals, etc.

ranger /'reɪndʒə/ *n.* a person employed to patrol a public reserve, wildlife park, etc.

rank[1] /ræŋk/ *n.* **1.** position or standing in the social scale or in any graded body, especially a high position. **2.** a row, line, or series of things or persons. – *v.t.* **3.** to assign to a particular position, station, class, etc. – *v.i.* **4.** to take up or occupy a place in a particular rank, class, etc.

rank[2] /ræŋk/ *adj.* **1.** growing with excessive luxuriance. **2.** having an offensively strong smell or taste. **3.** utter; unmistakable. **4.** grossly coarse or indecent.

rankle /'ræŋkəl/ *v.i.,* **-kled**, **-kling**. to produce or continue to produce within the mind keen irritation or bitter resentment.

ransack /'rænsæk/ *v.t.* to search thoroughly or vigorously through.

ransom /'rænsəm/ *n.* **1.** the redemption of a prisoner, slave, kidnapped person, captured goods, etc., for a price. **2.** the sum or price paid or demanded. – *v.t.* **3.** to redeem from captivity, bondage, detention, etc., by paying a price demanded.

rant /rænt/ *v.i.* to talk in a wild or vehement way.

rap /ræp/ *v.,* **rapped**, **rapping**, *n.* – *v.t.* **1.** to strike, especially with a quick, smart, or light blow. **2.** to utter sharply or vigorously (usually fol. by *out*). **3.** *Colloquial* to accelerate (a motor vehicle). – *v.i.* **4.** to knock smartly or lightly. – *n.* **5.** a quick, smart, or light blow.

rap dancing *n.* a form of street dancing involving jerky movements of the limbs.

rape /reɪp/ *n., v.,* **raped**, **raping**. – *n.* **1.** the crime of having sexual intercourse with a person against their will. – *v.t.* **2.** to commit the crime or act of rape on.

rapid /'ræpəd/ *adj.* **1.** moving or acting with great speed; swift. – *n.* **2.** (*usu. pl.*) a part of a river where the current runs very swiftly. – **rapidity**, *n.*

rapier /'reɪpiə/ *n.* a slender sword used only for thrusting.

rapport /ræ'pɔ/ *n.* relation; connection, especially harmonious or sympathetic relation.

rapt /ræpt/ *adj.* **1.** deeply engrossed or absorbed. **2.** transported with emotion; enraptured.

rapture /'ræptʃə/ *n.* ecstatic joy or delight; joyful ecstasy.

rare[1] /rɛə/ *adj.,* **rarer**, **rarest**. **1.** few in number. **2.** of low density or pressure. **3.** remarkable or unusual, especially in excellence or greatness.

rare[2] /rɛə/ *adj.,* **rarer**, **rarest**. (of meat) not thoroughly cooked; underdone.

rarefy /'rɛərəfaɪ/ *v.t., v.i.,* **-fied**, **-fying**. to make or become rare, more rare, or less dense. – **rarefaction**, *n.*

raring /'rɛərɪŋ/ *adj.* ready; eager.

rarity /'rɛərəti/ *n., pl.* **-ties**. something rare, unusual, or uncommon.

rascal /'raskəl/ *n.* a base, dishonest person.

rash[1] /ræʃ/ *adj.* acting too hastily or without due consideration.

rash[2] /ræʃ/ *n.* **1.** an eruption or efflorescence on the skin. **2.** a proliferation.

rasher /'ræʃə/ *n.* a thin slice of bacon.

rasp /rasp, ræsp/ *v.t.* **1.** to scrape or abrade with a rough instrument. **2.** to utter with a grating sound. – *v.i.* **3.** to scrape or grate. **4.** to make a grating sound. – *n.* **5.** a coarse form of file, having separate pointlike teeth.

raspberry[1] /'razbəri, -bri/ *n., pl.* **-ries**. a small red, black, or pale yellow berry.

raspberry[2] /'razbəri, -bri/ *n., pl.* **-ries**. *Colloquial* a sound expressing derision or contempt, made with the tongue and lips.

rat /ræt/ *n., v.,* **ratted**, **ratting**. – *n.* **1.** any of certain long-tailed rodents. **2.** *Colloquial* someone who abandons friends or associates, especially in time of trouble. **3. smell a rat,** *Colloquial* to be suspicious. – *v.i.* **4.** *Colloquial* to desert one's party or associates, especially in time of trouble. **5.** *Colloquial* to inform (on). **6. rat through,** to sort through in a careless or hasty manner.

ratatouille /rætə'tui/ *n.* a type of vegetable casserole or stew.

ratchet /'rætʃət/ *n.* a toothed bar with which a pawl engages.

rate /reɪt/ *n., v.,* **rated**, **rating**. – *n.* **1.** a certain quantity or amount of one thing considered in relation to a unit of another thing and used as a standard or measure. **2.** a fixed charge per unit of quantity. **3.** degree of speed, of travelling, working, etc. **4.** (*usu. pl.*) a tax on property, imposed by a local authority and used for the maintenance and supply of services. – *v.t.* **5.** to estimate the value or worth of; appraise. **6.** to fix at a certain rate, as of charge or payment. – *v.i.* **7.** to have value, standing, etc.

rateable value *n.* the value of a property assessed by a local authority on which the amount of rate charged is based.

rate of exchange *n.* the ratio at which the unit of currency of one country can be exchanged for the unit of currency of another country. Also, **exchange rate**.

rather /'raðə/ *adv.* **1.** more so than not; to a certain extent; somewhat. **2.** in preference; as a preferred or accepted alternative.

ratify /'rætəfaɪ/ *v.t.,* **-fied**, **-fying**. to confirm by expressing consent, approval, or formal sanction.

rating /'reɪtɪŋ/ *n.* **1.** classification according to grade or rank. **2.** a person's or firm's credit standing.

ratio /'reɪʃioʊ/ *n., pl.* **-tios**. proportional relation; rate; quotient of two numbers.

ration /'ræʃən/ *n.* **1.** a fixed allowance of provisions or food. – *v.t.* **2.** to put on, or restrict to, rations.

rational /'ræʃnəl, 'ræʃənəl/ *adj.* **1.** agreeable to reason; reasonable; sensible. **2.** endowed with the faculty of reason. **3.** proceeding or derived from reason, or based on reasoning. **4.** *Mathematics* expressible as the quotient of two integers. – **rationality**, *n.*

rationale /ræʃə'nal/ *n.* a reasoned exposition of principles.

rationalise = rationalize /'ræʃnəlaɪz/ *v.,* **-lised**, **-lising**. – *v.t.* **1.** *Psychology* to invent a rational, acceptable explanation for (behaviour). **2.** to reorganise (resources, the components of a business, etc.) to promote efficiency, economy, etc. – *v.i.* **3.** to employ reason; think in a rational or rationalistic manner. **4.** to reorganise and integrate (an industry). **5.** to justify one's behaviour by plausible explanations.

rat-race /'ræt-reɪs/ *n.* **1.** the struggle for success, especially in career, fiercely competitive and often unscrupulous. **2.** the frantic pace of city life.

ratshit /'ræt,ʃɪt/ *adj.* no good. Also, **R.S**.

rattan /rə'tæn/ *n.* the tough stems of certain palms, used for wickerwork, canes, etc.

rattle /'rætl/ *v.,* **-tled**, **-tling**, *n.* – *v.i.* **1.** to give out a rapid succession of short sharp sounds. – *v.t.* **2.** to cause to rattle. **3.** to utter or perform in a rapid or lively manner: *to rattle off a speech.* **4.** *Colloquial* to disconcert or confuse (a person). – *n.* **5.** a rapid succession of short, sharp sounds, as from the collision of hard bodies. **6.** an instrument contrived to make a rattling sound, as a child's toy.

rattlesnake /'rætlsneɪk/ *n.* any of various venomous American snakes with a rattling mechanism at the end of the tail.

raucous /'rɔkəs/ *adj.* hoarse; harsh-sounding, as a voice.

raunchy /'rɔntʃi/ *adj.* coarse; earthy; lusty.

ravage /'rævɪdʒ/ *n., v.,* **-aged**, **-aging**. – *n.* **1.** havoc; ruinous damage. – *v.t.* **2.** to work havoc upon; damage or mar by ravages.

rave /reɪv/ *v.,* **raved**, **raving**, *n., adj.* – *v.i.* **1.** to talk wildly, as in delirium. – *n.* **2.** extravagantly enthusiastic praise. – *adj.* **3.** praising with extravagant enthusiasm.

ravel /'rævəl/ *v.,* **-elled**, **-elling**. – *v.t.* **1.** to tangle or entangle. – *v.i.* **2.** to become disjoined thread by thread or fibre by fibre; fray. **3.** to become tangled.

raven /'reɪvən/ *n.* **1.** a large, glossy black bird with a loud harsh call. – *adj.* **2.** lustrous black.

ravenous /'rævənəs/ *adj.* extremely hungry.

ravine /rə'vin/ *n.* a long, deep, narrow valley, especially one worn by water.

ravioli /rævi'oʊli/ *pl. n.* small pieces of filled pasta.

ravish /'rævɪʃ/ *v.t.* **1.** to fill with strong emotion, especially joy. **2.** to seize and carry off by force.

ravishing /'rævəʃɪŋ/ *adj.* entrancing; enchanting.

raw /rɔ/ *adj.* **1.** not having undergone processes of preparing, dressing, finishing, refining, or manufacture. **2.** denoting figures, etc., before adjustments have been made. **3.** painfully open, as a sore, wound, etc. **4.** *Colloquial* harsh or unfair.

ray[1] /reɪ/ *n.* **1.** a narrow beam of light. **2.** *Mathematics* one of a system of straight lines emanating from a point.

ray[2] /reɪ/ *n.* a flat fish living on the sea bottom.

rayon /'reɪɒn/ *n.* a synthetic textile.

raze /reɪz/ *v.t.,* **razed**, **razing**. to tear down, demolish, or level to the ground.

razor /'reɪzə/ *n.* **1.** a sharp-edged instrument used especially for shaving hair from the skin. – *v.t.* **2.** to apply a razor to.

razorback /'reɪzəbæk/ *n.* a sharp ridge.

RBT /a bi 'ti/ random breath test.

RDO /a di 'oʊ/ rostered day off.

re /ri, reɪ/ *prep.* in the case of; with reference to.

're *v.* a contracted form of **are**.

re- **1.** a prefix indicating repetition. **2.** a prefix indicating withdrawal or backward motion.

reach /ritʃ/ *v.t.* **1.** to get to, or get as far as, in moving, going, travelling, etc. **2.** to stretch or extend so as to touch or meet. **3.** to establish communication with. – *v.i.* **4.** to make a stretch, as with the hand or arm. **5.** to extend in operation or effect. **6.** to stretch in space; extend in direction, length, distance, etc. – *n.* **7.** the act of reaching. **8.** the extent or distance of reaching. **9.** a continuous stretch or extent of something.

react /ri'ækt/ *v.i.* **1.** to act in return on an agent or influence; act reciprocally upon each other, as two things. **2.** to act in opposition, as against some force. – **reactor**, *n.* – **reactive**, *adj.*

reaction /ri'ækʃən/ *n.* **1.** the act or an instance of reacting. **2.** *Commerce* a drop in the market after an advance in prices.

read[1] /rid/ *v.,* **read** /rɛd/, **reading** /'ridɪŋ/ *n.* – *v.t.* **1.** to observe, and apprehend the meaning of (something written, printed, etc.). **2.** to render in speech (something written, printed, etc.). **3.** to understand or take (something read or observed) in a particular way. **4.** to introduce (something not expressed or directly indicated) into what is read or considered. **5.** to register or indicate, as a thermometer or other instrument. **6.** (of a computer) to take (information) from a peripheral device into the central computer. – *v.i.* **7.** to read or peruse writing, printing, etc., or papers, books, etc. **8.** to utter aloud, or render in speech, written or printed words that one is perusing. **9.** to obtain knowledge or learn of something by reading. **10.** to admit of being read or interpreted (as stated). **11.** (of a computer) to take in information. – *n.* **12.** the act or process of reading.

read[2] /rɛd/ *adj.* having knowledge gained by reading.

readout /ˈridaʊt/ *n.* → **digital display**.

read-write /rid-ˈraɪt/ *adj.* of or relating to a computer, etc., which reads and then restores memory data.

ready /ˈrɛdi/ *adj.*, **readier**, **readiest**, *v.*, **readied**, **readying**, *n.* – *adj.* **1.** completely prepared or in due condition for immediate action or use. **2.** willing. **3.** prompt or quick in perceiving, comprehending, speaking, writing, etc. **4.** present or convenient. – *v.t.* **5.** to make ready; prepare. – *n.* **6.** *Colloquial* ready money. **7.** the condition or position of being ready.

reagent /riˈeɪdʒənt/ *n.* a substance which, on account of the reactions it causes, is used in chemical analysis.

real /ril/ *adj.* **1.** true. **2.** genuine; not counterfeit, artificial, or imitation. **3.** *Law* denoting or relating to immoveable property of a freehold type, as lands and tenements excluding leaseholds (opposed to *personal*). – *adv.* **4.** *Colloquial* very.

real estate *n.* property in the form of land, buildings, etc.: *a valuable piece of real estate.*

real estate agent *n.* a person who acts as an intermediary between the buyer and the vendor of real estate; real estate broker.

realise = realize /ˈriəlaɪz/ *v.*, **-lised**, **-lising**. – *v.t.* **1.** to grasp or understand clearly. **2.** to make real, or give reality to (a hope, fear, plan, etc.). **3.** to convert into cash or money. **4.** to obtain as a profit or income for oneself by trade, labour, or investment. – *v.i.* **5.** to convert property or goods into cash or money. **6.** to realise a profit.

realism /ˈriəlɪzəm/ *n.* **1.** the taking of a practical rather than a moral view in human problems, etc. **2.** the tendency to view or represent things as they really are. – **realistic**, *adj.*

reality /riˈæləti/ *n.*, *pl.* **-ties**. **1.** the state or fact of being real. **2.** resemblance to what is real. **3.** that which is real. **4. in reality,** in fact; actually.

really /ˈrɪəli/ *adv.* **1.** in reality; actually. **2.** genuinely or truly. **3.** indeed.

realm /rɛlm/ *n.* the region, sphere, or domain within which anything rules or prevails.

real-time /ˈril-taɪm/ *adj.*, /ril-ˈtaɪm/ *n.* – *adj.* **1.** of or relating to an analytical or computing device which processes information and outputs results at the same rate at which the original information is presented. – *n.* **2.** a method using real-time processing.

realtor /ˈriəltə, -tɔ/ *n.* *Chiefly US* → **real estate agent**.

realty /ˈriəlti/ *n.* → **real estate**.

real wages *pl. n.* wages paid for work done, expressed in terms of purchasing power (opposed to *money wages*).

ream /rim/ *n.* a standard quantity among paper dealers meaning 20 quires or 500 sheets (formerly 480 sheets).

reap /rip/ *v.t.* to gather or take (a crop, harvest, etc.).

rear[1] /rɪə/ *n.* **1.** the back of anything, as opposed to the front. **2.** the space or position behind anything. – *adj.* **3.** situated at or relating to the rear.

rear[2] /rɪə/ *v.t.* **1.** to care for and support up to maturity. **2.** to raise to an upright position. – *v.i.* **3.** to rise on the hind legs, as a horse or other animal.

rearrange /riəˈreɪndʒ/ *v.t.* to place in a new order.

reason /ˈrizən/ *n.* **1.** a ground or cause, as for a belief, action, fact, event, etc. **2.** the mental powers concerned with drawing conclusions or inferences. **3.** sound judgment or good sense. – *v.i.* **4.** to think or argue in a logical manner. – *v.t.* **5.** to think out (a problem, etc.) logically (often fol. by *out*). **6.** to conclude or infer (fol. by *that*). **7.** to bring, persuade, etc., by reasoning.

reasonable /ˈrizənəbəl/ *adj.* **1.** endowed with reason. **2.** agreeable to reason or sound judgment. **3.** moderate, or moderate in price.

reassure /riəˈʃɔ/ *v.t.*, **-sured**, **-suring**. to restore (a person, etc.) to assurance or confidence.

rebate /ˈribeɪt/ *n.*, *v.*, **-bated**, **-bating**. – *n.* **1.** a return of part of an original amount paid for some service or merchandise. – *v.t.* **2.** to allow as a discount.

rebel /ˈrɛbəl/ *n.*, *adj.*; /rəˈbɛl/ *v.*, **-belled**, **-belling**. – *n.* **1.** someone who refuses allegiance to, resists, or rises in arms against, the established government or ruler. – *adj.* **2.** of or relating to rebels. – *v.i.* **3.** to rise in arms or active resistance against one's government or ruler. – **rebellious**, *adj.*

rebellion /rəˈbɛljən/ *n.* the act of rebelling.

rebound /rəˈbaʊnd/ *v.*, /ˈribaʊnd, rəˈbaʊnd/ *n.* – *v.i.* **1.** to bound or spring back from force of impact. – *n.* **2.** the act of rebounding; recoil.

rebuff /rəˈbʌf/ *n.* **1.** a peremptory refusal of a request, offer, etc.; a snub. **2.** a check to action or progress. – *v.t.* **3.** to give a rebuff to.

rebuke /rəˈbjuk/ *v.*, **-buked**, **-buking**, *n.* – *v.t.* **1.** to reprove or reprimand. – *n.* **2.** a reproof; a reprimand.

rebut /rəˈbʌt/ *v.t.*, **-butted**, **-butting**. to refute by evidence or argument. – **rebuttal**, *n.*

recalcitrant /rəˈkælsətrənt/ *adj.* **1.** resisting authority or control. – *n.* **2.** a recalcitrant person. – **recalcitrance**, **recalcitrancy**, *n.*

recall /rəˈkɔl/ *v.*, /ˈrikɔl/ *n.* – *v.t.* **1.** to recollect or remember. **2.** to call back; summon to return. – *n.* **3.** the act of recalling. **4.** memory; recollection.

recant /rəˈkænt/ *v.t.*, *v.i.* to withdraw or disavow (a statement, etc.), especially formally; retract.

recapitalisation = recapitalization /riˌkæpətəlaɪˈzeɪʃən/ *n.* a revision of a company's capital structure by an exchange of securities.

recapitalise = recapitalize /riˈkæpətəlaɪz/ *v.t.*, **-lised**, **lising**. to renew or change the capital of.

recapitulate /rikəˈpɪtʃəleɪt/ *v.*, **-lated**,

-lating. – *v.t.* **1.** to review by way of an orderly summary, as at the end of a speech or discourse. – *v.i.* **2.** to sum up statements or matters.

recede /rə'sid/ *v.i.*, **-ceded**, **-ceding**. **1.** to go or move back, to or towards a more distant point. **2.** to slope backwards.

receipt /rə'sit/ *n.* **1.** a written acknowledgment of having received money, goods, etc., specified. **2.** (*pl.*) the amount or quantity received. **3.** the state of being received. – *v.t.* **4.** to give a receipt for (money, goods, etc.). – *v.i.* **5.** to give a receipt, as for money or goods.

receive /rə'siv/ *v.*, **-ceived**, **-ceiving**. – *v.t.* **1.** to take into one's hand or one's possession. **2.** to take into the mind; apprehend mentally. **3.** to meet with; experience. **4.** to greet or welcome (guests, etc.) upon arriving. **5.** to accept as authoritative, valid, true, or approved. – *v.i.* **6.** to receive something. **7.** *Radio*, *TV* to convert incoming electromagnetic waves into the original signal.

recent /'risənt/ *adj.* lately happening, done, made, etc.

receptacle /rə'sɛptəkəl/ *n.* that which serves to receive or hold something.

reception /rə'sɛpʃən/ *n.* **1.** the act of receiving. **2.** a manner of being received. **3.** a function or occasion when people are formally received. **4.** a place, office, desk, or the like where callers are received, as in an office or hotel.

receptionist /rə'sɛpʃənəst/ *n.* a person employed to receive and direct callers, as in an office or hotel.

receptive /rə'sɛptɪv/ *adj.* able or quick to receive ideas, etc.

recess /rə'sɛs, 'risɛs/ *n.*, /rə'sɛs/ *v.* – *n.* **1.** a part or space that is set back or recedes. **2.** withdrawal or cessation for a time from the usual occupation, work, or activity. – *v.t.* **3.** to place or set in a recess. **4.** to make a recess or recesses in. – *v.i.* **5.** to take a recess.

recession /rə'sɛʃən/ *n.* **1.** a receding part of a wall, etc. **2.** a period of adverse economic circumstances, usually less severe than a depression.

recessive /rə'sɛsɪv/ *adj.* tending to recede; receding.

recipe /'rɛsəpi/ *n.* any formula, especially one for preparing a dish in cookery.

recipient /rə'sɪpiənt/ *n.* someone who or that which receives; a receiver.

reciprocate /rə'sɪprəkeɪt/ *v.*, **-cated**, **-cating**. – *v.t.* **1.** to give, feel, etc., in return. **2.** to give and receive reciprocally; interchange. – *v.i.* **3.** to make return, as for something given. – **reciprocity**, *n.* – **reciprocal**, *adj.*

recite /rə'saɪt/ *v.*, **-cited**, **-citing**. – *v.t.* **1.** to repeat the words of, as from memory, especially in a formal manner. – *v.i.* **2.** to recite or repeat something from memory.

reckless /'rɛkləs/ *adj.* utterly careless of the consequences of action.

reckon /'rɛkən/ *v.t.* **1.** to count, compute, or calculate as to number or amount. **2.** to esteem or consider (as stated). **3.** *Colloquial* to think or suppose. – *v.i.* **4.** to count; make a computation or calculation. **5.** to settle accounts, as with a person. **6.** to count, depend, or rely (*on*), as in expectation. **7.** to think; suppose.

reclaim /rə'kleɪm/ *v.t.* to bring (wild, waste, or marshy land) into a condition for cultivation or other use. – **reclamation**, *n.*

recline /rə'klaɪn, ri-/ *v.*, **-clined**, **-clining**. – *v.i.* **1.** to lean or lie back; rest in a recumbent position. – *v.t.* **2.** to cause to lean back on something.

recluse /rə'klus/ *n.* a person who lives in seclusion or apart from society, often for religious meditation.

recognise = recognize /'rɛkəgnaɪz/ *v.t.*, **-nised**, **-nising**. **1.** to identify from knowledge of appearance or character. **2.** to perceive as existing or true; realise. **3.** to acknowledge or treat as valid. – **recognition**, *n.*

recoil /rə'kɔɪl/ *v.*, /rə'kɔɪl, 'rikɔɪl/ *n.* – *v.i.* **1.** to draw back, as in alarm, horror, or disgust. **2.** to spring or fly back, as from force of impact, as a firearm. – *n.* **3.** the act of recoiling.

recollect /rɛkə'lɛkt/ *v.t.* to recall to mind, or recover knowledge of by an act or effort of memory; remember.

recommend /rɛkə'mɛnd/ *v.t.* to present as worthy of confidence, acceptance, use, etc. – **recommendation**, *n.*

recompense /'rɛkəmpɛns/ *v.*, **-pensed**, **-pensing**, *n.* – *v.t.* **1.** to make compensation to (a person, etc.); repay. – *v.i.* **2.** to repay or reward a person for service, aid, etc. – *n.* **3.** compensation made, as for loss, injury, or wrong.

reconcile /'rɛkənsaɪl/ *v.t.*, **-ciled**, **-ciling**. to bring into agreement or harmony; make compatible or consistent. – **reconciliation**, *n.*

recondition /rikən'dɪʃən/ *v.t.* to restore to a good or satisfactory condition; repair; overhaul.

reconnoitre /rɛkə'nɔɪtə/ *v.t.*, **-tred**, **-tring**. to examine or survey (a region, etc.) for engineering, geological, military, or other purposes. – **reconnaissance**, *n.*

record /rə'kɔd/ *v.*, /'rɛkɔd/ *n.*, *adj.* – *v.t.* **1.** to set down or register in some permanent form. – *v.i.* **2.** to record something. – *n.* **3.** an account in writing or the like preserving the memory or knowledge of facts or events. **4.** information or knowledge preserved in writing or the like. **5.** *Computers* a self-contained group of data. **6.** a disc or, formerly, a cylinder, or other device having characteristic markings for reproducing sound, especially for use with a record-player or a gramophone. **7.** the highest or farthest recorded degree attained. **8. off the record,** unofficially; without intending to be quoted. – *adj.* **9.** making or affording a record.

recorder /rə'kɔdə/ *n.* **1.** a recording or registering apparatus or device. **2.** a soft-toned flute played in vertical position.

recount /rə'kaʊnt/ *v.t.* to relate or narrate.

recoup /rə'kup/ *v.*, /'rikup/ *n.* – *v.t.* **1.** to obtain an equivalent for; compensate for. **2.** to regain or recover. **3.** to reimburse or indemnify. – *v.i.* **4.** to obtain an equivalent, as for something lost. – *n.* **5.** the act of recouping.

recourse /rə'kɔs/ *n.* **1.** resort or application to a person or thing for help or protection. **2.** *Commerce* the right to resort to a person for pecuniary compensation. An endorsement **without recourse** is one by which a payee or holder of a negotiable instrument merely transfers the instrument without assuming any liability upon it.

recover /rə'kʌvə/ *v.t.* **1.** to get again, or regain (something lost or taken away). **2.** to make up for or make good (loss, damage, etc., to oneself). **3.** to regain the strength, composure, balance, etc., of (oneself). – *v.i.* **4.** to regain a former (and better) state or condition. – **recovery**, *n.*

recreation /rɛkri'eɪʃən/ *n.* **1.** refreshment by means of some pastime, agreeable exercise, or the like. **2.** a pastime, diversion, exercise, or other resource affording relaxation and enjoyment. – **recreate**, *v.*

recriminate /rə'krɪməneɪt/ *v.t.*, **-nated**, **-nating**. to accuse in return.

recruit /rə'krut/ *n.* **1.** a newly secured member of any body or class. – *v.t., v.i.* **2.** to enlist (people) for service in the armed forces.

rectangle /'rɛktæŋgəl/ *n.* a parallelogram with all its angles right angles. – **rectangular**, *adj.*

recti- a word element meaning 'straight', 'right'. Also (*before vowels*), **rect-**.

rectify /'rɛktəfaɪ/ *v.t.*, **-fied**, **-fying**. **1.** to make, put, or set right; remedy; correct. **2.** *Electricity* to change (an alternating current) into a direct current.

rectitude /'rɛktətjud/ *n.* rightness of principle or practice.

rector /'rɛktə/ *n.* *Church of England* a minister who has the charge of a parish.

rectum /'rɛktəm/ *n., pl.* **-ta** /-tə/. the comparatively straight terminal section of the intestine, ending in the anus.

recumbent /rə'kʌmbənt/ *adj.* lying down; reclining; leaning.

recuperate /rə'kupəreɪt/ *v.*, **-rated**, **-rating**. **1.** to recover from sickness or exhaustion. **2.** to recover from pecuniary loss.

recur /ri'kɜ, rə-/ *v.i.*, **-curred**, **-curring**. to occur again, as an event, experience, etc.

recursive /rə'kɜsɪv/ *adj.* permitting or relating to an operation that may be repeated indefinitely.

recycle /ri'saɪkəl/ *v.t.*, **-cycled**, **-cycling**. to treat (waste, empty bottles, old tins, etc.) so that new products can be manufactured from them.

red /rɛd/ *adj.*, **redder**, **reddest**, *n.* – *adj.* **1.** of a spectral hue beyond orange in the spectrum. **2.** (*often cap.*) ultraradical politically, especially communist. – *n.* **3.** any of the hues adjacent to orange in the spectrum, such as scarlet, vermilion, cherry. **4.** red wine. **5. the red, a.** red ink as used in bookkeeping and accounting practice for recording deficits. **b.** loss or deficit.

-red a noun suffix denoting condition, as in *hatred, kindred.*

red-back /'rɛd-bæk/ *n.* a small, highly venomous, Australian spider.

red-blooded /'rɛd-blʌdəd/ *adj.* vigorous; virile.

red carpet *n.* highly favoured or deferential treatment.

redeem /rə'dim/ *v.t.* **1.** to buy or pay off; clear by payment. **2.** to recover (something pledged or mortgaged) by payment or other satisfaction. **3.** to convert (paper money) into specie. **4.** to make up for; make amends for. **5.** to obtain the release or restoration of, as from captivity, by paying a ransom. – **redemption**, *n.*

red-handed /rɛd-'hændəd/ *adj., adv.* in the very act of a crime or other deed.

red herring *n.* something to divert attention; a false clue.

red-letter day /rɛd-'lɛtə deɪ/ *n.* a memorable or especially happy occasion.

red light *n.* **1.** a red lamp, used as a signal to mean 'stop'. **2.** a warning signal. **3.** the symbol of a brothel.

redolent /'rɛdələnt/ *adj.* **1.** having a pleasant smell; fragrant. **2.** odorous or smelling (fol. by *of*). **3.** suggestive; reminiscent (fol. by *of*).

redoubtable /rə'daʊtəbəl/ *adj.* that is to be feared; formidable.

redound /rə'daʊnd/ *v.i.* to come back or recoil, as upon a person.

red-pencil /rɛd-'pɛnsəl/ *v.t.*, **-cilled**, **-cilling**. to correct or edit manuscript or typescript with or as with a red pencil.

redraft /'ridraft/ *n.* *Commerce* a draft on the drawer or endorser of a dishonoured and protested bill of exchange for the amount of the bill plus the costs and charges.

redress /rə'drɛs/ *n.* **1.** the setting right of what is wrong. **2.** compensation for wrong or injury. – *v.t.* **3.** to set right; remedy or repair (wrongs, injuries, etc.). **4.** to adjust evenly again, as a balance.

red tape *n.* **1.** excessive attention to formality and routine. **2.** official procedures

reduce /rə'djus/ *v.*, **-duced**, **-ducing**. – *v.t.* **1.** to bring down to a smaller extent, size, amount, number, etc. **2.** to lower in degree, intensity, etc. **3.** to lower in price. **4.** to bring to a certain state, condition, arrangement, etc. **5.** to bring under control or authority; subdue. **6.** to thin (paints, etc.) with oil or turpentine. – *v.i.* **7.** to become reduced.

reduction /rə'dʌkʃən/ *n.* **1.** the act of reducing. **2.** the amount by which something is reduced or diminished. **3.** a copy on a smaller scale.

redundant /rə'dʌndənt/ *adj.* **1.** being in excess. **2.** denoting or relating to an employee who is or becomes superfluous to the needs of the employer.

reed /rid/ *n.* **1.** the straight stalk of any of various tall grasses. **2.** anything made from such a stalk or from something similar.

reef /rif/ *n.* a narrow ridge of rocks or sand, often of coral debris, at or near the surface of water.

reefer /'rifə/ *n.* *Colloquial* a marijuana cigarette.

reef knot *n.* a kind of flat knot.

reek /rik/ *n.* **1.** a strong, unpleasant smell. – *v.i.* **2.** to smell strongly and unpleasantly.

reel[1] /ril/ *n.* **1.** a cylinder, frame, or other device, turning on an axis, on which to wind something. – *v.t.* **2.** to draw with a reel, or by winding. **3.** to say, write, or produce in an easy, continuous way (fol. by *off*).

reel[2] /ril/ *v.i.* **1.** to sway or rock under a blow, shock, etc. **2.** to sway about in standing or walking, as from dizziness, intoxication, etc.; stagger.

reel[3] /ril/ *n.* a lively dance popular in Scotland.

reel-to-reel /ril-tə-'ril/ *n.* **1.** a tape recorder which uses reels of tape rather than cassettes or cartridges. – *adj.* **2.** of or relating to such a system of recording.

re-enact /ri-ən'æɔt/ *v.t.* to act out again (a past event, especially one of historical importance). – **re-enactment**, *n.*

refectory /rə'fɛktri/ *n., pl.* **-ries**. a dining hall in an institution.

refer /rə'fɜ/ *v.,* **-ferred**, **-ferring**. – *v.t.* **1.** to direct for information or for anything required. **2.** to hand over or submit for information, consideration, decision, etc. **3.** to direct anyone for information, especially about one's character, abilities, etc. – *v.i.* **4.** to have relation; relate; apply. **5.** to direct a remark or mention. – **referral**, *n.*

referee /rɛfə'ri/ *n., v.,* **-reed**, **-reeing**. – *n.* **1.** one to whom something is referred, especially for decision or settlement; arbitrator; umpire. – *v.t.* **2.** to preside over as referee; act as referee in.

reference /'rɛfrəns/ *n.* **1.** the act or fact of referring. **2.** a directing of attention; allusion. **3.** direction or a direction to some source of information. **4.** use or recourse for purposes of information. **5.** a person to whom one refers for testimony as to one's character, abilities, etc. **6.** a written testimonial as to character, abilities, etc. **7.** relation, regard, or respect. **8. terms of reference,** the scope allowed to an investigating body.

referendum /rɛfə'rɛndəm/ *n., pl.* **-dums, -da** /-də/. the principle or procedure of referring or submitting measures proposed or passed by a legislative body to the vote of the electorate for approval or rejection.

refinance /ri'faɪnæns/ *v.,* **-nanced**, **nancing**. – *v.i.* **1.** to borrow money in order to meet maturing liabilities. – *v.t.* **2.** to provide (a company, enterprise, etc,) with money borrowed in order to meet its maturing liabilities.

refine /rə'faɪn/ *v.,* **-fined**, **-fining**. – *v.t.* **1.** to free from impurities. **2.** to make elegant or cultured. – *v.i.* **3.** to become pure. **4.** to become more fine, elegant, or polished.

reflect /rə'flɛkt/ *v.t.* **1.** to cast back (light, heat, sound, etc.) after incidence. **2.** to give back or show an image of; mirror. **3.** to reproduce; show. – *v.i.* **4.** to be turned or cast back, as light. **5.** to cast back light, heat, etc. **6.** to be reflected or mirrored. **7.** to serve or tend to bring reproach or discredit. **8.** to think, ponder, or meditate.

reflex /'riflɛks/ *adj.* **1.** occurring in reaction; responsive. **2.** bent or turned back. – *n.* **3.** *Physiology* a reflex action or movement.

reflexive /rə'flɛksɪv/ *adj. Grammar* **1.** (of a verb) having identical subject and object, as *shave* in *he shaved himself.* **2.** (of a pronoun) indicating identity of object with subject, as *himself* in the example above.

reform /rə'fɔm/ *n.* **1.** the improvement or amendment of what is wrong, corrupt, etc. – *v.t.* **2.** to improve by alteration, substitution, abolition, etc. **3.** to cause (a person) to abandon wrong or evil ways of life or conduct. – *v.i.* **4.** to abandon evil conduct or error.

reformatory /rə'fɔmətri/ *n., pl.* **-ries**. a penal institution for the reformation of young offenders. Also, **reform school**.

refraction /rə'frækʃən/ *n. Physics* the change of direction of a ray of light, heat, or the like, in passing obliquely from one medium into another.

refractory /rə'fræktəri/ *adj.* stubborn; unmanageable.

refrain[1] /rə'freɪn/ *v.i.* to forbear; keep oneself back (often fol. by *from*).

refrain[2] /rə'freɪn/ *n.* a phrase or verse recurring at intervals in a song or poem, especially at the end of each stanza; chorus.

refresh /rə'frɛʃ/ *v.t.* **1.** (*often reflexive*) to reinvigorate by rest, food, etc. **2.** to stimulate (the memory). – *v.i.* **3.** to become fresh or vigorous again; revive.

refreshment /rə'frɛʃmənt/ *n.* that which refreshes, especially food or drink.

refrigerate /rə'frɪdʒəreɪt/ *v.t.,* **-rated**, **-rating**. to make or keep cold or cool.

refrigerator /rə'frɪdʒəreɪtə/ *n.* a cabinet or room in which food, drink, etc., is kept cool.

refuge /'rɛfjudʒ/ *n.* shelter or protection from danger, trouble, etc.

refugee /rɛfju'dʒi/ *n.* someone who flees for refuge or safety, especially to a foreign country.

refund[1] /rə'fʌnd/ *v.,* /'rifʌnd/ *n.* – *v.t.* **1.** to give back or restore (especially money); repay. **2.** to make repayment to; reimburse. – *n.* **3.** a repayment.

refund[2] /ri'fʌnd/ *v.t. Finance* **1.** to meet (a matured debt structure) by new borrowing, especially through issuance of bonds. **2.** to replace (an old issue) with a new, especially with one bearing a lower rate of interest.

refurbish /ri'fɜbɪʃ/ *v.t.* to renovate.

refusal /rə'fjuzəl/ *n.* **1.** the act of refusing. **2.** priority in refusing or taking something; option.

refuse[1] /rə'fjuz/ *v.,* **-fused**, **-fusing**. – *v.t.* **1.** to decline to accept (something offered). **2.** to deny (a request, demand, etc.). **3.** to express a determination not (to do something). – *v.i.* **4.** to decline acceptance, consent, or compliance.

refuse[2] /'rɛfjus/ *n.* that which is discarded as worthless or useless; rubbish.

refute /rə'fjut/ *v.t.,* **-futed**, **-futing**. to prove to be false.

regal /'rigəl/ *adj.* **1.** of or relating to a king; royal. **2.** (of a woman) tall, dignified, and elegant.

regale /rə'geɪl/ *v.t.,* **-galed**, **-galing**. to entertain agreeably; delight.

regard /rə'gad/ *v.t.* **1.** to look upon or think of with a particular feeling. **2.** to have or show respect or concern for. **3.** to take into account; consider. **4.** to look at; observe. **5.** to relate to; concern. – *v.i.* **6.** to pay attention. – *n.* **7.** reference; relation. **8.** a point or particular. **9.** thought; attention; concern. **10.** look; gaze. **11.** respect; deference. **12.** kindly feeling; liking. **13.** (*pl.*) sentiments of esteem or affection.

regatta /rə'gætə/ *n.* a boat race.

regenerate /rə'dʒɛnəreɪt/ *v.*, **-rated**, **-rating** /rə'dʒɛnərət/. – *adj.* **1.** to re-create, reconstitute, or make over, especially in a better form or condition. – *v.i.* **2.** to come into existence or be formed again. **3.** to reform; become regenerate. – *adj.* **4.** reconstituted in a better form. **5.** reformed.

regent /'ridʒənt/ *n.* someone who exercises the ruling power in a kingdom during the minority, absence, or disability of the sovereign. – **regency**, *n.*

regime /reɪ'ʒim/ *n.* a mode or system of rule or government.

regimen /'rɛdʒəmən/ *n.* **1.** a prevailing system. **2.** a regulated course of diet, exercise, etc.

regiment /'rɛdʒəmənt/ *n.*, /'rɛdʒəmɛnt/ *v.* – *n.* **1.** *Military* a unit of ground forces. – *v.t.* **2.** to form into an organised body or group; organise or systematise. – **regimentation**, *n.* – **regimental**, *adj.*

regina /rə'dʒinə/ *n.* (*often cap.*) reigning queen.

region /'ridʒən/ *n.* **1.** any more or less extensive, continuous part of a surface or space. **2.** a district without respect to boundaries or extent.

register /'rɛdʒəstə/ *n.* **1.** a record of acts, occurrences, etc. **2.** *Commerce* a ship's official document of identification which must be produced when a ship is entering or leaving a port. **3.** a mechanical device by which data is automatically recorded, as a cash register. **4.** *Computers* a device capable of holding digital information until it is required. – *v.t.* **5.** to enter or have entered formally in a register. **6.** to indicate or show, as on a scale. **7.** to show (surprise, joy, anger, etc.). – *v.i.* **8.** to enter one's name, or cause it to be entered, in an electoral or other register; enrol. **9.** *Colloquial* to make an impression. – **registration**, *n.*

registered /'rɛdʒəstəd/ *adj.* *Commerce* officially listing the owner's name with the issuing company and suitably inscribing the certificate, as with bonds to evidence title.

registrar /'rɛdʒəstra/ *n.* **1.** someone who keeps a record; an official recorder. **2.** an employee of a limited company who is responsible for registering the issues of securities.

registry /'rɛdʒəstri/ *n.*, *pl.* **-tries**. a place where a register is kept; an office of registration.

regnant /'rɛgnənt/ *adj.* reigning; ruling.

regrate /ri'greɪt/ *v.t.*, **-grated**, **-grating**. to buy up (grain, provisions, etc.) in order to sell again at a profit in or near the same market.

regress /ri'grɛs/ *v.i.* to move in a backward direction; go back. – **regression**, *n.*

regressive /rə'grɛsɪv/ *adj.* **1.** moving backwards. **2.** denoting or relating to a form of taxation in which the rate decreases in proportion to the increase in taxable income.

regret /rə'grɛt/ *v.*, **-gretted**, **-gretting**, *n.* – *v.t.* **1.** to feel sorry about (anything disappointing, unpleasant, etc.). **2.** to think of with a sense of loss. – *n.* **3.** a sense of loss, disappointment, dissatisfaction, etc. **4.** the feeling of being sorry for some fault, act, omission, etc., of one's own.

regular /'rɛgjələ/ *adj.* **1.** usual; normal; customary. **2.** conforming in form or arrangement; symmetrical. **3.** adhering to rule or procedure. **4.** orderly; well-ordered. **5.** *Colloquial* complete; thorough. – *n.* **6.** *Colloquial* a regular customer.

regulate /'rɛgjəleɪt/ *v.t.*, **-lated**, **-lating**. **1.** to control or direct by rule, principle, method, etc. **2.** to adjust to some standard or requirement, as amount, degree, etc. – **regulation**, *n.*

regurgitate /rə'gɜdʒəteɪt/ *v.t.*, **-tated**, **-tating**. to cause to surge or rush back.

rehabilitate /rihə'bɪləteɪt/ *v.t.*, **-tated**, **-tating**. to restore to a good condition, or alter to an improved form.

rehash /ri'hæʃ/ *v.*, /'rihæʃ/ *n.* – *v.t.* **1.** to work up (old material) in a new form. – *n.* **2.** something rehashed.

rehearse /rə'hɜs/ *v.*, **-hearsed**, **-hearsing**. – *v.t.* **1.** to perform in private by way of practice. – *v.i.* **2.** to rehearse a play, part, etc. – **rehearsal**, *n.*

reign /reɪn/ *n.* **1.** the period or term of ruling, as of a sovereign. – *v.i.* **2.** to possess or exercise sovereign power or authority.

reimburse /riɪm'bɜs/ *v.t.*, **-bursed**, **-bursing**. to make repayment to for expense or loss incurred.

reimport /riɪm'pɔt/ *v.t.* to import back into the country of exportation.

rein /reɪn/ *n.* **1.** a long, narrow strap for guiding a horse. **2.** any means of curbing, controlling, or directing; a check; restraint. – *v.t.* **3.** to curb; restrain; control.

reincarnation /ˌriɪnka'neɪʃən/ *n.* rebirth of the soul in a new body.

reindeer /'reɪndɪə/ *n.*, *pl.* **-deer**, (*occasionally*) **-deers**. any of various species of large deer.

reinforce /riɪn'fɔs/ *v.t.*, **-forced**, **-forcing**. **1.** to strengthen; make more forcible or effective. **2.** to augment; increase.

reinstate /riɪn'steɪt/ *v.t.*, **-stated**, **-stating**. to put back or establish again, as in a former position or state.

reiterate /ri'ɪtəreɪt/ *v.t.*, **-rated**, **-rating**. to repeat; say or do again or repeatedly.

reject /rə'dʒɛkt/ *v.*, /'ridʒɛkt/ *n.* – *v.t.* **1.** to refuse to have, take, recognise, etc. **2.** to cast out or off. – *n.* **3.** something rejected, as an imperfect article.

rejoice /rə'dʒɔɪs/ *v.i.*, **-joiced**, **-joicing**. to be glad; take delight (*in*).

rejoinder /rə'dʒɔɪndə/ *n.* **1.** an answer to a reply; response. **2.** *Law* the defendant's answer to the plaintiff's replication.

rejuvenate /rə'dʒuvəneɪt/ *v.t.*, **-nated**, **-nating**. to make young again.

-rel a noun suffix having a diminutive or pejorative force.

relapse /rə'læps/ *v.*, **-lapsed**, **-lapsing**, *n.* – *v.i.* **1.** to fall or slip back into a former state, practice, etc. – *n.* **2.** the act of relapsing.

relate /rə'leɪt/ *v.*, **-lated**, **-lating**. – *v.t.* **1.** to tell. **2.** to bring into or establish association, connection, or relation. – *v.i.* **3.** to have reference (*to*). **4.** to have some relation (*to*).

relation /rə'leɪʃən/ *n.* **1.** an existing connection; a particular way of being related. **2.** connection between persons by blood or marriage. **3.** a relative. **4.** reference; regard; respect.

relative /'rɛlətɪv/ *n.* **1.** someone who is connected with another or others by blood or marriage. **2.** something having, or standing in, some relation to something else, as opposed to *absolute*. – *adj.* **3.** considered in relation to something else; comparative. **4.** having relation or connection. **5.** correspondent; proportionate.

relative atomic mass *n.* the average mass of the atoms of an element in its naturally occurring state, relative to the mass of an atom of the carbon-12 isotope taken as exactly 12. Cf. **atomic mass**. Also, **atomic weight**.

relativity /rɛlə'tɪvəti/ *n.* **1.** the state or fact of being relative. **2.** (*pl.*) the relative differences in wages between groups of workers.

relax /rə'læks/ *v.t.* **1.** to make lax, or less tense, rigid, or firm. **2.** to diminish the force of. – *v.i.* **3.** to become less tense, rigid, or firm. **4.** to become less strict or severe; grow milder. **5.** to slacken in effort, application, etc.; take relaxation.

relay /'rileɪ/ *n.*, /rə'leɪ, 'rileɪ/ *v.* – *n.* **1.** a set of persons relieving others or taking turns; a shift. **2.** an automatic device for operating the controls of a larger piece of equipment. – *v.t.* **3.** to carry forward by or as by relays.

release /rə'lis/ *v.*, **-leased**, **-leasing**, *n.* – *v.t.* **1.** to free from confinement, bondage, obligation, pain, etc. **2.** to allow to become known, be issued or exhibited. – *n.* **3.** liberation from anything that restrains or fastens. **4.** some device for effecting such liberation. **5.** the releasing of something for public exhibition or sale. **6.** the article so released.

relegate /'rɛləgeɪt/ *v.t.*, **-gated**, **-gating**. to send or consign to some obscure position, place, or condition.

relent /rə'lɛnt/ *v.i.* to soften in feeling, temper, or determination.

relevant /'rɛləvənt/ *adj.* bearing upon or connected with the matter in hand; to the purpose; pertinent. – **relevance**, *n.*

reliable /rə'laɪəbəl/ *adj.* that may be relied on; trustworthy.

reliant /rə'laɪənt/ *adj.* confident; trustful.

relic /'rɛlɪk/ *n.* **1.** a surviving memorial of something past. **2.** a surviving trace of something.

relief /rə'lif/ *n.* **1.** deliverance, alleviation, or ease through the removal of pain, distress, oppression, etc. **2.** something affording a pleasing change, as from monotony. **3.** the person or persons relieving another or others. **4.** prominence, distinctness, or vividness due to contrast.

relieve /rə'liv/ *v.t.*, **-lieved**, **-lieving**. **1.** to ease or alleviate (pain, distress, anxiety, need, etc.). **2.** to free from anxiety, fear, pain, etc. **3.** to make less tedious, unpleasant, or monotonous. **4.** to bring into relief or prominence. **5.** to release (one on duty) by coming as or providing a substitute. **6.** to take the place of (an absent worker). **7. relieve oneself,** to empty the bowels or bladder.

religion /rə'lɪdʒən/ *n.* recognition on the part of human beings of a controlling superhuman power entitled to obedience, reverence, and worship.

religious /rə'lɪdʒəs/ *adj.* **1.** of, relating to, or concerned with religion. **2.** scrupulously faithful; conscientious.

relinquish /rə'lɪŋkwɪʃ/ *v.t.* to renounce or surrender (a possession, right, etc.).

relish /'rɛlɪʃ/ *n.* **1.** pleasurable appreciation of anything; liking. **2.** something appetising or savoury added to a meal, as chutney. **3.** a taste or flavour. – *v.t.* **4.** to take pleasure in; like; enjoy.

relive /ˌri'lɪv/ *v.t.*, **-lived**, **-living**. to repeat former experiences, in fact or memory.

reluctant /rə'lʌktənt/ *adj.* unwilling; disinclined.

rely /rə'laɪ/ *v.i.*, **-lied**, **-lying**. to depend confidently; put trust in (fol. by *on* or *upon*).

remain /rə'meɪn/ *v.i.* **1.** to continue in the same state; continue to be (as specified). **2.** to stay in a place. **3.** to be left after the removal, departure, loss, etc., of another or others. – *n.* **4.** (*always pl.*) that which remains or is left; a remnant.

remainder /rə'meɪndə/ *n.* **1.** that which remains or is left. **2.** a copy of a book remaining in the publisher's stock when the sale has practically ceased, frequently sold at a reduced price. – *v.t.* **3.** to dispose of or sell as a publisher's remainder.

remand /rə'mænd, -'mand/ *v.t.* **1.** to send back, remit, or consign again. **2.** the state of being remanded.

remark /rə'mak/ *v.t.* **1.** to say casually, as in making a comment. **2.** to note; perceive. – *v.i.* **3.** to make a remark or observation (fol. by *on* or *upon*). – *n.* **4.** a casual or brief expression of thought or opinion.

remarkable /rə'makəbəl/ *adj.* worthy of remark or notice.

remedy /'rɛmədi/ *n.*, *pl.* **-dies**, *v.*, **-died**, **-dying**. – *n.* **1.** something that corrects or removes an evil of any kind. – *v.t.* **2.** to cure or heal. **3.** to put right, or restore to the natural or proper condition. – **remedial**, *adj.*

remember /rə'mɛmbə/ *v.t.* **1.** to recall to the mind by an act or effort of memory. **2.** to retain in the memory; bear in mind. **3.** to mention to another as sending kindly greetings. – *v.i.* **4.** to possess or exercise the faculty of memory. – **remembrance**, *n.*

remind /rə'maɪnd/ *v.t.* to cause to remember.

reminiscence /rɛmə'nɪsəns/ *n.* the act or process of remembering one's past. – **reminiscent**, *adj.* – **reminisce**, *v.*

remiss /rə'mɪs/ *adj.* characterised by negligence or carelessness.

remit /rə'mɪt/ *v.*, **-mitted**, **-mitting**, *n.* – *v.t.* **1.** to transmit or send (money, etc.) to a person or place. **2.** to refrain from exacting, as a payment or service. **3.** to slacken; abate. **4.** to give back. **5.** to put back into a previous position or condition. – *v.i.* **6.** to transmit money, etc., as in payment. **7.** to slacken; abate. – *n.* **8.** *NZ* a recommendation from a branch of an organisation to the main body or annual conference for possible adoption. – **remission**, *n.*

remittance /rə'mɪtns/ *n.* **1.** the remitting of money, etc., to a recipient at a distance. **2.** money or its equivalent sent from one place to another.

remix /'rimɪkʌ/ *n.* **1.** a recorded version of a piece of music containing a mix of the original recording tracks which is different from that used for the earlier published version. – *v.t.* **2.** to mix again.

remnant /'rɛmnənt/ *n.* a part, quantity, or number (usually small) remaining.

remonstrance /rə'mɒnstrəns/ *n.* a protest. – **remonstrate**, *v.*

remorse /rə'mɔs/ *n.* deep and painful regret for wrongdoing; compunction.

remote /rə'moʊt/ *adj.*, **-moter**, **-motest**. **1.** far apart; far distant in space. **2.** out-of-the-way; retired; secluded. **3.** distant in time. **4.** far off; removed. **5.** slight or faint. **6.** abstracted; cold and aloof.

remote control *n.* the control of a system from a point outside the system.

removal /rə'muvəl/ *n.* **1.** the act of removing. **2.** a change of residence, position, etc. **3.** dismissal, as from an office.

remove /rə'muv/ *v.*, **-moved**, **-moving**, *n.* – *v.t.* **1.** to move from a place or position; take away; take off. **2.** to take, withdraw, or separate (from). – *v.i.* **3.** to move from one place to another, especially to another locality or residence. – *n.* **4.** the act of removing. **5.** a step or degree, as in a graded scale.

removed /rə'muvd/ *adj.* remote; separate; not connected with; distinct from.

remunerate /rə'mjunəreɪt/ *v.t.*, **-rated**, **-rating**. to pay, recompense, or reward for work, trouble, etc. – **remuneration**, *n.* – **remunerative**, *adj.*

renal /'rinəl/ *adj.* of or relating to the kidneys.

rend /rɛnd/ *v.t.*, *v.i.*, **rent**, **rending**. to tear apart, split, or divide.

render /'rɛndə/ *v.t.* **1.** to make, or cause, to be or become. **2.** to do; perform. **3.** to present for consideration, approval, payment, action, etc., as an account. **4.** to pay as due (a tax, tribute, etc.). **5.** to give in return or requital. – **rendition**, *n.*

rendezvous /'rɒndeɪvu, rɒndeɪ'vu/ *n.* an appointment to meet at a fixed place and time.

renegade /'rɛnəgeɪd/ *n.* someone who deserts a party or cause for another.

renege /rə'nɛg, -'nɪg/ *v.i.*, **-neged**, **-neging**. *Colloquial* to go back on one's word.

renew /rə'nju/ *v.t.* **1.** to begin or take up again, as acquaintance, conversation, etc. **2.** to make effective for an additional period. **3.** to restore or replenish. – *v.i.* **4.** to begin again; recommence. **5.** to renew a lease, note, etc. – **renewal**, *n.*

renounce /rə'naʊns/ *v.t.*, **-nounced**, **-nouncing**. **1.** to give up or put aside voluntarily. **2.** to repudiate; disown.

renovate /'rɛnəveɪt/ *v.t.*, **-vated**, **-vating**. to make new or as if new again.

renown /rə'naʊn/ *n.* widespread and high repute; fame.

renowned /rə'naʊnd/ *adj.* celebrated; famous.

rent¹ /rɛnt/ *n.* **1.** a return or payment made periodically by a tenant to an owner or landlord for the use of land or building. **2.** profit or return derived from any differential advantage in production. – *v.t.* **3.** to grant the possession and enjoyment of (property) in return for payments to be made at agreed times. **4.** to take and hold (property) in return for payments to be made at agreed times. – *v.i.* **5.** to be leased or let for rent.

rent² /rɛnt/ *n.* **1.** an opening made by rending or tearing; slit; fissure. – *v.* **2.** past tense and past participle of **rend**.

rental /'rɛntl/ *n.* **1.** an amount received or paid as rent. **2.** an income arising from rents received. – *adj.* **3.** relating to rent. **4.** available for rent.

renunciation /rənʌnsi'eɪʃən/ *n.* the formal abandoning of a right, title, etc.

rep /rɛp/ *n. Colloquial* **1.** a travelling salesman. **2.** a union representative.

repair¹ /rə'pɛə/ *v.t.* **1.** to restore to a good or sound condition after decay or damage; mend. – *n.* **2.** the act, process, or work of repairing. **3.** the good condition resulting from repairing.

repair² /rə'pɛə/ *v.i.* to betake oneself or go, as to a place.

reparable /'rɛpərəbəl, 'rɛprəbəl/ *adj.* capable of being repaired or remedied.

reparation /rɛpə'reɪʃən/ *n.* the making of amends for wrong or injury done.

repartee /rɛpa'ti/ *n.* speech or talk characterised by quickness and wittiness of reply.

repast /rə'past/ *n.* a taking of food; a meal.

repatriate /ri'pætrieɪt/ *v.t.*, **-ated**, **-ating**. to bring or send back (a person) to his or her own country.

repay /rɪ'peɪ/ *v.t.*, **-paid**, **-paying**. **1.** to pay back or refund (money, etc.). **2.** to make return for.

repeal /rə'pil/ *v.t.* **1.** to revoke or withdraw formally or officially. – *n.* **2.** the act of repealing; revocation; abrogation.

repeat /rə'pit/ *v.t.* **1.** to say or utter again. **2.** to say or utter in reproducing the words, etc., of another. **3.** to do, make, perform, etc., again. – *v.i.* **4.** to do or say something again. **5.** something repeated. **6.** an order for goods identical to a previous order. **7.** a duplicate or reproduction of something.

repel /rə'pɛl/ *v.t.*, **-pelled**, **-pelling**. **1.** to drive or force back (an assailant, invader, etc.). **2.** to keep off or out; fail to mix with. **3.** to excite feelings of distaste or aversion in. – **repellent**, *adj.*, *n.*

repent /rə'pɛnt/ *v.i.* **1.** to feel self-reproach, compunction, or contrition for past conduct. – *v.t.* **2.** to feel sorry for; regret. – **repentance**, *n.*

repercussion /ripə'kʌʃən/ *n.* an after-effect, often an indirect result, of some event or action.

repertoire /'rɛpətwa/ *n.* the list of dramas, operas, parts, pieces, etc., which a company, actor, singer or the like, is prepared to perform.

repertory /'rɛpətri/ *n.*, *pl.* **-ries**. a theatrical company.

repetition /rɛpə'tɪʃən/ *n.* **1.** the act of repeating. **2.** a repeated action, performance, production, or presentation.

repetition strain injury *n.* → **RSI**. Also, **repetitive strain injury**.

repetitive /rə'pɛtətɪv/ *adj.* relating to or characterised by repetition.

replace /rə'pleɪs/ *v.t.*, **-placed**, **-placing**. **1.** to fill or take the place of; substitute for (a person or thing). **2.** to provide a substitute or equivalent in the place of. **3.** to restore to a former or the proper place. – **replacement**, *n.*

replenish /rə'plɛnɪʃ/ *v.t.* to bring back to a state of fullness or completeness.

replete /rə'plit/ *adj.* stuffed or gorged with food and drink.

replica /'rɛplɪkə/ *n.* any copy or reproduction.

replication /rɛplə'keɪʃən/ *n.* a reply to an answer.

reply /rə'plaɪ/ *v.*, **-plied**, **-plying**, *n.*, *pl.* **-plies**. – *v.i.* **1.** to make answer in words or writing; answer; respond. **2.** to respond by some action, performance, etc. – *v.t.* **3.** to return as an answer. – *n.* **4.** an answer or response.

report /rə'pɔt/ *n.* **1.** an account brought back or presented. **2.** a statement generally circulated; rumour. **3.** repute; reputation. **4.** a loud noise, as from an explosion. – *v.t.* **5.** to relate as what has been learned by observation or investigation. **6.** to give or render a formal account or statement of. **7.** to lay a charge against (a person), as to a superior. **8.** to relate or tell. – *v.i.* **9.** to make a report. **10.** to present oneself duly, as at a place.

reporter /rə'pɔtə/ *n.* **1.** someone employed to gather and report news for a newspaper, news agency, or broadcasting organisation. **2.** someone who prepares official reports, as of legal or legislative proceedings.

repose /rə'poʊz/ *n.*, *v.*, **-posed**, **-posing**. *-n.* **1.** the state of reposing or resting; rest; sleep. **2.** dignified calmness, as of manner or demeanour. – *v.i.* **3.** to lie at rest; take rest. – *v.t.* **4.** (*often used reflexively*) to lay to rest; rest; refresh by rest.

repository /rə'pɒzətri/ *n.*, *pl.* **-tories**. a receptacle or place where things are deposited, stored, or offered for sale.

repossess /ripə'zɛs/ *v.t.* **1.** to possess again; regain possession of. **2.** to put again in possession of something.

reprehensible /rɛprə'hɛnsəbəl/ *adj.* blameworthy.

represent /rɛprə'zɛnt/ *v.t.* **1.** to serve to express, designate, stand for, or denote, as a word, symbol, or the like; symbolise. **2.** to speak and act for by delegated authority. **3.** to present in words; set forth; describe; state. **4.** to serve as an example or specimen of; exemplify. **5.** to be the equivalent of; correspond to.

representative /rɛprə'zɛntətɪv/ *adj.* **1.** serving to represent; representing. **2.** representing a constituency or community or the people generally in legislation or government. **3.** characterised by, founded on, or relating to representation of the people in government. – *n.* **4.** someone who or that which represents another or others, especially in government. **5.** a commercial traveller; a travelling salesman. **6.** an agent or deputy.

repress /rə'prɛs/ *v.t.* to keep under control, check, or suppress.

reprieve /rə'priv/ *v.*, **-prieved**, **-prieving**, *n.* – *v.t.* **1.** to relieve temporarily from any evil. – *n.* **2.** respite from impending punishment, especially from execution of a sentence of death.

reprimand /'rɛprəmand, -mænd/ *n.* **1.** a severe reproof, especially a formal one by a person in authority. – *v.t.* **2.** to reprove severely, especially in a formal way.

reprisal /rə'praɪzəl/ *n.* retaliation, or an act of retaliation.

reproach /rə'proʊtʃ/ *v.t.* **1.** to find fault with (a person, etc.); blame; censure. – *n.* **2.** an expression of upbraiding, censure or reproof. **3.** a cause or occasion of disgrace or discredit.

reprobate /'rɛprəbeɪt/ *n.* **1.** an abandoned, unprincipled, or reprehensible person. – *adj.* **2.** morally depraved; unprincipled; bad.

reproduce /riprə'djus/ *v.*, **-duced**, **-ducing**. – *v.t.* **1.** to make a copy, representation, duplicate, or close imitation of. **2.** to produce another or more individuals of (some animal or plant kind). **3.** to produce, form, make, or bring about again or anew in any manner. – *v.i.* **4.** to reproduce its kind, as an animal or plant; propagate. **5.** to turn out (well, etc.) when copied. – **reproducible**, *adj.* – **reproduction**, *n.*

reproof /rə'pruf/ *n.* an expression of censure or rebuke.

reprove /rə'pruv/ *v.*, **-proved**, **-proving**. – *v.t.* **1.** to address words of disapproval to (a person, etc.); rebuke; blame. – *v.i.* **2.** to speak in reproof; administer a reproof. – **reproval**, *n.*

reptile /'rɛptaɪl/ *n.* any of various creeping or crawling animals, as the lizards, snakes, etc.

republic /rə'pʌblɪk/ *n.* a state, especially a democratic state, in which the head of the government is an elected or nominated president, not a hereditary monarch.

republican /rə'pʌblɪkən/ *adj.* **1.** of, relating to, or of the nature of a republic. **2.** favouring a republic. – *n.* **3.** someone who favours a republican form of government. – **republicanism**, *n.*

repudiate /rə'pjudieɪt/ *v.t.*, **-ated**, **-ating**. **1.** to reject as having no authority or binding force. **2.** to refuse to acknowledge and pay, as a debt (said specifically of a state, municipality, etc.).

repugnant /rə'pʌgnənt/ *adj.* distasteful or objectionable. – **repugnance**, *n.*

repulse /rə'pʌls/ *v.t.*, **-pulsed**, **-pulsing**. to drive back, or repel, as an assailant, etc. – **repulsion**, *n.* – **repulsive**, *adj.*

reputable /'rɛpjətəbəl/ *adj.* held in good repute; honourable.

reputation /rɛpjə'teɪʃən/ *n.* the estimation in which a person or thing is held.

repute /rə'pjut/ *n.* estimation in the view of others; reputation.

reputed /rə'pjutəd/ *adj.* accounted or supposed to be such.

request /rə'kwɛst/ *n.* **1.** the act of asking for something. – *v.t.* **2.** to ask for, especially politely or formally. **3.** to make request to, ask, or beg (a person, etc.) to do something.

requiem /'rɛkwiəm/ *n.* any musical service, hymn, or dirge for the repose of the dead.

require /rə'kwaɪə/ *v.t.*, **-quired**, **-quiring**. **1.** to have need of; need. **2.** to ask for authoritatively or imperatively; demand. **3.** to place under an obligation or necessity.

requisition /rɛkwə'zɪʃən/ *n.* **1.** an authoritative or official demand. **2.** the state of being required for use or called into service. – *v.t.* **3.** to require or take for use; press into service.

requite /rə'kwaɪt/ *v.t.*, **-quited**, **-quiting**. to give or do in return. – **requital**, *n.*

resale price maintenance *n.* the establishment of a fixed or minimum retail price for branded products, by agreement between manufacturer and retailer.

rescind /rə'sɪnd/ *v.t.* to invalidate (an act, measure, etc.) by a later action or a higher authority. – **recission**, *n.*

rescue /'rɛskju/ *v.*, **-cued**, **-cuing**, *n.* – *v.t.* **1.** to free or deliver from confinement, violence, danger, or evil. – *n.* **2.** the act of rescuing.

research /rə'sɜtʃ, 'risɜtʃ/ *n.* **1.** diligent and systematic inquiry or investigation into a subject in order to discover facts or principles. – *v.i.* **2.** to make researches; investigate carefully. – *v.t.* **3.** to investigate carefully. – *adj.* **4.** of or relating to research.

resemble /rə'zɛmbəl/ *v.t.*, **-bled**, **-bling**. to be like or similar to. – **resemblance**, *n.*

resent /rə'zɛnt/ *v.t.* to feel or show a sense of injury or insult.

reservation /rɛzə'veɪʃən/ *n.* **1.** the making of some exception or qualification. **2.** tract of public land set apart for a special purpose. **3.** the allotting or the securing of accommodation at a hotel, on a train or boat, etc.

reserve /rə'zɜv/ *v.*, **-served**, **-serving**, *n.*, *adj.* – *v.t.* **1.** to keep back or save for future use, disposal, treatment, etc. **2.** to secure or book in advance, as accommodation, theatre seats, etc. **3.** *Law* to delay handing down (a judgment or decision), especially to give time for better consideration of the issues involved. – *n.* **4.** an amount of capital retained by a company to meet contingencies. **5.** something reserved, as for some purpose or contingency; a store or stock. **6.** a tract of public land set apart for a special purpose, as a nature reserve. **7.** reticence or silence. **8.** → **reserve price**. – *adj.* **9.** kept in reserve; forming a reserve.

reserve bank *n.* the national banking organisation of a country, which administers the monetary policy of a government, receives revenue, pays government expenditure and issues money, both paper and coin, as legal tender.

reserved /rə'zɜvd/ *adj.* **1.** kept in reserve. **2.** characterised by reserve, as the disposition, manner, etc.

reserve price *n.* the lowest price at which a person is willing that their property shall be sold at auction. Also, **reserve**.

reservoir /'rɛzəvwa, 'rɛzevɔ/ *n.* a natural or artificial place where water is collected and stored for use.

reshuffle /ˌri'ʃʌfəl/ *v.i.*, **-fled**, **-fling**. to make a new allocation of jobs, especially within a government or cabinet.

reside /rə'zaɪd/ *v.i.*, **-sided**, **-siding**. **1.** to dwell permanently or for a considerable time. **2.** to rest or be vested, as powers, rights, etc. (fol. by *in*). – **resident**, *adj.*, *n.*

residence /'rɛzədəns/ *n.* **1.** the place, especially the house, in which one resides. **2.** a large house. **3. in residence,** living or staying in a place of official or other duty. **4.** the time during which one resides in a place. – **residential**, *adj.*

residency /'rɛzədənsi/ *n.*, *pl.* **-cies**. **1.** → **residence**. **2.** the dwelling place of officials or diplomats representing the heads of state of foreign countries.

residue /'rɛzədʒu/ *n.* that which remains after a part is taken, disposed of, or gone; remainder; rest. – **residual**, *adj.*

resign /rə'zaɪn/ *v.i.* **1.** to give up an office or position (often fol. by *from*). **2.** to submit; yield. – *v.t.* **3.** to give up (an office, position, etc.) formally. **4.** to submit (oneself, one's mind, etc.) without resistance. – **resignation**, *n.*

resilient /rə'zɪliənt, -'zɪljənt/ *adj.* **1.** returning to the original form or position after being bent, compressed, or stretched. **2.** readily recovering, as from sickness, depression, or the like; buoyant; cheerful. – **resilience**, *n.*

resin /'rɛzən/ *n.* any of a class of organic substances used in medicine and in the making of varnishes and plastics.

resist /rə'zɪst/ *v.t.* **1.** to withstand, strive against, or oppose. – *v.i.* **2.** to act in opposition; offer resistance.

resistance /rə'zɪstəns/ *n.* **1.** the opposition offered by one thing, force, etc., to another. **2.** *Electricity* the property of a device which opposes the flow of an electric current.

resolute /'rɛzəlut/ *adj.* firmly resolved or determined; set in purpose or opinion.

resolution /rɛzə'luʃən/ *n.* **1.** a resolve or determination. **2.** the mental state or quality of being resolved or resolute; firmness of purpose. **3.** the act or process of resolving or separating into constituent or elementary parts.

resolve /rə'zɒlv/ *v.*, **-solved**, **-solving**, *n.* – *v.t.* **1.** to fix or settle on by deliberate choice and will; determine (to do something). **2.** to separate into constituent or elementary parts. **3.** to convert or transform by any process (often reflexive). **4.** to settle, determine, or state formally in a vote or resolution, as of a deliberative assembly. **5.** to deal with (a question, a matter of uncertainty, etc.) conclusively; explain; solve (a problem). **6.** to clear away or dispel (doubts, etc.), as by explanation. – *v.i.* **7.** to come to a determination; make up one's mind; determine (often fol. by *on* or *upon*). **8.** to break up or disintegrate. – *n.* **9.** a resolution or determination made. **10.** determination; firmness of purpose.

resonance /'rɛzənəns/ *n.* **1.** the state or quality of being resonant. **2.** the prolongation of sound by reflection; reverberation.

resonant /'rɛzənənt/ *adj.* **1.** resounding or re-echoing, as sounds, places, etc. **2.** deep and full of resonance.

resonate /'rɛzəneɪt/ *v.i.*, **-nated**, **-nating**. to resound.

resort /rə'zɔt/ *v.i.* **1.** to have recourse for use, service, or help. – *n.* **2.** a place frequented, especially by the public generally. **3.** a resorting to some person or thing for aid, service, etc.; recourse. **4.** a person or thing resorted to for aid, service, etc.

resound /rə'zaʊnd/ *v.i.* **1.** to re-echo or ring with sound. **2.** to be echoed, or ring, as sounds. – *v.t.* **3.** to re-echo (a sound). **4.** to proclaim loudly (praises, etc.).

resource /rə'zɔs, rə'sɔs/ *n.* **1.** a source of supply, support, or aid. **2.** (*often pl.*) money, or any property which can be converted into money; assets. **3.** capability in dealing with a situation or in meeting difficulties.

resources boom *n.* an upsurge in the economic activity and general prosperity of a country as a result of the widespread development of mineral resources, as coal, nickel, etc.

respect /rə'spɛkt/ *n.* **1.** a particular, detail, or point (in phrases preceded by *in*). **2.** relation or reference (preceded by *in* or *with*). **3.** esteem or deferential regard felt or shown. **4.** (*pl.*) deferential, respectful, or friendly compliments. – *v.t.* **5.** to hold in esteem or honour. **6.** to treat with consideration; refrain from interfering with.

respectable /rə'spɛktəbəl/ *adj.* **1.** worthy of respect or esteem. **2.** having socially accepted standards of moral behaviour. **3.** of presentable appearance; decently clothed.

respective /rə'spɛktɪv/ *adj.* relating individually or severally to each of a number of persons, things, etc.; particular.

respectively /rə'spɛktɪvli/ *adv.* with respect to each of a number in the stated or corresponding order.

respiration /rɛspə'reɪʃən/ *n.* the inhalation and exhalation of air; breathing.

respite /'rɛspət, 'rɛspaɪt/ *n.*, *v.*, **-pited**, **-piting**. – *n.* **1.** a delay or cessation for a time, especially of anything distressing or trying; an interval of relief. – *v.t.* **2.** to relieve temporarily.

resplendent /rə'splɛndənt/ *adj.* shining brilliantly; gleaming; splendid.

respond /rə'spɒnd/ *v.i.* to answer; give a reply.

respondent /rə'spɒndənt/ *n.* *Law* a defendant, especially in appellate and divorce cases.

response /rə'spɒns/ *n.* answer or reply, whether in words, in some action, etc.

response time *n.* the time between the initiating of a computer operation and the receipt of the results at a terminal.

responsibility /rəspɒnsə'bɪləti/ *n.*, *pl.* **-ties**. **1.** the state or fact of being responsible. **2.** something for which one is responsible. **3.** ability to meet debts or payments.

responsible /rə'spɒnsəbəl/ *adj.* **1.** answerable or accountable, as for something within one's power, control, or management (often fol. by *to* or *for*). **2.** able to discharge obligations or pay debts. **3.** reliable in business or other dealings; showing reliability.

responsive /rə'spɒnsɪv/ *adj.* responding readily to influences, appeals, efforts, etc.

rest[1] /rɛst/ *n.* **1.** refreshing ease or inactivity after exertion or labour. **2.** relief or freedom, especially from anything that wearies, troubles, or disturbs. **3.** cessation or absence of motion. **4.** a pause or interval. **5.** a support, or supporting device. – *v.i.* **6.** to refresh oneself, as by sleeping, lying down, or relaxing. **7.** to be quiet or still. **8.** to cease from motion, come to rest, or stop. **9.** to remain without further action or notice. **10.** to lie, sit, lean, or be set (fol. by *in*, *on*, *against*, etc.). **11.** to be based or founded (fol. by *on* or *upon*). **12.** to be a responsibility, as something to be done (fol. by *in* or *with*). – *v.t.* **13.** to give rest to; refresh with rest. **14.** to base, or let depend, as on some ground of reliance. **15.** to bring to rest; halt; stop.

rest[2] /rɛst/ *n.* that which is left or remains; the remainder.

restaurant /'rɛstərɒnt/ *n.* an establishment where meals are served to customers.

restitution /rɛstə'tjuʃən/ *n.* the restoration of property or rights previously taken away or surrendered.

restive /'rɛstɪv/ *adj.* impatient of control, restraint, or delay.

restore /rə'stɔ/ *v.t.*, **-stored**, **-storing**. **1.** to bring back to a former, original, or normal condition. **2.** to put back to a former place, or to a former position, rank, etc. **3.** to give back. – **restoration**, *n.*

restrain /rə'streɪn/ *v.t.* to hold back from action; keep in check or under control.

restraint /rə'streɪnt/ *n.* **1.** a means of restraining. **2.** the state or fact of being restrained.

restraint of trade *n.* the restriction of business activity and freedom to compete.

restrict /rə'strɪkt/ *v.t.* to confine or keep within limits, as of space, action, choice, quantity, etc. – **restriction**, *n.* – **restrictive**, *adj.*

restrictive practice *n.* a practice on the part of the members of an association such as a trade union, tending to limit the freedom of choice of their coworkers or employers.

restrictive trade practice *n.* an agreement between trading companies which is contrary to the public interest, as resale price maintenance, exclusive dealing, price discrimination, etc.

result /rə'zʌlt/ *n.* **1.** that which results; the outcome, consequence, or effect. – *v.i.* **2.** to spring, arise, or proceed as a consequence. **3.** to terminate or end in a specified manner or thing.

resume /rə'zjum/ *v.*, **-sumed**, **-suming**. – *v.t.* **1.** to take up or go on with again after interruption. – *v.i.* **2.** to go on or continue after interruption.

résumé /'rɛzjəmeɪ/ *n.* **1.** a summing up; a summary. **2.** *Originally US* → **curriculum vitae**. Also, **resumé**.

resurrect /rɛzə'rɛkt/ *v.t.* **1.** to raise from the dead; bring to life again. – *v.i.* **2.** to rise from the dead.

resuscitate /rə'sʌsəteɪt/ *v.t.*, *v.i.*, **-tated**, **-tating**. to revive, especially from apparent death or from unconsciousness.

retail /'riteɪl/ *n.* **1.** the sale of commodities

to household or ultimate consumers, usually in small quantities (opposed to *wholesale*). – *adj.* **2.** relating to, connected with, or engaged in sale at retail. – *adv.* **3.** at a retail price or in a retail quantity. – *v.t.* **4.** to sell directly to the consumer. – *v.i.* **5.** to be sold at retail.

retail banking *n.* the section of banking services which is directed at the general public, including savings and cheque accounts, loans, credit cards, etc.

retain /rəˈteɪn/ *v.t.* **1.** to continue to use, practise, etc. **2.** to continue to hold or have. **3.** to keep in mind; remember. – **retention**, *n.*

retainer /rəˈteɪnə/ *n.* **1.** a fee paid to secure services, as of a barrister. **2.** a reduced rent paid during absence as an indication of future requirement.

retaliate /rəˈtælieɪt/ *v.i.*, **-ated**, **-ating**. to return like for like, especially evil for evil.

retard /rəˈtad/ *v.t.* **1.** to delay the progress of; hinder or impede. **2.** to delay or limit (a person's intellectual or emotional development).

retch /rɛtʃ/ *v.i.* **1.** to make efforts to vomit. – *n.* **2.** the act or an instance of retching.

retentive /rəˈtɛntɪv/ *adj.* **1.** tending or serving to retain something. **2.** having power or capacity to retain.

reticent /ˈrɛtəsənt/ *adj.* disposed to be silent; not inclined to speak freely.

retina /ˈrɛtənə/ *n.*, *pl.* **-nas**, **-nae** /-ni/. the innermost coat of the posterior part of the eyeball, serving to receive the image.

retinue /ˈrɛtənju/ *n.* a body of people in attendance upon an important personage.

retire /rəˈtaɪə/ *v.i.*, **-tired**, **-tiring**. **1.** to withdraw, or go away or apart, to a place of abode, shelter, or seclusion. **2.** to go to bed. **3.** to withdraw from office, business, or active life.

retirement /rəˈtaɪəmənt/ *n.* **1.** the state of being retired. **2.** repurchase of its own securities by a company.

retort /rəˈtɔt/ *v.t.* **1.** to reply in retaliation. – *n.* **2.** a severe, incisive, or witty reply.

retrace /rəˈtreɪs/ *v.t.*, **-traced**, **-tracing**. to trace back; go back over.

retract[1] /rəˈtrækt/ *v.t.* to draw back or in.

retract[2] /rəˈtrækt/ *v.t.* to withdraw or revoke (a decree, promise, etc.).

retread /ˌriˈtrɛd/ *v.*, **-treaded**, **-treading**, /ˈritrɛd/ *n.* – *v.t.* **1.** to recondition (a worn motor-vehicle tyre) by moulding a fresh tread on to it. – *n.* **2.** a retreaded tyre.

retreat /rəˈtrit/ *n.* **1.** the act of withdrawing, as into safety or privacy. **2.** a place of refuge, seclusion, or privacy. – *v.i.* **3.** to withdraw, retire, or draw back, especially for shelter or seclusion.

retrench /rəˈtrɛntʃ/ *v.t.* **1.** to sack or dismiss, as part of an effort to economise. – *v.i.* **2.** to economise; reduce expenses.

retribution /rɛtrəˈbjuʃən/ *n.* requital according to merits or deserts, especially for evil.

retrieve /rəˈtriv/ *v.t.*, **-trieved**, **-trieving**. **1.** to recover or regain. **2.** to bring back to a former and better state; restore.

retriever /rəˈtrivə/ *n.* any of several breeds of dog for retrieving game.

retro /ˈrɛtroʊ/ *adj.* of or relating to a style of fashion or music which remixes aspects of previous styles.

retro- a prefix meaning 'backwards'.

retroactive /rɛtroʊˈæktɪv/ *adj.* operative with respect to past occurrences, as a statute; retrospective.

retrograde /ˈrɛtrəgreɪd/ *adj.* **1.** moving backwards. **2.** returning to an earlier and inferior state.

retrogress /rɛtrəˈgrɛs/ *v.i.* to go backwards into a worse or earlier condition.

retrospect /ˈrɛtrəspɛkt/ *n.* contemplation of the past. – **retrospection**, *n.*

retrospective /rɛtrəˈspɛktɪv/ *adj.* **1.** looking or directed backwards. **2.** retroactive, as a statute.

retrospectivity /ˌrɛtroʊspɛkˈtɪvəti/ *n.* **1.** the quality of being retrospective. **2.** (in union or other agreements) the dating of the effectiveness of the agreement to a time prior to the date of the discussion concerning the agreement.

return /rəˈtɜn/ *v.i.* **1.** to go or come back, as to a former place, position, state, etc. **2.** to make reply; retort. – *v.t.* **3.** to put, bring, take, give, or send back. **4.** to yield (a profit, revenue, etc.), as in return for labour, expenditure, or investment. **5.** to elect, as to a legislative body. **6.** to turn back or in the reverse direction. – *n.* **7.** the act or fact of returning. **8.** response or reply. **9.** (*often pl.*) a yield or profit. **10.** the report or statement of financial condition. **11.** *Economics* yield per unit as compared to the cost per unit involved in a specific industrial process. **12. by return,** by the next post. – *adj.* **13.** sent, given, or done in return. **14.** done or occurring again.

returning officer *n.* an official responsible for the organisation of an election, the accuracy of the count, the reading of the results, etc.

reunion /riˈjunjən/ *n.* a gathering of relatives, friends, or associates after separation.

rev /rɛv/ *n.*, *v.*, **revved**, **revving**. – *n.* **1.** a revolution (in an engine or the like). – *v.t.* **2.** to change, especially to increase the speed of (in a specified way).

revalue /riˈvælju/ *v.t.*, **-ued**, **-uing**. to value again, especially to raise the legal value of (a currency).

revamp /riˈvæmp/ *v.t.* to renovate.

reveal /rəˈvil/ *v.t.* **1.** to make known; disclose; divulge. **2.** to lay open to view; display; exhibit. – **revelation**, *n.*

reveille /rəˈvæli/ *n.* a signal to waken soldiers or sailors for the day's duties.

revel /ˈrɛvəl/ *v.*, **-elled**, **-elling**, *n.* – *v.i.* **1.** to take great pleasure or delight (fol. by *in*). – *n.* **2.** (*often pl.*) an occasion of merrymaking or noisy festivity with dancing, etc. – **revelry**, *n.*

revenge /rəˈvɛndʒ/ *n.*, *v.*, **-venged**, **-venging**. – *n.* **1.** retaliation for injuries or wrongs; vengeance. – *v.t.* **2.** to take vengeance on behalf of (a person, etc.) or for (a wrong, etc.).

revenue /ˈrɛvənju/ *n.* **1.** the income of a government from taxation, excise duties, customs, or other sources, appropriated to the payment of the public expenses. **2.** the

return or yield from any kind of property; income. **3.** an amount of money regularly coming in.

reverberate /rə'vɜbəreɪt/ *v.i.*, **-rated**, **-rating**. to re-echo or resound.

revere /rə'vɪə/ *v.t.*, **-vered**, **-vering**. to regard with respect tinged with awe; venerate. – **reverence**, *n.* – **reverent**, *adj.*

reverend /'rɛvrənd, 'rɛvərənd/ *adj.* **1.** (*often cap.*) an epithet of respect for a member of the clergy. – *n.* **2.** *Colloquial* a member of the clergy.

reverie /'rɛvəri/ *n.* a state of dreamy meditation or fanciful musing.

reverse /rə'vɜs/ *adj.*, *n.*, *v.*, **-versed**, **-versing**. – *adj.* **1.** opposite or contrary in position, direction, order, or character. **2.** producing a rearward motion. – *n.* **3.** the opposite or contrary of something. **4.** the back or rear of anything. **5.** an adverse change of fortune. **6.** *Motor Vehicles* reverse gear. – *v.t.* **7.** to turn inside out or upside down. **8.** to turn in the opposite direction; send on the opposite course. **9.** to revoke or annul (a decree, judgment, etc.). **10.** to drive (a motor vehicle) backwards. – *v.i.* **11.** to turn or move in the opposite or contrary direction.

reverse gazump *v.t.* (of a buyer before entering upon a binding contract) to force (a vendor) to accept a price lower than that previously agreed upon.

reversionary bonus /rə'vɜʒənəri, -ʒənri/ *n.* a periodic free addition to the sum insured under a life insurance policy, made from surplus earned on the insurer's investments. See **terminal bonus**.

revert /rə'vɜt/ *v.i.* **1.** to return to a former habit, practice, belief, condition, etc. **2.** *Law* to go back or return to the former owner or his or her heirs. – **reversion**, *n.*

review /rə'vju/ *n.* **1.** a critical article or report on some literary work, film, play, opera, etc. **2.** a periodical publication containing articles on current events or affairs, books, art, etc. **3.** contemplation or consideration of past events, circumstances, or facts. **4.** a general survey of something, especially in words. – *v.t.* **5.** to view, look at, or look over again. **6.** to look back upon; view retrospectively. **7.** to present a survey of in speech or writing. **8.** to discuss (a book, etc.) in a critical review.

revile /rə'vaɪl/ *v.t.*, **-viled**, **-viling**. to address, or speak of, abusively.

revise /rə'vaɪz/ *v.t.*, **-vised**, **-vising**. **1.** to amend or alter. **2.** to go over (a subject, book, etc.) again or study in order to fix it in the memory, as before an examination. – **revision**, *n.*

revitalise = revitalize /ri'vaɪtəlaɪz/ *v.t.* to introduce new vigour and strength into. – **revitalisation**, *n.*

revive /rə'vaɪv/ *v.t.*, **-vived**, **-viving**. **1.** to bring back into notice, use, or currency. **2.** to restore to life or consciousness. – **revival**, *n.*

revocable /'rɛvəkəbəl/ *adj.* that may be revoked.

revoke /rə'voʊk/ *v.t.*, **-voked**, **-voking**. to take back or withdraw; annul, cancel, or reverse. – **revocation**, *n.*

revolt /rə'voʊlt/ *v.i.* **1.** to break away from or rise against constituted authority; rebel. **2.** to turn away in mental rebellion, utter disgust, or abhorrence. – *v.t.* **3.** to affect with disgust or abhorrence. – *n.* **4.** an insurrection or rebellion. **5.** the state of those revolting.

revolution /rɛvə'luʃən/ *n.* **1.** a complete overthrow of an established government or political system. **2.** procedure or course as if in a circuit. **3.** a single turn of this kind.

revolutionary /rɛvə'luʃənəri, -ʃənri/ *adj.*, *n.*, *pl.* **-ries**. – *adj.* **1.** subversive to established procedure, principles, etc. – *n.* **2.** someone who advocates or takes part in a revolution.

revolutionise = revolutionize /rɛvə'luʃənaɪz/ *v.t.*, **-nised**, **-nising**. to bring about a revolution in; effect a radical change in.

revolve /rə'vɒlv/ *v.i.*, **-volved**, **-volving**. **1.** to turn round or rotate, as on an axis. **2.** to move in a circular or curving course, or orbit.

revolver /rə'vɒlvə/ *n.* a pistol which can be fired repeatedly without reloading.

revolving fund *n.* any loan fund intended to be maintained by the repayment of past loans.

revue /rə'vju/ *n.* any group of skits, dances, and songs.

revulsion /rə'vʌlʃən/ *n.* **1.** a sudden and violent change of feeling or reaction in sentiment. **2.** a violent dislike or aversion for something.

reward /rə'wɔd/ *n.* something given or received in return or recompense for service, merit, hardship, etc.

rewarding /rə'wɔdɪŋ/ *adj.* giving satisfaction that the effort made was worth while.

rezone /ri'zoʊn/ *v.t.* to vary the zoning classification of (land, property, etc.).

-rhagia a word element meaning 'bursting forth'.

rhapsody /'ræpsədi/ *n.*, *pl.* **-dies**. an exalted or exaggerated expression of feeling or enthusiasm.

rheo- a word element meaning 'something flowing', 'a stream', 'current'.

rhetoric /'rɛtərɪk/ *n.* **1.** (in prose or verse) the use of exaggeration or display, in an unfavourable sense. **2.** (originally) the art of oratory.

rhetorical question *n.* a question designed to produce an effect and not to draw an answer.

rheumatism /'rumətɪzəm/ *n. Pathology* a disease commonly affecting the joints. – **rheumatic**, *adj.*

rhinestone /'raɪnstoʊn/ *n.* an artificial gem made of paste.

rhino /'raɪnoʊ/ *n.*, *pl.* **-nos**. → **rhinoceros**.

rhino- a word element meaning 'nose'. Also, **rhin-**.

rhinoceros /raɪ'nɒsərəs, raɪ'nɒsrəs/ *n.*, *pl.* **-roses**, (*esp. collectively*) **-ros**. any of various large mammals with one or two upright horns on the snout.

rhinoplasty /'raɪnoʊ,plæsti/ *n.* plastic surgery of the nose.

rhizo- a word element meaning 'root'.

rhizome /'raɪzoʊm/ *n.* a rootlike subterranean stem.

rhodium /ˈroʊdiəm/ *n.* a silvery-white metallic element of the platinum family. *Symbol*: Rh

rhodo- a word element meaning 'rose'. Also, **rhod-**.

rhododendron /roʊdəˈdɛndrən/ *n.* any of several evergreen and deciduous shrubs and trees much cultivated for ornament.

-rhoea a word element meaning 'flow', 'discharge'.

rhombus /ˈrɒmbəs/ *n., pl.* **-buses**, **-bi** /-baɪ/. an oblique-angled equilateral parallelogram.

rhubarb /ˈrubab/ *n.* **1.** a garden plant with edible leafstalks. **2.** the word supposedly spoken by actors to simulate noisy conversation in the background.

rhyme /raɪm/ *n., v.,* **rhymed**, **rhyming**. – *n.* **1.** agreement in the terminal sounds of lines of verse, or of words. **2.** a word agreeing with another in terminal sound. **3.** verse or poetry having correspondence in the terminal sounds of the line. **4. rhyme or reason,** logic; explanation; meaning. – *v.i.* **5.** to form a rhyme, as one word or line with another.

rhythm /ˈrɪðəm/ *n.* **1.** movement or procedure with uniform recurrence of a beat, accent, or the like. **2.** procedure marked by the regular recurrence of particular elements, phases, etc. – **rhythmic**, **rhythmical**, *adj.*

rib[1] /rɪb/ *n., v.,* **ribbed**, **ribbing**. – *n.* **1.** one of a series of long, slender, curved bones, occurring in pairs, more or less enclosing the thoracic cavity. **2.** some thing or part resembling a rib in form, position, or use, as a supporting or strengthening part. – *v.t.* **3.** to furnish or strengthen with ribs.

rib[2] /rɪb/ *v.t.,* **ribbed**, **ribbing**. *Colloquial* to tease; ridicule; make fun of.

ribald /ˈrɪbəld, ˈraɪ-/ *adj.* coarsely mocking or abusive; wantonly irreverent. – **ribaldry**, *n.*

ribbon /ˈrɪbən/ *n.* **1.** a woven strip or band of fine material, used for ornament, tying, etc. **2.** anything resembling or suggesting a ribbon or woven band. **3.** a band of material charged with ink, or supplying ink, for the impression in a typewriter.

riboflavin /raɪboʊˈfleɪvən/ *n.* vitamin B_2, one of the vitamins in the vitamin B complex.

rice /raɪs/ *n.* the starchy seeds or grain of a species of grass, an important food.

rice paper *n.* a thin, edible paper made from the straw of rice.

rich /rɪtʃ/ *adj.* **1.** abundantly supplied with resources, means, or funds. **2.** abounding in natural resources. **3.** abounding (fol. by *in* or *with*). **4.** of great value or worth; valuable. **5.** (of wine, gravy, etc.) strong and full flavoured. **6.** (of colour) deep, strong, or vivid. **7.** (of sound, the voice, etc.) full and mellow in tone. **8.** *Colloquial* ridiculous, absurd, or preposterous. – *n.* **9.** rich people collectively (usually preceded by *the*).

riches /ˈrɪtʃəz/ *pl. n.* wealth.

rickets /ˈrɪkəts/ *n. Pathology* a childhood disease, caused by malnutrition and often resulting in deformities.

rickety /ˈrɪkəti/ *adj.* liable to fall or collapse; shaky.

rickshaw /ˈrɪkʃɔ/ *n.* a small two-wheeled hooded vehicle drawn by one or more people.

ricochet /ˈrɪkəʃeɪ/ *n.* the motion of an object or projectile which rebounds one or more times from the surface or surfaces it strikes.

ricotta /rəˈkɒtə/ *n.* a soft cottage cheese with a fresh bland flavour.

rid /rɪd/ *v.,* **rid** *or* **ridded**, **ridding**, *adj.* – *v.t.* **1.** to clear, disencumber, or free of something objectionable (fol. by *of*). – *adj.* **2. get rid of,** to get free, or relieved of.

riddance /ˈrɪdns/ *n.* a relieving or deliverance from something.

ridden /ˈrɪdn/ *v.* past participle of **ride**.

riddle[1] /ˈrɪdl/ *n.* **1.** a question or statement so framed as to exercise one's ingenuity in answering it or discovering its meaning. **2.** a puzzling question, problem, or matter.

riddle[2] /ˈrɪdl/ *v.t.,* **-dled**, **-dling**. to pierce with many holes.

ride /raɪd/ *v.,* **rode**, **ridden**, **riding**, *n.* – *v.i.* **1.** to sit on and manage a horse or other animal in motion. **2.** to be carried on something as if on horseback. **3.** to be borne along on or in a vehicle or any kind of conveyance. **4.** to turn or rest on something. **5.** to work or move (*up*) from the proper position, as a skirt, or the like. **6.** to have a specified character for riding purposes. – *v.t.* **7.** to sit on and manage (a horse or other animal, or a bicycle or the like) so as to be carried along. **8.** to ride over, along or through (a road, boundary, region, etc.). **9. ride out,** to sustain or endure successfully. – *n.* **10.** a journey or excursion on a horse, etc., or on or in a vehicle.

rider /ˈraɪdə/ *n.* **1.** someone who rides. **2.** an addition or amendment to a document, etc.

ridge /rɪdʒ/ *n., v.,* **ridged**, **ridging**. – *n.* **1.** a long, narrow elevation of land, or a chain of hills or mountains. **2.** any raised narrow strip, as on cloth, etc. **3.** the horizontal line in which the tops of the rafters of a roof meet. – *v.t.* **4.** to provide with or form into a ridge or ridges.

ridicule /ˈrɪdəkjul/ *n., v.,* **-culed**, **-culing**. – *n.* **1.** words or actions intended to excite contemptuous laughter at a person or thing; derision. – *v.t.* **2.** to deride; make fun of.

ridiculous /rəˈdɪkjələs/ *adj.* absurd, preposterous, or laughable.

Riesling /ˈrizlɪŋ, ˈrislɪŋ/ *n.* (*often lower case*) a dry white wine.

rife /raɪf/ *adj.* of common or frequent occurrence; prevalent.

riffle /ˈrɪfəl/ *v.i.,* **-fled**, **-fling**. to flutter and shift, as pages.

riffraff /ˈrɪfræf/ *n.* worthless or low persons.

rifle[1] /ˈraɪfəl/ *n.* a shoulder firearm.

rifle[2] /ˈraɪfəl/ *v.t.,* **-fled**, **-fling**. to ransack and rob (a place, receptacle, etc.).

rift /rɪft/ *n.* a fissure; a cleft; a chink.

rig /rɪg/ *v.,* **rigged**, **rigging**, *n.* – *v.t.* **1.** to furnish or provide with equipment, etc.; fit (usually fol. by *out* or *up*). **2.** to prepare or put together, especially as a makeshift (often fol. by *up*). **3.** to manipulate fraudulently. – *n.* **4.** apparatus for some purpose; equipment; outfit. **5.** Also, **rig-out**. *Colloquial* costume or dress, especially when odd or conspicuous.

rigging /ˈrɪgɪŋ/ *n.* the ropes, chains, etc., employed to support and work the masts, yards, sails, etc., on a ship.

right /raɪt/ *adj.* **1.** in accordance with what is just or good. **2.** in conformity with fact, reason, or some standard or principle; correct. **3.** in good health or spirits, as persons. **4.** in a satisfactory state; in good order. **5.** most convenient, desirable, or favourable. **6.** belonging or relating to the side of a person or thing which is turned towards the east when the face is towards the north (opposed to *left*). **7.** belonging or relating to the political right. **8.** *Geometry* having the axis perpendicular to the base. **9.** *Colloquial* unquestionable; unmistakable; true. – *n.* **10.** a just claim or title, whether legal, prescriptive, or moral. **11.** that which is due to anyone by just claim. **12.** *Finance* **a.** the privilege, usually pre-emptive, which accrues to the owners of the stock of a company to subscribe for additional stock or shares at an advantageous price. **b.** (*often pl.*) a privilege of subscribing for a stock or bond. **13.** that which is ethically good and proper and in conformity with the moral law. **14.** that which accords with fact, reason, or propriety. **15.** the right side or what is on the right side. **16.** a body of persons, political party, etc., holding conservative views. – *adv.* **17.** quite or completely. **18.** immediately. **19.** exactly, precisely, or just. **20.** correctly or accurately. **21.** properly or fittingly. **22.** advantageously, favourably, or well. **23.** towards the right hand; to the right. **24.** very (used in certain titles). – *v.t.* **25.** to bring or restore to an upright or the proper position. **26.** to set in order or put right. **27.** to redress (wrong, etc.). – *v.i.* **28.** to resume an upright or the proper position.

right angle *n.* an angle of 90°.

righteous /ˈraɪtʃəs/ *adj.* **1.** characterised by uprightness or morality. **2.** in accordance with right; upright or virtuous.

right-handed /raɪt-ˈhændəd/ *adj.* preferring to use the right hand.

right of way *n.* **1.** the legal or customary right of a person, motor car or vessel to proceed ahead of another. **2.** a right of passage, as over another's land.

rights issue *n.* an issue of stocks or shares offered to members of a company at a preferential rate.

right wing *n.* the members of a conservative or reactionary political party or group. – **right-wing**, *adj.* – **right-winger**, *n.*

rigid /ˈrɪdʒəd/ *adj.* stiff or unyielding; not pliant or flexible; hard.

rigmarole /ˈrɪgməroʊl/ *n.* a long and complicated process.

rigor mortis /rɪgə ˈmɔtəs/ *n.* the stiffening of the body after death.

rigour = rigor /ˈrɪgə/ *n.* **1.** strictness, severity, or harshness, as in dealing with persons. **2.** severity of life; hardship. – **rigorous**, *adj.*

rile /raɪl/ *v.t.*, **riled**, **riling**. *Colloquial* to irritate or vex.

rim /rɪm/ *n.*, *v.*, **rimmed**, **rimming**. – *n.* **1.** the outer edge, border, or margin, especially of a circular object. – *v.t.* **2.** to furnish with a rim, border, or margin.

rime /raɪm/ *n.* a rough, white icy covering deposited on trees, etc.

rind /raɪnd/ *n.* a thick and firm coat or covering, as of fruits, cheeses, etc.

ring[1] /rɪŋ/ *n.*, *v.*, **ringed**, **ringing**. – *n.* **1.** a circular band of metal or other material, especially one for wearing on the finger. **2.** anything having the form of a circular band. **3.** a circular course. **4.** an enclosed circular or other area, as one in which some sport or exhibition takes place. **5.** a group of persons cooperating for selfish or illegal purposes. – *v.t.* **6.** to surround with a ring; encircle. **7.** to form into a ring. – *v.i.* **8.** to form a ring or rings. **9.** to move in a ring or a constantly curving course.

ring[2] /rɪŋ/ *v.*, **rang**, **rung**, **ringing**, *n.* – *v.i.* **1.** to give forth a clear, resonant sound when set in sudden vibration by a blow or otherwise, as a bell, glass, etc. **2.** to seem (true, false, etc.) in the effect produced on the mind. **3.** to cause a bell or bells to sound, especially as a summons. **4.** to be filled with sound; re-echo with sound, as a place. – *v.t.* **5.** to cause to ring. **6.** to proclaim, usher in or out, summon, signal, etc., by or as by the sound of a bell. **7.** to telephone. **8. ring a bell,** to arouse a memory; sound familiar. **9. ring off,** to end a telephone conversation. **10. ring the changes,** to vary the manner of performing an action. **11. ring up, a.** to telephone. **b.** to record (the cost of an item) on a cash register. – *n.* **12.** a resonant sound or note. **13.** a telephone call. **14.** a characteristic or inherent quality.

ringbark /ˈrɪŋbak/ *v.t.* to cut away the bark in a ring around a tree trunk or branch, in order to kill the tree or the affected part.

ringer[1] /ˈrɪŋə/ *n.* a station hand, especially a stockman or drover.

ringer[2] /ˈrɪŋə/ *n.* *Colloquial* **1.** an athlete, horse, etc., entered in a competition under false representations as to identity or ability. **2.** a person or thing that closely resembles another.

ringer[3] /ˈrɪŋə/ *n.* the fastest shearer of a group.

ring-in /ˈrɪŋ-ɪn/ *n.* *Colloquial* **1.** someone who or that which does not belong in a group or set. **2.** a person or thing substituted for another at the last moment, as a horse fraudulently substituted for another in a race.

ringlet /ˈrɪŋlət/ *n.* a curled lock of hair.

ringmaster /ˈrɪŋmastə/ *n.* one in charge of the performances in the ring of a circus.

ringside /ˈrɪŋsaɪd/ *n.* any place providing a close view.

ringworm /ˈrɪŋwɜm/ *n.* any of certain contagious skin diseases.

rink /rɪŋk/ *n.* **1.** a sheet of ice for skating. **2.** a smooth floor for roller-skating.

rinse /rɪns/ *v.*, **rinsed**, **rinsing**, *n.* – *v.t.* **1.** to put through clean water, as a final stage in cleansing. – *n.* **2.** an act or instance of rinsing. **3.** any liquid preparation used for impermanently tinting the hair.

riot /ˈraɪət/ *n.* **1.** any disturbance of the peace by an assembly of persons. **2.** an unbridled outbreak, as of emotions, passions, etc. **3.** a brilliant display. **4.** *Colloquial* someone who or that which causes great amusement, enthusiasm, etc. **5. run riot,** to act without control or restraint. – *v.i.* **6.** to take part in a riot or disorderly public outbreak. – **riotous**, *adj.*

rip[1] /rɪp/ *v.*, **ripped**, **ripping**, *n.* – *v.t.* **1.** to cut or tear apart or off in a rough or vigorous manner. – *v.i.* **2.** *Colloquial* to move along with violence or great speed. – *n.* **3.** a rent made by ripping; a tear.

rip[2] /rɪp/ *n.* a fast current, especially one at a beach, which can take swimmers out to sea.

ripcord /'rɪpkɔd/ *n.* a cord or ring which opens a parachute during a descent.

ripe /raɪp/ *adj.*, **riper**, **ripest**. complete in natural growth or development.

rip-off /'rɪp-ɒf/ *n.* an excessive charge or exorbitant price; swindle. – **rip off**, *v.*

riposte /rə'pɒst/ *n.* a quick, sharp return in speech or action. Also, **ripost**.

ripper /'rɪpə/ *n.* *Colloquial* something or someone exciting extreme admiration.

ripping /'rɪpɪŋ/ *adj.* *Colloquial* excellent, splendid, or fine.

ripple /'rɪpəl/ *v.i.*, **-pled**, **-pling**. to form small waves or undulations on the surface, as water.

rise /raɪz/ *v.*, **rose**, **risen**, **rising**, *n.* – *v.i.* **1.** to get up from a lying, sitting, or kneeling posture; assume a standing position. **2.** to get up from bed. **3.** to become active in opposition or resistance; revolt or rebel. **4.** to spring up or grow. **5.** to move from a lower to a higher position; move upwards; ascend. **6.** to come above the horizon, as a heavenly body. **7.** to extend directly upwards. **8.** to attain higher rank, importance, etc. **9.** to prove oneself equal to a demand, emergency, etc. **10.** to become animated or cheerful, as the spirits. **11.** to swell or puff up, as dough from the action of yeast. **12.** to increase in amount, as prices, etc. **13.** to increase in price or value, as commodities. **14.** to increase in degree, intensity, or force, as colour, fever, etc. **15.** to become louder or of higher pitch, as the voice. **16.** to adjourn, or close a session, as a deliberative body or court. – *v.t.* **17.** to cause to rise. – *n.* **18.** the act of rising; upward movement or ascent. **19.** appearance above the horizon, as of the sun or moon. **20.** elevation or advance in rank, position, fortune, etc. **21.** an increase in amount, as of wages, salary, etc. **22.** an increase in degree or intensity, as of temperature. **23.** origin, source, or beginning. **24.** extension upwards. **25.** upward slope, as of ground or a road. **26.** a piece of rising or high ground. **27. get** (or **take**) **a rise out of,** to provoke to anger, annoyance, etc., by banter, mockery, deception, etc.

risk /rɪsk/ *n.* **1.** a hazard or dangerous chance. **2.** *Insurance* **a.** the hazard or chance of loss. **b.** the amount which the insurance company may lose. **c.** the type of loss, as life, fire, theft, etc., against which insurance policies are drawn. – *v.t.* **3.** to expose to the chance of injury or loss, or hazard. **4.** to venture upon; take or run the risk of.

risk capital *n.* capital invested or available for investment in an enterprise, especially a speculative one.

risqué /'rɪskeɪ, rɪs'keɪ/ *adj.* daringly close to indelicacy or impropriety.

rissole /'rɪsoʊl/ *n.* a small fried ball, roll, or cake of minced meat or fish.

rite /raɪt/ *n.* a formal or ceremonial act or procedure prescribed or customary in religious or other solemn use.

ritual /'rɪtʃuəl/ *n.* **1.** an established or prescribed procedure, code, etc., for a religious or other rite. **2.** any solemn or customary action, code of behaviour, etc., regulating social conduct.

rival /'raɪvəl/ *n.*, *adj.*, *v.*, **-valled**, **-valling**. – *n.* **1.** someone who is in pursuit of the same object as another, or strives to equal or outdo another; a competitor. – *adj.* **2.** being a rival. – *v.t.* **3.** to strive to equal or outdo.

river /'rɪvə/ *n.* **1.** a considerable natural stream of water flowing in a definite course. **2.** any abundant stream or copious flow.

rivet /'rɪvət/ *n.* **1.** a metal pin or bolt. – *v.t.* **2.** to fasten or fix firmly.

rivulet /'rɪvjələt/ *n.* a small stream.

roach[1] /roʊtʃ/ *n.* → **cockroach**.

roach[2] /roʊtʃ/ *n.* *Colloquial* the butt of a cigarette or joint.

road /roʊd/ *n.* **1.** a way, usually open to the public for the passage of vehicles, persons, and animals. **2.** a way or course.

roadhog /'roʊdhɒg/ *n.* a motorist who drives without consideration for other road users.

roadhouse /'roʊdhaʊs/ *n.* an inn, hotel, restaurant, etc., on a main road.

roadie /'roʊdi/ *n.* *Colloquial* a person associated with a pop group who arranges road transportation, sets up equipment, etc.

road rage *n.* uncontrollable violent behaviour by a motorist, usually directed towards another motorist, resulting from the tensions and frustrations of driving.

roadrunner /'roʊdrʌnə/ *n.* a terrestrial cuckoo of the south western US.

road toll *n.* the tally of traffic accident deaths.

road train *n.* a group of articulated motor vehicles, used for transportation, especially of cattle.

roadway /'roʊdweɪ/ *n.* a way used as a road; a road.

roam /roʊm/ *v.i.* to walk, go, or travel about without fixed purpose or direction.

roan /roʊn/ *adj.* (chiefly of horses) brown sprinkled with grey or white.

roar /rɔ/ *v.i.* **1.** to utter a loud, deep sound, especially of excitement, distress, or anger. **2.** to laugh loudly or boisterously. **3.** to make a loud noise or din, as thunder, cannon, waves, wind, etc. – *v.t.* **4.** to utter or express in a roar. – *n.* **5.** the sound of roaring.

roast /roʊst/ *v.t.* **1.** to bake (meat or other food) by dry heat, as in an oven. **2.** to brown by exposure to heat, as coffee. **3.** *Colloquial* to criticise, rebuke or ridicule severely. – *n.* **4.** a piece of roasted meat; roasted meat.

rob /rɒb/ *v.t.*, **robbed**, **robbing**. to deprive of something by unlawful force or threat of violence; steal from.

robe[1] /roʊb/ *n.* any long, loose garment.

robe[2] /roʊb/ *n.* → **wardrobe**..

robin /'rɒbən/ *n.* **1.** any of various small Australian birds. **2.** any of several small birds of Europe and North America having a red or reddish breast.

robot /'roʊbɒt/ *n.* a mechanical self-controlling apparatus designed to carry out a specific task, normally performed by a human.

robust /'roʊbʌst, rə'bʌst/ *adj.* **1.** strong and healthy, hardy, or vigorous. **2.** suited to or requiring bodily strength or endurance.

rock[1] /rɒk/ **1.** *Geology* mineral matter of various composition, assembled in masses or considerable quantities in nature. **2.** stone in the mass. **3.** something resembling or suggesting a rock. **4.** a firm foundation or support. **5.** a stone of any size. **6. on the rocks, a.** *Colloquial* into or in a state of disaster or ruin. **b.** (of drinks) with ice-cubes.

rock[2] /rɒk/ *v.i.* **1.** to move or sway to and fro or from side to side. – *v.t.* **2.** to cause to rock. – *n.* **3.** → **rock music**. **4.** → **rock-and-roll**.

rock-and-roll /rɒk-ən-'roʊl/ *n.* a form of pop music of the 1950s which has a twelve bar blues form, and a heavily accented rhythm. Also, **rock**, **rock'n'roll**, **rock-'n'-roll**.

rock bottom *n.* the lowest level, especially of fortune.

rocker /'rɒkə/ *n.* **1.** one of the curved pieces on which a cradle or a rocking chair rocks. **2.** any of various devices that operate with a rocking motion. **3. off one's rocker,** *Colloquial* crazy; mad; demented.

rockery /'rɒkəri/ *n., pl.* **-ries**. a garden, or part of a garden, featuring rocks and plants which favour a rocky soil and are suited to dry, sunny conditions.

rocket /'rɒkət/ *n.* **1.** *Aeronautics* a structure propelled by an emission of heated gas from the rear. – *v.i.* **2.** to move like a rocket.

rocking chair *n.* a chair mounted on rockers, or on springs, so as to permit a rocking back and forth.

rocking horse *n.* a toy horse, mounted on rockers.

rockmelon /'rɒkmɛlən/ *n.* a type of melon with orange-coloured flesh; cantaloupe.

rock music *n.* contemporary music which is derived basically from the blues, but which has incorporated aspects of country and western, jazz, gospel music and bluegrass.

rock-salt /'rɒk-sɒlt/ *n.* a common salt (sodium chloride), occurring in extensive, irregular beds in rocklike masses.

rococo /rə'koʊkoʊ/ *adj.* tastelessly or clumsily florid.

rod /rɒd/ *n.* **1.** a stick, wand, staff, shaft, or the like, of wood, metal, or other material. **2.** a pole used in angling or fishing. **3.** a stick used as an instrument of punishment. **4.** a wand or staff carried as a symbol of office, authority, power, etc.

rode /roʊd/ *v.* past tense of **ride**.

rodent /'roʊdnt/ *n.* one of the order of gnawing or nibbling mammals, that includes the mice, squirrels, beavers, etc.

rodeo /roʊ'deɪoʊ, 'roʊdioʊ/ *n., pl.* **-deos**. an exhibition of the skills of cowboys.

roe /roʊ/ *n.* the mass of eggs, or spawn, of the female fish.

roger /'rɒdʒə/ *interj.* (an expression of agreement, comprehension, etc.).

rogue /roʊg/ *n.* **1.** a dishonest person. **2.** a playfully mischievous person; rascal; scamp. **3.** an elephant or other animal of savage disposition and solitary life.

roister /'rɔɪstə/ *v.i.* to act in a swaggering, boisterous, or uproarious manner.

role /roʊl/ *n.* **1.** the part or character which an actor presents in a play. **2.** proper or customary function.

roll /roʊl/ *v.i.* **1.** to move along a surface by turning over and over, as a ball or a wheel. **2.** to move or be moved on wheels, as a vehicle or its occupants (often fol. by *along*). **3.** to extend in undulations, as land. **4.** to continue with or have a deep, prolonged sound, as thunder, etc. **5.** to turn over, or over and over, as a person or animal lying down. **6.** to sway or rock from side to side, as a ship (opposed to *pitch*). **7.** to form into a roll, or curl up from itself. **8.** to spread out from being rolled up; unroll (fol. by *out*, etc.). **9.** to spread out as under a roller. – *v.t.* **10.** to cause to roll. **11.** to cause to turn round in different directions, as the eyes. **12.** to make by forming a roll. **13.** to wrap, enfold, or envelop, as in some covering. **14.** to operate upon so as to spread out, level, compact, or the like, as with a roller, rolling pin, etc. – *n.* **15.** a list, register, or catalogue. **16.** anything rolled up in cylindrical form. **17.** a small cake of bread. **18.** a deep, prolonged sound, as of thunder, etc. **19.** the continuous sound of a drum rapidly beaten. **20.** a single throw of dice. **21.** *Colloquial* a wad of paper currency.

rolled gold *n.* metal covered with a thin coating of gold.

roller /'roʊlə/ *n.* **1.** a cylinder, wheel, or the like, upon which something is rolled along. **2.** a cylinder of plastic, wire, etc., around which hair is rolled to set it. **3.** a cylindrical body for rolling over something to be spread out, levelled, crushed, compacted, impressed, linked, etc. **4.** any of various other revolving cylindrical bodies.

roller-skate /'roʊlə-skeɪt/ *n., v.,* **-skated, -skating**. – *n.* **1.** a form of skate running on small wheels or rollers. – *v.i.* **2.** to move on roller-skates.

rollicking /'rɒlɪkɪŋ/ *adj.* swaggering and jolly.

rolling strike *n.* industrial action by employees against their employer in which groups of employees go on strike consecutively.

rollover /'roʊloʊvə/ *adj.* having to do with the investment of a superannuation payout with a government-approved institution that allows the deferral of lump sum tax. Also, **roll-over**.

rollover provision *n.* an agreement made between a borrower and a lender in which each guarantees to renew a loan, when it matures, at a rate of interest based on the ruling rate of interest at the time of renewal.

roly-poly /ˌroʊli-'poʊli/ *adj., n., pl.* **-lies**. – *adj.* **1.** plump and podgy. – *n.* **2.** a type of pudding.

ROM /rɒm/ *n.* *Computers* read-only memory;

a computer storage device which holds data that can be read, but not altered, by program instructions.

romance /rə'mæns, 'roʊmæns/ *n.*, /rə'mæns/ *v.*, **-manced**, **-mancing**. – *n.* **1.** a tale depicting heroic or marvellous achievements. **2.** a made-up story; fanciful or extravagant invention or exaggeration. **3.** romantic character or quality. **4.** a romantic affair or experience; a love affair. – *v.i.* **5.** to think or talk romantically.

Roman numerals *pl. n.* the numerals in the ancient Roman system of notation, still used for certain limited purposes. The common basic symbols are I(=1), V(=5), X(=10), L(=50), C(=100), D(=500), and M(=1000). Examples: XLVII(=47), CXVI(=116), MCXX(=1120), MCMXIV (=1914). See Appendix.

romantic /rə'mæntɪk/ *adj.* **1.** of, relating to, or of the nature of romance. **2.** proper to romance rather than to real or practical life. **3.** displaying or expressing love, emotion, strong affection, etc. **4.** imaginary, fictitious, or fabulous. – *n.* **5.** a romantic person.

romanticise = romanticize /rə'mæntəsaɪz/ *v.*, **-cised**, **-cising**. – *v.t.* **1.** to invest with a romantic character. – *v.i.* **2.** to have romantic ideas.

romp /rɒmp/ *v.i.* **1.** to play or frolic in a lively or boisterous manner. **2. romp home** (or **in**), to win easily.

rompers /'rɒmpəz/ *pl. n.* a one-piece loose outer garment for a baby.

roneo /'roʊnioʊ/ *v.t.* to make a copy or copies of by cutting a stencil and duplicating it on a fluid-containing copier.

roo /ru/ *n. Colloquial* a kangaroo.

roof /ruf/ *n.*, *pl.* **roofs** /rufs, ruvz/ **1.** the external upper covering of a house or other building. **2.** something which in form or position resembles the roof of a house.

rook[1] /rʊk/ *n.* **1.** a black European crow. – *v.t.* **2.** to cheat; fleece; swindle.

rook[2] /rʊk/ *n.* a chess piece.

rookery /'rʊkəri/ *n.*, *pl.* **-ries**. **1.** a colony of rooks. **2.** any instance of cheating, sharp practice, exorbitant prices, etc.

rookie /'rʊki/ *n. Colloquial* a raw recruit.

room /rum/ *n.* **1.** a portion of space within a building or other structure, separated by walls or partitions from other parts. **2.** space, or extent of space, occupied by or available for something. **3.** opportunity or scope for or to do something. – *v.i.* **4.** to occupy a room or rooms; to share a room; lodge.

roomy /'rumi/ *adj.*, **-mier**, **-miest**. affording ample room; spacious; large.

roost /rust/ *n.* **1.** a perch upon which domestic fowls rest at night. – *v.i.* **2.** to settle or stay, especially for the night.

rooster /'rustə/ *n.* a domestic cock.

root[1] /rut/ *n.* **1.** a part of the body of a plant which grows downwards into the soil, fixing the plant and absorbing nutriment and moisture. **2.** the embedded or basal portion of a hair, tooth, nail, etc. **3.** the fundamental or essential part. **4.** the base or point of origin of something. **5.** (*pl.*) a person's real home and environment. **6.** *Mathematics* a quantity which, when multiplied by itself a certain number of times, produces a given quantity. – *v.i.* **7.** to send out roots and begin to grow. **8.** to become fixed or established. – *v.t.* **9.** to fix by, or as if by, roots. **10.** to pull, tear, or dig (fol. by *up*, *out*, etc.) by the roots. **11.** *Colloquial* to break; ruin. **12.** *Colloquial* to have sexual intercourse with.

root[2] /rut/ *v.i.* **1.** to poke, pry, or search, as if to find something (fol. by *around*). – *v.t.* **2.** to unearth; bring to light (fol. by *up*, etc.).

rope /roʊp/ *n.*, *v.*, **roped**, **roping**. – *n.* **1.** a strong, thick line or cord. **2.** death by hanging as a punishment. **3.** (*pl.*) methods; procedure; operations of a business, etc. – *v.t.* **4.** to tie, bind, or fasten with a rope. **5.** *Colloquial* to draw, entice, or inveigle into something (fol. by *in*).

ropeable = ropable /'roʊpəbəl/ *adj. Colloquial* angry; bad-tempered.

rort /rɔt/ *Colloquial* – *n.* **1.** an incident or series of incidents involving reprehensible or suspect behaviour, especially by officials or politicians. **2.** a wild party. – *v.t.* **3.** to gain control over (an organisation, as a branch of a political party) especially by falsifying records. **4.** to take wrongful advantage of; abuse: *to rort the system.*

rosary /'roʊzəri/ *n.*, *pl.* **-ries**. a string of beads used for counting prayers in reciting them.

rose[1] /roʊz/ *n.* **1.** any of various showy-flowered shrubs. **2.** the flower of any such shrubs. **3.** an ornament shaped like or suggesting a rose. **4.** the traditional reddish colour of the rose. **5.** a perforated cap or plate at the end of a water pipe or the spout of a watering can, etc., to break a flow of water into a spray.

rose[2] /roʊz/ *v.* past tense of **rise**.

rosé /roʊ'zeɪ/ *n.* a light wine of a translucent pale red colour.

rosella /roʊ'zɛlə/ *n.* any of a number of brilliantly coloured parrots.

rosemary /'roʊzməri/ *n.*, *pl.* **-maries**. an evergreen shrub used as a herb in cookery.

rosette /roʊ'zɛt/ *n.* any arrangement, part, object, or formation more or less resembling a rose.

rosin /'rɒzən/ *n.* a hard, brittle resin used in making varnish, for rubbing on violin bows, etc.

roster /'rɒstə/ *n.* a list of persons or groups with their turns or periods of duty.

rostrum /'rɒstrəm/ *n.*, *pl.* **-trums**, **-tra** /-trə/. any platform, stage, or the like, for public speaking.

rosy /'roʊzi/ *adj.*, **rosier**, **rosiest**. **1.** pink or pinkish red. **2.** (of persons, the cheeks, lips, etc.) having a fresh, healthy redness. **3.** bright or promising. **4.** cheerful or optimistic.

rot /rɒt/ *v.*, **rotted**, **rotting**, *n.* – *v.i.* **1.** to undergo decomposition; decay. – *v.t.* **2.** to cause to rot. – *n.* **3.** rotting or rotten matter. **4.** any of various diseases characterised by decomposition. **5.** *Colloquial* nonsense.

rotary /'roʊtəri/ *adj.* **1.** turning round as on an axis, as an object. **2.** having a part or parts that rotate, as a machine.

rotate /roʊ'teɪt/ *v.*, **-tated**, **-tating**. – *v.t.*

1. to cause to turn round like a wheel on its axis. – *v.i.* **2.** to turn round as on an axis. **3.** to proceed in a fixed routine of succession. – **rotation**, *n.*

rote /roʊt/ *n. in the phr.* **by rote,** in a mechanical way without thought of the meaning.

rotisserie /roʊ'tɪsəri/ *n.* a mechanical spit on which meat, poultry, and game can be cooked.

rotten /'rɒtn/ *adj.* **1.** in a state of decomposition or decay; putrid. **2.** *Colloquial* wretchedly bad, unsatisfactory, or unpleasant. **3.** contemptible. **4.** *Colloquial* extremely drunk.

rotund /roʊ'tʌnd/ *adj.* rounded; plump.

rotunda /rə'tʌndə/ *n.* a round building, especially one with a dome.

rouge /ruʒ/ *n., v.,* **rouged**, **rouging**. – *n.* **1.** any of various red cosmetics for colouring the cheeks or lips. – *v.t.* **2.** to colour with rouge.

rough /rʌf/ *adj.* **1.** uneven from projections, irregularities, or breaks of surface; not smooth. **2.** shaggy. **3.** acting with or characterised by violence. **4.** unmannerly or rude. **5.** *Colloquial* severe, hard, or unpleasant. **6.** without refinements, luxuries, or ordinary comforts or conveniences. **7.** requiring exertion or strength rather than intelligence or skill, as work. **8.** unpolished, as language, verse, style, etc. **9.** made or done without any attempt at exactness, completeness, or thoroughness. – *n.* **10.** that which is rough. **11.** the rough, hard, or unpleasant side or part of anything. – *adv.* **12.** in a rough manner; roughly. – *v.t.* **13.** to treat roughly or harshly (often fol. by *up*). **14.** to cut, shape, or sketch roughly (fol. by *in* or *out*).

rough-house /'rʌf-haʊs/ *n. Colloquial* noisy, disorderly behaviour or play.

roughly /'rʌfli/ *adv.* **1.** in a crude, harsh or violent manner. **2.** approximately; about.

rouleau /'ruloʊ/ *n., pl.* **-leaux**, **-leaus** /-loʊz/. a number of coins put up in cylindrical form in a paper wrapping.

roulette /ru'lɛt/ *n.* **1.** a gambling game played at a table. **2.** a small wheel, especially one with sharp teeth, mounted in a handle, for making lines of marks, dots, or perforations.

round /raʊnd/ *adj.* **1.** circular, as a disc. **2.** ring-shaped, as a hoop. **3.** curved like part of a circle, as an outline. **4.** spherical or globular, as a ball. **5.** free from angularity; curved, as parts of the body. **6.** full, complete, or entire. **7.** roughly correct. **8.** considerable in amount. – *n.* **9.** something round. **10.** any complete course, series, or succession. **11.** (*sometimes pl.*) a circuit of any place, series of places, etc., covered in a customary or predetermined way. **12.** a single outburst, as of applause, cheers, etc. **13.** a distribution of drink, etc., to all the members of a company. **14.** a standard cut of beef from the lower part of the butt. **15. a.** (of bread) a slice. **b.** a sandwich. – *adv.* **16.** in a circle, ring, or the like, or so as to surround something. **17.** on all sides, or about, whether circularly or otherwise. **18.** in a circular or rounded course. **19.** throughout, or from beginning to end of, a recurring period of time. **20.** by a circuitous or roundabout course. **21.** with change to another or opposite direction, course, opinion, etc. – *prep.* **22.** so as to encircle, surround, or envelop. **23.** around; about. **24.** in the vicinity of. **25.** so as to make a turn or partial circuit about or to the other side of. **26. round the bend** (or **twist**), *Colloquial* insane. – *v.t.* **27.** to free from angularity or flatness. **28.** to encircle or surround. **29. round up,** to collect (cattle, people, etc.) in a particular place or for a particular purpose. – *v.i.* **30.** to become free from angularity; become plump. **31.** to develop to completeness or perfection. **32. round on** (or **upon**), to attack, usually verbally, with sudden and often unexpected vigour.

roundabout /'raʊndəbaʊt/ *n.* **1.** → **merry-go-round**. **2.** a road junction at which the flow of traffic is facilitated by moving in one direction only round a circular arrangement. – *adj.* **3.** circuitous or indirect.

rounders /'raʊndəz/ *pl. n.* (*construed as sing.*) a game played with bat and ball.

roundly /'raʊndli/ *adv.* vigorously or briskly.

round table *n.* a number of persons assembled for conference or discussion of some subject, and considered as meeting on equal terms.

rouse[1] /raʊz/ *v.t., v.i.,* **roused**, **rousing**. to bring or come out of a state of sleep, unconsciousness, inactivity, fancied security, apathy, depression, etc.

rouse[2] /raʊs/ *v.i.* scold, upbraid (fol. by *on*, *at*).

rouseabout /'raʊsəbaʊt/ *n.* a general hand on a station, in a hotel, etc.

rout[1] /raʊt/ *n.* **1.** a defeat attended with disorderly flight. **2.** a clamour or fuss. – *v.t.* **3.** to defeat utterly.

rout[2] /raʊt/ *v.t.* to turn over or dig up with the snout, as swine.

route /rut/ *n.* a way or road taken or planned for passage or travel.

routine /ru'tin/ *n.* **1.** a customary or regular course of procedure. **2.** *Computers* a set of orders which cause a digital computer to perform some simple function. – *adj.* **3.** of the nature of, proceeding by, or adhering to routine.

rove /roʊv/ *v.i.,* **roved**, **roving**. to wander about without definite destination.

row[1] /roʊ/ *n.* a number of persons or things arranged in a straight line.

row[2] /roʊ/ *v.i.* **1.** to use oars or the like for propelling a boat. – *v.t.* **2.** to propel (a boat, etc.) by or as by the use of oars. – *n.* **3.** an act of rowing.

row[3] /raʊ/ *n.* **1.** a noisy dispute or quarrel; commotion. **2.** *Colloquial* noise or clamour.

rowdy /'raʊdi/ *adj.,* **-dier**, **-diest**. rough and disorderly.

rowlock /'rɒlək/ *n.* a device on which an oar rests and swings.

royal /'rɔɪəl/ *adj.* **1.** of or relating to a sovereign, king, queen, or the like, or sovereignty. **2.** established or chartered by, or existing under the patronage of, a sovereign.

royalist /'rɔɪələst/ *n.* a supporter or adherent of a king or a royal government.

royalty /'rɔɪəlti/ *n., pl.* **-ties**. **1.** royal persons collectively. **2.** royal status, dignity, or power; sovereignty. **3.** a compensation or portion of proceeds paid to the owner of a right, as a patent, for the use of it. **4.** an agreed portion of the proceeds from his or her work, paid to an author, composer, etc.

-rrhagia variant of **-rhagia**. Also, **-rrhage**, **-rrhagy**.

RSI /ar ɛs 'aɪ/ *n.* an injury resulting in inflammation of the tendon sheath of a muscle, caused by the excessive repetition of a movement over a period of time; repetition strain injury.

rub /rʌb/ *v.*, **rubbed**, **rubbing**, *n.* – *v.t.* **1.** to subject (an object) to pressure and friction, especially in order to clean, smooth, polish, etc. **2.** to move, spread, or apply (something) with pressure and friction over something else. **3.** to move (things) with pressure and friction over each other (fol. by *together*, etc.). **4.** to remove or erase by rubbing (fol. by *off*, *out*, etc.). **5.** to chafe or abrade. **6. rub it in,** to remind someone repeatedly of their mistakes, failures or shortcomings. – *v.i.* **7.** to exert pressure and friction on something. **8.** to admit of being rubbed (*off*, etc.). **9. rub off on,** to be transferred to, especially as a result of repeated close contact. – *n.* **10.** the act of rubbing. **11.** a difficulty; source of doubt or difficulty.

rubber[1] /'rʌbə/ *n.* **1.** an elastic material, derived from the latex of certain plants. **2.** a synthetic material resembling rubber. **3.** a piece of rubber for erasing pencil marks, etc.

rubber[2] /'rʌbə/ *n. Bridge, Whist, etc.* a set of games.

rubberneck /'rʌbənɛk/ *n. Colloquial* **1.** an extremely or excessively curious person. **2.** a tourist.

rubber plant *n.* an ornamental house plant.

rubber stamp *n.* **1.** a device of rubber for printing dates, etc., by hand. **2.** *Colloquial* someone who gives approval without consideration, or without demur.

rubbish /'rʌbɪʃ/ *n.* **1.** waste or refuse material; debris; litter. **2.** worthless stuff; trash. **3.** nonsense. – *v.t.* **4.** to speak of scornfully; criticise; denigrate.

rubble /'rʌbəl/ *n.* rough fragments of broken stone.

rubella /ru'bɛlə/ *n.* a contagious disease, usually mild, accompanied by fever, often some sore throat, and a rash resembling that of scarlet fever, causing birth defects in the first three months of pregnancy; German measles.

rubric /'rubrɪk/ *n.* a title, heading, direction, or the like, in a manuscript, book, etc.

ruby /'rubi/ *n.*, *pl.* **-bies**. **1.** a red gemstone. **2.** deep red; carmine. – *adj.* **3.** ruby-coloured. **4.** made from or containing a ruby.

ruck[1] /rʌk/ *n.* **1.** *Australian Rules* a group of three players who do not have fixed positions. **2.** *Rugby Football* a group of players struggling for the ball in no set pattern of play.

ruck[2] /rʌk/ *n.* a fold, crease, or wrinkle.

rucksack /'rʌksæk/ *n.* a kind of knapsack carried by hikers, etc.

ruction /'rʌkʃən/ *n. Colloquial* a disturbance, quarrel or row.

rudder /'rʌdə/ *n.* a board or plate of wood or metal hinged vertically at the stern of a boat or ship as a means of steering.

ruddy /'rʌdi/ *adj.*, **-dier**, **-diest**, *adv.* – *adj.* **1.** reddish. – *adv.* **2.** *Colloquial* extremely.

rude /rud/ *adj.*, **ruder**, **rudest**. **1.** discourteous or impolite. **2.** without culture, learning, or refinement.

rudiments /'rudəmənts/ *pl. n.* the elements or first principles of a subject.

rue[1] /ru/ *v.t.*, **rued**, **ruing**. to feel sorrow over; repent of; regret bitterly.

rue[2] /ru/ *n.* a yellow-flowered herb.

ruffian /'rʌfiən/ *n.* a violent, lawless man; a rough brute.

ruffle /'rʌfəl/ *v.*, **-fled**, **-fling**, *n.* – *v.t.* **1.** to destroy the smoothness or evenness of. **2.** to annoy, disturb, discompose, or irritate. **3.** to draw up (cloth, lace, etc.) into a ruffle by gathering along one edge. – *v.i.* **4.** to be or become ruffled. – *n.* **5.** a break in the smoothness or evenness of some surface. **6.** a strip of cloth, lace, etc., drawn up by gathering along one edge, and used as a trimming on dress, etc.

rug /rʌg/ *n.* **1.** a small, often thick, carpet. **2.** a thick, warm blanket. – *v.t.* **3.** to dress (oneself) in thick clothing, etc. (usually fol. by *up*).

Rugby football /'rʌgbi/ *n.* either of two forms of football, **Rugby League**, played by teams of thirteen players each, and **Rugby Union**, played by teams of fifteen players each.

rugged /'rʌgəd/ *adj.* **1.** roughly broken, rocky, hilly, or otherwise difficult of passage. **2.** severe, hard, or trying.

ruin /'ruən/ *n.* **1.** (*pl.*) the remains of a fallen building, town, etc., or of anything in a state of destruction or decay. **2.** a ruined building, town, etc. **3.** fallen and wrecked or decayed state; ruinous condition. **4.** the downfall, decay, or destruction of anything. **5.** the complete loss of means, position, or the like. – *v.t.* **6.** to reduce to ruin. – **ruinous**, *adj.*

rule /rul/ *n.*, *v.*, **ruled**, **ruling**. – *n.* **1.** a principle or regulation governing conduct, action, procedure, arrangement, etc. **2.** that which customarily or normally occurs or holds good. **3.** control, government, or dominion. – *v.t.* **4.** to control or direct; exercise dominating power or influence over. **5.** to declare judicially; decree. **6.** to mark with lines, especially parallel straight lines, with the aid of a ruler or the like. **7. rule out,** to exclude; refuse to admit. – *v.i.* **8.** to exercise dominating power or influence. **9.** to prevail or be current.

ruler /'rulə/ *n.* **1.** someone who or that which rules or governs. **2.** a strip of wood, metal, or other material with a graduated straight edge, used in drawing lines, measuring, etc.

rum /rʌm/ *n.* an alcoholic spirit.

rumble /'rʌmbəl/ *v.*, **-bled**, **-bling**, *n.* – *v.i.* **1.** to make a deep, heavy, continuous, resonant sound, as thunder, etc. **2.** to fight. – *n.* **3.** *Colloquial* a fight, especially between teenage gangs.

rumbustious /rʌm'bʌstʃəs/ *adj.* boisterous; noisy.

ruminant /'rumənənt/ *n.* any of the cloven-hoofed, cud-chewing quadrupeds, as cattle, sheep, goats, etc.

ruminate /ˈruməneɪt/ *v.i.*, **-nated**, **-nating**. to meditate or muse; ponder.

rummage /ˈrʌmɪdʒ/ *v.*, **-maged**, **-maging**, *n.* – *v.t.* **1.** to search thoroughly or actively through (a place, receptacle, etc.). **2.** to find (fol. by *out* or *up*) by searching. – *v.i.* **3.** to search actively, as in a place or receptacle. – *n.* **4.** miscellaneous articles; odds and ends. **5.** a rummaging search.

rummy /ˈrʌmi/ *n.* a card game.

rumour = rumor /ˈrumə/ *n.* **1.** a story or statement in general circulation without confirmation or certainty as to facts. – *v.t.* **2.** to circulate, report, or assert by a rumour.

rump /rʌmp/ *n.* the hinder part of the body of an animal.

rumple /ˈrʌmpəl/ *v.*, **-pled**, **-pling**. – *v.t.* **1.** to draw or crush into wrinkles; crumple. – *v.i.* **2.** to become wrinkled or crumpled.

rumpus /ˈrʌmpəs/ *n.* *Colloquial* disturbing noise; uproar.

run /rʌn/ *v.*, **ran**, **run**, **running**, *n.* – *v.i.* **1.** to move quickly on foot, so as to go more rapidly than in walking. **2.** to move easily or swiftly. **3.** to make a short, quick, or casual journey, as for a visit, etc. **4.** to stand as a candidate for election. **5.** to traverse a route, as a public conveyance. **6.** to melt and flow, as solder, varnish, etc. **7.** to flow, stream, or be wet with a liquid. **8.** to recur or be inherent. **9.** to come undone, as stitches or a fabric; ladder. **10.** to be in operation or continue operating. **11.** to exist or occur within a specified range of variation. **12.** to pass into a certain state or condition; become. – *v.t.* **13.** to cause (an animal, etc.) to move quickly on foot. **14.** to cause (a vehicle, etc.) to move. **15.** to traverse (a distance or course) in running. **16.** to perform by or as by running. **17.** to run or get past or through. **18.** to keep (livestock), as on pasture. **19.** to cause to move, especially quickly or cursorily. **20.** to convey or transport, as in a vessel or vehicle. **21.** to keep operating or in service, as a machine. **22.** to expose oneself to or be exposed to (a risk, etc.). **23.** to bring, lead, or force into some state, action, etc. **24.** to conduct, administer, or manage, as a business, an experiment, or the like. – *v.* **25. run down, a.** to slow up before stopping, as a clock or other mechanism. **b.** to knock down and injure, as a vehicle or driver; run over. **c.** to denigrate; make adverse criticism of. **d.** to reduce, as stocks. **e.** to find, especially after extensive searching. **26. run in, a.** to operate (new machinery, especially a motor vehicle) carefully for an initial period, so that the machine becomes ready for full operation without damage. **b.** *Colloquial* → **arrest**. **27. run off, a.** to depart or retreat quickly. **b.** to produce by a printing or similar process. **c.** to write or otherwise create quickly. **28. run over, a.** to knock down and injure, as a vehicle or driver. **b.** to exceed (a time-limit or the like). **c.** to review, rehearse, or recapitulate. **29. run up, a.** to amass or incur, as a bill. **b.** to make, especially quickly, as something sewn. – *n.* **30.** an act, instance, or spell of running. **31.** a running pace. **32.** an act or instance of escaping, running away, etc. **33.** a quick, short trip. **34.** the amount of something produced in any uninterrupted period of operation. **35.** a line or place in knitted or sewn work where a series of stitches have slipped or come undone; a ladder. **36.** freedom to range over, go through, or use. **37.** any rapid or easy course or progress. **38.** a continuous course of some condition of affairs, etc. **39.** a continuous series of something. **40.** any continued or extensive demand, call, or the like. **41.** a series of sudden and urgent demands for payment, as on a bank. **42.** the ordinary or average kind. **43.** an enclosure within which domestic animals may range about. **44.** the area and habitual route covered by a vendor who delivers goods to houses, etc. **45.** a large area of grazing land; a rural property. **46. in the long run,** ultimately. **47. the runs,** light diarrhoea.

rung[1] /rʌŋ/ *v.* past tense and past participle of **ring**[2].

rung[2] /rʌŋ/ *n.* **1.** one of the rounded cross-pieces forming the steps of a ladder. **2.** a rounded or shaped piece fixed horizontally, for strengthening purposes, as between the legs of a chair.

runnel /ˈrʌnəl/ *n.* a small channel, as for water.

runner /ˈrʌnə/ *n.* **1.** one acting as collector, agent, or the like for a bank, broker, etc. **2.** one whose business it is to solicit patronage or trade. **3.** something in or on which something else runs or moves, as the strips of wood that guide a drawer, etc. **4.** a long, narrow strip, as of material. **5.** → **sandshoe**.

runner-up /rʌnər-ˈʌp/ *n.* (*plural* **runners-up**) the competitor, player, or team finishing in second place.

running /ˈrʌnɪŋ/ *n.* **1. in the running,** having a chance of success. – *adj.* **2.** that runs; moving or passing rapidly or smoothly. **3.** creeping or climbing, as plants. **4.** slipping or sliding easily, as a knot or a noose. **5.** operating, as a machine. **6.** cursive, as handwriting. **7.** going or carried on continuously; sustained. **8.** following in succession (placed after the noun). **9.** discharging matter, especially fluid, as a sore.

running stitch *n.* a small, even stitch used for seams, gathering, quilting, etc.

runny /ˈrʌni/ *adj.* **1.** (of matter) fluid or tending to flow. **2.** tending to flow with or discharge liquid.

run-of-the-mill /ˈrʌn-əv-ðə-mɪl/ *adj.* ordinary; mediocre; commonplace.

runout campaign /ˈrʌnaʊt/ *n.* a vigorous program to sell previous model cars before the release of the latest model.

runt /ˈrʌnt/ *n.* the smallest in a litter.

run time *n.* the time required for a computer to complete a single, continuous program.

runway /ˈrʌnweɪ/ *n.* a paved or cleared strip on which aeroplanes land and take off; airstrip.

rupture /ˈrʌptʃə/ *n.*, *v.*, **-tured**, **-turing**. – *n.* **1.** the state of being broken or burst. – *v.t.* **2.** to break or burst (a blood vessel, etc.). **3.** to cause a breach of (relations, etc.).

rural /ˈrurəl/ *adj.* of, relating to, or characteristic of the country (as distinguished from towns or cities).

ruse /ruz/ *n.* a trick, stratagem, or artifice.

rush[1] /rʌʃ/ *v.i.* **1.** to move or go with speed, rash haste, or violence. – *v.t.* **2.** to send or drive with speed or violence. **3.** to perform, complete, or organise (some process or activity) with special haste. **4.** to attack with a rush. – *n.* **5.** the act of rushing; a rapid, impetuous, or headlong onward movement. **6.** a sudden coming or access. **7.** a hurried state, as from pressure of affairs. **8.** a period of intense activity. **9.** a great demand for a commodity, etc. (fol. by *on*). – *adj.* **10.** requiring or performed with haste. **11.** characterised by rush or press of work, traffic, etc.

rush[2] /rʌʃ/ *n.* **1.** any of several grasslike herbs with pithy or hollow stems, found in wet or marshy places. **2.** a stem of such a plant, used for making chair bottoms, mats, baskets, etc.

rusk /rʌsk/ *n.* a crisp cake, given especially to babies when teething, and invalids.

russet /ˈrʌsət/ *n., adj.* reddish brown; light brown; yellowish brown.

rust /rʌst/ *n.* **1.** the red or orange coating which forms on the surface of iron when exposed to air and moisture. **2.** rust colour; reddish brown or orange. – *v.i.* **3.** to grow rusty, as iron does; corrode. **4.** to deteriorate or become impaired, as through inaction or disuse. – *v.t.* **5.** to impair as if with rust.

rustic /ˈrʌstɪk/ *adj.* **1.** rural. **2.** made of roughly dressed limbs or roots of trees, as garden seats, etc. – *n.* **3.** an unsophisticated country person.

rustle /ˈrʌsəl/ *v.,* **-tled, -tling,** *n.* – *v.t.* **1.** to make a succession of slight, soft sounds, as of parts rubbing gently one on another, as leaves, silks, papers, etc. – *v.t.* **2.** to move or stir so as to cause a rustling sound. **3.** to steal (cattle, etc.). **4.** *Colloquial* to move, bring, get, etc., by energetic action (often fol. by *up*). – *n.* **5.** the sound made by anything that rustles.

rut[1] /rʌt/ *n.* **1.** any furrow, groove, etc. **2.** a fixed or established way of life; a dull routine.

rut[2] /rʌt/ *n.* the periodically recurring sexual excitement of the deer, goat, sheep, etc.

ruthless /ˈruθləs/ *adj.* without pity or compassion; pitiless; merciless.

-ry a suffix of abstract nouns of condition, practice and collectives.

rye /raɪ/ *n.* **1.** a widely cultivated cereal grass. **2.** its seeds or grain. **3.** an American whisky distilled from rye.

S s

S, s /ɛs/ *n., pl.* **S's** *or* **Ss**, **s's** *or* **ss**. the 19th letter of the English alphabet.

's[1] an ending which marks the possessive singular of nouns, as in *man's*.

's[2] an ending which marks the possessive plural of nouns, as in *men's*.

's[3] colloquial reduction of: **1.** is: *he's here*. **2.** has. **3.** does. **4.** us.

-s[1] a suffix serving to form adverbs, as *always*, *evenings*, *needs*, *unawares*. Cf. **-ways**.

-s[2] an ending which marks the third person singular indicative active of verbs, as in *hits*.

-s[3] **1.** an ending which marks the regular plural of nouns, as in *dogs*. **2.** a quasi-plural ending occurring in nouns for which there is no proper singular, as *trousers*, *shorts*, *scissors*.

sabbatical /sə'bætɪkəl/ *n.* (in certain universities, etc.) a period of freedom from teaching granted to a teacher, as for study or travel. Also, **sabbatical leave**.

sable /'seɪbəl/ *n.* **1.** a weasel-like mammal valued for its dark brown fur. – *adj.* **2.** made of the fur or hair of the sable. **3.** *Poetic* black; very dark.

sabotage /'sæbətaʒ/ *n., v.,* **-taged**, **-taging**. – *n.* **1.** malicious injury to work, tools, machinery, etc. **2.** any malicious attack on or undermining of a cause. – *v.t.* **3.** to injure or attack by sabotage. – **saboteur**, *n.*

sabre /'seɪbə/ *n.* **1.** a heavy one-edged sword. **2.** a light sword for fencing and duelling.

sac /sæk/ *n.* a baglike structure in an animal or plant, as one containing fluid.

sacchar- a word element referring to sugar or saccharine. Also, **saccharo-**.

saccharide /'sækəraɪd/ *n.* any sugar or other carbohydrate, especially a simple sugar.

saccharin /'sækərən, -krən/ *n.* a very sweet crystalline compound. Also, **saccharine**.

saccharine /'sækərən, -krən/ *adj.* **1.** of a sugary sweetness. – *n.* **2.** → **saccharin**.

sachet /'sæʃeɪ/ *n.* a small sealed bag used for packaging a variety of goods.

sack[1] /sæk/ *n.* **1.** a large bag of stout woven material. **2.** a woman's loose-fitting, unbelted dress. **3.** *Colloquial* dismissal or discharge, as from employment. – *v.t.* **4.** *Colloquial* to dismiss or discharge, as from employment.

sack[2] /sæk/ *v.t.* **1.** to pillage or loot after capture; plunder. – *n.* **2.** the plundering of a captured place; pillage.

sacrament /'sækrəmənt/ *n.* something regarded as possessing a sacred character or a mysterious significance.

sacred /'seɪkrəd/ *adj.* **1.** relating to or connected with religion (opposed to *profane* and *secular*). **2.** properly immune from violence, interference, etc., as a person or their office.

sacred site *n.* **1.** (in Australia) a site that is sacred to Aborigines or is otherwise of significance according to Aboriginal tradition. **2.** a site or institution that has particular religious, cultural or historical significance.

sacrifice /'sækrəfaɪs/ *n., v.,* **-ficed**, **-ficing**. – *n.* **1.** the offering of life (animal, plant, or human) or some material possession, etc., to a deity, as in propitiation or homage. **2.** the surrender or destruction of something prized or desirable for the sake of something considered as having a higher or more pressing claim. **3.** the thing so surrendered or devoted. **4.** a loss incurred in selling something below its value. – *v.t.* **5.** to make a sacrifice or offering of. **6.** to dispose of (goods, etc.) regardless of profit. – **sacrificial**, *adj.*

sacrilege /'sækrəlɪdʒ/ *n.* the violation or profanation of anything sacred or held sacred. – **sacrilegious**, *adj.*

sacro- a word element: meaning 'holy'.

sacrosanct /'sækrəsæŋkt/ *adj.* especially or superlatively sacred or inviolable.

sad /sæd/ *adj.,* **sadder**, **saddest**. **1.** sorrowful or mournful. **2.** causing sorrow.

saddle /'sædl/ *n., v.,* **-dled**, **-dling**. – *n.* **1.** a seat for a rider on the back of a horse or other animal. **2.** a similar seat on a bicycle, machine, etc. **3.** something resembling a saddle in shape or position. – *v.t.* **4.** to put a saddle upon (a horse, etc.). **5.** to load or charge, as with a burden.

sadism /'sædɪzəm, 'seɪ-/ *n.* **1.** sexual gratification gained through causing physical pain and humiliation. **2.** any morbid enjoyment in inflicting mental or physical pain.

sadomasochism /ˌseɪdoʊ'mæsəkɪzəm, ˌsædoʊ-/ *n.* a disturbed condition of the mind marked by the presence of sadistic and masochistic tendencies.

safari /sə'fari/ *n., pl.* **-ris**. a journey; an expedition, especially for hunting.

safari park *n.* a large park where wild animals are kept, uncaged, to be viewed by the public from cars, etc.

safe /seɪf/ *adj.,* **safer**, **safest**, *n., adv.* – *adj.* **1.** secure from liability to harm, injury, danger, or risk. **2.** involving no risk of mishap, error, etc. – *n.* **3.** any receptacle or structure for the storage or preservation of articles. – *adv.* **4.** **play safe,** to act cautiously.

safe-conduct /seɪf-'kɒndʌkt/ *n.* a conducting in safety.

safe-deposit /'seɪf-dəpɒzət/ *adj.* providing safekeeping for valuables.

safeguard /'seɪfgad/ *n.* **1.** something serving as a protection or defence, or ensuring safety. – *v.t.* **2.** to guard; protect; secure.

safe sex *n.* any sexual practices in which precautions are taken to prevent the transmission of sexually transmitted diseases, especially AIDS.

safety /'seɪfti/ *n., pl.* **-ties**. **1.** the state of being safe; freedom from injury or danger. **2.** the quality of insuring against hurt, injury, danger, or risk.

safety pin *n.* a pin bent back on itself to form a spring, with a guard to cover the point.

safflower /'sæflaʊə/ *n.* a thistlelike herb cultivated for its oil which is used in cookery, cosmetics, etc.

saffron /'sæfrən/ *n.* an orange-coloured plant product used to colour confectionery, for flavouring, etc.

sag /sæg/ *v.,* **sagged**, **sagging**, *n.* – *v.i.* **1.** to sink or bend downwards by weight or pressure, especially in the middle. **2.** to decline, as in price. – *n.* **3.** the degree of sagging. **4.** a place where anything sags; a depression. **5.** moderate decline in prices.

saga /'sagə/ *n.* any narrative or legend of heroic exploits.

sagacious /sə'geɪʃəs/ *adj.* having acute mental discernment and keen practical sense; shrewd. – **sagacity**, *n.*

sage[1] /seɪdʒ/ *n., adj.,* **sager**, **sagest**. – *n.* **1.** a profoundly wise person. – *adj.* **2.** wise, judicious, or prudent.

sage[2] /seɪdʒ/ *n.* a perennial plant used for seasoning in cookery.

sago /'seɪgoʊ/ *n.* a starchy foodstuff used in making puddings, and other dishes.

said /sɛd/ *v.* **1.** past tense and past participle of **say**. – *adj.* **2.** named or mentioned before.

sail /seɪl/ *n.* **1.** an expanse of canvas or similar material spread to the wind to make a vessel move through the water. **2.** some similar piece or apparatus. **3.** a voyage or excursion, especially in a sailing vessel. – *v.i.* **4.** to travel in a vessel conveyed by the action of wind, steam, etc. **5.** to move along in a manner suggestive of a sailing vessel. – *v.t.* **6.** to sail upon, over, or through. **7.** to navigate (a ship, etc.). – **sailor**, *n.*

saint /seɪnt/ *n.* a person of great holiness.

sake[1] /seɪk/ *n.* **1.** cause, account, or interest. **2.** purpose or end.

sake[2] /'saki/ *n.* a Japanese fermented alcoholic drink made from rice.

sal /sæl/ *n. Chiefly Pharmaceutical* salt.

salacious /sə'leɪʃəs/ *adj.* lustful or lecherous.

salad /'sæləd/ *n.* a dish of uncooked vegetables, typically served with a savoury dressing.

salad days *pl. n.* days of youthful inexperience.

salamander /'sæləmændə/ *n.* **1.** any of various tailed amphibians, most of which have an aquatic larval stage but are terrestrial as adults. **2.** a mythical being supposed to be able to live in fire.

salami /sə'lami/ *n.* a kind of sausage, originally Italian, often flavoured with garlic.

salary /'sæləri/ *n., pl.* **-ries**. a fixed periodical payment, usually monthly, paid to a person for regular work or services. – **salaried**, *adj.*

sale /seɪl/ *n.* **1.** the act of selling. **2.** the quantity sold. **3.** a special disposal of goods, as at reduced prices. **4.** transfer of property for money or credit. **5. for sale** or **on sale,** offered to be sold; offered to purchasers.

salesperson /'seɪlzpɜsən/ *n.* someone employed to sell goods, as in a shop, etc.

sales talk *n.* **1.** a line of reasoning or argument intended to effect a sale. **2.** any persuasive argument.

sales tax *n.* a tax imposed on the seller of goods in respect of goods sold, but generally passed on to the ultimate consumer in the retail price.

salient /'seɪliənt/ *adj.* prominent or conspicuous.

saline /'seɪlaɪn, -lin/ *adj.* **1.** containing or tasting like common table salt. – *n.* **2.** a saline health drink or medicine.

saliva /sə'laɪvə/ *n.* a fluid consisting of the secretions produced by glands which discharge into the mouth.

sallow /'sæloʊ/ *adj.* of a yellowish, sickly hue or complexion.

sally /'sæli/ *v.i.,* **-lied**, **-lying**. to set out briskly or energetically.

salmon /'sæmən/ *n., pl.* **-mons**, (*esp. collectively*) **-mon**. **1.** a marine and freshwater food fish with pink flesh. **2.** Also, **salmon pink**. light yellowish-pink.

salon /'sælɒn/ *n.* **1.** a drawing room or reception room in a large house. **2.** a fashionable business establishment or shop.

saloon /sə'lun/ *n.* a room or place for general use for a specific purpose.

salt /sɒlt, sɔlt/ *n.* **1.** a crystalline compound, sodium chloride, NaCl, occurring as a mineral, a constituent of sea water, etc., and used for seasoning food, as a preservative, etc. **2.** *Chemistry* a compound which upon dissociation yields cations (positively charged) of a metal, and anions (negatively charged) of an acid radical. **3.** (*pl.*) any of various salts used as purgatives. **4.** wit; pungency. – *v.t.* **5.** to season with salt. **6.** to cure, preserve, or treat with salt. – *adj.* **7.** containing salt; having the taste of salt. **8.** overflowed with or growing in salt water.

saltbush /'sɒltbʊʃ/ *n.* any of various drought-resistant plants used as grazing plants in arid areas.

saltcellar /'sɒltsɛlə/ *n.* a shaker or vessel for salt.

saltpan /'sɒltpæn/ *n.* a small basin flooded by salt deposits.

saltpetre /sɒlt'pitə/ *n.* a white salt used in making gunpowder, etc.

salubrious /sə'lubriəs/ *adj.* (especially of air, climate, etc.) favourable to health.

salutary /'sæljətri/ *adj.* promoting or conducive to some beneficial purpose.

salutation /sæljə'teɪʃən/ *n.* something uttered, written, or done by way of saluting.

salute /sə'lut/ *v.,* **-luted**, **-luting**, *n.* – *v.t.* **1.** to address with expressions of goodwill, respect, etc.; greet. **2.** *Military, Navy* to pay respect to or honour by some formal act, as by raising the right hand to the side of the headgear, presenting arms, firing cannon, dipping colours, etc. – *n.* **3.** an act of saluting. **4.** → **Australian salute**.

salvage /'sælvɪdʒ/ *n., v.,* **-vaged**, **-vaging**. **1.** the saving of anything from fire, danger, etc., or the property so saved. – *v.t.* **2.** to save from shipwreck, fire, etc.

salvation /sæl'veɪʃən/ *n.* **1.** the state of being saved or delivered. **2.** a source, cause, or means of deliverance.

salve /sav, sælv/ *n., v.,* **salved**, **salving**. – *n.* **1.** a healing ointment. – *v.t.* **2.** to soothe as if with salve.

salver /'sælvə/ *n.* a tray.

salvo /'sælvoʊ/ *n., pl.* **-vos**, **-voes**. a discharge of artillery or other firearms, often intended as a salute.

same /seɪm/ *adj.* **1.** identical with what is about to be or has just been mentioned. **2.** being one or identical, though having different names, aspects, etc. **3.** agreeing in kind, amount, etc.; corresponding. **4.** unchanged in character, condition, etc. – *pron.* **5.** the same person or thing. **6. the same,** with the same manner (used adverbially).

sample /'sæmpəl/ *n., adj., v.,* **-pled, -pling.** – *n.* **1.** a small part of anything or one of a number, intended to show the quality, style, etc., of the whole; a specimen. – *adj.* **2.** serving as a specimen. – *v.t.* **3.** to take a sample or samples of; test or judge by a sample.

sanatorium /sænə'tɔriəm/ *n., pl.* **-toriums, -toria** /-'tɔriə/. an establishment for the treatment of invalids, convalescents, etc.

sanctimonious /sæŋktə'moʊniəs/ *adj.* making a show of holiness; affecting sanctity.

sanction /'sæŋkʃən/ *n.* **1.** countenance or support given to an action, etc. **2.** something serving to support an action, etc. – *v.t.* **3.** to authorise, countenance, or approve. **4.** to ratify or confirm.

sanctity /'sæŋktəti/ *n., pl.* **-ties.** **1.** holiness, saintliness, or godliness. **2.** sacred or hallowed character.

sanctuary /'sæŋktʃəri, 'sæŋktʃuəri/ *n., pl.* **-ries.** **1.** a sacred or holy place. **2.** a place of protection from something. **3.** the protection given by such a place.

sand /sænd/ *n.* **1.** the more or less fine debris of rocks, consisting of small, loose grains, often of quartz. **2.** a dull reddish yellow colour. – *v.t.* **3.** to smooth or polish with sand or sandpaper.

sandal /'sændl/ *n.* any of various kinds of low shoes or slippers.

sandalwood /'sændlwʊd/ *n.* the fragrant heartwood of any of certain Asiatic and Australian trees.

sandbar /'sændba/ *n.* a bar of sand formed in a river or sea by the action of tides or currents.

sandpaper /'sændpeɪpə/ *n.* **1.** strong paper coated with a layer of sand or the like, used for smoothing or polishing. – *v.t.* **2.** to smooth or polish with or as with sandpaper.

sandshoe /'sænʃu, 'sændʃu/ *n.* a rubber-soled canvas shoe, worn especially for sports, etc.

sandsoap /'sændsoʊp/ *n.* a soap with mildly abrasive power.

sandstone /'sændstoʊn/ *n.* a rock formed by the consolidation of sand.

sandwich /'sænwɪtʃ, -wɪdʒ/ *n.* **1.** two slices of bread (or toast), plain or buttered, with a layer of meat, fish, cheese, or the like between. – *v.t.* **2.** to insert or hem in between two other things.

sane /seɪn/ *adj.,* **saner, sanest.** **1.** free from mental derangement. **2.** having or showing reason, sound judgment, or good sense. – **sanity,** *n.*

sang /sæŋ/ *v.* past tense of **sing**.

sangfroid /sõŋ'frwa/ *n.* coolness of mind; calmness; composure.

sanguine /'sæŋgwən/ *adj.* hopeful or confident.

sanitarium /sænə'tɛəriəm/ *n., pl.* **-tariums, -taria** /-'tɛəriə/. → **sanatorium**.

sanitary /'sænətri/ *adj.* **1.** of or relating to health. **2.** favourable to health; free from dirt, germs, etc.

sanitary napkin *n.* a soft, absorbent, disposable pad worn during menstruation to absorb the discharge from the uterus. Also, **sanitary pad**.

sanitation /sænə'teɪʃən/ *n.* a drainage system.

sank /sæŋk/ *v.* past tense of **sink**.

sap[1] /sæp/ *n.* **1.** the juice or vital circulating fluid, especially of a woody plant. **2.** *Colloquial* a fool or weak person.

sap[2] /sæp/ *v.t.,* **sapped, sapping.** to undermine; weaken or destroy insidiously.

sapling /'sæplɪŋ/ *n.* a young tree.

sapphire /'sæfaɪə/ *n.* **1.** a transparent blue gemstone. **2.** a deep blue. – *adj.* **3.** resembling sapphire; deep blue.

sapro- a word element meaning 'rotten'. Also (*before vowels*), **sapr-**.

sarc- a word element meaning 'flesh'. Also (*before consonants*), **sarco-**.

sarcasm /'sakæzəm/ *n.* harsh or bitter derision or irony. – **sarcastic,** *adj.*

sarcoma /sa'koʊmə/ *n., pl.* **-mata** /-mətə/. any of various malignant tumours originating in the connective tissue, attacking especially the bones.

sarcophagus /sa'kɒfəgəs/ *n., pl.* **-gi** /-gaɪ/, **-guses.** a stone coffin.

sardine /sa'din/ *n., pl.* **-dines,** (*esp. collectively*) **-dine.** the young of the common pilchard, often preserved in oil and canned for food.

sardonic /sa'dɒnɪk/ *adj.* bitterly ironical; sarcastic; sneering.

sari /'sari/ *n., pl.* **-ris.** a long piece of cotton or silk, the principal outer garment of Hindu women.

sarong /sə'rɒŋ/ *n.* a garment consisting of a piece of cloth enveloping the lower part of the body like a skirt.

sarsaparilla /saspə'rɪlə/ *n.* an extract or other preparation made of it.

sartorial /sa'tɔriəl/ *adj.* of or relating to clothes or dress, generally men's.

sash[1] /sæʃ/ *n.* a long band or scarf of silk, etc.

sash[2] /sæʃ/ *n.* a movable framework in which panes of glass are set, as in a window or the like.

sashay /'sæʃeɪ/ *v.i. Colloquial* to strut, move exaggeratedly.

sassafras /'sæsəfræs/ *n.* any of several Australian trees with fragrant bark.

sassy /'sæsi/ *adj.,* **-sier, -siest.** *Colloquial* saucy.

sat /sæt/ *v.* past tense and past participle of **sit**.

satanic /sə'tænɪk/ *adj.* characteristic of or befitting Satan; extremely wicked; diabolical. Also, **satanical**.

satchel /'sætʃəl/ *n.* a bag with a shoulder-strap, used for carrying schoolbooks.

sate /seɪt/ *v.t.,* **sated, sating.** to satisfy (any

appetite or desire) to the full.

satellite /ˈsætəlaɪt/ *n.* **1.** a small body which revolves round a planet; a moon. **2.** a human-made device for launching into orbit round the earth, another planet, or the sun, for purposes of communication, research, etc.

satiate /ˈseɪʃieɪt/ *v.t.*, **-ated**, **-ating**. to satisfy to the full.

satin /ˈsætn/ *n.* **1.** a very smooth, glossy fabric. – *adj.* **2.** smooth; glossy.

satire /ˈsætaɪə/ *n.* the use of irony, sarcasm, ridicule, etc., in exposing, denouncing, or deriding vice, folly, etc. – **satirical**, **satiric**, *adj.*

satirise = satirize /ˈsætəraɪz/ *v.t.*, **-rised**, **-rising**. to make the object of satire.

satisfaction /sætəsˈfækʃən/ *n.* **1.** the state of being satisfied. **2.** the cause of being satisfied. **3.** the opportunity of repairing a supposed wrong, as by a duel. **4.** payment, as for debt; discharge, as of obligations. – **satisfactory**, *adj.*

satisfy /ˈsætəsfaɪ/ *v.*, **-fied**, **-fying**. – *v.t.* **1.** to fulfil the desires, expectations, needs, or demands of. **2.** to fulfil (a desire, expectation, want, etc.). **3.** to discharge fully (a debt, etc.). **4.** to pay (a creditor). – *v.i.* **5.** to give satisfaction.

saturate /ˈsætʃəreɪt/ *v.t.*, **-rated**, **-rating**. to soak, impregnate, or imbue thoroughly or completely.

saturnine /ˈsætənaɪn/ *adj.* gloomy; taciturn.

satyr /ˈsætə, ˈseɪtə/ *n.* **1.** in classical mythology, a god, part human and part goat. **2.** a lascivious man.

sauce /sɔs/ *n.* **1.** any preparation, usually liquid or soft, eaten as a relish or appetising accompaniment to food. **2.** *Colloquial* impertinence; impudence.

saucepan /ˈsɔspən/ *n.* a container for boiling, stewing, etc.

saucer /ˈsɔsə/ *n.* a small, round, shallow dish to hold a cup.

saucy /ˈsɔsi/ *adj.*, **-cier**, **-ciest**. impertinent; insolent.

sauerkraut /ˈsaʊəkraʊt/ *n.* cabbage cut fine, salted, and allowed to ferment until sour.

sauna /ˈsɔnə/ *n.* **1.** a type of steam bath. **2.** a room or device for taking such a bath.

saunter /ˈsɔntə/ *v.i.* **1.** to walk with a leisurely gait; stroll. – *n.* **2.** a leisurely walk or ramble; a stroll.

-saur a word element meaning 'lizard'.

sauro- a word element meaning 'lizard'.

sausage /ˈsɒsɪdʒ/ *n.* minced meat packed into a special skin.

sauté /ˈsoʊteɪ/ *v.t.*, **-téed**, **-téing**. to cook in a small amount of fat; pan fry.

sauterne /soʊˈtɜn, sə-/ *n.* a rich sweet white table wine.

savage /ˈsævɪdʒ/ *adj.*, *n.*, *v.*, **savaged**, **savaging**. – *adj.* **1.** uncivilised; barbarous. **2.** fierce, ferocious, or cruel; untamed. – *n.* **3.** an uncivilised human being. – *v.t.* **4.** to assail violently; maul. – **savagery**, *n.*

save[1] /seɪv/ *v.*, **saved**, **saving**, *n.* – *v.t.* **1.** to rescue from danger. **2.** to avoid the spending, consumption, or waste of. **3.** to set apart, reserve, or lay by. **4.** to prevent the occurrence, use, or necessity of. – *v.i.* **5.** to accumulate or put aside money, etc., as the result of economy (often fol. by *up*). – *n.* **6.** the act or instance of saving, especially in sports.

save[2] /seɪv/ *prep.* **1.** except; but. – *conj.* **2.** except; but.

saveloy /ˈsævəlɔɪ/ *n.* → **frankfurt**.

saving /ˈseɪvɪŋ/ *adj.* **1.** that saves; rescuing; preserving. **2.** redeeming. – *n.* **3.** a reduction or lessening of expenditure or outlay. **4.** (*pl.*) sums of money saved by economy and laid away. – *prep.* **5.** except.

savings account *n.* an account with a savings bank or permanent building society on which a rate of interest is paid and money can be withdrawn at short notice.

savings bank *n.* a bank which mainly accepts deposits from individual customers and lends money for housing. In 1989, the distinction between trading banks and savings banks was removed in Australia.

saviour = savior /ˈseɪvjə/ *n.* someone who saves, rescues, or delivers.

savour = savor /ˈseɪvə/ *n.* **1.** a particular taste or smell. **2.** distinctive quality or property. – *v.t.* **3.** to perceive by taste or smell, especially with relish. **4.** to give oneself to the enjoyment of.

savoury = savory /ˈseɪvəri/ *adj.*, *n.*, *pl.* **-vouries**. – *adj.* **1.** piquant, pungent, or salty to the taste; not sweet. – *n.* **2.** an unsweet, usually salty, bite-sized morsel on a small biscuit or crouton.

savvy /ˈsævi/ *v.i.*, *v.t.*, **-vied**, **-vying**. *Colloquial* to know; understand.

saw[1] /sɔ/ *n.*, *v.*, **sawed**, **sawn** *or* **sawed**, **sawing**. – *n.* **1.** a tool or device for cutting, typically a thin blade of metal with a series of sharp teeth. – *v.t.* **2.** to cut or divide with a saw. – *v.i.* **3.** to cut as a saw does.

saw[2] /sɔ/ *v.* past tense of **see**[1].

sax /sæks/ *n.* *Colloquial* a saxophone.

saxophone /ˈsæksəfoʊn/ *n.* a musical wind instrument.

say /seɪ/ *v.*, **said**, **saying**, *n.* – *v.t.* **1.** to utter or pronounce; speak. **2.** to express in words; state; declare. **3.** to assume as a hypothesis or an estimate. – *v.i.* **4.** to speak; declare; express an opinion. – *n.* **5.** *Colloquial* the right or opportunity to say, speak or decide.

saying /ˈseɪɪŋ/ *n.* something said, especially a proverb.

scab /skæb/ *n.*, *v.*, **scabbed**, **scabbing**. – *n.* **1.** the encrustation which forms over a sore during healing. **2.** someone who continues to work during a strike. – *v.i.* **3.** to act or work as a scab.

scabbard /ˈskæbəd/ *n.* a sheath or cover for the blade of a sword, dagger, or the like.

scabies /ˈskeɪbiz, -biiz/ *n.* any of several infectious skin diseases occurring in sheep and cattle, and in humans, caused by parasitic mites; itch.

scads /skædz/ *pl. n.* *Colloquial* a large quantity.

scaffold /ˈskæfəld, -oʊld/ *n.* any raised framework or platform.

scald /skɔld/ *v.t.* **1.** to burn or affect painfully with, or as with, hot liquid or steam. **2.** to subject to the action of boiling or hot liquid. – *n.* **3.** a burn caused by hot liquid or steam.

scale[1] /skeɪl/ *n., v.,* **scaled**, **scaling**. – *n.* **1.** one of the thin, flat, horny or hard plates that form the covering of certain animals, as fishes. **2.** any thin platelike piece, lamina, or flake such as peels off from a surface. – *v.t.* **3.** to remove the scales or scale from.

scale[2] /skeɪl/ *n.* (*usu. pl.*) a balance, or any of various other more or less complicated devices for weighing.

scale[3] /skeɪl/ *n., v.,* **scaled**, **scaling**. – *n.* **1.** a succession or progression of steps or degrees. **2.** a graduated line, as on a map, representing proportionate size. **3.** an instrument with graduated spaces, for measuring, etc. **4.** the proportion which the representation of an object bears to the object. **5.** *Music* a succession of notes ascending or descending according to fixed intervals, especially such a series beginning on a particular note. – *v.t.* **6.** to climb by, or as by, a ladder; climb up or over. **7.** to reduce in amount according to a fixed scale or proportion (often fol. by *down*).

scallop /ˈskɒləp/ *n.* **1.** any of various bivalve molluscs having fluted shell valves. **2.** one of a series of rounded projections along the edge of pastry, a garment, cloth, etc. **3.** a thin slice of potato dipped in batter and deep-fried. – *v.t.* **4.** to finish (an edge) with scallops.

scallywag /ˈskæliwæg/ *n.* (*often used indulgently of children*) a scamp; rascal. Also, **scalawag**, **scallawag**.

scalp /skælp/ *n.* **1.** the skin of the upper part of the head. – *v.t.* **2.** to cut or tear the scalp from. **3.** *Colloquial* to buy and sell so as to make small, quick profits, as stocks. **4.** *Colloquial* to buy (tickets) cheap and sell at other than official rates.

scalpel /ˈskælpəl/ *n.* a light knife used in surgery.

scamp /skæmp/ *n.* a mischievous child.

scamper /ˈskæmpə/ *v.i.* to run or go hastily or quickly.

scan /skæn/ *v.,* **scanned**, **scanning**, *n.* – *v.t.* **1.** to glance at or run through hastily. **2.** *Radar* to sweep a region with a beam from a radar transmitter. **3.** *Computers* to examine every item in (a record or file). **4.** *Medicine* to examine an area, organ, or system of the body using a moving detector or moving beam of radiation to produce an image of that body part, sometimes after an injection of a radioactive substance which has the ability to enhance the image of a particular tissue. – *v.i.* **5.** (of verse) to conform to the rules of metre. – *n.* **6.** the act of scanning; close examination or scrutiny.

scandal /ˈskændl/ *n.* **1.** a disgraceful or discreditable action, circumstance, etc. **2.** damage to reputation; disgrace. **3.** malicious gossip.

scandalise = scandalize /ˈskændəlaɪz/ *v.t.,* **-lised**, **-lising**. to shock or horrify by something considered immoral or improper.

scant /skænt/ *adj.* **1.** barely sufficient in amount or quantity. **2.** barely amounting to as much as indicated.

-scape a suffix indicating a view or expanse of the particular location indicated.

scapegoat /ˈskeɪpgoʊt/ *n.* someone who is made to bear the blame for others.

scapula /ˈskæpjələ/ *n., pl.* **-lae** /-li/. *Anatomy* a shoulder-blade.

scar[1] /ska/ *n., v.,* **scarred**, **scarring**. – *n.* **1.** the mark left by a healed wound, sore, or burn. – *v.t.* **2.** to mark with a scar.

scar[2] /ska/ *n.* a precipitous rocky place; a cliff.

scarab /ˈskærəb/ *n.* a type of beetle.

scarce /skɛəs/ *adj.,* **scarcer**, **scarcest**. seldom met with; rare.

scarcely /ˈskɛəsli/ *adv.* barely; hardly.

scare /skɛə/ *v.,* **scared**, **scaring**, *n.* – *v.t.* **1.** to strike with sudden fear or terror. – *v.i.* **2.** to become frightened. – *n.* **3.** a sudden fright or alarm, especially with little or no ground.

scarecrow /ˈskɛəkroʊ/ *n.* an object, usually a figure of a man in old clothes, set up to frighten crows, etc., away from crops.

scarf /skaf/ *n., pl.* **scarfs**, **scarves** /skavz/. a long, broad strip of silk, wool, lace, etc., worn about the neck, shoulders, or head for ornament or protection.

scarify /ˈskærəfaɪ, ˈskɛər-/ *v.t.,* **-fied**, **-fying**. to make scratches or superficial incisions in.

scarlet /ˈskalət/ *n.* **1.** bright red colour inclining towards orange. – *adj.* **2.** of the colour scarlet.

scarlet fever *n.* a contagious disease, now chiefly of children.

scarp /skap/ *n.* a steep face on the side of a hill.

scarper /ˈskapə/ *v.i.* *Colloquial* to run away; depart suddenly, especially leaving behind debts or other commitments.

scat /skæt/ *v.i.,* **scatted**, **scatting**. *Colloquial* to go off hastily (usually in the imperative).

scathing /ˈskeɪðɪŋ/ *adj.* intended to hurt the feelings.

scato- a word element indicating faeces or excrement.

scatter /ˈskætə/ *v.t.* **1.** to throw loosely about; distribute at irregular intervals. **2.** to separate and drive off in various directions; disperse. – *v.i.* **3.** to separate and disperse; go in different directions. – *n.* **4.** the act of scattering. **5.** that which is scattered.

scavenge /ˈskævəndʒ/ *v.,* **-enged**, **-enging**. – *v.t.* **1.** to search for, and take (anything useable) from discarded material. – *v.i.* **2.** to search amongst refuse or any discarded material for anything useable, as food, clothing, etc.

scenario /səˈnarioʊ/ *n., pl.* **-narios**. an outline of the plot of a dramatic work.

scene /sin/ *n.* **1.** the place where any action occurs. **2.** any view or picture. **3.** an exhibition or outbreak of excited or violent feeling before others. **4.** a unit of dramatic action within a play. **5.** an episode, situation, or the like, as described in writing. **6.** the setting of a story or the like.

scenery /ˈsinəri/ *n., pl.* **-neries**. **1.** the general appearance of a place. **2.** hangings, draperies, structures, etc., on the stage to represent some place or furnish decorative background.

scenic /ˈsinɪk/ *adj.* of or relating to natural

scenery; having fine scenery.

scent /sɛnt/ *n.* **1.** distinctive smell, especially when agreeable. **2.** a track or trail as indicated by such a smell. **3.** → **perfume**. – *v.t.* **4.** to perceive or recognise by the sense of smell. **5.** to impregnate or sprinkle with perfume.

sceptic /'skɛptɪk/ *n.* someone who mistrusts and who maintains a doubting pessimistic attitude towards people, plans, ideas, etc.

sceptre /'sɛptə/ *n.* a rod or wand borne in the hand as an emblem of regal or imperial power.

schedule /'ʃɛdʒul/, *Chiefly US* /'skɛdʒul/ *n.*, *v.*, **-uled**, **-uling**. – *n.* **1.** a plan of procedure for a specified project. **2.** a list of items to be dealt with during a specified time. **3.** a timetable. – *v.t.* **4.** to enter in a schedule. **5.** to plan for a certain date.

schema /'skimə/ *n.*, *pl.* **-mata** /-mətə/. a diagram, plan, or scheme. – **schematic**, *adj.*

scheme /skim/ *n.*, *v.*, **schemed**, **scheming**. – *n.* **1.** a plan or design to be followed, as for building operations, etc. **2.** a policy or plan officially adopted by a company, business, etc., as for pensions, loans, etc. **3.** an underhand plot; intrigue. **4.** any system of correlated things, parts, etc., or the manner of its arrangement. – *v.t.* **5.** to devise as a scheme; plan. – *v.i.* **6.** to plot.

schism /'skɪzəm, 'ʃɪzəm, 'sɪzəm/ *n.* division or disunion, especially into mutually opposed parties.

schizo /'skɪtsoʊ/ *n.*, *adj.* *Colloquial* **1.** schizophrenic. **2.** (a person) having an unpredictable character.

schizo- a word element referring to cleavage. Also (*before vowels*), **schiz-**.

schizophrenia /skɪtsə'friniə/ *n.* a psychosis characterised by breakdown of integrated personality functioning, withdrawal from reality, emotional blunting and distortion, and disturbances in thought and behaviour. – **schizophrenic**, *n.*, *adj.*

schmalz /ʃmɔlts, ʃmælts/ *n.* *Colloquial* excessive sentimentality, especially in the arts. Also, **schmaltz**. – **schmalzy**, *adj.*

schnapper /'snæpə/ *n.* → **snapper**.

schnapps /ʃnæps/ *n.* a type of gin.

scholar /'skɒlə/ *n.* **1.** a learned or erudite person. **2.** a student; pupil.

scholarship /'skɒləʃɪp/ *n.* **1.** learning; knowledge acquired by study; the academic attainments of a scholar. **2.** the sum of money or other aid granted to a scholar.

scholastic /skə'læstɪk/ *adj.* of or relating to schools, scholars, or education.

school¹ /skul/ *n.* **1.** a place or establishment where instruction is given, especially one for children. **2.** a department or faculty in a university or similar educational institution. **3.** a body of scholars, artists, writers, etc., or who are united by a similarity of method, style, principles, etc. – *v.t.* **4.** to educate in or as in a school.

school² /skul/ *n.* a large number of fish, porpoises, whales, or the like, feeding or migrating together.

schoolyard /'skuljad/ *n.* the playground of a school.

schooner /'skunə/ *n.* **1.** a sailing vessel with two or more masts. **2.** a beer glass.

sciatica /saɪ'ætɪkə/ *n.* any painful disorder extending from the hip down the back of the thigh and surrounding area.

science /'saɪəns/ *n.* **1.** systematised knowledge in general. **2.** a particular branch of knowledge.

science fiction *n.* a form of fiction which draws imaginatively on scientific knowledge and speculation.

scientific /saɪən'tɪfɪk/ *adj.* **1.** of or relating to science or the sciences. **2.** systematic or accurate.

scientist /'saɪəntəst/ *n.* one versed in or devoted to science.

scintillate /'sɪntəleɪt/ *v.*, **-lated**, **-lating**. **1.** to twinkle, as the stars. **2.** to be witty, brilliant in conversation.

scion /'saɪən/ *n.* a descendant.

scissors /'sɪzəz/ *pl. n.* a cutting instrument consisting of two blades (with handles) so pivoted together that their edges work against each other (often called *a pair of scissors*).

sclero- a word element meaning 'hard'. Also (*before vowels*), **scler-**.

scoff¹ /skɒf/ *v.i.* to jeer (often fol. by *at*).

scoff² /skɒf/ *v.t.*, *v.i.* *Colloquial* to eat greedily and quickly.

scold /skoʊld/ *v.t.* **1.** to find fault with; chide. – *v.i.* **2.** to find fault; reprove. – *n.* **3.** a person, especially a woman, who is habitually abusive.

scone /skɒn/ *n.* **1.** a small light plain cake, usually eaten split open and spread with butter, etc. **2.** *Colloquial* the head.

scoop /skup/ *n.* **1.** a ladle or ladle-like utensil. **2.** an item of news, etc., published or broadcast in advance of, or to the exclusion of, rival newspapers, broadcasting organisations, etc. – *v.t.* **3.** to take up or out with, or as with a scoop.

scoot /skut/ *v.i.* *Colloquial* to dart; go swiftly or hastily.

scooter /'skutə/ *n.* a child's vehicle with two wheels, one in front of the other, and a tread between them, steered by a handlebar and propelled by pushing against the ground with one foot.

scope /skoʊp/ *n.* **1.** extent or range of view, operation, etc. **2.** space for movement or activity.

-scope a word element referring to instruments for viewing.

-scopy a word element for forming abstract action nouns related to *-scope*.

scorch /skɔtʃ/ *v.t.* **1.** to affect in colour, taste, etc., by burning slightly. **2.** to parch or shrivel with heat. – *v.i.* **3.** to be or become scorched.

score /skɔ/ *n.*, *v.*, **scored**, **scoring**. – *n.* **1.** the record of points made by the competitors in a game or match. **2.** the aggregate of points made by a side or individual. **3.** a notch or scratch. **4.** a group or set of twenty. **5.** account, reason, or ground. **6.** *Music* **a.** a written or printed piece of music. **b.** the background music to a film, play, etc. – *v.t.* **7.** to make a score of. **8.** to make notches, cuts, or lines in or on. – *v.i.* **9.** to make a point or points in a game or contest. **10.** to keep score, as of a game.

scorn /skɔn/ *n.* **1.** open or unqualified contempt; disdain. – *v.t.* **2.** to treat or regard with scorn.

scorpion /'skɔpiən/ *n.* any of numerous arachnids having a long narrow abdomen terminating in a venomous sting.

scotch /skɒtʃ/ *v.t.* to injure so as to make harmless.

scot-free /skɒt-'fri/ *adj.* free from penalty.

scoundrel /'skaʊndrəl/ *n.* an unprincipled, dishonourable person; a villain.

scour[1] /'skaʊə/ *v.t.* **1.** to cleanse or polish by hard rubbing. – *n.* **2.** act of scouring.

scour[2] /'skaʊə/ *v.t.* to range over, as in search.

scourge /skɜdʒ/ *n., v.,* **scourged, scourging**. – *n.* **1.** a cause of affliction or calamity. – *v.t.* **2.** to punish or chastise severely; afflict; torment.

scout /skaʊt/ *n.* **1.** a person sent out to obtain information. – *v.t.* **2.** *Colloquial* to seek; search for (usually fol. by *out* or *up*).

scowl /skaʊl/ *v.i.* **1.** to have a gloomy or threatening look. – *n.* **2.** a scowling expression, look, or aspect.

scrabble /'skræbəl/ *v.,* **-bled, -bling,** *n.* – *v.i.* **1.** to scratch or scrape, as with the claws or hands. **2.** to struggle to gain possession of something. – *n.* **3.** a scrabbling or scramble.

scraggly /'skrægli/ *adj.,* **-glier, -gliest**. irregular; ragged; straggling.

scraggy /'skrægi/ *adj.,* **-gier, -giest**. **1.** lean or thin. **2.** meagre.

scram /skræm/ *v.i.,* **scrammed, scramming**. *Colloquial* to get out quickly; go away.

scramble /'skræmbəl/ *v.,* **-bled, -bling,** *n.* – *v.i.* **1.** to make one's way hurriedly by use of the hands and feet, as over rough ground. **2.** to struggle with others for possession. **3.** to mix together confusedly. – *n.* **4.** a climb or progression over rough, irregular ground, or the like. **5.** any disorderly struggle or proceeding.

scrap[1] /skræp/ *n., adj., v.,* **scrapped, scrapping**. – *n.* **1.** a small piece or portion; a fragment. – *adj.* **2.** consisting of scraps or fragments. **3.** discarded or left over. – *v.t.* **4.** to discard as useless or worthless.

scrap[2] /skræp/ *n. Colloquial* a fight or quarrel.

scrape /skreɪp/ *v.,* **scraped, scraping,** *n.* – *v.t.* **1.** to free from an outer layer by rubbing a sharp instrument over the surface. **2.** to remove (an outer layer, adhering matter, etc.) in this way. **3.** to collect by or as by scraping, or laboriously, or with difficulty (fol. by *up* or *together*). **4.** to rub harshly on or across (something). – *v.i.* **5.** to scrape something. **6.** to practise laborious economy or saving. – *n.* **7.** a scraped place. **8.** an embarrassing situation. **9.** a fight; struggle; scrap.

scratch /skrætʃ/ *v.t.* **1.** to dig, scrape, or to tear (*out, off,* etc.) with the claws, the nails, etc. **2.** to rub or scrape lightly with the fingernails, etc., as to relieve itching. **3.** to erase or strike out (writing, a name, etc.). – *v.i.* **4.** to use the nails, claws, etc., for tearing, digging, etc. **5.** to relieve itching by rubbing with the nails, etc. **6.** to make a slight grating noise, as a pen. – *n.* **7.** a mark produced by scratching, such as one on the skin. **8.** an act of scratching. **9. from scratch,** from the beginning. **10. up to scratch,** satisfactory.

scrawl /skrɔl/ *v.t., v.i.* **1.** to write or draw in a sprawling awkward manner. – *n.* **2.** awkward or careless handwriting.

scrawny /'skrɔni/ *adj.,* **-nier, -niest**. lean; thin; scraggy.

scream /skrim/ *v.i.* **1.** to utter a loud, sharp, piercing cry or sound. – *n.* **2.** a loud, sharp, piercing cry or sound. **3.** *Colloquial* someone or something that is very funny.

screech /skritʃ/ *v.i.* **1.** to utter a harsh, shrill cry. – *n.* **2.** a harsh, shrill cry.

screed /skrid/ *n.* a long speech or piece of writing; harangue.

screen /skrin/ *n.* **1.** a covered frame or the like, movable or fixed, serving as a shelter, partition, etc. **2.** something affording a surface for displaying films, slides, etc. **3.** films collectively. **4.** anything that shelters, protects, or conceals. – *v.t.* **5.** to shelter, protect, or conceal with, or as with, a screen. **6.** to project (pictures, etc.) on a screen. **7.** to check the loyalty, character, ability, etc., of applicants, employees, (etc.).

screenplay /'skrinpleɪ/ *n.* the script of a film, including details of camera positions and movement, action, dialogue, lighting, etc.

screen-print /skrin-'prɪnt/ *n., v.t.* → **silkscreen**.

screw /skru/ *n.* **1.** a metal device to hold things together, having a slotted head and a tapering body with a helical ridge. **2.** something having a spiral form. **3.** *Colloquial* sexual intercourse. – *v.t.* **4.** to force, press, hold fast, stretch tight, etc., by or as by means of a screw. **5.** to work (a screw, etc.) by turning. **6.** to twist; contort; distort. **7.** to force. – *v.i.* **8.** to turn as or like a screw. **9.** to be adapted for being connected or taken apart by means of a screw or screws (fol. by *on, together, off,* etc.).

screwdriver /'skrudraɪvə/ *n.* a tool fitting into the slotted head of a screw for driving in or withdrawing it by turning.

scribble /'skrɪbəl/ *v.,* **-bled, -bling,** *n.* – *v.t.* **1.** to write hastily or carelessly. **2.** to make meaningless marks. – *n.* **3.** a hasty or careless piece of writing or drawing.

scribe /skraɪb/ *n.* a penman or copyist, as someone who, formerly, made copies of manuscripts, etc.

scrimp /skrɪmp/ *v.t.* to be sparing of or in; stint.

scrip /skrɪp/ *n.* **1.** a writing, especially a receipt or certificate. **2.** *Finance* shares or stock issued to existing shareholders in a scrip issue. **3.** *Finance* a certificate that part of the issue price of a debenture, bond, or share has been paid, and setting out the amounts and dates when further sums are due.

scrip issue *n.* an issue of stock, etc., where the purchase price is payable by instalments according to the terms of the prospectus.

script /skrɪpt/ *n.* the working text of a play, film, etc.

scripture /'skrɪptʃə/ *n.* any writing or book, of a sacred nature, especially (*cap.*) the Bible.

scroll /skroʊl/ *n.* **1.** a roll of parchment or

paper, especially one with writing on it. **2.** an ornament, having a spiral or coiled form.

scrooge /skrudʒ/ *n.* a miserly, ill-tempered person.

scrotum /'skroʊtəm/ *n., pl.* **-ta** /-tə/. the pouch of skin that contains the testicles.

scrounge /skraʊndʒ/ *v.t.,* **scrounged, scrounging**. to obtain by borrowing, foraging, or pilfering.

scrub[1] /skrʌb/ *v.,* **scrubbed, scrubbing**, *n.* – *v.t.* **1.** to rub hard with a brush, cloth, etc., or against a rough surface, in washing. **2.** *Colloquial* to cancel; get rid of. – *v.i.* **3.** to cleanse things by hard rubbing. – *n.* **4.** the act of scrubbing.

scrub[2] /skrʌb/ *n.* **1.** low trees or shrubs, collectively. **2.** tall, thick rainforest in eastern Australia.

scruff /skrʌf/ *n.* the nape or back of the neck.

scruffy /'skrʌfi/ *adj. Colloquial* unkempt or dirty; shabby.

scrumptious /'skrʌmpʃəs/ *adj. Colloquial* deliciously tasty; superlatively fine or nice; splendid.

scrupulous /'skrupjələs/ *adj.* punctiliously or minutely careful, precise, or exact.

scrutineer /skrutə'nɪə/ *n.* someone who is authorised, especially by a candidate at an election, to inspect the counting of votes by electoral officers.

scrutinise = scrutinize /'skrutənaɪz/ *v.t.,* **-nised, -nising**. to examine closely or critically. – **scrutiny**, *n.*

scuba /'skubə/ *n.* a portable breathing device for free-swimming divers.

scud /skʌd/ *v.i.,* **scudded, scudding**. to run or move quickly or hurriedly.

scuff /skʌf/ *v.t.* **1.** to mar by scraping or hard use, as shoes, furniture, etc. – *n.* **2.** a type of slipper or sandal without a back.

scuffle /'skʌfəl/ *v.,* **-fled, -fling**, *n.* – *v.i.* **1.** to struggle or fight in a scrambling, confused manner. – *n.* **2.** a confused struggle or fight.

scullery /'skʌləri/ *n., pl.* **-leries**. a small room where the rough, dirty work of a kitchen is done.

sculpture /'skʌlptʃə/ *n., v.,* **-tured, -turing**. – *n.* **1.** the fine art of forming figures or designs by carving, moulding, etc. **2.** a piece of such work. – *v.t.* **3.** Also, **sculpt**. to carve, make, or execute by sculpture. – **sculptor**, *n.*

scum /skʌm/ *n.* a film of foul or extraneous matter on a liquid.

scunge /skʌndʒ/ *n. Colloquial* dirt, mess, slime, etc.

scupper /'skʌpə/ *v.t.* to sink (a ship) deliberately.

scurrilous /'skʌrələs/ *adj.* grossly or indecently abusive.

scurry /'skʌri/ *v.,* **-ried, -rying**, *n., pl.* **-ries**. – *v.i.* **1.** to go or move quickly or in haste. – *n.* **2.** a scurrying rush.

scurvy /'skɜvi/ *n., adj.,* **-vier, -viest**. – *n.* **1.** *Pathology* a disease caused by a diet lacking in vitamin C. – *adj.* **2.** low, mean, or contemptible.

scuttle /'skʌtl/ *v.,* **-tled, -tling**, *n.* – *v.i.* **1.** to run with quick, hasty steps; hurry (often fol. by *off*, *away*, etc.). – *n.* **2.** an act of scuttling.

scythe /saɪð/ *n.* an agricultural implement for mowing grass, etc., by hand.

se- a prefix applied mainly to stems not used as words, having a general meaning of setting apart or taking away, as in *seclude*, *seduce*.

sea /si/ *n.* **1.** the salt waters that cover the greater part of the earth's surface. **2.** a division of these waters. **3.** a large lake or landlocked body of water. **4. at sea,** in a state of perplexity.

sea anemone /'si əˌnɛməni/ *n.* any of several marine coelenterates.

sea-breeze /'si-briz/ *n.* a thermally produced wind blowing during the day from the cool ocean surface on to the adjoining warm land.

seafood /'sifud/ *n.* any saltwater fish or shellfish which is used for food.

seafront /'sifrʌnt/ *n.* the side or edge of land and buildings bordering on the sea.

seagoing /'sigoʊɪŋ/ *adj.* designed or fit for going to sea, as a vessel.

seagrass matting /'sigras/ *n.* matting made using certain grass fibres.

seagull /'sigʌl/ *n.* a gull, especially any of the marine species.

seahorse /'sihɔs/ *n.* any of a number of small fishes with a prehensile tail and a beaked head that is turned at right angles to the body.

seal[1] /sil/ *n.* **1.** a device affixed to a document as evidence of authenticity or attestation. **2.** anything that effectively closes a thing. **3.** a road surface of hard material, as tar, bitumen, etc. – *v.t.* **4.** to approve, authorise, or confirm. **5.** to close by any form of fastening that must be broken before access can be had. **6.** to decide irrevocably. **7.** to surface a road with tar, bitumen, etc.

seal[2] /sil/ *n., pl.* **seals**, (*esp. collectively*) **seal**. any of several furred, amphibious mammals with flippers for limbs.

sea level *n.* the horizontal plane or level corresponding to the surface of the sea when halfway between mean high and low water.

seam /sim/ *n.* **1.** the line formed by sewing together pieces of cloth, leather, or the like. **2.** any line between abutting edges; a crack or fissure; a groove. – *v.t.* **3.** to join with a seam; sew the seams of. **4.** to furrow; mark with wrinkles, scars, etc. – *v.i.* **5.** to become cracked, fissured, or furrowed.

seamstress /'simstrəs/ *n.* a woman whose occupation is sewing. Also, **sempstress**.

seamy /'simi/ *adj.,* **-mier, -miest**. not pleasing or favourable; bad; sordid.

seance /'seɪɒns/ *n.* a meeting of people seeking to communicate with spirits of the dead with the help of a medium. Also, **séance**.

seaplane /'sipleɪn/ *n.* an aeroplane that can land on water.

sear /sɪə/ *v.t.* to burn or char the surface of.

search /sɜtʃ/ *v.t.* **1.** to go or look through carefully in seeking to find something. **2.** to examine (a person) for concealed objects by going through their pockets or the like. **3.** to bring or find (*out*) by a search. – *v.i.* **4.** to seek. – *n.* **5.** the act of searching. **6.** *Law* examination by a purchaser of records and registers at the Land Titles Office to find encumbrances affecting title to property.

search-warrant /'sɜtʃ-wɒrənt/ *n.* a court order authorising the searching of a house, etc., as for stolen goods.

seashell /'siʃɛl/ *n.* the shell of any marine mollusc.

seashore /'siʃɔ/ *n.* land along the sea or ocean.

seasickness /'sisɪknəs/ *n.* nausea caused by the motion of a vessel at sea.

season /'sizən/ *n.* **1.** a period of the year characterised by particular conditions of weather, temperature, etc. **2.** the period of the year when something is best or available. **3.** any period of time. **4.** a suitable, proper, fitting, or right time. **5.** *Agriculture* fertile period in female stock; time for mating. – *v.t.* **6.** to heighten or improve the flavour of (food) by adding condiments, spices, herbs, or the like. **7.** to dry and harden (timber) by due process. – *v.i.* **8.** to become seasoned, matured, hardened, or the like.

seasonable /'sizənəbəl/ *adj.* **1.** suitable to the season. **2.** timely; opportune.

seasonal /'sizənəl/ *adj.* periodical.

seasonally-adjusted /sizənəli-ə'dʒʌstəd/ *adj.* of or relating to sets of figures, as unemployment figures, which are altered to allow for seasonal fluctuations which would distort them.

seasoning /'sizənɪŋ/ *n.* something that seasons, especially salt, spices, herbs, or other condiments.

season ticket *n.* a ticket valid any number of times for a specified period, usually at a reduced rate.

seat /sit/ *n.* **1.** something for sitting on, as a chair or bench. **2.** the part of a chair or the like on which one sits. **3.** the part of the body on which one sits; the buttocks. **4.** manner of sitting, as on horseback. **5.** an established place or centre, as of government. **6.** site, location, or locality. **7.** a parliamentary constituency. – *v.t.* **8.** to place on a seat or seats. **9.** to find seats for.

seatbelt /'sitbɛlt/ *n.* a belt attached to the frame of a motor vehicle for securing a driver or passenger against sudden turns, stops, collision, etc. Also, **safety belt**.

seaweed /'siwid/ *n.* any plant or plants growing in the ocean, especially marine algae.

sebaceous /sə'beɪʃəs/ *adj.* **1.** relating to, of the nature of, or resembling tallow or fat. **2.** secreting a fatty substance.

secant /'sikənt/ *n.* *Mathematics* a straight line which cuts a circle or other curve.

secateurs /'sɛkətəz, sɛkə'tɜz/ *pl. n.* a scissor-like cutting instrument for pruning shrubs, etc.

secede /sə'sid/ *v.i.*, **-ceded**, **-ceding**. to withdraw formally from an alliance or association, as from a political or religious organisation. – **secession**, *n.*

seclude /sə'klud/ *v.t.*, **-cluded**, **-cluding**. to shut off or keep apart; place in or withdraw into solitude. – **seclusion**, *n.*

second[1] /'sɛkənd/ *adj.* **1.** next after the first in order, place, time, rank, value, quality, etc.; the ordinal of two. **2.** alternate. **3.** additional; further. – *n.* **4.** someone who or that which comes next to or after the first, in order, quality, rank, etc. **5.** (*sometimes pl.*) *Commerce* a product or material that is below the normal or required standard. – *v.t.* **6.** to support, back up, or assist. – *adv.* **7.** in the second place, group, etc.

second[2] /'sɛkənd/ *n.* **1.** a sixtieth part of a minute of time. **2.** *Geometry, etc.* the sixtieth part of a minute of a degree. **3.** a moment or instant.

second[3] /sə'kɒnd/ *v.t.* to transfer (a military officer or other) temporarily to another post, organisation, or responsibility.

secondary /'sɛkəndri/ *adj.* **1.** next after the first in order, place, time, importance, etc. **2.** derived or derivative; not primary or original. **3.** of or relating to the processing of primary products. **4.** of minor importance; subordinate; auxiliary.

secondary boycott *n.* a boycott placed by employees on dealings of their employer with another person, or an attempt by an employer to place a ban on or undermine free competition with another employer.

secondary school *n.* a school providing post-primary education; a high school.

secondary wage *n.* → **margin** (def. 6).

second cousin *n.* See **cousin**.

second-hand /'sɛkənd-hænd, sɛkənd-'hænd/ *adj.*, /sɛkənd-'hænd/ *adv.* – *adj.* **1.** previously used or owned. – *adv.* **2.** after having been owned by another person.

second mortgage *n.* a mortgage taken out in addition to an existing mortgage.

second nature *n.* habit, tendency, etc., so long practised that it is inalterably fixed in one's character.

second sight *n.* a supposed faculty of seeing distant objects and future events; clairvoyance.

second wind *n.* the restoration of more comfortable breathing after one has got over an initial stress.

secret /'sikrət/ *adj.* **1.** done, made, or conducted without the knowledge of others. – *n.* **2.** something secret, hidden, or concealed. **3.** the reason or explanation, not immediately or generally apparent. **4. in secret,** secretly. – **secretive**, *adj.*

secret agent *n.* a spy.

secretariat /sɛkrə'tɛəriət/ *n.* the officials or office entrusted with maintaining records and performing secretarial duties, especially for an international organisation.

secretary /'sɛkrətri, 'sɛkrətəri/ *n.*, *pl.* **-taries**. **1.** a person who conducts correspondence, keeps records, etc., for an individual or an organisation. **2.** → **private secretary**.

secretary-general /sɛkrətri-'dʒɛnrəl/ *n.*, *pl.* **secretaries-general**. the head of a secretariat.

secrete /sə'krit/ *v.t.*, **-creted**, **-creting**. **1.** *Biology* to separate off, prepare, or elaborate from the blood, as in the physiological process of secretion. **2.** to hide or conceal; keep secret. – **secretion**, *n.*

secret service *n.* official service of a secret nature.

sect /sɛkt/ *n.* a body of persons adhering to a particular religious faith; a religious denomination.

-sect a word element meaning 'cut', as in *intersect.*

section /'sɛkʃən/ *n.* **1.** one of a number of parts that fit together to make a whole. **2.** the act of cutting; separation by cutting. **3.** a representation of an object as it would appear if cut by a plane. **4.** → **block** (def. 7).

sector /'sɛktə/ *n.* any field or division of a field of activity.

secular /'sɛkjələ/ *adj.* of or relating to the world, or to things not religious, sacred, or spiritual; temporal; worldly.

secure /sə'kjuə/ *adj., v.,* **-cured**, **-curing**. *– adj.* **1.** free from or not exposed to danger; safe. **2.** not liable to fall, yield, become displaced, etc., as a support or a fastening. **3.** free from care; without anxiety. **4.** sure; certain. *– v.t.* **5.** to get hold or possession of; obtain. **6.** to make secure or certain. **7.** to assure a creditor of (payment) by the pledge or mortgaging of property.

sedan /sə'dæn/ *n.* a four-door passenger car. Also, **saloon car**.

sedate /sə'deɪt/ *adj., v.,* **-dated**, **-dating**. *– adj.* **1.** calm, quiet, or composed. *– v.t.* **2.** to calm or put to sleep by means of sedatives.

sedative /'sɛdətɪv/ *adj.* **1.** tending to calm or soothe. *– n.* **2.** a sedative agent or remedy.

sedentary /'sɛdəntri/ *adj.* characterised by or requiring a sitting posture.

sediment /'sɛdəmənt/ *n.* matter which settles to the bottom of a liquid.

sedition /sə'dɪʃən/ *n.* incitement of discontent or rebellion against the government.

seduce /sə'djus/ *v.t.,* **-duced**, **-ducing**. **1.** to induce to have sexual intercourse. **2.** to win over; entice. – **seduction**, *n.* – **seductive**, *adj.*

see[1] /si/ *v.,* **saw**, **seen**, **seeing**. *– v.t.* **1.** to observe, be aware of, or perceive, with the eyes. **2.** to perceive or be aware of with any or all of the senses. **3.** to have experience or knowledge of. **4.** to view, or visit or attend as a spectator. **5.** to discern with the intelligence; perceive mentally; understand. **6.** to ascertain, find out, or learn, as by enquiry. **7.** to visit. **8.** to accompany or escort. **9.** to ensure. *– v.i.* **10.** to have or use the power of sight. **11.** to understand; discern. **12.** to enquire or find out. **13.** to give attention or care.

see[2] /si/ *n.* the seat, centre of authority, office, or jurisdiction of a bishop.

seed /sid/ *n., pl.* **seeds**, **seed**, *v. – n.* **1.** the propagative part of a plant, especially as preserved for growing a new crop, including ovules, tubers, bulbs, etc. **2.** (*usu. pl.*) the germ or beginning of anything. **3.** a player who has been seeded. *– v.t.* **4.** to sow (land) with seed. **5.** to modify (the ordinary drawing of lots for position in a tournament, as at tennis) by distributing certain outstanding players so that they will not meet in the early rounds of play. *– v.i.* **6.** to produce or shed seed.

seedling /'sidlɪŋ/ *n.* a young plant developed from the embryo after germination of a seed.

seedy /'sidi/ *adj.,* **-dier**, **-diest**. rather disreputable or shabby.

seek /sik/ *v.t.,* **sought**, **seeking**. **1.** to go in search or quest of. **2.** to try or attempt (followed by an infinitive). **3.** to ask for; request.

seem /sim/ *v.i.* to appear to be; appear (to be, feel, do, etc.).

seemly /'simli/ *adj.,* **-lier**, **-liest**. fitting or becoming with respect to propriety or good taste; decent; decorous.

seep /sip/ *v.i.* to pass gradually, as liquid, through a porous substance; ooze.

seer /sɪə/ *n.* someone who foretells future events; a prophet.

seesaw /'si,sɔ/ *n.* **1.** a plank or beam balanced at the middle so that its ends may rise and fall alternately. *– v.i.* **2.** to move in the manner of a seesaw.

seethe /sið/ *v.i.,* **seethed**, **seething**. to surge or foam, as a boiling liquid.

segment /'sɛgmənt/ *n.,* /sɛg'mɛnt/ *v. – n.* **1.** one of the parts into which anything naturally separates or is naturally divided. *– v.t., v.i.* **2.** to separate or divide into segments.

segregate /'sɛgrəgeɪt/ *v.,* **-gated**, **-gating**. *– v.t.* **1.** to separate or set apart from the others or from the main body; isolate. *– v.i.* **2.** to separate or go apart.

seismic /'saɪzmɪk/ *adj.* relating to, of the nature of, or caused by an earthquake. Also, **seismal**, **seismical**.

seismo- a word element meaning 'seismic'.

seize /siz/ *v.,* **seized**, **seizing**. *– v.t.* **1.** to lay hold of suddenly or forcibly; grasp. **2.** to take possession of by legal authority; confiscate. **3.** to take advantage of promptly. *– v.i.* **4.** to become jammed or stuck solid, as an engine through excessive heat (fol. by *up*).

seizure /'siʒə/ *n.* **1.** the act of seizing. **2.** a sudden attack, as of disease.

seldom /'sɛldəm/ *adv.* rarely; infrequently; not often.

select /sə'lɛkt/ *v.t.* **1.** to choose in preference to another or others. *– adj.* **2.** selected; chosen in preference to others.

selection /sə'lɛkʃən/ *n.* **1.** the act of selecting or the fact of being selected; choice. **2.** a thing or a number of things selected. **3.** a range of things from which selection may be made.

seleno- a word element meaning 'moon', as in *selenology.*

self /sɛlf/ *n., pl.* **selves**, *pron., pl.* **selves**. *– n.* **1.** a person or thing referred to with respect to individuality; one's own person. *– pron.* **2.** myself, himself, etc.

self- prefixal use of **self**, expressing principally reflexive action or relation.

self-assurance /sɛlf-ə'ʃɔrəns/ *n.* self-confidence. – **self-assured**, *adj.*

self-centred /sɛlf-'sɛntəd/ *adj.* engrossed in one's self; selfish.

self-confidence /sɛlf-'kɒnfədəns/ *n.* confidence in one's own judgment, ability, power, etc., sometimes to an excessive degree.

self-conscious /sɛlf-ˈkɒnʃəs/ *adj.* excessively conscious of oneself as an object of observation to others.

self-contained /ˈsɛlf-kənteɪnd/ *adj.* containing in oneself or itself all that is necessary; independent.

self-control /sɛlf-kənˈtroʊl/ *n.* control of oneself or one's actions, feelings, etc.

self-defence /sɛlf-dəˈfɛns/ *n.* the act of defending one's own person, reputation, etc.

self-esteem /sɛlf-əsˈtim/ *n.* favourable opinion of oneself.

self-evident /sɛlf-ˈɛvədənt/ *adj.* evident in itself without proof; axiomatic.

self-government /sɛlf-ˈgʌvənmənt/ *n.* political independence of a country, people, region, etc.

self-important /sɛlf-ɪmˈpɔtnt/ *adj.* having or showing an exaggerated opinion of one's own importance; conceited or pompous.

self-interest /sɛlf-ˈɪntrəst/ *n.* regard for one's own interest or advantage, especially with disregard of others.

selfish /ˈsɛlfɪʃ/ *adj.* devoted to or caring only for oneself, one's welfare, interests, etc.

self-opinionated /sɛlf-əˈpɪnjəneɪtəd/ *adj.* obstinate in one's own opinion.

self-possessed /sɛlf-pəˈzɛst/ *adj.* having or showing control of one's feelings, behaviour, etc.

self-raising flour /sɛlf-ˈreɪzɪŋ flaʊə/ *n.* wheat flour with baking powder already added.

self-respect /sɛlf-rəˈspɛkt/ *n.* proper esteem or regard for the dignity of one's character.

selfsame /ˈsɛlfseɪm/ *adj.* (the) very same; identical.

self-satisfaction /ˌsɛlf-sætəsˈfækʃən/ *n.* satisfaction with oneself, one's achievements, etc.; smugness. – **self-satisfied**, *adj.*

self-seeking /sɛlf-ˈsikɪŋ/ *adj.* selfish.

self-service /sɛlf-ˈsɜvəs/ *adj.* (of a service station, restaurant, shop, etc.) operating on the principle that the customers perform part or all of the service themselves. Also, **self-serve**.

self-sufficient /sɛlf-səˈfɪʃənt/ *adj.* able to supply one's own needs.

sell /sɛl/ *v.,* **sold**, **selling**, *n.* – *v.t.* **1.** to give up or make over for a consideration; dispose of to a purchaser for a price. **2.** to deal in; keep for sale. – *v.i.* **3.** to sell something; engage in selling. **4.** to be on sale; find purchasers. **5. sell out, a.** to sell all of. **b.** *Colloquial* to betray. **6. sell up,** to liquidate by selling the assets (of). – *n.* **7.** *Colloquial* an act of selling or salesmanship. See **hard sell**, **soft sell**.

sellers' market *n.* a market in which the seller is at an advantage because of scarcity of supply.

selvage = selvedge /ˈsɛlvɪdʒ/ *n.* the edge of woven fabric finished to prevent fraying, often in a narrow tape effect, different from the body of the fabric.

selves /sɛlvz/ *n.* plural of **self**.

semantic /səˈmæntɪk/ *adj.* relating to meaning.

semaphore /ˈsɛməfɔ/ *n.* a system of signalling by hand, in which a flag is held in each hand at arm's length in various positions.

semblance /ˈsɛmbləns/ *n.* an outward aspect or appearance.

semen /ˈsimən/ *n.* the impregnating fluid produced by male reproductive organs; seed; sperm.

semester /səˈmɛstə/ *n.* (in educational institutions) one of two divisions of the academic year. See **term**.

semi- a prefix modifying the latter element of the word, meaning 'half' in its precise and less precise meanings, as in *semitone.*

semicolon /sɛmiˈkoʊlən, ˈsɛmikoʊlən/ *n.* a mark of punctuation (;) used to indicate a more distinct separation between parts of a sentence than that indicated by a comma.

semiconductor /ˌsɛmɪkənˈdʌktə/ *n.* **1.** a substance whose electrical conductivity at normal temperatures is intermediate between that of a metal and an insulator. **2.** a device, as a transistor, which is based on the electronic properties of such substances.

semiconductor memory *n.* a computer memory with storage elements formed by integrated semiconductor devices.

semidetached /ˌsɛmidəˈtætʃt/ *adj.* of or relating to a pair of houses joined by a common wall but detached from other buildings.

seminal /ˈsɛmənəl/ *adj.* highly original and influential.

seminar /ˈsɛmənа/ *n.* a meeting organised to discuss a specific topic.

seminary /ˈsɛmənri/ *n., pl.* **-naries**. *Roman Catholic Church* a college for the education of men for the priesthood or ministry.

semitone /ˈsɛmitoʊn/ *n. Music* the smallest interval in the chromatic scale of Western music.

semitrailer /sɛmiˈtreɪlə/ *n.* an articulated goods vehicle.

semolina /sɛməˈlinə/ *n.* the large, hard parts of wheat grains used for making puddings, etc.

senate /ˈsɛnət/ *n.* **1.** a legislative assembly of a state or nation. **2.** a governing, advisory, or disciplinary body, as in certain universities. – **senator**, *n.*

send /sɛnd/ *v.,* **sent**, **sending**. – *v.t.* **1.** to cause to go; direct or order to go. **2.** to cause to be conveyed or transmitted to a destination. **3.** to give (fol. by *forth*, *out*, etc.), as light, smell, or sound. **4. send up,** *Colloquial* to mock or ridicule; satirise. – *v.i.* **5.** to dispatch a message, messenger, etc.

senile /ˈsɛnaɪl, ˈsinaɪl/ *adj.* mentally or physically infirm due to old age.

senior /ˈsinjə/ *adj.* **1.** older or elder. **2.** of higher rank or standing, especially by virtue of longer service. – *n.* **3.** a person who is older than another. – **seniority**, *n.*

sensation /sɛnˈseɪʃən/ *n.* **1.** the operation or function of the senses; perception through the senses. **2.** a mental condition produced through or as through an organ of sense. **3.** a state of excited feeling or interest caused among a number of persons. **4.** a cause of such feeling or interest.

sensationalism /sɛnˈseɪʃənəlɪzəm/ *n.* the

exploitation of cheap emotional excitement by popular newspapers, novels, etc.

sense /sɛns/ *n.*, *v.*, **sensed**, **sensing**. – *n.* **1.** each of the special faculties connected with bodily organs by which human beings and other animals perceive external objects and their own bodily changes (commonly reckoned as sight, hearing, smell, taste, and touch). **2.** a feeling or perception produced through the organs of touch, taste, etc. **3.** any more or less vague perception or impression. **4.** sound practical intelligence; common sense. **5.** what is sensible or reasonable. **6.** the meaning, or one of the meanings, of a word, statement, or a passage. **7. in a sense,** according to one interpretation. – *v.t.* **8.** to perceive by or as by the senses.

sensibility /sɛnsə'bɪləti/ *n.*, *pl.* **-ties**. **1.** mental susceptibility or responsiveness. **2.** (*pl.*) emotional capacities.

sensible /'sɛnsəbəl/ *adj.* **1.** having, using, or showing good sense or sound judgment. **2.** cognisant; keenly aware (usually fol. by *of*).

sensitive /'sɛnsətɪv/ *adj.* **1.** readily affected by external agencies or influences. **2.** easily affected, pained, annoyed, etc. **3.** (of an issue, topic, etc.) arousing strong feelings or reaction.

sensory /'sɛnsəri/ *adj.* relating to sensation.

sensual /'sɛnʃuəl/ *adj.* relating to or given to the gratification of the senses or the indulgence of appetite.

sensuous /'sɛnʃuəs/ *adj.* readily affected through the senses.

sent /sɛnt/ *v.* past tense and past participle of **send**.

sentence /'sɛntəns/ *n.*, *v.*, **-tenced**, **-tencing**. – *n.* **1.** a word or a sequence of words arranged in a grammatical construction expressing an independent statement, inquiry, command, or the like, as, *Fire!* or *Summer is here* or *Who's there?* **2.** *Law* **a.** a judicial judgment or decree, especially the judicial determination of the punishment to be inflicted on a convicted criminal. **b.** the punishment itself. – *v.t.* **3.** to pronounce sentence upon.

sententious /sɛn'tɛnʃəs/ *adj.* moralising.

sentient /'sɛntiənt, 'sɛnʃənt/ *adj.* having the power of perception by the senses.

sentiment /'sɛntəmənt/ *n.* **1.** mental attitude with regard to something; opinion. **2.** refined or tender emotion. **3.** the thought or feeling intended to be conveyed by words.

sentimental /sɛntə'mɛntl/ *adj.* **1.** relating to or dependent on sentiment. **2.** weakly emotional.

sentimental value *n.* the value which something often of little or no monetary value has because of its ability to arouse sentiments.

sentinel /'sɛntənəl/ *n.* one on watch.

sentry /'sɛntri/ *n.*, *pl.* **-tries**. a soldier stationed at a place to keep guard; a sentinel.

sepal /'sipəl/ *n.* any of the individual leaves or parts of the calyx of a flower.

separate /'sɛpəreɪt/ *v.*, **-rated**, **-rating**, /'sɛprət/ *adj.* – *v.t.* **1.** to keep apart or divide, as by an intervening barrier, space, etc. **2.** to part or divide (an assemblage, mass, compound, etc.) into individuals, components, or elements. **3.** to take (fol. by *from* or *out*) by such parting or dividing. – *v.i.* **4.** to part company; withdraw from personal association (often fol. by *from*). **5.** become disconnected or disengaged. **6.** to become parted from a mass or compound, as crystals. – *adj.* **7.** separated, disconnected, or disjoined. **8.** unconnected or distinct.

sepia /'sipiə/ *n.* **1.** a brown pigment. **2.** *Photography* a brown-coloured image. – *adj.* **3.** of a brown similar to that from sepia ink.

sepsis /'sɛpsəs/ *n.* local or generalised bacterial invasion of the body.

sept- a prefix meaning 'seven'. Also, **septem-**, **septe-**, **septi-**.

septic /'sɛptɪk/ *adj.* relating to or of the nature of sepsis; infected.

septicaemia = septicemia /sɛptə'simiə/ *n.* the invasion and persistence of pathogenic bacteria in the bloodstream.

septic tank *n.* a tank in which solid organic sewage is decomposed and purified by bacteria.

septum /'sɛptəm/ *n.*, *pl.* **septa** /'sɛptə/. *Biology* a dividing wall, membrane, or the like in a plant or animal structure.

sepulchre /'sɛpəlkə/ *n.* a tomb, grave, or burial place.

sequel /'sikwəl/ *n.* **1.** a literary work, film, etc., complete in itself, but continuing a preceding work. **2.** an event or circumstance following something.

sequence /'sikwəns/ *n.* **1.** the following of one thing after another; succession. **2.** order of succession. **3.** a continuous or connected series.

sequester /sə'kwɛstə, si-/ *v.t.* to remove or withdraw into solitude or retirement; seclude. – **sequestration**, *n.*

sequin /'sikwən/ *n.* a small shining disc or spangle used to ornament a dress, etc.

serenade /sɛrə'neɪd/ *n.*, *v.*, **-naded**, **-nading**. – *n.* **1.** a song sung in the open air at night, as by a man under the window of his lover. – *v.t.* **2.** to entertain with a serenade.

serene /sə'rin/ *adj.* calm; peaceful; tranquil. – **serenity**, *n.*

serf /sɜf/ *n.* a person required to render services to a lord.

serge /sɜdʒ/ *n.* cotton, rayon, or silk in a twill weave.

serial /'sɪəriəl/ *n.* **1.** anything published, broadcast, etc., in instalments at regular intervals. – *adj.* **2.** published in instalments or successive parts. **3.** of, relating to, or arranged in a series.

serial number *n.* an individual number given to a particular person, article, etc., for identification.

series /'sɪəriz/ *n.*, *pl.* **-ries**. a number of things, events, etc., ranged or occurring in spatial, temporal, or other succession; a sequence.

serious /'sɪəriəs/ *adj.* **1.** of grave or solemn disposition or character; thoughtful. **2.** being in earnest; not trifling. **3.** weighty or important.

sermon /'sɜmən/ *n.* **1.** a discourse for the

purpose of religious instruction or exhortation, especially one based on a text of Scripture and delivered from a pulpit. **2.** a long, tedious speech.

sero- a word element representing **serum**.

serpent /'sɜpənt/ *n.* a snake. – **serpentine**, *adj.*

serrated /sə'reɪtəd/ *adj.* having a notched or grooved edge.

serum /'sɪərəm/ *n., pl.* **sera** /'sɪərə/, **serums**. the clear, pale yellow liquid which separates from the clot in the coagulation of blood.

servant /'sɜvənt/ *n.* a person in the service of another.

serve /sɜv/ *v.,* **served**, **serving**, *n.* – *v.i.* **1.** to act as a servant. **2.** to wait at table; hand food to guests. **3.** to render assistance; help. **4.** to go through a term of service. **5.** *Tennis, etc.* to put the ball in play. – *v.t.* **6.** to be in the service of; work for. **7.** to render service to; help. **8.** to go through (a term of service, imprisonment, etc.). **9.** to answer the requirements of; suffice. **10.** to wait upon; set food before. **11.** to set (food) on a table. **12.** (of a male animal) to mate with. **13.** *Law* to make legal delivery of (a process or writ). – *n.* **14.** the act, manner, or right of serving, as in tennis.

servery /'sɜvəri/ *n.* an area in which food is set out on plates.

service /'sɜvəs/ *n., adj., v.,* **-viced**, **-vicing**. – *n.* **1.** an act of helpful activity. **2.** the supplying or supplier of any articles, commodities, activities, etc., required or demanded. **3.** occupation or employment as a servant. **4.** *Military* (*pl.*) the armed forces. **5.** the act of servicing a piece of machinery, especially a motor vehicle. **6.** public religious worship according to prescribed form and order. **7.** *Tennis, etc.* the act or manner of putting the ball in play. – *adj.* **8.** of service; useful. **9.** of, relating to, or used by, servants, tradespeople, etc. **10.** of or relating to the armed forces. – *v.t.* **11.** to make fit for service; restore to condition for service. **12.** (of a male animal) to inseminate (a female animal). **13.** to meet interest and other payments on, as a government debt.

serviceable /'sɜvəsəbəl/ *adj.* capable of doing good service.

service industry *n.* an industry providing services such as transport or entertainment, as opposed to the manufacturing industry.

service lift *n.* a goods lift.

service station *n.* commercial premises selling petrol, oil, etc., for motor vehicles, and sometimes offering mechanical repairs. Also, **petrol station**.

serviette /sɜvi'ɛt/ *n.* a piece of cloth or paper used at table to protect the clothes, etc.; napkin; dinner napkin; table napkin.

servile /'sɜvaɪl/ *adj.* obsequious.

serving /'sɜvɪŋ/ *n.* a portion of food or drink; a helping.

servitude /'sɜvətjud/ *n.* slavery; bondage.

sesame /'sɛsəmi/ *n.* the small edible seeds of a tropical plant.

sesqui- a word element meaning 'one and a half'.

session /'sɛʃən/ *n.* a period of time during which a person or group of persons performs an activity.

set /sɛt/ *v.,* **set**, **setting**, *n., adj.* – *v.t.* **1.** to put in a particular place, position, condition or relation. **2.** to apply. **3.** to put (a price or value) upon something. **4.** to incite or urge to attack. **5.** to fix, appoint, or ordain. **6.** to prescribe or assign, as a task. **7.** to put in the proper position, order, or condition for use; adjust or arrange. **8.** to adjust according to a standard. **9.** to cause to sit; seat. **10.** to put into a fixed, rigid, or settled state, as the countenance, the muscles, or the mind. **11.** to cause (something, as mortar) to become firm or hard. **12.** to change into a curd. **13.** to cause (hair, etc.) to assume a desired shape, style, or form. **14.** *Surgery* to put (a broken or dislocated bone) back in position. **15.** *Music* to fit, as words to music. – *v.i.* **16.** to pass below the horizon; sink. **17.** to become set. – *v.* **18. set about,** to begin; start. **19. set off, a.** to explode. **b.** to cause to explode. **c.** to begin; start, as on a journey. **d.** to intensify or improve by contrast. **e.** *Banking* to hold a credit balance on (one account) against a debit balance on another account held by the same person, company, etc. **20. set out, a.** to arrange. **b.** to state or explain methodically. **c.** to start, as on a journey. **21. set to, a.** to apply oneself; start, as to work. **b.** to start to fight. – *n.* **22.** the act or state of setting. **23.** a number of things customarily used together or forming a complete assortment, outfit, or collection. **24.** a number or group of persons associating or classed together. **25.** fixed direction or bent, as of the mind, etc. **26.** a radio or television receiving apparatus. **27.** a construction representing a place in which action takes place in a film, television or theatre production, or the like. – *adj.* **28.** fixed beforehand. **29.** fixed; rigid. **30.** resolved or determined; habitually or stubbornly fixed. **31.** ready; prepared; organised. **32. dead set,** *Colloquial* true; certain.

seti- a word element meaning 'bristle'.

set-off /'sɛt-ɒf/ *n.* **1.** anything that counterbalances or makes up for something else. **2.** a counterbalancing debt or claim.

set square *n.* a flat piece of wood, plastic, or the like, in the shape of a right-angled triangle, used in mechanical drawing.

settee /sɛ'ti, sə'ti/ *n.* a seat for two or more persons.

setter /'sɛtə/ *n.* one of a breed of long-haired hunting dogs.

setting /'sɛtɪŋ/ *n.* **1.** the surroundings or environment of anything. **2.** the articles required for setting a single place at a table.

settle[1] /'sɛtl/ *v.,* **-tled**, **-tling**. – *v.t.* **1.** to agree upon (a time, price, conditions, etc.). **2.** to pay (a bill, account due, or the like). **3.** to close (an account) by payment. **4.** to take up residence in (a country, place, house, etc.). **5.** to cause to take up residence. **6.** to furnish (a place) with inhabitants or settlers. **7.** to establish in a way of life, a business, etc. **8.** to bring to rest; quiet (the nerves, stomach, etc.). **9.** to cause to sink down gradually. – *v.i.* **10.** to decide; arrange (often fol. by *on* or *upon*). **11.** to make a financial arrangement; pay (often fol. by *up*). **12.** to take up residence in a new country or place. **13.** to come to rest in a particular place. **14.** to sink to the bottom, as sediment.

settle² /'sɛtl/ *n.* a long seat or bench.

settlement /'sɛtlmənt/ *n.* **1.** the act of settling. **2.** a colony, especially in its early stages.

settlement of minutes *n.* a procedure in industrial relations, in which parties to proceedings agree upon and produce a written statement of the decision of a tribunal contained in an order or award.

settling day *n.* a day fixed for the settling of accounts and completion of transactions, especially with respect to bookmakers.

seven /'sɛvən/ *n.* a cardinal number, six plus one.

seventeen /sɛvən'tin/ *n.* a cardinal number, ten plus seven.

seventy /'sɛvənti/ *n., pl.* **-ties**. a cardinal number, ten times seven.

seventy-eight /sɛvənti-'eɪt/ *n.* a gramophone record which revolves seventy-eight times a minute when being played.

sever /'sɛvə/ *v.t.* **1.** to divide into parts, especially forcibly; cut; cleave. **2.** to break off or dissolve (ties, relations, etc.). – **severance**, *n.*

several /'sɛvrəl/ *adj.* **1.** being more than two or three, but not many. **2.** respective; individual. **3.** separate; different.

severance pay *n.* money paid by a firm to employees or directors in compensation for loss of employment.

severe /sə'vɪə/ *adj.,* **-verer**, **-verest**. **1.** harsh; harshly extreme. **2.** serious; stern. **3.** rigidly restrained in style or taste; simple; plain. **4.** rigidly exact, accurate, or methodical. – **severity**, *n.*

sew /soʊ/ *v.,* **sewed**, **sewn** *or* **sewed**, **sewing**. – *v.t.* **1.** to join or attach by a thread or the like, as with a needle. **2.** to make, repair, etc., (a garment) by such means. – *v.i.* **3.** to work with a needle and thread, or with a sewing machine.

sewage /'suɪdʒ/ *n.* the waste matter which passes through sewers.

sewer /'suə/ *n.* an artificial conduit, usually underground, for carrying off waste water and refuse, as from a town or city.

sewerage /'suərɪdʒ/ *n.* **1.** the removal of waste water and refuse by means of sewers. **2.** the pipes and fittings conveying sewage.

sex /sɛks/ *n.* **1.** the character of being either male or female: *persons of both sexes.* **2.** the sum of the anatomical and physiological differences with reference to which the male and the female are distinguished. **3.** men collectively or women collectively. **4. have sex,** *Colloquial* to have sexual intercourse. – *v.t.* **5.** to ascertain the sex of.

sex- a word element meaning 'six'.

sexist /'sɛksəst/ *adj.* **1.** of an attitude which stereotypes a person according to gender, or sexual preference, rather than judging on individual merits. – *n.* **2.** a person who displays sexist attitudes.

sexual /'sɛkʃuəl/ *adj.* **1.** of or relating to sex. **2.** occurring between or involving the two sexes.

sexual harassment *n.* persistent unwelcome sexual advances, especially when made by superiors in the workplace and when employment status is dependent upon compliance.

sexuality /sɛkʃu'æləti/ *n.* sexual character; possession of sex.

sexy /'sɛksi/ *adj.,* **-ier**, **-iest**. **1.** having or involving a predominant or intense concern with sex. **2.** sexually interesting or exciting; having sex appeal.

SGML /ɛs dʒi ɛm 'ɛl/ *n.* standard generalised markup language; a computer markup language designed a standard for multiple applications or operating systems.

shabby /'ʃæbi/ *adj.,* **-bier**, **-biest**. **1.** having the appearance impaired by wear, use, etc. **2.** meanly ungenerous or unfair; contemptible, as persons, actions, etc.

shack /ʃæk/ *n.* **1.** a rough cabin; shanty. – *v.i.* **2. shack up with,** to live with.

shackle /'ʃækəl/ *n., v.,* **-led**, **-ling**. – *n.* **1.** a ring or fastening of iron or the like for securing the wrist, ankle, etc.; a fetter. **2.** anything that serves to prevent freedom of procedure, thought, etc. – *v.t.* **3.** to put a shackle or shackles on; confine or restrain.

shade /ʃeɪd/ *n., v.,* **shaded**, **shading**. – *n.* **1.** the comparative darkness caused by the interception of rays of light. **2.** comparative obscurity. **3.** a spectre or ghost. **4.** anything used for protection against excessive light, heat, etc. **5.** degree of darkening of a colour. **6.** a slight variation, amount, or degree. – *v.t.* **7.** to produce shade in or on. **8.** to screen. – *v.i.* **9.** to pass or change by slight graduations, as one colour or one thing into another.

shadow /'ʃædoʊ/ *n.* **1.** a dark figure or image cast by a body intercepting light. **2.** an instance or area of comparative darkness. **3.** shelter; protection. **4.** a slight suggestion; a trace. – *v.t.* **5.** to follow (a person) about secretly. – *adj. Government* **6.** of or relating to members of the chief opposition party, as *shadow cabinet, shadow ministry.*

shaft /ʃaft/ *n.* **1.** a long pole or rod forming the body of various weapons, as a spear, lance, or arrow. **2.** something directed as in sharp attack. **3.** a ray or beam. **4.** the handle of a long implement. **5.** either of the parallel bars of wood between which the animal drawing a vehicle is placed. **6.** any vertical enclosed space, as in a building.

shag¹ /ʃæg/ *n.* rough, matted hair, wool, or the like.

shag² /ʃæg/ *n.* → **cormorant**.

shag³ /ʃæg/ *v.t.,* **shagged**, **shagging**. *Colloquial* to have sexual intercourse with.

shag pile *n.* carpet pile which is long and thick.

shah /ʃa/ *n.* a king (especially used as a title of the former rulers of Iran).

shake /ʃeɪk/ *v.,* **shook**, **shaken**, **shaking**, *n.* – *v.i.* **1.** to move or sway with short, quick, irregular vibratory movements. **2.** to tremble with emotion, cold, etc. **3.** to totter; become unsteady. – *v.t.* **4.** to shake (something). **5.** to bring, throw, force, rouse, etc., by or as by shaking. **6.** to agitate or disturb profoundly in feeling. – *n.* **7.** the act of shaking. **8.** tremulous motion. **9.** a drink made by shaking ingredients together. **10.** (*pl.*) *Colloquial* a state of trembling, especially that induced by alcoholism, drugs or nervous disorder.

shake-out /ˈʃeɪk-aʊt/ *n.* **1.** *Stock Exchange* a sharp drop in certain share values. **2.** *Commerce* the elimination of companies, products, etc., owing to increased competition in a declining market, or to rising standards of quality.

shall /ʃæl/, *weak form* /ʃəl/ *v. (aux), past* **should**. **1.** (used, generally in the first person, to indicate simple future time). **2.** (used, generally in the second and third persons, to indicate promise or determination).

shallot /ʃəˈlɒt/ *n.* a plant of the lily family whose bulblets are used in cookery.

shallow /ˈʃæloʊ/ *adj.* **1.** of little depth; not deep. – *n.* **2.** (*usu. pl.*) a shallow part of a body of water.

sham /ʃæm/ *n., adj., v.,* **shammed**, **shamming**. – *n.* **1.** something that is not what it purports to be; a spurious imitation. – *adj.* **2.** pretended; counterfeit. – *v.t.* **3.** to assume the appearance of.

shamble /ˈʃæmbəl/ *v.i.,* **-bled**, **-bling**. to walk or go awkwardly; shuffle.

shambles /ˈʃæmbəlz/ *n.* any place or thing in confusion or disorder.

shame /ʃeɪm/ *n., v.,* **shamed**, **shaming**. – *n.* **1.** the painful feeling arising from the consciousness of something dishonourable, improper, ridiculous, etc., done by oneself or another. **2.** disgrace; ignominy. – *v.t.* **3.** to cause to feel shame; make ashamed.

shampoo /ʃæmˈpu/ *v.,* **-pooed**, **-pooing**, *n.* – *v.t.* **1.** to wash, especially with a cleaning preparation. – *n.* **2.** a preparation used for shampooing.

shamrock /ˈʃæmrɒk/ *n.* a plant with three-lobed leaflets.

shandy /ˈʃændi/ *n.* a mixed drink of beer with ginger beer or lemonade.

shanghai[1] /ˈʃæŋhaɪ, ʃæŋˈhaɪ/ *v.t.,* **-haied**, **-haiing**. *Nautical* to obtain (a person) for the crew of a ship by unscrupulous means.

shanghai[2] /ˈʃæŋhaɪ/ *n.* a child's catapult.

shank /ʃæŋk/ *n.* that part of the leg in humans between the knee and the ankle.

shan't /ʃant/ *v. Colloquial* contraction of *shall not.*

shanty /ˈʃænti/ *n., pl.* **-ties**. a roughly built hut.

shape /ʃeɪp/ *n., v.,* **shaped**, **shaping**. – *n.* **1.** the quality of a thing depending on its outline or external surface. **2.** a particular or definite form or nature. **3.** something used to give form, as a mould or a pattern. – *v.t.* **4.** to give definite form, shape, or character to; fashion or form. – *v.i.* **5.** to develop; assume a definite form or character (often fol. by *up*).

shard /ʃad/ *n.* a fragment, especially of broken earthenware.

share /ʃɛə/ *n., v.,* **shared**, **sharing**. – *n.* **1.** the portion or part allotted or belonging to, or contributed or owed by, an individual or group. **2.** one of the equal fractional parts into which the capital stock of a limited company is divided. – *v.t.* **3.** to use, participate in, enjoy, etc., jointly.

sharebroker /ˈʃɛəbroʊkə/ *n.* → **stockbroker**.

share certificate *n.* a document showing the entitlement of its owner to a number of shares in a company.

shareholders' funds *pl. n.* in a company, the net amount owned by the shareholders.

share-pusher /ˈʃɛə-pʊʃə/ *n.* a dealer in stocks and shares who uses means, often fraudulent, to induce the public to buy them.

share register *n.* a register of all shareholders in a company, showing their names and addresses and the number of shares held by each.

shark /ʃak/ *n.* any of a group of elongate (mostly marine) fishes, certain species of which are large, ferocious, and dangerous to humans.

sharp /ʃap/ *adj.* **1.** having a thin cutting edge or a fine point; well adapted for cutting or piercing. **2.** terminating in an edge or point; not blunt or rounded. **3.** clearly outlined; distinct. **4.** keen or acute. **5.** shrewd to the point of dishonesty. **6.** stylish or elegant, especially in an ostentatious manner. – *adv.* **7.** keenly or acutely. **8.** abruptly or suddenly. **9.** punctually.

sharper /ˈʃapə/ *n.* a shrewd swindler.

shashlik /ˈʃæʃlɪk/ *n.* → **shish kebab**. Also, **shashlick**, **shaslick**.

shatter /ˈʃætə/ *v.t.* **1.** to break in pieces, as by a blow. – *v.i.* **2.** to break suddenly into fragments.

shave /ʃeɪv/ *v.,* **shaved**, **shaved** *or* **shaven**, **shaving**, *n.* – *v.t.* **1.** to remove hair from (the face, legs, etc.) **2.** to cut or scrape away the surface of with a sharp-edged tool. – *n.* **3.** a narrow miss or escape.

shaving /ˈʃeɪvɪŋ/ *n.* (*often pl.*) a very thin piece or slice, especially of wood.

shawl /ʃɔl/ *n.* a piece of material, worn as a covering for the shoulders, head, etc.

she /ʃi/ *pron., possessive,* **her**, *objective,* **her**, *pl.* **they**, *n., pl.* **shes**, *adj.* – *pron.* **1.** the female in question or last mentioned. – *n.* **2.** any woman or any female person or animal (correlative to *he*). – *adj.* **3.** female or feminine, especially of animals.

sheaf /ʃif/ *n., pl.* **sheaves**. any bundle, cluster, or collection.

shear /ʃɪə/ *v.,* **sheared** *or* **shorn**, **shearing**, *n.* – *v.t.* **1.** to remove by or as by cutting with a sharp instrument. **2.** to cut the hair, fleece, wool, etc., from. – *n.* **3.** (*pl.*) scissors of large size.

sheath /ʃiθ/ *n., pl.* **sheaths** /ʃiðz, ʃiθs/ **1.** a case or covering for the blade of a sword, dagger, or the like. **2.** any similar covering.

shed[1] /ʃɛd/ *n.* **1.** a slight or rough structure built for shelter, storage, etc. **2.** a large, strongly built structure, often open at the sides or end.

shed[2] /ʃɛd/ *v.t.,* **shed**, **shedding**. **1.** to emit and let fall (tears). **2.** to cast off or let fall by natural process (leaves, hair, feathers, skin, shell, etc.).

sheen /ʃin/ *n.* lustre; brightness; radiance.

sheep /ʃip/ *n., pl.* **sheep**. **1.** a ruminant mammal, closely allied to the goat, valuable for its flesh, fleece, etc. **2.** a meek, timid, or stupid person.

sheepish /ˈʃipɪʃ/ *adj.* awkwardly bashful or

embarrassed.

sheepshank /'ʃipʃæŋk/ *n.* a kind of knot, hitch, or bend made on a rope to shorten it temporarily.

sheer[1] /ʃɪə/ *adj.* **1.** transparently thin. **2.** unmixed with anything else. **3.** extending down or up very steeply.

sheer[2] /ʃɪə/ *v.i.* to deviate from a course, as a ship; swerve.

sheet /ʃit/ *n.* **1.** a large rectangular piece of linen, cotton, etc., used as an article of bedding, commonly one of a pair spread immediately above and below the sleeper. **2.** a broad, thin mass, layer, or covering. **3.** an oblong or square piece of paper.

shelf /ʃɛlf/ *n., pl.* **shelves**. **1.** a thin slab of wood or other material fixed horizontally to a wall, or in a frame, for supporting objects. **2.** a shelf-like surface or projection; a ledge.

shelf life *n.* the period in which a product may remain on the shelf before being purchased, and still be marketable.

shell /ʃɛl/ *n.* **1.** a hard outer covering of an animal, as the hard case of a mollusc. **2.** any of various objects resembling a shell in some respect. **3.** the material constituting any of various kinds of shells. **4.** the exterior surface of an egg. **5.** an enclosing case or cover suggesting a shell. **6.** a cartridge. – *v.t.* **7.** to take out of the shell, pod, etc. **8.** to remove the shell of.

shellfish /'ʃɛlfɪʃ/ *n., pl.* **-fishes**, (*esp. collectively*) **-fish**. an aquatic animal (not a fish in the ordinary sense) having a shell, especially molluscs such as oysters, mussels, etc., and (less commonly in Australia) crustaceans such as lobsters, prawns, etc.

shelter /'ʃɛltə/ *n.* **1.** something which affords protection or refuge; a place of refuge or safety. **2.** protection. – *v.t.* **3.** to be a shelter for; afford shelter to. – *v.i.* **4.** to take shelter; find a refuge.

shelve[1] /ʃɛlv/ *v.t.,* **shelved**, **shelving**. to lay or put aside from consideration.

shelve[2] /ʃɛlv/ *v.i.,* **shelved**, **shelving**. to slope gradually.

shepherd /'ʃɛpəd/ *n.* **1.** a person who minds sheep. **2.** someone who watches over or protects a group of people. – *v.t.* **3.** to tend or guard as a shepherd.

sherbet /'ʃɜbət/ *n.* **1.** a powdered confection. **2.** Also, **sorbet**. a frozen fruit-flavoured mixture.

sheriff /'ʃɛrəf/ *n. Law* an officer of the Supreme Court with duties relating to service and execution of processes, summoning of juries, etc.

sherry /'ʃɛri/ *n., pl.* **-ries**. a fortified and blended wine.

shiatsu /ʃi'ætsu/ *n.* → **acupressure**.

shied /ʃaɪd/ *v.* past tense and past participle of **shy**.

shield /ʃild/ *n.* **1.** anything used or serving to protect, especially a piece of armour carried on the left arm. **2.** *Heraldry* a shield-shaped escutcheon on which armorial bearings are displayed. – *v.t.* **3.** to protect with or as with a shield. – *v.i.* **4.** to act or serve as a shield.

shift /ʃɪft/ *v.i.* **1.** to move from one place, position, etc., to another. **2.** to transfer from one place, position, person, etc., to another. – *n.* **3.** a shifting from one place, position, person, etc., to another; a transfer. **4.** the portion of the day scheduled as a day's work when a factory, etc., operates continuously during the 24 hours, or works both day and night. **5.** an expedient; ingenious device. **6.** a woman's loose-fitting dress. **7. make shift,** to manage to get along or succeed.

shift allowance *n.* an allowance paid to employees on shift work as compensation for their having to work outside the usual span of hours fixed for day workers. Also, **shift loading**, **shift premium**.

shiftless /'ʃɪftləs/ *adj.* lacking in resource.

shift register *n.* a computer register in which binary bits are moved as a contiguous group a specified number of positions right or left.

shiftwork /'ʃɪftwɜk/ *n.* **1.** a system of work which is regularly carried out at hours outside the normal spread of hours in addition to work within the spread, so that work performed by one employee or group of employees during a shift (usually of eight hours) is continued by another employee or group for the following shift, etc. **2.** an arrangement of an employee's working hours under which, over a period of time, the employee works on different shifts. – **shiftworker**, *n.*

shifty /'ʃɪfti/ *adj.,* **-tier**, **-tiest**. furtive.

shilling /'ʃɪlɪŋ/ *n.* (formerly) a coin equal to $1/20$ of a pound.

shimmer /'ʃɪmə/ *n.* **1.** a subdued, tremulous light or gleam. – *v.i.* **2.** to shine with a shimmer.

shin /ʃɪn/ *n., v.,* **shinned**, **shinning**. – *n.* **1.** the front part of the leg from the knee to the ankle. – *v.t., v.i.* **2.** to climb by holding fast with the hands or arms and legs and drawing oneself up.

shine /ʃaɪn/ *v.,* **shone** *or* **shined**, **shining**, *n.* – *v.i.* **1.** to give forth, or glow with, light; shed or cast light. **2.** to be bright with reflected light; glisten; sparkle. **3.** to excel; be conspicuous. – *v.t.* **4.** to cause to shine. – *n.* **5.** radiance; light. **6.** lustre; polish. **7.** sunshine; fair weather. **8.** *Colloquial* a liking; fancy.

shiner /'ʃaɪnə/ *n. Colloquial* a black eye.

shingle[1] /'ʃɪŋgəl/ *n.* a thin piece of wood, slate, etc., used to cover the roofs and sides of houses.

shingle[2] /'ʃɪŋgəl/ *n.* small, water-worn stones or pebbles such as on the seashore.

shingles /'ʃɪŋgəlz/ *n.* (*sing. or pl.*) a disease of the skin.

ship /ʃɪp/ *n., v.,* **shipped**, **shipping**. – *n.* **1.** any vessel intended or used for navigating the water, especially one of large size and not propelled by oars, paddles, or the like. **2.** an airship or aeroplane. – *v.t.* **3.** to send or transport by ship, rail, etc. **4.** to bring (an object) into a ship or boat.

-ship a suffix of nouns denoting condition, character, office, skill, etc., as in *kingship*, *friendship*, *statesmanship*.

shipment /'ʃɪpmənt/ *n.* **1.** the act of shipping goods, etc. **2.** that which is shipped.

shipping agent *n.* the representative of a ship-owner, who transacts business on their behalf.

shipshape /'ʃɪpʃeɪp/ *adj.* in good order.

shire /'ʃaɪə/ *n.* an area of land delineated for the purposes of local government.

shirk /ʃɜk/ *v.t.* to evade (work, duty, etc.).

shirt /ʃɜt/ *n.* a garment for the upper part of the body.

shirtmaker /'ʃɜtmeɪkə/ *n.* a woman's dress with a collar, sleeves and buttoned front.

shirty /'ʃɜti/ *adj. Colloquial* bad-tempered.

shish kebab /'ʃɪʃ kəbæb/ *n.* a dish consisting of cubes of meat, marinated, and grilled on a skewer, often with onion, tomato, green pepper, etc. Also, **kebab**.

shit /ʃɪt/ *v.,* **shitted**, **shat** *or* **shit**, **shitting**, *n., interj. Colloquial – v.i.* **1.** to defecate. *– v.t.* **2.** to anger or disgust (often fol. by *off*). *– n.* **3.** faeces; dung; excrement. **4.** the act of defecating. *– interj.* **5.** (an exclamation expressing anger, disgust, disappointment, disbelief, etc.).

shithouse /'ʃɪthaʊs/ *Colloquial – n.* **1.** a toilet. *– adj.* **2.** foul; wretchedly bad.

shiver /'ʃɪvə/ *v.i.* **1.** to shake or tremble with cold, fear, excitement, etc. *– n.* **2. the shivers,** a fit or attack of shivering.

shoal[1] /ʃoʊl/ *n.* a sandbank or sandbar in the bed of a body of water, especially one which shows at low water.

shoal[2] /ʃoʊl/ *n.* a group of fish crowded fairly close together.

shock[1] /ʃɒk/ *n.* **1.** a sudden and violent blow, or impact, collision, or encounter. **2.** something that shocks mentally, emotionally, etc. **3.** *Pathology* a sudden collapse of the nervous mechanism caused by violent physical or psychic factors. **4.** the physiological effect produced by the passage of an electric current through the body. *– v.t.* **5.** to strike with intense surprise, horror, disgust, etc. **6.** to cause a shock in. *– adj.* **7.** causing intense surprise, horror, etc.

shock[2] /ʃɒk/ *n.* a thick, bushy mass, as of hair.

shoddy /'ʃɒdi/ *adj.,* **-dier**, **-diest**. of poor quality or badly made.

shoe /ʃu/ *n., pl.* **shoes**, *v.,* **shod**, **shoeing**. *– n.* **1.** an external covering, usually of leather, for the foot. **2.** some thing or part resembling a shoe in form, position, or use. *– v.t.* **3.** to provide or fit with a shoe or shoes.

shoehorn /'ʃuhɔn/ *n.* a shaped piece of horn, metal, or the like, inserted in a shoe at the heel to make it slip on more easily.

shone /ʃɒn/ *v.* past tense and past participle of **shine**.

shook /ʃʊk/ *v.* past tense of **shake**.

shoot /ʃut/ *v.,* **shot** /ʃɒt/, **shooting**, *n. – v.t.* **1.** to hit, wound, or kill with a missile discharged from a weapon. **2.** to send forth (arrows, bullets, etc.) from a bow, firearm, or the like. **3.** to send forth like an arrow or bullet. **4.** to pass rapidly along with. **5.** *Photography* to photograph or film. *– v.i.* **6.** to send forth missiles, from a bow, firearm, or the like. **7.** to move, start to move, or pass suddenly or swiftly; dart; be propelled (fol. by *ahead, away, into, off,* etc.). **8.** to grow, especially rapidly (often fol. by *up*). *– n.* **9.** an act of shooting with a bow, firearm, etc. **10.** a young branch, stem, twig, or the like.

shooting star *n.* a falling star.

shop /ʃɒp/ *n., v.,* **shopped**, **shopping**. *– n.* **1.** a building where goods are sold retail. **2.** a place for doing certain work; a workshop. **3. talk shop,** to discuss one's trade, profession, or business. *– v.i.* **4.** to visit shops for purchasing or examining goods.

shop committee *n.* a committee made up of members of all unions represented in an establishment, set up principally to coordinate union policy and to facilitate negotiations with the employer.

shop floor *n.* **1.** that part of a factory where the machines, etc., are situated. **2.** workers collectively, especially factory workers.

shopfront /'ʃɒpfrʌnt/ *n.* that part of an organisation which deals directly with the public.

shoplift /'ʃɒplɪft/ *v.t.* to steal (goods) from a shop while appearing to be a legitimate shopper.

shopping /'ʃɒpɪŋ/ *n.* **1.** the act of one someone who shops. **2.** the articles bought.

shop steward *n.* a trade-union official representing workers in a factory, workshop, etc.

shore[1] /ʃɔ/ *n.* land along the edge of a sea, lake, large river, etc.

shore[2] /ʃɔ/ *v.t.,* **shored**, **shoring**. to support or prop (usually fol. by *up*).

shorn /ʃɔn/ *v.* past participle of **shear**.

short /ʃɔt/ *adj.* **1.** having little length; not long. **2.** having little height; not tall; low. **3.** brief; not extensive. **4.** rudely brief; curt; hurting. **5.** below the standard in extent, quantity, duration, etc. **6.** deficient in (fol. by *on*). **7.** *Commerce* not possessing at the time of sale commodities or stocks that one sells. *– adv.* **8.** on the nearer side of an intended or particular point. **9.** *Commerce* without possessing at the time the stocks, etc., sold. *– n.* **10.** something that is short. **11. for short,** by way of abbreviation. **12. in short,** briefly. *– v.t.* **13.** *Colloquial* to short-circuit.

shortage /'ʃɔtɪdʒ/ *n.* deficiency in quantity.

shortbread /'ʃɔtbrɛd/ *n.* a thick, crisp biscuit, rich in butter.

short-change /ʃɔt-'tʃeɪndʒ/ *v.t.,* **-changed**, **-changing**. *Colloquial* to give less than proper change to.

short circuit *n.* an abnormal connection of relatively low resistance, whether made accidentally or intentionally, between two points of different potential in an electrical circuit.

shortcoming /'ʃɔtkʌmɪŋ/ *n.* a failure or defect in conduct, condition, etc.

short cut *n.* a shorter or quicker way.

shortening /'ʃɔtnɪŋ/ *n.* butter, lard, or other fat, used to make pastry, etc.

shorthand /'ʃɔthænd/ *n.* **1.** a method of rapid handwriting using extremely simple strokes in place of letters. *– adj.* **2.** using shorthand. **3.** written in shorthand.

shorthanded /ʃɔt'hændəd/ *adj.* not having the necessary number of workers, helpers, etc.

short list *n.* a list of especially favoured

candidates for a position, promotion, etc., who have been selected from a larger group of applicants.

shortly /'ʃɔtli/ *adv.* in a short time; soon.

shorts /ʃɔts/ *pl. n.* short trousers, not extending beyond the knee.

short-sighted /'ʃɔt-saɪtəd/ *adj.* unable to see far; near-sighted; myopic.

short-staffed /ʃɔt-'staft/ *adj.* not having the usual number of personnel present.

short-tempered /ʃɔt-'tɛmpəd/ *adj.* having a hasty temper; inclined to become angry on little provocation.

short-term /'ʃɔt-tɜm/ *adj.* **1.** covering a comparatively short period of time. **2.** having a maturity within a comparatively short time.

short-winded /ʃɔt-'wɪndəd/ *adj.* short of breath; liable to difficulty in breathing.

shot[1] /ʃɒt/ *n.* **1.** the act of shooting. **2.** small pellets of lead as used in a sportsman's gun. **3.** a person who shoots. **4.** anything like a shot. **5.** a heavy metal ball which competitors cast as far as possible in shot-putting contests. **6.** an aimed stroke, throw, or the like, as in games, etc. **7.** an attempt or try. **8.** *Colloquial* an injection of a drug, vaccine, etc. **9.** *Photography* a photograph.

shot[2] /ʃɒt/ *v.* **1.** past tense and past participle of **shoot**. – *adj.* **2.** woven so as to present a play of colours, as silk.

shotgun /'ʃɒtgʌn/ *n.* a smoothbore gun for firing small shot to kill small game.

shot-put /'ʃɒt-pʊt/ *n.* the athletic exercise of putting the shot. See **shot**[1] (def. 5).

should /ʃʊd/ *v.* **1.** past tense of **shall**. **2.** (specially used) **a.** to denote duty, propriety, or expediency. **b.** to make a statement less direct or blunt. **c.** to emphasise the uncertainty in conditional and hypothetical clauses.

shoulder /'ʃoʊldə/ *n.* **1.** either of two corresponding parts of the human body, situated at the top of the trunk and extending respectively from the right side and left side of the neck to the upper joint of the corresponding arm. **2.** a corresponding part in animals. **3.** a shoulder-like part or projection. **4.** either of two strips of land bordering a road. – *v.t.* **5.** to push, as with the shoulder, especially roughly. **6.** to take upon or support with the shoulder. **7.** to assume as a burden, or responsibility. – *v.i.* **8.** to push with the shoulder.

shoulder-blade /'ʃoʊldə-bleɪd/ *n. Anatomy* either of two flat bones forming the back part of the shoulder.

shout /ʃaʊt/ *v.i.* **1.** to call or cry out loudly and vigorously. – *v.t.* **2.** to express by a shout or shouts. **3.** to pay for something for (another person); treat. – *n.* **4.** a loud call or cry. **5.** one's turn to shout.

shove /ʃʌv/ *v.*, **shoved**, **shoving**, *n.* – *v.t.* **1.** to move along by force from behind. **2.** to push roughly or rudely; jostle. – *v.i.* **3.** to push. – *n.* **4.** an act of shoving.

shovel /'ʃʌvəl/ *n.*, *v.*, **-elled**, **-elling**. – *n.* **1.** an implement similar to a spade in use and appearance. – *v.t.* **2.** to take up and cast or remove with a shovel.

show /ʃoʊ/ *v.*, **showed**, **shown** *or* **showed**, **showing**, *n.* – *v.t.* **1.** to cause or allow to be seen; exhibit; display; present. **2.** to point out. **3.** to guide; escort. **4.** to indicate; register. **5.** to make evident by appearance, behaviour, etc. **6. show off,** to exhibit for approval or admiration, or ostentatiously. – *v.i.* **7.** to be seen; be or become visible. – *n.* **8.** a display. **9.** ostentatious display. **10.** an indication; trace. **11.** any undertaking, organisation, etc.; affair.

show business *n.* the entertainment industry, especially that part concerned with variety. Also, **show biz**.

showdown /'ʃoʊdaʊn/ *n.* a confrontation of parties for the final settlement of a contested issue.

shower /'ʃaʊə/ *n.* **1.** a brief fall, as of rain, hail, sleet or snow. **2. a.** an apparatus for spraying water for bathing. **b.** a washing of the body in the water sprayed from such an apparatus. – *v.t.* **3.** to pour (something) down in a shower. – *v.i.* **4.** to rain in a shower. **5.** (of a person) to take a shower (def. 2b).

shower tea *n.* → **kitchen tea**.

show-off /'ʃoʊ-ɒf/ *n. Colloquial* one given to pretentious display or exhibitionism.

showroom *n.* a room used for the display of goods or merchandise.

shrank /ʃræŋk/ *v.* past tense of **shrink**.

shrapnel /'ʃræpnəl/ *n.* **1.** shell fragments. **2.** *Colloquial* small change, especially silver.

shred /ʃrɛd/ *n.*, *v.*, **shredded** *or* **shred**, **shredding**. – *n.* **1.** a piece cut or torn off, especially in a narrow strip. – *v.t.* **2.** to cut or tear into small pieces, especially small strips; reduce to shreds. – *v.i.* **3.** to tear; be reduced to shreds.

shrew /ʃru/ *n.* **1.** any of various small, insectivorous mouse-like mammals. **2.** a woman of violent temper and speech.

shrewd /ʃrud/ *adj.* astute or sharp.

shriek /ʃrik/ *n.* **1.** a loud, sharp, shrill cry. – *v.i.* **2.** to cry out sharply in a high voice.

shrift /ʃrɪft/ *n. in the phr.* **short shrift,** little consideration in dealing with someone or something.

shrill /ʃrɪl/ *adj.* **1.** high-pitched and piercing. – *v.t.*, *v.i.* **2.** to cry shrilly.

shrimp /ʃrɪmp/ *n.* **1.** any of various small, long-tailed, chiefly marine, crustaceans, esteemed as a table delicacy. **2.** *Colloquial* a diminutive or insignificant person.

shrine /ʃraɪn/ *n.* any structure or place consecrated or devoted to some saint or deity.

shrink /ʃrɪŋk/ *v.*, **shrank** *or* **shrunk**, **shrunk** *or* **shrunken**, **shrinking**. – *v.i.* **1.** to draw back, as in retreat or avoidance. **2.** to become reduced in extent or compass. – *v.t.* **3.** to cause to shrink or contract. – **shrinkage**, *n.*

shrivel /'ʃrɪvəl/ *v.t.*, *v.i.*, **-elled**, **-elling**. to contract and wrinkle, as from great heat or cold.

shroud /ʃraʊd/ *n.* **1.** a white cloth or sheet in which a corpse is wrapped for burial. **2.** something which covers or conceals. – *v.t.* **3.** to cover; hide from view.

shrub /ʃrʌb/ *n.* a woody perennial plant smaller than a tree, usually having permanent stems branching from or near the ground.

shrug /ʃrʌg/ *v.*, **shrugged**, **shrugging**, *n.*

– *v.t., v.i.* **1.** to raise and lower (the shoulders), expressing indifference, disdain, etc. – *n.* **2.** this movement.

shudder /'ʃʌdə/ *v.i.* **1.** to tremble with a sudden convulsive movement, as from horror, fear, or cold. – *n.* **2.** such a movement.

shuffle /'ʃʌfəl/ *v.,* **-fled, -fling,** *n.* – *v.i.* **1.** to walk without lifting the feet. **2.** to move this way and that. **3.** to mix (cards in a pack) so as to change their relative position. – *n.* **4.** the act of shuffling.

shun /ʃʌn/ *v.t.,* **shunned, shunning.** to keep away from.

shunt /ʃʌnt/ *v.t.* to move or turn aside or out of the way.

shush /ʃʊʃ/ *interj.* hush (a command to be quiet or silent).

shut /ʃʌt/ *v.,* **shut, shutting.** – *v.t.* **1.** to put (a door, cover, etc.) in position to close or obstruct. **2.** to close the doors of (often fol. by *up*). **3.** to close by folding or bringing the parts together. **4.** to confine; enclose. **5.** to bar; exclude. – *v.i.* **6.** to become shut or closed; close. **7. shut up,** *Colloquial* to stop talking; become silent.

shutter /'ʃʌtə/ *n.* a hinged or otherwise movable cover for a window or other opening.

shuttle /'ʃʌtl/ *n., v.,* **-tled, -tling.** – *n.* **1.** the sliding container that carries the lower thread in a sewing machine. – *v.t., v.i.* **2.** to move quickly to and fro like a shuttle.

shuttlecock /'ʃʌtlkɒk/ *n.* a piece of cork, or similar light material, with feathers stuck in one end, intended to be struck to and fro.

shy /ʃaɪ/ *adj.,* **shyer, shyest** *or* **shier, shiest,** *v.,* **shied, shying.** – *adj.* **1.** bashful; retiring. **2.** easily frightened away; timid. – *v.i.* **3.** to draw back; recoil.

sibilant /'sɪbələnt/ *adj.* hissing.

sibling /'sɪblɪŋ/ *n.* a brother or sister.

sic /sɪk/ *adv.* so; thus (often used parenthetically to show that something, especially a mistake, has been copied exactly from the original).

sick /sɪk/ *adj.* **1.** affected with nausea. **2.** affected with any disorder of health; ill, unwell, or ailing. **3.** of or appropriate to sick persons. **4.** morbid; macabre. – *n.* **5.** vomit. – *v.t., v.i.* **6. sick up,** to vomit.

sickie /'sɪki/ *n. Colloquial* a day taken off work with pay, because of genuine or feigned illness.

sickle /'sɪkəl/ *n.* an implement for cutting grain, grass, etc., consisting of a curved, hooklike blade mounted in a short handle.

sick leave *n.* leave of absence granted because of illness.

side /saɪd/ *n., adj., v.,* **sided, siding.** – *n.* **1.** one of the surfaces or lines bounding a thing. **2.** one of the two surfaces of an object other than the front, back, top, and bottom. **3.** either of the two lateral (right and left) parts of a thing. **4.** the space immediately beside someone or something. **5.** one of two or more parties concerned in a case, contest, etc. – *adj.* **6.** being at or on one side. **7.** coming from one side. **8.** directed towards one side. **9.** subordinate. – *v.i.* **10. side with** (or **against**), to place oneself with (or against) a side or party to support or oppose an issue.

sideboard /'saɪdbɔd/ *n.* a piece of furniture for holding articles of table service.

sidecar /'saɪdka/ *n.* a small car attached on one side to a motorcycle and supported on the other by a wheel of its own; used for a passenger, parcels, etc.

side effect *n.* any effect produced other than those originally intended, especially an unpleasant or harmful effect.

sidelevers /'saɪdlivəz/ *pl. n.* short whiskers worn with an unbearded chin. Also, **sideboards, sideburns.**

sidelong /'saɪdlɒŋ/ *adj.* **1.** directed to one side. – *adv.* **2.** towards the side; obliquely.

sidero- a word element meaning 'iron', 'steel'. Also (*before vowels*), **sider-.**

sidestep /'saɪdstɛp/ *v.,* **-stepped, -stepping,** *n.* – *v.i.* **1.** to step to one side, as in avoidance. – *v.t.* **2.** to avoid by stepping to one side. – *n.* **3.** an act or instance of sidestepping.

sidetrack /'saɪdtræk/ *v.i., v.t.* **1.** to move from the main subject or course. – *n.* **2.** an act of sidetracking; a diversion; distraction. **3.** a temporary road constructed as a detour.

sideways /'saɪdweɪz/ *adv.* **1.** with the side foremost. **2.** towards or from one side. – *adj.* **3.** towards or from one side. Also, **sidewise** /'saɪdwaɪz/.

sidle /'saɪdl/ *v.i.,* **-dled, -dling.** to edge along furtively.

SIDS /sɪdz/ *n.* → **sudden infant death syndrome.**

siege /sidʒ/ *n.* the operation of reducing and capturing a fortified place by surrounding it, cutting off supplies, and other offensive operations.

siemens /'simənz/ *n., pl.* **siemens.** the SI unit of electrical conductance. *Symbol*: S

siesta /si'ɛstə/ *n.* a midday or afternoon rest or nap.

sieve /sɪv/ *n.* an instrument, with a meshed or perforated bottom, used for separating coarse from fine parts of loose matter, for straining liquids, etc.

sift /sɪft/ *v.t.* **1.** to separate the coarse parts of (flour, ashes, etc.) with a sieve. **2.** to scatter by means of a sieve. **3.** to examine closely.

sigh /saɪ/ *v.i.* **1.** to let out one's breath audibly, as from sorrow, weariness, relief, etc. **2.** to yearn or long. – *v.t.* **3.** to express with a sigh. – *n.* **4.** the act or sound of sighing.

sight /saɪt/ *n.* **1.** the power or faculty of seeing; vision. **2.** the act or fact of seeing. **3.** range of vision. **4.** a view; glimpse. **5.** something seen or to be seen; spectacle. – *v.t.* **6.** to get sight of.

sign /saɪn/ *n.* **1.** a token; indication. **2.** a symbol used technically instead of the word or words which it represents, as an abbreviation. **3.** an inscribed board, space, etc., serving for information, advertisement, warning, etc. – *v.t.* **4.** to affix a signature to. **5.** to communicate by a sign. – *v.i.* **6.** to write one's signature, as a token of agreement, obligation, receipt, etc. **7.** to make a sign or signal.

signal /'sɪgnəl/ *n., adj., v.,* **-nalled, -nalling.** – *n.* **1.** a gesture, act, light, etc., serving to warn, direct, command, or the like. **2.** an act, event, or the like, which precipitates an action. **3.** a token; indication. **4.** *Radio, etc.* the impulses, waves, sounds, etc., transmitted or received. – *adj.* **5.** serving as a sign. – *v.t.* **6.** to make a signal to. **7.** to make known by a signal. – *v.i.* **8.** to make communication by a signal or signals.

signatory /'sɪgnətri/ *adj., n., pl.* **-ries**. – *adj.* **1.** that has signed, or has joined in signing, a document. – *n.* **2.** a signer, or one of the signers, of a document, as a treaty.

signature /'sɪgnətʃə/ *n.* **1.** a person's name written by himself or herself or by a deputy, as in signing a letter or other document. **2.** the act of signing a document.

signet /'sɪgnət/ *n.* a small official seal.

significance /sɪg'nɪfəkəns/ *n.* **1.** importance; consequence. **2.** meaning; import. – **significant**, *adj.*

signify /'sɪgnəfaɪ/ *v.,* **-fied**, **-fying**. – *v.t.* **1.** to make known by signs, speech, or action. **2.** to be a sign of; mean; portend. – *v.i.* **3.** to be of importance or consequence.

silence /'saɪləns/ *n., v.,* **-lenced**, **-lencing**, *interj.* – *n.* **1.** absence of any sound or noise; stillness. – *v.t.* **2.** to put or bring to silence; still. – *interj.* **3.** be silent! – **silent**, *adj.*

silent partner *n.* a partner taking no active or public part in the conduct of a business.

silhouette /sɪlu'ɛt, sɪlə'wɛt/ *n.* a dark image outlined against a lighter background.

silic- a word element meaning 'flint', 'silica', 'silicon'. Also, **silici-**, **silico-**.

silicon /'sɪləkən/ *n.* a non-metallic element used in steel-making, etc.; widely used as a semiconductor in solid-state electronics. *Symbol*: Si

silicon chip *n.* a chip (def. 5) with a silicon base.

silk /sɪlk/ *n.* **1.** the fine, soft, lustrous fibre obtained from the cocoon of the silkworm. **2.** thread or cloth made of this fibre. **3.** any fibre or filamentous matter resembling silk. **4. take silk,** to become a Queen's Counsel. – *adj.* **5.** made of silk. **6.** of or relating to silk. – **silken**, *adj.*

silk-screen /'sɪlk-skrin/ *n.* **1.** a process of printing from stencils through a fine mesh of silk, metal or other material. – *v.t.* **2.** to print using this process.

sill /sɪl/ *n.* the horizontal piece or member beneath a window, door, or other opening.

silly /'sɪli/ *adj.,* **-lier**, **-liest**, *n., pl.* **-lies**. – *adj.* **1.** lacking good sense; foolish; stupid. **2.** absurd or ridiculous. – *n.* **3.** *Colloquial* a silly person.

silo /'saɪloʊ/ *n., pl.* **-los**. a tower-like structure for storing grain.

silt /sɪlt/ *n.* earthy matter, fine sand, or the like, carried by moving or running water and deposited as a sediment.

silver /'sɪlvə/ *n.* **1.** *Chemistry* a white ductile metallic element, used for making mirrors, coins, ornaments, table utensils, etc. *Symbol*: Ag (for *argentum*). **2.** coin made of silver or of a metal resembling silver; money. **3.** silverware; table articles made of or plated with silver. **4.** a lustrous greyish-white or whitish-grey; colour of metallic silver. – *adj.* **5.** consisting or made of silver; plated with silver. **6.** of or relating to silver. **7.** (of coins) made of a metal or alloy resembling silver. **8.** having the colour silver, or tinted with silver. **9.** indicating the 25th event of a series, as a wedding anniversary.

silver beet *n.* a form of beet with large, strongly veined leaves and a fleshy stalk, used as a vegetable.

silverfish /'sɪlvəfɪʃ/ *n., pl.* **-fishes**, (*esp. collectively*) **-fish**. any of certain small, wingless insects damaging to books, wallpaper, etc.

silver plate *n.* **1.** a thin silver coating deposited on the surface of another metal. **2.** silver-plated tableware.

silverside /'sɪlvəsaɪd/ *n.* a cut of beef from the outside portion of a full butt, usually boiled or pickled.

silver standard *n.* a monetary system with silver of specified weight and fineness as the unit of value.

similar /'sɪmələ/ *adj.* having likeness or resemblance, especially in a general way. – **similarity**, *n.*

simile /'sɪməli/ *n.* a figure of speech directly expressing a resemblance, in one or more points, of one thing to another, as *a man like an ox.*

similitude /sə'mɪlətjud/ *n.* **1.** likeness; resemblance. **2.** a likening or comparison; a parable or allegory.

simmer /'sɪmə/ *v.i., v.t.* **1.** to cook in a liquid just below the boiling point. **2. simmer down,** *Colloquial* to become calm or calmer. – *n.* **3.** state or process of simmering.

simper /'sɪmpə/ *v.i.* to smile in a silly, self-conscious way.

simple /'sɪmpəl/ *adj.,* **-pler**, **-plest**. **1.** easy to understand, deal with, use, etc. **2.** not elaborate or artificial. **3.** not complex or complicated. **4.** sincere; innocent. **5.** unlearned; ignorant. – **simplicity**, *n.*

simple interest *n.* interest which is not compounded, that is, payable only on the principal amount of a debt.

simpleton /'sɪmpəltən/ *n.* a fool.

simplistic /sɪm'plɪstɪk/ *adj.* characterised by extreme simplification; oversimplified.

simulation /sɪmjə'leɪʃən/ *n.* **1.** assumption of a particular appearance or form. **2.** *Computers* **a.** the technique of establishing a routine for one computer to make it function as nearly as possible like another computer. **b.** the representation of physical systems, phenomena, etc., by computers. **3.** the practice of constructing a model of a machine in order to test behaviour. – **simulate**, *v.*

simulcast /'sɪməlkast, 'saɪ-/ *n.* simultaneous broadcast by a radio and a television station.

simultaneous /sɪməl'teɪniəs/ *adj.* existing, occurring, or operating at the same time.

sin /sɪn/ *n., v.,* **sinned**, **sinning**. – *n.* **1.** transgression of divine law. **2.** an act regarded as such transgression. – *v.i.* **3.** to do a sinful act.

since /sɪns/ *adv.* **1.** from then till now (often preceded by *ever*). **2.** between a particular past time and the present; subsequently. **3.** ago; before now. – *prep.* **4.** continuously from or counting from. **5.** between (a past time or event) and the present. – *conj.* **6.** in the period following the time when. **7.** because; inasmuch as.

sincere /sɪn'sɪə, sən-/ *adj.*, **-cerer**, **-cerest**. free from any element of deceit, dissimulation, duplicity or hypocrisy. – **sincerity**, *n.*

sine /saɪn/ *n. Mathematics* a trigonometric function defined for an acute angle in a right-angled triangle as the ratio of the side opposite the angle to the hypotenuse.

sinecure /'sɪnəkjʊə, 'saɪnəkjʊə/ *n.* an office requiring little or no work, especially one yielding profitable returns.

sinew /'sɪnju/ *n.* **1.** a tendon. **2.** strength; vigour.

sing /sɪŋ/ *v.*, **sang** *or* **sung**, **sung**, **singing**, *n.* – *v.i.* **1.** to utter words or sounds in succession with musical modulations of the voice. **2.** to produce melodious sounds, as certain birds, insects, etc. **3.** to make a short ringing, whistling, or whizzing sound. – *v.t.* **4.** to utter with musical modulations of the voice, as a song. **5.** to bring, send, put, etc., with or by singing. – *n.* **6.** a singing, ringing, or whistling sound, as of a bullet.

singe /sɪndʒ/ *v.*, **singed**, **singeing**, *n.* – *v.i.*, *v.t.* **1.** to burn superficially. – *n.* **2.** a superficial burn.

single /'sɪŋgəl/ *adj.*, *v.*, **-gled**, **-gling**, *n.* – *adj.* **1.** one only; separate; individual. **2.** of or relating to one person, family, etc. **3.** alone; solitary. **4.** without a spouse or de facto spouse. **5.** consisting of one part, element, or member. **6.** sincere; honest. – *v.t.* **7.** to pick or choose out from others (usually fol. by *out*). – *n.* **8.** something single or separate; a single one.

single entry *n.* a simple accounting system in which each transaction is noted by only one entry.

single-handed /sɪŋgəl-'hændəd/ *adj.* acting or working alone or unaided.

single-minded /sɪŋgəl-'maɪndəd/ *adj.* having or showing undivided purpose.

singlet /'sɪŋlət, 'sɪŋglət/ *n.* a short garment, with or without sleeves, usually worn next to the skin.

singsong /'sɪŋsɒŋ/ *n.* **1.** an informal gathering at which the company sing; community singing. – *adj.* **2.** characterised by a regular rising and falling intonation.

singular /'sɪŋgjələ/ *adj.* **1.** being the only one of the kind; unique. **2.** separate; individual. **3.** *Grammar* designating the number category that normally implies one person, thing, or collection.

sinister /'sɪnəstə/ *adj.* threatening or portending evil; ominous.

sink /sɪŋk/ *v.*, **sank** *or* **sunk**, **sunk** *or* **sunken**, **sinking**, *n.* – *v.i.* **1.** to descend gradually to a lower level, as water, flames, etc. **2.** to become submerged. **3.** to pass or fall into some lower state, as of fortune, estimation, etc. **4.** to decrease in amount, extent, degree, etc., as value, prices, rates, etc. **5.** to enter or permeate the mind; become understood (fol. by *in*, *into*, etc.). **6.** to fall in; become hollow, as the cheeks. **7.** to be or become deeply absorbed in a mental state (usually fol. by *in* or *into*). – *v.t.* **8.** to cause to sink. **9.** to suppress; ignore; omit. **10.** to invest (money), now especially unprofitably. **11.** to make (a hole, shaft, well, etc.) by excavating or boring downwards; hollow out (any cavity). – *n.* **12.** a basin with a water supply and outlet. **13.** a low-lying area where waters collect. **14.** a place of vice or corruption.

sinker /'sɪŋkə/ *n.* a weight of lead, etc., for sinking a fishing line, fishing net, or the like in the water.

sinking fund *n.* a fund created to liquidate a debt by degrees.

sinuous /'sɪnjuəs/ *adj.* having many curves, bends, or turns; winding.

sinus /'saɪnəs/ *n.*, *pl.* **-nuses**. one of the hollow cavities in the skull connecting with the nasal cavities.

-sion a suffix having the same function as **-tion**, as in *compulsion*.

sip /sɪp/ *v.*, **sipped**, **sipping**, *n.* – *v.i.*, *v.t.* **1.** to drink a little at a time. – *n.* **2.** an act of sipping. **3.** a small quantity taken by sipping.

siphon = syphon /'saɪfən/ *n.* **1.** a tube through which liquid flows over the wall of a tank or reservoir to a lower elevation by atmospheric pressure. – *v.t.*, *v.i.* **2.** to convey or pass through a siphon.

sir /sɜ/ *n.* (a respectful term of address used to a man).

sire /'saɪə/ *n.*, *v.*, **sired**, **siring**. – *n.* **1.** the male parent of an animal. – *v.t.* **2.** to beget.

siren /'saɪrən/ *n.* **1.** *Classical Mythology* one of several sea nymphs, part woman and part bird, supposed to lure mariners to destruction by their seductive singing. **2.** a device used as a whistle, fog signal, warning sound on an ambulance, fire-engine, etc. – *adj.* **3.** of or like a siren.

sirloin /'sɜlɔɪn/ *n.* the portion of the loin of beef in front of the rump, used whole as a roast or cut into steaks.

sissy /'sɪsi/ *n.*, *pl.* **-sies**. a timid or cowardly person. Also, **cissy**.

sister /'sɪstə/ *n.* **1.** a daughter of the same parents. **2.** a female associate. **3.** a female member of a religious community. **4.** a senior nurse. – *adj.* **5.** being a sister; related by, or as by, sisterhood.

sister-in-law /'sɪstər-ɪn-lɔ/ *n.*, *pl.* **sisters-in-law**. **1.** a husband's or wife's sister. **2.** a brother's wife.

sit /sɪt/ *v.*, **sat**, **sitting**. – *v.i.* **1.** to rest on the lower part of the body; be seated. **2.** to be situated; dwell. **3.** to remain quiet or inactive. **4.** to fit or be adjusted, as a garment. **5.** to occupy a seat in an official capacity, as a judge or bishop. **6.** to be convened or in session, as an assembly. – *v.t.* **7.** to cause to sit; seat (often with *down*). **8.** to sit upon (a horse, etc.). **9.** to provide seating room for; seat.

sitar /'sɪta, 'sita/ *n.* a guitar-like instrument of India, having a long neck and usually three strings. Also, **sittar**.

sit-down strike *n.* a strike during which workers refuse either to leave their place of employment or to work or to allow others to work until the strike is settled. Also, **sit-down**.

site /saɪt/ *n.*, *v.*, **sited**, **siting**. – *n.* **1.** the area on which anything, as a building, is, has been or is to be situated. – *v.t.* **2.** to locate; place; provide with a site.

sito- a word element referring to food.

sitting duck *n.* any particularly easy mark to shoot at.

situate /ˈsɪtʃueɪt/ *v.t.,* **-ated**, **-ating**. to give a site to; locate.

situation /sɪtʃuˈeɪʃən/ *n.* **1.** manner of being situated; a location or position with reference to environment. **2.** a place or locality. **3.** the state of affairs; combination of circumstances. **4.** a position or post of employment.

SI unit /ɛs ˈaɪ junət/ *n.* a unit of the International System of Units.

six /sɪks/ *n.* a cardinal number, five plus one.

sixteen /sɪksˈtin/ *n.* a cardinal number, ten plus six.

sixth sense /sɪksθ ˈsɛns/ *n.* a power of perception beyond the five senses; intuition.

sixty /ˈsɪksti/ *n.* a cardinal number, ten times six.

size[1] /saɪz/ *n., v.,* **sized**, **sizing**. – *n.* **1.** the dimensions, proportions, or magnitude of anything. – *v.t.* **2.** to separate or sort according to size. **3.** to make of a certain size. **4. size up,** to form an estimate of.

size[2] /saɪz/ *n.* any of various gelatinous or glutinous preparations used for glazing or coating paper, cloth, etc.

sizzle /ˈsɪəl/ *v.,* **-zled**, **-zling**, *n.* – *v.i.* **1.** to make a hissing sound, as in frying or burning. – *n.* **2.** a sizzling sound.

skate /skeɪt/ *n., v.,* **skated**, **skating**. – *n.* **1.** a steel blade attached to the bottom of a shoe, enabling a person to glide on ice. **2.** → **roller-skate**. – *v.i.* **3.** to glide over ice, the ground, etc., on skates.

skateboard /ˈskeɪtbɔd/ *n.* a short plank on rollerskate wheels, ridden, usually standing up, as a recreation.

skein /skeɪn/ *n.* a length of thread or yarn wound in a coil.

skeleton /ˈskɛlətn/ *n.* **1.** the bones of a human or other animal body considered together. **2.** *Colloquial* a very lean person or animal. **3.** a supporting framework, as of a leaf, building, or ship. – *adj.* **4.** of or relating to a skeleton. – **skeletal**, *adj.*

skeleton key *n.* a key which may open various locks. Also, **pass key**.

skerrick /ˈskɛrɪk/ *n.* a very small quantity; a scrap.

sketch /skɛtʃ/ *n.* **1.** a simply or hastily executed drawing or painting. **2.** a rough design, plan, or draft, as of a literary work. **3.** a brief or hasty outline of facts, occurrences, etc. – *v.t.* **4.** to make a sketch of. – *v.i.* **5.** to make a sketch or sketches.

skew /skju/ *v.i.* **1.** to turn aside or swerve; take an oblique course. – *v.t.* **2.** to give an oblique direction to; shape or form obliquely.

skewer /ˈskjuə/ *n.* **1.** a long pin of wood or metal for putting through meat to hold it together or in place while being cooked. – *v.t.* **2.** to fasten with, or as with, skewers.

ski /ski/ *n., pl.* **skis**, **ski**, *v.,* **ski'd** *or* **skied**, **skiing**. – *n.* **1.** one of a pair of long, slender pieces of hard wood, metal, or plastic, one fastened to each shoe, used for travelling or gliding over snow, and often (especially as a sport) down slopes. – *v.i.* **2.** to travel on or use skis.

skid /skɪd/ *n., v.,* **skidded**, **skidding**. – *n.* **1.** a plank, bar, log, or the like, especially one of a pair, on which something heavy may be slid or rolled along. **2.** an act of skidding. – *v.i.* **3.** to slide along without rotating, as a wheel to which a brake has been applied. **4.** to slide forward under its own momentum, as a car when the wheels have been braked.

skill /skɪl/ *n.* the ability that comes from knowledge, practice, aptitude, etc., to do something well. – **skilful**, *adj.*

skilled /skɪld/ *adj.* **1.** showing, involving, or requiring skill, as work. **2.** of or relating to workers performing a specific operation requiring apprenticeship or other special training or experience.

skillet /ˈskɪlət/ *n.* a small frying pan.

skim /skɪm/ *v.,* **skimmed**, **skimming**, *n.* – *v.t.* **1.** to take up or remove (floating matter) from a liquid with a spoon, ladle, etc. **2.** to clear (liquid) thus. **3.** to move or glide lightly over or along the surface of (the ground, water, etc.). – *v.i.* **4.** to pass or glide lightly along over or near a surface. – *n.* **5.** the act of skimming. **6.** that which is skimmed off.

skim milk *n.* milk from which the cream has been removed. Also, **skimmed milk**.

skimp /skɪmp/ *v.t.* **1.** to be sparing with; scrimp. – *v.i.* **2.** to be extremely thrifty (often fol. by *on*).

skin /skɪn/ *n., v.,* **skinned**, **skinning**. – *n.* **1.** the external covering of an animal body, especially when soft and flexible. **2.** any outer coating, or surface layer, as an investing membrane, the rind or peel of fruit, or a film on liquid. – *v.t.* **3.** to strip or deprive of skin; flay; peel. **4.** to strip off, as or like skin.

skindiving /ˈskɪndaɪvɪŋ/ *n.* underwater swimming with an aqualung or snorkel, and foot fins.

skinflint /ˈskɪnflɪnt/ *n.* a mean person.

skink /skɪŋk/ *n.* any of various harmless, generally smooth-scaled lizards.

skinny /ˈskɪni/ *adj.,* **-nier**, **-niest**. **1.** lean; emaciated. **2.** of or like skin.

skint /skɪnt/ *adj. Colloquial* completely without money; broke.

skip /skɪp/ *v.,* **skipped**, **skipping**, *n.* – *v.i.* **1.** to spring, jump, or leap lightly; gambol. **2.** to pass from one point, thing, subject, etc., to another, disregarding or omitting what intervenes. **3.** to use a skipping-rope. – *v.t.* **4.** to jump lightly over. **5.** to miss out, as part of a continuum or one of a series. **6.** *Colloquial* to leave hastily, or flee from, as a place. – *n.* **7.** a skipping movement; a light jump.

skipper /ˈskɪpə/ *n.* a captain or leader, as of a team.

skirmish /ˈskɜmɪʃ/ *n.* **1.** any brisk encounter. – *v.i.* **2.** to engage in a skirmish.

skirt /skɜt/ *n.* **1.** the lower part of a garment, hanging from the waist. **2.** a separate garment, extending from the waist downwards. **3.** some part resembling or suggesting the skirt of a garment. **4.** *Colloquial* a woman or girl. – *v.t.* **5.** to pass along or around the border or edge of. – *v.i.* **6.** to be, lie, live, etc., on or along the edge of something.

skirting board *n.* a line of boarding protecting an interior wall next to the floor. Also, **skirting**.

skit /skɪt/ *n.* a slight parody, satire, or caricature, especially dramatic or literary.

skite /skaɪt/ *Colloquial* – *v.i.* **1.** to boast; brag. – *n.* **2.** a boast; brag. **3.** Also, **skiter**. a boaster; braggart.

skittish /'skɪtɪʃ/ *adj.* restlessly or excessively lively.

skittle /'skɪtl/ *n.*, *v.*, **skittled**, **skittling**. – *n.* **1.** (*pl.*) ninepins. – *v.t.* **2.** to knock over or send flying, in the manner of skittles.

skivvy /'skɪvi/ *n.* a close-fitting garment with long sleeves and a turtle neck, similar to a jumper, but usually made of machine-knitted cotton.

skulduggery /skʌl'dʌgəri/ *n.* dishonourable proceedings; mean dishonesty or trickery. Also, **skullduggery**.

skulk /skʌlk/ *v.i.* to lie or keep in hiding, as for some evil or cowardly reason.

skull /skʌl/ *n.* the bony framework of the head, enclosing the brain and supporting the face.

skunk /skʌŋk/ *n.* **1.** a small, striped, fur-bearing, bushy-tailed, North American mammal which ejects a fetid fluid when attacked. **2.** *Colloquial* a thoroughly contemptible person.

sky /skaɪ/ *n.* (*often pl.*) the region of the clouds or the upper air.

skydiving /'skaɪdaɪvɪŋ/ *n.* the sport of free-falling from an aeroplane for a great distance, controlling one's course by changes in body position, before releasing one's parachute.

skylark /'skaɪlak/ *v.i.* to frolic, sport or play about, especially boisterously or in high spirits; play tricks.

skylight /'skaɪlaɪt/ *n.* an opening in a roof or ceiling, fitted with glass, for admitting daylight.

skyrocket /'skaɪrɒkət/ *n.* **1.** a firework that ascends into the air and explodes at a height. – *v.i.* **2.** to move like a skyrocket.

skyscraper /'skaɪskreɪpə/ *n.* a tall building of many storeys, especially one for office or commercial use.

slab /slæb/ *n.* a broad, flat, somewhat thick piece of stone, wood, or other solid material.

slack /slæk/ *adj.* **1.** not tense or taut; loose. **2.** indolent; negligent; remiss. – *n.* **3.** a slack condition, interval, or part. – *v.t.* **4.** to be remiss in respect to (some matter, duty, right, etc.); shirk; leave undone. – *v.t.*, *v.i.* **5.** to make or become slack.

slacks /slæks/ *pl. n.* long trousers, worn by either men or women as informal wear.

slag /slæg/ *n.* matter separated during the reduction of a metal from its ore.

slain /sleɪn/ *v.* past participle of **slay**.

slake /sleɪk/ *v.t.*, **slaked**, **slaking**. to allay (thirst, desire, wrath, etc.) by satisfying.

slam /slæm/ *v.*, **slammed**, **slamming**, *n.* – *v.t.*, *v.i.* **1.** to shut with force and noise. **2.** to dash, strike, etc., with violent and noisy impact. – *n.* **3.** a violent and noisy closing, dashing, or impact.

slander /'slændə/ *n.* **1.** a malicious, false, and defamatory statement or report. – *v.t.* **2.** to utter slander concerning; defame.

slang /slæŋ/ *n.* language differing from standard or written speech in vocabulary and construction, involving extensive metaphor, ellipsis, humorous usage, etc., less conservative and more informal than standard speech, and sometimes regarded as being in some way inferior.

slant /slænt, slant/ *v.i.* **1.** to slope; be directed or lie obliquely. – *v.t.* **2.** to slope; direct or turn so as to make (something) oblique. **3.** to distort or give partisan emphasis to (a newspaper story, article, etc.). – *n.* **4.** slanting or oblique direction; slope. **5.** a mental leaning or tendency, especially unusual or unfair; bias.

slap /slæp/ *n.*, *v.*, **slapped**, **slapping**. – *n.* **1.** a smart blow, especially with the open hand or with something flat. – *v.t.* **2.** to strike with a slap.

slapdash /'slæpdæʃ/ *adv.*, *adj.* carelessly hasty or offhand.

slap-up /'slæp-ʌp/ *adj.* *Colloquial* first-rate; excellent.

slash /slæʃ/ *v.t.* **1.** to cut with a violent sweep or by striking violently and at random. **2.** to cut, reduce, or alter, especially drastically. – *v.i.* **3.** to make a sweeping, cutting stroke. – *n.* **4.** a sweeping stroke. **5.** a cut or wound made with such a stroke; a gash.

slat /slæt/ *n.*, *v.*, **slatted**, **slatting**. – *n.* **1.** a long, thin, narrow strip of wood, metal, etc., used as a support for a bed, as one of the horizontal laths of a venetian blind, etc. – *v.t.* **2.** to furnish or make with slats.

slate[1] /sleɪt/ *n.*, *v.*, **slated**, **slating**. – *n.* **1.** a fine-grained rock formed by the compression of mudstone, that tends to split along parallel cleavage planes, usually at an angle to the planes of stratification. **2.** a thin piece or plate of this rock or a similar material, used especially for roofing, or for writing on. **3.** a dull, dark bluish grey. – *v.t.* **4.** to write or set down for nomination or appointment.

slate[2] /sleɪt/ *v.t.*, **slated**, **slating**. to censure or reprimand severely.

slather /'slæðə/ *v.t.* **1.** to use in large quantities, to lavish. – *n.* **2.** **open slather,** complete freedom; free rein.

slaughter /'slɔtə/ *n.* **1.** the killing or butchering of cattle, sheep, etc., especially for food. **2.** the killing by violence of great numbers of persons. – *v.t.* **3.** to slaughter (people or animals).

slave /sleɪv/ *n.*, *v.*, **slaved**, **slaving**. – *n.* **1.** someone who is the property of and wholly subject to another. – *v.i.* **2.** to work like a slave; drudge. – **slavery**, *n.* – **slavish**, *adj.*

slaver /'slævə/ *v.i.* to let saliva run from the mouth; slobber.

slay /sleɪ/ *v.t.*, **slew**, **slain**, **slaying**. to kill by violence.

sleazy /'slizi/ *adj.*, **-zier**, **-ziest**. shabby, shoddy, untidy, or grubby.

sled /slɛd/ *n.* a vehicle mounted on runners for travelling over snow, etc.

sledge /slɛdʒ/ *n.* any of various vehicles mounted on runners for travelling or conveying loads over snow, ice, rough ground, etc.

sledge-hammer /ˈslɛdʒ-hæmə/ *n.* a large heavy hammer, often held with both hands, as used by blacksmiths, etc.; sledge.

sleek /slik/ *adj.* **1.** smooth; glossy, as hair, an animal, etc. **2.** well-fed or well-groomed. **3.** suave; insinuating.

sleep /slip/ *v.,* **slept**, **sleeping**, *n.* – *v.i.* **1.** to take the repose or rest afforded by the natural suspension, complete or partial, of consciousness. **2.** to be dormant, quiescent, or inactive, as faculties. – *v.t.* **3.** to have beds or sleeping accommodation for. **4.** to spend or pass (time, etc.) in sleep (fol. by *away* or *out*). – *n.* **5.** the state of a person, animal, or plant that sleeps. **6.** a period of sleeping. **7.** the mucous congealed in the corner of the eyes, especially after sleep.

sleeper /ˈslipə/ *n.* **1.** a timber, concrete, or steel beam forming part of a railway track, serving as a foundation or support for the rails. **2.** a bed, place, or compartment in a carriage on a passenger train. **3.** a small ring, bar, etc., worn in the ear lobe after piercing to prevent the hole from closing. **4.** *Colloquial* **a.** someone or something that unexpectedly achieves success or fame. **b.** a book, item of manufacture, etc., which has slow but constant sales.

sleeping partner *n.* → **silent partner**.

sleepwalking /ˈslipwɔkɪŋ/ *n.* the state or act of walking or performing other activities while asleep.

sleet /slit/ *n.* snow or hail and rain falling together.

sleeve /sliv/ *n., v.,* **sleeved**, **sleeving**. – *n.* **1.** the part of a garment that covers the arm, varying in form and length but commonly tubular. **2.** something resembling this.

sleigh /sleɪ/ *n.* a vehicle on runners, drawn by horses, dogs, etc., and used for transport on snow or ice.

sleight /slaɪt/ *n.* skill; dexterity.

slender /ˈslɛndə/ *adj.* **1.** small in circumference in proportion to height or length. **2.** small in size, amount, extent, etc.

sleuth /sluθ/ *n. Colloquial* a detective.

slew[1] /slu/ *v.* past tense of **slay**.

slew[2] /slu/ *v.t.* **1.** to turn or twist (something), especially upon its own axis or without moving it from its place. **2.** to cause to swing round. – *v.i.* **3.** to swerve awkwardly; swing round; twist. **4.** *Colloquial* to relax vigilance. – *n.* **5.** such a movement. **6.** the position reached by slewing.

slice /slaɪs/ *n., v.,* **sliced**, **slicing**. – *n.* **1.** a thin, broad, flat piece cut from something. **2.** any of various implements with a thin, broad blade or part, as for turning food in a frying pan, etc. – *v.t.* **3.** to cut into slices; divide into parts. **4.** to cut (*off, away, from,* etc.) as or like a slice.

slick /slɪk/ *adj.* **1.** smooth of manners, speech, etc. **2.** ingenious; cleverly devised. – *n.* **3.** a patch or film of oil or the like, as on the sea.

slicker /ˈslɪkə/ *n.* an account which balances correctly on the first calculation.

slide /slaɪd/ *v.,* **slid**, **slid** *or* **slidden**, **sliding**, *n.* – *v.i.* **1.** to move along in continuous contact with a smooth or slippery surface. **2.** to slip, as one losing foothold or as a vehicle skidding. **3.** to slip easily, quietly, or unobtrusively (fol. by *in, out, away,* etc.). – *v.t.* **4.** to cause to slide, as over a surface or with a smooth, gliding motion. – *n.* **5.** the act of sliding. **6.** a single image for projection in a projector; transparency. **7.** Also, **hair slide**. a clip for holding a woman's hair in place. **8.** that which slides, as part of a machine.

slide rule *n.* a device for rapid arithmetic calculation.

sliding scale *n.* a variable scale, especially of industrial costs, as wages, raw materials, etc., which may be adapted to demand.

slight /slaɪt/ *adj.* **1.** small in amount, degree, etc. **2.** frail; flimsy. – *v.t.* **3.** to treat with indifference; ignore or snub. – *n.* **4.** an instance of slighting treatment; an affront.

slim /slɪm/ *adj.,* **slimmer**, **slimmest**, *v.,* **slimmed**, **slimming**. – *adj.* **1.** slender, as in girth or form; slight in build or structure. – *v.i.* **2.** to make oneself slim, as by dieting, exercise, etc.

slime /slaɪm/ *n.* **1.** thin, glutinous mud. **2.** a viscous secretion of animal or vegetable origin. **3.** *Colloquial* servility; quality of being ingratiating. – **slimy**, *adj.*

sling /slɪŋ/ *n., v.,* **slung**, **slinging**. – *n.* **1.** an instrument for hurling stones, etc., by hand, consisting of a piece for holding the missile, with two strings attached. **2.** a strap, band, or the like forming a loop by which something is suspended or carried. – *v.t.* **3.** to throw, cast or hurl; fling, as from the hand. **4.** to suspend. – *v.i.* **5.** to give money as a bribe.

slingshot /ˈslɪŋʃɒt/ *n.* a catapult.

slink /slɪŋk/ *v.i.,* **slunk**, **slinking**. to move stealthily, as to evade notice.

slip[1] /slɪp/ *v.,* **slipped**, **slipping**, *n.* – *v.i.* **1.** to pass or go smoothly or easily; glide; slide. **2.** to slide suddenly and involuntarily, as on a smooth surface; to lose one's foothold. **3.** to move, slide, or start from place, position, fastening, the hold, etc. **4.** to go, come, get, etc., easily or quickly. **5.** to go quietly; steal. **6.** to make a slip, mistake, or error (often fol. by *up*). – *v.t.* **7.** to cause to slip, pass, put, draw, etc., with a smooth, easy, or sliding motion. **8.** to untie or undo (a knot). **9.** to escape (one's memory, notice, knowledge, etc.). – *n.* **10.** the act of slipping. **11.** a mistake, often inadvertent, as in speaking or writing. **12.** the eluding of a pursuer, etc. **13.** a woman's sleeveless underdress. **14.** a pillowcase.

slip[2] /slɪp/ *n.* **1.** any long, narrow piece or strip, as of wood, paper, land, etc. **2. a slip of a** (**person**), Also, **a slip of a thing**. a young person, especially one of slender form.

slipper /ˈslɪpə/ *n.* a light shoe into which the foot may be easily slipped for indoor wear.

slippery /ˈslɪpəri, ˈslɪpri/ *adj.,* **-perier**, **-periest**. **1.** tending to cause slipping or sliding, as ground, surfaces, things, etc. **2.** likely to slip away or escape.

slippery dip *n.* a construction bearing an inclined smooth slope for children to slide down for amusement; slide. Also, **slippery slide**.

slipshod /ˈslɪpʃɒd/ *adj.* untidy, or slovenly; careless or negligent.

slip-stitch /ˈslɪp-stɪtʃ/ *n.* one of a series of stitches used for dress hems, etc., in which only a few threads of material are caught up from the outer material, and the stitches which hold it are invisible from the outside.

slipstream /ˈslɪpstrim/ *n.* an air current behind any moving object.

slit /slɪt/ *v.*, **slit**, **slitting**, *n.* – *v.t.* **1.** to cut apart or open along a line; make a long cut, fissure, or opening in. – *n.* **2.** a straight, narrow cut, opening, or aperture.

slither /ˈslɪðə/ *v.i.* to slide down or along a surface, especially unsteadily or with more or less friction or noise.

sliver /ˈslɪvə/ *n.* a slender piece, as of wood, split, broken, or cut off, usually lengthwise or with the grain; splinter.

slob /slɒb/ *n. Colloquial* a stupid, clumsy, uncouth, or slovenly person.

slobber /ˈslɒbə/ *v.i.* **1.** to let saliva, etc., run from the mouth; slaver; dribble. **2.** to indulge in mawkish sentimentality. – *n.* **3.** saliva or liquid dribbling from the mouth; slaver.

slog /slɒg/ *v.*, **slogged**, **slogging**, *n. Colloquial* – *v.t.* **1.** to hit hard, as in boxing, cricket, etc. – *v.i.* **2.** to deal heavy blows. **3.** to toil. – *n.* **4.** a strong blow with little finesse. **5.** a spell of hard work or walking.

slogan /ˈsloʊgən/ *n.* a distinctive cry or phrase of any party, class, body, or person.

slop /slɒp/ *v.*, **slopped**, **slopping**, *n.* – *v.t.*, *v.i.* **1.** to spill or splash. – *n.* **2.** (*often pl.*) the dirty water, liquid refuse, etc., of a household or the like.

slope[1] /sloʊp/ *v.*, **sloped**, **sloping**, *n.* – *v.i.* **1.** to take or have an inclined or slanting direction, especially downwards or upwards from the horizontal. – *v.t.* **2.** to direct at a slope or inclination; incline from the horizontal. – *n.* **3.** inclination or slant, especially downwards or upwards. **4.** an inclined surface.

slope[2] /sloʊp/ *v.i.*, **sloped**, **sloping**. *Colloquial* to move or go.

sloppy /ˈslɒpi/ *adj.*, **-pier**, **-piest**. **1.** muddy, slushy, or very wet. **2.** *Colloquial* weak, silly, or maudlin. **3.** *Colloquial* loose, careless, or slovenly.

sloppy joe *n.* a loose, thick sweater.

slosh /slɒʃ/ *n.* **1.** → **slush**. – *v.i.* **2.** to splash in slush, mud, or water. – *v.t.* **3.** to pour, stir, spread, etc., a liquid or similar (often fol. by *in*, *on*, *round*, etc.).

sloshed /slɒʃt/ *adj. Colloquial* drunk.

slot /slɒt/ *n.*, *v.*, **slotted**, **slotting**. – *n.* **1.** a narrow, elongated depression or aperture, especially one to receive or admit something. **2.** a position within a system. – *v.t.* **3.** to provide with a slot or slots; make a slot in. **4.** to insert into a slot (usually fol. by *in*).

slothful /ˈsloʊθfəl/ *adj.* sluggardly; indolent; lazy. – **sloth**, *n.*

slouch /slaʊtʃ/ *v.i.* **1.** to sit, stand, or walk in an awkward, drooping posture. – *v.t.* **2.** to cause to droop or bend down. – *n.* **3.** a drooping or bending forward of the head and shoulders.

slouch hat *n.* an army hat of soft felt.

slough /slʌf/ *v.t.* to cast (fol. by *off*).

sloven /ˈslʌvən/ *n.* someone who is habitually untidy or dirty. – **slovenly**, *adj.*

slow /sloʊ/ *adj.* **1.** taking or requiring a comparatively long time. **2.** sluggish in nature, disposition, or function. **3.** dull of perception or understanding, as a person, the mind, etc. **4.** slack, as trade. **5.** showing a time earlier than the correct time, as a clock. – *adv.* **6.** in a slow manner; slowly. – *v.t.*, *v.i.* **7.** to make or become slow or slower.

slow-motion /ˈsloʊ-moʊʃən/ *adj.* denoting or relating to films in which the images move more slowly than their originals.

sludge /slʌdʒ/ *n.* mud, mire.

slug[1] /slʌg/ *n.* **1.** any of various slimy, elongated terrestrial gastropods related to the terrestrial snails, but having no shell or only a rudimentary one. **2.** a piece of lead or other metal for firing from a gun.

slug[2] /slʌg/ *v.*, **slugged**, **slugging**, *n.* – *v.t.* **1.** to strike heavily. – *n.* **2.** a heavy blow, especially with the fist.

sluggard /ˈslʌgəd/ *n.* someone who is habitually lazy.

sluggish /ˈslʌgɪʃ/ *adj.* inactive, slow, or of little energy or vigour.

sluice /slus/ *n.*, *v.*, **sluiced**, **sluicing**. – *n.* **1.** any contrivance for regulating a flow from or into a receptacle. **2.** a channel or a drain. – *v.t.* **3.** to flush or cleanse with a rush of water.

slum /slʌm/ *n.* (*often pl.*) an overpopulated, squalid part of a city, inhabited by the poorest people.

slumber /ˈslʌmbə/ *v.i.* **1.** to sleep, especially deeply. – *n.* **2.** (*often pl.*) sleep, especially deep sleep.

slump /slʌmp/ *v.i.* **1.** to drop heavily and limply. **2.** to fall suddenly and markedly, as prices, the market, etc. – *n.* **3.** a decline in prices or sales.

slur /slɜ/ *v.*, **slurred**, **slurring**, *n.* – *v.t.* **1.** to pass over lightly, or without due mention or consideration (often fol. by *over*). **2.** to pronounce (a syllable, word, etc.) indistinctly. – *n.* **3.** a disparaging remark; a slight. **4.** a blot or stain, as upon reputation.

slurp /slɜp/ *v.i.*, *v.t.* **1.** to eat or drink noisily. – *n.* **2.** the noise produced by eating in such a manner.

slush /slʌʃ/ *n.* **1.** snow in a partly melted state. **2.** *Colloquial* silly, sentimental, or weakly emotional writing, talk, etc.

slush fund *n.* money collected unofficially, sometimes by secret or deceitful means, by an individual or an organisation for a special purpose.

slut /slʌt/ *n.* a dirty, slovenly woman.

sly /slaɪ/ *adj.*, **slyer**, **slyest** *or* **slier**, **sliest**. cunning or wily.

smack[1] /smæk/ *n.* **1.** a taste or flavour, especially a slight flavour distinctive or suggestive of something. – *v.i.* **2.** to have a taste, flavour, trace, or suggestion (often fol. by *of*).

smack[2] /smæk/ *v.t.* **1.** to strike smartly, especially with the open hand or anything flat. **2.** to bring, put, throw, send, etc., with a sharp, resounding blow or a smart stroke. **3.** to come or strike smartly or forcibly, as against something. – *n.* **4.** a smart, resounding blow, especially with something flat. **5.** a resounding or loud kiss. **6.** *Colloquial* heroin. – *adv.* **7.** *Colloquial* directly; straight.

small /smɔl/ *adj.* **1.** of limited size; not big; little. **2.** not great in amount, degree, extent, duration, value, etc. **3.** of minor importance, moment, weight, or consequence. – *adv.* **4.** in a small manner. **5.** into small pieces. – *n.* **6.** that which is small. **7.** the lower central part of the back.

small fry *n.* young or unimportant persons or objects.

smallgoods /ˈsmɔlgʊdz/ *pl. n.* processed meats, as salami, frankfurts.

smallpox /ˈsmɔlpɒks/ *n.* an acute, highly contagious disease characterised by a pustular sore which often leaves permanent pits or scars.

smarmy /ˈsmami/ *n.* flattering; unctuous.

smart /smat/ *v.i.* **1.** to be a source of sharp local and usually superficial pain, as a wound. **2.** to suffer keenly from wounded feelings. – *adj.* **3.** sharp or keen, as pain. **4.** sharply severe, as blows, strokes, etc. **5.** sharply brisk, vigorous, or active. **6.** clever. **7.** dashingly or effectively neat or trim in appearance, as persons, dress, etc. **8.** socially elegant, or fashionable. – *n.* **9.** sharp local pain, usually superficial, as from a wound or sting.

smart card *n.* a plastic card with an in-built memory chip which keeps a record of financial transactions made using the card.

smash /smæʃ/ *v.t.* **1.** to break to pieces with violence and often with a crashing sound. – *v.i.* **2.** to break to pieces from a violent blow or collision. – *n.* **3.** a smashing or shattering, or the sound of it. **4.** a destructive collision.

smashed /smæʃt/ *adj. Colloquial* incapacitated as a result of taking drugs, alcohol, etc.

smashing /ˈsmæʃɪŋ/ *adj. Colloquial* excellent or extremely good; first-rate.

smattering /ˈsmætərɪŋ/ *n.* a slight or superficial knowledge of something.

smear /smɪə/ *v.t.* **1.** to rub or spread with oil, grease, paint, dirt, etc. **2.** to rub something over (a thing) so as to cause a smear. – *n.* **3.** a mark or stain made by, or as by, smearing.

smell /smɛl/ *v.*, **smelled** *or* **smelt**, **smelling**, *n.* – *v.t.* **1.** to perceive through the nose. **2.** to test by the sense of smell. **3.** to search or find as if by smell (fol. by *out*). **4.** to search or investigate (usually fol. by *around*). **5.** to give out an odour, especially as specified. **6.** to seem or be unpleasant or bad. – *n.* **7.** the faculty or sense of smelling. **8.** that quality of a thing which is or may be smelled; odour. **9.** the act of smelling.

smidgin /ˈsmɪdʒən/ *n.* a very small quantity; a bit. Also, **smidgen**, **smidgeon**.

smile /smaɪl/ *v.*, **smiled**, **smiling**, *n.* – *v.i.* **1.** to assume a facial expression, characterised especially by a widening of the mouth, indicative of pleasure, favour, kindliness, amusement, derision, scorn, etc. – *v.t.* **2.** to assume or give (a smile). **3.** to express by a smile. **4.** to look with favour, or support (fol. by *on* or *upon*). – *n.* **5.** the act of smiling; a smiling expression of the face.

smirch /smɜtʃ/ *v.t.* **1.** to discolour or soil with some substance, as soot, dust, dirt, etc., or as the substance does. – *n.* **2.** a dirty mark or smear.

smirk /smɜk/ *v.i.* **1.** to smile in a condescending or knowing way. – *n.* **2.** such a smile.

smite /smaɪt/ *v.t.*, **smote**, **smitten**, **smiting**. **1.** to strike or hit hard, as with the hand, a stick or weapon, etc. **2.** to affect suddenly and strongly with a specified feeling. **3.** to impress favourably; charm; enamour.

smith /smɪθ/ *n.* a worker in metal.

smithereens /smɪðəˈrinz/ *pl. n. Colloquial* small fragments.

smock /smɒk/ *n.* any loose overgarment.

smog /smɒg/ *n.* a mixture of smoke and fog.

smoke /smoʊk/ *n.*, *v.*, **smoked**, **smoking**. – *n.* **1.** the visible exhalation given off by a burning or smouldering substance. **2.** something resembling this, as vapour or mist, flying particles, etc. **3.** an act or spell of smoking tobacco, or the like. **4.** that which is smoked, as a cigar or cigarette. – *v.i.* **5.** to give off or emit smoke. **6.** to draw into the mouth and puff out the smoke of tobacco or the like. – *v.t.* **7.** to draw into the mouth and puff out the smoke of tobacco, etc., from (a cigarette, pipe, etc.). **8.** to expose to smoke.

smokescreen /ˈsmoʊkskrin/ *n.* a mass of dense smoke produced to conceal an area, vessel, or aeroplane from the enemy.

smooch /smutʃ/ *v.i. Colloquial* to kiss; cuddle.

smoodge /smudʒ/ *v.i. Colloquial* to kiss; caress.

smooth /smuð/ *adj.* **1.** free from projections or irregularities of surface such as would be perceived in touching or stroking. **2.** of uniform consistency. **3.** pleasant, agreeable, or ingratiatingly polite. – *v.t.* **4.** to make smooth of surface, as by scraping, planing, pressing, stroking, etc. (sometimes fol. by *down*). **5.** to remove (projections, etc.) in making something smooth (often fol. by *away* or *out*). **6.** a smooth part or place.

smorgasbord /ˈsmɔgəzbɔd/ *n.* a buffet meal of various dishes.

smother /ˈsmʌðə/ *v.t.* **1.** to stifle or suffocate, especially by smoke or by depriving of the air necessary for life. **2.** to extinguish or deaden (fire, etc.) by covering so as to exclude air. – *v.i.* **3.** to become stifled or suffocated. – *n.* **4.** an overspreading profusion of anything.

smoulder /ˈsmoʊldə/ *v.i.* **1.** to burn or smoke without flame. **2.** to exist or continue in a suppressed state or without outward demonstration. Also, *US*, **smolder**.

smudge /smʌdʒ/ *n.*, *v.*, **smudged**, **smudging**. – *n.* **1.** a dirty mark or smear. – *v.t.* **2.** to mark with dirty streaks or smears.

smug /smʌg/ *adj.*, **smugger**, **smuggest**. complacently proper, righteous, clever, etc.

smuggle /ˈsmʌgəl/ *v.t.*, **-gled**, **-gling**. to import or export (goods) secretly, without payment of legal duty or in violation of law.

smut /smʌt/ *n.* **1.** a black or dirty mark; a smudge. **2.** indecent talk or writing;

obscenity.

snack /snæk/ *n.* **1.** a small portion of food or drink; a light meal. **2.** *Colloquial* anything easily done.

snag[1] /snæg/ *n., v.,* **snagged**, **snagging**. – *n.* **1.** any sharp or rough projection. **2.** any obstacle or impediment. **3.** a small hole or ladder caused by a snag. – *v.t.* **4.** to ladder; catch upon, or damage by, a snag.

snag[2] /snæg/ *n. Colloquial* a sausage.

snag[3] /snæg/ *n. Colloquial* sensitive new-age guy; a man who displays sensitivity in personal relationships. Also, **SNAG**.

snail /sneɪl/ *n.* **1.** a mollusc of the class Gastropoda having a single, usually spirally coiled shell. **2.** a slow or lazy person; a sluggard.

snake /sneɪk/ *n., v.,* **snaked**, **snaking**. – *n.* **1.** a scaly, limbless, usually slender reptile, occurring in venomous and non-venomous forms. **2.** a treacherous person. **3.** something resembling a snake in form or manner. – *v.i.* **4.** to move, twist, or wind in the manner of a snake.

snap /snæp/ *v.,* **snapped**, **snapping**, *n., adj.* – *v.i.* **1.** to move, strike, shut, catch, etc. with a sharp sound, as a lid. **2.** to break suddenly, especially with a sharp, cracking sound. **3.** to make a quick or sudden bite or snatch. **4.** to utter a quick, sharp speech, reproof, retort, etc. – *v.t.* **5.** to seize with, or as with, a quick bite or snatch (usually fol. by *up* or *off*). **6.** to bring, strike, shut, open, operate, etc., with a sharp sound or movement. **7.** to break suddenly, especially with a crackling sound. **8.** *Photography* to take a snapshot of. – *n.* **9.** a sharp, crackling or clicking sound, or a movement or action causing such a sound. **10.** a catch or the like operating with such a sound. **11.** a quick or sudden bite or snatch, as at something. **12.** a short spell, as of cold weather. **13.** → **snapshot**. – *adj.* **14.** denoting devices closing by pressure on a spring catch, or articles using such devices. **15.** made, done, taken, etc., suddenly or offhand.

snapper /ˈsnæpə/ *n.* a marine food fish widely distributed in Australian and New Zealand coastal waters. Also, **schnapper**.

snapshot /ˈsnæpʃɒt/ *n.* a photograph taken quickly without any formal arrangement of the subject, mechanical adjustment of the camera, etc.

snare /snɛə/ *n.* anything serving to entrap, entangle, or catch unawares; a trap.

snarl[1] /snal/ *v.i.* **1.** to growl angrily or viciously, as a dog. – *n.* **2.** the act of snarling.

snarl[2] /snal/ *n.* **1.** a tangle, as of thread or hair. – *v.t.* **2.** to bring into a tangled condition, as thread, hair, etc; tangle.

snatch /snætʃ/ *v.i.* **1.** to make a sudden effort to seize something, as with the hand (usually fol. by *at*). – *v.t.* **2.** to seize by a sudden or hasty grasp (often fol. by *up*, *from*, *out of*, *away*, etc.). – *n.* **3.** the act of snatching. **4.** a bit, scrap, or fragment of something.

snazzy /ˈsnæzi/ *adj.,* **-zier**, **-ziest**. *Colloquial* very smart; strikingly fashionable; stylish.

sneak /snik/ *v.,* **sneaked** *or Colloquial* **snuck**, **sneaking**, *n.* – *v.i.* **1.** to go in a stealthy or furtive manner; slink; skulk (fol. by *about*, *along*, *in*, *off*, *out*, etc.). **2.** to act in a furtive, underhand, or mean way. – *v.t.* **3.** to move, put, pass, etc., in a stealthy or furtive manner. – *n.* **4.** someone who sneaks; a sneaking, underhand, or contemptible person.

sneaker /ˈsnikə/ *n.* a shoe with a rubber or other soft sole worn for sport or as part of informal fashion.

sneer /snɪə/ *v.i.* **1.** to smile or curl the lip in a manner that shows scorn, contempt, etc. – *n.* **2.** an act of sneering.

sneeze /sniz/ *v.,* **sneezed**, **sneezing**, *n.* – *v.i.* **1.** to emit air or breath suddenly, forcibly, and audibly through the nose and mouth by involuntary, spasmodic action. – *n.* **2.** an act or sound of sneezing.

snick /snɪk/ *v.t.* to cut, snip, or nick.

snicker /ˈsnɪkə/ *n.* → **snigger**.

snide /snaɪd/ *adj.* derogatory in a nasty, insinuating manner.

sniff /snɪf/ *v.i.* **1.** to draw air through the nose in short, audible inhalation. – *v.t.* **2.** to draw in or up through the nose by sniffing, as air, smells, liquid, powder, etc.; inhale. – *n.* **3.** an act of sniffing; a single short, audible inhalation.

sniffle /ˈsnɪfəl/ *v.i.,* **-fled**, **-fling**. to sniff repeatedly, as from a cold in the head or in repressing tearful emotion.

snigger /ˈsnɪgə/ *v.i.* to laugh in a half-suppressed, indecorous or disrespectful, manner.

snip /snɪp/ *v.,* **snipped**, **snipping**, *n.* – *v.t.* **1.** to cut with a small, quick stroke, or a succession of such strokes, with scissors or the like. – *n.* **2.** the act of snipping, as with scissors. **3.** a small cut, notch, slit, etc., made by snipping.

snipe /snaɪp/ *v.i.,* **sniped**, **sniping**. to shoot at individual soldiers, etc., as opportunity offers from a concealed or long-range position. – **sniper**, *n.*

snippet /ˈsnɪpət/ *n.* a small piece snipped off; a small bit, scrap, or fragment.

snivel /ˈsnɪvəl/ *v.i.,* **-elled**, **-elling**. **1.** to weep or cry with sniffing. **2.** to draw up mucus audibly through the nose.

snob /snɒb/ *n.* someone who affects social importance and exclusiveness.

snooker /ˈsnukə/ *n.* a game played on a billiard table with fifteen red balls and six balls of other colours.

snoop /snup/ *Colloquial* – *v.i.* **1.** to prowl or pry; go about in a sneaking, prying way; pry in a mean, sly manner. – *n.* **2.** an act or instance of snooping. **3.** someone who snoops.

snooze /snuz/ *v.,* **snoozed**, **snoozing**, *n.* *Colloquial* – *v.i.* **1.** to sleep; slumber; doze; nap. – *n.* **2.** a rest; nap.

snore /snɔ/ *v.,* **snored**, **snoring**, *n.* – *v.i.* **1.** to breathe during sleep with hoarse or harsh sounds. – *n.* **2.** an act of snoring, or the sound made.

snorkel /ˈsnɔkəl/ *n.* a tube enabling a person swimming underwater to breathe.

snort /snɔt/ *v.i.* **1.** to force the breath violently through the nostrils with a loud, harsh sound, as a horse, etc. **2.** to express contempt, indignation, etc., by such a sound. – *n.* **3.** the act or sound of snorting.

snot /snɒt/ *n. Colloquial* mucus from the nose.

snout /snaʊt/ *n.* the part of an animal's head projecting forward and containing the nose and jaws; the muzzle.

snow /snoʊ/ *n.* **1.** the aqueous vapour of the atmosphere precipitated in partially frozen crystalline form and falling to the earth in white flakes. **2.** something resembling snow. – *v.i.* **3.** (of snow) to fall: *it snowed last night.* **4.** to descend like snow. – *v.t.* **5.** to cover, obstruct, isolate, etc., with snow (fol. by *in, over, under, up,* etc.).

snub /snʌb/ *v.,* **snubbed**, **snubbing**, *n., adj.* – *v.t.* **1.** to treat with disdain or contempt. **2.** to check or rebuke sharply. – *n.* **3.** an act of snubbing; a sharp rebuke. – *adj.* **4.** (of the nose) short, and turned up at the tip.

snuff[1] /snʌf/ *n.* a preparation of powdered tobacco, usually taken into the nostrils by inhalation.

snuff[2] /snʌf/ *v.t.* to extinguish (fol. by *out*).

snuffle /'snʌfəl/ *v.,* **-fled**, **-fling**, *n.* – *v.i.* **1.** to speak through the nose or with a nasal twang. **2.** to sniff; snivel. – *n.* **3.** an act of snuffling.

snug /snʌg/ *adj.,* **snugger**, **snuggest**. **1.** comfortable or cosy, as a place, living quarters, etc. **2.** fitting closely, but comfortably, as a garment.

snuggle /'snʌgəl/ *v.,* **-gled**, **-gling**, *n.* – *v.i.* **1.** to lie or press closely, as for comfort or from affection; nestle; cuddle (often fol. by *up, in,* etc). – *n.* **2.** a cuddle; embrace.

so /soʊ/ *adv.* **1.** in the way or manner indicated, described, or implied. **2.** as stated or reported. **3.** to that extent; in that degree. **4.** for a given reason; hence; therefore. **5.** in the way that follows; in this way. **6. and so on,** et cetera. **7. or so,** about thus: *twenty or so.* – *conj.* **8.** *Colloquial* consequently; with the result that. **9.** under the condition that (often fol. by *that*). – *pron.* **10.** such as has been stated.

soak /soʊk/ *v.i.* **1.** to lie in and become saturated or permeated with water or some other liquid. **2.** to pass, as a liquid, through pores or interstices (usually fol. by *in, through, out,* etc.). – *v.t.* **3.** to place and keep in liquid in order to saturate thoroughly; steep. **4.** to permeate thoroughly, as liquid or moisture. **5.** to take in or up by absorption (often fol. by *up*). – *n.* **6.** the act of soaking. **7.** the liquid in which anything is soaked.

soap /soʊp/ *n.* **1.** a substance used for washing and cleansing purposes, usually made by treating a fat with an alkali (as sodium or potassium hydroxide), and consisting chiefly of the sodium or potassium salts of the acids contained in the fat. – *v.t.* **2.** to rub, cover or treat with soap.

soapbox /'soʊpbɒks/ *n.* a box, usually wooden, in which soap has been packed, especially one used as a temporary platform by speakers addressing a street audience.

soar /sɔ/ *v.i.* to fly at a great height, without visible movements of the pinions, as a bird.

sob /sɒb/ *v.,* **sobbed**, **sobbing**, *n.* – *v.i.* **1.** to weep with a sound caused by a convulsive catching of the breath. – *n.* **2.** the act of sobbing; a convulsive catching of the breath in weeping.

sober /'soʊbə/ *adj.* **1.** not intoxicated or drunk. **2.** quiet or sedate in demeanour, as persons. **3.** free from excess, extravagance, or exaggeration. – *v.i., v.t.* **4.** to make or become sober. – **sobriety**, *n.*

soccer /'sɒkə/ *n.* a form of football in which there are eleven players in a team, the ball is spherical, and the use of the hands and arms is prohibited except to the goalkeeper; association football.

sociable /'soʊʃəbəl/ *adj.* inclined to associate with or be in the company of others.

social /'soʊʃəl/ *adj.* **1.** relating to, devoted to, or characterised by friendly companionship or relations. **2.** of or relating to the life and relation of human beings in a community. – *n.* **3.** a social gathering or party.

socialise = socialize /'soʊʃəlaɪz/ *v.,* **-lised**, **-lising**. – *v.t.* **1.** to make social; educate to conform to society. – *v.i.* **2.** to go into society; frequent social functions.

socialism /'soʊʃəlɪzəm/ *n.* a theory or system of social organisation which advocates the vesting of the ownership and control of the means of production, capital, land, etc., in the community as a whole.

socialite /'soʊʃəlaɪt/ *n.* a member of the social elite, or someone who aspires to be such.

social sciences *pl. n.* a broad group of subjects, as economics, anthropology, sociology, etc., relating to human social function.

social security *n.* the provision by the state for the economic and social welfare of the public by means of old-age pensions, sickness and unemployment benefits.

social service *n.* organised welfare efforts carried on under professional rules by trained personnel.

social studies *pl. n.* a broad group of subjects, as economics, social history, sociology, etc., relating to man's function as a social being, especially as taught in schools. Also, **social science**.

social welfare *n.* a system of services set up by a state for the benefit of the community.

social work *n.* organised work directed towards the betterment of social conditions in the community, as by seeking to improve the condition of the poor, to promote the welfare of children, etc.

society /sə'saɪəti/ *n., pl.* **-ties**, *adj.* – *n.* **1.** a body of individuals living as members of a community. **2.** human beings collectively regarded as a body divided into classes according to worldly status. **3.** an organisation of persons associated together for religious, benevolent, literary, scientific, political, patriotic, or other purposes. **4.** any community. – *adj.* **5.** of or relating to polite society.

socio- a word element representing 'social', 'sociological'.

sociology /soʊsi'ɒlədʒi/ *n.* the science or study of the origin, development, organisation, and functioning of human society; the science of the fundamental laws of social relations, institutions, etc.

sock[1] /sɒk/ *n.* a short stocking reaching about halfway to the knee, or only above the ankle.

sock[2] /sɒk/ *v.t. Colloquial* to strike or hit hard.

socket /'sɒkət/ *n.* a hollow part or piece for receiving and holding some part or thing.

sod /sɒd/ *n.* a disagreeable person.

soda /'soʊdə/ *n.* **1.** sodium (in expressions such as *carbonate of soda*). **2.** soda-water. **3.** a drink made with soda-water, served with fruit or other syrups, ice-cream, etc.

soda-water /'soʊdə-wɔtə/ *n.* an effervescent beverage consisting of water charged with carbon dioxide.

sodden /'sɒdn/ *adj.* soaked with liquid or moisture.

sodium /'soʊdiəm/ *n.* a soft, silver-white metallic element which oxidises rapidly in moist air, occurring in nature only in the combined state. *Symbol*: Na

sodium chloride *n.* common salt, NaCl.

sodomy /'sɒdəmi/ *n.* **1.** anal intercourse. **2.** any sexual practice regarded as unnatural or perverted.

soever /soʊ'ɛvə/ *adv.* at all; in any case; of any kind; in any way (used with generalising force after *who, what, when, where, how, any, all*, etc., sometimes separated by intervening words, often in composition).

sofa /'soʊfə/ *n.* a long upholstered seat; couch.

soft /sɒft/ *adj.* **1.** yielding readily to touch or pressure; easily penetrated, divided, or altered in shape; not hard or stiff. **2.** smooth and agreeable to the touch; not rough or coarse. **3.** producing agreeable sensations. **4.** gentle, mild. **5.** not strong or robust; delicate. **6.** *Colloquial* not hard, trying, or severe; involving little effort. **7.** (of water) relatively free from mineral salts that interfere with the action of soap. **8.** (of drugs) non-addictive, as marijuana and LSD. – **softness**, *n.*

softball /'sɒftbɔl/ *n.* a form of baseball played with a larger and softer ball, in which the pitcher delivers the ball underarm.

soft dollars *pl. n.* (in finance) payment for services made other than with money.

soft drink *n.* a drink which is not alcoholic or intoxicating, as ginger beer, lemonade, etc.

soft goods *pl. n.* merchandise such as textiles, furnishings, etc.

soft loan *n.* (in finance) a loan at below market interest rates, usually by a government to foreign importers.

soft pedal *n.* a pedal, as on a piano, for lessening the volume.

soft sell *n.* a method of selling or advertising which is quietly persuasive and subtle. Cf. **hard sell**. – **soft-sell**, *v.*

software /'sɒftwɛə/ *n.* a collection of computer programs which will cause the computer to perform a desired operation or series of operations.

soggy /'sɒgi/ *adj.*, **-gier**, **-giest**. **1.** soaked; thoroughly wet. **2.** damp and heavy, as ill-baked bread.

soil[1] /sɔɪl/ *n.* **1.** that portion of the earth's surface in which plants grow. **2.** a particular kind of earth. **3.** the ground or earth.

soil[2] /sɔɪl/ *v.t., v.i.* to make or become dirty or foul, especially on the surface.

sojourn /'soʊdʒɜn, 'sɒdʒɜn, 'sʌdʒ-, -ən/ *v.i.* **1.** to dwell for a time in a place; make a temporary stay. – *n.* **2.** a temporary stay.

solace /'sɒləs/ *n., v.,* **-aced**, **-acing**. – *n.* **1.** comfort in sorrow or trouble. **2.** something that gives comfort. – *v.t.* **3.** to comfort, console, or cheer (a person, oneself, the heart, etc.).

solar /'soʊlə/ *adj.* **1.** of or relating to the sun. **2.** determined by the sun. **3.** proceeding from the sun, as light or heat. **4.** operating by the light or heat of the sun, as a mechanism.

solar plexus /'plɛksəs/ *n. Anatomy* a network of nerves situated at the upper part of the abdomen, behind the stomach and in front of the aorta.

solar system *n.* the sun together with all the planets, satellites, asteroids, etc., revolving around it.

sold /soʊld/ *v.* past tense and past participle of **sell**.

solder /'sɒldə/ *n.* **1.** any of various fusible alloys, applied in a melted state to metal surfaces, joints, etc., to unite them. – *v.t.* **2.** to unite with solder or some other substance or device.

soldier /'soʊldʒə/ *n.* **1.** someone who serves in an army for pay; one engaged in military service. – *v.i.* **2.** to act or serve as a soldier.

sole[1] /soʊl/ *adj.* **1.** being the only one or ones; only. **2.** belonging or relating to one individual or group to the exclusion of all others; exclusive.

sole[2] /soʊl/ *n.* **1.** the bottom or under surface of the foot. **2.** the corresponding under part of a shoe, boot, or the like.

sole[3] /soʊl/ *n., pl.* **soles**, (*esp. collectively*) **sole**. a flatfish with a hooklike snout.

solecism /'sɒləsɪzəm/ *n.* **1.** a use of language regarded as substandard or nonstandard. **2.** any error, impropriety, or inconsistency.

solemn /'sɒləm/ *adj.* **1.** grave, sober, or mirthless. **2.** serious or earnest. **3.** of a formal or ceremonious character. – **solemnity**, *n.*

solenoid /'sɒlənɔɪd/ *n. Electricity* an electrical conductor wound as a helix, a current passing through which establishes a magnetic field.

soli-[1] a word element meaning 'alone', 'solitary'.

soli-[2] a word element meaning 'sun'.

solicit /sə'lɪsət/ *v.t.* **1.** to seek for by entreaty, earnest or respectful request, formal application, etc. **2.** to entreat or petition (a person, etc.) for something or to do something. – *v.i.* **3.** to make petition or request, as for something desired. **4.** to accost another with immoral intention. **5.** to endeavour to obtain orders or trade, as for a business house. – **solicitation**, *n.*

solicitor /sə'lɪsətə/ *n.* a member of that branch of the legal profession whose services consist of advising clients, representing them before the lower courts, and preparing cases for barristers to try in the higher courts.

solicitor-general /səlɪsətə-ˈdʒɛnrəl/ *n., pl.* **solicitors-general**, **solicitor-generals**. usually the second legal officer of the government whose principal functions are to appear on behalf of the government in litigation to which the government is a party and to offer such legal advice to the government as is requested by the attorney-general.

solicitous /səˈlɪsətəs/ *adj.* anxious or concerned over something (fol. by *about, for,* etc., or a clause).

solid /ˈsɒləd/ *adj.* **1.** having three dimensions (length, breadth, and thickness), as a geometrical body or figure. **2.** having the interior completely filled up, free from cavities, or not hollow. **3.** without openings or breaks. **4.** firm, hard, or compact in substance. **5.** dense, thick, or heavy in nature or appearance. **6.** whole or entire. **7.** financially sound or strong. *– n.* **8.** a body or magnitude having three dimensions (length, breadth, and thickness). **9.** a solid substance or body.

solidarity /sɒləˈdærəti/ *n.* union or fellowship arising from common responsibilities and interests.

solid-state /ˈsɒləd-steɪt/ *adj. Electronics* of or relating to electronic devices which are composed of components in the solid state, as transistors, integrated circuits, etc.

soliloquy /səˈlɪləkwi/ *n., pl.* **-quies**. the act of talking when alone or as if alone.

solitaire /ˈsɒlətɛə/ *n.* **1.** a game played by one person alone. **2.** a precious stone set by itself.

solitary /ˈsɒlətri/ *adj.* **1.** quite alone. **2.** done without assistance or accompaniment. **3.** secluded, or lonely.

solitude /ˈsɒlətjud/ *n.* the state of being or living alone.

solo /ˈsoʊloʊ/ *n., pl.* **-los**, **-li** /-li/, *adj., adv. – n.* **1.** any performance, as a dance, by one person. *– adj.* **2.** performed alone; not combined with other parts of equal importance; not concerted. *– adv.* **3.** alone; without a companion or partner.

so long *interj. Colloquial* goodbye.

solstice /ˈsɒlstəs/ *n. Astronomy* the shortest (winter) or longest (summer) day of the year.

soluble /ˈsɒljəbəl/ *adj.* **1.** capable of being dissolved or liquefied. **2.** capable of being solved or explained.

solution /səˈluʃən/ *n.* **1.** a particular instance or method of solving; an explanation or answer. **2.** the fact of being dissolved; dissolved state. **3.** a homogeneous molecular mixture of two or more substances.

solve /sɒlv/ *v.t.,* **solved**, **solving**. **1.** to clear up or explain; find the answer to. **2.** to work out the answer or solution to (a mathematical problem).

solvent /ˈsɒlvənt/ *adj.* **1.** able to pay all just debts. **2.** having the power of dissolving; causing solution. *– n.* **3.** the component of a solution which dissolves the other component. – **solvency**, *n.*

somatic /soʊˈmætɪk/ *adj.* of the body; bodily; physical.

sombre /ˈsɒmbə/ *adj.* gloomily dark, shadowy, or dimly lit.

sombrero /sɒmˈbrɛəroʊ/ *n., pl.* **-ros**. a broad-brimmed hat, as worn in Mexico.

some /sʌm/, *weak form* /səm/ *– adj.* **1.** being an undetermined or unspecified one. **2.** certain (with plural nouns). **3.** of a certain unspecified number, amount, degree, etc. *– pron.* **4.** certain persons, instances, etc., not specified.

-some[1] suffix found in some adjectives showing especially a tendency, as in *quarrelsome, burdensome.*

-some[2] collective suffix used with numerals, as in *twosome, threesome, foursome.*

-some[3] a word element meaning 'body', as in *chromosome.*

somebody /ˈsʌmbɒdi, ˈsʌmbədi/ *pron., n., pl.* **-bodies**. *– pron.* **1.** some person. *– n.* **2.** a person of some note or importance.

somehow /ˈsʌmhaʊ/ *adv.* in some way not specified, apparent, or known.

someone /ˈsʌmwʌn/ *pron., n.* → **somebody**.

somersault /ˈsʌməsɔlt, -sɒlt/ *n.* an acrobatic movement of the body in which it describes a complete revolution, heels over head.

somewhat /ˈsʌmwɒt/ *adv.* in some measure or degree; to some extent.

somewhere /ˈsʌmwɛə/ *adv.* in, at or to some place not specified, determined, or known.

somnambulism /sɒmˈnæmbjəlɪzəm/ *n.* sleepwalking.

son /sʌn/ *n.* **1.** a male child or person in relation to his parents. **2.** any male descendant. **3.** one related as if by ties of sonship.

sonar /ˈsoʊna/ *n.* an echo sounder. Also, **SONAR**.

sonata /səˈnatə/ *n. Music* an extended instrumental composition.

song /sɒŋ/ *n.* **1.** a short metrical composition combining words and music. **2.** poetical composition; poetry. **3.** the musical or tuneful sounds produced by certain birds, insects, etc.

sonic /ˈsɒnɪk/ *adj.* **1.** of or relating to sound. **2.** denoting a speed approximating that of the propagation of sound.

son-in-law /ˈsʌn-ɪn-lɔ, -ən-/ *n., pl.* **sons-in-law**. the husband of one's daughter.

sonnet /ˈsɒnət/ *n. Prosody* a poem of 14 lines.

sonorous /ˈsɒnərəs/ *adj.* loud, deep, or resonant, as a sound.

-sonous a word element used in adjectives to refer to sounds.

sook /sʊk/ *n.* (usually of children) a timid, shy, cowardly person; a cry-baby.

soon /sun/ *adv.* **1.** within a short period after this (or that) time, event, etc. **2.** promptly or quickly.

soot /sʊt/ *n.* a black carbonaceous substance produced during the imperfect combustion of coal, wood, oil, etc.

soothe /suð/ *v.t.,* **soothed**, **soothing**. **1.** to tranquillise or calm. **2.** to mitigate, assuage, or allay, as pain, sorrow, doubt, etc.

sop /sɒp/ *n., v.,* **sopped**, **sopping**. *– n.* **1.** something given to pacify or quiet, or as a bribe. *– v.t.* **2.** to drench. **3.** to take up (water, etc.) by absorption (usually fol. by *up*). – *v.i.* **4.** to become or be soaking wet.

sophism /ˈsɒfɪzəm/ *n.* a specious but fallacious argument.

sophisticated /səˈfɪstəkeɪtəd/ *adj.* **1.** (of a person, ideas, tastes, manners, etc.) altered by education, experience, etc., worldly-wise; refined; artificial. **2.** of intellectual complexity; reflecting a high degree of skill, intelligence, etc.; subtle. – **sophisticate**, *n.*

sophistication /səfɪstəˈkeɪʃən/ *n.* **1.** sophisticated character, ideas, tastes, or ways. **2.** advanced refinement or complexity.

-sophy a word element referring to systems of thought, as in *philosophy*.

soporific /sɒpəˈrɪfɪk/ *adj.* causing or tending to cause sleep.

soppy /ˈsɒpi/ *adj.*, **-pier**, **-piest**. *Colloquial* excessively sentimental; mawkish; silly.

soprano /səˈpranoʊ/ *n., pl.* **-pranos**, **-prani** /-ˈprani/. the highest singing voice in women and boys.

sorbet /ˈsɔbeɪ, ˈsɔbət/ *n.* a light frozen dish made with fruit, eggwhites, etc., served between the courses of a meal to clear the palate or as a dessert.

sorcery /ˈsɔsəri/ *n., pl.* **-ceries**. the art, practices, or spells of a sorcerer; magic, especially black magic.

sordid /ˈsɔdəd/ *adj.* **1.** dirty or filthy; squalid. **2.** morally mean or ignoble.

sore /sɔ/ *adj.*, **sorer**, **sorest**, *n.* – *adj.* **1.** physically painful or sensitive, as a wound. **2.** suffering bodily pain. **3.** causing very great suffering, misery, hardship, etc. – *n.* **4.** a sore spot or place on the body.

sorrow /ˈsɒroʊ/ *n.* **1.** distress caused by loss, affliction, disappointment, etc. **2.** a cause or occasion of grief or regret. – *v.i.* **3.** to feel sorrow; grieve.

sorry /ˈsɒri/ *adj.*, **-rier**, **-riest**. **1.** feeling regret, compunction, sympathy, pity, etc. **2.** of a deplorable, pitiable, or miserable kind.

sort /sɔt/ *n.* **1.** a particular kind, species, variety, class, group, or description, as distinguished by the character or nature. **2. of sorts,** of a mediocre or poor kind. **3. out of sorts,** not in a normal condition of good health, spirits, or temper. **4. sort of,** to a certain extent; in some way; as it were. – *v.t.* **5.** to arrange according to sort, kind, or class; separate into sorts; classify. **6.** to separate or take (*out*) from other sorts, or from others.

SOS /ɛs oʊ ˈɛs/ *n.* any call for help.

so-so /ˈsoʊ-soʊ, soʊ-ˈsoʊ/ *adj.* indifferent; neither very good nor very bad.

sotto voce /sɒtoʊ ˈvoʊtʃeɪ/ *adv.* in a low tone intended not to be overheard.

sou' /saʊ/ *n., adj., adv. Chiefly Nautical* south.

soufflé /ˈsufleɪ/ *n.* a light baked dish made fluffy with beaten eggwhites combined with egg yolks, white sauce, and fish, cheese, or other ingredients.

sought /sɔt/ *v.* past tense and past participle of **seek**.

soul /soʊl/ *n.* **1.** the spiritual part of a human being as believed to survive death. **2.** the seat of the feelings or sentiments. **3.** the embodiment of some quality. **4.** a human being; person.

sound[1] /saʊnd/ *n.* **1.** the sensation produced in the organs of hearing when certain vibrations (**soundwaves**) are caused in the surrounding air. **2.** a noise, vocal utterance, musical note, or the like. **3.** mere noise, without meaning. – *v.i.* **4.** to make or emit a sound. **5.** to be heard, as a sound. **6.** to convey a certain impression when heard or read. – *v.t.* **7.** to cause (an instrument, etc.) to make or emit a sound. **8.** to give forth (a sound).

sound[2] /saʊnd/ *adj.* **1.** free from injury, defect, etc. **2.** financially strong, secure, or reliable. – *adv.* **3.** in a sound manner.

sound[3] /saʊnd/ *v.t.* **1.** to measure or try the depth of (water, a deep hole, etc.) by letting down a lead or plummet at the end of a line or by some equivalent means. **2.** to seek to elicit the views or sentiments of (a person) by indirect inquiries, suggestive allusions, etc. (often fol. by *out*).

sound[4] /saʊnd/ *n.* an inlet, arm, or recessed portion of the sea.

soundtrack /ˈsaʊndtræk/ *n.* **1.** a strip at the side of a cinema film which carries the sound recording. **2.** such a recording, especially when transferred on to a CD or cassette.

soup /sup/ *n.* **1.** a liquid food made with various ingredients, by boiling or simmering. – *v.t.* **2. soup up,** *Colloquial* to modify (an engine, especially of a motor car) in order to increase its power.

soupçon /ˈsupsɒn/ *n.* a very small amount.

sour /ˈsaʊə/ *adj.* **1.** having an acid taste, such as that of vinegar, lemon juice, etc.; tart. **2.** rendered acid or affected by fermentation; fermented. **3.** distasteful or disagreeable; unpleasant.

source /sɔs/ *n.* any thing or place from which something comes, arises, or is obtained; origin.

souse /saʊs/ *v.*, **soused**, **sousing**, *n.* – *v.t.* **1.** to plunge into water or other liquid. – *n.* **2.** *Colloquial* a drunkard.

south /saʊθ/ *n.* **1.** a cardinal point of the compass directly opposite to the north. – *adj.* **2.** lying or proceeding towards the south. **3.** coming from the south, as a wind. – *adv.* **4.** towards or in the south. **5.** from the south. Also, *especially Nautical,* **sou'** /saʊ/. – **southerly**, *adj., n.* – **southern**, *adj.*

southern lights *pl. n.* the aurora of the Southern Hemisphere.

souvenir /suvəˈnɪə/ *n.* something given or kept for remembrance; a memento.

sovereign /ˈsɒvrən/ *n.* **1.** a monarch; a king or queen. **2.** a former British gold coin. – *adj.* **3.** belonging to or characteristic of a sovereign or sovereignty.

sow[1] /soʊ/ *v.*, **sowed**, **sown** *or* **sowed**, **sowing**. – *v.t.* **1.** to scatter (seed) over land, earth, etc., for growth; plant (seed, and hence a crop). **2.** to scatter seed over (land, earth, etc.) for the purpose of growth. – *v.i.* **3.** to sow seed, as for the production of a crop.

sow[2] /saʊ/ *n.* an adult female pig.

soya bean /ˈsɔɪjə bin/ *n.* a leguminous plant

with an oil-yielding seed used as food. Also, **soy**, **soybean**.

soya sauce *n.* a salty dark brown sauce, made by fermenting soya beans in brine. Also, **soy sauce**.

spa /spa/ *n.* **1.** a mineral spring, or a locality in which such springs exist. **2.** a spa bath or spa pool.

spa bath *n.* a bath equipped with submerged water jets which create water turbulence.

space /speɪs/ *n., v.,* **spaced**, **spacing**. – *n.* **1.** the unlimited or indefinitely great general receptacle of things, commonly conceived as an expanse extending in all directions. **2.** that part of the universe which lies outside the earth's atmosphere. **3.** extent or area; a particular extent of surface. **4.** the area or position for a person to stand, sit, etc. **5.** extent, or a particular extent, of time. – *v.t.* **6.** to set some distance apart.

space age *n.* the period in human history when exploration of and travel in space has been possible.

spacecraft /'speɪskraft/ *n.* a vehicle capable of travelling in space.

space shuttle *n.* a re-useable rocket-propelled spacecraft designed to transport equipment and personnel between earth and a satellite.

spacious /'speɪʃəs/ *adj.* containing much space, as a house, room, court, street, etc.; amply large.

spade[1] /speɪd/ *n.* **1.** a tool for digging. **2.** some implement, piece, or part resembling this.

spade[2] /speɪd/ *n.* a black figure shaped like an inverted heart with a short stem at the cusp opposite the point, used on playing cards.

spadework /'speɪdwɜk/ *n.* preliminary or initial work, especially of a laborious or tedious nature.

spaghetti /spə'geti/ *n.* a kind of pasta.

span /spæn/ *n., v.,* **spanned**, **spanning**. – *n.* **1.** the distance between the tip of the thumb and the tip of the little finger when the hand is fully extended. **2.** the distance or space between two supports of a bridge, beam, or similar structure. **3.** the full extent, stretch, or reach of anything. – *v.t.* **4.** to encircle with the hand or hands, as the waist. **5.** to extend over or across (a space, a river, etc.).

spangle /'spæŋgəl/ *n., v.,* **-gled**, **-gling**. – *n.* **1.** any small, bright drop, object, spot, or the like. – *v.t.* **2.** to decorate with spangles.

spaniel /'spænjəl/ *n.* a small dog usually with a long, silky coat and drooping ears.

spank[1] /spæŋk/ *v.t.* **1.** to strike (a person, usually a child) with the open hand, a slipper, etc., especially on the buttocks, as in punishment. – *n.* **2.** a blow given in spanking; a smart or resounding slap.

spank[2] /spæŋk/ *v.i.* to move quickly, vigorously, or smartly.

spanner /'spænə/ *n.* a tool for catching upon or gripping and turning or twisting the head of a bolt, a nut, a pipe, or the like, commonly consisting of a bar of metal with fixed or adjustable jaws.

span of hours *n.* a formula prescribing a period in each day during which an employee's hours of work are to be performed, and outside which no work is to be performed except at overtime rates. Also, **spread of hours**.

spa pool *n.* a small pool, sometimes part of a larger pool, in which heated water is agitated and aerated to massage the bather's muscles.

spar[1] /spa/ *n. Nautical* a stout pole such as those used for masts, etc.; a mast, yard, boom, gaff, or the like.

spar[2] /spa/ *v.i.,* **sparred**, **sparring**. to box with light blows, especially while seeking an opening in an opponent's defence.

spare /spɛə/ *v.,* **spared**, **sparing**, *adj.,* **sparer**, **sparest**, *n.* – *v.t.* **1.** to refrain from harming or destroying. **2.** to save from strain, discomfort, annoyance, or the like. **3.** to part with or let go, as from a supply, especially without inconvenience or loss. **4.** to use economically or frugally. – *v.i.* **5.** to use economy; be frugal. – *adj.* **6.** kept in reserve, as for possible use. **7.** being in excess of present need; free for other use. **8.** lean or thin, as a person. – *n.* **9.** a spare thing, part, etc., as an extra tyre for emergency use.

spare part *n.* a part which replaces a faulty, worn, or broken part of a machine, especially a motor vehicle. Also, **spare**.

spark /spak/ *n.* **1.** an ignited or fiery particle such as is thrown off by burning wood, etc., or produced by one hard body striking against another. **2.** *Electricity* the light produced by a sudden discontinuous discharge of electricity. – *v.i.* **3.** to emit or produce sparks.

sparkle /'spakəl/ *v.,* **-kled**, **-kling**, *n.* – *v.i.* **1.** to emit little sparks, as burning matter. **2.** to shine with little gleams of light. **3.** to effervesce, as wine. – *n.* **4.** a little spark or fiery particle.

spark plug *n.* a device inserted in the cylinder of an internal-combustion engine, containing two terminals between which passes the electric spark for igniting the explosive gases. Also, **sparking plug**.

sparrow /'spæroʊ/ *n.* a small, hardy, pugnacious bird, introduced into Australia as a destroyer of insects.

sparse /spas/ *adj.,* **sparser**, **sparsest**. thinly scattered or distributed.

spasm /'spæzəm/ *n.* a sudden, involuntary muscular contraction. – **spasmodic**, *adj.*

spastic /'spæstɪk/ *n.* a person who has cerebral palsy.

spat[1] /spæt/ *n.* a petty quarrel.

spat[2] /spæt/ *v.* past tense and past participle of **spit**.

spate /speɪt/ *n.* a sudden, almost overwhelming, outpouring.

spatial /'speɪʃəl/ *adj.* of or relating to space.

spatio- a word element meaning 'space'.

spatter /'spætə/ *v.t.* **1.** to scatter or dash in small particles or drops. **2.** to splash with something in small particles.

spatula /'spætʃələ/ *n.* a broad, flexible blade, used for mixing and spreading.

spawn /spɔn/ *v.i.* **1.** to shed the sex cells, especially as applied to animals that shed eggs and sperm directly into water. – *v.t.* **2.** to give birth to; give rise to.

spay /speɪ/ *v.t.* to remove the ovaries of (a female animal).

SP bookmaker *n.* an unlicensed bookmaker operating off racetracks paying the starting price odds.

speak /spik/ *v.*, **spoke**, **spoken**, **speaking**. – *v.i.* **1.** to utter words or articulate sounds with the ordinary (talking) voice. **2.** to deliver an address, discourse, etc. **3.** to make communication by any means. – *v.t.* **4.** to utter orally and articulately. **5.** to use, or be able to use, in oral utterance, as a language.

speaker /'spikə/ *n.* **1.** (*usu. cap.*) the presiding officer of the lower house of a parliament, as in the House of Representatives. **2.** a loudspeaker.

spear /spɪə/ *n.* **1.** a weapon for thrusting or throwing, being a long staff with a sharp head, as of iron or steel. – *v.t.* **2.** to pierce with or as with a spear.

spearmint /'spɪəmɪnt/ *n.* an aromatic herb much used for flavouring.

spec builder /spɛk 'bɪldə/ *n.* someone who builds houses, etc., as a speculative enterprise, rather than under contract.

special /'spɛʃəl/ *adj.* **1.** of a distinct or particular character. **2.** being a particular one. **3.** relating or peculiar to a particular person, thing, instance, etc. **4.** extraordinary; exceptional. – *n.* **5. on special,** *Colloquial* available at a bargain price.

special drawing rights *pl. n.* credits which central banks in the western world extend to each other.

specialise = specialize /'spɛʃəlaɪz/ *v.*, **-lised**, **-lising**. – *v.i.* **1.** to pursue some special line of study, work, etc. – *v.t.* **2.** to invest with a special character, function, etc. **3.** to adapt to special conditions. **4.** to restrict payment of (a negotiable instrument) by endorsing over to a specific payee. – **specialisation**, *n.*

specialist /'spɛʃələst/ *n.* someone who is devoted to one subject, or to one particular branch of a subject or pursuit.

speciality /spɛʃi'æləti/ *n.*, *pl.* **-ties**. **1.** an article of unusual or superior design or quality. **2.** an article with such strong consumer demand that it is at least partially removed from price competition. Also, **specialty**.

specialty /'spɛʃəlti/ *n.*, *pl.* **-ties**. **1.** a special study, line of work, or the like. **2.** an article particularly dealt in, manufactured, etc. **3.** → **speciality**.

specie /'spiʃi/ *n.* coin; coined money.

species /'spisiz, -ʃiz/ *n.*, *pl.* **-cies**. a group of individuals having some common characteristics or qualities; distinct sort or kind.

speciesism /'spisizɪzəm/ *n.* human discrimination against other animal species, especially in regard to the exploitation of certain animals for human benefit.

specific /spə'sɪfɪk/ *adj.* **1.** specified, precise, or particular. **2.** peculiar or proper to something, as qualities, characteristics, effects, etc. **3.** of a special or particular kind. **4.** *Commerce* denoting customs or duties levied in fixed amounts per unit (number, volume, weight, etc.). – *n.* **5.** something specific, as a statement, quality, etc. – **specificity**, *n.*

specification /spɛsəfə'keɪʃən/ *n.* **1.** the act of specifying. **2.** a statement of particulars.

specify /'spɛsəfaɪ/ *v.t.*, **-fied**, **-fying**. **1.** to mention or name specifically or definitely; state in detail. **2.** to name or state as a condition.

specimen /'spɛsəmən/ *n.* a part or an individual taken as exemplifying a whole mass or number.

specious /'spiʃəs/ *adj.* apparently good or right but without real merit; superficially pleasing.

speck /spɛk/ *n.* **1.** a small spot differing in colour or substance from that of the surface or material upon which it appears. – *v.t.* **2.** to mark with, or as with, a speck or specks.

speckle /'spɛkəl/ *n.*, *v.*, **-led**, **-ling**. – *n.* **1.** a small speck, spot, or mark, as on skin. – *v.t.* **2.** to mark with, or as with, speckles.

spectacle /'spɛktəkəl/ *n.* **1.** anything presented to the sight or view, especially something of a striking kind. **2.** (*pl.*) a device to aid defective vision or to protect the eyes from light, dust, etc., consisting usually of two glass lenses set in a frame which rests on the nose. – **spectacular**, *adj.*

spectator /spɛk'teɪtə, 'spɛkteɪtə/ *n.* someone who looks on; an onlooker.

spectra /'spɛktrə/ *n.* plural of **spectrum**.

spectre /'spɛktə/ *n.* a ghost; phantom.

spectro- a word element representing **spectrum**.

spectrum /'spɛktrəm/ *n.* **1.** *Optics* the band of colours (red, orange, yellow, green, blue, indigo, violet) observed when white light passes through a prism. **2.** a range of interrelated values, objects, opinions, etc.

speculate /'spɛkjəleɪt/ *v.i.*, **-lated**, **-lating**. **1.** to engage in thought or reflection, or meditate (often fol. by *on*, *upon*, or a clause). **2.** to indulge in conjectural thought. **3.** *Commerce* to buy and sell commodities, shares, etc., in the expectation of profit through a change in their market value. – **speculation**, *n.* – **speculative**, *adj.* – **speculator**, *n.*

sped /spɛd/ *v.* past tense and past participle of **speed**.

speech /spitʃ/ *n.* **1.** the faculty or power of speaking; oral communication. **2.** that which is spoken. **3.** a form of communication in spoken language, made by a speaker before an audience for a given purpose. **4.** the form of utterance characteristic of a particular people or region; a language or dialect. **5.** manner of speaking, as of a person.

speed /spid/ *n.*, *v.*, **sped** *or* **speeded**, **speeding**. – *n.* **1.** rapidity in moving, going, travelling. **2.** *Physics* the ratio of the distance covered by a moving body to the time taken. **3.** *Colloquial* amphetamines. – *v.t.* **4.** to increase the rate of speed of (usually fol. by *up*). – *v.i.* **5.** to move, go, pass, or proceed with speed or rapidity. **6.** to drive a vehicle at a rate exceeding the maximum permitted by law. **7.** to increase the rate of speed or progress (fol. by *up*).

speedometer /spi'dɒmətə/ *n.* a device attached to a motor vehicle or the like to indicate the rate of travel. Also, **speedo**.

speleology /spili'ɒlədʒi/ *n.* the exploration and study of caves. Also, **spelaeology**.

spell[1] /spɛl/ *v.,* **spelt** *or* **spelled**, **spelling**. – *v.t.* **1.** to name, write, or otherwise give (as by signals), in order, the letters of (a word, syllable, etc.). **2.** (of letters) to form (a word, syllable, etc.). – *v.i.* **3.** to name, write, or give the letters of words, etc.

spell[2] /spɛl/ *n.* a form of words supposed to possess magic power.

spell[3] /spɛl/ *n.* **1.** a continuous course or period of work or other activity. **2.** *Colloquial* an interval or space of time, usually indefinite or short. **3.** an interval or period of rest. – *v.t.* **4.** to give an interval of rest to.

spellchecker /'spɛltʃɛkə/ *n.* a computer program which checks the spelling of words.

spelling /'spɛlɪŋ/ *n.* the manner in which words are spelt.

spencer /'spɛnsə/ *n.* a kind of woman's vest, worn for extra warmth.

spend /spɛnd/ *v.,* **spent**, **spending**. – *v.t.* **1.** to pay out, disburse, or expend; dispose of (money, wealth, resources, etc.). – *v.i.* **2.** to spend money, etc.

spendthrift /'spɛndθrɪft/ *n.* someone who spends their possessions or money extravagantly or wastefully; a prodigal.

sperm /spɜm/ *n.* a male reproductive cell; a spermatozoon.

sperm- a word element representing **sperm**. Also, **spermo-**.

-sperm a terminal combining form of **sperm**, as in *angiosperm.*

spermatozoon /ˌspɜmətoʊ'zoʊɒn/ *n., pl.* **-zoa** /-'zoʊə/. a mature male reproductive cell.

spew /spju/ *v.i.* **1.** to discharge the contents of the stomach through the mouth; vomit. – *v.t.* **2.** to eject from the stomach through the mouth; vomit.

SPF /ɛs pi 'ɛf/ *n.* the effectiveness of a sunscreen preparation in protecting the skin from ultraviolet radiation, indicated on a scale, usually from 2 to 15. Also, **sun protection factor**.

sphere /sfɪə/ *n.* **1.** a round body whose surface is at all points equidistant from the centre. **2.** any rounded body approximately of this form; a globular mass, shell, etc. **3.** a field of activity or operation.

-sphere a word element representing **sphere**.

spherical /'sfɛrəkəl/ *adj.* **1.** having the form of a sphere; globular. **2.** of or relating to a sphere or spheres.

sphincter /'sfɪŋktə/ *n. Anatomy* a circular band of voluntary or involuntary muscle which encircles an orifice of the body or one of its hollow organs.

spice /spaɪs/ *n., v.,* **spiced**, **spicing**. – *n.* **1.** any of a class of pungent or aromatic substances of vegetable origin, as pepper, cinnamon, cloves, and the like, used as seasoning, preservatives, etc. **2.** piquancy, or interest. – *v.t.* **3.** to prepare or season with a spice or spices. – **spicy**, *adj.*

spick-and-span /spɪk-ən-'spæn/ *adj.* **1.** neat and clean. **2.** perfectly new; fresh. Also, **spick and span**.

spider /'spaɪdə/ *n.* **1.** any of the eight-legged wingless, predatory, insectlike arachnids most of which spin webs that serve as nests and as traps for prey. **2.** any of various things resembling or suggesting a spider. **3.** an aerated soft drink to which ice-cream is added.

spiel /spil, ʃpil/ *n.* a salesperson's, conjurer's, or swindler's patter.

spiff /spɪf/ *n.* a form of incentive given to sales people, usually in the form of money or goods to an appropriate value.

spiflicate /'spɪfləkeɪt/ *v.t.,* **-cated**, **-cating**. *Colloquial* (*often humorous*) to destroy or kill. Also, **spifflicate**.

spigot /'spɪgət/ *n.* a small peg or plug for stopping the vent of a cask, etc.

spike /spaɪk/ *n., v.,* **spiked**, **spiking**. – *n.* **1.** a stiff, sharp-pointed piece or part. – *v.t.* **2.** to fasten or secure with a spike or spikes. **3.** to pierce with or impale on a spike. **4.** to set or stud with something suggesting spikes. **5.** to make ineffective, or frustrate the action or purpose of. **6.** *Colloquial* to add alcoholic liquor to a drink.

spill[1] /spɪl/ *v.,* **spilt** *or* **spilled**, **spilling**, *n.* – *v.t.* **1.** to cause or allow (liquid, or any matter in grains or loose pieces) to run or fall from a container, especially accidentally or wastefully. – *v.i.* **2.** (of a liquid, loose particles, etc.) to run or escape from a container, especially by accident or in careless handling. – *n.* **3.** a spilling, as of liquid. **4.** a quantity spilt. **5.** a throw or fall from a horse, vehicle, or the like. **6.** *Politics* the declaring vacant of a number of positions when one of them falls vacant.

spill[2] /spɪl/ *n.* a slender piece of wood or twisted paper, for lighting candles, lamps, etc.

spin /spɪn/ *v.,* **spun**, **spinning**, *n.* – *v.t.* **1.** to make (yarn) by drawing out, twisting, and winding fibres. **2.** to form (any material) into thread. **3.** to cause to turn round rapidly, as on an axis; twirl; whirl. **4.** to produce, fabricate, or evolve in a manner suggestive of spinning thread, as a story. – *v.i.* **5.** to turn round rapidly, as on an axis, as the earth, a top, etc. **6.** to produce a thread from the body, as spiders, silkworms, etc. – *n.* **7.** a spinning motion given to a ball or the like when thrown or struck. **8.** a rapid run, ride, drive, or the like, as for exercise or enjoyment.

spinach /'spɪnɪtʃ/ *n.* **1.** an annual herb cultivated for its succulent leaves; English spinach. **2.** → **silver beet**.

spindle /'spɪndl/ *n.* **1.** the rod on a spinning wheel by which the thread is twisted and on which it is wound. **2.** any similar rod or pin.

spindly /'spɪndli/ *adj.,* **-dlier**, **-dliest**. long or tall and slender.

spin-dry /spɪn-'draɪ/ *v.t.,* **-dried**, **-drying**. to dry (laundry) by spinning it in a tub.

spine /spaɪn/ *n.* **1.** the vertebral or spinal column; the backbone. **2.** any backbone-like part. **3.** a stiff, pointed process or appendage. **4.** *Bookbinding* the part of a book's cover that holds the front and back together. – **spinal**, *adj.*

spinechilling /'spaɪntʃɪlɪŋ/ *adj.* terrifying.

spinifex /ˈspɪnəfɛks/ *n.* spiny-leaved tussock-forming grasses of inland Australia.

spinnaker /ˈspɪnəkə/ *n.* a large triangular sail with a light boom (**spinnaker boom**).

spinning wheel *n.* a device for spinning wool, flax, etc., into yarn or thread consisting essentially of a single spindle driven by a large wheel operated by hand or foot.

spin-off /ˈspɪn-ɒf/ *n.* **1.** an object, product or enterprise derived as an incidental or secondary development of a larger enterprise. **2.** *Economics* a new company formed by an already existing company, with shareholders in the existing company entitled to subscribe for shares in the new company.

spinster /ˈspɪnstə/ *n.* a woman who has never been married.

spiny anteater /ˈspaɪni/ *n.* → **echidna**.

spiral /ˈspaɪrəl/ *n., adj., v.,* **-ralled**, **-ralling**. – *n.* **1.** a plane curve traced by a point which runs continuously round and round a fixed point or centre while constantly receding from or approaching it. **2.** a spiral or helical object, formation, or form. **3.** *Economics* a reciprocal interaction of price and cost changes forming an overall economic change upwards (**inflationary spiral**) or downwards (**deflationary spiral**). – *adj.* **4.** resembling or arranged in a spiral or spirals. – *v.i.* **5.** to take a spiral form or course. – *v.t.* **6.** to cause to take a spiral form or course.

spire /ˈspaɪə/ *n.* a tall, tapering structure, generally an elongated, upright cone or pyramid, erected on a tower, roof, etc.

spirit /ˈspɪrət/ *n.* **1.** the vital principle in human beings, animating the body or mediating between body and soul. **2.** the incorporeal part of a human being. **3.** a supernatural, incorporeal being. **4.** (*pl.*) feelings with respect to exaltation or depression. **5.** fine or brave vigour or liveliness; mettle. **6.** the true or general meaning or intent of a statement, etc. (opposed to *letter*). **7.** (*often pl.*) a strong distilled alcoholic liquor. **8.** *Pharmaceutical* a solution in alcohol of an essential or volatile principle. – *adj.* **9.** relating to something which works by burning alcoholic spirits. – *v.t.* **10.** to carry (*away, off,* etc.) mysteriously or secretly. – **spirited**, *adj.*

spiritual /ˈspɪrətʃuəl, -tʃəl/ *adj.* **1.** of, relating to, or consisting of spirit or incorporeal being. – *n.* **2.** a traditional religious song, especially of American Negroes.

spiro-[1] a word element referring to respiration.

spiro-[2] a word element meaning 'coil', 'spiral'.

spit[1] /spɪt/ *v.,* **spat** *or* **spit**, **spitting**, *n.* – *v.i.* **1.** to eject saliva from the mouth. **2.** to sputter. **3.** to fall in scattered drops or flakes, as rain or snow. – *v.t.* **4.** to eject (saliva, etc.) from the mouth. **5.** to throw out or emit, especially violently. – *n.* **6.** saliva, especially when ejected. **7.** the act of spitting. **8. dead spit,** *Colloquial* the image, likeness, or counterpart of a person, etc.

spit[2] /spɪt/ *n., v.,* **spitted**, **spitting**. – *n.* **1.** any of various rods, pins, or the like used for particular purposes. **2.** a narrow point of land projecting into the water. – *v.t.* **3.** to thrust a spit into or through, as roasting meat.

spite /spaɪt/ *n., v.,* **spited**, **spiting**. – *n.* **1.** a keen, ill-natured desire to humiliate, annoy, or injure another. **2. in spite of,** in disregard or defiance of; notwithstanding. – *v.t.* **3.** to annoy or thwart, out of spite.

spittle /ˈspɪtl/ *n.* saliva; spit.

spittoon /spɪˈtun/ *n.* a bowl, etc., for spitting into.

splash /splæʃ/ *v.t.* **1.** to wet or soil by dashing masses or particles of water, mud, or the like; spatter. **2.** to dash (water, etc.) about in scattered masses or particles. **3.** *Colloquial* to display or print very noticeably, as in a newspaper. – *v.i.* **4.** to dash a liquid or semiliquid substance about. **5.** to fall, move, or go with a splash or splashes. – *n.* **6.** the act of splashing. **7.** the sound of splashing. **8.** a striking show, or an ostentatious display; sensation or excitement.

splat /splæt/ *n.* a slapping sound as made with something wet.

splatter /ˈsplætə/ *v.i., v.t.* to splash.

splay /spleɪ/ *v.t.* **1.** to spread out, expand, or extend. – *v.i.* **2.** to spread or flare.

spleen /splin/ *n.* **1.** *Anatomy* a highly vascular, glandlike but ductless organ, situated in humans near the cardiac end of the stomach, in which the blood undergoes certain corpuscular changes. **2.** ill humour, peevish temper, or spite. – **splenetic**, *adj.*

splendid /ˈsplɛndəd/ *adj.* **1.** gorgeous; magnificent; sumptuous. **2.** strikingly admirable or fine.

splendour = splendor /ˈsplɛndə/ *n.* brilliant or gorgeous appearance, colouring, etc.

splice /splaɪs/ *v.t.,* **spliced**, **splicing**. to join together or unite, especially by the interweaving of strands.

splint /splɪnt/ *n.* **1.** a thin piece of wood or other rigid material used to immobilise a fractured or dislocated bone. – *v.t.* **2.** to support as if with splints.

splinter /ˈsplɪntə/ *n.* **1.** a rough piece of wood, bone, etc., usually comparatively long, thin, and sharp, split or broken off from a main body. – *v.t., v.i.* **2.** to split or break into splinters.

split /splɪt/ *v.,* **split**, **splitting**, *n., adj.* – *v.t.* **1.** to divide into distinct parts or portions. **2.** to separate (a part) by such division. **3.** to make (a vote) less effective by offering more than one candidate with a similar policy. – *v.i.* **4.** to break or part lengthways, or suffer longitudinal division. **5.** to part, divide, or separate in any way. **6.** to become separated off by such a division, as a piece or part from a whole. **7.** *Colloquial* to leave hurriedly. – *n.* **8.** the act of splitting. **9.** a crack, rent, or fissure caused by splitting. **10.** (*usu. pl.*) the feat of separating the legs while sinking to the floor, until they extend at right angles to the body. – *adj.* **11.** that has undergone splitting; parted lengthwise; cleft.

split-level /ˈsplɪt-lɛvəl/ *adj.* denoting or relating to a building or room with a floor at more than one level.

splotch /splɒtʃ/ *n.* a large, irregular spot; blot; stain.

splurge /splɜdʒ/ *v.i.,* **splurged**, **splurging**.

Colloquial to be extravagant.

splutter /ˈsplʌtə/ *v.i.* **1.** to talk hastily and confusedly or incoherently, as in excitement or embarrassment. **2.** to fly or fall in particles or drops; spatter, as a liquid.

spoil /spɔɪl/ *v.*, **spoiled** *or* **spoilt**, **spoiling**, *n.* – *v.t.* **1.** to damage or impair (a thing) irreparably. **2.** to impair in character or disposition. – *v.i.* **3.** to become spoiled, bad, or unfit for use. – *n.* **4.** (*often pl.*) booty, loot, or plunder taken in war or robbery. **5.** treasures won or accumulated.

spoilsport /ˈspɔɪlspɔt/ *n.* someone who interferes with the pleasure of others.

spoke[1] /spoʊk/ *v.* past tense of **speak**.

spoke[2] /spoʊk/ *n.* one of the bars, rods, or rungs radiating from the hub of a wheel and supporting the rim.

spoken /ˈspoʊkən/ *v.* **1.** past participle of **speak**. – *adj.* **2.** (in compounds) speaking, or using speech, as specified.

spokesperson /ˈspoʊkspɜsən/ *n.* someone who speaks for another or others.

sponge /spʌndʒ/ *n.*, *v.*, **sponged**, **sponging**. – *n.* **1.** the light, yielding, porous, fibrous skeleton or framework of certain animals, or colonies of this group, from which the living matter has been removed, characterised by readily absorbing water, and becoming soft when wet while retaining toughness. **2.** someone who or that which absorbs something freely, as a sponge does water. **3.** a light, sweet cake. – *v.t.* **4.** to wipe or rub with a wet sponge, as in order to clean or moisten. **5.** to remove with a wet sponge (fol. by *off*, *away*, etc.). – *v.i.* **6.** *Colloquial* to live at the expense of others.

sponsor /ˈspɒnsə/ *n.* **1.** someone who vouches or is responsible for a person or thing. **2.** a person, firm, or other organisation that finances a radio or television program in return for advertisement. – *v.t.* **3.** to act as sponsor for.

spontaneous /spɒnˈteɪniəs/ *adj.* **1.** natural and unconstrained. **2.** independent of external agencies.

spoof /spuf/ *n.* *Colloquial* parody; hoax.

spook /spuk/ *n.* *Colloquial* a ghost; a spectre.

spooked /spukt/ *adj.* frightened; on edge; nervous.

spool /spul/ *n.* any cylindrical piece or appliance on which something is wound.

spoon /spun/ *n.* **1.** a utensil consisting of a bowl or concave part and a handle, for taking up or stirring liquid or other food, or other matter. – *v.t.* **2.** to take up or transfer in or as in a spoon. – *v.i.* **3.** *Colloquial* to show affection, especially in an openly sentimental manner.

spoonerism /ˈspunərɪzəm/ *n.* a slip of the tongue whereby initial or other sounds of words are transposed, as in 'our queer old dean' for 'our dear old queen'.

spoor /spɔ/ *n.* a track or trail, especially that of a wild animal pursued as game.

sporadic /spəˈrædɪk/ *adj.* appearing or happening at intervals; occasional.

spore /spɔ/ *n.* a germ, germ cell, seed, or the like.

sporo- a word element meaning 'seed'. Also, **spor-**.

sporran /ˈspɒrən/ *n.* (in Scottish Highland costume) a large pouch, commonly of fur, worn hanging from the belt over the front of the kilt.

sport /spɔt/ *n.* **1.** an activity pursued for exercise or pleasure, usually requiring some degree of physical prowess. **2.** pleasant pastime. **3.** something sported with or tossed about like a plaything. **4.** *Colloquial* (a term of address, usually between males). **5.** *Colloquial* someone who is interested in pursuits involving betting or gambling. – *v.i.* **6.** to amuse oneself with some pleasant pastime or recreation. – *v.t.* **7.** to have or wear, especially ostentatiously, proudly, etc.

sporting /ˈspɔtɪŋ/ *adj.* **1.** exhibiting qualities especially esteemed in those who engage in sports, such as fairness, good humour when losing, etc. **2.** willing to take a chance. **3.** even or fair; involving reasonable odds, as a gamble.

sports /spɔts/ *adj.* **1.** of, relating to, or devoted to a sport or sports. **2.** (of garments, etc.) suitable for outdoor or informal use.

sports car *n.* a high-powered car with stylish lines, usually a two-seater.

sportsman /ˈspɔtsmən/ *n.*, *pl.* **-men**. **1.** a man who engages in sport, especially in an open-air sport and with some expertise. **2.** one who exhibits sporting qualities.

sportsperson /ˈspɔtspɜsən/ *n.*, *pl.* **-people**. a person who engages in sport, usually with a degree of expertise.

sportswoman /ˈspɔtswʊmən/ *n.*, *pl.* **-women**. a woman who engages in sport, especially in an open-air sport and with some expertise.

spot /spɒt/ *n.*, *v.*, **spotted**, **spotting**, *adj.* – *n.* **1.** a mark made by foreign matter; a stain. **2.** a blemish of the skin, as a pimple. **3.** a relatively small, usually roundish, part of a surface differing from the rest in appearance or character. **4.** a moral blemish; flaw. **5.** a place or locality. **6.** *Colloquial* a small quantity of something. **7.** *Colloquial* a predicament. – *v.t.* **8.** to stain with spots. **9.** to see or perceive, especially suddenly, by chance, or when it is difficult to do so. – *v.i.* **10.** to make a spot; cause a stain. – *adj.* **11.** *Commerce* made, paid, delivered, etc., at once.

spot check *n.* **1.** an inspection made without warning, as of motor vehicles, etc. **2.** a check made on a random sample, as of manufactured articles.

spotlight /ˈspɒtlaɪt/ *n.* *Theatre* a strong light with a narrow beam thrown upon a particular spot on the stage.

spot-on /spɒt-ˈɒn/ *adj.* *Colloquial* absolutely right or accurate; excellent.

spot price *n.* (in commodities trading) the price agreed on for immediate delivery of the commodity.

spouse /spaʊs, spaʊz/ *n.* one's husband or wife.

spout /spaʊt/ *v.t.* **1.** to discharge or emit (a liquid, etc.) in a stream, with some force. – *v.i.* **2.** to discharge a liquid, etc., in a jet or continuous stream. **3.** to issue with force, as liquid through a narrow orifice. – *n.* **4.** a tube by which a liquid is discharged or poured.

sprain /spreɪn/ *v.t.* to overstrain or wrench (a joint) so as to injure without fracture or dislocation.

sprang /spræŋ/ *v.* past tense of **spring**.

sprat /spræt/ *n.* a small, herring-like marine fish.

sprawl /sprɔl/ *v.i.* **1.** to be stretched out in irregular or ungraceful movements, as the limbs. **2.** to lie or sit with the limbs stretched out in a careless or ungraceful posture. **3.** to spread out in a straggling or irregular manner, as vines, buildings, handwriting, etc. – *v.t.* **4.** to stretch out (the limbs) as in sprawling.

spray[1] /spreɪ/ *n.* **1.** water or other liquid broken up into small particles and blown or falling through the air. – *v.t.* **2.** to scatter in the form of fine particles. **3.** to direct a spray of particles, missiles, etc., upon. – *v.i.* **4.** to scatter spray; discharge a spray. **5.** to issue as spray.

spray[2] /spreɪ/ *n.* a single flower or small bouquet of flowers designed to be pinned to one's clothes as an adornment.

spread /sprɛd/ *v.,* **spread**, **spreading**, *n.* – *v.t.* **1.** to draw or stretch out to the full width. **2.** to distribute in a sheet or layer. **3.** to overlay, cover, or coat with something. **4.** to diffuse or disseminate, as knowledge, news, disease, etc. – *v.i.* **5.** to become stretched out or extended. **6.** to admit of being spread or applied in a thin layer, as a soft substance. **7.** to become diffused or disseminated. – *n.* **8.** expansion; extension; diffusion. **9.** a stretch, expanse, or extent of something. **10.** a cloth covering for a bed, table, or the like, especially a bedspread. **11.** any food preparation for spreading on bread, etc. **12.** *Stock Exchange* **a.** the difference between the highest and the lowest prices at which business has been done during one day. **b.** the difference between the prices quoted by a stockjobber for buying and selling. **13.** a pair of facing pages of a book, magazine, or the like, or any part of them.

spread-eagle /sprɛd-ˈigəl/ *v.t.* to stretch out. – **spread-eagled**, *adj.*

spreadsheet /ˈsprɛdʃit/ *n.* a computer program for organising large amounts of numerical data in tabular formats.

spree /spri/ *n.* a session or period of indulgence.

sprig /sprɪg/ *n.* a shoot, twig, or small branch.

sprightly /ˈspraɪtli/ *adj.,* **-lier**, **-liest**. animated or vivacious; lively.

spring /sprɪŋ/ *v.,* **sprang** *or* **sprung**, **sprung**, **springing**, *n., adj.* – *v.i.* **1.** to rise or move suddenly and lightly as by some inherent power. **2.** to go or come suddenly as if with a leap. **3.** to come into being; rise or arise (often fol. by *up*). – *v.t.* **4.** to cause to spring. **5.** to bring out, disclose, produce, make, etc., suddenly. **6.** to equip or fit with springs. **7.** to leap over. **8.** to make a surprise attack on (someone). – *n.* **9.** a leap, jump, or bound. **10.** elasticity or springiness. **11.** an issue of water from the earth. **12.** a beginning or cause of origin. **13.** the season of the year between winter and summer. **14.** the first and freshest period. **15.** an elastic contrivance which recovers its shape after being compressed, bent, etc. – *adj.* **16.** of, relating to, characteristic of, or suitable for the season of spring. **17.** resting on or containing springs.

springboard /ˈsprɪŋbɔd/ *n.* **1.** a projecting semiflexible board used for diving. **2.** a flexible board used as a take-off in vaulting, tumbling, etc., to increase the height of leaps.

spring roll *n.* a Chinese delicacy consisting of a savoury filling wrapped in a thin dough and deep fried.

sprinkle /ˈsprɪŋkəl/ *v.,* **-kled**, **-kling**, *n.* – *v.t.* **1.** to scatter, as a liquid or a powder, in drops or particles. **2.** to disperse or distribute here and there. **3.** to overspread with drops or particles of water, powder, or the like. – *n.* **4.** a sprinkling.

sprint /sprɪnt/ *v.i.* **1.** to race at full speed, especially for a short distance, as in running, rowing, etc. – *n.* **2.** a short race at full speed.

sprite /spraɪt/ *n.* **1.** an elf, fairy, or goblin. **2.** an icon which moves around a screen in computer graphics.

spritzig /ˈsprɪtsɪg/ *adj.* (of wine) showing a slight degree of gassiness.

sprocket /ˈsprɒkət/ *n. Machinery* one of a set of projections on the rim of a wheel which engage the links of a chain.

sprout /spraʊt/ *v.i.* **1.** to begin to grow. **2.** (of a seed, plant, the earth, etc.) to put forth buds or shoots. – *n.* **3.** a shoot of a plant. **4.** → **brussels sprout**.

spruce[1] /sprus/ *n.* an evergreen tree with short angular needle-shaped leaves.

spruce[2] /sprus/ *adj.,* **sprucer**, **sprucest**, *v.,* **spruced**, **sprucing**. – *adj.* **1.** smart in dress or appearance. – *v.i.* **2.** to make oneself spruce (usually fol. by *up*).

sprung /sprʌŋ/ *v.* past tense and past participle of **spring**.

spry /spraɪ/ *adj.,* **spryer**, **spryest** *or* **sprier**, **spriest**. active; nimble; brisk.

spud /spʌd/ *n. Colloquial* a potato.

spume /spjum/ *n.* foam; froth; scum.

spun /spʌn/ *v.* past tense and past participle of **spin**.

spun glass *n.* → **fibreglass**.

spunk /spʌŋk/ *n. Colloquial* **1.** pluck; spirit; mettle. **2.** a good-looking person.

spur /spɜ/ *n., v.,* **spurred**, **spurring**. – *n.* **1.** a pointed device attached to a horseman's boot heel, for goading a horse onwards, etc. **2. on the spur of the moment,** suddenly; without premeditation. – *v.t.* **3.** to prick with, or as with, spurs or a spur, as in order to urge on.

spurious /ˈspjuriəs/ *adj.* not genuine or true.

spurn /spɜn/ *v.t.* to reject with disdain.

spurt /spɜt/ *v.i.* **1.** to gush or issue suddenly in a stream or jet, as a liquid. **2.** to show marked activity or energy for a short period. – *n.* **3.** a forcible gush of water, etc., as from a confined place. **4.** a sudden outburst, as of feeling.

sputnik /ˈspʌtnɪk, ˈspʊtnɪk/ *n.* an artificial satellite, especially an early Soviet one.

sputter /ˈspʌtə/ *v.i.* **1.** to emit particles of anything in an explosive manner, as a candle does in burning. – *v.t.* **2.** to emit (anything) in small particles, as if by spitting.

spy /spaɪ/ *n., pl.* **spies**, *v.,* **spied**, **spying**. – *n.* **1.** someone who keeps secret watch on the actions of others. **2.** one employed by a government to obtain secret information or intelligence. – *v.i.* **3.** to make secret observations. – *v.t.* **4.** to find (*out*) by observation or scrutiny. **5.** to catch sight of; see.

spyglass /ˈspaɪglas/ *n.* a small telescope.

squabble /ˈskwɒbəl/ *v.,* **-bled**, **-bling**, *n.* – *v.i.* **1.** to engage in a petty quarrel. – *n.* **2.** a petty quarrel.

squad /skwɒd/ *n.* any small group or party of persons engaged in a common enterprise, etc.

squadron /ˈskwɒdrən/ *n.* an air force unit.

squalid /ˈskwɒləd/ *adj.* foul and repulsive.

squall[1] /ˈskwɔl/ *n.* a sudden strong wind which dies away rapidly.

squall[2] /skwɔl/ *v.i.* to cry out loudly; scream violently.

squalor /ˈskwɒlə/ *n.* filth and misery.

squander /ˈskwɒndə/ *v.t.* to spend (money, time, etc.) extravagantly or wastefully (often fol. by *away*).

square /skwɛə/ *n., v.,* **squared**, **squaring**, *adj.,* **squarer**, **squarest**, *adv.* – *n.* **1.** a four-sided plane having all its sides equal and all its angles right angles. **2.** anything having this form or a form approximating it. **3.** *Mathematics* the second power of a number or quantity. **4.** *Colloquial* someone who is ignorant of or uninterested in the latest fads. – *v.t.* **5.** to reduce to square, rectangular, or cubic form. **6.** *Mathematics* to multiply (a number or quantity) by itself. **7.** to make straight, level, or even (often fol. by *off*). – *v.i.* **8.** to accord or agree (often fol. by *with*). **9. square up,** to pay or settle a bill, debt, etc. – *adj.* **10.** of the form of a right angle; having some part or parts rectangular. **11.** at right angles, or perpendicular. **12.** designating a unit representing an area in the form of a square. **13.** of a specified length on each side of a square. **14.** leaving no balance of debt on either side; having all accounts settled. **15.** just, fair, or honest. **16.** conservative. – *adv.* **17.** so as to be square; in square or rectangular form.

square bracket *n.* either of the two parenthetical marks: [ ].

square dance *n.* a dance by couples arranged in a square or in some set form.

square root *n.* *Mathematics* the quantity of which a given quantity is the square.

squash[1] /skwɒʃ/ *v.t.* **1.** to press into a flat mass or pulp; crush. – *n.* **2.** the act or sound of squashing. **3.** the fact of being squashed. **4.** something squashed or crushed. **5.** Also, **squash racquets**. a game for two players, played in a small walled court with light racquets and a small rubber ball.

squash[2] /skwɒʃ/ *n.* a vegetable similar to the pumpkin.

squat /skwɒt/ *v.,* **squatted** *or* **squat**, **squatting**, *adj., n.* – *v.i.* **1.** to assume a posture close to the ground with the knees bent and the back more or less straight. **2.** to occupy a building without title or right. – *adj.* **3.** low and thick or broad. – *n.* **4.** a squatting position or posture.

squatter /ˈskwɒtə/ *n.* **1.** (formerly) someone who settled on crown land to run stock. **2.** someone who occupies a building without right or title.

squaw /skwɔ/ *n.* a North American Indian woman or wife.

squawk /skwɔk/ *v.i.* **1.** to utter a loud, harsh cry, as a duck. – *n.* **2.** a loud, harsh cry or sound.

squeak /skwik/ *n.* **1.** a short, sharp, shrill cry. – *v.i.* **2.** to utter or emit a squeak or squeaky sound.

squeal /skwil/ *n.* **1.** a more or less prolonged, sharp, shrill cry, as of pain, fear, etc. – *v.i.* **2.** to utter or emit a squeal or squealing sound.

squeamish /ˈskwimɪʃ/ *adj.* easily nauseated or sickened.

squeeze /skwiz/ *v.,* **squeezed**, **squeezing**, *n.* – *v.t.* **1.** to press forcibly together; compress. **2.** to apply pressure to as in order to extract something. **3.** to thrust forcibly; force by pressure; cram. **4.** to force out, extract, or procure by pressure (usually fol. by *out* or *from*). – *v.i.* **5.** to exert a compressing force. **6.** to force a way through some narrow or crowded place (fol. by *through, in, out,* etc.). – *n.* **7.** the act of squeezing. **8.** a restriction, demand, or pressure, as imposed by a government. **9.** a small quantity or amount of anything obtained by squeezing.

squelch /skwɛltʃ/ *v.t.* **1.** to strike or press with crushing force; crush down; squash. – *v.i.* **2.** to make a splashing sound.

squid /skwɪd/ *n., pl.* **squids**, (*esp. collectively*) **squid**. any of various slender cephalopods with ten tentacles.

squint /skwɪnt/ *v.i.* **1.** to look with the eyes partly closed. **2.** to look or glance obliquely or sideways; look askance. – *v.t.* **3.** to close (the eyes) partly. – *n.* **4.** *Pathology* a disorder of the eye. **5.** a looking obliquely or askance. – *adj.* **6.** looking obliquely.

squire /ˈskwaɪə/ *n., v.,* **squired**, **squiring**. – *n.* **1.** a personal attendant, as of a person of rank. – *v.t.* **2.** to attend as or in the manner of a squire.

squirm /skwɜm/ *v.i.* to wriggle or writhe.

squirrel /ˈskwɪrəl/ *n.* **1.** any of various arboreal, bushy-tailed rodents. **2.** *Colloquial* a person who hoards objects of little value.

squirt /skwɜt/ *v.i.* **1.** to eject liquid in a jet from a narrow orifice. **2.** to issue in a jetlike stream. – *v.t.* **3.** to cause (liquid) to issue in a jet from a narrow orifice. **4.** to wet or bespatter with a liquid so ejected. – *n.* **5.** a jet, as of water.

SRAM /ˈɛsræm/ *n.* *Computers* static random access memory; RAM which maintains its memory even when the power is turned off. Cf. **dynamic random access memory**. Also, **Sram**.

stab /stæb/ *v.,* **stabbed**, **stabbing**, *n.* – *v.t.* **1.** to pierce or wound with, or as with, a pointed weapon. **2.** to thrust or plunge (a knife, etc.) into something. – *v.i.* **3.** to thrust with or as with a knife or other pointed weapon. – *n.* **4.** the act of stabbing. **5.** a sudden, usually painful sensation.

stable[1] /ˈsteɪbəl/ *n., v.,* **-bled**, **-bling**. – *n.* **1.** a building for the lodging and feeding of horses, cattle, etc. **2.** a collection of animals belonging in such a building. **3.** any centre of production or connected group of such centres, as a group of newspapers, car factories, etc. – *v.t.* **4.** to put or lodge in or as in a stable.

stable[2] /ˈsteɪbəl/ *adj.* not likely to fall or give way, as a structure, support, foundation, etc.; firm; steady. – **stability**, *n.* – **stabilise = stabilize**, *v.*

staccato /stəˈkatoʊ/ *adj. Music* detached, disconnected, or abrupt.

stack /stæk/ *n.* **1.** any more or less orderly pile or heap. **2.** *Colloquial* a great quantity or number. **3.** that part of a library in which the main holdings of a library are kept. – *v.t.* **4.** to pile or arrange in a stack. **5.** to cover or load with something in stacks or piles. **6.** to bring a large number of one's own supporters to (a meeting) in order to outvote those of opposing views. **7.** to crash (a motor vehicle, bicycle, etc.). – *v.i.* **8.** to accumulate; add up (fol. by *up*).

stadium /ˈsteɪdiəm/ *n., pl.* **-diums**, **-dia** /-diə/. a sporting facility, often, though not necessarily, enclosed, comprising an arena, tiers or seats for spectators, parking, etc.

staff /staf/ *n., pl.* **staffs** *for defs 1–2;* **staffs**, **staves** /steɪvz/ *for def. 3*; *v.* – *n.* **1.** something which serves to support or sustain. **2.** a body of persons charged with carrying out the work of an establishment or executing some undertaking. **3.** *Music* → **stave** (def. 1). – *v.t.* **4.** to provide with a staff.

stag /stæg/ *n.* **1.** an adult male deer. – *adj.* **2.** *Colloquial* for or of men only.

stage /steɪdʒ/ *n., v.,* **staged**, **staging**. – *n.* **1.** a single step or degree in a process; a particular period in a process of development. **2.** a raised platform or floor. **3.** the theatre, the drama, or the dramatic profession. **4.** the scene of any action. – *v.t.* **5.** to put, represent, or exhibit on or as on a stage. **6.** to arrange; set up, as for a particular event.

stagecoach /ˈsteɪdʒkoʊtʃ/ *n.* a coach that runs regularly over a fixed route.

stagflation /stægˈfleɪʃən/ *n.* a situation in the economy in which stagnant economic growth is accompanied by inflation.

stagger /ˈstægə/ *v.i.* **1.** to walk, move, or stand unsteadily; sway. – *v.t.* **2.** to cause to reel, as with shock. **3.** to arrange in some other order or manner than the regular, uniform, or usual one, especially at such intervals that there is a continuous overlapping. – *n.* **4.** the act of staggering.

stagnant /ˈstægnənt/ *adj.* not running or flowing, as water, air, etc.

stagnate /ˈstægneɪt, stægˈneɪt/ *v.i.,* **-nated**, **-nating**. **1.** to become foul from standing, as a pool of water. **2.** to become inactive, sluggish, or dull. **3.** to make no progress; stop developing.

staid /steɪd/ *adj.* of settled or sedate character; not flighty or capricious.

stain /steɪn/ *n.* **1.** a semipermanent discolouration produced by foreign matter; a spot. **2.** a cause of reproach; blemish. **3.** a solution or suspension of colouring matter in water, spirit, or oil. – *v.t.* **4.** to discolour with spots or streaks of foreign matter. – *v.i.* **5.** to become stained; take a stain.

stair /stɛə/ *n.* a series or flight of steps; a stairway.

staircase /ˈstɛəkeɪs/ *n.* a flight of stairs.

stairwell /ˈstɛəwɛl/ *n.* the vertical shaft or opening containing a stairway.

stake[1] /steɪk/ *n., v.,* **staked**, **staking**. – *n.* **1.** a stick or post pointed at one end, for driving into the ground. **2.** a post, especially one to which a person is bound for execution, usually by burning. – *v.t.* **3.** to mark with stakes (often fol. by *off* or *out*). **4.** to protect, separate, or close off by a barrier of stakes. **5.** to support with a stake or stakes, as a plant. **6.** to surround (a building, etc.) for the purposes of a raid, a siege or keeping watch (fol. by *out*).

stake[2] /steɪk/ *n., v.,* **staked**, **staking**. – *n.* **1.** that which is wagered in a game, race, or contest. **2.** an interest held in something. **3. at stake,** involved; in a state of being staked or at hazard. – *v.t.* **4.** to put at risk upon the result of a game, the event of a contingency, etc.; wager.

stalactite /ˈstæləktaɪt/ *n.* a calcium deposit shaped like an icicle, hanging from the roof of a cave.

stalagmite /ˈstæləgmaɪt/ *n.* a calcium deposit shaped like an inverted stalactite, formed on the floor of a cave.

stale /steɪl/ *adj.* not fresh; flat, as beverages; dry or hardened, as bread.

stalemate /ˈsteɪlmeɪt/ *n.* any position in which no action can be taken; a deadlock.

stalk[1] /stɔk/ *n.* the stem or main axis of a plant.

stalk[2] /stɔk/ *v.i.* **1.** to pursue or approach game, etc., stealthily. **2.** to walk with slow, stiff, or haughty strides. – *v.t.* **3.** to pursue (game, a person, etc.) stealthily.

stall /stɔl/ *n.* **1.** a compartment in a stable or shed, for the accommodation of one animal. **2.** a booth, bench, table, or stand on which merchandise is displayed or exposed for sale. – *v.t.* **3.** to bring to a standstill; check the progress or motion of, especially of a vehicle or an engine by unintentionally overloading it or giving an inadequate fuel supply. – *v.i.* **4.** to come to a standstill; be brought to a stop, especially unintentionally.

stallion /ˈstæljən/ *n.* a male horse not castrated.

stamina /ˈstæmənə/ *n.* strength of physical constitution.

stammer /ˈstæmə/ *v.i.* **1.** to speak with spasmodic repetitions of syllables or sounds. – *n.* **2.** a stammering mode of utterance.

stamp /stæmp/ *v.t.* **1.** to strike or beat with a forcible downward thrust of the foot. **2.** to bring (the foot) down forcibly or smartly on the ground, floor, etc. **3.** to impress with a particular mark or device, as to indicate genuineness, approval, ownership, etc. **4.** to impress (a design, figure, words, etc.) on something; imprint deeply or permanently on anything. **5.** to affix an adhesive paper stamp to (a letter, etc.). – *v.i.* **6.** to bring the foot down forcibly or smartly, as in crushing something, expressing rage, etc. – *n.* **7.** the act or an instance of stamping. **8.** a die, engraved block, or the like, for impressing a design, characters, words, or marks. **9.** an official mark indicating genuineness, validity, etc., or payment of a duty or charge. **10.** a small adhesive piece of paper printed with a distinctive design, issued by a government for a fixed sum, for attaching to documents, goods subject to duty, letters, etc., to show that a charge has been paid. **11.** a similar piece of paper issued privately for various purposes.

stamp duty *n.* a tax imposed on certain legal documents, as cheques, receipts, conveyances, etc., on which a stamp is impressed or affixed.

stampede /stæm'pid/ *n., v.,* **-peded, -peding.** – *n.* **1.** a sudden scattering or headlong flight, especially of a body of cattle or horses in fright. – *v.i.* **2.** to scatter or flee in a stampede. – *v.t.* **3.** to cause to stampede.

stance /stæns/ *n.* the position or bearing of the body while standing.

stand /stænd/ *v.,* **stood, standing,** *n.* – *v.i.* **1.** to take or keep an upright position on the feet (opposed to *sit, lie,* etc.). **2.** to have a specified height when in this position. **3.** to cease moving; halt; stop. **4.** to take a position or stand as indicated. **5.** to adopt a certain course or attitude. **6.** (of things) to be in an upright position (opposed to *lie*). **7.** (of an account, score, etc.) to show a specified position of the parties concerned. **8.** to resist change, decay, or destruction. **9.** to become or be a candidate, as for parliament. – *v.t.* **10.** to cause to stand; set upright; set. **11.** to endure or undergo without hurt or damage, or without giving way. **12.** to tolerate: *I will stand no nonsense.* – *v.* **13. stand by, a.** to wait in a state of readiness. **b.** to aid, uphold, or sustain. **14. stand down, a.** to withdraw, as from a contest. **b.** to dismiss (employees) who are not involved in direct strike action but who are not able to carry out their normal duties as a result. **15. stand in,** to act as a substitute or representative. **16. stand out,** to be prominent or conspicuous. – *n.* **17.** the act of standing. **18.** a coming to a position of rest. **19.** a determined opposition to or support for some cause, circumstance, or the like. **20.** a raised platform or other structure. **21.** a framework on or in which articles are placed for support, exhibition, etc. **22.** a standing growth, as of grass, wheat, etc.

stand-alone /'stænd-əloʊn/ *adj.* **1.** of or relating to any computerised device which does not need to be linked up to a larger computer system. – *n.* **2.** such a device.

standard /'stændəd/ *n.* **1.** anything taken by general consent as a basis of comparison; an approved model. **2.** a certain commodity in which the basic monetary unit is stated, historically usually either gold or silver. **3.** a grade or level of excellence, achievement, or advancement. **4.** a level of quality which is regarded as normal, adequate, or acceptable. **5.** *Military* any of various military or naval flags. **6.** an upright support or supporting part. – *adj.* **7.** serving as a basis of weight, measure, value, comparison, or judgment. **8.** of recognised excellence or established authority. **9.** normal, adequate, acceptable, or average.

standard deviation *n. Statistics* the square root of the average of the squares of a set of deviations about an arithmetic mean.

standardise = standardize /'stændədaɪz/ *v.t.,* **-dised, -dising. 1.** to bring to or make of an established standard size, weight, quality, strength, or the like. **2.** to compare with or test by a standard.

stand-by /'stænd-baɪ/ *n., pl.* **-bys. 1.** something or someone upon which one can rely; a chief support. **2.** something kept in a state of readiness for use, as for an emergency.

stand-in /'stænd-ɪn/ *n.* a substitute.

standing /'stændɪŋ/ *n.* **1.** position or status, as to rank, credit, reputation, etc. **2.** good position, financial viability, or credit. **3.** length of existence, continuance, residence, membership, experience, etc. – *adj.* **4.** performed in or from a stationary or an erect position. **5.** continuing in operation, force, use, etc.

standing committee *n.* **1.** a committee that may be appointed without a term, to oversee an aspect of the running of an institution. **2.** *Parliamentary Procedure* a committee, the members of which are appointed at the beginning of each parliamentary session, which has a continuing responsibility for a general sphere of government activity.

standing order *n.* any of the rules ensuring continuity of procedure during the meetings of an assembly, especially the rules governing the conduct of business in parliament.

standpoint /'stændpɔɪnt/ *n.* **1.** the point at which one stands to view something. **2.** the mental position from which one views and judges things.

stank /stæŋk/ *v.* a past tense of **stink**.

stanza /'stænzə/ *n.* a group of lines of verse, forming a regularly repeated metrical division of a poem.

staphylococcus /stæfələ'kɒkəs/ *n., pl.* **-cocci** /-'kɒksaɪ/. any of certain species of bacteria.

staple[1] /'steɪpəl/ *n., v.,* **-pled, -pling.** – *n.* **1.** a bent piece of wire used to bind papers, sections of a book, etc., together. – *v.t.* **2.** to secure or fasten by a staple or staples.

staple[2] /'steɪpəl/ *n., adj., v.,* **-pled, -pling.** – *n.* **1.** a principal commodity grown or manufactured in a locality. **2.** a principal item, thing, feature, element, or part. – *adj.* **3.** principally used.

stapler /'steɪplə/ *n.* a stapling machine.

star /sta/ *n., adj., v.,* **starred, starring.** – *n.* **1.** any of the heavenly bodies appearing as apparently fixed luminous points in the sky at night. **2.** (*pl.*) a horoscope. **3.** a conventional figure considered as representing a star of the sky. **4.** a prominent actor, singer, or the like. – *adj.* **5.** brilliant, prominent, or distinguished; chief. – *v.t.* **6.** to set with, or as with, stars; spangle. **7.** to present or feature (an actor, etc.) as a star. **8.** to mark with a star or asterisk, as for special notice. – *v.i.* **9.** (of an actor, etc.) to appear as a star.

starboard /'stabəd/ *n. Nautical* the side of a ship to the right of a person looking towards the bow (opposed to *port*).

starch /statʃ/ *n.* **1.** a white, tasteless solid, chemically a carbohydrate, occurring in the form of minute grains in the seeds, tubers, and other parts of plants. **2.** a commercial preparation of this substance. **3.** stiffness or formality, as of manner. – *v.t.* **4.** to stiffen or treat with starch.

star-crossed /ˈsta-krɒst/ *adj.* having much bad luck, as if brought about by the influence of the stars.

stare /stɛə/ *v.,* **stared**, **staring**, *n.* – *v.i.* **1.** to gaze fixedly, especially with the eyes wide open. **2.** to stand out boldly or obtrusively to view. – *n.* **3.** a staring gaze; a fixed look with the eyes wide open.

starfish /ˈstafɪʃ/ *n., pl.* **-fishes**, (*esp. collectively*) **-fish**. a marine animal having the body radially arranged, usually in the form of a star.

stark /stak/ *adj.* **1.** sheer, utter, downright, or arrant. **2.** harsh, grim, or desolate to the view, as places, etc. – *adv.* **3.** utterly, absolutely, or quite.

starling /ˈstalɪŋ/ *n.* a small bird, introduced and now widespread in eastern Australia.

start /stat/ *v.i.* **1.** to begin to move, go, or act. **2.** to begin any course of action or procedure. **3.** (of a process or performance) to begin. **4.** to move with a sudden, involuntary jerk or twitch, as from a shock of surprise, alarm, or pain. – *v.t.* **5.** to set moving, going, or acting. **6.** to set in operation; establish. **7.** to enter upon or begin. – *n.* **8.** the beginning or outset of anything. **9.** the first part of anything. **10.** a sudden, involuntary jerking movement of the body. **11.** a lead or advance of specified amount, as over competitors or pursuers. **12.** a spurt of activity.

starting price *n.* the betting odds on a horse, greyhound, etc., at the time when a race begins.

startle /ˈstatl/ *v.,* **-tled**, **-tling**. – *v.t.* **1.** to cause to start involuntarily, as under a sudden shock. – *v.i.* **2.** to start involuntarily, as from a surprise or alarm.

starve /stav/ *v.,* **starved**, **starving**. – *v.i.* **1.** to die or perish from hunger. **2.** to pine or suffer for lack of something specified (fol. by *for*). – *v.t.* **3.** to cause to starve. – **starvation**, *n.*

-stat a word element meaning 'standing', 'stationary'.

state /steɪt/ *n., adj., v.,* **stated**, **stating**. – *n.* **1.** the condition of a person or thing, as with respect to circumstances or attributes. **2.** condition with respect to constitution, structure, form, phase, or the like. **3.** a particular condition of mind or feeling. **4.** a particularly tense, nervous, or excited condition. **5.** a body of people occupying a definite territory and organised under one government, especially a sovereign government. – *adj.* **6.** of or relating to the supreme civil government or authority. **7.** characterised by, attended with, or involving ceremony. – *v.t.* **8.** to declare definitely or specifically. **9.** to set forth formally in speech or writing.

stately /ˈsteɪtli/ *adj.,* **-lier**, **-liest**. dignified or majestic; imposing in magnificence, elegance, etc.

statement /ˈsteɪtmənt/ *n.* **1.** something stated. **2.** *Commerce* an abstract of an account, as one rendered to show the balance due.

statesman /ˈsteɪtsmən/ *n., pl.* **-men**. someone who exhibits ability of the highest kind in directing the affairs of a government or in dealing with important public issues. – **statesmanlike**, *adj.* – **stateswoman**, *n. fem.*

static /ˈstætɪk/ *adj.* **1.** relating to or characterised by a fixed or stationary condition. **2.** *Economics* relating to fixed relations, or different combinations of fixed quantities. – *n.* **3.** Also, **atmospherics**. *Radio* extraneous noises, crackling, etc., caused by electrical currents picked up by the receiver.

station /ˈsteɪʃən/ *n.* **1.** the place in which anything stands. **2.** the place at which something stops. **3.** a place equipped for some particular kind of work, service, or the like. **4.** a sheep run or cattle run. **5.** standing, as of persons or things, in a scale of estimation, rank, or dignity. **6.** the wavelength on which a radio or television program is broadcast; a frequency or channel. – *adj.* **7.** of or relating to a sheep or cattle station. – *v.t.* **8.** to assign a station to; place or post in a station or position.

stationary /ˈsteɪʃənri, ˈsteɪʃənəri/ *adj.* standing still; not moving.

stationery /ˈsteɪʃənri, ˈsteɪʃənəri/ writing materials, as pens, pencils, paper, etc. – **stationer**, *n.*

station wagon *n.* a car with an extended interior, allowing extra space behind the rear seat, and a door or tailgate at the back.

statistics /stəˈtɪstɪks/ *n.* **1.** (*construed as sing.*) the science which deals with the collection, classification, and use of numerical facts or data, bearing on a subject or matter. **2.** (*construed as pl.*) the numerical facts or data themselves. – **statistician**, *n.* – **statistical**, *adj.*

statue /ˈstætʃu/ *n.* a representation in the round of a person or an animal.

stature /ˈstætʃə/ *n.* **1.** the height of an animal body, especially of a human. **2.** degree of development or achievement attained.

status /ˈsteɪtəs, ˈstætəs/ *n.* **1.** condition, position, or standing socially, professionally, or otherwise. **2.** the relative standing, position, or condition of anything.

status quo *n.* the existing or previously existing state or condition.

statute /ˈstætʃut/ *n.* **1.** a law made by a legislature. **2.** a permanent rule established by an institution, corporation, etc., for the conduct of its internal affairs. – **statutory**, *adj.*

statutory declaration /ˈstætʃətri/ *n.* a written statement declared before and witnessed by an authorised official.

statutory reserve deposit *n.* the minimum deposit which each trading bank is required to maintain with the Reserve Bank.

staunch[1] /stɔntʃ/ *v.t.* to stop the flow of (a liquid, especially blood).

staunch[2] /stɔntʃ/ *adj.* characterised by firmness or steadfastness.

stave /steɪv/ *n., v.,* **staved** *or* **stove**, **stav-**

ing. – *n.* **1.** Also, **staff**. *Music* a set of horizontal lines on which music is written. – *v.t.* **2.** to break a hole in; crush inwards (often fol. by *in*). **3. stave off,** to put, ward, or keep off, as by force or evasion.

stay[1] /steɪ/ *v.i.* **1.** to remain in a place, situation, company, etc. **2.** to pause or wait, as for a moment. **3.** to hold back, detain, or restrain. **4.** to remain through or during (a period of time, etc.). **5.** to remain to the end of. – *n.* **6.** a sojourn or temporary residence.

stay[2] /steɪ/ *n.* **1.** a prop; a brace. **2.** (*pl.*) a corset.

stay[3] /steɪ/ *n.* *Chiefly Nautical* rope used to support a mast.

STD /ɛs ti 'di/ *n.* any disease such as syphilis, gonorrhoea, AIDS, herpes, etc., which is transmitted through sexual contact; sexually transmitted disease.

stead /stɛd/ *n.* the place of a person or thing as occupied by a successor or substitute.

steadfast /'stɛdfast, -fəst/ *adj.* **1.** firm in purpose, resolution, faith, attachment, etc., as a person. **2.** unwavering, as resolution, faith, adherence, etc.

steady /'stɛdi/ *adj.*, **steadier**, **steadiest**, *n.*, *pl.* **steadies**, *v.*, **steadied**, **steadying**, *adv.* – *adj.* **1.** firmly placed or fixed; stable. **2.** uniform; continuous. **3.** settled, staid, or sober. – *n.* **4.** *Colloquial* a regular boyfriend or girlfriend. – *v.t.* **5.** to make steady, as in position, movement, action, character, etc. – *v.i.* **6.** to become steady. – *adv.* **7.** in a firm or steady manner.

steak /steɪk/ *n.* a slice of meat or fish, usually cut thick and across the grain of the muscle.

steal /stil/ *v.*, **stole**, **stolen**, **stealing**, *n.* – *v.t.* **1.** to take or take away dishonestly or wrongfully, especially secretly. **2.** to move, bring, convey, or put secretly or quietly (fol. by *away*, *from*, *in*, *into*, etc.). – *v.i.* **3.** to commit or practise theft. **4.** to move, go, or come secretly, quietly, or unobserved. – *n.* **5.** *Colloquial* something acquired at a cost well below its true value.

stealth /stɛlθ/ *n.* secret, clandestine, or surreptitious procedure. – **stealthy**, *adj.*

steam /stim/ *n.* **1.** water in the form of gas or vapour. **2.** water changed to this form by boiling, and extensively used for the generation of mechanical power, for heating purposes, etc. – *v.i.* **3.** to emit or give off steam or vapour. **4.** to become covered with condensed steam, as a surface. – *v.t.* **5.** to expose to or treat with steam, as in order to heat, cook, soften, renovate, or the like. – *adj.* **6.** heated by or heating with steam. **7.** operated by steam.

steamroller /'stimroulə/ *n.* a heavy locomotive, originally steam-powered, having a roller or rollers, for crushing or levelling materials in road-making.

steed /stid/ *n.* a horse, especially one for riding.

steel /stil/ *n.* **1.** iron in a modified form, artificially produced, and possessing a hardness, elasticity, strength, etc., which vary with the composition and the heat treatment. – *adj.* **2.** relating to or made of steel. **3.** like steel in colour, hardness, or strength. – *v.t.* **4.** to cause to resemble steel in some way.

steel wool *n.* fine threads or shavings of steel, tangled into a small pad, and used for scouring, polishing, etc.

steep[1] /stip/ *adj.* **1.** having a relatively high gradient, as a hill, an ascent, stairs, etc. **2.** *Colloquial* unduly high, or exorbitant, as a price or amount.

steep[2] /stip/ *v.t.* **1.** to soak in water or other liquid. – *v.i.* **2.** to lie soaking in a liquid.

steeple /'stipəl/ *n.* a lofty tower, especially one with a spire, attached to a church, temple, or the like, and often containing bells.

steeplechase /'stipəltʃeɪs/ *n.* a horserace over a course furnished with artificial ditches, hedges, and other obstacles.

steer[1] /stɪə/ *v.t.* **1.** to guide the course of (anything in motion) by a rudder, helm, wheel, etc. – *v.i.* **2.** to direct the course of a vessel, vehicle, aeroplane, or the like by the use of a rudder or other means. **3.** (of a vessel, etc.) to admit of being steered.

steer[2] /stɪə/ *n.* a castrated male bovine, especially one raised for beef; ox; bullock.

steerage /'stɪərɪdʒ/ *n.* (in a passenger ship) the part allotted to the passengers who travel at the cheapest rate.

steering committee *n.* a committee, especially one of a legislative body, entrusted with the preparation of the agenda of a conference, session, etc.

stego- a word element meaning 'cover'.

stein /staɪn/ *n.* an earthenware mug, especially for beer.

stellar /'stɛlə/ *adj.* **1.** of or relating to the stars; consisting of stars. **2.** starlike.

stem /stɛm/ *n.*, *v.*, **stemmed**, **stemming**. – *n.* **1.** the ascending part of a plant which ordinarily grows in an opposite direction to the root. **2.** something resembling or suggesting the stem of a plant, flower, etc. – *v.t.* **3.** to remove the stem from (a fruit, etc.). – *v.i.* **4.** to originate (usually fol. by *from*).

stem cell *n.* an undifferentiated form of cell which can develop into various specific cell types, such as blood cells, ova, etc.

stench /stɛntʃ/ *n.* an offensive smell; stink.

stencil /'stɛnsəl/ *n.*, *v.*, **-cilled**, **-cilling**. – *n.* **1.** a thin sheet of paper, cardboard or metal cut through so as to reproduce a design, letters, etc., when colour is rubbed through it. **2.** the letters, designs, etc., produced. – *v.t.* **3.** to produce (letters, etc.) by means of a stencil.

steno- a word element meaning 'little', 'narrow'.

stenograph /'stɛnəgræf, -graf/ *n.* **1.** a character written in shorthand. **2.** any of various keyboard instruments, somewhat resembling a typewriter, used for writing in shorthand, as by means of phonetic or arbitrary symbols. – **stenography**, *n.* – **stenographer**, *n.*

stenotype /'stɛnətaɪp/ *n.* a keyboard instrument resembling a typewriter, used in a system of phonetic shorthand.

step /stɛp/ *n.*, *v.*, **stepped**, **stepping**. – *n.* **1.** a movement made by lifting the foot and setting it down again in a new position, as in walking, running, marching, or dancing. **2.** the space passed over or measured by one movement of the foot in stepping. **3.** pace uniform with that of another or others, or in time with music. **4.** a move or proceeding, as towards some end or in the general course of action. **5.** a degree on a scale. **6.** a support for the foot in ascending or descending. – *v.i.* **7.** to move by a step or steps. **8.** to tread (*on* or *upon*), by intention or accident. **9.** to move or set (the foot) in taking a step. **10.** to measure (a distance, ground, etc.) by steps (sometimes fol. by *off* or *out*). **11.** to make or arrange in the manner of a series of steps. **12. step down, a.** to decrease. **b.** to resign; relinquish a position, etc.

step- a prefix indicating connection between members of a family by the remarriage of a parent, and not by blood.

stepladder /'stɛplædə/ *n.* a ladder having flat steps or treads in place of rungs and a hinged support to keep it upright.

steppe /stɛp/ *n.* an extensive plain, especially one without trees.

stepping stone *n.* **1.** a stone in shallow water, a marshy place, or the like, used for stepping on in crossing. **2.** any means of advancing or rising.

-ster a suffix of personal nouns, often derogatory, referring especially to occupation or habit, as in *songster, gamester, trickster,* also having less apparent connotations, as in *youngster, roadster.*

stereo /'stɛrioʊ, 'stɪərioʊ/ *n., pl.* **stereos,** *adj.* – *n.* **1.** stereophonic sound reproduction. **2.** any system, equipment, etc., for reproducing stereophonic sound. – *adj.* **3.** relating to stereophonic sound, stereoscopic photography, etc.

stereo- a word element referring to hardness, solidity, three-dimensionality. Also (*before some vowels*), **stere-**.

stereophonic /stɛriə'fɒnɪk, stɪə-/ *adj.* **1.** of or relating to a three-dimensional auditory perspective. **2.** of or relating to the multichannel reproduction or broadcasting of sound which simulates three-dimensional auditory perspective.

stereotype /'stɛriətaɪp, 'stɪə-/ *n., v.,* **-typed, -typing.** – *n.* **1.** a process for making metal plates for use in printing from moulds. **2.** a plate made by this process. **3.** a standardised idea or concept. – *v.t.* **4.** to make a stereotype of.

sterile /'stɛraɪl/ *adj.* **1.** free from living germs or micro-organisms. **2.** incapable of producing, or not producing, offspring. – **sterility,** *n.* – **sterilise = sterilize,** *v.*

sterling /'stɜlɪŋ/ *adj.* **1.** consisting of or relating to British money. **2.** (of silver) being of standard quality, 92½ per cent pure silver.

stern[1] /stɜn/ *adj.* firm, strict, or uncompromising.

stern[2] /stɜn/ *n.* the hinder part of anything.

sternum /'stɜnəm/ *n., pl.* **-nums, -na** /-nə/. *Anatomy* the breastbone.

stet /stɛt/ *v.i.,* **stetted, stetting.** let it stand (a direction on a printer's proof, a manuscript, or the like to retain cancelled matter).

stetho- a word element meaning 'chest'. Also (*before vowels*), **steth-**.

stethoscope /'stɛθəskoʊp/ *n.* an instrument used to convey sounds in the chest or other parts of the body to the ear of the examiner.

stevedore /'stivədɔ/ *n.* a firm or individual engaged in the loading or unloading of a vessel.

stew /stju/ *v.t.* **1.** to cook (food) by simmering or slow boiling. – *v.i.* **2.** to undergo cooking by simmering or slow boiling. – *n.* **3.** a preparation of meat, fish or other food cooked by stewing.

steward /'stjuəd/ *n.* **1.** someone who manages another's property or financial affairs. **2.** any attendant on a ship or aircraft who waits on passengers. – *v.i.* **3.** to act or serve as steward.

stick[1] /stɪk/ *n.* **1.** a relatively long and slender piece of wood. **2.** an elongated, stick-like piece of some material. **3. the sticks,** remote and little developed areas.

stick[2] /stɪk/ *v.,* **stuck, sticking.** – *v.t.* **1.** to pierce or puncture with a pointed instrument, as a dagger, spear, or pin; stab. **2.** to thrust (something pointed) in, into, through etc. **3.** to fasten in position by, or as by, something thrust through. **4.** to place in a specified position. **5.** to fasten or attach by causing to adhere. **6.** to endure; tolerate. – *v.i.* **7.** to have the point piercing, or embedded in something. **8.** to remain attached by adhesion. **9.** to remain firm in resolution, opinion, statement, attachment, etc. **10.** to keep steadily at a task, undertaking, or the like (fol. by *at* or *to*). **11.** to be at a standstill, as from difficulties. **12.** to be thrust, or extend, project, or protrude (fol. by *through, from, out, up,* etc.). – *v.* **13. stick up,** *Colloquial* to rob, especially at gunpoint. **14. stick up for,** to speak or act in favour of; defend; support.

sticker /'stɪkə/ *n.* an adhesive label, usually with an advertisement, publicity slogan, or other message printed on it.

stick insect *n.* any of certain insects with long, slender, twig-like bodies.

stickler /'stɪklə/ *n.* a person who insists on something unyieldingly (fol. by *for*).

stickybeak /'stɪkibik/ *n.* someone who pries.

stiff /stɪf/ *adj.* **1.** rigid or firm in substance. **2.** not moving or working easily. **3.** rigidly formal. **4.** lacking ease and grace; awkward. **5.** severe, as a penalty. **6.** relatively firm in consistency, as semisolid matter. – *n.* *Colloquial* **7.** a dead body; corpse. – *adv.* **8.** in a rigid state.

stifle /'staɪfəl/ *v.,* **-fled, -fling.** – *v.t.* **1.** to kill by impeding respiration; smother. **2.** to suppress, crush, or stop. – *v.i.* **3.** to become stifled or suffocated.

stigma /'stɪgmə/ *n., pl.* **stigmata** /'stɪgmətə/, **stigmas.** a mark of disgrace; a stain, as on one's reputation. – **stigmatic,** *adj.*

stile /staɪl/ *n.* a series of steps or the like for ascending and descending in getting over a fence, etc., which remains closed to cattle.

stiletto /stə'lɛtoʊ/ *n.* a dagger having a narrow blade, thick in proportion to its width.

still[1] /stɪl/ *adj.* **1.** remaining in place or at rest. **2.** free from sound or noise. **3.** tranquil; calm. **4.** not effervescent or sparkling, as wine. – *n.* **5.** a single photographic picture, especially a print of one of the frames of a film. – *adv.* **6.** up to this or that time. **7.** even or yet (with comparatives or the like). **8.** even then; yet; nevertheless. – *conj.* **9.** and yet; but yet; nevertheless. – *v.t.* **10.** to calm, appease, or allay.

still² /stɪl/ *n.* a distilling apparatus.

stillbirth /'stɪlbɜθ/ *n.* the birth of a dead child or organism.

still life *n., pl.* **still lifes** /stɪl 'laɪfs/. a picture representing inanimate objects, such as fruit, flowers, etc.

stilt /stɪlt/ *n.* **1.** one of two poles, each with a support for the foot at some distance above the ground. **2.** one of several high posts underneath any structure built above land or over water.

stilted /'stɪltəd/ *adj.* stiffly dignified or formal, as speech, literary style, etc.; pompous.

stimulant /'stɪmjələnt/ *n.* any beverage or food that stimulates.

stimulate /'stɪmjəleɪt/ *v.,* **-lated, -lating.** – *v.t.* **1.** to rouse to action or effort. **2.** to invigorate by an alcoholic or other stimulant. – *v.i.* **3.** to act as a stimulus or stimulant.

stimulus /'stɪmjələs/ *n., pl.* **-li** /-li, -laɪ/ **-luses**. something that incites to action or exertion, or quickens action, feeling, thought, etc.; an incentive.

sting /stɪŋ/ *v.,* **stung, stinging,** *n.* – *v.t.* **1.** to affect painfully or irritatingly. – *v.i.* **2.** to use or have a sting, as bees. **3.** to cause a sharp, smarting pain, as some plants, an acrid liquid or gas, etc. **4.** to feel a smarting pain, as from the sting of an insect or from a blow. – *n.* **5.** any sharp or smarting wound, hurt, or pain (physical or mental). **6.** anything, or an element in anything, that wounds, pains, or irritates.

stingy /'stɪndʒi/ *adj.,* **-gier, -giest**. reluctant to give or spend; niggardly.

stink /stɪŋk/ *v.,* **stank** *or* **stunk, stunk, stinking,** *n.* – *v.i.* **1.** to emit a strong offensive smell. – *n.* **2.** a strong offensive smell; stench.

stint /stɪnt/ *v.t.* **1.** to limit, often unduly. – *v.i.* **2.** to be sparing or frugal. – *n.* **3.** a period of time, usually short, allotted to a particular activity.

stipend /'staɪpɛnd/ *n.* fixed or regular pay; periodic payment; salary.

stipendiary magistrate /staɪˌpɛndəri 'mædʒəstreɪt/ *n.* a legally qualified paid magistrate who may do alone all acts authorised to be done by two justices of the peace.

stipple /'stɪpəl/ *v.t.,* **-pled, -pling**. to paint, engrave, or draw by means of dots or small touches.

stipulate /'stɪpjəleɪt/ *v.,* **-lated, -lating.** – *v.i.* **1.** to make an express demand or arrangement (*for*), as a condition of agreement. – *v.t.* **2.** to require as an essential condition in making an agreement.

stir /stɜ/ *v.,* **stirred, stirring,** *n.* – *v.t.* **1.** to move or agitate (a liquid, or any matter in separate particles or pieces). **2.** to move, especially in some slight way. **3.** to rouse from inactivity (often fol. by *up*). **4.** to affect strongly; excite. – *v.i.* **5.** to move, especially slightly or lightly. **6.** to touch on controversial topics in a deliberate attempt to incite a heated discussion. – *n.* **7.** the act of stirring or moving, or the sound made. **8.** a state or occasion of general excitement; a commotion.

stirrup /'stɪrəp/ *n.* a loop, ring, or other contrivance of metal, wood, leather, etc., suspended from the saddle of a horse to support the rider's foot.

stitch /stɪtʃ/ *n.* **1.** a loop or portion of thread disposed in place by one movement in sewing, knitting, etc., or the mode of disposing it. **2.** a sudden, sharp pain in the side, brought on by physical exertion. – *v.t.* **3.** to work upon, join, or fasten with stitches.

stoat /stoʊt/ *n.* the ermine in its brown summer phase.

stock /stɒk/ *n.* **1.** an aggregate of goods kept on hand by a merchant, business firm, manufacturer, etc., for the supply of customers. **2.** a quantity of something accumulated, as for future use. **3.** a race or other related group of animals or plants. **4.** the handle of a whip, etc. **5.** a long stick used in skiing. **6.** the raw material from which anything is made. **7.** *Finance* **a.** the capital of a company converted from fully paid shares. **b.** the shares of a particular company. **8. take stock, a.** to make an inventory of stock on hand. **b.** to make an appraisal of resources, prospects, etc. – *adj.* **9.** having as one's job the care of a concern's goods: *a stock clerk.* **10.** of the common or ordinary type; in common use. **11.** designating or relating to livestock raising; stock farming. **12.** *Theatre* relating to repertory plays or pieces. **13.** to furnish with stock, as a farm with horses, cattle, etc. **14.** to fasten to or provide with a stock, as a rifle, plough, bell, anchor, etc.

stockade /stɒ'keɪd/ *n.* a defensive barrier consisting of strong posts or timbers fixed upright in the ground.

stock and station agent *n.* one engaged in the business of buying and selling rural properties and stock.

stock book *n.* a ledger for recording amounts of goods bought and sold.

stockbroker /'stɒkbroʊkə/ *n.* a broker who buys and sells stocks and shares for customers for a commission.

stock certificate *n.* a certificate evidencing ownership of one or more shares of a company's stock.

stock exchange *n.* **1.** (*often caps*) a building or place where stocks and shares are bought and sold. **2.** an association of brokers, jobbers, and dealers in stocks and bonds, who meet to transact business according to fixed rules.

stocking /'stɒkɪŋ/ *n.* a close-fitting covering for the foot and leg.

stock-in-trade /stɒk-ɪn-'treɪd/ *n.* goods, assets, etc., necessary for carrying on a business.

stockjobber /'stɒkdʒɒbə/ *n.* a stock exchange dealer who acts as an intermediary between brokers and buyers but does not deal directly with the public.

stock market *n.* a market where stocks and shares are bought and sold; a stock exchange.

stockpile /'stɒkpaɪl/ *n., v.,* **-piled, -piling**.

– *n.* **1.** a large supply of essential materials, held in reserve for use during a period of shortage, etc. – *v.t.* **2.** to accumulate for future use.

stock-still /stɒk-ˈstɪl/ *adj.* motionless.

stocky /ˈstɒki/ *adj.*, **-ier**, **-iest**. of solid and sturdy form or build; thickset, often short.

stoic /ˈstoʊɪk/ *n.* someone who maintains or affects a mental attitude of austere fortitude.

stoke /stoʊk/ *v.*, **stoked**, **stoking**. – *v.t.* **1.** to poke, stir up, and feed (a fire). **2.** to tend a fire or furnace. – **stoker**, *n.*

stole[1] /stoʊl/ *v.* past tense of **steal**.

stole[2] /stoʊl/ *n.* a type of long scarf.

stolen /ˈstoʊlən/ *v.* past participle of **steal**.

stolen generations *pl. n.* (in Australia) Aboriginal children who were removed from their families and communities, by government or non-government agencies, in order to enforce integration into white society; the practice continued in some areas until the 1960s. Also, **stolen generation**.

stolid /ˈstɒləd/ *adj.* not easily moved or stirred mentally; impassive; unemotional.

stomach /ˈstʌmək/ *n.* **1.** (in humans and other vertebrates) a sac-like enlargement of the alimentary canal, forming an organ of storage, dilution, and digestion. **2.** the part of the body containing the stomach; the belly or abdomen. – *v.t.* **3.** to take into or retain in the stomach. **4.** to endure or tolerate.

stomato- a word element referring to the mouth. Also (*before vowels*), **stomat-**.

-stome a word element referring to the mouth.

stomp /stɒmp/ *v.i. Colloquial* to stamp.

stone /stoʊn/ *n.*, *pl.* **stones**, **stone** *for def. 3, adj., v.*, **stoned**, **stoning**. – *n.* **1.** the hard substance of which rocks consist. **2.** a piece of rock of small or moderate size. **3.** a unit of mass in the imperial system, equal to 14 lb avoirdupois, or approx. 6.35 kg. **4.** something resembling a small stone or pebble. – *adj.* **5.** made of or relating to stone. – *v.t.* **6.** to throw stones at; drive by pelting with stones. **7.** to free from stones, as fruit.

stoned /stoʊnd/ *adj. Colloquial* completely drunk or under the influence of drugs.

stood /stʊd/ *v.* past tense and past participle of **stand**.

stooge /studʒ/ *n.* someone who acts on behalf of another, especially in an obsequious, corrupt, or secretive fashion.

stool /stul/ *n.* **1.** a seat without arms or a back. **2.** the mass of matter evacuated at each movement of the bowels; faeces.

stoop /stup/ *v.i.* **1.** to bend the head and shoulders, or the body generally, forwards and downwards from an erect position. **2.** to condescend; deign. – *v.t.* **3.** to bend (oneself, one's head, etc.) forwards and downwards. – *n.* **4.** the act of stooping; a stooping movement. **5.** a stooping position or carriage of body.

stop /stɒp/ *v.*, **stopped** *or Poetic* **stopt**, **stopping**, *n.* – *v.t.* **1.** to cease from, leave off, or discontinue. **2.** to cause to cease; put an end to. **3.** to cut off, intercept, or withhold. **4.** to prevent from proceeding, acting, operating, continuing, etc. **5.** to block, obstruct, or close (a passageway, channel, opening, duct, etc.) (often fol. by *up*). **6.** *Banking* to notify a banker not to honour (a cheque) on presentation. – *v.i.* **7.** to cease moving, proceeding, speaking, acting, operating, etc.; to pause; desist. **8.** to cease; come to an end. **9.** to stay. **10. stop by,** to call somewhere briefly on the way to another destination. – *n.* **11.** the act of stopping. **12.** a stay or sojourn made at a place, as in the course of a journey. **13.** a place where buses or other vehicles halt. **14.** any piece or device that serves to check or control movement or action in a mechanism. **15.** *Banking* an order to stop a cheque. **16.** → **full stop**.

stopcock /ˈstɒpkɒk/ *n.* a valve, with a tapered plug operated by a handle, used to control the flow of a liquid or gas from a receptacle or through a pipe.

stoploss /ˈstɒplɒs/ *adj.* (of a share trading system) designed to prevent or minimise financial loss to the trader.

stoploss order *n.* an order given by a share trader to a stockbroker to buy or sell shares at a particular price.

stopover /ˈstɒpoʊvə/ *n.* any brief stop in the course of a journey.

stop payment *n. Banking* an order by the drawer of a cheque to his or her bank not to pay a specified cheque.

stopper /ˈstɒpə/ *n.* a plug or piece for closing a bottle, tube, or the like.

stop press *n.* news inserted in a newspaper after printing has begun.

stopwatch /ˈstɒpwɒtʃ/ *n.* a watch in which the timing mechanism can be stopped or started at any instant.

stop-work meeting *n.* a meeting of employees held during working time to consult with unions or management over conditions of work, etc.

storage /ˈstɔrɪdʒ/ *n.* **1.** the state or fact of being stored. **2.** *Computers* the capacity of a device to hold information. **3.** a place where something is stored.

store /stɔ/ *n.*, *v.*, **stored**, **storing**. – *n.* **1.** a large shop with many departments or branches. **2.** a supply or stock (of something), especially one for future use. **3.** a shop. **4.** measure of esteem or regard. **5.** a computer memory. – *v.t.* **6.** to lay up or put away, as a supply for future use (often with *up* or *away*).

storehouse /ˈstɔhaʊs/ *n.* a house or building in which things are stored.

storey /ˈstɔri/ *n.*, *pl.* **-reys**. a complete horizontal section of a building, having one continuous or approximately continuous floor.

stork /stɔk/ *n.* one of the long-legged, long-necked, long-billed wading birds.

storm /stɔm/ *n.* **1.** a disturbance of the normal condition of the atmosphere, manifesting itself by winds of unusual force or direction, often accompanied by rain, snow, hail, thunder and lightning, or flying sand or dust. **2.** a violent assault on a fortified place, strong position, or the like. **3.** a violent outburst or outbreak. – *v.i.* **4.** to rage or complain with violence or fury. **5.** to rush to an assault or attack. – *v.t.* **6.** to subject to or as to a storm.

stormwater /ˈstɔmwɔtə/ *n.* a sudden, excessive run-off of water following a storm.

story /ˈstɔri/ *n., pl.* **-ries**. **1.** narrative designed to interest or amuse the hearer or reader; a tale. **2.** the plot, or succession of incidents of a novel, poem, drama, etc. **3.** *Media* a news item. **4.** *Colloquial* a lie; a fib.

stout /staʊt/ *adj.* **1.** bulky or thickset. **2.** bold, hardy, or dauntless. – *n.* **3.** any of various beers brewed by the top-fermentation method but darker and heavier than ales.

stove[1] /stoʊv/ *n.* an apparatus for furnishing heat, as for comfort, cooking, or mechanical purposes.

stove[2] /stoʊv/ *v.* a past tense and past participle of **stave**.

stow /stoʊ/ *v.t.* to put in a place or receptacle as for storage or reserve; pack.

straddle /ˈstrædl/ *v.,* **-dled**, **-dling**. – *v.i.* **1.** to walk, stand, or sit with the legs wide apart. – *v.t.* **2.** to walk, stand, or sit with one leg on each side of.

strafe /straf, streɪf/ *v.t.,* **strafed**, **strafing**. to bombard heavily.

straggle /ˈstrægəl/ *v.i.,* **-gled**, **-gling**. **1.** to stray from the road, course, or line of march. **2.** to go, come, or spread in a scattered, irregular fashion.

straight /streɪt/ *adj.* **1.** without a bend, crook, or curve. **2.** (of a line) lying evenly between its points. **3.** evenly formed or set. **4.** honest, honourable, or upright. **5.** *Colloquial* **a.** conforming to orthodox forms of behaviour, as avoidance of illegal drugs, etc. **b.** heterosexual. **6.** right or correct. **7.** undiluted, as an alcoholic beverage; neat. – *adv.* **8.** in a straight line. **9.** honestly, honourably, or virtuously. **10.** in the proper order or condition, as a room. – *n.* **11.** a straight form or position. **12.** *Colloquial* a conservative person.

straightaway /streɪtəˈweɪ/ *adv.* immediately.

straightforward /streɪtˈfɔwəd/ *adj.* **1.** free from crookedness or deceit; honest. **2.** without difficulty, uncomplicated.

strain[1] /streɪn/ *v.t.* **1.** to exert to the utmost. **2.** to impair, injure, or weaken by stretching or overexertion, as a muscle. **3.** to make excessive demands upon. **4.** to pass (liquid matter) through a filter, sieve, or the like, in order to hold back the denser or solid constituents. – *v.i.* **5.** to stretch one's muscles, nerves, etc., to the utmost. – *n.* **6.** any force or pressure tending to alter shape, cause fracture, etc. **7.** an injury to a muscle, tendon, etc., due to excessive tension or use; a sprain. **8.** severe, trying, or wearing pressure or effect. **9.** (*sing. or pl., often collective pl.*) a passage of music or song as rendered or heard.

strain[2] /streɪn/ *n.* **1.** any of the different lines of ancestry united in a family or an individual. **2.** a variety, especially of microorganisms.

strainer /ˈstreɪnə/ *n.* a filter, sieve, or the like for straining liquids.

strait /streɪt/ *n.* **1.** (*often pl. with sing. sense*) a narrow passage of water connecting two large bodies of water. **2.** (*often pl.*) a position of difficulty, distress, or need.

straitened /ˈstreɪtənd/ *adj.* difficult, especially financially.

straitjacket /ˈstreɪtdʒækət/ *n.* a kind of coat for confining the arms of violently insane persons, etc. Also, **straightjacket**.

straitlaced /ˈstreɪtleɪst/ *adj.* excessively strict in conduct or morality; puritanical; prudish.

strand[1] /strænd/ *v.t.* **1.** (*usu. in the passive*) to bring into a helpless position. – *v.i.* **2.** to be driven or run ashore, as a ship, etc.; run aground. – *n.* **3.** *Poetic* the seashore.

strand[2] /strænd/ *n.* **1.** each of a number of strings or yarns which are twisted together to form a rope, cord, or the like. **2.** a thread of the texture of anything, as cloth.

strange /streɪndʒ/ *adj.,* **stranger**, **strangest**. **1.** unusual, extraordinary, or curious; odd; queer. **2.** situated, belonging, or coming from outside one's own or a particular locality.

stranger /ˈstreɪndʒə/ *n.* **1.** a person with whom one has, or has hitherto had, no personal acquaintance. **2.** a person or thing that is unaccustomed or new (fol. by *to*).

strangle /ˈstræŋgəl/ *v.t.,* **-gled**, **-gling**. to kill by stopping the breath.

strap /stræp/ *n., v.,* **strapped**, **strapping**. – *n.* **1.** a long, narrow piece or object; strip; band. – *v.t.* **2.** to fasten or secure with a strap or straps.

strapping /ˈstræpɪŋ/ *adj.* *Colloquial* tall, robust, and strongly built.

strata /ˈstratə/ *n.* a plural of **stratum**.

stratagem /ˈstrætədʒəm/ *n.* a plan, scheme, or trick for deceiving the enemy.

strata title *n.* a system of registration of strata of air space in multistorey buildings, similar to the registration of titles under the Torrens system.

strategic /strəˈtidʒɪk/ *adj.* important in strategy.

strategy /ˈstrætədʒi/ *n., pl.* **-gies**. the method of conducting operations, especially by the aid of manoeuvring or stratagem.

strati- a word element representing **stratum**.

stratify /ˈstrætəfaɪ/ *v.t.,* **-fied**, **-fying**. to form in strata or layers.

strato- a word element meaning 'low and horizontal'.

stratum /ˈstratəm/ *n., pl.* **strata** /ˈstratə/, **stratums**. a layer of material, formed either naturally or artificially, often one of a number of parallel layers placed one upon another.

straw /strɔ/ *n.* **1.** a single stalk or stem, especially of certain species of grain, chiefly wheat, rye, oats, and barley. **2.** a mass of such stalks, especially after drying and threshing, used as fodder, as material for hats, etc. **3.** a hollow paper tube, plant stem, etc., used in drinking some beverages, etc. – *adj.* **4.** of, relating to, or made of straw.

strawberry /ˈstrɔbəri, -bri/ *n., pl.* **-ries**. a small, red, fleshy fruit.

straw company *n.* a company set up not to produce anything but simply as a legal device to obtain some benefit, especially tax benefits.

straw vote *n.* an unofficial vote taken to obtain some indication of the general drift of opinion. Also, **straw poll**.

stray /streɪ/ *v.i.* **1.** to wander (fol. by *away*, *off*, *from*, *into*, *to*, etc.). **2.** to deviate, as from the set or right course; go astray; get lost. – *n.* **3.** a domestic animal found wandering at large or without an owner. – *adj.* **4.** straying, or having strayed, as a domestic animal. **5.** found or occurring apart from others, or as an isolated or casual instance.

streak /strik/ *n.* **1.** a long, narrow mark, smear, band of colour, or the like. **2.** a vein, strain, or admixture of anything. – *v.t.* **3.** to mark with a streak or streaks. – *v.i.* **4.** to become streaked. **5.** to flash or go rapidly, like a streak of lightning.

stream /strim/ *n.* **1.** a body of water flowing in a channel or bed. **2.** any flow of water or other liquid or fluid. **3.** prevailing direction; drift. – *v.i.* **4.** to flow, pass, or issue in a stream, as water, tears, blood, etc. **5.** to send forth or throw off a stream; run or flow (fol. by *with*). – *v.t.* **6.** to send forth or discharge in a stream.

streamer /ˈstrimə/ *n.* **1.** a long, narrow flag or pennant. **2.** a long, narrow strip of paper, usually brightly coloured, thrown in festivities, or used for decorating rooms or the like.

streamlined /ˈstrimlaɪnd/ *adj.* **1.** having a shape designed to offer the least possible resistance in passing through the air, etc. **2.** designed for smooth running and optimum efficiency.

street /strit/ *n.* a public way or road, paved or unpaved, in a town or city, sometimes including a pavement or pavements, with houses, shops, etc., along it.

strength /strɛŋθ/ *n.* **1.** the quality or state of being strong; bodily or muscular power; vigour, as in robust health. **2.** something that makes strong; a support or stay.

strenuous /ˈstrɛnjuəs/ *adj.* characterised by vigorous exertion.

stress /strɛs/ *v.t.* **1.** to lay stress or emphasis on; emphasise. – *n.* **2.** importance or significance attached to a thing; emphasis. **3.** emphasis in music, rhythm, etc. **4.** the physical pressure, pull, or other force exerted on one thing by another. **5.** a disturbing physiological or psychological influence which produces a state of severe tension in an individual.

-stress a feminine equivalent of **-ster**.

stretch /strɛtʃ/ *v.t.* **1.** to draw out or extend. **2.** to lengthen, widen, distend, or enlarge by tension. **3.** to extend or force beyond the natural or proper limits; strain. – *v.i.* **4.** to recline at full length (usually fol. by *out*). **5.** to extend the hand, or reach, as for something. **6.** to extend over a distance, area, period of time, or in a particular direction. **7.** to stretch oneself by extending the limbs, straining the muscles, etc. **8.** to become stretched, or admit of being stretched, to greater length, width, etc., as any elastic material. – *n.* **9.** the act of stretching. **10.** the state of being stretched. **11.** capacity for being stretched. **12.** a continuous length, distance, tract, or expanse. **13.** an extent in time or duration. – *adj.* **14.** made to stretch in order to fit different shapes and sizes, as clothing.

stretcher /ˈstrɛtʃə/ *n.* **1.** a light, folding bed. **2.** a bed-like device designed for transporting an ill or injured person.

strew /stru/ *v.t.*, **strewed**, **strewed** *or* **strewn**, **strewing**. to let fall in separate pieces or particles over a surface; scatter or sprinkle.

stricken /ˈstrɪkən/ *adj.* smitten or afflicted, as with disease, trouble, or sorrow.

strict /strɪkt/ *adj.* **1.** characterised by or acting in close conformity to requirements or principles. **2.** closely or rigorously enforced or maintained. **3.** exact or precise.

stricture /ˈstrɪktʃə/ *n.* a remark or comment, especially an adverse criticism.

stride /straɪd/ *v.*, **strode**, **stridden**, **striding**, *n.* – *v.i.* **1.** to walk with long steps. **2.** to take a long step. – *v.t.* **3.** to walk with long steps along, on, through, over, etc. **4.** to pass over or across by one stride. – *n.* **5.** a long step in walking. **6.** (*pl.*) *Colloquial* trousers.

strident /ˈstraɪdnt/ *adj.* making or having a harsh sound; grating; creaking.

strife /straɪf/ *n.* conflict, discord, or variance.

strike /straɪk/ *v.*, **struck**, **striking**, *n.* – *v.t.* **1.** to deal a blow or stroke to. **2.** to deal or inflict (a blow, stroke, etc.). **3.** to drive or thrust forcibly. **4.** to produce (fire, sparks, light, etc.) by percussion, friction, etc. **5.** to cause (a match) to ignite by friction. **6.** to come into forcible contact or collision with. **7.** to fall upon (something), as light or sound. **8.** to enter the mind of; occur to. **9.** to impress strongly. **10.** to come upon or find (ore, oil, etc.) in prospecting, boring, or the like. **11.** to send down or put forth (a root, etc.), as a plant, cutting, etc. **12.** to balance (a ledger, etc.). **13.** (in various technical uses) to make level or smooth. **14.** to efface or cancel with, or as with, the stroke of a pen (fol. by *off*, *out*, etc.). **15.** to remove or separate with a cut (usually fol. by *off*). **16.** to indicate (the hour of day) by a stroke or strokes, as a clock. **17.** to assume (an attitude or posture). **18.** to reach by agreement, as a compromise. **19.** to enter upon or form (an acquaintance, etc.) (usually fol. by *up*). – *v.i.* **20.** to deal or aim a blow or stroke. **21.** come into forcible contact. **22.** to make an impression on the mind, senses, etc., as something seen or heard. **23.** (of an orchestra or band) to begin to play. **24.** to take root, as a slip of a plant. **25.** to go, proceed, or advance, especially in a new direction. **26.** (of an employee or employees) to engage in a strike. – *n.* **27.** an act of striking. **28.** a concerted stopping of work or withdrawal of workers' services in order to compel an employer to accede to demands.

string /strɪŋ/ *n.*, *v.*, **strung**, **stringing**. – *n.* **1.** a line, cord, or thread, used for tying parcels, etc. **2.** a number of objects, as beads or pearls, threaded or arranged on a cord. **3.** any series of things arranged or connected in a line or following closely one after another. **4.** (in musical instruments) a tightly stretched cord or wire which produces a note when caused to vibrate. – *v.t.* **5.** to furnish with or as with a string or strings. **6.** to extend or stretch (a cord, etc.) from one point to another. **7.** to thread on, or as on, a string. **8.** to connect in, or as in, a line; arrange in a series or succession. **9.** to deprive of a string or strings; strip the strings from. **10. string along** (or **on**), *Colloquial* to deceive (someone) in a progressive series of falsehoods; con. – *v.i.* **11.** to form into a string or strings, as glutinous substances do when pulled.

stringent /ˈstrɪndʒənt/ *adj.* **1.** narrowly binding; rigorously exacting; strict; severe. **2.** (of the money market) tight; characterised by a shortage of loan money.

strip[1] /strɪp/ *v.*, **stripped**, **stripping**. – *v.t.* **1.** to deprive of covering. **2.** to deprive of clothing; make bare or naked. **3.** to take away or remove. **4.** to deprive or divest. – *v.i.* **5.** to strip something; especially, to strip oneself of clothes.

strip[2] /strɪp/ *n.* a narrow piece, comparatively long and usually of uniform width.

stripe /straɪp/ *n.*, *v.*, **striped**, **striping**. – *n.* **1.** a relatively long, narrow band of a different colour, appearance, weave, material, or nature from the rest of a surface or thing. **2.** a strip, or long, narrow piece of anything. – *v.t.* **3.** to mark or furnish with a stripe or stripes.

stripling /ˈstrɪplɪŋ/ *n.* a youth just passing from boyhood to manhood.

striptease /ˈstrɪptiz/ *n.* an act in which someone strips before an audience.

strive /straɪv/ *v.i.*, **strove**, **striven**, **striving**. **1.** to make strenuous efforts towards any end. **2.** to struggle vigorously, as in opposition or resistance.

strobe lighting /stroʊb/ *n.* flashing light of great intensity, as at a dance, etc.

strode /stroʊd/ *v.* past tense of **stride**.

stroke[1] /stroʊk/ *n.* **1.** an act of striking; a blow. **2.** something likened to a blow in its effect, as an attack of apoplexy or paralysis. **3.** a single complete movement, especially one continuously repeated in some process. **4.** a movement of a pen, pencil, brush, or the like. **5.** a mark traced by or as if by a pen, pencil, brush, or the like.

stroke[2] /stroʊk/ *v.*, **stroked**, **stroking**, *n.* – *v.t.* **1.** to pass the hand or an instrument over (something) lightly or with little pressure; rub gently, as in soothing or caressing. – *n.* **2.** the act or an instance of stroking; a stroking movement.

stroll /stroʊl/ *v.i.* **1.** to walk leisurely as inclination directs; ramble. – *n.* **2.** a leisurely walk; a ramble; a saunter.

stroller /ˈstroʊlə/ *n.* a light collapsible chair on wheels, used for carrying small children. Also, **pushchair**, **pusher**.

strong /strɒŋ/ *adj.* **1.** physically vigorous or robust. **2.** mentally powerful or vigorous. **3.** of great moral power, firmness, or courage. **4.** powerful in influence, authority, resources. **5.** well-supplied or rich in something specified. **6.** of great force, effectiveness, potency, or cogency. **7.** containing alcohol, or much alcohol. **8.** intense, as light or colour. **9.** strenuous or energetic; forceful or vigorous. **10.** of an unpleasant or offensive flavour or smell. **11.** *Commerce* characterised by steady or advancing prices. – *adv.* **12.** in a strong manner. **13.** in number: *the team was fifteen strong.*

stronghold /ˈstrɒŋhoʊld/ *n.* a strong or well-fortified place; a fortress.

strop /strɒp/ *n.*, *v.*, **stropped**, **stropping**. – *n.* **1.** material used for sharpening razors. – *v.t.* **2.** to sharpen on, or as on, a strop.

stroppy /ˈstrɒpi/ *adj.* *Colloquial* rebellious and difficult to control.

strove /stroʊv/ *v.* past tense of **strive**.

struck /strʌk/ *v.* past tense and a past participle of **strike**.

structure /ˈstrʌktʃə/ *n.*, *v.*, **-tured**, **-turing**. – *n.* **1.** arrangement of parts, elements or constituents. **2.** something built or constructed. **3.** anything composed of parts arranged together in some way; an organisation. – *v.t.* **4.** to give form or organisation to. – **structural**, *adj.*

struggle /ˈstrʌgəl/ *v.*, **-gled**, **-gling**, *n.* – *v.i.* **1.** to contend with an adversary or opposing force. – *n.* **2.** the act or process of struggling.

strum /strʌm/ *v.*, **strummed**, **strumming**. – *v.t.* **1.** to play on (a stringed musical instrument) unskilfully or carelessly. **2.** to play (chords, etc., especially on a guitar) by sweeping across the strings with the fingers or with a plectrum. – *v.i.* **3.** to play chords on a stringed instrument unskilfully or as a simple accompaniment.

strumpet /ˈstrʌmpət/ *n.* a prostitute.

strung /strʌŋ/ *v.* past tense and past participle of **string**.

strut[1] /strʌt/ *v.i.*, **strutted**, **strutting**. to walk with a vain, pompous bearing, as with head erect and chest thrown out, as if expecting to impress observers.

strut[2] /strʌt/ *n.* a structural part designed to take pressure.

strychnine /ˈstrɪknin, -nən/ *n.* a colourless crystalline poison.

stub /stʌb/ *n.*, *v.*, **stubbed**, **stubbing**. – *n.* **1.** a short remaining piece. – *v.t.* **2.** to strike, as one's toe, against something projecting from a surface. **3. stub out,** to extinguish (a cigarette) by pressing the lighted end against a hard surface.

stubble /ˈstʌbəl/ *n.* any short, rough growth, as of beard.

stubborn /ˈstʌbən/ *adj.* unreasonably obstinate; obstinately perverse.

stubby /ˈstʌbi/ *adj.*, **-bier**, **-biest**, *n.*, *pl.* **-bies**. – *adj.* **1.** short and thick or broad. – *n.* **2.** a small squat beer bottle.

stuck /stʌk/ *v.* past tense and past participle of **stick**[2].

stud[1] /stʌd/ *n.*, *v.*, **studded**, **studding**. – *n.* **1.** a boss, knob, nailhead, or other protuberance projecting from a surface or part, especially as an ornament. **2.** a kind of small button or fastener. – *v.t.* **3.** to set with or as with studs, bosses, or the like. **4.** to set or scatter (objects) at intervals over a surface.

stud[2] /stʌd/ *n.* **1.** an establishment in which horses cattle, etc., are kept for breeding. **2.** retained for breeding purposes.

student /ˈstjudnt/ *n.* someone who studies.

studio /ˈstjudioʊ/ *n.*, *pl.* **-dios**. **1.** a room or place in which some form of art is pursued. **2.** a room or set of rooms specially equipped for broadcasting radio or television programs or making recordings.

study /ˈstʌdi/ *n., pl.* **studies**, *v.,* **studied**, **studying**. – *n.* **1.** application of the mind to the acquisition of knowledge, as by reading, investigation, or reflection. **2.** a thorough examination and analysis of a particular subject. **3.** a room, in a house or other building, set apart for private study, reading, writing, or the like. **4.** something produced as an educational exercise. – *v.i.* **5.** to apply oneself to the acquisition of knowledge, as by reading, investigation, practice, etc. – *v.t.* **6.** to apply oneself to acquiring a knowledge of (a branch of learning, science, or art, or a subject), especially systematically. **7.** to examine or investigate carefully and in detail. – **studious**, *adj.*

stuff /stʌf/ *n.* **1.** the material of which anything is made. **2.** material to be worked upon, or to be used in making something. **3.** matter or material indefinitely. **4.** worthless matter or things. – *v.t.* **5.** to fill (a receptacle), especially by packing the contents closely together. **6.** to fill (a chicken, turkey, piece of meat, etc.) with seasoned breadcrumbs or other savoury matter. **7.** to thrust or cram (something) tightly into a receptacle, cavity, or the like. **8.** to stop up or plug; block or choke (usually fol. by *up*). **9.** *Colloquial* to cause to fail; render useless. – *v.i.* **10.** to cram oneself with food.

stuffing /ˈstʌfɪŋ/ *n.* that with which anything is or may be stuffed.

stuffy /ˈstʌfi/ *adj.,* **stuffier**, **stuffiest**. **1.** close or ill-ventilated, as a room; oppressive from lack of freshness, as the air, etc. **2.** conceited. **3.** old-fashioned; immune to new ideas.

stumble /ˈstʌmbəl/ *v.,* **-bled**, **-bling**, *n.* – *v.i.* **1.** to strike the foot against something in walking, running, etc., so as to stagger or fall; trip. **2.** to walk or go unsteadily. **3.** to come accidentally or unexpectedly (fol. by *on, upon, across,* etc.). – *n.* **4.** the act of stumbling.

stump /stʌmp/ *n.* **1.** something left after a part has been cut off, as of a tree, leg, etc. **2.** a short remnant of a pencil, candle, cigar, etc. **3.** *Cricket* each of the three upright sticks which, with the two bails laid on the top of them, form a wicket. – *v.t.* **4.** to clear of stumps, as land. **5.** to nonplus, embarrass, or render completely at a loss. – *v.i.* **6.** to walk heavily or clumsily, as if with a wooden leg.

stun /stʌn/ *v.t.,* **stunned**, **stunning**. **1.** to deprive of consciousness or strength by or as by a blow, fall, etc. **2.** to strike with astonishment; astound; amaze.

stung /stʌŋ/ *v.* past tense and past participle of **sting**.

stunt[1] /stʌnt/ *v.t.* to check the growth or development of.

stunt[2] /stʌnt/ *n.* a performance serving as a display of strength, activity, skill, or the like, as in athletics, etc.; a feat.

stupefy /ˈstjupəfaɪ/ *v.t.,* **-fied**, **-fying**. to put into a state of stupor.

stupendous /stjuˈpɛndəs/ *adj.* such as to cause amazement.

stupid /ˈstjupəd/ *adj.* lacking ordinary activity and keenness of mind; dull.

stupor /ˈstjupə/ *n.* a state of suspended or deadened sensibility.

sturdy /ˈstɜdi/ *adj.,* **-dier**, **-diest**. strongly built, stalwart, or robust.

stutter /ˈstʌtə/ *v.t., v.i.* **1.** to utter (sounds) in which the rhythm is interrupted by blocks or spasms, repetitions, or prolongation. – *n.* **2.** unrhythmical and distorted speech.

sty[1] /staɪ/ *n., pl.* **sties**. a pen or enclosure for pigs.

sty[2] /staɪ/ *n., pl.* **sties**. a small inflammation on the eyelid. Also, **stye**.

style /staɪl/ *n., v.,* **styled**, **styling**. – *n.* **1.** a particular kind, sort, or type, as with reference to form, appearance, or character. **2.** a particular, distinctive, or characteristic mode of action. **3.** a mode of fashion, as in dress, especially good or approved fashion; elegance; smartness. **4.** the features of a literary composition belonging to the form of expression other than the content. **5.** a manner or tone adopted in speaking to others. **6.** the rules of spelling, punctuation, capitalisation, etc., observed by a publishing house, newspaper, etc. **7.** a descriptive or distinguishing appellation, especially a recognised title. – *v.t.* **8.** to call by a particular style or appellation (as specified). **9.** to design in accordance with a given or new style. – **stylistic**, *adj.* – **stylish**, *adj.*

stylise = stylize /ˈstaɪlaɪz/ *v.t.,* **-lised**, **-lising**. to bring into conformity with a particular style.

stylus /ˈstaɪləs/ *n.* **1.** a needle tipped with diamond, sapphire, etc., for reproducing the sound of a gramophone record. **2.** any of various pointed instruments used in drawing, tracing, stencilling, etc.

suave /swav/ *adj.* (of persons or their manner, speech, etc.) smoothly agreeable or polite; agreeably or blandly urbane.

sub /sʌb/ *n.* **1.** subeditor. **2.** submarine. **3.** subscription.

sub- a prefix meaning 'under', 'not quite', or 'somewhat', also attached to stems not used independently, with various extensions of meaning (*subject, subtract, subvert*).

subcommittee /ˈsʌbkəˌmɪti/ *n.* a secondary committee appointed out of a main committee.

subconscious /sʌbˈkɒnʃəs/ *adj.* **1.** existing or operating beneath or beyond consciousness. – *n.* **2.** the totality of mental processes of which the individual is not aware; unreportable mental activities.

subcontract /sʌbˈkɒntrækt/ *n.,* /sʌbkənˈtrækt/ *v. Law* – *n.* **1.** a contract by which one agrees to render services or to provide materials necessary for the performance of another contract. – *v.i., v.t.* **2.** to make a subcontract (for). – **subcontractor**, *n.*

subculture /ˈsʌbkʌltʃə/ *n. Sociology* a distinct network of behaviour, beliefs and attitudes existing within a larger culture.

subcutaneous /sʌbkjuˈteɪniəs/ *adj.* situated or lying under the skin, as tissue.

subdivide /ˈsʌbdəvaɪd, sʌbdəˈvaɪd/ *v.,* **-vided**, **-viding**. – *v.t.* **1.** to divide (a part, or an already divided whole) into smaller parts; divide anew after a first division. – *v.i.* **2.** to become separated into subdivisions.

subdue /səbˈdju/ *v.t.,* **-dued**, **-duing**. **1.** to overpower by superior force; overcome. **2.** to bring into mental subjection. **3.** to reduce the intensity, force, or vividness of.

subeditor /sʌb'ɛdətə/ *n.* **1.** *Journalism* someone who edits and corrects material written by others. **2.** an assistant or subordinate editor.

subheading /'sʌbhɛdɪŋ/ *n.* **1.** a title or heading of a subdivision or subsection in a chapter, treatise, essay, newspaper article, etc. **2.** a subordinate division of a heading or title. Also, **subhead**.

subject /'sʌbdʒɛkt/ *n., adj.*; /səb'dʒɛkt/ *v.* – *n.* **1.** something that forms a matter of thought, discourse, investigation, etc. **2.** a branch of knowledge organised into a system so as to form a suitable course of study. **3.** someone who is under the dominion or rule of a sovereign, state, etc. **4.** *Grammar* the word or words of a sentence which represent the person or object performing the action expressed in the predicate, as, *she* in *she raised her hat.* **5.** someone who or that which undergoes, or may undergo, some action. – *adj.* **6.** being under domination, control, or influence (often fol. by *to*). **7.** being under dominion, rule, or authority. **8.** open or exposed (fol. by *to*). **9.** being dependent or conditional upon something (fol. by *to*). – *v.t.* **10.** to make subject (usually fol. by *to*). – **subjection**, *n.*

subjective /səb'dʒɛktɪv/ *adj.* belonging to the thinking subject rather than to the object of thought (opposed to *objective*).

sub judice /sʌb 'dʒudəsi/ *adv.* before a judge or court of law; under judicial consideration.

subjugate /'sʌbdʒəgeɪt/ *v.t.,* **-gated**, **-gating**. to bring under complete control or into subjection; subdue; conquer.

sublet /sʌb'lɛt/ *v.t.,* **-let**, **-letting**. to let to another person, the party letting being himself or herself a lessee.

sublimate /'sʌbləmeɪt/ *v.t.,* **-mated**, **-mating**. *Psychology* to deflect (sexual or other biological energies) into socially constructive or creative channels.

sublime /sə'blaɪm/ *adj.* **1.** supreme or perfect. – *n.* **2.** that which is sublime.

subliminal /sə'blɪmənəl/ *adj. Psychology* (of stimuli, etc.) being or operating below the threshold of consciousness or perception.

submarine /'sʌbmərin, sʌbmə'rin/ *n.* **1.** a type of vessel that can be submerged and navigated under water. – *adj.* **2.** situated, occurring, operating, or living under the surface of the sea.

submerge /səb'mɜdʒ/ *v.,* **-merged**, **-merging**. – *v.t.* **1.** to cover with or as with water; immerse. – *v.i.* **2.** to sink or plunge under water.

submissive /səb'mɪsɪv/ *adj.* **1.** inclined or ready to submit. **2.** marked by or indicating submission.

submit /səb'mɪt/ *v.,* **-mitted**, **-mitting**. – *v.t.* **1.** to yield in surrender, compliance, or obedience. **2.** to state or urge with deference (usually followed by a clause). **3.** to refer to the decision or judgment of another or others. – *v.i.* **4.** to yield in surrender, compliance, obedience, etc.

subordinate /sə'bɔdənət/ *adj., n.*; /sə'bɔdəneɪt/ *v.,* **-nated**, **-nating**. – *adj.* **1.** of lesser importance; secondary. **2.** subject to or under the authority of a superior. – *n.* **3.** a subordinate person or thing. – *v.t.* **4.** to place in a lower order or rank. **5.** to make subordinate.

subpoena /sə'pinə/ *n., v.,* **-naed**, **-naing**. *Law* – *n.* **1.** the usual writ process for the summoning of witnesses. – *v.t.* **2.** to serve with a subpoena.

subroutine /'sʌbrutin/ *n. Computers* a section of a program which can be called up as required from various points in the main program, returning the user to the point at which it was called up.

subscribe /səb'skraɪb/ *v.,* **-scribed**, **-scribing**. – *v.t.* **1.** to write or inscribe (something) beneath or at the end of a thing; sign (one's name) to a document, etc. – *v.i.* **2.** to obtain a subscription to a magazine, newspaper, etc. **3.** to give or pay money as a contribution, payment, etc. **4.** to assent by, or as by, signing one's name.

subscript /'sʌbskrɪpt/ *n.* something written below.

subscription /səb'skrɪpʃən/ *n.* **1.** a monetary contribution towards some object or a payment for shares, a book, a periodical, etc. **2.** the dues paid by a member of a club, society, etc. **3.** something subscribed.

subsequent /'sʌbsəkwənt/ *adj.* occurring or coming later or after.

subservient /səb'sɜviənt/ *adj.* (of persons, their conduct, etc.) servile; excessively submissive; obsequious.

subside /səb'saɪd/ *v.i.,* **-sided**, **-siding**. to sink to a low or lower level.

subsidiary /səb'sɪdʒəri/ *adj.* **1.** serving to assist or supplement. **2.** subordinate or secondary.

subsidiary company *n.* a company the controlling interest in which is owned by another company.

subsidise = subsidize /'sʌbsədaɪz/ *v.t.,* **-dised**, **-dising**. to furnish or aid with a subsidy.

subsidy /'sʌbsədi/ *n., pl.* **-dies**. a direct pecuniary aid furnished by a government to a private industrial undertaking, a cultural organisation, or the like.

subsist /səb'sɪst/ *v.i.* to continue alive; live, as on food, resources, etc., especially when these are limited.

subsistence /səb'sɪstəns/ *n.* **1.** the state or fact of subsisting. **2.** means of supporting life; a living or livelihood.

substance /'sʌbstəns/ *n.* **1.** that of which a thing consists; matter or material. **2.** a species of matter of definite chemical composition. **3.** substantial or solid character or quality. **4.** the meaning or gist, as of speech or writing.

substantial /səb'stænʃəl/ *adj.* **1.** of a corporeal or material nature; real or actual. **2.** of ample or considerable amount, quantity, size, etc. **3.** of solid character or quality; firm, stout, or strong. **4.** wealthy or influential.

substantiate /səb'stænʃieɪt/ *v.t.,* **-ated**, **-ating**. to establish by proof or competent evidence.

substantive /sʌb'stæntɪv, 'sʌbstəntɪv/ *n.* **1.** *Grammar* a noun, pronoun, or other word or phrase having nominal function in a sentence. – *adj.* **2.** *Grammar* of or relating to substantives. **3.** real or actual. **4.** of considerable amount or quantity. **5.** *Law* relating to the rules of right which courts are called on to apply, as opposed to rules of procedure.

substitute /'sʌbstətjut/ *n., v.,* **-tuted, -tuting**. – *n.* **1.** a person or thing acting or serving in place of another. – *v.t.* **2.** to put (one person or thing) in the place of another. – *v.i.* **3.** to act as substitute.

subsume /səb'sjum/ *v.t.,* **-sumed, -suming**. **1.** to consider (an idea, term, proposition, etc.) as part of a more comprehensive one. **2.** bring (a case, instance, etc.) under a rule.

subter- a prefix meaning 'position underneath', with figurative applications, as in *subterfuge*.

subterfuge /'sʌbtəfjudʒ/ *n.* an artifice or expedient employed to escape the force of an argument, to evade unfavourable consequences, hide something etc.

subterranean /sʌbtə'reɪniən/ *adj.* existing, situated, or operating below the surface of the earth; underground.

subtitle /'sʌbtaɪtl/ *n.* **1.** a secondary or subordinate title of a literary work, usually of explanatory character. **2.** *Film* one of a series of captions projected on to the lower part of the screen which translate and summarise the dialogue of foreign language films.

subtle /'sʌtl/ *adj.* **1.** fine or delicate, often when likely to elude perception or understanding. **2.** requiring mental acuteness, penetration, or discernment. **3.** insidious in operation, as poison, etc. – **subtlety**, *n.*

subtract /səb'trækt/ *v.t.* **1.** to withdraw or take away, as a part from a whole. – *v.i.* **2.** to take away something or a part, as from a whole. – **subtraction**, *n.*

sub-underwrite /sʌb-'ʌndəraɪt/ *v.t.,* **-wrote, -written, -writing**. *Economics* to subcontract the obligation of an underwriter.

suburb /'sʌbɜb/ *n.* a more or less self-contained district of a town or city. – **suburban**, *adj.*

suburbia /sə'bɜbiə/ *n.* the suburbs collectively especially as they embody the middle range of community standards and values.

subvert /səb'vɜt/ *v.t.* to cause the downfall, ruin, or destruction of.

subway /'sʌbweɪ/ *n.* an underground passage or tunnel enabling pedestrians to cross beneath a street, railway line, etc.

succeed /sək'sid/ *v.i.* **1.** to turn out or terminate according to desire. **2.** to accomplish what is attempted or intended. **3.** to follow or replace another by descent, election, appointment, etc. (often fol. by *to*). **4.** to come next after something else in an order or series. – *v.t.* **5.** to come after and take the place of, as in an office or estate. **6.** to come next after in an order or series, or in the course of events; follow. – **succession**, *n.* – **successive**, *adj.*

success /sək'sɛs/ *n.* **1.** the favourable or prosperous termination of attempts or endeavours. **2.** the gaining of wealth, position, or the like. **3.** a thing or a person that is successful.

successor /sək'sɛsə/ *n.* someone who or that which succeeds or follows.

succinct /sək'sɪŋkt/ *adj.* characterised by conciseness or verbal brevity.

succour = succor /'sʌkə/ *n.* help; relief; aid; assistance.

succulent /'sʌkjələnt/ *adj.* full of juice; juicy.

succumb /sə'kʌm/ *v.i.* to give way to superior force; yield.

such /sʌtʃ/ *adj.* **1.** of the kind, character, degree, extent, etc., of that or those indicated or implied. **2.** (preceding an adjective used attributively) so, or in such a manner or degree. **3.** (used as an intensifier) to a high degree: *he is such a nice man.* **4.** (with omission of an indication of comparison) of so extreme a kind; so great, good, bad, etc.: *she is such a liar.* **5.** being the person or thing, or the persons or things, indicated. **6.** Also, **such and such**. being definite or particular, but not named or specified. – *pron.* **7.** the person or thing, or the persons or things, indicated. **8. as such, a.** as being what is indicated; in that capacity. **b.** in itself or themselves.

suck /sʌk/ *v.t.* **1.** to draw into the mouth by action of the lips and tongue which produces a partial vacuum. **2.** to draw (water, moisture, air, etc.) by any process resembling this. **3.** to apply the lips or mouth to, and draw upon by producing a partial vacuum, especially for extracting fluid contents. **4.** to hold in the mouth and dissolve in the saliva, assisted by the action of the tongue, etc. – *v.i.* **5.** to draw or be drawn by, or as by, suction. – *n.* **6.** the act or instance of sucking.

sucker /'sʌkə/ *n.* *Colloquial* a person easily deceived or imposed upon; dupe.

suckle /'sʌkəl/ *v.,* **-led, -ling**. – *v.t.* **1.** to nurse at the breast. – *v.i.* **2.** to suck at the breast.

sucrose /'sukroʊz, -oʊs/ *n.* the sugar obtained from the sugar cane, the sugar beet, etc.

suction /'sʌkʃən/ *n.* **1.** the act, process, or condition of sucking. **2.** the tendency to suck a substance into an interior space when the atmospheric pressure is reduced in the space. **3.** the act or process of sucking a gas or liquid by such means.

sudden /'sʌdn/ *adj.* **1.** happening, coming, made, or done quickly, without warning or unexpectedly. **2. all of a sudden,** suddenly.

sudden infant death syndrome *n.* the sudden unexplained death of an apparently healthy baby, usually while asleep; cot death. Also, **SIDS**.

suds /sʌdz/ *pl. n.* soapy water; lather.

sue /su/ *v.,* **sued, suing**. – *v.t.* **1.** to institute process in law against. – *v.i.* **2.** to institute legal proceedings, or bring suit.

suede /sweɪd/ *n.* kid or other leather finished on the flesh side with a soft, napped surface.

suet /'suət/ *n.* hard animal fat used in cookery, etc.

suffer /'sʌfə/ *v.i.* **1.** to undergo or feel pain or distress. **2.** to endure patiently or bravely. – *v.t.* **3.** to undergo, experience, or be subjected to. **4.** to tolerate or allow.

sufferance /'sʌfərəns, 'sʌfrəns/ *n. in the phr.* **on sufferance,** reluctantly tolerated.

suffice /sə'faɪs/ *v.i.,* **-ficed**, **-ficing**. to be enough or adequate.

sufficient /sə'fɪʃənt/ *adj.* that suffices. – **sufficiency**, *n.*

suffocate /'sʌfəkeɪt/ *v.,* **-cated**, **-cating**. – *v.t.* **1.** to kill by preventing the access of air to the blood. – *v.i.* **2.** to become suffocated; stifle; smother.

suffrage /'sʌfrɪdʒ/ *n.* the right of voting, especially in political elections.

suffuse /sə'fjuz/ *v.t.,* **-fused**, **-fusing**. to overspread with or as with a liquid, colour, etc.

sugar /'ʃʊgə/ *n.* **1.** a sweet crystalline substance extensively used for food purposes. **2.** a member of the same class of carbohydrates. – *v.t.* **3.** to cover, sprinkle, mix, or sweeten with sugar.

sugar beet *n.* a variety of beet cultivated for the sugar it yields.

sugar cane *n.* a tall grass of tropical and warm regions, constituting the chief source of sugar. Also, **sugarcane**.

suggest /sə'dʒɛst/ *v.t.* **1.** to place or bring (an idea, proposition, plan, etc.) before a person's mind for consideration or possible action. **2.** to propose (a person or thing) as suitable or possible.

suggestible /sə'dʒɛstəbəl/ *adj.* capable of being influenced by suggestion.

suggestive /sə'dʒɛstɪv/ *adj.* such as to suggest something improper or indecent.

suicide /'suəsaɪd/ *n., v.,* **-cided**, **-ciding**. – *n.* **1.** someone who intentionally takes their own life. **2.** the intentional taking of one's own life. – *v.i.* **3.** to commit suicide. – **suicidal**, *adj.*

suit /sut/ *n.* **1.** a set of garments, vestments, or armour, intended to be worn together. **2.** the act or process of suing in a court of law; legal prosecution. **3.** a number of things forming a series or set. – *v.t.* **4.** to make appropriate, adapt, or accommodate, as one thing to another. **5.** to be appropriate or becoming to. – *v.i.* **6.** to be appropriate or suitable; accord. **7.** to be satisfactory, agreeable, or acceptable.

suitable /'sutəbəl/ *adj.* such as to suit; appropriate; fitting; becoming.

suitcase /'sutkeɪs/ *n.* a portable rectangular travelling bag, usually with stiffened frame, for carrying clothes, etc.

suite /swit/ *n.* **1.** a company of followers or attendants; a train or retinue. **2.** a number of things forming a series or set.

sulfur /'sʌlfə/ *n. Chemistry* a non-metallic element which exists in several forms. *Symbol*: S Also, *Obsolescent*, **sulphur**. – **sulfuric**, *adj.* – **sulfurous**, *adj.*

sulk /sʌlk/ *v.i.* to hold aloof in a sullen, morose, ill-humoured, or offended mood.

sullen /'sʌlən/ *adj.* showing ill humour by a gloomy silence or reserve.

sully /'sʌli/ *v.t.,* **-lied**, **-lying**. to soil, stain, or tarnish.

sulphur /'sʌlfə/ *n.* → **sulfur**.

sultan /'sʌltən/ *n.* the sovereign of a Muslim country.

sultana /sʌl'tanə, səl-/ *n.* **1.** a wife of a sultan. **2.** a small, green, seedless grape. **3.** a raisin made from such a grape.

sultry /'sʌltri/ *adj.,* **-trier**, **-triest**. oppressively hot and close or moist; sweltering.

sum /sʌm/ *n., v.,* **summed**, **summing**, *adj.* – *n.* **1.** the aggregate of two or more numbers, magnitudes, quantities, or particulars as determined by mathematical process. **2.** a quantity or amount, especially of money. **3.** a series of numbers or quantities to be added up. **4.** the total amount, or the whole. – *v.t.* **5.** to combine into an aggregate or total (often fol. by *up*). **6.** to bring into or contain in a brief and comprehensive statement. – *adj.* **7.** denoting or relating to a sum.

sum- occasional variant of **sub-** (by assimilation) before *m.*

summary /'sʌməri/ *n., pl.* **-ries**, *adj.* – *n.* **1.** a brief and comprehensive presentation of facts or statements. – *adj.* **2.** brief and comprehensive; concise. **3.** direct and prompt; unceremoniously fast. **4.** (of legal proceedings, jurisdiction, etc.) conducted without or exempt from the various steps or delays of full proceedings. – **summarise = summarize**, *v.*

summer /'sʌmə/ *n.* **1.** the warmest season of the year, between spring and autumn. – *adj.* **2.** of, relating to, or characteristic of summer.

summit /'sʌmət/ *n.* **1.** the highest point or part. **2.** a meeting or conference between heads of state or the heads of any other organisation. – *adj.* **3.** (in diplomacy) between heads of state.

summon /'sʌmən/ *v.t.* **1.** to call as with authority. **2.** to call into action; rouse; call forth (often fol. by *up*).

summons /'sʌmənz/ *n., pl.* **-monses**. an authoritative command, message, or signal by which one is summoned.

sump /sʌmp/ *n.* a pit, well, or the like in which water or other liquid is collected.

sumptuous /'sʌmptʃuəs/ *adj.* luxuriously fine; splendid or superb.

sun /sʌn/ *n., v.,* **sunned**, **sunning**. – *n.* **1.** the star which is the central body of the solar system. **2.** sunshine. **3.** something likened to the sun in brightness, splendour, etc. **4.** to warm, dry, etc., in the sunshine. – *v.i.* **5.** to expose oneself to the sun's rays.

sunbake /'sʌnbeɪk/ *v.i.,* **-baked**, **-baking**. to expose one's body to the sun.

sunblock /'sʌnblɒk/ *n.* → **sunscreen** (def. 2).

sunburn /'sʌnbɜn/ *n., v.,* **-burnt** *or* **-burned**, **-burning**. – *n.* **1.** superficial inflammation of the skin, caused by excessive or too sudden exposure to the sun's rays. – *v.t., v.i.* **2.** to affect or be affected with sunburn.

suncream /'sʌnkrim/ *n.* → **sunscreen** (def. 2).

sundae /'sʌndeɪ/ *n.* a portion of ice-cream with fruit or other syrup poured over it.

sunder /'sʌndə/ *v.t., v.i.* to separate; part; divide.

sundial /'sʌndaɪəl/ *n.* an instrument for indicating the time of day by the position of a shadow cast by the sun.

sundries /'sʌndriz/ *pl. n.* sundry things or

items.

sundry /'sʌndri/ *adj.* **1.** various. – *pron.* **2. all and sundry,** everyone collectively and individually.

sunflower /'sʌnflaʊə/ *n.* a tall plant grown for its showy flowers, and for its seeds, valuable as a source of oil.

sung /sʌŋ/ *v.* past tense and past participle of **sing**.

sunglasses /'sʌnglasəz/ *pl. n.* spectacles having tinted, darkened, or polaroid lenses to protect the eyes from the glare of the sun.

sunk /sʌŋk/ *v.* a past tense and past participle of **sink**.

sunrise /'sʌnraɪz/ *n.* the rise or ascent of the sun above the horizon in the morning.

sunrise industry *n.* industry based on innovative local technology, especially electronic.

sunscreen /'sʌnskrin/ *n.* **1.** an awning, etc., which provides a screen against the sun. **2.** Also, **sunblock**, **suncream**, **blockout**. a lotion or cream which, when applied to the skin, protects it against damage from the rays of the sun.

sunset /'sʌnsɛt/ *n.* the setting or descent of the sun below the horizon in the evening.

sunset clause *n.* a clause in a bill which terminates the act or brings it up for review at the end of a specified period.

sunset legislation *n.* legislation which includes a sunset clause.

sunshine /'sʌnʃaɪn/ *n.* **1.** the shining of the sun; the direct light of the sun. **2.** cheerfulness, happiness, or prosperity.

sunspot /'sʌnspɒt/ *n.* **1.** one of the relatively dark patches which appear periodically on the surface of the sun. **2.** a discolouration and roughening of part of the skin, usually as a result of exposure to the sun.

sunstroke /'sʌnstroʊk/ *n.* a condition caused by excessive exposure to the sun, marked by prostration.

suntan /'sʌntæn/ *n.* brownness of the skin induced by exposure to the sun.

sup[1] /sʌp/ *v.i.,* **supped**, **supping**. to eat the evening meal; take supper.

sup[2] /sʌp/ *v.t., v.i.,* **supped**, **supping**. to take (liquid food, or any liquid) into the mouth in small quantities, as from a spoon or a cup.

super /'supə/ *n. Colloquial* **1.** → **superannuation**. **2.** high-grade petrol. **3.** a superintendent. **4.** a supervisor. – *adj.* **5.** of a superior quality, grade, size, etc.

super- a prefix meaning 'superior to' or 'over-', applied variously.

superannuate /supər'ænjueɪt/ *v.t.,* **-ated**, **-ating**. to allow to retire from service or office on a pension, on account of age or infirmity.

superannuation /ˌsupərænju'eɪʃən/ *n.* **1.** a pension or allowance to a superannuated person. **2.** a sum paid periodically as contribution to a superannuation fund.

superannuation fund *n.* a retirement fund to which an employee (and usually also his or her employer) contributes during the period of his or her employment, and which provides benefits during illness and after retirement. Also, **provident fund**.

superb /sə'pɜb, su-/ *adj.* admirably fine or excellent.

supercilious /supə'sɪliəs/ *adj.* haughtily disdainful or contemptuous.

superficial /supə'fɪʃəl/ *adj.* **1.** being at, on, or near the surface. **2.** concerned with or comprehending only what is on the surface or obvious. **3.** shallow; not profound or thorough. **4.** apparent, rather than real.

superfluous /su'pɜfluəs/ *adj.* being over and above what is sufficient or required.

superimpose /supərɪm'poʊz/ *v.t.,* **-posed**, **-posing**. **1.** to impose, place, or set on or over something else. **2.** to put or join as an addition (fol. by *on* or *upon*).

superintend /supərɪn'tɛnd, suprɪn-/ *v.t., v.i.* to oversee and direct (work, processes, affairs, etc.). – **superintendent**, *n.*

superior /sə'pɪəriə, su-/ *adj.* **1.** higher in station, rank, degree, or grade. **2.** of higher grade or quality. **3.** greater in quantity or amount. **4.** showing a consciousness or feeling of being above others in such respects. – *n.* **5.** one superior to another or others. – **superiority**, *n.*

superlative /su'pɜlətɪv/ *adj.* surpassing all other or others.

supermarket /'supəmakət/ *n.* a large, usually self-service, retail store or market.

supernatural /supə'nætʃrəl, -'nætʃərəl/ *adj.* **1.** not explicable in terms of natural laws or phenomena. **2.** of or relating to supernatural beings, as ghosts, spirits, etc. **3.** abnormal; extraordinary; unprecedented. – *n.* **4.** supernatural forces, effects, and beings collectively.

superordinate /supər'ɔdənət/ *adj.* **1.** higher in rank, degree, etc. – *n.* **2.** someone who or something which is superordinate.

superscript /'supəskrɪpt/ *adj.* **1.** written above, as a diacritical mark or a correction of a word. – *n.* **2.** a superscript or superior letter, figure, etc.

supersede /supə'sid/ *v.t.,* **-seded**, **-seding**. **1.** to set aside, as void, useless, or obsolete, now usually in favour of something mentioned. **2.** to succeed to the position, function, office, etc., of; supplant.

supersonic /supə'sɒnɪk/ *adj.* (of velocities) above the velocity of sound in the medium.

superstar /'supəsta/ *n.* a singer, actor, or show business personality who is very famous.

superstition /supə'stɪʃən/ *n.* **1.** a belief or notion entertained, regardless of reason or knowledge, of the ominous significance of a particular thing, circumstance, occurrence, proceeding, or the like. **2.** any blindly accepted belief or notion.

superstructure /'supəstrʌktʃə/ *n.* all of an edifice above the basement or foundation.

supertax /'supətæks/ *n.* **1.** a tax in addition to a normal tax, as one upon income above a certain amount. **2.** → **surtax**.

supervise /'supəvaɪz/ *v.t.,* **-vised**, **-vising**. to oversee (a process, work, workers, etc.) during execution or performance. – **supervision**, *n.* – **supervisor**, *n.*

supper /'sʌpə/ *n.* **1.** a light meal taken late at night. **2.** *Chiefly Brit and US* the evening meal. **3.** any evening meal often one forming part of a social entertainment.

supplant /sə'plænt/ *v.t.* to take the place of (another).

supple /'sʌpəl/ *adj.* bending readily or easily.

supplement /'sʌpləmənt/ *n.*, /'sʌpləmɛnt/ *v.* – *n.* **1.** something added to complete a thing, supply a deficiency, or reinforce or extend a whole. – *v.t.* **2.** to complete, add to, or extend by a supplement; form a supplement or addition to. – **supplementary**, *adj.*

supplicate /'sʌpləkeɪt/ *v.i.*, **-cated**, **-cating**. to pray humbly; make humble and earnest entreaty or petition.

supply /sə'plaɪ/ *v.*, **-plied**, **-plying**, *n.*, *pl.* **-plies**. – *v.t.* **1.** to furnish (a person, establishment, place, etc.) with what is lacking or requisite. **2.** to furnish or provide (something wanting or requisite). – *v.i.* **3.** to fill the place of another, temporarily, or as a substitute. – *n.* **4.** the act of supplying, furnishing, providing, satisfying, etc. **5.** a quantity of something provided or on hand, as for use; a stock or store. **6.** *Economics* the quantity of a commodity, etc., that is in the market and available for purchase, or that is available for purchase at a particular price.

supply-side economics *n.* management of the national economy which seeks to overcome a recession by stimulating the production of goods and the supply of services.

support /sə'pɔt/ *v.t.* **1.** to sustain or withstand (weight, etc.) without giving way. **2.** to undergo or endure, especially with patience or submission; tolerate. **3.** to sustain (a person, the mind, spirits, courage, etc.) under trial or affliction. **4.** to maintain (a person, family, establishment, institution, etc.) by supplying with things necessary to existence; provide for.. **5.** to uphold (a person, cause, policy, etc.). – *n.* **6.** the act of supporting. **7.** the state of being supported. **8.** maintenance, as of a person, family, etc., with necessities, means, or funds. **9.** a thing or a person that supports.

suppose /sə'poʊz/ *v.*, **-posed**, **-posing**. – *v.t.* **1.** to assume (something), without reference to its being true or false, for the sake of argument or for the purpose of tracing the consequences. **2.** to assume as true, or believe, in the absence of positive knowledge or of evidence to the contrary. **3.** to think, with reference to mere opinion. **4.** (of facts, circumstances, etc.) to require logically; imply; presuppose. – *v.i.* **5.** to assume something; presume; think. – **supposition**, *n.*

supposed /sə'poʊzd, sə'poʊzəd/ *adj.* merely thought to be such.

suppository /sə'pɒzətri/ *n.*, *pl.* **-ries**. a medicinal substance inserted into the rectum or vagina to be dissolved therein.

suppress /sə'prɛs/ *v.t.* **1.** to keep in or repress. **2.** to quell; crush; vanquish or subdue.

suppurate /'sʌpjəreɪt/ *v.i.*, **-rated**, **-rating**. to produce or discharge pus.

supra /'suprə/ *adv.* above.

supra- a prefix meaning 'above', equivalent to **super-**, but emphasising situation or position.

supra protest *adv.* upon or after protest (a phrase used with reference to an acceptance or a payment of a bill by a third person for the honour of the drawer after protest for non-payment by the drawee).

supreme /su'prim, sə-/ *adj.* **1.** highest in rank or authority. **2.** greatest, utmost, or extreme. – **supremacy**, *n.*

sur-[1] a prefix corresponding to **super-**.

sur-[2] occasional variant of **sub-** (by assimilation) before *r*.

surcharge /'sɜtʃadʒ/ *n.*, /'sɜtʃadʒ, sɜ'tʃadʒ/ *v.*, **-charged**, **-charging**. **1.** an additional sum added to the usual cost, in restaurants, etc. – *v.t.* **2.** to subject to an additional or extra charge (for payment). **3.** to show an omission in (an account) of something that operates as a charge against the accounting party.

sure /ʃɔ/ *adj.*, **surer**, **surest**, *adv.* – *adj.* **1.** free from apprehension or doubt as to the reliability, character, action, etc., of something. **2.** confident, as of something expected. **3.** worthy of confidence; reliable. **4.** firm or stable. **5.** unerring; never missing, slipping, etc. **6.** inevitable. – *adv.* **7.** *Colloquial* surely, undoubtedly, or certainly.

surely /'ʃɔli/ *adv.* **1.** in a sure manner. **2.** (in emphatic utterances that are not necessarily sustained by fact) assuredly. **3.** inevitably or without fail.

surety /'ʃɔrəti, 'ʃurəti/ *n.*, *pl.* **-ties**. security against loss or damage; security for the fulfilment of an obligation, the payment of a debt, etc.; a pledge, guarantee, or bond.

surf /sɜf/ *n.* **1.** the swell of the sea which breaks upon a shore or upon shoals. – *v.i.* **2.** to engage in surfing. – *v.t.* **3.** *Computers* to explore (an information network): *to surf the Internet.*

surface /'sɜfəs/ *n.*, *adj.*, *v.*, **-faced**, **-facing**. – *n.* **1.** the outer face, or outside, of a thing. **2.** extent or area of outer face; superficial area. – *adj.* **3.** of, on, or relating to the surface. **4.** superficial; external; apparent, rather than real. **5.** of, on, or relating to land and/or sea. – *v.t.* **6.** to finish as to surface; give a particular kind of surface to; make even or smooth. – *v.i.* **7.** to rise to the surface.

surfboard /'sɜfbɔd/ *n.* a long, narrow board used by surfers in riding waves towards the shore.

surfeit /'sɜfət/ *n.* **1.** excess; an excessive amount. **2.** general disgust caused by excess or satiety.

surfing /'sɜfɪŋ/ *n.* **1.** the sport in which one paddles a surfboard out over the surf, and then attempts to ride on or with a wave towards the shore. **2.** Also, **body-surfing**. the sport of swimming in the surf, and especially of riding waves, allowing oneself to be carried along by the force of the water.

surge /sɜdʒ/ *n.*, *v.*, **surged**, **surging**. – *n.* **1.** a strong forward or upward movement, rush, or sweep, like that of swelling or rolling waves. – *v.i.* **2.** to rise or roll in waves, or like waves.

surgeon /'sɜdʒən/ *n.* a medical practitioner or physician qualified to practise surgery.

surgery /'sɜdʒəri/ *n.*, *pl.* **-geries**. **1.** the art, practice, or work of treating diseases, injuries, or deformities by manual operation or instrumental appliances. **2.** the consulting room of a medical practitioner, dentist, or the like. – **surgical**, *adj.*

surgical appliance /ˈsɜdʒɪkəl/ *n.* any device designed to be worn to support a damaged or deformed part of the body.

surly /ˈsɜli/ *adj.*, **-lier**, **-liest**. churlishly rude or ill-humoured.

surmise /sɜˈmaɪz/ *v.*, **-mised**, **-mising** /sɜˈmaɪz, ˈsɜmaɪz/ *n.* – *v.t.* **1.** to think or infer without certain or strong evidence. – *n.* **2.** a matter of conjecture.

surmount /sɜˈmaʊnt/ *v.t.* **1.** to get over or across (barriers, obstacles, etc.). **2.** to be on top of or above.

surname /ˈsɜneɪm/ *n.* the name which a person has in common with the other members of his or her family, as distinguished from his or her Christian or first name; a family name.

surpass /sɜˈpas/ *v.t.* to go beyond in amount, extent, or degree.

surplus /ˈsɜpləs/ *n.* **1.** that which remains above what is used or needed. **2.** *Accounting* the excess of assets over liabilities accumulated throughout the existence of a business, excepting assets against which stock certificates have been issued.

surprise /səˈpraɪz/ *v.*, **-prised**, **-prising**, *n.*, *adj.* – *v.t.* **1.** to catch (a person, etc.) in the act of doing something; discover (a thing) suddenly. **2.** to assail, attack, or capture suddenly or without warning. **3.** to strike with a sudden feeling of wonder. – *n.* **4.** a sudden and unexpected event, action, or the like. **5.** the state or feeling of being surprised as by something unexpected. – *adj.* **6.** sudden and unexpected.

surrender /səˈrɛndə/ *v.t.* **1.** to yield (something) to the possession or power of another. – *v.i.* **2.** to give oneself up, as into the power of another or of an emotion, course of action, etc.; submit or yield. – *n.* **3.** the act of surrendering.

surreptitious /sʌrəpˈtɪʃəs/ *adj.* obtained, done, made, etc., by stealth.

surrogate /ˈsʌrəgət/ *n.*, /ˈsʌrəgeɪt/ *v.*, **-gated**, **-gating**. – *n.* **1.** a substitute. – *v.t.* **2.** to put into the place of another as a successor, substitute, or deputy; substitute for another.

surround /səˈraʊnd/ *v.t.* **1.** to enclose on all sides, or encompass. – *n.* **2.** a border which surrounds.

surtax /ˈsɜtæks/ *n.* **1.** one of a graded series of additional taxes levied on incomes exceeding a certain amount. **2.** an additional or extra tax on something already taxed.

surveillance /sɜˈveɪləns/ *n.* watch kept over a person, etc.

survey /sɜˈveɪ, ˈsɜveɪ/ *v.*, /ˈsɜveɪ/ *n.*, *pl.* **-veys**. – *v.t.* **1.** to take a general or comprehensive view of. **2.** to view in detail, especially to inspect or examine formally or officially in order to ascertain condition, value, etc. **3.** to collect sample opinions, facts, figures or the like in order to estimate the total overall situation. – *n.* **4.** the act of surveying; a comprehensive view. **5.** a formal or official examination. **6.** a partial poll or gathering of sample opinions, facts or figures in order to estimate the total or overall situation.

survive /səˈvaɪv/ *v.*, **-vived**, **-viving**. – *v.i.* **1.** to remain alive or in existence after the death of someone or after the cessation of something or the occurrence of some event; continue to live. – *v.t.* **2.** to outlive. – **survivor**, *n.* – **survival**, *n.*

susceptible /səˈsɛptəbəl/ *adj.* **1.** capable of receiving, admitting, undergoing, or being affected by, something (fol. by *of* or *to*). **2.** impressionable. – **susceptibility**, *n.*

suspect /səˈspɛkt/ *v.*, /ˈsʌspɛkt/ *n.*, *adj.* – *v.t.* **1.** to imagine to be guilty, false, counterfeit, undesirable, defective, bad, etc., with insufficient proof or with no proof. **2.** to imagine to be the case or to be likely; surmise. – *v.i.* **3.** to imagine something, especially something evil, wrong, or undesirable, to be the case; have suspicion. – *n.* **4.** one suspected; a person suspected of a crime, offence, or the like. – *adj.* **5.** suspected; open to suspicion.

suspend /səˈspɛnd/ *v.t.* **1.** to hang by attachment to something above. **2.** to defer or postpone. **3.** to cause to cease, or bring to a stop or stay, usually for a time. **4.** to debar, usually for a time, from the exercise of an office or function or the enjoyment of a privilege. – *v.i.* **5.** to come to a stop, usually temporarily; cease from operation for a time. **6.** to stop payment; be unable to meet financial obligations.

suspender /səˈspɛndə/ *n.* a strap with fastenings to support women's stockings.

suspense /səˈspɛns/ *n.* a state of mental uncertainty, as in awaiting a decision or outcome, usually with more or less apprehension or anxiety.

suspense account *n.* an account in which items are entered which, for some reason, cannot at once be placed in the account to which they are intended to go.

suspension /səˈspɛnʃən/ *n.* **1.** the act of suspending. **2.** the state of being suspended. **3.** stoppage of payment of debts, etc., through financial inability, or insolvency. **4.** something on or by which something else is hung. **5.** the arrangement of springs, shock absorbers, hangers, etc., in a motor vehicle.

suspicion /səˈspɪʃən/ *n.* **1.** the act of suspecting; imagination of the existence of guilt, fault, falsity, defect, or the like, on slight evidence or without evidence. **2.** a vague notion of something. **3.** a slight trace. – **suspicious**, *adj.*

suss /sʌs/ *v.t.* *Colloquial* to attempt to determine the possibilities of a situation.

sustain /səˈsteɪn/ *v.t.* **1.** to hold or bear up from below. **2.** to bear (a burden, charge, etc.). **3.** to undergo, experience, or suffer (injury, loss, etc.). **4.** to keep up or keep going, as an action or process. **5.** to supply with food and drink, or the necessities of life, as persons. **6.** to support by aid or countenance, as a person or cause.

sustainable development *n.* economic development designed to meet present needs while also taking into account future costs, including costs to the environment and depletion of natural resources.

sustenance /ˈsʌstənəns/ *n.* means of sustaining life; nourishment.

suture /'sutʃə/ *n.*, *v.*, **-tured**, **-turing**. – *n.* **1.** a sewing together, or a joining as by sewing. – *v.t.* **2.** to unite by or as by a suture.

svelte /svɛlt, sfɛlt/ *adj.* slender, especially gracefully slender in figure; lithe.

swaddle /'swɒdl/ *v.t.*, **-dled**, **-dling**. to bind (an infant, especially a newborn infant) with long, narrow strips of cloth.

swag /swæg/ *n.* **1.** a bundle or roll containing the bedding and personal belongings of a traveller through the bush, a miner, etc. **2.** *Colloquial* an unspecified but large number or quantity.

swagger /'swægə/ *v.i.* to walk or strut with a defiant or insolent air.

swallow[1] /'swɒloʊ/ *v.t.* **1.** to take into the stomach through the throat or gullet (oesophagus), as food, drink, or other substances. **2.** to take in so as to envelop. **3.** *Colloquial* to accept without question or suspicion. – *v.i.* **4.** to perform the act of swallowing. – *n.* **5.** the act of swallowing.

swallow[2] /'swɒloʊ/ *n.* a small, migratory, long-winged passerine bird notable for its swift, graceful flight.

swam /swæm/ *v.* past tense of **swim**.

swamp /swɒmp/ *n.* **1.** a piece or tract of wet, spongy land. – *v.t.* **2.** to flood or drench with water or the like.

swan /swɒn/ *n.* a large, stately swimming bird with a long, slender neck.

swank /swæŋk/ *n.* *Colloquial* dashing smartness, as in bearing, appearance, etc.; style.

swap /swɒp/ *v.*, **swapped**, **swapping**, *n.* – *v.t.* **1.** to exchange, barter, or trade, as one thing for another. – *v.i.* **2.** to make an exchange. – *n.* **3.** an exchange. Also, **swop**.

swarm[1] /swɔm/ *n.* **1.** a body of bees settled together, as in a hive. **2.** a great number of things or persons, especially in motion. – *v.i.* **3.** to move about, along, forth, etc., in great numbers, as things or persons. **4.** (of a place) to be thronged or overrun; abound or teem (fol. by *with*).

swarm[2] /swɔm/ *v.i.*, *v.t.* to climb (a tree, pole, or the like) by clasping it with the hands or arms and legs and drawing oneself up; shin (usually fol. by *up*).

swarthy /'swɔði/ *adj.*, **-thier**, **-thiest**. dark-coloured, now especially as the skin, complexion, etc., of a person.

swashbuckler /'swɒʃbʌklə/ *n.* a swaggering swordsman or bully. Also, **swasher**.

swat /swɒt/ *v.t.*, **swatted**, **swatting**. *Colloquial* to hit with a smart or violent blow.

swathe /sweɪð/ *v.*, **swathed**, **swathing**, *n.* – *v.t.* **1.** to wrap, bind, or swaddle with bands of some material. – *n.* **2.** a band of linen or the like in which something is wrapped; a wrapping; a bandage.

sway /sweɪ/ *v.i.* **1.** to move to and fro, as something fixed at one end or resting on a support; swing to and fro. **2.** to fluctuate or vacillate, as in opinion. – *v.t.* **3.** to cause to sway. **4.** to cause (the mind, etc., or the person) to incline or turn in a specified way. – *n.* **5.** rule; dominion. **6.** dominating power or influence.

swear /swɛə/ *v.*, **swore**, **sworn**, **swearing**. – *v.i.* **1.** to make a solemn declaration with an appeal to God or some superhuman being in confirmation of what is declared. **2.** to engage or promise on oath or in a solemn manner. **3.** to use profane or taboo oaths or language. – *v.t.* **4.** to declare or affirm by swearing by a deity, some sacred object, etc. **5.** to affirm or say with solemn earnestness or great emphasis. **6.** to promise or undertake on oath or in a solemn manner; vow. **7.** **swear in,** to admit to office or service by administering an oath.

sweat /swɛt/ *v.*, **sweat** *or* **sweated**, **sweating**, *n.* – *v.i.* **1.** to excrete watery fluid through the pores of the skin, as from heat, exertion, etc.; perspire, especially freely or profusely. **2.** *Colloquial* to exert oneself strenuously; work hard. – *v.t.* **3.** to exude (moisture, etc.) in drops or small particles. **4.** to send forth or get rid of with or like perspiration (often fol. by *out* or *off*). **5.** **sweat it out,** *Colloquial* to hold out; endure until the end. – *n.* **6.** the process of sweating or perspiring. **7.** the secretions of sweat glands; the product of sweating.

sweated /'swɛtəd/ *adj.* underpaid and overworked.

sweater /'swɛtə/ *n.* a knitted jumper, usually of wool.

sweatshirt /'swɛtˌʃɜt/ *n.* a loose pullover.

sweep /swip/ *v.*, **swept**, **sweeping**, *n.* – *v.t.* **1.** to move, drive, or bring, by passing a broom, brush, or the like over the surface occupied, or as the broom or other object does. **2.** to pass or draw (something) over a surface, or about, along, etc., with a steady, continuous stroke or movement. **3.** to clear or clean (a floor, room, chimney, path, etc.) of dirt, litter, etc., by means of a broom or the like. – *v.i.* **4.** to sweep a floor, room, etc., as with a broom, or as a broom does. **5.** to move steadily and strongly or swiftly (fol. by *down*, *over*, etc.). **6.** to walk in long, trailing garments. **7.** to extend in a continuous or curving stretch, as a road, a shore, fields, etc. – *n.* **8.** the act of sweeping, especially a moving, removing, clearing, etc., by or as by the use of a broom. **9.** a swinging or curving movement or stroke, as of the arm or a weapon, oar, etc. **10.** a continuous extent or stretch. **11.** the motion of the spot across the screen of a cathode-ray tube.

sweepstake /'swipsteɪk/ *n.* a method of gambling, as on the outcome of a horserace, in which each participant contributes a stake, usually by buying a numbered ticket entitling the winner to draw the name of a competitor, the winnings being provided from the stake money. Also, **sweepstakes**.

sweet /swit/ *adj.* **1.** pleasing to the taste, especially having the pleasant taste or flavour characteristic of sugar, honey, etc. **2.** pleasing or agreeable; yielding pleasure or enjoyment; delightful. **3.** pleasant in disposition or manners; amiable; kind or gracious as a person, action, etc. **4.** dear; beloved; precious. – *adv.* **5.** in a sweet manner; sweetly. – *n.* **6.** that which is sweet. **7.** Also, **sweetie**. any of various small confections made wholly or partly from sugar. **8.** (*often pl.*) any sweet dish, as a pudding, tart, etc., served at the end of a meal. **9.** a beloved person; darling; sweetheart.

sweetbread /'switbrɛd/ *n.* **1.** the pancreas

of an animal, especially a calf or a lamb, used for food. **2.** the thymus gland likewise so used.

sweet corn *n.* the unripe and tender ears of maize, especially when used as a table vegetable and when the kernels have been removed from the cob.

sweetheart /'swithat/ *n.* a beloved person (often used in affectionate address).

sweetmeat /'switmit/ *n.* a sweet delicacy.

sweet potato *n.* a plant cultivated for its edible root.

sweet tooth *n. Colloquial* a strong liking for sweets, sweet dishes, etc.

swell /swɛl/ *v.,* **swelled**, **swollen** *or* **swelled**, **swelling**, *n., adj.* – *v.i.* **1.** to grow in bulk, as by absorption of moisture, by inflation or distention, by addition of material in the process of growth, or the like. **2.** to rise in waves, as the sea. **3.** to grow in amount, degree, force, or the like. **4.** to increase in amount, degree, force, etc. **5.** to puff up with pride. – *n.* **6.** increase in bulk; inflation or distention. **7.** a part that bulges out, or a protuberant part. **8.** a wave, especially when long and unbroken, or such waves collectively. **9.** a gradually rising elevation of the land. **10.** increase in amount, degree, force, etc. **11.** a person of high social standing. – *adj. Colloquial* **12.** (of things) stylish; elegant; grand. **13.** first-rate; excellent.

swelling /'swɛlɪŋ/ *n.* a swollen part; a protuberance or prominence.

swelter /'swɛltə/ *v.i.* to suffer or languish with oppressive heat.

swept /swɛpt/ *v.* past tense and past participle of **sweep**.

swerve /swɜv/ *v.i.,* **swerved**, **swerving**. to turn aside abruptly in movement or direction.

swift /swɪft/ *adj.* **1.** moving with great speed or velocity; fleet; rapid. – *n.* **2.** any of several rapidly flying birds.

swill /swɪl/ *n.* **1.** liquid or partly liquid food for animals, especially kitchen refuse given to pigs. **2.** any liquid matter; slops. – *v.t.* **3.** to wash or cleanse by flooding with water.

swim /swɪm/ *v.,* **swam**, **swum**, **swimming**, *n.* – *v.i.* **1.** to move on or in water or other liquid in any way, especially on the surface. **2.** to be immersed or steeped in, or overflowed or flooded with, a liquid. **3.** to be dizzy or giddy; have a whirling sensation; seem to whirl. – *v.t.* **4.** to perform (a particular stroke) in swimming. – *n.* **5. in the swim,** actively engaged in current affairs, social activities, etc.

swimmingly /'swɪmɪŋli/ *adv.* without difficulty; with great success.

swindle /'swɪndl/ *v.,* **-dled**, **-dling**, *n.* – *v.t.* **1.** to cheat (a person) out of money, etc. – *n.* **2.** a fraudulent transaction or scheme.

swine /swaɪn/ *n., pl.* **swine**. **1.** the domestic pig. **2.** a contemptible person.

swing[1] /swɪŋ/ *v.,* **swung**, **swinging**, *n.* – *v.t.* **1.** to cause to move to and fro, sway, or oscillate, as something suspended from above. **2.** to cause to move in alternate directions, or in either direction, about a fixed point or line of support, as a door on its hinges. **3.** to suspend so as to hang freely, as a hammock or a door. **4.** to sway, influence, or manage as desired. – *v.i.* **5.** to move to and fro, as something suspended from above, as a pendulum. **6.** to move to and fro on a swing, as for amusement. **7.** to move in alternate directions, as a gate on its hinges. **8.** to move in a curve as if about a central point, as around a corner. **9.** to change or shift one's attention, opinion, interest, etc.; fluctuate. **10.** to aim at or hit something with a sweeping movement of the arm. – *n.* **11.** the act or the manner of swinging; movement in alternate directions, or in a particular direction. **12.** the amount of such movement. **13.** active operation. **14.** a seat suspended from above as in a loop of rope or between ropes or rods, in which one may sit and swing to and fro for amusement.

swing[2] /swɪŋ/ *n., v.,* **swung**, **swinging**. – *n.* **1.** Also, **swing music**. a smooth, orchestral type of jazz popular in the 1930s, often arranged for big bands. – *v.i.* **2.** *Colloquial* to be lively or modern.

swipe /swaɪp/ *n., v.,* **swiped**, **swiping**. – *n.* **1.** *Colloquial* a sweeping stroke; a stroke with full swing of the arms, as in cricket or golf. – *v.t.* **2.** *Colloquial* to strike with a sweeping blow. **3.** *Colloquial* to steal. **4.** to move (a card with a magnetic strip) through the slot of an electronic device. – *v.i.* **5.** *Colloquial* to make a sweeping stroke.

swirl /swɜl/ *v.i.* to move about or along with a whirling motion.

swish /swɪʃ/ *v.i.* **1.** to move with or make a sibilant sound. – *n.* **2.** a swishing movement or sound. – *adj.* **3.** Also, **swishy**. *Colloquial* smart; stylish; glamorous.

switch /swɪtʃ/ *n.* **1.** a slender, flexible shoot, rod, etc., used especially in whipping, beating, etc. **2.** *Electricity* a device for turning on or off or directing an electric current, or making or breaking a circuit. **3.** *Colloquial* → **switchboard**. – *v.t.* **4.** to whip or beat with a switch or the like; lash. **5.** to move, swing, or whisk (a cane, a fishing line, etc.) like a switch or with a swift, lashing stroke. **6.** to exchange; shift. **7. switch on,** to cause (an electric current) to flow or (an electric appliance) to operate. **8. switch off,** to cause an electric current or appliance to stop. – *v.i.* **9.** to strike with or as with a switch. **10.** to change direction or course; turn, shift, or change.

switchboard /'swɪtʃbɔd/ *n.* an arrangement of switches, plugs, and jacks mounted on a board or frame enabling an operator to make temporary connections between telephone users.

swivel /'swɪvəl/ *n.* a fastening device which allows the thing fastened to turn round freely upon it.

swollen /'swoʊlən/ *v.* past participle of **swell**.

swoon /swun/ *v.i.* to faint; lose consciousness.

swoop /swup/ *v.i.* **1.** to sweep through the air, as a bird or a bat, especially down upon prey. **2.** to come down in a sudden swift attack (often fol. by *down* or *on* or *upon*). – *v.t.* **3.** to take, lift, or remove, with, or as with, a sweeping motion (often fol. by *up*). – *n.* **4.** the act of swooping; a sudden, swift descent. **5. at one fell swoop,** all at once.

sword /sɔd/ *n.* a weapon with a long, straight or slightly curved blade, sharp-edged on one side or both sides, with one end pointed and the other fixed in a hilt or handle.

swore /swɔ/ *v.* past tense of **swear**.

sworn /swɔn/ *v.* **1.** past participle of **swear**. – *adj.* **2.** bound by or as by an oath.

swot /swɒt/ *v.*, **swotted**, **swotting**, *n. Colloquial* – *v.i.* **1.** to study hard. – *n.* **2.** someone who studies hard.

swum /swʌm/ *v.* past participle of **swim**.

swung /swʌŋ/ *v.* past tense and past participle of **swing**.

sy- variant of **syn-**.

sycophant /'sɪkəfənt, 'saɪ-, -fænt/ *n.* a self-seeking flatterer; a fawning, servile parasite.

syl- variant of **syn-** (by assimilation) before *l.*

syllable /'sɪləbəl/ *n.* **1.** *Phonetics* a segment of speech uttered with a single impulse of air pressure from the lungs. **2.** the least portion or amount of speech or writing. – **syllabic**, *adj.*

syllabus /'sɪləbəs/ *n.*, *pl.* **-buses**, **-bi** /-baɪ/. an outline or summary of a course of studies, lectures, etc.

sym- variant of **syn-**, before *b*, *p*, and *m*, as in *sympathy*.

symbiosis /sɪmbi'oʊsəs, -baɪ-/ *n. Biology* the living together of two species of organisms. – **symbiotic**, *adj.*

symbol /'sɪmbəl/ *n.* something used or regarded as standing for or representing something else; an emblem, token, or sign. – **symbolic**, *adj.*

symbolise = symbolize /'sɪmbəlaɪz/ *v.t.*, **-lised**, **-lising**. **1.** to be a symbol of; stand for, or represent, as a symbol does. **2.** to represent by a symbol or symbols.

symmetry /'sɪmətri/ *n.*, *pl.* **-tries**. the correspondence, in size, form, and arrangement, of parts on opposite sides of a plane, line, or point. – **symmetrical**, *adj.*

sympathetic /sɪmpə'θɛtɪk/ *adj.* **1.** characterised by, proceeding from, exhibiting, or feeling sympathy; sympathising; compassionate. **2.** looking with favour or liking upon (often fol. by *to* or *towards*).

sympathise = sympathize /'sɪmpəθaɪz/ *v.i.*, **-thised**, **-thising**. **1.** to feel a compassionate sympathy, as for suffering or trouble (often fol. by *with*). **2.** to agree, correspond, or accord.

sympathy /'sɪmpəθi/ *n.*, *pl.* **-thies**. **1.** community of or agreement in feeling. **2.** the fact or the power of entering into the feelings of another. **3.** agreement, consonance, or accord. **4.** *Physiology*, *Pathology* the relation between parts or organs whereby a condition, affection, or disorder of one part induces some effect in another.

symphony /'sɪmfəni/ *n.*, *pl.* **-nies**. *Music* an elaborate instrumental composition written for an orchestra.

symposium /sɪm'poʊziəm/ *n.*, *pl.* **-siums**, **-sia** /-ziə/. a meeting or conference for discussion of some subject.

symptom /'sɪmptəm/ *n.* a sign or indication of something.

symptomatic /sɪmptə'mætɪk/ *adj.* of the nature of or constituting a symptom; indicative (often fol. by *of*).

syn- a prefix in learned words having the same function as **co-** (def. 1), as in *synthesis*, *synoptic*. Also, **sy-**, **syl-**, **sym-**, **sys-**.

synagogue /'sɪnəgɒg/ *n.* a Jewish house of worship.

synchronise = synchronize /'sɪŋkrənaɪz/ *v.*, **-nised**, **-nising**. – *v.i.* **1.** to occur at the same time, or coincide or agree in time. – *v.t.* **2.** to cause to synchronise. – **synchronisation**, *n.*

syndic /'sɪndɪk/ *n.* a person chosen to represent and transact business for a society, corporation, or the like.

syndical /'sɪndɪkəl/ *adj.* denoting or relating to a union of persons engaged in a particular trade.

syndicate /'sɪndɪkət/ *n.*, /'sɪndɪkeɪt/ *v.*, **-cated**, **-cating**. – *n.* **1.** a combination of persons, as business associates, commercial firms, etc., formed for the purpose of carrying out some project, especially one requiring large resources of capital. – *v.t.* **2.** to combine into a syndicate. **3.** *Journalism* to publish simultaneously, or supply for simultaneous publication, in a number of newspapers or other periodicals in different places.

syndrome /'sɪndroʊm/ *n.* the pattern of symptoms in a disease or the like; a number of characteristic symptoms occurring together.

synonym /'sɪnənɪm/ *n.* a word having the same, or nearly the same, meaning as another in the language, as *joyful*, *elated*, *glad*.

synopsis /sə'nɒpsəs/ *n.*, *pl.* **-opses** /-ɒpsiz/. a brief or condensed statement giving a general view of some subject.

synoptic chart /sə'nɒptɪk/ *n.* a chart showing distribution of meteorological conditions over a region at a given moment.

syntax /'sɪntæks/ *n. Grammar* the patterns of formation of sentences and phrases from words in a particular language.

synthesis /'sɪnθəsəs/ *n.*, *pl.* **-theses** /-θəsiz/. **1.** the combination of parts or elements, as material substances or objects of thought, into a complex whole (opposed to *analysis*). **2.** a complex whole made up of parts or elements combined.

synthesise = synthesize /'sɪnθəsaɪz/ *v.t.*, **-sised**, **-sising**. **1.** to make up by combining parts or elements. **2.** to combine into a complex whole. **3.** *Chemistry* to manufacture (a complex product, especially a product resembling one of natural origin) by combining simple substances.

synthetic /sɪn'θɛtɪk/ *adj.* **1.** of, relating to, or involving synthesis (opposed to *analytic*). **2.** (of materials, etc.) made by chemical process, as opposed to being of natural origin.

syphilis /'sɪfələs/ *n.* a chronic, infectious venereal disease communicated by contact or heredity.

syphon /'saɪfən/ *n.*, *v.i.*, *v.t.* → **siphon**.

syringe /sə'rɪndʒ, 'sɪrɪndʒ/ *n. Medicine* a small tube used for injecting fluids into the body, etc.

syrup /'sɪrəp/ *n.* any of various sweet, more or less viscid liquids.

sys- variant of **syn-**, before *s.*

system /'sɪstəm/ *n.* **1.** an assemblage or combination of things or parts forming a complex or unitary whole. **2.** a coordinated body of methods, or a complex scheme or plan of procedure. **3.** *Biology* the entire human or animal body. **4.** a method or scheme of classification. **5.** (*also pl.*) *Computers* (in data-processing) the interrelation of personnel, procedure, hardware, and software, which combine to accomplish a set of specific functions. **6.** *Colloquial* society at large or an organisation within it.

systematic /sɪstə'mætɪk/ *adj.* having, showing, or involving a system, method, or plan.

systematise = systematize /'sɪstəmətaɪz/ *v.t.*, **-tised**, **-tising**. to arrange in or according to a system; reduce to a system; make systematic.

systems analysis *n.* the analysis of an activity or project, usually with the aid of a computer, to determine its aims, methods and effectiveness. – **systems analyst**, *n.*

systems engineer *n.* an engineer who is concerned with the design of systems in the light of systems analysis and information theory.

T t

T, t /ti/ *n., pl.* **T's** *or* **Ts**, **t's** *or* **ts**. the 20th letter of the English alphabet.

-t a suffix forming the past tense or past participle of certain verbs; an equivalent of **-ed**.

tab /tæb/ *n.* **1.** a small flap, strap, loop, or similar appendage, as on a garment, etc. **2.** a stiffened projecting piece from file, paper, or the like, for ready identification; tag.

tabby /ˈtæbi/ *n., pl.* **-bies**. a cat with a striped or brindled coat.

tabernacle /ˈtæbənækəl/ *n.* **1.** the tent used by the Jews as a portable sanctuary before their final settlement in Palestine. **2.** any place of worship, especially one designed for a large congregation.

table /ˈteɪbəl/ *n., v.,* **-bled**, **-bling**. – *n.* **1.** an article of furniture consisting of a flat top resting on legs or on a pillar. **2.** a flat or plane surface; a level area. **3.** an arrangement of words, numbers, or signs, or combinations of them, as the multiplication tables, to exhibit a set of facts or relations in a definite, compact, and comprehensive form. – *v.t.* **4.** to enter in or form into a table or list. **5.** to place or lay on a table.

tableau /ˈtæbloʊ/ *n., pl.* **-leaux**, **-leaus**. a picturesque grouping of persons or objects; a striking scene.

tableland /ˈteɪbəllænd/ *n.* an elevated and generally level region.

tablespoon /ˈteɪbəlspun/ *n.* a large spoon.

tablet /ˈtæblət/ *n.* **1.** a number of sheets of writing paper or the like fastened together at the edge; a pad. **2.** a small, flat slab or surface, especially one bearing or intended to bear an inscription, carving, or the like. **3.** a small, flat or flattish, cake or piece of some solid or solidified substance, as a drug, chemical or the like.

tabloid /ˈtæblɔɪd/ *n.* a newspaper, about one half the ordinary page size, emphasising pictures and concise writing.

taboo /təˈbu, tæ-/ *adj., n., pl.* **-boos**, *v.,* **-booed**, **-booing**. – *adj.* **1.** forbidden to general use; placed under a prohibition or ban. – *n.* **2.** a prohibition or interdiction of anything; exclusion from use or practice. – *v.t.* **3.** to put under a taboo; prohibit or forbid.

tabular /ˈtæbjələ/ *adj.* **1.** relating to or of the nature of a table or tabulated arrangement. **2.** having the form of a table, tablet, or tablature.

tabulate /ˈtæbjəleɪt/ *v.t.,* **-lated**, **-lating**. to put or form into a table, scheme, or synopsis; formulate tabularly.

tacit /ˈtæsət/ *adj.* **1.** silent; saying nothing. **2.** not openly expressed, but implied.

taciturn /ˈtæsətɜn/ *adj.* inclined to silence, or reserved in speech.

tack /tæk/ *n.* **1.** a short, sharp-pointed nail or pin. **2.** a long temporary stitch. **3.** *Nautical* **a.** the direction or course of a ship in relation to the position of its sails. **b.** a course obliquely against the wind. **4.** a course of action or conduct, especially one differing from some preceding or other course. **5.** the equipment collectively which pertains to the saddling and harnessing of horses. – *v.t.* **6.** to fasten by a tack or tacks. **7.** to append or annex (usually fol. by *on* or *on to*). – *v.i.* **8.** *Nautical* to change the course of a ship by bringing its head into the wind and then causing it to fall off on the other side.

tackle /ˈtækəl/ *n., v.,* **-led**, **-ling**. – *n.* **1.** equipment, apparatus, or gear, especially for fishing. **2.** a mechanism or apparatus, as a rope and block or a combination of ropes and blocks, for hoisting, lowering, and shifting objects or materials. **3.** an act of tackling, as in football. – *v.t.* **4.** to undertake to deal with, master, solve, etc. **5.** *Rugby Football, etc.* to seize and pull down (an opponent having the ball).

tacky /ˈtæki/ *adj.,* **-ier**, **-iest**. *Colloquial* **1.** shabby; dowdy. **2.** superficially attractive but lacking quality or craftsmanship.

tact /tækt/ *n.* a keen sense of what to say or do to avoid giving offence.

tactic /ˈtæktɪk/ *n.* a plan or procedure for achieving a desired end.

tactile /ˈtæktaɪl/ *adj.* of or relating to the organs or sense of touch.

tad /tæd/ *n.* a small amount.

tadpole /ˈtædpoʊl/ *n.* the aquatic larva or immature form of frogs, toads, etc.

tag[1] /tæg/ *n., v.,* **tagged**, **tagging**. – *n.* **1.** a piece or strip of strong paper, leather, or the like, for attaching by one end to something as a mark or label. **2.** any small hanging or loosely attached part or piece; tatter. – *v.t.* **3.** to append as a tag to something else. – *v.i.* **4.** to follow closely; go along or about as a follower (usually fol. by *along*).

tag[2] /tæg/ *n.* a type of wrestling.

tail[1] /teɪl/ *n.* **1.** the hindmost part of an animal especially when forming a distinct flexible appendage to the trunk. **2.** something resembling or suggesting this in shape or position. **3.** the hinder, bottom, or concluding part of anything; the rear. **4.** *Colloquial* (*pl.*) the reverse of a coin. **5.** *Colloquial* the buttocks. **6.** *Colloquial* a person who follows another, especially someone who is employed to do so in order to observe or hinder escape. – *v.t.* **7.** to dock the tail of. **8.** *Colloquial* to follow in order to hinder escape or to observe.

tail[2] /teɪl/ *n.* *Law* the limitation of an estate to a person and the heirs of his or her body, or some particular class of such heirs.

tailor /ˈteɪlə/ *n.* **1.** someone whose business it is to make or mend outer garments, especially for men. **2.** Also, **tailer**, **taylor**. an Australian sport fish.

taint /teɪnt/ *n.* **1.** a trace of infection, contamination, or the like. – *v.t.* **2.** to infect, contaminate, or corrupt. **3.** to sully or tarnish.

taipan /ˈtaɪpæn/ *n.* a long-fanged, highly venomous snake.

take /teɪk/ *v.,* **took**, **taken**, **taking**, *n.* – *v.t.* **1.** to get into one's hands, possession, control, etc. **2.** to seize, catch, or capture. **3.** to select; pick out from a number. **4.** to obtain by making payment. **5.** to carry off or remove (fol. by *away*, etc.). **6.** to subtract or deduct. **7.** to carry or convey. **8.** to have recourse to (a vehicle, etc.) as a means of progression or travel. **9.** to conduct or lead. **10.** to absorb or become impregnated with (a colour, etc.). **11.** to proceed to deal with in some manner. **12.** to proceed to occupy. **13.** to occupy, use up, or consume (space, material, time, etc.). **14.** to attract and hold. **15.** to write down (notes, a copy, etc.). **16.** to make (a reproduction, picture, or photograph of something). **17.** to make or perform (a measurement, observation, etc.). **18.** to assume the obligation of (a vow, pledge, etc.); perform or discharge (a part, service, etc.). **19.** to assume or adopt as one's own (a part or side in a contest, etc.); assume or appropriate as if by right. **20.** to accept and comply with (advice, etc.). **21.** *Grammar* to have by usage, either as part of itself or with it in construction (a particular form, accent, etc., or a case, mode, etc.), as a word or the like. – *v.i.* **22.** to catch or engage, as a mechanical device. **23.** to strike root, or begin to grow, as a plant. **24.** to adhere, as ink, etc. **25.** to have the intended result or affect as a medicine, inoculation, etc. **26.** to become (sick or ill). **27. take off, a.** to remove, as of clothing; to undress. **b.** to leave the ground, as an aeroplane. **c.** *Colloquial* to imitate or mimic. **28. take place,** to happen; occur. – *n.* **29.** an act or instance of taking. **30.** that which is taken. **31.** the quantity of fish, etc. taken at one time. **32.** *Film, etc.* a scene or a portion of a scene photographed at one time without any interruption or break. **33.** *Colloquial* a cheat; swindle.

takeover /'teɪkoʊvə/ *n.* acquisition of control, especially of a business company, by the purchase of the majority of its shares.

takings /'teɪkɪŋz/ *pl. n.* receipts.

talc /tælk/ *n.* a soft greenish grey mineral used in making lubricants, talcum powder, electrical insulation, etc. Also, **talcum** /'tælkəm/.

talcum powder *n.* powdered talc or soapstone, usually perfumed for toilet use.

tale /teɪl/ *n.* a narrative purporting to relate the facts about some real or imaginary event.

talent /'tælənt/ *n.* a special natural ability or aptitude.

talisman /'tæləzmən/ *n., pl.* **-mans**. any amulet or charm.

talk /tɔk/ *v.i.* **1.** to speak or converse; perform the act of speaking. **2.** to make known by means of spoken words. – *v.t.* **3.** to express in words. **4.** to discuss. – *n.* **5.** the act of talking; speech; conversation, especially of a familiar or informal kind. **6.** a lecture or informal speech. **7.** report or rumour; gossip.

tall /tɔl/ *adj.* of more than average height.

tallow /'tæloʊ/ *n.* the fatty tissue or suet of animals.

tally /'tæli/ *n., pl.* **-lies**, *v.,* **-lied**, **lying**. – *n.* **1.** anything on which a score or account is kept. – *v.t.* **2.** to count or reckon up.

talon /'tælən/ *n.* a claw, especially of a bird of prey.

tambourine /tæmbə'rin/ *n.* a small drum with several pairs of metal discs (jingles) inserted into the frame.

tame /teɪm/ *adj.,* **tamer**, **tamest**, *v.,* **tamed**, **taming**. – *adj.* **1.** changed from the wild or savage state; domesticated. **2.** tractable, docile, or submissive, as a person, the disposition, etc. **3.** spiritless or pusillanimous. – *v.t.* **4.** to make tame; domesticate; make tractable; subdue. **5.** to soften; tone down.

tam-o'-shanter /tæm-ə-'ʃæntə/ *n.* a cap, of Scottish origin.

tamp /tæmp/ *v.t.* to force in or down by repeated, somewhat light strokes.

tamper /'tæmpə/ *v.i.* to meddle, especially for the purpose of altering, damaging, misusing, etc. (fol. by *with*).

tampon /'tæmpɒn/ *n.* **1.** a plug of cotton or the like inserted into an orifice, wound, etc., as to stop haemorrhage. **2.** a similar device used internally to absorb menstrual flow.

tan /tæn/ *v.,* **tanned**, **tanning**, *n.* – *v.t.* **1.** to convert (a hide) into a leather, especially by soaking or steeping in a bath prepared from bark, as wattle, etc., or synthetically. **2.** to make brown by exposure to ultraviolet rays, as of the sun. **3.** *Colloquial* to beat or thrash. – *n.* **4.** the brown colour imparted to the skin by exposure to the sun or open air; suntan.

tandem /'tændəm/ *adv.* **1.** one behind another; in single file. – *n.* **2.** a bicycle for two riders, having twin seats, pedals, etc.

tang /tæŋ/ *n.* **1.** a strong taste or flavour. **2.** a pungent or distinctive smell.

tangent /'tændʒənt/ *adj.* **1.** touching. – *n.* **2.** a sudden divergence from one course, thought, etc., to another.

tangerine /tændʒə'rin/ *n.* a small, loose-skinned variety of mandarin.

tangible /'tændʒəbəl/ *adj.* **1.** discernible by the touch; material or substantial. **2.** real or actual, rather than imaginary or visionary. **3.** (of an asset) capable of being possessed or realised; having the form of real property or chattels.

tangle /'tæŋgəl/ *v.,* **-gled**, **-gling**, *n.* – *v.t.* **1.** to bring together into a mass of confusedly interlaced or intertwisted threads, strands, or other like parts; snarl. – *v.i.* **2.** to be or become tangled. – *n.* **3.** a tangled condition.

tango /'tæŋgoʊ/ *n., pl.* **-gos**, *v.,* **-goed**, **-going**. – *n.* **1.** a dance of Spanish-American origin. – *v.i.* **2.** to dance the tango.

tank /tæŋk/ *n.* **1.** a large receptacle or structure for holding water or other liquid or a gas. **2.** *Military* an armoured, self-propelled combat vehicle, armed with cannon, and machine-guns and moving on caterpillar tracks.

tankard /'tæŋkəd/ *n.* a large drinking cup, now usually with a handle and (sometimes) a hinged cover.

tanker /'tæŋkə/ *n.* a ship, aircraft, road or rail vehicle designed to carry oil or other liquid in bulk.

tannin /'tænən/ *n.* a substance used in tanning.

tantalise = tantalize /'tæntəlaɪz/ *v.t.,* **-lised**, **-lising**. to torment with, or as with, the sight of something desired but out of reach; tease by arousing expectations that are repeatedly disappointed.

tantamount /'tæntəmaʊnt/ *adj.* equivalent,

as in value, force, effect, or signification.

tantrum /'tæntrəm/ *n.* a fit of ill temper or passion.

tap[1] /tæp/ *v.*, **tapped**, **tapping**, *n.* – *v.t.* **1.** to strike lightly but audibly; strike with slight blows. – *n.* **2.** a light but audible blow.

tap[2] /tæp/ *n.*, *v.*, **tapped**, **tapping**. – *n.* **1.** any device for controlling the flow of liquid from a pipe or the like by opening or closing an orifice; a cock. **2.** an instrument for cutting the thread of a female screw. – *v.t.* **3.** to draw off (liquid) by drawing out or opening a tap, or by piercing the container; draw liquid from (any vessel or reservoir). **4.** to gain or effect secret access to. **5.** to open outlets from (power lines, roads, pipes, etc.).

tape /teɪp/ *n.*, *v.*, **taped**, **taping**. – *n.* **1.** a long narrow strip of linen, cotton, or the like, used for tying garments, etc. **2.** a long narrow strip of paper, metal, etc. **3.** the ribbon of white paper on which a ticker prints quotations or news. – *v.t.* **4.** to furnish with a tape or tapes. **5.** to tape-record.

tape machine *n.* a telegraphic instrument which automatically prints share prices, market reports, etc., on a tape (**ticker tape**).

tape measure *n.* a long strip or ribbon, as of linen or steel, marked with subdivisions of the foot or metre for measuring.

taper /'teɪpə/ *v.i.* **1.** to become gradually slenderer towards one end. – *v.t.* **2.** to make gradually smaller towards one end. **3.** to reduce gradually. – *n.* **4.** gradual diminution of width or thickness in an elongated object. **5.** gradual decrease of force, capacity, etc. **6.** a long wick coated with wax, tallow, or the like, as for use in lighting candles or gas.

tape-reader /'teɪp-ridə/ *n.* *Computers* a machine that converts information on punched paper tape into electrical impulses as the tape is drawn through the machine.

tape recorder /'teɪp rəkɔdə/ *n.* a device for recording an electrical signal, especially one produced by sound.

tapestry /'tæpəstri/ *n.*, *pl.* **-tries**. a fabric consisting of a warp upon which coloured threads are woven by hand to produce a design, often pictorial, and used for wall hangings, furniture coverings, etc.

tape unit *n.* a machine that handles magnetic tape in a computer system.

tapeworm /'teɪpwɜm/ *n.* a parasitic flat or tapelike worm.

tapioca /tæpi'oʊkə/ *n.* a granular farinaceous food substance used for making puddings, etc.

taproot /'tæprut/ *n.* *Botany* a main root descending downwards from the radicle and giving off small lateral roots.

tar[1] /ta/ *n.*, *v.*, **tarred**, **tarring**. – *n.* **1.** any of various dark-coloured viscid products obtained by the destructive distillation of certain organic substances, such as coal, wood, etc. – *v.t.* **2.** to smear or cover with, or as with, tar.

tar[2] /ta/ *n.* *Colloquial* a sailor.

tarantula /tə'ræntʃələ/ *n.*, *pl.* **-las**, **-lae** /-li/. a large spider.

tardy /'tadi/ *adj.*, **-dier**, **-diest**. **1.** moving or acting slowly; slow; sluggish. **2.** late or behindhand.

tare /tɛə/ *n.* **1.** the weight of the wrapping, receptacle, or conveyance containing goods. **2.** the weight of a vehicle without cargo, passengers, etc.

target /'tagət/ *n.*, *v.*, **-eted** *or* **-etted**, **-eting** *or* **-etting**. – *n.* **1.** a device, usually marked with concentric circles, to be aimed at in shooting practice or contests. **2.** a goal to be reached. – *v.t.* **3.** to have as a target: *nuclear submarines can target the US.*

tariff /'tærəf/ *n.* **1.** an official list or table showing the duties or customs imposed by a government on exports or, especially, imports. **2.** any duty in such a list or system.

tarmac /'tamæk/ *n.* **1.** → **tarmacadam**. **2.** a road or airport runway.

tarmacadam /tamə'kædəm/ *n.* a road-surfacing mixture consisting of small stones or gravel bound together with tar or a mixture of tar and bitumen.

tarnish /'tanɪʃ/ *v.t.* **1.** to dull or alter the lustre of (especially a metallic surface by oxidation, etc.); discolour. **2.** to diminish or destroy the purity of; stain; sully. – *n.* **3.** tarnished condition; discolouration; alteration of the lustre.

tarot /'tæroʊ/ *n.* a pack of cards, usually used in fortune-telling.

tarpaulin /ta'pɔlən/ *n.* a protective covering of canvas or other material waterproofed with tar, paint, or wax.

tarragon /'tærəgən/ *n.* a herb with aromatic leaves used for flavouring.

tarry /'tæri/ *v.i.*, **-ried**, **-rying**. **1.** to remain or stay, as in a place. **2.** to delay or be tardy in acting, starting, coming, etc.; linger or loiter. **3.** to wait.

tart[1] /tat/ *adj.* sour or acid.

tart[2] /tat/ *n.* a saucer-shaped shell of pastry, filled with cooked fruit or other sweetened preparation, and having no top crust.

tart[3] /tat/ *Colloquial* – *n.* **1.** a prostitute. – *v.i.* **2. tart up,** to adorn; make attractive, especially with cheap ornaments and cosmetics.

tartan /'tatn/ *n.* a woollen or worsted cloth woven with stripes of different colours and widths crossing at right angles, worn chiefly by the Scottish Highlanders.

tartar /'tatə/ *n.* **1.** a hard substance deposited on the teeth. **2.** the deposit from wines.

task /task/ *n.* **1.** a definite piece of work assigned or falling to a person; a duty. **2.** a matter of considerable labour or difficulty. – *v.t.* **3.** to subject to severe or excessive labour or exertion.

Tasmanian devil /tæz'meɪniən/ *n.* a carnivorous marsupial of Tasmania having a black coat with white markings.

tassel /'tæsəl/ *n.* **1.** a clasp consisting commonly of a bunch of threads, small cords, or strand hanging from a roundish knob or head. **2.** something resembling this.

taste /teɪst/ *v.*, **tasted**, **tasting**, *n.* – *v.t.* **1.** to try the flavour or quality of (something) by taking some into the mouth. **2.** to eat or drink a little of. **3.** to perceive or distinguish the flavour of. **4.** to have or get experience, especially a slight experience. – *v.i.* **5.** to smack or savour (usually fol. by *of*). – *n.* **6.** the act of tasting food, drink, or the like. **7.** the sense by which the flavour or savour of things is perceived when they are brought into contact with special organs of the tongue. **8.** a small quantity tasted; a morsel, bit, or sip. **9.** a relish, liking, or predilection for something. **10.** the sense of what is fitting, harmonious, or beautiful; the perception and enjoyment of what constitutes excellence in the fine arts, literature, etc. **11.** a slight experience or a sample of something.

tastebud /'teɪstbʌd/ *n.* any of a number of small, flask-shaped bodies on the tongue, etc., the special organs of taste.

tasty /'teɪsti/ *adj.*, **tastier**, **tastiest**. pleasing to the taste; savoury; appetising.

tatter /'tætə/ *n.* **1.** a torn piece hanging loose from the main part, as of a garment, etc. **2.** a separate torn piece.

tatting /'tætɪŋ/ *n.* the process or work of making a kind of knotted lace of cotton or linen thread with a shuttle.

tattle /'tætl/ *v.i.*, **-tled**, **-tling**. to let out secrets.

tattoo[1] /tæ'tu/ *n.*, *pl.* **-toos**. an outdoor military pageant or display.

tattoo[2] /tæ'tu/ *n.*, *pl.* **-toos**. an indelible pattern made on the skin.

taught /tɔt/ *v.* past tense and past participle of **teach**.

taunt /tɔnt/ *v.t.* to reproach or provoke in a sarcastic or insulting manner.

taupe /tɔp, toʊp/ *n.* dark grey.

taut /tɔt/ *adj.* tightly drawn; tense.

tautology /tɔ'tɒlədʒi/ *n.*, *pl.* **-gies**. needless repetition of an idea.

tavern /'tævən/ *n.* premises where food and alcoholic drink are served.

taw /tɔ/ *n.* a choice or fancy marble.

tawdry /'tɔdri/ *adj.*, **-drier**, **-driest**. (of finery, etc.) gaudy; showy and cheap.

tawny /'tɔni/ *adj.*, **-nier**, **-niest**. dark yellowish or yellowish brown colour.

tax /tæks/ *n.* **1.** a compulsory monetary contribution demanded by a government for its support and levied on incomes, property, goods purchased, etc. – *v.t.* **2.** to impose tax on. **3.** to lay a burden on; make serious demands. – **taxable**, *adj.*

taxation /tæk'seɪʃən/ *n.* **1.** the act of taxing. **2.** the revenue raised by taxes.

tax avoidance *n.* the taking of lawful measures to minimise one's tax liabilities. Cf. **tax evasion**.

tax-deductible /'tæks-dədʌktəbəl/ *adj.* of or relating to any expense, loss, etc., which can be legally claimed as a deduction from taxable income. – **tax-deduction**, *n.*

tax evasion *n.* the taking of illegal steps to deprive the revenue of fiscal dues.

tax haven *n.* a country or territory in which resident individuals and resident companies pay little or no tax.

taxi /'tæksi/ *n.*, *pl.* **taxis**, *v.*, **taxied**, **taxiing** *or* **taxying**. – *n.* **1.** Also, **taxicab**. a motor car for public hire. – *v.i.* **2.** (of an aeroplane) to move over the surface of the ground or water under its own power.

taxidermy /'tæksəˌdɜmi/ *n.* the art of preparing and preserving the skins of animals, and stuffing and mounting them in lifelike form. – **taxidermist**, *n.*

tax indexation *n.* the indexing of tax scales in accordance with certain economic variables such as the consumer price index.

tax lurk *n.* a scheme or trick by which one avoids paying tax. Also, **tax dodge**.

taxonomy /tæk'sɒnəmi/ *n.* classification, especially in relation to its principles or laws.

tax return *n.* a statement of personal income required annually by tax authorities, used in assessing a person's tax liability.

tax shelter *n.* an investment, allowance, etc., used by a person or company to reduce or avoid tax liability.

tea /ti/ *n.* **1.** the dried and prepared leaves of the shrub, *Thea sinensis*, from which a somewhat bitter, aromatic beverage is made by infusion in boiling water. **2.** any of various infusions prepared from the leaves, flowers, etc., of other plants, and used as beverages or medicines. **3.** a light meal taken in the late afternoon. **4.** the main evening meal.

teach /titʃ/ *v.*, **taught**, **teaching**. – *v.t.* **1.** to impart knowledge of or skill in; give instruction in. **2.** to impart knowledge or skill to; give instruction to. – **teacher**, *n.*

teak /tik/ *n.* a large East Indian tree with a hard, durable, yellowish brown, resinous wood.

teal /til/ *n.*, *pl.* **teals**, (*esp. collectively*) **teal**. a small freshwater duck.

team /tim/ *n.* **1.** a number of persons associated in some joint action, especially one of the sides in a match. **2.** two or more horses, oxen, or other animals harnessed together to draw a vehicle, plough or the like. – *v.t.* **3.** to join together in a team.

team spirit /tim 'spɪrət/ *n.* the camaraderie and loyalty which members of a team display towards each other.

tear[1] /tɪə/ *n.* a drop of fluid appearing in or flowing from the eye, chiefly as the result of emotion, especially grief.

tear[2] /tɛə/ *v.*, **tore**, **torn**, **tearing**, *n.* – *v.t.* **1.** to pull apart or in pieces by force, especially so as to leave ragged or irregular edges. **2.** to pull or pluck violently or with force. **3.** to rend or divide. – *v.i.* **4.** to become torn. **5.** *Colloquial* to move or go with violence or great haste. – *n.* **6.** the act of tearing. **7.** a rent or fissure.

tease /tiz/ *v.*, **teased**, **teasing**, *n.* – *v.t.* **1.** to worry or irritate by persistent petty requests, trifling raillery, or other annoyances often in jest. **2.** to pull apart or separate the adhering fibres of. **3.** to flirt. – *n.* **4.** the act of teasing. **5.** the state of being teased. **6.** someone who or that which teases or annoys.

teat /tit/ *n.* **1.** the protuberance on the breast or udder in female mammals (except the monotremes), where the milk ducts discharge; a nipple. **2.** something resembling a teat, especially for feeding a baby from a bottle.

tech /tɛk/ *n.* *Colloquial* a technical college or school.

technical /'tɛknɪkəl/ *adj.* **1.** belonging or relating to an art, science, or the like. **2.** skilled in, or familiar in a practical way with, a particular art, trade, etc., as a person. **3.** relating to or connected with the mechanical or industrial arts and the applied sciences.

technical college *n.* a state institution providing technical education at the tertiary level.

technicality /tɛknə'kæləti/ *n., pl.* **-ties**. a literal, often narrow-minded interpretation of a rule, law, etc.; quibble.

technician /tɛk'nɪʃən/ *n.* **1.** one skilled in the technique of an art, as music or painting. **2.** a person skilled and knowledgeable in a particular technical area: *a telephone technician.*

technicolour = technicolor /'tɛknɪkʌlə, -nə-/ *n.* a process of making cinema films in colour by superimposing the three primary colours to produce a final coloured print.

technique /tɛk'nik/ *n.* method of performance; way of accomplishing.

technocracy /tɛk'nɒkrəsi/ *n.* government by experts in technical fields, as engineering, economics, etc. – **technocrat**, *n.*

technology /tɛk'nɒlədʒi/ *n.* the branch of knowledge that deals with science and engineering, or its practice, as applied to industry; applied science.

technology park *n.* an industrial park devoted to high-technology industries. Also, **high technology park**.

tectonic /tɛk'tɒnɪk/ *adj.* of or relating to building or construction.

teddy bear /'tɛdi/ *n.* a stuffed toy bear.

tedium /'tidiəm/ *n.* the state of being wearisome. – **tedious**, *adj.*

tee /ti/ *n., v.,* **teed**, **teeing**. – *n.* **1.** *Golf* the starting place, usually a hard mound of earth, at the beginning of each fairway. **2.** *Golf* a small heap of sand, or a rubber, plastic, or wooden object, on which the ball is placed and from which it is driven at the beginning of a hole. – *v.i.* **3.** *Golf* to strike the ball from a tee (fol. by *off*).

teem[1] /tim/ *v.i.* to abound or swarm; be prolific or fertile (fol. by *with*).

teem[2] /tim/ *v.i.* **1.** to empty or pour out; discharge. **2.** to rain very hard.

teenager /'tineɪdʒə/ *n.* a person in his or her teens. – **teenage**, *adj.*

teens /tinz/ *pl. n.* the period of one's life between the ages of 12 and 20.

teeter /'titə/ *v.i.* **1.** to seesaw. **2.** to move unsteadily.

teeth /tiθ/ *n.* plural of **tooth**.

teethe /tið/ *v.i.,* **teethed**, **teething**. to grow teeth; cut one's teeth.

teetotal /'titoutl, ti'toutl/ *adj.* of or relating to, advocating, or pledged to total abstinence from intoxicating drink. – **teetotaller**, *n.* – **teetotally**, *adv.*

teflon /'tɛflɒn/ *n.* a lining for saucepans, frying pans, etc., to which food does not adhere.

tele- 1. a word element meaning 'distant', especially 'transmission over a distance', as in *telegraph.* **2.** a word element referring to *television* or *telephone.*

telecast /'tɛləkast, 'tɛli-/ *v.,* **-cast** *or* **-casted**, **-casting**, *n.* – *v.i., v.t.* **1.** to broadcast by television. – *n.* **2.** a television broadcast.

telecommunications /ˌtɛləkəmjunə'keɪʃənz, ˌtɛli-/ *pl. n.* the science or technology of telegraphic or telephonic communications by line or radio transmission.

teleconference /tɛli'kɒnfərəns/ *n.* a conference in which the people at locations remote from each other can take part using an audio and video telecommunications system. – **teleconferencing**, *n.*

telegram /'tɛləgræm/ *n.* a communication sent by telegraph; a telegraphic message.

telegraph /'tɛləgræf, -graf/ *n.* **1.** an apparatus for transmitting messages or signals to a distance. – *v.t.* **2.** to transmit or send (a message, etc.) by telegraph. – **telegraphic**, *adj.* – **telegraphy**, *n.*

telegraphic transfer *n.* the transfer, by telegraph, radio, or telephone, of credit from one person or firm to another.

telemarketing /'tɛlimakətɪŋ/ *n.* the selling of goods or services by contacting potential customers on the telephone.

telemovie /'tɛlimuvi/ *n.* a film produced especially for television.

teleology /tili'ɒlədʒi, tɛl-/ *n.* **1.** the doctrine of final causes or purposes. **2.** the belief that purpose and design are a part of, or are apparent in, nature.

telepathy /tə'lɛpəθi/ *n.* communication of one mind with another by some means other than the normal use of the senses.

telephone /'tɛləfoun/ *n.* an apparatus, system, or process for transmission of sound or speech to a distant point, especially by an electrical device. – **telephonist**, *n.* – **telephony**, *n.*

telephoto /'tɛlifoutou, 'tɛlə-/ *adj.* denoting or relating to a form of photographic lens which produces magnified images.

teleprinter /'tɛliprɪntə, 'tɛlə-/ *n.* an instrument having a typewriter keyboard which transmits and receives messages by telegraphic transmission, or to and from a computer. Also, **teletype**.

teleprocessing /'tɛliˌprousɛsɪŋ/ *n.* the processing of information held at another place, by means of an online computer.

telescope /'tɛləskoup/ *n., v.,* **-scoped**, **-scoping**. – *n.* **1.** an optical instrument for making distant objects appear nearer and larger. – *v.t.* **2.** to force together, one into another, or force into something else, in the manner of the sliding tubes of a jointed telescope. **3.** to condense; shorten. – *v.i.* **4.** to slide together, or into something else in the manner of the tubes of a jointed telescope. – **telescopic**, *adj.*

teletype /'tɛlitaɪp, 'tɛlə-/ *n.* → **teleprinter**.

televise /'tɛləvaɪz/ *v.t.,* **-vised**, **-vising**. to broadcast by television.

television /'tɛləvɪʒən/ *n.* **1.** the broadcasting of a still or moving image via radio waves to receivers which project it on a picture tube. **2.** a television receiver; television set.

television station *n.* an organisation engaged in broadcasting, on a fixed channel, television programs of news, entertainment, propaganda, etc.

telex /ˈtɛlɛks/ *n.* an international two-way communications system which uses the public telecommunications network to link teleprinters at remote locations.

tell /tɛl/ *v.,* **told, telling**. – *v.t.* **1.** to give an account or narrative of; narrate; relate (a story, tale, etc.). **2.** to make known by speech or writing (a fact, news, information, etc.); communicate. **3.** to utter (the truth, a lie, etc.). **4.** to recognise or distinguish. – *v.i.* **5.** to give an account or report. **6.** to give evidence or be an indication (fol. by *of*). **7.** to disclose something secret or private; play the informer (usually fol. by *on*). **8.** to produce a marked or severe effect.

teller /ˈtɛlə/ *n.* someone employed in a bank to receive or pay out money over the counter.

tellurian /tɛlˈjuriən, təˈlu-/ *adj.* of or characteristic of the earth or an inhabitant of the earth.

telluric /tɛlˈjurɪk, təˈlu-/ *adj.* of or relating to the earth; terrestrial.

tellurium /tɛlˈjuriəm, təˈlu-/ *n.* a rare silver-white element. *Symbol*: Te

temerity /təˈmɛrəti/ *n.* reckless boldness.

temper /ˈtɛmpə/ *n.* **1.** a particular state of mind or feelings. **2.** heat of mind or passion, shown in outbursts of anger, resentment, etc. **3.** *Metallurgy* the particular degree of hardness and elasticity imparted to steel, etc., by tempering. – *v.t.* **4.** to moderate or mitigate. **5.** to bring to a proper, suitable, or desirable state by, or as by, blending or admixture. **6.** to heat and cool or quench (metal) to bring to the proper degree of hardness, elasticity, etc.

tempera /ˈtɛmpərə/ *n.* paint made from pigment ground in water and mixed with an emulsion of egg yolk or some similar substance.

temperament /ˈtɛmprəmənt/ *n.* the individual peculiarity of physical organisation by which the manner of thinking, feeling, and acting of every person is permanently affected; natural disposition.

temperamental /tɛmprəˈmɛntl/ *adj.* **1.** moody, irritable or sensitive. **2.** liable to behave erratically; unstable; unreliable.

temperance /ˈtɛmpərəns, ˈtɛmprəns/ *n.* **1.** habitual moderation. **2.** total abstinence from alcoholic drink.

temperate /ˈtɛmpərət, ˈtɛmprət/ *adj.* **1.** moderate or self-restrained. **2.** not excessive.

temperature /ˈtɛmprətʃə/ *n.* **1.** a measure of the degree of hotness or coldness of a body or substance. **2.** *Physiology, Pathology* **a.** the degree of heat of a living body, especially the human body. **b.** the excess of this above the normal (which in the adult human being is about 37°C or about 98.4°F).

tempest /ˈtɛmpəst/ *n.* a violent storm.

template /ˈtɛmplət, -leɪt/ *n.* **1.** a formula or exemplum. **2.** a pattern, mould, or the like, usually consisting of a thin plate of wood, metal, or plastic, used as a guide in mechanical work or for transferring a design onto a work surface, etc.

temple[1] /ˈtɛmpəl/ *n.* an edifice erected as a place of worship; a church, especially a large or imposing one.

temple[2] /ˈtɛmpəl/ *n.* the flattened region on either side of the human forehead.

tempo /ˈtɛmpoʊ/ *n., pl.* **-pos, -pi** /-pi/. *Music* relative rapidity or rate of movement.

temporal /ˈtɛmpərəl, ˈtɛmprəl/ *adj.* **1.** of or relating to time. **2.** relating to or concerned with the present life or this world; worldly.

temporary /ˈtɛmpri, -prəri/ *adj.* lasting, existing, serving, or effective for a time only; not permanent.

temporise = temporize /ˈtɛmpəraɪz/ *v.i.,* **-rised, -rising**. **1.** to act indecisively or evasively to gain time or delay matters. **2.** to comply with the time or occasion; yield temporarily or ostensibly to the current of opinion or circumstances.

tempt /tɛmpt/ *v.t.* **1.** to induce or persuade by enticement or allurement. **2.** to render strongly disposed (to do something). – **temptation**, *n.*

ten /tɛn/ *n.* a cardinal number, nine plus one. – **tenth**, *adj., n.*

tenable /ˈtɛnəbəl/ *adj.* capable of being held, maintained, or defended, as against attack or objection.

tenacious /təˈneɪʃəs/ *adj.* **1.** holding fast; characterised by keeping a firm hold (often fol. by *of*). **2.** highly retentive. **3.** pertinacious, persistent, stubborn, or obstinate. – **tenacity**, *n.*

tenant /ˈtɛnənt/ *n.* someone who holds land, a house, or the like, of another (the landlord) for a period of time, as a lessee or occupant for rent. – **tenancy**, *n.*

tend[1] /tɛnd/ *v.i.* to be disposed or inclined in action, operation, or effect (to do something). – **tendency**, *n.*

tend[2] /tɛnd/ *v.t.* **1.** to attend to by work or services, care, etc. **2.** to look after.

tendentious /tɛnˈdɛnʃəs/ *adj.* having or showing a definite tendency, bias, or purpose.

tender[1] /ˈtɛndə/ *adj.* **1.** soft or delicate in substance; not hard or tough. **2.** weak or delicate in constitution; not strong or hardy; fragile. **3.** gentle. **4.** acutely or painfully sensitive.

tender[2] /ˈtɛndə/ *v.t.* **1.** to present formally for acceptance; make formal offer of. – *n.* **2.** the act of tendering; an offer of something for acceptance. **3.** *Commerce* an offer made in writing by one party to another to execute certain work, supply certain commodities, etc., at a given cost.

tendon /ˈtɛndən/ *n. Anatomy* a cord or band of dense, tough, inelastic, white fibrous tissue, serving to connect a muscle with a bone or part; a sinew. – **tendinous**, *adj.*

tendril /ˈtɛndrəl/ *n. Botany* a leafless curly organ of climbing plants.

tenement house /ˈtɛnəmənt/ *n.* a house divided into flats, especially one in the poorer, crowded parts of a large city.

tenet /ˈtɛnət/ *n.* any opinion, principle, doctrine, dogma, or the like, held as true.

tennis /ˈtɛnəs/ *n.* a game in which a ball is hit with racquets backwards and forwards over a net.

tenon /ˈtɛnən/ *n.* a projection shaped on an end of a piece of wood, etc., for insertion in a corresponding cavity (mortice) in another piece.

tenor /ˈtɛnə/ *n.* **1.** the course of thought or meaning which runs through something written or spoken; purport; drift. **2.** *Music* the highest natural male voice.

tense[1] /tɛns/ *adj.*, **tenser**, **tensest**, *v.*, **tensed**, **tensing**. – *adj.* **1.** stretched tight, as a cord, fibre, etc.; drawn taut; rigid. **2.** in a state of mental or nervous strain, as a person. – *v.t.*, *v.i.* **3.** to make or become tense.

tense[2] /tɛns/ *n. Grammar* a category of verb inflection found in some languages which specifies the time and length of occurrence of the action or state expressed by the verb.

tensile /ˈtɛnsaɪl/ *adj.* **1.** of or relating to tension. **2.** capable of being stretched or drawn out; ductile. – **tensility**, *n.*

tension /ˈtɛnʃən/ *n.* **1.** the act of stretching or straining. **2.** mental or emotional strain; intense suppressed anxiety, suspense, or excitement. **3.** *Electricity* electromotive force; potential.

tent /tɛnt/ *n.* a portable shelter of skins or coarse cloth, especially canvas.

tentacle /ˈtɛntəkəl/ *n. Zoology* any of various slender, flexible processes or appendages in animals, especially invertebrates, which serve as organs of touch, prehension, etc.; a feeler.

tentative /ˈtɛntətɪv/ *adj.* **1.** of the nature of, or made or done as, a trial, experiment, or attempt; experimental. **2.** hesitant; cautious; diffident.

tenterhooks /ˈtɛntəhʊks/ *pl. n. in the phr.* **on tenterhooks,** in a state of painful suspense or anxiety.

tenuous /ˈtɛnjuəs/ *adj.* flimsy; lacking a firm or sound basis; weak; vague.

tenure /ˈtɛnjə/ *n.* **1.** the holding or possessing of anything. **2.** a period of office or employment that terminates, possibly subject to certain conditions, only on resignation or retirement. **3.** the period or terms of holding something.

tepee /ˈtipi/ *n.* a tent or wigwam of the North American Indians.

tepid /ˈtɛpəd/ *adj.* moderately warm.

terbium /ˈtɜbiəm/ *n.* a rare-earth, metallic element. *Symbol*: Tb

tercentenary /tɜsənˈtinəri, -ˈtɛn-/ *adj.* of or relating to a 300th anniversary.

term /tɜm/ *n.* **1.** any word or group of linguistic forms naming something, especially as used in some particular field of knowledge. **2.** the time or period through which something lasts or is fixed to last. **3.** each of certain stated periods of the year into which instruction is regularly organised for students or pupils in universities, colleges, and schools. **4.** (*pl.*) conditions with regard to payment, price, charge, rates, wages, etc. **5.** (*pl.*) footing or standing. **6. a contradiction in terms,** a statement which is self-contradictory. – *v.t.* **7.** to apply a particular term or name to; name; call; designate.

term deposit *n.* a deposit that can be withdrawn by the depositor only after he or she has given advance notice or after a period of time agreed upon has elapsed. Also, **time deposit**.

terminal /ˈtɜmənəl/ *adj.* **1.** situated at or forming the end or extremity of something. **2.** relating to, situated, at or forming the terminus of a railway. **3.** occurring at or causing the end of life. – *n.* **4.** a terminal part or structure; end or extremity. **5.** the end of a railway line, shipping route, air route, etc., at which large scale loading and unloading of passengers, goods, etc., takes place. **6.** *Electricity* the mechanical device by means of which an electrical connection to an apparatus is established. **7.** → **computer terminal**. **8.** *Architecture, etc.* a carving or the like at the end of something.

terminal bonus *n.* a free addition to the sum assured on a policy to reflect the excess of the market value of the life insurance company's assets over their book value. It is paid once only, when the policy matures. See **reversionary bonus**.

terminate /ˈtɜməneɪt/ *v.*, **-nated**, **-nating**. – *v.t.* **1.** bring to an end; put an end to. – *v.i.* **2.** to end, conclude, or cease. – **terminable**, *adj.*

terminating building society *n.* an association of individuals who make regular payments to a common fund, from which each obtains a housing loan, the order usually being determined by ballot; the society is terminated when the last house is paid for.

terminology /tɜməˈnɒlədʒi/ *n.*, *pl.* **-gies**. the system of terms belonging to a science, art, or subject; nomenclature.

terminus /ˈtɜmənəs/ *n.*, *pl.* **-nuses**, **-ni** /-naɪ/. the station or town at the end of a railway line, bus route, etc.

termite /ˈtɜmaɪt/ *n.* a social insect, sometimes very destructive to buildings, etc.; white ant.

tern /tɜn/ *n.* a seabird.

ternary /ˈtɜnəri/ *adj.* consisting of or involving three; threefold; triple.

terrace /ˈtɛrəs/ *n.* **1.** one of a series of flat levels formed across a slope, mountain side, etc., usually for the purposes of cultivation. **2.** an open (usually paved) area connected with a house and serving as an outdoor living area. **3.** a row of adjoining, identical houses, or a house in such a row.

terracotta /tɛrəˈkɒtə/ *n.* a hard, usually unglazed earthenware of fine quality.

terrain /təˈreɪn/ *n.* a tract of land, especially as considered with reference to its natural features, military advantages, etc.

terra nullius /tɛrə ˈnʊliəs/ *n.* territory belonging to no state, that is, not inhabited by a community with a social and political organisation.

terrestrial /təˈrɛstriəl/ *adj.* **1.** relating to, consisting of, or representing the earth. **2.** of or relating to the land as distinct from the water.

terrible /ˈtɛrəbəl/ *adj.* **1.** exciting or fitted to excite terror or great fear; dreadful; awful. **2.** *Colloquial* very bad.

terrier /ˈtɛriə/ *n.* a small dog.

terrific /təˈrɪfɪk/ *adj.* **1.** causing terror; terrifying. **2.** *Colloquial* very good.

terrify /ˈtɛrəfaɪ/ *v.t.*, **-fied**, **-fying**. to fill with terror; make greatly afraid.

territory /ˈtɛrətri, -təri/ *n.*, *pl.* **-ries**. **1.** any tract of land; region or district. **2.** the land and waters belonging to or under the jurisdiction of a state, sovereign, etc. **3.** any separate tract of land belonging to a nation. **4.** the field of action, thought, etc.; domain or province of something. – **territorial**, *adj.*

terror /'tɛrə/ *n.* **1.** intense, sharp, overpowering fear. **2.** *Colloquial* a person or thing that is a particular nuisance.

terrorise = terrorize /'tɛrəraɪz/ *v.t.*, **-rised**, **-rising**. to fill or overcome with terror.

terrorism /'tɛrərɪzəm/ *n.* **1.** the use of terrorising methods. **2.** a method of resisting a government or of governing by deliberate acts of armed violence. – **terrorist**, *n., adj.* – **terroristic**, *adj.*

terry /'tɛri/ *n., pl.* **-ries**. the loop formed by the pile of a fabric when left uncut.

terse /tɜs/ *adj.*, **terser**, **tersest**. **1.** neatly or effectively concise; brief and pithy, as language. **2.** abrupt or bad-tempered, especially in one's speech.

tertiary /'tɜʃəri/ *adj.* of the third order, rank, formation, etc.; third.

tertiary education *n.* all forms of formal education beyond secondary education.

terylene /'tɛrəlin/ *n.* a synthetic polyester fibre.

tessellate /'tɛsəleɪt/ *v.t.*, **-lated**, **-lating**. to form of small squares or blocks, as floors, pavements, etc.; form or arrange in a chequered or mosaic pattern.

test /tɛst/ *n.* **1.** that by which the presence, quality, or genuineness of anything is determined; a means of trial. **2.** *Education* a form of examination for evaluating the performance and capabilities of a student or class. – *v.t.* **3.** to subject to a test of any kind; try.

testament /'tɛstəmənt/ *n.* **1.** *Law* a formal declaration, usually in writing, of a person's wishes as to the disposition of his or her property after his or her death. **2.** (*cap.*) either of the two main divisions of the Bible.

testate /'tɛsteɪt, 'tɛstət/ *adj.* *Law* having made and left a valid will. – **testacy**, *n.* – **testator**, *n.* – **testatrix**, *fem. n.*

testes /'tɛstiz/ *n.* plural of **testis**.

testicle /'tɛstɪkə/ *n.* the male sex gland, either of two oval glands situated in the scrotal sac.

testify /'tɛstəfaɪ/ *v.*, **-fied**, **-fying**. – *v.i.* **1.** to bear witness; give or afford evidence. **2.** to make solemn declaration. – *v.t.* **3.** to bear witness to; affirm as fact or truth.

testimonial /tɛstə'moʊniəl/ *n.* **1.** a writing certifying to a person's character, conduct, or qualifications. **2.** something given or done as an expression of esteem, admiration, or gratitude.

testimony /'tɛstəməni/ *n., pl.* **-nies**. **1.** *Law* the statement or declaration of a witness under oath or affirmation, usually in court. **2.** evidence.

testis /'tɛstəs/ *n., pl.* **-tes** /-tiz/. → **testicle**.

test tube *n.* a hollow cylinder of thin glass with one end closed, used in chemical tests.

testy /'tɛsti/ *adj.*, **-tier**, **-tiest**. touchy.

tetanus /'tɛtnəs, 'tɛtənəs/ *n.* *Pathology* an infectious, often fatal disease, marked by spasms and muscle rigidity.

tether /'tɛðə/ *n.* **1.** a rope, chain, or the like, by which an animal is fastened, as to a stake, so that its range of movement is limited. **2. the end of one's tether,** the limit of one's possibilities, patience, or resources. – *v.t.* **3.** to fasten or confine with or as with a tether.

tetra- a word element meaning 'four'.

tetragon /'tɛtrəgən, -gɒn/ *n.* a plane figure having four angles; a quadrangle.

text /tɛkst/ *n.* **1.** the main body of matter in a book or manuscript. **2.** the actual wording of anything written or printed. **3.** a short passage of Scripture. – **textual**, *adj.*

textbook /'tɛkstbʊk/ *n.* a book used by students for a particular branch of study.

textile /'tɛkstaɪl/ *n.* a woven material.

texture /'tɛkstʃə/ *n.* **1.** the characteristic appearance or essential quality of something, especially as conveyed to the touch. **2.** the structure of the surface of any work of art, or the simulation of the surface structure of the skin, garment, etc., of the object represented in paint, stone, or other medium.

-th[1] a noun suffix referring to condition, quality, or action, added to words (*warmth*) and to stems related to words (*depth*, *length*).

-th[2] the suffix of ordinal numerals (*fourth*, *tenth*, *twentieth*), the form *-th* being added in one or two cases to altered stems of the cardinal (*fifth*, *twelfth*).

than /ðæn/, *weak form* /ðən/ – *conj.* **1.** a particle used after comparative adjectives and adverbs and certain other words, such as *other*, *otherwise*, *else*, etc., to introduce the second member of a comparison. – *prep.* **2.** in comparison with.

thank /θæŋk/ *v.t.* **1.** to give thanks to; express gratitude to. – *n.* **2.** (*usu. pl.*) the expression of grateful feeling, or grateful acknowledgment of a benefit or favour, by words or otherwise.

that /ðæt/ *weak form* /ðət/. *pron., pl.* **those**, *adj., pl.* **those**, *adv., conj.* – *pron.* **1.** (a demonstrative pronoun used to indicate: **a.** a person, thing, idea, etc., as pointed out or present, before mentioned, about to be mentioned, supposed to be understood, or by way of emphasis: *that is my husband.* **b.** of two or more persons, things, etc., already mentioned, to the one more remote in place, time, or thought (often opposed to *this*): *that is the one I want*). **2.** (a relative pronoun used as the subject or object of a relative clause: *how old was the car that was stolen?*). – *adj.* **3.** (a demonstrative adjective used to indicate: **a.** a person, place, thing, idea, etc., as pointed out or present, before mentioned, supposed to be understood, or by way of emphasis: *that man is my husband.* **b.** of two or more persons, things, etc., already mentioned, the one more remote in place, time, or thought (opposed to *this*): *it was that one, not this one.*). – *adv.* **4.** (an adverb used with adjectives and adverbs of quality or extent to indicate precise degree or extent: *that much*; *that far*). – *conj.* **5.** (a conjunction used to introduce a clause as the subject or object of the principal verb or as the necessary complement to a statement made: *that he will come is certain*; *I know that you will do it*).

thatch /θætʃ/ *n.* **1.** a material, as straw, rushes, leaves, or the like, used to cover roofs, haystacks, etc. – *v.t.* **2.** to cover with or as with thatch.

thaw /θɔ/ *v.i.* to pass from a frozen to a liquid or semi-liquid state; melt.

the[1] /ði/, *before a vowel* /ðə/, *before a consonant – definite article* **1.** (used before nouns with a specifying or particularising effect, opposed to *a* or *an*). **2.** (used before adjectives substantively and denoting an individual, a class or number of individuals, or an abstract notion).

the[2] /ði/, *before a vowel* /ðə/, *before a consonant – adv.* (used to modify an adjective or adverb in the comparative degree: **1.** signifying 'in or by that', 'on that account', 'in or by so much', or 'in some or any degree': *he looks the better for his holiday.* **2.** used correlatively, in one instance with relative force and in the other with demonstrative force, and signifying 'by how much . . . by so much' or 'in what degree . . . in that degree': *the more, the merrier.*)

theatre /'θɪətə, 'θiətə/ *n.* **1.** a building or room designed to house dramatic presentations, stage entertainments, or the like. **2.** dramatic performances as a branch of art; the drama. **3.** a room or hall, fitted with tiers of seats rising like steps, as used for lectures, anatomical demonstrations, etc. **4.** a room in a hospital or elsewhere in which surgical operations are performed. **5.** a place of action; field of operations. – **theatrical**, *adj.*

theatrette /'θɪətərɛt/ *n.* a small theatre.

theft /θɛft/ *n.* the act of stealing.

their /ðɛə/ *adj.* the possessive form of **they** used before a noun.

theirs /ðɛəz/ *pron.* the possessive form of **they** used predicatively or without a noun following.

theism /'θiɪzəm/ *n.* the belief in one god as the creator and ruler of the universe.

them /ðɛm/, *weak form* /ðəm/ – *pron.* the objective case of **they**.

theme /θim/ *n.* a subject of discourse, discussion, meditation, or composition; a topic.

themselves /ðəm'sɛlvz/ *pl. pron.* **1.** a reflexive form of **they**. **2.** an emphatic form of **them** or **they**.

then /ðɛn/ *adv.* **1.** at that time. **2.** next in order of time. **3.** in that case; in those circumstances.

thence /ðɛns/ *adv.* **1.** from that place. **2.** from that time. **3.** from that source; for that reason; therefore.

theocracy /θi'ɒkrəsi/ *n., pl.* **-cies**. a form of government in which a deity is recognised as the supreme civil ruler.

theodolite /θi'ɒdəlaɪt/ *n. Surveying* an instrument for measuring horizontal or vertical angles.

theology /θi'ɒlədʒi/ *n., pl.* **-gies**. the science or study of divine things or religious truth; divinity. – **theologian**, *n.*

theorem /'θɪərəm/ *n.* a rule or law, especially one expressed by an equation or formula.

theoretical /θiə'rɛtɪkəl/ *adj.* **1.** of, relating to, or consisting in theory; not practical. **2.** existing only in theory; hypothetical.

theorise = theorize /'θiəraɪz/ *v.i.,* **-rised**, **-rising**. **1.** to form a theory or theories. **2.** to speculate or conjecture.

theory /'θɪəri/ *n., pl.* **-ries**. **1.** a coherent group of general propositions used as principles of explanation for a class of phenomena. **2.** that department of a science or art which deals with its principles or methods, as distinguished from the practice of it. **3.** conjecture or opinion.

therapeutic /θɛrə'pjutɪk/ *adj.* relating to the treating or curing of disease.

therapy /'θɛrəpi/ *n., pl.* **-pies**. the treatment of disease, disorder, defect, etc., as by some remedial or curative process. – **therapist**, *n.*

there /ðɛə/ *adv.* **1.** in or at that place. **2.** into or to that place; thither.

there- a word element meaning 'that (place)', 'that (time)', etc., used in combination with certain adverbs and prepositions.

thereby /ðɛə'baɪ, 'ðɛəbaɪ/ *adv.* by that; by means of that.

therefore /'ðɛəfɔ, ðɛə'fɔ/ *adv.* in consequence of that; as a result; consequently.

thereupon /ðɛərə'pɒn, 'ðɛərəpɒn/ *adv.* immediately following that.

thermal /'θɜməl/ *adj.* of or relating to heat or temperature. Also, **thermic**.

thermodynamics /,θɜmoʊdaɪ'næmɪks/ *n.* the science concerned with the relations between heat and mechanical energy or work, and the conversion of one into the other.

thermometer /θə'mɒmətə/ *n.* an instrument for measuring temperature.

thermonuclear /,θɜmoʊ'njukliə/ *adj.* designating, or capable of producing, extremely high temperatures resulting from, caused by, or associated with nuclear fusion.

thermonuclear reaction *n.* a nuclear fusion reaction that takes place between atomic nuclei which form part of a substance which has been heated to a temperature of several million degrees centigrade.

thermos /'θɜmɒs, -məs/ *n.* a vessel which keeps its contents at a constant temperature. Also, **thermos flask**.

thermostat /'θɜməstæt/ *n.* a device which establishes and maintains a desired temperature automatically.

thesaurus /θə'sɔrəs/ *n., pl.* **-ruses** /-rəsəz/. a dictionary of synonyms and antonyms.

these /ðiz/ *pron., adj.* plural of **this**.

thesis /'θisəs/ *n., pl.* **theses** /'θisiz/. **1.** a proposition laid down or stated, especially one to be discussed and proved or to be maintained against objections. **2.** a subject for a composition or essay. **3.** a dissertation, as one presented by a candidate for a diploma or degree, especially a postgraduate degree.

thew /θju/ *n.* (*usu. pl.*) muscle or sinew.

they /ðeɪ/ *pron., pl. possessive* **theirs**, *objective* **them**. nominative plural of **he**, **she** and **it**.

thiamine /'θaɪəmin/ *n.* a vitamin (B_1) required by the nervous system.

thick /θɪk/ *adj.* **1.** having relatively great extent from one surface or side to its opposite; not thin. **2.** measuring as specified between opposite surfaces, or in depth, or in a direction perpendicular to that of the length and breadth. **3.** set close together; compact; dense. **4.** having relatively great consistency; viscous. **5.** (of an accent or dialect) very pronounced.

thicket /ˈθɪkət/ *n.* a thick or dense growth of shrubs, bushes, or small trees; a thick coppice.

thief /θif/ *n., pl.* **thieves**. someone who steals.

thieve /θiv/ *v.t.,* **thieved**, **thieving**. to take by theft; steal. – **thievery**, *n.*

thigh /θaɪ/ *n.* that part of the leg between the hip and the knee in humans.

thimble /ˈθɪmbəl/ *n.* a small cap, usually of metal, worn on the finger to push the needle in sewing.

thin /θɪn/ *adj.,* **thinner**, **thinnest**, *v.,* **thinned**, **thinning**. – *adj.* **1.** having relatively little extent from one surface or side to its opposite; not thick. **2.** of small cross-section in comparison with the length; slender. **3.** having little flesh; spare; lean. **4.** not dense; sparse; scanty. **5.** having relatively slight consistency, as a liquid; fluid; rare or rarefied, as air, etc. **6.** easily seen through, transparent, or flimsy. – *v.t.* **7.** to make thin or thinner (often fol. by *down*, *out*, etc.).

thing /θɪŋ/ *n.* **1.** a material object without life or consciousness; an inanimate object. **2.** that which is or may become an object of thought, whether material or ideal, animate or inanimate, actual, possible, or imaginary.

think /θɪŋk/ *v.,* **thought**, **thinking**. – *v.t.* **1.** to form or conceive in the mind; have in the mind as an idea, conception, or the like. **2.** to form or have an idea or conception of (a thing, fact, circumstance, etc.). **3.** to hold as an opinion; believe; suppose. **4.** to consider (something) to be (as specified). – *v.i.* **5.** to use the mind, especially the intellect, actively; cogitate or meditate. **6.** to form or have an idea or mental image (fol. by *of*). **7.** to reflect upon the matter in question. **8.** to have a belief or opinion as indicated.

third /θɜd/ *adj.* **1.** next after the second in order, place, time, rank, value, quality, etc. (the ordinal of three). – *n.* **2.** someone who or that which comes next after the second. **3.** a third part, especially of one.

third party *n.* any person other than the principals to some transaction, proceeding, or agreement.

thirst /θɜst/ *n.* **1.** an uneasy or painful sensation of dryness in the mouth and throat caused by need of drink. **2.** strong or eager desire; craving. – **thirsty**, *adj.*

thirteen /θɜˈtin/ *n.* a cardinal number, ten plus three. – **thirteenth**, *adj., n.*

thirty /ˈθɜti/ *n., pl.* **-ties**.– *n.* a cardinal number, ten times three. – **thirtieth**, *adj., n.*

this /ðɪs/ *pron., pl.* **these**, *adj., pl.* **these**, *adv.* – *pron.* **1.** (a demonstrative pronoun used to indicate: **a.** a person, thing, idea, etc., as pointed out, present, or near, as before mentioned or supposed to be understood, as about to be mentioned, or by way of emphasis: *this is my husband.* **b.** one of two or more persons, things, etc., already mentioned, referring to the one nearer in place, time, or thought: *this is the one*). – *adj.* **2.** (a demonstrative adjective used to indicate: **a.** a person, place, thing, idea, etc., as pointed out, present, or near, before mentioned, supposed to be understood, or by way of emphasis: *this man is my husband.* **b.** one of two or more persons, things, etc., already mentioned, referring to one nearer in place, time, or thought: *this one, not that one*). – *adv.* **3.** (an adverb used with adjectives and adverbs of quality or extent to indicate precise degree or extent: *this much*; *this far*).

thistle /ˈθɪsəl/ *n.* any of various prickly plants.

thither /ˈðɪðə/ *adv.* to or towards that place or point.

thong /θɒŋ/ *n.* **1.** a narrow strip of hide or leather, used as a fastening, as the lash of a whip, etc. **2.** a sandal held loosely on the foot by two strips of leather, rubber, etc., passing between the first and second toes and over either side of the foot.

thorax /ˈθɔræks/ *n., pl.* **thoraces** /ˈθɔrəsiz, θɔˈreɪsiz/, **thoraxes**. *Anatomy* (in humans and the higher vertebrates) the part of the trunk between the neck and the abdomen, containing the cavity (enclosed by the ribs, etc.) in which the heart, lungs, etc., are situated; the chest. – **thoracic**, *adj.*

thorn /θɔn/ *n.* a sharp-pointed excrescence on a plant; a prickle.

thorough /ˈθʌrə/ *adj.* **1.** carried out through the whole of something; fully executed; complete or perfect. **2.** thoroughgoing in action or procedure; leaving nothing undone.

thoroughfare /ˈθʌrəfɛə/ *n.* a road, street, or the like, open at both ends, especially a main road.

those /ðoʊz/ *pron., adj.* plural of **that**.

thou /ðaʊ/ *pron., objective* **thee** *Archaic* the personal pronoun of the second person, in the singular number and nominative case, now little used (being replaced by *you*, which is in origin plural and takes a plural verb).

though /ðoʊ/ *conj.* **1.** (introducing a subordinate clause, which is often marked by ellipsis) notwithstanding that; in spite of the fact that. **2.** even if; granting that. **3.** if (usually in *as though*). – *adv.* **4.** for all that; however. Also, **tho'**.

thought[1] /θɔt/ *n.* **1.** the product of mental activity; that which one thinks. **2.** the capacity or faculty of thinking. **3.** meditation.

thought[2] /θɔt/ *v.* past tense and past participle of **think**.

thousand /ˈθaʊzənd/ *n.* a cardinal number, ten times one hundred.

thrall /θrɔl/ *n.* someone who is in bondage.

thrash /θræʃ/ *v.t.* **1.** to beat soundly by way of punishment; administer a beating to. – *v.i.* **2.** to beat, toss, or plunge wildly or violently about.

thread /θrɛd/ *n.* **1.** a fine cord, especially that used for sewing. **2.** the helical ridge of a screw. **3.** that which runs through the whole course of something, connecting successive parts, as the sequence of events in a narrative. – *v.t.* **4.** to pass the end of a thread through the eye of (a needle). **5.** to fix (beads, etc.) upon a thread that is passed through; string.

threadbare /ˈθrɛdbɛə/ *adj.* **1.** having the nap worn off so as to lay bare the threads of the warp and woof, as a fabric, garment, etc. **2.** meagre, scanty, or poor.

threat /θrɛt/ *n.* **1.** a declaration of an intention or determination to inflict punishment, pain or loss on someone. **2.** an indication of probable evil to come. – **threaten**, *v.*

three /θri/ *n.* a cardinal number, two plus one.

3-D /θri-'di/ *adj.* **1.** three-dimensional. – *n.* **2.** a three-dimensional form or appearance.

three-dimensional /θri-daɪ'mɛnʃənəl, -də'mɛn-/ *adj.* **1.** having or seeming to have, the dimension of depth as well as height and breadth. **2.** realistic; lifelike.

thresh /θrɛʃ/ *v.t.* to separate the grain or seeds from (a cereal plant, etc.) by some mechanical means, as by beating with a flail or by the action of a threshing machine.

threshold /'θrɛʃhoʊld/ *n.* **1.** the entrance to a house or building. **2.** any place or point of entering or beginning. **3.** *Psychology, Physiology* the point at which a stimulus becomes perceptible or is of sufficient intensity to produce an effect.

threw /θru/ *v.* past tense of **throw**.

thrice /θraɪs/ *adv.* three times.

thrift /θrɪft/ *n.* economical management; economy; frugality. – **thrifty**, *adj.*

thrill /θrɪl/ *v.t.* **1.** to effect with a sudden wave of keen emotion, so as to produce a tremor or tingling sensation through the body. – *v.i.* **2.** to be stirred by a thrill of emotion or excitement. – *n.* **3.** a tremor or tingling sensation passing through the body as the result of sudden keen emotion or excitement. **4.** thrilling property or quality, as of a story.

thriller /'θrɪlə/ *n.* a book, play, or film, dealing with crime, mystery, etc., in an exciting or sensational manner

thrive /θraɪv/ *v.i.*, **throve** *or* **thrived**, **thrived** *or* **thriven** /'θrɪvən/, **thriving**. to grow or develop vigorously; flourish.

throat /θroʊt/ *n.* **1.** the passage from the mouth to the stomach or to the lungs. **2.** the front of the neck below the chin and above the collarbones.

throb /θrɒb/ *v.*, **throbbed**, **throbbing**, *n.* – *v.i.* **1.** to beat with increased force or rapidity, as the heart under the influence of emotion or excitement; palpitate. – *n.* **2.** the act of throbbing. **3.** any pulsation or vibration.

throe /θroʊ/ *n.* **1.** a violent spasm or pang; a paroxysm. **2. in the throes of,** engaged in; fully preoccupied with.

thrombosis /θrɒm'boʊsəs/ *n.* coagulation of the blood in the heart, arteries, veins, or capillaries.

throne /θroʊn/ *n.* the chair or seat occupied by a sovereign, bishop, or other exalted personage on ceremonial occasions.

throng /θrɒŋ/ *n.* a multitude of people crowded or assembled together; a crowd.

throttle /'θrɒtl/ *n.*, *v.*, **-tled**, **-tling**. – *n.* **1.** a lever, pedal, or other device to control the amount of fuel being fed to an engine. – *v.t.* **2.** to stop the breath of by compressing the throat; strangle.

through /θru/ *prep.* **1.** in at one end, side, or surface, and out at the other, of. **2.** by the means or instrumentality of. **3.** by reason of or in consequence of. – *adv.* **4.** in at one end, side, or surface and out at the other. **5.** from the beginning to the end. **6.** to the end. – *adj.* **7.** that extends, goes, or conveys through the whole of a long distance with little or no interruption, obstruction, or hindrance. Also, **thro**, **thro'**, **thru**.

throughout /θru'aʊt/ *prep.* **1.** in or to every part of; everywhere in. – *adv.* **2.** in every part.

throw /θroʊ/ *v.*, **threw**, **thrown**, **throwing**, *n.* – *v.t.* **1.** to project or propel forcibly through the air by a sudden jerk or straightening of the arm; propel or cast in any way. **2.** to put hastily. **3.** to shape on a potter's wheel. **4.** to deliver (a blow or punch). **5.** to cast (dice). **6.** (of a horse, etc.) to cause to fall off. **7.** *Colloquial* to astonish; disconcert; confuse. **8.** to arrange or host (a social event). – *n.* **9.** an act of throwing or casting; a cast or fling.

throwback /'θroʊbæk/ *n.* reversion to an ancestral type or character.

thru /θru/ *prep.*, *adv.*, *adj.* → **through**.

thrush[1] /θrʌʃ/ *n.* any of numerous passerine birds.

thrush[2] /θrʌʃ/ *n.* *Pathology* a disease, especially in children, characterised by whitish spots and ulcers on the membranes of the mouth, throat, etc., due to a parasitic fungus; monilia.

thrust /θrʌst/ *v.*, **thrust**, **thrusting**, *n.* – *v.t.* **1.** to push forcibly; shove; put or drive with force. – *v.i.* **2.** to push against something. **3.** to make a thrust, lunge, or stab at something. – *n.* **4.** the act of thrusting; a forcible push or drive; a lunge or stab.

thud /θʌd/ *n.*, *v.*, **thudded**, **thudding**. – *n.* **1.** a dull sound, as of a heavy blow or fall. – *v.i.*, *v.t.* **2.** to beat or strike with a dull sound of heavy impact.

thug /θʌg/ *n.* a brutal, vicious, or murderous ruffian, robber, or gangster.

thumb /θʌm/ *n.* **1.** the short, thick inner digit of the human hand, next to the forefinger. – *v.t.* **2.** to soil or wear with the thumbs in handling, as the pages of a book. **3.** to run through (the pages of a book, etc.) quickly (often fol. by *through*).

thump /θʌmp/ *n.* **1.** a blow with something thick and heavy, producing a dull sound; a heavy knock. – *v.t.* **2.** to strike or beat with something thick and heavy, so as to produce a dull sound; pound. **3.** *Colloquial* to punch; thrash severely.

thunder /'θʌndə/ *n.* **1.** the loud noise which accompanies a flash of lightning, due to violent disturbance of the air by a discharge of electricity. – *v.i.* **2.** to speak in a very loud tone.

thus /ðʌs/ *adv.* **1.** in the way just indicated; in this way. **2.** accordingly; consequently.

thwack /θwæk/ *v.t.* to strike or beat vigorously with something flat; whack.

thwart /θwɔt/ *v.t.* **1.** to oppose successfully; prevent from accomplishing a purpose; frustrate (a purpose, etc.); baffle. – *adj.* **2.** adverse; unfavourable.

thy /ðaɪ/ *pron.*, *adj.* the possessive form of **thou**.

thyme /taɪm/ *n.* any of various plants of the mint family with aromatic leaves used for seasoning.

thymus /ˈθaɪməs/ *n. Anatomy* a ductless gland lying near the base of the neck.

thyroid gland /ˈθaɪrɔɪd/ *n. Anatomy* a two-lobed gland lying on either side of the trachea. Its internal secretion is important in regulating body growth.

tiara /tiˈarə/ *n.* a jewelled ornamental coronet worn by women.

tibia /ˈtɪbiə/ *n., pl.* **tibias**, **tibiae** /ˈtɪbii/. *Anatomy* the inner of the two bones of the lower leg, extending from the knee to the ankle; shinbone.

tic /tɪk/ *n. Pathology* a sudden, painless, purposeless muscular contraction in the face or extremities.

tick[1] /tɪk/ *n.* **1.** a slight, sharp recurring click or beat, as of a clock. **2.** a small mark, as a dash (often formed by two small strokes at an acute angle). *– v.i.* **3.** to emit or produce a tick, like that of a clock. *– v.t.* **4.** to mark (an item, etc.) with a tick, as to indicate examination or correctness. **5. tick off,** to rebuke; scold.

tick[2] /tɪk/ *n.* a blood-sucking mitelike animal.

ticker tape /ˈtɪkə/ *n.* the paper tape on which the tape machine prints its information.

ticket /ˈtɪkət/ *n.* **1.** a slip, usually of paper or cardboard, serving as evidence of the holder's title to some service, right, or the like. **2.** a label or tag. **3.** a list of candidates nominated or put forward by a political party, faction, etc. **4.** a summons issued for a traffic or parking offence. **5.** a preliminary recording of transactions prior to their entry into more permanent books of account. **6. be the ticket,** *Colloquial* to be the correct, right, or proper thing: *that's the ticket!*

tickle /ˈtɪkəl/ *v.t.,* **-led**, **-ling**. **1.** to touch or stroke lightly with the fingers, a feather, etc., so as to excite a tingling or itching sensation in; titillate. **2.** to poke in some sensitive part of the body so as to excite spasmodic laughter.

ticklish /ˈtɪklɪʃ/ *adj.* **1.** sensitive to tickling. **2.** requiring careful handling or action; risky; difficult. **3.** unstable or easily upset, as a boat; unsteady.

tidal wave /ˈtaɪdəl/ *n.* a large destructive ocean wave produced by an earthquake or the like.

tiddler /ˈtɪdlə/ *n.* a very small fish.

tiddly /ˈtɪdli/ *n. Colloquial* slightly drunk.

tide /taɪd/ *n., v.,* **tided**, **tiding**. *– n.* **1.** the periodic rise and fall of the waters of the ocean and its inlets, about every 12 hours and 26 minutes, due to the attraction of the moon and sun. **2.** a tendency, trend, current, etc., as of events, ideas, public opinion, etc. *– v.t.* **3. tide over,** to get (a person, etc.) over a period of difficulty, distress, etc.; enable (a person, etc.) to cope. – **tidal**, *adj.*

tidings /ˈtaɪdɪŋz/ *pl. n.* (*sometimes construed as sing.*) news, information, or intelligence.

tidy /ˈtaɪdi/ *adj.,* **-dier**, **-diest**, *v.,* **-died**, **-dying**. *– adj.* **1.** neat; trim; orderly. **2.** *Colloquial* considerable. *– v.t., v.i.* **3.** to make tidy or neat (often fol. by *up*).

tie /taɪ/ *v.,* **tied**, **tying**, *n. – v.t.* **1.** to bind or fasten with a cord, string, or the like, drawn together and knotted. **2.** to draw together the parts of with a knotted string or the like. **3.** to draw together into a knot, as a cord. **4.** to fasten, join, or connect in any way. **5.** to confine, restrict, or limit. **6.** to bind or oblige, as to do something. *– v.i.* **7.** to make the same score; be equal in a contest. *– n.* **8.** that with which anything is tied. **9.** a narrow, decorative band, as of cotton or silk, worn round the neck, commonly under a collar, and tied in front. **10.** anything that fastens, secures, or unites. **11.** something that restricts one's freedom of action. **12.** a state of equality in points, votes, etc., as among competitors.

tier /tɪə/ *n.* a row, range, or rank.

tiff /tɪf/ *n.* a slight or petty quarrel.

tiger /ˈtaɪgə/ *n.* a large, carnivorous feline.

tiger snake *n.* a highly venomous snake of southern Australia.

tight /taɪt/ *adj.* **1.** firmly or closely fixed in place; not easily moved; secure. **2.** drawn or stretched so as to be tense; taut. **3.** fitting closely, especially too closely. **4.** of such close or compacted texture, or fitted together so closely, as to be impervious to water, air, steam, etc. **5.** strict; firm; rigid. **6.** *Colloquial* stingy; parsimonious. **7.** *Colloquial* drunk; tipsy. **8.** *Commerce* (of a commodity) difficult to obtain. **9.** *Finance* (of credit) not easily obtained.

-tight a suffix meaning 'impervious to', as in *watertight.*

tightrope /ˈtaɪtroʊp/ *n.* a rope or wire stretched tight, on which acrobats perform feats of balancing.

tights /taɪts/ *pl. n.* a close-fitting garment covering the body from the waist downwards, and the legs.

tiki /ˈtiki/ *n.* a carved image representing an ancestor, worn as an amulet in some Polynesian cultures.

tile /taɪl/ *n., v.,* **tiled**, **tiling**. *– n.* **1.** a thin slab or shaped piece of baked clay used for covering roofs, lining walls, paving floors, etc. *– v.t.* **2.** to cover with or as with tiles.

till[1] /tɪl/ *prep.* **1.** up to the time of; until. **2.** (with a negative) before. *– conj.* **3.** to the time that or when; until. **4.** (with a negative) before.

till[2] /tɪl/ *v.t.* to work (land); cultivate.

till[3] /tɪl/ *n.* (in a shop, etc.) a container as a box, drawer, or the like, in which cash is kept.

tilt /tɪlt/ *v.t.* **1.** to cause to lean, incline, slope or slant. *– v.i.* **2.** to move into or assume a sloping position or direction. **3.** to strike, thrust, or charge with a lance or the like (fol. by *at*). *– n.* **4.** an act or instance of tilting. **5.** the state of being tilted; a sloping position.

timber /ˈtɪmbə/ *n.* wood, especially when suitable for building houses, ships, etc., or for use in carpentry, joinery, etc.

timbre /ˈtɪmbə, ˈtæmbə/ *n.* the characteristic quality of a sound.

time /taɪm/ *n., adj., v.,* **timed**, **timing**. *– n.* **1.** the system of those relations which any event has to any other as past, present, or future; indefinite continuous duration regarded as that in which events succeed one another. **2.** a limited extent of time, as between two successive events. **3.** (*often pl.*) the period or era now (or then) present. **4.** a prescribed or allotted period, as of one's life, for payment of a debt, etc. **5.** a particular or definite point in time. **6.** a particular part of a year, day, etc. **7.** the period in which an action is completed, especially a performance in a race. **8.** each occasion of a recurring action or event. **9.** (*pl.*) used as a multiplicative word in phrasal combinations expressing how many instances of a quantity or factor are taken together. **10.** *Music, etc.* tempo; relative rapidity of movement. – *adj.* **11.** of, relating to, or showing the passage of time. **12.** *Commerce* payable a stated period of time after presentment. – *v.t.* **13.** to ascertain or record the time, duration, or rate of. **14.** to appoint or choose the moment or occasion for.

time allowance *n.* an amount of time allowed off the normal working week without loss of pay, in consideration for working under certain unpleasant conditions.

time and a half (quarter, etc.) *n.* a rate of pay for overtime work equal to one and a half (quarter, etc.) times the regular hourly rate.

timely /ˈtaɪmli/ *adj.*, **-lier**, **-liest**. occurring at a suitable time; seasonable; opportune; well-timed.

timepiece /ˈtaɪmpis/ *n.* a clock or a watch.

time share /ˈtaɪm ʃɛə/ *n.* a share in a holiday resort property, entitling the owner to occupy the resort unit for a specified time each year. – **timeshare**, *adj.*

time-sharing /ˈtaɪm-ʃɛərɪŋ/ *n.* the handling by a computer of several programs at the same time.

time sheet *n.* a sheet or card recording the hours worked by an employee.

timetable /ˈtaɪmteɪbəl/ *n.* **1.** a schedule showing the times at which railway trains, buses, aeroplanes, etc., arrive and depart. **2.** any plan listing the times at which certain things are due to take place.

timid /ˈtɪməd/ *adj.* **1.** subject to fear; easily alarmed; timorous; shy. **2.** characterised by or indicating fear.

timing /ˈtaɪmɪŋ/ *n.* **1.** the controlling of the speed of an action, event, etc. **2.** the mechanism which ensures that the valves in an internal-combustion engine open and close at the correct time.

timorous /ˈtɪmərəs/ *adj.* **1.** full of fear; fearful. **2.** subject to fear; timid.

timpani /ˈtɪmpəni/ *pl. n., sing.* **-no** /-noʊ/. a set of kettledrums.

tin /tɪn/ *n., v.,* **tinned, tinning**. – *n.* **1.** a low-melting, metallic element. *Symbol*: Sn (for *stannum*). **2.** any shallow metal pan, especially one used in baking. **3.** a hermetically sealed container for food, especially one made of tin plate. – *v.t.* **4.** to cover or coat with a thin deposit of tin. **5.** to pack or preserve in tins, as foodstuffs.

tincture /ˈtɪŋktʃə/ *n. Pharmaceutical* a solution of a medicinal substance in alcohol.

tinder /ˈtɪndə/ *n.* any dry substance that readily takes fire from a spark.

tine = tyne /taɪn/ *n.* a sharp projecting point or prong, as of a fork or deer's antler.

tinea /ˈtɪniə/ *n.* any of several skin diseases caused by fungi.

ting /tɪŋ/ *v.t., v.i.* to cause to make, or to make, a high, clear, ringing sound.

tinge /tɪnʒ/ *v.,* **tinged**, **tingeing** *or* **tinging**, *n.* – *v.t.* **1.** to impart a trace or slight degree of some colour to; tint. – *n.* **2.** a slight degree of colouration.

tingle /ˈtɪŋgəl/ *v.,* **-gled**, **-gling**, *n.* – *v.i.* **1.** to have a sensation of slight stings or prickly pains, from a sharp blow or from cold. – *n.* **2.** a tingling sensation.

tinker /ˈtɪŋkə/ *n.* **1.** a mender of pots, kettles, pans, etc., usually an itinerant. – *v.i.* **2.** to busy oneself with something, especially a machine or an appliance, usually without useful results.

tinkle /ˈtɪŋkəl/ *v.,* **-kled**, **-kling**, *n.* – *v.i.* **1.** to give forth or make a succession of short, light, ringing sounds. – *n.* **2.** a tinkling sound.

tinny[1] /ˈtɪni/ *adj.,* **-nier**, **-niest**. characteristic of tin, as sounds; lacking resonance.

tinny[2] /ˈtɪni/ *adj. Colloquial* lucky.

tinsel /ˈtɪnsəl/ *n.* an inexpensive glittering metallic substance used in pieces, strips, threads, etc., to produce a sparkling effect.

tint /tɪnt/ *n.* **1.** a colour, or a variety of a colour; hue. **2.** a colour diluted with white. – *v.t.* **3.** to apply a tint or tints to; colour slightly or delicately; tinge.

tiny /ˈtaɪni/ *adj.,* **-nier**, **-niest**. very small; minute; wee.

-tion a suffix used to form abstract nouns. Also, **-ation**, **-cion**, **-ion**, **-sion**, **-xion**.

tip[1] /tɪp/ *n.* **1.** a slender or pointed extremity, especially of anything long or tapered. **2.** the top, summit, or apex.

tip[2] /tɪp/ *v.,* **tipped**, **tipping**, *n.* – *v.t.* **1.** to cause to assume a slanting or sloping position; incline; tilt. **2.** to overthrow, overturn, or upset (often fol. by *over* or *up*). – *v.i.* **3.** to tumble or topple (usually fol. by *over* or *up*). – *n.* **4.** a rubbish dump.

tip[3] /tɪp/ *n., v.,* **tipped**, **tipping**. – *n.* **1.** a small present of money given to someone, as a waiter, porter, etc., for performing a service; a gratuity. **2.** a useful hint or idea. – *v.t.* **3.** to give a small present of money to.

tipple /ˈtɪpəl/ *v.t.,* **-pled**, **-pling**. to drink (wine, spirits, etc.), especially repeatedly.

tipsy /ˈtɪpsi/ *adj.,* **-sier**, **-siest**. slightly intoxicated.

tiptoe /ˈtɪptoʊ/ *n., v.,* **-toed**, **-toeing**. – *n.* **1.** the tip or end of a toe. – *v.i.* **2.** to move or go on tiptoe, as with caution or stealth.

tirade /taɪˈreɪd, təˈreɪd/ *n.* a prolonged outburst of denunciation.

tire /ˈtaɪə/ *v.,* **tired**, **tiring**. – *v.t.* **1.** to reduce or exhaust the strength of, as by exertion; make weary; fatigue (sometimes fol. by *out*). – *v.i.* **2.** to have the strength reduced or exhausted, as by labour or exertion; become fatigued. **3.** to have one's appreciation, interest, patience, etc., exhausted; become or be weary (usually fol. by *of*).

'tis /tɪz/ contraction of *it is.*

tissue /ˈtɪʃu/ *n.* **1.** *Biology* the substance of which an organism or part is composed. **2.** a woven fabric, especially one of light or gauzy texture, originally woven with gold or silver. **3.** any of several kinds of soft gauzelike papers used for various purposes. **4.** a paper handkerchief.

tit[1] /tɪt/ *n.* a small bird.

tit[2] /tɪt/ *n. Colloquial* a female breast.

titanium /taɪ'teɪniəm/ *n.* a metallic element. *Symbol*: Ti

titbit /'tɪtbɪt/ *n.* **1.** a delicate bit of food. **2.** a choice or pleasing bit of anything.

tithe /taɪð/ *n.* (*often pl.*) the tenth part of the annual produce of agriculture, etc., due or paid as a tax.

titian /'tɪʃən, 'ti-/ *n.* a reddish brown colour.

titillate /'tɪtəleɪt/ *v.t.*, **-lated**, **-lating**. **1.** to tickle; excite a tingling or itching sensation in, as by touching or stroking lightly. **2.** to excite agreeably.

titivate /'tɪtəveɪt/ *v.*, **-vated**, **-vating**. *Colloquial* – *v.i.* **1.** to make oneself smart or spruce. – *v.t.* **2.** to make smart or spruce.

title /'taɪtl/ *n.* **1.** the distinguishing name of a book, poem, picture, piece of music, or the like. **2.** a descriptive or distinctive appellation, especially one belonging to a person by right of rank, office, attainment, etc. **3.** *Sport* the championship. **4.** established or recognised right to something. **5.** *Law* **a.** legal right to the possession of property, especially real property. **b.** the instrument constituting evidence of such right.

title deed *n. Law* a deed or document containing or constituting evidence of ownership.

titter /'tɪtə/ *v.i.* to laugh in a low, half-restrained way, as from nervousness or in ill-suppressed amusement.

tittle-tattle /'tɪtl-tætl/ *n.* gossip.

titular /'tɪtʃələ/ *adj.* **1.** of, relating to, or of the nature of a title. **2.** existing or being such in title only.

tizz /tɪz/ *n. Colloquial* a state of somewhat hysterical confusion and anxiety, often expressed in frantic but ineffectual activity.

tizzy /'tɪzi/ *adj. Colloquial* gaudy, vulgar.

to /tu/, *weak form* /tə/ – *prep.* **1.** expressing motion or direction towards something. **2.** indicating limit of movement or extension. **3.** expressing a point or limit in time. **4.** expressing aim, purpose, or intention. **5.** expressing limit in degree or amount. **6.** indicating addition or amount. **7.** expressing comparison or opposition. **8.** expressing reference or relation. **9.** expressing relative position. **10.** indicating proportion or ratio. **11.** connecting transitive verbs with their indirect or distant objects, and adjectives, nouns, and intransitive or passive verbs with a following noun which limits their action or application. **12.** used as the ordinary sign or accompaniment of the infinitive. – *adv.* **13.** towards a person, thing, or point implied or understood. **14.** to consciousness; to one's senses.

toad /toʊd/ *n.* a terrestrial amphibian similar to a frog.

toadstool /'toʊdstul/ *n.* a usually poisonous fungus, similar to a mushroom.

toast[1] /toʊst/ *n.* bread in slices browned on both surfaces by heat.

toast[2] /toʊst/ *n.* **1.** a person whose health is proposed and drunk. **2.** a call on another or others to drink to some person or thing. **3.** words of congratulation, appreciation, loyalty, etc., spoken before drinking. – *v.t.* **4.** to drink to the health of, or in honour of.

tobacco /tə'bækoʊ/ *n., pl.* **-cos**, **-coes**. a plant whose leaves are prepared for smoking or chewing or as snuff.

toboggan /tə'bɒgən/ *n.* a light sledge with low runners.

today /tə'deɪ/ *n.* **1.** this present day. – *adv.* **2.** on this present day.

toddle /'tɒdl/ *v.i.*, **-dled**, **-dling**. to go with short, unsteady steps, as a child or an old person.

toddy /'tɒdi/ *n., pl.* **-dies**. a drink made of spirits and hot water.

to-do /tə-'du/ *n., pl.* **-dos**. *Colloquial* bustle; fuss.

toe /toʊ/ *n.* **1.** (in humans) one of the terminal members or digits of the foot. **2.** an analogous part in other animals. **3.** a part resembling a toe in shape or position.

toff /tɒf/ *n. Colloquial* a rich, upper-class, usually well-dressed person; a gentleman.

toffee /'tɒfi/ *n.* a sweet made of sugar or treacle.

tofu /'toʊfu/ *n.* a curd made from white soya beans, usually formed into small blocks; bean curd.

toga /'toʊgə/ *n., pl.* **-gas**. the loose outer garment of the citizens of ancient Rome.

together /tə'gɛðə/ *adv.* **1.** into or in one gathering, company, mass, place, or body. **2.** at the same time; simultaneously. **3.** in cooperation; with united action. – *adj.* **4.** capable and calm.

toggle /'tɒgəl/ *n.* **1.** a transverse pin, bolt, or rod placed through an eye of a rope, link of a chain, or the like, for various purposes. **2.** *Computers* a key or command that has the reverse effect on each successive use.

togs /tɒgz/ *pl. n. Colloquial* clothes.

toil /tɔɪl/ *n.* **1.** hard and continuous work; exhausting labour or effort. – *v.i.* **2.** to engage in severe and continuous work; labour arduously.

toilet /'tɔɪlət/ *n.* **1.** a disposal apparatus of any type used for urination and defecation, especially a water closet. **2.** the act or process of dressing, including bathing, arranging the hair, etc.

toiletry /'tɔɪlətri/ *n., pl.* **-tries**. an article or substance used in dressing or hygiene.

token /'toʊkən/ *n.* **1.** something serving to represent or indicate some fact, event, feeling, etc.; sign. **2.** a characteristic mark or indication; symbol. **3.** a ticket, metal disc, etc., certified as having a particular value, for payment or exchange, as for ferry fares, at a nominal value much greater than its commodity value. **4.** a particular act or event, especially as an instance of a class or type.

told /toʊld/ *v.* **1.** past tense and past participle of **tell**. **2. all told,** in all.

tolerate /'tɒləreɪt/ *v.t.*, **-rated**, **-rating**. **1.** to allow; permit. **2.** to bear without repugnance; put up with. **3.** *Medicine* to endure or resist the action of (a drug, poison, etc.). – **tolerable**, *adj.* – **tolerance**, *n.* – **tolerant**, *adj.* – **toleration**, *n.*

toll[1] /toʊl/ *v.t.* **1.** to cause (a large bell) to sound with single strokes slowly and regularly repeated, as for summoning a congregation to church, or especially for announcing a death. – *v.i.* **2.** to sound with single strokes slowly and regularly repeated, as a bell.

toll[2] /toʊl/ *n.* **1.** Also, **tollage**. a payment exacted by the state, the local authorities, etc., for some right or privilege, as for passage along a road or over a bridge. **2.** exaction, cost or the like, especially in terms of death or loss.

tom /tɒm/ *n.* the male of various animals.

tomahawk /'tɒməhɔk/ *n.* a small, short-handled axe.

tomato /tə'matoʊ/ *n., pl.* **-toes**. a widely cultivated plant bearing a slightly acid, pulpy fruit, commonly red, sometimes yellow, used as a vegetable.

tomb /tum/ *n.* an excavation in earth or rock for the reception of a dead body.

tomboy /'tɒmbɔɪ/ *n.* a boisterous, romping girl.

tombstone /'tumstoʊn/ *n.* a stone, usually bearing an inscription, set to mark a tomb or grave.

tome /toʊm/ *n.* any volume, especially a ponderous one.

tomfoolery /tɒm'fuləri/ *n., pl.* **-eries**. foolish or silly behaviour.

tomorrow /tə'mɒroʊ/ *n.* **1.** the day after this day. – *adv.* **2.** on the morrow; on the day after this day.

tom-tom /'tɒm-tɒm/ *n.* a type of drum.

ton /tʌn/ *n.* **1.** a unit of mass in the imperial system equal to 2240 lb. **2.** → **tonne**. – **tonnage**, *n.*

tone /toʊn/ *n., v.,* **toned**, **toning**. – *n.* **1.** any sound considered with reference to its quality, pitch, strength, source, etc. **2.** quality or character of sound. **3.** a particular quality, way of sounding, modulation, or intonation of the voice. **4.** stress of voice on a syllable of a word. **5.** *Music* an interval equivalent to two semitones. **6.** a variety of colour; a tint; a shade. **7.** *Physiology* the state of tension or firmness proper to the organs or tissues of the body. **8.** style, distinction, or elegance. – *v.t.* **9.** to sound with a particular tone. **10.** to give the proper tone to. **11.** to modify the tone or character of. – *v.i.* **12.** to harmonise in tone or colour (fol. by *with* or *in with*). – **tonal**, *adj.*

tongs /tɒŋz/ *pl. n.* (*sometimes construed as sing.*) any of various implements consisting of two arms fastened together, for seizing, holding, or lifting something.

tongue /tʌŋ/ *n.* **1.** an organ in humans and most vertebrates occupying the floor of the mouth and often protrusible and freely movable, being the principal organ of taste, and, in humans, of articulate speech. **2.** the faculty or power of speech. **3.** the language of a particular people, country, or locality. **4.** something resembling or suggesting an animal's tongue in shape, position, or function.

tonic /'tɒnɪk/ *n.* **1.** a medicine that invigorates or strengthens. **2.** anything invigorating physically, mentally, or morally. **3.** *Music* the first degree of the scale; the keynote. – *adj.* **4.** relating to, maintaining, increasing, or restoring the tone or healthy condition of the system or organs, as a medicine. **5.** invigorating physically, mentally, or morally. **6.** characterised by distinctions of tone or accent.

tonic water *n.* effervescent water with quinine, often added to spirits.

tonight /tə'naɪt/ *n.* **1.** this present or coming night; the night of this present day. – *adv.* **2.** on this present night; on the night of this present day.

tonne /tɒn/ *n.* a unit of mass equal to 1000 kilograms. *Symbol*: t

tonsil /'tɒnsəl/ *n.* *Anatomy* either of two prominent oval masses of lymphoid tissue situated one on each side of the throat.

tonsure /'tɒnʃə/ *n.* the shaving of the head, or of some part of it, as a religious practice or rite.

tontine /'tɒntin, tɒn'tin/ *n.* **1.** a scheme in which subscribers to a common fund share an annuity with the benefit of survivorship, the shares of the survivors being increased as the subscribers die, until the whole goes to the last survivor. **2.** any of various forms of life insurance in which the chief benefits accrue to participants who are alive and whose policies are in force at the end of a specified period.

too /tu/ *adv.* **1.** in addition; also; furthermore; moreover. **2.** to an excessive extent or degree.

took /tʊk/ *v.* past tense of **take**.

tool /tul/ *n.* **1.** an instrument, especially one held in the hand, for performing or facilitating mechanical operations, as a hammer, saw, file, etc. **2.** a person used by another for that person's own ends. – *v.t.* **3.** to work or shape with a tool.

toot /tut/ *v.i.* **1.** (of a horn) to give forth its characteristic sound. – *v.t.* **2.** to cause (a horn, etc.) to sound by blowing it.

tooth /tuθ/ *n., pl.* **teeth** /tiθ/. **1.** (in most vertebrates) one of the hard bodies or processes usually attached in a row to each jaw, used for chewing, etc. **2.** any projection resembling or suggesting a tooth.

tootle /'tutl/ *v.i.,* **-tled**, **-tling**. *Colloquial* to go, walk, or drive.

top[1] /tɒp/ *n., adj., v.,* **topped**, **topping**. – *n.* **1.** the highest point or part of anything. **2.** the highest or leading place, position, rank, etc. **3.** the highest point, pitch, or degree. **4.** a covering or lid, as of a box, motor car, carriage, etc. **5.** a blouse, skivvy, jumper, jacket or other outer garment, sometimes with sleeves, to cover the torso. – *adj.* **6.** relating to, situated at, or forming the top; highest; uppermost; upper. **7.** highest in degree; greatest. **8.** foremost, chief, or principal. **9.** *Colloquial* the best; excellent. – *v.t.* **10.** to furnish with a top; put a top on. **11.** to be at or constitute the top of. **12.** to reach the top of. **13.** to surpass, excel, or outdo. **14.** to remove the top of; crop; prune.

top[2] /tɒp/ *n.* a child's toy, having a point on which it is made to spin.

topaz /'toʊpæz/ *n.* a mineral occurring in crystals of various colours, and used as a gem.

topiary /'toʊpiəri/ *adj.* (of hedges, trees, etc.) clipped or trimmed into (fantastic) shapes.

topic /'tɒpɪk/ *n.* a subject of conversation or discussion.

topical /ˈtɒpɪkəl/ *adj.* **1.** relating to or dealing with matters of current or local interest. **2.** relating to the subject of a discourse, composition, or the like.

topnotch /ˈtɒpnɒtʃ/ *adj. Colloquial* first-rate.

topo- a word element meaning 'place'.

topography /təˈpɒgrəfi/ *n., pl.* **-phies**. the relief features or surface configuration of an area.

topple /ˈtɒpəl/ *v.i.,* **-pled**, **-pling**. to fall forwards as having too heavy a top.

topsoil /ˈtɒpsɔɪl/ *n.* the surface or upper part of the soil.

topsy-turvy /tɒpsi-ˈtɜvi/ *adj.* turned upside down; inverted; reversed.

tor /tɔ/ *n.* a rocky eminence; a hill.

torch /tɔtʃ/ *n.* **1.** a small portable electric lamp powered by dry batteries. **2.** a flame carried in the hand to give light. **3.** any of various lamplike devices which produce a hot flame and are used for soldering, burning off paint, etc.

tore /tɔ/ *v.* past tense of **tear**[2].

toreador /ˈtɒriədɔ/ *n.* a bullfighter.

torment /tɔˈmɛnt/ *v.,* /ˈtɔmɛnt/ *n.* – *v.t.* **1.** to afflict with great bodily or mental suffering. – *n.* **2.** a state of great bodily or mental suffering; agony; misery. **3.** a source of pain, anguish, trouble.

torn /tɔn/ *v.* past participle of **tear**[2].

tornado /tɔˈneɪdoʊ/ *n., pl.* **-does**, **-dos**. a violent whirlwind.

torpedo /tɔˈpidoʊ/ *n., pl.* **-does**, *v.,* **-doed**, **-doing**. – *n.* **1.** a self-propelled cigar-shaped missile containing explosives. – *v.t.* **2.** to damage, or destroy with a torpedo or torpedoes.

torpor /ˈtɔpə/ *n.* lethargic dullness or indifference; apathy. – **torpid**, *adj.*

torque /tɔk/ *n. Mechanics* that which produces or tends to produce torsion or rotation.

Torrens title /ˈtɒrənz/ *n.* a system whereby title to land is evidenced by one document issued by a government department.

torrent /ˈtɒrənt/ *n.* a stream of water flowing with great rapidity and violence. – **torrential**, *adj.*

torrid /ˈtɒrəd/ *adj.* **1.** oppressively hot, parching, or burning. **2.** ardent; passionate.

torsion /ˈtɔʃən/ *n.* **1.** the act of twisting. **2.** the resulting state. **3.** *Mechanics* **a.** the twisting of a body by two equal and opposite torques. **b.** the internal torque so produced.

torso /ˈtɔsoʊ/ *n., pl.* **-sos**. the trunk of the human body.

tort /tɔt/ *n. Law* **1.** any wrong other than a criminal wrong, as negligence, defamation, etc. **2.** (*pl.*) the field of study of torts.

tortoise /ˈtɔtəs/ *n.* a slow-moving reptile, with a hard shell into which it can retract its head and feet.

tortoiseshell /ˈtɔtəʃɛl/ *n.* a hard, brown, mottled substance obtained from the shell of a type of tortoise, or a synthetic equivalent.

tortuous /ˈtɔtʃuəs/ *adj.* **1.** full of twists, turns, or bends. **2.** not direct or straightforward.

torture /ˈtɔtʃə/ *n., v.,* **-tured**, **-turing**. – *n.* **1.** the act of inflicting excruciating pain, especially from sheer cruelty or in hatred, revenge, or the like. **2.** extreme anguish of body or mind; agony. – *v.t.* **3.** to subject to torture. – **torturous**, *adj.*

toss /tɒs/ *v.t.* **1.** to throw, pitch, or fling, especially to throw lightly or carelessly. – *v.i.* **2.** to pitch, rock, sway, or move irregularly, as a flag or plumes in the breeze. **3.** to move restlessly about. – *n.* **4.** the act of tossing.

tot[1] /tɒt/ *n.* a small child.

tot[2] /tɒt/ *v.t.,* **totted**, **totting**. *Colloquial* to add (often fol. by *up*).

total /ˈtoʊtl/ *adj., n., v.,* **-talled**, **-talling**. – *adj.* **1.** constituting or comprising the whole; entire; whole. **2.** complete in extent or degree; absolute; unqualified; utter. – *n.* **3.** the total amount; sum; aggregate. – *v.t.* **4.** to bring to a total; add up. **5.** to reach a total of; amount to.

totalisator = totalizator /ˈtoʊtəlaɪˌzeɪtə/ *n.* a form of betting, as on horseraces, in which those who bet on the winners divide the bets or stakes, less a percentage for the management, taxes, etc.

totalitarian /toʊˌtæləˈtɛəriən/ *adj.* of or relating to a centralised government in which those in control grant neither recognition nor tolerance to parties of differing opinion.

totality /toʊˈtæləti/ *n., pl.* **-ties**. **1.** the state of being total. **2.** that which is total.

tote /toʊt/ *v.t.,* **toted**, **toting**. *Colloquial* to carry, as on the back or in the arms, as a burden or load.

totem /ˈtoʊtəm/ *n.* an object or natural phenomenon, often an animal, assumed as the token or emblem of a clan, family, or related group. – **totemic**, *adj.*

totter /ˈtɒtə/ *v.i.* **1.** to walk or go with faltering steps, as if from extreme weakness. **2.** to sway or rock on the base or ground, as if about to fall.

toucan /ˈtukæn/ *n.* a strikingly coloured bird with a huge beak.

touch /tʌtʃ/ *v.t.* **1.** to put the hand, finger, etc., on or into contact with (something) to feel it. **2.** to come into or be in contact with. **3.** to come up to; reach; attain. **4.** to affect with some feeling or emotion. **5.** to be a matter of importance to; make a difference to. **6.** *Colloquial* to apply to for money. – *v.i.* **7.** to come into or be in contact with something. **8.** to speak or write briefly or casually (fol. by *on* or *upon*) in the course of a discourse, etc. – *n.* **9.** the act of touching. **10.** that sense by which anything material is perceived by means of the contact with it of some part of the body. **11.** the sensation or effect caused by touching something, regarded as a quality of the thing. **12.** a slight stroke or blow. **13.** a slight attack, as of illness or disease. **14.** manner of execution in artistic work. **15.** a slight amount. **16.** *Colloquial* a person from whom one can obtain money as a gift or loan.

touch-type /ˈtʌtʃ-taɪp/ *v.i.,* **-typed**, **typing**. to type without looking at the keys of the typewriter or computer keyboard.

touchy /ˈtʌtʃi/ *adj.,* **touchier**, **touchiest**.

1. irritable. **2.** risky.

tough /tʌf/ *adj.* **1.** not easily broken or cut. **2.** capable of great endurance; sturdy; hardy. **3.** difficult to perform, accomplish, or deal with; hard, trying, or troublesome. **4.** vigorous; severe; violent.

toupee /ˈtupeɪ/ *n.* a wig worn to cover a bald spot.

tour /tʊə, ˈtuə, tɔ/ *v.i.* **1.** to travel from place to place. – *n.* **2.** a travelling around from place to place. **3.** a long journey including the visiting of a number of places in sequence. **4.** *Chiefly Military* a period of duty at one place.

tourism /ˈtʊərɪzəm, ˈtuə-, ˈtɔ-/ *n.* the occupation of providing local services, as entertainment, lodging, food, etc., for tourists.

tourist /ˈtʊərəst, ˈtuə-, ˈtɔ-/ *n.* someone who tours, especially for pleasure.

tournament /ˈtɔnəmənt/ *n.* **1.** a meeting for contests in athletic or other sports. **2.** a trial of skill in some game, in which competitors play a series of contests.

tourniquet /ˈtɔnəkeɪ, ˈtʊə-/ *n.* any device for arresting bleeding by forcibly compressing a blood vessel.

tousle /ˈtaʊzəl/ *v.t.*, **-sled**, **-sling**. **1.** to disorder or dishevel. **2.** to handle roughly.

tout /taʊt/ *v.i.* **1.** to solicit business, employment, votes, etc., importunately. **2.** *Racing* to sell betting information, take bets, etc., especially in public places. – *n.* **3.** someone who touts.

tow /toʊ/ *v.t.* **1.** to drag or pull (a boat, car, etc.) by means of a rope or chain. – *n.* **2.** the act of towing.

towards /təˈwɔdz, tɔdz/ *prep.* **1.** in the direction of (with reference to either motion or position). **2.** with respect to; as regards. **3.** as a help or contribution to. Also, **toward**.

towel /ˈtaʊəl, taʊl/ *n.* a cloth or the like for wiping and drying something wet.

towelling /ˈtaʊəlɪŋ/ *n.* any of various absorbent fabrics used for towels, and also for beachwear and the like.

tower /ˈtaʊə/ *n.* **1.** a building or structure high in proportion to its width. **2.** any of various tower-like structures, contrivances, or objects. – *v.i.* **3.** to rise or extend far upwards. **4.** to surpass, as in ability, etc. (fol. by *over*, *above*, etc.).

town /taʊn/ *n.* **1.** a distinct densely populated area of considerable size, having some degree of self-government, usually smaller than a city. **2.** urban life, opposed to rural. **3.** the main shopping, business, or entertainment centre of a large town, contrasted with the suburbs. **4.** an urban community; the people of a town.

town clerk *n.* an appointed official of a council who is in charge of all responsibilities of local government.

town hall *n.* a hall or building belonging to a town, used for the transaction of the town's business, etc., and often also as a place of public assembly.

town house *n.* a house designed as part of a small block of such, each with ground floor access.

township /ˈtaʊnʃɪp/ *n.* a small town or settlement.

toxicology /tɒksəˈkɒlədʒi/ *n.* the science of poisons, their effects, antidotes, detection, etc.

toxin /ˈtɒksən/ *n.* a specific poisonous product generated by a disease-producing micro-organism. – **toxic**, *adj.* – **toxicity**, *n.*

toy /tɔɪ/ *n.* **1.** an object for playing with, usually by children; a plaything. – *adj.* **2.** of or like a toy, especially in size. – *v.i.* **3.** to act idly, absentmindedly, or without seriousness. **4.** to trifle; deal with as unimportant (usually fol. by *with*).

trace[1] /treɪs/ *n.*, *v.*, **traced**, **tracing**. – *n.* **1.** a mark, token, or evidence of the former presence, existence, or action of something; a vestige. **2.** a mark, indication, or evidence. **3.** a scarcely discernible quantity of something; a very small amount. **4.** a record traced by a self-registering instrument. – *v.t.* **5.** to follow the footprints, track, or traces of. **6.** to follow the course, development, or history of. **7.** to copy (a drawing, plan, etc.) by following the lines of the original on a superimposed transparent sheet. **8.** to make a plan, diagram, or map of.

trace[2] /treɪs/ *n.* each of the two straps, ropes, or chains by which a carriage, wagon, or the like is drawn by a harness horse or other draught animal.

trace element *n.* *Biochemistry* a chemical element, found in plants and animals in minute quantities, which is a critical factor in physiological processes.

tracery /ˈtreɪsəri/ *n.*, *pl.* **-ries**. any delicate interlacing work of lines, threads, etc.

trachea /trəˈkiə/ *n.*, *pl.* **-cheas**, **-cheae** /-ˈkii/. the principal passage for conveying air to and from the lungs; the windpipe.

track /træk/ *n.* **1.** a road, path, or trail. **2.** the structure of rails, sleepers, etc., on which a railway train or the like runs; a railway line. **3.** the mark, or series of marks, left by anything that has passed along. **4.** a rough roadway or path. **5.** a route, usually only roughly defined. **6.** an endless jointed metal band around the wheels of some heavy vehicles. **7.** a course of action or conduct; a method of proceeding. **8.** a course laid out for running or racing. **9.** one of the distinct sections of a gramophone record containing a piece, or section of music, etc. – *v.t.* **10.** to hunt by following the tracks of. **11.** to catch or find, after pursuit or searching (fol. by *down*). **12.** to follow (a track, course, etc.).

track record *n.* an account of a person's successes or failures in a specific field.

tracksuit /ˈtræksut/ *n.* a loose, two-piece overgarment worn by athletes in training, between events, etc.

tract[1] /trækt/ *n.* a stretch or extent, as of land, water, etc.

tract[2] /trækt/ *n.* a brief treatise or pamphlet suitable for general distribution, especially one dealing with some topic of practical religion.

tractable /ˈtræktəbəl/ *adj.* easily managed, or docile.

traction /ˈtrækʃən/ *n.* **1.** the act of drawing or pulling. **2.** the adhesive friction of a body, as of a wheel on a rail.

tractor /ˈtræktə/ *n.* a motor vehicle, usually

fitted with deeply treaded tyres, used to draw farm implements.

trade /treɪd/ *n.*, *v.*, **traded**, **trading**. – *n.* **1.** the buying and selling, or exchanging, of commodities, either by wholesale or by retail, within a country or between countries. **2.** market: *the tourist trade.* **3.** commercial occupation (as against professional). – *v.t.* **4.** to give in return; exchange; barter. **5. trade in,** to give in part exchange, as in a transaction. – *v.i.* **6.** to carry on trade.

trade cycle *n.* the recurrent alternation of boom-time and depression in a country's economy.

trade gap *n.* the difference between the value of a country's imports and of its exports, when the former is a larger figure.

trademark /'treɪdmak/ *n.* the name, symbol, figure, letter, word, or mark adopted and used by a manufacturer or merchant in order to designate the goods he or she manufactures or sells, and to distinguish them from those manufactured or sold by others. Any mark entitled to registration under the provisions of a statute is a trademark. Also, **trade mark**.

trade name *n.* **1.** the name or style under which a firm does business. **2.** a word or phrase used in trade whereby a business or enterprise or a particular class of goods is designated, but which is not technically a trademark, either because it is not susceptible of exclusive appropriation as a trademark or because it is not affixed to goods sold in the market. **3.** the name by which an article or substance is known to the trade.

trade-off /'treɪd-ɒf/ *n.* a concession made in a negotiation in return for one given.

trade price *n.* the price at which goods are sold to members of the same trade, or to retail dealers by wholesalers.

trade reference *n.* **1.** an individual or company in business to which one is referred for information concerning an applicant's credit standing. **2.** the reference itself.

trade union *n.* an organisation of employees for mutual aid and protection, and for dealing collectively with employers. Also, **trades union**. – **trade unionism**, *n.* – **trade unionist**, *n.*

trading bank /'treɪdɪŋ/ *n.* a bank which offers a wide variety of financial services to both individual and corporate customers, and able to compete freely with merchant banks and other financial institutions. In 1989, the distinction between trading banks and savings banks was removed in Australia.

trading stamp *n.* a stamp with a certain value given as a premium by a seller to a customer, specified quantities of these stamps being exchangeable for various articles when presented to the issuers of the stamps.

trading stock *n.* stock not held for permanent investment.

tradition /trə'dɪʃən/ *n.* the handing down of statements, beliefs, legends, customs, etc., from generation to generation, especially by word of mouth or by practice. – **traditional**, *adj.*

traduce /trə'djus/ *v.t.*, **-duced**, **-ducing**. to speak evil or maliciously and falsely of.

traffic /'træfɪk/ *n.*, *v.*, **-ficked**, **-ficking**. – *n.* **1.** the coming and going of persons, vehicles, ships, etc., along a way of passage or travel. **2.** trade; buying and selling; commercial dealings. **3.** dealings or exchanges of anything between parties, people, etc. – *v.i.* **4.** to carry on dealings of an illicit or improper kind.

tragedy /'trædʒədi/ *n.*, *pl.* **-dies**. **1.** a dramatic composition of serious or sombre character, with an unhappy ending. **2.** a disaster or calamity. – **tragic**, *adj.*

trail /treɪl/ *v.t.* **1.** to draw or drag along behind. – *v.i.* **2.** to be drawn or dragged along the ground or some other surface, as when hanging from something moving. **3.** to hang down loosely from something. – *n.* **4.** a path or track made across a wild region, over rough country, or the like, by the passage of people or animals. **5.** the track, scent, or the like, left by an animal, person, or thing, especially as followed by a hunter, hound, or other pursuer.

trailer /'treɪlə/ *n.* **1.** a vehicle designed to be towed by a motor vehicle, and used in transporting loads. **2.** *Film* an advertisement for a forthcoming film, usually consisting of extracts from it.

train /treɪn/ *n.* **1.** a set of railway carriages or wagons, whether self-propelled or connected to a locomotive. **2.** a line or procession of persons, vehicles, etc., travelling together. **3.** an elongated part of a skirt or dress trailing behind on the ground. **4.** a succession or series of proceedings, events, circumstances, etc. **5.** a succession of connected ideas; a course of reasoning. – *v.t.* **6.** to make proficient by instruction and practice, as in some art, profession, or work. **7.** to make (a person, etc.) fit by proper exercise, diet, etc., as for some athletic feat or contest. **8.** to discipline and instruct (an animal) to perform specified actions. – *v.i.* **9.** to undergo discipline and instruction, drill, etc. **10.** to get oneself into condition by exercise, etc.

trainee /treɪ'ni/ *n.* **1.** one receiving training. – *adj.* **2.** receiving training.

traipse /treɪps/ *v.i.*, **traipsed**, **traipsing**. to walk (about) aimlessly.

trait /treɪ, treɪt/ *n.* a distinguishing feature or quality; characteristic.

traitor /'treɪtə/ *n.* someone who betrays their country by violating their allegiance; one guilty of treason.

trajectory /trə'dʒɛktəri/ *n.*, *pl.* **-ries**. the curve described by a projectile in its flight.

tram /træm/ *n.* a passenger vehicle moving on tracks laid in urban streets. Also, **tramcar**.

trammel /'træməl/ *n.* (*usu. pl.*) anything that impedes or hinders free action; a restraint.

tramp /træmp/ *v.i.* **1.** to tread or walk with a firm, heavy, resounding step. **2.** to go about as a vagabond or tramp. – *n.* **3.** the act of tramping. **4.** a person who travels about on foot from place to place, especially a vagabond living on occasional jobs or gifts of money or food.

trample /'træmpəl/ *v.t.*, **-pled**, **-pling**. to tread heavily, roughly, or carelessly on or over.

trampoline /'træmpəlin, træmpə'lin/ *n.* a sheet of canvas attached by resilient cords to a horizontal frame used as a springboard when performing acrobatics.

trance /træns, trans/ *n.* **1.** a dazed or bewildered condition. **2.** a fit of complete mental absorption or deep musing. **3.** an unconscious hypnotic condition.

tranche /træntʃ, trantʃ/ *n.* an additional block of stock, as bonds, etc., supplementary to an already existing issue.

tranquil /'træŋkwəl/ *adj.*, **-quiller**, **-quillest**. **1.** free from commotion or tumult; peaceful; quiet; calm. **2.** free from or unaffected by disturbing emotions; unruffled. – **tranquillity**, *n.* – **tranquillise = tranquillize**, *v.*

trans- a prefix meaning 'across', 'beyond'.

transact /trænz'ækt/ *v.t.* to carry through (affairs, business, negotiations, etc.) to a conclusion or settlement.

transaction /trænz'ækʃən/ *n.* **1.** the act of transacting. **2.** an instance or process of transacting something. **3.** that which is transacted; an affair; a piece of business.

transcend /træn'sɛnd/ *v.t.* to go or be above or beyond; surpass or exceed. – **transcendent**, *adj.*

transcendental /trænsɛn'dɛntl/ *adj.* transcending ordinary or common experience, thought, or belief.

transcribe /træn'skraɪb/ *v.t.*, **-scribed**, **-scribing**. **1.** to make a copy of in writing. **2.** to reproduce in writing or print as from speech. **3.** to write out in other characters; transliterate. – **transcript**, *n.* – **transcription**, *n.*

transfer /træns'fɜ/ *v.*, **-ferred**, **-ferring** /'trænsfɜ/. *n.* – *v.t.* **1.** to convey or remove from one place, person, etc., to another. **2.** *Law* to make over or convey – *n.* **3.** the means or system of transferring. **4.** the act of transferring. **5.** a drawing, pattern, etc., which may be transferred to a surface, especially by direct contact. **6.** *Law* a conveyance, by sale, gift, or otherwise, of real or personal property, to another. **7.** *Finance* the act of having the ownership of a stock or registered bond transferred upon the books of the issuing company or its agent. **8.** *Finance* a deed completed when stocks and shares change hands, which is registered with the company issuing the shares. – **transferable**, *adj.* – **transference**, *n.* – **transferral**, *n.*

transfigure /træns'fɪgə/ *v.t.*, **-ured**, **-uring**. to change in outward form or appearance; transform, change, or alter.

transfix /træns'fɪks/ *v.t.* **1.** to pierce through, as with a pointed weapon, or as the weapon does. **2.** to make motionless with amazement, terror, etc.

transform /træns'fɔm/ *v.t.* **1.** to change in form. **2.** to change in appearance, condition, nature, or character, especially completely or extensively. – **transformation**, *n.*

transformer /træns'fɔmə/ *n.* *Electricity* an electric device which transforms electric energy from circuit to circuit, usually also changing voltage and current.

transfuse /træns'fjuz/ *v.t.*, **-fused**, **-fusing**. **1.** to pour from one container into another. **2.** *Medicine* to transfer (blood) from the veins or arteries of one person or animal into those of another. – **transfusion**, *n.*

transgress /trænz'grɛs/ *v.t.* to go beyond the limits imposed by (a law, command, etc.). – **transgression**, *n.*

transient /'trænziənt/ *adj.* **1.** not lasting or enduring. **2.** remaining for only a short time, as a guest at a hotel. – *n.* **3.** someone who or that which is transient. – **transience**, *n.*

transistor /træn'zɪstə/ *n.* **1.** *Electronics* a miniature solid-state device for amplifying or switching. **2.** a radio equipped with transistors.

transit /'trænzət/ *n.* **1.** the act or fact of passing across or through; passage from one place to another. **2.** conveyance from one place to another, as of persons or goods.

transition /træn'zɪʃən/ *n.* passage from one position, state, stage, etc., to another.

transitive verb /'trænzətɪv/ *n.* **1.** a verb which can only be used with a direct object. **2.** a verb used with a direct object, as *drink* in the sentence *she drinks water* where *water* is the direct object. Cf. **intransitive verb**.

transitory /'trænzətri/ *adj.* passing away; not lasting, enduring, permanent or eternal.

translate /trænz'leɪt/ *v.t.*, **-lated**, **-lating**. **1.** to turn (something written or spoken) from one language into another. **2.** to express in other terms; interpret; explain. – **translation**, *n.*

transliterate /trænz'lɪtəreɪt/ *v.t.*, **-rated**, **-rating**. to change (letters, words, etc.) into corresponding characters of another alphabet or language.

translucent /trænz'lusənt/ *adj.* transmitting light imperfectly, as frosted glass.

transmission /trænz'mɪʃən/ *n.* **1.** the act of transmitting. **2.** that which is transmitted. **3.** *Machinery* **a.** the transmitting or transferring of motive force. **b.** a device for this purpose, especially the mechanism for transmitting power from the engine to the wheels of a motor vehicle.

transmit /trænz'mɪt/ *v.t.*, **-mitted**, **-mitting**. **1.** to send over or along, as to a recipient or destination; forward, dispatch, or convey. **2.** to communicate, as information, news, etc. **3.** to broadcast (a radio or television program). **4.** to convey or pass along.

transmogrify /trænz'mɒgrəfaɪ/ *v.t.*, **-fied**, **-fying**. to change as by magic; transform.

transmute /trænz'mjut/ *v.t.*, **-muted**, **-muting**. to change from one nature, substance, or form into another; transform.

transnational /trænz'næʃənəl/ *adj.* **1.** operating on a nationwide basis. **2.** → **multinational**.

transom /'trænsəm/ *n.* a lintel.

transparency /træns'pɛərənsi, -'pær-/ *n.*, *pl.* **-cies**. **1.** Also, **transparence**. the property or quality of being transparent. **2.** a transparent positive photographic image used for projection.

transparent /træns'pɛərənt, -'pær-/ *adj.* **1.** having the property of transmitting rays of light through its substance so that bodies situated beyond or behind can be distinctly seen. **2.** open, frank, or candid. **3.** easily seen through or understood.

transpire /træns'paɪə/ *v.i.*, **-spired**, **-spiring**.

1. to occur, happen, or take place. **2.** to emit or give off waste matter, etc., through the surface, as of the body, of leaves, etc.

transplant /træns'plænt, -'plant/ *v.,* /'trænsplænt, -plant/ *n.* – *v.t.* **1.** to remove (a plant) from one place and plant it in another. **2.** *Surgery* to transfer (an organ or a portion of tissue) from one part of the body to another or from one person or animal to another. – *n.* **3.** a transplanting. **4.** something transplanted.

transport /træns'pɔt, 'trænspɔt/ *v.,* /'trænspɔt/ *n.* – *v.t.* **1.** to carry or convey from one place to another. **2.** to carry away by strong emotion. – *n.* **3.** the act or method of transporting or conveying; conveyance. **4.** a system of conveying passengers or freight. **5.** a means of transporting or conveying, as a ship, large truck, aeroplane, etc. **6.** strong emotion; ecstatic joy, bliss, etc. – **transportation**, *n.*

transpose /træns'poʊz/ *v.t.,* **-posed**, **-posing**. **1.** to alter the relative position or order of (a thing in a series, or a series of things). **2.** to cause (two or more things) to change places; interchange. **3.** *Music* to reproduce in a different key.

transsexual = transexual /trænz'sɛkʃuəl/ *adj.* **1.** of or relating to someone who has changed sex. – *n.* **2.** someone who has undergone a sex change operation. **3.** someone who feels himself or herself, though physically of one sex, to be of the other sex in psychological disposition.

transverse /'trænzvɜs, trænz'vɜs/ *adj.* lying or being across or in a crosswise direction.

transvestism /trænz'vɛstɪzəm/ *n.* the abnormal desire to wear clothing appropriate to the opposite sex. – **transvestite**, *n., adj.*

trap /træp/ *n., v.,* **trapped**, **trapping**. – *n.* **1.** a contrivance used for catching game or other animals, as a mechanical device that springs shut suddenly. **2.** any device, stratagem, or the like for catching someone unawares. **3.** any of various mechanical contrivances for preventing the passage of steam, water, etc. **4.** a carriage, especially a light two-wheeled one. – *v.t.* **5.** to catch in a trap.

trapdoor /'træpdɔ/ *n.* a door or the like, flush, or nearly so, with the surface of a floor, ceiling, roof, etc.

trapdoor spider *n.* a burrowing spider.

trapeze /trə'piz/ *n.* an apparatus for gymnastics, consisting of a short horizontal bar attached to the ends of two suspended ropes.

trapezium /trə'piziəm/ *n., pl.* **-ziums**, **-zia** /-ziə/. a quadrilateral plane figure in which only one pair of opposite sides is parallel.

trapezoid /'træpəzɔɪd/ *n. Geometry* a quadrilateral plane figure of which no two sides are parallel.

trappings /'træpɪŋz/ *pl. n.* articles of equipment or dress, especially of an ornamental character.

trash /træʃ/ *n.* anything worthless or useless; rubbish.

trauma /'trɔmə/ *n., pl.* **-mas**, **-mata** /-mətə/. **1.** *Pathology* a bodily injury. **2.** *Psychology* a startling experience which has a lasting effect on mental life; a severe shock. – **traumatic**, *adj.*

travail /'træveɪl/ *n.* physical or mental toil or exertion, especially when painful.

travel /'trævəl/ *v.,* **-elled**, **-elling**, *n.* – *v.i.* **1.** to move or go from one place or point to another. – *n.* **2.** the act of travelling; journeying, especially in distant or foreign places. **3.** (*pl.*) journeys. **4.** *Machinery* the complete movement of a moving part in one direction, or the distance traversed. – **traveller**, *n.*

traverse /trə'vɜs, 'trævɜs/ *v.,* **-ersed**, **-ersing**, *n., adj.* – *v.t.* **1.** to pass across, over, or through. **2.** to go to and fro over or along, as a place. **3.** *Law* to deny formally, in pleading at law. – *n.* **4.** the act of traversing. **5.** something that crosses, obstructs, or thwarts; obstacle. **6.** a place where one may traverse or cross; a crossing. – *adj.* **7.** lying, extending, or passing across; cross; transverse.

travesty /'trævəsti/ *n., pl.* **-ties**. any grotesque or debased likeness or imitation.

trawl /trɔl/ *n.* **1.** Also, **trawl net**. a strong fishing net dragged along the sea bottom in trawling. – *v.i.* **2.** to fish with a trawl. **3.** to troll.

tray /treɪ/ *n.* a flat container or receptacle with slightly raised edges used for carrying things.

treachery /'trɛtʃəri/ *n., pl.* **-eries**. violation of faith; betrayal of trust; treason. – **treacherous**, *adj.*

treacle /'trikəl/ *n.* the dark, viscous, uncrystallised syrup obtained in refining sugar.

tread /trɛd/ *v.,* **trod**, **trodden** *or* **trod**, **treading**, *n.* – *v.t.* **1.** to step or walk on, about, in, or along. **2.** to trample or crush underfoot. **3.** to domineer harshly over; crush. – *n.* **4.** a treading, stepping, or walking, or the sound of this. **5.** manner of treading or walking. **6.** a single step as in walking. **7.** the horizontal upper surface of a step. **8.** that part of a wheel, tyre, or runner which touches the road, rail, etc.

treadle /'trɛdl/ *n.* a lever or the like worked by the foot, as to impart motion to a machine.

treadmill /'trɛdmɪl/ *n.* a monotonous or wearisome round, as of work or life.

treason /'trizən/ *n.* violation by a subject of his or her allegiance to his or her sovereign or to the state; high treason.

treasure /'trɛʒə/ *n., v.,* **-ured**, **-uring**. – *n.* **1.** wealth or riches stored or accumulated, especially in the form of precious metals or money. **2.** any thing or person greatly valued or highly prized. – *v.t.* **3.** to regard as precious; prize; cherish.

treasurer /'trɛʒərə/ *n.* **1.** someone who has charge of the funds of a company, private society, or the like. **2.** an officer of a state, city, etc., entrusted with the receipt, care, and disbursement of public money.

treasury /'trɛʒəri/ *n., pl.* **-uries**. **1.** a place where public revenues, or the funds of a company, etc., are deposited, kept, and disbursed. **2.** (*cap.*) the department of government which has control over the collection, management, and disbursement of the public revenue.

Treasury note *n.* security issued with three and six month maturities by the Australian

Government, to acknowledge a borrowing obligation.

Treasury note rediscount rate *n.* the yield at which the Reserve Bank is prepared to buy back its Treasury notes before they are due to mature.

treat /trit/ *v.t.* **1.** to act or behave towards in some specified way. **2.** to deal with. **3.** to subject to some agent or action in order to bring about a particular result. – *v.i.* **4.** to carry on negotiations with someone, with a view to a settlement, discuss terms of settlement, or negotiate. – *n.* **5.** *Colloquial* anything that affords particular pleasure or enjoyment. **6.** one's turn to pay, as for a joint outing, etc. – **treatment**, *n.*

treatise /'tritəs/ *n.* a book or writing dealing with some particular subject.

treaty /'triti/ *n., pl.* **-ties**. a formal agreement between two or more independent states in reference to peace, alliance, commerce, etc.

treble /'trɛbəl/ *adj.* **1.** threefold; triple. **2.** *Music* of the highest pitch or range, as a voice part, voice, singer, or instrument.

tree /tri/ *n.* a perennial plant having a permanent, woody, self-supporting main stem or trunk, usually growing to a considerable height, and usually developing branches at some distance from the ground.

trek /trɛk/ *n.* a journey, especially a difficult one on foot.

trellis /'trɛləs/ *n.* a frame or structure of latticework; a lattice.

tremble /'trɛmbəl/ *v.i.*, **-bled**, **-bling**. **1.** (of persons, the body, etc.) to shake involuntarily with quick, short movements, as from fear, excitement, weakness, cold, etc. **2.** to be tremulous, as light, sound, etc.

tremendous /trə'mɛndəs/ *adj.* *Colloquial* **1.** extraordinarily great in size, amount, degree, etc. **2.** extraordinary; unusual; remarkable.

tremor /'trɛmə/ *n.* **1.** involuntary shaking of the body or limbs, as from fear, weakness, etc.; a fit of trembling. **2.** any tremulous or vibratory movement; a vibration. **3.** a trembling or quivering effect, as of light, etc. **4.** a tremulous sound or note.

tremulous /'trɛmjələs/ *adj.* **1.** (of persons, the body, etc.) characterised by trembling. **2.** (of things) vibratory or quivering.

trench /trɛntʃ/ *n.* a deep furrow, ditch, or cut.

trenchant /'trɛntʃənt/ *adj.* incisive or keen, as language or a person; cutting.

trencher /'trɛntʃə/ *n.* → **mortarboard**.

trend /trɛnd/ *n.* **1.** the general course, drift, or tendency. **2.** style; fashion. – **trendy**, *adj.*

trepidation /trɛpə'deɪʃən/ *n.* tremulous alarm or agitation; perturbation.

trespass /'trɛspəs/ *n.* **1.** *Law* **a.** an unlawful act causing injury to the person, property, or rights of another, committed with force or violence, actual or implied. **b.** a wrongful entry upon the lands of another. **2.** an encroachment or intrusion. – *v.i.* **3.** to commit trespass.

tress /trɛs/ *n.* (*usu. pl.*) any long lock or curl of hair.

-tress a suffix forming some feminine agent-nouns, corresponding to masculine nouns in *-ter*, *-tor*.

trestle /'trɛsəl/ *n.* a frame used as a support, consisting typically of a horizontal beam or bar fixed at each end to a pair of spreading legs.

trevally /trə'væli/ *n.* a sport and food fish.

tri- a word element meaning 'three'.

triad /'traɪæd/ *n.* a group of three.

triage /'triaʒ/ *n.* the sorting of casualties according to the urgency of treatment required.

trial /'traɪəl, traɪl/ *n.* **1.** *Law* **a.** the examination before a judicial tribunal of the facts put in issue in a cause (often including issues of law as well as of fact). **b.** the determination of a person's guilt or innocence by due process of law. **2.** the act of trying or testing, or putting to the test. **3.** a contest or competition. **4.** an attempt or effort to do something. **5.** tentative or experimental action in order to ascertain results; an experiment. **6.** an affliction or trouble.

trial balance *n.* *Accounting* a statement of all the open debit and credit items, made preliminary to balancing a double-entry ledger.

triangle /'traɪæŋgəl/ *n.* **1.** a geometrical plane figure formed by three (usually) straight lines which meet two by two in three points, thus forming three angles. **2.** *Music* a triangular percussion instrument. – **triangular**, *adj.*

tribe /traɪb/ *n.* any aggregate of people united by ties of descent from a common ancestor, community of customs and traditions, adherence to the same leaders, etc. – **tribal**, *adj.*

tribulation /trɪbjə'leɪʃən/ *n.* grievous trouble; severe trial or experience.

tribunal /traɪ'bjunəl/ *n.* **1.** a body set up to investigate and resolve disputes. **2.** a court of justice. **3.** a place or seat of judgment.

tributary /'trɪbjətri/ *n., pl.* **-taries**, *adj.* – *n.* **1.** a stream contributing its flow to a larger stream or other body of water. – *adj.* **2.** furnishing subsidiary aid; contributory; auxiliary. **3.** paying or required to pay tribute.

tribute /'trɪbjut/ *n.* **1.** a personal offering, testimonial, compliment, or the like given as if due, or in acknowledgment of gratitude, esteem, or regard. **2.** a stated sum or other valuable consideration paid by one sovereign or state in acknowledgment of submission or as the price of peace, security, protection, or the like.

trice /traɪs/ *n.* a very short time.

trick /trɪk/ *n.* **1.** a crafty or fraudulent device, expedient, or proceeding. **2.** the art or knack of doing something. **3.** a clever or dexterous feat, as for exhibition or entertainment. **4.** *Cards* the cards collectively which are played and won in one round. – *v.t.* **5.** to deceive by trickery. – **trickery**, *n.*

trickle /'trɪkəl/ *v.*, **-led**, **-ling**, *n.* – *v.i.* **1.** to flow or fall by drops, or in a small, broken, or gentle stream. **2.** to come, go, pass, or proceed bit by bit, slowly, irregularly, etc. – *n.* **3.** a trickling flow or stream.

tricycle /'traɪsɪkəl/ *n.* a cycle with three wheels.

trident /'traɪdnt/ *n.* a three-pronged instrument or weapon.

tried /traɪd/ *v.* past tense and past participle of **try**.

triennial /traɪ'ɛniəl/ *adj.* **1.** lasting three years. **2.** occurring every three years.

trifle /'traɪfəl/ *n., v.,* **-fled**, **-fling**. – *n.* **1.** an article or thing of small value. **2.** a small, inconsiderable amount; a matter of slight importance. **3.** a dessert of sponge, jelly, cream, etc. – *v.i.* **4.** to deal lightly or without due seriousness or respect (usually fol. by *with*). – **trifling**, *adj.*

trigger /'trɪgə/ *n.* **1.** (in firearms) a small projecting piece which when pressed by the finger liberates the mechanism and discharges the weapon. – *v.t.* **2.** to start or precipitate (something), as a chain of events or a scientific reaction (often fol. by *off*).

trigonometry /trɪgə'nɒmətri/ *n.* the branch of mathematics that deals with the relations between the sides and angles of triangles and the calculations, etc., based on these.

trill /trɪl/ *v.i.* **1.** to resound vibrantly, or with a rapid succession of sounds, as the voice, song, laughter, etc. **2.** to execute a shake or trill with the voice or on a musical instrument. – *n.* **3.** the act or sound of trilling.

trillion /'trɪljən/ *n.* **1.** a million times a million, or 10^{12}. **2.** (becoming obsolete) a million times a million times a million, or 10^{18}.

trilogy /'trɪlədʒi/ *n., pl.* **-gies**. a series or group of three related dramas, operas, novels, etc.

trim /trɪm/ *v.,* **trimmed**, **trimming**, *n., adj.,* **trimmer**, **trimmest**. – *v.t.* **1.** to reduce to a neat or orderly state by clipping, paring, pruning, etc. **2.** to modify (opinions, etc.) according to expediency. **3.** to decorate or deck with ornaments, etc. **4.** to upholster and line the interior of motor cars, etc. – *n.* **5.** proper condition or order. **6.** dress, array, or equipment. **7.** material used for decoration; decorative trimming. **8.** a trimming by cutting, clipping, or the like. **9. a.** the upholstery, knobs, handles, and other equipment inside a motor car. **b.** ornamentation on the exterior of a motor car, especially in chromium or a contrasting colour. – *adj.* **10.** pleasingly neat or smart in appearance. **11.** in good condition or order.

trimaran /'traɪməræn/ *n.* a boat with a main middle hull and two outer hulls.

trinity /'trɪnəti/ *n., pl.* **-ties**. a group of three; a triad.

trinket /'trɪŋkət/ *n.* **1.** any small fancy article, bit of jewellery, or the like, usually of little value. **2.** anything trifling.

trio /'triou/ *n., pl.* **trios**. any group of three persons or things.

trip /trɪp/ *n., v.,* **tripped**, **tripping**. – *n.* **1.** a journey or voyage. **2.** *Colloquial* a period under the influence of a hallucinatory drug. **3.** a stumble. – *v.i.* **4.** to stumble. **5.** to make a slip or mistake, as in a statement; make a wrong step in conduct. **6.** to step lightly or nimbly; skip; dance. – *v.t.* **7.** to cause to stumble (often fol. by *up*). **8.** to cause to make or catch in a slip or error (often fol. by *up*).

tripartite /traɪ'patait/ *adj.* divided into or consisting of three parts.

tripe /traɪp/ *n.* **1.** the first and second divisions of the stomach of a ruminant, especially of the ox kind, prepared for use as food. **2.** *Colloquial* anything poor or worthless, especially written work; nonsense; rubbish.

triple /'trɪpəl/ *adj.* threefold; consisting of three parts.

triplet /'trɪplət/ *n.* **1.** one of three children born at one birth. **2.** any group or combination of three. **3.** a thin bar of opal set between two layers of plastic, or one layer of potch and one of crystal.

triplicate /'trɪpləkeɪt/ *v.,* **-cated**, **-cating**, /'trɪpləkət/ *adj.* – *v.t.* **1.** to make threefold; triple. – *adj.* **2.** threefold; triple; tripartite.

tripod /'traɪpɒd/ *n.* **1.** a stool, pedestal, or the like with three legs. **2.** a three-legged stand, as for a camera.

triptych /'trɪptɪk/ *n. Art* a set of three panels or compartments side by side, bearing pictures, carvings, or the like.

trite /traɪt/ *adj.,* **triter**, **tritest**. hackneyed by constant use or repetition.

triumph /'traɪʌmf, 'traɪəmf/ *n.* **1.** the act or fact of being victorious, or triumphing; victory; conquest. **2.** a notable achievement; striking success. – *v.i.* **3.** to achieve success. – **triumphal**, *adj.*

triumphant /traɪ'ʌmfənt/ *adj.* having achieved victory or success; victorious.

trivet /'trɪvət/ *n.* a small metal plate with short legs put under a hot platter or dish at the table.

trivia /'trɪviə/ *pl. n.* inessential, unimportant, or inconsequential things; trifles.

trivial /'trɪviəl/ *adj.* of little importance; trifling; insignificant. – **triviality**, *n.*

-trix a suffix of feminine agent-nouns, as in *executrix*. Cf. **-or**².

trochee /'trouki/ *n. Prosody* a metrical foot of two syllables, a long followed by a short, or an accented followed by an unaccented. – **trochaic**, *adj.*

trod /trɒd/ *v.* past tense and past participle of **tread**.

trodden /'trɒdn/ *v.* past participle of **tread**.

troglodyte /'trɒglədaɪt/ *n.* a caveman or cave-dweller.

troll /troul/ *v.i.* to fish with a moving line, as one worked up and down in fishing for pike with a rod, or one trailed behind a boat.

trolley /'trɒli/ *n., pl.* **-leys**. any of various kinds of low carts or vehicles.

trollop /'trɒləp/ *n.* **1.** an untidy or slovenly woman; a slattern. **2.** an immoral woman; prostitute.

trombone /trɒm'boun/ *n.* a musical wind instrument consisting of a cylindrical metal tube expanding into a bell and bent twice in U shape, usually equipped with a slide. – **trombonist**, *n.*

troop /trup/ *n.* **1.** an assemblage of persons or things; a company or band. **2.** (*pl.*) a body of soldiers, marines, etc. – *v.i.* **3.** to walk as if on a march.

trope /troup/ *n. Rhetoric* a figure of speech.

trophy /'troufi/ *n., pl.* **-phies**. anything taken in war, hunting, etc., especially when preserved as a memento; a spoil or prize.

tropic /'trɒpɪk/ *n. Geography* **1.** either of two corresponding parallels of latitude on the terrestrial globe, one (**tropic of Cancer**) about 23½° north, and the other (**tropic of Capricorn**) about 23½° south of the equator, being the boundaries of the Torrid Zone. **2. the tropics,** the regions lying between and near these parallels of latitude. – **tropical**, *adj.*

trot /trɒt/ *v.*, **trotted, trotting,** *n.* – *v.i.* **1.** (of a horse, etc.) to go at a gait between a walk and a run. **2.** to go at a quick, steady gait; move briskly, bustle, or hurry. – *n.* **3.** a jogging gait between a walk and a run. **4.** (*pl.*) races for trotting or pacing horses; a trotting meeting. **5.** (*pl.*) *Colloquial* diarrhoea.

troth /troʊθ/ *n.* one's word or promise.

trotter /'trɒtə/ *n.* **1.** an animal which trots; a horse bred and trained for harness racing. **2.** the foot of an animal, especially of a sheep or pig, used as food.

troubadour /'trubədɔ/ *n.* a minstrel.

trouble /'trʌbəl/ *v.*, **-bled, -bling,** *n.* – *v.t.* **1.** to disturb in mind; distress; worry. **2.** to put to inconvenience, exertion, pains, or the like. – *n.* **3.** molestation, harassment, annoyance, or difficulty. **4.** unfortunate position or circumstances; misfortunes. **5.** disturbance; disorder; unrest. **6.** disturbance of mind, distress, or worry. – **troublesome**, *adj.*

trough /trɒf/ *n.* **1.** an open, boxlike receptacle, usually long and narrow, as for containing water or food for animals, or for any of various other purposes. **2.** *Meteorology* an elongated area of relatively low pressure.

trounce /traʊns/ *v.t.*, **trounced, trouncing.** to beat or thrash severely.

troupe /trup/ *n.* a troop, company, or band, especially of actors, singers, or the like.

trousers /'traʊzəz/ *pl. n.* an outer garment covering the lower part of the trunk and each leg separately, extending to the ankles.

trousseau /'trusoʊ/ *n., pl.* **-seaux, -seaus** /-soʊz/. a bride's outfit of clothes, linen, etc.

trout /traʊt/ *n., pl.* **trouts,** (*esp. collectively*) **trout**. a game and food fish.

trowel /'traʊəl/ *n.* any of various tools consisting of a plate of metal or other material, usually flat, fitted into a short handle, used for spreading, shaping, or smoothing plaster or the like.

troy weight /trɔɪ/ *n.* an imperial system for measuring the mass of precious metals and gems.

truant /'truənt/ *n.* a pupil who stays away from school without permission. – **truancy**, *n.*

truce /trus/ *n.* a suspension of hostilities, as between armies, by agreement, for a specified period; an armistice.

truck[1] /trʌk/ *n.* **1.** any of various vehicles for carrying goods, etc. **2.** a motor vehicle with cab (def. 2) and tray or compartment for carrying goods; lorry. – *v.t.* **3.** to transport by a truck or trucks.

truck[2] /trʌk/ *n.* dealings.

truculent /'trʌkjələnt/ *adj.* **1.** fierce; cruel. **2.** aggressive; belligerent.

trudge /trʌdʒ/ *v.i.*, **trudged, trudging**. to walk laboriously or wearily.

true /tru/ *adj.*, **truer, truest,** *adv.* – *adj.* **1.** being in accordance with the actual state of things; conforming to fact; not false. **2.** real or genuine. **3.** firm in allegiance; loyal; faithful; trusty. **4.** exact, correct, or accurate. **5.** legitimate or rightful. **6.** exactly or accurately shaped, formed, fitted, or placed, as a surface, instrument, or part of a mechanism. **7.** *Navigation* (of a bearing) fixed in relation to the earth's axis rather than the magnetic poles. – *adv.* **8.** in a true manner; truly or truthfully. **9.** exactly or accurately. – **truly**, *adv.*

true-blue /'tru-blu/ *adj.* **1.** unchanging; unwavering; staunch; true. **2.** staunchly conservative.

truffle /'trʌfəl/ *n.* any of various subterranean edible fungi.

truism /'truɪzəm/ *n.* a self-evident, obvious truth. – **truistic, truistical,** *adj.*

trump /trʌmp/ *n. Cards* **1.** any playing card of a suit that for the time outranks the other suits, such a card being able to take any card of another suit. – *v.t.* **2.** *Cards* to take with a trump.

trumpet /'trʌmpət/ *n.* **1.** *Music* any of a family of musical wind instruments with a penetrating, powerful tone, consisting of a tube, now usually metallic, and commonly once or twice curved round upon itself, having a cup-shaped mouthpiece at one end and a flaring bell at the other. – *v.t.* **2.** to sound on a trumpet.

truncate /trʌŋ'keɪt, 'trʌŋkeɪt/ *v.t.*, **-cated, -cating**. to shorten by cutting off a part; cut short; mutilate.

truncheon /'trʌnʃən/ *n.* a short club carried by a police officer.

trundle /'trʌndəl/ *v.*, **-dled, -dling**. – *v.t.* **1.** to cause (a ball, hoop, etc.) to roll along; roll. – *v.i.* **2.** *Colloquial* to walk in a leisurely fashion.

trunk /trʌŋk/ *n.* **1.** the main stem of a tree, as distinct from the branches and roots. **2.** a box or chest for holding clothes and other articles, as for use on a journey. **3.** the body of a human being or of an animal, excluding the head and limbs. **4.** (*pl.*) shorts, either tight-fitting or loose, worn by swimmers, athletes, etc. **5.** the long, flexible, cylindrical nasal appendage of the elephant.

trunk line *n. Telecommunications* a telephone line or channel between two exchanges in different parts of a country or of the world, which is used to provide connections between subscribers making long-distance calls.

truss /trʌs/ *v.t.* **1.** to tie, bind, or fasten. – *n.* **2.** *Building Trades, etc.* a combination of members, as beams, bars, ties, or the like, so arranged as to form a rigid framework and support. **3.** *Medicine* an apparatus for maintaining a hernia in a reduced state.

trust /trʌst/ *n.* **1.** reliance on the integrity, justice, etc., of a person, or on some quality or attribute of a thing; confidence. **2.** confident expectation of something; hope. **3.** the state of being relied on, or the state of one to whom something is entrusted. **4.** the obligation or responsibility imposed on one in whom confidence or authority is placed. **5.** *Law* **a.** a fiduciary relationship in which one person (the trustee) holds the title to property (the **trust estate** or **trust property**) for the benefit of another (the beneficiary). **b.** a fund of securities, cash or other assets, held by trustees on behalf of a number of investors. **6.** *Commerce* **a.** a combination of industrial or commercial companies having a central committee or board of trustees, controlling a majority or the whole of the stock of each of the constituent companies, thus making it possible to manage the concerns so as to economise expenses, defeat competition, etc. **b.** a monopolistic organisation or combination in restraint of trade whether in the form of a trust (def. 6a), contract, association or otherwise. – *v.t.* **7.** to have trust or confidence in; rely on. **8.** to expect confidently, hope (usually followed by a clause or an infinitive).

trust corporation *n.* a corporation organised to exercise the functions of a trustee.

trust deed *n.* the legal document which appoints trustees and defines their power.

trustee /trʌs'ti/ *n.* *Law* **1.** a person, usually one of a body of persons, appointed to administer the affairs of a company, institution, etc. **2.** a person who holds the title to property for the benefit of another.

trust instrument *n.* the document which sets out the trusts upon which the person entitled to the enjoyment of land holds the estate.

trustworthy /'trʌstwɜði/ *adj.* worthy of trust or confidence; reliable.

truth /truθ/ *n.* **1.** that which is true; the true or actual facts of a case. **2.** a verified or indisputable fact, proposition, principle, or the like.

try /traɪ/ *v.,* **tried**, **trying**, *n., pl.* **tries**. – *v.t.* **1.** to attempt to do or accomplish. **2.** to test the quality, value, fitness, accuracy, etc, of. **3.** *Law* to examine and determine judicially, as a cause; determine judicially the guilt or innocence of (a person). **4.** to put to a severe test; strain the endurance, patience, etc., of; subject to grievous experiences, affliction, or trouble. – *n.* **5.** an attempt, endeavour, or effort. **6.** *Rugby* a score of four points (League) or five points (Union) earned by placing the ball on the ground in the opponent's in-goal area.

trying /'traɪɪŋ/ *adj.* annoying; distressing.

tryst /trɪst/ *n.* an appointment, especially between lovers.

tsar /za/ *n.* **1.** an emperor or king. **2.** (*usu. cap.*) the emperor of Russia.

T-shirt /'ti-ʃɜt/ *n.* a lightweight top, usually short-sleeved and collarless, made from a knitted fabric. Also, **tee-shirt**.

tub /tʌb/ *n.* **1.** a vessel or receptacle for bathing in; a bathtub. **2.** any of various vessels resembling or suggesting a tub.

tuba /'tjubə/ *n., pl.* **-bas**, **-bae** /-bi/. a brass wind instrument of low pitch.

tubby /'tʌbi/ *adj.,* **-bier**, **-biest**. short and fat.

tube /tjub/ *n.* **1.** a hollow usually cylindrical body of metal, glass, rubber, or other material, used for conveying or containing fluids, and for other purposes. **2.** a small, collapsible, metal cylinder closed at one end and having the open end provided with a cap, for holding paint, toothpaste, or other semiliquid substance to be squeezed out by pressure. – **tubular**, *adj.*

tuber /'tjubə/ *n.* *Botany* a fleshy, usually oblong or rounded thickening or outgrowth (as the potato) of a subterranean stem or shoot.

tubercle /'tjubəkəl/ *n.* **1.** a small rounded projection. **2.** *Pathology* **a.** a small, firm, rounded nodule or swelling. **b.** such a swelling as characteristic of tuberculosis. – **tubercular**, *adj.*

tuberculosis /təbɜkjə'lousəs/ *n.* an infectious disease, especially of the lungs.

tuck /tʌk/ *v.t.* **1.** to thrust into some narrow space or close or concealed place. **2.** to draw up in folds or a folded arrangement. – *n.* **3.** a tucked piece or part. **4.** *Sewing* a fold, or one of a series of folds, made by doubling cloth upon itself, and stitching parallel with the edge of the fold.

tucker[1] /'tʌkə/ *n.* *Colloquial* food.

tucker[2] /'tʌkə/ *v.t.* *Colloquial* to weary; tire.

-tude a suffix forming abstract nouns.

tuft /tʌft/ *n.* a bunch of small, usually soft and flexible things, as feathers, hairs, etc., fixed at the base with the upper part loose.

tug /tʌg/ *v.t.,* **tugged**, **tugging**. to pull at with force or effort.

tugboat /'tʌgbout/ *n.* a strongly-built vessel with a powerful engine, designed for towing other vessels.

tuition /tju'ɪʃən/ *n.* teaching or instruction, as of pupils.

tulip /'tjuləp/ *n.* a plant with large, showy, cup-shaped or bell-shaped flowers of various colours.

tumble /'tʌmbəl/ *v.,* **-bled**, **-bling**, *n.* – *v.i.* **1.** to roll or fall over or down as by losing footing, support, or equilibrium. **2.** to fall rapidly, as stock market prices. – *n.* **3.** an act of tumbling; a fall; a downfall. **4.** tumbled condition; disorder or confusion.

tumefy /'tjuməfaɪ/ *v.t., v.i.,* **-fied**, **-fying**. to make or become swollen or tumid.

tumescent /tju'mɛsənt/ *adj.* swelling.

tummy /'tʌmi/ *n.* *Colloquial* stomach.

tumour = tumor /'tjumə/ *n.* *Pathology* an abnormal or morbid swelling in any part of the body.

tumult /'tjumʌlt/ *n.* **1.** the commotion or disturbance of a multitude, usually with noise; an uproar. **2.** agitation of mind; a mental or emotional disturbance. – **tumultuous**, *adj.*

tuna /'tjunə/ *n.* a large, fast-swimming, marine food fish.

tundra /'tʌndrə/ *n.* one of the vast, nearly level, treeless plains of the arctic regions of Europe, Asia, and North America.

tune /tjun/ *n., v.,* **tuned**, **tuning**. – *n.* **1.** a succession of musical sounds forming an air or melody, with or without the harmony accompanying it. **2.** the state of being in the proper pitch. **3.** accord; agreement. – *v.t.* **4.** to adjust (a musical instrument) to a correct or given standard of pitch (often fol. by *up*). **5.** to bring into harmony. **6.** to adjust (an engine, machine or the like) for proper or improved running (often fol. by *up*). **7.** *Radio* to adjust a receiving apparatus so as to receive (the signals of a sending station).

tuner /ˈtjunə/ *n.* the part of a radio receiver which produces an output suitable for feeding into an amplifier.

tungsten /ˈtʌŋstən/ *n.* a rare metallic element *Symbol*: W (for *wolframium*).

tunic /ˈtjunɪk/ *n.* **1.** a coat worn as part of a military or other uniform. **2.** a loose, sleeveless dress, especially as worn by girls as part of a school uniform.

tunnel /ˈtʌnəl/ *n.*, *v.*, **-nelled**, **-nelling**. – *n.* **1.** an underground passage. – *v.t.* **2.** to make or form a tunnel through or under.

tunny /ˈtʌni/ *n.*, *pl.* **-nies**, (*esp. collectively*) **-ny**. a marine food fish.

turban /ˈtɜbən/ *n.* a form of headdress consisting of a scarf wound around the head.

turbid /ˈtɜbəd/ *adj.* **1.** (of liquids) opaque or muddy with particles of extraneous matter. **2.** disturbed; confused.

turbine /ˈtɜbaɪn/ *n.* any of a class of hydraulic motors in which a vaned wheel or runner is made to revolve by the impingement of a free jet of fluid (**impulse turbine** or **action turbine**) or by the passage of fluid which completely fills the motor (**reaction turbine** or **pressure turbine**).

turbo- /ˈtɜboʊ-/ *adj* a prefix indicating: **1.** driven by a turbine. **2.** of or relating to a turbine.

turbulent /ˈtɜbjələnt/ *adj.* disturbed; agitated; troubled; stormy. – **turbulent**, *n.*

turd /tɜd/ *n.* *Colloquial* **1.** a piece of excrement. **2.** (*derogatory*) an unpleasant person.

tureen /təˈrin, tju-/ *n.* a large deep dish with a cover, for holding soup, etc.

turf /tɜf/ *n.*, *pl.* **turfs**, **turves** /tɜvz/, *v.* – *n.* **1.** the covering of grass, etc., with its matted roots, forming the surface of grassland. **2.** a piece cut or torn from the surface of grassland, with the grass, etc., growing on it; a sod. – *v.t.* **3.** to cover with turf or sod. **4. turf out,** *Colloquial* to throw out; eject.

turgid /ˈtɜdʒəd/ *adj.* **1.** pompous or bombastic, as language, style, etc. **2.** swollen; distended.

turkey /ˈtɜki/ *n.* a large gallinaceous bird.

turmeric /ˈtɜmərɪk/ *n.* **1.** the aromatic rhizome of an East Indian plant. **2.** a powder prepared from it, used as a condiment (especially in curry powder), a yellow dye, a medicine, etc.

turmoil /ˈtɜmɔɪl/ *n.* a state of commotion or disturbance; tumult; agitation; disquiet.

turn /tɜn/ *v.t.* **1.** cause to move round on an axis or about a centre; rotate. **2.** to reverse the position or posture of. **3.** to change or alter the course of; to divert; deflect. **4.** to change or alter the nature, character, or appearance of. **5.** to change or convert (fol. by *into* or *to*). **6.** to put or apply to some use or purpose. **7.** to get beyond or pass (a certain age, time, amount, etc.). **8.** to bring into a rounded or curved form. **9.** to form or express gracefully. **10.** to cause to go; send; drive. **11.** to maintain a steady flow or circulation of (money or articles of commerce). **12.** to curve, bend, or twist. – *v.i.* **13.** to move round on an axis or about a centre; rotate. **14.** to direct the face or gaze towards or away from something, or in a particular direction. **15.** to direct or set one's course towards or away from something or in a particular direction. **16.** to apply one's efforts, interest, etc., to something; devote oneself to something. **17.** to shift the body about as if on an axis. **18.** to assume a curved form; bend. **19.** to be affected with nausea, as the stomach. **20.** to change or alter, as in nature, character, or appearance. **21.** to become sour, fermented, or the like, as milk, etc. **22.** to be changed, transformed, or converted (fol. by *into* or *to*). – *v.* **23. turn down, a.** to fold. **b.** to lessen the intensity of; moderate. **c.** to refuse or reject (a person, request, etc.). **24. turn off, a.** to stop the flow of (water, gas, etc.) as by closing a valve, etc. **b.** to switch off (a radio, light, etc.). **c.** to branch off; diverge; change direction. **d.** to arouse antipathy or revulsion in. **25. turn on, a.** to cause (water, gas, etc.) to flow as by opening a valve, etc. **b.** to switch on (a radio, light, etc.). **c.** Also, **turn upon**. to become suddenly hostile to; attack without warning. **d.** *Colloquial* to excite or interest (a person). **26. turn out, a.** to extinguish or put out (a light, etc.). **b.** to come to be; become ultimately. **27. turn over, a.** to move or be moved from one side to another. **b.** to meditate; ponder. **c.** *Commerce* to purchase and then sell (goods or commodities). **d.** *Commerce* to do business or sell goods to the amount of (a specified sum). **e.** *Commerce* to invest or recover (capital) in some transaction or in the course of business. – *n.* **28.** a movement of rotation, whether total or partial. **29.** the time for action or proceeding which comes in due rotation or order to each of a number of persons, etc. **30.** a place where a road, river, or the like turns. **31.** a single revolution, as of a wheel. **32.** change or a change in nature, character, condition, circumstances, etc. **33.** a passing or twisting of one thing round another as of a rope round a mast. **34.** a distinctive form or style imparted. **35.** a short walk, ride, or the like which includes a going and a returning, especially by different routes. **36.** natural inclination, bent, tendency, or aptitude. **37.** a spell or bout of action. **38.** an attack of illness or the like. **39.** an act of service or disservice (with *good*, *bad*, *kind*, etc.). **40.** *Colloquial* a nervous shock, as from fright or astonishment. **41.** Also, **turnout**. a social entertainment; party.

turnaround /ˈtɜnəraʊnd/ *n.* **1.** a reversal in circumstances, as debit to credit, loss to profit, or in sport, especially as losing to winning. **2.** the time taken to perform a task, as maintenance, unloading, etc. Also, **turnround**.

turnip /ˈtɜnəp/ *n.* a plant with a thick, fleshy, edible root.

turnover /ˈtɜnoʊvə/ *n.* **1.** the aggregate of worker replacements in a given period in a given business or industry. **2.** the total amount of business done in a given time. **3.** the rate at which items are sold or stock used up and replaced.

turnstile /ˈtɜnstaɪl/ *n.* a horizontally revolving gate which allows people to pass one at a time.

turntable /ˈtɜnteɪbəl/ *n.* the rotating disc on which the record in a gramophone rests.

turpentine /ˈtɜpəntaɪn/ *n.* a resin derived

from various trees, yielding a volatile oil.

turpitude /'tɜpətʃud/ *n.* **1.** shameful depravity. **2.** a depraved or shameful act.

turquoise /'tɜkwɔɪz/ *n.* **1.** a sky blue or greenish blue compact opaque mineral. **2.** a greenish blue or bluish green.

turret /'tʌrət/ *n.* a small tower, usually one forming part of a larger structure.

turtle /'tɜtl/ *n.* any of various reptiles having the body enclosed in a shell from which the head, tail, and four legs protrude.

tusk /tʌsk/ *n.* (in certain animals) a tooth developed to great length, usually as one of a pair, as in the elephant, walrus, wild boar, etc.

tussive /'tʌsɪv/ *adj.* of or relating to a cough.

tussle /'tʌsəl/ *v.*, **-sled**, **-sling**, *n.* – *v.i.* **1.** to struggle or fight roughly or vigorously; wrestle; scuffle. – *n.* **2.** a rough struggle as in fighting or wrestling; a scuffle.

tussock /'tʌsək/ *n.* a tuft or clump of growing grass or the like.

tutelage /'tjutəlɪdʒ/ *n.* **1.** the office or function of a guardian; guardianship. **2.** instruction. – **tutelary**, *adj.*

tutor /'tjutə/ *n.* **1.** one employed to instruct another in some branch or branches of learning, especially a private instructor. **2.** a university teacher who supervises the studies of certain undergraduates assigned to him or her. – *v.t.* **3.** to act as a tutor to.

tutorial /tju'tɔriəl/ *n.* a period of instruction given by a university tutor to an individual student or a small group of students.

tutti-frutti /tuti-'fruti/ *n.* **1.** a preserve of chopped mixed fruits, often with brandy syrup. **2.** a variety of fruits (usually candied and minced), used in ice-cream, confections, etc.

tutu /'tutu, 'tjutju/ *n.* a short, full, ballet skirt.

tuxedo /tʌk'sidoʊ/ *n.*, *pl.* **-dos**. a dinner jacket.

twain /tweɪn/ *adj.*, *n.* *Archaic* two.

twang /twæŋ/ *v.i.* **1.** to give out a sharp, ringing sound, as the string of a musical instrument when plucked. – *n.* **2.** the sharp, ringing sound produced by plucking or suddenly releasing a tense string. **3.** a sharp, nasal tone, as of the human voice.

twat /twɒt/ *n.* *Colloquial* (*offensive*) **1.** the vagina. **2.** a despicable or unpleasant person.

tweak /twik/ *v.t.* to seize and pull with a sharp jerk and twist.

twee /twi/ *adj.* *Colloquial* affected; excessively dainty.

tweed /twid/ *n.* a coarse wool cloth in a variety of weaves and colours.

tweezers /'twizəz/ *pl. n.* small pincers or nippers for plucking out hairs, taking up small objects, etc.

twelve /twɛlv/ *n.* a cardinal number, ten plus two. – **twelfth**, *adj.*, *n.*

twenty /'twɛnti/ *n.*, *pl.* **-ties**. a cardinal number, ten times two. – **twentieth**, *adj.*, *n.*

twi- a word element meaning 'two', or 'twice'.

twice /twaɪs/ *adv.* two times.

twiddle /'twɪdl/ *v.t.*, **-dled**, **-dling**. to turn round and round, especially with the fingers.

twig[1] /twɪg/ *n.* **1.** a slender shoot of a tree or other plant. **2.** a small dry, woody piece fallen from a branch.

twig[2] /twɪg/ *v.i.*, **twigged**, **twigging**. to understand.

twilight /'twaɪlaɪt/ *n.* the light from the sky when the sun is below the horizon, especially in the evening.

twill /twɪl/ *n.* a fabric woven with the weft threads so crossing the warp as to produce an effect of parallel diagonal lines.

twin /twɪn/ *n.* **1.** one of two children or animals born at a single birth. – *adj.* **2.** being two, or one of two, children or animals born at the same birth. **3.** being two persons or things closely related or associated or much alike; forming a pair or couple.

twine /twaɪn/ *n.*, *v.*, **twined**, **twining**. – *n.* **1.** a strong thread or string composed of two or more strands twisted together. – *v.t.* **2.** to twist together. – *v.i.* **3.** to wind in a sinuous or meandering course.

twinge /twɪndʒ/ *n.* a sudden, sharp pain.

twinkle /'twɪŋkəl/ *v.*, **-kled**, **-kling**, *n.* – *v.i.* **1.** to shine with quick, flickering, gleams of light, as stars, distant lights, etc. **2.** to sparkle in the light. **3.** (of the eyes) to be bright with amusement, pleasure, etc. – *n.* **4.** a twinkling with light. **5.** a twinkling brightness in the eyes.

twin-set /'twɪn-sɛt/ *n.* a cardigan and matching jumper, worn by women.

twirl /twɜl/ *v.t.* **1.** to cause to rotate rapidly; spin; whirl; swing circularly. – *v.i.* **2.** to rotate rapidly; whirl.

twist /twɪst/ *v.t.* **1.** to combine, as two or more strands or threads, by winding together. **2.** to entwine (one thing) with or in another; wind or twine (something) about a thing. **3.** to alter in shape, as by turning the ends in opposite directions, so that parts previously in the same straight line and plane are situated in a spiral curve. **4.** to change the proper form or meaning; pervert. – *v.i.* **5.** to be or become intertwined. **6.** to wind or twine about something. **7.** to take a spiral form or course; wind, curve, or bend. **8.** to turn or rotate, as on an axis. – *n.* **9.** a curve, bend, or turn. **10.** a peculiar bent, bias, or the like, as in the mind or nature. **11.** a sudden, unexpected alteration to the course of events, as in a play. **12.** a vigorous dance of the 1960s.

twisted pair *n.* (in a computer) two insulated conductors twisted together helically and having useful properties for the transmission of digital data.

twit[1] /twɪt/ *v.*, **twitted**, **twitting**. – *v.t.* **1.** to taunt, gibe at, or banter by references to anything embarrassing. **2.** to reproach or upbraid.

twit[2] /twɪt/ *n.* *Colloquial* a fool.

twitch /twɪtʃ/ *v.t.* **1.** to give a short, sudden pull or tug at; jerk. – *n.* **2.** a quick, jerky movement of the body, or of some part of it.

twitter /'twɪtə/ *v.i.* to utter a succession of small, tremulous sounds, as a bird.

two /tu/ *n.* a cardinal number, one plus one.

two-dimensional /tu-daɪ'mɛnʃənəl, tu-də-/ *adj.* having two dimensions, as height and width.

2, 4-D /tu fɔ-'di/ *n.* a substance used as a weedkiller.

2, 4, 5-T /tu fɔ faɪv-'ti/ *n.* a substance used as a weed-killer.

two-up /'tu-ʌp/ *n.* a gambling game in which two coins are spun in the air and bets are laid on whether they fall heads or tails.

-ty[1] a suffix of numerals denoting multiples of ten, as *twenty*.

-ty[2] a suffix of nouns denoting quality, state, etc., as *unity*, *enmity*.

tycoon /taɪ'kun/ *n.* a businessperson having great wealth and power.

tyke[1] /taɪk/ *n. Colloquial* a mischievous child.

tyke[2] /taɪk/ *n. Colloquial* a Roman Catholic.

type /taɪp/ *n., v.,* **typed**, **typing**. *– n.* **1.** a kind, class, or group as distinguished by a particular characteristic. **2.** the general form, style, or character distinguishing a particular kind, class or group. **3.** the pattern or model from which something is made. **4.** *Printing* **a.** a rectangular piece or block, now usually of metal, having on its upper surface a letter or character in relief. **b.** a printed character or printed characters. *– v.t.* **5.** to write (a letter, etc.) by means of a typewriter. **6.** to be a type or symbol of. *– v.i.* **7.** to write by means of a typewriter.

typecast /'taɪpkast/ *v.t.,* **-cast**, **-casting**. to cast (an actor, etc.) continually in the same kind of role, especially because of some physical characteristic.

typeface /'taɪpfeɪs/ *n.* → **face** (def. 7).

typescript /'taɪpskrɪpt/ *n.* a typewritten copy of a literary composition, a document, or the like.

typeset /'taɪpsɛt/ *v.t.,* **-set**, **-setting**. *Printing* to set in type.

typewriter /'taɪpraɪtə/ *n.* a machine for writing mechanically in letters and characters.

typho- a word element representing **typhus** and **typhoid**.

typhoid fever /taɪfɔɪd 'fivə/ *n.* an infectious, often fatal, fever. Also, **typhoid**.

typhoon /taɪ'fun/ *n.* a tropical cyclone or hurricane.

typhus /'taɪfəs/ *n.* an acute infectious disease marked by great prostration, severe nervous symptoms, and a characteristic eruption of reddish spots on the body, now regarded as due to a specific micro-organism transmitted by lice and fleas. Also, **typhus fever**. – **typhous**, *adj.*

typical /'tɪpɪkəl/ *adj.* **1.** relating to, of the nature of, or serving as a type or emblem; symbolic. **2.** of the nature of or serving as a type or representative specimen. **3.** conforming to the type.

typify /'tɪpəfaɪ/ *v.t.,* **-fied**, **-fying**. to serve as the typical specimen of; exemplify.

typist /'taɪpəst/ *n.* someone who operates a typewriter.

typo /'taɪpoʊ/ *n. Colloquial* a typographical error.

typography /taɪ'pɒgrəfi/ *n.* **1.** the work or process of printing with types. **2.** the general character of printed matter. – **typographical**, *adj.*

tyranny /'tɪrəni/ *n., pl.* **-nies**. **1.** arbitrary or unrestrained exercise of power; despotic abuse of authority. **2.** the government or rule of a tyrant or absolute ruler. **3.** undue severity or harshness. – **tyrannical**, *adj.* **tyrannise = tyrannize**, *v.*

tyrant /'taɪrənt/ *n.* **1.** a king or ruler who exercises power oppressively or unjustly. **2.** any person who exercises power despotically.

tyre /'taɪə/ *n.* a band of metal or (usually inflated) rubber, fitted round the rim of a wheel as a running surface.

tzar /za/ *n.* → **tsar**.

U u

U, u /ju/ *n., pl.* **U's** *or* **Us**, **u's** *or* **us**. the 21st letter of the English alphabet.

ubiquity /ju'bɪkwəti/ *n.* the state or capacity of being everywhere at the same time; omnipresence. – **ubiquitous**, *adj.*

udder /'ʌdə/ *n.* a mammary gland, especially when pendulous and with more than one teat, as in cows.

UFO /ju ɛf 'oʊ, 'jufoʊ/ *n.* unidentified flying object.

ugly /'ʌgli/ *adj.*, **-lier**, **-liest**. **1.** repulsive; offensive to the sense of beauty. **2.** troubling; threatening disadvantage or danger.

ukulele = ukelele /jukə'leɪli/ *n.* a small guitar-like musical instrument.

ulcer /'ʌlsə/ *n. Pathology* a sore open either to the surface of the body or to a natural cavity, and accompanied by the disintegration of tissue and the formation of pus, etc. – **ulcerous**, *adj.* – **ulcerate**, *v.*

-ule a diminutive suffix of nouns.

-ulent an adjective suffix meaning 'abounding in'.

ulna /'ʌlnə/ *n., pl.* **-nae** /-ni/, **-nas**. *Anatomy* that one of the two bones of the forearm which is on the side opposite to the thumb.

-ulose variant of **-ulous** in scientific terms.

-ulous a suffix forming adjectives meaning 'tending to'.

ulterior /ʌl'tɪəriə/ *adj.* intentionally kept concealed.

ultimate /'ʌltəmət/ *adj.* **1.** forming the final aim or object. **2.** coming at the end, as of a course of action, a process, etc. – *n.* **3.** the final point; final result. **4.** a fundamental fact or principle.

ultimatum /ʌltə'meɪtəm/ *n., pl.* **-tums**, **-ta** /-tə/. a final proposal or statement of conditions.

ultimo /'ʌltəmoʊ/ *adv.* in or of the month preceding the present.

ultra- a prefix meaning: **1.** beyond (in space or time). **2.** excessive; excessively.

ultramarine /ʌltrəmə'rin/ *n.* a deep blue colour.

ultrasound /'ʌltrəsaʊnd/ *n.* sound vibrations above the audible limit, used in medicine as a means of diagnosis or therapy, as in the imaging of internal organs of the body or deep-heat treatment.

ultraviolet /ʌltrə'vaɪələt, -'vaɪlət/ *adj.* beyond the violet, as the invisible rays of the spectrum lying outside the violet end of the visible spectrum.

ululate /'juljəleɪt/ *v.i.*, **-lated**, **-lating**. to howl, as a dog or wolf.

umbel /'ʌmbəl/ *n. Botany* a flower cluster in which several stalks or pedicels spread from a common cluster. – **umbelliferous**, *adj.*

umber /'ʌmbə/ *n.* a brown pigment.

umbilical cord /ʌm'bɪləkəl, ʌmbə'laɪkəl/ *n. Anatomy* a cord connecting the embryo or foetus with the placenta of the mother, and transmitting nourishment from the mother.

umbrage /'ʌmbrɪdʒ/ *n.* offence given or taken; resentful displeasure.

umbrella /ʌm'brɛlə/ *n.* **1.** a portable shade or screen for protection from sunlight, rain, etc. **2.** any general protection or cover.

umpire /'ʌmpaɪə/ *n.* **1.** a person selected to see that a game is played in accordance with the rules. **2.** a person to whose decision a controversy between parties is referred; an arbiter or referee.

un-[1] a prefix meaning 'not', freely used as an English formative, giving a negative or opposite force. Note: Of the words in **un-**[1], only a selected number are separately entered, since in most formations of this class, the meaning, spelling, and pronunciation may readily be determined by reference to the simple word from which each is formed.

un-[2] a prefix freely used in English to form verbs expressing a reversal of some action or state, or removal, deprivation, release, etc.

unaccountable /ʌnə'kaʊntəbəl/ *adj.* not to be accounted for or explained.

unanimous /ju'nænəməs/ *adj.* of one mind; in complete accord; agreed.

unassuming /ʌnə'sjumɪŋ/ *adj.* unpretending; modest.

uncalled-for /ʌn'kɔld-fɔ/ *adj.* unnecessary and improper; unwarranted.

uncanny /ʌn'kæni/ *adj.* **1.** such as to arouse superstitious uneasiness; unnaturally strange. **2.** abnormally good.

uncle /'ʌŋkəl/ *n.* **1.** a brother of one's father or mother. **2.** an aunt's husband.

unconscionable /ʌn'kɒnʃənəbəl/ *adj.* **1.** unreasonably excessive. **2.** not in accordance with what is just or reasonable. **3.** not guided by conscience; unscrupulous.

unconscious /ʌn'kɒnʃəs/ *adj.* **1.** not conscious; unaware. **2.** temporarily devoid of consciousness. **3.** occurring below the level of conscious thought. **4.** unintentional. – *n.* **5. the unconscious,** *Psychology* an organisation of the mind containing all psychic material not available in the immediate field of awareness.

uncouth /ʌn'kuθ/ *adj.* awkward, clumsy, or unmannerly, as persons, behaviour, actions, etc.

uncovered /ʌn-'kʌvəd/ *adj.* not protected by security, as a debt.

uncrossed *adj.* (of a cheque) not crossed; negotiable.

unction /'ʌŋkʃən/ *n.* the act of anointing, especially for medical purposes or as a religious rite.

unctuous /'ʌŋkʃuəs/ *adj.* oily; greasy.

under /'ʌndə/ *prep.* **1.** beneath and covered by. **2.** at a point or position lower than or farther down than. **3.** subject to. **4.** below in degree, amount, price, etc.; less than. **5.** below in rank, dignity, or the like. **6.** authorised, warranted, or attested by. **7.** in accordance with. – *adv.* **8.** under or beneath something. **9.** in a lower place. **10.** in a lower degree, amount, etc. **11.** in a subordinate position or condition. **12. go under,** *Colloquial* **a.** to sink in or as in water. **b.** to fail, especially of a business.

under- a prefixal attributive use of *under*, as to indicate **a.** a place or situation below or beneath, as in *underbrush*, *undertow*, or lower in grade or dignity, as in *understudy*. **b.** a lesser degree, extent, or amount, as in *undersized*. **c.** an insufficiency, as in *underfeed*.

underachieve /ʌndərəˈtʃiv/ *v.i.* to fail to perform as well as one's innate ability suggests.

underarm /ˈʌndəram/ *adj. Cricket, Tennis, etc.* executed with the hand below the shoulder as in bowling, service, etc.

undercapitalise = undercapitalize /ʌndəˈkæpətəlaɪz/ *v.t.*, **-lised**, **-lising**. to provide insufficient capital for (a business venture).

undercarriage /ˈʌndəkærɪdʒ/ *n.* the portions of an aeroplane beneath the body.

undercurrent /ˈʌndəkʌrənt/ *n.* **1.** a current below the surface. **2.** an underlying or concealed condition or tendency.

undercut /ʌndəˈkʌt/ *v.t.*, **-cut**, **-cutting**. to sell or work at a lower price than.

underdeveloped /ʌndədəˈvɛləpt/ *adj.* less fully developed than average.

underdog /ˈʌndədɒg/ *n.* **1.** a victim of oppression. **2.** the loser or expected loser in a competitive situation, fight, etc.

underfelt /ˈʌndəfɛlt/ *n.* a thick felt laid under a carpet to make it more resilient.

undergo /ʌndəˈgoʊ/ *v.t.*, **-went**, **-gone**, **-going**. **1.** to be subjected to; experience; pass through. **2.** to endure; sustain; suffer.

undergraduate /ʌndəˈgrædʒuət/ *n.* a student in a university or college who has not completed a first degree.

underground /ˈʌndəgraʊnd/ *adj.* **1.** existing, situated, operating, or taking place beneath the surface of the ground. **2.** hidden or secret; not open. – *n.* **3.** the place or region beneath the surface of the ground; the underworld. **4.** a secret organisation, etc.

underground economy *n.* cash economy, operating as a means of tax evasion.

undergrowth /ˈʌndəgroʊθ/ *n.* shrubs or small trees growing beneath or among large trees.

underhand /ˈʌndəhænd/ *adj.* secret and crafty or dishonourable.

underlie /ʌndəˈlaɪ/ *v.t.*, **-lay**, **-lain**, **-lying**. **1.** to lie under or beneath. **2.** to be at the basis of. – **underlying**, *adj.*

underline /ʌndəˈlaɪn/ *v.t.*, **-lined**, **-lining**. to mark with a line or lines underneath, as writing, etc.

undermine /ʌndəˈmaɪn, ˈʌndəmaɪn/ *v.t.*, **-mined**, **-mining**. to weaken insidiously; destroy gradually.

underneath /ʌndəˈniθ/ *prep.* **1.** under; beneath. – *adv.* **2.** beneath; below. – *adj.* **3.** lower.

underpants /ˈʌndəpænts/ *pl. n.* an article of underwear in the form of close-fitting short trousers, with or without legs.

underprivileged /ʌndəˈprɪvəlɪdʒd/ *adj.* denied the enjoyment of the normal privileges or rights of a society because of poverty and low social status.

undersecretary /ʌndəˈsɛkrətri/ *n.*, *pl.* **-taries**. the permanent head in certain government departments.

undersigned /ˈʌndəsaɪnd/ *n.* the person or persons who have signed at the end of a document.

understand /ʌndəˈstænd/ *v.*, **-stood**, **-standing**. – *v.t.* **1.** to perceive the meaning of; grasp the idea of; comprehend. **2.** to be thoroughly familiar with; apprehend clearly the character or nature of. **3.** to regard or take as a fact, or as settled. – *v.i.* **4.** to perceive what is meant.

understanding /ʌndəˈstændɪŋ/ *n.* **1.** the act of someone who understands; comprehension; personal interpretation. **2.** superior intelligence; superior power of recognising the truth. **3.** a mutual comprehension of each other's meaning, thoughts, etc. **4.** a mutual agreement of a private or unannounced kind. – *adj.* **5.** sympathetically discerning; tolerant.

understate /ʌndəˈsteɪt/ *v.t.*, **-stated**, **-stating**. to state or represent less strongly than is desirable or necessary; state with too little emphasis. – **understatement**, *n.*

understorey /ˈʌndəstɔri/ *n.* lower-level growth in forests, especially the plants and seedlings protected by the forest canopy.

understudy /ˈʌndəstʌdi/ *n.* an actor or actress who stands by to replace a performer when the latter is unable to appear.

undertake /ʌndəˈteɪk/ *v.t.*, **-took**, **-taken**, **-taking**. **1.** to take on oneself (some task, performance, etc.); attempt. **2.** to lay oneself under a formal obligation to perform or execute (some task, duty, etc.).

undertaker /ˈʌndəteɪkə/ *n* one whose business it is to prepare the dead for burial and to take charge of funerals.

undertaking /ˈʌndəteɪkɪŋ/ *n.* a task, enterprise, etc., undertaken.

undertone /ˈʌndətoʊn/ *n.* **1.** a low or subdued tone, as of utterance. **2.** an underlying quality, element, or tendency.

undertow /ˈʌndətoʊ/ *n.* the backward flow or draught of the water, below the surface, from waves breaking on a beach.

underwear /ˈʌndəwɛə/ *n.* clothes worn under outer clothes, especially those worn next to the skin.

underworld /ˈʌndəwɜld/ *n.* **1.** the lower, degraded, or criminal part of human society. **2.** the lower or nether world.

underwrite /ˈʌndəraɪt, ʌndəˈraɪt/ *v.t.*, **-wrote**, **-written**, **-writing**. **1.** to agree to meet the expense of; undertake to finance. **2.** to guarantee the sale of (shares or bonds to be offered to the public for subscription). **3.** *Insurance* to write one's name at the end of (a policy of insurance), thereby becoming liable in case of certain losses specified therein.

undo /ʌnˈdu/ *v.t.*, **-did**, **-done**, **-doing**. **1.** to unfasten and open (something closed, locked, barred, etc.). **2.** to untie or loose (strings, etc.). **3.** to reverse the doing of; cause to be as if never done. **4.** to bring to ruin or disaster; destroy.

undress /ʌnˈdrɛs/ *v.t.*, *v.i.* to remove the clothes (of).

undulate /ˈʌndʒəleɪt/ *v.i.*, **-lated**, **-lating**. to have a wavy motion.

unearned income /ʌnˈɜnd/ *n.* income, from investments, inheritance, property, etc., which is not earned as salary, and is sometimes taxed at a higher level than earned income.

unearned increment *n.* the increase in the value of land, etc., due to natural causes, as growth of population, rather than to any labour or expenditure by the owner.

unearth /ʌn'ɜθ/ *v.t.* to uncover or bring to light by digging, searching, or discovery.

uneasy /ʌn'izi/ *adj.*, **-easier**, **-easiest**. not easy in body or mind; disturbed.

unemployed /ʌnəm'plɔɪd/ *adj.* without work or employment.

unerring /ʌn'ɜrɪŋ/ *adj.* **1.** not erring; without error or mistake. **2.** unfailingly right, exact, or sure.

unexplored /ʌnək'splɔd/ *adj.* **1.** not explored; uncharted. **2.** not analysed; unknown.

unfeeling /ʌn'filɪŋ/ *adj.* unsympathetic; callous; hard-hearted.

unforeseen /ʌnfɔ'sin, -fə-/ *adj.* not predicted; unexpected.

unfreeze /ʌn'friz/ *v.t.*, **-froze**, **-frozen**, **-freezing**. **1.** to relax restrictions on (prices, incomes, credit, etc.). **2.** to lift controls from the manufacture of or dealing in (a commodity or the like).

ungainly /ʌn'geɪnli/ *adj.* not graceful.

unguent /'ʌŋgwənt/ *n.* any soft preparation or salve; an ointment.

uni /'juni/ *n. Colloquial* a university.

uni- a word element meaning 'one', 'single'.

unicorn /'junəkɔn/ *n.* a mythological animal with a single long horn.

uniform /'junəfɔm/ *adj.* **1.** having always the same form or character; unvarying. **2.** regular; even. **3.** agreeing with one another in form, character, appearance, etc.; alike; of the same form, character, etc., with another or others. – *n.* **4.** a distinctive dress of uniform style, materials, and colour worn by and identifying all the members of a group or organisation. – **uniformity**, *n.*

unify /'junəfaɪ/ *v.t.*, **-fied**, **-fying**. to form into one; make a unit of; reduce to unity. – **unification**, *n.*

unilateral /juni'lætərəl, -'lætrəl, junə-/ *adj.* **1.** relating to, occurring on, or affecting one side only. **2.** affecting one side, party, or person only. **3.** concerned with or considering only one side of a matter or question; one-sided.

unimpressed /ʌnɪm'prest/ *adj.* **1.** not impressed; unmoved: *unimpressed by the sales pitch.* **2.** (*ironic*) definitely displeased: *decidedly unimpressed with the opposition.*

uninterested /ʌn'ɪntrəstəd/ *adj.* **1.** having or showing no feeling of interest; indifferent. **2.** not personally concerned in something.

union /'junjən/ *n.* **1.** the act of uniting two or more things into one. **2.** the state of being so united; conjunction; combination. **3.** something formed by uniting two or more things; a combination. **4.** a number of persons, societies, states, or the like, joined together or associated for some common purpose. **5.** a trade union.

union delegate *n.* a trade union official elected to represent employees in a place of work.

unionise = unionize /'junjənaɪz/ *v.t.*, **-nised**, **-nising**. to organise into a trade union.

unionist /'junjənəst/ *n.* a trade unionist.

unique /ju'nik/ *adj.* **1.** of which there is only one; sole. **2.** having no like or equal.

unisex /'junisɛks/ *adj.* of a style of dress, etc., which does not adhere to the traditional differentiations between the sexes.

unison /'junəsən/ *n.* **1.** coincidence in pitch of two or more notes, voices, etc. **2.** accord or agreement.

unit /'junət/ *n.* **1.** a single thing or person; any group of things or persons regarded as an individual. **2.** any specified amount of a quantity, as of length, volume, force, momentum, time, by comparison with which any other quantity of the same kind is measured or estimated. **3.** (in a block of flats or motel) a self-contained suite of rooms.

unite /ju'naɪt/ *v.*, **united**, **uniting**. – *v.t.* **1.** to join so as to form one connected whole; join, combine, or incorporate in one; cause to be one. **2.** to associate (persons, etc.) by some bond or tie; join in action, interest, opinion, feeling, etc. – *v.i.* **3.** to join together so as to form one connected whole; become one; combine.

unit holder *n.* someone with a holding in a unit trust.

unit price *n.* a price per agreed unit, as per kilogram, per dozen, etc.

unit trust *n.* **1.** a trust whose management purchases shares from a number of companies. The portfolio of such shares is divided into equal units for sale to the public, whose interests are served by an independent trustee company. **2.** the units issued for sale by such a trust.

unity /'junəti/ *n.*, *pl.* **-ties**. **1.** the state or fact of being one; oneness. **2.** the oneness of a complex or organic whole or of an interconnected series. **3.** freedom from diversity or variety. **4.** oneness of mind, feeling, etc., as among a number of persons; concord, harmony, or agreement.

universal /junə'vɜsəl/ *adj.* **1.** extending over, including, proceeding from, all or the whole (of something specified or implicit); without exception. **2.** applicable to many individuals or single cases; general. **3.** affecting, concerning, or involving all. **4.** of or relating to the universe, all nature, or all existing things. **5.** *Machinery, etc.* adapted or adaptable for all or various uses, angles, sizes, etc. – *n.* **6.** that which may be applied throughout the universe to many things.

Universal Product Code *n.* → **bar code**.

universe /'junəvɜs/ *n.* **1.** all of space, and all the matter and energy which it contains; the cosmos. **2.** a world or sphere in which something exists or prevails.

university /junə'vɜsəti/ *n.*, *pl.* **-ties**. an institution of higher learning, conducting teaching and research at the undergraduate and postgraduate level.

unkempt /ʌn'kɛmpt/ *adj.* in an uncared-for, neglected, or untidy state; rough.

unless /ʌn'lɛs, ən-/ *conj.* except on condition that; except when; if ... not.

unload /ʌn'loʊd/ *v.t.* to take the load from; remove the burden, cargo, or freight from.

unnerve /ʌn'nɜv/ *v.t.*, **-nerved**, **-nerving**. to

deprive of nerve, strength, or physical or mental firmness; break down the self-control of; upset.

unorthodox /ʌn'ɔθədɒks/ *adj.* not conventional in ideology, method, behaviour, etc.

unravel /ʌn'rævəl/ *v.t.*, **-elled**, **-elling**. to disentangle; disengage the threads or fibres of (a woven or knitted fabric, a rope, etc.).

unreal /ʌn'ril/ *adj.* **1.** not real; not substantial; imaginary; artificial; unpractical or visionary. **2.** *Colloquial* **a.** unbelievably awful. **b.** unbelievably wonderful.

unrequited /ʌnrə'kwaɪtəd/ *adj.* (used especially of affection) not returned or reciprocated.

unrest /ʌn'rɛst/ *n.* strong, almost rebellious, dissatisfaction and agitation.

unruly /ʌn'ruli/ *adj.* not submissive or conforming to rule; ungovernable. – **unruliness**, *n.*

unsavoury = unsavory /ʌn'seɪvəri/ *adj.* socially or morally unpleasant or offensive.

unscrupulous /ʌn'skrupjələs/ *adj.* untroubled by conscience; lacking sound moral principles.

unsecured /ʌnsə'kjuəd/ *adj.* **1.** not made secure or fastened. **2.** not insured against loss, as by a mortgage, bond, pledge, etc.

unsecured note *n.* a certificate acknowledging a loan made for fixed period of time at a fixed rate of interest, not secured by a charge over the company's assets, and ranking after debentures for payment in a winding-up.

unsettle /ʌn'sɛtl/ *v.t.*, **-tled**, **-tling**. to shake or weaken (beliefs, feelings, etc.); derange (the mind, etc.).

unsightly /ʌn'saɪtli/ *adj.* not pleasing to the sight; forming an unpleasing sight.

untenable /ʌn'tɛnəbəl/ *adj.* incapable of being maintained against arguments, as an opinion, scheme, etc.

unthinkable /ʌn'θɪŋkəbəl/ *adj.* **1.** inconceivable; unimaginable. **2.** not to be considered; utterly out of the question.

until /ʌn'tɪl/ *conj.* **1.** up to the time that or when; till. **2.** (with negatives) before: *not until he's finished.* – *prep.* **3.** onward to, or till (a specified time); up to the time of (some occurrence). **4.** (with negatives) before: *not until evening.*

unto /'ʌntu/ *prep. Archaic* to (in its various uses, except as the accompaniment of the infinitive).

untoward /ʌntə'wɔd, ʌn'touəd/ *adj.* **1.** unfavourable or unfortunate. **2.** unseemly.

unwieldy /ʌn'wildi/ *adj.* **1.** not readily handled or managed in use or action, as from size, shape, or weight. **2.** ungainly; awkward.

unwitting /ʌn'wɪtɪŋ/ *adj.* unaware; unconscious.

unwritten law *n.* **1.** law which rests for its authority on custom, judicial decision, etc., as distinguished from law originating in written command, statute, or decree. **2.** a custom or social convention.

up /ʌp/ *adv., prep., adj., v.,* **upped**, **upping**, *interj.* – *adv.* **1.** to, towards, or in a more elevated position. **2.** into the air. **3.** to or in an erect position. **4.** out of bed. **5.** to or at any point that is considered higher, as the north, a capital city, or the like. **6.** to or at a higher point or degree in a scale, as of rank, size, value, pitch, etc. **7.** to or at a point of equal advance, extent, etc. **8.** well advanced or versed, as in a subject. **9.** to a state of maturity. **10.** to a state of completion; to an end. – *prep.* **11.** to, towards, or at a higher place on or in. **12.** to, towards, near, or at a higher station, condition, or rank in. – *adj.* **13.** upwards; going or directed upwards. **14.** travelling towards a terminus or centre. **15.** standing and speaking. **16.** out of bed. **17.** well informed or advanced, as in a subject. **18.** (especially of a computer) operational. **19.** appearing before a court or the like on some charge. **20.** in a leading or advanced position. – *v.t. Colloquial* **21.** to make larger; step up. **22.** to go better than (a preceding wager). – *interj.* **23.** (a command to rise or stand up).

up- a prefixal, attributive use of *up*, in its various meanings.

upbraid /ʌp'breɪd/ *v.t.* to reproach for some fault or offence; reprove severely; chide.

upbringing /'ʌpbrɪŋɪŋ/ *n.* the bringing up or rearing of a person from childhood.

up-country /'ʌp-kʌntri/ *adj.* **1.** being or living remote from the coast or border; interior. – *adv.* **2.** towards or in the interior of a country.

update /ʌp'deɪt/ *v.t.*, **-dated**, **-dating**. to bring up to date.

up-end /ʌp-'ɛnd/ *v.t.* **1.** to set on end. **2.** to upset.

up-front /'ʌp-frʌnt/ *adj.* **1.** placed in a position of leadership or responsibility. **2.** straightforward; open; extroverted. **3.** (of money) payable in the early stages of a project: *an up-front advance.*

upgrade /ʌp'greɪd/ *v.t., v.i.,* **-graded**, **-grading**. to improve.

upheave /ʌp'hiv/ *v.t.*, **-heaved**, **-heaving**. **1.** to heave or lift up; raise up or aloft. **2.** to disturb or change violently or radically. – **upheaval**, *n.*

uphold /ʌp'hould/ *v.t.*, **-held**, **-holding**. to support or maintain, as by advocacy or agreement.

upholstery /ʌp'houlstri, -stəri/ *n., pl.* **-ries**. the cushions, furniture coverings and other material used to stuff and cover furniture and cushions.

upkeep /'ʌpkip/ *n.* (the cost of) the maintenance of an establishment, machine, etc.

uplift /ʌp'lɪft/ *v.t.* **1.** to lift up; raise; elevate. **2.** to exalt emotionally or spiritually.

up-market /'ʌp-makət/ *adj.* **1.** of or relating to commercial services and goods of superior status, quality and price. **2.** superior in style or production; pretentious. See **down-market**.

upon /ə'pɒn/ *prep.* **1.** up and on; upwards so as to get or be on. **2.** on, in any of various senses.

upper /'ʌpə/ *adj.* **1.** higher (than something implied) or highest, as in place, or position, or in a scale. **2.** forming the higher of a pair of corresponding things or sets. **3.** (of a surface) facing upwards. – *n.* **4.** anything which is higher (than another, as of a pair) or highest. **5.** the part of a shoe or boot above the sole.

upper class *n.* the class of people socially and conventionally regarded as being higher or highest in the social hierarchy and commonly identified by wealth or aristocratic birth.

upright /'ʌpràɪt/ *adj.* **1.** erect or vertical, as in position or posture. **2.** righteous, honest, or just.

uprising /'ʌpraɪzɪŋ, ʌp'raɪzɪŋ/ *n.* an insurrection or revolt.

uproar /'ʌprɔ/ *n.* violent and noisy disturbance.

uproarious /ʌp'rɔriəs/ *adj.* **1.** characterised by or in a state of uproar; tumultuous. **2.** extremely funny.

upset /ʌp'sɛt/ *v.,* **-set**, **-setting**; /'ʌpsɛt/ *n.*; /'ʌpsɛt/, *especially in predicative use* /ʌp'sɛt/ *adj.* – *v.t.* **1.** to overturn; knock or tip over; capsize. **2.** to disturb (someone) mentally or emotionally; distress. **3.** to defeat (a competitor or opponent), especially contrary to expectation. – *n.* **4.** a physical upsetting or being upset; overthrow. **5.** an emotional disturbance. **6.** a defeat, especially unexpected. – *adj.* **7.** emotionally disturbed; distressed.

upshot /'ʌpʃɒt/ *n.* the final issue, the conclusion, or the result.

upstage /ʌp'steɪdʒ/ *adv.,* /ʌp'steɪdʒ/ *v.,* **-staged**, **-staging**. – *adv.* **1.** on or to the back of the stage. – *v.t.* **2.** to steal attention (from another) by some manoeuvre.

upstairs /ʌp'stɛəz/ *adv.,* /'ʌpstɛəz/ *adj.* – *adv.* **1.** up the stairs; to or on an upper floor. **2.** to or in a higher rank or office. – *adj.* **3.** on or relating to an upper floor.

upstanding /'ʌpstændɪŋ/, *especially in predicative use* /ʌp'stændɪŋ/ – *adj.* straightforward, open, or independent; upright; honourable.

upstart /'ʌpstat/ *n.* someone who has risen suddenly from a humble position to wealth or power, or to assumed consequence.

upstream /ʌp'strim/ *adv.* towards or in the higher part of a stream; against the current.

uptake /'ʌpteɪk/ *n.* the action of understanding or comprehension; mental grasp.

uptight /'ʌptaɪt/ *adj. Colloquial* tense, nervous, or irritable.

up-to-date /'ʌp-tə-deɪt/ *adj.* extending to the present time; including the latest facts.

upturn /'ʌptɜn/ *n.* an upward turn, or a changing and rising movement, as in prices, business, etc.

upvalue /'ʌpvælju/ *v.t.,* **-ued**, **-uing**. to revalue (a currency) upwards.

upward /'ʌpwəd/ *adj.* **1.** directed, tending, or moving towards a higher point or level; ascending. – *adv.* **2.** upwards.

upwards /'ʌpwədz/ *adv.* **1.** towards a higher place or position; in a vertical direction. **2.** towards a higher level, degree, or standard.

upwind /ʌp'wɪnd/ *adv.* towards or in the direction from which the wind is blowing.

uranium /ju'reɪniəm/ *n.* a white, lustrous, radioactive, metallic element, one isotope of which is the basis of the atomic bomb and nuclear reactors. *Symbol*: U

urano- a word element meaning 'heaven'.

urban /'ɜbən/ *adj.* of, relating to, or comprising a city or town.

urbane /ɜ'beɪn/ *adj.* having the refinement and manners considered to be characteristic of city-dwellers; civilised; sophisticated.

urchin /'ɜtʃən/ *n.* a small boy or youngster, especially someone who is mischievous and impudent, or ragged and shabbily dressed.

-ure a suffix of abstract nouns indicating action, result, and instrument, as in *legislature, pressure.*

urea /ju'riə, 'juriə/ *n.* a colourless crystalline substance occurring in the urine of mammals, amphibians, and some fishes and reptiles.

urethra /ju'riθrə/ *n., pl.* **-thrae** /-θri/, **-thras**. *Anatomy* the membranous tube which extends from the bladder to the exterior. In the male it conveys semen as well as urine.

urge /ɜdʒ/ *v.,* **urged**, **urging**, *n.* – *v.t.* **1.** to endeavour to induce or persuade; entreat or exhort earnestly. **2.** to press, push, or hasten (the course, activities, etc.). – *n.* **3.** the fact of urging or being urged. **4.** an involuntary, natural, or instinctive impulse.

urgent /'ɜdʒənt/ *adj.* **1.** pressing; compelling or requiring immediate action or attention; imperative. **2.** insistent or earnest in solicitation. – **urgency**, *n.*

-urgy a word element meaning 'a technology', as in *metallurgy.*

urinal /'jurənəl, ju'raɪnəl/ *n.* a fixture, room, or building for discharging urine in.

urinate /'jurəneɪt/ *v.i.* to discharge urine.

urine /'jurən, -aɪn/ *n.* the secretion of the kidneys (in mammals, a fluid). – **urinary**, *adj.*

URL /ju ar 'ɛl/ *n. Computers* the address of a document on the Internet.

urn /ɜn/ *n.* **1.** a kind of vase, of various forms, especially one with a foot or pedestal. **2.** a vessel with a tap, used for heating water, tea, coffee, etc., in quantity.

ursine /'ɜsaɪn/ *adj.* **1.** of or relating to a bear or bears. **2.** bearlike.

us /ʌs/, *weak forms* /əs, əz/ – *pron.* objective case of **we**.

usage /'jusɪdʒ, 'juzɪdʒ/ *n.* **1.** customary way of doing; a custom or practice. **2.** customary manner of using a language or any of its forms, especially standard practice in a given language. **3.** usual conduct or behaviour. **4.** the act or fact of using or employing; use.

usance /'juzəns/ *n.* **1.** *Commerce* the length of time, exclusive of days of grace, allowed by custom or usage for the payment of foreign bills of exchange. **2.** *Economics* the income of benefits of every kind derived from the ownership of wealth.

use /juz/, *for def. 6 also* /jus/ *v.,* **used, using**; /jus/ *n.* – *v.t.* **1.** to employ for some purpose; put into service. **2.** to avail oneself of; apply to one's own purposes. **3.** to act or behave towards, or treat (a person) in some manner. **4.** to exploit (a person) for one's own ends. **5.** to operate or put into effect. – *v.i.* **6.** to be accustomed, wont, or customarily found (with an infinitive expressed or understood, and, except in archaic use, now only in the past). – *n.* **7.** the act of employing or using, or putting into service. **8.** the state of being employed or used. **9.** a way of being employed or used; a purpose for which something is used. **10.** the power, right, or privilege of employing or using something. **11.** help; profit; resulting good. **12.** custom; practice. **13.** way of using or treating; treatment.

use-by date *n.* the date by which the manufacturer of a product recommends that it should be used, usually stamped onto the packaging.

used /just/ *adj.* accustomed; habituated; inured (fol. by *to*).

useful /'jusfəl/ *adj.* being of use or service; serving some purpose.

user-friendly /'juzə-frɛndli/ *adj.* of or relating to equipment, especially computer programs or equipment, designed to provide minimal difficulty for the inexperienced operator.

user-pays principle *n.* the principle that the cost of a government service should be borne mainly by the people who benefit from it.

usher /'ʌʃə/ *n.* **1.** someone who escorts persons to seats in a church, theatre, etc. **2.** an attendant who keeps order in a law court. – *v.t.* **3.** to act as an usher to; conduct or show (fol. by *in*, *into*, *out*, etc.).

usherette /ʌʃə'rɛt/ *n.* a female attendant, especially someone who shows people to their seats in a cinema or theatre.

usual /'juʒuəl/ *adj.* **1.** habitual or customary. **2.** such as is commonly met with or observed in experience; ordinary. **3.** in common use; common. – *n.* **4.** that which is usual or habitual. – **usually**, *adv.*

usurp /ju'zɜp/ *v.t.* to seize and hold (an office or position, power, etc.) by force or without right.

usury /'juʒəri/ *n., pl.* **-ries**. **1.** an exorbitant amount or rate of interest, especially one in excess of the legal rate. **2.** the lending, or practice of lending money at an exorbitant rate of interest.

utensil /ju'tɛnsəl/ *n.* any instrument, vessel, or implement.

uterus /'jutərəs/ *n., pl.* **uteri** /'jutəraɪ/. that portion of the female reproductive system in which the fertilised ovum implants itself and develops until birth; womb. – **uterine**, *adj.*

utilise = utilize /'jutəlaɪz/ *v.t.,* **-lised**, **-lising**. to put to use; turn to profitable account.

utilitarian /juˌtɪlə'tɛəriən/ *adj.* **1.** relating to or consisting in utility; concerning practical or material things. **2.** having regard to utility or usefulness rather than beauty, ornamentality, etc.

utility /ju'tɪləti/ *n., pl.* **-ties**. **1.** the state or character of being useful. **2.** something useful; a useful thing. **3.** a public service, as a bus or railway service, gas or electricity supply, or the like. **4.** Also, **utility truck**, **ute**. a small truck with an enclosed cabin and a rectangular tray which has sides and is sometimes covered by a tarpaulin. **5.** *Economics* the capacity of an object for satisfying a human want.

utility program *n.* *Computers* a computer program designed to carry out a routine process, as sorting data, copying files, etc.

utility truck *n.* → **utility** (def. 4).

utmost /'ʌtmoʊst/ *adj.* **1.** of the greatest or highest degree, quantity, or the like; greatest. **2.** being at the farthest point or extremity; farthest. – *n.* **3.** the greatest degree or amount. **4.** the highest, greatest, or best of one's power. Also, **uttermost**.

utopia /ju'toʊpiə/ *n.* (*sometimes cap.*) a place or state of ideal perfection. – **utopian**, *adj.*

utter[1] /'ʌtə/ *v.t.* **1.** to give audible expression to (words, etc.); speak or pronounce. **2.** to express or make known in any manner. **3.** to make publicly known; publish. **4.** to put into circulation, as coins, notes, etc., and especially counterfeit money, forged cheques, etc. – **utterance**, *n.*

utter[2] /'ʌtə/ *adj.* complete; total; absolute. – **utterly**, *adv.*

UV ultraviolet.

uvula /'juvjələ/ *n., pl.* **-las**, **-lae** /-li/. the small, fleshy, conical body projecting downwards from the middle of the soft palate. – **uvular**, *adj.*

uxorious /ʌk'sɔriəs/ *adj.* excessively or foolishly fond of one's wife.

V v

V, v /vi/ *n., pl.* **V's** *or* **Vs, v's** *or* **vs**. the 22nd letter of the English alphabet.

vacant /'veɪkənt/ *adj.* **1.** having no contents; empty; void. **2.** having no occupant. **3.** free from work, business, etc., as time. – **vacancy**, *n.*

vacate /və'keɪt, veɪ'keɪt/ *v.t.,* **-cated, -cating**. **1.** to make vacant; cause to be empty or unoccupied. **2.** to give up the occupancy of.

vacation /və'keɪʃən, veɪ'keɪʃən/ *n.* **1.** a part of the year when law courts, universities, etc., are suspended or closed. **2.** *Originally US* a holiday.

vaccinate /'væksəneɪt/ *v.t.,* **-nated, -nating**. **1.** to inoculate with the vaccine of cowpox, so as to render the subject immune to smallpox. **2.** to inoculate with the modified virus of any of various other diseases, as a preventive measure.

vaccine /'væksin, væk'sin/ *n.* **1.** the virus of cowpox used in vaccination against smallpox. **2.** the modified virus of any of various other diseases, used for preventive inoculation.

vacillate /'væsəleɪt/ *v.i.,* **-lated, -lating**. **1.** to sway unsteadily; waver; stagger. **2.** to fluctuate.

vacuous /'vækjuəs/ *adj.* **1.** empty; without contents. **2.** empty of ideas or intelligence; stupidly vacant. – **vacuity**, *n.*

vacuum /'vækjum/ *n., pl.* **vacuums, vacua** /'vækjuə/. **1.** a space entirely void of matter. **2.** an enclosed space from which air (or other gas) has been removed, as by an air pump. **3.** Also, **vacuum cleaner**. an apparatus for cleaning carpets, floors, etc., by suction.

vagabond /'vægəbɒnd/ *n.* someone who is without a fixed abode and wanders from place to place.

vagary /'veɪgəri/ *n., pl.* **-ries**. **1.** an extravagant idea or notion. **2.** a wild, capricious, or fantastic action; a freak. **3.** uncertainty: *the vagaries of life.*

vagina /və'dʒaɪnə/ *n., pl.* **-nas, -nae** /-ni/. *Anatomy* the passage leading from the uterus to the vulva in a female mammal. – **vaginal**, *adj.*

vagrant /'veɪgrənt/ *n.* **1.** someone who wanders from place to place and has no settled home or means of support; tramp. – *adj.* **2.** wandering or roaming from place to place. – **vagrancy**, *n.*

vague /veɪg/ *adj.,* **vaguer, vaguest**. **1.** not definite in statement or meaning; not explicit or precise. **2.** indistinct to the sight or other sense, or perceptible or recognisable only in an indefinite way. **3.** (of persons, etc.) indefinite in statement; not clear in thought or understanding.

vain /veɪn/ *adj.* **1.** without real value or importance; hollow, idle or worthless. **2.** futile; useless; ineffectual. **3.** having an excessive pride in one's own appearance, qualities, gifts, achievements, etc.; conceited.

vainglory /veɪn'glɔri/ *n.* inordinate elation or pride in one's achievements, abilities, etc. – **vainglorious**, *adj.*

valance /'væləns/ *n.* a short curtain.

valediction /vælə'dɪkʃən/ *n.* a bidding farewell; a leave-taking. – **valedictory**, *adj.*

valency /'veɪlənsi/ *n., pl.* **-cies**. *Chemistry* the combining capacity of an atom.

-valent a word element meaning 'having worth or value', used especially in scientific terminology to refer to valency.

valerian /və'lɛəriən, -'lɪə-/ *n.* **1.** a herb with white or pink flowers. **2.** a drug consisting of or made from its root, used as a nerve sedative and antispasmodic.

valet /'vælei, 'vælət/ *n.* **1.** a manservant who is his employer's personal attendant, caring for the employer's clothing, etc. **2.** someone who performs similar services for patrons of a hotel, etc.

valetudinarian /,vælətjudə'nɛəriən/ *n.* **1.** an invalid. **2.** someone who is constantly or excessively concerned about the state of their health.

valiant /'væliənt/ *adj.* brave, courageous, or stout-hearted, as persons.

valid /'væləd/ *adj.* **1.** sound, just, or well-founded. **2.** having force, weight, or cogency; authoritative. **3.** legally sound, effective, or binding. – **validity**, *n.* – **validate**, *v.*

valley /'væli/ *n., pl.* **-leys**. an elongated depression, usually with an outlet, between uplands, hills, or mountains, especially one following the course of a stream.

valour = valor /'vælə/ *n.* bravery or heroic courage, especially in battle.

valuable /'væljuəbəl, 'væljubəl/ *adj.* **1.** of monetary worth. **2.** of considerable use, service, or importance.

valuation /vælju'eɪʃən/ *n.* an estimating or fixing of the value of a thing.

value /'vælju/ *n., v.,* **-ued, -uing**. – *n.* **1.** that property of a thing because of which it is esteemed, desirable, or useful, or the degree of this property possessed; worth, merit, or importance. **2.** the worth of a thing as measured by the amount of other things for which it can be exchanged, or as estimated in terms of a medium of exchange. **3.** force, import, or significance. – *v.t.* **4.** to estimate the value of; rate at a certain value or price; appraise. **5.** to consider with respect to worth, excellence, usefulness, or importance. **6.** to regard or esteem highly.

valuer general *n.* a government official in charge of making valuations of property.

valuta /və'lutə/ *n.* the value of a currency in terms of another currency.

valve /vælv/ *n.* **1.** any device for closing or modifying the passage through a pipe, outlet, inlet, or the like, in order to control the flow of liquids, gases, etc. **2.** *Anatomy* a membranous fold or other structure which permits blood to flow in one direction only. **3.** *Electronics* an electrical device which can be used for controlling a flow of electricity.

vamp[1] /væmp/ *n.* **1.** the front part of the upper of a shoe or boot. **2.** anything patched up or pieced together. – *v.t.* **3.** to patch up or repair; renovate (often fol. by *up*).

vamp[2] /væmp/ *n. Colloquial* a woman who uses her charms to seduce and exploit men.

vampire /'væmpaɪə/ *n.* **1.** a supernatural being, in the common belief a reanimated corpse of a person improperly buried, supposed to suck blood of sleeping persons at night. **2.** Also, **vampire bat**. a bat which feeds on the blood of animals including humans.

van /væn/ *n.* a covered vehicle, usually large in size, for moving furniture, goods, etc.

vanadium /və'neɪdiəm/ *n.* a rare element used as an ingredient of steel. *Symbol*: V

vandal /'vændl/ *n.* someone who wilfully or ignorantly destroys or damages anything. – **vandalism**, *n.* – **vandalise = vandalize**, *v.*

vane /veɪn/ *n.* a flat piece of metal, etc., especially one which moves with the wind and indicates its direction.

vanguard /'væŋgad/ *n.* the leading position in any field.

vanilla /və'nɪlə/ *n.* a tropical orchid whose pod-like fruit yields an extract used in flavourings, perfumery, etc.

vanish /'vænɪʃ/ *v.i.* to disappear from sight, or become invisible, especially quickly.

vanity /'vænəti/ *n., pl.* **-ties** the quality of being personally vain.

vanquish /'væŋkwɪʃ/ *v.t.* to conquer or defeat in battle or conflict.

vantage point /'væntɪdʒ, 'van-/ *n.* a position or place affording an advantageous or clear view or perspective.

vapid /'væpəd/ *adj.* having lost life, sharpness, or flavour; insipid; flat.

vaporise = vaporize /'veɪpəraɪz/ *v.t.*, **-rised**, **-rising**. to cause to pass into the gaseous state.

vapour = vapor /'veɪpə/ *n.* **1.** a visible exhalation, as fog, mist, condensed steam, smoke, etc. **2.** a substance in the gaseous state; a gas.

variable /'vɛəriəbəl/ *adj.* **1.** apt or liable to vary or change; changeable. **2.** inconsistent or fickle, as a person. – *n.* **3.** something variable. **4.** *Mathematics* a symbol, or the quantity or function which it signifies, which may represent any one of a given set of numbers and other objects. – **variability**, *n.*

variance /'vɛəriəns/ *n.* the state or fact of varying; divergence or discrepancy.

variant /'vɛəriənt/ *adj.* **1.** being an altered or different form of something. – *n.* **2.** a variant form.

variation /vɛəri'eɪʃən/ *n.* **1.** the act or process of varying; change in condition, character, degree, etc. **2.** amount or rate of change. **3.** a different form of something; a variant.

varicose /'værəkous, -kəs/ *adj.* abnormally or unusually enlarged, swollen, or dilated.

variegate /'vɛəriəgeɪt, 'vɛərə-/ *v.t.*, **-gated**, **-gating**. to make varied in appearance; mark with different colours, tints, etc.

variety /və'raɪəti/ *n., pl.* **-ties**. **1.** the state or character of being various or varied; diversity, or absence of uniformity or monotony. **2.** a number of things of different kinds. **3.** a kind or sort. **4.** a different form, condition, or phase of something.

various /'vɛəriəs/ *adj.* **1.** differing one from another, or of different kinds, as two or more things. **2.** several or many.

varnish /'vanɪʃ/ *n.* **1.** a preparation which, when applied to the surface of wood, metal, etc., dries and leaves a hard, more or less glossy, usually transparent coating. – *v.t.* **2.** to apply varnish to.

vary /'vɛəri/ *v.*, **-ried**, **-rying**. – *v.t.* **1.** to change or alter, as in form, appearance, character, substance, degree, etc. **2.** to cause to be different, one from another. **3.** to diversify (something); relieve from uniformity or monotony. – *v.i.* **4.** to be different, or show diversity. **5.** to undergo change in form, appearance, character, substance, degree, etc. **6.** to change in succession, follow alternately, or alternate. **7.** to diverge; deviate (usually fol. by *from*).

vas /væs/ *n., pl.* **vasa** /'veɪsə/. *Anatomy, Zoology, Botany* a vessel or duct.

vascular /'væskjələ/ *adj.* relating to, composed of, or provided with vessels or ducts which convey fluids, as blood, lymph, or sap.

vas deferens /væs 'dɛfərɛnz/ *n., pl.* **vasa deferentia** /ˌveɪsə dɛfə'rɛnʃiə/. *Anatomy* the duct of the testicle which transports sperm to the penis.

vase /vaz/ *n.* a hollow vessel used as a container for flowers.

vasectomy /və'sɛktəmi/ *n., pl.* **-mies**. the surgical excision of the vas deferens, or of a portion of it as a contraceptive measure.

vassal /'væsəl/ *n.* (in the feudal system) a person holding lands by the obligation to render military service or its equivalent to a superior.

vast /vast/ *adj.* of very great extent or area; very extensive, or immense.

vat /væt/ *n.* a large container for liquids.

vaudeville /'vɔdvɪl, 'vɔdəvɪl/ *n.* a theatrical piece of light or amusing character, interspersed with songs and dances.

vault[1] /vɔlt, vɒlt/ *n.* **1.** an arched space, chamber, or passage. **2.** a strongroom for storing and safeguarding valuables.

vault[2] /vɔlt, vɒlt/ *v.i.* to leap or spring, as to or from a position or over something.

vaunt /vɔnt/ *v.t.* **1.** to speak boastfully of. – *n.* **2.** boastful utterance.

V-chip /'vi-tʃɪp/ *n.* a computerised device installed in a TV set which responds to a signal accompanying a television program identified as being violent, and which can be activated to prevent the showing of the program.

VCR /vi si 'a/ *n.* → **video cassette recorder**.

veal /vil/ *n.* the flesh of the calf as used for food.

vector /'vɛktə/ *n.* **1.** *Mathematics* a quantity which possesses both magnitude and direction. **2.** *Computers* the address of an entry in a memory which is conceptually organised into position-dependent entries of fixed length. **3.** *Biology* an insect or other organism transmitting germs or other agents of disease.

veer /vɪə/ *v.i.* to turn or shift to another direction; change from one direction or course to another.

vegetable /ˈvɛdʒtəbəl/ *n.* **1.** any herbaceous plant whose fruits, seeds, roots, tubers, bulbs, stems, leaves, or flower parts are used as food. **2.** *Colloquial* a person who, due to physical injury or mental deficiency, is entirely dependent on the agencies of others for subsistence.

vegetarian /vɛdʒəˈtɛəriən/ *n.* someone who lives on vegetable food only.

vegetate /ˈvɛdʒəteɪt/ *v.i.,* **-tated**, **-tating**. **1.** to grow in the manner of plants; increase as if by vegetable growth. **2.** to live in an inactive, passive, or unthinking way.

vegetation /vɛdʒəˈteɪʃən/ *n.* plants collectively; the plant life of a particular region considered as a whole.

vehement /ˈviəmənt/ *adj.* **1.** eager, impetuous, or impassioned. **2.** (of actions) marked by great energy, exertion, or unusual force.

vehicle /ˈviɪkəl, ˈviəkəl/ *n.* **1.** any receptacle, or means of transport, in which something is carried or conveyed, or travels. **2.** a medium by which ideas or effects are communicated. – **vehicular**, *adj.*

veil /veɪl/ *n.* **1.** a piece of material worn over the head or face, as to conceal the face or to protect it from the sun or wind. **2.** something that covers, screens, or conceals. – *v.t.* **3.** to cover or conceal with or as with a veil.

vein /veɪn/ *n.* **1.** one of the system of branching vessels or tubes conveying blood from various parts of the body to the heart. **2.** one of the strands or bundles of vascular tissue forming the principal framework of a leaf. **3.** any body or stratum of ore, coal, etc., clearly separated or defined. **4.** a strain or quality traceable in character or conduct, writing, etc.

velcro /ˈvɛlkroʊ/ *n.* a type of tape used as a fastening, comprising two strips of fabric, one with a dense arrangement of small nylon hooks and the other with a nylon pile, so that when the strips are pressed together one hooks into the other. Also, **Velcro**.

vellum /ˈvɛləm/ *n.* a sheet of calfskin prepared as parchment for writing or bookbinding.

velocity /vəˈlɒsəti/ *n., pl.* **-ties**. **1.** rapidity of motion or operation; swiftness; quickness. **2.** *Physics* rate of motion, especially when the direction of motion is also specified.

velodrome /ˈvɛlədroʊm/ *n.* an arena with a banked track for cycle races.

velour /vəˈluə/ *n.* any of various fabrics with a fine, raised finish. Also, **velours**.

velvet /ˈvɛlvət/ *n.* **1.** a fabric with a thick, soft pile. **2.** something likened to the fabric velvet in softness, etc.

venal /ˈvinəl/ *adj.* accessible to bribery; corruptly mercenary.

vend /vɛnd/ *v.t.* to dispose of by sale.

vendetta /vɛnˈdɛtə/ *n.* any prolonged or persistent quarrel, rivalry, etc.

veneer /vəˈnɪə/ *n.* **1.** a thin layer of wood or other material used for facing or overlaying wood. **2.** a superficially pleasing appearance or show.

venerable /ˈvɛnrəbəl, -nərəbəl/ *adj.* worthy of veneration or reverence, as on account of high character or office.

venerate /ˈvɛnəreɪt/ *v.t.,* **-rated**, **-rating**. to regard with reverence, or revere. – **veneration**, *n.*

venereal disease /vəˈnɪəriəl/ *n.* any of those diseases which are transmitted by sexual intercourse with an infected person, especially syphilis and gonorrhoea.

vengeance /ˈvɛndʒəns/ *n.* the avenging of wrong, injury, or the like, or retributive punishment. – **vengeful**, *adj.*

venial /ˈviniəl/ *adj.* that may be forgiven or pardoned.

venison /ˈvɛnəsən, ˈvɛnzən/ *n.* the flesh of a deer or similar animal.

venom /ˈvɛnəm/ *n.* the poisonous fluid which some animals, as certain snakes, spiders, etc., secrete, and introduce into the bodies of their victims by biting, stinging, etc. – **venomous**, *adj.*

vent[1] /vɛnt/ *n.* an opening or aperture serving as an outlet for air, smoke, fumes, etc.

vent[2] /vɛnt/ *v.t.* to give free course or expression to (an emotion, passion, etc.).

ventilate /ˈvɛntəleɪt/ *v.t.,* **-lated**, **-lating**. **1.** to provide (a room, mine, etc.) with fresh air. **2.** to submit (a question, etc.) to free examination and discussion.

ventral /ˈvɛntrəl/ *adj.* of or relating to the belly; abdominal.

ventricle /ˈvɛntrɪkəl/ *n. Anatomy* **1.** any of various hollow organs or parts in an animal body. **2.** one of the two main cavities of the heart.

ventriloquism /vɛnˈtrɪləkwɪzəm/ *n.* the art or practice of speaking in such a manner that the voice appears to come from some other source, as a dummy. Also, **ventriloquy**. – **ventriloquist**, *n.*

venture /ˈvɛntʃə/ *n., v.,* **-tured**, **-turing**. – *n.* **1.** any undertaking or proceeding involving uncertainty as to the outcome. **2.** a business enterprise or proceeding in which loss is risked in the hope of profit. – *v.i.* **3.** to make a venture. **4.** to take a risk; dare or presume (often fol. by *on* or *upon* or an infinitive).

venturous /ˈvɛntʃərəs/ *adj.* **1.** disposed to venture; bold; daring; adventurous. **2.** hazardous; risky.

venue /ˈvɛnju/ *n.* the scene of any action or event, as a hall for a concert, meeting, etc.

veracious /vəˈreɪʃəs/ *adj.* truthful. – **veracity**, *n.*

veranda = verandah /vəˈrændə/ *n.* an open or partly open portion of a house or other building, outside its principal rooms, but roofed usually by the main structure.

verb /vɜb/ *n. Grammar* one of the major form classes, or parts of speech, comprising words which express the occurrence of an action, existence of a state, and the like.

verbal /ˈvɜbəl/ *adj.* **1.** of or relating to words. **2.** expressed in spoken words; oral rather than written. **3.** *Grammar* of, relating to, or derived from a verb.

verbalise = verbalize /ˈvɜbəlaɪz/ *v.t.,* **-lised**, **-lising**. to express in words.

verbatim /vɜˈbeɪtəm/ *adv.* word for word, or in exactly the same words.

verbiage /ˈvɜbiɪdʒ/ *n.* abundance of useless words, as in writing or speech; wordiness.

verbose /vɜ'boʊs/ *adj.* expressed in, characterised by the use of, or using many or too many words; wordy.

verdant /'vɜdnt/ *adj.* green with vegetation; covered with growing plants or grass.

verdict /'vɜdɪkt/ *n.* **1.** *Law* the finding or answer of a jury given to the court concerning a matter submitted to their judgment. **2.** a judgment or decision.

verdure /'vɜdʒuə/ *n.* greenness, especially of fresh, flourishing vegetation.

verge /vɜdʒ/ *n.*, *v.*, **verged**, **verging**. – *n.* **1.** the edge, rim, or margin of something. **2.** the limit or point beyond which something begins or occurs. – *v.i.* **3.** to be on the verge or border, or touch at the border. **4.** to come close to, approach, or border on some state or condition (usually fol. by *on* or *upon*).

verger /'vɜdʒə/ *n.* an official who takes care of the interior of a church and acts as attendant.

verify /'vɛrəfaɪ/ *v.t.*, **-fied**, **-fying**. **1.** to prove (something) to be true, as by evidence or testimony; confirm or substantiate. **2.** to ascertain the truth or correctness of, especially by examination or comparison. – **verification**, *n.*

verisimilitude /ˌvɛrisə'mɪlətʃud/ *n.* appearance or semblance of truth. – **verisimilar**, *adj.*

veritable /'vɛrətəbəl/ *adj.* being truly such; genuine or real.

verity /'vɛrəti/ *n.*, *pl.* **-ties**. quality of being true, or in accordance with fact or reality.

vermiform /'vɜməfɔm/ *adj.* like a worm in form; long and slender.

vermiform appendix *n.* *Anatomy* ' **appendix** (def. 2).

vermilion /və'mɪljən/ *n.* brilliant scarlet red.

vermin /'vɜmən/ *n.* (*pl. or sing.*) noxious, troublesome, or objectionable animals collectively.

vermouth /'vɜməθ, və'muθ/ *n.* a white wine in which herbs, roots, barks, bitters, and other flavourings have been steeped.

vernacular /və'nækjələ/ *adj.* **1.** native or originating in the place of its occurrence or use, as language or words (often as opposed to *literary* or *learned* language). – *n.* **2.** the native speech or language of a place.

vernal /'vɜnəl/ *adj.* of or relating to spring.

vernix /'vɜnɪks/ *n.* a greasy substance protecting the skin of a foetus.

versatile /'vɜsətaɪl/ *adj.* capable of or adapted for turning with ease from one to another of various tasks, subjects, etc.; many-sided in abilities. – **versatility**, *n.*

verse /vɜs/ *n.* **1.** (not in technical use) a stanza or other subdivision of a metrical composition. **2.** one of the lines of a poem. **3.** a short division of a chapter in the Bible.

versed /vɜst/ *adj.* experienced; practised; skilled (fol. by *in*).

version /'vɜʒən/ *n.* **1.** a particular account of some matter, as from one person or source, as contrasted with some other account or accounts. **2.** a translation.

versus /'vɜsəs/ *prep.* against (used especially in law to indicate an action brought by one party against another, and in sport to denote a contest between two teams or players). *Abbrev.*: v., vs.

vertebra /'vɜtəbrə/ *n.*, *pl.* **-bras**, **-brae** /-bri/. *Anatomy* any of the bones or segments composing the spinal column.

vertebrate /'vɜtəbreɪt, -brət/ *n.* **1.** a vertebrate animal. – *adj.* **2.** having vertebrae; having a backbone or spinal column.

vertex /'vɜtɛks/ *n.*, *pl.* **-tices** /-təsiz/, **-texes**. the highest point of something; the apex; the top; the summit.

vertical /'vɜtɪkəl/ *adj.* **1.** being in a position or direction perpendicular to the plane of the horizon; upright. **2.** of or relating to the consolidation of businesses or industries that are closely related in the manufacture or sale of a certain commodity. – *n.* **3.** a vertical line, plane, or the like.

vertigo /'vɜtəgoʊ/ *n.*, *pl.* **vertigos**, **vertigines** /vɜ'tɪdʒəniz/. a disordered condition in which an individual, or whatever is around him or her, seems to be whirling about; dizziness.

verve /vɜv/ *n.* enthusiasm or energy, as in literary or artistic work.

very /'vɛri/ *adv.*, *adj.*, **-rier**, **-riest**. – *adv.* **1.** in a high degree, extremely, or exceedingly. – *adj.* **2.** precise or identical. **3.** mere. **4.** actual. **5.** true, genuine, or real.

vesicle /'vɛsɪkəl/ *n.* a little sac or cyst.

vessel /'vɛsəl/ *n.* **1.** a craft for travelling on water. **2.** a hollow or concave article, as a cup, bowl, pot, pitcher, vase, bottle, etc., for holding liquid or other contents. **3.** *Anatomy*, *Zoology* a tube or duct, as an artery, vein, or the like, containing or conveying blood or some other body fluid.

vest /vɛst/ *n.* **1.** a short, warm undergarment with sleeves, usually worn next to the skin under a shirt; a singlet. **2.** a waistcoat. – *v.t.* **3.** to clothe, dress, or robe. **4.** to place or settle (something, especially property, rights, powers, etc.) in the possession or control of a person or persons (usually fol. by *in*). **5.** to invest or endow (a person, etc.) with something, especially with powers, functions, etc.

vestal /'vɛstl/ *adj.* virginal; chaste.

vestibule /'vɛstəbjul/ *n.* a passage, hall, or room between the outer door and the interior parts of a house or building.

vestige /'vɛstɪdʒ/ *n.* a mark, trace, or visible evidence of something which is no longer present or in existence. – **vestigial**, *adj.*

vestment /'vɛstmənt/ *n.* an official or ceremonial robe.

vestry /'vɛstri/ *n.*, *pl.* **-tries**. a room in or a building attached to a church.

vet /vɛt/ *n.*, *v.*, **vetted**, **vetting**. *Colloquial* – *n.* **1.** a veterinary surgeon. – *v.t.* **2.** to examine (a person). **3.** to examine (a product, proposal, or the like) with a view to acceptance, rejection, or correction.

vetch /vɛtʃ/ *n.* any of various leguminous plants cultivated for forage and soil improvement.

veteran /'vɛtərən, 'vɛtrən/ *n.* **1.** someone who has seen long service in any occupation or office. – *adj.* **2.** experienced through long service or practice; having served for a long period; grown old in service.

veterinary science /ˈvɛtənri, ˈvɛtərənri/ *n.* that branch of medicine that concerns itself with the study, prevention, and treatment of animal diseases. Also, **veterinary medicine**.

veterinary surgeon /ˈvɛtənri, ˈvɛtərənri/ *n.* someone who practises veterinary science or surgery.

veto /ˈvitoʊ/ *n., pl.* **-tos**, **-toes**, *v.,* **-toed**, **-toing**. – *n.* **1.** the power or right of preventing action by a prohibition. – *v.t.* **2.** to prevent (a proposal, legislative bill, etc.) being put into action by exercising the right of veto. **3.** to refuse to consent to.

vex /vɛks/ *v.t.* to irritate; annoy; provoke; make angry. – **vexatious**, *adj.*

VHS /vi eɪtʃ ˈɛs/ *adj.* having to do with a unique format for coding and playing a videotape for a video cassette recorder.

via /ˈvaɪə/ *prep.* **1.** by way of; by a route that passes through. **2.** by means of.

viable /ˈvaɪəbəl/ *adj.* **1.** capable of living. **2.** practicable; workable.

viaduct /ˈvaɪədʌkt/ *n.* a bridge for carrying a road, railway, etc., over a valley, ravine, or the like.

vial /ˈvaɪəl/ *n.* → **phial**.

vibes /vaɪbz/ *pl. n. Colloquial* the quality, mood or atmosphere of a place or person.

vibrant /ˈvaɪbrənt/ *adj.* **1.** moving to and fro rapidly; vibrating. **2.** full of vigour; energetic; powerful; forceful.

vibrate /vaɪˈbreɪt/ *v.i.,* **-brated**, **-brating**. **1.** to move to and fro, as a pendulum; oscillate. **2.** to move to and fro or up and down quickly and repeatedly; quiver; tremble. – **vibratory**, *adj.* – **vibration**, *n.* – **vibrator**, *n.*

vibrato /vəˈbratoʊ/ *n., pl.* **-tos**. *Music* a pulsating effect produced in the singing voice or in an instrumental tone by rapid small oscillations in pitch about the given note.

vicar /ˈvɪkə/ *n.* a member of the clergy acting as priest of a parish.

vicarious /vəˈkɛəriəs, vaɪ-/ *adj.* performed, exercised, received, or suffered in place of another.

vice[1] /vaɪs/ *n.* **1.** an immoral or evil habit or practice; a grave moral fault. **2.** immoral conduct or life; indulgence in impure or degrading practices.

vice[2] /vaɪs/ *n.* any of various devices used to hold an object firmly while work is being done upon it.

vice- a prefix denoting a substitute, deputy, or subordinate.

viceroy /ˈvaɪsrɔi/ *n.* one appointed to rule a country or province as the deputy of the sovereign.

vice versa /vaɪsə ˈvɜsə, vaɪs, vaɪsi/ *adv.* conversely; the order being changed (from that of a preceding statement).

vicinity /vəˈsɪnəti/ *n., pl.* **-ties**. the region near or about a place.

vicious /ˈvɪʃəs/ *adj.* **1.** addicted to or characterised by vice or immorality; depraved; profligate. **2.** spiteful or malignant. **3.** unpleasantly severe.

vicissitude /vəˈsɪsətjud/ *n.* **1.** a change or variation, or something different, occurring in the course of something. **2.** (*pl.*) changes, variations, successive or alternating phases or conditions, etc., in the course of anything.

victim /ˈvɪktəm/ *n.* a sufferer from any destructive, injurious, or adverse action or agency.

victimise = victimize /ˈvɪktəmaɪz/ *v.t.,* **-mised**, **-mising**. **1.** to make a victim of. **2.** to discipline or punish selectively, especially as a result of an industrial dispute.

victory /ˈvɪktəri, -tri/ *n., pl.* **-ries**. **1.** the ultimate and decisive superiority in a battle or any contest. **2.** any success or successful performance achieved over an adversary or opponent, opposition, difficulties, etc. – **victor**, *n.* – **victorious**, *adj.*

video /ˈvɪdioʊ/ *adj. TV* relating to or employed in the transmission or reception of a televised image, or to images displayed on television screens as in the video terminal of a computer.

video camera *n.* a camera designed for filming on videotape. Also, **video-camera**.

video cassette *n.* a cassette enclosing a length of videotape for video recording or playback. Also, **videocassette**.

video cassette recorder *n.* a videotape recorder which allows for playback through or recording from a television set, the videotape being held in a video cassette. Also, **VCR**.

video clip *n.* a short video recording, as one showing a performance of a popular song, a spectacular news event, etc.

videophone /ˈvɪdioʊfoʊn/ *n.* a telephone which allows visual, as well as verbal, communication.

videotape /ˈvɪdioʊteɪp/ *n.* magnetic tape upon which a video signal is recorded, used for storing a television program or film.

video terminal *n.* a computer terminal in which information is displayed on a television screen.

vie /vaɪ/ *v.i.,* **vied**, **vying**. to strive in competition or rivalry with another; to contend for superiority.

view /vju/ *n.* **1.** a seeing or beholding; an examination by the eye. **2.** range of sight or vision. **3.** a sight or prospect of some landscape, scene, etc. **4.** aim, intention, or purpose. **5.** a conception, notion, or idea of a thing; an opinion or theory. – *v.t.* **6.** to see or behold. **7.** to look at, survey, or inspect. **8.** to contemplate mentally; consider.

viewpoint /ˈvjupɔɪnt/ *n.* a point of view; an attitude of mind.

vigil /ˈvɪdʒəl/ *n.* a keeping awake for any purpose during the normal hours of sleep.

vigilant /ˈvɪdʒələnt/ *adj.* keenly attentive to detect danger; wary. – **vigilance**, *n.*

vigilante /vɪdʒəˈlænti/ *n. Chiefly US* a member of an unauthorised body organised for the maintenance of order.

vigour = vigor /ˈvɪgə/ *n.* **1.** active strength or force, as of body or mind. **2.** healthy physical or mental energy or power. **3.** active or effective force. – **vigorous**, *adj.*

vile /vaɪl/ *adj.,* **viler**, **vilest**. **1.** wretchedly bad. **2.** repulsive or disgusting, as to the senses or feelings; despicably or revoltingly bad. **3.** of mean or low condition, as a person.

vilify /'vɪləfaɪ/ *v.t.*, **-fied**, **-fying**. to speak evil of; defame; traduce.

villa /'vɪlə/ *n.* a country residence, usually of some size and pretensions.

village /'vɪlɪdʒ/ *n.* a small assemblage of houses in a country district.

villain /'vɪlən/ *n.* a wicked person; scoundrel. – **villainous**, *adj.* – **villainy**, *n.*

vim /vɪm/ *n. Colloquial* force; energy; vigour in action.

vindicate /'vɪndəkeɪt/ *v.t.*, **-cated**, **-cating**. **1.** to clear, as from a charge, imputation, suspicion, or the like. **2.** to uphold or justify by argument or evidence. – **vindicatory**, *adj.*

vindictive /vɪn'dɪktɪv/ *adj.* disposed or inclined to revenge; revengeful.

vine /vaɪn/ *n.* **1.** a long, slender stem that trails or creeps on the ground or climbs by winding itself about a support or holding fast with tendrils or claspers. **2.** a plant bearing such stems.

vinegar /'vɪnɪgə, -nə-/ *n.* a sour, acidic liquid used as a condiment, preservative, etc.

vineyard /'vɪnjəd/ *n.* a plantation of grapevines, for producing grapes for winemaking, etc.

vintage /'vɪntɪdʒ/ *n.* **1.** the wine from a particular harvest or crop. **2.** an exceptionally fine wine from the crop of a good year, designated and sold as the produce of that year. **3.** the season of gathering grapes, or of winemaking. – *adj.* **4.** of or relating to wine or winemaking. **5.** (of wines) designated and sold as the produce of a specified year. **6.** of high quality; exceptionally fine. **7.** old-fashioned; out of date.

vintner /'vɪntnə/ *n.* a dealer in wine; a wine merchant.

vinyl /'vaɪnəl/ *n. Chemistry* a type of plastic.

viol /'vaɪəl/ *n.* a musical instrument similar to the violin.

viola /vi'oulə/ *n.* a four-stringed musical instrument slightly larger than the violin.

violate /'vaɪəleɪt/ *v.t.*, **-lated**, **-lating**. **1.** to break, infringe, or transgress (a law, rule, agreement, promise, instructions, etc.). **2.** to deal with or treat in a violent or irreverent way; desecrate or profane.

violent /'vaɪələnt/ *adj.* **1.** acting with or characterised by uncontrolled, strong, rough force. **2.** intense in force, effect, etc.; severe; extreme. – **violence**, *n.*

violet /'vaɪələt/ *n.* **1.** a small plant with purple, blue, yellow, white, or variegated flowers. **2.** a bluish purple colour.

violin /vaɪə'lɪn/ *n.* a bowed instrument held nearly horizontal by the player's arm, with the lower part supported against the collarbone or shoulder; a fiddle.

violoncello /vaɪələn'tʃɛlou/ *n.*, *pl.* **-los**, **-li** /-li/. → **cello**.

viper /'vaɪpə/ *n.* a venomous snake.

virago /və'ragou/ *n.*, *pl.* **-goes**, **-gos**. a turbulent, violent, or ill-tempered, scolding woman; a shrew.

viral /'vaɪrəl/ *adj.* relating to or caused by a virus.

virement /'vaɪəmənt/ *n. Accounting* the authority to transfer funds between different accounts of an organisation, etc.

virgin /'vɜdʒən/ *n.* **1.** a person, especially a young woman, who has had no sexual intercourse. – *adj.* **2.** being a virgin. **3.** pure; unsullied; undefiled. **4.** untouched, untried, or unused.

virginal[1] /'vɜdʒənəl/ *adj.* of, relating to, characteristic of, or befitting a virgin.

virginal[2] /'vɜdʒənəl/ *n.* a small harpsichord of rectangular shape.

virile /'vɪraɪl/ *adj.* **1.** of, relating to, or characteristic of a man, as opposed to a woman or a child; masculine or manly; natural to or befitting a man. **2.** having or exhibiting in a marked degree masculine strength, vigour, or forcefulness. – **virility**, *n.*

virology /vaɪ'rɒlədʒi/ *n.* the study of viruses and the diseases caused by them.

virtual /'vɜtʃuəl/ *adj.* being such in power, force, or effect, although not actually or expressly such.

virtual reality *n.* the artificial world created by an interactive computer technology which gives the user the illusion that he or she has entered and is acting in this constructed reality.

virtue /'vɜtʃu/ *n.* **1.** moral excellence or goodness. **2.** a particular moral excellence, as justice, prudence, etc. **3.** an excellence, merit, or good quality. **4. by** (or **in**) **virtue of,** by reason of.

virtuoso /vɜtʃu'ousou, -'ouzou/ *n.*, *pl.* **-sos**, **-si** /-si, -zi/ someone who has special knowledge or skill in any field, as in music. – **virtuosity**, *n.*

virtuous /'vɜtʃuəs/ *adj.* morally excellent or good; conforming or conformed to moral laws.

virulent /'vɪrələnt/ *adj.* **1.** actively poisonous, malignant, or deadly. **2.** *Medicine* highly infective; malignant or deadly.

virus /'vaɪrəs/ *n.* **1.** an infective agent smaller than a common micro-organism, and requiring living cells for multiplication. **2.** any disease caused by a virus. **3.** a rogue program introduced into a computer network.

visa /'vizə/ *n.* an endorsement made on a passport, permitting passage to the country making the endorsement.

visage /'vɪzɪdʒ/ *n.* the face.

viscera /'vɪsərə/ *pl. n.*, *sing.* **viscus**. the soft interior organs in the cavities of the body, especially such of these as are confined to the abdomen.

viscid /'vɪsəd/ *adj.* sticky, adhesive, or glutinous; of a glutinous consistency; viscous.

viscount /'vaɪkaunt/ *n.* a nobleman next below an earl or count and next above a baron. – **viscountess**, *fem. n.*

viscous /'vɪskəs/ *adj.* sticky, adhesive, or glutinous; of a glutinous character or consistency; thick. – **viscosity**, *n.*

visibility /vɪzə'bɪləti/ *n.*, *pl.* **-ties**. **1.** the state or fact of being visible; capability of being seen. **2.** *Meteorology* visual range.

visible /'vɪzəbəl/ *adj.* capable of being seen; perceptible by the eye.

vision /'vɪʒən/ *n.* **1.** the act of seeing with the eye; the power, faculty, or sense of sight. **2.** the act or power of perceiving what is not actually present to the eye, whether by some supernatural endowment or by natural intellectual acuteness. **3.** a mental view or image, whether of supernatural origin or merely imaginative, of what is not actually present in place or time. **4.** something seen; an object of sight. – *v.t.* **5.** to show, or to see, in or as in a vision.

visionary /ˈvɪʒənri/ *adj., n., pl.* **-ries**. – *adj.* **1.** given to or characterised by radical, often unpractical ideas, views, or schemes. **2.** given to or concerned with seeing visions. – *n.* **3.** someone who sees visions. **4.** someone who is given to novel ideas or schemes which are not immediately practicable; an unpractical theorist or enthusiast.

visit /ˈvɪzət/ *v.t.* **1.** to go to see (a person, place, etc.) in the way of friendship, ceremony, duty, business, curiosity, or the like. **2.** (in general) to come or go to. **3.** to come upon or assail. – *n.* **4.** an act of visiting. – **visitor**, *n.*

visitation /vɪzəˈteɪʃən/ *n.* **1.** the act of visiting; a visit. **2.** a visiting or a visit for the purpose of making an official inspection or examination. **3.** an affliction or punishment from God.

visor /ˈvaɪzə/ *n.* **1.** the movable front parts of a helmet, covering the face, especially the uppermost part which protects the eyes. **2.** a small shield attached to the inside roof of a car, which may be swung down to protect the driver's eyes from glare or sunlight.

vista /ˈvɪstə/ *n.* a view or prospect.

visual /ˈvɪʒjuəl/ *adj.* **1.** of or relating to sight. **2.** perceptible by the sight; visible.

visual display unit *n.* a computer terminal which displays information on a screen. Also, **visual display terminal**.

visualise = visualize /ˈvɪzjuəlaɪz/ *v.t.,* **-lised**, **-lising**. to form a mental image of.

vital /ˈvaɪtl/ *adj.* **1.** of or relating to life. **2.** having remarkable energy, enthusiasm, vivacity. **3.** necessary to life. **4.** necessary to the existence, continuance, or wellbeing of something; indispensable; essential. **5.** of critical importance.

vitality /vaɪˈtæləti/ *n., pl.* **-ties**. exuberant physical vigour; energy; enthusiastic vivacity.

vitamin /ˈvaɪtəmən, ˈvɪt-/ *n.* any of a group of food factors essential in small quantities to maintain life, but not themselves employing energy. The absence of any one of them results in a characteristic deficiency disease.

vitiate /ˈvɪʃieɪt/ *v.t.,* **-ated**, **-ating**. **1.** to impair the quality of; make faulty; mar. **2.** to contaminate; corrupt; spoil. **3.** to make legally defective or invalid; invalidate.

viticulture /ˈvɪtikʌltʃə/ *n.* the culture or cultivation of the grapevine; grape-growing.

vitreous /ˈvɪtriəs/ *adj.* of the nature of glass; resembling glass, as in transparency, brittleness, hardness, etc.; glassy.

vitri- a word element meaning 'glass'.

vitrify /ˈvɪtrəfaɪ/ *v.t., v.i.,* **-fied**, **-fying**. **1.** to convert or be converted into glass. **2.** to make or become vitreous.

vitriol /ˈvɪtriɒl/ *n.* **1.** sulfuric acid. **2.** something highly caustic, or severe in its effects, as criticism. – **vitriolic**, *adj.*

vituperate /vəˈtjupəreɪt, vaɪ-/ *v.t.,* **-rated**, **-rating**. **1.** to find fault with abusively. **2.** to address abusive language to.

vivacious /vəˈveɪʃəs/ *adj.* lively, animated, or sprightly. – **vivacity**, *n.*

vivid /ˈvɪvəd/ *adj.* **1.** strikingly bright, as colour, light, objects, etc. **2.** lively or intense, as feelings, etc. **3.** clearly perceptible to the eye or mind.

vivify /ˈvɪvəfaɪ/ *v.t.,* **-fied**, **-fying**. to enliven; render lively or animated; brighten.

viviparous /vəˈvɪpərəs/ *adj. Zoology* bringing forth living young (rather than eggs), as most mammals and some reptiles and fishes.

vivisect /ˈvɪvəsɛkt, vɪvəˈsɛkt/ *v.t.* to dissect the living body of. – **vivisection**, *n.*

vixen /ˈvɪksən/ *n.* a female fox.

viyella /vaɪˈɛlə/ *n.* (*also cap.*) a soft fabric made of cotton and wool.

vocabulary /vəˈkæbjələri/ *n., pl.* **-ries**. **1.** the stock of words used by a people, or by a particular class or person. **2.** a list or collection of the words of a language, book, author, branch of science, or the like, usually in alphabetical order and defined; a wordbook, glossary, dictionary, or lexicon.

vocal /ˈvoʊkəl/ *adj.* **1.** of or relating to the voice; uttered with the voice; oral. **2.** rendered by or intended for singing, as music.

vocal cords *pl. n. Anatomy* folds of mucous membrane projecting into the cavity of the larynx, the edges of which can be drawn tense and made to vibrate by the passage of air from the lungs, thus producing vocal sound.

vocalic /voʊˈkælɪk/ *adj.* of or relating to a vowel or vowels; vowel-like.

vocalise = vocalize /ˈvoʊkəlaɪz/ *v.t.,* **-lised**, **-lising**. to make vocal; form into voice; utter or articulate; sing.

vocalist /ˈvoʊkələst/ *n.* a singer.

vocation /voʊˈkeɪʃən/ *n.* a particular occupation, business, or profession; a trade or calling. – **vocational**, *adj.*

vocative /ˈvɒkətɪv/ *adj. Grammar* relating to, or used in, addressing or calling (someone).

vociferous /vəˈsɪfərəs/ *adj.* crying out noisily; clamorous.

vodka /ˈvɒdkə/ *n.* an alcoholic drink of Russian origin.

vogue /voʊg/ *n.* the fashion, as at a particular time.

voice /vɔɪs/ *n., v.,* **voiced**, **voicing**. – *n.* **1.** the sound or sounds uttered through the mouth of living creatures, especially of human beings in speaking, shouting, singing, etc. **2.** such sounds considered with reference to their character or quality. **3.** expressed opinion or choice. **4.** the right to express an opinion or choice; vote; suffrage. **5.** *Phonetics* the sound produced by vibration of the vocal cords. **6.** *Grammar* **a.** (in some languages, as Latin) a group of categories of verb inflection denoting the relationship between the action expressed by the verb and the subject of the sentence (e.g., as acting or as acted upon). **b.** any one of such categories or constructions in a particular language, as the *active* and *passive* voices in Latin. – *v.t.* **7.** to give voice, utterance, or expression to (an emotion, opinion, etc.); express;

declare; proclaim.

voice mail *n.* **1.** Also, **voice mail system**. a system for recording messages over the telephone for later playback. **2.** a message received on such a system.

voice messaging *n.* a system which records a spoken message for replay later, now often integrated in computer transfer of spoken information as well as data.

void /vɔɪd/ *adj.* **1.** *Law* without legal force or effect; not legally binding or enforceable. **2.** useless; ineffectual; vain. **3.** completely empty; devoid; destitute (fol. by *of*). – *n.* **4.** an empty space. **5.** a place without the usual or desired occupant. **6.** emptiness; vacancy. – *v.t.* **7.** to make void or of no effect; invalidate; nullify. **8.** to empty or discharge (contents); evacuate (excrement, etc.).

voile /vɔɪl/ *n.* a semitransparent dress fabric.

volatile /'vɒlətaɪl/ *adj.* **1.** evaporating rapidly; passing off readily in the form of vapour. **2.** light and changeable of mind; frivolous; flighty. **3.** relating to information in the memory bank of a computer which is lost when power is disconnected.

volcano /vɒl'keɪnoʊ/ *n., pl.* **-noes**, **-nos**. an opening in the earth's crust through which molten rock (lava), steam, ashes, etc., are expelled from within, either continuously or at irregular intervals. – **volcanic**, *adj.*

vole /voʊl/ *n.* a type of rodent.

volition /və'lɪʃən/ *n.* the act of willing; exercise of choice to determine action.

volley /'vɒli/ *n., pl.* **-leys**, *v.*, **-leyed**, **-leying**. – *n.* **1.** the discharge of a number of missiles or firearms simultaneously. **2.** a burst or outpouring of many things at once or in quick succession. **3.** *Tennis, etc.* **a.** a return of the ball before it touches the ground. **b.** a succession of such returns. – *v.t.* **4.** to discharge in or as in a volley. **5.** *Tennis, Soccer, etc.* to return, kick, etc., (the ball) before it strikes the ground. – *v.i.* **6.** to fly or be discharged together, as missiles. **7.** to move or proceed with great rapidity, as in a volley.

volleyball /'vɒlibɔl/ *n.* a game in which a large ball is struck from side to side over a high net with the hands or arms.

volt /voʊlt/ *n.* the derived SI unit of electric potential. *Symbol*: V

voltage /'voʊltɪdʒ/ *n.* electromotive force or potential expressed in volts.

voluble /'vɒljəbəl/ *adj.* characterised by a ready and continuous flow of words.

volume /'vɒljum/ *n.* **1.** a collection of written or printed sheets bound together and constituting a book. **2.** the size, measure, or amount of anything in three dimensions; the space occupied by a body or substance in cubic units; the SI unit of volume is the cubic metre (m^3). **3.** a mass or quantity, especially a large quantity, of anything. **4.** loudness or softness.

volumetric /vɒljə'metrɪk/ *adj.* denoting, relating to, or depending upon measurement by volume. Also, **volumetrical**.

voluminous /və'lumənəs/ *adj.* of ample size, extent, or fullness, as garments, draperies, etc.

voluntary /'vɒləntri, -ləntəri/ *adj., n., pl.* **-taries**. – *adj.* **1.** done, made, brought about, undertaken, etc., of one's own accord or by free choice. **2.** *Physiology* subject to or controlled by the will. – *n.* **3.** a piece of music performed as a prelude to a larger work.

volunteer /vɒlən'tɪə/ *n.* **1.** someone who enters into any service of their own free will, or who offers himself or herself for any service or undertaking. – *v.i.* **2.** to offer oneself for some service or undertaking.

voluptuary /və'lʌptʃuəri/ *n., pl.* **-aries**. one given up to luxurious or sensuous pleasures.

voluptuous /və'lʌptʃuəs/ *adj.* **1.** full of, characterised by, or ministering to pleasure or luxurious or sensual enjoyment. **2.** directed towards luxurious or sensual enjoyment. **3.** sensually pleasing or delightful. **4.** (of the female figure) curvaceous.

volute /və'ljut/ *n.* a spiral or twisted formation or object.

vomit /'vɒmət/ *v.i.* **1.** to eject the contents of the stomach by the mouth; spew; be sick. **2.** to be ejected or come out with force or violence. – *v.t.* **3.** to throw up or eject from the stomach through the mouth; spew. **4.** to cast out or eject as if in vomiting; to send out with force or copiously.

voodoo /'vudu/ *n.* a class of mysterious rites or practices, of the nature of sorcery or witchcraft.

voracious /və'reɪʃəs/ *adj.* devouring or craving food in large quantities.

-vorous a word element meaning 'eating'

vortex /'vɔteks/ *n., pl.* **-texes**, **-tices** /-təsiz/. a whirling movement or mass of water, as a whirlpool.

votary /'voʊtəri/ *n., pl.* **-ries**. someone who is bound by a vow, especially one bound by vows to a religious life.

vote /voʊt/ *n., v.*, **voted**, **voting**. – *n.* **1.** a formal expression of will, wish, or choice in some matter, signified by voice, by ballot, etc. **2.** the right to such expression; suffrage. **3.** an expression of feeling, as approval, or the like. – *v.i.* **4.** to express or signify choice in a matter undergoing decision, as by a voice, ballot, or otherwise. – *v.t.* **5.** to enact, establish, or determine by vote; bring or put (*in*, *out*, *down*, etc.) by vote; grant by vote.

votive /'voʊtɪv/ *adj.* offered, given, dedicated, etc., in accordance with a vow.

vouch /vaʊtʃ/ *v.i.* **1.** to answer (*for*) as being true, certain, reliable, justly asserted, etc. **2.** to give one's own assurance, as surety or sponsor (fol. by *for*).

voucher /'vaʊtʃə/ *n.* **1.** a document, receipt, stamp, or the like, which proves the truth of a claimed expenditure. **2.** a ticket used as a substitute for cash, as a gift voucher, luncheon voucher, etc.

vouchsafe /vaʊtʃ'seɪf/ *v.t.*, **-safed**, **-safing**. to grant or give, by favour, graciousness, or condescension.

vow /vaʊ/ *n.* **1.** a solemn promise, pledge, or personal engagement. **2.** a solemn, religiously binding promise made to God or to any deity or saint, as to perform some act, make some offering or gift, or enter some service or condition. – *v.t.* **3.** to make a vow of; promise by a vow, as to God or a saint. **4.** to pledge oneself to do, make, give, observe, etc.; make a solemn threat or resolution of.

vowel /ˈvauəl/ *n. Phonetics* a voiced speech sound during the articulation of which air from the lungs is free to pass out through the middle of the mouth without causing undue friction.

voyage /ˈvɔɪɪdʒ/ *n., v.,* **-aged**, **-aging**. *– n.* **1.** a passage, or course of travel, by sea or water, especially to a distant place. *– v.i.* **2.** to make or take a voyage; travel by sea or water.

voyeur /vɔɪˈɜ, vwaˈjɜ/ *n.* someone who attains sexual gratification by looking at sexual objects or situations. – **voyeurism**, *n.* – **voyeuristic**, *adj.*

vulcanology /vʌlkəˈnɒlədʒi/ *n.* the scientific study of volcanoes and volcanic phenomena.

vulgar /ˈvʌlgə/ *adj.* **1.** marked by ignorance of or want of good breeding or taste, as manners, actions, language, dress, display, etc. **2.** crude; coarse; unrefined. **3.** ostentatious; unsubtle. **4.** belonging to or constituting the common people of society. **5.** common or ordinary. – **vulgarity**, *n.*

vulnerable /ˈvʌlnrəbəl, -nərəbəl/ *adj.* **1.** susceptible to being wounded; liable to physical hurt. **2.** not protected against emotional hurt; highly sensitive. – **vulnerability**, *n.*

vulpine /ˈvʌlpaɪn/ *adj.* relating to, like, or characteristic of a fox.

vulture /ˈvʌltʃə/ *n.* a large, carrion-eating bird related to the eagle.

vulva /ˈvʊlvə/ *n., pl.* **-vae** /-vi/, **-vas**. the external female genitalia.

vying /ˈvaɪɪŋ/ *adj.* that vies; competing.

W w

W, w /ˈdʌbəlju/ *n., pl.* **W's** *or* **Ws, w's** *or* **ws**. the 23rd letter of the English alphabet.

wad /wɒd/ *n.* **1.** a small mass or lump of anything soft. **2.** a roll or bundle, especially of banknotes.

wadding /ˈwɒdɪŋ/ *n.* any fibrous or soft material for stuffing, padding, packing, etc.

waddle /ˈwɒdl/ *v.i.,* **-dled**, **-dling**. to walk with short steps and swaying or rocking from side to side, as a duck.

waddy /ˈwɒdi/ *n., pl.* **-dies**. an Aboriginal heavy wooden war club.

wade /weɪd/ *v.i.,* **waded**, **wading**. to walk through any substance, as water, snow, sand, etc., that impedes free motion.

wafer /ˈweɪfə/ *n.* **1.** a thin, crisp cake or biscuit. **2.** any of various other thin, flat cakes, sheets, or the like.

waffle[1] /ˈwɒfəl/ *n.* a kind of batter cake.

waffle[2] /ˈwɒfəl/ *v.i.,* **-fled**, **-fling**. *Colloquial* to speak or write vaguely, pointlessly, and at considerable length.

waft /wɒft/ *v.t.* **1.** to bear or carry through the air or over water. **2.** to bear or convey lightly as if in flight. – *v.i.* **3.** to float or be carried, especially through the air.

wag[1] /wæg/ *v.,* **wagged**, **wagging**, *n.* – *v.t.* **1.** to move from side to side, forwards and backwards, or up and down, especially rapidly and repeatedly. **2.** *Colloquial* to be absent from (school, etc.) without permission. – *v.i.* **3.** to be moved from side to side or one way and the other, especially rapidly and repeatedly, as the head or the tail. – *n.* **4.** the act of wagging.

wag[2] /wæg/ *n.* a humorous person; joker.

wage /weɪdʒ/ *n., v.,* **waged**, **waging**. – *n.* **1.** (*often pl.*) that which is paid for work or services, as by the day or week; hire; pay. **2.** (*pl.*) *Economics* the share of the products of industry received by labour for its work, as distinct from the share going to capital. – *v.t.* **3.** to carry on (a battle, war, conflict, etc.).

wager /ˈweɪdʒə/ *n.* **1.** something staked or hazarded on an uncertain event; a bet. – *v.t.* **2.** to hazard (something) on the issue of a contest or any uncertain event or matter; stake; bet.

waggle /ˈwægəl/ *v.,* **-gled**, **-gling**, *n.* – *v.t., v.i.* **1.** to wag with short, quick movements. – *n.* **2.** a waggling motion.

wagon /ˈwægən/ *n.* any of various kinds of four-wheeled vehicles, especially one designed for the transport of heavy loads, delivery, etc.

wagtail /ˈwægteɪl/ *n.* a small bird with a long, narrow tail.

waif /weɪf/ *n.* a person without home or friends, especially a child.

wail /weɪl/ *v.i.* **1.** to utter a prolonged, inarticulate, mournful cry. – *n.* **2.** the act of wailing. **3.** a wailing cry, as of grief, pain, etc.

wainscot /ˈweɪnskət, -koʊt/ *n.* wooden panels serving to line the walls of a room, etc. – **wainscoting**, *n.*

waist /weɪst/ *n.* the part of the human body between the ribs and the hips.

waistcoat /ˈweɪstkoʊt/ *n.* a close-fitting, sleeveless garment which reaches to the waist.

wait /weɪt/ *v.i.* **1.** to stay or rest in expectation; remain in a state of quiescence or inaction, as until something expected happens (often fol. by *for*, *till*, or *until*). **2. wait on** (or **upon**), **a.** to perform the duties of an attendant or servant for. **b.** to supply the wants of (a person) at table. – *v.t.* **3.** to continue stationary or inactive in expectation of; await. – *n.* **4.** the act of waiting or awaiting; delay; halt. **5.** a period or interval of waiting.

waiter /ˈweɪtə/ *n.* someone who waits at table, as in a restaurant, hotel, etc.

waitress /ˈweɪtrəs/ *n.* a woman who waits at table, as in a restaurant, hotel, etc.

waive /weɪv/ *v.t.,* **waived**, **waiving**. to forbear to insist on; relinquish; forgo.

waiver /ˈweɪvə/ *n.* an intentional relinquishment of some right, interest, or the like.

wake[1] /weɪk/ *v.,* **woke**, **woken**, **waking**. – *v.i.* **1.** to become roused from sleep; awake (often fol. by *up*). – *v.t.* **2.** to rouse from sleep; awake (often fol. by *up*). – *n.* **3.** a watching, or a watch kept, especially for some solemn or ceremonial purpose. **4.** a watch, especially at night, near the body of a dead person before burial, often accompanied by drinking and feasting.

wake[2] /weɪk/ *n.* the track left by a ship or other object moving in the water.

walk /wɔk/ *v.i.* **1.** to go or travel on foot at a moderate pace; to proceed by steps, or by advancing the feet in turn. – *v.t.* **2.** to proceed through, over, or upon by walking. **3.** to cause to walk; lead, drive, or ride at a walk, as an animal. – *n.* **4.** the act or course of walking, or going on foot. **5.** a spell of walking for exercise or pleasure. **6.** the gait or pace of a person or animal that walks. **7.** a department or branch of activity, or a particular line of work.

walkabout /ˈwɔkəbaʊt/ *n.* a period of wandering as a nomad, especially as undertaken by Aborigines.

walkie-talkie /wɔki-ˈtɔki/ *n.* a combined radio transmitter and receiver, light enough to be carried by one person, widely used by police, medical services, etc.

walkman /ˈwɔkmən/ *n.* a small portable transistor radio, cassette player, etc., with earphones. Also, **Walkman**.

walkout /ˈwɔkaʊt/ *n.* **1.** a strike by workers. **2.** the act of leaving or boycotting a conference, meeting, etc., especially as an act of protest.

walkover /ˈwɔkoʊvə/ *n.* *Colloquial* an unopposed or easy victory.

wall /wɔl/ *n.* **1.** an upright work or structure of stone, brick, or similar material, serving for enclosure, division, support, protection, etc. **2.** anything which resembles or suggests a wall. – *v.t.* **3.** to enclose, shut off, divide, protect, etc., with or as with a wall (often fol. by *in* or *off*).

wallaby /ˈwɒləbi/ *n., pl.* **-bies**, (*esp. collectively*) **-by**. any of various animals, many resembling small kangaroos.

wallaroo /wɒləˈru/ *n.* a stocky, coarse-haired

kangaroo.

wallet /ˈwɒlət/ *n.* a small, booklike folding case for carrying papers, paper money, etc., in the pocket.

walleyed /ˈwɔlaɪd/ *adj.* having an eye or the eyes with little or no colour.

wallop /ˈwɒləp/ *v.t. Colloquial* to beat soundly; thrash.

wallow /ˈwɒloʊ/ *v.i.* to roll the body about, or lie, in water, snow, mud, dust, or the like, as for refreshment.

wallpaper /ˈwɔlpeɪpə/ *n.* paper, commonly with printed decorative patterns in colour, for pasting on and covering the walls or ceilings of rooms, etc.

walnut /ˈwɔlnʌt/ *n.* **1.** an edible nut. **2.** a tree bearing this nut and also yielding valuable timber.

walrus /ˈwɔlrəs, ˈwɒlrəs/ *n., pl.* **-ruses**, (*esp. collectively*) **-rus**. either of two large marine mammals of arctic seas, related to the seals, and having flippers, a pair of large tusks, and a thick, tough skin.

waltz /wɔls, wɒls/ *n.* **1.** a ballroom dance in which the dancers move in a series of circles. – *v.i.* **2.** to dance a waltz.

wan /wɒn/ *adj.,* **wanner**, **wannest**. of an unnatural or sickly pallor; pallid.

wand /wɒnd/ *n.* a slender stick or rod, especially one used by a conjurer, or supposedly by a magician or fairy to work magic.

wander /ˈwɒndə/ *v.i.* **1.** to ramble without any certain course or object in view; roam. **2.** to stray from a path, companions, etc.

wane /weɪn/ *v.,* **waned**, **waning**, *n.* – *v.i.* **1.** (of the moon) to decrease periodically in the extent of its illuminated portion after the full moon (opposed to *wax*). **2.** to decline in power, importance, prosperity, etc. – *n.* **3.** gradual decline in strength, intensity, power, etc.

wangle /ˈwæŋgəl/ *v.t.,* **-gled**, **-gling**. *Colloquial* to bring about, accomplish, or obtain by contrivance, scheming, or often, indirect or insidious methods.

wank /wæŋk/ *v.i. Colloquial* to masturbate.

wannabe /ˈwɒnəbi/ *n. Colloquial* someone who aspires to be something or someone specified: *a Madonna wannabe.*

want /wɒnt/ *v.t.* **1.** to feel a need or a desire for; wish for. **2.** to be without or be deficient in. – *v.i.* **3.** to wish; like; feel inclined to (often fol. by *to*). **4.** to be deficient by the absence of some part or thing, or fall short (sometimes fol. by *for*). **5.** to be in a state of destitution or poverty. **6.** to be lacking or absent, as a part or thing necessary to completeness. – *n.* **7.** something wanted or needed; a necessity.

wanton /ˈwɒntən/ *adj.* **1.** done, shown, used, etc., maliciously or unjustifiably. **2.** reckless or disregardful of right, justice, humanity, etc., as persons. **3.** lawless or unbridled with respect to sexual behaviour; loose, lascivious, or lewd.

war /wɔ/ *n., v.,* **warred**, **warring**. – *n.* **1.** a conflict carried on by force of arms, as between nations or states, or between parties within a state. **2.** active hostility or contention; conflict; contest. – *v.i.* **3.** to make or carry on war; fight.

waratah /wɒrəˈta, ˈwɒrəta/ *n.* a shrub or small tree with a dense globular head of red flowers.

warble /ˈwɔbəl/ *v.i.,* **-bled**, **-bling**. to sing with trills, quavers, or melodic embellishments.

ward /wɔd/ *n.* **1.** a division or district of a municipality, city or town, as for administrative or representative purposes. **2.** a division of a hospital or the like, as for a particular class of patients. **3.** each of the separate divisions of a prison. **4.** *Law* a person, especially a minor, who has been legally placed under the care or control of a legal guardian. – *v.t.* **5.** to avert, repel, or turn aside, as danger, an attack, assailant, etc. (usually fol. by *off*).

-ward an adjectival and adverbial suffix indicating direction, as in *onward, seaward, backward.*

warden /ˈwɔdn/ *n.* **1.** one charged with the care or custody of something; a keeper. **2.** the head of certain colleges, schools, hospitals, youth hostels, etc.

warder[1] /ˈwɔdə/ *n.* → **prison officer**.

warder[2] /ˈwɔdə/ *n.* a truncheon or staff of office or authority, used in giving signals.

wardrobe /ˈwɔdroʊb/ *n.* **1.** a stock of clothes or costumes, as of a person or of a theatrical company. **2.** a piece of furniture for holding clothes, now usually a tall, upright, cupboard fitted with hooks, shelves, etc.

-wards an adverbial suffix indicating direction, as in *onwards, seawards, backwards.*

ware /wɛə/ *n.* (*usu. pl.*) articles of merchandise or manufacture, or goods.

warehouse /ˈwɛəhaʊs/ *n.* a storehouse for wares or goods.

warfare /ˈwɔfɛə/ *n.* **1.** the act of waging war. **2.** armed conflict.

warlock /ˈwɔlɒk/ *n.* someone who practises magic arts by the aid of the devil; a sorcerer or wizard.

warm /wɔm/ *adj.* **1.** having or communicating a moderate degree of heat, as perceptible to the senses. **2.** keeping or maintaining warmth. **3.** (of colour, effects of colour, etc.) suggestive of warmth; inclining towards red or orange, as yellow (rather than towards green or blue). **4.** characterised by or showing lively feelings, passions, emotions, sympathies, etc. **5.** strongly attached, or intimate. – *v.t.* **6.** to make warm; heat (often fol. by *up*). **7.** to excite ardour, enthusiasm, or animation in. **8.** to inspire with kindly feeling; affect with lively pleasure. – *v.i.* **9.** to become warm (often fol. by *up*). **10. warm up,** to prepare for a sporting event, musical or theatrical performance, etc. – **warmth,** *n.*

warn /wɔn/ *v.t.* **1.** to give notice or intimation to (a person, etc.) of danger, impending evil, possible harm, or anything unfavourable. **2.** to admonish or exhort as to action or conduct. **3.** to give notice to (a person, etc.) to go, stay, or keep (away, off, etc.). **4.** to give authoritative or formal notice to, order, or summon. – **warning,** *n.*

warp /wɔp/ *v.t.* **1.** to bend or twist out of shape, especially from a straight or flat form. **2.** to distort from the truth, fact, true meaning, etc.; bias or pervert. – *v.i.* **3.** to become bent or twisted out of shape. **4.** to turn or change from the natural or proper course, state, etc. – *n.* **5.** a bend or twist in something, as in wood that has dried unevenly. **6.** a mental twist or bias. **7.** yarns placed lengthwise in the loom, across the weft or woof, and interlaced.

warrant /ˈwɒrənt/ *n.* **1.** authorisation, sanction, or justification. **2.** that which serves to give reliable or formal assurance of something; a guarantee. **3.** a writing or document certifying or authorising something, as a certificate, receipt, licence, or commission. – *v.t.* **4.** to give authority to; authorise. **5.** to afford warrant or sanction for, or justify. **6.** to give a formal assurance, or a guarantee or promise, to or for; guarantee.

warranty /ˈwɒrənti/ *n., pl.* **-ties**. **1.** the act of warranting; warrant; assurance. **2.** *Law* an engagement, express or implied, in assurance of some particular in connection with a contract, as of sale.

warren /ˈwɒrən/ *n.* a place where rabbits breed or abound.

warrigal /ˈwɒrəgəl/ *n.* **1.** a dingo. **2.** a wild horse. **3.** an Aborigine living in the traditional manner. – *adj.* **4.** wild; untamed. Also, **warragul**, **warregal**.

warrior /ˈwɒriə/ *n.* someone engaged or experienced in warfare; soldier.

wart /wɔt/ *n.* **1.** a small, usually hard, abnormal elevation on the skin, caused by a virus. **2.** a small protuberance.

wary /ˈwɛəri/ *adj.,* **warier**, **wariest**. watchful, or on one's guard, especially habitually; on the alert; cautious; careful.

was /wɒz/ *v.* first and third person singular past tense indicative of **be**.

wash /wɒʃ/ *v.t.* **1.** to apply water or some other liquid to for the purpose of cleansing; cleanse by dipping, rubbing, or scrubbing in water, etc. **2.** to flow over or against. – *v.i.* **3.** to wash oneself. **4.** *Colloquial* to stand being put to the proof; bear investigation. **5.** to be worn by the action of water, as a hill (often fol. by *away*). – *n.* **6.** the act of washing with water or other liquid. **7.** a quantity of clothes, etc., washed, or to be washed, at one time. **8.** a liquid with which something is washed, wetted, coloured, overspread, etc. **9.** the flow, sweep, dash, or breaking of water. **10.** a broad, thin layer of colour applied by a continuous movement of the brush, as in watercolour painting.

washer /ˈwɒʃə/ *n.* **1.** a flat ring used to give tightness to a joint, to prevent leakage, and to distribute pressure (as under the head of a bolt, under a nut, etc.). **2.** Also, **washrag**, **washcloth**. a small piece of towelling or similar material used for washing the face or body; facecloth; flannel.

wasn't /ˈwɒzənt/ *v.* contraction of *was not.*

wasp /wɒsp/ *n.* a stinging insect.

waspish /ˈwɒspɪʃ/ *adj.* quick to resent a trifling affront or injury.

wastage /ˈweɪstɪdʒ/ *n.* loss by use, wear, decay, wastefulness, etc.

waste /weɪst/ *v.,* **wasted**, **wasting**, *n., adj.* – *v.t.* **1.** to consume, spend, or employ uselessly or without adequate return; squander. **2.** to fail to use, or let go to waste. **3.** to wear down or reduce, especially in health or strength. **4.** to destroy or devastate. – *v.i.* **5.** to become physically wasted (often fol. by *away*). **6.** to diminish gradually, as wealth, power, etc. (often fol. by *away*). – *n.* **7.** useless consumption or expenditure, or use without adequate return. **8.** neglect, instead of use. **9.** gradual destruction or decay. **10.** a place in ruins. **11.** anything left over, as excess materials, etc. – *adj.* **12.** not used or in use. **13.** (of land, etc.) uninhabited and wild; desolate. **14.** left over or superfluous. **15.** *Physiology* relating to material unused by or unusable to the organism.

wastrel /ˈweɪstrəl/ *n.* a wasteful person; spendthrift.

watch /wɒtʃ/ *v.i.* **1.** to be on the lookout, look attentively, or be closely observant. **2.** to look or wait attentively and expectantly (usually fol. by *for*). – *v.t.* **3.** to keep under attentive view or observation, as in order to see or learn something; view attentively or with interest. **4.** to guard for protection or safekeeping. – *n.* **5.** close, constant observation for the purpose of seeking or discovering something. **6.** a lookout, as for something expected. **7.** vigilant guard, as for protection, restraint, etc. **8.** a small, portable timepiece.

watchful /ˈwɒtʃfəl/ *adj.* vigilant or alert; closely observant.

water /ˈwɔtə/ *n.* **1.** the liquid which in a more or less impure state constitutes rain, oceans, lakes, rivers, etc., and which in a pure state is a transparent, odourless, tasteless liquid, a compound of hydrogen and oxygen. **2.** (*pl.*) a body of water. **3.** any liquid or aqueous organic secretion. – *v.t.* **4.** to sprinkle, moisten, or drench with water. **5.** to supply (animals) with water for drinking. **6.** to dilute or adulterate with water (often fol. by *down*). **7.** to weaken (fol. by *down*). **8.** *Finance* to issue (shares of stock) without receiving a corresponding amount of cash or property. **9.** to produce a wavy lustrous pattern, marking, or finish on (fabrics, metals, etc.). – *v.i.* **10.** to discharge, fill with, or secrete water or liquid, as the eyes, or as the mouth at the sight or thought of tempting food. – **watery**, *adj.*

waterbed /ˈwɔtəbɛd/ *n.* a heavy durable plastic bag filled with water, used as a mattress often in a supporting wooden frame.

water buffalo /ˈwɔtə bʌfəloʊ/ *n.* a large buffalo widely used as a draught animal. Also, **water ox**.

water chestnut *n.* an aquatic plant bearing an edible, nutlike fruit.

water closet /ˈwɔtə klɒzət/ *n.* a receptacle in which human excrement is flushed down a drain by water from a cistern. Also, **WC**.

watercolour = watercolor /ˈwɔtəkʌlə/ *n.* **1.** a pigment dispersed in water-soluble gum. **2.** the art or method of painting with such pigments. **3.** a painting or design executed by this method.

watercourse /ˈwɔtəkɔs/ *n.* **1.** a stream of water, as a river or brook. **2.** the bed of such a stream.

watercress /ˈwɔtəkrɛs/ *n.* a plant, usually growing in clear, running water, and bearing pungent leaves used in salads, etc.

waterfall /ˈwɔtəfɔl/ *n.* a steep fall or flow of

water from a height; a cascade.

waterfront /'wɔtəfrʌnt/ *n.* **1.** land abutting on a body of water. **2.** (*collectively*) workers in industries using wharf facilities.

waterlily /'wɔtəlɪli/ *n.* an aquatic plant having floating leaves and showy, often fragrant, flowers.

waterlog /'wɔtəlɒg/ *v.t.*, **-logged**, **-logging**. to soak or saturate with water.

watermark /'wɔtəmak/ *n.* **1.** a mark indicating the height to which water rises or has risen, as in a river, etc. **2.** a figure or design impressed in the fabric in the manufacture of paper and visible when the paper is held to the light.

watermelon /'wɔtəmɛlən/ *n.* a large melon with pink, juicy flesh.

water polo /'wɔtə-poʊloʊ/ *n.* a water game played by two teams, each having seven swimmers, in which the object is to carry or pass the ball over the opponent's goal line.

watershed /'wɔtəʃɛd/ *n.* the ridge or crest line dividing two drainage areas; divide.

waterside worker /'wɔtəsaɪd ˌwɜkə/ *n.* wharf labourer. Also, **watersider**.

waterski /'wɔtəski/ *n.*, *v.*, **-ski'd** *or* **-skied**, **-skiing**. – *n.* **1.** a type of ski used for gliding over water. – *v.i.* **2.** to glide over water on waterskis by grasping a rope towed by a speedboat.

watertable /'wɔtəteɪbəl/ *n.* in an aquifer, the upper limit of the portion of ground saturated with water.

watertight /'wɔtətaɪt/ *adj.* **1.** impervious to water. **2.** without fault; irrefutable; flawless.

waterway /'wɔtəweɪ/ *n.* a river, canal, or other body of water as a route or way of travel or transport.

watt /wɒt/ *n.* the derived SI unit of power, defined as one joule per second. *Symbol*: W

wattle /wɒtl/ *n.* **1.** (*pl. or sing.*) rods or stakes interwoven with twigs or branches of trees, used for making fences, walls, roofs, etc. **2.** any of the very numerous Australian acacias, with spikes or globular heads of yellow or cream flowers, the branches of which were used as wattles. **3.** a fleshy lobe or appendage hanging down from the throat or chin.

wattle and daub *n.* wattles (interwoven rods) plastered with mud or clay and used as a building material.

wave /weɪv/ *n.*, *v.*, **waved**, **waving**. – *n.* **1.** a disturbance of the surface of a liquid body, as the sea or a lake, in the form of a ridge or swell. **2.** a swell, surge, or rush, as of feeling, excitement, prosperity, etc. **3.** a widespread movement, feeling, opinion, tendency, etc. **4.** *Physics* a progressive vibrational disturbance propagated through a medium, as air, without corresponding progress or advance of the parts or particles themselves, as in the transmission of sound or electromagnetic energy. – *v.i.* **5.** to move loosely to and fro or up and down; flutter. **6.** to curve alternately in opposite directions; have an undulating form. – *v.t.* **7.** to cause to move loosely to and fro or up and down. – **wavy**, *adj.*

wavelength /'weɪvlɛŋθ/ *n. Physics* the length of each cycle of a wave (def. 4).

waver /'weɪvə/ *v.i.* **1.** to sway to and fro; flutter. **2.** to feel or show doubt or indecision, or vacillate.

wax[1] /wæks/ *n.* **1.** any of a group of solid, non-greasy, insoluble substances which have a low melting or softening point, especially mixtures of the higher hydrocarbons, as paraffin wax. **2.** a substance secreted by certain insects and plants. **3.** something suggesting wax as being readily moulded, worked upon, handled, managed, etc. – *v.t.* **4.** to rub, smear, stiffen, polish, etc., with wax; treat with wax.

wax[2] /wæks/ *v.i.*, **waxed**, **waxed** *or Poetic* **waxen**, **waxing**. **1.** to increase in extent, quantity, intensity, power, etc. **2.** (of the moon) to increase in the extent of its illuminated portion before the full moon (opposed to *wane*). **3.** to grow or become (as stated).

waxwork /'wækswɜk/ *n.* figures, ornaments, etc., made of wax, or one such figure.

way /weɪ/ *n.* **1.** manner, mode, or fashion. **2.** a course, plan, or means for attaining an end. **3.** respect or particular. **4.** direction. **5.** passage or progress on a course. **6.** a path or course leading from one place to another. **7.** (*often pl.*) a habit or custom. **8.** range of experience or notice. **9.** course of life, action, or experience. **10. by the way,** incidentally; in the course of one's remarks. **11. give way to, a.** to yield to. **b.** to lose control of (one's emotions, etc.). **12. in the way,** forming an obstruction or hindrance. **13. make one's way,** to proceed. **14. make way for, a.** to allow to pass. **b.** to give up or retire in favour of. **15. under way,** in motion or moving along.

wayfarer /'weɪfɛərə/ *n.* a traveller.

waylay /weɪ'leɪ/ *v.t.*, **-laid**, **-laying**. to fall upon or assail from ambush, as in order to rob, seize, or slay.

-ways a suffix of manner creating adverbs, as in *sideways*, *lengthways*. See **-wise**.

wayside /'weɪsaɪd/ *n.* the side of the way; the border or edge of the road or highway.

wayward /'weɪwəd/ *adj.* turned or turning away from what is right or proper; perverse.

WC /dʌbəlju 'si/ *n. Colloquial* a toilet. Also, **wc**.

we /wi/ *pron., pl. possessive* **our** *or* **ours**, *objective* **us**. nominative plural of 'I'.

weak /wik/ *adj.* **1.** liable to yield, break, or collapse under pressure or strain; fragile; frail; not strong. **2.** deficient in bodily strength or healthy vigour, as from age, sickness, etc.; feeble; infirm. **3.** lacking in force, potency, or efficacy. **4.** deficient in amount, volume, loudness, intensity, etc.; faint; slight. **5.** *Commerce* characterised by falling prices.

weakling /'wiklɪŋ/ *n.* a weak or feeble creature (physically or morally).

weal /wil/ *n.* **1.** a small burning or itching swelling on the skin. **2.** a welt.

wealth /wɛlθ/ *n.* **1.** a great store of valuable possessions, property, or riches. **2.** a rich abundance or profusion of anything. **3.** *Economics* **a.** all things having a value in money, in exchange, or in use. **b.** anything having utility and capable of being appropriated or exchanged. – **wealthy**, *adj.*

wean /win/ *v.t.* to accustom (a child or animal) to food other than its mother's milk.

weapon /'wɛpən/ *n.* any instrument for use in attack or defence in combat, fighting, or war, as a sword, rifle, cannon, etc.

wear /wɛə/ *v.*, **wore**, **worn**, **wearing**, *n.* – *v.t.* **1.** to carry or have on the body or about the person as a covering, equipment, ornament, or the like. **2.** to bear or have in the aspect or appearance. **3.** to impair, deteriorate, or consume gradually by use or any continued process. **4.** to make (a hole, channel, way, etc.) by such action. **5. wear out, a.** to wear or use until no longer fit for use. **b.** to exhaust by continued use, strain, or any gradual process. – *v.i.* **6.** to undergo gradual impairment, diminution, reduction, etc., from wear, use, attrition, or other causes (often fol. by *away*, *down*, *out*, or *off*). **7.** to hold out or last under wear, use, or any continued strain. – *n.* **8.** gradual impairment, wasting, diminution, etc., as from use.

weariless /'wɪərilәs/ *adj.* unwearying.

wearisome /'wɪərisәm/ *adj.* tedious.

weary /'wɪəri/ *adj.*, **-rier**, **-riest**, *v.*, **-ried**, **-rying**. – *adj.* **1.** exhausted physically or mentally by labour, exertion, strain, etc.; fatigued; tired. **2.** impatient or dissatisfied at excess or overlong continuance (often fol. by *of*). – *v.t.*, *v.i.* **3.** to make or become weary; fatigue or tire. **4.** to make or grow impatient or dissatisfied at having too much of something (often fol. by *of*).

weasel /'wizəl/ *n.* a small carnivore having a long, slender body, and feeding largely on small rodents.

weather /'wɛðə/ *n.* **1.** the state of the atmosphere with respect to wind, temperature, cloudiness, moisture, pressure, etc. – *v.t.* **2.** to bear up against and come safely through (a storm, danger, trouble, etc.). – *v.i.* **3.** to undergo change, as discolouration or disintegration, as the result of exposure to atmospheric conditions.

weatherboard /'wɛðəbɔd/ *n.* one of a series of thin boards nailed on an outside wall or a roof to form a protective covering.

weathervane /'wɛðəveɪn/ *n.* a vane for indicating the direction of the wind.

weave /wiv/ *v.*, **wove** *or especially for defs 2 and 4* **weaved**, **wove** *or* **woven**, **weaving**, *n.* – *v.t.* **1.** to interlace (threads, yarns, strips, fibrous material, etc.) so as to form a fabric or texture. **2.** to follow in a winding course; to move from side to side. – *v.i.* **3.** to weave cloth, etc. **4.** to move from side to side. – *n.* **5.** a manner of interlacing yarns.

web /wɛb/ *n.*, *v.*, **webbed**, **webbing**. – *n.* **1.** something formed as by weaving or interweaving. **2.** a thin silken fabric spun by spiders, and also by the larvae of some insects. **3.** a tangled intricate state of circumstances, events, etc. **4.** *Zoology* a membrane which connects the digits of some animals and birds.

web site /'wɛb saɪt/ *n.* a location on the World Wide Web which can be accessed by others on the Internet. Also, **website**.

wed /wɛd/ *v.t.*, **wedded** *or* **wed**, **wedding**. **1.** to bind oneself to (a person) in marriage; take for husband or wife. **2.** to unite (a couple) or join (one person to another) in marriage or wedlock; marry.

we'd /wid/ contraction of *we had*, *we should* or *we would*.

wedding /'wɛdɪŋ/ *n.* the act or ceremony of marrying; marriage.

wedge /wɛdʒ/ *n.*, *v.*, **wedged**, **wedging**. – *n.* **1.** a device consisting of a piece of hard material with two principle faces meeting in a sharply acute angle. **2.** a piece of anything of like shape. **3.** something that serves to part, divide, etc. – *v.t.* **4.** to pack or fix tightly by driving in a wedge or wedges. **5.** to thrust, drive, or fix (in, between, etc.) like a wedge. – *v.i.* **6.** to force a way (in, etc.) like a wedge.

wedlock /'wɛdlɒk/ *n.* the state of marriage; matrimony.

wee /wi/ *adj.* little; very small.

weed /wid/ *n.* **1.** a plant growing wild, especially in cultivated ground to the exclusion or injury of the desired crop. **2.** a thin or weakly person, especially one regarded as stupid or infantile. – *v.t.* **3.** to free from weeds or troublesome plants. **4.** to rid of what is undesirable or superfluous.

week /wik/ *n.* **1.** a period of seven successive days, commonly understood as beginning (unless otherwise specified or implied) with Sunday, followed by Monday, Tuesday, Wednesday, Thursday, Friday, and Saturday. **2.** the working days or working portion of the seven-day period. **3.** seven days after a specified day: *Tuesday week*.

weekend /wik'ɛnd/ *n.* the end of the working week, especially the period from Friday night or Saturday to Monday, as a time for recreation.

weekly /'wikli/ *adj.*, *adv.*, *n.*, *pl.* **-lies**. – *adj.* **1.** relating to a week, or to each week. **2.** done, happening, appearing, etc., once a week, or every week. – *adv.* **3.** once a week. **4.** by the week. – *n.* **5.** a periodical appearing once a week.

weep /wip/ *v.*, **wept**, **weeping**. – *v.i.* **1.** to shed tears, as from sorrow, unhappiness, or any overpowering emotion; cry. **2.** to exude water or liquid, as soil, rock, a plant stem, a sore, etc. – *v.t.* **3.** to shed (tears, etc.).

weevil /'wivəl/ *n.* a type of beetle destructive to nuts, grain, fruit, etc.

weft /wɛft/ *n.* **1.** *Textiles* woof or filling yarns which interlace with warp running from selvage to selvage. **2.** a woven piece.

weigh /weɪ/ *v.t.* **1.** to ascertain the weight of by means of a balance, scale, or other mechanical device. **2.** to bear (down) by weight, heaviness, oppression, etc. **3.** to balance in the mind; consider carefully in order to reach an opinion, decision, or choice (sometimes fol. by *up*). **4.** to raise or lift (now chiefly in the phrase *to weigh anchor*). – *v.i.* **5.** to have weight or heaviness.

weight /weɪt/ *n.* **1.** amount of heaviness; amount a thing weighs. **2.** a body of determinate mass, as of metal, for using on a balance or scale in weighing objects, substances, etc. **3.** any heavy mass or object, especially an object used because of its heaviness. **4.** importance, moment, consequence, or effective influence. – *v.t.* **5.** to add weight to; load with additional weight.

weighting /ˈweɪtɪŋ/ *n.* **1.** an additional quantity or value attributed to any particular factor or factors in a complex situation. **2.** an increased amount, as of salary or the like, to balance the higher cost of living in a particular area.

weight-lifting /ˈweɪt-lɪftɪŋ/ *n.* the sport of lifting barbells of specified weights, in competition or for exercise.

weighty /ˈweɪti/ *adj.*, **-tier**, **-tiest**. having considerable weight; heavy.

weir /wɪə/ *n.* a dam in a river or stream to stop and raise the water.

weird /wɪəd/ *adj.* **1.** involving or suggesting the supernatural; unearthly or uncanny. **2.** *Colloquial* startlingly or extraordinarily singular, odd, or queer.

welcome /ˈwɛlkəm/ *n.*, *v.*, **-comed**, **-coming**, *adj.* – *n.* **1.** a kindly greeting or reception. – *v.t.* **2.** to greet the coming of (a person, etc.) with pleasure or kindly courtesy. – *adj.* **3.** gladly received.

weld /wɛld/ *v.t.* to unite or fuse (pieces of metal, etc.), especially with the use of heat.

welfare /ˈwɛlfɛə/ *n.* the state of faring well; wellbeing.

well[1] /wɛl/ *adv.*, *adj.*, *comparative* **better**, *superlative* **best**. – *adv.* **1.** in a satisfactory, favourable, or advantageous manner; fortunately or happily. **2.** in a good or proper manner. **3.** thoroughly or soundly. **4.** easily; clearly. **5.** to a considerable extent or degree. **6. as well,** in addition. **7. as well as,** in addition to; no less than. **8. very well, a.** with certainty; undeniably. **b.** (a phrase used to indicate consent, often with reluctance). **c.** (*ironic*) satisfactory; pleasing. – *adj.* **9.** in good health, or sound in body and mind. **10.** satisfactory or good.

well[2] /wɛl/ *n.* **1.** a hole drilled into the earth, generally by boring, for the production of water, petroleum, natural gas, brine, or sulfur. **2.** a spring or natural source of water. – *v.i.* **3.** to rise, spring, or gush, as water, from the earth or some source (often fol. by *up*, *out*, or *forth*).

we'll /wil/ contraction of *we will* or *we shall.*

wellbeing /ˈwɛlbiɪŋ/ *n.* good or satisfactory condition of existence; welfare.

well-heeled /ˈwɛl-hild/ *adj.* *Colloquial* wealthy; prosperous.

wellington boot /ˈwɛlɪŋtən but/ *n.* a waterproof knee-high boot; a gumboot.

well-mannered /ˈwɛl-mænəd/ *adj.* polite; courteous.

well-meaning /ˈwɛl-minɪŋ/ *adj.* meaning or intending well.

well-off /ˈwɛl-ɒf/ *adj.* in good or easy circumstances as to money or means; moderately rich.

well-read /ˈwɛl-rɛd/ *adj.* **1.** having read much. **2.** having an extensive and intelligent knowledge of books or literature.

well-spoken /ˈwɛl-spoʊkən/ *adj.* **1.** having a cultured, refined accent. **2.** speaking well, fittingly, or pleasingly.

well-to-do /wɛl-tə-ˈdu/ *adj.* having a sufficiency of means for comfortable living; well-off or prosperous.

welsh /wɛlʃ/ *v.t.*, *v.i.* *Colloquial* to cheat by evading payment, especially of a gambling debt (sometimes fol. by *on*).

welt /wɛlt/ *n.* **1.** a ridge on the surface of the body, as from the stroke of a stick or whip. **2.** a strengthening or ornamental finish along a seam, the edge of a garment, etc.

welter /ˈwɛltə/ *n.* **1.** a rolling or tumbling about. **2.** commotion, turmoil, or chaos.

wen /wɛn/ *n.* a benign tumour of the skin, especially on the scalp.

wench /wɛntʃ/ *n.* **1.** a girl, or young woman. **2.** a rustic or working girl.

wend /wɛnd/ *v.t.* to direct or pursue (one's way, etc.).

went /wɛnt/ *v.* past tense of **go**.

wept /wɛpt/ *v.* past tense and past participle of **weep**.

were /wɜ/ *v.* past tense indicative plural and subjunctive singular and plural of **be**.

we're /wɪə, wɜ, wɛə/ contraction of *we are.*

weren't /wɜnt/ contraction of *were not.*

werewolf /ˈwɪəwʊlf, ˈwɜ-, ˈwɛə-/ *n.*, *pl.* **-wolves** /-wʊlvz/. (in old superstition) a human being turned into a wolf.

west /wɛst/ *n.* **1.** a cardinal point of the compass (90° to the left of north) corresponding to the point where the sun is seen to set. – *adj.* **2.** lying or proceeding towards the west. **3.** coming from the west. – *adv.* **4.** in the direction of the sunset; towards or in the west. **5.** from the west (as of wind). – **westerly**, *adj.*, *n.*

western /ˈwɛstən/ *adj.* **1.** lying towards or situated in the west. **2.** directed or proceeding towards the west. **3.** coming from the west, as a wind. – *n.* **4.** (*usu. cap.*) a story or film about frontier life in the American west.

wet /wɛt/ *adj.*, **wetter**, **wettest**, *n.*, *v.*, **wet** *or* **wetted**, **wetting**. – *adj.* **1.** covered or soaked, wholly or in part, with water or some other liquid. **2.** moist, damp, or not dry. **3.** rainy; having a rainy climate. – *n.* **4.** that which makes wet, as water or other liquid; moisture. **5.** rain. – *v.t.* **6.** to make wet.

wet blanket *n.* a person or thing that has a discouraging or depressing effect.

wet cell *n.* an electric cell whose electrolyte is in liquid form and free to flow.

wether /ˈwɛðə/ *n.* a ram castrated when young.

wetlands /ˈwɛtlændz, ˈwɛtləndz/ *pl. n.* an area in which the soil is frequently or permanently saturated with or under water, as a swamp, marsh, etc.

wet nurse *n.* a woman hired to suckle another's infant.

wetsuit /ˈwɛtsut/ *n.* a tight-fitting rubber suit worn by divers, surfers, etc.

we've /wiv/, *unstressed* /wəv/ contraction of *we have.*

whack /wæk/ *v.t.* *Colloquial* to strike with a smart, resounding blow or blows.

whale[1] /weɪl/ *n.* *Zoology* any of numerous large cetaceans with fishlike bodies, modified foreflippers, and a horizontally flattened tail.

whale[2] /weɪl/ *v.i.*, **whaled**, **whaling**. *Colloquial* **1.** to throw oneself into something energetically (fol. by *into*). **2. a.** to beat up, bash. **b.** to attack verbally, berate (fol. by *into*).

whalebone /ˈweɪlboʊn/ *n.* an elastic horny substance growing in place of teeth in the upper jaw of certain whales used in strips, especially for stiffening corsets, etc.

wham /wæm/ *v.i., v.t.,* **whammed, whamming**. to hit forcefully, especially with a single loud noise.

wharf /wɔf/ *n., pl.* **wharves, wharfs**. a structure built on the shore of, or projecting out into, a harbour, stream, etc., so that vessels may be moored alongside to load or unload or to lie at rest; a quay.

what /wɒt/ *interrogative pron.* **1.** (asking for the specifying of some impersonal thing): *what is your name?* **2.** (enquiring as to the nature, character, class, origin, etc., of a thing or person): *what is that animal?* **3.** (enquiring as to the worth, usefulness, force, or importance of something): *what is wealth without health?* **4.** (asking, often elliptically, for repetition or explanation of some word or words used, as by a previous speaker): *you need five what?* **5.** how much?: *what did it cost?* **6.** (often used interjectionally to express surprise, disbelief, indignation, etc.). **7. what for?,** for what reason or purpose. – *relative pron.* **8.** (as a compound relative) that which: *that is what he says.* **9.** the kind of thing or person that, or such: *the old man is not what he was.* **10.** anything that, or whatever: *take what you like.* **11.** (in parenthetic clauses) something that: *he came, and what is more, he stayed.* **12.** (used adjectively) that or any ... which; such ... as: *take what time you need.*

whatever /wɒtˈɛvə/ *pron., indefinite relative pron.* **1. a.** anything that: *do whatever you like.* **b.** any amount or measure (of something) that. **c.** no matter what: *whatever happens, don't go.* – *adj.* **2.** any ... that: *whatever time I have.*

what's /wɒts/ contraction of *what is.*

wheat /wit/ *n.* the grain of a widely distributed cereal grass, used extensively in the form of flour.

wheedle /ˈwidl/ *v.t.,* **-dled, -dling**. to endeavour to influence (a person) by smooth, flattering, or beguiling words.

wheel /wil/ *n.* **1.** a circular frame or solid disc arranged to turn on an axis, as in vehicles, machinery, etc. **2.** any instrument, machine, apparatus, etc., shaped like this, or having such a frame or disc as an essential feature. **3.** anything resembling or suggesting a wheel. **4.** (*pl.*) moving, propelling, or animating agencies. **5.** (*pl.*) *Colloquial* a motor vehicle. **6.** a wheeling or circular movement. **7.** *Colloquial* a person of considerable importance or influence. – *v.t.* **8.** to cause to turn, rotate, or revolve, as on an axis. **9.** to move, roll, or convey on wheels, castors, etc. – *v.i.* **10.** to turn on or as on an axis or about a centre; rotate, revolve. **11.** to move in a circular or curving course. **12.** to turn or change in procedure or opinion (often fol. by *about* or *round*). **13.** to roll along on, or as on, wheels; to travel along smoothly.

wheelbarrow /ˈwilbæroʊ/ *n.* a barrow supported at one end by a wheel on which it is pushed along.

wheelchair /ˈwiltʃɛə/ *n.* a chair mounted on large wheels, and used by invalids and those unable to walk.

wheeze /wiz/ *v.i.,* **wheezed, wheezing**. to breathe with difficulty and with a whistling sound.

whelk /wɛlk/ *n.* any of various large spiral-shelled marine gastropods.

whelp /wɛlp/ *n.* the young of the dog, or of the wolf, bear, lion, tiger, seal, etc.

when /wɛn/ *adv.* **1.** at what time: *when are you coming?* – *conj.* **2.** at what time: *to know when to be silent.* **3.** at the time that: *when we were young, life was fun.* **4.** while on the contrary, or whereas: *you rush ahead, when you should think first.* – *pron.* **5.** what time: *since when?* **6.** which time: *they left on Monday, since when we have heard nothing.*

whenever /wɛnˈɛvə/ *conj.* at whatever time; at any time when: *come whenever you like.*

where /wɛə/ *adv.* **1.** in or at what place?: *where is he?* **2.** in what position or circumstances?: *where are you, without money?* **3.** to what place, point, or end?: *where are you going?* **4.** from what source, or whence: *where did you get that notion?* – *conj.* **5.** in or at what place, part, point, etc.: *find where he is.* **6.** in or at the place, part, point, etc., in or at which: *it's where you left it.* **7.** in or at which place; and there: *they came to the town, where they stayed overnight.* – *pron.* **8.** what place: *from where?*

where- a word element meaning 'what' or 'which'.

whereabouts /ˈwɛərəbaʊts/, *interrogatively* /wɛərəˈbaʊts/ – *adv.* **1.** about where? where? – *conj.* **2.** near or in what place. – *pl. n.* **3.** (*sometimes construed as sing.*) the place where a person or thing is; the locality of a person or thing.

whereas /wɛərˈæz/ *conj.* **1.** while on the contrary. **2.** it being the case that, or considering that (especially used in formal preambles).

whereby /wɛəˈbaɪ/ *adv., conj.* by what or by which.

whereupon /wɛərəˈpɒn/ *conj.* at or after which.

wherever /wɛərˈɛvə/ *conj.* in, at, or to whatever place.

wherewithal /ˈwɛəwɪðɔl, -θɔl/ *n.* means or supplies for the purpose or need, especially money.

whet /wɛt/ *v.t.,* **whetted, whetting**. **1.** to sharpen (a knife, tool, etc.) by grinding or friction. **2.** to make keen or eager.

whether /ˈwɛðə/ *conj.* a word introducing the first of two or more alternatives (used in correlation with *or*).

whetstone /ˈwɛtstoʊn/ *n.* a stone for sharpening cutlery, etc., by friction.

whey /weɪ/ *n.* milk serum, separating as a watery liquid from the curd after coagulation, as in cheese-making.

which /wɪtʃ/ *interrogative pron.* **1.** what one (of a certain number mentioned or implied)?: *which do you want?* – *relative pron.* **2.** (a simple relative with an antecedent which is a thing or body of persons): *I read the book, which was short.* **3.** (in parenthetic clauses) a thing that: *and, which is worse, you've done it wrongly.* – *adj.* **4.** what one of (a certain number mentioned or implied): *which book do you want?*

whichever /wɪtʃ'ɛvə/ *pron.* **1.** any one (of those in question) that: *take whichever you like.* **2.** no matter which: *whichever you choose, someone will be offended.* – *adj.* **3.** no matter which: *whichever book you like.*

whiff /wɪf/ *n.* **1.** a slight blast or puff of wind or air. **2.** a puff or waft of scent or smell.

while /waɪl/ *n., conj., v.,* **whiled, whiling.** – *n.* **1.** a space of time. – *conj.* Also, **whilst. 2.** during or in the time that. **3.** throughout the time that, or as long as. **4.** at the same time that (implying opposition or contrast). – *v.t.* **5.** to cause (time) to pass, especially in some easy or pleasant manner (usually fol. by *away*).

whim /wɪm/ *n.* an odd or fanciful notion; a freakish or capricious fancy or desire.

whimper /'wɪmpə/ *v.i.* **1.** to cry with low, plaintive, broken sounds, as a child, a dog, etc. – *n.* **2.** a whimpering cry or sound.

whimsical /'wɪmzɪkəl/ *adj.* of an odd, quaint, or comical kind.

whimsy /'wɪmzi/ *n., pl.* **-sies.** an odd or fanciful notion.

whine /waɪn/ *v.,* **whined, whining,** *n.* – *v.i.* **1.** to utter a nasal, complaining cry or sound, as from uneasiness, discontent, peevishness, etc. – *n.* **2.** a whining utterance, sound, or tone.

whinge /wɪndʒ/ *v.i.,* **whinged, whingeing.** to complain; whine. – **whinger,** *n.*

whinny /'wɪni/ *v.i.,* **-nied, -nying.** (of a horse) to utter its characteristic cry; neigh.

whip /wɪp/ *v.,* **whipped** *or* **whipt, whipping,** *n.* – *v.t.* **1.** to strike with quick, repeated strokes of something slender and flexible; lash. **2.** to beat with a whip or the like, especially by way of punishment or chastisement; flog; thrash. **3.** to move quickly and suddenly; pull, jerk, snatch, seize, put, etc., with a sudden movement (fol. by *away, out, up, into,* etc.). **4.** to beat (eggs, cream, etc.) to a froth with a whisk, fork, or other implement in order to incorporate air and produce expansion. **5. whip up, a.** to create quickly. **b.** to arouse to fury, intense excitement, etc. – *v.i.* **6.** to move or go quickly and suddenly (*away, off, out, in,* etc.); dart; whisk. **7.** to beat or lash about, as a pennant in the wind. – *n.* **8.** an instrument to strike with, as in driving animals or in punishing, typically consisting of a lash or other flexible part with a more rigid handle. **9.** a party manager in a legislative body, who supplies information to members about the government business, secures their attendance for voting, supplies lists of members to serve on committees and keeps the leaders informed as to the trend of party opinion.

whiplash /'wɪplæʃ/ *n.* an injury to the spine, usually in the cervical area, caused by sudden movement forwards or backwards, as in a motor accident.

whippet /'wɪpət/ *n.* a dog similar to a small greyhound.

whirl /wɜl/ *v.i.* **1.** to turn round, spin, or rotate rapidly. **2.** to move, travel, or be carried rapidly along on wheels or otherwise. – *v.t.* **3.** to cause to turn round, spin, or rotate rapidly. – *n.* **4.** the act of whirling; rapid rotation or gyration. **5.** a short drive, run, walk, or the like, or a spin. **6.** a rapid round of events, affairs, etc. **7.** a state marked by a dizzying succession or mingling of feelings, thoughts, etc.

whirlpool /'wɜlpul/ *n.* a whirling eddy or current, as in a river or the sea.

whirlwind /'wɜlwɪnd/ *n.* a mass of air rotating rapidly round and towards a more or less vertical axis.

whirr /wɜ/ *v.i.,* **whirred, whirring.** to go, fly, dart, revolve, or otherwise move quickly with a vibratory or buzzing sound.

whisk[1] /wɪsk/ *v.t.* **1.** to sweep (dust, crumbs, etc.) or a surface with a brush, or the like. **2.** to move with a rapid, sweeping stroke.

whisk[2] /wɪsk/ *v.t.* **1.** to whip (eggs, cream, etc.) to a froth with a whisk or beating implement. – *n.* **2.** a small bunch of grass, straw, hair, or the like, especially for use in brushing. **3.** an implement, in one form a bunch of loops of wire held together in a handle, for beating or whipping eggs, cream, etc.

whisker /'wɪskə/ *n.* **1.** (*pl.*) the beard generally. **2.** a single hair of the beard.

whisky /'wɪski/ *n., pl.* **-kies.** a distilled spirit made from grain.

whisper /'wɪspə/ *v.i.* **1.** to speak with soft, low sounds, using the breath, lips, etc., without vibration of the vocal cords. **2.** (of trees, water, breezes, etc.) to make a soft, rustling sound. – *v.t.* **3.** to utter with soft, low sounds, using the breath, lips, etc. – *n.* **4.** the mode of utterance, or the voice, of someone who whispers. **5.** confidential information; rumour.

whist /wɪst/ *n.* a card game.

whistle /wɪsl/ *v.,* **-tled, -tling,** *n.* – *v.i.* **1.** to make a kind of clear musical sound, or a series of such sounds, by the forcible expulsion of the breath through a small orifice formed by contracting the lips, or through the teeth, together with the aid of the tongue. **2.** to make such a sound or series of sounds otherwise, as by blowing on a particular device. – *n.* **3.** an instrument for producing whistling sounds as by the breath, steam, etc., as a small wooden or tin tube or a small pipe. **4.** a sound produced by or as by whistling.

white /waɪt/ *adj.,* **whiter, whitest,** *n., v.,* **whited, whiting.** – *adj.* **1.** of the colour of pure snow, reflecting all or nearly all the rays of sunlight. **2.** having a light skin; marked by comparatively slight pigmentation of the skin. **3.** pallid or pale, as from fear or other strong emotion, or pain or illness. **4.** (of wines) light-coloured or yellowish (opposed to *red*). **5.** (of coffee) with milk or cream. – *n.* **6.** an achromatic visual sensation of relatively high luminosity. A white surface reflects light of all hues completely and diffusely. **7.** lightness of skin pigment. **8.** something white, or a white part of something. **9.** a pellucid viscous fluid which surrounds the yolk of an egg. **10.** the white part of the eyeball. – *v.t.* **11.** *Printing* to make white by leaving blank spaces (often fol. by *out*). **12.** to reduce the daylight visibility of, as a result of snow or fog (fol. by *out*).

white ant *n.* any of various species of wood-eating insects.

white-collar /'waɪt-kɒlə/ *adj.* belonging or relating to non-manual workers, as those in professional and clerical work.

white flag *n.* an all-white flag, used as a symbol of surrender, etc.

white gold *n.* any of several gold alloys possessing a white colour due to the presence of nickel or platinum.

whitegoods /ˈwaɪtgʊdz/ *pl. n.* electrical goods as fridges, washing machines, etc., which have a white enamel surface.

white heat *n.* an intense heat at which a substance glows with white light.

white lie *n.* a lie uttered from polite, amiable, or pardonable motives.

white light *n.* light which contains all the wavelengths of the visible spectrum at approximately the same intensity.

white meat *n.* any light-coloured meat, as veal, the breast of chicken, etc., (distinguished from *red meat*).

white noise *n.* an electronically produced noise in which all frequencies are represented with equal energy in each equal range of frequencies.

white paper *n.* an official report or policy proposal of a government on a specific subject.

whitewash /ˈwaɪtwɒʃ/ *n.* **1.** a composition used for whitening walls, woodwork, etc. **2.** anything used to cover up defects, gloss over faults or errors, or give a specious semblance of respectability, honesty, etc.

whither /ˈwɪðə/ *adv. Archaic* (*now replaced by where*) to what place?

whiting /waɪtɪŋ/ *n.* any of numerous species of estuarine and surf fishes, highly prized for sport and table.

whitlow /ˈwɪtloʊ/ *n.* an inflammation of the deeper tissues of a finger or toe.

whittle /ˈwɪtl/ *v.t.*, **-tled**, **-tling**. **1.** to cut, trim, or shape (a stick, piece of wood, etc.) by taking off bits with a knife. **2.** to cut by way of reducing amount (especially fol. by *down*). – **whittler**, *n.*

whiz[1] /wɪz/ *v.i.*, **whizzed**, **whizzing**. to make a humming or hissing sound, as an object passing rapidly through the air.

whiz[2] /wɪz/ *n. Colloquial* a person who shows outstanding ability in a particular field or who is notable in some way; expert.

who /hu/ *pron.*, *possessive* **whose**, *objective* **whom**. – *interrogative pron.* **1.** what person? **2.** (of a person) what as to character, origin, position, importance, etc. – *relative pron.* **3.** (as a compound relative): the or any person that; any person, be it who it may. **4.** (as a simple relative, with antecedent a person, or sometimes an animal or a personified thing expressed): **a.** in clauses conveying an additional idea: *we saw men who were at work.* **b.** used in clauses defining or restricting the antecedent.

who'd /hud/ contraction of *who would.*

whoever /huˈɛvə/ *pron.*, *possessive* **whosever**, *objective* **whomever**. – *indefinite relative pron.* **1.** whatever person, or anyone that. – *interrogative pron.* **2.** *Colloquial* who ever? who? (used emphatically).

whole /hoʊl/ *adj.* **1.** comprising the full quantity, amount, extent, number, etc., without diminution or exception; entire, full, or total. **2.** undivided, or in one piece. **3.** uninjured, undamaged, or unbroken; sound; intact. **4.** being fully or entirely such. – *n.* **5.** the whole assemblage of parts or elements belonging to a thing; the entire quantity, account, extent, or number. **6.** a thing complete in itself, or comprising all its parts or elements. – **wholly**, *adv.*

wholehearted /ˈhoʊlhatəd/ *adj.* hearty; cordial; earnest; sincere.

wholemeal /ˈhoʊlmil/ *adj.* prepared with the complete wheat kernel, as flour or the bread baked with it.

whole number *n. Mathematics* an integer as 0, 1, 2, 3, 4, 5, etc.

wholesale /ˈhoʊlseɪl/ *n., adj., adv., v.,* **-saled**, **-saling**. – *n.* **1.** the sale of commodities in large quantities, as to retailers or jobbers rather than to consumers directly (distinguished from *retail*). – *adj.* **2.** extensive and indiscriminate. – *adv.* **3.** in a wholesale way. – *v.t., v.i.* **4.** to sell by wholesale. – **wholesaler**, *n.*

wholesale banking *n.* the section of banking services which includes the provision or arrangement of corporate finance and operations in the money market.

wholesome /ˈhoʊlsəm/ *adj.* **1.** conducive to moral or general wellbeing; salutary; beneficial. **2.** conducive to bodily health; healthful; salubrious.

who'll /hul/ contraction of *who will* or *who shall.*

whom /hum/ *pron.* objective case of **who**.

whoop /wup, hup/ *n.* **1.** a loud cry or shout, as one uttered by children or warriors. – *v.i.* **2.** to utter a loud cry or shout (originally the syllable whoop, or hoop), as a call, or in enthusiasm, excitement, frenzy, etc.

whooping cough /ˈhupɪŋ kɒf/ *n.* an infectious disease of the respiratory mucous membrane, especially of children.

whoops /wʊps/ *interj.* (an exclamation of mild surprise, dismay, etc.). Also, **whoops-a-daisy**.

whoosh /wʊʃ/ *n.* a loud rushing noise, as of water or air.

whopper /ˈwɒpə/ *n. Colloquial* **1.** something uncommonly large of its kind. **2.** a big lie.

whore /hɔ/ *n.* a prostitute.

who're /ˈhuə/ contraction of *who are.*

whorl /wɜl/ *n.* **1.** a circular arrangement of like parts, as leaves, flowers, etc., round a point on an axis. **2.** anything shaped like a coil.

who's /huz/ contraction of *who is* or *who has.*

whose /huz/ *pron.* **1.** possessive case of the relative and interrogative pronoun **who**. **2.** possessive case of the relative pronoun **which** (historically, of **what**).

who've /huv/ contraction of *who have.*

why /waɪ/ *adv.* **1.** for what? for what cause, reason, or purpose? – *conj.* **2.** for what cause or reason.

wick /wɪk/ *n.* a bundle or loose twist or braid of soft threads, or a woven strip or tube, as of cotton, which in a candle, lamp, oilstove, or the like serves to draw up the melted tallow or wax or the oil or other flammable liquid to be burned at its top end.

wicked /ˈwɪkəd/ *adj.* evil or morally bad in principle or practice; iniquitous; sinful.

wickerwork /ˈwɪkəwɜk/ *n.* work consisting of plaited or woven twigs or osiers; articles made of wicker.

wicket /ˈwɪkət/ *n.* **1.** a small door or gate, especially one beside, or forming part of, a larger one. **2.** *Cricket* **a.** either of the two frameworks, each consisting of three stumps with two bails in grooves across their tops, at which the bowler aims the ball. **b.** the area between the wickets, especially with reference to the state of the ground. **c.** the achievement of a batsman's dismissal by the fielding side.

wide /waɪd/ *adj.*, **wider**, **widest**, *adv.* – *adj.* **1.** having considerable or great extent from side to side; broad; not narrow. **2.** having a certain or specified extent from side to side. **3.** of great range or scope; embracing a great number or variety of subjects, cases, etc. **4.** open to the full or a great extent; expanded; distended. – *adv.* **5.** to a great, or relatively great, extent from side to side. **6.** to the full extent of opening. **7.** away from or to one side of a point, mark, purpose, or the like; aside; astray. – **width**, *n.*

widespread /ˈwaɪdsprɛd/ *adj.* **1.** spread over or occupying a wide space. **2.** distributed over a wide region, or occurring in many places or among many persons or individuals. Also, **widespreading**.

widow /ˈwɪdoʊ/ *n.* a woman whose husband has died and who has not married again.

widower /ˈwɪdoʊə/ *n.* a man who has lost his wife by death and has not married again.

wield /wild/ *v.t.* **1.** to exercise (power, authority, influence, etc.), as in ruling or dominating. **2.** to manage (a weapon, instrument, etc.) in use; handle or employ in action.

wife /waɪf/ *n., pl.* **wives** /waɪvz/. a woman joined in marriage to a man as husband.

wig /wɪg/ *n.* an artificial covering of hair for the head, worn to conceal baldness, for disguise, theatricals, etc., or formerly as an ordinary head covering.

wiggle /ˈwɪgəl/ *v.*, **-gled**, **-gling**, *n.* – *v.i.* **1.** to move or go with short, quick, irregular movements from side to side; wriggle. – *v.t.* **2.** to cause to wiggle; move quickly and irregularly from side to side. – *n.* **3.** a wavy line. – **wiggly**, *adj.*

wigwam /ˈwɪgwɒm/ *n.* an American Indian hut or lodge, usually of rounded or oval shape.

wild /waɪld/ *adj.* **1.** living in a state of nature, as animals that have not been tamed or domesticated. **2.** growing or produced without cultivation or the care of humans, as plants, flowers, fruit, honey, etc. **3.** of unrestrained violence, fury, intensity, etc.; violent; furious. **4.** unrestrained, untrammelled, or unbridled. **5.** extravagant or fantastic. **6.** disorderly or dishevelled. **7.** *Colloquial* intensely eager or enthusiastic. – *adv.* **8.** in a wild manner; wildly. – *n.* **9.** (*often pl.*) an uncultivated, uninhabited, or desolate region or tract; a waste; a wilderness; a desert.

wild-card /ˈwaɪld-kad/ *adj.* having to do with a computer search of text for a character string which has one or more variable elements indicated by an asterisk or other non-textual character.

wildcat strike /waɪldkæt/ *n.* a strike which has not been called or sanctioned by officials of a trade union; unofficial strike.

wildebeest /ˈwɪldəbist/ *n., pl.* **-beests**. any of several African antelopes characterised by an oxlike head, curved horns, and a long, flowing tail; gnu.

wilderness /ˈwɪldənəs/ *n.* a wild region, as of forest or desert; a waste; a tract of land inhabited only by wild animals.

wildlife /ˈwaɪldlaɪf/ *n.* animals living in their natural habitat.

wile /waɪl/ *n.* a trick, artifice, or stratagem.

wilful /ˈwɪlfəl/ *adj.* **1.** willed, voluntary, or intentional. **2.** self-willed or headstrong.

will[1] /wɪl/, *weak forms* /wəl, l/ *v. (aux), past* **would**, (*imperative and infinitive lacking*) **1.** am (is, are, etc.) about or going to (in future constructions, denoting in the first person promise or determination, in the second and third persons mere futurity). **2.** am (is, are, etc.) disposed or willing to. **3.** am (is, are, etc.) determined or sure to (used emphatically).

will[2] /wɪl/ *n., v.*, **willed**, **willing**. – *n.* **1.** the faculty of conscious and especially of deliberate action. **2.** the power of choosing one's own actions. **3.** wish or desire. **4.** purpose or determination, often hearty determination. **5.** disposition (good or ill) towards another. **6.** *Law* a legal declaration of a person's wishes as to the disposition of his or her (real) property, etc., after death, usually in writing. – *v.t.* **7.** to give by will or testament; to bequeath or devise. **8.** to influence by exerting willpower. **9.** to purpose, determine on, or elect, by act of will.

willing /ˈwɪlɪŋ/ *adj.* **1.** disposed or consenting (without being particularly desirous). **2.** cheerfully consenting or ready.

willow /ˈwɪloʊ/ *n.* a tree or shrub with tough, pliable twigs or branches which are used for wickerwork, etc.

willpower /ˈwɪlpaʊə/ *n.* control over one's impulses and actions.

wilt /wɪlt/ *v.i.* to become limp and drooping, as a fading flower; wither.

wily /ˈwaɪli/ *adj.*, **-lier**, **-liest**. crafty.

wimp /wɪmp/ *n.* *Colloquial* a weak, timorous and ineffectual person.

wimple /ˈwɪmpəl/ *n.* a woman's headcloth drawn in folds about the chin, as worn by some nuns.

win /wɪn/ *v.*, **won**, **winning**, *n.* – *v.i.* **1.** to succeed by striving or effort (sometimes fol. by *out*). **2.** to gain the victory. **3.** to be placed first in a race or the like. – *v.t.* **4.** to get by effort, as through labour, competition, or conquest. **5.** to gain (a prize, fame, etc.). **6.** to be successful in (a game, battle, etc.). – *n.* **7.** an act of winning; a success; a victory. – **winner**, *n.*

wince /wɪns/ *v.i.*, **winced**, **wincing**. to shrink, as in pain or from a blow; start; flinch.

winch /wɪntʃ/ *n.* the crank or handle of a revolving machine.

wind[1] /wɪnd/ *n.* **1.** air in natural motion, as along the earth's surface. **2.** any stream of air, as that produced by a bellows, a fan, etc. **3.** a hint or intimation. **4.** gas generated in the stomach and bowels. – *v.t.* **5.** to expose to wind or air. **6.** to deprive momentarily of breath, as by a blow.

– **windy**, *adj.*

wind² /waɪnd/ *v.*, **wound**, **winding**. – *v.i.* **1.** to change direction; bend; turn; take a frequently bending course; meander. **2.** to have a circular or spiral course or direction. **3.** to proceed circuitously or indirectly. **4.** to undergo winding, or winding up. – *v.t.* **5.** to encircle or wreathe, as with something twined, wrapped, or placed about. **6.** to roll or coil (thread, etc.) into a ball or on a spool or the like (often fol. by *up*). **7.** to twine, fold, wrap, or place about something. **8.** to adjust (a mechanism, etc.) for operation by some turning or coiling process (often fol. by *up*). **9.** to make (one's or its way) in a winding or frequently bending course. **10. wind up,** to terminate or conclude (affairs, a business, etc.).

windbreak /'wɪndbreɪk/ *n.* a growth of trees, a structure of boards, or the like, serving as a shelter from the wind.

windcheater /'wɪntʃitə/ *n.* a fleecy-lined garment for the upper part of the body designed to give protection against the wind.

windfall /'wɪndfɔl/ *n.* an unexpected piece of good fortune.

windfall profits *pl. n.* profits made unexpectedly as a result of events not directly related to the company, as fluctuations in the currency or on the stock exchange, changes in government policy affecting the market, etc. Also, **windfall gains**.

wind instrument *n.* a musical instrument sounded by the player's breath or any current of air.

windlass /'wɪndləs/ *n.* a device for raising weights, etc.

windmill /'wɪndmɪl, 'wɪn-/ *n.* a mill or machine, as for grinding or pumping, operated by the wind, usually by the wind acting on a set of arms, vanes, sails, or slats attached to a horizontal axis so as to form a vertical revolving wheel.

window /'wɪndoʊ/ *n.* **1.** an opening in the wall or roof of a building, the cabin of a boat, etc., for the admission of air or light, or both, commonly fitted with a frame in which are set movable sashes containing panes of glass. **2.** anything likened to a window in appearance or function, as a transparent section in an envelope, displaying the address. **3.** a boxed-off section of a visual display unit screen in which secondary text or information is shown.

windpipe /'wɪndpaɪp, 'wɪn-/ *n.* the trachea of an air-breathing vertebrate.

windscreen /'wɪndskrin, 'wɪn-/ *n.* the sheet of glass which forms the front window of a motor vehicle.

windsock /'wɪndsɒk, 'wɪn-/ *n.* a wind-direction indicator, installed at airports and elsewhere, consisting of an elongated truncated cone of textile material, flown from a mast.

wine /waɪn/ *n.* the fermented juice of the grape, in many varieties (red, white, sweet, dry, still, sparkling, etc.) used as a beverage and in cookery, religious rites, etc.

wing /wɪŋ/ *n.* **1.** either of the two appendages, of most birds and bats, which are adapted for flight. **2.** a similar structure. **3.** *Aeronautics* that portion of a main supporting surface confined to one side of an aeroplane. **4.** *Architecture* a part of a building projecting on one side of, or subordinate to, a central or main part. **5.** (*pl.*) the insignia or emblem worn by a qualified pilot. **6. a.** *Australian Rules* either of the two centre-line positions on each side of the centre. **b.** *Hockey*, *Rugby*, *Soccer*, *etc.* either of the two areas of the pitch near the touchline and ahead of the halfway line, known as the left and right wings respectively, with reference to the direction of the opposing goal. **c.** a player in one of these positions. **7.** *Theatre* the platform or space on the right or left of the stage proper. – *v.t.* **8.** to equip with wings. **9.** to enable to fly, move rapidly, etc.; lend speed or celerity to. **10.** to wound or disable (a bird, etc.) in the wing. **11.** to wound (a person) in an arm or other non-vital part. – *v.i.* **12.** to travel on or as on wings; fly; soar.

wink /wɪŋk/ *v.i.* **1.** to close and open the eyes quickly. **2.** to close and open one eye quickly as a hint or signal or with some sly meaning (often fol. by *at*). **3.** to shine with little flashes of light, or twinkle. – *v.t.* **4.** to close and open (the eyes or an eye) quickly; execute or give (a wink). – *n.* **5.** the act of winking. **6.** the time required for winking once; an instant or twinkling.

winnow /'wɪnoʊ/ *v.t.* **1.** to free (grain, etc.) from chaff, refuse particles, etc., by means of wind or driven air. **2.** to subject to some process of separating or distinguishing; analyse critically; sift.

winsome /'wɪnsəm/ *adj.* winning, engaging, or charming.

winter /'wɪntə/ *n.* **1.** the coldest season of the year. **2.** a period like winter, as the last or final period of life, a period of decline, decay, inertia, dreariness, or adversity. – *adj.* **3.** of, relating to, or characteristic of winter. **4.** suitable for wear or use in winter.

wipe /waɪp/ *v.*, **wiped**, **wiping**, *n.* – *v.t.* **1.** to rub lightly with or on a cloth, towel, paper, the hand, etc., in order to clean or dry. **2.** to remove by rubbing with or on something (usually fol. by *away*, *off*, *out*, etc.) **3.** to destroy or eradicate, as from existence or memory. **4. wipe out,** to destroy completely. – *n.* **5.** the action of wiping.

wire /'waɪə/ *n.*, *v.*, **wired**, **wiring**. – *n.* **1.** a piece of slender, flexible metal, ranging from a thickness that can be bent by the hand only with some difficulty down to a fine thread, and usually circular in section. **2.** a length of such material used as a conductor of electricity, usually insulated in a flex. **3.** *Originally US Colloquial* a telegram. **4.** *Originally US Colloquial* the telegraphic system. – *v.t.* **5.** to furnish with a wire or wires. **6.** to install an electric system of wiring, as for lighting, etc. **7.** *Colloquial* to send a telegraphic message to.

wireless /'waɪələs/ *n.* radio.

wiry /'waɪəri/ *adj.*, **wirier**, **wiriest**. lean and sinewy.

wisdom /'wɪzdəm/ *n.* the quality or state of being wise; knowledge of what is true or right coupled with just judgment as to action; sagacity, prudence, or common sense.

wise /waɪz/ *adj.*, **wiser**, **wisest**. **1.** having the power of discerning and judging properly as to what is true or right. **2.** possessed of or characterised by scholarly knowledge or learning; learned; erudite. **3.** having knowledge or information as to facts, circumstances, etc.

-wise a suffix denoting: **1. a.** attitude or direction: *lengthwise*; *clockwise*. **b.** with reference to; in respect of. **2.** See **-ways**.

wish /wɪʃ/ *v.t.* **1.** to want; desire. – *v.i.* **2.** to have a desire, longing, or yearning. – *n.* **3.** a distinct mental inclination towards the doing, obtaining, attaining, etc., of something; a desire, felt or expressed. **4.** that which is wished.

wishbone /ˈwɪʃboʊn/ *n.* the forked bone in front of the breastbone in most birds.

wishy-washy /ˈwɪʃi-wɒʃi/ *adj.* lacking in substantial qualities; without strength or force; weak, feeble, or poor.

wisp /wɪsp/ *n.* **1.** a handful or small bundle of straw, hay, or the like. **2.** anything small or thin, as a shred, bundle, or slip of something, sometimes used as a brush or whisk.

wisteria /wɪsˈtɪəriə, wəs-/ *n.* a climbing shrub with handsome purple flowers.

wistful /ˈwɪstfəl/ *adj.* **1.** pensive or melancholy. **2.** showing longing tinged with melancholy; regretful; sad.

wit /wɪt/ *n.* **1.** keen perception and cleverly apt expression of connections between ideas which may arouse pleasure and especially amusement. **2.** a person endowed with or noted for such wit. **3.** (*pl.*) mental faculties, or senses.

witch /wɪtʃ/ *n.* a person, now especially a woman, who professes or is supposed to practise magic, especially black magic or the black art; a sorceress. – **witchery**, *n.*

witchetty grub /ˈwɪtʃəti grʌb/ *n.* any of various large, white, edible, wood-boring grubs that are the larvae of certain Australian moths and beetles.

with /wɪð, wɪθ/ *prep.* **1.** accompanied by or accompanying. **2.** in some particular relation to (especially implying interaction, company, association, conjunction, or connection). **3.** (expressing similarity or agreement). **4.** characterised by or having. **5.** (of means or instrument) by the use of. **6.** (of manner) using or showing. **7.** in correspondence or proportion to. **8.** against, as in opposition or competition.

with- limited prefixal use of *with*, separative or opposing, as in *withdraw*, *withstand*.

-with a suffix indicating conjunction.

withdraw /wɪðˈdrɔ, wɪθ-/ *v.*, **-drew**, **-drawn**, **-drawing**. – *v.t.* **1.** to draw back or away; take back; remove. – *v.i.* **2.** to retire; retreat; go apart or away. **3.** to retract a statement or expression. – **withdrawal**, *n.*

wither /ˈwɪðə/ *v.i.* **1.** to shrivel; fade; decay. – *v.t.* **2.** to make flaccid, shrunken, or dry, as from loss of moisture; cause to lose freshness, bloom, vigour, etc.

withers /ˈwɪðəz/ *pl. n.* the highest part of a horse's or other animal's back, behind the neck.

withhold /wɪðˈhoʊld, wɪθ-/ *v.t.*, **-held**, **-holding**. **1.** to hold back; restrain or check. **2.** to refrain from giving or granting. – **withholder**, *n.*

withholding tax *n.* that part of one's tax liability withheld by the employer, and paid directly to the government.

within /wɪðˈɪn, wɪθˈɪn/ *adv.* **1.** in or into the interior or inner part, or inside. – *prep.* **2.** in or into the interior of or the parts or space enclosed by. **3.** at or to some amount or degree not exceeding.

without /wɪðˈaʊt, wɪθ-/ *prep.* **1.** not with; with no; with absence, omission, or avoidance of; lacking (as opposed to *with*). **2.** beyond the compass, limits, range, or scope of (now used chiefly in opposition to *within*).

withstand /wɪðˈstænd, wɪθ-/ *v.*, **-stood**, **-standing**. – *v.t.* **1.** to stand or hold out against; resist or oppose, especially successfully. – *v.i.* **2.** to stand in opposition.

witness /ˈwɪtnəs/ *v.t.* **1.** to see or know by personal presence and perception. **2.** to be present at (an occurrence) as a formal witness or otherwise. – *n.* **3.** someone who, being present, personally sees or perceives a thing; a beholder, spectator, or eyewitness. **4.** a person or thing that affords evidence. **5.** someone who gives testimony, as in a court of law. **6.** someone who signs a document in attestation of the genuineness of its execution.

witticism /ˈwɪtəsɪzəm/ *n.* a witty remark.

witty /ˈwɪti/ *adj.*, **-tier**, **-tiest**. possessing wit in speech or writing; amusingly clever in perception and expression.

wives /waɪvz/ *n.* plural of **wife**.

wizard /ˈwɪzəd/ *n.* someone who professes to practise magic; a magician or sorcerer.

wizened /ˈwɪzənd/ *adj.* dried-up; withered; shrivelled.

wobbegong /ˈwɒbigɒŋ/ *n.* a shark with a flattened body and mottled skin.

wobble /ˈwɒbəl/ *v.i.*, **-bled**, **-bling**. **1.** to incline to one side and to the other alternately, as a wheel, top, or other rotating body, when not properly balanced. **2.** to move unsteadily from side to side.

woe /woʊ/ *n.* grievous distress, affliction, or trouble. – **woeful**, *adj.*

woebegone /ˈwoʊbəgɒn/ *adj.* beset with woe; mournful or miserable; affected by woe, especially in appearance.

wog[1] /wɒg/ *n.* *Colloquial* (*derogatory*) a person of Mediterranean extraction, or of similar complexion and appearance.

wog[2] /wɒg/ *n.* *Colloquial* **1.** a germ, especially one leading to a minor disease such as a cold or a stomach upset. **2.** such a cold, stomach upset, etc. **3.** a small insect.

woke /woʊk/ *v.* a past tense of **wake**.

woken /ˈwoʊkən/ *v.* past participle of **wake**.

wolf /wʊlf/ *n.*, *pl.* **wolves** /wʊlvz/. *v.* – *n.* **1.** a large, wild carnivore, *Canis lupus*, of Europe, Asia, and North America, belonging to the dog family, a swift-footed, cunning, rapacious animal, destructive to game, sheep, etc. **2.** *Colloquial* a man who is boldly flirtatious or amorous towards many women. – *v.t.* **3.** *Colloquial* to eat ravenously.

wolves /wʊlvz/ *n.* plural of **wolf**.

woman /ˈwʊmən/ *n.*, *pl.* **women** /ˈwɪmən/. **1.** a female human being (distinguished from *man*). **2.** an adult female person (distinguished from *girl*).

womanise = womanize /ˈwʊmənaɪz/ *v.t.*, **-nised**, **-nising**. (of a man) to have numerous casual affairs; philander.

womb /wum/ *n.* the uterus of the human female and some of the higher mammalian quadrupeds.

wombat /'wɒmbæt/ *n.* a large, heavily-built burrowing marsupial with short legs and a rudimentary tail.

women /'wɪmən/ *n.* plural of **woman**.

women's liberation *n.* the movement which seeks to free women from sexist discrimination and make available to them the opportunity to play any role in society. Also, **women's lib** /wɪmənz 'lɪb/.

won /wʌn/ *v.* past tense and past participle of **win**.

wonder /'wʌndə/ *v.i.* **1.** to think or speculate curiously. **2.** to be affected with wonder; marvel (often fol. by *at*). – *v.t.* **3.** to be curious about; be curious to know (followed by a clause). **4.** to feel wonder at (now only followed by a clause as object). – *n.* **5.** something strange and surprising; a cause of surprise, astonishment, or admiration. **6.** the emotion excited by what is strange and surprising; a feeling of surprised or puzzled interest, sometimes tinged with admiration.

wonderful /'wʌndəfəl/ *adj.* excellent; delightful; extremely good or fine.

wondrous /'wʌndrəs/ *adj.* wonderful.

wonky /'wɒŋki/ *adj. Colloquial* **1.** shaky; unsound. **2.** unwell; upset.

wont /woʊnt/ *adj.* **1.** accustomed; used: *he is wont to digress.* – *n.* **2.** custom; habit; practice.

won't /woʊnt/ *v.* contraction of *will not.*

woo /wu/ *v.t.* **1.** to seek the favour, affection, or love of, especially with a view to marriage. **2.** to seek to win.

wood /wʊd/ *n.* **1.** the hard, fibrous substance composing most of the stem and branches of a tree or shrub, and lying beneath the bark. **2.** the trunks or main stems of trees as suitable for architectural and other purposes; timber or lumber. **3.** *Music* a wooden wind instrument. **4.** (*often pl.*) a large and thick collection of growing trees, usually less extensive than a forest. **5.** *Golf* a club with a wooden head. **6.** *Tennis, etc.* the frame part of a racquet, usually made of wood. – *adj.* **7.** made of wood; wooden. **8.** used to cut, carve, or otherwise shape wood. – *v.t.* **9.** to cover or plant with trees. – **woody**, *adj.*

wooden /'wʊdn/ *adj.* **1.** consisting or made of wood. **2.** stiff, ungainly, or awkward. **3.** without spirit or animation.

woodpecker /'wʊdpɛkə/ *n.* a bird with a hard, chisel-like bill for boring into wood after insects.

woodpigeon /'wʊdpɪdʒən/ *n.* a large wild pigeon.

wood-turning /'wʊd-tɜnɪŋ/ *n.* the forming of wood articles upon a lathe.

woodwind /'wʊdwɪnd/ *n.* (*sing., sometimes construed as pl.*) the group of wind instruments which comprises the flutes, clarinets, oboes, and bassoons.

woodwork /'wʊdwɜk/ *n.* **1.** the interior wooden fittings of a house or the like. **2.** the art or craft of working in wood; carpentry.

woof[1] /wʊf/ *n.* yarns which travel from selvage to selvage in a loom, interlacing with the warp; weft.

woof[2] /wʊf/ *n.* the sound of a dog barking, especially deeply and loudly.

wool /wʊl/ *n.* **1.** a fibre produced from sheep's fleece or the like, that may be spun into yarn, or made into felt, upholstery materials, etc. **2.** any finely fibrous or filamentous matter suggestive of the wool of sheep.

wool clip /'wʊl klɪp/ *n.* the amount of wool yielded from the annual shearing season (by a station, district, etc.). Also, **clip**.

woollen /'wʊlən/ *adj.* made or consisting of wool.

woolly /'wʊli/ *adj.*, **-lier**, **-liest**. **1.** consisting of wool. **2.** resembling wool. **3.** not clear or firm, as thinking, expression, depiction, etc.; blurred, confused, or indistinct.

woolshed /'wʊlʃɛd/ *n.* a large shed for shearing and baling of wool.

woomera /'wʊmərə/ *n.* a type of throwing stick with a notch at one end for holding a dart or spear, thus giving increased leverage in throwing, used by Australian Aborigines. Also, **womera**.

woozy /'wuzi/ *adj. Colloquial* **1.** muddled, or stupidly confused. **2.** out of sorts physically, as with dizziness, nausea, or the like.

word /wɜd/ *n.* **1.** a sound or a combination of sounds, or its written or printed representation, used in any language as the sign of a concept. **2.** a speech element which signifies; a term used to describe or refer. **3.** (*pl.*) contentious or angry speech; a quarrel. **4.** warrant, assurance, or promise. **5.** intelligence or tidings. **6.** *Computers* a unit of information, usually consisting of a number or of a group of alphanumeric characters, in the memory of a computer. – *v.t.* **7.** to express in words, or phrase; select words to express.

wordbreak /'wɜdbreɪk/ *n.* the point of division in a word which runs over from one line to the next.

word processor *n.* a computer usually with keyboard and visual display unit, designed especially for storing and editing text. – **word processing**, *n.*

wordy /'wɜdi/ *adj.*, **wordier**, **wordiest**. characterised by or given to the use of many, or too many, words; verbose.

wore /wɔ/ *v.* past tense of **wear**.

work /wɜk/ *n., v.,* **worked** *or* **wrought**, **working**. – *n.* **1.** exertion directed to produce or accomplish something; labour; toil. **2.** that on which exertion or labour is expended; something to be made or done; a task or undertaking. **3.** productive or operative activity. **4.** *Physics* the product of the force acting upon a body and the distance through which the point of application of force moves. The derived SI unit of work is the joule. **5.** employment; a job, especially that by which one earns a living. **6.** (*pl. often construed as sing.*) a place or establishment for carrying on some form of labour or industry. **7.** (*pl.*) *Theology* acts performed in obedience to the law of God, or righteous deeds. – *v.i.* **8.** to do work, or labour; exert oneself (contrasted with *play*). **9.** to be employed, as for one's livelihood.

10. to be in operation, as a machine. **11.** to act or operate effectively. **12.** to get (*round, loose,* etc.), as if by continuous effort. **13.** to have an effect or influence, as on a person or on the mind or feelings. – *v.t.* **14.** to use or manage (an apparatus, contrivance, etc.) in operation. **15.** to bring, put, get, render, etc., by work, effort, or action (fol. by *in, off, out,* or other completive words). **16.** to effect, accomplish, cause, or do. **17.** to expend work on; manipulate or treat by labour. **18.** to operate (a mine, farm, etc.) for productive purposes. **19.** to make, fashion, or execute by work. **20.** to arrange or contrive. **21.** to move, stir, or excite in feeling, etc. (often fol. by *up*). – *v.* **22. work at,** to attempt to achieve or master (something) with application and energy. **23. work out, a.** to effect or achieve by labour. **b.** to solve (a problem) by a reasoning process. **c.** to cause to finish up, turn out, or culminate (satisfactorily, unless otherwise specified). **d.** to develop; elaborate. **e.** to undergo training or practice, especially intensively, as an athlete.

workable /'wɜkəbəl/ *adj.* practicable or feasible.

workaday /'wɜkədeɪ/ *n.* humdrum.

worker /'wɜkə/ *n.* **1.** one employed in manual or industrial labour. **2.** an employee, especially as contrasted with a capitalist or a manager.

workers' compensation *n.* payments by employers to employees as compensation for injuries incurred while engaged in the employers' business.

work force *n.* the total of all those engaged in employment.

working capital *n.* **1.** the amount of capital needed to carry on a business. **2.** *Accounting* current assets minus current liabilities. **3.** *Finance* liquid as distinguished from fixed capital assets.

working class *n.* the class of people composed chiefly of manual workers and labourers; the proletariat.

working memory *n. Computers* a high-speed memory unit used to hold intermediate results during a calculation.

workload /'wɜkloʊd/ *n.* the amount of work done or to be done in a specified time.

workmanship /'wɜkmənʃɪp/ *n.* **1.** skill in working or execution. **2.** quality or mode of execution, as of a thing made.

works committee /'wɜks kə,mɪti/ *n.* **1.** an elected body of employee representatives which deals with management regarding grievances, working conditions, wages, etc., and which is consulted by management in regard to labour matters. **2.** a joint council or committee representing employer and employees which discusses working conditions, wages, etc., within a factory or office. Also, **works council**.

workstation /'wɔksteɪʃən/ *n.* an area in an office which is assigned to a user of electronic equipment such as a computer terminal, etc. Also, **work station**.

work-to-rule /wɜk-tə-'rul/ *n.* **1.** a deliberate curtailment of output by workers, by meticulous observation of rules, as an industrial sanction. **2.** → **go-slow**.

world /wɜld/ *n.* **1.** the earth or globe. **2.** a particular section of the world's inhabitants. **3.** humankind; humanity. **4.** a particular class of humankind, with common interests, aims, etc. **5.** any sphere, realm, or domain, with all that pertains to it. **6.** the entire system of created things; the universe; the macrocosm.

world-class /'wɜld-klas/ *adj.* sufficiently good to be acceptable anywhere in the world.

worldly /'wɜldli/ *adj.,* **-lier**, **-liest**, *adv.* – *adj.* **1.** earthly or mundane (as opposed to *heavenly, spiritual,* etc.). **2.** devoted to, directed towards, or connected with the affairs, interests, or pleasures of this world. **3.** secular (as opposed to *ecclesiastic, religious,* etc.). – *adv.* **4.** in a worldly manner. – **worldliness**, *n.*

world-weary /'wɜld-wɪəri/ *adj.* weary of the world or of existence and its pleasures; blasé.

World Wide Web *n.* the global communications system made possible by the Internet. Also, **WWW**.

worm /wɜm/ *n.* **1.** *Zoology* a long, slender, soft-bodied invertebrate. **2.** (in popular language) any of numerous small creeping animals with more or less slender, elongated bodies, and without limbs or with very short ones, including individuals of widely differing kinds, as earthworms, tapeworms, insect larvae, adult forms of some insects, etc. **3.** something resembling or suggesting a worm in appearance, movement, etc. **4.** a grovelling, abject, or contemptible person. **5.** (*pl.*) *Pathology* any disease or disorder arising from the presence of parasitic worms in the intestines or other tissues. – *v.i.* **6.** to move or act like a worm; creep, crawl, or advance slowly or stealthily. – *v.t.* **7.** to make, cause, bring, etc., along by creeping or crawling, or by stealthy or devious advances.

worn /wɔn/ *v.* **1.** past participle of **wear**. – *adj.* **2.** impaired by wear or use. **3.** wearied or exhausted. – **wornness**, *n.*

worrisome /'wʌrisəm/ *adj.* worrying, annoying, or disturbing; causing worry.

worry /'wʌri/ *v.,* **-ried**, **-rying**, *n., pl.* **-ries**. – *v.i.* **1.** to feel uneasy or anxious; fret; torment oneself with or suffer from disturbing thoughts. – *v.t.* **2.** to cause to feel uneasy or anxious; trouble; torment with annoyances, cares, anxieties, etc.; plague, pester, or bother. **3.** to harass by repeated biting, snapping, etc. – *n.* **4.** worried condition or feeling; uneasiness or anxiety.

worse /wɜs/ *adj.* (*used as comparative of bad*) **1.** bad or ill in a greater or higher degree; inferior in excellence, quality, or character. – *n.* **2.** that which is worse. – *adv.* **3.** in a more disagreeable, evil, wicked, severe, or disadvantageous manner. **4.** with more severity, intensity, etc.; in a greater degree. **5.** in a less effective manner.

worship /'wɜʃəp/ *n., v.,* **-shipped**, **-shipping**. – *n.* **1.** reverent honour and homage paid to God, a god, or a sacred personage, or to any object regarded as sacred. **2.** adoring reverence or regard. **3.** (with *your, his,* etc.) a title of honour used in addressing or mentioning certain magistrates and others of rank or station. – *v.t.* **4.** to render religious reverence and homage to.

worst /wɜst/ *adj.* (*used as superlative of bad*) **1.** bad or ill in the greatest or highest degree. **2.** most faulty, unsatisfactory, or objectionable. – *n.* **3.** that which or someone who is worst or the worst part. – *adv.* **4.** in the most evil, wicked, or disadvantageous manner. **5.** with the most severity, intensity, etc.; in the greatest degree. **6.** in the least satisfactory, complete or effective manner.

worsted /ˈwʊstəd/ *n.* (cloth woven from) a type of woollen yarn.

wort /wɜt/ *n.* a plant; herb.

worth /wɜθ/ *adj.* **1.** good or important enough to justify (what is specified). **2.** having a value of, or equal in value to, as in money. – *n.* **3.** excellence of character or quality as commanding esteem. **4.** usefulness or importance, as to the world, to a person, or for a purpose. **5.** value, as in money. **6.** a quantity of something, of a specified value.

worthwhile /wɜθˈwaɪl/ *adj.* such as to repay one's time, attention, interest, work, trouble, etc.

worthy /ˈwɜði/ *adj.*, **-thier**, **-thiest**, *n.*, *pl.* **-thies**. – *adj.* **1.** of adequate merit or character. **2.** of commendable excellence or merit; deserving (often fol. by *of*, an infinitive, or occasionally a clause). – *n.* **3.** a person of eminent worth or merit or of social importance. **4.** (*often humorous*) a person.

would /wʊd/, *weak forms* /wəd, d/ – *v.* past tense of **will**[1] used: **1.** specially in expressing a wish: *I would it were true.* **2.** often in place of *will*, to make a statement or question less direct or blunt.

would-be /ˈwʊd-bi/ *adj.* **1.** wishing or pretending to be. **2.** intended to be.

wouldn't /ˈwʊdənt/ *v.* contraction of *would not.*

wound[1] /wund/ *n.* **1.** an injury to an organism due to external violence or some mechanical agency rather than disease. – *v.t.* **2.** to inflict a wound upon; injure; hurt.

wound[2] /waʊnd/ *v.* past tense and past participle of **wind**[2].

wove /woʊv/ *v.* past tense and occasional past participle of **weave**.

woven /ˈwoʊvən/ *v.* past participle of **weave**.

wow /waʊ/ *interj. Colloquial* (an exclamation of surprise, wonder, pleasure, dismay, etc.).

wowser /ˈwaʊzə/ *n. Colloquial* a prudish teetotaller; a killjoy.

wraith /reɪθ/ *n.* a visible spirit.

wrangle /ˈræŋgəl/ *v.i.*, **-gled**, **-gling**. to argue or dispute, especially in a noisy or angry manner.

wrap /ræp/ *v.*, **wrapped** *or* **wrapt**, **wrapping**, *n.* – *v.t.* **1.** to enclose, envelop, or muffle in something wound or folded about (often fol. by *up*). **2.** to wind, fold, or bind (something) about as a covering. **3.** to surround, envelop, shroud, or enfold. **4. wrap up,** *Colloquial* to conclude or settle. – *n.* **5.** something to be wrapped about the person, especially in addition to the usually indoor clothing, as a shawl, scarf, or mantle.

wrapped /ræpt/ *adj. Colloquial* enthused (about).

wrath /rɒθ/ *n.* strong, stern, or fierce anger; deeply resentful indignation; ire.

wreak /rik/ *v.t.* to inflict or execute (vengeance, etc.).

wreath /riθ/ *n.*, *pl.* **wreaths** /riðz/. something twisted or bent into a circular form; a circular band of flowers, foliage, or any ornamental work.

wreathe /rið/ *v.t.*, **wreathed**, **wreathing**. **1.** to encircle or adorn with or as with a wreath or wreaths. **2.** to surround in curving or curling masses or form.

wreck /rɛk/ *n.* **1.** a vessel in a state of ruin from disaster at sea, on rocks, etc. **2.** the ruin or destruction of anything. – *v.t.* **3.** to cause the wreck of (a vessel), as in navigation; shipwreck. **4.** to cause the ruin or destruction of; spoil.

wren /rɛn/ *n.* a small passerine bird with long legs and a long, almost upright tail.

wrench /rɛntʃ/ *v.t.* **1.** to twist suddenly and forcibly; pull, jerk, or force by a violent twist. – *n.* **2.** a wrenching movement; a sudden, violent twist. **3.** a sharp, distressing strain, as to the feelings, especially on parting or separation. **4.** a spanner.

wrest /rɛst/ *v.t.* **1.** to twist or turn; pull, jerk, or force by a violent twist. **2.** to take away by force.

wrestle /ˈrɛsəl/ *v.i.*, **-tled**, **-tling**. **1.** to engage in wrestling. **2.** to contend, as in a struggle for mastery; grapple.

wrestling /ˈrɛslɪŋ/ *n.* an exercise or sport in which two persons struggle hand to hand, each striving to throw or force the other to the ground.

wretch /rɛtʃ/ *n.* a deplorably unfortunate or unhappy person.

wretched /ˈrɛtʃəd/ *adj.* very unfortunate in condition or circumstances; miserable; pitiable.

wrick /rɪk/ *v.t.* to wrench or strain.

wriggle /ˈrɪgl/ *v.i.*, **-gled**, **-gling**. to twist to and fro, writhe, or squirm.

wring /rɪŋ/ *v.t.*, **wrung**, **wringing**. **1.** to twist forcibly, as something flexible. **2.** to twist and compress, or compress without twisting, in order to force out moisture (often fol. by *out*). **3.** to clasp (one's hands) together, as in grief, etc.

wrinkle /ˈrɪŋkəl/ *n.*, *v.*, **-kled**, **-kling**. – *n.* **1.** a ridge or furrow on a surface, due to contraction, folding, rumpling, or the like; corrugation; slight fold; crease. – *v.t.* **2.** to form a wrinkle or wrinkles in; corrugate; crease.

wrist /rɪst/ *n.* the part of the arm between the forearm and the hand.

writ /rɪt/ *n. Law* a formal order under seal, issued in the name of a sovereign, government, court, etc.

write /raɪt/ *v.*, **wrote**, **written**, **writing**. – *v.t.* **1.** to express or communicate in writing; give a written account of. **2.** to compose and produce in words or characters duly set down. **3.** to produce as author or composer. **4.** *Computers* to store (information) on a medium, such as magnetic tape or disk. – *v.i.* **5.** to trace or form characters, words, etc., with a pen, pencil, or other instrument or means, or as a pen or the like does. **6.** to be a writer, journalist, or author for one's living. **7.** to write a letter or letters, or communicate by letter. – *v.* **8. write down,** *Commerce* to reduce the book value of. **9. write off,** to cancel, as an entry in an account, as by an offsetting entry. **10. write up,** *Accounting* to make an excessive valuation of (an asset). – **writer**, *n.*

write-off /'raɪt-ɒf/ *n.* **1.** *Accounting* something written off from the books. **2.** *Colloquial* something irreparably damaged.

write-up /'raɪt-ʌp/ *n.* a written description or account, as in a newspaper or magazine.

writhe /raɪð/ *v.i.*, **writhed**, **writhing**. to twist the body about, or squirm, as in pain, violent effort, etc.

wrong /rɒŋ/ *adj.* **1.** not in accordance with what is morally right or good. **2.** deviating from truth or fact; erroneous. **3.** not correct in action, judgment, opinion, method, etc., as a person; in error. **4.** not suitable or appropriate. – *n.* **5.** that which is wrong, or not in accordance with morality, goodness, justice, truth, or the like; evil. **6.** an unjust act; injury. – *adv.* **7.** in a wrong manner; not rightly; awry or amiss. – *v.t.* **8.** to do wrong to; treat unfairly or unjustly; injure or harm. **9.** to impute evil to unjustly. – **wrongly**, *adv.*

wrought /rɔt/ *v.* **1.** *Archaic* a past tense and past participle of **work**. – *adj.* **2.** fashioned or formed; resulting from or having been subjected to working or manufacturing. **3.** produced or shaped by beating with a hammer, etc., as iron or silver articles. **4.** ornamented or elaborated. **5.** not rough or crude.

wrung /rʌŋ/ *v.* past tense and past participle of **wring**.

wry /raɪ/ *adj.*, **wryer**, **wryest** *or* **wrier**, **wriest**. **1.** produced by the distortion of the facial features, usually to indicate dislike, dissatisfaction, or displeasure. **2.** ironically or bitterly amusing. **3.** abnormally bent or turned to one side; twisted or crooked. **4.** devious in course or purpose; misdirected. **5.** distorted or perverted, as in meaning.

wuss /wʊs/ *n.* *Colloquial* an overly timid or ineffectual person, especially a male; wimp.

WWW *n.* → **World Wide Web**.

WYSIWYG /'wɪziwɪg/ *n.* a computer system which displays text and images on screen exactly as it will appear in printed output. Also, **what-you-see-is-what-you-get**.

X, x /ɛks/ *n., pl.* **X's** *or* **Xs**, **x's** *or* **xs**. **1.** the 24th letter of the English alphabet. **2.** a term often used to designate a person, thing, agency, factor, or the like, whose true name is unknown or withheld.

xanthorrhoea /zænθə'riə/ *n.* any plant of the genus Xanthorrhoea, native to Australia, as the grasstree.

xeno- a word element meaning 'alien', 'strange', 'foreign'.

xenon /'zinɒn/ *n.* a heavy, colourless, chemically unreactive gaseous element. *Symbol:* Xe

xenophobia /zɛnə'foubiə/ *n.* fear or hatred of foreigners.

xero- a word element meaning 'dry'.

xerography /zɪə'rɒgrəfi/ *n.* a method of photographic copying. – **xerograph**, *n.* – **xerographic**, *adj.*

xerox /'zɪərɒks/ *n.* **1.** a xerographic process. **2.** a copy obtained by this process. – *v.t., v.i.* **3.** to obtain copies (of) by this process.

X generation /'ɛks dʒɛnə,reɪʃən/ *n.* → **generation X**.

-xion variant of **-tion**.

XL /ɛks 'ɛl/ *adj.* (as a clothing size) extra large.

Xmas /'ɛksməs, krɪsməs/ *n.* Christmas.

X-ray /'ɛks-reɪ, ɛks-'reɪ/ *n.* **1.** *Physics (often pl.)* electromagnetic radiation of shorter wavelength than light, which is able to penetrate solids, expose photographic plates, etc. **2.** a picture produced by the action of X-rays. – *v.t.* **3.** to examine by means of X-rays.

xylo- a word element meaning 'wood'.

xylophone /'zaɪləfoun/ *n.* a musical instrument consisting of a graduated series of wooden bars, usually sounded by striking with small wooden hammers.

Y y

Y, y /waɪ/ *n., pl.* **Y's** *or* **Ys**, **y's** *or* **ys**. the 25th letter of the English alphabet.

-y[1] a suffix of adjectives meaning 'characterised by or inclined to' the substance or action of the word or stem to which the suffix is attached, as in *juicy, dreamy, chilly.* Also, **-ey**[1].

-y[2] a diminutive suffix, often affectionate, common in names, as in *Billy, pussy.* Also, **-ey**[2], **-ie**.

-y[3] a suffix forming action nouns from verbs, as in *inquiry,* also found in other abstract nouns, as *carpentry, infamy.*

yabber /'jæbə/ *Colloquial* – *v.i.* **1.** to talk; converse. – *n.* **2.** talk; conversation.

yabby /'jæbi/ *n.* an Australian freshwater crayfish.

yacht /jɒt/ *n.* a sailing vessel used for private cruising, racing, or other like non-commercial purposes.

yahoo /'jahu, ja'hu/ *n.* **1.** a rough, coarse, or uncouth person. – *v.i.* **2.** to behave in a rough, uncouth manner (fol. by *around*). – *interj.* **3.** (an exclamation expressing enthusiasm or delight).

yak[1] /jæk/ *n.* a long-haired wild ox.

yak[2] /jæk/ *v.i.*, **yakked**, **yakking**. to talk or chatter, especially pointlessly and continuously.

yakka /'jækə/ *n.* *Colloquial* work. Also, **yacker**, **yakker**.

yam /jæm/ *n.* the starchy, tuberous root of certain climbing vines.

yank /jæŋk/ *Colloquial* – *v.t., v.i.* **1.** to pull or move with a sudden jerking motion; tug sharply. – *n.* **2.** a jerk or tug.

yap /jæp/ *v.i.*, **yapped**, **yapping**. **1.** to yelp; bark snappishly. **2.** *Colloquial* to talk snappishly, noisily, or foolishly.

yard[1] /jad/ *n.* **1.** a common unit of linear measure in the imperial system equal to 3ft or 36 in., defined as 0.9144 metres. **2.** *Nautical* a long cylindrical spar slung crosswise to a mast and suspending a sail.

yard[2] /jad/ *n.* **1.** a piece of enclosed ground for use as a garden, for animals, or for some other purpose. **2.** an enclosure within which any work or business is carried on.

yardarm /'jadam/ *n.* either end of a yard of a square sail.

yardstick /'jadstɪk/ *n.* any standard of measurement.

yarmulke /'jamulkə/ *n.* a skullcap worm by Jewish males, especially on religious occasions.

yarn /jan/ *n.* **1.** thread made by twisting fibres, as nylon, cotton or wool, and used for knitting and weaving. **2.** *Colloquial* a story or tale of adventure, especially a long one about incredible events. **3.** a talk, chat. – *v.i.* **4.** *Colloquial* to spin a yarn; tell stories. **5.** to talk, chat.

yaw /jɔ/ *v.i.* **1.** to deviate temporarily from the straight course, as a ship. **2.** (of an aircraft, rocket, etc.) to have a motion about its vertical axis.

yawn /jɔn/ *v.i.* **1.** to open the mouth involuntarily with a prolonged, deep intake of breath, as from drowsiness or weariness. **2.** to open wide like a mouth. – *n.* **3.** the act of yawning.

ye /ji/ *pron. Archaic* you (especially plural).

yea /jeɪ/ *interj.* yes.

yeah /jɛə/ *adv. Colloquial* yes.

year /jɪə/ *n.* **1.** a period of 365 or 366 days, divided into 12 calendar months, now reckoned as beginning 1 January and ending 31 December (**calendar year**). **2.** a space of 12 calendar months reckoned from any point. **3.** the true period of the earth's revolution round the sun. **4.** a full round of the seasons. **5.** a level or grade in an academic program, usually indicating one full year's study. **6.** (*pl.*) age, especially of a person. **7.** (*pl.*) time, especially a long time.

yearling /jɪəlɪŋ/ *n.* an animal one year old or in the second year of its age.

yearly /'jɪəli/ *adj., adv., n., pl.* **-lies**. – *adj.* **1.** relating to a year, or to each year. **2.** done, made, happening, appearing, coming, etc., once a year, or every year. – *adv.* **3.** once a year; annually. – *n.* **4.** a publication appearing once a year.

yearn /jɜn/ *v.i.* to have an earnest or strong desire; long.

yeast /jist/ *n.* a substance consisting of the aggregated cells of certain minute fungi, used to induce fermentation in the manufacture of alcoholic drink, especially beer, and as a leaven to make bread, etc., light and spongy, and also used in medicine.

yell /jɛl/ *v.i.* **1.** to cry out with a strong, loud, clear sound. – *n.* **2.** a cry uttered by yelling.

yellow /ˈjɛloʊ/ *adj.* **1.** of a bright colour like that of butter, lemons, etc.; between green and orange in the spectrum. **2.** *Colloquial* cowardly; mean or contemptible. **3.** *Colloquial* (of newspapers, etc.) sensational, especially morbidly or offensively sensational. – *n.* **4.** a hue between green and orange in the spectrum.

yellowcake /ˈjɛloʊkeɪk/ *n.* uranium oxide in an unprocessed form, which has low radioactivity.

yellow fever /jɛloʊ ˈfivə/ *n.* a dangerous, often fatal, infectious febrile disease.

yellow pages *pl. n.* (*sometimes construed as sing.*) a telephone directory listing businesses, professional people, organisations, etc.

yelp /jɛlp/ *v.i.* **1.** to give a quick, sharp, shrill cry, as dogs, foxes, etc. – *n.* **2.** a quick, sharp bark or cry.

yen /jɛn/ *n. Colloquial* desire; longing.

yep /jɛp/ *interj. Colloquial* → **yes**.

yes /jɛs/ *interj., n., pl.* **yeses**. – *interj.* **1.** (used to express affirmation or assent). – *n.* **2.** an affirmative reply.

yesterday /ˈjɛstədeɪ, -di/ *adv.* **1.** on the day preceding this day. – *n.* **2.** the day preceding this day.

yet /jɛt/ *adv.* **1.** at the present time. **2.** up to a particular time, or thus far. **3.** in the time still remaining, or before all is done. **4.** now or then as previously; still. **5.** in addition, or again. **6.** moreover. **7.** even or still (with comparatives). **8.** though the case be such; nevertheless. – *conj.* **9.** and yet; but yet; nevertheless.

yew /ju/ *n.* an evergreen coniferous tree with thick, dark foliage.

yield /jild/ *v.t.* **1.** to give forth or produce by a natural process or in return for cultivation. **2.** to produce or furnish as payment, profit, or interest. **3.** to give up, as to superior power or authority. – *v.i.* **4.** to give a return, as for labour expended; produce or bear. **5.** to give way to influence, entreaty, argument, or the like. – *n.* **6.** the action of yielding or producing. **7.** that which is yielded. **8.** the quantity or amount yielded. **9.** *Stock Exchange* dividend return on investment outlay, usually expressed as a percentage.

yob /jɒb/ *n. Colloquial* a loutish, aggressive, or surly youth. Also, **yobbo** /ˈjɒboʊ/.

yodel /ˈjoʊdl/ *v.t., v.i.,* **-delled**, **-delling**. to sing with frequent changes from the natural voice to falsetto and back again.

yoga /ˈjoʊgə/ *n.* the use of meditation, often with unfamiliar movements and postures, to attain the withdrawal of the senses from all external objects.

yoghurt = yogurt /ˈjoʊgət, ˈjɒgət/ *n.* a prepared food of custard-like consistency, sometimes sweetened or flavoured, made from milk that has been curdled by the action of enzymes or other cultures. Also, **yoghourt**.

yogi /ˈjoʊgi/ *n., pl.* **-gis** /-giz/. someone who practises yoga.

yoke /joʊk/ *n., v.,* **yoked**, **yoking**. – *n.* **1.** a contrivance for joining a pair of draught animals, especially oxen, for pulling a cart, etc. **2.** something resembling a yoke in form or use. **3.** a shaped piece in a garment from which the rest of the garment hangs. – *v.t.* **4.** to put a yoke on.

yokel /ˈjoʊkəl/ *n.* a countryman or rustic.

yolk /joʊk/ *n.* the yellow and principal substance of an egg, as distinguished from the white.

yonder /ˈjɒndə/ *adj.* **1.** being the more distant, or farther. **2.** being in that place or over there, or being that or those over there. – *adv.* **3.** at, in, or to that place (specified or more or less distant); over there.

yonks /jɒŋks/ *n. Colloquial* a long time.

yore /jɔ/ *n.* time long past, now only in the phrase **of yore**.

you /ju/, *weak form* /jə/ *pron., possessive* **your** *or* **yours**, *objective* **you**. **1.** (used to refer the person addressed). **2.** one; anyone; people in general.

you'd /jud/, *weak form* /jəd/ contraction of *you had* or *you would.*

you'll /jul/, *weak form* /jəl/ contraction of *you will* or *you shall.*

young /jʌŋ/ *adj.* **1.** being in the first or early stage of life, or growth; youthful; not old. **2.** of or relating to youth. **3.** not far advanced in years in comparison with another or others. – *n.* **4.** young offspring. **5.** young people collectively.

youngster /ˈjʌŋstə/ *n.* a young person.

your /jɔ/ *pron.* **1.** the possessive form of **you**, **ye**, used before a noun. **2.** (used to indicate all members of a particular group). Cf. **yours**.

you're /jɔ/ contraction of *you are.*

yours /jɔz/ *pron.* form of **your** used predicatively or without a noun following.

yourself /jɔˈsɛlf/ *pron., pl.* **-selves**. **1.** a reflexive form of **you**: *you've cut yourself.* **2.** an emphatic form of **you** or **ye** used: **a.** as object. **b.** in apposition to a subject or object. **3.** your proper or normal self.

youth /juθ/ *n., pl.* **youths** /juðz/. (*collectively youth*) **1.** the condition of being young; youngness. **2.** the time of being young; early life. **3.** the first or early period of anything. **4.** a young person, especially a young man. – **youthful**, *adj.*

you've /juv/ contraction of *you have.*

yowl /jaʊl/ *v.i.* to utter a long distressful or dismal cry.

yoyo /ˈjoʊjoʊ/ *n., pl.* **-yos**. a toy, consisting of a round, flat-sided block of wood, plastic, etc., with a groove round the edge, in which a string is wound. The yoyo is spun out and reeled in by the string, one end of which remains attached to the finger.

yuk = yuck /jʌk/ *interj.* **1.** (an expression of disgust). – *adj.* **2.** repulsive; disgusting.

yule /jul/ *n.* Christmas, or the Christmas season.

yuppie /ˈjʌpi/ *n.* *Originally US* a young urban professional person, typified as having a good income and available cash to spend on luxury consumer goods. Also, **yuppy**.

Z z

Z, z /zɛd/ *US* /zi/ *n., pl.* **Z's** *or* **Zs**, **z's** *or* **zs**. the 26th letter of the English alphabet.

zany /ˈzeɪni/ *adj.* **1.** extremely comical; clownish. **2.** slightly crazy; fantastic or ludicrous.

zarzuela /zaˈzweɪlə/ *n.* a type of traditional Spanish light opera with spoken dialogue.

zeal /zil/ *n.* ardour for a person, cause, or object; eager desire or endeavour; enthusiastic diligence. – **zealous**, *adj.*

zealot /ˈzɛlət/ *n.* **1.** someone who displays zeal. **2.** someone carried away by excess of zeal. **3.** *Colloquial* a religious fanatic.

zebra /ˈzɛbrə/, *US* /ˈzibrə/ – *n.* a wild, horselike animal, with regular black and white stripes over its entire body.

zebra crossing *n.* a crossing place on a road, marked with broad black and white stripes parallel to the kerb, and used by pedestrians.

zenith /ˈzɛnəθ/ *n.* **1.** *Astronomy* the point in the heavens vertically above any place or observer. **2.** any highest point or state; culmination. – **zenithal**, *adj.*

zephyr /ˈzɛfə/ *n.* a soft, mild breeze.

zeppelin /ˈzɛpələn/ *n.* a large dirigible.

zero /ˈzɪəroʊ/ *n., pl.* **-ros**, **-roes**, *v.,* **-roed**, **-roing**. – *n.* **1.** the figure or symbol 0, which stands for the absence of quantity. **2.** the origin of any kind of measurement; line or point from which all divisions of a scale (as a thermometer) are measured in either a positive or a negative direction. **3.** naught or nothing. **4.** the lowest point or degree. – *v.t.* **5.** to adjust to a zero point. – *v.i.* **6. zero in, a.** to focus attention (fol. by *on*). **b.** to arrive at a conclusion, etc., by a process of elimination (fol. by *on*).

zest /zɛst/ *n.* **1.** anything added to impart flavour or cause relish. **2.** an agreeable or piquant flavour imparted. **3.** piquancy, interest, or charm. – *v.t.* **4.** to give zest, relish, or piquancy to.

zigzag /ˈzɪgzæg/ *n.* a line, course, or progression characterised by sharp turns first to one side and then to the other.

zilch /ˈzɪltʃ/ *n.* *Colloquial* nothing.

zinc /zɪŋk/ *n.* *Chemistry* a bluish-white metallic element used in making alloys, and as a protective covering for roofs, etc. *Symbol:* Zn

zinnia /ˈzɪniə/ *n.* an annual plant with colourful flowers.

zip /zɪp/ *n., v.,* **zipped**, **zipping**. **1.** Also, **zipper**. a fastener consisting of an interlocking device set along two edges, which unites (or separates) them when an attached piece sliding between them is pulled, and used in place of buttons, hooks, etc. **2.** energy or vim. – *v.i.* **3.** *Colloquial* to move with zip; hurry. **4.** to proceed with energy. – *v.t.* **5.** to fasten with a zip (fol. by *up*).

zircon /ˈzɜkɒn/ *n.* a common mineral, transparent varieties of which are valued as a gem.

zither /ˈzɪðə/ *n.* a stringed musical instrument, played horizontally.

-zoa plural combining form naming zoological groups.

zodiac /ˈzoʊdiæk/ *n.* *Astronomy* an imaginary belt of the heavens, containing twelve constellations and hence twelve divisions (called *signs*). – **zodiacal**, *adj.*

zombie /ˈzɒmbi/ *n.* **1.** a dead body brought to life by a supernatural force. **2.** (*derogatory*) a person having no independent judgment, intelligence, etc. Also, **zombi**.

zone /zoʊn/ *n.* **1.** any continuous tract or area, which differs in some respect, or is distinguished for some purpose, from adjoining tracts or areas, or within which certain distinguishing circumstances exist or are established. **2.** an area or district under special restrictions or where certain conditions or circumstances prevail. – **zonal**, *adj.*

zone allowance *n.* an allowance paid to employees as an inducement to work in remote areas.

zoning /ˈzoʊnɪŋ/ *n.* the marking out of an area of land with respect to its use.

zoo /zu/ *n.* a park or other large enclosure in which live animals are kept for public exhibition; a zoological garden.

zoo- a word element meaning 'living being'.

zoogamy /zoʊˈɒgəmi/ *n.* sexual reproduction. – **zoogamous**, *adj.*

zooid /ˈzoʊɔɪd/ *n.* *Biology* any organic body or cell which is capable of spontaneous movement and of an existence more or less apart from or independent of the parent organism.

zoological garden /zoʊəˌlɒdʒɪkəl ˈgadn/ *n.* (*often pl.*) a zoo.

zoology /zoʊˈɒlədʒi/ *n., pl.* **-gies**. **1.** the science that deals with animals or the animal kingdom. **2.** the animals existing in a particular region. – **zoological**, *adj.*

zoom /zum/ *v.i.* **1.** to make a continuous humming sound. **2.** to move with this sound. **3.** (of prices) to rise rapidly. **4.** *Film, TV, etc.* to use a lens which makes an object appear to approach (often fol. by *in*) or recede (often fol. by *out*) from the viewer.

zoophile /ˈzoʊəfaɪl/ *n.* someone who loves animals, especially someone who is opposed to vivisection or other such experimentation.

zot /zɒt/ *v.,* **zotted**, **zotting**. *Colloquial* – *v.i.* **1.** to depart quickly (usually fol. by *off*). – *v.t.* **2.** to knock, or kill.

zounds /zaʊndz, zundz/ *interj.* *Archaic* (an emphatic exclamation, as of surprise, indignation, or anger).

zucchini /zəˈkini, zu-/ *n., pl.* **-ni**, **-nis**. a small vegetable marrow; courgette.

zygote /ˈzaɪgoʊt, ˈzɪgoʊt/ *n.* *Biology* the cell produced by the union of two gametes. – **zygotic**, *adj.*

Appendixes

World times

(at noon Eastern Standard Time)

Subtract 30 minutes for South Australia, and 2 hours for Western Australia

Adelaide	11.30 a.m.	**New York**	*9.00 p.m.
Athens	4.00 a.m.	**Oslo**	3.00 a.m.
Beijing	10.00 a.m.	**Ottawa**	*9.00 p.m.
Bombay	7.30 a.m.	**Panama**	*9.00 p.m.
Buenos Aires	*10.00 p.m.	**Paris**	3.00 a.m.
Cairo	4.00 a.m.	**Perth WA**	10.00 a.m.
Calcutta	7.30 a.m.	**Quebec**	*9.00 p.m.
Capetown	4.00 a.m.	**Rangoon**	8.30 a.m.
Chicago	*8.00 p.m.	**Rio de Janeiro**	*11.00 p.m.
Copenhagen	3.00 a.m.	**Rome**	3.00 a.m.
Gibraltar	2.00 a.m.	**Rotterdam**	3.00 a.m.
Islamabad	7.00 a.m.	**San Francisco**	*6.00 p.m.
Istanbul	4.00 a.m.	**Singapore**	9.30 a.m.
Karachi	7.00 a.m.	**St Petersburg**	5.00 a.m.
Lisbon	3.00 a.m.	**Stockholm**	3.00 a.m.
London	2.00 a.m.	**Suez**	4.00 a.m.
Madras	7.30 a.m.	**Tokyo**	11.00 a.m.
Madrid	3.00 a.m.	**Vancouver**	*6.00 p.m.
Malta	3.00 a.m.	**Vienna**	3.00 a.m.
Mauritius	6.00 a.m.	**Washington DC**	*9.00 p.m.
Montreal	*9.00 p.m.	**Wellington, NZ**	2.00 p.m.
Moscow	5.00 a.m.	**Winnipeg**	*8.00 p.m.
New Orleans	*8.00 p.m.	**Yokohama**	11.00 a.m.

*Denotes previous day. (Adjust for local summertime where applicable.)

Countries - languages, capitals, currencies

Country	People	Official main language(s)	Capital	Main unit of currency
Afghanistan	Afghan, Afghani	Pashto, Dari (Persian)	Kabul	afghani
Albania	Albanian	Albanian	Tirana	lek
Algeria	Algerian, Algerine	Arabic	Algiers	Algerian dinar
Andorra	Andorran	Catalan, French, Spanish	Andorra la Vella	French franc, Spanish peseta
Angola	Angolan	Portuguese	Luanda	kwanza
Antigua and Barbuda	Antiguan	English	St John's	East Caribbean dollar
Argentina	Argentine, Argentinian	Spanish	Buenos Aires	peso
Armenia	Armenian	Armenian	Yerevan	dram
Australia	Australian	English	Canberra	Australian dollar
Austria	Austrian	German	Vienna	schilling
Azerbaijan	Azerbaijani	Azerbaijani	Baku	manat
Bahamas, the	Bahamian	English	Nassau	Bahamian dollar
Bahrain	Bahraini	Arabic	Manama	Bahrain dinar Bangladesh
Barbados	Barbadian	English	Bridgetown	Barbados dollar
Belarus	Belarusian	Belarusian	Minsk	rubel
Belgium	Belgian	Dutch, French, German	Brussels	Belgian franc
Belize	Belizean	English, Spanish, Carib, Maya	Belmopan	Belize dollar
Benin	Beninese	French	Porto Novo	CFA franc
Bhutan	Bhutanese	Dzongkha	Thimphu	ngultrum, Indian rupee
Bolivia	Bolivian	Spanish, Quechua, Aymará	Sucre and La Paz	boliviano

Bosnia and Herzegovina	Bosnian	Bosnian	Sarajevo	Bosnian dinar
Botswana	Botswanan	Tswana, English	Gaborone	pula
Brazil	Brazilian	Portuguese	Brasília	real
Brunei	Bruneian	Malay, English	Bandar Seri Begawan	Brunei dollar
Bulgaria	Bulgarian	Bulgarian	Sofia	lev
Burkina Faso	–	French, Mossi	Ouagadougou	CFA franc
Burma (Myanmar)	Burmese	Burmese	Rangoon (Yangon)	kyat
Burundi	Burundian	French, Kirundi	Bujumbura	Burundi franc
Cambodia	Cambodian	Khmer, French	Phnom Penh	riel
Cameroon	Cameroonian	French, English	Yaoundé	CFA franc
Canada	Canadian	English, French	Ottawa	Canadian dollar
Cape Verde Islands	Cape Verdean	Portuguese	Praia	Cape Verde escudo
Central African Republic	–	French, Sangho	Bangui	CFA franc
Chad	Chadian	French, Arabic	N'Djamena	CFA franc
Chile	Chilean	Spanish	Santiago	Chilean peso
China	Chinese	Chinese (Mandarin)	Beijing	yuan
Colombia	Colombian	Spanish	Bogotá	Colombian peso
Comoros	Comorian, Comoran	French, Arabic, Comorian	Moroni	Comorian franc
Congo, Democratic Republic of	Congolese	French	Kinshasa	zaire
Congo, Republic of	Congolese	French	Brazzaville	CFA franc
Costa Rica	Costa Rican	Spanish	San José	Costa Rican colón
Côte d'Ivorie (Ivory Coast)	–	French	Abidjan, Yamoussoukro	CFA franc
Croatia	Croat, Croatian	Croatian	Zagreb	kuna
Cuba	Cuban	Spanish	Havana	Cuban peso
Cyprus	Cypriot	Greek, Turkish	Nicosia	Cyprus pound
Czech Republic	Czech	Czech	Prague	Czech koruna
Denmark	Dane	Danish	Copenhagen	Danish krone

Country	People	Official main language(s)	Capital	Main unit of currency
Djibouti	Djibouti	Arabic, French	Djibouti	Djibouti franc
Dominica	Dominican	English	Roseau	East Caribbean dollar
Dominican Republic	Dominican	Spanish	Santo Domingo	Dominican peso
Ecuador	Ecuadorian	Spanish, Quechua	Quito	sucre
Egypt	Egyptian	Arabic	Cairo	Egyptian pound
El Salvador	Salvadoran	Spanish	San Salvador	colón
Equatorial Guinea	Guinean	Spanish	Malabo	CFA franc
Eritrea	Eritrean	Tigrinya	Asmara	Ethiopian birr
Estonia	Estonian	Estonian	Tallinn	kroon
Ethiopia	Ethiopian	Amharic	Addis Ababa	birr
Fiji	Fijian	English, Fijian, Hindi	Suva	Fiji dollar
Finland	Finn, Finlander, Finnish	Finnish, Swedish	Helsinki	markka
France	French	French	Paris	French franc
Gabon	Gabonese	French, Fang	Libreville	CFA franc
Gambia, the	Gambian	English	Banjul	dalasi
Georgia	Georgian	Georgian	Tbilisi	lari
Germany	German	German	Berlin	deutschmark
Ghana	Ghanian	English	Accra	cedi
Greece	Greek	Greek	Athens	drachma
Grenada	Grenadian	English	St George's	East Caribbean dollar
Guatemala	Guatemalan	Spanish	Guatemala City	quetzal
Guinea	Guinean	French	Conakry	Guinean franc
Guinea-Bissau	Guinean	Portuguese	Bissau	Guinea-Bissau peso
Guyana	Guyanan	English	Georgetown	Guyana dollar
Haiti	Haitian	French, Haitian Creole	Port-au-Prince	gourde
Honduras	Honduran	Spanish, English	Tegucigalpa	lempira

Hungary	Hungarian	Hungarian	Budapest	forint
Iceland	Icelandic	Icelandic	Reykjavik	krona
India	Indian	Hindi, English	New Delhi	Indian rupee
Indonesia	Indonesian	Bahasa Indonesia	Jakarta	rupiah
Iran	Iranian	Farsi (Persian)	Teheran	Iranian rial
Iraq	Iraqi	Arabic, Kurdish	Baghdad	Iraqi dinar
Ireland, Republic of	Irish	Irish (Gaelic), English	Dublin	Irish pound (punt)
Israel	Israeli	Hebrew, Arabic	Jerusalem	new shekel
Italy	Italian	Italian	Rome	lira
Jamaica	Jamaican	English	Kingston	Jamaica dollar
Japan	Japanese	Japanese	Tokyo	yen
Jordan	Jordanian	Arabic	Amman	Jordan dinar
Kazakhstan	Kazakh	Kazakh	Almaty	tenge
Kenya	Kenyan	Swahili, English	Nairobi	Kenya shilling
Kiribati	–	I-Kiribati, English	Bairiki	Australian dollar
Korea, North	North Korean	Korean	Pyongyang	won
Korea, South	South Korean	Korean	Seoul	won
Kuwait	Kuwaiti	Arabic	Kuwait City	Kuwaiti dinar
Kyrgyzstan	Kyrgyz	Kyrgyz, Russian	Bishkek	som
Laos	Laotian	Lao	Vientiane	new kip
Latvia	Latvian	Latvian	Riga	lats
Lebanon	Lebanese	Arabic	Beirut	Lebanese pound
Lesotho	–	English, Sesotho	Maseru	loti
Liberia	Liberian	English	Monrovia	Liberian dollar
Libya	Libyan	Arabic	Tripoli	Libyan dinar
Liechtenstein	–	German	Vaduz	Swiss franc
Lithuania	Lithuanian	Lithuanian	Vilnius	litas
Luxembourg	–	French, German	Luxembourg	Luxembourg franc

Country	People	Official main language(s)	Capital	Main unit of currency
Macedonia	Macedonian	Macedonian	Skopje	denar
Madagascar	Madagascan	Malagasy, French	Antananarivo	Malagasy franc
Malawi	–	English, Chichewa	Lilongwe	kwacha
Malaysia	Malaysian	Malay, English	Kuala Lumpur	ringgit
Maldives	Maldivian	Divehi	Malé	rufiyaa
Mali	Malian	French	Bamako	CFA franc
Malta	Maltese	Maltese, English	Valletta	Maltese lira
Marshall Islands	Marshallese	Marshallese, English	Majuro	US dollar
Mauritania	Mauritanian	French, Arabic	Nouakchott	ouguiya
Mauritius	Mauritian	English, French Creole	Port Louis	Mauritian rupee
Mexico	Mexican	Spanish	Mexico City	peso
Micronesia, Federated States of	Micronesian	English	Palikir	US dollar
Moldova	Moldovan	Romanian	Chişinău	leu
Monaco	Monacan, Monegasque	French	Monaco-Ville	French franc
Mongolia	Mongolian	Khalkha Mongolian	Ulan Bator	tugrik
Morocco	Moroccan	Arabic	Rabat	dirham
Mozambique	–	Portuguese	Maputo	metical
Namibia	Namibian	English	Windhoek	Namibian dollar
Nauru	Nauruan	Nauruan, English	Nauru	Australian dollar
Nepal	Nepalese, Nepali	Nepali	Katmandu	Nepalese rupee
Netherlands, the	Dutch	Dutch	Amsterdam	Netherlands guilder
New Zealand	New Zealander	English, Maori	Wellington	NZ dollar
Nicaragua	Nicaraguan	Spanish	Managua	córdoba oro
Niger	–	French	Niamey	CFA franc
Nigeria	Nigerian	English	Abuja	naira

Norway	Norwegian	Norwegian	Oslo	Norwegian krone
Oman	Omani	Arabic	Muscat	rial omani
Pakistan	Pakistani	Urdu	Islamabad	Pakistan rupee
Palau	Palauan	Palauan, English	Koror	US dollar
Panama	Panamanian	Spanish	Panama City	balboa
Papua New Guinea	Papua New Guinean	Neo-Melanesian, Pidgin, Motu, English	Port Moresby	kina
Paraguay	Paraguayan	Spanish, Guaraní	Asunción	guaraní
Peru	Peruvian	Spanish, Quechua	Lima	nuovo sol
Philippines, the	Filipino	Pilipino, English	Manila	Philippine peso
Poland	Pole, Polish	Polish	Warsaw	zloty
Portugal	Portuguese	Portuguese	Lisbon	escudo
Qatar	Qatari	Arabic	Doha	Qatar riyal
Romania	Romanian	Romanian	Bucharest	leu
Russia	Russian	Russian	Moscow	rouble
Rwanda	Rwandan	French, Rwanda	Kigali	Rwanda franc
San Marino	San Marinese	Italian	San Marino	Italian lira
São Tomé and Príncipe	–	Portuguese	São Tomé	dobra
Saudi Arabia	Saudi Arabian, Saudi	Arabic	Riyadh	Saudi riyal
Senegal	Senegalese	French	Dakar	CFA franc
Seychelles	–	English, French, Creole	Victoria	Seychelles rupee
Sierra Leone	Sierra Leonean	English	Freetown	leone
Singapore	Singaporean	Malay, Chinese, English, Tamil	Singapore	Singapore dollar
Slovakia	Slovak, Slovakian	Slovak	Bratislava	Slovak koruna
Slovenia	Slovene, Slovenian	Slovene	Ljubljana	Slovene tolar
Solomon Islands	Solomon Islander	English, Neo-Melanesian, Pidgin	Honiara	Solomon Islands dollar

Country	People	Official main language(s)	Capital	Main unit of currency
Somalia	Somali, Somalian	Somali, Arabic, English, Italian	Mogadishu	Somali shilling
South Africa	South African	English, Afrikaans, and 9 other official African languages	Pretoria, Cape Town, and Bloemfontein	rand
Spain	Spaniard, Spanish	Spanish	Madrid	Spanish peseta
Sri Lanka	Sri Lankan, Sinhalese	Sinhalese, Tamil, English	Colombo, and Sri Jayawardenapura Kotte	Sri Lanka rupee
St Kitts and Nevis	–	English	Basseterre	East Caribbean dollar
St Lucia	St Lucian	English	Castries	East Caribbean dollar
St Vincent and the Grenadines	–	English	Kingstown	East Caribbean dollar
Sudan	Sudanese	Arabic	Khartoum, Omdurman	Sudanese dinar
Suriname	Surinamese	Dutch, English	Paramaribo	Suriname guilder
Swaziland	Swazi	English, Swazi	Mbabane, Lobamba	emalangeni
Sweden	Swede, Swedish	Swedish	Stockholm	Swedish krona
Switzerland	Swiss	German, French, Italian	Bern	Swiss franc
Syria	Syrian	Arabic	Damascus	Syrian pound
Taiwan	Taiwanese	Chinese (Mandarin)	Taipei	New Taiwan dollar
Tajikistan	Tajik	Tajik	Dushanbe	Tajik rouble
Tanzania	Tanzanian	Swahili, English	Dodoma	Tanzanian shilling
Thailand	Thai	Thai	Bangkok	baht
Togo	Togolese	French	Lomé	CFA franc
Tonga	Tongan	Tongan, English	Nuku'alofa	pa'anga
Trinidad and Tobago	Trinidadian	English	Port of Spain	Trinidad and Tobago dollar
Tunisia	Tunisian	Arabic, French	Tunis	Tunisian dinar

Turkey	Turk, Turkish	Turkish	Ankara	Turkish lira
Turkmenistan	Turkmen	Turkmen	Ashgabat	manat
Tuvalu	Tuvaluan	Tuvaluan, English	Vaiaku (on Funafuti atoll)	Australian dollar, Tuvaluan dollar
Uganda	Ugandan	Swahili, English	Kampala	Uganda shilling
Ukraine	Ukrainian	Ukrainian	Kiev	hryvnia
United Arab Emirates	–	Arabic	Abu Dhabi	dirham
United Kingdom	Briton, British	English	London	pound sterling
United States of America	American	English	Washington	US dollar
Uruguay	Uruguayan	Spanish	Montevideo	Uruguayan peso
Uzbekistan	Uzbek	Uzbek	Tashkent	sum
Vanuatu	Vanuatuan	Bislama, French, English	Vila	vatu
Venezuela	Venezuelan	Spanish	Caracas	bolívar
Vietnam	Vietnamese	Vietnamese	Hanoi	dông
Western Samoa	Western Samoan	Samoan, English	Apia	tala
Yemen	Yemeni	Arabic	Sana'a	Yemeni rial
Yugoslavia	Yugoslav, Yugoslavian	Serbian	Belgrade	Yugoslav new dinar
Zambia	Zambian	English	Lusaka	kwacha
Zimbabwe	Zimbabwean	English	Harare	Zimbabwe dollar

Australian honours, awards and medals

(in order of precedence)

VC	Victoria Cross
GC	George Cross
CV	Cross of Valour
KG	Knight of the Garter
KT	Knight of the Thistle
GCB	Knight Grand Cross or Dame Grand Cross of the Order of the Bath
OM	Order of Merit
Bt	Baronet
AK	Knight of the Order of Australia
AD	Dame of the Order of Australia
GCMG	Knight Grand Cross or Dame Grand Cross of the Order of St Michael and St George
GCVO	Knight Grand Cross or Dame Grand Cross of the Order of the Royal Victorian Order
GBE	Knight Grand Cross or Dame Grand Cross of the Order of the British Empire
AC	Companion of the Order of Australia
CH	Companion of Honour
KCB	Knight Commander of the Order of the Bath
DCB	Dame Commander of the Order of the Bath
KCMG	Knight Commander of the Order of St Michael and St George
DCMG	Dame Commander of the Order of St Michael and St George
KCVO	Knight Commander of the Royal Victorian Order
DCVO	Dame Commander of the Royal Victorian Order
KBE	Knight Commander of the Order of the British Empire
DBE	Dame Commander of the Order of the British Empire
KB	Knight Bachelor
AO	Officer of the Order of Australia
CB	Companion of the Order of the Bath
CMG	Companion of the Order of St Michael and St George
CVO	Companion of the Royal Victorian Order
CBE	Companion of the Order of the British Empire
SC	Star of Courage
DSO	Companion of the Distinguished Service Order
AM	Member of the Order of Australia
MVO	Member of the Royal Victorian Order (4th Class)
OBE	Officer of the Order of the British Empire
ISO	Companion of the Imperial Service Order
MVO	Member of the Royal Victorian Order (5th Class)
MBE	Member of the Order of the British Empire
RRC	Member of the Royal Red Cross (1st Class)
DSC	Distinguished Service Cross
MC	Military Cross
DFC	Distinguished Flying Cross
AFC	Air Force Cross
ARRC	Royal Red Cross (2nd Class)
OAM	Medal of the Order of Australia
CGStJ	Bailiff Grand Cross of the Order of St John of Jerusalem
DCM	Distinguished Conduct Medal
CGM	Conspicuous Gallantry Medal

GM George Medal
BM Bravery Medal
QPM Queen's Police Medal for Gallantry
QFSM Queen's Fire Service Medal for Gallantry
DSM Distinguished Service Medal
MM Military Medal
DFM Distinguished Flying Medal
AFM Air Force Medal
QGM Queen's Gallantry Medal
BEM British Empire Medal
QPM Queen's Police Medal for Distinguished Service
QFSM Queen's Fire Service Medal for Distinguised Service
Commendation for Brave Conduct
Queen's Commendation for Brave Conduct
War Medals - in order of the date of Campaign for which they were awarded
Polar Medals - in order of date
RVM Royal Victorian Medal
Imperial Service Medal
Defence Force Service Medal
Reserve Force Decoration
Reserve Force Medal
National Medal
Coronation, Jubilee and other commemorative medals
Long Service Medals
Army Emergency Reserve Decoration
TD Territorial Decoration
ED Efficiency Decoration
VRD Decoration for Officers of RAN Volunteer Reserve
Queen's Medal (Champion shot in Military Forces)
Cadet Medal
Papua New Guinea Independence Medal

Denominations above one million

American system

Name	Value in powers of ten	Number of zeros	Number of groups of three 0's after 1000
billion	10^{9}	9	2
trillion	10^{12}	12	3
quadrillion	10^{15}	15	4
quintillion	10^{18}	18	5
sextillion	10^{21}	21	6
septillion	10^{24}	24	7
octillion	10^{27}	27	8
nonillion	10^{30}	30	9
decillion	10^{33}	33	10
undecillion	10^{36}	36	11
duodecillion	10^{39}	39	12
tredecillion	10^{42}	42	13
quattourdecillion	10^{45}	45	14
quindecillion	10^{48}	48	15
sexdecillion	10^{51}	51	16
septendecillion	10^{54}	54	17
octodecillion	10^{57}	57	18
novemdecillion	10^{60}	60	19
vigintillion	10^{63}	63	20
centillion	10^{303}	303	100

British system

Name	Value in powers of ten	Number of zeros	Powers of 1 000 000
milliard	10^{9}	9	–
billion	10^{12}	12	2
trillion	10^{18}	18	3
quadrillion	10^{24}	24	4
quintillion	10^{30}	30	5
sextillion	10^{36}	36	6
septillion	10^{42}	42	7
octillion	10^{48}	48	8
nonillion	10^{54}	54	9
decillion	10^{60}	60	10
undecillion	10^{66}	66	11
duodecillion	10^{72}	72	12
tredecillion	10^{78}	78	13
quattuordecillion	10^{84}	84	14
quindecllion	10^{90}	90	15
sexdecillion	10^{96}	96	16
septendecillion	10^{102}	102	17
octodecillion	10^{108}	108	18
novemdecillion	10^{114}	114	19
vigintillion	10^{120}	120	20
centillion	10^{600}	600	100

Note: To avoid ambiguity, the US system of naming these denominations is increasingly being adopted in Australia and elsewhere in the world, including Britain.

Roman numerals

NUMBER	ROMAN NUMERAL	NUMBER	ROMAN NUMERAL
1	I	43	XLIII
2	II	50	L
3	III	54	LIV
4	IV	60	LX
5	V	65	LXV
6	VI	70	LXX
7	VII	76	LXXVI
8	VIII	80	LXXX
9	IX	87	LXXXVII
10	X	90	XC
11	XI	98	XCVIII
12	XII	100	C
13	XIII	101	CI
14	XIV	115	CXV
15	XV	150	CL
16	XVI	200	CC
17	XVII	300	CCC
18	XVIII	400	CD
19	XIX	500	D
20	XX	600	DC
21	XXI	700	DCC
30	XXX	800	DCCC
32	XXXII	900	CM
40	XL	1000	M

Phonetic alphabet used in communications

A	Alpha	N	November
B	Bravo	O	Oscar
C	Charlie	P	Papa
D	Delta	Q	Quebec
E	Echo	R	Romeo
F	Foxtrot	S	Sierra
G	Golf	T	Tango
H	Hotel	U	Uniform
I	India	V	Victor
J	Juliet	W	Whisky
K	Kilo	X	X-ray
L	Lima	Y	Yankee
M	Mike	Z	Zulu

Paper sizes

The following sizes are those recommended by the International Organization for Standardization (ISO).

ISO RA1	610 mm × 860 mm
ISO RA2	610 mm × 430 mm
ISO SRA1	640 mm × 900 mm
ISO SRA2	640 mm × 450 mm

A *series*

A0	841 mm × 1189 mm
A1	841 mm × 594 mm
A2	420 mm × 594 mm
A3	420 mm × 297 mm
A4	210 mm × 297 mm
A5	210 mm × 148 mm
A6	105 mm × 148 mm
A7	105 mm × 74 mm
A8	52 mm × 74 mm

B *series*

B0	1000 mm × 1414 mm
B1	1000 mm × 707 mm
B2	500 mm × 707 mm
B3	500 mm × 353 mm
B4	250 mm × 353 mm
B5	250 mm × 176 mm
B6	125 mm × 176 mm
B7	125 mm × 88 mm
B8	62 mm × 88 mm

C *series*

C0	917 mm × 1297 mm
C1	917 mm × 648 mm
C2	458 mm × 648 mm
C3	458 mm × 324 mm
C4	229 mm × 324 mm
C5	229 mm × 162 mm
C6	114 mm × 162 mm
C7	114 mm × 81 mm
C8	57 mm × 81 mm

The thickness of paper is measured in micrometres (μm).

Its density, or substance, is measured in grams per square metre (gsm).

Abbreviations

A *or* **amp.** ampere
AA Australian Army; Automobile Association; Alcoholics Anonymous
AAEC Australian Atomic Energy Commission
AAP Australian Associated Press
AAR against all risk
AASE Australian Associated Stock Exchange
AAT Australian Antarctic Territory; Administrative Appeals Tribunal
ab. *or* **abt** about
abb. *or* **abbr.** *or* **abbrev.** abbreviated; abbreviation
ABC Australian Broadcasting Corporation
ABS Australian Bureau of Statistics
AC Companion of the Order of Australia
AC *or* **a.c.** alternating current
A/C account current
A/C *or* **acc.** *or* **Acc** *or* **acct** account
ACA Australian Consumers' Association
acc. acceleration; accent; acceptance; according; account; accusative
ACC Australian Chamber of Commerce
ACCEC Australian Chamber of Commerce Export Council
accel. (*Music*) accelerando (quickening)
accom. accommocation; accompaniment
acct account; accountant
ACMA Associated Chambers of Manufacturers of Australia
ACN Australian Company Number
ACT Australian Capital Territory
ACTU Australian Council of Trade Unions
AD in the year of our Lord (Latin: *Anno Domini*)
ADA Australian Dental Association
adag. (*Music*) adagio (leisurely)
add. addendum
adj. adjective
ad lib. at pleasure, to the extent desired (Latin: *ad libitum*)
ad loc. at the place (Latin: *ad locum*)
Adm Admiral
admin. administration
ADP automatic data processing
adv. *or* **advb** adverb
advert. *or* **advt** advertisement
AEC Atomic Energy Commission
a.f. advance freight
AFIA Association of Federal Institute of Accountants (Aust.)
aft. after; afternoon
aftn *or* **aft.** afternoon
AG Attorney-General
AGM Annual General Meeting
agric. agriculture
AH *or* **a.h.** after hours
AI artificial intelligence; artificial insemination
AIAS Australian Institute of Agricultural Science
AIDC Australian Industry Development Corporation
AIDS acquired immune deficiency syndrome
AIIA Australian Institute of International Affairs
AIM Australian Institute of Management
AK Knight of the Order of Australia
alg. algebra
ALP Australian Labor Party
al seg. (*Music*) al segno (to the sign)
alt. alternative; altitude
a.m. before noon (Latin: *ante meridiem*)
AM Member of the Order of Australia; amplitude modulation
AMA Australian Medical Association
AMF Australian Military Forces
amp. amperage; ampere
amt amount
anat. anatomical; anatomy
and. (*Music*) andante (moderately slow)
ann. annual
anniv. anniversary
anon. anonymous
ANRC Australian National Research Council
ans. answer
ANTA Australian National Travel Association
anth. anthology
ANZAAS Australian and New Zealand Association for the Advancement of Science
ANZAC Australian and New Zea-

land Army Corps
AO (*Films, TV*) adults only; Officer of the Order of Australia
AOB any other business
Ap *or* **Apl** *or* **Apr** April
AP Associated Press
APA Australian Publishers Association
app. appended; appendix; appointed; approval
approx. approximate; approximately
appt. appointment
apptd appointed
AR annual return; account rendered
A/R all risks
arch. architect; architecture; archipelago
arith. arithmetic
arr. arranged; arrived
ASA Australian Society of Accountants
ASAP *or* **a.s.a.p.** as soon as possible
ASC Australian Securities Commission
ASEAN Association of South-East Asian Nations
ASIO Australian Security Intelligence Organisation
ASIS Australian Secret Intelligence Service
Assn *or* **assn** association
Assoc associate; associated; association
asst. assistant
astr. *or* **astron.** astronomer; astronomical; astronomy
astrol. astrologer; astrological; astrology
ASX Australian Stock Exchange
ATO Australian Taxation Office
atm. atmosphere; atmospheric
ATM automatic teller machine
attrib. attributed
at.wt atomic weight
Aug August
Aust Australia; Australian
aux. auxiliary
Av *or* **Ave** Avenue
av. *or* **avg.** *or* **avge** average
AVA Australian Veterinary Association
AWB air waybill
AWU Australian Workers' Union
B Bachelor; British
b. born; bowled; breadth; billion; book
BA Bachelor of Arts
BAgrSc Bachelor of Agricultural Science
bal. balance
BAppSc Bachelor of Applied Science
BArch Bachelor of Architecture
Bapt Baptist
b. & b. bed and breakfast
BBQ barbecue
BBS Bachelor of Business Studies
BC Before Christ
BCA Business Council of Australia
bch beach; branch
BD Bachelor of Divinity
B/D *or* **b/d** bank draft
Bde Brigade
bdg binding; building
BDS Bachelor of Dental Surgery
B/E *or* **b/e** bill of exchange
BEc Bachelor of Economics
BEd Bachelor of Education
BENELUX Belgium/ Netherlands/ Luxembourg
b/f brought forward
BH *or* **b.h.** business hours
Bib Bible; Biblical
biol. biological; biologist; biology
bk bank; book
bkpt bankrupt
B/L *or* **b/l** bill of lading
bldg building
Blvd *or* **Boul** Boulevard
BM Bravery Medal (Aust)
BO body odour
bot. botanical; botanist; botany; bottle
BPharm Bachelor of Pharmacy
Br British
Brig Brigadier
bros brothers
BS Bachelor of Surgery
B/S *or* **b/s** bill of sale
BSc Bachelor of Science
bus. business
BVSc Bachelor of Veterinary Science
B/W black and white
BYO bring your own
BYOG bring your own grog
C Cape; Celsius; Centigrade; century; coulomb
C/- care of
c. cent; centigrade; centimetre; century; about (Latin: *circa*)
CA chartered accountant

C/A capital account; commercial account; credit account; current account
CAD cash against documents
cal. (*Music*) calando (slowing gradually and decreasing volume); calibre; calorie
Cantab of Cambridge University
Cap *or* **Capt** Captain
cap. capital letter
car. carat
cas. casual
Cath Catholic
c.c. carbon copy; cubic centimetre
cd candela
CD certificate of deposit; cash discount; compact disc
c/d carried down; cum dividend
Cdr Commander; conductor
cent. centigrade; central; century
CEO Chief Executive Office
cert. certain; certificate; certified
CES Commonwealth Employment Service
cf. compare (Latin: *confer*)
c/f (*Accounting*) carried forward, carry forward
c. & f. cost and freight
c. & i. cost and insurance
c.g.s. centimetre-gram-second (system)
ch. *or* **chap.** chapter
CHOGM Commonwealth Heads of Government Meeting
chq. cheque
C/I certificate of insurance
CIB Criminal Investigation Branch
CIF *or* **c.i.f.** cost, insurance and freight
C-in-C Commancer-in-Chief
CIP cataloguing-in-publication
circ. about (Latin: *circa*)
CIS Commonwealth of Independent States
cit. citation; cited (Latin: *citato*)
CJ Chief Justice
CN credit note
Co *or* **Coy** company
c/o care of
CO Commanding Officer; certificate of origin
COD cash on delivery
co-ed co-educational
C of C Chamber of Commerce
C of E Church of England
Col Colonel
col. colour; column
colloq. colloquial
com. committee
Com Commission; Commissioner
comm. commerce; commercial; commission
comp. compiled; composition; compound
compl. complimentary
con. consolidated
cond. condition
conf. conference
conj. conjunction
cont. *or* **contd** continued
cop. copper
COPQ Committee on Overseas Professional Qualifications
Corp corporation
CP charter party
CPA certified practising accountant
CPI consumer price index
Cpl Corporal
CPO Chief Petty Officer
c.p.s. cycles per second
CPU central processor unit
Cr credit; creditor; councillor
Cres Crescent
cres. (*Music*) crescendo (gradually louder)
CSIRO Commonwealth Scientific and Industrial Research Organisation
CST Central Standard Time
ct carat; caught
ctge cartage
Cth Commonwealth (Australia)
cu. cubic
c.v. curriculum vitae
CV curriculum vitae; Cross of Valour (Aust)
CWA Country Women's Association
C'wlth Commonwealth (Australia)
cwt hundredweight
CWO cash with order
d. daughter; deci; density; diameter
DAgrSc Doctor of Agricultural Science
DAppSc Doctor of Applied Science
dB decibel
DBA Doctor of Business Administration
dbl. double
DC (*Music*) da capo (repeat); direct durrent; Double ertificated
d.c. direct current
dcd *or* **dec.** deceased

dd. delivered
d.d. deferred delivery; given as a gift (Latin: *dono dedit*)
DD Doctor of Divinity
DDS Doctor of Dental Surgery DE Doctor of Engineering
deb. debenture
Dec December
dec. deceased; (*Music*) decrescendo (becoming softer)
DEd Doctor of Education
def. deferred
deg. degree
del. delegate; delivery; delivered
dep. deposit; depart; deputy; deposed
dept department
dict. dictionary
dip. diploma
dir. director
disc. discount
div. dividend
DLitt Doctor of Letters
DLP Democratic Labor Party
DMus Doctor of Music
DMZ demilitarised zone
D/N debit note; delivery note
DNA deoxyribonucleic acid
do. ditto, the same
DOB date of birth
doc. document
doz. dozen
DP document against payment; displaced person
D/P deferred payment
dpt department
Dr Doctor; Drive (in street names)
DSc Doctor of Science
dup. duplicate
DVSc Doctor of Veterinary Science
d.w. dead weight; delivered weight
D/W dock warrant; dead weight
d.w.t. dead weight tonnage
E east; eastern; English
ea. each
EB enterprise bargaining
EC European Community
ecol. ecological; ecology
econ. economics; economist; economy
ECT electroconvulsive therapy
ed. *or* **edit.** edited; edition; editor
edn edition
EEC European Economic Community
EEO equal employment opportunity
EFTA European Free Trade Association
EFTPOS electronic funds transfer at point of sale
e.g. for example (Latin: *exempli gratia*)
enc. *or* **encl.** enclosed
enl. enlarged
ENT Ear, Nose and Throat
env. envelope
E&OE errors and omissions excepted
EPAC Economic Planning Advisory Council
e.p.s. earnings per share
eq. equal
equiv. equivalent
esp. especially
ESP extrasensory perception
Esq. Esquire
est. established
EST Eastern Standard Time
estab. established
ETA estimated time of arrival
et al. and others (Latin: *et alii*)
etc. and so on (Latin: *et cetera*)
et seq. and that which follows (Latin: *et sequentia*)
Exc Excellency
exc. except
exch exchange; exchequer
excl excluding; exclusive
exec. executive; executor
ex lib. from the library of (Latin: *ex libris*)
exp. expenses; experienced; export; express
ext. extension; external; extra
exx. examples
F Fahrenheit; Fellow; freeway
f (*Music*) forte (loud)
f. folio; following; franc
FAA free of all average
FAM free at mill
FAO Food and Agriculture Organisation
FAQ *or* **f.a.q.** fair average quality
FAS *or* **f.a.s.** free alongside ship
FBI Federal Bureau of Investigtion
FBT fringe benefits tax
FCL full container load
fcp foolscap
FD forward delivery
Feb February
fed. federal
fem. female; feminine

ff folios; following; (*Music*) fortissimo (very loud)
fict. fiction
FID financial institutions duty
FIFO first in first out
fig. figurative; figure
figs figures
fin. financial
FIRB Foreign Investment Review Board
FIS *or* **f.i.s.** free into store
Flt Lt Flight Lieutenant
fn *or* **f.n.** footnote
FO Foreign Office; field officer
FOB *or* **f.o.b.** free on board
FOC *or* **f.o.c.** free of charge
FOI freedom of information
fol. folio; following
FOR *or* **f.o.r.** free on rail
Fr Father; Friday
freq. frequent; frequently
Fri *or* **Fr** *or* **Frid** Friday
ft foot; feet
f.v. on the back of the page (Latin: *folio verso*)
fwd forward
f.w.d. four wheel drive
G (*Films, TV*) for general exhibition; the constant of gravitation
g gram, gravity
gal. gallon(s)
GATT General Agreement on Tariffs and Trade
GB Great Britain
GDP Gross Domestic Product
gds goods
Gen General
gen. gender; general; genus
geog. geographer; geographical; geography
geol. geological; geologist; geology
geom. geometrical; geometry
ger. gerund; gerundive
GG Governor-General
GHQ General Headquarters
gloss. glossary
GM General Manager
GMT Greenwich Mean Time
GNE gross national expenditure
GNP gross national product
Govt *or* **govt** government
GP general practitioner
Gp Capt Group Captain
GPO General Post Office
GRT gross registered tonnage
gr. wt gross weight
GSO General Staff Officer
GST Goods and Services Tax
gtd. guaranteed
h. height; hour
ha hectare
h.c.f. highest common factor
hcp handicap
hdqrs headquarters
HE His/Her Excellency; His/Her Eminence
hist. historical; history
HM Her (or His) Majesty
HMAS Her (or His) Majesty's Australian Ship
HO Head Office
Hon honorary; honorable
hosp. hospital
HP hire purchase
hp *or* **h.p.** horse power
HQ headquarters
hr hour
HR House of Representatives
HRH His/Her Royal Highness
HSC Higher School Certificate
Hts Heights
I information
ibid in the same place (Latin: *ibidem*)
i/c in charge; in command
IC Industries Commission
ICAA Institute of Chartered Accountants of Australia
ICFTU International Confederation of Free Trade Unions
id the same (Latin: *idem*)
ID identification
IDD International Direct Dialling
i.e. that is (Latin: *id est*)
ILC irrevocable letter of credit
ILO International Labour Organisation
illus. illustrated; illustration
IMF International Monetary Fund
imp. imperial; import
imperf. imperfect; imperforate
in. inch(es)
inc. included; including; inclusive; incorporated; increase
incl. included; including; inclusive
incorp. *or* **inc.** incorporated
incr. *or* **inc.** increase
ind. independent
info. information
init. at the beginning; initially
in loc. cit. in the place cited (Latin: *in loco citato*)

Insp Inspector
inst. in or of the present month
intro. *or* **introd.** introduced; introduction
I/O input/output
IOU I owe you
IPA International Phonetic Alphabet
Is *or* **is.** *or* **isl.** Island; Isle
ISBN International Standard Book Number
Isth *or* **isth.** Isthmus
ital. italics (type)
ITO International Trade Organisation
J journal; Judge; Justice; joule
Jan *or* **Ja** January
Jn *or* **Jun** June
jnr *or* **jr** junior
JP Justice of the Peace
jt. joint
Jul *or* **Jl** *or* **Jy** July
K (*Computers*) 2^{10} (1024); (*Physics*) kelvin
kd killed
kg kilogram
kit. kitchen
km/h kilometres per hour
kn international knot
Kt knight
kt karat; carat; knot
L litre; learner (driver)
l. left; length; litre
LA Legislative Assembly
L/A letter of authority
LAC Leading Aircraftman
lang. language
lat. latitude
lb pound (Latin: *libra*); pounds (Latin: *librae*)
lbs pounds
l.b.w. leg before wicket
l.c. lower case; letter of credit
L/C letter of credit
l.c.m. lowest common multiple
l.h.s. left hand side
lic'd licensed
LIFO last in first out
LLB Bachelor of Laws
LLD Doctor of Laws
LLM Master of Laws
LLR lender of last resort
loc. cit. in the place cited (Latin: *loco citato*)
log. logarithm
long. longitude
LPG liquefied petroleum gas
LS Leading Seaman
l.s.d. pounds, shillings and pence (Latin: *librae, solidi, denarii*)
Lt Lieutenant
Lt-Col Lieutenant-Colonel
Ltd limited
Lt-Gen Lieutenant-General
M (*Films, TV*) for mature audiences (15 years and over); Member; money supply; Majesty; Monsieur
m. male; married; masculine; mass; noon (Latin: *meridiem*); metre; million; minim; minute; month
MA Master of Arts; (*Films, TV*) for mature audiences (15 years and over - restricted viewing below this age)
mag. magazine; magnetism; magnitude
MAgrSc Master of Agricultural Science
Maj Major
Maj Gen Major General
MAppSc Master of Applied Science
Mar *or* **Mch** March
MArch Master of Architecture
masc. masculine
math. *or* **maths** mathematical; mathematics
matric. matriculation
max. maximum
MB Bachelor of Medicine
MBA Master of Business Administration
MC Military Cross; Master of Ceremonies
MCPS megacycles per second
MD Managing Director; Doctor of Medicine
MDS Master of Dental Surgery
ME Master of Engineering
MEc Master of Economics
med. medical; medicine; medium
MEd Master of Education
Messrs plural of *Mr* (French: *Messieurs*)
met. metropolitan
meth. methylated
mf (*Music*) mezzo-forte (rather loud)
mfd manufactured
mfg manufacturing
mfr manufacture; manufacturer
Mgr *or* **mgr** Manager
m.g.s. metre-gram-second

MHA Member of the House of Assembly
MHR Member of the House of Representatives
mid. middle; midnight
mil. military
mill. million; millions
min. minimum; minute; minutes
mins minutes
misc. miscellaneous
m.k.s. metre-kilogram-second (system)
mktg marketing
ml millilitre
MLA Member of the Legislative Assembly
MLC Member of the Legislative Council
MLG Member of Local Government
MLitt Master of Letters
MLR minimum lending rate
mm millimetre
mo. month
MO mail order; medical officer, money order
mod. moderate; (*Music*) moderato
mol. molecular; molecule
Mon Monday
mp (*Music*) mezzo-piano (moderately soft)
MP Member of Parliament; Military Police
m.p.g. miles per gallon
m.p.h. *or* **mph** miles per hour
m.p.s. miles per second
ms manuscript
MS Master of Surgery; manuscript; multiple sclerosis
MSc Master of Science
MSS manuscripts
Mt mount; mountain
Mus museum; music; musical; musician
MV merchant vessel; motor vessel
MVSc Master of Veterinary Science
N north; northern; newton
n. born (Latin: *natus*)
n/a *or* **n.a.** not applicable; not available
NASA National Aeronautics and Space Administration (USA)
nat. national; native; natural
NATO North Atlantic Treaty Organisation
naut. nautical
nav. naval; navigation; navy
navig. navigation; navigator
NB note well (Latin: *nota bene*)
NCDC National Capital Development Commission
NCO Non-Commissioned Officer
NE north-east; north-eastern
neg. negation; negative
NL no liability
NLCC National Labour Consultative Council
No *or* **no.** number
Nos *or* **nos** numbers
Nov November
n.p. new paragraph
NP National Party
NPV net present value
nr near
NRMA National Roads and Motorists' Association (of New South Wales)
NSF not sufficient funds
NSW New South Wales
NT Northern Territory
nt.wt. net weight
NW north-west; north-western
NWCC National Women's Consultative Council
NZ New Zealand
O order; owner; ohm
o/a on account of
O/A offer accepted
OAM Medal of the Order of Australia
obs. observation; observatory; obsolete
OBU offshore banking unit
occas. occasion
Oct October
O/D overdraft; overdrawn; on demand
OECD Organisation for Economic Cooperation and Development
off. office; officer; official
OHMS On Her (or His) Majesty's Service
OK all correct
OM Order of Merit
o.n.o. or nearest offer
op. operation; opus
o.p. out of print
op. cit. in the work cited (Latin: *opere citato*)
OPEC Organisation of Petroleum Exporting Countries
opp. opposite
opt. option

o.r. owner's risk; official receiver
OR operations research; operational research
orch. orchestra
ord. order; ordinary
orig. origin; original
o/s out of stock
o.s. overseas
o/t overtime
Oxon of Oxford University; Oxfordshire (UK)
oz ounce; ounces
ozs ounces
P provisional (driver's licence); President
p. page; (*Music*) softly (It. *piano*)
p.a. yearly (Latin: *per annum*)
PA personal assistant; power of attorney
PABX private automatic branch exchange
para. paragraph
Parl *or* **Parlt** Parliament
partn. partnership
pass. passenger; passive
pat. patent
PAYE pay as you earn
p.c. per cent
p/c petty cash
pd paid
p/d postdated
PD prompt delivery
Pen peninsula
perm. permanent
per pro. *or* **per proc.** on behalf of (Latin: *per procurationem*)
pers. person; personal
pg. *or* **p.** page
PG (*Films, TV*) parental guidance (recommended for children under 15)
PhD Doctor of Philosophy
photog. photographic; photography
phr. phrase
phys. physical; physics
phys. ed. physical education
PIN personal identification number
pizz. (*Music*) pizzicato (plucked strings)
Pk Park
pkg package
pkt packet
Pl Place (in street names)
PL partial loss
pl. *or* **plur.** plural
PLC Public Limited Company
PLR public lending right
p.m. afternoon (Latin: *post meridiem*)
PM Prime Minister; postmaster; post-mortem; Police Magistrate; paymaster
PMG Postmaster-General
p.n. promissory note
PNG Papua New Guinea
PO post office; postal order; Petty Officer
POA price on application
pol. political; politics
pop. population
POW prisoner of war
pp. pages; (*Music*) pianissimo (very softly); on behalf of (Latin: *per procurationem*)
PPS additional postscript (Latin: *post post scriptum*); prescribed payments system
pr pair
PR public relations
pref. preference; preferred
prelim. preliminary
prep. preparation
Pres President
Prof Professor
pronunc. pronunciation
prop. proprietor
pro tem. for the time being (Latin: *pro tempore*)
prox. in or of the next or coming month (Latin: *proximo*)
PS postscript; private secretary
PSA Prices Surveillance Authority; Public Service Association
PSB Public Service Board
psychol. psychology
pt point; pint; part; payment
p.t. part time; for the time being (Latin: *pro tempore*)
Pte Private
PTO *or* **p.t.o.** please turn over
Pty proprietary
p.w. per week
Q Queen; Queensland
q. quarto; question
QC Queen's Counsel
QED which was to be proved (Latin: *quod erat demonstrandum*)
Qld *or* **Q** *or* **Qd** Queensland
qq. questions
qr quarter
qt quart
qt. quantity

qto quarto
qtr quarter; quarterly
qual. qualified; quality
quin. quintuplet
quot. quotation
q.v. which see (Latin: *quod vide*)
R (*Films, TV*) unsuitable for people under 18 years of age (restricted exhibition)
r. radius; right; (*Cricket*) runs
RA Royal Academy
RAAF Royal Australian Air Force
rad. radian
rall. (*Music*) rallentando (becoming gradually slower)
RAN Royal Australian Navy
RBA Reserve Bank of Australia
RC Roman Catholic; Red Cross
Rd Road
R/D refer to drawer
R&D research and development
RDO rostered day off
Rear-Adm. Rear Admiral
rec. receipt; record
recd received
ref. reference; referred
reg. registration; registered; regulation
Regt Regiment
relig. religion; religious
rep. representative
res. research; reserve; residence; resigned
ret. *or* **retd** returned; retired
rev. reverse; revised; revenue; review
Rev. Reverend
RH Royal Highness
r.h.s. right hand side
rit. *or* **ritard.** (*Music*) ritardando (slower, holding back)
riv. river
RLO returned letter office
rm room; ream
RNA ribonucleic acid
ROI return on investment
r.p.m. revolutions per minute
r.p.s. revolutions per second
RRP recommended retail price
RSL Returned Services League (of Australia)
RSPCA Royal Society for the Prevention of Cruelty to Animals
RSVP please reply (French: *repondez s'il vous plait*)
Rt Hon Right Honourable
RVSVP please reply quickly (French: *repondez vite, s'il vous plait*)
S south; southern; Society
s. singular; second(s); south; southern
s.a. subject to approval; semi-annual; without year or date (Latin: *sine anno*)
SA South Australia
s.a.e. stamped adressed envelope
Sat Saturday
SB short bill (payable on demand or sight)
SBN standard book number
sc. that is to say, namely (Latin *scilicet*)
s.c. single column; small capitals
sch. school
sci. science; scientific
SD sight draft; short delivery; sea damaged; standard deviation
SE south-east; south-eastern
S/E Stock Exchange
SEATO South-East Asia Treaty Organisation
sec. second; secondary; secretary; section
sect. section
secy or sec. secretary
sen. *or* **snr** *or* **sr** senior
Sep *or* **Sept** September
sep. *or* **separ.** separate
Sergt *or* **Sgt** Sergeant
sf *or* **s.f.** science fiction
s.g. specific gravity
SGC Superannuation Guarantee Charge
sgd signed
shd should
shpt shipment
shr share
SI International System of Units (French: *Systeme International d'Unites*)
sic so; thus (used parenthetically to show that something has been copied exactly)
sig. signature
sing. singular
SM Stipendiary Magistrate
snr senior
SO staff officer; seller's option
Soc society
sop. soprano
SOR sale or return
sp. special; species

spec. *or* **sp.** special
spp. species (pl.)
sq. square
Sqn Ldr Squadron Leader
Sr senior
S/R sale or return
SRD statutory reserve deposit
SS steamship
St Saint; Strait; Street
STD Subscriber Trunk Dialling
ster. sterling
Sth south
Sthn southern
stn station
sub. sub-editor, subject
subj. subject
Sun *or* **Sund** Sunday
Super. Superintendent
suppl. supplement; supplementary
surg. surgeon; surgery; surgical
SW south-west; south-western
sym. symbol; symbolic; symmetrical; symphony
sz. size
t tonne
TAFE Technical and Further Education
Tas Tasmania
TB trial balance
tbs. *or* **tbsp.** tablespoon
TEC Tertiary Education Commission
tech. technical; technology
tel. telephone; telegram; telegraph
telecom. telecommunications
temp. temperature; temporary
theat. theatre; theatrical
Thu *or* **Thurs** Thursday
t.l. total loss
TPC Trade Practices Commission
tr. transitive; translate *or* translated; translator
trad. traditional
trans. transcript; translated; translation; translator
Treas Treasurer; Treasury
trig. trigonometric; trigonometry
trop. tropical
tsp. *or* **t.** teaspoon
Tues *or* **Tue** *or* **Tu** Tuesday
TT telegraphic transfer
TUC Trade Union Congress
TUTA Trade Union Training Authority
TV television
U union; united; university
u.c. upper case
u.h.f. *or* **UHF** ultra high frequency
UK United Kingdom
ult. in or of the preceding month (Latin: *ultimo*)
UN United Nations
UNCTAD United Nations Commission on Trade and Development
UNESCO United Nations Educational, Scientific and Cultural Organisation
uni. university
UNICEF United Nations International Children's Emergency Fund
univ. universal
USA United States of America
US United States
usu. usually
UV ultra violet
UW *or* **U/W** underwriter
v. velocity; verb; verse; versus; volume
vac. vacancy; vacant; vacation
var. variant; variation; variety
VAT value added tax
vb verb
VC Victoria Cross; Vice Chairman; Vice Chancellor
VDT visual display terminal
VDU visual display unit
vel. velocity
VG Valuer-General; Vicar-General
v.h.f. *or* **VFH** very high frequency
Vic Victoria
vid. see (Latin: *vide*)
VIP very important person
viz. namely (Latin: *videlicet*)
vol. volume
VP Vice President
vs. versus; verse
vv. verses
v.v. vice versa
W west; western
w. watt(s); week; weight; west; western; wide; width; with
WA Western Australia
WB waybill
w.c. without charge
wd word; would
WEA Workers' Educational Association
Wed Wednesday
WFTU World Federation of Trade Unions
Wg Cdr Wing Commander
WHO World Health Organisation

wk week; work
wkly weekly
wkt wicket
W/M weight or measurement
WMO World Maritime Organisation; World Meteorological Organisation
WO Warrant Officer
WP without prejudice
WPA without particular average
w.p.b. waste paper basket
w.p.m. *or* **wpm** words per minute
WR warehouse receipt
WRAAF Women's Royal Australian Air Force
WRAN Women's Royal Australian Navy
WRO war risk only
WST Western Standard Time
wt weight
WW warehouse warrant
WWI First World War
WWII Second World War
WWW World Wide Web
X Cross; (*Videotapes*) restricted viewing
Xmas Christmas
X ref. cross reference
y. yard; year
yd yard
yds yards
YHA Youth Hostels Association
YMCA Young Men's Christian Association
yr year; your
yrs yours
YWCA Young Women's Christian Association
Z *or* **z** zero; zone
zool. zoology